Chief Executive's Handbook

Edited by

JOHN DESMOND GLOVER

Lovett-Learned Professor of
Business Administration
Harvard University

and

GERALD A. SIMON

Managing Director
Cambridge Research Institute

1976

Dow Jones-Irwin, Inc.   Homewood, Illinois   60430

First Printing, January 1976

ISBN 0-87094-104-6
Library of Congress Catalog Card No. 75–11387
Printed in the United States of America

PREFACE

THIS BOOK is about the important aspects of the job of the Chief Executive Officer of a corporation. To attempt to provide a practical handbook for the CEO does pose problems. What the Chief Executive Officer needs to know is not at all a straightforward summation of everything that everyone else in the organization knows—the marketers, the money people, the production people, personnel manager, director of research, and the rest. No one person could know all that, but the CEO must evaluate what these people say and recommend; he must gauge their performance. The CEO must synthesize the many, and sometimes contending views into an integrated, and integrating whole. This commonplace observation determined the specifications for, and the constraints upon the contents of this book.

This is not an "academic" book, written by and for students and scholars. It is not based upon statistical or clinical research. It does not bristle with footnotes citing "authorities." The contributors *are* authorities. Their chapters set forth their views—almost always judicious and detached; often personal; sometimes, indeed, controversial. Here are ideas, insights, hunches, observations, and thoughtful ruminations of people who have competed for position, who know what it is to face personal and institutional challenge, to exercise power and authority, and to be held responsible.

Why publish a book that focuses on the concerns and interests of chief executives? By the time companies are large enough to have shares listed and traded, in theory and in practice, ownership and management have been separated. These firms have become *institutions* with lives apart from the lives of any owners or managers. They are *public* institutions. They are no longer mere extensions of the proprietors or owner-managers. By law, they are no longer *private*. Their affairs are public, and an increasing array of disclosures must be made of intimate details of the business. The stockholders of these publicly held corporations number into the thousands or even hundreds of thousands. These stockholders can and do bring the company's directors, officers, auditors, and attorneys to account. The directors and managers of these companies are dealing with other people's money. The chief executives of these companies need a guide to dealing with not only the competitive market places but also the many external entities that surround all business organizations. This book is intended to meet that need.

What all institutions have in common is that they must have mechanisms of management—including people—to supplement the perceptions, the thoughts, the knowledge, and the reflexes of the individual who is the *chief* executive. Working through people is very different from doing things by yourself. The chapters in this book reflect that understanding.

Our intended audience surely includes executive officers of the thousands of our sizeable not-for-profit organizations: governments, educational institutions, hospitals, foundations, and such. Many of these are larger, and in many cases, more complex than many businesses. For instance, a 500-bed modern hospital is as large or larger (as measured by its budget, the value of its assets, or the number of its people) than many business corporations listed on the stock exchanges. Also, it is as complex, in terms of the numbers of technologies and different kinds of skills that must be brought to bear in its management and its workings.

This book should be of value to the junior people who aspire to manage our public institutions. In time, the abler—and the luckier—of them will be invited to join *top* management. Some will become CEOs. Reading these chapters should prove one useful step they can take in a pattern of efforts to get an early feel for the concerns and unique perspectives of the top management team and, even, of the Chief Executive Officer.

We hope to meet the needs of readers around the world. In our experience—and this has been confirmed by European, Asian, and American businessmen alike—the "technology" of management is becoming increasingly trans-national and "culture-free." In proof of this, reading the chapters of this book will show that only a very few—certainly not more than 3 or 4—are so particularly North American as to be of little interest to chief executives elsewhere. In further proof, if such be needed, our readers of all nationalities will find—as we found—that the chapters contributed by outstanding people in countries other than the United States are every bit as interesting and pertinent as those which come from the U.S.

ACKNOWLEDGMENTS

We are honored to be able to acknowledge our indebtedness to so many very distinguished people for producing what the reader will find here. Never before has such a "panel" of able people been assembled to give of their ideas to such an audience.

We are beholden to our Editorial Advisory Board for their ideas and help in designing this volume. Some of them were willing to go even further: to contribute chapters of their own. The quality of their writings speaks for itself and attests to qualifications for serving as we asked them to do.

Most of our authors are products of universities and business schools. What they learned there surely helped them on their way; and some of that education no doubt still flows through what they have written here. We must all—readers and authors alike—be grateful to those estimable institutions. But we editors have a special debt to the Harvard Business School of which we ourselves are products, and which has touched, directly, close to one-half of the authors here brought together. No doubt, present and past members of the faculty of the Harvard Business School will recognize many touches of themselves in these pages.

We are pleased to voice our thanks to members of the staff of the Cambridge Research Institute, especially to David Kiser, D.B.A., an Associate of the firm, and Ms. Frances Harrington, Assistant Secretary, as well as to Ms. Claire M. Tebo, Professor Glover's secretary.

Cambridge, Massachusetts   J.D.G.
December 1975   G.A.S.

CONTRIBUTING AUTHORS

ROBERT ANDERSON
  President and Chief Executive Officer, Rockwell International Corporation

LAWRENCE A. APPLEY
  Chairman Emeritus, American Management Associations

FRANK E. BARNETT*
  Chairman of the Board and Chief Executive Officer, Union Pacific Corporation

ALBERT BARRAUD
  President, Société D.B.A.

SAMUEL G. BARTON
  President; Webber, Barton, Jolitz, Shaw, Inc.

ENRICO BIGNAMI
  Managing Director and Vice Chairman (Retired), Nestlé Alimentana, S.A. (Switzerland)

WILLIAM BLACKIE
  Senior Partner, Lehman Brothers; *Chairman (Retired),* Caterpillar Tractor Co.

MARVIN BOWER
  Director, McKinsey & Company, Inc.

COURTNEY C. BROWN
  Dean Emeritus, Columbia University, Graduate School of Business

WERNER C. BROWN
  President, Hercules Incorporated

ALEXANDER CALDER, JR.
  Chairman, Union Camp Corporation

ALFRED D. CHANDLER, JR.
  Isidor Straus Professor of Business History, Harvard Business School

GEORGE A. CHANDLER
  President, Winchester Group, Olin Corporation

---

* Joint author.

ROBERT B. CLARK
President and Chief Executive Officer, Hoffmann-La Roche Inc.

RICHARD F. COLE
President, Cryogenic Technology, inc.

ABRAM T. COLLIER
Chairman, New England Mutual Life Insurance Company

WILLIAM C. CONNER*
Chairman of the Board, Alcon Laboratories, Inc.

JOHN T. CONNOR
Chairman of the Board, Allied Chemical Corporation

GORDON R. COREY
Vice Chairman, Commonwealth Edison Company

HERSHNER CROSS
Senior Vice President, General Electric Company

ALEX DIBBS
Director and Chief Executive Officer, National Westminster Bank Limited

GEORGE H. DIXON*
Chairman and President, First National Bank of Minneapolis

EDWARD DONLEY
President, Air Products and Chemicals, Inc.

BERNARD EDISON
President, Edison Brothers Stores, Inc.

WILLIAM M. ELLINGHAUS*
President, New York Telephone Company

GENE E. ENGLEMAN
Chairman, Union Bank of Fort Worth

JOHN P. FISHWICK
President and Chief Executive Officer, Norfolk and Western Railway Company

JOHN M. FOX
President, H. P. Hood Inc.

MORTIMER J. FOX, JR.
Vice President (Retired), Schering Corporation

GAYLORD FREEMAN
Chairman of the Board, First Chicago Corporation/The First National Bank of Chicago

N. W. FREEMAN
Chairman, Tenneco Inc.

---

* Joint author.

RICHARD L. GELB
  President, Bristol-Myers Company

RICHARD C. GERSTENBERG
  Chairman of the Board (Retired), General Motors Corporation

E. BURKE GIBLIN
  Chairman and Chief Executive Officer, Warner-Lambert Company

JOHN DESMOND GLOVER
  Lovett-Learned Professor of Business Administration, Harvard Business School

ROY M. GOODMAN
  New York State Senator; Former Corporate President and New York City Finance Commissioner

ALBERT H. GORDON
  Chairman of the Board; Kidder, Peabody, Inc.

STANLEY M. GORTIKOV
  President, Recording Industry Association of America, Inc.; *Former President,* Capitol Records

JOSEPH B. HALL
  Chairman of the Board (Retired), The Kroger Company

DR. ARMAND HAMMER
  Chairman of the Board and Chief Executive Officer, Occidental Petroleum Corporation

DANIEL J. HAUGHTON
  Chairman of the Board, Lockheed Aircraft Corporation

JAMES L. HAYES
  President and Chief Executive Officer, American Management Associations

YOSHIZO IKEDA
  President, Mitsui & Co., Ltd.

EDWIN L. KENNEDY
  Managing Director, Lehman Brothers

DAVID B. KISER
  Associate, Cambridge Research Institute

PIETER KUIN
  Former Director, Unilever N.V., and Unilever, Ltd.

CHARLES M. LEIGHTON*
  Chairman and Chief Executive Officer, CML Group, Incorporated

PHILLIP LIFSCHULTZ
  Vice President—Taxes, Montgomery Ward

---

* Joint author.

TOM LILLEY
  Former Director, Export-Import Bank

SOL M. LINOWITZ
  Partner, Coudert Brothers; *Former Chairman of the Board,* Xerox Corporation

LOUIS B. LUNDBORG
  Chairman of the Board (Retired), Bank of America

ROBERT E. McDONALD
  President and Chief Operating Officer, Sperry Rand Corporation

WILLIAM J. McDONALD*
  Senior Vice President—Law, Union Pacific Corporation

MYLES L. MACE
  Professor of Business Administration (Emeritus), Harvard Business School

JOHN K. McKINLEY
  President, Texaco Inc.

DONALD S. MacNAUGHTON
  Chairman and Chief Executive Officer, The Prudential Insurance Company of America

TED L. MARSTON*
  Vice President—Personnel, Cummins Engine Company

GERALD B. MITCHELL
  President, Dana Corporation

ROGER F. MURRAY
  S. Sloan Colt Professor of Banking and Finance, Columbia University

JAMES F. OATES, JR.
  Chairman (Retired), The Equitable Life Assurance Society of the United States

JOHN J. O'CONNELL
  Vice President—Industrial Relations, Bethlehem Steel Corporation

BARBARA NEGRI OPPER*
  Financial Economist, The Travelers Insurance Companies

DONALD S. PERKINS
  Chairman, Jewel Companies, Inc.

JESSE PHILIPS
  Chairman and Chief Executive Officer, Philips Industries, Inc.

BERT E. PHILLIPS
  President, Clark Equipment Company

---

* Joint author.

SIMON RAMO
Vice Chairman, TRW Inc.

J. DONALD RAUTH
President, Martin Marietta Corporation

DELBERT D. REICHARDT
Executive Vice President—Finance and Administration, Great American Management Corporation

MILTON L. ROCK
Managing Partner, Hay Associates

HERBERT ROTH, JR.
President, LFE Corporation

MICHAEL L. SANYOUR
Executive Vice President, Science Management Corporation; *Former President,* Subaru of America, Inc.

HENRY B. SCHACHT*
President, Cummins Engine Company

EDGAR H. SCHOLLMAIER*
President, Alcon Laboratories, Inc.

JOHN SCHREINER*
Chairman, Department of Finance, University of Minnesota

PETER G. SCOTESE
President and Vice Chairman, Springs Mills, Inc.

ELI SHAPIRO*
Chairman, Finance Committee, and Director, The Travelers Insurance Companies

WILLIAM G. SHARWELL*
Executive Vice President, Operations, New York Telephone Company

GERALD A. SIMON
Managing Director, Cambridge Research Institute

JAYNE BAKER SPAIN
Vice Chairman, U.S. Civil Service Commission

CHARLES D. TANDY
Chairman of the Board and Chief Executive Officer, Tandy Corporation

WILLIAM R. TINCHER
Chairman and President, Purex Corporation

---

* Joint author.

G. ROBERT TOD*
President, CML Group, Incorporated

LYNN TOWNSEND
Chairman and Chief Executive Officer, Chrysler Corporation

JACK VALENTI
President, Motion Picture Association of America, Inc.

JESSE WERNER
Chairman and President, GAF Corporation

JAMES W. WILCOCK
President, Joy Manufacturing Company

T. F. WILLERS
Former Chairman and Chief Executive Officer, Champion International, Inc.

ROBERT C. WILSON
Chairman, Memorex Corporation; *Former President,* Collins Radio Company

SAMUEL H. WOOLLEY
Chairman (Retired), The Bank of New York

J. DAVID WRIGHT
Chairman of the Board (Retired), TRW Inc.

MICHAEL Y. YOSHINO
Professor of Business Administration, Harvard Business School

---

* Joint author.

CONTENTS

Part IV
DIRECTING THE FUNCTIONS OF THE BUSINESS

A.   DEVELOPMENT ENGINEERING AND RESEARCH

B.   PRODUCTION

Part V
MANAGING THE COMPANY'S EXTERNAL RELATIONSHIPS

PART I
Overview

THE MANY ROLES OF THE CHIEF EXECUTIVE

by John Desmond Glover

Lovett-Learned Professor of Business Administration,
Harvard Business School

In GREEK mythology there was a god called Proteus. He was a son of Poseidon, the god of the sea. Poseidon was brother to Zeus. In this way, Proteus was nephew to the chief executive of the oligarchy that ran things from the top of Mount Olympus. Proteus lived, so some say, on an island in the Aegean between Crete and Rhodes, Karpathos by name. He was the protector of sea animals; seals and dolphins, for instance. More important: he knew everything. But *everything*. Past. Present. Future. Everything that ever was, is, or would be. And that's one reason he makes one think of the Chief Executive Officer of the modern corporation, who is supposed to know everything in this book. And much, much more. And to be able to put it all into action.

There's another reason. Proteus could and did, they say, assume any shape he wanted to or that the situation called for. He could become a lion, a wolf, a leopard, a seal, a snake, a bird, a tree. Anything.

And that's how it is with the chief executive of an organization, say, a company, a university, a hospital, a government agency, a nation. If you believe the textbooks, he—or she—is supposed to *know everything* and to *be everything*. To be an entrepreneur; a canny merchant; an administrator, a decision-maker; an organization-builder; a pillar of the community; a trenchant analyst of baffling complexities; a solver of technical problems; a setter of goals; a strategist; a tactician in the infighting of the marketplaces, just for instance. A charismatic leader. A raconteur. All those things. A man—or woman—for all seasons.

3

And the textbooks are not wrong. He should be. He should be a Proteus of the modern world, able to fill many very different roles. Whether he wants to, or whether he can, his position and function and circumstances force him to try to assume and play—well or badly, as his bent and talents allow—the many and different roles of the chief executive.

In this book, many chief executives speak to others, out of their experience and thought, trying to put into words many of the things they feel the chief executive should know. In doing so, they touch upon roles he must fill, the many roles that require all this know-how and know about. In this chapter, I shall try to set down some thoughts about these many Protean roles. As we think of them, we should bear in mind what the corporation is, over which the Chief Executive Officer presides.

THE BUSINESS CORPORATION OF THE CHIEF EXECUTIVE

This book is about the job of the chief executive of the *business* corporation. John T. Connor, Chairman of Allied Chemical, points out in his chapter in this book that basic concepts and theories as to the nature of the corporation and its relationship with the outside world evolved from the Middle Ages onward with the development of earlier organizations: bishoprics, monasteries and convents, hospitals, and colleges.[1] All of these were institutions in which—quite apart from any individuals associated with them at any given time— were vested various rights and powers; which had various obligations and responsibilities; and which had indefinite lives of their own. Although these institutions, themselves, only incidentally had anything to do with business enterprises, these concepts and theories found application in the development of the business corporation.[2]

Along with concepts and theories about the corporate institution, as such, there evolved a body of thought and doctrine concerning its internal governance and the nature and extent of the prerogatives and authority of their heads: bishops, canons, abbotts, abbesses,

---

[1] "The Legal, Ideological, and Philosophical Foundations of the Corporate Presidency."

[2] Some of these institutions, such as the "Bishop of Durham," did engage extensively in agricultural, commercial, and industrial undertakings, even mining.

"wardens," "principals," and "presidents."[3] These early administrators, also, had many roles. But the institutions they headed were far simpler than the business corporation of today.

Alfred D. Chandler, Jr., Professor of Business History at the Harvard Business School, tells in his chapter how the office of the business chief executive evolved over the past century in response to the growing and developing management needs of the modern business entity as it was transformed from a proprietorship, or partnership, identified with one or a few owners, into a large, continuing corporation.[4] He tells of how the concept of the corporate presidency evolved in response to the increasing size and complexity and institutional character of the modern corporation. In sum, the "president," or chief executive, was transformed from an autocrat, essentially responsible to no one, into a Chief Executive Officer responsible, at least in theory, to a board of directors and presiding in a collegial fashion over a group of professional peers.

It is with the roles of that kind of chief executive of the modern corporation that we are here concerned.

The Chief Executive Officer, in the minds of most of the authors of the chapters of this book, is the top manager of a "typical" modern business corporation. This implied company is sizeable. It employs hundreds, thousands, or tens of thousands of people. It utilizes millions of dollars worth of assets. It employs thousands, perhaps scores of thousands of dollars worth of physical and financial capital per worker. It brings to bear in its operations what we think of as modern industrial technology. It applies in its workings and management an expanding array of increasingly sophisticated disciplines and techniques based on both "hard" sciences—such as mathematics, physics, chemistry, and biology—in R&D and production, and "soft" sciences —such as economics, psychology, sociology, regional analysis, and demography—in management.[5] The modern corporation is so large that the total management job must be divided among many persons. It is so complex that these people must be capable in many different ways. It is so large *and* so complex that its internal goverance presents

---

[3] The "chief executive" of the Harvard corporation, "The President and Fellows of Harvard College" by name, which was founded in 1636 and is now the oldest corporation in North America, was called "President" from the outset.

[4] See his chapter, "The Office of the Chief Executive in Historical Perspective."

[5] See the chapter by J. D. Glover, "Strategic Decision-Making: Planning, Manning, Organization."

important problems of its own and needs to be institutionalized in formal statements of "policy" and the like.

This corporation, more often than not, is publicly held. Its shares of ownership are traded in stock exchanges and over the counter. It has hundreds or thousands of stockholders. This corporation is governed —at least in theory—by a board of directors and it is run by managers who, altogether, hold at most only a small fraction of its ownership.

The modern corporation, like earlier ecclesiastical organizations, is an *institution*. It has rights, powers, responsibilities, and obligations. It has acquired an identity and a life of its own.

In the United States, there are somewhere around 4,500 to 5,000 such publicly held corporations, and there are about another 10,000 that are privately held. As measured by the value of their assets, they range in size upward from $25 million. Together, these companies hold over $2 trillion of assets out of a total something of the order $2.5 trillion of all corporate assets. They produce somewhere around one half of the Gross National Product.

It is through and because of the workings of these private-sector, publicly held institutions and sizeable privately owned corporations that, for better or worse, the economy and the society of the United States are characteristically different from those of any other country —even other industrial nations. No other industrial community is so deeply characterized by large-scale capital intensivity, modernity of technology, public ownership, and institutionalized governance and management.[6]

---

[6] In addition to publicly held, institutionalized corporations, there are some thousands of sizeable, closely held, mostly "unlisted" corporations in the United States. Aside from their rather private nature, these companies have characteristics similar to those of the large institutionalized corporations that, naturally, have far greater visibility on the American scene.

While thinking about these sizeable companies, public and private, it is useful to remember that well over 90 percent of the number of corporations in the United States —about 1,800,000—have assets valued at less than $500,000; in fact, 56 percent, about 1,000,000 companies, have assets valued at less than $100,000. In many ways, these far more numerous smaller companies are very different from the larger ones that tend to come to mind when one thinks of "American Business."

Typically, these smaller companies are "family" businesses. Apart from their corporate form and clothing, they are in substance not greatly different from proprietorships and partnerships. They are small enough that all significant decisions conceivably can be, and tend to be, made by one man or a group of two or three. Relevant technologies are generally such that the top man or men can master and apply them all.

Among smaller companies, ownership *and* management, at least to a majority position, if not entirely, vest in the same person or persons. For this reason, continuity of ownership and management presents problems not faced by the institutionalized corporation. Publicly held companies, by their very nature—through the *separateness* of ownership and management—have provided for such continuity. For the privately held

It is those basic facts that define, shape, and color the job—the functions, the tasks, and the roles—of the corporate Chief Executive Officer of the modern corporation.

The many specific roles of the chief executive can be thought of as falling into three categories: (1) those having to do with the workings of the corporation as an entity that produces goods or services; (2) those having to do with the relationships of the corporation with the outside world; and (3) those having to do with the internal direction and governance of the people who run the business and make it work.

It is to the first category that we now turn.

THE CEO AS PRODUCER OF VALUES

The socio-ideological rationale of private ownership of productive entities rests upon the ideas, among others, that these entities are more efficient than would be publicly owned means of production and that they respond better to freely expressed desires of the community. Equally important with these economic reasons is the belief that privately owned productive entities, along with individuals and households, are independently viable counterpoises that stand as actual or potential checks against inherently oppressive powers of government. This implies, among other things, that the business corporation will function efficiently and be able to live healthily in competitive marketplaces. It also now implies, I think, that, in a changing environment, the corporation can evolve and change over time and thus survive, so that economic values and opportunities created in the past shall not be wasted and lost, not only to the owners, but to society at large.

There is another element in the rationale of private enterprise that has to do with the role of the CEO, one often taken for granted or, more seriously, overlooked. A prime role of the classic "entrepreneur" —the bourgeois businessman of Adam Smith and the other classic economists—was just that: to undertake projects, to do something

---

company, continuity of ownership and management, in fact continuity of existence as an entity, is provided through inheritance or, if this is not possible or practical, through sale of the company. In fact, many thousands of small corporations are liquidated or sold off every year in consequence of the death or incapacity of owners. Lack of institutionalization can be, and is, a source of management problems, financial problems, tax problems, personal and human problems.

These smaller companies are a species of social organization much different from the "modern" corporation. They are close kin to the private family businesses that one typically still finds today in less industrial countries.

that was not being done; to initiate change, in other words.[7] The businessman was a prime dynamic force in society. He was an agent of change: economic, technological, political, and social change. Early in the Industrial Revolution, this businessman was perceived by the old aristocracy, quite correctly, as a threat to the Established Order. Acting on his own, outside the "Establishment," he mustered resources, allocated and reallocated them, and organized them into a productive entity. He was a pragmatist in an era of doctrine and dogma. As heir, in the 20th century, of the classic businessman, the corporation in ideology and in fact is a productive agent of change. And in this institution there is a corresponding role to be played, that of innovator-in-chief. And that is one of the more important roles of the CEO. We shall return to this point.

The CEO, as the responsible head of the corporation, therefore has an implicit social mandate to see that the economic values intended to be produced by the company are, in fact, generated; that they are produced efficiently through efficient use of the resources available; and that they continue to be so produced over time. In a manner of speaking, an essential role of the corporate CEO, therefore, is that of a *producer*—"chief producer"—in a productive organization whose function it is to produce a stream of economic values. To do so, he has to perform well a role as producer of innovations.

THE CEO AS CHIEF TACTICIAN

First, as to ongoing processes and problems of current production. Under the organizing corporate form, there has been put together by each company a productive apparatus wherewith various kinds of purchased and hired "inputs" are converted into "outputs" for sale. It's a kind of "machine." The whole apparatus is what engineers might call a "conversion system." In a changeless world—what a bizarre idea!—this conversion system, being at least reasonably well designed, could work along all by itself indefinitely.

In fact, in a dynamic world, all kinds of adjustments need constantly to be made. For example, the pace of production has to be speeded up or slowed down. This means, among other things, that

---

[7] The function of the firm as agent of change through innovation was set forth by Joseph A. Schumpeter in his extraordinary work *The Theory of Economic Development*; Cambridge, Mass.: Harvard University Press; 1936 and 1961; and in *Capitalism, Socialism, and Democracy*; New York: Harper and Bros.; 1942.

the work force and inventories have to be expanded or contracted. New sources of inputs—people, materials, or equipment—need to be sought out or become available. Customers become displeased, or want to accelerate or decelerate delivery, or want something different. Competitors cut or raise prices and offer new products and services. New competitors appear. Government agencies issue new regulations that require that something different be done. More or less capital than before is needed for current purposes. All that sort of thing. Minor "seismological shocks" constantly course through the whole organization. Telephones ring; teletypes and typewriters chatter; people come and go. And chatter. When things get hectic enough, there are lots of sweaty palms around.

Just directing the company to respond to current opportunities, contingencies, and exigencies within the basic policy or strategic framework of the company, demands a continuing stream of "tactical" adjustments.

This is the world of day-to-day, of "on-line" perceptions, assessments, and decisions of adjustment. This is where most CEOs and most of their teammates spend most of their time.

In this mode of action, the CEO tends to perform the role of chief tactician. In doing so, he—or she—may draw upon his own demonstrated expertness as an "operator"—as a marketer, or production or financial person; comptroller, house counsel, or whatever it was he was so successful in doing that he moved into upper management and then into the CEO slot. In this mode, he is a "problem solver," figuring out what to do "now." He "knows the territory." He has good ideas as to what is going on and why and what works.

He draws upon something like a merchant's instinct that knows how to respond quickly to vagaries in marketplaces. Or upon something akin to a tinkerer's skill that knows how to keep things going.

THE CEO AS CHIEF STRATEGIST

In its ongoing tactical maneuvers, the corporation necessarily acts within a whole set of limits and constraints. These are created by "strategic" decisions, commitments, and allocations of resources made in the past. These strategic or basic "policy" decisions define—with some room for maneuver—the function of the firm. This function is defined at any one time in terms of the goods and services it produces, for what customers and where; by the scale of its operations;

by the kinds of inputs it uses, including materials, equipment, people, and capital; by where these are obtained, from whom and under what conditions; by its productive apparatus.

In a concrete sense, such matters as these define *what* the company *is* as of any moment of time. They set limits and constraints, more or less flexible, as to what can be done by way of short-run tactical maneuver.

As time goes on and the world changes, any or all of these aspects of the business become less and less well suited to external realities: changing customer wants; technological change; changes in the money markets; changes in government regulation; depletion of resources; changes in labor markets and demands; new sources and forms of competition; and so on. The company, or at least some aspects of it, come to need redefinition, sometimes in a major way. A new strategy is needed. Generally, for the kinds of companies we are talking about in this book, managements have to work against pretty long time-horizons. For instance, one petroleum company has a 15-year plan according to which it will not only grow, but will shift its emphasis from 12 percent petrochemicals to 50 percent. A diversified company has been following for some years already a strategy of phasing out of nonferrous metals and expanding and broadening its other quite different lines of business.

In the reevaluation and reformulation of company strategy, the CEO plays the role of chief strategist. This topic of corporate strategy and the CEO is developed elsewhere in this book.[8] Accordingly, just a few comments will do for now.

The making of strategy calls for very different skills, perspectives, and sensitivities from the making of tactics. It calls increasingly for appreciation of the possible contributions of social sciences useful in detecting, measuring, and forecasting changing externalities. Successful dynamic strategy-making is greatly helped by a capacity for cool detachment and for seeing above and beyond the changes and pressures of the day. It requires an imaginative aptitude for foreseeing future states of affairs that are coming about. It calls for a knack in seeing the opportunities in that future and how to take advantage of them. It demands a creative capacity for designing specific, quan-

---

[8] See the chapter by Marvin Bower, "The Chief Executive as Chief Strategist"; and that by Alexander Calder, "Strategy and Planning: Some Personal Observations of a Chief Executive."

tified, and time-phased plans for doing what needs to be done to meet those opportunities. Carried out, these plans will determine the limits and constraints, in fact, the very nature of the tactical maneuvers available to the company as options in the future.

At some risk of oversimplification, one can say that the role of tactician calls for a *doer*. The role of strategist calls for a *visionary*. He gets ready for what will be and what *can* be.

THE CHIEF EXECUTIVE AS LEGATE

As "legate" of the corporation, the Chief Executive Officer is deputed to represent and to speak and act for the corporation as he goes about his many functions. He is armed with the great authority vested in the corporation as an institution and, through it, in him, by law, by the corporate bylaws, votes of the board of directors, and by custom in the community at large and within the individual corporation. In this role, the CEO is a sort of full-time plenipotentiary at large.[9]

To the outside world, the chief executive is the personification of the corporation. If anyone goes looking for "the corporation," he will not find it in the corporate charter or bylaws; nor in bricks and mortar. Actually, he won't find "it" anywhere. But he can find the CEO. The corporation's CEO, by the very nature of the position, is the apparent embodiment of the "company." If someone wants to talk to the company, that's the CEO. If the "company" is to talk back, that's the CEO.

A "legate," in the sense that we are using the word, is the spokesman *of* the corporation. But it means much more: it also means spokesman *for* the corporation. But it means still more, yet. The CEO, as legate, *stands for* the corporation. Formally, morally, psychologically, and otherwise, he can, he does, commit the corporation. He forms the "image" of the corporation in the minds of outside parties.

It's no wonder that some CEOs—especially if they need ego-buildup, or if they have been around too long—come to think they *are* the corporation. No. They're not. Just its *legate*.

To what outside parties is the CEO the company's legate? Well, to stockholders. To the financial community: commercial and invest-

---

[9] See "Legate," *The Oxford English Dictionary; The Compact Edition;* vol. 1, page 1,599.

ment bankers, brokerage houses, pension funds, security analysts.[10] To customers, certainly important ones. To members of Congress; to state governors and legislators; to mayors and other city officials. To cabinet members. To important people in regulatory commissions.[11] To suppliers, distributors, union leaders. To important personages of governments in foreign countries where the company is, or wants to be, active. To CEOs of other companies which may be or are involved in merger discussions. Those are a few of the parties.

The CEO as "Salesman" and "Advocate"

In his general capacity as legate, the CEO has several particular roles to fill. In some situations, as in making a speech before an important audience, he is an advocate. Before a consumer group he will be, intentionally or otherwise, a "salesman" trying to "sell" the company, its interests, point of view, products or services. Before an industry group he will be trying to sell a point of view, a program. He may appear in the role of petitioner before a legislative committee to urge legislation, or before a government department to urge the adoption of a new ruling or the modification of an old one.

In some situations, the CEO may be called—even subpoenaed—to appear as a defender of a corporate act, or as a witness to answer questions. In a cordial inquiry, he may act as an educator, providing information and ideas sincerely sought by lawmakers or government administrators.

The CEO as Negotiator

In other situations, the CEO appears in the role of negotiator. This he does in working out terms of loans with bankers; provisions of important contracts with important suppliers; franchise agreements with distributors; license agreements.

The CEO as "Receptor"

In working with outside parties, the CEO has many opportunities to act as a receiver of information. For some purposes and for some

---

[10] See the chapter by Jesse Philips, "What to Expect from Your Bankers."

[11] See the chapter by Jayne Baker Spain, "The Chief Executive and Government Relations at the National Level"; and that by Roy M. Goodman, "The CEO and State and Local Governments."

people, he is the only one they want to talk with. They are people, perhaps important, with something to say that they want to get through. Here, he is a *listener*—not only to what is said, but how it is said; and he listens especially hard for what is not said.

In many instances, the CEO is the receiver of petitions. It may be a request for support from some nonprofit organization. An individual —a customer, for instance—who feels aggrieved may carry a plea for redress to the very top of the organization. It may be an important government official asking that the company follow a certain action felt to be in the public interest or, for a similar reason, to forebear doing something within the company's rights.

In contrast to receiving petitions and such, CEOs have been known to find themselves in the role of receiving criticism—sometimes harsh —for actions of the company. Every president of the United States from Franklin Roosevelt to Gerald Ford has lectured and jawboned chief executives of corporations—mostly large ones, but small ones, too. Some of these "receiving" sessions have been memorable, it appears.

The CEO as Manager of External Relations

A sizeable company has a slew of relationships with outside parties. As legate, the CEO has overall responsibility for the handling of these relationships. Every day, many interactions take place. The CEO can't handle everything himself. He must organize and delegate the management and handling of much of this work. The kinds of people he selects, the guidelines he sets for them, in addition to what he does himself—these things will determine what kind of external relationship and "image" the company has. This is not just a "public relations" matter, to be passed off.[12] The way these relationships are handled may make or break the CEO, himself, if not the corporation.

THE CHIEF EXECUTIVE AS "CHIEFTAIN"

If the corporation is to function at all, it has to be through people, of course. People do the work, make decisions. In fact, it is not uncommon to think that these people collectively, or at least some of

---

[12] See the chapter by Jack Valenti, "What Is Public Relations?"; that by John J. O'Connell, "What the CEO Needs to Know about Labor Relations"; and that by John P. Fishwick, "The CEO and the Media."

them—say the "bosses"—*are* the company. One hears of such-and-such a company referred to as "The folks who bring you _____." In a legal sense that's incorrect, of course. But in a practical sense, there is something to such an idea.

Because there are people working together; because they perform jobs that are interrelated; because they fill roles and fit into a system of mutual and reciprocal expectations; because they become interdependent in working relationships on the job; because of such things, these people become more than just so many individuals. They develop, and become members of a *social system*.

This social system has many aspects and attributes. Here are just a few of them: The individuals included develop certain more or less clearly recognized rights and obligations as regards others and the group as a whole. They perform expected roles, and these relate to the roles of others in more or less clearly recognized ways. Some of these roles have to do with the jobs and tasks to be done. The individuals also relate to others as persons and, accordingly, some of the roles have to do with filling human needs and requirements of people as individuals. There is a decision-making structure into which various individuals fit in particular ways. There is a communication network. There is a more or less clearly recognized pattern of succession whereby, when individuals move out or up, their previous roles are filled by others. There are shared values and points of view. There is a collective sense of "right" and "wrong." The group takes care of its own. It parcels out rewards for jobs well done and for service to the group. It punishes transgressions against "the system": failure to do assigned tasks to standard, to fulfill obligations, to uphold shared values.

In short, these people in their membership and behavior in the group constitute something of a tribe or a clan. And the CEO is its chieftain.

THE CEO AS "CHIEF MAGISTRATE"

In many organizations, much of all this is unwritten. People "just know" what it's all about. This is the "informal organization."[13] It is very real; very powerful. But, increasingly, over the last couple of decades, many aspects and attributes of the social system are being set

---

[13] See Roethlisberger, Fritz J., and Dickson, William R.; *Management and Worker*; Cambridge, Mass.: Harvard University Press; 1939; chapters 23 and 24.

down in labor contracts; in policy manuals; in standard operating procedures; in organization charts; in directives; and such. The social system comes to be less based on an internal tradition and a sort of "common law." The organization becomes, instead, more formal, more codified, more explicit, more self-aware, more deliberate. And impersonal. The social system, the informal organization is given formal content and structure. In a manner of speaking, it gets "legitimized."

In the process, the social system—the whole organization—comes to resemble more a "republic" than a clan. And as it does, the CEO becomes less its "Chieftain" and more its "Chief Magistrate."

In many corporations, the social system is in transition. For some matters, it still acts like a tribe; in others, more like a republic. In some instances, there is fumbling uncertainty between the old and passing and the new and emergent.

Chieftain or magistrate, the CEO has many particular roles to fill in the internal governance of the organization. Let's mention just a few. None is more important than the dispensing of "justice" and equity, as these matters are perceived and defined in the particular organization. It is the CEO, as final arbiter, who sees to it that individuals get what is coming to them: rewards; discipline; compassion; assignment; promotion; transfer; termination.

As the CEO is the personification of the corporation to the external world, so is he the apparent embodiment of the organization—in both its formal and informal aspects—to those who are part of its own social system.

As chieftain, the CEO is expected to maintain and defend—to strengthen—all of those aspects and attributes of the informal organization: its sense of identity and worth; its system of expectations of loyalty and obligation; its shared values, norms, and beliefs. Such things. Like kings of old—who were chieftains of nations—he is expected to be, for the group, its "defender of the faith." For the formal organization, as president or principal magistrate, he is expected to defend and uphold its "laws" and "constitution." He demonstrates this at dedications of new buildings, annual stockholders' meetings, banquets for retiring oldsters, and other such "tribal" or "civic" ceremonies.

Far more important, he discharges this role of magistrate many times a week as he does his job. And in so doing, he affirms, reinforces, builds, modifies, the social system. If he is insensitive, inept, clumsy but powerful, he may undermine or even destroy the social system; if he is weak, he may be toppled and ejected by the system as it acts to protect itself. The CEO is, or ought to be, its chief designer and builder. He establishes a hierarchy of authority and power. He selects his lieutenants. He sets performance standards. Formally, as through organization charts and policy and procedures manuals and informally, through day-to-day patterns of behavior, interaction, and communication, he molds the organization. His actions, more than his words, express values and he dispenses rewards and discipline. He has final say-so as to who will do what and with what resources, including people.

Some chieftains, chief magistrates, some heads of state, and some Chief Executive Officers of corporations have been known to betray their trust.

If the CEO wants to know more about his role as chieftain, he can read in the literature of anthropology. If he wants to know more about his role as chief magistrate, he can read in the literature of politics and government.

THE CEO AS TECHNOCRAT

Whether a master member of a medieval merchant or craft guild, a merchant adventurer of the 16th century, an entrepreneur of the 18th, a bourgeois or middle-class businessman of the 19th, or a CEO of a modern corporation, the chief executive has always had to *know* at least something, if not many things, better than those who worked for or with him. But *what* they knew or know, how they learned or learn it, and how they applied or apply this knowledge have evolved in very significant ways. And in the course of this evolution, an important role of the chief executive has also evolved. It was and has been one of his roles to *know* things; and this knowledge has been and is an important part of his claim to authority.

I suppose if one went back far enough, say back to the workshop of a member of a medieval guild, one would find that the master of the establishment knew literally everything that had to be known about the business: its technology, economics, procurement, selling, and all the rest. Through long years of apprenticeship on the job followed by years as a journeyman for hire, the master came to know the whole of what was needed to be known. He learned it on the job through observation, through being taught, by thinking about what he was doing, and, especially, by doing. He was a store of knowledge and the master of skills. In this, he was not different from the independent businessman of later centuries. Even up to the present, many able business people have developed their knowledge in this way.

When the scale and complexity of business developed rapidly and enormously, around the turn of the 20th century, more knowledge came to be needed to run the enterprise than any one person could command. People began to concentrate their efforts on particular aspects of the business. Specialized knowledge, and people who applied it, appeared. And a very important innovation emerged: schools in which people could learn some of this knowledge and develop some of the special skills now needed. The day of the chief executive who knew everything was passing.

After World War I, young men went back into business, having learned something about organization structures and procedures in the course of their military experience. Organization charts, job descriptions, manuals of procedures began to appear in corporate management. Separate *functions* came to be widely recognized, such as production, marketing, control, finance. Significantly, and in response to the needs of the times, the curriculum of business schools as at Harvard, began, in the early 1920s, to be built around those *functions* rather than, as they were before that war, around industries. It was scarcely possible, any more, to learn everything that was needed to run a company in its industry; it was difficult enough to get on top of one function.

As managers of the older generation died away, their places typically were taken by people who had spent most of their careers in one particular function. Again, typically, this was the function that the old CEO or his directors regarded as *key* to the success of the business. More often than not, this meant the selling or marketing end of the business. But in some industries, utilities and railroads for example, this often meant the financial end.

After World War II—and this still happens—some new types of CEOs appeared. In some instances, the second or third generation of directors judged that a particular kind of skill had come to be required at the top different from those just needed in running or even building the business. In this way, lawyers were sometimes tapped because of the real or felt need for people to be at the very apex of the management who had that background and who could cope with antitrust problems, for example, and problems of working with regulatory agencies. Accountants were sometimes put in at the top to oversee the development of control systems for companies that had grown rather like Topsy, to the discomfort of auditors, directors, and investment bankers. In certain cases, finance people were put up or brought in because of a sensed need for someone at the top who could deal with new and urgent money problems. In some instances, scientific and engineering people were put in top slots because of a sensed need for mastery of relevant new technology in the top slot.

These CEOs, it is fair to say, were specialists. Superspecialists, in many cases; but specialists nonetheless. Extremely talented in their particular way, many of these CEOs did not well understand and could not discharge with great effectiveness the several unique roles of the Chief Executive Officer. The roles involved in running large, complex institutions came to call more and more for aptitudes and skills of their own, different from both functional and special skills.

THE MULTIPLE-PERSON "OFFICE" OF THE CEO

Recognition by directors and corporate officers that the demands of the job of the CEO of the modern corporation call for something more than expertise in a particular field frequently has led to the use of the device of a multiple-person office of the chief executive.[14] The people who fill this office almost invariably have different backgrounds and strengths; thus, it is felt, they complement each other. Members of such a "team" often adhere to a clear division of involvement and authority along lines of their special competences. This "office" device, it would seem, represents an effort to compensate for a recognized inadequacy, in dealing with the several roles the CEO has to fill, of the specialized strengths of persons who have spent a lifetime each dealing with a particular category of problems.

Aside from such a rationale, I suspect that some of these multiple-person arrangements have represented political compromises or "stand-offs" in situations where no one person was able to achieve a clear mandate from those who shared power. This "collegial" sort of leadership seems to be a necessary step in management succession in the Kremlin. Eventually, one of that group emerges as *the* "CEO"; through what processes of accommodation or intrigue one can only

---

[14] See the chapter by J. David Wright, "The Team Concept for the Chief Executive Office."

speculate. So in business corporations having collegial, committee-type leadership, I would guess, one person, in time, tends to move to the fore, overshadowing the others, some or all of whom may move out.

There is no apparent standard number of persons in the multiple-person *office* of the chief executive. In a recent case, it was reported that a group of *five* had been named to such an "office." I suspect this is unusual. A "troika" of three sometimes appears. A more common number may be two.

The *troika* or *duo* arrangement has often been noted by students of management, and has sometimes been called a "constellation." It is more than coincidence that the two-man group that once headed a large and prominent multinational was known both inside and outside the company as "The Heavenly Twins." Which of these Gemini was Castor and which was Pollux, I do not know.

Duos as CEO

Often the relationship and division of labor of such duos have fallen into one of two patterns. Frequently, one person has been "Mr. Outside"; and the other, of course, "Mr. Inside." Mr. Outside handled government relations; relations with institutions in the money markets, large customers and large suppliers; industry and trade associations. Often he was the chief strategist. Mr. Inside handled internal operations, budgets, organization, and personnel. He was often the chief tactician. Mr. Outside seems to have been usually, but not always, *the* head man when it came to a choice of ultimate authority.

Another pattern, which some have observed—perhaps with psychoanalytic perception—was for one of a duo to assume a "father-figure" role in the informal organization, the other being a "mother-figure." *Father* "laid down the law"; demanded performance and results; tried to maintain "standards" in the face of human inclinations to ease up. *Mother* dispensed rewards, consolation, and sympathy; interceded, and generally tempered the fatherly but chill wind as it blew upon the shorn lambs. I suspect that "father" was usually Number One, but I know of at least two cases where "mother" was.

It is my hunch that multiple-person devices are interim arrangements, making do in a period of transition from one stage to the next in the evolution of management technology. Time will tell.

THE GENERALIST CEO

In recent years, we have seen the emergence of a new type of CEO. He is the generalist-manager or generalist-administrator. He may, and often does have an outstanding track record in some particular function of the business. But that was not the decisive reason for his being chosen as chief executive. He was chosen for his ability, real or supposed, for running a large, complex enterprise. This ability includes organization building, selection and evaluation of people; working with directors and through committees. He is skillful at getting people to work together. He grasps the nascent technology of how to be an effective Chief Magistrate. He does, or is presumed to know how to work with outside groups and persons—regulators, the press, money-market people, representatives of foreign governments, important customers and suppliers. He knows how to be the *Legate* of the corporation. He understands management information systems; and how to control operations through line-item, functional, program, or divisional budgets, and how to analyze and appraise performance. He knows how to *get* productive performance. He knows a great deal about the growing art of strategy formulation. Preferably, he has something of the visionary about him. He knows that analysis of the changing environment requires its own disciplines, just as planning for the future, using such disciplines, now needs its own skills also. He knows how to get these disciplines and skills applied. In short, he is a master of the technology of general management in a large, complex organization. He really is a *technocrat* in the sense that his technology is *management*. That's his specialty. That's what he knows. He may or may not know much about the technology of production, or of research, or of selling, or how to design a control system. But he knows how to work with people and groups who do.

Coming along behind him are younger people who are growing up in this new tradition. They have rotated in assignments among the several functions of the business and among its several, often unlike divisions. They have attended executive development programs produced in-house, given by industry groups—such as the Conference Board and the American Management Associations—and by universities and business schools. They are active in business groups. They keep up with management literature. Many will have read books like this one. They are the managers of the future—true professionals.

In the meantime, an increasing number of Chief Executive Officers of important corporations merit the label of *Chief* Technocrat. This mantle fits very well indeed upon the shoulders of some of the distinguished executives who have contributed chapters to this volume.

The role of the Chief Technocrat is to exercise the ultimate executive authority and to assume the ultimate executive responsibility for the management of the corporation. He sees that it operates well in the here and now. He sees that strategy and its implementing plans are developed appropriately for the future. He sees that appropriate subdivisions of modern management technology are applied all through the organization. And that his future successors—if not actually in sight, as preferably they would be—are at least in the process of development.

As we said. The modern Chief Executive Officer is a Protean being. A man—or woman—for all seasons.

THE LEGAL, IDEOLOGICAL, AND PHILOSOPHICAL FOUNDATIONS OF THE CORPORATE PRESIDENCY

by John T. Connor[1]

Chairman of the Board, Allied Chemical Corporation

EVOLUTION OF THE OFFICE OF THE PRESIDENCY

THE WORD "president" comes from the same Latin roots as does "preside": *prae* and *sedēre*, together meaning literally "to sit in front of," as a president does before the body over which he presides. The use of the same word to denote one who heads a corporation and one who presides over a legislative assembly is perhaps an accident of history, but, as I shall discuss later, it is coming to acquire a rationale that brings full cycle the role of corporate president.

We tend to think of our social structures as the product of a natural evolution in which what works best has survived: Armies are commanded by generals and corporations are headed by presidents because otherwise they could not survive. The need for a single source of power and responsibility in a corporation is not, however, as universally recognized as might be thought. In Japan and Sweden, for example, it is not uncommon for top management power and responsibility formally to reside in a committee rather than an individual, and it seems to work well. Nevertheless, I do not intend to cover in this chapter any form of business leadership other than the presidency as it exists in the United States.

The foundations of present-day corporation law, as of other areas, developed only in response to need. By far the most important social unit of the Middle Ages was that built around the feudal lord.

---

[1] The author accepts full responsibility for the philosophy expressed and experiences cited, but this chapter would not have been possible without the many contributions of his associate, Christian O. Basler.

England at that time was engaged almost exclusively in farming and fighting, and the lord served well as the basis of both. Groups of men associated for some other purpose and having no lord as the source and embodiment of group unity were then rare, and the common law began its evolution without much notice of them. By the time they surpassed feudal structures in importance, they were woven into the English legal tapestry without so much as a loose thread to show the agony of the weavers.

The earliest groups to be taken account of by the law were religious groups, towns, and, somewhat later, guilds. The problems they presented had to do basically with the application to them of law formulated in terms of individuals who could be identified, touched, served, killed, or what have you. There was thus an inherent legal as well as practical need for presidents or similar officers through whom they could act or be acted upon. Such problems as how to serve process on, or how to give property rights to a corporation find their solutions in centuries of experience and scholarship.

Early royal charters or grants to cities or towns, paralleling grants made to individuals, were made *habendum* to the townsmen and their heirs, and later to the townsmen, their heirs and successors, by the king and his heirs. Thus was recognition given to the perpetual identity of a city as an entity, though the identity of its mortal inhabitants would change. By the time of Henry VI's Charter to Southampton in 1445, the grant included language to the effect that the town "shall be forever incorporate," and "shall be one perpetual community incorporate in word and deed."[2]

Long before there were king's courts, the canon lawyers had definite theories about the legal nature of churches, abbeys, and other religious groups. The unity and perpetuity of these groups was recognized early by canon law, but the king's judges were reluctant to adopt the theories. Perhaps the greatest contribution of canon law was the principle of personification, both of an organization and of the jobs within it, such as the office of bishop. With this concept, one could think of the office as a separate entity—apart from the person who held the office at a particular moment. It may be taken for granted today, but it was a difficult bit of conceptualization at the time. With it, we are able to formulate rules for dealing with an or-

---

[2] "Charters of the Borough of Southampton," vol. 1; pp. 55–57; reprinted in Smith, Joseph H., *Development of Legal Institutions;* 1965; pp. 629–30.

ganization through its officers even though identity of the individual holders of office is constantly changing.

The canonists in turn had derived the germ of the personification theory from Roman law. Roman law was divided into the *ius publicum*, public law, and the *ius privatum*, private law. Public law dealt with the Roman State and the institutions of which it was constituted. Private law dealt with relationships between individuals. Under public law, associations of persons were treated as units while under private law they were at first reduced to the rights and duties of the majority of their subjects. An individual under private law was thought of as a "person" (*persona*), a concept which focused on the exercise of the powers of individual will. As Roman law developed, a public law unit came to be placed in a series of relationships with individuals under private law (principally in the field of property law), which later would be called "juristic persons." It was also basic to Roman public law that an association needed state authorization; i.e., it could only be received into the *ius publicum* as a unified *corpus* by virtue of a legislative act.

The canonists were the first to apply the name of "person" to the unitary legal subject. In addition to Roman law, they had the early Christian traditions of conceiving of the church as wife, betrothed, or mother, and the theological or legal distinctions between the concepts "person" and "man." It was a relatively easy step from thinking of the church as a person to thinking of all corporations as such.

The absorption of these Roman and Canon law concepts into the English common law was probably the inevitable result of the early contact between clerics and the king's judges, but it may have been hastened by the policy begun by Edward I (1239–1307) of increasing the king's power over the rights of associations. By the time of Edward III (1312–1377) this had resulted in changes in the form of franchises granted to reflect the notion that the association was a *corpus*, which, under Roman law, only the state could create. The language described above in Henry VI's Charter to Southampton in 1445 was the result. The absorption was subtle and gradual, and it is difficult to discern because the common-law judges liked to preserve the appearance that their decisions were grounded in native soil.

Early English law on corporations had nothing to do with commercial institutions or, for that matter, with institutions that would today even be thought of as corporations. Single persons having perpetual succession and the capacity of suing and being sued in their political capacity were called "corporations sole," such as the king, archbishops and bishops, and certain deans. "Corporations aggregate," consisting of more than one person, were further divided into corporations aggregate of many persons capable, and corporations aggregate of one person capable and the rest incapable or dead in law. A master and fellows of a college were examples of the former; an abbot and monks of an abbey were examples of the latter. Those of the former sued and were sued in their aggregate name, but the abbot alone sued and was sued in the right of his house.

Many aggregate corporations were composed of several distinct parts thought of as integral parts without which the corporation would be incomplete and incapable of action. An example of this would be a mayor and aldermen, neither of whom could act without the other. In most aggregate corporations, there was one particular person, called the "head," who formed one of its integral parts, such as the chancellor of a university or the master of a college. This led to the general rule of law that

> (W)here a corporation aggregate has, by its constitution, a head, a grant to that corporation in the vacancy of the headship is void . . . and the reason is, that without the head the corporation is incomplete, and the only act it can do, during the vacancy, is to elect another.[3]

This bit of law was fortunately not carried over into the modern corporation law applicable to the function of presidents.

The first commercial corporations were little more than groups of traders seeking protection or extraordinary powers under a corporate charter. Such were the Levant and Muskovy companies of the late 16th and 17th centuries. Under their charters, they had monopolies on the trade with their respective areas and rights to exercise quasi-governmental power in their pursuit. Joint stock companies, the most famous of which were the East India Companies, differed little from these earlier trading companies except in their method of raising capital. The language of the first East India Company's charter, granted by Elizabeth I in 1600, gives some idea of the organization. The grant provided that George, Earl of Sunderland, and 215 others,

> ". . . from henceforth be one body corporate and politic . . . by the name of the 'Governor and Company of Merchants of London, trading into the East Indies,' " have corporate succession with power

---

[3] Kyd, Stewart; *Treatise on the Law of Corporations*; 1793; p. 106; citing 13 Ed. 4 8

to admit and expel members, be capable of receiving, holding and granting property, sue and be sued in the corporate name and use a common seal. "The direction of the voyages, . . . the provisions of the shipping and merchandise thereto belonging, . . . the sale of all merchandise returned in the voyages, . . . and the managing and handling of all other things belonging to the company" were reposed in a governor, deputy governor and twenty-four committees (directors) elected annually by the members of the Company. . . .[4]

Early American colonial corporations were of the same noncommercial types then found in England, with the exception that the colonies themselves were corporations. As in England, the unincorporated association was the prevalent form taken by business enterprises. The corporate device was used all through the 18th century, however, for numerous large-scale "public service" enterprises, such as construction of canals.

The earliest general incorporation laws for commercial enterprises were passed around 1800, before which time a special legislative act was required to create a corporation. The organization of each corporation would thus depend upon the specific provisions of the act. New York enacted a general incorporation law for manufacturing companies in 1811 which provided that the concerns of the company incorporated be managed by trustees elected by the stockholders. Further details of management organization were left to the trustees:

(T)he trustees of such company . . . shall have power to make and prescribe such bylaws, rules and regulations as they shall deem proper respecting the management and disposition of the stock, property and estate of such company, the duties of the officers, artificers and servants by them to be employed, the election of trustees, and all such matters as appertain to the concerns of said company, to appoint such and so many officers, clerks and servants for carrying on the business of said company, and with such wages as to them shall seem reasonable. . . .[5]

PRESENT LAW

Modern corporation laws generally follow the common-law pattern in regard to the role of the president, usually containing only requirements as to the manner of his election. Most states require that offi-

---

[4] Davis, John P.; *Corporations*; vol. 2; 1905; p. 115; quoting from *Court Records of East India Company*.

[5] *Laws of New York*; 34th Session; 1811; ch. 67; section 6.

cers be elected by the board of directors, but several, including New York, New Jersey, and Delaware, permit election by the stockholders. The trend has been away from stockholder election, but the New York provision permitting it was added only recently in order to give more flexibility to closely held corporations.[6] Most states require corporations to have certain specified officers, but there may be a trend in the other direction. Delaware amended its law in 1970 to permit corporations to have officers as stated in the bylaws, though a proviso requires that it have either a president or a vice president and other officers to sign stock certificates.[7] In states requiring a president, such other officers as provided in the bylaws are generally permitted.[8] In such states it is thus possible to have an officer with the title "president" who is in fact not the Chief Executive Officer, in which case the Chief Executive Officer will usually be the chairman of the board. I shall continue to use the term "president" as synonymous with "Chief Executive Officer" for purposes of this chapter, even though "chairman of the board" is increasingly being recognized as such.

No state general corporation law attempts to spell out the powers of the president. Under statute law, he theoretically has only such power as is provided in the bylaws or by the board of directors. There are two lines of cases growing out of situations in which a president has exceeded such authority, in which the corporation is held to be bound or not bound by his acts. In 1891 a New Hampshire court stated what is known as the strict rule as follows:

> (T)he president has no implied authority, as such, to act as the agent of the corporation, but, like other agents, he must derive his power from the board of directors, or from the corporation.[9]

The other line of cases is illustrated by a New York case of the same period:

> (T)he president or other general officer of a corporation has power, prima facie, to do any act which the directors could authorize or ratify.[10]

This power is sometimes called "inherent," sometimes "apparent," depending upon the reasoning used to justify it, but its effect is to

---

[6] *New York Business Corporation Law* §715 (b).

[7] *Delaware General Corporation Law* §142.

[8] See, e.g.; *New York Business Corp. Law* §715 (a).

[9] *Wait v. Nashua Armory Ass'n.*, 23 Atl. 77, 78 (N.H. 1891).

[10] *Hastings v. Brooklyn Life Insurance Co.*, 138 N.Y. 473 (1893).

bind a corporation in relation to an outsider who believed the president to have the necessary authority. This rule is sometimes limited to acts of the president done in the ordinary course of business, but this factor would in any case be relevant to what an outsider could reasonably believe to be the president's power. The law books are full of cases on this point, and indeed most of what is said there about the powers of a president is based on these decisions, but they are not instructive for any but the limited use dictated by their peculiar fact situations. In describing what should be, or what generally are the powers of a president, we must look to other than legal sources.

The ultimate source of power in a stock corporation resides in the stockholders, and though they are theoretically capable of acting directly in the management of its affairs, the use of a board of directors or some other form of governing body has been, and is, almost universal. Because of the concept of the corporation as a unified entity, the directors are thought of as agents not of the stockholders but (if at all) of the corporation. Considered as agents, they are often said to be subject to the old legal maxim, *delegatus non potest delegare*, i.e., a trust delegated by a principal to his agent cannot be subdelegated, particularly where the exercise of discretion is involved. When courts follow this reasoning, however, it is softened by the addition of an exception for principals that are not natural persons capable of acting for themselves, in which case power to subdelegate is to some extent implied. Further, the doctrine that an agent cannot delegate his powers does not apply where he is expressly authorized to do so.

Most state corporation laws expressly provide that the business of a corporation shall be managed by its board of directors,[11] but they also provide that they may delegate power to officers. New York law provides in this respect as follows:

> All officers as between themselves and the corporation shall have such authority and perform such duties in the management of the corporation as may be provided in the bylaws or, to the extent not so provided, by the board.[12]

There does not appear to be any limit in the statute on the board's power to delegate to officers, but in fact a limit is implied by the more

---

[11] *New York Business Corp. Law*; e.g., §701. (This section also permits certain other arrangements for management of close corporations if set forth in the certificate of incorporation.)

[12] *New York Business Corp. Law*; §715 (g).

basic provision that the board of directors shall manage the business. It is well established in case law that the board cannot delegate *all* of its power to the president, but any more precise delineation is difficult to make. The cases generally arise out of actions to enforce a contract in situations involving excessive delegation, or out of actions by creditors or stockholders against directors for failure adequately to supervise the president. As with the cases on inherent or apparent authority of a president, they are not a sound basis for considering what in fact is, or would be a good division of power.

Complementing the law's recognition of the realities of the distribution of power between the president and the directors is its imposition of liability for failure properly to exercise such power. With respect to liability to stockholders and creditors, both directors and officers are in most jurisdictions held to a standard of ordinary care and diligence; but what amounts to ordinary care or a lack of it depends upon the facts of the particular case, especially upon the degree of authority actually exercised by an officer.[13] The standard applicable to directors reflects the rule that they cannot relinquish all control to the president. The president is naturally held to a very high standard, but very seldom is he held liable in the absence of bad faith or breach of trust.

Recent Securities Act cases, such as the celebrated *BarChris* case,[14] illustrate the law's different treatment of the president and directors. In *BarChris*, officers and directors were sued for misstatements and omissions in a prospectus. In these cases, the exercise of "due diligence" is a defense, and what constitutes due diligence varies with the responsibility of the position held by the particular defendant. The court summed up the president's status as follows:

> In short, Russo knew all the relevant facts. He could not have believed that there were no untrue statements or material omissions in the prospectus. Russo has no due diligence defenses.[15]

Personal criminal liability is rarely imposed on corporation presidents for corporate acts in which they took no direct part. The standard applied to determine personal liability in antitrust cases, for example, is whether the corporate officer "knowingly participates in

---

[13] See 3 Fletcher; Cyc. Corp. (Perm. ed. 1965) §§1035–1038; and *New York Business Corp. Law* §717.

[14] *Escott* v. *BarChris Constr. Corp.*, 283 F. Supp. 643 (S.D.N.Y. 1968).

[15] 283 F. Supp. at 684.

effecting the illegal contract, combination, or conspiracy—be he one who authorizes, orders or helps perpetrate the crime—regardless of whether he is acting in a representative capacity."[16] There is occasionally a public outcry for more criminal liability at the top of corporations in areas like pollution control and health, even absent personal involvement, but there is no indication that the law will take such a turn.

EVOLUTION OF THE PRESIDENCY: PROFESSIONALIZATION OF MANAGEMENT

The evolution of the role of a corporation's chief executive has come almost full circle. In the early corporations, the abbots of monasteries or the headships of colleges were in a position of first among equals. Their function was to a large extent to *preside* over their brethren in the literal sense of the word. Had they existed in isolation, they might have managed without any individualized leadership, but with rough feudal lords for neighbors, they needed an effective way to interact with the world on its own terms. When the corporate form was adopted by the early trading companies, they naturally had need for a more formidable chief executive. The "governor" of the first East India Company indeed governed more than he presided. This was entirely appropriate for a corporation that literally waged war to win new business, and George, Earl of Sunderland, its first governor, would have settled for no less, whatever legal form the company had taken.

Before this century, businesses were almost always run directly by their owners. Corporations were different only in that they tended to be bigger. Given the complete freedom of action afforded by ownership, a corporation president tended to make his corporation an extension of his personality. In the economic atmosphere that prevailed, it was the rugged hard-driving individualist who made his corporation grow. They were at heart entrepreneurs and swashbucklers, admired by the public as "captains of industry." If one came to dominate in his industry, he was likely to have deserved the title of "robber baron."

Though the captains of industry were ideally suited to the early growth of our modern corporations, they fared no better than dino-

---

[16] *U.S.* v. *Wise,* 370 U.S. 405, 416 (1960).

saurs would have if they had lived to survive their era. The decline of the Ford Motor Company and of Montgomery Ward in the 30s dramatically illustrated that the captains-of-industry era was past. With few exceptions, large mature corporations were simply not susceptible to the autocratic rule that had nurtured them through adolescence. Their size and complexity have brought them well past the point of single-handed manageability.

The professionalization of management has been the inevitable outcome of this increase in size and complexity. As John Kenneth Galbraith described it in *The New Industrial State,*

> Technology, with its own dynamic, later added its demands for capi-
> tal and for specialized talent with need for more comprehensive plan-
> ning. Thus what the entrepreneur created passed inexorably beyond
> the scope of his authority. He could build. And he could exert in-
> fluence for a time. But his creation, were it to serve the purposes for
> which it was brought into being, required his replacement. What the
> entrepreneur created, only a group of men sharing specialized infor-
> mation could ultimately operate.[17]

Galbraith called the group of men sharing this specialized informa-
tion the "technostructure." A corporation president is a part of, as well as above the technostructure. As Galbraith describes it, and as it in fact is, much responsibility is of necessity delegated downward. Even high-level problems and long-range planning are handled by committees of the technostructure.*

PRESIDENTIAL "CONTROL" AND MANAGEMENT SUCCESSION

The separation of management from ownership has been the sub-
ject of much legal and philosophical discourse since the study of Adolf Berle and Gardiner Means showed that, in 1930, 44 percent of the 200 largest nonfinancial corporations (58 percent, as measured by corporate wealth) were effectively controlled by their management.[18] In a later development of this basic thesis, Berle refers to management

---

[17] Galbraith, John Kenneth; *The New Industrial State*; Boston: Houghton Mifflin Company; 1967; pp. 100–101.

* [Ed. Note: See also the chapter by Alfred D. Chandler, "The Chief Executive's Office in Historical Perspective."]

[18] Berle, Adolf A., Jr., and Means, Gardiner C.; *The Modern Corporation and Private Property*; New York: The Macmillan Company; 1934; p. 94.

has having become "an automatic self-perpetuating oligarchy."[19] Berle and Means were not, and are not alone in holding such views.

In short, there are those who tend to see the "modern" corporate chief executive as head man of a small group who, although owning only a negligible amount of the assets (even of the equity of the corporation), actually control it. Not only do they control at the moment, they control also, in an ongoing way indefinitely into the future, the very processes by which the controlling group, itself, is perpetuated; they do so by virtue of their control of the departure of members who are getting too old or are inadequate for any other reason whatever (as the "in-group" sees matters), and through their control of the selection of successors.

According to this view, the professional, essentially propertyless managers, not the stockholders, control, by themselves, the selection of the management.

Going only a short step farther, people of such persuasion can readily perceive the chief executive as the prime controller, head oligarch, or "king-maker," who, in addition to his other functions, actually controls not only the workings of the company, but the selection of the successor who follows him and his fellow oligarchs of the future.

This perceived evolution of the chief executive from chief owner, as he was in the past, to chief oligarch, as he seems to some to be now, is thought by such observers to represent a significant departure from "true" capitalism, or even from democracy.

In my own view, this is a great oversimplification which ends up by being a serious misapprehension of the facts.

I have no statistics on the matter, but my own experience indicates that the process whereby management is selected, replaced, and renewed is far from automatic and that management is "self" perpetuating only if we define it to mean persons of competence and integrity who are seeking others of that description. In fact, the trend seems to be to place more responsibility for this matter with outside directors. Both Allied Chemical and General Motors, on whose board I sit as an outside director, have, for example, established nominating committees composed of outside directors. The nominating committee of the General Motors board, composed of six outside directors, has the responsibility of obtaining from all interested sources the

---

[19] Berle, Adolf A., Jr.; *Economic Power and the Free Society*; New York: Fund for the Republic; 1957; p. 9.

names of persons considered to be qualified as prospective directors. Thereafter, the committee members review the suggestions with the Chief Executive Officer and other directors who are not members of the committee and obtain information about the suggested nominees from knowledgeable people outside the corporation. In due course, the committee makes appropriate recommendations to the full board for discussion and final decision as to nominations to be presented to the stockholders for election. The nominating committee not only deals with the question of who should sit on the board, but how many. It is within the committee's responsibilities to recommend enlarging or reducing the board membership if either course seems appropriate.

In the relatively short time the General Motors nominating committee has been in existence it has proved to be of great help to the full board in fulfilling its responsibilities. Certainly it has been an effective answer to the untrue charge made by some critics that the board members are always hand picked by the Chief Executive Officer so that they will rubber stamp his decisions and actions. That criticism has always amused me because of my own experience of becoming Chief Executive Officer in two different companies where I had to start working with boards composed of individuals selected over the years by the respective boards without my personal participation in any way. I am prepared to testify that neither board could in any way qualify for the term "rubber stamp."

In fact, I would like to take this opportunity to put to rest the widely stated legend that board actions are always taken unanimously. My experience on many corporate boards has included innumerable situations in which outside directors have objected to management recommendations with the result that, even though no formal votes were taken, proposals were withdrawn. After further consideration and discussion, a revised proposal usually is submitted and adopted by the board, but I can recall quite a few situations where the matter was never heard of again. My point is that the formal official vote quite frequently does not tell the whole story. Even so, in my life as a corporate director, I can recall several occasions when one or more outside directors insisted upon being recorded as voting against the final management proposal.

This independence and multiplicity of views find expression in things having to do with "succession" just as they do in other matters.

To an outsider, management may appear to be "an automatic self-perpetuating oligarchy" because primary responsibility for management succession, like the rest of the corporation's business, lies with management, and because only the results of the process are publicized. Corporate employees and officers, unlike the corporation they serve, are self-centered and mortal. They will sometimes move on to better opportunities despite the best interests of the corporation, and they will always eventually retire. How well management handles these facts for the good of the corporation is a measure of its professionalism at all levels.

This area of a president's responsibility does not lend itself well to description or quantification. Personal reaction and intuition are, indeed, much relied upon in the selection of managers, but professionalism requires that the selection be recognizably based upon objective criteria. In my own experience, managements—and this certainly goes for chief executives—are advancing very considerably in their skills of managing the selection and development of a continuing succession of competent professional managers.

In *The Power Elite*, C. Wright Mills describes "big-propertied cliques and political influence"[20] as determinative factors in the selection of corporate management. So far as I can see, this is no truer of corporation managements than of the university faculties with which Mills had more direct experience; but to an outsider unable to discern the subtleties of judgment involved, it may appear so. Corporation presidents whom I consider to be professional, and that includes the vast majority of presidents of large corporations, conscientiously try to base their management selections on merit. Any other course would eventually reflect upon their own performance. The choice of his own successor is really no more than a continuation and extension of a president's building of a top management team.

It is in connection with succession that the board of directors is called upon to perform its most important duty. The choice of a chief executive is nondelegable. If the directors have confidence in the current chief executive, they naturally seek and are guided by his recommendation, but they want to be satisfied that his recommendation is based on merit. This is especially true if the directors are themselves drawn from the ranks of professional managers, either inside or outside the corporation. What I said above about the independence of directors holds true, of course, when the proposal being considered is

---

[20] Mills, C. Wright; *The Power Elite*; New York: Oxford University Press; 1956; p. 136.

of this magnitude; and I am personally aware of quite a few instances in which the board of directors has taken the lead away from management in selecting a new president. Its relative infrequency is evidence more of the professionalism of management in fulfilling its succession responsibility than of the passivity of directors.

THE PRESIDENT AS PUBLIC TRUSTEE

Most of the productive wealth of the United States is held by its large corporations. These are in turn so widely held, either directly or through institutions, that the line between capitalism and socialism has become less distinct. The public nature of modern large corporations has been recognized since the depression of the 1930s forced it upon us. The Securities Act of 1934, and the other regulatory legislation we live with today are expressive of the public's determination that business is too important to be left exclusively to businessmen. As public institutions, corporations must justify their existence by serving the public.

Until a few years ago it was assumed that corporations could best serve the public interest by tending to the business of producing goods and services efficiently, but corporations have behaved no better than individuals in our society and in tending to business have contributed their share to some rather monumental problems. This has given rise to a demand by some social critics for "corporate responsibility"[21] as a means of solving the problems. Responsibility, whether corporate or individual, cannot exist without corresponding power. We cannot meaningfully say that corporations have a responsibility to accomplish what they have no power to accomplish any more than we say that of individuals, and if corporations accept social challenges without corresponding power they will dissipate their efforts without solving the social problems and perhaps without continuing to produce goods and services efficiently.

As I see it, a corporate president's duty with respect to corporate responsibility is threefold. First, he must accept and define responsibility where the corporation does have the power to effect a social good. This of course includes compliance with the spirit as well as the letter of the law where laws exist for guidance. It also includes making the corporation follow the same high standards that an ethical in-

---

[21] See Burck, Gilbert; "The Hazards of Corporate Responsibility"; *Fortune*; June 1973; p. 114.

dividual businessman would follow. Thus a corporation would not sell the public a worthless or dangerous product even though it might legally do so. It is peculiarly within the province of the president to set the standard here, because it requires a balancing of the stockholders' interest in a return on their investment against everyone's interest in the public welfare. He must say, in effect, "In managing your property we will not violate our personal standards of conduct."

Second, the corporation president has a duty to the stockholders not to dissipate the corporation's property in a quixotic tilting at social evils. For example, no corporation can clean up the environment single-handedly, and corporations collectively lack the power to set and police industrywide standards. Acting alone will have little effect on the overall problem and may in the long run simply delay the day that industrywide standards are set.

Third, the corporation president has a duty to ensure that the corporation contributes in a fair way to the formulation of legislation and regulations. It is important to the survival of our free enterprise system that the benefit of industry's expertise be made available to legislators undiluted by bias and self-interest. Again using environmental concerns as an example, legislators need to know what pollution control technology is or will be available and at what cost. Anything less than full and honest cooperation could rightfully be called corporate irresponsibility. As above, balancing profits against public welfare is the duty of the president.

THE PRESIDENT AS HEAD OF A COMMUNITY

With the growth of suburbs and the increase in mobility of our population, we tend to identify less with our geographic communities. More and more the corporation is the focal point of those who work for them. Their social orientation is naturally taken from the place where they spend so much of their lives, and though it is generally not consciously exercised by a corporation president, he personally can have a profound influence over that orientation. I recently read a biography of Thomas J. Watson, Chief Executive Officer of IBM during its formative years, and was struck with the realization of just how extreme that influence can be in unusual situations.[22] Considering the publicity given this type of corporate living in such popular

---

[22] Rodgers, William; *Think: A Biography of the Watsons and IBM*; New York: Stein and Day; 1969.

books as W. H. Whyte's *The Organization Man,* it is not surprising that so many young Americans think working for any corporation after college would stifle their individualities. My own policy in this regard is to avoid giving any overt guidance whatsoever. I recognize that what Whyte calls the "subtle pressures to conform" do exist, but I don't think that I mislead by saying that at two corporations where I have been Chief Executive Officer a great diversity of life styles have been able to coexist without noticeable friction.

It is common enough to think of the president, along with the directors, as having a duty to represent the interest of the stockholders. He also has a duty, not often stated as such, to represent the employees. Exploitation of the workers belonged to the era of the robber barons. A professional management has a responsibility to see to it that employees are being fairly compensated. I am referring here not just to the level of compensation but to the manner in which it is given. I believe that every employee has the right to an honest appraisal of his compensation expectations and a good faith effort on the part of his superiors to insure that he is not misled. This may in many cases require a higher level of compensation than could otherwise be maintained, and as the point of contact between the interests of employees and stockholders, only the president can strike the fair balance.

The president's power to exert subtle influence on those below him is most important in the area of, for lack of a better word, ethics. Today all chief executives will give lip service to fair play and compliance with the law, but from time to time we see some who are willing to wink at, if not covertly encourage, other behavior. Other officers and employees are quick to notice whether a president is serious about his public statements. In this respect, it is important to bear in mind that employees generally sincerely believe, and with good reason, that their superiors all the way up the line really know what is going on and that they therefore must condone improper conduct, as well as approve meritorious actions. This feeling on the part of employees generally imposes a special burden of responsibility on the president to consider the ethical as well as the business and legal aspects of a proposed course of action. He should let his associates know that he expects them to do "the right thing," even in situations where there may be no business advantage in so doing. Such an approach, and that kind of thinking, is reflected in attitudes and, more than any other factor, helps to determine and maintain the good name of the corporation—an almost invaluable corporate asset.

THE CHIEF EXECUTIVE'S OFFICE IN HISTORICAL PERSPECTIVE

by Alfred D. Chandler, Jr.*

Isidor Straus Professor of Business History, Harvard Business School

RISE OF THE MODERN CORPORATION

THE MODERN corporation, it must be remembered, is historically a new institution. A century ago, except for railroads, nearly all businesses were small and nearly all were partnerships. There were very few salaried managers. The owners managed their enterprises. A handful of partners or stockholders handled the details of day-to-day operations as well as providing overall supervision and long-term planning for their enterprises. There were no corporate headquarters and no salaried managers with the title of chief executive. A brief look at the rise of the modern industrial corporation and with it the modern corporate headquarters can then help give perspective to the activities and responsibilities of the modern chief executive's office.

The modern industrial corporation appeared in the United States with dramatic suddenness in the last years of the 19th and the first of the 20th century. It came in two ways. One was through the growth of manufacturers who began to use brand new mass production techniques and to create national and often global sales organizations to market and distribute their products. The other was by merger. The two different routes to size led to quite different styles of management and quite different types of corporate headquarters. The modern general office and position of the chief executive evolved more from the experiences of the firms that grew large by merger rather than from those that expanded initially by creating an extensive sales organization.

---

* [Ed. Note: Professor Chandler is author of a leading study of the development of modern corporate organization: *Strategy and Structure: Chapters in the History of the American Industrial Enterprise*; Cambridge, Mass.: The M.I.T. Press; 1962. Chandler is also editor of *The Harvard Studies in Business History*.]

The first modern industrial enterprises were, however, those that grew large by internal growth rather than merger. They were the firms that found themselves forced to build large networks of sales offices if they were to sell their products in volume. As a result these enterprises were the first to integrate the processes of mass production with those of mass distribution (and also of mass purchasing). Such enterprises appeared almost simultaneously in the decade of the 1880s in a number of industries producing semiperishable packaged goods including cigarettes (Duke's American Tobacco), matches (Diamond Match), breakfast cereals (Quaker Oats), canned goods (Campbell, Heinz, and Borden), soap (Procter & Gamble), soft drinks (Coca-Cola), and photographic equipment (Eastman Kodak). There also first appeared at almost precisely the same time large companies in industries using new refrigerated techniques to distribute perishable products in the national market. These included meat packers (Armour and Swift), and brewers (Pabst, Schlitz, and Anheuser Busch). Still more innovative were the manufacturers of mass produced machinery who built sales departments to provide specialized marketing services such as demonstration, after-sales service, and repair, and consumer credit essential for mass distribution of their machines. These included the makers of sewing machines (Singer), complex agricultural machinery (McCormick Harvester, John Deere, J. I. Case), and newly invented office machinery (Remington Typewriter, National Cash Register). At the same time firms producing heavier machinery (such as Otis Elevator, Western Electric, Westinghouse, Edison General Electric, Babcock & Wilcox, and Worthington Pump) built similar global marketing organizations in those same years.

All these companies appeared in much their modern form in the single decade of the 1880s. Others quickly followed. For example, in the 1890s, office machinery makers such as A. B. Dick (makers of mimeograph machines), Burroughs Adding Machine, and Tabulating Machine Company (the forerunner of IBM) built similar enterprises based on similar sales networks. Then, in the first years of the new century, companies that were formed to mass produce and mass distribute the automobile—the Ford Motor Company, Dodge Motor Company, and William C. Durant's Buick, and then his Chevrolet company—followed the same pattern of growth.

All these enterprises were managed and financed in the same way. All were financed internally. The high volume of cash flow generated by effective integration of mass production with mass distribution provided the funds needed for both working and fixed capital. These firms rarely had any need to go to the capital markets for other than occasional very short-term loans. Therefore, all these enterprises continued to be controlled fully by the entrepreneur who founded the firm, his family, and a few close associates. So, although their activities quickly became global in scope—these were the country's first multinationals—they continued to be managed at the top in a personal way. Middle management which supervised the functional activities remained thin; top management tiny.

In such companies, corporate headquarters consisted of three or four senior executives, usually large stockholders, assisted by little more than a small clerical staff. These entrepreneurs and their successors often continued to involve themselves in day-to-day activities. They made little attempt to develop sophisticated accounting and statistical controls and gave little attention to long-term strategic planning and to the systematic allocation of managerial and capital resources to carry out such plans. Such firms can be termed *entrepreneurial enterprises.* And for all such entrepreneurial enterprises the continuing challenge was to create an effective headquarters headed by a knowledgeable and professional chief executive. Many were successful in meeting the challenge but some of the largest, including Armour, Westinghouse, and Ford, failed to do so.

A larger number of modern industrial corporations came into being by following the second route to size—that of merger—than by the means of creating a mass marketing organization. Those that took the route of mergers all moved in much the same way: Legal consolidation of a number of small manufacturing firms (first in the form of a trust or holding company) was followed by administrative centralization. The manufacturing or processing facilities of the constituent companies were placed under the control of a single production or manufacturing department. Next, the company integrated forward by building an extensive sales network; and then backward by setting up a large buying organization and often obtaining control of raw and semifinished materials. The final result was a centralized functionally departmentalized organizational structure very similar to that developed by the first large entrepreneurial firms. It was not until well into the 20th century, when mergers of already integrated companies began to occur, that the constituent companies of a merger continued to operate as autonomous divisions under the control of headquarters.

The modern enterprises that grew large through the merger route also first appeared in the 1880s. At first, they were few in number, and were all in industries where continuous process operations permitted high volume output and economies of large scale. These included petroleum (Standard Oil), sugar (American Sugar Refining), lead (National Lead), whiskey, cotton seed oil, and linseed oil. In the early 1890s, more mergers took place in rubber (U.S. Rubber), starch, cordage, lead, and, for the first time, in machinery industries, including electrical equipment (General Electric). Then, after the country pulled out of the deep economic depression of the 1890s, came the first and still the greatest merger movement in American history. There were hundreds of mergers in a wide variety of industries. Many failed. Those that were the most successful were in industries where high volume production could be integrated with mass distribution such as iron and steel, nonferrous metals, machinery, rubber, glass, paper, chemicals, and certain foods. In all these industries, the enterprises that first appeared in the giant merger movement that took place at the turn of the century still remain leading firms. Examples are United States Steel, Bethlehem, Anaconda, American Smelting and Refining, International Nickel, International Harvester, American Can, Continental Can, American Car & Foundry, Pittsburgh Plate Glass, Du Pont, International Paper, Distillers Securities, United Fruit, and Corn Products Refining.

The firms which became large through merger came to be managed and financed quite differently from the entrepreneurial enterprises that had grown initially by building extensive marketing organizations. These mergers usually led to the reorganization of production and distribution processes and facilities in large sectors of many major industries. Older and smaller factories were dismantled, new ones built, others consolidated. Nationwide sales and purchasing organizations had to be created overnight. All this required more capital than could be funded by current cash flow. For the first time American industrial firms began to rely heavily on capital markets for funds. Stock ownership, already somewhat scattered by the process of merger, became still more dispersed. At the same time, salaried managers had to be hired to run the new functional departments, and salaried executives moved into the new central executive offices. The firms resulting from merger therefore had a larger number of middle and top managers than did the entrepreneurial firms of that day. In these merged enterprises, ownership became separated from management from almost the very beginning. Such firms can be properly termed *managerial enterprises.*

THE RISE OF MODERN MANAGEMENT

It was in these managerial enterprises that modern general management methods and procedures were first developed. In nearly all cases, top management became collegiate or collective. Decisions came to be made more systematically and rationally than they were in the personally managed entrepreneurial firms. The top management group, usually meeting as an executive committee, included the president and the chairman of the board and the heads of the functional departments. Later when mergers of already integrated enterprises occurred in which the constituent firms continued to operate autonomous divisions, the top committee came to be made up of managers in charge of regional and product divisions rather than of heads of departments.

One of the very first tasks faced by these new top management groups was to build an effective corporate headquarters. Attention was initially concentrated on developing statistical and financial information and controls. The new financial staffs developed modern corporate accounting. In fact, as a result of the mergers, standardized modern accounting appeared for the first time in many American industries. Moreover, as these firms began to carry out programs of plant expansion and of integrating backward to control raw and semifinished materials, their financial offices began to develop rigorous criteria for determining rate of return on investment. Du Pont, for example, devised by World War I a complex formula, based on turnover as well as on the ratio of earnings to sales, for determining R.O.I. That formula is still widely used today. In addition, these new financial offices began to develop long-range forecasts to assist in determining long-term investment of plant and personnel. Once the financial staffs were operating effectively, these same companies enlarged their corporate headquarters by creating offices to handle such specialized services as legal, personnel, public relations, real estate, and most important of all, research and development.

As the new financial and advisory staffs worked out improved procedures to coordinate, evaluate, and plan for the activities of these merged and integrated enterprises, their senior executives began to concern themselves with the *processes* by which they made their decisions. All agreed that collegiate management, although necessary, created difficulties. The very makeup of the executive committee created obvious problems. Because the committee consisted of heads of functional departments (or, later, of product divisions), policy rarely resulted from objective *analysis*. Instead it was determined by *negotiations* between the heads of different operating units. These operating vice presidents quite naturally tended to put the interests of their departments and divisions ahead of that of the company as a whole. To remedy this weakness, the executive committee or top decision-making group came to be made up of general executives responsible for the welfare and activities of the entire corporation as a whole rather than of some one operating unit. These men, vice presidents or group executives, were relieved of all day-to-day operating responsibilities. Instead, they were to concentrate on evaluating the performance of the operating units, on coordinating their activities, and most important of all on planning long-term strategy and allocating capital and managerial resources necessary to implement such plans.

Another weakness inherent in the working of early group management led to the creation of the title and office of the chief executive. Some one person in the top management group had to have the final authority and responsibility for the decisions of the group. Someone had to be able to make a decision when the group could not agree. Someone had to personify the impersonal corporation to its many constituencies—workers, stockholders, customers, and larger outside local and national communities. In most companies, such duties and responsibilities were at first divided between the president and the chairman of the board and even, in some cases, the chairman of the executive committee. As time passed, the manager holding one of these positions was also given the title of Chief Executive Officer. He became formally and officially the company's leader.

The precise role and functions of the Chief Executive Officer varied from corporation to corporation, and within one company from one chief executive to the next. His responsibilities were rarely carefully and specifically designed, primarily because leadership could hardly be defined by a job description in an organization manual. It had to reflect the personality and experience of the leader.

The most successful corporations were those whose Chief Executive Officers were able to lead effectively by acting as firsts among equals. This was true of Pierre du Pont and Walter Carpenter at

Du Pont, of Alfred Sloan at General Motors, of Gerard Swope at General Electric, and even of John D. Rockefeller at Standard Oil. The success of these men and of the companies they managed reflected their ability to work closely with others. They did not command by using their formal or legal authority. They almost never gave direct orders. Their authority was based instead on knowledge, analytical ability, and on the intellectual force of their analyses and proposals.

In time, the entrepreneurial enterprises—those which grew large by creating marketing organizations rather than from mergers—had to build general offices similar to those first created by managerial firms. Although the *group* style of management of the latter had its weaknesses, it was usually less of a handicap than those inherent in the individual and personal management that was characteristic of the entrepreneurial firm. Group management often became cumbersome and unresponsive. Corporate headquarters might become overstaffed. Chief Executive Officers might fail to lead. Nevertheless, the larger corporate headquarters provided the manpower essential to carry out the basic functions of complex tasks of top management of evaluation, coordination, and policy planning. And where leadership was lacking, the public relations department at least could create an image of leadership. On the other hand, a single entrepreneur with a few close associates or members of his family simply was not able to provide the professional skills essential to the corporation's short-term health and long-term growth.

So, by the mid-20th century, nearly all large American corporations of whatever origin had their general offices made up of general executives who were corporate generalists rather than functional specialists. All operated through collegiate management, and nearly all had a chief executive, a first among equals, who was both its symbolic and its actual head.

EVOLUTION OF THE CHIEF EXECUTIVE'S OFFICE IN THE AUTOMOBILE INDUSTRY

The developments outlined are well illustrated by the experience of the automobile industry which, for most of the 20th century, has been one of the nation's largest and most important. Ford provides a classic example of the *entrepreneurial* firm, and General Motors an illustration of an innovative *managerial* one. The electrical, steel, chemical, rubber, and other industries provide comparable stories, but none are as dramatic and illuminating.

From the time of the introduction of the "Model T" until the mid-1920s, the Ford Motor Company was one of the most successful and best known of American business enterprises. Its achievement resulted from more than just the development of an excellent product. In the years after 1908, Ford followed the lead of earlier mass producers of sewing, agriculture, and office machinery by building a marketing and distributing organization that quickly covered the nation and then the world. The powerful demand engendered by the sales organization created a tremendous pressure to speed up the manufacturing process. Finally, in 1914, Ford engineers completed the first modern moving assembly line. That basic symbol of modern mass production came—it must be stressed—after, and, indeed, it resulted from Ford's highly effective national and global marketing organization.

By 1923, Ford's huge integrated enterprise sold 1.7 million cars in a single year and enjoyed 46.1 percent of the market; during the depression year of 1921, Ford's share had reached 55.7 percent of the market. Ford cars had become the cheapest in the world; his workers the highest paid in the world; and Ford, himself, had become one of the richest men in the world. He still owned the company he managed, and he was proud to command it personally through a small informal organization. He boasted that his company had "no organization, no specific duties attached to any position, no line of succession of authority, very few titles and no conferences."

After the mid-1920s, however, Ford's story was one of unmitigated disaster. His profits and share of the market plummeted. By 1929, when the "Model A" replaced the "Model T," his share had fallen to 31.3 percent and by 1940 to 18.9 percent, a figure well below that of a relatively new firm, Chrysler, as well as below that of General Motors. In spite of the excellent sales during the first two years after the appearance of the "A" and of its successor the "V8," Ford recorded a net loss of $16 million for the decade between 1927 and 1937. In some years, the losses ran as high as $70 million. By the 1930s Ford no longer built the lowest priced car. His labor relations had become the worst in the industry.

During this period of sharp decline, Henry Ford continued to run his company from a tiny headquarters. He had hired hundreds of executives to manage his worldwide enterprise. But these managers received little guidance, evaluation, or support from Detroit. Their suggestions and achievements were ignored. Many left; as many were fired. Ford found it psychologically impossible to seek or take advice as to how to run his firm. He lost touch with the market. Planning became irregular and erratic; control authoritarian. By the mid-1930s, Ford was managing his enterprises with two assistants—Charles E. Sorenson, a tough-minded production man, and Harry Bennett, a former prize fighter and small-time gangster. Ford continued to be a powerful owner-manager operating informally through a small central office. The result was disaster.

The rapid rise of General Motors was a very different matter. Ford's failure contributed, of course, to its success. There were, however, significant managerial reasons for the swift rise of General Motors to the top in the 1920s. Formed in 1908 by William C. Durant, a talented entrepreneur, General Motors continued to be run, like Ford, as a one-man show until 1921. Durant made Buick, by 1906, and Chevrolet, some years later, into leading firms by building national and global sales organizations. Durant's interest, however, was not in expanding the activities of these individual firms. He turned their management over to able executives, including Charles W. Nash and Walter P. Chrysler. Instead, Durant concentrated on merging many automobile, truck, bus, and parts and accessories companies into one huge integrated but sprawling industrial empire. Corporate headquarters remained little more than Durant and some secretarial assistants. Control and planning became unpredictable and erratic. Nash, Chrysler, and other senior executives left the corporation. With little planning and little long-term market and financial information, General Motors was totally unprepared for the sudden and sharp postwar recession of 1920–21. In 1921, its share of the market dropped to 12.7 percent. Its losses soared; $83 million had to be written off in inventory alone. Durant's losses in the stock market during the recession amounted to over $30 million. These corporate and personal losses forced Durant to leave General Motors.

Pierre du Pont then took Durant's place as president. He did so at the request of the Du Pont Company, which had invested millions of its war profits in the automobile firm, and of the bankers who had helped to finance the final phase of General Motors' postwar expansion. Du Pont began immediately to transform Durant's sprawling, heterogeneous business empire into one of the most successful industrial enterprises of all time. To assist him, he relied increasingly on the talents of Alfred P. Sloan, Jr. In 1923, after reorganization had assured recovery, Pierre appointed Sloan as president and Chief Executive Officer, retaining the position of chairman of the board for himself.

For du Pont and Sloan, the central task at General Motors was to build an effective general office. To provide the essential statistical and financial controls, Pierre recruited from the Du Pont Company an experienced financial staff headed by that company's former treasurer, Donaldson Brown. By 1924, as a result of the work of Brown and his assistants, all major operating decisions by the product divisions, including output, size of working force, materials purchased, and price, were based on short-term annual market forecasts adjusted every ten days to market demand. Long-term investments in plant, equipment, and other facilities became tied to long-range market and financial forecasts.

In these same years, Sloan concentrated on building up the corporate advisory staff. By 1923, a wide variety of staff offices had been created and manned by experts in different functional activities. These staff officers for marketing, advertising, purchasing, production, traffic, legal matters, public relations, personnel, and research and development advised both the operating divisions and the general office. In addition, they provided information and controls to the top management through their regular "auditing" of the functional activities within each of the divisions. To coordinate the work of the staff and of the functional executives in the divisions, and of the functional managers of the divisions and of the senior executives in the general office, Sloan created Interdivisional Relations committees each with its own permanent secretary and staff. These committees later became known as Policy Groups.

Sloan, Brown, Pierre du Pont, and John J. Raskob (du Pont's closest business associate) with four group executives managed General Motors as its Executive Committee. Each of the group vice presidents had general oversight of a number of operating divisions, but no day-to-day operating duties. Nor had the other four general executives. The committee spent much of its time systematically evaluating the performance of the divisions. Its primary concern, however, was the formulation of long-term strategy and providing capital and managerial resources to carry out these plans. These decisions were group ones based on extensive data provided by the financial and advisory staff, and were made usually only after extended discussion and debate.

It was in this atmosphere of collegiate command and group decision making that Sloan defined his role as the corporation's Chief Executive Officer. Like Pierre du Pont, he rarely gave an order. Issues were argued and decisions were made on the basis of long-term rate of return on investment, determined by analyses and interpretations of information which had been carefully collected, collated, and checked. In addition to his regular duties of evaluation and planning, Sloan kept a watchful eye on specific trouble spots. In the early 1920s, he concentrated on product development; in the depressed years of the early 1930s, on improving dealer methods and morale; in the late 1930s, on labor relations; and then on wartime conversion, expansion, and reconversion. In addition, all through these years, Sloan continued to be a vigorous spokesman for the corporation to the stockholders, customers, suppliers, and local and national audiences.

The success of the Sloan regime is legendary. By 1927, General Motors had already taken 43.3 percent of the market. In the following year, its profits of $267.5 million were the largest ever reported by an American industrial corporation. During the decade when Ford's losses were $16 million, General Motors' profits totalled over $2 billion.

The lessons of the profit and loss accounts ultimately had an effect on Ford. In 1944, after the death of his son Edsel, 81-year-old Henry finally began to turn the company over to his grandson, Henry Ford II. The young Ford soon brought in a team of General Motors executives headed by Ernest R. Breech. Their first task was, in the words of *Fortune,* "to clap the General Motors organizational garment on the Ford manufacturing frame." In a short time, Ford had a general office comparable to that of General Motors and it became for the first time in almost 20 years a powerful competitor to its two major rivals.

The story of success and failure at Ford and General Motors tells much about the personalities of the top executives of those two companies. It says even more about the evolution of the general corporate office in the United States and with it the office of the chief executive. It emphasizes that personal rule by the founder, his family, and close associates has little place in the operation of a large modern corporation. Continuing effective overall coordination, evaluation, and planning all demand the creation of sizeable financial and advisory staffs and the placing of final responsibility in the hands of a small group of general executives without specific day-to-day operating duties. Within this group, one man still must have the final responsibility for decision and action, must make the decisions when consensus fails, and must act as spokesman for the corporation with groups within and outside of the enterprise.

The personality of style and abilities of the chief executive continue to be one of the most critical factors in a corporation's present health and future growth. As these attributes are rarely the same in any two executives, the specific role and function of a chief executive office vary as different managers move in and out of the position. In nearly all cases, however, the successful chief executive has been a first among equals. And the effective chief executive is one who is first in fact as well as name. He must be able to work closely and intimately with his colleagues and at the same time to lead them by the force of his intellect and talent rather than from the authority of his position.

ESTABLISHING AND EXERCISING EXECUTIVE AUTHORITY AND POWER[1]

by James F. Oates, Jr.
Chairman (Retired), The Equitable Life Assurance Society of the United States

THE ESTABLISHMENT of the authority and power of the Chief Executive Officer (CEO) is frequently accomplished by the preparation of descriptive statements and through the use of diagrams, organization charts, and other like material. These statements and diagrams should be developed with the participation of those responsible corporate officials primarily affected. Such statements attain top influence when accepted and approved by the entire officer force and by the management board. The descriptive material should be explicit, unambiguous, comprehensive, and readily available.

Special problems can arise where a new CEO is brought to office from the outside without familiarity with or responsibility for the descriptive statements, charts, and other like material then existing and constituting the establishment of the authority and power of the CEO. Indeed, one of the most powerful arguments in support of promotion from within is the recognition that the stranger is handicapped or delayed in effectiveness by his lack of familiarity with the customs and traditions of the past which are many times invisible.

The new incumbent, therefore, has the special task of appraising

---

[1] The following material has been prepared to deal only with the establishment and exercise of authority and power by the Chief Executive Officer of a business corporation. The CEO has been viewed as the chief corporate mobilizer, motivator, strategist, interpreter, and overseer.

No attempt is made to differentiate the subject matter between different grades of officers or to apply business principles and philosophy peculiarly appropriate for the CEO of business corporations to subordinate supervisory officers of lower ranks or to other forms of business organizations.

existing material as to executive authority in relation to his established point of view and business philosophy. The new incumbent would be well advised not to strike out all existing material but to endeavor to select the most promising and that which is the most consistent with his faith and business philosophy. To the extent that the material and views developed in the past are consistent with the business philosophy of the new entrant, this congeniality should be underscored to emphasize the support they will be given by the new CEO. In the final analysis, the *mechanism* of fulfilling corporate objectives is unimportant as compared with the *quality* of the business philosophy and standards of performance which the material reflects. A new entrant CEO, particularly, must embrace opportunities to point out and confess his faith in the importance and influence of business objectives and practices of high quality and standing. If the new entrant is convinced that the basic existing philosophy of authority is sound and basically consistent with his point of view and "faith," then only loopholes need to be filled and inconsistencies eliminated. If not, the incongenial should be stricken out, and the organization put to work in a cooperative effort to rebuild and to rewrite objectives and rededicate allegiance to familiar principles.

In many cases, the new entrant will be well advised to salvage existing descriptive material through the process of correction or clarification, having in mind the great strength and value of tradition and past experience. In many cases, also, if not in most, the basic initial objective of the new entrant should be to conserve and improve existing dogma and not to destroy and rebuild.

There is a very real distinction between technical authority and operative power. The mere statement of technical authority does not guarantee power to any person. It is the effective exercise of duly established and approved authority that creates and builds power.

The initial task of the Chief Executive Officer (CEO) is to seek and achieve agreement upon basic corporate objectives. The indispensable initial step to the effective exercise of top executive authority is the development of an agreed pronouncement which declares the fundamental purpose, business objectives, and implicit goals of the business.

To be successful in creating power, the exercise of authority must be in fulfillment of understood, accepted, and respected corporate objectives.

The agreed statement of objectives must be simply expressed, well understood, and generally accepted by the entire organization. This involves a careful development over a period of time to assure broad participation by all interested parties and to produce a result which is adequate, workable, and entitled to respect. It is most important to recognize, however, that such an agreed-to statement must always be subject to modification and change in order to reflect the varying conditions and needs of our society and the business enterprise in question.

Appropriate levels of operating officials and responsible staff officers should participate in defining those corporate objectives, the attainment of which will be their direct and immediate responsibility. The lessons of the past and established workable routines should be preserved to every appropriate and feasible degree. However, enlightened innovation must be boldly embraced when demonstrated to be sound and consistent.

The daily operations in pursuit of agreed objectives should be consistent with high principles. Formal "Codes to Work By" are helpful guidelines for such a philosophy.[2]

Fair and respected operating philosophy should be the agreed and acceptable objective of all. A personnel policy based on the dignity of the individual lies therefore at the heart of the exercise of authority. Each CEO should accept and respect the view that his number one job is to be the best possible and most effective assistant to his immediate subordinates. The individual tasks are thus done by the subordinates at the direction and with the help of the CEO. The value of this concept and concomitant attitude is very great. Every person is primarily interested in his own job and wants to do his work himself and not simply obey the directives of his supervisor. This policy always works and quietly builds morale. Support for the CEO can only come from below.

All operating corporate officials must be deeply involved in personnel policy. The area of greatest sensitivity in corporate management has to do with the relations between the officers, supervisors, and the general employees. All supervisors, particularly the CEO, must recognize and feel sincerely that all men and women in the business organization need more than pecuniary rewards that provide food, shelter, clothing, and so on. They need a working environment where they can realize a substantial percentage of their dreams. No

---

[2] See the Appendix to this chapter.

one, certainly no corporate official, can trample on the human personality with impunity. True gratification in personal relations comes from human communion and not merely the joint solution of common problems.

Business operations of all kinds and at every level involve inevitably the actions of numerous corporate supervisors and employees. Since all accomplishments are made by people and not by things, the most fundamental philosophy of the CEO must be the genuine recognition of the dignity and integrity of the individual person.

It is suggested that all supervisors, particularly the CEO, must be sure that the entire corporate family, including each employee, is kept fully informed respecting all matters of current or future interest in which they have a vital concern. Everyone so far as practical should not only be informed respecting the corporate status but encouraged to participate in making suggestions or performing special assignments.

Furthermore, the CEO must take as his own the responsibility to create the sentiment and understanding throughout the entire organization that all individual employees and all operating groups are mutually dependent upon each other. For the business to succeed as a whole, every department must succeed. The business will fail if the departments fail.

Operating practices which are in accord with the highest of living philosophies inevitably lead the Chief Executive Officer to engage in numerous activities, which include the following.[3]

A. The CEO must consciously, continuously, and sincerely seek out and pursue personal contacts throughout the entire organization. Every natural opportunity to establish such relations should be promptly utilized.

It is a human fact of life that the CEO should seek consciously to impress upon the members of the organization his recognition that the success of the enterprise depends entirely upon the spirit and talents of the individual men and women who perform the all-important operating functions and thereby achieve the standards and objectives of the business.

Throughout each business day there arise endless incidents where a smile, a handshake, an inquiry, and an expression of commendation, taking only a moment, reach scores and scores of people who are glad

---

[3] These grow in importance and effectiveness through use.

that the organization is led by officers who recognize and believe in the common humanity of all men.

B. Painstaking, detailed study should be made by the CEO of each of the main areas of corporate operations. The chief operating officers of each of the principal operating and staff organizations of the corporation should meet regularly with the CEO and review with him performance, progress, failures, problems, and complaints. The CEO invariably at these meetings should demonstrate that his familiarity with the company's principal concerns is the result of personal study and sincere interest.

It is recommended that all new entrants to the ranks of CEO should give top priority to the task of fully understanding in depth the nontechnical aspects of all major corporate operations. One of the methods most effective in such educational efforts is the regular holding of periodic meetings with the top operating officials of each of the principal departments of the business. These meetings provide the opportunity for discussions between department heads and the CEO as to the objectives of the department in question, how it is organized to attain such objectives, who are its most effective members, what are its principal problems, and how can the department operate more effectively and economically. Nothing is more effective than a CEO who genuinely and sincerely shows interest and knowledge about the operations of a department and its most valuable leaders and demonstrates his intention and objective to help the department heads make a better record for themselves.

C. Disappointments, failures, business defeats, trying problems, and so on, indeed all bad news, should be brought from the point of origin via the hierachy to the CEO immediately for his understanding and participation in cure or correction.

D. The CEO should respond to all new problems at once, if at all possible. It is obvious but frequently overlooked that the CEO should take every available step to be sure that all adverse developments, all mistakes, all frustrations, all failures, and all defeats are brought to his attention at once to the end that he can participate in ameliorating their adverse effects and demonstrate his desire to help the organization remedy the problem and eliminate further concern. These circumstances provide opportunities to build morale, to study and interpret corporate policy, and to avoid the repetition of many problems. The value of CEO familiarity with trouble will be lost if delays follow the communication to the chief. Remedies, if any, should be promptly discussed and applied, reassurance given to those involved and worried, meetings held by all interested parties to the end that cures can be found and repetition avoided; and all of this should be done so promptly that no one will be misled into the belief that the effort is not genuine.

E. The CEO should be visible and readily available to all official representatives and supervisors. It is generally recognized that the corporate leader who is either invisible or unavailable is greatly handicaped in the fulfillment of his own best talents and potentials. The "open door" is a very simple but very obvious illustration of the attitude and point of view of the man behind the desk. If you can't get to him, if he is never visible, if he is always too busy, then his organization from the top to the bottom loses confidence and faith in the management at all levels. It is amazing how valuable and immediate are the favorable results of a few minutes spared to discuss a relatively unimportant matter with someone greatly worried and upset. The corollary sometimes overlooked and disbelieved is that the "open door" policy can be fully fulfilled by the use of a relatively brief period of time provided that during that period of time the corporate leader is truly absorbed and anxious to listen to and comment upon the views of his caller.

F. In the solution of problems the CEO should insist first on finding the facts and then in selecting the criteria of value which should guide the exercise of judgment on such facts.

Business life consists importantly of a series of questions to be answered and problems to be solved. An endless procession of hard questions to answer and confused difficulties to unwind constitute the contents of the CEO's desk. Experience has taught that there are two basic steps to the solution of these problems and to finding answers to these questions. The first step is the historical one where the relevant facts must be found. It is amazing how many problems solve themselves when the disclosure of all the facts has been realized. Finding the facts, however, is more difficult than it sounds. What are the facts! Not what you think they are, wish they were, hope that they could be, or even what they should be. No—what *are* the facts! When the facts are ascertained and disclosed, you can take the second or philosophical step which is always required in the answer to questions and the solution to problems. This step involves the selection of that set of values you wish to use in exercising judgment on facts.

What are your criteria of value? What do you believe in? Do you believe in justice and beauty? What is important and what is unimportant to you? Who is your God? Through countless years of corporate experience, businessmen have learned instinctively to insist on the discovery of facts and to nourish and apply criteria of value which they have faith will ultimately prevail.

G. As soon as may be, the CEO should build a sentiment throughout the entire organization that a top objective of the overall operation is to serve the interests and meet the needs of our fellow citizens. High morale and pride is created when the officers and employees join in recognizing the corporation to be a good and respected corporate citizen.

H. The CEO should seek general support for the ultimate conviction that because individual men are the source of all success, each must give the best that is in him.

Many thoughtful men including active corporate executives have been troubled, confused, and concerned by the seeming dilemma of our society in terms of the basic principles of constitutional equality. The dilemma arises from the apparent conflict between the basic national belief that all men are created free and equal on the one hand and the national devotion to the concept "may the best man win" on the other. This has stimulated the philosophers of business to seek a reconciliation. Such a solution has been found in the widely accepted view that individual men do have different capacities, qualities, and talents. However, they are equal, and happily so, if each man is charged with the obligation of giving to society the best that is in him.

The constitutional objective is thus attained through the availability for all of equality of opportunity. Because no man can give more than the best of which he is capable, all men from emperors to slaves can enjoy a life of satisfaction if each has given the best that is in him. Thus, equality of opportunity as the true right of the American citizen reconciles our dilemma and gives full promise of human satisfaction in the fulfillment of such individual life.

I. In the furtherance and attainment of high quality corporate citizenship for the enterprise, all employees should be encouraged to serve both local communities and the nation through acceptance of responsibility in fields of religious, charitable, and educational activity.

Final corporate authority is exercised not only by operations thereunder but by delegation from the CEO to other officers and supervisors. The delegation of authority does not diminish either authority or responsibility. Actually it is evidence of a most effective use of authority. Delegation demonstrates confidence in those subordinates who are thereby enriched and developed and it always can be revoked if and when necessary or desirable.

Authority can never be irrevocably delegated since the top and final executive responsibility and power as fixed by the bylaws and approved by the directors has been placed in the hands of the CEO.

Although authority *can be delegated revocably, final responsibility can never be assigned.* This means that the CEO must answer for all of the operations of those to whom he has delegated authority or assigned responsibility. The CEO who delegates authority while retaining responsibility stimulates a sense of confidence and pride in all subordinates, supervisors, and managers.

Corporate officers of all ranks are inescapably subject to the temptation to confuse the *incumbent* officer with the "job itself." The job itself as defined in the organization manuals is the controlling guideline. The incumbent is always bound by and subject to the limitations of the job. The CEO particularly must recognize that until modified by proper action, his conduct must be clearly within the controlling limitations fixed by board action, executive orders, etc.

The credibility of each top office is greatly enhanced if the incumbent in that office clearly recognizes that the power held by the *office* is subject to limitations which he must understand and respect. Top decisions, if at all possible, should be consistent with traditional conduct particularly that which has been found successful in the past. The CEO consequently should capitalize on the past, and change established practice as little as possible. This evidences respect for the job and not overindulgence in self-importance.

ACTION AND PERFORMANCE

In the final analysis, sound objectives, high principles, sincere motives, constant self-discipline are all tools of performance. The CEO must never for one minute lose sight of the fact that his job is to promptly dispose of business brought to his desk either by his own motivation or by the action of others in order thereby to keep "the whole effort" incessantly rolling along.

He should strive for prompt disposition of an impressive volume of work. There should be little, if any, backlog and nothing should be delayed beyond that point which is readily recognized as absolutely necessary. Progress can be stimulated and a backlog avoided through the prompt request for further facts and by arrangements for additional study and research. Such further research can and should call on the experience of the past and seek advice and guidance from all those who have had an involvement in such matters. The thoughtful and careful direction of further investigation involves the use of more talent and builds men. It necessarily develops in the organization a renewed understanding of the value of the spirit of unity.

BOARD OF DIRECTORS AND CEO

The existence of a board of directors lies at the very heart of the legal effectiveness and operating strength of the enterprise. In virtually all business enterprises today, the management is reposed by law in a board of directors. All vital and important business actions are invariably taken with the approval of the directors on the recommendation of the CEO. The board of directors is a most important and highly useful corporate feature. It is exceptionally helpful to the CEO because he soon finds that the board contains men who have had a great wealth of experience in both broad and narrow fields.

The very existence of the board motivates the CEO to be sure that high standards of conduct and common sense are consistently observed. The board functions as a very powerful influence and guide.

The directors individually have the broad obligation to speak up at any and all times, and the influence of a board "question" provokes corrective action even though the board seldom takes explicit unfavorable action at meetings.

The CEO is possessed of a highly valuable and practical opportunity to reveal tentative proposals of magnitude to board members for their guidance and reaction; particularly those board members having peculiar knowledge of the subject at hand. Thus, the subject matter of all major corporate actions can be carefully scrutinized and tested, while in tentative form, by those members of the board who are known to have extensive knowledge of the field. This procedure provides for a thoughtful appraisal and sophisticated refinement of the proposal before being presented to the board for action. Thus, when the proposal is formally presented to the board for action, it is realized that the proposal has already been carefully scrutinized by formal or informal committees of highly qualified board representatives. A favorable board action under these circumstances is not that of a rubber stamp but an informed action taken under conditions which assure the observance of the highest standards of propriety, prudence, and common sense.

The board has and exercises final authority in the basic matters of corporate existence, direction, and status. It actually possesses final authority which it always exercises in the event of a crisis. This is important, among other reasons, because no one else in our governmental or corporate structure has this final power. It is highly important that trusted private machinery exists so that action in the event of a crisis can be taken by some group which has the unquestioned right and duty to do so.

The board and only the board can make sure that the corporation participates in the solution of social problems and ills where such solutions are essential for the future corporate success of the enterprise.

The CEO and the board are not antagonists, although it is a primary obligation of the board to keep the conduct and views of the CEO consistent with all current and high standards of corporate conduct. The CEO and the board must act as a team pulling a common load. The board's alertness to contemporary problems which arise in their respective individual fields of life is a great asset to the corporation. The CEO can call upon them and gain the value of their informed judgment, in wide areas of technical and complex problems.

BASIC PHILOSOPHY AND FAITH

As stated heretofore, the establishment and exercise of executive authority and power is assisted and implemented through the use of familiar and helpful tools and mechanisms, including organization manuals, statements of personnel policies such as "A Code to Work By" (see the Appendix), and the development and articulation of corporate principles, goals, and objectives. It must, however, be emphasized in closing that the mere mechanism of fulfilling corporate objectives is unimportant as compared with the quality of the business philosophy and the attitude of the executive.

It is a matter of fundamental business philosophy to embrace the view that since all accomplishments are made by people and not by things, all policies, particularly those relating to personnel, must be based on belief in the common.dignity and integrity of the individual man. Indeed, the success of all enterprise depends upon the spirit and talents of the individuals involved and the genuine recognition by executives of the common humanity of all men.

Actually, the whole of life, certainly business life, is based upon human dynamics and humanistic behavior and not on materialistic equipment or physical tools.

This means that an executive cannot have faith in a specific organization manual alone—the manual can and must be changed or dropped when the human beings using or relying upon it sense and feel the necessity to change in the interests of the individuals affected.

The underlying human conviction of what is good, right, just and noble must prevail. This faith we gladly confess!

APPENDIX: A CODE TO WORK BY

"A Code to Work By" is a set of principles on which officers and employees strive to base their relationships with each other. These principles are summarized as follows:

1. To recognize and respect the dignity and individuality of each employee and to treat him courteously and considerately.
2. To attract, select, place, and promote employees, based on their qualifications for work requirements, without discrimination.[4]
3. To maintain fair and consistent standards of performance, objectively reflecting these standards in decisions concerning the promotion, compensation, and retention of each employee.
4. To use the ability of each employee as fully as possible by work assignments in line with individual interest, aptitude, and experience, and by recognition of constructive ideas and suggestions.
5. To encourage individual growth and development both for improvement of present performance and for promotion.

---

[4] The words "without discrimination" cover discrimination because of race, sex, creed, color, age, or national origin, as well as discrimination based on any other factors unrelated to ability. This policy covers applicants for all jobs and promotions at all levels, including applicants for executive training programs. Placement officers of educational institutions and employment agencies should be periodically advised of this policy.

6. To maintain fair pay by considering job requirements, prevailing salaries for similar work in other organizations, and job performance.

7. To maintain a benefit program that provides each employee with the opportunity to protect himself against the major economic uncertainties of life.

8. To maintain working conditions conducive to health, comfort, and efficiency.

9. To give clear information to each employee about job duties, job performance, and to the greatest extent practicable, the corporation's policies and activities that affect him.

10. To emphasize continuously the interdependence of the individual employees, the units, and the departments of the corporation.

PART II

Organization,
Motivation,
Accomplishment

PART II-A

The
Board
of
Directors

MANNING AND ORGANIZATION OF THE BOARD OF DIRECTORS

by Lawrence A. Appley

Chairman Emeritus, American Management Associations

WHAT A BOARD OF DIRECTORS IS

WITH FULL recognition of the important influence of the community within which an organization functions, the stockholders are the top and final authority in the chain of command. Because it is unrealistic for a large number of stockholders to give the business the detailed attention it requires, they elect a board of directors and give that board considerable authority. The board, therefore, becomes second in command and is responsible to the stockholders for the successful operation of the business. The stockholders elect outside auditors to assure that they are properly informed as to how the company is operating.

A board of directors normally consists of "inside directors" (management employees) and "outside directors" (nonemployees of the corporation). There are still a number of corporations that have no outside directors. When that is the case, they really do not have a board of directors, they have a management committee even though they may call it by another name.

"Insiders" serve on a board of directors for a number of reasons. The Chief Executive Officer, of course, has to be a member of the board because he is the most influential person in the running of the business, and as such should take part in the board's deliberations. He is the leader and gives direction to the affairs of the corporation. Other full-time officers keep the Chief Executive Officer "honest" in his representation of company operations to the board. Their presence gives outside directors immediate contact with operating officials and also enables them to evaluate management's depth— particularly the executive material available for possible succession to the chief executive office.

There are other reasons why it is important to have some management directors on a board: it makes them more effective in their own jobs; it gives them a sense of accountability to an authority higher than the Chief Executive Officer; it adds prestige to their positions.

"Outside" directors are absolutely essential for the proper operation of any board. They make varying types and degrees of expertise available to the company, they increase the feeling of accountability to a higher authority as far as the Chief Executive Officer is concerned and, especially, they offer a Chief Executive Officer an opportunity to discuss certain important matters which he cannot discuss with members of his own management group. It is unrealistic to believe that an officer of a company can work for a Chief Executive Officer on one day and then, as a member of an "inside" board, sit in judgment of that officer on the next day.

In view of the tremendously increasing exposure of directors to law suits, it is amazing that corporations these days can get outsiders to serve on their boards. There are boards, however, that are still attractive. If a board of directors has several outsiders on it, then each director has broad contacts with the experience of many corporations —not just the one represented by the board. Service on other boards of directors is a very broadening experience for any individual.

It is rather commonly said that the type of person you want as an outside director "is not interested in financial remuneration." That is what I label as a management cliché. Regardless of how independently wealthy a person may be, he considers his time as worth something, and it is also important to him what kind of value is placed on his time by those who seek him out as a director. If nothing else, director compensation is a "status symbol." Even though a person did not need anything in the way of retainers or meeting fees, he or she would be much more impressed with a directorship that paid $12,000 a year than with one paying $3,000 a year.

In my opinion, a director represents just one major interest: the stockholders—not one, not five—*all!* A director is elected by all of the stockholders and therefore must represent *all* stockholders.

There is a great deal of difference between managing a company and representative government. There are certain decisions which the law requires that boards of directors make. By far the greatest majority of decisions in connection with running a corporation, however, are made by the full-time management team, headed by the Chief Executive Officer. There is absolutely no justification for any special representation by, or catering to, the interests of any particular segment of our society. There is only one basic consideration within a corporation and that is "What's good for the stockholders within the framework of corporate plans, policies, the law, and ethics."

Because of this strong feeling on my part, I do not agree that any particular stockholder should be on a board of directors to represent *his* block of stock and neither do I believe that anybody else should be on the board as his deputy. I cannot see why a woman should be on the board just to have a woman on the board, or why organized labor, a brokerage firm, a bank, or a legal firm should be specially represented. Any member of the board should represent *all* the stockholders and nobody else. That's repetitious, but it is important.

It is extremely important to keep in mind that a board of directors is neither a management nor an operating committee. It paints with a broad brush. It cannot, and should not deal with the types of problems that usually are reflected by special interests. These problems are handled by full-time management within the day-to-day operations of the business.

At the very moment I am dictating this, a board of directors of which I am a member is being pressured by one director to spin-off a certain division and divide the proceeds among the stockholders. This particular director is on that board specifically to represent the interest of one large stockholder. The recommendation does not take into account the welfare of the entire business, and it could not reasonably be made if that director really understood what the management has in mind for the future.

SIZE OF THE BOARD

The size of the board of directors does not necessarily vary with the size of the business. I am on the board of a relatively small corporation which has 25 directors. I am also on the board of one of the largest corporations in this nation and there are only 15 directors. The number of directors to be elected should be determined by the nature of the work to be done by the board. If many areas of specialization are desirable, if there is a great deal of special committee work, if extra time of the directors is desired, then a larger board would seem advisable. If on the other hand, the work of the board is rather ordinary except in time of crises, a smaller number would be adequate.

In my opinion, instances are very rare when any board of directors should have more than 15 members on it. Never, in my opinion, should there be less than 5. The ideal number in almost any situation is 9 to 12, except in the case of a very small company.

KINDS OF PEOPLE NEEDED

Aside from the Chief Executive Officer, the "heir apparent," if there is one, should be a management director. Beyond that it is entirely up to the Chief Executive Officer as to whether key management people should serve. They should not be elected because of the position held, or tradition. Management directors should be on the board because of their potential and actual contributions to the deliberation of the board and because of any help it may give them in the performance of their tasks.

Outside directors should be former CEOs, present CEOs, or potential CEOs. By "potential" is meant a person it is generally agreed within his management will be the next CEO of the corporation for which he works.

Because an outside director offers a corporation relatively "cheap" consultation, special areas of expertise are usually considered. An acknowledged high-ranking financial expert, engineer, scientist, or educator could be very helpful. Many boards include proven experts in professional management. Executives experienced in the particular type of business or industry of the corporation involved can be very helpful.

One of the most desirable qualifications for an outside director is his or her ability to ask perceptive questions. Someone once said, "It isn't the person with the right answers that is important, but rather the person with the right questions."

SECURING AND SEVERING DIRECTORS

George S. Dively, long-time president, chairman of the board, and Chief Executive Officer of The Harris Corporation, who took that company from less than $10 million a year sales volume to $450 million a year sales volume, has given the functioning of a board of directors more deep and continuing consideration than any other executive within my knowledge or experience. It has been my privilege to have served on his board for over 20 years. On many occasions George Dively has said, "The board of directors is the weakest link in the management chain of command." He deliberately planned and implemented plans to see that this was not the case in his corporation.

There is probably no group or activity in management where the practices are more varied than in the case of boards of directors. A considerable amount of research is being done and study given to this subject, however, and specific patterns are beginning to emerge. One of these is away from the selection of the "safe director" toward the "working director."

The "safe director" is the fraternity brother, the old college chum, the golf partner, bridge partner, fellow club member, or head of a corporation on whose board you serve. He is expected to be "loyal," to "go along," to "not be difficult." Such a situation often leads to reciprocal arrangements—"You scratch my back and I'll scratch yours."

One board I served on many years ago had a 92-year-old director whose chauffeur brought him to the meetings in a wheelchair. He usually was asleep when he arrived. By some intuition he always managed to awaken long enough to say "Aye" and then go back to sleep again. On another board on which I served was a gentleman whom the president always told how to vote. It was perfectly obvious that he did not know what was going on, and did not have intelligence enough to know what kind of a vote was expected. He filled a place at the board table, however.

Professionalism in management has been increasing in leaps and bounds over the last quarter of a century. Professional management does not permit these kinds of practices. The professional manager knows that he must accomplish preestablished objectives to which he is committed and which the board of directors has approved. In order to do this, he recognizes his dependence upon a competent and contributing board of directors. Because of the increasing number of Chief Executive Officers who are now trained professional managers, much more careful attention is being given to the selection and severence of directors.

In the professionally managed company, you will usually find a "management development" or "corporate development" committee of the board. This committee is charged by the Chief Executive Officer and the other directors with the task of assuring the competence of the top management team and with having the depth of reserves required for succession. Such a committee sets the climate for, and assists the Chief Executive Officer in the administration of a formal manager development program.

The Chief Executive Officer who is a professional manager (trained and skilled in the principles, practices, and character of professional management) uses the management development committee to help him in the selection of new directors. Qualifications are drawn up. Good sources are carefully identified. Contacts and interests are ascertained. Many discussions are held and checks are made. Ultimately candidates are submitted to the full board after thorough research by the management development committee.

The professional manager welcomes a competent board of directors that will keep him on his toes. A responsible person seeks accountability to a higher authority and wants that to be a competent and helpful authority.

A position description should be written for the board of directors and by the board of directors. This position description should outline the full responsibilities and functions of the board. It should differentiate between the functions of inside directors and outside directors. It should also differentiate between the contributions that can be made and are expected to be made by inside directors as compared to outside directors. Such a position description should be developed in a series of full board discussions with the benefit of considerable research and staff work.

In my finest experience in this regard, the board of directors met first for a full weekend. They went to an appropriate place with their wives, and mixed some relaxation with work. An initial draft of a position description prepared by the staff and contributed to by the Chief Executive Officer was presented for discussion. Corrections and additions were worked out on the blackboard. The final result was used as a tentative position description for one year. Another weekend was scheduled to review and perfect this position description.

This practice has continued now for 15 years and has developed one of the finest boards of directors that it has been my privilege to serve on, and I have served on more than 30. This practice has established a fellowship and esprit de corps along with dedication, understanding, and competence. It has assured opportunities for individual members of the board to make contributions and to sense their importance. Service on such a board is also a great challenge to personal growth.

When director candidates are told the story and shown the position description that has been worked out, they are unusually impressed with the opportunity and not so inclined to give it an initial "no."

This kind of a climate is also conducive to the development of standards of performance for directors. This is another management technique which, although not new, is gaining momentum in usage. Little along these lines has been done with boards of directors, but I know of at least two experiences that have been very gratifying. In order to arrive at standards of performance, all one has to do is to ask the directors the question, "What is supposed to happen in the company because there is a board of directors that would not happen if there were not one?" This can be brought down to specific annual targets.

Although it is not common, I know of instances where there is a standard practice that each director schedule a specific appointment with the Chief Executive Officer to discuss his relationships with, and contribution to the board. These discussions are handled on an annual basis, and they provide an automatic situation within which understandings can be arrived at. There should also be time set aside at one meeting a year for a discussion with the full board as to the value of its service.

It is unfortunate in human relationships that so many people lack the intestinal fortitude and the ability to tell others when they are not pleased with them and to do so while maintaining mutual respect. Because of this we have built-in, automatic procedures that have been both wasteful and unjust.

Seniority rules are a case in point. Because somebody lacks the courage and the ability to select people for promotion on merit, the easiest way to do it is to select those with the longest service. Another device is a compulsory retirement age. Because most chief executives cannot measure up to telling close associates and friends they are losing their effectiveness, an automatic time for their retirement is established. This leads to the loss of exceptional talent and experience in many cases, and to individuals being maintained on the payroll beyond the end of their effectiveness in many other cases.

There are directors who have lost their effectiveness, if they ever had any, by the age of 60. There are others who maintain their forcefulness and capacity for contribution at 80. I serve on a board right now with a director who is 86 and I hope I have his mental alertness and capacity for contribution when I am that age.

However, because we shall probably never attain enough courage and ability to ask individual directors to continue or retire, depending on the particular circumstances, compulsory age limits will increase in practice. There are two ways at least of putting this into practice: the use of a "grandfather clause"; and the establishment of "directors' pensions." A "grandfather clause" excuses present directors from the age limit. The "directors' pension" continues a director on a consulting basis at approximately half his previous compensation. In the latter case, he may continue to come to board meetings but does not have the right to vote.

The idea of a "directors' pension" is a new one as far as I know. It may have been done in individual cases, but I know of only two where it is a company policy for all outside directors. I shall in time be the beneficiary of one of these.

BOARD LEADERSHIP AND SERVICE

In any event, the responsibility for the quality and character of the board of directors rests upon the Chief Executive Officer. He takes the initiative in matters having to do with the selection, severence, and compensation of directors. He is really the leader of the board, even though it may have a chairman who is not the chief executive.

The officers of a board of directors are the chairman of the board, sometimes a vice chairman of the board, a president, and a corporate secretary. If the chairman is not the Chief Executive Officer, his principal function, other than that of a director, is to preside at board meetings. The leadership of board discussions should be furnished by the Chief Executive Officer because he is the one being advised in the management of the business.

The corporate secretary is a very important position. Any group is dependent upon competent detail and staff work. Agenda and other materials have to be mailed on time and in the proper form. Meeting facilities and setups have to be carefully arranged. Meticulous and careful records must be kept, and from time to time proper procedures ruled upon.

Common practice is to have a lawyer as the corporate secretary, but I have never seen any particular reason for this. In the many board meetings in which I have served, legal questions have rarely arisen. When they do, it is perfectly easy to call upon general counsel, and in many cases there is a lawyer who is a director. The important thing about a corporate secretary is that he or she be a *competent* one. In many instances, I have known a woman to be an assistant secretary and to do most of the work. Actually she should have been the corporate secretary.

COMMITTEES—SCOPE, AUTHORITY

The first committee of any board of directors is the executive committee. It usually has the authority to act for the board between board meetings; but it should not act upon matters that can be effectively held for, and handled by the full board. One exception to the authority of the executive committee should be in the selection of the Chief Executive Officer. That authority must be reserved for the board as a whole. Clear differentiation has to be made between an executive committee and a management committee. The executive committee should not deal in matters which are not appropriate for the Board to deal with.

A finance committee of the board is, at times, the same as the executive committee. At other times, it is a subcommittee of the executive committee. In most cases, however, the finance committee stands on its own feet as responsible representative of the board on financial matters which require more discussion and study in depth than is practical at a board meeting. Suffice it to say that the finance committee deals with the financing of the business and the utilization of its funds.

We have referred to the management development committee before. Committees of this sort are few in number but they are very important. The most important and first duty of a board of directors is to see that there is a competent Chief Executive Officer and to determine his functions, his tenure of office, and his compensation, and to evaluate the quality of his performance. Secondarily, the board is interested in the management team that helps the Chief Executive Officer in his work. The selection and development of management talent requires skill, time, and top-side attention. The only way an organization is going to get it is when the board of directors actively participates in it.

A management development committee of the board of directors, therefore, sits with the Chief Executive Officer at regular intervals to examine the management talent within the organization by divisions, subsidiaries, and corporate departments. Usually the management development committee also deals with matters of incentives and base compensation.

Lower echelons of management do what upper echelons inspect—

not what they expect. If, therefore, the board of directors wants adequate development of management talent within a corporation, it must provide for the inspection of what talent there is and what is being done toward further development.

An audit committee of the board also has a very important function. The stockholders should ratify the appointment of outside auditors. A committee of outside directors should have regular meetings with the outside auditors to review the scope of the audit, procedures to be followed, the results of the audit, and the auditors' recommendations to management. The committee should also make sure that there are no important disagreements between the outside auditors and the management, and that the outside auditors have complete access to any information within the corporation which they desire. The audit committee also determines the competence of the outside auditors and the fairness of their fees. The full board must rely very heavily on the audit committee.

MEETINGS

Regular meetings of the board of directors should be scheduled in advance. It is highly preferable to have them on the same day each month or each quarter, as the case may be. Personally, I do not know how any corporation can function without a board of directors meeting at least every two months.

The board meeting should generally be held at the headquarters of the corporation. Once or twice a year, however, it is desirable to meet at field locations such as division headquarters or subsidiaries or plants. It is good, once in a while, to have an annual stockholders' meeting at a field location. A great deal of employee relations and public relations mileage can be gained thereby.

Unless there is unusual business to be handled, a regular board of directors meeting should not require more than half a day, including a breakfast or a luncheon, at which some special staff presentation might be made. Meetings for the review of the annual budget and for the review of long-range plans would take longer by two or three hours. A regular board meeting that takes no more than an hour is, in my opinion, quite superficial and a symptom of a "rubber stamp" board.

"Homework" is a symbol of an effective contributing board of directors. No board should be caught by surprise. No director should be permitted to come into a meeting without being fairly well informed on the questions coming up for discussion. There should, therefore, be advance reports, studies, and recommendations on questions coming before the board.

Reports to the board must be well and clearly presented. Visual aids are the signs of a professional presentation. Annual statements of the five-year plan (or other long-range term), quarterly presentations of the annual plan, and monthly reviews of performance against plan are required reports. Annual reports on insurance coverage, capital expenditures against commitments, progress in research and development projects, et cetera, are important parts of keeping a board of directors well informed.

In addition to annual retainer fees which are paid to outside directors regardless of meeting attendance, regular meeting fees should be paid. Such meeting fees should be respectable. Well do I recall 50 years ago when my uncle used to return from bank board meetings with his ten-dollar gold piece. If directors' fees these days could be in gold they would be more meaningful, but because that is not readily available,[1] checks or paper money are perfectly acceptable.

A meeting fee of less than $200 does not have much stature in the directorship community. A fee of from $300 to $500 is more appropriate and significant. Fees should be paid for board meetings and committee meetings but on a "half-day" basis. In other words, if there are two or three committee meetings and a board meeting within the same half-day, there should be one single fee. If any part of the second half of the day is required, another single fee should be paid. If a committee meeting is held on days other than board meeting days, a separate fee should be paid. If a single committee meeting takes more than one half-day, a double fee should be paid. Frequently, there are extra annual retainer fees for service on board committees. In no case should inside (full-time management) directors receive any director fees.

IN CONCLUSION

Let there be much more thought, care, and professional attention given to the manning and organization of the board of directors. The board of directors is an important part of the whole American business system, and such attention will pay off in terms of the enhanced effectiveness of that system.

---

[1] As of 1974.

WORKING WITH THE
BOARD OF DIRECTORS

by Myles L. Mace

*Professor of Business Administration (Emeritus),
Harvard Business School*

THE EXTENT to which a board of directors serves to represent the stock-holder owners and fulfills an important role at the highest level of a corporate business organization depends upon the desires of the Chief Executive Officer. In a large, widely held company, the CEO and members of the board typically own little of the company's stock. Instead, the ownership is dispersed among thousands of unorganized (and essentially unorganizable) stockholders. With this absence of control or influence by the corporate owners, the CEO has de facto powers to control the enterprise and, accordingly, determines what the board of directors does or does not do. At the other end of the company-size spectrum, in the small family company, ownership and the management are identical; powers of control are in the family owners and the CEO, as the principal owner, determines what the board does or does not do. Thus, in both cases, the CEO determines whether he wants an involved, function-fulfilling board or a board that complies with the legal requirements by being in existence, meeting periodically, but serving completely subservient and obedient to the decision-making process of the CEO.

If the CEO chooses to regard the board as an important and involved element in corporate management, and there seems to be a growing trend in this direction, he must communicate to board members through word and behavior that their participation is required. Some managements have prepared written statements of business functions to define specifically the respective roles and relationships of the CEO and the board of directors. The board's position description in Omark Industries, for example, covered seven major areas of function.

I shall include a select few of the many roles in each area to illustrate the specific job defined.

Shareholder relations:

. . . approve policy governing quarterly, annual, and special reports to shareholders to ensure that the contents are fair representations to the investors.

. . . approve policy regarding tender offer strategy and determination of levels of "fight value."

Financial structure and actions:

. . . approve changes in capital structure and basic changes in debt policy.

. . . approve annually the maximum limits of short-term debt, receive quarterly reports on short-term borrowings, and be advised of borrowings and lines of credit by the individual bank of the parent and its subsidiaries.

. . . approve all long-term loans.

Purpose, objectives, policies, plans:

. . . approve long-range corporate objectives normally initiated by the Chief Executive Officer.

. . . review the annual operating budget, which will have been related to the longer-range objectives of the corporation.

. . . receive annually a special R&D report (products or manufacturing processes) listing major projects by divisions.

. . . review annually the long-range strategy of the company; confirm its direction or proposed changes of direction.

. . . receive on request periodic compliance audits concerning conformance to major corporate policy.

Management:

. . . appraise performance of the Chief Executive Officer and the chairman, and review with them their annual personal objectives; the Chief Executive Officer will inform the board annually of his appraisal of the executive vice president.

. . . provide for the orderly succession to the position of CEO.

Employee relations:

. . . approve basic corporate benefit plans.

. . . be promptly advised by the CEO via special letter of any position or decision likely to lead to a strike in any direction.

Control:

. . . recognize and identify the board's need for company information, and arrange for its timely supply.

. . . review company performance against purpose, policies, objectives, and plans.

. . . inquire into causes of measured deficiencies in performance.

The board:

. . . propose the size of the board.

. . . fix the age limit of board membership.

. . . recruit new members to the board, and elect them as authorized by the bylaws.

. . . remove members from the board for just cause.

Generally board members are honorable, competent men and women, who are willing to devote the time, energy, and help requested by the CEO; but the essential factor is the leadership of the CEO in asking the board to perform in order to truly represent the best interests of the stockholders.

To enable board members to be knowledgable and effective, an information and reporting system is basic. Usually the monthly or quarterly reports prepared for the board are designed to measure the company's performance against an operating budget and against last year's results. There is no single form or model as to the amount of detail, for this is determined by the size, organization structure, and complexity of each company. Care must be exercised to assure that board members receive accounting and financial data in sufficient detail to provide an understanding of the company's situation, but not in such volume that a "blizzard of paper" discourages study. One company management, for example, overwhelms its board members with a monthly financial report that varies in thickness from six to eight inches.

Financial reports on a company's operations as well as management proposals involving major policies should be provided to board members a reasonable time prior to the scheduled meeting. Thoughtful analysis requires time, and except for emergency incidents requiring board action, board members need to evaluate company performance and policy proposals prior to a meeting so that a discussion at a board meeting can be focused on the issues rather than reviewing the facts of the problem.

Here, too, in the board discussion, say of last month's results, the attitude and behavior of the CEO determine board interest and involvement. When questions by board members are encouraged, and management representatives are responding openly, the board and management are working together effectively to promote the best interests of the company.

Some CEOs have adopted the practice of writing a "president's letter" to accompany the financial data forwarded to directors prior to a meeting. In the letter, the CEO comments on the performance of the principal product categories, divisions, or subsidiaries of the company, identifies problems, and indicates what action is being taken to correct the particular difficulties of the operating units. Analysis of company operations by the CEO is helpful not only to board members, but it also serves as an effective management discipline in that the CEO must analyze each operating unit's performance in order to comment perceptively on his subordinate's performance.

Board members' contributions to the management of corporations are not limited to the time spent in board meetings. Involved and responsible members of the board are responsive to changes in the business environment which might affect the company they serve and are expected to communicate relevant observations to the CEO. Also, the CEO calls upon individual members or all members between meetings to elicit comments and suggestions on company problems. The informal working relationships between the CEO and board members are fully as important as those found in the board's formal meetings.

Some CEOs are reluctant to seek board advice between meetings. As one said, "We do not compensate our directors at all well and I don't want to take advantage of them—I don't want my questions to be an imposition." Other CEOs say that one of their greatest management resources is the availability of able, interested, involved, and motivated directors. A telephone or luncheon chat provides the CEO with an external point of view, thereby multiplying the inputs needed on major management decisions. "The outside directors," stated one CEO, "give me many windows to the outside world—windows of information to add to the effective resolution of tough problems in an uncertain world."

Although there has been some increase in the compensation level of outside directors in recent years, the average is still well below what would be paid to senior consultants on a per diem basis. Directors are typically conscientious persons who, compensated on appropriate levels, contribute beyond the call of duty. Also, additional rewards to directors encourage CEOs to call upon the unique composite of professional advice and counsel found on boards.

Compensation policies for directors have come a long way from the early corporate practice of distributing gold pieces to directors at the end of each meeting. Current compensation practices by industry and size of company are reported upon periodically by several professional organizations. One such organization, The Conference Board, reports that outside directors of few companies serve without compensation today—"3 percent of the manufacturers and 2 percent of nonmanufacturing firms."[1] The Conference Board also reports that

> . . . per-meeting fees are still more common than annual retainers as a means of compensating outside directors for board service. Fees paid to outside directors by a manufacturing company range from $15 to $1,000 per meeting, but amounts of $100 and $200 are by far the most frequently reported. Among nonmanufacturing companies, fees of $100 and $200 are also the most commonly used, but the range of fees in these industries is relatively narrow.[2]

Outside directors, who are well aware of, and sensitive to the increasing legal liabilities requiring a higher standard of care in the performance of the board functions and who generally desire to fulfill their roles as involved and responsible directors, need to be compensated appropriately. The practice of one company is not enough, where the CEO said, "We pay our directors $25 for each half-day meeting, we don't have to pay them any more because it is an honor to be on our board."

The CEO who recognizes the dual role of board members (1) to represent the owners—the stockholders—by monitoring and measuring his performance and (2) to serve as sources of advice and counsel to him, can design the optimum composition of the boards so as to best serve the unique requirements of the company. To illustrate:

The CEO of a manufacturer of ladies' fashion consumer products added to his board a woman editor of a ladies' fashion magazine and the president of a consumer products company which expends annually substantial sums on advertising and promotion. Another CEO, embarking on a company growth program in international markets, and identifying the continuing need for counsel in this area, invited an experienced world marketer from the United Kingdom to serve on his board. Thus, both of these CEOs defined the optimum characteristics of board members and designed programs for board membership for use when vacancies occurred.

---

[1] The Conference Board; "Corporate Directorship Practices"; *Studies in Business Policy*; no. 125; p. 29.

[2] Ibid; "Highlights for the Executive."

Changes in board makeup often are relatively infrequent, but when opportunities arise for new candidates CEOs can strengthen their boards through planning their ideal board and adding those who meet the predefined specifications.

Also, CEOs can strengthen the composition of their boards by limiting the number of inside-officer directors and increasing the number of outsiders. This is a controversial issue and CEOs generally have firm convictions. Some believe strongly that the board should be dominated by insiders who live with the business on a day-to-day basis; others state equally strongly that representation of stockholders can best be accomplished by having the CEO and one or two other insiders on the board with the remainder made up of outsiders. Still other CEOs take a middle-ground position that the ideal board consists of a balance of insiders and outsiders, without stating what "balance" really means.

There are many plausible reasons for having a considerable number of insiders on the board—e.g., board membership gives prestige to the insiders and contributes to high morale throughout the organization; membership on the board contributes to the insiders' education by allowing them to participate in the top-level management process; outside directors are enabled to calibrate insiders as potential candidates for the presidency; and insiders at board meetings can answer queries raised with regard to their respective areas of responsibility.

I believe that the objectives of the reasons cited for having insiders on boards may be accomplished through other means. Populating a board with insiders whose advice and counsel are available through existing working relationships reduces the number of outsiders whose additional objective advice and counsel would be unaffected by the superior-subordinate lines of authority within the organization. Subordinates of CEOs are effectively precluded from monitoring and measuring the performance of their superiors.

CONCLUSION

Boards of directors of business corporations, as well as those of nonprofit organizations, can perform useful, responsible, and constructive roles only when the CEO works with the board and permits, encourages, and insists upon their involvement. The interests of the corporation, represented by its stockholders, employees, and directors, are served well when this is the case.

LEGITIMACY, OBJECTIVITY, AND VITALITY OF THE BOARD OF DIRECTORS OF THE LARGE COMPANY

by Courtney C. Brown*

Dean Emeritus, Columbia University,
Graduate School of Business

OVER THE YEARS, I have heard and read many things relating to the function, legitimacy, objectivity and vitality of the board of directors of the publicly held corporation, especially the *large* corporation. Also, over the years, it has been my pleasure, and a source of great interest to me to know many directors of large companies, to observe the boards of directors of companies and indeed to serve on some boards. On the whole, my experience has been reassuring. But I must say that not everything that I have heard, read, observed and thought has been entirely laudatory of the board of directors as an institution, nor of the workings of boards of directors of particular companies. Out of all this, I have distilled a few ideas of my own that may be worth passing along.

THE PLACE AND ROLE OF THE DIRECTOR; AMBIGUITY, UNCERTAINTY, AND DOUBT

The world of the director, these days, is a place of ambiguity, uncertainty, and doubt. A number of court cases, which need not be reviewed here, have opened up—or reopened—important questions as to the responsibilities and liabilities of directors. Not all of these ques-

---

* [Ed. Note: Courtney Brown is a director, or former director of Columbia Broadcasting System, Inc.; Borden, Inc.; Union Pacific Corporation; American Electric Power Co.; Associated Dry Goods Corp.; American Standard; Uris Buildings Corp.; Esso Standard Oil; New York Stock Exchange.]

tions are easily settled. A number of critics of the workings of large corporations have questioned the legitimacy and efficacy of the board of directors, as they see it—or think they see it—as an institution. They raise questions as to what the board is really *supposed* to do and as to what it actually *does* do. It isn't easy to give them clear-cut answers.

Even many directors, themselves, and managers, too, ask themselves what *is* the role of the board in the large publicly held corporation? How *should* the board be constituted and organized? How should it work? Conscientious and thoughtful directors, however, probably more than judges on the bench or critics on the sidelines, are aware of the ambiguities, uncertainties, doubts surrounding the board of directors of the large corporation—to say nothing of the tremendous diversity, from company to company, as to composition, working, and plain effectiveness of boards.

A WORD ABOUT SOME CRITICISM

A couple of comments about people who believe that the large corporation should now become something of a quasi-public institution: They often base their case largely on what they see as the "unrepresentativeness" of the board of directors of the typical large company. The board, they say, typically represents only itself and not even the stockholders. They say the board is dependent on management favor for the selection of its members. They say that the board is in no position at all to function as an independent agent. They see the board as "unrepresentative" of any constituency and as nothing more than a creature of the management.

Some who raise questions as to the legitimacy of the boards of large companies hold that a basic change in the allocation of power within the corporation is required to correct the situation. They sometimes suggest that boards should include representatives of the public, government, or special interest groups.

Personally, I don't go along with such proposals. It seems to me that such measures would simply lead to political tension, or even conflict where it has no real place. Too, I believe that the corporation has a *job* to do and should not be diverted by political wrangle. More especially, it seems to me that such measures would make the board's role and function even more ambiguous than it is already.

Nevertheless, it must be conceded that all of us citizens are interested in having our large corporations well run. And if we hope to sustain and even strengthen our private enterprise system, we recognize that it must ultimately be based on public approval and sanction. And the approval, of course, must include the board of directors, as an institution. To that end, as well as for the purpose of possibly contributing to the health and prosperity of the corporation, we must do what we can to clarify the role of the board and to make it as effective as we can.

It is with thoughts such as these in mind that I put forward some ideas designed to make the board as effective and as responsive to changing circumstances as possible.

SEPARATION OF DIRECTORS AND MANAGEMENT

One basic reason for the shortcomings of boards of directors, it seems to me, is that their functions have not been clearly defined and, especially, kept separate from those of the management. It seems to me that a very important step in strengthening the position and role of the board is to make sure that it is *separate from the management—* both in function and in manning.

Functions of the Board and Management

First as to function. In a period of growing complexity, any single definition of the role and responsibilities of directors will be an oversimplification. It does seem to me, however, that one basic distinction is valid; indeed, it is a distinction that may ultimately be regarded as essential to the effective discharge of the board's collective responsibilities and for the healthy future development of the corporation. Something that really helps increase the usefulness of the board as an institution and strengthens its legitimacy is also in the ultimate interest of management. The distinction: The board of directors is the appropriate unit for the establishment of broad policies and procedures and for reviewing performance. Management is the agency delegated by the board to make those policies and procedures effective, subject to board review. Conversely, intervention by board members in the *execution* of policy, apart from prior approval and review, can be and has proved to be debilitating. On the other hand, the *making of policy* by management through the accumulation of day-today decisions can cause a company to lose its sense of direction and motivation. Thoughtless practice by both directors and managers has tended to blur the distinction between the two bodies.

In legal terms, the responsibility of the directors is clear. They are elected by the voting stockholders of the company to represent the interest of stockholders with due diligence and prudence. It is that simple. A major task of the board is to select competent people to manage the property, including the Chief Executive Officer or officers, and to arrange for a reasonably continuous and comprehensive review of the operations. Another task is to establish broad guidelines for administering and protecting the assets of the enterprise. Still another is to settle compensation of the officers of the corporation. A specific responsibility is to see to it that there is no conflict of interest between the corporation and the stockholders, on the one hand, and the management on the other. It is not the function of the directors to run the company day-to-day.

A second major function of the board is to guide the corporation in those matters related to social responsibility that the public has come to expect of business organizations. It is unfair to expect management, whose success is measured by return on investment, to deliberately take sustained actions that increase costs without board encouragement and even initiative.

There is much more that could be said as to the functions of the directors and how they differ from those of the management. But it is clear that there are essential differences. It is also clear that difficulties and ambiguity will arise if and when the membership of the directors and management become too closely identified.

Membership of the Board and Management

The second aspect of preserving separation between the board and the management, so that there will not be confusion as to their respective functions, is to make sure that there is a very clear-cut separation between membership on the board and membership in management.

I take it for granted that in many large companies people who have been, and are, intimately associated with the corporation will be included on its board. This makes excellent sense, for the activities, economics, technology, financial requirements, and all the rest, of the large corporation are very complex, and considerable first-hand knowledge and experience with the industry and the workings of the company are indispensible. But having corporate officers with ongoing operating responsibilities also serve as directors on the board for extended periods of time can be a source of ambiguity and confusion and can operate to reduce the effectiveness of both management and board.

"Outsiders" by definition, are separate from management. But "insiders" should also be separate and independent from management. If not, there will be confusion with all the consequent results.

The separation of board and management should start at the very top. In recent years the practice has grown of electing a single individual to the several posts of chairman of the board, president, and Chief Executive Officer; in which case he is the senior officer of both the board and of the management of the company. A variation is to elect one person as chairman of the board and chief *executive* officer and another person as president and chief *operating* officer. In both cases, there is an obvious difficulty of separating out the functions and responsibilities of the chief executive of the company when he sits as a member of the board from those which he has when he acts as chief executive of the *management*. Ambiguity of the role of the total board can start right there.

The cure for this is simple: Make sure that the chairman has *no* responsibility for day-to-day management, and that his sole job is to be, literally, the chairman of the board. If such is the case, he has no occasion for getting confused as to whether he is acting, or should act as a member of the board or as a member of the management. And that goes for all the other "insiders" as well.

The common confusion between board and management can be avoided if, after joining the board, former officers of the management are relieved as soon as possible of all *operating* responsibilities. The one exception would be the president, whose principle function is managing the ongoing workings of the company. In that event, "insiders" would no longer be "inside directors" as that term is now understood, but rather officers of the *board*. In that role and in that position they could bring to bear a rich fund of knowledge and experience about the company's affairs.

This practice has precedents, even if the nomenclature is not quite the same. Exxon, formerly Standard Oil Company (New Jersey), for many years was said to have a totally "inside board," even though the board members, recruited exclusively from executive officers of the organization, were, in fact, relieved of all *operating* responsibilities after election. Their task was, and, I believe, still is to help develop policy and procedures and to counsel with operating officers of the company in the review of performance. In recent years several outside directors without Exxon experience have been added to that board.

There is nothing in this dichotomy to imply conflict of interest or of purpose between management and board, except perhaps in those instances where management is concerned with the short-term showing and the board looks further ahead. But arrangements that clarify the respective, and separate functions and responsibilities of both board and management, and that provide a system of checks and balances between the two, will do much to minimize mistakes and maximize successes.

A NEW CONCEPT OF THE FUNCTION OF BOARD CHAIRMAN

The dichotomy between board and management—the clear separation of the two—does imply a new and different concept of the role of the chairman of the board. Although in most cases, the chairman would be elected by the board after a successful career in the company, he would no longer be an officer of the management. He would be the senior officer of the board. The Chief Executive Officer would not report to the chairman directly but rather to the collective board, of which the chairman is but one member.

The chairman's main function would be to organize the work of the board, which—certainly for most of our large, complex corporations—if effectively done would require a full-time or nearly full-time commitment. In collaboration with the Chief Executive Officer, the chairman would schedule, organize, and propose the agenda for regular or special board meetings, including prior review of the adequacy of documentary material sent to other board members. Subject to the board's review, he would establish the procedures to govern the board's work; he would assign specific tasks to members of the board; and assure adequate lead time for effective study and discussion of matters under consideration. He would have under continuous review the flow of information to board members, and he would propose to the board for its approval a committee structure, together with the assignments of fellow members of the board to effectuate the board's work.

BOARD COMMITTEES

The legitimate functions and concerns of the board of directors of one of our large, complex, often multinational, companies are so multifarious and difficult, and the burdens of handling them well so heavy, that special attention needs to be given to setting up board committees and helping them to do their work properly without interfering with the ongoing work of management—and without being interfered with!

Among the board committees that may be needed to cover adequately the board's activities in larger corporations are the following: an executive committee; a finance and budget committee; a compensation and pension committee; an audit committee, that may also be concerned with corporate organization and administration; a conflicts-of-interest and "legalities" committee; and, possibly, a personnel, appointments, and succession committee. These suggested committees encompass the major areas of concern internal to the company on which the board's attention will from time to time be focused. Areas of interest are at least six in number: (1) the allocation of resources; (2) the systems of internal reporting and communications for audit and control; (3) the types of administrative structures best adapted to the nature of the business or businesses; (4) possible conflicts of interest within the management and on the board; (5) compensation, fringe benefits, and pension arrangements for both wage and salary personnel; and (6) last, but not least, the problem of assuring competent management in depth, and arranging for orderly succession at all senior levels including the Chief Executive Officer.

A special point might be made about the comprehensive opportunities of the personnel, appointments, and succession committee, which does not appear in the usual roster. It is generally true that the entry to, and exit from, board membership is today informal, and apart from age retirement, more dependent on the judgment and desire of the Chief Executive Officer than upon ownership of stock or formal approval of stockholders. The influence on a board member's degree of independence is self evident. A screening procedure for both entry and exit of board members, administered by a board subcommittee on personnel, appointments, and succession, could contribute constructively to objective policy determination.

Some companies have subcommittees concerned with technology and with public policy issues, but others feel that these are areas of interest to all committees and to the whole board.

ORGANIZATION OF THE BOARD

Even though the respective functions of the board and management of the large, complex corporation may have been clarified, there remains the matter of organizing the board, determining its procedures, and recruiting and renewing its membership. What are the most likely sources of a chairman of the board, of chairmen of the respective subcommittees, and of board members not previously associated with the company? What physical facilities should be made available to the board, if any, and where should they be located? To what extent should the board be provided with staff? How much time should board members commit to their work? What kind of prerequisites and compensation are appropriate and how should they be determined? There are as many ways to answer each of these questions as there are corporations. Again, it is possible only to provide general observations.

Usually the board's work should be processed in the office of the chairman. Specific matters might originate with him, with the president, or with a subcommittee. Occasionally, they might originate with an individual board member. Background documentation should be developed on assignment by the appropriate subcommittee in collaboration with the company officers involved, or by the chairman's office if the matter falls outside a subcommittee's designated interest. It would then go on the agenda, with appropriate documentation, of a meeting of the full board, with or without recommendation. Submission without recommendation should not imply disapproval but rather that, in the specific instance, a discussion by the full board without prejudice is desirable.

This pattern of work would obviously require office space and secretarial assistance. Probably a board member assistant to the chairman of the board would expedite the work. Both of these officers of the board should be prepared to assign a major part of their time, if not all of their time, to their respective tasks. They must, of course, be thoroughly familiar with the traditions and operations of the organization.

Other chairmen of subcommittees need not necessarily make the same commitment of time. Depending on circumstances and the personalities and talents involved, they may or may not have had a career in the company. For example, an experienced lawyer or accountant would qualify for the conflict of interest and "legalities" committee, or for the audit committee. The personnel subcommittee would possibly benefit from experience external to the company, as would the compensation subcommittee. None of these chairmanships would require full time; they could be filled by directors with limited or no previous company experience. Advantages accrue from the thinking and points of view of those with broad contacts in numerous activities.

Generally speaking, a greater participation in the determination of policy, and procedures, and in the review of performance, implies commitment of more time and attention than is the present practice of most directors of most boards of our very large companies. Guidance in matters related to social responsibility imposes an additional dimension. A corresponding increase in compensation is implied. Indeed, the quality of board members and their work will be enhanced with a clarification of their functions and an increase in their rewards. Those board members recruited from officers of the company would necessarily retire from operating responsibilities at earlier ages, perhaps in their early or mid-fifties. Membership on one or more boards would become a full-time career for some, and a part-time career for most. Under such a procedure the distinction between "inside" and "outside" directors would become obsolete. In a real sense, all but the president (who would be the Chief Executive Officer) would really be "outside"—that is outside of, and independent of, the management.

BOARD INDEPENDENCE AND LEGITIMACY REVIEWED

Having come to this point, we can now return to our starting concern: How to assure the legitimacy, representativeness, objectivity, and vitality of the boards of directors of our large companies.

The search for greater independence of board members has led some companies to accept the notion of specialized representation: women, ethnic minorities, consumers, labor, clergy, and so on. It is not clear to me how the conflicting interests of multiple and diverse constituencies will, in the long run, be reconciled with the best interest of the basic constituency of the board, which is, of course, the *company*, itself. To be sure, we must recognize that there now exists a certain lethargy among many boards of directors of large companies in responding to changing practices and expectations and to modifications in the scale of values of a dynamic contemporary society. An aggressive woman with a vital interest in equality for members of her sex or an outspoken black or clergyman no doubt may be desirable or necessary to serve for a period as a "catfish in the herring tank." In the long run, however, a board consisting predominantly of members serving specialized interests could not be expected to maximize the development of the total enterprise.

It seems to me, rather, that the current concern for specialized representation may prove to be more of an unstated recognition of the *need* for greater *independence* among all board members than a *solution* to the problem. It is more important to have a vigorous and informed review of proposals from the point of view of the general interest than it is to have contending and specialized individuals on the board trying to represent the particular interests of limited constituencies. Conflict on the board would make effective action difficult. Service to a particular group may constitute a conflict of interest with the very institution board members are elected to help govern. Over time, I would judge, the interests of the several parties involved in the enterprise will be best served by the balanced and healthy *total* development of the enterprise as a whole.

That is not to say that specialized interests should be unsponsored. With a requisite degree of independence, *all* members of the board will espouse causes from time to time, and not always the same cause. This is true of all who are worthy of board membership, whether female, black, or of primarily religious background. The sex or the ethnic, vocational, or religious affiliation of the individual board member should be irrelevant. The *quality* of the individual is what really is paramount.

A reconceptualization of the board's function and structure is a far more promising way of assuring independence of its posture. Especially is this true of efforts to separate clearly the "legislative" functions of the board from the "executive" functions of the management, and to establish and maintain a clear demarcation between the memberships of the two groups. Such steps should provide for the technical competence required in both bodies as well as for their ability to look at themselves and each other with objectivity. Those steps, alone, should do much to assure the "legitimacy" of the corporation, its direction, and its management.

Numerous books and articles critical of the effectiveness of directors in the discharge of this and that aspect of their responsibilities have appeared in recent years. Many business leaders are now persuaded that revitalization of the board of directors can do much to assure the continued development of the corporation as a constructive influence in contemporary society. Although there is, I am sure, no single prescription for that revitalization, I am equally persuaded that a clarification and implementation of the respective separate functions of board members and of management can make a major contribution to that important purpose.

CONCLUSION

There is much more, of course, that could be said on this topic. Only a limited reference has been made, for instance, about meeting the changing social responsibilities of the corporation. Clearly, these will have to be met if the privately owned and privately run corporation is to retain its legitimacy in the modern scheme of things. Clear separation between the board and the management may make it easier for these new responsibilities to be perceived, evaluated, and responded to. There are new areas of concern external to the corporation itself that need to be recognized, including the environment; conservation; alleviation of community tensions, particularly those arising from discrimination and poverty. Moreover, external communications are needed to assure that effective internal and external performance become widely known by the public at large. In all such matters, a clear division of function between board and management, combined with a tradition of mutually helpful collaboration between them, should facilitate recognition of new opportunities and needs and the design of new policies responsive to the times.

PITFALLS OF BEING A DIRECTOR

by Edwin L. Kennedy

Managing Director, Lehman Brothers

WHEN I first accepted membership on boards of directors, I formulated certain rules to apply to such membership. I believe they have served me well; I pass them on in the hope they may be of help to others. These basic principles have been:

1. Accept an invitation to join a corporation as a director only when you are really convinced that the management is of good character and subscribes to a code of high ethical standards.

2. Regardless of the circumstances which cause the invitation to be given, I was, and I am persuaded that a board member must, without pause and without reservation, represent *all* stockholders. Membership in a board of directors where views on corporate problems or policies are shaped by the attitudes of a single or a special-interest stockholder are not compatible with the basic thesis of corporate democracy. Furthermore, a narrow special-interest representation that dominates a corporation's affairs may lead to unwarranted risks in the field of directors' liability.

3. I assumed, and I take it as unarguable that one must not serve on a board unless one is both able to and committed to give sufficient time to become a knowledgeable director. Absences from directors' meetings should be minimal. Maintaining a position as a knowledgeable director involves much more time and work than merely attending meetings.

4. A board member should have a direct ownership of sufficient stock of the corporation to give him a meaningful personal stake in the board decisions in which he participates. A meaningful, personal stake does not necessarily mean a large number of shares. We know able directors who do not have great personal wealth for whom ownership of 100 shares meets the requirement, and we know of others

for whom a much larger position does not meet the requirement. Ownership should be more than a token one as measured, not by the number of shares owned, but in relation to the director's total financial picture.

5. A board member, clearly, must keep himself continuously informed about the problems, trends, and managerial performance of the company with which he is associated as a director. He avoids getting into the area of operating decisions except as management may inform him while considering broad matters of policy. His most important function is evaluation of managerial performance. He performs his duties in a background that presumes his general support of management. But his support of management is not automatic or rubber-stamp. It comes from independent thinking and analysis. When a director's judgment, carefully determined, differs too often on major issues from that of management, the director must reassess the situation to determine whether *he* is misplaced in his director's position or whether *management* should be strengthened. This may pose a hard decision; if so, I believe it should be faced and made.

The basic principles enumerated above were not mere abstractions but rather hard-core working philosophy from the beginning of my activity as a director. Because I have been guided by them, I believe that I have been less concerned than many others about the growing risks associated with being a director. As standards of performance have changed with greater exposure to liability, I have, to be sure, made adjustments in procedure and details to assure my serious intent and diligent conduct; but major changes, alterations, or additions to the above basic principles were not required. I have, however, more carefully applied the thesis stated in my number one "basic principle," above, before accepting new directorships, and I have continuously reassessed my position in this regard with respect to existing boards. Many of the heavily publicized corporate events, which have led to critical problems for board members, sadly but simply unearthed weakness of character, of ethics, of judgment in management or elsewhere in a corporation's governance. Although it is not possible to predict what people will do under all conditions, a prudent person of maturity and experience—and that's the kind of person a director should be—should be able in very many instances to sense warning signals. The working rule that I have followed in this respect is: *If in doubt, don't* accept membership on a board of directors.

Much has been written in recent years about the changing role of the director in a world of accelerating turmoil and change. Especially the director's exposure to liability has been and is the subject of voluminous comments and queries as legislators and the courts have broadened and deepened the area of punitive sanctions for negligence, nonperformance, or malfeasance. There is no question that directors today are exposed to greater liabilities than 25 years ago. Hence, insurance or indemnification against these liabilities is much more prevalent. In my judgment a board member should insist that the company he serves make available the protection that insurance provides. He should do so, however, with full understanding that insurance, in and of itself, is limited in the protection that it provides against liability, if the director does not diligently discharge his duties as a director.

DIRECTORSHIPS AND SOCIAL RESPONSIBILITY

A corporation serves many constituencies: customers, employees, investors, governments, the general public. A director, holding a position of fiduciary responsibility for the corporation's affairs, necessarily bears responsibility to each of these constituencies. His obligation to each is to protect and serve its interests with good judgment and fairness. This, of course, is more easily stated than applied in practice because the wishes of the constituent groups frequently are conflicting. For example, at a time of high interest rates and rising capital expenditures, financial officers of corporations are likely to oppose liberalization of dividend policy in line with improving earnings. Yet, stockholders are victims of soaring living costs due to the same forces of inflation that invite financial officers to reinvest earnings rather than pay them out as dividends. Fairness to investors and hence to the general public, because they are the general public, requires, as a minimum, that the guidelines of past dividend policy continue to be followed as profits move upward.

It may be noted that my statement of basic principles did not include a specific reference to the public interest. This was neither an oversight nor an omission. It simply is included in the emphasis I place on a director's responsibility to represent all stockholders in decisions that are rational and fair to the constituencies a corporation serves. Every decision that directors make involves, in greater or less amounts, elements of social responsibility. Wage policy, dividend policy, product pricing policy, and so on, involve decisions of special interest to one of a corporation's constituent groups. Yet, these decisions are only in degree less important to the other constituent groups than they are to the group directly involved. A director's social responsibility is not something that can be compartmentalized or neatly boxed as a separate package to appear as a separate item on the agenda of a directors' meeting. It is inherent in every problem discussed and every decision made.

Earlier I indicated that I strongly subscribe to the principle of ownership by each and every board member. I react negatively to board rosters that show no stockholdings or merely trivial stockholdings to meet requirements for qualification. I have also indicated a cautious view toward a situation where a corporation's decisions are dominated by a single or special-interest stockholder or stockholders. These views are not inconsistent. Substantial ownership by management and directors encourages sound judgment from the prudent action that self-interest stimulates. But this does not carry to a point where concentrated ownership dominates decisions to the exclusion of other stockholders, the public interest, or the constituencies that a corporation serves. The greater the stock ownership by men in areas of responsibility, the better; provided that ownership is held by men who give priority to their social responsibility in all decision making.

I have observed that, in some cases, serious problems arise for "outside" directors when a business moves from a position of being fully privately owned or closely held to one of partial public ownership. Usually such businesses have been developed by strong individuals who did not have to live with the greater constraints, controls, and regulation that accompanies public ownership. The psychological background of running a family corporation sometimes carries beyond a transition period of adjustment to a point where management continues to operate the business, after it is opened up to public ownership, with attitudes not greatly changed from the period before that took place.

DIRECTORS AND THE PUBLIC INTEREST

At a time of rapid social and economic change, it is not surprising that the role of business in our complex society should be increasingly discussed, evaluated, and criticized. The focal point of this critical discussion is often boards of directors, because directorship as an institution has represented the apex of authority and responsibility—boards of governors, overseers, trustees, or directors—since trading companies were established by sovereign grant in the 16th and 17th centuries. Views range all the way from the thesis that directors are insignificantly important to the opposite view that their record of top responsibility, over a period that provided the greatest progress ever in meeting mankind's wants, shows them to be highly effective. In other words, directorship has met the crucial pragmatic test; it has worked well. It has shown an ability to adapt to changing circumstances as shown by survival from the early days of the Industrial Revolution to this time of high-technology business.

With increasing frequency, a view is expressed between these extreme positions that boards of directors should represent more broadly the public in general and minorities in particular. This has led to the election to some boards of individuals who have little of the expertise, skills, or proven business judgment that usually are the ingredients sought in a candidate before an invitation to membership is issued. This is being done in the hope that public representation on boards will insure that members of society, on which corporations have a widespread social and economic impact, have their full say about corporate conduct. Public representation may be sought by the appointment of individuals responsive to the rather indefinite concept of the "general interest" or representatives of special groups such as environmentalists, minority groups, women, students, etc.

In my view, there is no question about the desirability of achieving widespread recognition of the social responsibility of business. I have serious reservations, however, about accepting fully the view that adding special interest groups to boards of directors will achieve the objectives of broader public representation without interfering, at the same time, with the ability of business to pay employees and finance government and all the other segments of our society that depend on the economic viability of business for their continued support. Can representatives of special interest or limited points of view function objectively in their areas of knowledge as they are required to do as directors? A special pleader for a group who joins a board of directors is not relieved of his legal responsibility and liability in areas other than his special interest. Can he function knowledgeably and fairly in these areas, or must he depend on other members of the board to make the right decisions? If one special group is granted board membership, can other minority or social groups be denied equal treatment? Should special interest representation displace other board members or should the size of the board be expanded to accommodate them, even if expansion goes beyond optimum size?

Directors have responsibility clearly expressed in statutory requirements, regulations, court decisions, etc. Adding special points of view does not relieve any director from accountability to all the constituencies of a corporation, which, in effect, add up to society as a whole.

CONFLICT OF INTEREST

Of all the potential problems that may be troublesome to directors, I have found the exposure to conflict of interest situations to be one of the most easily handled. This requires continuous and active sensitivity, early, to determine conditions where the problem may arise. Sensing such a problem before it actually arises is important because it permits action to be taken on a rational basis. Determining that there is no actual conflict is not sufficient, if there remains to people outside the company the appearance of conflict.

The basic principle of my approach to the question is personal integrity with whatever documentation is required in each case. In many instances, a declaration of interest followed by nonparticipation to be recorded in the minutes of the meeting is ample. In other cases, withdrawal from the meeting, while the other board members discuss the issue, is advisable. In extreme cases of extraordinary importance, such as a merger, resignation may be advisable. This may not be necessary if both sides give written consent to continuance without change. In my record, there were two cases in which I thought it advisable to submit my resignation. In each case, however, both sides to the transaction asked that I remain active in the situation. In another case I was requested to be chairman of a negotiating team for a corporation which had agreed with a company, where I held board membership, that acquisition was in the interest of both concerns. Despite requests not to do so, I resigned board membership before negotiations began.

As a partner of a banking firm, I am sometimes asked how I resolve the conflict question when the banking firm of which I am a part negotiates financing terms with a client company where I serve as a board member. I simply take the side of the client firm, with notice to my banking associates, that I shall so participate in such negotiations.

FULL FLOW OF INFORMATION

Legally, directors bear top responsibility to stockholders for the conduct of a company's affairs. The meaning of this statement has changed over the years, since the corporate device began to be used extensively. More frequently than not, in its early history, management, ownership, and directorship were commingled and the separate functions of each were substantially carried on by the same men. Today, operations are carried on by professional managers who are far more skilled and competent to make day-to-day decisions in running the business than directors and owners. It does not minimize the importance of directors to say that they, as a group, are less competent to operate than the group of professionals they have chosen for that purpose. Rather it limits their activity to the broad areas that make up the direction of the business.

The first responsibility of boards of directors is to monitor the results of the operating management. Few, if any, managements have the capacity for impersonal and objective self-appraisal. No matter how good a management may be in making operating profits, there may be areas of less competence, particularly in the broader phases of charting the longer range objectives, how the objectives will be achieved, assurance of future management in depth, etc. A board blessed with good management should structure its role accordingly; to supplement where necessary, and above all to assure good management into the future. Sometimes innovative opportunities are more firmly and accurately grasped by outsiders than by operating management. The recent erratic and sometimes disastrous results of diversification, especially through acquisitions and mergers, reflect on management, but even more so on the failure of directors to act in an independent, informed, and objective manner.

Just as every corporation and its management differs from all others, each board—its make up, its problems, its methods of meeting its responsibilities—differs from all other boards. Furthermore, the varying internal factors and changing external circumstances emphasize that a board cannot consider its role as a fixed and unchanging one.

Under these conditions how can a board function effectively? The answer emphasizes that it has little chance to do so, *unless* there is a continuous, accurate, and full *flow of information* from management to the board. Each director, particularly each independent director, must decide the extent and kinds of information that he requires to discharge his duty to stockholders and protect himself in those extreme cases where the phrase "knew or should have known" becomes the controlling factor.

A full flow of information is not to be confused with a plethora of operating statistics that consume time and smother a director in a mass of detail. Operating information should be limited to data necessary to show trends of the business on a continuous basis, to be supplemented by more detailed data as required for specific problems. This information and financial data should flow regularly to board members on a time schedule that enables it to be studied before meetings take place. An alert management will schedule agenda items over a period of time to include special presentations about divisions of the business, major projects, budget and finances, and problem areas. Management should not hesitate to supply the board with studies and reports on developing projects, or ideas. Board members should feel free to discuss the business with officers and employees (with the approval of management).

All of this must take place against a background of cooperative understanding and mutual respect that avoids an adversary atmosphere. Needless to say, not every board member has the skill and the tact to carry it off successfully.

AUDIT COMMITTEES

Audit committees composed of "outside" members of the board of directors are becoming recognized parts of good corporate practice. I strongly support this trend.

At their minimum, audit committee functions include: participation in the selection of independent auditors, pre-audit consultation with the independent auditors, and review of their findings after the audit is completed. Other responsibilities usually are added to the minimal ones. Of these the most important are reviews of internal audit activities, internal accounting controls, and related matters of asset security.

The principal purpose of an audit committee is the establishment of a direct line of communication between the independent auditing firm and the board of directors. This increases the likelihood of early awareness of any special problems. The audit committee assists directors to fulfill their fiduciary responsibilities relating to accounting, auditing, and reporting practices.

A director can reasonably well satisfy himself as to the adequacy of the flow of information from management to the board. It is more difficult to determine its accuracy, not so much with respect to statistical correctness but to accounting policy, reserve sufficiency, effect of governmental regulations (often ambiguous) on operating results, etc. An audit committee can assist materially in all the background factors that enter into the determination of accurate information, as well as the preparation of the material itself.

Important as providing accurate information to a board of directors is as a basis for decision making, it is even more important in all matters pertaining to regulation under the Securities Acts. Here, an audit committee can assist in achieving a maximum of due diligence, which is the minimum acceptable level of performance.

An audit committee, properly set up and diligently used, can provide significant protection to all parties bearing responsibility in corporate governance, in particular, boards of directors, management, and independent auditors. However, when an audit committee is established only to lapse into inactivity and ineffectiveness, the situation then is worse than no committee at all. All parties, especially the public, are deceived into believing that a watchdog is on duty, when in fact it is not. In such cases, directors' exposure to liability increases very sharply because they are stripped of the protection provided by exercising the care "that a prudent man would use in the conduct of his own affairs."

MISCELLANEOUS OBSERVATIONS

There is no definite number representing the optimum size of the board of a business corporation. My preference is a board size of 11 or 13 members. In most cases this is sufficient to achieve a board with adequate diversity of skills and representation effectively to operate for all stockholders.

A majority of a board should be outside representatives not associated with the company's management.

A director should not use a company's plane if commercial service is available. Under no circumstances should a plane be used for personal convenience except in cases of unusual emergency.

The day has gone when being a director was similar to membership in a gentlemen's club meeting monthly. Today, it is a committment to hard work and service accompanied with a great deal of risk.

I oppose strongly any attitudes or actions of management or directors that may be promotional to market action of the stocks of the corporations they serve.

In my years of service as a director I have not had any serious problems of adequate flow of information from management, probably because of the care exercised before accepting an invitation to membership on a board. Several times I have been privately consulted by friends who have been confronted with this problem in a serious way. In each instance I have advised prompt resignation from the offending situation.

As I have observed over a period of years men serving as directors, I have noted that the good ones have a common denominator of personal integrity, deep interest, independent thinking, due diligence, and hard work.

PART II-B

The
Top-Management
Team

THE PROBLEM OF ORGANIZATIONAL CLIMATE

by Abram T. Collier

Chairman, New England Mutual Life Insurance Company

THE DANISH aphorist Piet Hein once wrote: "Problems worthy of attack/Prove their worth by hitting back." By such a test the problem of organizational climate is a worthy one. It is seldom understood and rarely solved. It is frequently not what it is thought to be. It can be particularly dangerous when it is ignored.

What is it? Or better perhaps, what isn't it? The problem of organizational climate, as we see it, transcends the setting of the organization's objectives, its conscious decision-making process, its methods or procedures. It is rather an interstitial problem. It is the problem of what members of the organization do when they *don't know* what to do. They may know what they are instructed to do in this or that circumstance, but since each specific situation faced is, to some extent, new and different, what is done often depends less on specific authorized instruction than on what the organizational climate seems to require.

An organization by its very nature involves two or three or more persons who have agreed to work together toward some common objectives. They can agree with considerable precision on their goals and their methods of achieving them; and yet success or failure may depend on the actions of individuals with respect to matters that have not been precisely agreed. It is in this area that "the organizational climate" can become critical.

"Organizational climate" is often equated with "organizational style." As we see it, however, "style" has to do with the way a given organization manages to get things done. Are matters typically handled formally or informally, orally or in writing? Are people treated courteously, with deference, or bluntly without guile? Are lines of authority and office hours followed strictly or only generally? For the most part, these are largely surface matters; they say a good deal about the tone and atmosphere of an organization but little about its "climate." "Climate," in the sense that we would use the term, applies more to those common and influential values and beliefs that grow and spread through an organization often without its members being aware of them. Climate concerns the general understandings and attitudes of the members—those understandings and attitudes that determine how they behave with regard to many of the important things the organization does.

To examine into the character of these values, attitudes, and beliefs, it may be useful to address ourselves to three questions:

What are the key variables in this climate?

How is the climate determined for a particular organization?

How may a climate be changed?

KEY VARIABLES OF ORGANIZATIONAL CLIMATE

Although wind, heat, rain, humidity, and similar measures enable us to define our physical climate, the climates in our organizations are defined by factors just as powerful but much more difficult to measure. We have no wind gauges, no thermometers to tell us how an organization may be oriented with respect to risk, to efficiency, to employees, to customers, to competitors, or to government, yet we know that these are among the key variables in defining the climate in which managements work. Nonetheless, let us suggest six climatic variables as being worth exploring.

Risk Orientation. Any organization that is not moribund is taking risks every day. It is, for example, paying someone to do work that may or may not prove to be useful. It is selling to a customer who may or may not pay his bills. These risks may seem small, compared to the risk of embarking on a new line of business, yet they suggest that mere organizational survival entails daily risks, while opportunities for growth in size and strength entail risks of great magnitude. The climate for risk-taking varies between companies, between levels of a given organization, and between one set of external circumstances and another.

In the life insurance business hundreds of millions of dollars are invested each year. The stated objective for each company is simple enough: the highest possible return with the least amount of risk.

What happens in fact, of course, is that there develops in each company a climate for risk-taking that suits the judgment of the head of the investment operations and the members of his finance committee. That climate is discovered by investment bankers and mortgage bankers who engage in the brokering of deals: They learn which investors will be interested in what types of loans. Many companies will *say* they are interested in any loan if they are compensated for the risk, but this statement, like so many others, is conditioned by the climate for risk that actually exists within the organization.

Efficiency Orientation.   In every organization there is also a spectrum of attitudes or beliefs concerning efficiency and effectiveness. At one end of the spectrum there is utmost concern with quality of service or product without regard for cost, and, at the other, utmost concern for costs without regard for quality. Every member of the organization daily makes judgments within the sphere of his own work guided by the organizational climate.

A few years ago one of the major companies in the field of electronics decided that its television sets were not selling as well as before and that it was losing its market share. A new vice president was brought in to correct the situation. The scenario was predictable. He cut production costs to lower selling prices; volume rose along with a large increase in complaints about defective sets; top management became worried over the company's reputation for quality; the new vice president was fired.

What had happened, it seems, is that the climate for the proper balance between quality and costs had not in fact changed. The men and women on the production line did not, or would not, adapt to high-volume, low-cost work; and top management was not really ready to adapt, either.

People Orientation.   Another variable in the organizational climate may be seen in the relative emphasis given to people and to things. In some organizations prime and overwhelming priorities are accorded the technical problems of accomplishing company objectives. Attention is given to research, to manufacture, to finance, to selling techniques. These "things" claim attention to the exclusion of people. In others, the interests of people demand attention almost to the exclusion of their common business objectives. "Let us be sure everyone is happy and has a chance for personal fulfillment," is the cry. Indeed, a strong case is made that the organization which does not fulfill its members will itself fail.

In the navy the distinction is often made between the "tight" ship and the "happy" ship. In the first, "SOP" (standard operating procedure) rules; in the second, the crew has a lot more freedom and makes up in morale what it lacks in discipline.

The climate of a business organization toward people may vary from ruthlessness to indifference to paternalism. The important consideration is not which kind of climate is most effective, but rather that the climate—whatever it is—permeates the behavior attitudes and decisions of all the organizational members regardless of their "normal" disposition.

Customer Orientation. Two articles of faith seem to underlie American business. The first is that the customer is right and should be favored regardless of the effect on the profits of the company. The second is that companies are in business to make a profit and that customers are to be used in order to maximize that profit. While neither article is absolutely true or false, business organizations tend to lean in one direction or the other. A general climate exists which suggests to members of the business organization how they should make these often-difficult judgments.

For companies with monopolies or market domination, the orthodox view is that they care little for customers and much for profit. When Henry Ford first dominated the small car market, he gave his customers any color they wanted so long as it was black. On the other hand, IBM has dominated the business machine market and at the same time has built its entire marketing strategy around the concept that no sale is complete until the special needs of the particular customer have been met.

Mutual companies and cooperatives are set up specifically in the interests of customers—as purchasers *and* owners—but they must still be concerned with the competitive market and with sufficient "profits" so as to stay competitive and to maintain their essential capital. No business can long survive without customer satisfaction, but the ways in which customers are satisfied seem to depend on a climatic factor in the organization.

Industry Orientation. In any industry where competition is strong, one eye is usually watching what the competitors are doing. If competitors steal a march, you cannot be far behind. Better still, of course, you want to be first, so you can strengthen your market position. Circumstances vary widely by industry, but your sensitivity to competitors' decisions, the speed with which you decide to follow competitive trends, whether you follow them at all, and the friendly or hostile relations you have with your competitors, is yet another climatic consideration—not usually spelled out in any manual or strategic document.

In a financial business such as banking, ideas are not patentable, thus new ways of doing business spread quickly from one firm to another. When the idea of a credit card, for example, was first adopted by one bank, many others quickly followed suit. Not only did they adopt the credit card idea, but nearly all followed the very unbanker-like practice of promoting their use by sending cards in the mail to millions of persons who had not asked for them. The result, of course, was untold fraud and losses running into many millions of dollars. Here the action was taken knowingly—in awareness of the risks—but the climate prevailing in various banks must also have been a factor. Some banks had the unstated conviction that if a service was offered by one "full-service" bank, they could not fail to offer it and still be a "full-service" bank. In some other banks the climate was such, however, that management felt little urge to follow the fad and enter the business. If they did, they did so later on a sounder basis.

Government and Community Orientation.   Every business must operate within legal limitations and within one or more communities. It must be aware of taxes, regulations, the attitudes of legislators, and the public at large. Nonetheless, even with a given industry there are widely different attitudes toward these matters. Without much conscious thought, the climate in some organizations seems to require meticulous compliance with laws and regulations, while in others there may be magnificent indifference. In some organizations, climate suggests keen sensitivity to community opinion, while in others it suggests a happy unconcern with respect to legal requirements.

At one time or another, nearly every industry seems to have had a bad time in its public and governmental relations. The steel industry in its price disputes, the auto industry in regard to safety and emission control, the paper industry with its polluted rivers, the oil industry in recent times, are all examples of industries that have been brought up short due to some degree of insensitivity to the political problems they had earlier ignored. It is reasonable to assume that an attitude or climate exists within the industry and within particular companies, of which key members are often unaware, and that such a climate of opinion—of "the way to do things"—affects key judgments in these affairs. Management may not say "the public be damned," it may even think it is "public-minded"; yet unless it *really* believes it exists only at sufferance of the public, it is unlikely to be quick to respond to its political problems.

DETERMINANTS OF A PARTICULAR CLIMATE

If these are some of the key variables in the climate of an organization, is it possible to make any generalizations about them? How is it decided, where in the spectrum of each climatic variable a particular organization has landed or should land? What are the main influences which create the climate for particular organizations? These are large questions, but let us suggest three lines of inquiry:

The Nature of the Enterprise. It is obvious, but not often remarked, that the climate of an organization depends in part on the nature of its mission. An army or a navy must be ready to take huge risks, but they are risks taken at the highest levels of authority; the latitude of its lower members is severely restricted. Similarly, a utility which is given a franchise to provide sure sources of power and light, lives in an environment where risk-taking is restricted, where efficiency is highly rated, and where its customer orientation is affected by a price relationship fixed less by the company than by government authority. In a highly competitive business, on the other hand, where customers have in fact many options, authority over price, service, and other considerations may be extended to agents or employees who are free to adapt their responses to local conditions.

Explicit Corporate Objectives. Organizational objectives, although not directly creating the climate, clearly create it indirectly. If, for instance, a business undertakes as a major objective to serve a particular segment of the market for a product, that decision may say a lot about the quality of workmanship it looks for. If it sets high goals for growth, it will determine, within limits, what level of risk it is ready to take. If it decides to build its business on new products, that decision also will say something about the resulting climate with respect to efficiency and innovation. If the business places great store by the achievement of specific profit goals for specific future years, this decision may affect its judgments about profits today, perhaps at the expense of profits tomorrow.

The Personality of the Chief Executive Officer. Of all the determinants of the organizational climate, the personality of the CEO, or others who occupy comparable roles, *seems* most evident. For in the CEO, there can be observed almost daily approval or disapproval of certain kinds of judgments. If he applauds risk-taking, and especially if he does not punish a risk-taker's failures, risk-taking will tend to be encouraged throughout the organization. If he is greatly upset by shoddy workmanship, there may be a tendency to improve quality at the expense of efficiency. If he promotes people who are strongly people-oriented, the climate will be thereby affected, as it is when he insists on customer satisfaction regardless of its affect on profits.

A cartoon some years ago showed a personnel manager interviewing a job applicant who looked like a twin brother. The caption read: "Jones, you're just the kind of man we like around here!" The CEO is, of course, the selector of the people he thinks will best serve the business. He may not always have the kinds of choices he would like (and it may be just as well he does not), but all things being equal, he may tend to duplicate his own attitudes, beliefs, and values. If he is, himself, an aggressive man, he will tend not to favor for high office a submissive man. If he is an outgoing and gregarious person, he will tend not to favor those who are retiring or withdrawn. If he is slow and deliberate, he may react adversely to those who are quick and temperamental. If he is sensitive and responsive, he may not care for those who are tough and unyielding.

Countering these tendencies, is the fact that every CEO worth his salt tries to select as his associates men who complement him in temperament and in skills. Still, the climate of an organization is to a degree a reflection of the values of the CEO. He is the person others are trying to please. And often others will try to do for him not only what they *know* he wants, but also what they *think* he would like to have them do even though they know he would frown on the action in question. Events in Washington during the spring of 1972, revealed in 1973, certainly bear this interpretation; many close observers believe they took place only because the individuals involved believed they were doing what they thought the President desired.

CHANGING THE ORGANIZATIONAL CLIMATE

To change the climate of an organization which has been in existence for any length of time is perhaps not possible without changing the CEO. Even when a new CEO is installed and he makes new declarations with respect to markets and policy, and secures commitments to achieve new goals, he may not be able to change the basic beliefs which were created or conditioned by the previous climate. Government bureaucracies are notoriously difficult to move; and many business bureaucracies are equally skillful in avoiding change. With the passage of time, it is easy to see how each member of the organization develops strong feelings about what he should do and what he can do.

What happens is that individuals tend not to analyze their own job attitudes. If a person is asked to do things differently or to think differently, *his* beliefs, *his* values, and *his* identity are challenged. Thus the mere installation of a new CEO does not guarantee that the climate will change. In more than a few instances, it is the CEO who changes and adapts to the environment he finds.

The more I have lived in organizations and the more I have thought about them, the more I have come to believe each permanent organization develops a life of its own. The special combination of people and challenges that occur at a particular time and place determines how the organization will act and react. Even people familiar with the organization may not make very good predictions of what those actions and reactions will be. More often than not, however, the interior climate of the business will have a major if not a controlling effect on the outcome of various problems and crises. For the climate has previously tested the vigor, the drive, the adroitness, the sensitivity, the shrewdness of the management—individually and collectively.

The CEO and his lieutenants may think they can control the climate—but they are themselves a part of the climate. Whether they spread sunshine or rain, whether they blow up a hard storm or a soft breeze, whether they appear cold or warm, is for most CEOs not a matter of deliberate choice: It is part of their very being. People are themselves, but they are also creatures of the atmosphere in which they live. It is the interplay of these people and their organizational climate that largely determines the heritage they leave.

MANAGING EXECUTIVE COMPENSATION

by Milton L. Rock
Managing Partner, Hay Associates

In my 25 years in counseling major industrial, commercial, and financial enterprises throughout the world, the question of interest to thinking CEOs has been not "how to" or "how much" to pay executives, but "why" do we pay them? Recently, a new CEO of a multibillion-dollar industrial company said he wanted to change the style of the organization. He felt that the potential of greatness was present, but direction, discipline, the zest for excellence were gone. He wanted his executives committed to performance, to value accountability for end results, and to get his company moving again. He hoped that, among other things, a reward management system emphasizing pay for performance would reinforce this management style change.

A few years ago in New York, another CEO said, "We have a great company built on the premise of pay-for-performance, but we are changing. For years, we emphasized getting things done now—making the budget—and the long-range just took care of itself. We did what had to be done, and we did it well. Now, our world is changing and the old ways no longer suffice. For example, I want to achieve a sustained growth element; a better mix between this year's incentive and longer-range incentive."

A third CEO in the Midwest who manages a billion-dollar conglomerate said he wanted his presidents to have the opportunity to become millionaires, based on corporate performance. "I want heavy emphasis on equity and a total cash compensation program that will pay out fast."

A European CEO, when questioned whether an incentive program should be installed in his traditional family-oriented company, said he didn't think his executives would want it, but still, it was an idea that should be considered.

I cite these examples to show the ongoing concern that Chief Executive Officers must exhibit in attracting, retaining, and motivating their top corps of managers.

Executives contend they don't work for money—at least, not for money alone—but they won't work without it, and they seem to work better if their salary is internally equitable and externally competitive. Executives of companies in highly competitive industrial, commercial, or financial markets seem to achieve more and better if their total compensation is tied to their performance, their unit's performance, and their company's performance. Many say that tying their incentives to measured end results is most useful, because it is an incentive to manage as well as a management incentive—it is not only the money, it is the scorekeeping aspect. Cash *now* is the predominant desire of most executives, but as executives mature, they start to change their compensation mix priorities to achieve retirement security—e.g., stock, pensions, benefits. So the executive compensation package should be a many-splendored thing in the eyes of the beholder. The mix differs from manager to manager, but one essential of the core of executive compensation—cash salary—is that it be equitable and competitive. The other elements can be mixed differently at different times and for different people. This chapter deals with several basics: (1) analysis of the climate to determine the proper mix of the other elements; (2) core (base) compensation; (3) incentive (cash); (4) equity; (5) benefits.

MANAGEMENT CLIMATE

In order to assure that your managerial compensation program reinforces your corporate strategy, you must get commitment from your people. Commitment evolves from the values and perceptions of the executives. An evaluation of the management climate gives you the feel of why you pay. It will give indications of the relationships between base salary and benefits. It will also indicate whether your present management and management systems will benefit from equity and incentive programs. It will show up gaps and differences in perception with respect to where your company is and where you want it to go; it is the first step in assessing these values and perceptions.

Managers, like everyone else, respond to what they see and sense.

Their perceptions of the organization, its structures, its style and processes not only influence their actions on the job but often determine these actions and the relative success they achieve.

So, if the chief executive wants to understand why things happen the way they do, and why managers act and behave as they do, it makes sense to analyze the ways managers perceive how the forces within the organization are acting upon them. It is the sum total of these perceptions that make up management climate.

Reward Systems as an Element of Climate

Not all perceptions have equal impact on individual managers nor, through their collective actions, is there equal impact on overall management behavior. There are, generally speaking, eight key positively identified elements or dimensions which constitute the measurement and analysis of management climate: delegation (or freedom to act), organization integration, clarity of objectives, organizational vitality, planning processes, conflict resolution, manpower development, and, not the least important of these, the organization's reward systems.

All of these interrelate with one another, but the element with which we are concerned here is the last-named one, reward systems.

This element of climate is defined as the degree to which the total reward system (cash, noncash, benefits, promotional opportunities, career development, etc.) contributes to performance and satisfaction. If managers are dissatisfied with the recognition and rewards they feel they deserve, they are rarely motivated to perform well or to contribute to organizational success.

Only after management climate is analyzed can the CEO know, for a fact, how his executives view the reward system, and how these perceptions are affecting organizational performance and achievement of corporate objectives. An understanding of the management climate, as it exists, lends direction to revising or devising appropriate management reward systems. Effective reward systems will motivate the executive corps to aim for *achievement*—as opposed to aiming for security—and therefore, greatly enhance the organization's chances for overall success.

Necessary Factors

Before the reward system may be expanded to include equity and cash executive incentives, however, three factors must be present.

1. A High Degree of Individual Motivation. Managers to be covered by the executive reward system should be achievement-oriented individuals willing to take personal risks to realize these achievements. Such people normally respond quite positively to reward systems in which part of their total compensation is risked on the job results they attain. Managers principally motivated by security needs are more likely to resist a variable compensation scheme; and, if one is installed in which personal risks are substantial, considerable anxiety ensues which may inhibit, rather than enhance, performance.

2. Effective Organizational Processes. If an executive reward system is to work equitably and to the organization's benefit, there must be means of measuring the performance of those covered by the system, and this involves the process of goal-setting and setting standards of achievement against these goals. Measures must be effectively devised and clearly understood so the individual executive has confidence that, because they are used to determine his compensation, they will accurately reflect his contribution. Additionally, there must be significant emphasis on performance improvement, since much of the reward will be based on increased profitability of the corporation.

3. Sufficient Delegation of Authority. The management structure must be so designed that significant authority is delegated to those covered by the executive reward system. If the manager cannot —because of the nature of his accountabilities—markedly affect the profitability or other objectives of the organization, then the reward system is merely a mechanism for payout rather than a device for mobilizing assertive, positive efforts toward the accomplishment of organizational objectives.

Resultant Benefits

Once the climate and, more specifically, the executives' perceptions of the reward system have been determined—and the conditions just described are for the most part met—necessary changes are more clearly seen and easily resolved. The executive reward system will then assure management performance. It will also clarify and help resolve such difficult problem areas as:

Specific provisions of the system (proportion of base, incentive, equity, and benefit elements).

Who (or what level of management) will be included in the executive reward system.

Standards of achievement.

Processes for individual measurement and performance planning.

Stages and timing of reward system implementation.

BASE COMPENSATION STANDARDS

Everyone employed has a base pay standard, be it by an hourly, piecework, or salary method. Almost universally, of course, executives are paid by the salary method, and salary constitutes the core, or base, of the total reward system and is that part around which all other elements are built. Usually, it is also by far the largest element in the total compensation package. (There are occasional, sometimes striking, exceptions to this, such as the remarkably large incentive or stock option payoffs in high profit years in some industries.)

But if the company or organization is to retain its high-talent executives, avoid internal dissatisfaction within the executive suite, and eliminate the danger of raids by outside parties, a key rule must be scrupulously and systematically followed: *The salary structure must remain internally equitable and externally competitive.*

All too often, we see organizations whose executive salaries are set by what the chief executive or top management committee perceives to be the going rate, or a little better if the executive in question is an exceptional performer. Other times, the salary structure may have, like Topsy, just grown. Fortunately, today most progressive companies eschew such unscientific, seat-of-the-pants management reward approaches. Such organizations elect, instead, to erect executive base salary structures that meet externally competitive and internally equitable standards by following proven, scientific integrated approaches.

But such structures don't just happen. The executive salary should be fair (in relation to other jobs in the executive corps), competitive (in comparison with like jobs in other organizations and industries), and large enough to be effectively motivating. To achieve these necessary ends, certain basics are essential

1. Job descriptions for everyone (including the chief executive and operating officers).
2. Job content evaluation (of the *job*, not of the incumbent).

3. Job comparisons (with the same or like jobs—not titles—on the outside).

Job Descriptions

It is a source of unending amazement to management authorities how many executive jobs are literally "orphans" when it comes to clear, concise, up-to-date, accurate job descriptions. In many concerns, jobs of the lowest level have detailed, complete job descriptions, but these seem to grow scarcer as job levels ascend until, at the top, position guides simply don't exist. According to some experienced observers, the most frequently missing position guides are those for the chief executive and operating officers.

In my view, job descriptions are essential before any kind of logical, reasoned, effective reward system can be devised. Without them, job evaluations based on measured job content, accountabilities, and activities and functions—upon which competitive and equitable base salary systems are (or should be) founded—are almost impossible to determine.

Job Evaluations

Numerous methodologies and techniques have been devised to evaluate jobs. Obviously, high-level executive positions are intrinsically different and far more complex than the vast preponderance of other jobs. However, no matter what method of evaluation is employed, the process must include three elements: know-how; problem-solving; and accountability.

Stripped to their bare essentials, definitions of these three elements may be stated in this way: *Know-how* is the sum total of every kind of skill, however acquired, required for acceptable job performance. It comprises technical depth, managerial know-how, and human relations skills. *Problem-solving*, the second element, is the original "self-starting" thinking required by the position to: (1) identify, and (2) resolve a problem. Ideas are put together from something already there. Therefore, problem-solving is treated as a percentage utilization of know-how. The third and final element, *accountability*, is the answerability for action and for the consequences of such action. It is the measured effect of the job on end results. It comprises: (1) freedom to act; (2) job impact on end results (i.e., remote, contributory, shared, or primary); and (3) magnitude of area most clearly affected by the job.

A good bit of technique is involved in a sophisticated program of job evaluation, and no attempt is made here to describe the detailed technology. But two principles are fundamental to the approach:

1. A thorough understanding of the content of the job to be measured.
2. A direct comparison of one job's content with another to determine relative value.

Although the process, once learned, is relatively simple, there is no question about the need for careful coaching in the concepts and applications of the method. It is not a do-it-yourself technique, and the chief executive should make sure that at least one individual has been thoroughly trained in the method before attempting its use.

Job Comparisons

It is obvious that jobs to be evaluated in any one company or organization cannot be treated as though existing in a vacuum. Comparison with similar jobs evaluated in similar-type outside organizations are needed to determine whether salaries are competitive—in effect, obtaining the "going price."

Evaluation of job content, if well done, assures internal equity. The placing of a salary policy line in relation to a survey of salary policy lines of competitive companies is the best method to assure competitiveness. An ideal survey system would be one that evaluates all jobs by the same method on the basis of job content, normalizing the lines and placing them on one chart.

The CEO then has to decide where his company's salary line should be in relation to all other company lines. At what level will the company's executive reward system be competitive: median, one-fourth quartile, three-fourth quartile—where? Most chief executives would prefer to have their company's pay line relate to corporate performance. In some situations, pay lines may be higher than corporate performance would indicate in order to attract better people to achieve desired company performance.

Placement of the base, total cash, and benefit lines must be competitive and generally in keeping with corporate performance; and the mix of these three elements is essential in assuring proper executive motivation. In my view, all this requires very careful and professional advice.

EXECUTIVE INCENTIVES

Base salaries are, naturally, the major element in compensating executives—or, for that matter, any salaried employee. Incentive compensation plans are common in American business, and the great majority of industrial companies participating in the well-known executive compensation surveys do employ incentives in their executive reward programs. The trend has been present for many years, and is still growing. More recently, the practice has increased remarkably among financial institutions, and today we even see some service concerns adopting the practice. A major contributing factor to this development are changes in federal tax legislation as embodied in the Tax Reform Act of 1969, which lent fresh impetus to the trend.

As every chief executive knows, the effect of bonuses and incentives on overall executive compensation levels can be dramatic; some industrials' bonuses in recent years have gained a degree of notoriety. The fact remains, however, that the nonincentive company existing in a market or industry where incentive-paying firms are the norm may find rough sledding in acquiring and retaining highly effective executive performers who, so often, are achievement-oriented, risk-taking individuals, attracted by the possibility of reaping significant rewards commensurate with their contributions to organizational success.

Why Incentives?

A well-designed and well-administered incentive plan is based purely and simply on performance: corporate, divisional, unit, and individual. Performance objectives are established before the fact; performance is measured against these objectives after the fact; and rewards are distributed on the basis of that measured performance. Thus, incentive compensation can be a most effective aid in achieving the aims of corporate strategy; the purpose of incentives is to motivate the executive to the achievement of goals. He is then rewarded on the basis of his contributions.

It is noted that an incentive compensation device—particularly the year-end bonus variety—should not be devised, or considered, as a supplement to an *inadequate base salary* arrangement (though, in fact, it may be that to the recipient), since this negates the incentive element in the payout.

Eligibility

One of the most perplexing, sensitive, and potentially explosive factors facing the chief executive is the determination of those to participate in "cutting the melon." Eligibility in most executive incentive plans is usually confined to a certain level of management and above, the cutoff level being determined by the ability to measure the individual executive's contribution to stated and predetermined objectives.

There are several bases upon which eligibility may be based. Four are enumerated here, with my personal observations following each.

1. Wholly Discretionary. In my experience, this is not a desirable criterion, since eligibility is based on the chief executive's, or the management committee's, "feel" for jobs and individuals. It constitutes a hit-or-miss method of trying to somehow determine the worthiness and contributions in a heterogeneous assortment of performances, jobs, individuals, and grasped (or missed) opportunities.

2. Organizational Level. This system of determining eligibility in management incentive plans sounds logical and workable—e.g., all people reporting to group vice presidents or general managers. In fact, it is neither. It is difficult to achieve equal opportunity for all participants, an indispensable element in an equitable plan. For example, the third-level job in a large division may be of more importance in achieving corporate objectives than the second-level in a small division. To exclude the former while including the latter is simply not an equitable arrangement.

3. Salary Level. This system does offer some rationale for defining eligibility since, presumably, the executive earning a specified salary or more is in a position to measurably affect organizational performance. However, salary levels may have evolved on the basis of past performance, length of service, or past or present favorable or adverse top management attitudes. Or, the individual earning such a salary may possess rare, technical and/or critically-needed expertise which commands a high price in the marketplace, but which has little or no measurable effect on overall organizational performance.

4. Job Evaluation. In my judgment, this is the only fair eligibility test. Any method of job evaluation makes some measurement of the relative importance of jobs. By its very nature, it avoids the distortion inherent in salary levels and organization levels. It focuses on job content alone, discounting non-job-content elements present in salaries and taking account of organizational levels only as they are an actual aspect of job content.

Many management incentive plans are designed to establish objectives and payouts for a calendar or fiscal year and are, therefore, limited by short-term objectives. Since measurement of results cannot be confined to one year, significant targets to assure sustained achievement of corporate goals should be established on a long-term cycle— i.e., three years or five years—and associated with long-range plans.

Normally, only officers and key executives clearly responsible for long-range impact on corporate results are given the opportunity for awards for sustained goal achievement.

Example of a Management Incentive Plan

Executive Vice President (800 accountability points)
Commendable—$10 per accountability point
Distinguished—$20 per accountability point

Incentive Opportunity Weighting		*Performance Rating*		
		Competent	*Commendable*	*Distinguished*
Corporate	25%	0	$2,000	$ 4,000
Unit	50	0	4,000	8,000
Individual	25	0	2,000	4,000
Total opportunity	100%	0	$8,000	$16,000
			$14,000	

Performance: Corporate —Commendable
Unit   —Distinguished
Individual—Distinguished

Incentive payout: $14,000

The payment of incentive for sustained performance is simply a bonus on a bonus. It ties executive performance to longer-range business objectives and pays off for their achievement. For example, an executive achieves results that qualify him for a bonus in this year. Three years prior to this, sustained performance objectives were established for him. He earned an incentive payment on this year's performance goals and his cumulative performance objectives over the last three years were also achieved, entitling him to an additional bonus. The sustained performance payoff can be cash, cash and stock, or stock, depending upon specific company management styles.

Performance Agreements

Various forms of executive performance agreements have been employed by companies for many years. Under this arrangement, the extent of an executive's participation in the incentive compensation plan is determined by his performance as measured against stated, predetermined elements contained in the agreement. In essence, the performance contract (performance agreement) is a written agreement between an executive and those executives reporting to him.

The specifics of the device bring together the elements by which the executive's performance is to be measured. They vary, of course, from individual to individual. A typical performance contract most often contains some combination of these elements:

Results areas—e.g., profitability/cost effectiveness, quality, growth, market penetration, market acceptance (or positioning), special assigned projects.

Measures—performance on results areas relative to historical patterns, competitive data, performance over the near and longer-term, opportunity of the participant to effect desired results.

Standards—specifics of measurement grades (distinguished, commendable, acceptable performance).

Weighting—a measurement of performance based on the proportion of corporate, group, divisional, departmental or other unit bases (e.g., 100 percent corporate; 25 percent corporate and 75 percent group).

Performance contracts must (1) be agreed upon and accepted by both parties, and (2) reflect what both executives believe are the most important tasks to be carried out and achievements to be realized during the coming year. Although organizations utilizing performance contracts naturally strive to make them as quantifiable and precise as possible, "managerial judgment" cannot be eliminated and is an acceptable—indeed, an indispensable—element of the procedure.

A typical example of performance contracts—one for a large financial institution—is shown in the following table.

Corporate Results, Measures, Goals, and Standards (bank president)

Results Area	Measures	Goals (suggested)	Standards
Profitability	Net profit before security transactions —current year—divided by net profit before security transactions in prior year(s)	Threshold of 10% net Better than X reference banks Better than Y reference banks	Distinguished Commendable Acceptable
Quality	Adjusted net profit before secutity transactions divided by capital base *	Threshold of $-\%$ Better than X reference banks Better than Y reference banks	Distinguished Commendable Acceptable
Growth	Increase in total assets—current year versus prior year(s)	Better than X reference banks Better than Y reference banks	Distinguished Commendable Acceptable
Penetration	a. Commercial and industrial loans b. Demand deposits c. Consumer loans d. Overseas income (absolute)	a.—c. X share of clearing house banks a.—c. Y share of clearing house banks d. Position relative to X, Y, Z banks	Distinguished Commendable Acceptable
Positioning	One to three plan statements		Distinguished Commendable Acceptable
Sustained growth (three-year target)	Performance against plan	Compound earnings growth rate of $X\%$ and in final year a growth rate better than Y reference banks	Distinguished Commendable Acceptable

* Adjusted net profit before security transactions plus the after-tax effect of interest on all long-term debt. A 50 percent tax rate is assumed. Capital base = stockholders' equity plus all long-term debt at the end of each period.

EQUITY

The question of providing adequate opportunity for building equity during the executive's productive years is one of the most frustrating, complex, and perplexing problems with which the Chief Executive Officer must deal today. A model compensation package fashioned 20, 10 or even 5 years ago, effectively motivating executives at the time, may now offer little as inflationary pressures and rapidly shifting tax and pension legislation cloud the outlook and erode eventual payout at retirement time.

This particularly concerns younger managers, whom the chief executive must recruit, attract, and retain, if any kind of management continuity is to be assured. Deferred compensation, to take one simple example, holds little attraction when the younger manager realizes that it is possible that deferred dollars may—and most likely *will*—be decimated in value when the time comes to collect.

However, there are several still useful avenues that top management may utilize in helping the executive build equity. Some of these follow.

Stock Arrangements

Stock option plans, both qualified and nonqualified (as defined by the Tax Reform Act of 1969), still afford the executive one of his most promising opportunities for building an estate. Only outstanding executives should be made eligible for this benefit. Small grants at intervals of one or two years have found more favor than one-shot grants of sizable amounts, because this gives the executive some leverage in gyrating securities markets.

Stock options have been declining in favor slightly among industrial companies, but more and more financials are now offering them. According to a 1974 Hay Noncash Compensation Survey, two thirds of the 233 participating industrial companies reported having option plans; this was down slightly from a high water mark of 70 percent two years earlier. Among stock-issuing financial/service firms, just over one third offered this extra to executives at specified levels.

Although it is beyond the scope of this chapter to enter into the details of the matter, it is worth noting that there are significant advantages and disadvantages inherent in the different kinds of stock option plans available. These plans are, as follows: qualified, nonqualified, phantom shares, and performance (bonus) share awards.[1]

A stock option plan should contain the following five general provisions.

1. Eligibility. Options may be granted to officers and other key employees at the discretion of the board of directors.

---

[1] A "qualified" stock option is one which is granted after December 31, 1963, and which meets certain requirements (such as having to be exercised within five years) that "qualify" it for beneficial tax treatment by the Internal Revenue Service. A "nonqualified" option simply results in fully taxable ordinary income.

2. *Types of Options.*   Options granted may be qualified, non-qualified, or both at the discretion of board of directors.

3. *Option Price.*   The purchase price of stock under each option, whether qualified or nonqualified, will be not less than 100 percent of the market value of stock at the time the option is granted.

4. *Exercise of Option.*   Options will be exercised in whole or in part at any time following the first anniversary of the date they are granted; fifth anniversary of date of the option; etcetera.

The size of grants should have some relationship to ability to pay: e.g., five to eight times salary converted to number of shares; or should be tied to a management incentive plan, e.g., management incentive plan award times two divided by market value, rounded to the nearest 50 shares.

Deferred Compensation

The intention of deferring some of the executive's current earnings is to put off receipt until a later and more beneficial date—i.e., when the executive is retired and presumably in a lower tax bracket. This can be an attractive benefit for a top manager, and it may have substantial value as a tax minimization instrument.

Private Investment Opportunities

These should be approached gingerly, because many executives investing in syndicates formed for such items as cattle raising, oil drilling, and real estate ventures may be getting into the conflict-of-interest area. Moreover, not all such investments have been highly profitable. Although these must by necessity remain personal matters and are privately arranged, they may consolidate the executive's economic interests and may have the effect of substantially reducing taxes and creating capital gains.

BENEFITS

For the most part, the same security elements are available, in varying degrees, to the bulk of all salaried employees. The difference for the upper managerial level lies in the larger and more expanded benefits extended to it. These elements include pensions, various forms of insurance, and different types of income maintenance. They are basic security items, intended to give executives a sense of freedom so that they may concentrate on their jobs, not being distracted by concerns of "what would happen if. . . ."

Pensions

The pension continues to be the nearest thing to a guarantee of ultimate economic comfort and, when combined with social security benefits, forms the foundation of retirement income. U.S. pension legislation enacted in the mid-1970s and the unceasing erosion of the purchasing power of currency worldwide—plus charges of mismanagement or negligence of administration of pension funds in some quarters—have recently focused attention on this very basic item. For these reasons, frequent review and close supervision of pension plans are essential.

There are alternatives—e.g., the purchase of additional annuities for individual executives, help in formulating estate-building and estate conservation plans, stock payoffs, stock purchase plans, and many others. Again, however, because of the vast complexity and combinations of options available, I feel that expert advice and counsel—especially legal—is highly advisable for those companies wishing to achieve some degree of certainty in gaining financial security in retirement for their top managers.

Health and Life Insurance

Another benefit now almost universally available to all salaried employees lies in the insurance area. For top-tier executives, total coverage amounts are usually larger, reflecting, for one thing, their larger incomes (because insurance coverage amounts are most frequently related to base salary figures). Major medical insurance for the executive and his dependents now runs to the hundreds of thousands of dollars; million-dollar coverage for the "typical" family of four is increasingly common. Health insurance is relatively inexpensive—unless the individual executive is a known high-risk case. Accordingly, this is an area where the organization can normally afford to be generous.

The same might be said for life insurance: $500,000 basic life is not now unusual for upper-level managers. Supplemental plans are available at nearly all firms; in these, the executive usually assumes part or all of the extra costs involved. Of course, at retirement, life insurance coverage usually ceases or tapers off rapidly.

Disability Income

For top managers, most companies are self-insuring, paying full salary for the short term (up to six months, as a rule) and part salary for longer periods (i.e., some fixed percentage—often half—of the salary for prolonged periods).

Post-Employment Agreements

These agreements provide for the continuance of salary, either partial or total, after an executive has left his position. The intent is to delay legal and complete termination for a variety of reasons: e.g., to prevent the departing executive from engaging in competing activities; to permit vesting in order to qualify for benefits; and, from the point of view of the executive, to provide for some insurance against sudden dismissal.

Executive Financial Counseling

One of the most desirable extras offered to upper-level executives today, including chief executive and chief operating officers, is executive financial counseling. As total compensation grows more and more complex and individualized, few executives have the time or know-how to act intelligently on the multiple confusing alternatives available. This specialized tailored service comprises three basics—compensation planning, estate planning, and estate building—and how to get the most out of each.

The CEO, in particular, can stress the importance, and help instigate the concept and practice, of personal financial planning among the top executive group as a part of the company's ongoing continuous management education program.

Executive Perquisites

Executive perquisites, or "perks," are a matter of continuing and intense interest to top management, constituting a very sensitive area (especially when it boils down to who are the "have" and "have-not" executives). For many years, top managers have enjoyed certain privileges which accrue to such managers by virtue of their position and the accountabilities they shoulder.

But perks are not primarily designed to set the high level executive apart from lesser mortals, but rather as aids to the busy and pressured executive, to help him get through the time-consuming and annoying mechanics of day-to-day living, leaving him more productive time, bearing in mind that he is one of the organization's more costly human resources.

Executive Automobiles. One of the most common perks generally available is the executive car, a benefit whose expense of purchase, maintenance, and operation are borne by the organization. According to some recent surveys, cars are made available to the top executive layer by about half of both industrial and financial/service firms, but eligibility requirements vary all over the lot. Generally, however, eligibility is most often restricted to CEOs, officers, and "key" executives. Normally, of course, the larger the firm, the more likely is this perquisite made available. Although no really reliable figures as to this practice by individual industry have come to my attention, large banks in particular, in the financial sector, commonly appear to maintain executive auto programs for top officials.

Chauffeur-driven limousines are not generally provided by organizations having executive auto programs. But among those that do provide drivers, the perk is most frequently limited to officers bearing titles of CEO, COO, president, and chairman. As to levels below these, this practice drops off sharply.

Geography also affects the incidence of this practice. In New York, for example, executive automobiles are relatively rare. But when they do appear, they are generally chauffeur-operated and limited to the top two or three officials of very large concerns headquartered in that city. Naturally, there are exceptions: Chauffeur-driven limousines are sometimes provided to make up for other amenities which a particular company may lack. One case that comes to mind is that of a prominent New York City industrial that furnishes individual chauffeur-driven limousines—as well as certain other privileges—to a relatively large group of officers. This is attributable to the fact that the firm's executive suite is located in an industrial and less accessible section of the city and in a building that also houses some of the firm's manufacturing operations.

In recent years, the use of executive autos has tended to decline sharply and abruptly in less prosperous times due to the high visibility factor, rather than to cost factors which, for large concerns, are relatively minor items in the overall budget.

Company Airplanes.   Company-operated airplanes, sometimes termed "executive aids," are now so common that they may scarcely be considered true executive perquisites. Such craft range from single-engine four-seaters, used for short hops or inspection work, to large, jet-powered custom-outfitted airliners, designed for ferrying large groups of executives and their business associates and customers.

Often, companies operating executive fleets have facilities in locations served infrequently or not at all by commercial airlines. Although top managers and their parties normally have first call on space—flying at times to fit their own schedules—most organizations permit all company personnel traveling on legitimate company business to board flights, so long as space is available, on a first-come, first-served basis, regardless of which high-level executives may have ordered the plane.

Operating company planes is expensive, but the incomparable convenience provided is enough to offset cost factors, in the opinion of most firms maintaining the practice.

Executive Health Benefits.   Executive physical examinations are another frequently-encountered benefit, although such physicals are really more of a company benefit than an executive or employee one. In a way, they fall into the "maintenance" category of expense. Despite fears of some managers that findings will somehow be used against the individual, a company will benefit primarily from having the manager consider his or her health on a regular, routine basis, and from the encouragement therefrom to take corrective action, if or as appropriate.

Nearly always, this benefit is made available to a larger group of managers than just the very top, and, according to a recent comprehensive survey, three out of four participants report they have such programs in force.

Special executive medical expense reimbursement programs are one of a rapidly-diminishing type of tax-sheltered benefit still available to an executive group. Such benefits can be especially valuable to high-salaried individuals, who are already faced with considerable pressures for the best medical treatment—regardless of cost—and who probably do not wish to haggle about fees and charges. The reason for the declining popularity of this type of benefit apparently may be traced to the vastly liberalized medical benefits programs extended in recent years to all salaried employees. In this connection, however, it should be noted that many top managers now have major medical insurance coverage paid by the employer. This coverage, which may run into the hundreds of thousands of dollars, is frequently extended to all dependents.

Other Perquisites. Executive dining rooms, subsidized partially or totally by the organization, are found in little more than one in four organizations, according to recent figures. Companies providing this perk are often headquartered in areas away from many acceptable restaurants, such as those located in suburban executive parks. Paid country and/or luncheon club memberships fare a bit better (35 percent of participants offer both) in the same survey. However, a third of reporting organizations provide neither.

CONCLUSION

Compensation, for better or worse, is the chief means of attracting, retaining, and motivating all the various populations present in the organization. And, like any other living process, the total reward-management system requires constant care and feeding. A healthy performance measurement system, a sound promotion policy, and well thought-out career pathing are all required to keep the base salary program vital. For this, annually updated knowledge of the weather outside (competition), and the weather inside ("climate" of the firm), is necessary. In times of high inflation, government controls, or rapid management style change, more frequent analyses are needed.

Things never happen exactly as you expect. There will be times when an incentive program doesn't pay off because of circumstances beyond management's control; or a well-designed stock option program goes underwater because of the Wall Street blues; or, on the other side, a sharp increase in incentive payments occurs in good market years or a bonanza in stock prices develops.

A good reward-management system reflects the reality that, in the short and long run, established policies must be adhered to under most circumstances. An essential ingredient of the system, however, is a degree of flexibility so that unforeseen circumstances can be channeled and directed to achieve desired effects. Keeping your executive reward-management system in order pays off under all circumstances and at all seasons.

THE TEAM CONCEPT FOR THE CHIEF EXECUTIVE OFFICE

by J. David Wright

Chairman of the Board (Retired), TRW Inc.

THE BOARD OF DIRECTORS customarily assigns to the Chief Executive Officer of a corporation responsibility for essentially all activities of the business, from policy and planning to operations. In fact, unless a crisis, or at the least, a severely troubled situation has arisen, the board of directors is likely to favor the approach of maximum legally permissible decentralization of its authority to the Chief Executive Officer. The board then concentrates its attention on adequate audits and review to ensure to its satisfaction that the Chief Executive Officer is discharging those responsibilities competently. It acts on those matters where legal approval is required by the board and it ponders only the most vital, far-reaching and consequential issues. Even on these its pattern is to start by hearing the Chief Executive Officer's proposal for action. This proposal is usually accepted when this officer has the confidence of the board, which usually means his record of performance suggests that his further recommendations will turn out well. In any case, it is widely, if not generally assumed that his analyses and proposals are the result of adequate study of all alternatives, for which study he is presumed to be far better equipped than outside board members.

In a typically large and complex corporation, as well as in many smaller ones with challenging problems or opportunities, the responsibilities of the top officer encompass so wide a range of matters and issues that no single executive, however experienced and brilliant, can be considered personally expert and adequate in all. Moreover, he does not have the time to be informed with depth on all of the pertinent details. This obvious condition leads to the use on his part of the concept of delegation of authority and responsibility. In particular, he usually sets up divisions and/or profit centers by product lines, areas, or functions for operating control and, in addition, employs a staff of experts and general assistants. But some responsibilities and authority he retains directly for himself. One commonly observes two general approaches for handling those duties which the Chief Executive Officer retains for himself.

THE SINGLE-EXECUTIVE CEO

In one method, he keeps for himself, personally, all of the true Chief Executive Officer's decision-making. He delegates pieces of his function, but never the *integration* of those pieces. He alone reaches the final judgment and issues the command. In this approach, he may make use of advice that will *influence* integration, decision, and action. He may utilize information and analyses served up to him by many members of the overall organization. He will be dependent, in part then, as he reaches his decisions and issues his orders, on the quality of effort by others. However, no one shares with the Chief Executive Officer the *power* of decision at corporate level. The authorities of all others are limited to specific, defined segments, short of such power. This is the single-executive CEO, as rather traditionally conceived.

THE TEAM CEO

In the other approach, labeled in this essay "the team approach to the chief executive office," a small group of individuals constitute the chief executive office in such a way as to share the duties. In an increasing fraction of existing large and complex companies this team approach is being applied. Where it is successfully used, it is not the result of accident but of a proper selection of both the individuals and the management system for the utilization of the concept. Where such an approach seems to be unsuccessful, it may, nevertheless, still be true that the team concept, properly conceived and implemented, will be appropriate or best for that company's management needs. It may be only that the approach has not been correctly conceived and implemented. The team concept for the chief executive office is not a fixed one and is susceptible of many variations in its application.

The concept of the *team* chief executive office generally applies to the employment of two or more executives—seldom more than four— who share the duties and responsibilities usually imputed to the chief executive. One variation might involve a two-man office with a chairman concentrating his time and energy on policy, future planning, and communications with the shareholders, the financial community, and the rest of the outside world, while a president acts as chief administrative officer or chief operating officer, being responsible for the success of the ongoing, current business of the company. Another variation might involve similar duties for the chairman with a vice chairman for future planning and a president as administrator. Some large companies have used, in addition to chairman and president, several vice chairmen, chairmen of executive or other committees of the board, vice president and general manager, and numerous other titles. Obviously, the matter of titles is not key. What is important is how the team concept works at its best and how it differs in its operation and in its potential for superior management from the first approach which places essentially total emphasis on decision-making by one individual.

NOT "MANAGEMENT BY COMMITTEE"

Many companies which could benefit from the use of the *team* concept do not use it because of the misconception that it is synonymous with committee operation of the company with no clear leader possessing ultimate power of decision. Many experienced leaders of organizations strongly believe that *decisions* should not be *made* by committees, especially at the very top. In the proper use of the team concept for the chief executive office, the company is not "run by *committee*." To be sure, the several team members will meet very frequently to ponder matters. They will "put their heads together" to try to move along the understanding of an issue or to reach a major decision. But when engaged in this kind of "committee" activity, the Chief Executive Officer will be clearly the chairman. He will be accepted as the boss and final arbitrator and *"decider"* just as much as when the single-individual chief executive office is the pattern.

Members of the team will ideally bring together varied capabilities that span the requirements of the particular issues under discussion. Both a conservative and a visionary might be included. Strong financial, technical, manufacturing, marketing, legal, international, or other backgrounds may be seen as paramount for inclusion in the team depending on the nature of the company. The team will participate in appraising current operations, in developing plans for the future, and in establishing broad corporate policies—in short, in all the functions of the chief executive office.

In such management deliberations, the ideas, experience, and information of a number of executives are brought together. There is a big difference, however, between the situation of the single-individual CEO and the team CEO. In the former, everyone pursues his assignment as an "assistant" to the single decision-maker. The *assistant's* role is to support, to set up for, perhaps to interpret and communicate. To exaggerate only slightly, the assistant dare not assume the authority of the CEO without very specific, clearly announced delegation of such authority. Each delegation is understood to be an ad hoc one, an exception. By contrast, in the team approach, on a broad, long-term, and widely understood basis, the individual members of the chief executive office have designated areas of *authority*, known to all company executives as the authority of the CEO. It is the exception when the Chief Executive Officer chooses to intercede and overrule, as he is understood to be privileged to do. The entire organization, but particularly those who report to the chief executive office, come to recognize that the team is in tight communication; that the members have arranged a separation and sharing of the CEO; and that when they speak, they speak with the authority of the CEO as though each one, on that particular issue, *is* the Chief Executive Officer. It is the organizational pattern that, when an issue arises requiring personal decision, guidance, or auditing by the Chief Executive Officer, the other chief executive office team members will know precisely that. They will have brought him into the situation properly through the team's system of communication and sharing of authority.

Thus, each team member actually does make decisions for the company in *assigned* and understood areas. In addition, in the best utilization of the team concept, each team member is authorized and expected to make prompt decisions for the others in appropriate instances. For example, in the event of unavailability of the team member most prepared or most accustomed to speaking for the CEO in that particular area, another member of the CEO who is reachable will take on the assignment of "being" the CEO. Either he will make the decision with confidence as though he were the Chief Executive Officer, even if he is some other team member, or he will know that it is wise in this particular instance to defer the decision, waiting for a more appropriate member of the team to be available, such as the

Chief Executive Officer himself, or to confer with other team members as might be sensible for that particular issue.

QUALIFICATIONS OF TEAM MEMBERS

It is important to emphasize that in a successful team approach to the chief executive office the individual members are not to be regarded merely as functional specialists, the synthesis of whose brains makes one outstanding total brain, but with the individual segments unprepared to deal with broad issues. (A corporate staff will serve the CEO team to provide that kind of specialized expertise—legal, accounting, public relations, etc.—in precisely the same way as a corporate staff serves the single-individual CEO.) Instead, every member of the team of the CEO should be a broad-gauge person, himself generally qualified to be a chief executive, although not necessarily the best one for that company at that time. A well-selected team constitutes an outstandingly capable chief executive office in part, to be sure, as a result of combining the judgments of several individuals whose talents and background are varied. But benefitting by this variation does not dominate over the necessity for *each* member to be prepared to act for the chief executive office.

It becomes imperative that all team members understand and accept the broad policies of the company in the same way, with unanimous agreement on how to implement all of the key aspects even though, if left to himself as a single-individual Chief Executive Officer, each member might have arrived at somewhat different policies. All members should be familiar with the potentials, problems, habits, strengths, and weaknesses of the key executives reporting to the chief executive office. They should know how the company works and should have the same kind of general familiarity with details of the operations that the single-individual CEO would be expected to have. It goes without saying that the team members must have cooperative attitudes, like to work with each other, and feel satisfaction in being members of the team and in supplementing each other's abilities. They must, of course, be in very close communication.

EVOLUTION TOWARD THE TEAM APPROACH

Although formal reference to the team approach is relatively recent, evolution toward this approach undoubtedly had its beginning with the transition from predominantly entrepreneurial management of single-purpose companies to the large diversified multinational companies of today. Granted decentralized operations with their general managers and specialized functional corporate staff (law, finance, public relations, etc.), the Chief Executive Officer, on behalf of the company as a whole, still must be prepared to handle policy, strategy, audit of performance, organizational change, big and little crises, and interfaces with the outside world. He must compare and select main alternatives, lead, inspire, stimulate, and integrate. Clearly, a single, strong chief executive—even if smart enough—will not have the time nor can he be in all the places required at once to do the job if the company is large and complex and geographically widespread. Also, the probability is that he will not be smart enough. His knowledge and experience will not span all of the requirements and he cannot remedy this shortcoming fully by setting up a supporting staff. So long as it is understood that he alone is the point of decision, and he does not truly share the authority and responsibility of his office with others, then he is very likely to become the prime bottleneck. Moreover, there is the danger (in fact, it is quite common to find) that his assistants will be of much lower caliber in individual competence, courage, aggressiveness, and breadth than is required. The single strong executive surrounded by "yes-men" is not only a familiar character in fiction. He exists in real life.

Some defend the single-individual approach as the only good one to aspire to, or at least the best one, provided only that the right individual can be found. They argue that under this approach bureaucracy is swept aside. Single, clear, rapid communications, they say, may be expected by the sole occupant of the CEO. Actually, it is more likely, in a large and complex situation, that the single individual, one who makes quick decisions and eliminates all bureaucracy, will also make a substantial fraction of very wrong decisions. Or, unbeknownst to that Chief Executive·Officer, a great many important matters will pile up, waiting for *him* because no one else dares to take action. Or he will tend to accept as normal and inevitable a situation in which information flow, analysis, surveying of alternatives, decisions, and actions queue up to wait for his initiative. The system of bringing things to him for decision does not appear to be slow to *him* because, although he is the actual bottleneck, he sits in the center of action as he sees it, calling all the shots.

LIMITATIONS OF THE TEAM APPROACH

It is, of course, true that serious limitations and considerable opportunity for unsatisfactory operation exist in the use of the team concept. A poor selection of the CEO team members, inadequate chairmanship of the team by the Chief Executive Officer, confused and committee-type operations—all can easily vitiate the value of the team concept. So could lack of credibility regarding the sharing of authority stemming from frequent reversals by the Chief Executive Officer of decisions made by team members. The team concept must be planned, implemented, and operated with great care and intelligence if its worth is to be realized. However, a company which manages to assemble an outstanding CEO team has a tremendous advantage, especially over companies headed by an individualist who tries to run a "one-man show."

AN ILLUSTRATIVE EXAMPLE OF THE TEAM CEO

Many of the points in the preceding paragraphs are well illustrated by the use of the team approach to the CEO at TRW Inc., where for a number of years the author was chairman of the board and Chief Executive Officer, and where the chief executive office included, in addition, Simon Ramo, with the title of vice chairman of the board, and Horace Shepard, with the title of president.

During the roughly ten years in which this three-man CEO team led the company, the expansion was very great, both through internal developments and through acquisitions. During that time, the activities of TRW spread geographically into most parts of the free world. To an increasing extent, the company's products became dependent on new and advanced technology and the company's growth in volume and in earnings per share was highly dependent on competent management of diversification. This diversification, according to a prime policy which the team established, was limited, highly selective, and related. The fields in which the company chose to engage were confined to those where the evidence was strong that benefit would result from common membership in a single corporate entity. Also it was required that no area be entered if it was not exceedingly well understood by the corporate leadership.

The organizational pattern of TRW Inc., included substantial decentralization of day-to-day operations to the operating managers assigned to the various units of the corporation. At the same time, the

CEO team reserved to itself the setting of goals, product area boundaries, and the basic strategy for the management of each entity. As a first approximation, an attempt was made to free the CEO team from participation in operating details. However, the CEO team was definitely involved in operations whenever the operating results indicated either: (*a*) substantial deviation from the approved plan; (*b*) some basic problem or an unanticipated major opportunity; (*c*) an unforeseen trend with repercussions on the corporation as a whole or on other decentralized divisions. The CEO team reviewed operating results of all domestic and international activities in monthly meetings with the operating executives.

The divisional managers were given wide latitude to operate in a manner suitable to their particular product lines, markets, customer relations, and geographical area, without requiring penalizing standardizations or bureaucratic and delaying approval mechanisms. But the CEO team produced clear objectives and worked out with the operating executives a detailed forecast for all key aspects of near-term operations, including sales, profits, margins, capital expenditures, profit plow-back, cash flow, and, in addition many nonquantitative accomplishments anticipated in the scheduled period.

Each of the three team members of the CEO had had years of line operating management experience before joining the team. These experiences covered technological operations in the volume range of hundreds of millions a year, with general management responsibility over all aspects of the activities. We differed, of course, in detailed background and areas of proven expertise. Accordingly, this influenced the tasks each team member took on as the "lead" member of the CEO team. Although all three participated in goals, policy, and organizational decisions, Shepard, for instance, was most active in auditing operating results and in following those events that might cause deviations from near-term forecasts. Ramo was more heavily involved in longer-term and technological matters. The author, as the third member of the team, gave more attention to the more general corporate policy, financing, stockholder relations, and legal aspects. The team members' attention to the needs of the decentralized managers was also partly determined on a geographical basis, with Ramo often being a substitute for Shepard in guiding activities or auditing operations whose operating managers happened to reside, as did he, on the West Coast. Shepard equally often acted for Ramo on long-range issues of interest to the managers located in the Cleveland area.

The assignment of CEO team effort was also in part by customers or area of product endeavor, with Shepard more likely to be the logical one to take on a CEO issue if the key customers on that issue were of the aircraft industry, Ramo if they were electronics, and Wright if they were automotive.

Each of us pondered all major corporate issues and opportunities, knew what were the predominant areas being investigated by the other two, and what key problems were being thrust at the CEO by all operating division heads or corporate staff functional specialists. We coordinated on selection of issues for individual attention and transferred assignments from one to another as the nature of the problems passed through phases. Our aim was to be in such tight communication that any one of the three of us could make a decision for guidance or redirection of the work of any of the major executives below the CEO level, with confidence that it would be the correct decision, not likely to require overturning when at a later time the three of us put our heads together for further consideration of the problem.

Our travel schedules were highly coordinated. Each could and did represent the company, speaking for the CEO, to explain the same policies, goals, needs, strategies, or company progress to our divisional personnel around the world, government and business leaders, the investment community, or the media. One individual could not have maintained the degree of communication internally and externally which was necessary and desirable and which the team of three provided.

If an attempt had been made to overdefine and divide up the areas of dominance of the three members of the team, then it would not have worked so successfully. That is, to have rigidly labeled Shepard, for example, as near-term and Ramo as long-term, both "internal," and Wright as "external," would have been both inaccurate and unworkable. A fundamental advantage of a team CEO is to produce the equivalent of a much wiser, more versatile, more perceptive and creative Chief Executive Officer. Such an officer would recognize that short- and long-term activities are inextricably bound together, as are technical, marketing, international, financing, organizational, and personnel matters.

With this balancing of a substantial degree of management decentralization and independence for the separate operating entities, and yet centralized control and setting of plans and goals, we believed that we came as close as is practical in the real world to a superior "multi-brained" CEO as regard breadth, competence, perception, and wisdom in decision-making. But none of this could have worked if we had not persevered at the creating of a controlled operation as seen by the operating entities. A foundation pillar in this control was a three-year operating forecast updated four times a year for each division covering, as indicated earlier, all pertinent operating parameters quantitatively stated. Another pillar was the maintaining of longer-range plans for each entity, usually including quantitative estimates of these same operating parameters out over a longer number of years than the operating forecast. Also utilized were frequent and regular planning sessions between the CEO and operating divisions in which alternatives for growth (or, indeed, for deliberate plateauing, spinoff, sale, or even liquidation of some product lines) were portrayed, selected, agreed upon, and made the basic plan which each entity was committed to follow.

Successful implementation of the team concept required an extraordinary degree of communication among the three team members of the CEO, with the four executive vice presidents, and with the several key corporate officers. This broader team of a dozen or so individuals had to understand company goals, strategy, problems, and opportunities well enough from the overall corporate viewpoint so that proposals for handling issues within the decentralized segments of the company could be presented and understood with a commonness of language, thought, and objectives. These individuals had incentive to wear a corporate hat. They knew that status, salary, and opportunities for further advancement and growth depended in substantial part on demonstrated appreciation for more than the narrow segment of activities under their individual close, decentralized control.

We recognized that, if we had been much more diversified than we actually were—please remember that we tried to keep the several divisions of the company pretty well related to each other and to the fields of our competence—we should have had to be much more decentralized. Then the CEO could not have participated so intimately in the running of the several activities of TRW. The CEO would then have been much more akin to an "investment manager" with a "portfolio" invested in essentially independent and unlike businesses. These would have had to be headed by managers with whom the CEO would have had little liaison as to operating matters. Under those circumstances, a CEO team might not be particularly useful. Perhaps an extremely diversified company with very dissimilar businesses—say, for instance, in high-style consumer goods and heavy industrial equipment—might better be headed by an individual CEO served by a group of specialized assistants.

We recognized, also, that a single individual acting as CEO operating with a staff of such specialized assistants as needed might be better than our CEO team for a much smaller and less complex company with a single line of business or a cluster of very closely related businesses. We were also aware that a company operating much more in a "steady-state" fashion in a technologically and economically more stable industry might find the single-executive CEO quite adequate even though we were convinced that it would not suffice for us in our circumstances.

But many corporations find themselves in circumstances not unlike that of TRW—sizeable; somewhat diversified, but not heterogeneous; dynamic and in the midst of rapid and deep changes. For them, the CEO team method is likely to be as useful as it was for us.

WORKING WITH CREATIVE PEOPLE

by Stanley M. Gortikov

President, Recording Industry Association of America, Inc.;
Former President, Capitol Records

THE NATURE OF CREATIVITY

CREATIVITY comes from what creative people make, or do, or think, or are, in infinitely varying ways. This chapter accents how you, as Chief Executive Officer, can best live productively with those creative people for their advantage and yours. And if you, the CEO, are especially fortunate, you'll be one of those creative people, too.

One predictable facet of creativity is its unpredictability. It is rarely constant, infrequently uniform, and undependably available. Dozens of books can give you dozens of definitions for creativity. They're mostly all appropriate, but you need not look for one single definition to carve in bronze. The multiplicity of descriptions is itself clue to the diversity of creativity's sources and uses.

There is no spot on your balance sheet reserved for "creativity," but there should be. Creativity can be a nondepleting resource if you'll just baby it a little. It's as close as you'll ever get to a business cure-all. Creativity can pop you out of your traditional molds. It can help you leap, not creep.

Sometimes the whole idea of creativity sounds rather forbidding to a chief executive. It smacks of "another world" where things might be too different for comfort. This chapter will help you deal with those "differences," even though it will not always be cozy to do so.

CREATIVE PEOPLE—A PROFILE

There is no "typical" creative person. But the characteristics of the creatives are usually more intense than in other people. Their highs are higher, their lows lower, their behavior more expressive, their moods and personalities visible with bolder accents.

My observations also support a belief that there is a positive correlation between creativity and intelligence. With that coupling usually comes a variety of behavioral patterns which influence the individual's performance in a company. This intelligent/creative person will be more observant than most, more aware of problems and realities, and certainly more immune to bullshit from any source. He sees and hears more, absorbs more, learns more, concludes more . . . and does all these more quickly than most.

Creative people are usually "special" people in so many ways, and this characteristic baffles and intimidates many with whom they work, including chief executives. As a result, they often are overtly treated like "oddballs" . . . ignored, avoided, snickered at, or resignedly accepted. Yes, creative people need to be treated in a special way at times, but treated as "leapers" not "lepers."

The ideal Chief Executive Officer is a master in relating to wide variations in human personality and deportment. But creative personalities often require from the boss an even more extensive sensitivity in human relations. Eccentricity is not infallibly found in creative people, but its prevalence is certainly common, along with emotional extremes and petulance. They "feel" more strongly than their noncreative brethren. They perceive life in a different way. Their productivity is more likely to spurt rather than flow.

Creative employees rather uniformly respect honesty and forthrightness. They are more likely to fall into relationships with others of creative inclinations, and with these they manage more trusting interrelationships. They are apt to rely on the judgment and objectivity of other creative people. But they tend not to be very objective about themselves and their own work.

They are intense in their demonstrations of sensitivity. They are rarely content with cursory responses, or dismissals, or avoidance. They want a hearing for what they have to say or show. Often they prefer no qualitative reaction to their presentation, only acknowledgement; only some form of responsive communication that says: "I hear you . . . I understand you . . . I appreciate your position." That's quite a different posture from the conventional seeker of response who hungers for judgmental approval.

It is neither "good" nor "bad" that creative people tend to be "different." But it is definitely "bad" if the CEO fails to know that.

THE FORMS OF CREATIVE OUTPUT

Creativity has much in common with venereal disease—you find it in all kinds of people, both sexes and all ages . . . it emerges from a pleasurable experience . . . at first you may not know you have it . . . it's contagious . . . and eventually results become apparent.

"Creativity" is one of those fuzzy words. But if you don't know what it is, how do you know when you've got it or even if you want it? Creativity in the company must cease being fuzzy and eventually must become very specific, very realistic, and very visible. Creativity in any business enterprise cannot long remain ethereal but must be both actionable and profitable. So the final shapes of creativity, emerging from creative people in the creative process, must crystallize into recognizable forms:

1. Creativity may take a very specific form such as a product, invention, design, or graphic form.
2. It may be conceptual in nature—ideas, philosophies, directions, plans, objectives.
3. It may be qualitative—flair, uniqueness, innovation.
4. It may be exploitative—copying or applying or enhancing the notions of others, even competitors.
5. Creativity may be very confined in its application—to sales, or engineering, or manufacturing, or administration, or finance.
6. Or broad—to science, or mankind, or America, or your industry, or the world, or management.
7. Creativity can be transient and relative—like doing an ordinary job or project extraordinarily.

CREATIVE MOTIVATIONS AND DETERRENTS

How does the Chief Executive Officer motivate creative people? I don't know. It's vital that you "not know" too, or else you may be tempted to impel them in the same simple prototyped way as everybody else. Because creative people themselves are so diverse, so are the forces that motivate them.

They literally march to the beat of different drummers. Therein is the key to working with creative people productively. You must be prepared to live comfortably with their individuality. You must be chameleon-like in adapting to their uniqueness if you expect to influence and optimize their performance. Money turns some on, others couldn't care less. Some work best when insulated and isolated, others when wallowing in the mainstream. Thus, you must deal with all the different forms of their energy.

The best single input to creative output is not a handy-dandy technique. It lies in the nature of the environment in which creators work. That atmospheric condition more than anything else can beneficially (or negatively) condition creative people. By "environment" or "atmosphere," I don't mean the physical surroundings alone. Instead, I relate to the quality of the human conditions of work—the attitudes, the responses, the acceptance. Creative people are constantly looking for affirmation of their worth . . . not just a pat on the head, but honest, positive responsiveness and reinforcement to their value and yield.

Time is a funny kind of factor in the creative motivational process. Unfortunately, there is no predictable gestation period for a creative result. It will happen when it will happen. Your deadlines, schedules, and logical exhortations won't dependably hasten the creative process. Press too hard, Mr. Boss-Man, and you start the counter-creative process. So your motivational influence must start with your sensitivity to the character of the particular creative people from whom you seek a particular result at a particular time. Not much motivation will take place if you or your cohorts are insensitive to sensitive people and clumsy in knowing when to encourage forward motion and when to stand aside and just watch. "Pull" works better than "push."

If all that helps motivate creative people, what roadblocks deter their accomplishment? Just the opposite. Take all the positive statements just made, articulate the negative to each one, and then you've built a foolproof formula for stifling creativity. The biggest killer of all is the strong negative response. Creative people break easily and mend slowly. They are least likely to flourish in an undynamic environment. They wither in bland, sterile, neat 'n tidy surroundings. Creativity tends to thrive under conditions of interaction, not sodden uniformity. Creative people respond expansively to dynamism in their colleagues, to altering patterns, changes of pace, often even to strife and crisis.

So, after all that, how does the chief executive motivate creative people? Know who they are . . . what they do best . . . be sensitive to their individual uniqueness . . . be responsive to their communication . . . recognize . . . appreciate . . . acknowledge . . . provide individuality in their environment.

ADAPTING VERSUS RESISTING

One predictable dilemma will emerge for the Chief Executive Officer who lives with creative people. Should you attempt to bend these creative individuals to existing company practices, policies, and traditions? Or should you adapt those hallowed practices to the uniqueness of the creative ones? Do the latter . . . most of the time, anyway. If you need a guideline, ask yourself: Which alternative best assures long-run innovation and productivity?

Of course, no responsible executive will abdicate his prerogatives and negate all precedent. This is not advocacy of business anarchy. It is, however, a plea for you as CEO to live comfortably and naturally with those differences which creative talents frequently manifest—whether it be dress, hair, thought process, life styles, values. Allow creative people an opportunity to be themselves; that's the best mode of harnessing their performance and creativity for your needs.

But a chief executive alone does not a company make. Apart from the flexibility of that chief, can the company hierarchy itself accommodate to the uniqueness of creative people, despite the traditional orientation of its staffs and procedures? It must learn how. Creativity is as much a natural resource as petroleum or a precious metal. Just as the corporation must learn how best to utilize its other natural resources, so must it determine the best accommodation to optimize its creative assets.

Your responsibility as Chief Executive Officer is not satisfied by developing your personal skills in dealing with creative people. Those capabilities must extend beyond your own person and office. You must be sure that all subordinate executives likewise have requisite sensitivity and skills in interfacing with creative people. Since most chief executives personally "touch" so few individuals within their realms, you are dependent on a coterie of other managers and functionaries. So personal accomplishment in dealing with creative people is far from enough; instead, you must deal with those people who deal with people who are creative.

All your noble aspirations in refining your skills in creative dealings can fall apart dismally unless those capacities permeate throughout the management hierarchy.

You may already be a chief executive, and, presumably, already a genius. Yet, the whole thrust of this book and this chapter is to make you even greater. Unless you pull up to your own new heights all those around you, company conditions down among the troops may remain just like they always have been. These "working-with-creative-people" comments relate to all levels of your company—the managers as well as the managed. And the counsel applies equally to those in the highest echelons nearest you—your top general executives . . . your division and subsidiary heads . . . your functional specialty executives. They certainly share your own responsibility companywide for exploiting all creative resources within their own domains and dealing as sensitively with creative people as if they were an extension of yourself.

In the process of this exploitation, even your own board of directors is not to be overlooked. Tap their creativity too . . . and encourage them to tap yours.

MEASURING CREATIVE PERFORMANCE

By what standards do you judge the creative person's performance and output? In a business organization, here is where the creator must make contact with the real world. Your judgment, as Chief Executive Officer, may ultimately be based on contribution to profit. That contribution may be direct or indirect, long-range or short, clearly or marginally measurable, commercial or institutional, but it must at some point relate to profitability. The profitability criterion, I know, is arguably simplistic. But even a corporation's pro bono efforts —for civil rights, community betterment, peace, or whatever—impact that company's institutional image . . . and thus its profit-making potential. And so it is that creativity in a business entity ultimately links up with dollars.

There are nuances of criteria for judging performance that can vary widely from traditional norms, however. One creative individual, for example, may clearly justify his compensation if he yields but one idea or one design or one approach in a year, rather than a daily outpouring of productive increments. So the creative person conceivably may be judged by different values, individually structured to suit the objectives of his employment. The challenge for the chief executive, of course, is to be able to live with these atypical criteria and accept varying judgment patterns for varying individuals of varying creative talents.

Just because creators may be "different" does not insulate them from an obligation to produce, though their production pattern may be understandably and even deliberately irregular. This irregularity imposes a need for performance monitoring so that inadequacies can ultimately be detected after reasonable time. There's another good reason for such monitoring, too. The kinds of output of some creative people can become "typed" or "dated"—frozen in time, rigid in direction. Some creators are expert in what they can create today, but they become incapable of adapting to change or of altering the direction of their creative thrust.

This puts an obligation on the chief executive to initiate turnover of creative personnel so that your company is always staffed with that type of creator who can meet the changing needs of today and tomorrow. Yesterday's creative genius may be today's human Edsel.

COMMUNICATING WITH CREATORS

Creative people speak the same language you do . . . sometimes. The need for communication is inescapable, but your mode can go far either in alienating or winning rapport with creative employees. Talking usually works—more successfully than writing. Listening is better than talking. Listen! It's a rare capability, but it's an imperative indulgence for any CEO who wants genuine communication with the creators in his realm. Verbalizing seems to be less intimidating than writing for the creative person and allows free articulation of thoughts and images.

When the CEO patiently listens, he also can gently encourage verbal flow, and show eye-to-eye interest and responsiveness. This allows important coloration to enrich otherwise sterile words. The chief executive also is better able deftly to alter the creator's course, or reshape his concepts, or exploit a breakthrough that may subtly and momentarily appear in conversation.

Formal written reports are anathema to so many creators, whether they are the initiators or the receivers. Corporate gobbledygook is a turn-off, but it typifies so many company communications.

Of course, directions, instructions, and limitations must be transmitted to creators, particularly to initiate work. But the best sequence is to do it verbally, give a chance for oral feedback, questions, and refinement. Then follow up with written confirmation on the understandings reached.

CONTROLLING THE CREATOR

It is often quite an impossible challenge to make creative specialists into "good businessmen" with dependable capabilities in cost control, profit orientation, and administrative discipline. So what! That condition must be completely acceptable if you are interested in maximum yield. Work around these deficiencies through other skilled supportive and administrative personnel who can help the creators and protect you.

Certainly we can stipulate—and even most creative people will affirm—that those in creative work need expenditures kept in line, budgets monitored, paper flow expedited, interdepartmental coordination achieved, and communications accomplished. The creators usually, however, are not the ideal guys to do this. They will work best free of the fetters of such procedural routines. Simple administrative practices, processed by truly understanding specialists, can relieve the creators of uncomfortable, distasteful tasks that complicate and hinder their output.

The staff chosen to do such work needs more than professional competence, however. They must be perceptive to the patterns of creative people and able to blend discretion and sensitivity along with their administrative activities and objectives. They must even view themselves more as a "support" staff rather than as a "control" staff. That subtle difference in attitude will maximize their accomplishments and rapport. The conventional administrative "watchdog" can be a disruptive force rather than a provider of benefits.

HANDLING THE CREATIVE CRISIS

It probably will happen when you least expect or when you least want it to occur. But it will happen. I speak of the inevitable creative crisis that will emerge from deep within the creative personality. That creative crisis may take any one of many forms, clearly articulated by its victim: "I quit" . . . "I can't go on like this" . . . "Screw all of you" . . . "Nobody understands me" . . . "This place bugs me."

Everybody has a boiling point, but in the creative person it is often reached more quickly than in most . . . and for more causes than in most. The result within the company is the same—a human relations crisis. It's so easy for "executive types" to respond in kind—with emotion, rancor, impatience, positiveness. It's so easy to heap full blame on "that prima donna."

When the pot so boils, I offer these soothing admonitions:

1. Volatility may be as predictable a trait in some creative people as their talent itself. If you value the latter, be willing to live with the former.

2. At times of crisis, avoid finality and harshness in the counter response. Seek a buffer of time and delay, no matter how brief. It's the best pacifier.

3. Don't "throw out the baby with the bathwater." As a priority, realize that rescuing the creative talent involved in the crisis will probably be more vital than any temporal right-wrong determination.

4. Listen . . . but with compassion and understanding. Find your own way to restore "face" and dignity to the distressed.

5. When all is calm, then you have your only chance to probe dispassionately into the real causes and considerations.

6. And after all that is over, you can be sure of one truth—it *will* happen again.

CREATIVITY UNMASKED

Creativity shows itself in unpredictable ways. Sure, from a creative artist or designer, you naturally would expect creative output. But commercially fruitful creativity can emerge, not just from creative "types," but from absolutely anybody. Not everyone in your employ is qualified to walk around wearing an "I Am a Creative Person" button. One of your greatest challenges will be to bring the creativity out of anybody and everybody.

The broadest creativity resource in your company today is probably virtually untapped or only marginally utilized. It is a phantom resource that is everywhere around you, yet almost invisible. This undeveloped, unexploited creativity pool resides in those whom you have employed for noncreative reasons. They constitute a hidden asset that could be activated at this very moment with capability of early, visible results.

Here's where to look for creative people who don't look like creative people . . . and creativity that is camouflaged behind other familiar facades:

1. The Routine Worker. Those in workaday jobs—the secretaries, bookkeepers, clerks, factory employees, warehousemen, and on and on. You tend to think of them solely in those limited identifications. But they are not just one homogeneous mass of employee categories. Every individual has some degree of uniqueness, and that uniqueness just may be creativity, even though it would be understandably far more limited than in creative specialists. They may have much stored up to say merely because nobody ever thinks to ask them. They offer objectivity and perspective that come from being ignored so long. Their potential creative output may be wide-ranging, varying from their own speciality to areas remote from their narrow daily concentration.

2. *Field and Branch Personnel.* No one feels more isolated, unloved, and "out of it all" than those "brain centers" that are geographically and operationally remote from home office. They are seldom heard from and narrowly solicited. You are using only a small specialized part of each of these people, and rarely is their creativity tapped or shared.

3. *Technical Specialists.* You hired them for a precise purpose, and, by God, that's what you use them for. Solely! But they have other buttons to press beyond their specific expertise. Creativity, anyone?

4. *Senior Citizens.* The "old Charlies," those in or near retirement, are so taken for granted. They peaked in their output long ago, and now they are reluctantly tolerated, in the shadow of those more zealous and those less tired. But, oh, do they have a treasure of unleashed creative bonuses. The unlocking is easy. China reveres their elderly and respects all they offer. Maybe you could "reorient" too.

5. *Ethnic Personnel.* Long used to being ignored, suppressed, or tokenized, they understandably respond in kind. But there are uncut gems among them, undeveloped sources of fresh creativity.

6. *The Youthful.* Don't underrate new employees, those just out of school, those deemed too young to know anything yet. Grab them before they are traditionalized and robotized. Here's really raw creative potential that may already be revolutionary in concepts and ideas.

7. *Women.* Possibly the greatest single underutilized resource you have is female. It's not all your fault that they have been low in profile. Women have been so conditioned by their male environment for so long, that they naturally gravitate toward secondary roles. Free their creative souls, and watch them soar.

8. *Executives.* Yes, even those VPs so close to you have become overlaid by layers and layers of distractions. Given the right time, oc-

casion, environment, and freedom, you're bound to find they're far more creative than either you or they ever thought.

A CREATIVE CHIEF EXECUTIVE?

While you're concerned with effectively handling creativity in others, don't overlook yourself. Creativity can be a precious commodity in any chief executive. But it's so simple to suppress creativity under your other tasks, responsibilities, and priorities. How do you bring it out . . . keep it viable . . . nourish it . . . harness it?

Your creative output may emerge in many forms—ideas, fresh approaches to old problems, unique planning, abandonment of fixations, unfettered new attitudes. If you have the talents to become a chief executive, you've undoubtedly relied significantly on your creative skills. But now that you're at the top, don't smother those precious sparks under other burdens. Personal creativity in you requires time for thoughtful reflection as well as time for idea interaction with others. If you are creative yourself, then you also become more credible and attractive to the creative personnel within your organization.

CREATIVITY—SOURCE FOR AN INDUSTRY

Creativity is alive and well and living in the recording industry. Here's a business sphere in which creativity literally can pervade virtually every aspect with positive results. Here is reinforcement for all of the principles and preachments of this chapter and their achievability in actual on-the-job practice . . . and a possible model for you.

I come from the recording industry and have lived on a daily basis with all of its creative forms and people. This is an arena where industry executives and subexecutives live comfortably and flexibly with the eccentricities of the recording artists and specialists from whom talent and dollars flow.

Creativity in the recording industry—and you may find the same practice elsewhere—is not consistently profitable and productive. Creative waste is a hallmark. About 75 percent of all recordings produced fail to recover their basic costs, which can mean oblivion for all those creators of the nonsuccesses. So with creativity, entrepreneurs must play the odds and percentages just as carefully as if they were dealing in the commodities market.

In the recording business, creativity is endemic, but it also can be the byproduct of an "explosion." A perfect example of the latter occurred with The Beatles, who stormed suddenly onto the creative musical scene. They precipitated a revolutionary impact on musical trends, consumer reactions, and sales levels. The Beatles brought a freshness and uniqueness in sound as well as in songwriting, and the industry has never been the same since. Creativity in that case begat other creativity, because their appearance unleashed an entire new stream of international talent, all catalyzed by their success and musical innovation. And never were those four young men a constant, predictable factor. Every year their own creative profiles changed, and when they ultimately broke up as a cohesive act, each retained his own special forms of creative capability.

Rock recording stars don't come out of a mold, contrary to popular belief. They all are individuals, each with creative uniqueness, and they each require special relationships with the company personnel with whom they deal. Those who interface with rock stars need not be finger-popping, long-haired prototypes of record company "swingers." One of the most successful artist relations specialists in one major company was a short-haired, mild-mannered, bespectacled, conservative gentleman who quickly earned the respect and confidence of all those creative types with whom he dealt. His word was good, he followed through, and he was alert and sensitive to their moods and needs.

Dealing with creative people does not necessarily imply blind acquiescence to all their wishes. It is just as important to say "no." John Lennon of The Beatles early in his career recorded an album with nude photographs of himself and his wife on the front and back cover of the jacket with all their respective "equipment" in full public view. The prospect of selling that package to the Sears, Penney's, and Woolworth stores throughout the Bible Belt was just too underwhelming, and our company refused the release wishes of our most important recording artist. But we allowed him to take his product-in-the-buff to a competing company. Had that album been released but a few years later in the days of the streakers and X-rated movies, the release decision might have been altogether different because the sales environment might have been altogether different. (Incidentally, the "nude" album sold poorly, thankfully.)

On another occasion, one of our prominent country music artists recorded a song extolling the virtues of Lt. Calley, famed for leading the presumed massacre of Vietnam villagers. The record touted his patriotic virtues and willingness to follow his country's "orders." Despite the cost investment and despite the wishes of this important artist, a decision was made not to release that particular record, because of the principle involved. Later, the artist himself, although originally incensed, expressed his later conviction that the "no" was right.

The true extent of creative potential is often difficult to discern, and someone in your company must forever be watchful in monitoring where it may lie. Today its form may be subtle or only marginally visible, but if you recognize and nourish it, the result can flourish into overwhelming importance. Glen Campbell, for example, was not always a number-one recording and TV star. For a long time he was a skilled guitarist on routine recording dates, accompanying other big stars with his instrumental expertise or backing up their voices as part of a background chorus. Somebody recognized his star potential and even had to convince Glen Campbell himself to exploit his own latent potential. In that case, the creativity lay both within Glen Campbell and the individual who was sharp enough to see the future in the present.

It is great to deal with creative people when they are malleable and responsive, but you have to be ready to face their tough side too. Life was not so easy when one famed recording star, irritated with his recording company, showed up at his recording sessions wearing a necktie embellished with an embroidered "fuck you"! And it was peculiar to have to explain to another recording group that they just couldn't drag the American flag around the floor of the recording studio. And it was tough to convince a famed opera soprano to record her arias on the many occasions when she just petulantly did not feel like it.

No matter how carefully you relate with creative people, you can't always expect to win the battle, as was demonstrated in the following vignette. Because recording artists are "night people," they prefer to record in studios during late hours of darkness. Therefore, those massive, expensive studios stand vacant throughout the daylight, and it behooves every cost-conscious recording company to maximize utilization during those dormant periods. Once, a well-known big band leader, equally famous for his musical and alcoholic capabilities, was humbly requested to record his next album during daylight morning hours. His adamant response and rejection was, "Are you kidding? Hell, I don't even start vomiting until noon!"

CONCLUSION

You, as chief executive, have many choices. Within your company you may seek creativity or not. You may find and recognize it or fail to. You may expand its current level or perpetuate what you have.

But the penetration of creativity can strongly sway the growth, profitability, and uniqueness of your company. And of you.

The title of this chapter is "Working with Creative People." But transcending that particular process is your boundless opportunity to discover creativity, nurture it, harness it, optimize its application, and maximize its productivity. Creative people can become your own special conduit to resourcefulness, innovation, extraordinary performance, and personal distinction.

PART II-C
Organization
Structure

BASIC ORGANIZATION STRUCTURE

by Donald S. MacNaughton

*Chairman and Chief Executive Officer, The Prudential Insurance
Company of America*

RECENT RESEARCH on organization has shown that the best form of organization for any particular company depends heavily on such variables as the technology employed, the size of the company, and the pace of change in its markets. Be warned, therefore, that my views on organization are strongly influenced generally by the experience of the insurance industry and, specifically, by the experience of Prudential.

One characteristic of an insurance company is that it typically doesn't own many "things." Its "assets" are for the most part policy reserves, which the company must hold in order to meet its future obligations to pay claims. It has little machinery, raw materials, and stocked supplies. By far its greatest true asset is the abilities of its employees, particularly its management staff. Thus, you will find that my opinions on organization reflect an over-riding concern for the impacts of structure on the behavior and development of employees.

Let me also state at the outset my personal management philosophy. It is fairly simple. A company, no matter how large, is made up of individuals. Individuals work best and produce most when they: (1) know what their job is; (2) know how it fits into the total picture and overall goals; and (3) are permitted to carry it out with a minimum of interference from anyone else. People tend to work best when they feel they are working for themselves. You will find this special bias of mine reflected in the discussion that follows.

Organizations—made up of humans and human relationships—are so complex that any discussion of them within a finite space necessarily involves oversimplification. Recognizing this, and nevertheless, here is the frame of reference I have chosen for this brief essay on basic organization structure.

161

DIMENSIONS OF ORGANIZATION

This frame of reference involves three of the basic dimensions along which business organizations can differ.

The first is the basis used for departmentalization. By this, I mean the principle the company has used to subdivide its organization. Of particular interest in a discussion of basic structure is the way the company has allocated responsibilities among the major organizational subdivisions found at one or two levels below that of the chief executive's office. The principal bases used for departmentalization appear to be function, market, and product. Within the overall structures of large companies, the use of all three bases usually can be discerned. Here the important thing is their relative significance in shaping the basic structure.

The second dimension is administrative decentralization. This refers to the degree to which decision-making authority has been delegated downward and outward throughout the organization. Although neither highly visible nor strictly measurable, administrative decentralization, in its effects on behavior of employees, is probably the most significant of the three dimensions to be discussed.

Third of the dimensions is geographic dispersion, i.e., the extent to which a company's facilities are split among separate locations. Unlike the first and second dimensions, this variable seems to receive little attention in the literature on organization. In our company's experience, however, geographic dispersion as a variable has had effects sufficiently important to justify including it in my frame of reference for this discussion.

I think it is apparent that these dimensions are interdependent to a considerable extent. Change along one of them may facilitate or hinder change along the others.

HISTORY OF CHANGES IN PRUDENTIAL'S
BASIC STRUCTURE

Because my views on basic organization structure rely so heavily on the experience of Prudential, let me recount briefly the major changes in our company's organization structure during the last 25 years.

In 1946, the Prudential was basically organized around major functions, as it had been since its founding in 1875. Home office operations were entirely concentrated in Newark. Carroll Shanks acceded to the presidency of the company in 1947 and announced a program of regionalization. Under this program, regional home offices would be set up each with responsibility for insurance sales and service, as well as investment operations, in a number of states. These regional home offices would enjoy a considerable degree of autonomy. Each would be headed by a senior vice president and have its own actuarial, accounting, personnel, and legal staffs.

By 1964, seven regional home offices had been established, each within its particular region, including one in Canada. Only New Jersey and a few other Mid-Atlantic states remained outside the regional home office structure. The Newark home office continued to be a collection of functional departments. These departments exercised three kinds of responsibilities: (1) overall policy-setting and control for the company; (2) other companywide functions of various types that had not been assigned to the regional home offices, e.g., auditing, product design and pricing, investments in bonds and stocks, and national union negotiations; and (3) sales, service, and other day-to-day operations in New Jersey and the few other states not served by regional home offices. Thus, at this point, the fundamental structure of the company had been changed from one primarily based on function to one based on a combination of function and market, with market geographically defined.

Orville Beal became the chief executive of the Prudential in 1963 and as a first step commissioned a study of company organization. As a result of this study, a reorganization took place in 1965 that established a separate corporate office having overall policy-making, long-range planning, and control functions for the company, as well as responsibility for the various centrally directed functions such as auditing. At this time, an Eastern Home Office was also created to serve the remaining states not covered by the then existing regional home offices. Later it was divided in two to bring the number of regional home offices to a total of nine.

The internal structure of the corporate office in 1965, although designed primarily along functional lines, also reflected recent movement toward product as a basis for departmentalization. For example, both the Group Insurance and Group Pension Departments now had their own actuarial staffs and their own computer programming staffs. The heads of these departments also informally had profit responsibility for their respective lines of business—this even though substantial parts of the sales and service operations for these lines were formally assigned to the regional home offices.

In 1971, the Prudential made the decision to enter the property and casualty field and a subsidiary company was formed to handle all operations related to these products except the functions that are performed by the agent himself. Prudential agents, operating under the direction of our regional home offices, sell the property and casualty lines and provide certain services to our property and casualty policyholders. The property and casualty subsidiary, however, has full profit responsibility for its products. Also, in 1971, a reinsurance subsidiary was formed and given full profit responsibility for the services it sells.

In 1972, without changing the Prudential's formal organization structure, we overlaid that structure with a system of financial control that, for each of the businesses we see ourselves as being in, gives profit responsibility to a "corporate activity head." As you might expect, these corporate activity heads are usually the senior officers of the corporate office departments having primary functional responsibility for particular types of business. Thus, for example, the head of the Corporate Computer and Insurance Services Department is the activity head for the data processing activity and has profit responsibility for data processing operations throughout the company. As another example, the head of the Corporate Group Insurance Department has full profit responsibility for our group insurance lines.

With this history available for reference, let me now turn to basic organization structure in general, the assigned subject of this essay. As mentioned earlier, I have arbitrarily chosen, as the framework for my presentation, three of the ways in which organizations can vary. These dimensions are: (1) basis for departmentalization, (2) administrative decentralization, and (3) geographic dispersion.

BASIS FOR DEPARTMENTALIZATION

The three primary bases for departmentalization seem to me to be function, product, and market.

Function is the primordial basis of organization. It is grounded in the nature of human learning ability. It pervades every organization. In small companies, it almost certainly will be the primary basis for subdividing the organization. In large organizations, even though product or market may be used as the basis for allocating responsibilities at the first or second level below the chief executive, function, as a basis, will invariably soon reappear as one follows down the successive levels of the structure.

The principal reasons for the pervasiveness of function as a basis of subdividing work are economic. For example, many small insurance companies find it prohibitively expensive to employ even one full-time actuary. Even fairly large insurance companies have no choice but to group their actuaries in an actuarial department, for this is the way to realize the maximum value for this expensive and scarce resource.

This is an age of increasing specialization. At the time the Prudential established its early regional home offices, computers had not yet appeared on the scene. Each of the regional home offices was capable of using the technology then available to develop and maintain its information processing systems. With the advent of computers, it became necessary for the Prudential to move in the direction of concentrating in the corporate office the design and development of data processing systems—this in order to minimize the requirement for an extremely expensive commodity, computer analysts and programmers and the talent needed to direct them.

At the lower levels of an organization, specialization by function has a similar economic rationale. The more specialized or narrow the tasks assigned to a clerical employee, the less the apparent costs of training the employee.

Although one cannot imagine an organization structure for a business enterprise that did not reflect function as one important basis for assigning responsibilities or tasks, overreliance on specialization by function can produce serious problems of coordination, motivation, and personnel development.

Although most insurance companies have felt that the greatest economy of operation could be achieved by grouping various kinds of functional specialists within major departments organized on the basis of the respective major functions, this economy has not been achieved without offsetting costs, some of them not so obvious.

It is most difficult to establish operational goals for many types of functional departments and to hold them accountable for results. It is often nearly impossible to fix the responsibility of major functional departments for the results achieved by the company. Where performance cannot be measured, much delegation of authority is not likely to occur. Furthermore, functional units such as the actuarial, sales, underwriting, or claim departments sometimes tend to evolve their own goals that deviate from those of the company.

Another negative feature of functional organization is that many, if not most, major company decisions do not fall neatly within the boundaries of one functional department. Automatically, therefore, these major decisions are pushed upward until they find an office with authority and responsibility for all major aspects of the matter involved. Too often this office turns out to be that of the Chief Executive Officer.

Opportunities for providing the kinds of broad experience needed to qualify for top management positions tend to be limited in the purely functional organization. One of the major benefits to Prudential of our regional home office structure has been in the increased ability it gives us to expose high-talent individuals to general management responsibilities at points fairly early in their careers. On the other hand, and as one would expect, the functional organization structure favors the growth of functional specialists in their particular areas of technical competence.

The use of product or market as the primary basis for departmentalization generally is confined to large companies for the reason previously noted. Both bases tend to require additional numbers of expensive staff specialists. As the size of the company increases, this factor becomes less burdensome.

Compared with function, the great advantage of product or market as bases for departmentalization is that they enable wider sharing of responsibility for end results. If responsibilities are grouped so that certain subordinate managers can also be held accountable for end results within particular markets or for certain products, this provides one of the two conditions under which the chief executive can delegate much of the authority that otherwise would have to be exercised by him alone. The other condition is, of course, that these subordinate managers are sufficiently competent to handle the authority given them.

It seems to me that a key point here—although perhaps an obvious one—is that the product or market bases of departmentalization provide the chief executive with some subordinate managers whose behavior will be conditioned by measures of performance that are similar to those used to evaluate the chief executive's own performance, i.e., final operating outcomes. With sufficient grants of authority—and if they are provided with the resources needed—these subordinate managers can perform many of the activities that would otherwise fall to the Chief Executive Officer. Within their particular areas, the subordinate managers can take the actions needed to ensure a flexible and effective response to the marketplace. They can coordinate the functional subunits within their respective divisions. In short, they can handle most of the day-to-day operating problems. In effect several persons will be doing the functions formerly performed by the Chief Executive Officer. The greater time and effort devoted to these functions should tend to improve the effectiveness with which they are performed.

Under this arrangement, if the necessary conditions are met, the chief executive and his corporate staff can turn their full attention to questions of basic company strategy, long-range plans, and other kinds of fundamental decisions affecting the company. This is the theory. As I can attest, this theoretical ideal can only be approached—more or less.

Nevertheless, there is enough substance behind the theoretical advantages described above to have caused most large companies to adopt either product or market, or both, as a primary basis for departmentalization. Typically, this leads the company to the "divisionalized" form of organization of which General Motors was a progenitor. One characteristic of this structure is a "corporate" office that has as its primary mission setting overall policy for the operating divisions, exercising overall control, and doing long-range planning for the company. The corporate office also performs centrally those kinds of staff services that are too expensive to be provided in each division or that should not be placed within the divisions for some other reason. Typical examples of the latter category would include auditing and negotiations with national unions that cut across division lines.

The Prudential has found substantial advantages in having corporate staff units solely devoted to overall policymaking, planning, and control. As March and Simon have noted, there is a sort of corporate counterpart to Gresham's Law which says that daily routine drives out planning (for most people, day-to-day activities automatically take precedence over longer-range kinds of responsibilities) and that, therefore, the only way to ensure that the longer-range kind of work is done is to assign it to units that are not hampered by day-to-day operating responsibilities.[1]

---

[1] March, James S., and Simon, Herbert A.; *Organizations*; New York: John Wiley & Sons, Inc.; 1958; p. 185.

A few additional words on the subject of planning: Our experience, as well as that of other companies I have observed, indicates that planning—other than for the short run—is not likely to be effective without the active participation and involvement of top management. Put another way, planning, intermediate or long-range, is one type of work which does not seem to lend itself to delegation. There are numerous examples that bear this out. Typically, in these instances, top management establishes a "long-range planning department" but the top managers themselves remain wholly preoccupied with day-to-day problems. Under these circumstances, the long-range planning department tends to operate in a vacuum. Its "plans," lacking the commitment by management which comes from participation, are largely ignored by the rest of the company. Some time goes by, perhaps several years, and, then, one day the planning department is quietly disbanded.*

Many issues that arise in planning are so fundamental that work done in the absence of active participation and direction by top managers is likely to be of little use. Further, in these fundamental areas, one cannot rely on the complete objectivity of lower-level management since planning of this kind often involves widespread changes in job responsibility and traditional operational methods. Third, a company often must have a willingness and desire to persist in this kind of work, even though for long periods of time it may appear unproductive and expensive.

Under the divisionalized form of organization, the Chief Executive Officer should have more time to devote to planning. This perhaps is the greatest advantage of this structure.

The divisionalized structure has attractions in addition to those mentioned above. It provides conditions favorable to heightened motivation of division executives. It also lends itself to geographic dispersion of the company, a topic to be discussed later.

Make no mistake, however, there is a price to be paid for these benefits. Only to the extent that the divisions are provided with most of the key staff and other resources needed to carry out their responsibilities can they be held accountable for end results of their operations. This means that, except for the large company, divisionalization is an expensive way to organize.

A different kind of cost incurred by the divisionalized company is the complexity of this form of organization. There is usually what

---

* [Ed. Note: See the chapter by John D. Glover, "Strategic Decision-Making: Planning, Manning, Organization."]

amounts to an institutionalized conflict between the corporate staff and the divisions—the corporate staff representing the overall and long-range interests of the company and the divisions representing the divisional, short-range interests. There is nothing wrong with such built-in conflict and it is, in fact, a highly useful device to ensure that diverse objectives are explicitly represented in the councils of the organization. On the other hand, the conflict of objectives can spill over into other areas. In Prudential, we pay a lot of attention to maintaining effective relationships between the corporate office and our regional home offices.

A final word on the product and market bases for departmentalization: An advantage that can be claimed for product, as opposed to market, as a basis for departmentalization is that decentralization of profit responsibility—delegation of part of the entrepreneurial function itself—is facilitated by having product-based divisions. On the other hand, if it is highly important to ensure an integrated and timely response by the company to the special needs of particular markets or regions, then it is advantageous to form market- or region-based divisions. This latter consideration led the Prudential to establish its regional home offices.

ADMINISTRATIVE DECENTRALIZATION

So far as I know, no one has developed a satisfactory, objective measure of administrative decentralization, or, if you wish, delegation of authority. That it cannot be precisely measured, however, makes it no less real as one of the basic ways in which organizations differ. I observe great differences between companies and within companies in the extent to which decision-making authority devolves downward.

The degree of administrative decentralization in a company is affected by various forces, of which management's philosophy and style are only one. Companies within the insurance industry, for example, generally seem to tend toward the centralized end of the centralization-decentralization spectrum. One can speculate that this is the result of their general use of function as a primary basis for departmentalization, as well as the nature of the relationship of the companies to their customers.

It is significant to me, however, that within the insurance industry and, indeed, between individual companies that are alike in practically every major respect, there do exist what seem to be major differences in the degree of administrative decentralization. If this is so, the way the companies are managed must make the difference.

What are the reasons why a company should seek to move authority downward and outward throughout its structure? First, people tend to work best when they feel they are working for themselves, when they have work that is meaningful and that involves responsibility.

Second, development of a company's future managers and executives requires that employees be given ability-stretching amounts of responsibility and authority early in their careers.

Third, management's most critical responsibility is planning. As change in the environment intensifies, executives and managers will have to spend more time in planning. The only way they will find the needed time is through greater delegation of authority.

Perhaps it also would be useful to consider the specific structural conditions under which effective delegation to a unit, or an individual, can occur. There are three such conditions:

1. The unit must have a reasonably well-defined objective or output, so that output can be measured.
2. The unit must be relatively self-contained, or self-sufficient, having within its control most of the resources and abilities needed for the achievement of its objectives—or at least enough of these resources to permit holding management of the unit accountable for results.
3. There must be sufficient technical competence on the part of unit management and confidence in that competence by higher management.

And, of course, whether or not delegation will occur will also depend on the approach and style of the higher level managers.

There are several forces at work that will tend to result in greater delegation of authority in the insurance industry and perhaps in business organizations generally. Concurrently, however, there are other, countervailing forces that are pushing in the direction of greater centralization of decision-making. Whether the net effect of these various forces will be greater or less delegation of authority is an open question.

Consider the increasing size and diversity of companies. The basic impetus for delegation of authority comes from the finite nature of human information-handling and decision-making capacities. As these capacities in managers are taxed toward their limit, they must delegate work to subordinates. As consumer demand for insurance products grows increasingly sophisticated, the diversity of company operations will naturally increase. If companies enter new lines of business, particularly noninsurance types of business, diversity and variety alone will compel unusual amounts of delegation to the management of the divisions or subsidiaries responsible for these new lines.

The impact on decision-making of the developing computer and communications technologies seems overwhelmingly in the direction of centralization. There are several aspects to this impact.

One use of computers by life insurance companies—the main use so far—is in processing insurance and investment contract transactions. This is the work which traditionally has occupied the bulk of the employees in a home office. This area of work has always been characterized by extensive use of rules and procedures; but, as long as the processing systems were primarily manual, there was room for, and indeed need for, considerable individual discretion by lower level employees. As the systems progressively have been mechanized, it has been necessary to bring their human components under the discipline demanded by the machines. The design and control of the systems, moreover, continues to pass from line middle managers to central systems and programming staffs.

The extent of use of computers and their allied disciplines as a means of improving the information of higher managers—and thereby expanding their decision-making capacities—has so far failed to live up to the widely-held expectations of a few years ago. The difference, however, has been one of the degree of change from that expected, not of its nature or direction. Further, much of what is being done along these lines has not been widely reported.

Computers and data-communications aside, greater general ease of communication over long distances is permitting decisions to be made at higher levels. In this regard, improvements or cost reductions in air transportation or voice telephone service are probably just as significant as computers.

Also favoring centralization of decision-making are the growth of specialization and the economics of employing specialists. These factors, taken together with increasing cost competition, will probably make it more and more difficult for companies to afford duplication in many types of technical and professional positions. For example, as noted earlier, one reason for centralizing processing systems design and development is to minimize the requirement for computer analysts and programmers and the talent needed to direct them.

There is another, somewhat contradictory side to the rise of specialization, however. This lies in the phenomenon of professionalism. As the specialist becomes a professional, his demand for autonomy in his work usually heightens. His commitment to the standards of his profession often grows at the expense of his allegiance to his particular company or its management. Obviously, these factors will tend to encourage some delegation of authority—to the professional positions at any rate.

Increases in governmental regulation of companies often lead them to centralize authority for decisions related to compliance and for dealing with the agency of government involved. For example, an unintended effect of the Civil Rights Act of 1964 was aggrandizement of the power, within their companies, of personnel departments throughout the land.

Companies can come under stronger regulation in two ways. First, the intensity or scope of regulation of existing operations may be increased, either through legislative or executive action. Second, the companies may enter new lines of business which are now subject to stringent regulation, for example, sale of equity-based products. Both types of regulatory increase seem likely to occur in the future, with their consequent centralizing effects. It is the degree of this future change that is unclear, not its direction.

GEOGRAPHIC DISPERSION

The significance of geographic dispersion—the extent to which a company's facilities are divided among separate locations—naturally is greatest when one considers very large companies.

The change, over the last 25 years, in the geographic dispersion of Prudential has been of enormous importance in achieving the company's objectives. Through geographic dispersion we have been able better to meet what we see as the social and economic responsibilities of a national company that owes its success to (and, in fact, is owned by) policyholders who live in every region of the United States and Canada. In addition to our field offices, which number almost 1,000, Prudential now has throughout the U.S. and Canada 22 major offices with staffs ranging from 200 to 3,000. These major offices provide employment and otherwise contribute to the economies of every region of the country. In addition, we intend that our offices play a strong and positive role as corporate citizens in each of the communities, states, and regions where they are found. I believe this intention is fully realized.

The value of any insurance to a policyholder depends on how well and in what spirit the insurer provides the services that the policyholder has purchased. From its regional home offices, Prudential has realized significant gains in the quality and responsiveness of the service it provides to its policyholders. Not only are communications and attitudes enhanced by the closer proximity of our home office service staffs to our agents and to our customers, but also by their common regional affiliation.

Our company's experience indicates that productivity and morale are functions of the size of an office. Beyond some point, the adverse effects of large size overtake economies of scale—at least they do in the kind of business we are in. By limiting the size of our offices, we gain the major benefits of simpler administrative routines, shorter lines of communication, and a higher sense of identification and purpose by our staff.

Finally, although not a necessary consequence, greater administrative decentralization is encouraged by greater geographic dispersion. Through dispersion of its home offices, the Prudential has been able better to realize the motivational and personnel development advantages that accrue from effective delegation of authority.

Perhaps the most significant cost of geographic dispersion is in the creation of additional barriers to personnel transfers. Movement between widely-separated geographic locations is often costly to the employee and his family in terms of their pattern of living and their relationships with friends, relatives, and schools. And interoffice transfers are exceedingly expensive from a financial standpoint, to the company, if not also to the employee.

There is another kind of barrier to interoffice mobility that we note in our company. One of the reasons why we realize gains in morale in the office of limited size is the greater cohesiveness developed among the staff. The other side of this coin, however, is an excessive tendency to promote from within to the exclusion of candidates from other offices. Local management is loyal to its own.

These additional barriers to intracompany mobility represent real, although not insurmountable, problems in achieving the most effective utilization and development of personnel in a geographically-dispersed company.

CONCLUDING NOTE

Of the many ways organization structures can differ, only three have been discussed here. These particular three variables—the basis selected for departmentalization, administrative decentralization, and geographic dispersion—have been emphasized in organization planning at Prudential. Thus, they were a natural frame of reference for describing the effects that we ascribe to changes in the company's organization structure during the last three decades.

Perhaps the outstanding characteristic of large organizations is their complexity; any discussion of them involves oversimplification. Furthermore, organizational variables are inextricably linked to other operational or environmental variables, such as the kind of technology employed by a company. For these reasons, those planning structural changes have little assurance that their experience will parallel closely those reported by others who have made similar changes. If reports of others' experience, such as this one, are useful it is mainly as a help in questioning the way a company is now organized and as a source of ideas for change.

LINE AND STAFF

by Alex Dibbs

*Director and Chief Executive Officer, National
Westminster Bank Limited*

DEFINITION AND EVOLUTION

TERMINOLOGY is often a cause of confusion in writings and discussions on management. "Line" and "staff" are particularly difficult to define because concepts of this separation of the elements of management can vary widely between different types of enterprise and may change within a single enterprise over time. Nevertheless, in formulating an organisation structure, the distinction between line and staff has to be made so that relationships as well as responsibilities can be clearly defined. The reasoning behind the distinction, which itself is divisive, needs therefore to be fully understood if the paramount principle of the unity of management is not to be undermined.

The terms, originally borrowed from the military, have acquired somewhat different meanings in ordinary usage and in applications to the management field. "Line" referred to the military formations likely to be directly engaged in combat with the enemy. It was also used to describe the main chain of command in which superior/subordinate relationships and responsibilities for making decisions were precisely defined. In large military formations there are several principal chains of command corresponding to the main arms, for example, armour, infantry, and artillery. The analogy can be applied to business enterprises where there will be one or more principal chains of command determined by, and closely identifiable with, the principal objectives of the enterprise. In a manufacturing company the principal chains of command, and hence the "line" activities, are likely to be production and marketing. In a service industry, "line" activities will usually be those directly providing the specific services to customers and who, therefore, have direct contact with customers.

175

"Staff," on the other hand, generally describes the officers or functions in an organisation which provide services to those in the main chains of command. The positions and the services given to "line" arise primarily from specialised knowledge or experience which is germane to the working and effectiveness of the organisation as a whole. In the military analogy these would be, for example, ordnance, transport, and medical services. In business enterprises they might be advisory and ancillary services, such as accounting, personnel, organisation and methods, etc.

The term, "staff" does, however, have other connotations. In industry it frequently means employees with a particular status. In government service it usually refers to all employees. In the title, "Staff Officer," widely applied in the armed forces and sometimes in industry, it refers to one who has general jurisdiction, within the scope of the responsibilities carried by his superior, which is a full reflection of his superior's authority.

To avoid additional confusions of terminology, "line and staff" are, therefore, sometimes described by other terms such as "operational and functional," "operational and supportive," or "executive and advisory."

It was probably the need for advice that first led to the distinction between line and staff—the acknowledgment by men of action that they could not themselves possess all the knowledge and information necessary to make vital decisions and be assured of successful outcomes. In ancient times no king or general would consider entering into battle without first consulting his oracle or seer to check that the omens and portents were favourable. Other examples arose in national planning. Pharaoh was fortunate enough to have on his staff one Joseph, who, as an interpreter of dreams, was able to predict the cycle of seven years of plenty followed by seven years of famine and to plan accordingly. Later Pharaohs usually sought the advice of the priests of the Nile temples on Egypt's harvest prospects. The forecasts were made on a more scientific basis, for the priests had made painstaking records of the rising and falling of the sacred river from which they could predict the flooding of the Nile with great accuracy. Nevertheless, they were careful to conceal the reality behind their calculations and to preserve their reputation for divinely-inspired prophecy.

The keeping of records as the basis for sound advice was, therefore, an early development of the staff function. Recording business transactions and wealth, for the purposes of control and co-ordination, probably followed close behind as the "line" activities and delegated authority of State, Church, and baron extended throughout the land. Accounting became a specialisation reserved for those with sufficient education to be able to count, read, and write. An accounting unit, separate from the policy-implementing "line," became a necessary adjunct for an operating unit of any size.

The rapid development of trade and commerce and the increasing complexities of business life in more recent centuries produced the need for additional specialisation. Every business enterprise today has to thread its way through a maze of legal requirements and cope with problems arising from rapid changes in technology and the whole economic environment in which it operates. A point is soon reached in the life of a growing company when the recurrence of problems in particular fields makes it worthwhile to separate out some of the elements of management for expert attention by specialised individuals or departments. Except in very small enterprises, some form of specialist activity is nearly always present. The pure "line" type of organisation is, therefore, seldom found in practice, whereas the "line and staff," in simple or complex form, tends to be the usual pattern. In effect, this separation of line and staff functions is little more than the extension of the division of labour which not only splits up the load but takes advantage of specialisation and specialised abilities. Like other forms of division of labour, it requires an understanding of the interdependence of, and the need for co-operation between, individuals and units for full advantage to be achieved. But as businesses grow larger and specialisations proliferate in the face of social, political, and economic pressures, the underlying principles tend to get obscured.

IS THE DISTINCTION IMPORTANT?

Some interdivisional or interdepartmental competition can be a healthy sign of corporate awareness and conducive to overall efficiency and morale. However, the divisive forces which separate line from staff are very strong and can easily produce frictions and counterproductive conflict within an enterprise.

Friction usually arises from poorly defined, or poorly understood, authority and responsibility relationships. The primary objective in the design of organisation structure should, therefore, be to make clear the respective responsibilities and relationships of line and staff even though this may appear to accentuate the distinction between them. We should perhaps start by substituting "operational" and "supportive" for "line" and "staff," as more closely reflecting their activities (although this may be open to a number of objections) and regard the activities as grouped in "divisions."

In the organisation structure, the operational divisions, as mentioned earlier, will be those most closely identified with the principal objectives of the enterprise. Upon them will rest the primary responsibility for profitability. If the enterprise is to be able to react quickly and flexibly to a changing environment, there must be a clear chain of command down which orders can be transmitted from the chief executive to employees in direct contact with customers. To ensure that directions get down to lower levels and that information comes up to higher levels easily and quickly, the channels of communication need to be clear and definite. The usual form of organisation for operational divisions is, therefore, hierarchical and, because the route from top to bottom must be as short as possible, the supportive divisions are excluded from the chain of command.

The supportive divisions are likely to be labelled as "cost centres" for the purposes of budgetary control. They may have similar chains of command in the exercise of their expertise, but outside the main pyramids. The relationships with the operational divisions are essentially lateral so that any operational division can seek advice and assistance without cutting across the authority of any other operational division. Supportive divisions, although not assuming any of the process of command in the operational divisions, are, nevertheless, instrumental in formulating the orders and instructions pertinent to their respective fields of specialisation, that pass through the direct, vertical links. These instructions may, for example, relate to methods and procedures or may specify matters that must be referred to particular supportive divisions for advice, recommendations or even for decision if considered to be outside the jurisdiction of the operational division. In any event, whether reference is mandatory or otherwise, it must be made clear where, and at what level, responsibility for decision and action lies.

This, of course, is merely a broad outline to illustrate the need for the distinction between operational and supportive activities. It assumes that decision-making will, invariably, be the prerogative of the operational executive; but it is becoming increasingly common for decisions, particularly on matters of greatest importance, to be arrived at by groups in which operational and supportive divisions both participate.

Good organisation structure, with clearcut definitions of responsibilities and areas of decision, can help to reduce causes of friction but cannot be expected to remove them entirely. A factor that this organisation approach cannot overcome is simply that the people found in operational activities are likely to have different personalities and characteristics from those in supportive groups.

There is a general belief that people can be categorised as "doers" or "thinkers" or as "practical" or "theoretical"; the former in each case being more temperamentally suited to operational and the latter to supportive activities. It is assumed that the two qualities are not to be found in the same person. This, of course, is not true. Indeed, the cynical "thinker" would say that it is a falsehood perpetuated by the "doers" to preserve their sense of superiority and to limit their numbers. But, although it is possible for a reflective person to become a sound decision-maker through gradual exposure to responsibility, it is much more difficult for a more impetuous one to accept and fill the supportive role. The tendency in the long run, through inclination, aptitude, or merely the opportunities presented, may well be that "doers" do gravitate to the operational divisions and "thinkers" to the supportive.

Because the main characteristics of the supportive or advisory division is the possession of specialist expertise, the educational standards required are likely to be higher than for operational. Training may be long and expensive. Professional or academic qualifications may be necessary, and these may have market values that do not fit readily into an existing salary structure. Some valuable branches of knowledge are in short supply in consequence of the increasing need for information as industry spreads into new markets and crosses more national frontiers and as new techniques and facilities have developed for using new kinds of knowledge and information in decision-making. Indeed, information technology, itself, has introduced new dimensions into the relationship between line and staff by extending the range of some of the supportive groups and increasing their importance within the organisation. All of this produces problems of status, rewards, and other forms of recognition which may have to include compensation for limited career paths.

SOME OF THE PROBLEMS

In the case of larger enterprises, the supportive divisions may employ sufficiently large numbers to offer a career path within the particular specialisation. But here a difficulty may emerge as a byproduct of size itself. The pattern and scale of the activity may tend to mask the service or ancillary role of the division. To those within it, the "work" may have every appearance of being a self-contained activity. Internal management, preoccupied with the coordination of subordinates' tasks and duties, may lose sight of the fact that the various "end-products" are merely the tools of management of the enterprise as a whole.

Where there is lack of cooperation between operational and supportive divisions, it is very often because of a "communications gap." Sideways communication and contact at as many levels as possible are essential if the two sides are to understand their respective roles and work together in unity of purpose.

Communication difficulties are greatest where, for one reason or another, people cannot easily move between the two types of activity to gain experience of the work and some appreciation of the other point of view. This may be because of the personal characteristics mentioned earlier, or because of geographical remoteness. The latter is most likely to occur in larger enterprises where specialist activities are highly centralised at headquarters, usually in an urban commercial or industrial centre, while operational units may be spread around the country. Transfers across divisional boundaries then involve all the problems of labour mobility: housing difficulties, arranging schooling for children, and a disruption of family and social life.

If the dispersed operational units are sufficiently large, one way of overcoming the geographical barriers to communication and to physical mobility is to decentralise the specialist activities; leaving the top strata at headquarters and placing subordinate specialists, perhaps locally recruited and trained, on the staff of the regional operational executive. This brings the supportive into close contact with operational management, and advice and assistance will be more readily accepted because of the specialists' knowledge of local conditions and operational realities. However, it involves the fragmentation of expertise and may have other disadvantages.

The supportive's prime responsibility will be to the operational manager, but he also has a reporting relationship to his superior in the particular specialisation which involves maintaining centrally-defined policy in that sphere. Management experts tend to dwell on the possibility of conflict between supportive and operational in the decentralised unit and, indeed, this can occur if responsibilities and relationships are ill-defined. Human nature being what it is, what is more likely to happen is that the supportive, through loyalty to the local unit, may develop a parochialism that may not be in the best interests of the enterprise as a whole. So, although decentralisation of both activities may bring operational and supportive divisions closer together, it can cause remoteness and communication problems within the supportive division. As is so often the case, overcoming one problem is apt to produce others but, it may be hoped, of lesser importance and more easy to solve.

A common communication difficulty is the "language barrier." Operational management often finds it hard to define its problems in terms that enable specialist, supportive divisions to grasp their practical significance and to give the advice and information that is really needed to solve them. Specialist divisions, for their part, often fail to give advice and information in terms that operational management can understand. Lawyers, accountants, economists, and most specialists, including management experts, have their own jargon. To them, the terminology is perfectly clear and is a convenient form of "shorthand" for summarising ideas and topics that may be very complex. They become so familiar with their jargon that very often they do not realise that they are using it. But no advice, however profound, or information, however valuable, is much use unless it is intelligible to those who need it for decision-making. However, the specialist who can speak to operational management in terms that are clear and readily understood has already gone a long way towards dispersing the fog of mystique that divides the two activities. It is, at least, the first step towards removing three other causes of dissension: (*a*) operational managers' lack of knowledge of the help and assistance available from supportive divisions; (*b*) the belief of operational managers that to seek specialist assistance questions their competence and reduces their authority; and (*c*) the reluctance of operational managers to accept specialist advice because the specialists are believed to be too theoretical and because they do not, in any event, have responsibility for the outcome of decisions based upon their advice.

WHAT CAN BE DONE TO EASE THESE PROBLEMS?

Although the problems outlined are likely to be met in greater or lesser degree in all enterprises, there is no universal set of rules for solving them. Well designed organisation structures can bring line and staff closer together and remove causes of friction between them;

but what may be an appropriate structure for one enterprise may be quite inappropriate for another of a different technology or scale of operations. And whatever framework is set up, a great deal depends upon the people who work within it—people of infinite variety in background, education, likes and dislikes, and hopes and fears.

I would like to emphasize, although it may not be necessary, that my views are largely based on experience in a major banking group in the United Kingdom employing some 50,000 people. The ways in which we have tried to ease the problems may not be open to other kinds of enterprise; but they may, nevertheless, illustrate some of the principles involved.

Of our three operational divisions—Domestic Banking, Related Banking Services, and International Banking—the first is by far the largest and conducts its operations through a network of some 3,400 branches which also act as retail outlets for the services of the other two. Each of these divisions has within itself some supportive elements which, in the two smaller divisions, are brought into close contact with operational management in company and activity groupings. The Domestic Banking Division is subdivided into seven geographical regions, three of which are centred on London and the other four in provincial cities. The supportive services of financial control, management services, personnel, and premises are represented at each regional centre to assist the Regional Executive Directors in these particular aspects of management. The heads of the supportive divisions, who are responsible for sectional policy throughout the organisation are, with their central departments, located at the London headquarters. In many respects they act as specialist staff officers to the chief executive while their subordinates in the regions act in similar capacities to the Regional Executive Directors.

It will be apparent from this thumbnail sketch that we look to subdivision of units and the decentralisation of both operational and supportive activities as a means of maintaining close working relationships between line and staff, and of obtaining their mutual cooperation through local loyalties that are capable of being welded into a corporate loyalty.

One of the well known features of organisation in banking is the ability to work on centrally-determined procedures and yet grant a considerable degree of authority to local management. What is perhaps less well known is the part that comprehensive "Books of Instructions," or "operating manuals," as they might be called in other industries, play in this.

Over the years, management will have met constantly recurring problems of a similar kind, and multiple experience will have provided solutions. Originally, many of these problems will have been referred to the supportive divisions for expert advice but, by codifying experience for the benefit of all, the solutions may be capable of being reduced to definite procedures that can be incorporated into the operating manual. It is possible to extend and refine this process to give an operational manager well down the line a high degree of independence; reducing his need to seek specialist assistance but making it clear that in certain circumstances it is essential that he should do so. This helps him to appreciate the role of the supportive division. Its rules and procedures are less likely to be regarded as irksome controls and he can see that specialist help, sought as necessary, in no way undermines his own authority. The supportive divisions themselves have an incentive to contribute to the process, because it reduces the number of routine matters referred to them and allows them to concentrate upon problems that require expert attention.

An example from my own bank is the authority we are able to delegate to the managers of our 3,400 branches, not only to grant advances, or assume other risks on behalf of the bank up to certain amounts without reference to superiors, but also in taking and perfecting security for loans and advances. The types of security available and the circumstances under which it may be offered range so widely that, in earlier years, expert legal assistance would frequently have been needed to draw up documents and to deal with the technicalities for ensuring that the security could be legally enforced in case of need. From many years of experience, the bank has developed its own forms of charge appropriate to particular circumstances, revising and adapting them in the light of changes in legislation and decisions under case law. It has also been able to reduce the technicalities to well-defined instructions to branches on the step-by-step measures to be taken to validate the bank's title and priority to the security of whatever kind. In some cases, however, particular complexities may arise, for example, in taking security from a company liquidator. Expert advice is then essential, and branch managers are specifically instructed to refer to the specialist department for guidance.

Similar examples of wide discretion being given to branch managers under standardised procedures, but in which we indicate where reference must be made to specialist departments, occur also in bank administration, accounting, premises, and personnel management.

On a wider front, supportive divisions should be encouraged to contribute articles to internal publications describing their activities and the assistance they can provide. Opportunities should also be given for officers to meet and talk to people in the operational fields.

The most effective way of bridging the gap between line and staff is, however, by transfers across divisional boundaries. This is perhaps easier in banking than in most other industries because the educational standards of entrants are relatively high, and because mobility, both geographical and functional, is accepted as necessary for career progress.

A senior management development programme, which aims to select and train people for the top executive posts, should certainly include experience in supportive as well as operational divisions. In view of the importance of the operational side and its main responsibility for profitability, the chief executive is more likely than not to have emerged from its ranks. If at some stage in his career he has worked in a supportive division, he is much more likely to be able to appreciate both points of view and it will be clear to all that his judgment is unlikely to be clouded by any elements of partisanship.

It is equally desirable that specialists should have some experience of operational activities; and if it is possible to draw some of them from the larger ranks of the operational divisions and train them in the particular specialisations, so much the better. A great deal depends, of course, on the degree of specialisation and the length and type of training required. Given a reasonable standard of education and a willingness on the part of the individual to further his, or her, education and to broaden experience, there can be much greater mobility from line to staff than is generally supposed. The number of highly qualified specialists required may, in fact, be relatively small; and if scarce expertise can be bought in on a contract basis, this will frequently suit both the expert practitioner and the employer, and be more readily acceptable to career staff.

Insofar as it is not possible to give all managers experience in both types of activity, in-company training programmes must be so designed that operational and supportive people participate together to exchange views, to cross-fertilise ideas, and to gain an appreciation of each others' roles in achieving corporate objectives. For those destined for higher posts in either activity, external business school courses can be particularly valuable, not only in bringing them up to date with developments in management techniques, but also by demonstrating, perhaps more clearly and convincingly than would otherwise be possible, the interdependence of operational and supportive roles in the enterprise as a whole.

Training of the kind that requires groups of individuals from different branches of management to pool their knowledge in solving problems has its direct counterpart in modern business. When decisions are required on matters of major importance—for example, acquisitions or the extension of operations into new areas or the development of new products—it is becoming the usual practice to set up project teams to examine proposals in detail and to make recommendations. Members of the team will be drawn from both operational and supportive divisions and will be backed by divisional resources of experience, skills, and information, so that every aspect is fully considered and all the implications taken into account. There is, in fact, growing recognition that, in to-day's complex business world, sound decisions are more likely to "emerge" from a combination of the skills of both line and staff than if "made" by line management on the basis of individual knowledge and judgment. This principle of teamwork needs to be extended as far as practicable for, indeed, it is the ideal that the whole organisation should be striving for. Direct involvement in the decision-making process makes the supportive role much more satisfying and there are the added advantages of commitment by both sides to decisions arrived at jointly.

So far the emphasis has been upon the formal lateral relationships and channels of communication between line and staff, but the importance of informal relationships should not be underestimated. Many of the problems discussed here arise from personal differences, and the solutions lie in finding common ground in the working environment. Equally, good personal relationships can be fostered by facilities for sharing mutual interests in social, cultural, and recreational activities. These facilities can range from shared catering arrangements for lunch and coffee breaks to sports grounds and country clubs. What is necessary, or appropriate, will vary from one enterprise to another. But although every encouragement should be given to clubs and societies which enable line and staff to meet together for shared interests in off-duty hours, care must be taken, in the western world at any rate, to prevent this being interpreted as paternalism.

CONCLUSION

This outline of the concept of line and staff, of problems arising from the distinction between them, and of ways of bringing them closer together in unity of purpose, inevitably leaves out many and, perhaps, more pertinent observations that could be made by chief executives in other industries and enterprises. There are, however, some conclusions that few will dispute. First, that there will be a certain amount of friction between line and staff; and, second, that with the increasing degree of specialisation in the modern business world there are greater dangers of counter-productive conflict.

Good organisation can reduce the causes of friction and make effective provision for resolving such conflicts as arise; but personal attitudes will still govern the level of success. Although a changing world and the ever-shifting pattern of personal relationships within an enterprise will make perfect harmony unattainable, the Chief Executive Officer has a great influence upon the general climate. By recognising the complementary roles of line and staff and by being seen to maintain a fair balance between them, he will set the example that will condition attitudes throughout the whole enterprise.

DECENTRALIZATION AND THE CHIEF EXECUTIVE OFFICER

by Charles M. Leighton

Chairman and Chief Executive Officer, CML Group, Incorporated

and G. Robert Tod

President, CML Group, Incorporated

APPROXIMATELY 85 percent of the *Fortune* "500" companies utilize some form of decentralized divisional organization. This form has been particularly attractive to diversification-oriented companies because it permits separate management of several different types of business within one corporation. It also enables smaller merged or acquired entrepreneur-managed companies to make a smooth transition into a larger parent organization. But the benefits of decentralization, although it is certainly not recommended as a panacea, are equally attractive to other types of companies. Throughout this chapter, we shall attempt to suggest how decentralization increases flexibility, stimulates management development, facilitates performance measurement, and encourages a future-oriented management style at every level of the organization.*

Because every Chief Executive Officer is a "manager of managers," he must at one time or another delegate some authority and responsibility for achieving corporate objectives to other managers whose judgment he chooses to trust. This distribution of authority and responsibility is the root of decentralization. Whether or not this activity is compatible with a CEOs personal goals will determine whether or not he will be comfortable with decentralization as a comprehensive organizational form. After the CEO has analyzed how decentraliza-

---

* [Ed. Note: Compare this chapter with that of Robert C. Wilson, "Delegation of Authority in a Decentralized Company."]

tion works, he will want to ask not only "Will it help my company?" but "Is it right for *me?*" In the discussion that follows, decentralization is considered both in terms of what it means for the organization and what it implies about personal leadership style.

One of the Chief Executive Officer's greatest challenges in a decentralized company is to coordinate activities in such a way that the benefits of decentralization are realized without losing the internal cooperation necessary to achieve corporate goals. Alfred P. Sloan of General Motors defined the task:

> Good management rests on a reconciliation of centralization and decentralization with coordinated control. . . . From decentralization we get initiative, responsibility, development of personnel, decisions close to the facts, flexibility—in short, all the qualities necessary for an organization to adapt to new conditions. From coordination we get efficiencies and economies. It must be apparent that coordinated decentralization is not an easy concept to apply.[1]

In a decentralized company, successful coordination of corporate and divisional goals depends to a large extent on the flexibility as well as the management skill of the CEO and the corporate staff. In a centralized company, the CEO may think of himself as a manager of ideas. In a decentralized organization he must be a manager of people. He may have to hire a divisional manager whose style is totally different from his own, someone with whom he may find it difficult to work because of differences in temperament. But if they are right for the divisions they manage, the CEO must be able to work with many different types of people and must value and encourage their independence. And he must choose corporate staff with the same flexibility. In short, if he prefers his managers to be replicas of himself, decentralization is not for him.

In the remainder of this article, we shall discuss what we think are the primary keys to effective coordination in a decentralized organization: (1) simplicity *of form* of the organization; (2) a clear and effective corporate *leadership style;* (3) the awareness on the part of the CEO and his staff of the essential *tasks* of decentralized management; and (4) the effective utilization of management *"roles"* for achieving these tasks. Finally, we shall enlarge upon some of the benefits to be derived from this type of organization.

---

[1] Sloan, Alfred P., Jr.; *My Years with General Motors;* New York: Doubleday and Company, Inc.; 1964.

ORGANIZATIONAL FORM

Our experience suggests that the best form of decentralized organizational structure is the simplest—one that enables the company to fulfill its corporate needs while providing sufficient autonomy to managers to allow them to test their ideas, develop independent management skills, and be highly visible. This visibility serves a twofold purpose. Because their performance can be readily evaluated by corporate staff, divisional managers achieve the recognition they crave. At the same time, top management quickly learns whether corporate goals as well as divisional objectives are being achieved.

For a medium-sized company the corporate staff might comprise the CEO, one or more home office operating executives, a financial staff, and, in some cases, in-house legal counsel. The head of each decentralized division would report directly to the appropriate corporate executive. Divisions could be assigned to group vice presidents on the basis of geography, industry, product lines, distribution channels, capital intensity, markets served, or whatever variable is critical to management success. Depending on their size, each group may have its own controller or other staff. The CEO may also wish to develop corporate level staffs to handle audit review, analysis, legal matters, insurance, EDP, or other specialized work needed by the divisions. Above all, however, the CEO should not allow his organization to become top-heavy. Cumbersome layers of bureaucracy inhibit frank communication and lead to duplication of effort, diffusion of responsibility and authority, and, inevitably, inertia and a state of atrophy. The CEO should keep his corporate staff organization simple, aggressive, and lean, with as few layers of management as possible between him and his division heads.

LEADERSHIP STYLE

We have already emphasized that the CEO's leadership style will have a strong bearing on the success of the divisions and the company as a whole. Yet the art of leading a decentralized organization is perhaps one of the most difficult management challenges. To insure that corporate objectives are being realized while he is developing managers who have the ability, confidence, and freedom to act independently, the CEO must do everything he can to promote open, honest, two-way communication. This means that both corporate and divisional goals must be clearly defined and interpreted so that they are understood and agreed upon at every level. Not only must the CEO and corporate staff delegate responsibility and motivate and monitor performance, they must create the kind of atmosphere in which divisional managers feel, on the one hand, that their independence is respected and, on the other hand, that they can turn to corporate staff for advice and assistance without risking a loss of face, or autonomy.

The CEO and his corporate staff should work with and through divisional managers, not around them. After goals and evaluation systems have been agreed upon by all concerned, corporate staff must seek to minimize anxieties about "interference from the top." Even in small matters, independence should be encouraged; e.g., letting divisional managers communicate divisional messages to employees and the public on their own letterheads. Corporate staff and operating management should avoid any tendency toward self-aggrandizement. Whenever possible, for example, they should travel to the division offices for meetings rather than asking division heads to come to headquarters. This small gesture demonstrates that top management appreciates the value of the division leaders' time. In the same vein, corporate personnel, including the CEO, should make it clear that they don't expect to be met at airports or chauffered and entertained during their visits. In short, diplomacy is a key ingredient of leadership style in a decentralized organization, as important as the dispensation of tangible rewards for successful performance.

MANAGEMENT TASKS OF THE CEO

The CEO is responsible for insuring that the essential tasks involved in managing a decentralized organization are accomplished. Among these are: (1) strategic planning and allocation of resources; (2) the selection and development of key managers; (3) the design and implementation of motivational systems for management; (4) the creation and maintenance of an atmosphere that nurtures growth; and (5) constant evaluation of performance. Although these tasks are not unique to a decentralized organization, this type of management structure presents peculiar demands, opportunities, and problems of implementation.

Strategic Planning and Allocation of Resources

Determining strategy, communicating it effectively, and winning a commitment to its attainment are the CEO's primary tasks. He must work with his corporate staff to determine how and where the company will utilize its resources in relation to short- and long-term objectives, competition, the economic and technical characteristics of the industries involved, anticipated trends, government regulation, and the basic goals and aspirations of key management. Because decentralized organizations are frequently highly diversified, the planning/allocation tasks are exceedingly more complex than in a "monolithic" organization. But there are also more opportunities for spreading risks and for increasing organizational flexibility in solving problems.

To match corporate resources with strategy, we recommend that the CEO and his board of directors first formulate corporate objectives and then involve each division's management in the development of short- and long-term strategies and budgets that will implement both corporate and divisional goals. These strategies and budgets should then be integrated at the corporate level. Modifications should be communicated by corporate staff to divisional managers, but the feedback process should not stop here. There should be a continual two-way communication and strategy refinement.

One way to formalize this two-way interchange is to ask each divisional manager to develop a long-range forecast. In our case we use three years. This should be carefully reviewed by the CEO and corporate executives. Then, the corporate operating officer and his financial officer should meet with each divisional manager to discuss the plan—avoiding a posture of judgment or censure or any semblance of attempting to dictate strategy. It should be made clear as each plan is analyzed and evaluated that corporate staff is there to listen and learn as well as to advise. In addition, when effective two-way communication has been established by personal contact, it is unlikely that the divisional long-range plan will contain major surprises for top management. The divisional manager and the corporate staff can then review the final plans, with special emphasis on the operating plan for the year ahead plus longer-term personnel and capital needs.

Management Development

One of the great strengths of decentralized management is in the area of management selection and development. By creating numerous autonomous management positions within the corporation and isolating the performance of each unit, decentralization provides the ideal climate for management development; i.e., performance is the major criterion for compensation and promotion. Of course—and here we return to leadership style—the CEO must be willing to take risks in delegating responsibility and must also be willing to encourage and accept innovation. These risks more often than not pay off richly. When a CEO is willing to take a chance on a divisional manager's ideas even when he has some misgivings, he demonstrates his faith in the manager's judgment and his commitment to divisional autonomy. Even if the idea is unsuccessful, the divisional manager will be grateful for the support he has received and will attempt to prove his loyalty and ability with increased efforts to succeed. He will also be more likely to accept advice than if he had not been given the opportunity to test his own theories.

The task of management development may itself be decentralized. For example, corporate staff might first identify the type of candidates they think are qualified for divisional management job openings. Then they should give the task of personnel selection and management development to the divisions, leaving the responsibility for final choices to the managers to whom personnel will report. The CEO and his corporate staff can then use the measurement and control techniques discussed in the following sections to evaluate the performance of individual managers.

Finally, in order to provide an atmosphere in which diverse personalities with a variety of personal and management goals and needs will flourish, the CEO must place a high priority on flexibility, tolerance, and moral integrity—both for his corporate staff and his divisional managers. He himself must set the example, making it clear that he expects others to follow.

Motivation

The CEO must take advantage of the achievement-orientation and need for recognition that characterize the entrepreneurial type of personality who is attracted to a decentralized organization. Such a manager is usually best motivated by being given the responsibility and authority to do the job required, and appropriate rewards—including recognition—when success is achieved. A decentralized organization provides a milieu especially suited to this type of motivational system. Because performance within his own division is the measure of his success, the manager can concentrate on his own batting average rather than working toward promotion within the organizational hierarchy. If he knows that the CEO is evaluating his performance in terms of corporate as well as divisional goals, moreover, his own standards will be realistic.

Understandable and mutually acceptable standards of performance measurement are a critical element of any motivational system because the criteria will determine where managers concentrate their energies (*and what they may neglect*). Compensation plans established to reward divisional managers should correspond to the performance measurement criteria selected and should reflect corporate and divisional objectives as well as the needs of the managers themselves. Corporate staff incentives must also be in harmony with divisional incentives so that the two levels of management will concentrate on the same goals.

Because each division in a decentralized organization has different needs, characteristics, and potential, incentives must be individually tailored. The CEO and corporate staff must avoid inflexible standards, reporting formats, and management homilies that tend to ignore differences rather than capitalizing on them. A simple financial bonus formula in different variations that we have used successfully increases the divisional manager's salary in some proportionate relationship to the percentage of profit increase he achieves and his return on managed assets. Several of our divisions have tripled profits in less than three years while maintaining their return on managed assets. The responsible managers were rewarded accordingly.

A Growth-Oriented Atmosphere

The CEO and his corporate staff must create and maintain a setting in which growth of the business and its people is supported and encouraged. Just as *he* must take risks in the delegation of operating responsibility and authority in order to test and develop management talent, the CEO must welcome risk-taking and testing of new ideas at the divisional level. This has a double advantage: The difficulties and hazards of corporate-wide trial of new concepts are avoided and, at the same time, the organization can move aggressively on to the frontiers of new opportunity. We, for example, encourage our divisional managers to investigate acquisitions of attractive businesses that complement their activities or will assist them in internal expansion. The corporate staff negotiates the specific acquisition terms, but the responsibility for the performance of the acquired company is given to the divisional manager. You may wish to have him measured on percentage growth of profits and return on assets employed. We do not believe his performance should be measured against the acquisition cost if he was not responsible for negotiating the purchase price.

In attempting to create a stimulating and growth-oriented atmosphere, the CEO should encourage cross-fertilization between divisions. Synergy doesn't just happen—it must be cultivated by the CEO and his operating personnel. We bring our divisional managers together at regularly scheduled meetings to discuss common opportunities, techniques, and problems. At our annual executive meetings, held away from office surroundings, each divisional manager presents his prior-year results and his forecasts for the coming fiscal year to the other divisional managers as well as the corporate officers and the board of directors. Not only is he stimulated by other managers' performance records and plans, but the exposure to his peers challenges him to his best efforts.

We have found, however, that forced synergy doesn't work. Even when the economics looks good on paper, joint activities initiated by corporate staff will not work unless the divisions involved are enthusiastic about the enterprise. When a joint marketing effort between two recently acquired companies made sense, for example, our corporate headquarters decided not to form a central marketing organization or to merge two sets of diverse production operations and management personalities. Instead, we left the two companies intact and encouraged them to set up an arms-length joint venture, a single captive sales/merchandising force. Both firms share in the profits generated by the sales company on a basis agreed upon by contractual arrangement between the companies' managers. Both managements will make the joint effort work because they can realize tangible rewards for their cooperation while retaining their individual prerogatives.

Performance Evaluation

A decentralized organization cannot succeed unless its methods for measuring performance are sound. In this type of company, the term "control" is less meaningful than "performance evaluation" because corporate staff seeks not to *dictate* divisional activities but to *communicate* corporate goals. These must be carefully explained and interpreted and, finally, codified into divisional strategies that will motivate managers to succeed. The performance evaluation system should measure management activities in terms of both corporate and divisional goals and should provide feedback on both goals and performance so that either or both can be modified as appropriate.

The quality of the performance evaluation system depends, in the final analysis, on the reliability of the division manager and his controller. The single most important rule is: *There should never be any surprises for top management, whether good or bad.* Corporate groups frequently praise and/or reward division managers who report "surprise" profits at year-end. This is extremely unwise. We have little faith in a manager who surprises us with "excess" profit. Next year his surprise may be of a less pleasant nature. To give a reward in this case is to invite distortion or abuse of the information system. Managers eager for recognition might, for example, intentionally understate their budgets, try to overstate profitability, attempt to manipulate company accounts, and/or create hidden "profit pockets" in good periods as a hedge against future losses.

By the same token, corporate staff should create an environment in which managers whose divisions cannot meet their budgets or who are confronted with unexpected adversity will not fail to bring their problems to top management's attention as quickly as possible. Such news should stimulate corporate staff to make every effort to advise and assist, never to berate or censure. Otherwise, managers may be hesitant to give timely warnings of changes in costs, cash usage, profits, or other operational problems.

As a general rule, divisional managers should be responsible only for those areas over which they exercise authority, so that accountability can be clearly defined. To ensure fair performance measurement, our company does not allocate corporate overhead charges to the divisions unless they themselves control the expense variables. Examples of costs that are controllable at the division level are auditors' fees, which the division can reduce by adequate advance preparation, and working capital, on which interest should be paid or charged, depending on usage. After divisional statements are submitted to corporate headquarters, costs can be accounted for with one general charge against consolidated income before federal taxes. The CEO should remember that there may be an important strategic advantage to deciding not to allocate costs to divisions, when he wants to encourage them to use corporate services they might otherwise resist.

BUDGETS AND REPORTING

The budgeting process is a key planning mechanism. There should be regular give and take between the corporate executives and divisional managers in developing written strategy and financial pro formas with distinct short- and long-term planning cycles. These meetings should include a review of past operating results, with the aim of developing realistic projections for the coming period. The final budget, however, should be the divisional manager's. He must believe in it or he won't take responsibility for it. If the CEO thinks it is too optimistic, he should let it stand for divisional purposes but make adjustments before submitting it to bankers, boards, etc. Be patient. Remember that it takes time to get inside the budgeting process. Remember, too, that division budgets established at corporate headquarters are almost meaningless to divisional personnel.

Reporting should be designed to give top management the information it needs to assess divisions without unduly straining divisional manpower resources. Monthly "P & L" and balance sheets compared to budget and previous year performance are a good starting point. In addition, it is important to monitor cash flow as closely as possible. Such a review can provide an excellent early warning system to alert corporate staff to potential problems. Finally, top management should define indicators that diagnose the health and activity of each decentralized division and should monitor these as well. Possible indicators might be: orders, inquiries, shipments, production backlog, inventory turnover (dollar or item quantity), and sales per employee.

As CEO, however, you should never forget that people are behind the numbers. Don't rely solely on financial statements and statistics when you are evaluating division performance, no matter how well designed and prepared these may be. Evaluate the strengths and weaknesses of your managers thoroughly. Get to know them through personal contact, well enough to anticipate their feelings, reactions, and needs, and to understand their capabilities. It is this appreciation of the human element that distinguishes a truly effective manager of managers from a mere manipulator.

Monthly review of financial reports at each divisional headquarters can be a good way to develop personal contact with managers and to assure them of top management's interest in them. Going to the divisions for monthly review, rather than asking division managers to come to headquarters, also gives corporate staff a chance to look around the plant and to size up inventories, backlogs, personnel attitudes, etc., on a regular basis. Following most meetings, it is a good idea to have operating executives write a summary of the discussion and send it to the division head. This gives corporate management the opportunity to reemphasize key points. The summary can be used as a follow-up agenda for the next meeting. It minimizes the divisional managers' paperwork chores, too.

Controllers

The reliability of regular financial reports can be improved by structuring reporting systems so that the divisional controller has a dual responsibility. The division head is his direct supervisor, but the controller must certify monthly statements to the corporate controller with the clear understanding that he will be held accountable if reports are inaccurate. Be certain he understands that he has a fiduciary responsibility similar to that of the financial vice president who certifies financial statements for external release.

Regular internal audits by a corporate controller provide an additional check on divisional reports. His analysis of the status of the business and of divisional and corporate accounting practices can be particularly useful to divisional management. The corporate auditor should write a report addressed to the division head and his controller, summarizing findings and, if appropriate, suggestions—remembering that his relationship to the divisional auditor should be supportive rather than dictatorial.

The performance evaluation system should provide information rapidly, thereby assisting divisional managers to control their operations by increasing their sensitivity to the effects of changes in labor, material costs, etc. A good evaluation system should stimulate improved communication between the divisions and corporate headquarters.

Finally, in order to be truly useful to divisional managers as well as to corporate staff, the control system for each unit must be tailored to its particular needs. For example, a company that makes $100,000 sailboats needs a different control system from a company making $50 backpacks, and both may be different from a direct mail retailer. It would be a mistake to use the same criteria for measuring all three, nor is it reasonable to ask all three to conform to an inflexible corporate reporting format, since the critical variables of performance are unique for each.

MANAGEMENT ROLES OF THE CEO

There are several roles that the CEO must assume in carrying out the tasks described above. He may fill all these roles himself or he may delegate some of them to members of the corporate staff. These roles include: the listener and learner, the advisor, the change catalyst, and the boss.

Listener and Learner

Headquarters personnel must have a comprehensive understanding of each division and its business in order to evaluate its strategy, its performance, and its capital expenditure and working capital proposals. To arrive at this understanding, the CEO and other corporate executives must develop the habit of asking divisional managers: "What do *you* think?" They may also want to research the industry or product area from the corporation's point of view. Then, during budget review sessions, they should ask each manager to explain the risks and opportunities that his division faces. Make him back up fund requests, and so on, with hard information. Most important, show that you believe you have something to learn. The CEO who is in touch with his managers *will* learn.

Advisor

The CEO and other corporate personnel should "sell rather than tell" managers when it comes to their own ideas because they will get the best results if divisional managers are convinced of the value of a new approach. If a manager hesitates to accept a new idea, let the corporate staff research and test it (e.g., a pricing policy, a marketing study, a cost system) and do a first-rate job. Then, have them submit a report to the divisional manager to use as he deems appropriate. Almost certainly, change will be accepted if and when its merits have been proven. This approach builds confidence and strengthens the CEO's relationship with each division.

The CEO can also help his divisions by taking an "outsider's" look at the divisional organization. He should play the devil's advocate—always in a positive and constructive way. At the same time, he should not make comparisons with other divisions or discuss corporate activities unless divisional managers make specific inquiries. It is important to concentrate on the manager's own division because he wants to talk about his own success or solicit help on his particular problems.

Change Catalyst

It is not news that people generally resist change—it can be threatening. So change doesn't just happen. It requires a great deal of planning, effort, and consideration of others' perspectives. If divisional change is expected, make it known as early as possible. Become familiar with the needs of the personnel involved. Above all, don't *force* change. Demonstrate that it is needed and provide rewards for adapting to new situations.

One of our divisions, for example, balked at incurring the expense of installing a computer we thought it obviously needed to replace an outmoded mailing list processing system. Corporate headquarters paid for operating the computer parallel to the old system for one year. Eventually everyone in the company was convinced that it provided a better system, and resistance disappeared. Employees now talk about the days before the computer as if they were "hard times." The division manager has taken over responsibility for the computer and for its expenses.

The Boss

Because the CEO is a manager of managers, he must balance the roles of listener and learner, advisor, and change catalyst into his necessary role as the boss. Provided that corporate administration is fair, flexible, and never arbitrary, divisional managers will appreciate the unequivocal exercise of authority when it is necessary. The person in the boss role must prevent conflicts of interest from developing within the organization and must ensure that standards of performance are maintained as corporate goals and strategies are achieved.

Though a clear written policy defining conflicts of interest will prevent many problems, managers may still need help. One of our divisional managers recently proposed that he privately build a warehouse that could be leased by his division at a lower cost than the company could obtain elsewhere. Another manager was being pressured by his son-in-law for use of the division's mail order customer lists for a political campaign. Both managers requested a corporate decision. We responded negatively in each case. Both accepted the answer gratefully—the first because he knew where we stood on conflict of interest; the second because it relieved family pressure without embarrassment. In disputes between divisions—e.g., an unresolved argument over the internal transfer price of an item or service without clear external market value—the top management must act as the final arbiter, while trying not to compromise its commitment to decentralization of management responsibility and authority.

The extent to which the CEO chooses to use his authority will depend on personalities, company situations, and most important, whether corporate and divisional goals are being met. If a divisional manager does not perform as expected—even after corporate management has made every possible effort to assist him—the CEO must respond to the situation and implement personnel and/or other changes that will ensure that the division maintains a successful performance record.

WHY DECENTRALIZATION

In a decentralized organization, where divisional managers are encouraged to take risks and make independent decisions, the company is uniquely prepared to respond rapidly to environmental changes and challenges. It has already established a framework within which individual planning and initiative are encouraged at the level where opportunities and problems occur. Furthermore, when managers feel that their autonomy is "safe," there is likely to be a more creative flow and interchange of ideas within the whole organization. This dynamic process stimulates a flexible approach to problems at every management level.

Career possibilities within a decentralized organization are open-ended. This means that the company can attract aggressive managers with a need to achieve. Because measurement of individual performance focuses on the results of independent management decisions, the manager is encouraged to take actions that bear his personal signature and demonstrate his ability. As he proves himself, he will be given greater responsibility and authority. This mobility will tend to mean fewer disgruntled, restless managers and less turnover.

Furthermore, because he knows that he will be judged by his division's performance on a long-term as well as a month-to-month basis, the divisional manager will not go for short-term solutions that will not really enhance his division's long-range growth. In other words, individual ambitions will not take precedence over corporate and divisional goals.

At the same time, managers do not have to play politics. Even if his division were to grow bigger than every other division, the divisional manager would not be restricting anyone else's options or independence. He knows he is not going to have artificial barriers set up to curtail his personal or professional growth. This, too, motivates him to evaluate his management actions realistically, in the light of long-term divisional and corporate goals.

This future orientation need not be confined to the divisional level; indeed, it is a dividend of decentralization that should be particularly appealing to the CEO. When responsibility for the implementation of corporate plans is decentralized, the CEO and top corporate staff are freed to concentrate on development of long-range goals, strategies, motivational systems, external corporate relations, and more effective allocation of resources.

Once he has studied the challenges and benefits that are particular to decentralization, the CEO must take an honest look at his own leadership style, particularly in the area of person-to-person relationships. Decentralization is not for the CEO who prefers to work in a secluded office; but it is especially attractive if he enjoys working with people—people of all types—as much as with information systems and budgets. He will have to choose unusually capable managers, both because so much authority is delegated and because so much depends on the quality of the relationships between corporate staff and divisional managers. He must also be able to design and interpret strategies and evaluation systems that will motivate talented managers and ensure their autonomy without compromising corporate goals. He must be able to listen and learn, and to stimulate rather than dictate change, as well as to advise and direct.

In the final analysis, the CEO remains the man on the spot. The success of decentralization will depend on how well the company takes advantage of this form of organizational structure to achieve its goals. This performance criterion will be the ultimate test of the effectiveness of decentralization *and* of the CEO.

DELEGATION OF AUTHORITY IN A DECENTRALIZED COMPANY

by Robert C. Wilson

Chairman, Memorex Corporation; Former President,
Collins Radio Company

INTRODUCTION—THE NEED FOR DELEGATION

DELEGATION of authority is at the heart of the successful management of anything—a business, a school, or an army. The determination of the proper amount and type of delegation is more like an art form than an absolute science. Overdelegation can easily become abdication, and underdelegation can mean no real delegation at all. The purpose of delegation is to attain company objectives most effectively by enabling human resources to initiate promptly effective action at the most appropriate organizational level.

Accountability always accompanies delegation. Every individual must be accountable for his performance; every manager must be accountable for the most effective utilization of all available resources. At the same time, no one can be held accountable for absolute end results unless he has been delegated appropriate authority or given the opportunity to exert considerable influence.

Delegation is necessitated by growth, beginning with expansion from the one-man enterprise. From the moment the single entrepreneur decides to add one employee, he must resolve delegation issues. True, the entrepreneur himself continues to be responsible for the entire operation, but through an interesting paradox, he cannot properly exercise that authority without sharing it. Only through effective delegation of authority can he obtain the performance required for the success of the business.

The nature and degree of delegation vary with the situation—the size of the organization, the complexity of the activities, geography, personalities, and even the circumstances under which the organization expands. For example, special questions arise when growth is achieved by acquisition. No two companies have identical management styles, methods of operation, or even language. If the acquired company has been an established success, it is hardly prudent to strip its management of the freedom which it has exercised so well. On the other hand, those accustomed to being unbridled will certainly run with the wind—and an organization of free agents is no organization at all. The length of the rope may vary, but there must be a rope.

Modern technical aids to management, such as computerized information, have not reduced the need for delegation. Advances in communication and transportation have vastly increased the ability of the chief executive to be seen and heard. There are those who have visualized a single individual seated at some sort of cosmic console making all of the decisions for a far-flung enterprise. Unfortunately, industry has been increasing in complexity at a more rapid rate than technology can simplify it. The demands on today's executive are social as well as economic, global as well as domestic. Accordingly, the basic issue is not whether to delegate—delegation is increasingly essential—but rather how to delegate effectively. Effective delegation cannot be achieved without mutuality of understanding and without accountability for end results.

PLANNING AND STRATEGY

All human beings want to contribute and all of them want to be part of a team. In organized sports, the objective of the team is easy to communicate and easy to understand. Thus, each of the players can take individual initiative consistent with the objectives of the total team. In business, it is much more difficult for the employee to understand the objectives of the business and the manner in which these objectives are to be attained. Before effective delegation can take place in a complex organization, there must be adequate written plans, strategies, and objectives. These, in effect, establish the name of the game and the ground rules under which it is to be played. In a large, complex industry, there may be literally hundreds of games being played simultaneously with little relationship between the nature of the game or the competition encountered. To the extent practicable, those to whom authority is to be delegated should participate in the formulation of the plans, strategies, and objectives. This will assure their understanding and hence the ability to responsibly accept increased delegation. These documents should clearly spell out the markets to be served, the business activities to be engaged in, the expected performance (objectives), and the strategy to be pursued.

In most organizations, there is a limited availability of resources with respect to available opportunities. Restrictions on resource availability should be made a part of plans and strategies. Although different resources may be limiting for different businesses, cash is a universal resource. Cash can usually be converted into the other resources required by the business. Thus, cash flow objectives and cash allocations should always be included as part of the overall business documentation. When properly prepared, these documents will create a broad framework of understanding between the chief executives and the other members throughout the enterprise who together must carry out the overall purposes of the business.

ESTABLISHING THE ORGANIZATIONAL STRUCTURE

In many respects, delegation cannot be separated from the design of the organizational structure. Once the plans, objectives, and strategies have been established, the responsibility for execution and attainment should be delegated to managers of specific organization entities. In a multimarket company, these organizations should be oriented toward serving distinct customer—or market—needs.

Because the best single, overall measurement of performance is profit, the organization should be structured along profit center lines to the extent practicable. Each profit center manager should be allocated the resources necessary to compete effectively within the competitive environment of his assigned marketplace.

The Functional Organization

When the enterprise services only a single marketplace, delegation will be along functional lines. Under these circumstances, it is essential that measurements and incentives motivate the functional manager to make decisions which are in the best interests of the total business—not necessarily in the best interests of the function which he represents.

When a single entrepreneur enterprise begins to grow, it is natural to organize it along functional lines—by adding a salesman, a designer, or a foreman. As the business grows and diversifies into different market segments, the functional type of organization begins to outlive its usefulness. Unless management is alert, the functional organization perpetuates itself out of sheer inertia. It is a wise manager who knows the right time to shift from a functional to a profit center, market-oriented organization structure.

The Profit Center, Division Organization

What activities should be included within his customer-oriented profit division? The overriding consideration is its ability to compete effectively. Ordinarily, the organization would include all of the primary functions of marketing, manufacturing, engineering, finance, and industrial relations. (Treasury and legal services are most often reserved to corporate activities.) Along with the functional activities, the division should be assigned the resources needed to attain and maintain profitable growth. Thus, the manager and his functional team have a clearly assigned customer grouping to be served and a good understanding of the competition encountered in serving those customers. They also have a number of excellent measures of their success in serving those customers. Two of the most important are market position and profit.

The delegation of authority into profit-making organizational entities is seldom a neat and simple task. On the one hand, each new profit center must develop a profit-oriented business teamwork among its several functional groups. This places a great burden on the new general manager to motivate each functional head to be a businessman first and a functional head second. It requires considerable skill to integrate the functions of a business into a cohesive entity.

On the other hand, there is likely to be a need to optimize the overall corporate structure by retaining some functions and some activities at the corporate level. The basic rule should be that all functions will be decentralized to the profit center divisions unless there is a clear indication that they can be performed more effectively on a central basis. The profit centers are competing in the marketplace with strong and active competitors, thus their efficiencies are constantly being tested and measured. On the other hand, staff activities are in many ways an in-house "monopoly" and are not being tested in the competitive marketplace. Accordingly, the lack of a strong measurement system alone indicates the desirability of minimizing central staff.

What about Financial Controls?   Although decentralized profit centers may object to strong central financial control, these same controls are essential to decentralization. The Chief Executive Officer must assure himself that the operating statements have integrity and that the assets of the corporation are fully protected. This means strong centralized financial control. It means that each of the financial employees in the decentralized profit centers must be responsible not only to his general manager, but to the central financial organization. Thus, the financial personnel throughout the company serve two masters and either of the two should be able to remove them from their positions. Without strong central financial control, delegation becomes abdication. It is through the "power of the purse" that the CEO can maintain ultimate control.

What about Personnel?   The most important resource a corporation has is its people. The Chief Executive Officer must continuously satisfy himself that a professional job is being done throughout the company of attracting, retaining, developing, and motivating personnel. He must also identify and participate in the development of the high potential individuals who will provide continuity of leadership.

What about Corporate Functions?   There are a number of functions which can be performed most effectively at the corporate level and uniquely represent the total corporation. Corporate strategic planning must not only look at the existing corporation and the elements there but what the corporation should be in the future. Corporate strategic plans must provide for the entering of new markets and the withdrawal from old ones. Where resource allocation is required, the corporate planning office must make the appropriate recommendations. In addition, external relations involving the corporation as a whole, such as those involved in treasury, shareowners' activities, legal activities, and corporate image, should be performed at the corporate level.

What about Pooled Services?   There may be activities which can be performed more efficiently and more economically on a centrally pooled basis than within the individual decentralized divisions. These may encompass such activities as purchasing, data processing, sales, manufacturing process, or research and development. When pooled services are established, the burden of proof should be continuously placed upon them to demonstrate performance and economy relative to what could be achieved by decentralized activities.

IMPORTANCE OF FEEDBACK

One of the most important requirements for effective delegation is that of effective feedback. The establishment of good balance, and strategies and objectives coupled with sound organization structure, set the stage for good delegation. The establishment of effective financial controls and measurements throughout the organization will be essential to keep that delegation from becoming abdication. The one additional element that is required is a continuous feedback from all levels of the organization. No matter how effective a paperwork or control system may be, it does not represent a substitute for voluntary communication throughout the organization. It is essential that the Chief Executive Officer establish a climate wherein open communication takes place from the top to the bottom. Organization structure with a minimum number of levels can be helpful but there is no substitute for people talking to people. One technique is to have the Chief Executive Officer meet frequently with varying groups and individuals throughout the company. For example, it may be possible for him to meet with one or two of the high-potential individuals on every plant visit. Only by coupling good feedback mechanisms with the other tools of delegation will a Chief Executive Officer be able to avoid surprises and thus effectively discharge his obligations.

AUTHORITIES TO BE DELEGATED

Once the organization has been established, what are the specific authorities to be delegated to the divisions? Each division should have a written charter statement outlining the boundaries of its sphere of operations—one which is distinct from the spheres of the other divisions. As previously indicated, the spheres would be determined by the markets served and the competition within those markets. They would be accompanied by an equally clear-cut statement of strategy, objectives, and commitment of corporate resources.

Concurrently, the division should receive a written delegation of its designated authorities. These should be clearly differentiated from those retained by the chief executive and his staff. The authorities should be sufficiently detailed to specify the pooled services and corporate services to be retained at the corporate level as well as those elements which are to be performed within the division.

Delegation and Financial Planning

In the area of financial planning, the division must be responsible for preparing annual operating plans. This must be done within the ground rules established by corporate finance. Once the annual plan has been agreed upon, it too forms the basis for additional delegation. As long as the division operates within the limits of the annual operating plan, it should proceed relatively independently. However, any substantial deviations should require more and more corporate involvement. It is important to note that the annual operating plan does not mean automatic approval of discretionary expenditures included therein. Discretionary expenditures above a designated dollar value should be reviewed and approved by the Chief Executive Officer.

The preparation annually of a five-year plan will enable the total company to obtain a much better perspective on the available opportunities and the available demands for resources. When properly integrated at the corporate level, the approval of these five-year plans will give the operating divisions assurance that there will be corporate support for the courses of action which they propose to follow.

Transfer Pricing between Divisions

One of the most wasteful practices within multidivisional companies is that of debating the basis of transfers or charges between divisions in the corporation. The policies established by the company should clearly spell out the relationships between the various elements of the total company and the basis for charges between them. Once these have been established, they should be reviewed annually to make sure that they are equitable. With clean-cut decisions in this regard, there should be no reason for substantial debate between various elements in the company.

Centralization or Decentralization of Technical Activities

Technology provides an excellent opportunity to combine the benefits of centralization and decentralization. Frequently, the same technology is utilized by many different elements of the overall company. Where this is true, a centralized corporate center of excellence may be established; or it may be desirable to select one of the line operating divisions and designate it as a center of technology for the whole company. Where a division is so designated, corporate funding may be provided to support the technological activities. By properly identifying areas responsible for leadership in technology, the company can achieve its technical purposes at minimum cost.

Centralization or Decentralization of International Activities

Another area where delegation is frequently misunderstood is the sphere of international activities. There is a tendency for the international operations to build a fence around their geography. In contrast, and often in opposition, the domestic divisions tend to claim worldwide responsibility for their products. The fact is that both approaches have considerable merit. The domestic product divisions have direct responsibility for their domestic operations and a strong functional responsibility for the international. The international divisions have direct operating responsibility for their geography but a strong functional responsibility to the domestic divisions and their product lines. Excellent planning and strategizing are required to coordinate effectively the responsibilities of the two. Each must respect the total interests of the corporation and attempt to coordinate activities in such a manner as to reflect the best corporate interests. Where this is not accomplished over a period of time, there should be a change of personnel or a change of organizational structure. Once a domestic business achieves a substantial portion of its business outside of the United States, it may be desirable to assign to it direct responsibility for international activities.

GENERAL CRITERIA FOR DELEGATION

Controls, Information, and Feedback

How are delegations of authority defined and controlled? The first requirement is the use of adequate controls. Performance cannot be evaluated without agreed-upon measurements. The division head and his managers must understand what the measurements are and how they will be applied. Indeed, they should participate in the development of the appropriate measures. There must be close agreement on the timing and nature of the reports that will be made to indicate performance. They should recognize that an essential element in good performance is timeliness. Even the best of products can lose its value if not available at the time needed.

Integral to the control system is the feedback from the chief executive and his staff to the divisions. Successful delegation demands continuing two-way communications on a two-way basis. Here the warmth of two-way relationships becomes the wonderful intangible which no written book can define. Most of all, the chief executive needs to maintain the climate of reasonableness.

Subordinates must feel that they can safely report bad news. One of the major reasons for a complete catastrophe is the bottling up of bad news at lower levels in the organization until a minor problem grows into a major emergency. Sometimes this is due to the subordinate's confidence that he can solve the problem without getting his superior involved. Good judgment in deciding whether or not to report a problem is one of the true indications of a professional manager. His decision should not be influenced by fear of the boss's reaction—the proper relationship can only be established in an atmosphere of continual understanding.

Need for Continuous Forecasting

Another factor which determines the success of delegation of authority is forecasting. A continuous forward projection of operating results is a form of reporting in advance. It gives the division head and the Chief Executive Officer the opportunity of taking corrective action before the problem actually occurs. All too often accounting data simply record history. The operating forecasts provide increasing confidence in the delegation of authority and still permit timely assistance to be given when required.

Participation in Goal Setting

The Chief Executive Officer will work with his division managers in establishing specific future goals. It is important that they accept those as their goals and not as his goals. In his reminiscences, Alfred Sloan of General Motors wrote that in all his business career he had never given a direct order. His direction was expressed in discussions with others in which pros and cons were considered and decisions reached through logic that was apparent to all. The day of arbitrary orders in the corporate world is past. Experience has shown that human beings, having the capacity for thought, must be brought into the decision-making process if they are to contribute most effectively.

The Behavior of the Corporate Staff

Another guideline or consideration in determining the amount of delegated authority is the impact of the corporate staff on division performance. A highly efficient corporate staff can keep itself well informed of the activities within the divisions which parallel their own. This can be done while maintaining a constructive, supportive approach to their counterparts in the division. Where this is done properly, it can give the chief executive additional confidence in his ability to delegate.

GENERALIZING DELEGATION

Despite the many rules that are available on delegation, one can never go strictly by the book. Delegation of authority must vary considerably depending upon the situation. The abilities and temperament of the individual manager being delegated to is perhaps the most significant consideration. There is too often a tendency to delegate the same amount to all individuals at the same organizational level. If a manager is new and untried in his position, he should be given less authority than a seasoned veteran. Other criteria include (*a*) the magnitude of the potential impact on the total business if delegation is abused; (*b*) the excellence of the information system with respect to current and future results; and (*c*) the general volatility of the business and the industry. It could be said that if a business is risking too little, it is not delegating enough and, conversely, if the exposure to potential disaster is too great, it may be overdelegating.

REWARD SYSTEM

Finally, what are the rewards inherent in delegation—that is, what does a division head receive in return for the personal risk he assumes in accepting such responsibility? Certainly such incentives accomplish more when they are on the positive side rather than on the negative side. The inherent satisfaction that goes with success is important, and the assigned tasks should always be percentaged as having at least a 40 percent probability of success by the division head. He should also feel that he has a financial stake in corporate results. This should be stated in tangible terms that make him interested in the success of other divisions as well as of his own. The compensation structure should be such that the division head should be able to communicate these effectively with his team and enable them to share in the rewards that come with successful accomplishment.

CONCLUSIONS

A summary of the delegation process must start with the premise that delegation itself is essential. As we have seen, no successful operation of any size can be dominated by a single individual. The most effective application of human resources involves individual initiative and creativity. Effective delegation is not an isolated act but requires a full range of managerial skills. It involves good direction but it also requires being a good listener. It requires both trust and skepticism and a realization that some things must be sacrificed in order to achieve greater things. In short, effective delegation is part art and part science. And although rules and guidelines are useful, effective delegation must be tailored to the type of business, to the economic conditions affecting that business, to the personalities of the givers and receivers of the delegation, and to the complex situation in which they are continuously involved. In short, it depends upon the actors, the audience, the stage, and the script.

A GROUP PRESIDENT
LOOKS AT HIS JOB

by George A. Chandler
President, Winchester Group, Olin Corporation

SPEAKING from personal experience, I can say that there are aspects of the jobs of group president and of division president (which I believe are similar to one another) that are rather different from almost any other executive position in a corporation. And this is so for a number of reasons. This distinctiveness needs to be recognized—explicitly—by those *in* the position, by the CEO, and also those reporting to the group or division president. Otherwise, the odds for success of the group or division president are not great.

I intend in this chapter to concentrate attention on those aspects of the job of group president that make the job different without ignoring general executive qualities that are particularly important in this job. (Reference is made, interchangeably, to group president and to division president.)

Division president is actually a top line operating job. In Olin, or any large diversified corporation, it is impossible for the Chief Executive Officer to be on top of the day-to-day activities of each division. The bigger and more diverse the company, the less likely it is that the chief executive can be part of daily operations and decisions. This is the reason for, and responsibility of, the division president.

A corporate Chief Executive Officer generally should spend most of his time on procedures, planning, finances—broad-based policy decisions. And, although planning and numbers are part of any high-level executive's job, the group president tends to be closer to the product or service that the company sells and further from general policy setting. And, of course, he generally has little or no direct involvement in stockholder relations.

Olin's organizational structure is conventional. There is a chair-

213

man, a president, and a chief financial officer. On the corporate level, there is a senior staff for legal affairs, personnel, communications, and so on. Olin's five group presidents, including myself, report directly to the chief executive office.

While the other Olin divisions are basically industrial or chemical, the Winchester Group, which I head, is basically consumer oriented. Winchester is diversified: It includes an international arms and ammunition business; recreational products—skis, tents, sleeping bags, and so on; a worldwide fastening for the construction industry; and Weaver® scopes. All key executives in the group report to me directly.

RELATIONSHIP WITH CHIEF EXECUTIVE OFFICER

Regular contact between a group president and his chief executive is essential to keep both up-to-date on pertinent developments in the other's sphere of responsibility.

Too often, both the chief executive and the group presidents are so busy with the day-to-day responsibilities of their respective jobs that they don't make the time to sit down together. Problems can arise purely as a result of this lack of communication between the two. Although a group president wants and needs the freedom to run his operation without interference from above, at least once a month—I think—he should meet with the chief executive to exchange information.

The actual frequency of such meetings will vary greatly from company to company. Management styles, the press of other business, geographic distance, severity of problems—all these things are factors in deciding frequency. The key point is to see that both chief executive and group president are communicating the information each must have to function at his (or her) best.

I've found it useful after such meetings to confirm in writing to my chief executive any important matters which have been discussed. This assures that if both interpretations of the meeting are not the same, misconceptions will not go on indefinitely and be discovered only after the damage is done.

As a group president, I consider it my responsibility to keep the chief executive informed about what goes on in my group. He hasn't the time to pursue aggressively what's happening in each division. It is up to me to keep him informed. The chief executive sets general policy and approves general plans and major expenditures; the group president then has the freedom to operate within these limits. The group president has a great deal of freedom, but it is freedom within defined limits.

A chief executive should not give specific day-to-day instructions to a group president. He's not close enough to each group's operation to do that effectively. If he *feels* he has to do that, maybe he needs another man; or maybe he needs to learn how to delegate; or—and this is a real possibility—maybe the group president isn't doing a good job of keeping the chief executive informed and focused on the really *important* matters that do require his attention.

RELATIONSHIP WITH CORPORATE STAFF

The corporate staff can provide vital services to a division head, and there is no reason for him not to use them. A full-time tax man, as an example of a staff officer who provides specialized service, would not earn his salary in most divisions; but by assisting all of them, plus the corporation, he can earn his keep. The corporate legal staff is usually very competent. A key specialist at the corporate staff may have been through situations similar to that a group president is facing; it would only be wise for the latter to draw upon this knowledge.

Sometimes a group president may find it hard to get the time and effort that he needs from the corporate staff. This calls for aggressive persistence on his part and perhaps a nudge from higher corporate levels.

Occasionally corporate staff members feel their job is to second-guess the group president rather than work with him. It is valid— and productive—for a corporate staff man to tell the group president if he doesn't agree with an action or policy. In my opinion the most effective corporate staff men are those that make an extra effort to be helpful to the group president.

I think it is fair to say that people at the group or division level sometimes get a little defensive about asking for, or receiving from staff people at the corporate level. And sometimes they get a little parochial and get to thinking that *their* business is so "different" that no "guidelines" can be helpful. Too much of attitudes like that may signal the chief executive that he needs to do a little straightening of his group people.

I try to keep my operation an open book for the corporate staff, and I invite them to discuss any questions about it with me. It is not their function to give orders to my staff or in any other way try to run my group. That is my responsibility alone. Giving advice and assistance, and giving orders and trying to run things are very different. The first is helpful and it is what corporate staff are paid for. The second can be confusing and counterproductive.

HOW A GROUP PRESIDENT SPENDS HIS TIME

The group president has an action job, and I spend about half my time on the road. I visit our own plants, both here and overseas, and I visit our customers. In a recent three-week period, I visited our two largest ammunition customers, our three largest fastener customers, and our largest tent customer. It is also my personal belief that a man should live his business to some degree. If I don't go out and shoot and use other products, I can't talk the language, and I consider it vital that I do so.

Whether on the road or in my office, a good 50 percent of my working hours are spent talking with people. And this generally means people in my own organization, but also includes customers, suppliers, other people in my industry. Any company can get inbred, and exposure to outside ideas helps keep the executive and the company fresh.

Another 25 percent of my time is spent planning and motivating. Both these functions may be accomplished during conversations. Motivation is crucial, because in big operations, it is impossible for one man to do everything. He must have people supporting and working with him and moving in the same direction. It is the group president's responsibility—and challenge—to achieve that.

Planning, too, may be worked out partially through conversation. There is a need for formal written plans, such as the major planning document we develop annually, but the planning process means much more. It is a continual reinforcement of the direction the company is going, both for the top executive and for the people who work with him.

The other 25 percent of my job is devoted to numbers. I, personally, don't find this aspect as exciting as the others; but knowing the numbers is essential, so I try to do my paperwork as quickly and efficiently as possible and to keep it to a minimum. I'd rather talk with my people than read reports from them. Some things must be put on paper; but I think too much time and money can be wasted sending memos back and forth across the hall. A group president has to be on top of things on a day-to-day basis, and it seems more effective to be there in person whenever possible.

This emphasis on personal contact rather than paperwork may be a matter of personal style. But I believe group presidents should generally operate this way.

BACKGROUND FOR THE JOB

My own background is manufacturing. I've been with Olin 19 years and have been president of this group four years. Before that, I was general manager of another group, and before that a plant manager.

Specific background is probably not as important to this position as motivation. In general, a division manager is his own boss, and he must have a strong desire to achieve.

A division manager is, by the nature of his job, in the thick of things, and he should be anxious to take profit responsibility. The essence of business is profit, and taking on that responsibility means getting involved in all phases of the operation—products, costs, people, pricing, community relations—everything.

The need for personal involvement in the product and the company is one reason I believe that the best route to a group presidency is to come up through line operating jobs. The head of our Brass Group, for instance, has been with the company almost 25 years, working his way up. He knows that business from all angles. Looking to succession, it is the responsibility of a group president to develop talent on all levels, to pick out and develop a person or persons who will eventually be able to run the division.

KNOWING THE OPERATION'S STRENGTHS AND WEAKNESSES

His employees are one of the areas in which a group president must develop a full knowledge of his organization's strengths and weaknesses. Because he is closer to the actual divisional operation than is the chief executive of the corporation, the group president needs that detailed knowledge more. For one reason, it is extremely important that a group head know how to keep his operation from getting involved in projects beyond its capabilities.

The task of providing objective and informed advice by the CEO—and of the group president in getting that kind of help—can be a difficult one in a multidivision company. The corporate head may have come up through a discipline unrelated to a particular group or division and, for that reason, may not be familiar with a particular group's operational details. If so, that means there may be no one in the company to double check the division president, or to offer assistance with specific problems.

There are various ways a group president can deal with this problem. In some cases, it may become necessary to hire a person with a specific expertise, or to bring in a temporary consultant. Some firms, like our former Olinkraft Group (now a separate company) have set up nonofficial advisory boards of directors. A board of five or six people with broad experience in the division's business can be an invaluable help in coping with day-to-day problems or more major decisions. They may be able to tell the group president things he should know in a way his subordinates perhaps cannot. Often they have already fought certain battles and can save a younger man from making serious mistakes.

The advisory board concept ties in with what I believe are the basics of running a business—solving problems and exploiting opportunities. Where the emphasis lies depends to a large degree on where you are in the business cycle. If you're in a turnaround situation, which is at least partially the case in my own group at present, you have to focus on identifying and solving problems. There are some executives who thrive on this activity, who excel at putting out fires. That may be their sole interest in the job, rather than finding a challenge in going on the offensive and creating new things. I personally find the latter to be the greater challenge and more fun, but you can't create until you have solved the problems.

THE NUMBERS DON'T TELL THE WHOLE STORY

Before talking about "nonfinancial indicators," I should clearly state that my strongest demand from my chief financial officer is quick, concise sales and earnings reports and estimates for the future. These are absolutely essential to good control and operation of any business.

However, many times high profits result from circumstances or targets of opportunity. A group executive (and the chief executive and his staff) must look further into his operations for key indicators.

For instance, in a manufacturing operation, a good indicator is the safety record. When that starts to fall off, it usually means the whole operation may not be far behind. It may be employee attitudes, faulty equipment, poor management control, or any combination of those. When the safety record improves, it usually means more attention is being paid to detail, and the rest of the operation can be expected to improve soon after.

Quality, as reflected in a growing number of internal rejections or external returns, is also an indication of big problems coming. A loss of a number of personnel in a short time span also spells trouble.

What this means is that financial data don't tell the whole story. The group president has to be aware of what those numbers do *not* reveal—before it's too late.

DIVISION GOALS AND ORGANIZATION VERSUS CORPORATE GOALS AND ORGANIZATION

Thorough understanding of objectives is especially important in a multidivisional company like Olin, where the goals of the corporation and the individual division may not be the same. This makes mutual understanding of both sets of goals that much more important. Corporate planners often think in terms of large aggregates and abstractions, and over longer time-spans; line people, in concrete terms of specifics, and, very often, in the "here-and-now." Spelling out objectives in detail, sometimes in both physical and financial terms, is one way to bring the two closer together.

This understanding is particularly important today when business changes are happening much faster than ever before. The group president is responsible for recognizing those changes and adjusting his organization to meet them. In a multi-industry company, no one organizational concept is going to work for all groups. Olin tried it some years ago, and it just didn't work. In fact, one of the main reasons for dividing a company into groups is that there *are* these basic differences. We have more sales people, for instance, than the other Olin divisions—but that's normal for a consumer business.

We are currently working, within the division, with a business "team" concept. The arms business team, for example, includes a business manager, a plant manager, a sales manager, an engineering manager. The business manager gets the team working together to maximize profit on a daily level. The others don't work for him; he's the coordinator.

But this is only one of many possible organizational set-ups, and as business changes, we will probably change too. The group president has to be attuned to which factors call for change; change for its own sake doesn't produce results. An insufficient profit, or technological or market changes, may call for something new in the organizational concept. At least a close evaluation of the current operation will be needed. Today there are also pressures regarding the environment, minority hiring, involvement in local politics, or lobbying. These are all important, to be sure, but it is also worthwhile to weight them against the organization's profit and efficiency and try to achieve the best balance.

DOMESTIC JOINT VENTURES

by John K. McKinley
President, Texaco Inc.

FOR MANY years in the United States, the joint venture has been utilized across the breadth of business as a proven method of achieving corporate goals.

In the petroleum industry, the joint venture has been found to be effective in developing raw material resources, in certain areas of manufacturing, and in some methods of transportation. These have been projects where capital requirements were very high, and where the degree of risk was high.

Basic tasks that face the executive interested in the joint venture method of doing business include: recognizing the need for a joint venture and identifying goals best achieved through this technique; selecting a participant; organizing and financing the joint venture; and operating the joint venture.

But first, a clear delineation of the business objectives to be achieved through the joint venture technique is essential. Although the distant future cannot be foreseen, it is usually better to define the boundaries or the business areas of the joint venture as clearly as possible before it is launched.

WHEN IS A JOINT VENTURE INDICATED?

Before proceeding to investigate the formation of a joint venture, one should first consider one's own capabilities for achieving the desired objective alone, without association with others. Go it alone if you reasonably can.

Bear in mind that a joint venture automatically imposes two serious restrictions: profits will be shared, and the desires of a second participant must be considered. These are important considerations, and their short- and long-term ramifications should be carefully analyzed before moving ahead. You may decide, upon analysis, that you cannot achieve your goal through your own resources. Analysis may show that achieving the goal independently would have such an impact on your organization that it would not be feasible. Then, a joint venture should be investigated.

Some of the corporate objectives that could involve a joint venture include reaching a specific market, developing a product, acquiring or developing a property—including raw material properties, or entering a new area of business unrelated to your usual activities. The attractiveness of a joint venture can come, for instance, from the marriage of your strengths in technology, raw materials, manufacturing facilities, marketing abilities, or personnel with the strengths of a second participant. The desire to spread the risk of a project that involves substantial uncertainty, or to obtain needed resources for projects beyond individual capability, would also make a joint venture attractive, even though your strengths were not different from those of the other participant.

GOALS BEST ACHIEVED THROUGH
THE JOINT VENTURE

Joint ventures have been utilized so widely it is not possible to list all situations where they might be applicable. However, there are some broad areas which can be defined:

Situations where a specific capability, not now held by yourself, can be economically achieved only by joining with a participant.

A situation could arise in manufacturing where one may have developed the capability and technical expertise to supply products for a particular market, but lacks the detailed knowledge of product requirements to move forward. Take, for example, a chemical company that wishes to supply products to the building trades but lacks a detailed knowledge of the product applications and of building code regulations. A joint venture with a firm with the needed product knowledge could be beneficial.

Expansion plans for a product could also be hampered by a restricted marketing capability. For instance, an instrument designed by an industrial supplier may have promise as a consumer item, but the development of the required mass marketing capability may be so foreign to the industrial-oriented concern that a joint venture with a firm having this consumer expertise is logical.

Situations where complementary strengths can be pooled by joining with a participant.

This is not an unusual situation. The marriage of a technological strength to a raw material strength would be an example of this type. There are others, of course, including market access and manufacturing capability, specialized personnel and manufacturing, and so forth.

Situations where the risks involved exceed corporate guidelines.

A good case can be made for a joint venture when the risk of failure is high but the potential rewards are correspondingly high. If the degree of risk exceeds established guidelines, a joint venture enables one to reduce the risk to an acceptable level, yet anticipate a share of the potential rewards. In the oil industry, exploration and development of unproven potential petroleum reserves would be an example of a situation where a joint venture should be considered.

Situations where the capital requirements exceed your own capabilities.

Although there are other ways to obtain capital, a joint venture can be an appropriate tool, especially if there are other factors—such as degree of risk—that also favor the use of a joint venture. Analysis of the desirability of a joint venture should establish the continuing capital requirements, as well as the initial capital needs. Many joint ventures have been formed when all participants like the odds but none of them can raise the entry fee alone.

In addition to determining if commercial conditions indicate the attractiveness of a joint venture, it is important to confirm that the situation will remain attractive over the target period. Usually, joint ventures are not easily dissolved and the management effort required to form and then dissolve the joint venture may outweigh the anticipated advantages.

As joint ventures often last for decades, careful thought must be given to future prospects of earnings before the joint venture is formed.

Very early in the considerations, potential antitrust problems should be resolved. The degree of management involvement and the necessary exchange of information required during the initial stages certainly indicate that this should be an early checkpoint. There are certain areas of activity where antitrust considerations will rule out entirely the possibility of joining with a participant in a joint venture. Thus, there must always be careful legal review. In today's business world, not only antitrust considerations but also the possible impact that pertinent governmental regulatory agency rulings may have on the joint venture should be carefully weighed.

SELECTING A PARTICIPANT

The basic considerations examined in making the decision that a joint venture is preferable also tend to narrow the field of prospective participants. In a specific situation, there will seldom be more than two or three prime candidates for this type of business marriage.

Joint ventures often will be long-term associations. Try to assess the willingness, desire, and dedication of the prospective participant to contribute to the venture, since these are as important as the ability to do so. Economic values of the proportionate capital and physical assets to be contributed by each are relatively easy to determine. The intangible contributions are more difficult to assess.

The management of the joint venture can be faced with difficult problems if the participants do not seem to take a strong and approximately equal interest in the venture.

Another sensitive area may be in the handling of patents and technology. A joint venture can be aborted by the efforts of one or both to use the area of these intangibles to secure a significantly greater advantage in the relationship. These matters may involve licenses to the joint venture by either partner or the arrangements by which the partner may use the technology developed by the joint venture.

Corporate good health depends a lot on the trust and confidence a company enjoys with its customers and the business community in general. Accordingly, integrity must be the hallmark in a joint venture if the undertaking is to receive a warm reception from the business world. Corporate integrity should be supplemented by the personal reputation and integrity of the principal officers in the participant firms as well.

Awareness of the public concern for ecological values and adherence to these values has recently become another very important factor. Serious violations in this area by a prospective participant raise the spectre of imputed guilt by association if the joint venture is formed. Actions of a joint venture corporation can also damage the reputation of a participant corporation even in situations where the participant corporation has no direct control or direct influence. This is a very serious stigma in today's environmentally conscious society, and one which is difficult to erase.

Finally, look closely at the managerial record of the other prospective participants. A history of chronic labor problems, work stoppages, or strikes raises at the very least some serious questions concerning the associate's administrative and industrial relations abilities.

Just remember: As in any good marriage gone sour, annulment or divorce can be painful and expensive.

ORGANIZING THE JOINT VENTURE

When the joint venture is reviewed from a legal viewpoint, it is essential to examine the proposed venture in terms of its future, as well as of its initial objectives. This will encourage a full discussion of alternative legal formats available and how best to organize the joint venture.

One approach often used is to form a new corporation in which the participants each have stock ownership. The important advantage to this approach is the protection of limited liability for the participants.

Another approach is to conduct the venture on the basis of a joint operating agreement. Under this arrangement, one participant serves as "operator" and conducts the physical operations of the venture for the benefit of all the participants.

The joint operating agreement approach is usually less involved. The operating participant can use its existing organization to operate the venture, thus avoiding an additional independent administrative organization.

If a joint operating approach is chosen, it is easier to decide which participant will become the operator if other similar ventures exist or are contemplated by the participants involved. The nonoperator in one venture can be the operator in another and thus average out the relative advantages and disadvantages. Even if the contemplated venture is the only one, an equitable balance between the advantages and disadvantages of being operator or nonoperator can be achieved.

The equitable balance should be built around the generally accepted premise that the operator should experience neither financial advantage nor financial loss from serving as operator other than reasonable compensation for operating services rendered. If necessary, the participants can also provide for a periodic rotation of the operator's functions among all participants. An alternative to periodic rotation is a provision that the participant who will contract to perform most economically will be the operator.

Tax Considerations

Hand in hand with the legal organization of a joint venture is the equally important initial consideration of its tax form. The basic organization of the venture can directly affect the taxes, particularly federal income taxes, that will be payable by the participants. Generally, the form most often recommended by tax advisors is one that will be taxable as a partnership, rather than as a corporation, for federal tax purposes.

A partnership is a reporting entity for income tax purposes, with gains or losses distributable to the participants. The start-up of most joint ventures will throw off a tax loss. In the construction of a facility, for example, it is likely that a major portion of its cost will be financed through borrowings. Interest on such borrowings during the construction period is deductible for tax purposes, even though it may be capitalized for book purposes. Other items—sales taxes, for instance—are likewise deductible for tax purposes.

If investment credit is allowable on the completion of the facility, this credit will be distributable to the participants and available against their income. Likewise, accelerated depreciation under the tax law can be claimed with benefits distributed among the participants.

If a corporate format is used, the so-called tax losses can still be realized in a corporate tax return. But their ultimate utilization will have to await the successful outcome of the venture through the carry-forward of its net operating loss.

For tax purposes, some of the additional advantages of using the partnership route include the handling of audits, and the avoidance of the double tax on the venture's earnings. When earnings are distributed as dividends by a corporation, the shareholder incurs an additional tax on the receipt of the dividends. This tax is not paid on earnings distributed under a partnership.

Admittedly, dividends may not have to be paid by a corporation currently. But eventually, in any successful operation, dividends have to be paid to shareholders in order to avoid tax penalties for the non-declaration of dividends. Tax advisors point out that, if the joint venture fails, a further complication arises under the corporate format: Such a failure generally results in capital loss, with substantially less benefit than in a partnership where failure results in an ordinary loss.

A further consideration is that it may not be feasible, under the tax laws, to establish a joint venture that will be recognized as a partnership for tax purposes. For example, creating a partnership for a large manufacturing and marketing operation with many participants may be impractical.

However, the partnership organizational format has been used in many joint ventures in this country, including operations in the oil and gas industries, real estate ventures, and even Broadway shows.

FINANCING THE JOINT VENTURE

Although there are attractive tax features to the partnership form, the advantages of limiting liability and other financial considerations often dictate the corporate organizational form. The following comments on financing the joint venture, therefore, will assume that the venture is to be organized under a corporate structure.

Once the decision has been reached to form a joint venture, the financial compatibility of the participants becomes a vital factor. If both participants are in sound financial condition and of approximately equal strength, the financing problems may be relatively simple.

However, when one participant is significantly weaker, problems and inequities may occur if capital is to be raised from outside sources. For example, a stronger company usually can borrow at a lower cost than a weaker one. In many joint ventures, the stronger participant indirectly subsidizes the weaker by accepting relatively high interest costs in the joint venture, because of the lower credit rating of its associate.

Conversely, the weaker participant often enjoys lower interest costs through the joint venture than its own credit rating would justify. In some instances, one participant may be required to guarantee the performance of the other participant in order to provide marketability for securities of the joint venture. This situation should be approached with caution. The desirable arrangement would not provide financial guarantees jointly and severally, but each participant would guarantee the loan in proportion to his ownership.

During organization and initial operation of the joint venture, there may be cases where the financial interests of the participants some-times conflict or, at least, do not coincide. For example, differences may arise over debt/equity ratios, timing of long-term financing, off-balance sheet or on-balance sheet financing, possible guarantee of debt by the parent companies, selection of investment bankers, and many other items. Under such conditions, it is a real problem to structure finances of the venture in such a way as to protect the individual par-ticipants and still provide a viable venture.

In most instances, the Chief Executive Officer of the joint venture will be well advised to provide a formal means by which financial ac-tivities of the venture are monitored and directed. One way to ac-complish this objective is to make sure the organizational structure includes a finance committee with representatives of the parent com-panies as members. Important financial activities of the joint venture —including long- and short-term financing, cash management, em-ployee plans policies, and dividend policy—should be screened by this committee.

Perhaps the best advice is to see that financial operations of a joint venture are brought under the supervision of the chief financial officers of the parent companies at an early date. Thus, decisions made in this area will receive the same review—including that of the parent com-panies' Chief Executive Officers, where necessary—as if the operation were a wholly owned one. For example, clearly defined agreement is needed on the policies relating to dividends and to the various defini-tions by which economic payout is measured. Some very difficult prob-lems can be avoided if this businesslike approach is taken.

OPERATING THE JOINT VENTURE

Regardless of the legal form a joint venture may take, the agree-ment under which it is operated should be carefully constructed to spell out the obligations and protect the rights of the participants.

The agreement should define the participant voting percentage re-quired to achieve a given result, such as commitment to capital invest-ment. In the event that one or more of the participants should desire to expand a facility, and other participants do not, agreement provi-sion could be made to allow the interested participants to proceed separately, with, perhaps, an optional provision for later back-in of the nonparticipating parties.

It is essential that this agreement make it clear who is to manage the venture, and provide for a board of directors and clearly state its makeup and procedures for succession. The legal form of the venture should be structured to allow it to be operated tightly, yet with the necessary flexibility to adjust to changes which will undoubtedly occur.

Participants in the joint venture should have a defined avenue for policy input provided for in the operating agreement. Providing for policy input at the board of directors level in the agreement, for example, would eliminate the need for participants to distract the active managers of the joint venture with constant operational policy directives.

Once the operating agreement has been written and an information flow between the participants and the joint venture has been established, specific policies for management control must be stated. These policies can and often do draw upon the valuable experience of the participants, where appropriate.

The chain of authority and limitations upon that authority must be established to permit the full utilization of the venture's management talents. It is equally important that the flow of authority be effectively communicated to management. When properly used, this authority will help maintain appropriate control and discipline throughout the joint venture.

A competitive personnel policy also must be established when organizing the joint venture. This policy will set the guidelines for reviewing the necessary employees required in the venture. The personnel policy should be highly comprehensive in such areas as compensation, employee benefits, and training. A word of caution: Joint venture management may attempt to adopt the best features of compensation and benefit plans of the various participants, and in a matter of time the joint venture could enjoy a set of benefit plans better than that of any one of the participants. Following the competitive personnel policy, qualified personnel will be hired at a level commensurate with their abilities. Where appropriate, recruit a number of key employees from the participants—employees with the ability to adjust quickly for the benefit of both the participants and the venture.

Intensified personnel training—offered by the participants or through outside educational institutions—is frequently required at the outset of a new joint venture. This may be on-the-job training or a more formal type.

An important aspect of staffing a new joint venture is to determine first the minimum number of employees that will be required to accomplish the goals of the venture. Then maintain this level of manpower unless there are strong and factual reasons for adjustment. Run a tight ship; joint ventures can easily become wasteful.

The venture's employees should—and will—become one of its most important assets. Staffing of the joint venture should be given as much time and talent as an executive feels necessary to insure a lasting and effective level of competence.

Despite the care and professionalism used in structuring the venture, and despite the broadness and completeness of management, personnel, and authority policies, there still will be differences between the participants. These differences usually occur because of different basic operating attitudes of the participants, or because the basic goals of the participating companies change with time. Disagreements quite frequently arise when a participant is buying from or selling to the joint venture.

The most popular formal means for settling differences is by arbitration, using the arbitration laws of the state in which the joint venture operates. The inclusion of an arbitration clause in the operating agreement is standard operating procedure in the organization of most joint ventures.

An effective—and less formal—means of settling differences is to preface any formal provision set forth in the operating agreement for the settling of differences with a clause to the effect that all participants will use their best efforts to resolve conflicts before resorting to any other remedies that may be provided for in the agreement. The spirit in which this clause is included in the operating agreement can prevail at the most difficult times, and often results in a resolution of differences among the participants that more formal and costly procedures may fail to achieve.

CONCLUSION

In summary, joint venture approaches to business endeavors offer a promising solution in selective situations. In the case of strong companies, joint ventures should be evaluated very cautiously and conservatively. In the case of large strong companies of diverse interests, there should be predominant and overriding reasons for proceeding jointly as compared to going it alone.

MANAGING A UNITED STATES SUBSIDIARY OF A FOREIGN CORPORATION

by Robert B. Clark
President and Chief Executive Officer, Hoffman-La Roche Inc.

SOME GENERAL CONSIDERATIONS

THE SCOPE and nature of the role of managing a U.S. subsidiary or affiliate of a foreign corporation can vary widely depending on many factors, some of which are the following:

(1) *The length of time the U.S. company has been in operation and the degree of success it has achieved.* In my own case, the American company achieved its present status in relation to the parent in the late 1920s and, under the guidance of three distinguished predecessors, has an established record of performance. This results in a relationship with the parent which is based on mutual respect and familiarity with the respective achievements and problems on both sides of the ocean. On the other hand, a new U.S. manager in a company just established would clearly have problems of developing credibility, performance, and a network of mutual relations *de novo*.

(2) *The nature of the U.S. operation.* If the U.S. company is an operating entity standing essentially on its own with respect to raw materials, production, and marketing, a high degree of autonomy may be possible, within the basic operating philosophy of the parent. On the other hand, if a U.S. corporation, particularly one newly started, is dependent upon the parent for raw materials, finished goods, marketing techniques and experience, or financing, quite a different relationship will be involved.

(3) *The purpose of the U.S. corporation.* Is the U.S. corporation intended to be a largely autonomous unit working with the resources and marketing operations of the largest producing and marketing

231

country in the world, or is the U.S. corporation designed to be part of a highly coordinated, regional or worldwide operation for which direction basically comes from overseas?

Therefore, the philosophic concepts of the parent corporation arising out of present intent and past performance, if any, will be controlling in establishing the relationships with its U.S. associate.

AUTONOMY AND COORDINATION

It is obvious from the above that it is difficult to generalize about the management of a U.S. corporation owned or controlled by a foreign corporation. However, one generality impossible to ignore is the large role which the United States as an economic force and entity must inevitably play in the plans of any foreign corporation that desires to locate here. Despite current problems, the United States, as a major producer of many essential raw materials, still enjoys an enviable independence in this regard possessed by few, if any, foreign countries. Further, in practically any market to which a company directs its attention, the United States will be the largest because of our population, economy, and disposable income. Therefore, although a number of factors may effect the relations which exist between the U.S. corporation and its parent, in the long run the parent will be wise to recognize that the conditions prevailing in this country almost mandate a high degree of autonomy for any U.S. operation, if not immediately, then at some point when the child is ready to stand on its own feet.

This degree of autonomy can be expressed through a recognition that the magnitude of the U.S. market requires adoption of plans, budgetary and organizational, adjusted to its particular and peculiar situations. Clearly, the parent must play a large role in establishing objectives and goals, both initially and on a continuing basis; in financing the new venture; in developing broad guidelines for continuing relationships in such areas as product selection, marketing strategies, diversification, and research; and in evolving a pattern of dividend remittances consistent with the development needs of the U.S. company. It is particularly important that these relationships be established on the basis of the mutual trust and respect that flows from any productive and successful collaboration. But, in the last analysis, it is my firm conviction that a necessary ingredient of any successful initial or continuing U.S. operation is a recognition by the parent of the inevitable importance which the size of the U.S. economy and market bestows on its U.S. corporation, from which should flow the corollary recognition of the need to permit its U.S. company to achieve a healthy and lusty growth of its own.

In my experience, such a result is not difficult to achieve, because organizational patterns, motivation, and accomplishment goals tend to be very similar between U.S. corporations and most progressive foreign parents with which I am familiar (in my own case, of course, the parent company is Swiss). After all, many modern foreign top managers have become thoroughly familiar with American marketing and other business concepts at several of our business schools. Likewise, U.S. managers have frequently become familiar with foreign concepts of business by either serving with an American company having extensive foreign interests or, in some instances, having actually worked overseas. It is my general impression, to which many exceptions can be found, that American corporations have tended to emphasize aggressive marketing concepts sooner and in a more innovative fashion than our foreign friends. Similarly, the tradition of European research, particularly in the chemical fields with which I am familiar, has frequently shown the way to many of us in the United States, although a strong, equalizing trend has emerged in the past decades. But speaking in a broad conceptual sense, the basic driving forces here and abroad have, in this era of instant travel and communication, become strikingly common.

A question may arise as to the staffing of the U.S. company. It might be expected that a company being established here would be provided with a top executive from the parent company familiar with the American scene. I think it would be highly likely, however, that staffing in subordinate roles, whether marketing, technical, or administrative, can best be done by hiring competent American personnel, since, in my experience, organizations function best when direct line supervision is familiar with the working habits and patterns of the resident country. A case may be made for achieving coordination of research activities by staffing research operations (if, in fact, they are to be conducted here), with someone from the home country familiar with research policies and practices. But, here again, staffing at a lower level probably should be with American personnel. In the long run, however, I firmly believe that any organization is best served by having the chief executive a native, or certainly a long-time resident, of the country.

Many examples might be cited of the advantages in according the U.S. company the degree of autonomy discussed above. Probably one of the most striking in the experience of my company arose in considering the question of marketing Librium, a well known minor tranquilizer. At the time consideration was being given to initial marketing of this product, another product was under consideration in the parent company. Very wisely, the chairman of the parent resisted suggestions for a common marketing effort and agreed that the product in which the parent company was interested would be marketed overseas and that Librium would be marketed in the United States. The rest is history, since Librium went on to become the largest-selling prescription drug in the industry. This result obviously would not have come to pass if a rigid degree of authority had been enforced.

ORGANIZATION

There is an initial tendency in any organization where an important affiliate is remote from the parent to channel communications through the chief executive of the affiliate. Frequently, this results in clogged channels and places on the executive the burden of many details with which he is not, and should not, be familiar. Clearly, the channel between the chief American executive and his counterpart in the parent should be open at all times in the frankest possible manner. But, equally clearly, administrative details in an affiliate of any substantial size, as most U.S. affiliates are, should be handled at the administrative level, subject to only the most general supervision. In my experience, this result can best be promoted by developing an organization in which control points correspond very closely with the counterparts in the parent, thus permitting the respective counterparts to interact at their own levels of expertise. Periodic meetings for exchange of information, discussion of mutual problems, and, most importantly, to coordinate future development and expansion, greatly facilitate this interchange. Obviously, individual national circumstances will necessitate development of specific plans in all areas of corporate activity to achieve the agreed-upon goals of the national enterprise, in accordance with the concept of autonomy above expressed. But, in the broader sense, unless there are compelling necessities for structuring the U.S. corporation differently from the parent, it would seem that prudent management would indicate proceeding as above.

This does not mean, however, that there is not a very real need to develop an American personality for the U.S. affiliate—quite the contrary. An early task of any successful American executive is to "educate" the parent corporation to the realities of American corporate life, both as they relate to conduct of the business in the United States and as to appropriate motivational factors.

SOME THOUGHTS ON ANTITRUST LAWS

Although the legal concept of the corporation and its relationship to the state are basically similar on both sides, one of the foremost "educational" problems clearly lies in the field of antitrust laws. There is some evidence that the European Economic Community is adopting many of the principles of American antitrust law. Nevertheless, it is my impression these concepts are just beginning to be an integral part of the thinking and planning of most European or other foreign managers. As Americans, we are clearly dedicated to upholding our antitrust laws both in practice and in concept. Our whole business training has geared us to accept these laws as a way of life and our economic and legal reflexes are so attuned. The reverse situation usually prevailed in the past with a non-American parent corporation. To me, this situation clearly creates an important problem of communication on a two-way basis. On the one side, it is imperative that Americans not attempt to interfere with, or in any way impose our concepts of competition on the successful and productive economies of our associates except insofar as they might affect United States commerce. It is even worse for the American to moralize the issue— it is an economic and legal issue, not a moral one. But it is equally imperative that the non-American parent corporation understand the very real problems and risks to which an American businessman is exposed in the antitrust field and not involve him or themselves in any operations overseas, however legitimate, which might represent violations of domestic United States laws.

Therefore, the parent corporation must be constantly reminded of the peculiar and severe antitrust exposure to which any American corporation and its officials are subjected and that this exposure can result in criminal sanctions.

This educational process must be continually repeated and emphasized because of the dynamic character of our antitrust laws and because recent trends make clear that they can involve not only the United States corporation and its domestic personnel, but also its foreign parent.

MUTUAL EDUCATION

I do not mean to imply from the above, however, that there is not an equal need for "reverse education," i.e., the American company learning from the parent. I have already mentioned the strong desirability of molding the pattern of organization of the American company along the lines of the parent. There is another area of "learning" which must also occur early in the career of the American executive we are now discussing. Most American businessmen tend to think globally from past experience in a company whose home office is in the United States. But this global thinking frequently causes the new executive to project himself into areas which, in the new circumstance, are not part of his responsibility. His primary function by definition is to manage the American affiliate of a foreign corporation; although it is not unusual for the territory of an American affiliate to possibly encompass Canada and maybe one or two other countries, clearly his responsibility terminates at these boundaries and his natural tendency to project himself worldwide must be resisted if relations are to remain smooth. An example may arise in the negotiation of a license agreement with another U.S. company which will cover the entire world— obviously, the parent corporation will expect to provide input in these negotiations for its own territory. For many reasons, therefore, organizationally and otherwise, it is prudent for the American executive to refrain from interfering with, or committing the parent to a course of action on which it has its own and, not infrequently, different ideas.

At the same time, however, it is also vital for an American executive to try to appreciate and understand the global view of the parent corporation, as it may be revealed or displayed to him. Usually the parent corporation knows far more about problems outside the United States than does our American executive. Furthermore, the parent corporation has usually painstakingly and with great effort built a network of relations and lines of communications which the American will violate at his peril. The prudent American executive, therefore, particularly one newly on the scene, would do well to keep his eyes and ears open, observe organization channels, and appreciate that the success of the parent corporation, which usually provided the basis for the origins of the U.S. affiliate, was probably not achieved by accident.

BUDGETARY CONSIDERATIONS

Because of the size of the U.S. market and the need to nurture its growth, capital budgets, particularly of a growing American affiliate, become of substantial importance to the parent. The ideal situation, of course, is that in which capital expenditures in the United States are paid out of its own income. Although this may occur in a mature corporation, it seldom happens in a fledgling one. It is obvious in either event that capital budgets of the parent and affiliate must be closely coordinated over a long-range period to achieve the necessary ordering of priorities and to make the optimum use of the funds of the total corporation. In situations where the same product may be made in different countries of the world, it is essential that the parent make the ultimate decision as to plant location, depending on its overall interests and taking into consideration such factors as freight costs, tax considerations, raw material sources, and the like. Closest possible coordination in the construction and implementation of capital budgets is thus mandatory between the parent and the affiliate. Once this coordination is achieved, annual capital budget considerations can proceed on a country-by-country basis, inasmuch as the phenomenon of inflation, fortunately or otherwise, is worldwide and well known to executives in all countries.

Annual sales forecasts and expense budgets should present fewer problems of coordination, since these are normally products of the local economy. In my experience, it is rare that the progressive executive of a parent will attempt to impose judgments on the marketing experience and knowledge of the executive in charge of the American company. This does not mean, of course, that the usual budgetary "give and take" will not occur, but in the final analysis responsibility for forecasts and results should rest primarily with the American executive, subject, of course, to the usual review and comparison with results achieved in other countries to the extent these may be pertinent.

A final word on the budgetary process as it relates to long-range planning. Here, of course, close coordination with the parent corporation is imperative. It may not necessarily result that the parent and its

American affiliate proceed along the same lines or even to the same goals, but it is essential that the parent and its affiliate closely understand what their respective goals are, be they similar or different. This can best be achieved by a highly coordinated long-range planning process usually, out of necessity, directed by the parent but one in which the American affiliate because of its inevitable importance should participate fully and frequently. Periodic meetings for review of long-range plans and goals are highly desirable.

COMPENSATION

A word as to appropriate compensation of executives of an American affiliate may be in order. It is axiomatic, of course, that employees of American affiliates of foreign corporations must be paid in accordance with American compensation standards. Thus, salaries, fringe benefits, and the like will be set in accordance with American practice rather than imposing foreign standards of compensation. What is sometimes not so well appreciated, however, is that most American executives either have participated in or are aware of the benefits of compensation plans involving accumulation of an equity position in the company, such as a stock option plan. In an American affiliate of a foreign parent, however, such plans are frequently not available, or, if so, only on terms which may not be meaningful in the American scene. In my opinion, therefore, accepting the assumption that the parent corporation will desire to compensate its American executives fairly and competitively, consideration must be given to alternate forms of compensation. These are many and varied and include savings plans with appropriate company contributions, deferred compensation plans, and many others. The important point to emphasize is the need for recognition of this aspect of compensation in some form.

In conclusion, may I say that there is one hidden and subtle benefit in being the American chief executive of a foreign corporation which is not necessarily apparent at first sight. Multinational American corporations are the subject of inquiry and interest all over the world, much of which is not always favorable. In the United States grave questions are being raised by labor groups and governmental officials who see in the multinational corporation a possible means of manipulating currency, employment, and other related matters. To my mind, the citizenship record of the multinational American corporations should need no defense, in view of the jobs which they have generated, and the income produced in this country, by virtue of their overseas activities. However, if you are the American chief executive of a foreign corporation, you find yourself in the role of importing jobs and business opportunities from overseas into the United States. From the viewpoint of the United States and the various contending factions in this country, you are in the reverse role of the multinational American corporation. I have found this most pleasurable and enjoyable.

MANAGING AN OVERSEAS SUBSIDIARY OF AN AMERICAN CORPORATION

by Albert Barraud
*President, Société D.B.A.**

I WOULD be glad if the ideas in the following article turned out to be helpful to other managers of American affiliates around the world and to their Chief Executive Officers "back home" in the United States. I suspect, although I cannot tell, of course, that ideas like these may be useful to overseas managers of affiliates of companies of other nationalities—say English, German, Dutch, Japanese, or even French.

But for the present purpose, let's just talk of managing an overseas subsidiary or affiliate of an American corporation.

For over 20 years, I have worked in executive positions in American companies and overseas affiliates. I have worked in the United States and abroad. I am a proud citizen of a proud nation. But I also have a great affection for America and, perhaps I flatter myself, I do believe I understand and appreciate the merits and strengths of the "American way" and American business methods. I also know what it is to be an overseas manager of an American affiliate. Not surprisingly, I have come by ideas concerning the problems one faces in such a position.

SOME GENERAL CONSIDERATIONS

In talking about the problems of managing an overseas subsidiary of an American corporation there are so many things one could discuss! I am going to pick out just three topics, because my experience suggests they are of fundamental importance:

---

* The Société D.B.A. is a French corporation in which the American company, Bendix Corporation, holds a majority equity interest. Prior to joining "D.B.A.," Mr. Barraud spent many years in the United States and in France as an executive with a large American-based, multinational oil company.

How to choose the affiliate's Chief Executive Officer.

How to handle the continuing relationship between the parent company and the affiliate both downward and upward.

What the most important risks are in this relation and how to avoid them.

But before I get to those particular topics, there are several general considerations of doing business abroad that CEOs and managers should bear in mind, for they color every aspect of the business of the overseas affiliate. And they are the source—or potential source—of tensions for the affiliate itself, and between the overseas company and the parent organization. To be sure, there are problems and tensions between parent organizations and their domestic subsidiaries. And many, if not all of those problems and tensions find their counterparts in the relationships between parent organizations and foreign subsidiaries and affiliates. That is a point worth remembering: Not all of the problems arise simply because of national differences! The foreign affiliates present *additional* kinds of problems and that is especially a point worth remembering! Because, if not carefully handled, these differences can become important causes of failure.

First of all—and this is especially important for American managers —in most foreign countries, the local central government controls strictly every investment made by American and other foreign parent companies. The kind and depth of control can differ depending upon the country concerned or the activity of the business, or the size of the corporation. Because the American tradition has always been to avoid governmental intervention, American managers must remind themselves that it is absolutely necessary that before making any decision on investing abroad, they and their advisors study carefully all the information available in the field of governmental intervention and policy which can reduce considerably the freedom of future managers in charge of the investment envisaged.

Second, the complex network of laws and customs existing in each country as a result of the particular laws concerning corporations, of the more and more complicated social legislation, and even of the special local ways and means of financing business activity, deserves a thorough study. However, even when all those enquiries have been made and answers obtained, the differences between the American business environment and the foreign one will not appear immediately.

Many problems will be discovered little by little *after* the investment is made and they will be sources of many of the specific tensions between the home office and management abroad.

One other problem which may be underestimated by an American corporation is the language barrier. In spite of the great progress made by American corporations in training international managers who can speak several languages, the difficulties of speaking the same *business* language will appear rapidly at each level of management in most American subsidiaries overseas.

Last but not least, the local habits of doing business and managing a company are not necessarily the same as the American ones. Even if the main principles of capitalism are identical in the United States, France, Germany, or Japan, the day-to-day application of those principles is different, mostly because of different traditions, education, history, or political factors.

Because these kinds of tensions are additive to the normal problems arising in any business group, it is necessary, first, to understand them and, second, to develop between the American company and its subsidiary abroad a satisfactory system for rendering them bearable. Better still, both domestic and overseas managements should try to utilize these differences for the benefit of both ends of the relationship. In this field, the chief executive of the affiliated company abroad has the most important role to play and the choice of the most capable person is essential to the success of the venture. It is for that reason I place so much emphasis on the Chief Executive Officer of the foreign affiliate.

HOW TO CHOOSE THE AFFILIATE'S CHIEF EXECUTIVE OFFICER

Even if everyone is aware of the extreme importance of this choice, I consider that I must underline with maximum strength that solving this problem in a satisfactory way is the key to the success of the foreign affiliate. Therefore, neither money nor effort should be spared in making the best choice possible.

Generally, he should be a national citizen of the country where the affiliate is operating.[1] An American citizen should very rarely be

---

[1] In saying "he," I am aware that in the United States more and more women are entering and rising in management. This is also happening, but more slowly, in other countries. But let "he" stand for either sex.

recommended. Even if he has great experience in the country and perfect knowledge of the language, he will always be regarded by the local government, by the business community at large, and by his colleagues and employees, as a direct representative of the parent company and not as the chief representative of the local organization and operating units.

Therefore, the choice of the local chief executive is a very delicate one. He should know the local environment and be well acquainted in the various circles of the business and administrative community. He should speak English fluently in order to be able to communicate without difficulty with his partners in the parent U.S. company, most of them being unable to speak his own national language. Furthermore, he should have an above-average knowledge of the United States. If he has acquired a wide acquaintance with the American business community through successive business trips in the United States and if he has had the very valuable opportunity of attending an American business school of good reputation, it will be a great asset in his duty as an intermediary between the parent company and the local affiliate. His day-to-day role consists mainly in explaining to those in both the United States and in his own country the differences in legislation, in habits, in business philosophy, and other recurring problems. Therefore, he will have to exert a kind of diplomatic talent requiring great qualities of understanding, of patience, of persuasion, and of flexibility, which are all necessary for the success of his important task.

It is extremely desirable that the affiliate's chief executive be well acquainted, not only with the business activity of the parent U.S. group, but also with the most important executives who will be his normal correspondents in America. To this end, it is advisable in most cases to provide him, before his appointment, with a sufficiently long training period with the parent company to develop his knowledge of the business, of its philosophy and outlook, and of the key people in the various areas of responsibility.

If the local chief executive possesses these qualities and experiences, there is some chance that the relations between the U.S. headquarters and the local affiliate will develop in the best possible climate.

Finally, the replacement of the chief executive should be planned a long time before he reaches retirement age. The selection of the potential candidate should be made preferably inside the company. A long training period should be given to two or three candidates in order to evaluate their qualities, the final choice should be made, if pos-sible, two or three years ahead of the actual replacement time.

HOW TO HANDLE COMMUNICATIONS BETWEEN
THE PARENT COMPANY AND THE AFFILIATE

Downward Communication

The CEO of the local affiliate should be the sole and unique inter-mediary to transmit the most important messages from the U.S. parent company to the local one. Any infringement of this basic prin-ciple will generally be extremely detrimental to the morale and there-fore to the efficiency of the management of the affiliate company.

The chief executive should have the entire responsibility, with his managerial group, for implementing locally the policy of the parent company. This policy should have been previously explained to him in the United States, criticized by him if he thinks it advisable, modified according to his advice, and agreed upon in an open discussion with his correspondents in the United States.

It is necessary here to underline the much too common practice of American companies, which consists of taking very important deci-sions concerning their affiliated companies without any prior and ef-fective consultation with their chief executives abroad. Very often the affiliate has only the possibility of choosing the best possible ways of implementing the decision already made, without any participation in the decision itself. This common error has the consequence of diminishing rapidly the authority of the local chief executive, of dis-couraging him, and of inducing him to abandon his position in order to find a more satisfactory way of developing his talents.

Assuming that the most important decisions are taken in what I consider the proper way, the local chief executive has the duty of convincing his direct colleagues and the local hierarchy and employees of the usefulness of those decisions and of having them implemented. It is not a simple duty even when both countries have the same gen-eral philosophy of capitalism. As a matter of fact, the local Chief Executive Officer has to take into account the local habits, which are very different from the American ones; he has to persuade the people working for him to change their attitude in order to be more efficient, to accept new organizational structures, new concepts, and new ways of reporting their results. This is always a long process, because it requires a lot of time for the people to recognize the real value of the changes for them as well as for the corporation.

The great danger of too rapid change or too strong pressure to adopt important modifications is failure. Examples of American failures abroad are numerous. The consequences are generally very severe, not only for the affiliated company abroad, but also for the parent company because its credibility is put in jeopardy. Therefore, it is necessary to study carefully the consequences of such lack of success ahead of time. But what is more important, the American company will generally be better off to adopt, after the necessary criticism and improvements, the initiatives and the proposals of the local chief executive and its management group in the field of new investments or new ventures. In any case, it is necessary to obtain, before any important decision, the enthusiastic support of the local chief executive and his direct colleagues.

It is very helpful for the chief executive to have visits to his operation from time to time by parent company executives. These visits should be planned ahead of time and carefully prepared locally. They help in developing an appreciation of the efforts of the local team, and generally create a new spirit of emulation to show to the visiting group the results achieved by each manager in his field of activity. Criticism and encouragement should be given as they are deserved, and there should be regular follow-up to maintain the enthusiasm and attention of the local people.

The basic strategy of the parent company should be known by the affiliate's chief executive abroad in spite of the fact that this strategy is often considered as a most important secret of the parent company. If he is informed confidentially, it will help the chief executive of the affiliate to better understand and to improve the application of the methods recommended to achieve this strategy locally. The danger of indiscretion by this executive is much less great than the risk of a lack of understanding by him of the main goals of the group in which he is working. The best way should be to develop in common a strategy for the parent company and the affiliate abroad.

Too frequent changes of policy adopted by American companies— sometimes for good reasons, sometimes only because of a new business fashion—becomes extremely puzzling for the local managers abroad who are not in close contact day-to-day with the American headquarters. These changes should generally be tried and proven as valuable in the United States before being exported to foreign countries Change only for the sake of change can be very detrimental.

The great technical advance of American companies compared with others in the world is a great asset which should be utilized by the chief executive abroad in two ways to improve the efficiency of his operating unit. One is to ask the mother company to send abroad some carefully chosen technicians in various fields such as finance, accounting, manufacturing, marketing, etc. This supposes, besides the basic qualifications in his speciality, that the technician sent abroad is also open-minded enough to adapt his knowledge to the requirements of the local affiliate so that he does not act in the foreign country as if he were in his normal American environment. It goes without saying that when the American parent company sends abroad poor managers or technicians in order simply to get rid of them, the results are generally catastrophic.

Conversely, the other way is to send to the United States junior local managers who have already proven their high potential so that they may spend some time with the corresponding activity in the parent company or its divisions. They will learn on the spot and more rapidly the American way of doing business and will return to their countries with more experience and more knowledge. Some of them may even complete their training period in an American business school.

Finally—maybe before all—the success of American companies abroad is often a consequence of their better behavior with their employees, with the authorities, and with the community at large. As a matter of fact, some American local affiliates make a point of compensating their employees a little better than their local competitors or of giving incentive remuneration along the lines of what is adopted in the United States, although these may not necessarily be the same. They are often more generous with their workers in case of necessary layoffs. They encourage and participate in artistic or cultural activities in order to gain a good reputation. The chief executive of the affiliate abroad is consequently more appreciated as the representative of a generous American corporation, and the social climate in the company is substantially improved.

Upward Communication

The success or failure of the local affiliates is judged by the American parent company through the written reports sent weekly, monthly, quarterly, and annually by the various local divisions or departments.

It is well known that some of these reports are absolutely necessary for accounting reasons; some are useful, especially the manufacturing and marketing reports; and some are completely useless and are maintained only because nobody bothers to question why they were initiated and who is supposed to look at them. It is wise to review with the local chief executive occasionally the reasons why these reports are kept, who back home looks at them and why, and the advantages of simplifying or eliminating some of them.

Besides the necessary accounting or technical reports, the most important report should be either a monthly or, preferably, a quarterly report by the affiliate's chief executive to the parent company dealing with the principal matters for which he is responsible. This report should contain, first, an explanation of the recent success or failure in trying to meet the objectives of the local affiliate. It should also, and above all, indicate the present and future trend of the business and of developing opportunities in order to advise the American company in due time of moves which might be advantageous for the success of its business abroad. Unfortunately, experience has proven that either the chief executive does not carefully prepare this report or that, if he does, the American executives receiving it do not pay any attention to it. The only consequence is that after a while this most important channel of communication is abandoned to the detriment of each party.

The best channel of communication between the affiliate and the parent company is generally a visit of the chief executive of the affiliate to the American headquarters. However, here again, these visits should be well planned in order to be efficient. He should not be thrown into a large conference where he is lost among other local or foreign managers. The contact should be short, but direct, in order to focus exclusively on the most important subjects of the period concerned. Such meetings should occur, for instance, twice a year and should give both parties an opportunity to review carefully the most important questions, such as management development and the evolution of business in the particular country or in the larger region where the affiliate operates, such as the EEC, the Middle East, Latin America, etc. More than the usual business conferences or seminars, these meetings are essential to maintain confidence between the American headquarters and the affiliate.

Of course, these contacts do not preclude other more technical visits by some of the most important functional managers such as the treasurer, the marketing and manufacturing managers, and the employee relations manager. But these meetings should be kept at a more technical level than the visits of the CEOs.

Some American companies also utilize the services of a permanent "shareholder representative" living abroad. His duties consist of counseling both sides: the affiliate on the evolution of the parent company, and the latter on the problems of the affiliate. I have seen such an arrangement work very efficiently due to the personality of the shareholder representative. However, two dangers can arise. Sometimes the American representative is too much aware of the wishes of the American company, which he tries to impose no matter what the consequences for the affiliate. Conversely, it can happen that he is so pleased with life abroad that he becomes too much involved in the environment of the affiliate and finally does not care enough about the parent company. If a shareholder representative is used, it is a good practice to change his assignment abroad every three or four years.

In all these various modes of communication, it is advisable to keep in mind that the chief executive of the U.S. affiliate abroad is the most knowledgeable as far as the problems of the affiliate are concerned. Therefore, the best contacts should be maintained with him in order to ensure harmony between the parent company and the affiliate.

IMPORTANT RISKS TO AVOID

It is well known that among the most successful American companies are the "multinationals." Generally, their success has not been very rapid. Most of these American companies invested abroad a long time ago, over the last 80 years. Except in some special cases, their development has been slow, with ups and downs.

Very often their original foreign investment was created through acquisition of a minority interest in an existing company abroad. In this way, the American parent company gradually developed its experience through a joint venture with foreign businessmen or a company well acquainted with the local customs. It appears that such an approach is best for an American corporation having no experience in any foreign country. Sometimes also it is more easily accepted by the foreign government concerned, especially when the American corporation is in a position to help the foreign national company either financially or technically or in the fields of organization and management. However, such cases should be handled carefully as far as the non-

American shareholders are concerned. Inasmuch as the normal tendency of the American corporation will be to acquire as soon as possible a controlling or a majority interest or even total control, the manner in which it acquires the outstanding shares must be considered early enough so as to avoid two dangers: paying too high a price for the minority shares if, as is common, the profitability of the business is improving; or paying too low a price if the new American management is impairing the profitability of the foreign affiliate by charging it with too heavy a burden for allocated costs or by failing to charge costs appropriately to the American parent.

Conversely, American companies that are well established abroad generally choose to approach foreign investment through the creation of a *new* business, with the construction of *new* plants. They know the difficulties and the problems, they have great experience, they can calculate the economies of their investment carefully, and can accept a loss compensated by profits elsewhere. Because foreign governments already have some knowledge of the activities—and, one can say, proclivities—of prominent American companies, these governments may be inclined either to give them special advantages to attract them or to impose special constraints on them beyond those imposed on other foreign investments.

These two ways of investing abroad help American companies to maximize their profits. The objective is certainly a sound one in the capitalistic system, but its implementation can lead to certain excesses which deserve a few words.

Much too often American companies consider foreign affiliates as if they were inexhaustible cows to be milked. Not only are 100 percent of the profits of the affiliate transferred, sometimes before the end of the fiscal year; also, royalty fees are exaggerated and other miscellaneous fees are charged to the foreign subsidiary, a practice which is hardly acceptable by the local government. The affiliate is obliged to use double accounting procedures, one that follows the local accounting rules, another in line with the parent company requirements. Chartered American accountants are utilized for the benefit of the parent company, but charged to the affiliated company in spite of the fact that they are additional to the controls normally imposed by the country of operation. All these common practices can substantially burden the affiliate, making any comparison of its performance with that of the parent company either impossible or false.

Furthermore, such practices become generally well known to local management, not only to the local CEO but down the line among the local managers and supervisors. If these various ways of distorting financial results are not firmly rejected by the local chief executive, he may gradually loose his authority and his prestige and be considered a mere puppet in the hands of his American shareholder. Far better for all concerned that he be known as a person of character and independent judgment.

CONCLUSION

The Chief Executive Officer of an American affiliate abroad will prove his worth if, on the one hand, he uses the most important strengths of the parent company to develop its local operation and to increase the return on the foreign investment under his charge; and if, on the other hand, he exemplifies the generous behavior of most American corporations operating abroad.

The most successful American companies in foreign countries are, generally speaking, the companies which have acquired strong technical and financial support in the United States, and which behave abroad as well as, or even better than, the corporations of the foreign country with which they have to compete.

DECISION-MAKING IN LARGE JAPANESE CORPORATIONS

by Michael Y. Yoshino

Professor of Business Administration,
Harvard Business School

INTRODUCTION

IN RECENT YEARS, Japan's economic growth has attracted much attention. No other nation in the world achieved such a rapid rate of growth as she did during 1950s and 60s. Although the Japanese case is fascinating in many respects, perhaps the most remarkable fact is that, to date, Japan is the only non-Western nation which has attained an advanced state of industrialization. Modern industries always impose certain objective requirements, notably as regards forms and specifications of raw materials, technologies, and economical scale. However, one critical ingredient varies considerably among societies: the manner in which human activities are organized and managed for large-scale and complex industrial undertakings.

The Japanese experience provides an excellent case in point. During the past two decades, Japan has developed some of the largest corporations in the world. On *Fortune's* list of the 200 largest, non-U.S. industrial firms, 1 out of 4 is Japanese. In fact, in automobiles, machinery, chemicals, synthetic fibers, and shipbuilding, Japanese corporations now rank among the dozen or so leading firms in the world. In terms of size, technology, scale, and efficiency, Japan's major corporations are hardly distinguishable from their international competitors. But the management system of these corporations is peculiarly Japanese. It is a system that has made a selective and skillful use of ingrained traditional values. Judged by its results, the system, which the Japanese have evolved during the past century, has been an extraordinarily effective one. It has facilitated a successful absorption of high technology and the concept of large-scale organization, rather

251

rapidly, without serious social disruptions. The Japanese have approached managerial tasks with quite a different set of assumptions than those in the West, and particularly those prevalent in the United States. This is nowhere more apparent than in the process of decision-making.

THE *RINGI* SYSTEM

The Japanese decision-making process, commonly followed in large organizations, is known as the *Ringi system.*[1] The system is often described as the "approval-seeking process" where the proposal, known as *ringisho*, prepared by a lower functionary, works itself up through the organizational hierarchy, in a highly circuitous manner, often at a snail's pace. At each step, it is said, the proposal is examined by the proper officials, who indicate approval by affixing a seal. Somehow, in this process, a decision emerges. Such a description, although partially correct, does not capture the essence of the system; it describes only a procedural aspect whereby the decision already reached is formally approved. The far more dynamic substance of the Ringi system is the aspect that is relevant to the present consideration.

The comprehension of the dynamics of the Ringi system requires an understanding of other closely related elements in the Japanese managerial system. Looking first at the Japanese concept of organization, we note that the basic unit of organization is the group. A task is defined on the basis of the group; the assignment is carried out by the group; and the responsibility is shared by the group's members. This emphasis on the group is consistent with traditional Japanese values. The individual, at least historically, existed solely as a member of the group and not as a distinct entity. This is in striking contrast to the Western pattern, where the basic building block of an organization consists of the individual's position and accountability.

Roots in Japanese History

For centuries prior to industrialization, Japan had been a country of small, localized farming communities. An agrarian economy, based on the cultivation of rice, required close, cooperative relationships.

---

[1] The term "ringi" consists of two parts—*rin*, meaning "submitting a proposal to one's superior and receiving his approval"; and *gi*, meaning deliberations and decisions. The Ringi system has, indeed, all of these features.

Moreover, the nation, being physically isolated, confined to a small land area, and under tight political control during the centuries of the feudal era, offered its populace virtually no opportunity for mobility. Thus, farming settlements took on permanency. Families remained for many generations in the same community.

In every aspect of village life—political, social, and economic—one was tightly bound to a group. The norms and standards of the group shaped the thought and actions of each of its members. There was little room for individual initiative, or innovations. Any initiatives taken, or innovations made, represented group efforts. This differs fundamentally from the strong emphasis given to individual motivation, initiative, and freedom of action and thought in American society. The Japanese culture had little tolerance for "rugged individualism." The most important of all groups was the family. In the traditional Japanese setting, the family had a greater significance than as a purely biological kinship group, for it came to serve as a model for structuring all types of secondary groups, including large-scale industrial activities.

The Permanent Employment System

Another remarkable feature of Japanese management is the so-called permanent employment system. This permanent relationship between the corporation and its employees is not a contractual one but, in fact, it is more binding and uncompromising than any legalistic arrangement. An employee spends his entire career in one firm. His fate and wellbeing are indeed bound to those of the corporation. Short of serious moral misconduct, an employee is not dismissed. Incompetence does not constitute an adequate ground for dismissal. In return for an implicit guarantee of lifetime security, the organization demands an almost total commitment from a person, not only as regards his technical or professional energies, but more importantly, as to his emotional identification.

Hierarchical Organization Structure

Still another distinct aspect of Japanese management is that, in keeping with the tradition of Japanese society, organization has a strong hierarchical orientation. The status of each individual member is meticulously defined, and the criterion for status determination is seniority. Although there is no doubt about the considerable rigidity of such a system, it is compensated by the fact that one's function in the organization is very loosely defined. Indeed, one cannot help but note a striking contrast between the strictness with which someone's status in the organization is defined and the very looseness of his functional assignment. Thus, the group has a great deal of flexibility in determining how, and by whom, a particular task is to be performed.

Importance of the Group

An individual's assignment is determined largely on a case-by-case basis, by such factors as the nature of a particular task, its relative importance, and the competence and qualifications of the individuals involved. Indeed, Japanese organizations make clear distinction between status and functional roles. This kind of organization requires a peculiar type of leadership. The strong sense of individual initiative and direction, so important to the American style of leadership, is not needed, for the japanese managerial philosophy places the utmost emphasis on maximizing the *group's* output. A leader must distribute work to group members according to their ability and experience, giving each freedom of action, yet at the same time maintaining harmony within the group. Under these arrangements a capable individual in the Japanese system enjoys considerable freedom in his actions and may enjoy influence with little regard to his formal status, subject to three conditions: (1) he must work within the overall guidelines set by the group; (2) he must pay appropriate formal reverence to those who have senior status; and (3) he must not seek personal recognition for his contributions.

THE PROCESS OF DECISION-MAKING IN THE *RINGI* SYSTEM

This is the organizational setting in which the Ringi system works. Indeed, the Ringi system defies a neat and clear definition. It has been characterized as a bottom-up, group-oriented, and consensus-seeking process. True, the Ringi system possesses all of these elements. But its essence is found in the dynamic interaction of all these elements. It is bottom-up in the sense that the need for decision is first recognized by those at the operating level, typically the middle management. It is group-oriented and consensus-seeking because the various interest groups which may be affected by a decision, as well as those who must implement it, participate in the decision-making. A final decision emerges in this process of group interactions, instead of being made explicitly by an individual who occupies the formal leadership role. Discussion, consultations, persuasions, bargaining, or arm-twisting are all carried on through subtle, informal, interpersonal interactions. Dynamic, though informal, interactions which characterize every stage of decision-making, are the very essence of the Ringi system. From the earliest stage during which a decision itself is being shaped, different ideas and various alternatives are explored, different interests are accommodated, and compromises are sought. At the same time, the process of education, persuasion, and coordination among various groups takes place.

Role of the Leader

Another elusive element in the Ringi system is the role of the formal leader. In this system, the formal leader is not a decision-maker in the classic sense. His role in the decision-making process is little differentiated from that of other members of the organization; he participates with his subordinates in the decision-making process. Thus, the degree to which the leader's view is incorporated into a decision depends largely on his relationship with his subordinates, how well he is accepted and respected by them.

CONDITIONS FOR EFFECTIVENESS OF THE SYSTEM

For the Ringi system to operate effectively, certain conditions must prevail. First, as observed earlier, a heavy reliance is placed on informal personal relations. Much of the discussion, negotiation, bargaining, and persuasion are performed through mobilization of networks of personal relationships.

To make this possible, the organizational and physical setting must encourage regular and frequent face-to-face interactions. Such opportunities are necessary for the process of making a specific decision; more important, they are essential to building and maintaining the personal relations upon which the system is based. The need for frequent and close contacts is further reinforced by the very nature of interpersonal relationship in the Japanese cultural setting.

Shared Understanding and Values

Another basic condition that makes the Ringi system effective is the compelling presence of shared understanding and values among participants. Employees are also expected to be totally familiar with the climate of an organization, and to have an unswerving loyalty to it. Inasmuch as anything important is unlikely to be explicitly defined, the participants in the system are expected to have a good feel for what is acceptable and possible within a given organizational context, how a decision is to be presented, who must be consulted, and how each must be approached. Moreover, communications often take the most subtle forms. In a system where individuals are bound to an organization for their entire working career, disagreements and conflicts on a particular issue must be managed in such a way as not to disturb any subsequent relationship. Communications under these circumstances must be subtle, discreet, and indirect; therefore participants are required to understand the implication of the most oblique cues. They must be able to read a real meaning into what may seem to outsiders a most casual comment. To be able to do this requires the aforementioned sense of shared understanding and common interest. In the large Japanese corporate organizations, such a shared understanding and organizational commitment are developed in a most elaborate manner.

Recruitment

The process begins with the recruitment system, and is subsequently reinforced through personnel practices. Young men are carefully selected, from among graduates of outstanding universities, who have survived a series of rigorous screening processes, and who are already highly homogeneous in their ability, training, background, and values. From the very first day of joining the company, they go through an intensive socialization process during which they are indoctrinated with the value orientation of the particular firm. As, over a number of years, a man goes through the well-structured advancement system, he develops a high degree of shared understanding and commitment.

CONTROL

Just as much of the decision-making works in an informal way, so does control. Unlike the management of a typical large American corporation, in the Ringi system there is no explicit control mechanism. This does not mean that the system does not have an effective mechanism for control. Once again, the Ringi system makes an effective use of informal means, relying heavily on understanding and commitment as a control mechanism, instead of on formal measurement. Given the pervasive presence of this shared understanding and commitment, carefully and painstakingly nurtured by the organization through the socialization process, participants in the Ringi system have a reasonably certain assurance that the decision, once approved, will be implemented in the best interest of the group. Equally important is the fact that, given the tightness of Japanese corporate organization, coupled with a close communication network, everyone is aware that the eventual outcome of the decision becomes known to those concerned in the decision. Such knowledge would, no doubt, become an important input for others to evaluate a subsequent decision proposed by the particular group. Those who are credited with excellent decisions can enhance their standing and reputation within the organization. Because of the ambiguity and the highly diffused nature of task assignments in a typical Japanese corporation, persons of established reputations can enjoy considerable maneuverability in the organization. Thus, it is important for an employee to build a consensus concerning his competence and capability within the organization. Moreover, because power and influence are highly diffused among various ranks, he must build such a consensus, not only among his superiors and peers, but even among his subordinates. Such a consensus, however, cannot be built overnight. It is a result of accumulated evidence, of many years of a sustained record of excellent performance.

CRITICISM OF THE *RINGI* SYSTEM

A perennial criticism heard from American managers who have dealt with Japanese corporations is that the Japanese style of decision-making is a terribly time-consuming process. The criticism is well justified in some ways, because the Ringi system usually is a complex, time-consuming process, and one that is indeed puzzling to an outsider.

In contrast, a decision in an American corporation, the critics of the Japanese method would argue, is made much more rapidly because it is typically done by one person, without resort to drawn-out consultation. This contrast is not completely accurate, however, if the decision-making is considered in a broader context, beginning with the recognition of a potential decision to be made, all the way through to the implementation of that decision. In American corporations, it is not unusual that a decision, once made by a senior executive, must be communicated and explained to subordinates. Not infrequently, subordinates manifest an amazing degree of resistance to a decision imposed from above. They must be persuaded, sometimes even pressured, to accept the decision. In this process, conflicting views must be accommodated and compromises may be sought, *after* the decision seemingly was made. These steps are often essential for smooth implementation of a decision. In contrast, in the Ringi system, these steps are all part of the decision-making process itself. Once the decision is formally approved, the only remaining step, though it is an extremely critical one, is that of implementation. Thus, if the decision-making process is viewed in a broader context, from inception to implementation, the frequent criticism of the slowness of the Ringi apparatus is not always justified.

FUTURE OF THE *RINGI* SYSTEM

So far, the Ringi system has worked well for Japanese enterprises, but it is not without actual or potential liabilities. The cumbersome quality of this process has been already mentioned. The Ringi system is somewhat piecemeal in that it tends to deal with problems only as they come up. It is reactive and much less anticipatory. Also, it could be stifling. Those who are consulted do not always give full attention to the problem because of the pressure of other matters which are of more immediate concern to them. Sometimes, the system encourages political reciprocity among various interest groups, whereby one group may agree to a proposal from another group in return for a reciprocal favor. Thus, there is possible danger of sacrificing long-term interests for immediate expediency. Finally, the particularly heavy reliance of the Ringi system on personal contacts tends to inhibit multinationalization of Japanese enterprises, which surely must be an important future thrust for leading Japanese corporations. The Ringi system is too "culture-bound" to be effective outside of Japan. Furthermore, the lack of an explicit form of communication makes it difficult for managers who do not have frequent opportunities for face-to-face contacts to become effective participants in the Ringi system.

Similarities to American Management

A relevant question to be addressed relates to the matter of uniqueness of the Japanese style of decision-making. Surely, it does reflect deeply entrenched, specifically Japanese cultural values. And yet, as we gain further insights into the decision-making processes in large complex corporations in the West, particularly in the United States, we become aware of the fact that the widely accepted notion that decision-making is a rational, discrete act is not necessarily accurate. There is a growing body of evidence that decision-making in large American firms is much more an interactive, consultative—even "political"—process than generally conceived. This suggests that the differences between American and Japanese styles may be simply a matter of degree rather than that of kind.*

Need for Adaptation

Direct applicability of the Ringi system to American settings is highly problematic. But it does offer an important lesson. There is, surely, no universally effective managerial system. Management is a human and social process. As such, of necessity, it reflects human and social elements present in the particular environment in which the process takes place. The effectiveness of the process depends on the "fit," that is, the degree of compatibility, between a particular practice or process and the human and social values surrounding it. At least to date, the Japanese system has been compatible with Japanese culture. But there is a growing body of evidence that suggests the environment in Japan is undergoing a transition, calling for dynamic revision of the traditional managerial system. Indeed, a number of thoughtful observers have come to believe that the continued success of Japan's industrial system will depend, to an important degree, on the capacity of Japanese managers to innovate new managerial practices and to adapt their traditional system to a changing environment.

* [Ed. Note: See, e.g., Allison, Graham T.; *The Essence of Decision: Explaining the Cuban Missile Crisis*; Boston: Little, Brown and Company; 1974; and Bower, Joseph L.; *Managing the Resource Allocation Process: A Study of Corporate Planning and Investment*; Boston: Division of Research; Harvard Business School; 1970; and Homewood, Ill.: Richard D. Irwin, Inc.; 1972.]

PART II-D

Changing
the
Organization
Structure

UPDATING ORGANIZATION STRUCTURE TO RESPOND TO GROWTH, INCREASED COMPLEXITY, AND NEW EXTERNAL CONSTRAINTS

by William C. Conner
Chairman of the Board, Alcon Laboratories, Inc.

and Edgar H. Schollmaier
President, Alcon Laboratories, Inc.

MAINTAINING an organizational structure capable of achieving the short-term, intermediate-, and long-term objectives of the enterprise is one of the most important, if not the most important, continuing responsibilities of the chief executive. The major emphasis in this statement must be on the word continuing. In this era of rapid change, it is evident that any organizational design is well on the way to becoming obsolete even before it is fully implemented. Thus the key to maintaining effective organization is not the design but the management system by which the CEO constantly assesses progress against objectives and "tunes" his organizational structure to increase its effectiveness.

ADAPTING THE ORGANIZATION TO CHANGE

Because change, even relatively rapid or dramatic change, invariably takes place gradually over a prolonged period of time, it is easy to become oblivious of it. As a result, we frequently tend to ignore the potential implications of change or to adopt the dangerous assumption that the organization will automatically adjust as necessary.

The varieties of change that affect an enterprise are infinite. Let your mind wander briefly over the last year, two years, five years of your business experience and this point will come into sharp focus. A good starting point for the CEO is the assumption that in the future, the process of change will be continual and profound. It then becomes the chief executive's function to identify the nature of change and to organize his resources accordingly.

For example, we at Alcon, a couple of years ago, became convinced that the regulatory climate in which we of the pharmaceutical industry operate was going to change in important ways. Among other changes we foresaw was that the number of approvals by the Food and Drug Administration of new pharmaceutical products would probably decline. Apparently, many people in the pharmaceutical industry found the idea so unpleasant that they simply couldn't accept it. But we felt sure it was going to happen and that on the whole, it was probably for the best for all parties. But the development could work to slow down corporate growth; and for a company committed, as Alcon is, to growth, that would be an unfortunate turn of events. Accordingly, we decided to look for channels for growth that would not be impeded by such a development. We found one answer in the development of a new line of surgical, nonpharmaceutical products needed by our primary market, the opthalmologists.

In order to build that business, we established a new division, our Surgical Division. This new structure was established as separate from our pharmaceutical business so that it could get the full attention of its own management—a field sales manager and a product manager— and its own sales force. We funded the new division at a level that we thought would enable them to get off to a good start and that would express an important commitment of the company to the new direction.

The division has grown to a $5 million-dollar-a-year business in four years. We have bought some new products to build up the line. We believe the quality of the line has enhanced the company's reputation with its customers. And it has been very profitable.

The important points here were these: recognizing a trend; perceiving *opportunity* in the trend and not merely frustration; and setting up a new division with its own charter, funds, people, and "p and l" responsibility.

Of course, the chief executive must accept that the full responsibility and accountability for organizing and adapting the organization to effectively meet problems and opportunities is his. Naturally, assignments may be given and certain decision-making passed to others, but the fact remains that the accountability for organizational effectiveness cannot be delegated. Moreover, if we recognize that we basically organize to attempt to achieve desired results and concede that organizational ineffectiveness (obsolescence) is a prime contributor to negative deviations, organizing must clearly be considered as one of the major reasons for the CEO's existence.

To effectively carry out this responsibility, the CEO must achieve certain understandings with both his board of directors and his top management group. It must be obvious to both groups that the chief executive accepts full accountability for this responsibility and is committed to effectively performing this function.

It must be recognized that most businesses have increased both in size and in complexity in recent years. Whether a company has expanded from a local to a regional or national basis; gone into added related or unrelated product lines; moved into diverse international markets; experienced merger or acquisition; sought other avenues of growth or increased prosperity—the organizational planning task has become increasingly difficult and important. Many companies have experienced several or all of these kinds of changes almost simultaneously. When other factors are mixed in, such as the mobility of executives, lack of management personnel experienced in the various segments of a business, management development lead times, intrapersonal conflicts, work-force discontent, labor union demands, inflation and recession, accelerated technological innovation, longer lead times on equipment and materials, rapidly increasing consumer vocalism and power, and the myriad of restrictions placed on ways of doing business by various governments throughout the world, it is easy to see that the chief executive's job is not getting any easier.

There is no longer such a thing as simple organizational concepts, because the objectives, direction, and forces acting upon most business enterprises are in no way simple. The situation is analogous to that of an army fighting on a number of fronts, having long supply lines, experiencing a variety of terrains and varying degrees of enemy resistance, while at the same time being attacked on its flanks. If survival and ultimate victory are to be achieved, the interdependence of various units must be recognized. Extremely effective communication and coordination must be achieved. Likewise, the CEO of a business organizes his troops so as to maximize effective communication, intradependent support, and coordination.

The chief executive has a variety of inputs to assist him in continually analyzing the forces of change acting on his organization. The annual planning and budgeting process, if done in sufficient depth, can be extremely revealing. The CEO cannot merely be satisfied in ending up with acceptable plans and budgets, but he must be a good observer of the pushing and pulling that takes place in arriving at the end product. In this way valuable insights can be gained into stress factors, agreed-upon needs, areas of uncertainty, fears and anxieties, and the assumptions which go into establishing the short-term course of his company. He must find the time, take the time, to think through the organizational implications, i.e., the strengths and weaknesses, areas needing attention, etc., in the profit plan he is approving. This analysis will also go a long way toward helping him define his role in the months ahead.

Ongoing reviews during the year (either monthly or quarterly) of performance deviations versus the planned expectations are also essential. The question, "Where are we as compared to where we expected to be and what are the fundamental factors causing the variances?" must be raised. Naturally, the deviations can be either positive or negative, and it is important to analyze where opportunities or problems are greater than had been anticipated. Incidentally, it is an important responsibility of the CEO to insist that his management team carry out both the planning and review process in considerable depth, clearly spelling out and amending the fundamental assumptions being made. It is also his responsibility to challenge these assumptions and to see that additional informational inputs are provided where necessary. Again, the CEO must discipline himself to analyze the organizational implications of performance deviations, especially when repetitive variances occur.

Some time ago, we reached the conclusion that our "R&D" organization and activities simply weren't productive enough. The fact that a lot of companies were in the same boat was no consolation. We were determined to do something about it. As we of the top management team thought and talked about the matter, we concluded that our R&D efforts should be more sharply focused to support our present business; more closely coordinated with other technical departments—such as production and quality control—and with our line divisions. They had been, we thought, too unrelated to our ongoing problems and for that reason we weren't getting our money's worth.

Alcon's R&D were restructured away from seeking new areas to giving better support and closer attention to our basic areas of commitment.

We brought all of our technical and technology-based operations together in a Science and Technology Division. This included Research and Development, Quality Control, Manufacturing, and Regulatory Affairs. And to make sure they stayed together and worked together, kept their focus, and became more productive, we put a first-rate, proven executive in charge. This will surprise you: He's a *marketer!* He knows people and he knows how to run an organization. Proof of the pudding is that within two years we had an expanded flow of new product introductions. And all of management, including our scientific people as well as our marketers, have a high level of confidence in our technical future.

It is terribly important that the CEO create the type of environment with his top management team in which he and they can openly discuss organizational questions and alternatives. This should not be expected to happen easily or quickly. The members must believe that such discussion is not intended as a threat to their positions within the hierarchy, but is truly intended to explore ways and means of strengthening their effectiveness. Frequently, suggestions will be proposed that the CEO had rejected because he did not feel they would be accepted. Even impractical proposals will provide important insights into how members of this group see the needs of the organization. Over a period of time, this freedom of discussion greatly increases the organizational alternatives open to the CEO and the organization's willingness to accept his leadership.

This type of organizational discussion can be especially meaningful if done in conjunction with the top management review of longer-term objectives and plans. Ideally, this should be done on a yearly basis, separate from the approval of the annual plans and budgets. It should require inputs of all key operational managers, as well as staff, as to major assumptions regarding fundamental change forces anticipated in the years ahead. The point is frequently made that management cannot be expected to be all-knowing in this respect and that it is inadequate merely to survey their understanding and knowledge. This conclusion has only limited validity. If we accept the premise that all change, even profound change, is relatively gradual and continual, it can be assumed that experienced and capable members of a top management group will have considerable insight into the forces that can be expected to effect their future. It is, of course, important to realize that in many instances they will recognize only symptoms rather than the underlying force and that there will be occasional blind spots. As a general rule, they will know a lot more than they don't know. Of course, it is important to point out that we are discussing an ongoing process and that focus will sharpen as time goes on. It is the CEO's role to make sure that the old adage, "Everyone talks about the weather, but no one does anything about it," doesn't apply to his business. It is his responsibility to insure that the basic plans of the company adapt to meet the changed requirements on the horizon.

We had a subsidiary that just wasn't performing up to expectations and budgets. We all kept thinking about this and concluded that there were some fundamental weaknesses in the picture: The method of selling and the channels of distribution would have to be changed. The board of directors came to doubt whether the very business of the subsidiary was truly consistent with the company's long-term corporate objectives. They directed the management not only to get the short-term problems of the subsidiary under control, but to undertake a study of whether, even if the subsidiary were to do well, it was something the company wanted to stay with.

The corporate marketing vice president was given full authority and freedom to act. He was authorized to, and did draw upon staff support from other divisions or temporary or "task force" assignments. The subsidiary got turned around and restored to profitability. But the experience and the greater understanding of the problems that had been encountered were fully discussed and we all, including the board, came to the conclusion that the subsidiary should be disposed of, which it was, on favorable terms.

It is my opinion that the type of organizational discussion we engaged in relating to the longer-term objectives and plans of a company must take place away from the day-to-day activities of the office. Enough time must also be allowed so that ideas may be explored in depth. This will not just happen. The CEO must plan for this activity and see that it takes place. It is also important that each of the top managers know well in advance that organizational needs will be discussed and that his views will be welcomed, assuming that he has adequately prepared himself to make a meaningful contribution.

The chief executive's role in these discussions is quite clear—to listen! It is important that he gain full understanding of the present and future organizational needs of the company as his top management team sees them. In this role, he should feel free to ask probing questions, to test assumptions, to explore alternative courses of action. In order to maximize its value, this type of group exploration must run its full course. The CEO must be careful not to attempt to draw conclusions too quickly or to try to sell a specific approach to the group. Likewise, he should not be concerned if there is a lack of agreement in the group. This frequently develops because managers tend to want to get to conclusions, i.e., drawing organizational charts, without spending adequate time gaining mutual understanding as to the fundamental underlying needs of the organization. For all of these reasons, it is important that these discussions not be cut off too quickly. Again it should be emphasized that the CEO should not feel an obligation to make any decisions at this time. This is merely an important part of the process by which he works at his responsibility of organizational structure planning.

Whether or not the chief executive carries out this essential activity should be the subject of one of his self-imposed annual performance standards. He should also undertake to appraise himself as to how effectively he is handling the task of organizational planning. Of course, ultimately he must be appraised as to how capably his organization is dealing with the forces of change in achieving its objectives.

Most chief executives will concede that self-appraisal is often not a potent enough source of discipline. This is where the CEO's working relationship with the board of directors comes into play. He should insist (and most boards will be delighted to accommodate him) that he annually establish with them agreed-upon performance standards against which the board will appraise his performance. This exercise will only have meaning and be productive if the board actually spends the time reviewing and agreeing upon the standards. It is extremely important that in addition to the generally accepted standards relating to profit and sales performance, there be specific standards relating to the organizational development responsibilities of the chief executive. These can be stated in a variety of acceptable ways and can encompass subjective as well as objective measurements. For example, included could be such standards as:

> Responsible for annually reviewing with the board a projected two-to-five-year plan, with underlying assumptions and alternatives.

Responsible for maintaining an organization (structure) capable of achieving short-, intermediate-, long-term corporate sales and profit objectives.

Responsible for annually reviewing organizational strengths and weaknesses with the board of directors.

Responsible for reviewing major organizational changes, in advance, with the board of directors.

Quite naturally, a board of directors will only carry out this type of activity if the CEO willingly imposes a high degree of visibility and discipline upon himself. This requires appropriate scheduling of board activities; proposing meaningful performance standards; and preparing detailed, in-depth, critical self-appraisals. Thus not only must the board be able to serve as a conscience (i.e., "Jiminy Cricket") for the CEO, but a relationship must be created in which the members of a balanced, experienced board can effectively counsel the chief executive. All concerned must keep in clear focus that accountability for organizational development rests with the CEO. He is accountable and he must expect to be held accountable.

It is a valuable exercise for the CEO to prepare annually, even in rough outline form, a two-to-five-year organization plan. The plan should include details of the projected major forces of change and various alternative approaches. In effect, this organizational plan becomes an addendum to the CEO's longer-term corporate objectives and plans. He will certainly want to share his thinking with his board of directors and receive their advice and counsel. Whether or not the CEO shares his preliminary plans with his top management team probably depends on the stage of their relationship. If they have accepted that it is the CEO's job to maintain organizational viability they will seek in a positive way to be part of his planning process.

By treating organizational planning as part of the overall longer-term corporate planning process, reorganization can be a gradual and constant process—minimizing organizational obsolescence and reducing the need to undertake massive reorganization attempts.

Ideally, this permits changes in organizational structure to be made when they can best be implemented, not when frustration forces action. It must be pointed out that organizational changes, while obviously intended to bring strength, in themselves can create stresses in an organization. Thus the time to implement changes is when you are ready to do so properly. In other words, when you have clearly defined roles and expectations; when you have appropriate candidate(s) available; and when you yourself have adequate time to frequently reinforce role and relationship definitions.

For many years we have given a great deal of what we believe is constructive thought to the problem of working with government agencies, the most important of which for a company in our industry must be the Food and Drug Administration. A number of years ago, we were convinced that, complex as the relationships were between pharmaceutical companies and the FDA, they were going to increase still further in complexity and importance and that contacts would increase greatly in frequency. A couple of years ago we concluded that the time had come to set up a new organization—a high corporate line—to deal exclusively with regulatory affairs. We split the function off from corporate legal affairs and put the office in charge of an able attorney. He has a full-time staff. Under our Vice President of Science and Technology, who was mentioned above, our Director of Regulatory Affairs can and does call on the scientific and technical people he needs for working effectively with the FDA.

He has established very effective working relationships within our S&T division and with the FDA. Working full time, and with highly qualified people, he has been able to resolve quietly numerous problems on a one-time basis. We have significantly shortened the time necessary for getting new product approvals through an FDA which is more demanding than ever.

It is important not to expect miracles from organizational changes. Fundamental changes take time and must be properly reinforced while the learning process takes hold. Further "tuning" is frequently necessary as implementation rarely duplicates conceptualization. In this regard, it is helpful if an organizational structure can be kept fairly fluid at all times. This does not mean an absence of clear role definitions, rather a willingness to experiment where it may be productive. This type of environment makes for greater acceptance of change, encourages further adjustments as necessary, and permits individuals to see changes in their status in a broader, more helpful perspective.

It is good counsel to avoid "organizing around a man," whenever possible. By over-concentrating on the skills and capabilities of a particular executive, it sometimes happens that a proper job is not done in clearly establishing objectives, recognizing forces of change, assessing needed changes, and so on. We must never lose sight of the concept that we organize to achieve desired results. This does not mean that you should hesitate to use your most competent, established managers in changing roles and for taking on new organizational responsibilities. This type of flexibility has many potential advantages. In addition to giving importance to the changes and helping to win broad support, it brings a known force to bear on a situation and utilizes established relationships and integrating skills. In many cases, it simplifies recruitment in that a replacement for the tapped manager may already be available. It may also help to prevent over-commitment to a position in terms of status, reporting relationships, compensation, etc. These comments do not mean to imply that new blood should not be introduced into the top management structure of an enterprise. It does suggest that carefully planned infusion is far superior to sudden transfusions.

The Chief Executive Officer must recognize that the "monkey" of organizational effectiveness falls clearly on his shoulders and that he must work at it . . . continually. His effectiveness, as well as his company's ability to survive and prosper, depends on it.

AS THE FAMILY BUSINESS GROWS, OR WHY DIDN'T GRANDFATHER TELL US?

by Bernard Edison

President, Edison Brothers Stores, Inc.

DEDICATION

(1) *You are Walter D. Throckmorton III, president of Throck-morton Throttles, Inc. Also in the business are: (2) your cousin, Will Throckmorton, executive vice president, financial executive, thorough, solid, dependable, you can trust him with your life (his wife, Laura, deals him a fit); (3) your son, Throcky IV, handsome, charming, customers love him (in fact, everybody likes him), has a 2 handicap, hits the ball a mile; (4) Will's son Paul, quiet, works hard (wonder how capable Paul really is?); (5) your sister Alice's son, Jimmy, or J. Throckmorton Brown as he signs his name now (can you tell Alice what you really think of Jimmy? Will was always close to Alice. Maybe Will can tell her); oh, and perhaps (6) Will's youngest daughter, Penny, getting her MBA in marketing this June, doesn't know a throttle from a thimble but thinks she knows something about business, pushy like her mother, yet some of her questions are damned sharp, and she can really talk that computer lingo with Schneider.*

You and I have only seen each other occasionally since we were roommates in college, but the old mutual respect is still there, a lot of the old affection. So Throcky, old boy, this is for you.

INTRODUCTION

Even a Family Member Can Be a Professional

Because you are reading this book, the fundamental assumption of this chapter will be that you want to improve your professional skills as a business manager, even though as one of the owners you could get by without doing so.

This chapter will speak to you with particular bluntness. You are part of the family management of your business, so it may be difficult for other associates to speak to you forthrightly about some sensitive subjects. And it may be difficult for you to listen if they try. If you find that some statements in this chapter make you a little uncomfortable, pay particular attention to those statements. If you find some things in this chapter that you would not want other members of your family (in or out of the business) to read, or that you would not want non-family executives in your business to read, pay particular attention to those statements also. Because if you have either reaction, you have probably identified an area in which *your* family business could do with some improvement.

Definition

For the purpose of this chapter, a family business will be considered to be one in which (1) members of a family own a controlling interest in the business, and (2) members of the family comprise all or a substantial portion of the top-management group, and (3) more than one generation of the family are active in the business, or are likely to be active in the future.

Incidentally, don't neglect the potential of female members of the family. For simplicity, the masculine gender is used mostly, but it represents both sexes.

Scope

This chapter will be directed toward those family businesses which are large enough to require more executives than the family alone can supply, or which have the potential to become of such size. It will also be directed primarily toward those family businesses which are experiencing more than nominal growth, or have the potential to do so. The special advantages and disadvantages of a family business become more significant in such situations.

Emphasis

The emphasis of this chapter will be on aspects of management in which a family business may differ from other businesses, either outright or in degree. Also emphasized will be some aspects of management in which family businesses rather unexpectedly do not differ much from other businesses.

Limitation

A family business can easily be an extension of the personality and character of an individual or a small number of closely related individuals. A wider range of variations may exist in family businesses than in others as to organizational form, management style, and motivation of top management.

If your company is one of those unusual or unorthodox ones, that doesn't necessarily mean it should change. If it works well, really well, and if it is likely to continue working well after you are no longer around, then perhaps you should not tinker with success. Just be sure you are being honest with yourself as to how well things are really going.

ADVANTAGES OF A FAMILY BUSINESS—USE THEM

Love

Yes, love. Don't be afraid to think of love in a business context. The real kind of love in which one truly cares about the other person's fulfillment can be a great asset to the relationship. It can provide extra loyalty, extra motivation, extra trust. (The Rothschilds, Rockefellers, Kennedys seem to draw extra strength from their family ties.)

Love, of course, does not always exist among family members in a business. Sometimes far from it. And it can grow between associates who are not related in any way. But love often exists in a family business.

> ADVICE: *If love does exist, don't try to repress it or ignore it. Recognize it as a source of strength and motivation. Encourage it. Engaging in a common endeavor toward common goals can strengthen the bonds among you, and strengthen the enterprise.*

A Potential Source of Capable Management

Most businesses have had the experience of trying to recruit an outstanding young prospect, only to lose him to "his family's business." Some have hired a talented young person, only to have him leave later for "his father's business." This illustrates clearly the special pull a family business can have.

The reasons are obvious enough: More likely to get to the top. Greater responsibility earlier. Immediate access to top management's ear for his ideas. More security. A business he probably already knows something about.

The advantages to the business of hiring a capable young family member may not be quite so obvious, but they are real. To begin with, capable, interested young people are not easy to locate. Here is one you may find easier to hire. He will probably start off already identifying himself with the company, and the company's prosperity with his own best interests. He is likely to stay, if he is handled properly (more about this later). And he probably comes to work with more knowledge about the business and its management philosophy than either you or he realize, gleaned from numberless dinner table or living room conversations. In summary, he probably begins with some headstart as to availability, involvement, loyalty, and training.

> ADVICE: *Make an appropriate recruiting effort to get capable young family members to join the business.*

Continuity of Management

Finance. Someday you are going to die or retire. Hopefully, that will be a distant event, but you know it is a certain one. If there are family members to assume at least a portion of the reins, those heirs who are not in the business will probably feel more secure in leaving their investment in the company. If the nonmanagement heirs are fairly treated by the family management, you may well avoid pressure to sell or liquidate the business. But without family members to "look after our interests," heirs may be understandably reluctant to leave what could be the bulk of their net worth invested in a single enterprise.

> ADVICE: *Recognize in advance the financial implications of succession. Talk about it with family members in and out of the company. Decide in advance what you are going to do.*

Direction. The closeness of a family group can help soften the abruptness of changes in management philosophy and corporate direction that may come when there is a change in top management.

ADVICE: *Encourage group discussions of major aspects of corporate philosophy and direction with other members of management, both family and nonfamily. Let them understand your thinking. Really listen to theirs. Try to evolve a direction that you and they accept. This will avoid some abrupt changes when you take your leave.*

Important Suppliers or Customers

Some important suppliers, customers, bankers, or other folks with whom you do business will be impressed if they meet, deal with, or are entertained by a member of the family whose name is part of the company name. Some will enjoy it themselves, and some will enjoy telling wives or associates about it. This use of the family can be overdone, but when it is significant, it can be very helpful indeed.

ADVICE: *Use this wherever it will help. Just be sure you are massaging the customer's ego, not your own. Encourage company executives to call on you, or to emphasize a point they have been trying to make, whenever they feel it will be useful. Put the family at the organization's disposal. Be sure to include the initiating executive in the activity or in the conversation.*

Organizational Esprit—If They Liked Throckmorton, Will They Love Son of Throckmorton?

Probably yes! Not just in business, but in politics, the entertainment fields, even medicine and law, people often tend to anticipate that they will find in the son what they found in the father. If they liked and trusted one, they will often start off by liking and trusting the other. Conversely, they will expect that respect they have earned from the father will have been communicated to the son. This advantage can be quickly dissipated, of course, if Son of Throckmorton is not at all as likeable or considerate as his father. Then the expectation can actually backfire, and the comparison be more unfavorable to the junior member than if he had not been a family member.

ADVICE: *(to the younger family members) People will ultimately evaluate you exactly as you merit, based on your ability, character, and the consideration and integrity with which you treat them. However, you can get an important headstart on their acceptance and cooperation. Let them know that their vested rights to respect and recognition have been transmitted to you by the senior members of the family. For example: "My father told me about the throttle-polishing process you developed. Would you show me how it works?" Or, similarly, "I remember when I was ten years old, hearing my uncle tell how you sold the King of Kadoot a million-dollar order by having a solid-gold throttle made with his picture on it. How did it happen?" Extremely important: Don't fake it! Don't patronize! People can tell, and will despise you for it. But if you are aware of the respect your father has for someone, and if you sincerely share it, show that you do and you will start off with some of the rapport they have achieved. You will probably already know whom in the organization the senior members of the family particularly respect, and why. If you don't, ask them!*

All for One and One for All

One of the great potential strengths of a family business is the possibility of avoiding internal power struggles and politics. "All for one and one for all!" "United we stand, divided we fall!" "A house divided against itself cannot stand." Trite sayings. Extremely true. Although they were not originally written about family business, they should have been!

> ADVICE: *More than any other single aspect, this is the heart of the matter. Be loyal to each other. Don't try to conceal differences of opinion, of course. They are natural and wholesome. But keep personal criticisms and uncomplimentary evaluations strictly within the family. Don't let anyone divide you, by individual flattery or otherwise. Share decision-making power and financial compensation as uniformly as you can justify. If some members of the family have more ownership control or more ability than others, they may consciously have to accept somewhat less individual authority and reward than might be their due on merit alone. But they will be amply compensated for their forbearance by the increased strength and success of the business as a whole.*

DISADVANTAGES OF A FAMILY BUSINESS—MINIMIZE THEM

Nepotism—We Are Not All Created Equal

For the purpose of this article, nepotism is defined as: The process whereby an executive, because he is a member of the family, is advanced to or retained in a position beyond his ability to perform well. *This is one of the two great dangers in family businesses!*

We are not all created equal, at least not in abilities and interests. Not everyone is cut out to be a business executive. Not everyone is cut out to be part of top management. And not everyone is really interested, either. It is not a source of shame to have different abilities or interests. A business needs middle management and junior management. The world needs artists, teachers, and dreamers.

> ADVICE: *Face it! If someone really isn't cut out for business, or for this business, he shouldn't stay. It is no long-range kindness to him to encourage or permit him to stay. The miscast person in the wrong career is seldom happy. Be ruthlessly honest in your judgment, and overwhelmingly kind in how you express it. Be patient, don't insist on action this week (barring a crisis). You may need to supplement his income, either from the business if it is privately owned, or from other members of the family. But do obtain the separation.*
>
> *If you have a family member who does an acceptable job at a moderate level of responsibility, but who really cannot handle bigger things, do not give him bigger things than he can do well! It will unfavorably affect both results and organizational morale if you do. A title is O.K., an office, and some of the visible signs of respect, such as inclusion in group meetings. These are part of the family loyalty to each other that will be accepted and even appreciated. But not real responsibility beyond capacity. Here, too, supplementary income may be provided, from the company if it is privately owned, or from other family members.*
>
> *Note that throughout this section, we are talking about capacity, not compatibility. Do not use the avoidance of nepotism as a pretext for separating a capable family member who may be somewhat hard to get along with. Usually in such cases, it will be worthwhile to make repeated attempts to improve the working relationship and salvage his motivation and contribution.*

Possible Difficulty of Attracting Capable Nonfamily Executives

This is a real potential problem in a family business. Good top-management people are ambitious. If they see all the top positions to which they aspire occupied now, and prospectively in the future, by family members, they will look elsewhere. For executives who aspire only to middle-management positions, this will not be such an important handicap, except in very small companies. They may actually be attracted by the extra security and continuity a family management often provides. But for the top-notch executive, it will be a matter of legitimate concern.

>ADVICE: *Level with him. Don't kid him. He will find out anyway. Tell him what he may realistically aspire to, in position, in participation, in compensation, in title. If your business is large enough, or if you want it to become so, try to structure your management so as to provide opportunities for nonfamily executives to become genuinely part of the top management group. (More about this later.)*

Objectivity—"But It Carries the Throckmorton Name!"

True objectivity is one of the hardest things to achieve. When the business is a family one, there is an extra ego involvement that can act powerfully to cloud your judgment. Have Throckmorton throttles always been known as the highest quality in the industry? But maybe the big market today is in the medium-grade, mass market, and that's where your competition is cleaning up. And the inefficient foundry at Ironton, shouldn't you have closed that money-loser long ago? But the people up there have worked for Throckmorton for years, and some of them wouldn't want to move down here to the main plant. Why Jake, the sweeper, was hired 40 years ago by Grandfather himself, for crying out loud!

>ADVICE: *Try, try, try to be honest with yourself about your motivations. "Know thyself." Some presidents have even found professional counseling helpful in understanding themselves.*

THE FAMILY EXECUTIVE—HE IS A PERSON, TOO

Don't Push Him into the Business—Recruit Him

You say that you want your son to come into the business. Think it over. Do you really? Will he be fulfilled and happy? (Remember love.) Will he be good at it? If the answers are "yes," in your opinion, they still may not be clearly so in his mind. Remember that initial motivation is one of the advantages of family management. This motivation will obviously be greater if the choice has been completely voluntary rather than made under pressure.

Conversely, if your son wants to come into the business, he has an obligation to prepare himself as well as possible for the profession of business management. And today that means attending and doing well at the best graduate school of business administration he can get admitted to. After all, if you were a doctor and wanted your son to practice with you, you would want him to go to medical school, wouldn't you?

> ADVICE: *A family member considering entering the business should prepare himself professionally. You should make clear that he is wanted, but not pressured. Have an open discussion about the advantages and disadvantages, from his point of view and from the company's. Level with him. Tell him what he can expect, and what will be expected from him. Then really let him decide. If he chooses to try something else, accept the decision gracefully. Leave the door open for him to join the family business later. This often happens, so try again to recruit him after he has been in the other job a year or so.*

Participation

One of the most satisfying rewards of any executive is being part of the important decisions and events. Knowing what is going on, what is being considered, and having an opportunity to express one's self on these matters. Early participation of this kind is one of the big inducements to going into a family business. And to continued motivation after joining. It is also the best possible training for future top-management responsibilities.

> ADVICE: *Include the younger family members as early as possible in as many planning discussions as possible. They will have to be discreet about their "inside" knowledge, and not flaunt it.*

Advancement, and the Opposite

You want any management person to develop as rapidly as he is able to. This is particularly true of family members. But you do not want them pushed beyond their capacity, for this will harm results and morale.

> ADVICE: *Expose the new family member to as much training and experience as he can absorb. A perfect executive for him to work under would be a nonfamily executive who is (1) a good teacher, (2) secure enough not to regard the young family member as a threat*

*or rival, (3) honest enough to tell you frankly how the young exec-
utive is doing. Then let the nonfamily executive make the decision as
to when the family executive can handle more responsibility. Also,
he should tell you if the young man is over his head or miscast, and
you should act on that advice.*

Pay

Pay can be a tough issue, with no universally right or wrong answer.

ADVICE: *Generally, it is better to be on the conservative side of
a fair pay range for the responsibilities a family member has. Far too
little is as wrong as far too much. But, it is better to pay the family a
shade too little than a shade too much. This is most true where the
company is large, publicly owned, and has a number of nonfamily
executives. And less true otherwise.*

Social Life, Including Spouses

Preferences will vary greatly as to the extent to which one's social
life should be involved with other members of the family. Some
people enjoy the warmth and closeness of frequently being with the
family socially. Others benefit from the change of pace of being with
friends who are not part of the business. Some wives resent it if their
social events consist of the husbands talking shop. Others enjoy it.
Frustrations and dissatisfactions in this area can be unusually hard
on marriages and on job satisfaction.

ADVICE: *As chief executive, you should recognize clearly that
preferences differ as to the extent of family socializing, including the
preferences of the spouses, and that these preferences should be respected. Particularly avoid making attendance at frequent family
social events a quasi-job-related duty. One good way is to let much
of the initiative for such events come from the younger family members. Do not express any displeasure or disappointment if they do not
seem to want to be with family as often as you might like. Since
social arrangements are often made by the wives, you will need your
wife's cooperation in this area. If you are unable to obtain her cooperation, you will need to disassociate yourself clearly from any
connotation that family social events are in any subtle sense a business obligation.*

THE TREATMENT OF NONFAMILY EXECUTIVES— YOU MAY OWN ALL THE STOCK, BUT YOU DON'T OWN ALL THE BRAINS

Participation

Paradoxically, a top management executive may find that he has more real participation in major discussions and decisions in a family business than he might have in a nonfamily business. The chief executive of a nonfamily business may perceive an outstanding number two or number three executive as a threat, a potential challenger to his own position. Consciously or not, he may limit this potential rival's access to important information or people, and his participation in major decisions.

But the chief executive whose family owns control of the company has such a secure position he need not be concerned about the other executive as a rival. He can afford him the complete working openness of a partner. This enables the nonfamily executive to perform in a superior way, and to take greater responsibility. It also is a powerful motivator. Everyone likes to be in the know. Everyone is more committed to company goals when he has had a part in formulating the goals. Moreover, you will make better decisions if other people have a chance to contribute their ideas. Remember: *You may own all the stock, but you don't own all the brains.*

> ADVICE: *Include as many executives as possible, rather than as few as possible, in corporate planning meetings. Make sure that as many people as possible know what is going on, what is being considered, and have an opportunity to contribute their thoughts to the decisions. Avoid "family only" meetings, especially on company premises and company time.*

Pay and Perquisites—Fair and Equal

> ADVICE: *Make sure that nonfamily executives are paid equally as well as family executives for equivalent responsibilities, taking into account seniority and other relevant factors other than family membership. This is a must. Additional family income should come from dividends out of profits. The same philosophy should apply to fringe benefits and perquisites. Key nonfamily executives should also be given an opportunity to obtain some stock ownership in the company.*

Advancement—Ability and Honesty

If the choice for the president's job is between a family member of average ability and a nonfamily executive of outstanding ability, everyone will be better off if you choose the better person. Everyone, particularly the family, whose investment in the company will be enhanced.

However, people can accept reality more easily than insincerity. If a family member is slated to be the next president, and if he is capable of doing the job well, people can understand and accept that. But a nonfamily executive will resent being told that he has an equal chance to become president if it isn't true.

Responsibilities can often be divided so that an extremely capable nonfamily executive can have an important area of authority and relative autonomy in which to make a major contribution. And the company will be stronger for it.

> ADVICE: *Pick the president on the basis of ability first, and family membership only second. Be honest with nonfamily executives about any limits to their potential advancement at the time they are hired and subsequently in their careers. Structure organization and responsibilities to give major areas of authority to capable executives, both family and nonfamily.*

Sensitivity and Tact—Don't Fake It

You have ownership control of the company. It is a fact. It is not a secret. You do not need to rub it in, or even to mention it. To do so is an indication of insecurity on your part, and demeaning to other executives who hear you do so.

There will be, on very rare occasions, decisions which are primarily ownership decisions. These are limited to such issues as possible sale of the company, selling stock to the public, or selection of a new chief executive. Here, again, people can accept the reality that these few decisions are the responsibility and the prerogative of ownership. Pretense that it is otherwise will usually be seen to be insincere, and resented more than the decision itself.

> ADVICE: *Reference by a family executive to the family's ownership control of the company for the purpose of supporting a decision or strengthening a personal position should always be avoided. Decisions should be discussed on the merits. In the unlikely event that a*

real challenge ιo authority is made, it should be met in terms of executive responsibility as chief executive rather than as owner.

In the case of the rare ownership decision, other executives should be consulted as much as is practical, because their insights will contribute to sound judgment. This is particularly true in assessing the impact of a decision on the organization. However, it is neither necessary nor wise to pretend that the decision will be made by the executive group in the same way that major operating decisions are made unless that is actually the case.

SOME PARTICULAR SITUATIONS AS THE WORLD CHANGES

Changing the Corporate Direction

The world and the corporate environment change constantly. Some of the changes come with startling rapidity. Once in a great while changes in fundamental corporate direction or philosophy may be required.

The process of changing the corporate direction can be either hindered or helped by the fact of being a family business. Which it will be depends on how the chief executive and the family group regard their special identification with the company. If they are emotionally involved with a certain aspect of the business, or with a certain way of doing things, or a particular image, this can be a great impediment to changing those areas when change is needed. However, if they identify with the process of change, with being flexible and progressive, their leadership can be particularly influential in directing the organization away from ideas they formerly espoused and have been identified with.

> ADVICE: *Don't let yourself get overinvolved in your own mind, and identified, with a particular idea, approach or direction. Be identified with it fully so long as it is appropriate, of course. But let your overriding identification be with progressiveness, adaptability, and the ability to recognize and adjust to the changes that occur constantly around us.*

It's Not Your Business Any More!

After a period of time even a family business makes at least a partial transition from the private possession of the chief executive (founder) to the property of others. If stock has been sold to even a limited number of people, they have the right to expect management that will be primarily concerned with enhancing the value of their investment.

Even if no stock has been sold, after a generation or two there will probably be family members who have inherited stock but who are not in the business. They have similar rights to expect management to be primarily concerned with their investment.

> ADVICE: *Whenever your own motives and desires are in conflict with the welfare of the business and the stockholders, resolve the conflict in the direction of what is best for the business and all its stockholders. Be brutally honest with yourself about your own motives. If you personally cannot tolerate what you recognize to be best for the company, turn the reins over to someone who can take the business in the necessary direction.*

Succession

The key concepts for succession in a family business are objectivity and planning. If you have a family member or group of family members who can run the company very well, you need not be squeamish about making that choice. People will expect it. And there are advantages of continuity and confidence and involvement in family management. But if you do not have a really competent family management to succeed you, realize that everyone will be better off if you choose a competent nonfamily person to be in charge.

The hard part is to be objective about your own descendants. Trust the evaluations that honest people in the company give you. If the potential successor does not have the respect of his associates, it is because he has not earned it. The matter is that simple. And he has not, therefore, qualified for leadership, since earning the respect of one's associates is one of the necessary prerequisites for leadership. Have the courage, if necessary, to face the bruised feelings of those who are disappointed. This is one of the real tests of your own competence. If you don't have the courage to make this choice objectively, you are not a fully competent chief executive. This evaluation should be an ongoing process over the years, not a sudden decision to be made when the event is at hand. Because it takes longer to grow a successor than to hire one, and because fate sometimes intervenes unkindly, family management succession must be planned further in advance than in a nonfamily business. Twenty years ahead is not too far to be doing some preliminary thinking about possible successors. This has the corollary advantage of leading to earlier and longer involvement of the future management, making for depth and orderly transition.

> ADVICE: *Succession must be professionally competent. Family succession is fine, if it is good. Otherwise, pick someone good. Be very objective. Recognize that objectivity in this decision is one of the major tests of your own competence. Respect the evaluations of associates. Plan far, far ahead.*

Civil War—when the Family Falls Out

Deep and lasting discord among the family is one of the two special potential disasters in a family business. (The other is nepotism, or the promotion of incompetent family members to top leadership.) If you have a serious family fight, don't look here for easy or happy solutions. There aren't any.

Perspective can be important. This isn't the first time it ever happened. Or the worst such experience. Examples are in the press every year. And do you remember Adam & Sons? That earliest family agribusiness suffered considerably when intense rivalry arose between the son who managed the Crops Division, and the son who managed the Animal Husbandry Division. Similar troubles once beset Denmark, Inc. There, also, family squabbles resulted in a considerable loss of top-management personnel.

The damage can be lessened if the areas of disagreement can be limited to differences of judgment and policy, and personalities avoided. Explicitly reminding oneself and the others of the large amount of common interest that exists can help keep the differences in perspective.

> ADVICE: *The only important advice about serious family fights is to avoid them, at almost any cost, short of irreparable harm to the company. If one is unavoidable, try to limit the damage by keeping the perspective and discussion to issues, not personalities. A mutually-respected outside arbiter or advisor can sometimes be helpful. And if one person or group has to depart, try to see that it is done in a mutually fair way, minimizing the harm to the company.*

Are You Mediocre?

Is that an impossible question to answer about oneself? Perhaps. But you can get some clues. Mediocrity can arise in a number of ways. Lack of talent. Lack of drive or motivation. Motivation which is misdirected toward goals other than the professional success of the business. Or the passage of time; a very competent executive can become less so if he fails to adapt his ideas appropriately to change.

> ADVICE: *Use as much formal analysis as you can. Let the numbers tell you as much as possible about what is working and what is not. How does your return on investment compare with others? How is your rate of growth? Be particularly suspicious of what is comfortable, or pleasurable, your fondest boast. Ask yourself what your organization's real strengths are, its real weaknesses.*
>
> *Question: Do other executives tell you when they think you are wrong? If not, you aren't encouraging them properly to do so. You really don't think you are always right, do you? Or that they always think so? Or that people don't enjoy expressing their own ideas when they feel secure in doing so?*
>
> *A useful exercise: Pretend that you are one of the two contenders for the vacant job of president. Each of you is presenting his program to a board of directors which truly represents the stockholders. They are asking, "What have you done for us lately? What will you do for us tomorrow?" The other fellow is aggressive, has given a lot of thought to how to make the company grow, become more profitable. Imagine what his program is. And imagine that you describe to the board your present plans and program. O.K.? Did you get the job?*

What to Do about Your Own Mediocrity

If you come to the realization that your own leadership is mediocre, what should you do about it? Well, you really already know the answer to that, don't you? There is no dishonor in recognizing one's own limitations. Quite the contrary. The decision to remove oneself in favor of someone better is one of the classiest examples of character and integrity that a man can exhibit!

If you helped found or build the company, you are entitled to appropriate continuing rewards. These can be in the form of pay, fringe benefits, respect, even a symbolic title. But you are not entitled to continue running the company when another executive or team could clearly do it better.

ADVICE: *If you arrive at the conclusion (or even a strong suspicion) that your results are mediocre, decide whether you want to retire or to try to improve. If you want to give it one last try, put yourself on probation. Set a definite time period, perhaps a year. Set precise, measurable goals. And tell someone you trust and respect what you have decided. And stick to it.*

When the time comes to retire, you should recognize it before the others do. That should be a source of pride to you. Let the objective selection of the best possible successor be another source of pride. You will then have ended your executive career on a very high professional note.

SUMMARY—EVEN A MEMBER OF THE FAMILY CAN BE A PROFESSIONAL

You can be a professional manager. Just expect of yourself and other family members the same excellence you would expect of a top-flight, nonfamily executive. Consider: training, motivation, objectivity, integrity.

Train yourself and other family members for the profession of business management as you would for the professions of law and medicine. For the family member newly out of college, this means the best graduate school of business administration he can get into. For older family members, it may mean one of the shorter courses for middle-management at those same institutions. For all, it means continuing study to maintain professional competence.

Align your motivations with professional criteria for the success of the business. Would you choose a career in medicine with the goal, "I want to become a mediocre doctor?" Of course not. Nor would you in law, teaching, or the arts. So don't do it in the profession of business management. Be first rate in your chosen field. Run a very successful company.

Objectivity will be a special requirement for a chief executive of a family business, because the family ownership partially shields him from the usual consequences of incompetence. So make a special effort to evaluate other family members and particularly yourself with complete objectivity. And then take the action appropriate to your evaluation.

Yours is a family business. Face the special advantages and special requirements of that fact with integrity and openness, and with a fair regard for the legitimate expectations of the family and nonfamily executives and stockholders. You will take advantage of the strengths and limit the potential weaknesses of being a family business.

As the head of a family business, you have a great opportunity. You have an opportunity to achieve prosperity for yourself, for other members of the family, and for nonfamily people in the business as employees, executives, and stockholders. You have an opportunity to contribute to a successful enterprise. And you have an opportunity to achieve the special satisfaction that comes from knowing you have handled a challenging job with high professional excellence. Don't waste those opportunities!

REDUCTIONS IN FORCE

by Daniel J. Haughton
Chairman of the Board, Lockheed Aircraft Corporation

MY OWN management experience has been confined to the aerospace industry. Whatever else it is, aerospace is an excellent way to qualify any executive as an expert in workforce reduction. I know of no other industry, with the possible exception of construction, that can match ours in terms of employment fluctuations. Aerospace industry employment levels react dramatically to a wide variety of circumstances—changing national defense and space budgets, international political and technical developments, new directions in national policy, the rise and fall of airline reequipment cycles, and other factors. Not only does the industry as a whole experience these peaks and valleys in employment but individual companies within the industry normally have their own ups and downs. Loss of a major follow-on contract can mean mass layoffs or even plant closings. Program stretchouts may mean a more gradual but equally severe drop in employment. We have had plenty of both.

NEED FOR DECISIVE ACTION

So I have to plead guilty to a great deal of experience in presiding over workforce reductions, and I hope I have learned something from it all. One fundamental lesson is worth stressing right at the beginning. It is this—unpleasant as it is to have to get rid of people, when necessary, you must do it quickly, decisively, and thoroughly. There's no good in putting it off or taking halfway measures.

This doesn't sound like any profound discovery, and of course it isn't. I imagine most executives will find it an obvious truth. But, obvious as it is in theory, it's not always easy to apply in practice. There always seem to be reasons why you should drag your heels.

291

Maybe business will pick up. Maybe we shouldn't be too anxious to break up good teams. Maybe we should go slowly to avoid cutting too deep. Maybe we ought to try to hang on to our people for a while, especially our good people.

There is, of course, something to be said for all these arguments. I'm not suggesting that there aren't times when it is worth keeping excess people temporarily in anticipation of new business. Nor am I suggesting we have no responsibility for trying to retain employees. What I am saying is that it is always easy to find some reason to avoid an unpleasant duty, and reducing the workforce certainly comes in that category. But, no matter how hard it is, we shouldn't yield to the temptation to let anything get in the way of sound business practice. The chief executive's first responsibility is for the health and preservation of the enterprise, and if getting rid of excess people is the way to maintain that health, then that is what he must do. In this case as in so many others, the businesslike approach turns out to be the most responsible approach. And the most humane one. By getting rid of some people, you save the jobs of others. It is going to do nobody any good if the whole enterprise collapses.

In our corporation and, I am sure, in most corporations, reduction of direct employees—those employees whose time is charged to specific contracts—is almost automatic. Normally, direct jobs are broken down into standard hours, easily converted into a head count. Careful and continual tracking of actual hours against standard hours and forecast hours almost automatically signals the need for workforce changes. With tracking performed at frequent and regular intervals, there should be no lag in reducing direct manpower in concert with declining workloads.

Where the problem usually comes is in indirect or support services, services that are not automatically controlled and that in any case have a way of building up like barnacles on a ship. A good scraping is useful at any time. In time of declining business it is imperative.

Tom Jones, president of Northrop Corporation, uses a dramatic example to illustrate the consequence of not moving rapidly enough to reduce indirect costs along with reduction in direct cost. Suppose, he points out, you are faced with a sales reduction from $100 million to $50 million over a year's time. And suppose also these sales include a pretax profit of 7 percent and that remaining costs are equally divided between direct and indirect. If you reduce indirect costs along with direct, operating income for the year will be $5.3 million. If you delay the decision to reduce indirect costs by just two months and then reduce them at the same rate, year-end operating income will be $2.7 million—down by about half. And if you delay four months, you end up in the red![1]

The lesson is obvious—you have to go after these indirect people and you have to go after them fast. Of course you will get objections from outraged department heads who insist their own functions are absolutely necessary to the enterprise or that they can't possibly get along with fewer people. Most functions may well be necessary. There may even be some that cannot safely be reduced. But I maintain a healthy skepticism in both areas and insist on proof, and I would advise any Chief Executive Officer to adopt the same seemingly hardheaded attitude. Without it, things quickly get out of control.

Aerospace companies generally establish ratios of indirect to direct labor as a way of controlling indirect labor costs, which may come to as much as 50 percent of all indirect costs. These ratios understandably differ from company to company and even from plant to plant. In my own corporation, for example, we have some divisions with 8 percent indirect labor and others that run as high as 59 percent. The trick is to find the ratio that is appropriate for your own organization and then to stick with it. I have sometimes been accused of being too inflexible in applying these ratios, and maybe I am. But I would rather err on the side of too much control rather than too little. I have seen too many examples of good systems invalidated by variances justified by good intentions.

ALTERNATIVES TO REDUCTION

"Get More Business"

Ideally, we would all just as soon avoid the necessity of layoffs. With this article in mind, I asked one of my associates if he thought there was an answer to the layoff problem and he replied, "Sure, get more business."

It's not quite as glib an answer as it sounds, and we ought to think about it before we dismiss it lightly. It suggests at least the need for advance planning to attempt to see trouble before it arrives. Back in the late 1960s, when my own corporation could foresee a decline in national defense spending and was faced with the decision of whether or not to try to get back into the growing commercial airliner business

---

[1] "Managing the Controllable", an address before the Armed Forces Management Association's 17th Annual Conference; Los Angeles; August 21, 1970.

with a new airplane, we recognized that one of the benefits of doing so was that it would help us keep some of our plants open and provide jobs for an otherwise declining workforce. I am bound to say that this was not a conclusive reason for our decision. On the other hand, it is inescapable that today's business decisions do have a profound effect on tomorrow's workforce, and the better those decisions are, the less we will need to be concerned with force reduction in the future.

Along with other companies, we try to look ahead some five or ten years to see how the situation looks for established product lines and to determine whether we should be in new ones. In the time period closer to hand, we track existing workloads closely against new business prospects. I don't mean to suggest that this solves all our problems, but it does help us obtain and schedule work to relieve employment fluctuations.

Other Strategies

There are other strategies. Subcontracting can help avoid undesirably high workload peaks, and in times of declining business it is often possible to bring subcontracted work back into your own shops. Contract labor is another device. We have used this technique with particularly good results in the case of engineers, for whom our need is greatest in the early design phase of a new aerospace vehicle and then declines to a sort of maintenance level as the vehicle moves into fabrication and assembly. Supplementing our regular force with contract engineers has helped us get the job done without the necessity for layoffs after it is finished. It's an extension of the Kelly Girl concept to engineering, an idea that I think deserves greater consideration.

When these and other techniques are insufficient, as they often are, it is sometimes possible to effect minor workplace reductions without resorting to layoffs. Some employees may be encouraged to take early retirement. Others may be transferred to other divisions or plants within the organization. Excess employees may even be loaned to other companies. A few years ago we developed an industry program to lend excess people back and forth to other companies in the industry to smooth out peaks and valleys. These loaned employees remained on their original company payroll and retained all seniority, benefit, and other rights during the period of their employment in the borrowing company. The lending company simply billed the borrowing company for their services.

Planning

Much of what I have been discussing about avoiding or minimizing the need for workforce reduction comes under the heading of manpower planning—forecasting manpower needs, planning for effective use of manpower, conserving it when it is possible to do so. Manpower planning is not a panacea, but it can help alleviate manpower problems, including layoffs, and it seems to me a vital part of the chief executive's job to see that this kind of planning takes place. It is just as important as planning for the use of financial, plant, or other resources.

WHEN THE CRUNCH COMES

Still, no matter how carefully you plan, there always seems to come the day when you are hit by the unexpected. Two recent examples stand out in my own experience. In 1971 our commercial engine supplier, Rolls-Royce Ltd., went into bankruptcy with no previous warning. It hit us immediately and very hard. We were forced to halt production on our new L-1011 commercial jet transport and lay off some 9,200 people in our Southern California plants within a matter of weeks. Though Rolls-Royce later resumed engine production and we were able to start up the line again, the disruption to our operations was extremely serious—something it took us a couple of years to recover from completely. Much of this disruption, of course, came from the necessity to rehire and retrain people in all manner of classifications. It made me realize once again the extreme damage that sudden mass layoffs can do and the importance of doing everything you can to avoid them.

The second example is even more recent. Late in 1973 we experienced a serious cash flow problem as a result of some airlines deferring deliveries on their planes, continued high jetliner production costs, soaring interest costs, and some other problems. As a result of this we instituted an emergency "action plan" in which we established a 20 percent manpower reduction goal for our Lockheed-California Company and corporate offices, to be achieved within six months. We examined every operation to determine if we needed it at all and, if we did, how deeply we could cut into it without losing its effectiveness and without endangering our remaining operations or immediate sales prospects. It was a purely judgmental exercise in many cases, based on rock-ribbed premises and involving hardnosed evaluations. I am sure that we may have cut too deeply in some areas —an error we later corrected—but, on the whole, it was an extremely successful operation. It was successful not only because we set up definite goals and established the mechanism to achieve them, but primarily because we insisted on its being done with no excuses, no variations, no exceptions, no special consideration for rank or title or anything else apart from the basic guideline of need. This kind of insistence, I am convinced, is the key to success in most campaigns of this kind—and it is a job that falls right on the chief executive's shoulders because he is the only one who can make it work. It isn't enough to have a system, even the best system in the world. As the top man, you have to commit yourself to see that the system is made to work.

DANGERS TO AVOID

No reduction in force should be undertaken, of course, without giving consideration to the long-term effect. In the case I mentioned above, short-term needs were crucial, and we did in fact reduce long-term functions to a dangerously low level. However, we did so with full consciousness of what we were doing and with full realization that, once the crisis was past, we would probably have to strengthen some of these activities later.

One obvious long-term danger is the dilution of technical and managerial strength. Any organization is built around people, and there is always a core of key people who, I believe, must be retained even in the most trying circumstances. Most of you will recognize this as the "heartland" concept. In our corporation we go to great lengths to identify these high-potential people and to keep them on whatever our problems. We did so in the rather serious reduction I have just mentioned, and I think if we had not, we would have seriously compromised our entire corporate future.

A second danger, especially in deep reductions, is that of producing an undesirable distortion of the work force age structure, particularly in managerial and technical areas. Usually this distortion is toward the side of an overage workforce. The natural tendency is to release those with least experience and seniority, who are of course usually the youngest. And there is often a corresponding bias to retain the older and more experienced. This bias, I might add, is an understandable managerial failing. It is the supervisor or department head who is usually faced with the tough decisions of whom to keep, whom to let go. And if his choice is between a youngster with no family responsibilities and an older employee whom he has known for years and who is struggling to support six children, it's not hard to guess where his sympathies are going to lie. Letting one bright young man or woman go is not going to hurt the company's future. But letting 50 or 100 or 500 probably will. To prevent this from happening I think it is essential, especially when mass reductions are involved, to have these supervisory decisions reviewed at higher levels where there is a broader viewpoint and less emotional involvement.

Perhaps a word of caution is in order here. It is of course illegal to discriminate against older employees in layoffs or any other work situation, and the federal government appears to be putting increasing emphasis on enforcing this law. Just recently, as I write this, Standard Oil of California has agreed to pay $2 million in back wages to older employees laid off between 1971 and 1973. It may be too early to assess the implications of the law or its interpretation in other cases, but I believe almost all executives would agree with it in principle. I do not believe it should constitute a serious bar to maintaining a balanced age structure. Qualifications to do the job remain a basic and legitimate test, and I think we can always count on the young to be competitive. I think it is quite possible to maintain a properly age-balanced workforce in ways that are equitable and not discriminatory.

I have been talking about areas, chiefly managerial and technical, where you have a choice. But where union-represented employees are concerned, you have no choice. Layoff procedures are spelled out in union agreements, usually in some detail, and these procedures almost always protect the employee with high seniority. With all the problems this entails—and we have had cases where complicated bumping rights have replaced entire work teams as many as two or three times in a month—old industrial relations hands point out that there are undoubted advantages in having mutually agreed-upon procedures, applied under the watchful eye of the union. In fact, one of my associates maintains that without them a mass layoff would be chaos. I keep an open mind on this, but I am realist enough to recognize the advantages of union participation as well as disadvantages, and I am sure the wisest course by far is to work closely and cooperatively with the union. It saves you a lot of grief.

RESPONSIBILITIES

I view the chief executive's job as one of fulfilling responsibilities to a number of groups—stockholders, employees, management, customers, suppliers, the community, and the nation. Often the interests of these groups come in conflict as they make competing claims on the corporation's resources. This is certainly the case in times of workforce reduction, and though I have been emphasizing responsibility to the corporation and its future, there are other responsibilities that simply cannot be overlooked.

One of these, certainly, is to the employees—those who remain and those who are leaving. I think we can best exercise our responsibility to the first group by effecting the reduction with as little confusion as possible and as little disturbance to their morale as possible. Communication plays an important part here—communication about the reasons for the workforce reduction, communication about its nature and extent, and communication about the company's position and prospects after the reduction is accomplished. Perception of fairness in the layoff procedure is also a must even for those unaffected; it's an unsettling event for everybody, and equitable handling buttressed by good communications is a fine prescription against possible morale problems.

For those who have been caught in the reduction much can and should be done. Perhaps we have a special responsibility here. It is easy to forget what a devastating experience a layoff can be to the individual. It strikes not only at his income but quite often at his sense of personal worth and sometimes brings real tragedy in its wake.

At the very least, laid-off employees deserve an explanation of why they are being laid off and a thorough explanation of such important matters as their reemployment rights, benefits from the company, and unemployment compensation.

Actually, they deserve much more than this. What they really need is help in finding another job. Many large corporations, including those in the aerospace and airline industries, do this routinely. When the airlines reduced employment drastically in response to the fuel crisis late in 1973, many of them went to great lengths to find employment for laid-off employees. Eastern Airlines credited newspaper ads and special placement offices in five cities with producing 1,000 job listings. TWA obtained numerous job offerings for secretarial, clerical, sales, and engineering people. Pan American's ads in five papers drew 3,000 responses.[2]

In our own corporation we routinely extend a vast amount of job placement help. During our 1973–74 layoff we got in touch with about 100 companies, developed job opportunities lists, counseled employees on writing resumes, scheduled group presentations and individual interviews with representatives from other companies, worked with state and local agencies as well as technical associations, and even held job help seminars. A Lockheed booklet providing advice on job hunting has been adopted for widespread use by a number of technical associations and other companies. I am not sure all of this is enough, but it is just about as much as we can possibly do to help in a bad situation, and I am sure we would never be satisfied with doing less.

Finally, there is the community to consider. A mass layoff or even a plant closing in a large city may have a minimal effect on the community, but it's a different matter for a small town that depends on your operations. For such a town a plant closing can be a disaster.

Back in the early 1950s my own company along with other aerospace companies established some large jet aircraft assembly operations in Palmdale, a small town of about 7,000 in the Antelope Valley north of Los Angeles. With the cooperation of enthusiastic—sometimes overly enthusiastic—townsfolk, a large expansion got under way to take care of the influx of new employees. Hundreds of new homes were built; new businesses moved in; and facilities like schools, hospitals, and recreation areas were increased. Several years later the aerospace industry entered one of its dry periods, and some of us had to close down our activities there. Houses stood empty, supporting businesses declined, school attendance and revenues dropped off sharply, and the town was left with large problems and bitter memories. Fortunately it survived, and today we are back with a civilian aircraft program that has solid promise of being enduring.

Although we tried to phase out our operations in as orderly a way as we could, and although we were able to place some of our people in a remaining aircraft company there, there was not a lot we could do to alleviate the problem. Looking back on it now, I think the time to do something is before collapse happens. We should perhaps have made it plainer to civic officials and leading businessmen that aerospace was a very uncertain business and that it was imperative for them to try

---

[2] *Wall Street Journal*; February 19, 1974.

to expand their industrial base by bringing other types of business in. We could perhaps have tried harder to help them do this during the years we were there. But the hard fact is that no company is in a position to avert serious damage to a small community when it is forced to pull out. The best it can do is to try to withdraw in an orderly fashion and with adequate explanations, and perhaps maintain a presence in the community afterwards to try to help solve some of the problems its withdrawal has created.

Priorities: Business and People

I mentioned responsibilities a little earlier. The necessity of force reduction brings the whole matter of priorities among responsibilities into sharp focus. There is no question that first priority must be assigned to the needs of the business. This means that people must be treated as a resource along with other resources like money, materials, tools, plant, and equipment.

Treating people as a resource is a difficult thing to do, especially in these times of emphasis upon human values and the organization's responsibility to provide opportunities for self-fulfillment. Nevertheless, the business leader must of necessity take this point of view— and so, incidentally, must leaders in other fields, who are sometimes called upon to sacrifice the good of the individual to the good of the whole. It is hard decisions like this that leadership is all about, whether it is in statescraft, the military, athletics, or business.

And yet, if we are required to look at people as a resource, we must acknowledge that they are our most important resource. One of our prime concerns in force reduction certainly must be to keep our "people resource" functioning well and efficiently; and this is why I think it is so important to retain a hard core of key people, make sure layoff procedures are fairly conducted and perceived, communicate openly and frankly about the need and the method, and try to maintain a high level of morale and motivation among those who remain.

Self-interest as well as basic human considerations dictates we must extend every consideration to those who are being released. The way we treat these people will have a tremendous effect upon our reputation in the community and among our remaining employees. Our ability to fill future manpower needs will depend to a large extent on how well we deal with people in times of force reduction.

What it all boils down to is treating people as what we always say they are—our most important resource.

PART III
Corporate
Strategy

THE CHIEF EXECUTIVE AS CHIEF STRATEGIST

by Marvin Bower*

McKinsey & Company, Inc.

CURRENTLY, and in the years ahead, no responsibility of the Chief Executive Officer of any business is more important than strategic planning. So the CEO should know what strategic planning is, why it is important, and how he should approach the task.

As used here, "approach" does not mean the mechanics of strategic planning (which are usually given too much emphasis anyway) but rather how the CEO should (1) think about strategy; (2) provide conceptual and day-to-day leadership for strategic planning; and (3) ensure that strategic plans are not only formulated but carried out. In view of forces operating now and in the years ahead, business success —even business survival—will depend in large measure on how well the CEO does his strategic job.

NATURE OF STRATEGIC PLANNING

The very definition of strategic planning not only demonstrates the importance of this managing activity but also suggests how to approach it successfully. Planning—any kind of planning—is decision-making: deciding what to do; how to do it; at what time, speed and cost; and with what investment in time, manpower, and money. As always, the chief executive can think of himself in his dual role of decision maker and leader (but leadership also involves decision-mak-

---

* [Ed. Note: Marvin Bower is a consultant with McKinsey & Company, international management consultants. From 1950 to 1967, he was managing director of the firm. His practice has been concerned with strategic planning for some of the largest national and multinational firms in the United States and Europe. Mr. Bower is recognized as a leader of the consulting profession. He is author of *The Will to Manage*; New York: McGraw-Hill; 1966.]

ing). Strategic planning, however, is only one phase of corporate planning; the other phases, including budgeting, can be grouped as operational planning.

The term "strategy," of course, comes from military science, and relates to generalship and maneuver. The dictionary defines it as "the science and art of employing the political, economic, psychological, and military forces of a nation or group of nations to afford the maximum support to adopted policies in peace or war." This military definition can be converted to business terms: Strategic planning is the science and art (chiefly the latter) of deploying all the resources of the business (men, materials, money, and management) in achieving established goals and objectives successfully (e.g., profitably) in the face of competition.

The military definition suggests an important ingredient for business strategy: concern with fundamental issues, both external and internal, which affect the business as an integrated whole. The CEO not only has responsibility for thinking about the business "as an integrated whole" but is in the best position to do so; and he should do this in terms of fundamental (not trivial) external and internal issues.

The CEO should, therefore, identify the company's market opportunity; understand its present and potential resources, strengths, and weaknesses; recognize the aspirations, personal values, and sense of public responsibility, of the key executives; and determine how company resources can (within limits and restraints that cannot be removed) best be fashioned into an effective strategy. The resulting strategic plan becomes a framework for decision-making throughout the company. With such a framework, the management no longer needs to let the business drift with the tides of its environment. Through established managing processes, it can better control the destiny of the enterprise.

If there is no overall plan to guide decision-making and action, the company's destiny will be determined by ad hoc operating decisions. Each executive will simply tell his people what he believes they should do, based on his personal understanding of what seems best. Thus, the destiny of the business will be determined by a multitude of individual decisions which will inherently jell into an overall company or division plan. Even worse, company destiny will be shaped by individual *reactions* to competitive thrusts—in effect by the decisions of *others*.

In recognition of these realities, during the past decade there has been an upsurge in the determination of top managements to develop strategic plans that will reduce corporate drift, avoid simply reacting to competitive thrusts, and help to control the destiny of the business. As a consequence, most major U.S. companies have some form of systematic strategic planning.

But no system of planning will be effective unless the CEO himself thinks deeply about the business as an integrated whole; stimulates others to do that, too; and exercises the will and the leadership to ensure that specific plans are made *and* carried out. Only then can the management hope to control the destiny of the business.

This role of the CEO is well summarized in these words of Professor Kenneth R. Andrews of Harvard Business School, an authority on strategic planning:

> The strategist is concerned with combining what a company *might do* in terms of alternatives discernable in the changing environment, what it *can do* in terms of resources and power, what it *wants to do* in terms of management values, and what it *ought to do* in recognition of the responsibility of the private firm to society.[1]

STRATEGIC VERSUS LONG-RANGE PLANNING

The sophisticated CEO should know the difference between *strategic* planning and *long-range* planning. These terms are not synonymous, because "long-range" refers to the time dimension rather than the type of planning. Strategic planning is, of course, concerned with the long-range development of the business, but a sound strategic plan may call for immediate action, e.g., divestment of a losing division or product line.

Unfortunately, too, "long-range" plans have typically taken the form of relatively useless profit projections, often extending as much as ten years ahead. And often these plans involve large amounts of paper work and limited amounts of strategic thinking. Use of the term "strategic planning" in a company will usually stimulate more productive thinking about the fundamentals determining business success and how they should govern decision-making.

---

[1] From "New Developments in Corporate Strategy"; speech to Harvard Business School Club of New York; May 27, 1968. This concept is developed more fully in Mr. Andrews's book *The Concept of Corporate Strategy*; Homewood, Ill.: Dow Jones-Irwin, Inc.; 1971, which every CEO should find conceptually and practically worthwhile.

PHASES OF STRATEGIC PLANNING

Strategic planning for a particular company is concerned with the development of *courses of action* that are "contrived"—in the literal sense—or determined to be the best for that company in present and foreseeable circumstances. The strategy must then be communicated throughout the company so that people will follow the plan in making day-to-day decisions. Unfortunately, strategic planning terms are neither precise nor uniformly used. But there can be agreement within a company on what the terms are to mean there. Some suggestions follow.

Setting the Goals

The dictionary treats "goal" and "objective" as synonymous. But the individual management group can decide to use each term in a different sense. There is value in doing so. I personally find it useful to think of a goal as a long-term, probably unattainable, purpose or mission that is sufficiently worthwhile to encourage people to commit themselves to its attainment.

The first goal to fix upon is the kind of business the company should pursue, such as manufacturing a particular class of products or providing a particular type of service. Thus Xerox, an office copier manufacturer, entered the educational field through an acquisition. So did IBM. Exxon entered the motel business in Europe through internal expansion. In all three cases, the "goals" of the company were changed.

Usually the goals of a manufacturing business will be concerned with leadership in serving customers (i.e., consumers and other ultimate users) with particular types of products and with growth in volume, share-of-market, stature, and profits. In a PepsiCo, Inc., top-management seminar, Andrall Pearson, the president, put it this way: "We must develop distinctive goals that will separate us from all other successful multinational corporations. . . . In my experience, behind every outstanding organization is a set of unifying goals or concepts which give it distinctiveness, consistency, and impact."

Some form of growth is usually an advisable goal in order to attract, hold, and motivate high-caliber people—the ones best able to achieve the goals.

Determining Objectives

The value of using "goal" *and* "objective" in different senses is found in using "objective" as a secondary or subgoal geared to the primary goal. The goal may be unattainable—the North Star on which eyes are constantly fixed—but an objective should be an attainable subgoal. As part of the overall strategy, an objective is established as a step toward the goals, usually to be completed within a specific time, such as a specified increase in share-of-market within a specified time.

Strategies

Both goals and objectives should be supported by strategies for achieving them. For example, the objective of increasing share-of-the-market by a specified percentage within a specified period should be accompanied by a strategic plan giving specific ways by which this increase is to be attained, together with the capital and/or other costs for achieving the expected results. These strategies should not be generalities but realistic ways by which part of the market volume can be wrested from competitors.

In fashioning a strategy there should be a careful evaluation of company resources and capabilities for carrying out the strategy. Does the company have the technological competence to improve the product in the specified period? Does it have (or can it employ) the executive ability? Does it have the financial resources? An overestimation of the "can do" will lead to failure or frustration.

Sub-Planning Units

Usually better results will be obtained if responsibility for strategic planning is fixed below the corporate level. This may be done at the division level if it is a single business (i.e., a single grouping of products and markets) or at the level of some other grouping if it is not.

The General Electric Company uses the term "strategic business unit" as a label for such groups. In a speech at the University of Chicago (November 3, 1971), R. H. Jones, now GE chairman, defined the "SBU" in substantially these terms: A grouping of products and markets which: (1) has a unique business mission independent of any component; (2) has a clearly identified set of competitors; (3) can be strategically planned relatively independently of other SBUs in the company in terms of products, services, markets, facilities, and organization; and (4) for which the general manager can be given authority over (and hence can be fairly held accountable for) the activities crucial to its success, including (as a minimum) technology, marketing, manufacturing, and cash management.

The general manager of the SBU should present the SBU's strategy to his CEO in terms of alternate courses of action, i.e., more than one way of achieving the SBU's goals and objectives. This provides the CEO with a better basis for evaluation and better enables him to contribute to strategic decision-making.

Although the SBU concept helps the CEO break down strategic planning into a more manageable task, the CEO must be the chief strategist. And certainly he should not be content with a company strategy that is simply the sum of the SBU strategies. He (perhaps with the assistance of a small staff) should determine, on his own, what the *overall* company strategy should be. And it may call for divesting an SBU which is no longer advancing the company toward its goals; for developing, or acquiring an entirely new SBU which offers opportunity; and for nurturing a new and promising SBU. The CEO (with staff assistance) is responsible for determining where corporate resources can best be invested, considering the relative long-term profitability of each SBU; in which one resources should be increased, held steady, or reduced; and which, for any of a number of reasons, should be divested or liquidated.

THINKING ABOUT STRATEGY[2]

If the CEO is to be the company strategist, he should train himself to think deeply and conceptually about the business and how to translate his thoughts into goals, objectives, and strategies. In any business the best thinking can be done in terms of the ultimate customer—the consumer or other user. This approach—which makes the marketing function the competitive cutting edge of the business—focuses on specific reasons why the ultimate user should buy the company's product rather than the products of competitors.

This user-strategy will be most effective if fact gathering and thinking are concentrated on four strategic elements: (1) product performance; (2) service; (3) brand acceptance (or confidence in the com-

---

[2] See my book, *The Will to Manage;* chapter 3; "Strategic Planning: Shaping the Destiny and Competitive Cutting Edge of the Business."

pany); and (4) price. If the user does not recognize authentic reasons for buying the company's particular value combination of product performance, service, and brand acceptance, then the company will have to price the product lower. Put another way, a competitive price is simply a reflection of the relative combined competitive strength of product performance, service, and brand acceptance—the company's particular "user-value package."

This approach does not mean that marketing dominates everything —certainly the research and development, manufacturing, personnel, and finance functions are important, too. The concept of making marketing the competitive cutting edge of the business simply means that strategic thinking begins with thinking about the customer or user. Who makes and/or influences the ultimate buying decision? What is —or can be—the relative influence of product performance, service, brand acceptance, and price on the ultimate buying decision?

Product Performance

The company should typically seek superior product performance that the consumer or other user can easily detect for himself. Distinctiveness in product performance is usually the best way to ensure strategic advantage. This can be done through one, or a combination, of three basic approaches:

1. Becoming a creative, technological leader—aiming to be the first in the industry to discover, develop, and market new products at the leading edge of moving technology. This strategy will usually call for a heavier investment in research and development than that of other companies in the industry.
2. Becoming an early imitator and adapter of successful innovation by industry leaders. The entry must be early, or the company will enter the market so late as to encounter the inevitable price-reduction phase of the market.
3. Becoming a low-price, low-cost producer, sacrificing the high margins (and high risks) of innovation for the high volume (and limited risks) of low-price imitation. (In any strategic approach low-cost manufacture is, of course, a desirable ingredient.)

Basically, the customer (ultimate user) buys a company's product (or service) because it will do more for him than competitive products—give him more tangible benefits, more intangible satisfactions, and (overall) greater value.

Service

Customers may buy a company's products because it, or the company organization, provides better service—more convenience, more objective help in buying the product, more help in using the product, better deliveries, and better return or repair service when product performance is unsatisfactory to the user. International Business Machines bases its strategy not only on superior product performance but also on better service all along the line.

Service strategy is frequently used for commodities and commodity-type products. But superior service also strengthens the strategy of companies with distinctive products. For example, General Foods and Johnson & Johnson have developed superior warehouse and delivery systems.

Brand Acceptance

Many companies, especially well-established ones, can base their strategies, at least in part, on the confidence of potential customers in the company itself. This confidence is developed through prior successful experience with other company products; through advertising that establishes a quality image which is backed up by good product performance; and through effective product performance and good service over time.

General Motors and General Electric have developed broad public confidence in their companies that enables them to launch new products with greater chance of success and to get better customer understanding when product performance is unsatisfactory.

Price

Unless a company can offer some other competitive sales appeal, it must depend on price to ensure customer value. Lower prices, narrower gross profit margins, and lower return on investment are competitive penalties that any business must pay if it cannot give the user a competitive value-package in some other way.

Thus the CEO of the company or the general manager of an SBU should look first to the research and development and marketing functions—working together—to provide specific reasons (other than price) why users should buy the company's products rather than the products of competitors.

EXTERNAL FORCES WITH SIGNIFICANT IMPACT

Every company should plan its strategy to cope with major external forces. As examples, here are nine major forces that have gathered momentum during the past decade and that promise to continue at work far into the future:

1. Broad and urgent demand for improving the quality of the environment.
2. Serious drain on the nation's natural resources.
3. Further expansion of consumerism.
4. Changing social attitudes and values.
5. Growing involvement of government in business decision-making.
6. Growing sense of social responsibility in business decision-makers.
7. Continuing increases in foreign competition.
8. Continued growth of the multinational (or transnational) corporation.
9. Increasing tempo and impact of technology.

Collectively these forces have substantive and diverse impacts on most companies. They are more than sufficient to illustrate a suggested approach.[3]

First, it is important for the CEO to recognize that ours is indeed a technological society. It is difficult to identify any major force that either is not a direct result of technology or has not been indirectly influenced by it. The atom bomb, jet travel, instant communications (telephone, radio, TV), the Pill, and the automobile are obvious examples of major technological causes or influencers of major forces with which society and every business must cope. Coping with forces such as these will involve changes in a company's strategy, structure, policies, and management style. By learning approaches for coping with these nine forces, a company will be prepared to deal with almost any external force that may be detected.

---

[3] A suggested approach to coping with forces such as these is developed more fully in "Gearing a Business to the Future" written by me and my partner, C. Lee Walton, Jr., Section Four of *Challenge to Leadership: Managing in a Changing World*; a Conference Board book; New York: The Free Press; 1973.

As the chief strategist, the CEO is the executive who must ultimately be responsible for keeping the business adjusted to the external forces affecting the business. And to do so successfully in today's and tomorrow's world, he must constantly "think deeply," "think forward," and "think outward." Even in his attention to current activities (which is also essential) he should concentrate on those that have *future impact*.

Each external force should be analyzed in a deep, factual, and tough-minded manner; and specific decisions should be made on how that particular force will affect the company as a whole or the SBU. Then specific plans should be made on how to cope with that force and, if possible, capitalize on it.

The CEO should see that every relevant external force is really grappled with—not overlooked, disregarded, or treated as something that will "go away." Since relevant forces will have their impact anyway, procrastination in dealing with them usually means that the company loses some of its decision options.*

INTERNAL DEVELOPMENTS AND FORCES

Most CEOs are more comfortable in looking inward than outward. Even so, major internal developments and changes in attitudes and values are often overlooked as factors to be considered in formulating corporate or SBU strategy.

The best approach to dealing with internal factors is to focus first on people: What developments, what changes in attitudes and values, will affect the capacity of the company to attract, hold, and motivate capable people? For example, there is considerable current public discussion of the lowered motivational value of the work ethic, and it is claimed that interest in acquiring material wealth is being eroded by a greater interest in the quality of life outside of work. If the CEO concludes that these forces are indeed real factors in motivating his people, can he develop the strategy, policies, and style of management that will gear the business more fully to worthwhile goals and objectives that will better motivate company people?

These social changes are difficult to assess and measure in the particular company; and it is even more difficult to make decisions that will cope with them effectively. But the CEO, as chief strategist,

---

* [Ed. Note: See the chapter by Alexander Calder, "Strategy and Planning: Some Personal Observations of a Chief Executive."]

should treat every significant internal development and identifiable change in people's attitudes and values as a factor to be weighed in changing corporate or SBU strategy.

ILLUSTRATIONS OF SUCCESSFUL STRATEGIC PLANNING

The CEO's role as chief strategist can be illustrated more concretely through experiences of companies that for some years have emphasized strategic planning as a managing function.

Xerox

Strategic planning emphasis in this company is reflected in a statement in 1963 by Joseph C. Wilson, president and CEO, who put the goals of Xerox in these words:[4]

> For the long term, that is, for the time more than five years away, we seek to be a leader throughout the world in the field of graphic communications concerned particularly with copying, duplicating, recording, and displaying images primarily of documentary subjects. We intend to find new ways of seeing and sensing images, of copying and duplicating them, of sending them, and recording them. Therefore, at the very heart of our business are the processes of imaging.

Then he stated the shorter-term objective in these words:

> . . . to be a leader throughout the world in the applications of xerography to the field of graphic communications. We also intend to be a strong participant in the field of documentary reproduction through the use of silver halide photography, the business on which we were founded. Throughout this time, of course, we will be seeking to take advantage of unusual and unforeseen opportunities.

Financial objectives were established as "seeking to grow in sales and profit at an average rate of 20 percent annually and earn more than 15 percent on net worth."

Mr. Wilson then outlined the strategy for achieving these goals and objectives in these words:

> In general, our plan to attain these ends is based on philosophy. Through developing, making, selling, and servicing reliable products and services of high quality, we want to offer new and worthwhile

---

[4] From a speech to the Investment Analysts Society of Chicago; February 28, 1963.

values. It is important for you to understand the breadth of this objective. Our prime policy is to conceive, invent, develop, make, sell, and service—the whole gamut. Through the attainment of these objectives, we hope to enlist the devoted loyalty of a sophisticated group of shareholders and creditors. Through sound, yet progressive and creative employment practives, we want to make Xerox an attractive place for the best people to work.

We have adopted a series of written operating policies to gain these ends, of which the most significant perhaps are these:

—We shall be guided by our customers' needs, not wedded to a particular product or process or technology, not even xerography itself. This requires a great effort intellectually to determine customers' needs and to translate them into compatible concepts perhaps before the customers are aware of them. We must continue to use imagination to identify products and services, like the 914, which are a giant step or two ahead of the services others are providing.

—We intend to maintain an aggressive, well-trained sales and service organization, backed by imaginative, powerful advertising and sales promotion.

—Another of our basic policies is to maintain a creative, strong research, development, and engineering organization and program and to spend about 10 percent of sales on research.

—We expect to grow primarily through the development of our own products, although acquisitions of companies or products will be sought to complement or supplement our present activities.

—We intend to continue a progressive, competent, quality and cost conscious manufacturing organization, capable of making complex, mechanical, electrical, and optical equipment and highly-specialized supplies requiring sophisticated chemical and physical techniques and to carry out these activities in modern, well-equipped plants.

—We are planning and operating now with a worldwide concept. Our opportunities overseas are not less promising than those in North America and we intend to serve well the surging economies throughout the rest of the world.

The new products and services which we intend to offer will in general have these characteristics:

—They must fill an important existing or clearly defined future need of business or government. We may well expand our business to include consumers by the way. They will be highly profitable for a reasonable time. Our targets are lofty; 30 percent profit before taxes on sales and a return of 20 percent on investment.

—We prefer that they be compatible with our present methods of distribution through our own sales and service organization operating within the business equipment industry.

—We are seeking services and products which are not subject to early obsolescence, for example, that are protected by patents or by know-how or by unusual advantages of distribution.

—This next is perhaps the most important point of all. We are seeking products and services with clearly defined substantial advantages over those of others. We have learned through the lesson of the 914's great success that large reward comes to him with the wit and courage and skill to plow new ground. We are not seeking products like those already offered.

It will be noted how closely this strategy follows the general principles discussed earlier. The record of Xerox shows how effective dedication to basic principles can spell success.

In 1970, the Xerox strategy was reaffirmed and further advanced and refined by the next president and CEO, C. Peter McColough, who put it this way:[5]

The basic purpose of Xerox Corporation is to find the best means to bring greater order and discipline to information. Thus our fundamental thrust, our common denominator, has evolved toward establishing leadership in what we call "the architecture of information."

We are still dedicated to growth and to technological innovation. Our belief in a direct marketing force concerned principally with the customer's problems it must solve, rather than with the product it sells, remains firm. And perhaps more important is our continuing conviction that we must provide an internal environment in which the full talents of the individual can be realized, recognized, and rewarded.

We seek to anticipate and to serve valid human needs profitably and within the scope of our strengths.

And although it might appear that we are now an organization offering multiple services in multiple markets and nations, there can be found beneath the surface of our efforts a common denominator, a concept, if you will, which defines our business, guides our actions, and sets our goals.

Xerox today is a company of extraordinary vitality, central to that much-discussed phenomenon called "the knowledge explosion."

Thus two CEOs of Xerox thought deeply about external and internal factors and developed specific goals, objectives, and strategies

---

[5] From a speech, "The Architecture of Information," to New York Society of Security Analysts; March 3, 1970.

for coping with them and capitalizing on them—and then made the strategy effective in day-to-day operations.

Texas Instruments

More than a decade ago, Texas Instruments (TI) began to formalize management philosophies with a principal system entitled, Objectives, Strategies and Tactics System (OST). (The company treats "goals" and "objectives" as being synonymous.) Mark Shepherd, Jr., president and CEO, has said:

> The first and most important precept is that the objectives of the enterprise must be clearly defined, must be stated in measurable terms where possible, and must be realistic but challenging. Without clearly stated objectives, progress cannot be measured and meaningful performance values are impossible.[6]

Mr. Shepherd went on to state, "Strategies for these objectives must be carefully conceived and clearly stated. . . . Strategies provide the 'how' to go with the 'what' of the objectives."

Third, priorities must be defined for objectives and strategies, and the people who will carry out the plans must be involved early and often. Then regular management reviews must be held to modify plans as needed. Resource allocations must be balanced between long-range and short-range goals, because "without adequate controls, short-range requirements tend to capture more than their rightful share of resources."

Finally, Mr. Shepherd said, the consequences of intermediate results must be evaluated in terms of their future effect on the total system—that is, everyone involved must be aware of each individual accomplishment and change in conditions so that revisions in strategic plans can be made.

In TI, the planning of research and development is an integral part of the overall business planning system, and R&D planning flows naturally from the statement of objectives.

The OST system is a structure of considered goals at all levels, backed by strategic courses of action to achieve these goals. Instead of having SBUs, TI has product-customer centers (PCCs) which "operate like complete small business organizations with each PCC man-

---

[6] From a speech, "Innovative Management in the Management of Innovation," at the 1st International Process Conference; Tokyo; October 1970.

ager having responsibility for the creative marketing and manufacturing functions to serve a particular class of customers in specific product areas."

Mr. Shepherd said that TI is trying to preserve the environment of the decentralized product-customer centers, but at the same time to knit them tightly together with an overall goal structure. "A major role of the general management is to shape the goal structure toward opportunities and problems which are the right scale for the total corporation."

The TI approach to management is strongly focused on performance and results to achieve objectives in accordance with prescribed strategies. This is accomplished in a number of ways, including the coupling of R&D to business planning and by involving R&D personnel directly in the planning process. The monthly profit and loss statement for each PCC shows actuals incurred versus the plan for both operating and OST expense categories. Strategic plans are stated in measurable terms so that performance can be monitored through management reviews.

General Electric

Under the leadership of Fred Borch, who was then chairman and CEO, GE undertook an intensive effort to improve strategic planning. Four senior vice presidents, who formed the corporate executive staff (CES) were charged with "the specific responsibility of helping to shape the future thrust and organization of the company at the corporate level."[7]

Their joint task was to formulate and recommend corporate objectives and to identify resources and other considerations that need to be committeed in view of economic threats, human and financial resources, technologies, and legal and political restraints in meeting these objectives.

Another responsibility of the CES was to shape the company's responses "to new social and environmental thrusts, soundly based within a competitive framework. . . . The trick is to accommodate these requirements within a competitive cost structure, while continuing our old job of improving our present products and developing new ones."

---

[7] *GE Investor*; vol. 1; no. 5; 1970.

Using this approach, GE top management keeps track of the growth opportunities and profitableness of the many SBUs, so that resources can be allocated to the most profitable ones and the least profitable divested or liquidated. At the same time, the Corporate Executive Staff helps the CEO establish a total corporate strategy which is not simply a sum of the strategies of SBUs.

As in the case of Xerox and TI, GE places strong emphasis on managing performance and monitoring results to ensure that corporate and SBU strategies are carried out effectively. And Reginald H. Jones, the succeeding chairman and CEO, who had a major part in establishing GE's strategic planning program, is following through to ensure its effectiveness.

Alcon Laboratories

This company, much smaller than the others discussed, follows the same basic approach to its strategic planning. William C. Conner, chairman, and CEO, has said:

> We're not a company to follow the crowd. We found out early what works for us, and have stuck to our basic philosophy for 25 years. . . . Alcon has established a record of outstanding growth in this span of years. You must suspect that we have developed a strategy of survival and growth that contains certain specific elements and a philosophy which permeates clear-eyed, self-assessment and which governs the overall pattern of how we operate.[8]

The chairman added that the company goal is to remain a publicly owned, independent company "with full opportunity to pursue our aspirations and plans . . . by continuing to be successful. This independent course will mean greater personal opportunities for employees and higher capital appreciation for our shareholders." The company's goal also includes "growth in sales and earnings per share at rates which outperform the industry averages."

The president, Mr. Schollmaier, explained that, "Since we are a relatively small company in a large-company industry, we have no intention of slugging it out with the marketing heavyweights." Instead, Alcon concentrates its marketing efforts on clearly defined, relatively

---

[8] From a presentation by Mr. Conner and Edgar Schollmaier, president, to New York Society of Security Analysts; October 25, 1972. [Ed. Note: See the chapter by W. C. Conner and E. H. Schollmaier, "Updating Organization Structure to Conform to Facts of Growth, Increased Complexity, New External Constraints."]

small, specialist-oriented market segments, both with pharmaceuticals and with other closely-related lines.

The president said: "This is what we call our 'think small' concept. No matter how you define a market, it can be subdivided by some characteristics into smaller segments. . . . [By] concentrating entirely on such relatively small market segments—as Alcon has done—it is possible to achieve a dominant position over a period of time."

The president explained that in the field of opthamology Alcon has carried this strategy several steps further by adding other requirements of that field, surgical products, electronic diagnostic instruments, contact lens care products, and the like to the marketing program. "At the same time," he said, "we have carried the strategy to 77 other countries, becoming the largest supplier of ocular therapeutics in the world."

In developing this strategy, Alcon recognizes its limitations. The president explained: "Frankly, we lack the resources or size necessary to undertake major basic research, so we give top priority to highly specialized product development activities in the specific health care fields where our marketing efforts are committed. Because of this approach, we have some of, and will have more of, the world's top scientific experts in our speciality fields working at Alcon."

The Alcon strategy includes an active program for seeking out products originated by others, but which fit into its specialized fields. In this effort there have also been selective acquisitions. "We select for acquisition and merger very carefully. We believe Alcon's objectives and capabilities should determine our acquisitions—not the other way around."

Alcon's strategy also calls for divestments. "We are much more concerned with what kind of company we are than with how large we are. Therefore, we are not averse to divesting parts of the business that become inconsistent with our overall objectives."

As in the case of other successful companies, Alcon emphasized execution. "Managerial accountability is clearly defined and fully accepted; and we work to make results consistent with committed expectations. Much of Alcon's success stems from this approach."

SUMMARY OF APPROACH

These illustrations confirm that successful strategic planning requires conceptual and intuitive thinking; perception of external and internal forces at work and analysis of their significance to the enterprise; imagination to perceive market opportunities; realistic evaluations of the company's resources, strengths, and weaknesses; correct assessment of the personal values, aspirations, ideals, capabilities, and even the interests of key people; and, finally, the judgment to bring forth from the various alternative courses of action that are the fruit of these intellectual efforts an optimal, specific, realistic, and attainable strategic plan.

These illustrations also confirm that when the intellectual work has been completed, the managing work must continue. There must be the will, the decisions, and the leadership (in Alcon's words) "to make results consistent with committed expectations."*

---

* [Ed. Note: See the chapter by John D. Glover, "Strategic Decision-Making: Planning, Manning, Organization."]

STRATEGY AND PLANNING: SOME PERSONAL OBSERVATIONS OF A CHIEF EXECUTIVE

by Alexander Calder, Jr.

Chairman, Union Camp Corporation

UNDER THE well-known doctrine of "The Buck Stops Here," the Chief Executive Officer is ultimately responsible for all company functions and activities; but his responsibilities as chief corporate planner are more specifically and uniquely his for the simple reason that anyone else in the organization would be severely handicapped in tackling many of the most important aspects of the job. Unless the CEO is intimately involved in strategy formulation and planning, it is difficult if not impossible for anyone else to accomplish much in these areas.

Without further specific documentation at this point as to why the chief executive must be the corporate planner, let's examine the key facets of the planning job. Such examination will inevitably provide further documentation.

THE CEO'S ORIENTATION TO THE FUTURE

In the first place, planning must necessarily involve trying to visualize the shape of the world decades ahead. One doesn't create a corporation to operate five or ten years or even a few decades and then liquidate. From the point of view of stockholder, employee, and customer alike, it should be a continuing thing. The determination of opportunities, avoiding hazards, and goal-setting generally clearly involves trying to understand and anticipate change—and we have long been told that one of the few certainties is that change is inevitable. Therefore the chief planner must be aware of Toffler's *Future Shock* or Kahn and Wiener's *The Year 2000* or their counterparts.[1] He does

---

[1] Toffler, Alvin; *Future Shock*; New York: Random House, Inc.; 1970; and Kahn Herman; and Wiener, Anthony; *The Year 2000: A Framework for Speculation on the Next Thirty-Three Years*; London: Macmillan Company; 1967.

not have to agree with their conclusions, but he must have gone through the discipline of knowing why he doesn't agree and in the process reached other conclusions which he finds more plausible. In a word, he must get in the game of being able to "visualize change."

Not only need he be able to visualize change in the world at large; the CEO needs to be able to answer "So what?" kinds of questions about changes he believes are coming: "What does this, what does that mean for our company?" In a word, the CEO must be a dealer in *implications*.

Getting Others to Participate

Let's assume the chief planner has achieved some concept of the shape of things to come. Does this mean he sits right down and writes his corporation's long-range strategic plan? Hardly. Heavy inputs are necessary from many avenues. Within the company, the whole "top management team," division managers, corporate marketing, R&D— all are valuable sources of ideas. A good board of directors' varied skills and backgrounds is another excellent source. However, the chief planner (i.e., chief executive) must test, probe, refine, and ultimately crystallize this material into the goals and programs for reaching them that constitute the plan. Getting himself and his principal colleagues oriented to the future is an important step.

An Eye to the Future in Day-by-Day Operations

It is often asserted that strategic planning is a vital corporate necessity, and I believe this to be true. However, an often overlooked result from planning is that the mere discipline of constructing a strategic plan has the byproduct benefit for all concerned, starting with the CEO, himself, of developing the information and insight necessary to do a good job of making the myriad operating decisions which confront a corporation day by day and year by year. Certain guideposts emerge which are useful in the process.

INVOLVEMENT OF PEOPLE

It is evident that forming a sound, well-conceived plan is only one facet of the chief executive's task as corporate strategist. He must also ensure that the plan is put into action; a key element here is people.

Lack of the proper skills and experience in a company and the manner in which talent is deployed within the organization can be as big a block to attaining an important corporate goal as shortage of raw materials, government restrictions, or whatever. At the same time, I believe few would argue against the thesis that one of the chief executive's key responsibilities is building the organization and determining how it should be structured. Although we all have personnel departments which make important professional contributions to effective company operation, the chief executive must realize that he is in effect the chief personnel officer. And only he can provide the model, the incentives, and—if need be—the pressure of example to get others involved.

At this point, it might be well to emphasize a second important point in carrying out a corporate growth program, the communications aspect of planning, and at the same time provide another documentation of the chief executive's indispensability in the function. The implementation of the best strategic plan is impossible unless the board of directors understands it and backs it. They hold the purse strings. The chief executive is responsible to the board for the operations of the company and therefore has to be the key man in developing board understanding and backing of whatever course the company is to follow.

In addition, it is equally clear that the organization itself must understand what course they are supposed to be following. An important corollary to this is that an organization operates most effectively if it understands the reasoning behind a given direction rather than just blindly trying to follow an edict from the front office. The chief executive is by definition "The Boss"; but perhaps more importantly he— or she—must also be the leader and inspirer. To get the entire organization to understand what they are striving for and why and that it all makes sense is a communications job of critical importance. This, the chief executive cannot delegate.

Although we all complain that there are too many meetings in our corporate existence, I have found that regular gatherings of a key management group with the chief executive on a not overstructured basis is a must in communicating where we are going and why. This is an important part of the whole strategy-making process. Just filtering "the word" down the organization chart doesn't seem to work all that well.

ALLOCATION OF CAPITAL

Strategic plans obviously vary all the way from very general selections of potential areas of growth to very specific plans which spell out just how this growth should take place and how fast. Whatever type plan your corporation has, the heart of positive implementation rests upon the allocation of capital. Whether your corporate plan is very specific or merely generally directional, the annual capital expenditure budget itself sets priorities. This again emphasizes the chief executive's responsibility, because it is he who must determine which of all the capital expenditure requests are to be recommended to the board for approval. Most companies try to plan this capital allocation on a long-range basis by developing five-year operating plans for each major activity complete with the estimates of the capital required to carry out these plans. The further out in time this planning goes, the more it is subject to change.* The point to be made, however, is that, again, the chief executive by assigning priorities in the allocation of corporate capital is the key to positive implementation of corporate strategic planning.

OBTAINING THE CAPITAL FOR
IMPLEMENTING STRATEGY

In addition to providing the orientation toward, and interest in planning for the future, to getting people involved, and to allocating capital for purposes called for by the strategic plan, the CEO must take a leading part in getting the capital funds. This entails dealing with the difficult question of "creating" the capital pool to be allocated. Here, the element of risk becomes a vital consideration. What is the responsible limit to the use of debt in creating this capital pool? In terms of timing, when should the more difficult avenue of increasing equity be utilized? Although he will draw upon the views of many people, the CEO's own judgments in this area are decisive. The use of debt-to-equity standards is undoubtedly necessary in order to give the rating agencies (Moody's, Standard & Poor's) certain guidelines to develop a common denominator for appraising the risk of any debt issue. However, a word should be said about the vagaries of balance sheet accounting in the development of these ratios. The forest products industry is only one example of where the asset values of land and timber as shown on the balance sheet are understated to

---

*[Ed. Note: See the chapter by Hershner Cross, "Capital Project Approval."]

the tune of hundreds of millions of dollars. This of course distorts the debt ratios which are perhaps too often used as immutable standards in determining whether a company is overextended. On the other side of the fence, for reasons growing out of its long history of government control, the railroad industry is probably an example of the overstatement of balance sheet assets. The CEO in making such judgments must draw upon a deep knowledge of the economics of his industry as well as certain prevailing attitudes in financial circles.

REEVALUATION AND REALLOCATION

Closely allied to the process whereby strategic priorities are affirmed through capital appropriations is the obvious requirement that strategic plans and projected allocations of capital funds must be constantly reappraised and altered in the face of changing conditions. The tremendous surge of environmental concern in the past few years, together with the emergence of such concepts as "zero growth," for example, would certainly make any company in the land development business—among many others—go back and reappraise its goals. The energy crisis and the prospects of substantially higher costs for energy from all sources will have a substantial impact on future prospects for many industries.

The CEO must show himself as flexible and ready to take the lead in such reassessments that become necessary because of external events.

I think few would disagree with what I just said about the need for reappraising strategic plans in the light of changing conditions. It is perhaps equally obvious that there is a timing advantage in recognizing an incipient change before it has already become the new way of life—but that is much easier said than done!

I have found that the hardest types of change to visualize are those that go against my own most deep-seated convictions. For instance, our company has been buying land and regenerating forests for decades in order to create a perpetual source of raw material for our basic paper and wood products. The cost of doing this can be calculated and the resulting values created can be estimated within fairly reasonable tolerances, even though the time frame is a long one, many years, in fact. What can upset this apple cart?

Not long ago, one of my associates wondered out loud whether a private company would be allowed to own and operate millions of acres of timberland 25 years from now—and if not, was it smart to continue to tie up scarce capital in this manner? My mental reflex is one of outrage at such a thought because of a deep-seated and long-standing conviction that private ownership of property is at the heart of the free enterprise system and our country's future.

But the fact is I only have one vote in our political system and seem to be getting out-voted more and more of late. Yet, as a responsible chief executive of a sizeable corporation, I must build our company's strategic plan on what is likely to happen, not what I believe should happen. Current land-use legislation now being introduced in the Congress may be just the beginning. The potential pitfall of going along with wishful thinking rather than with hard-headed objective thinking is real and omnipresent in the life of a chief executive. One way to guard against it is simply to be acutely aware that it is a pitfall and understand yourself well enough to know why. Another safeguard is to avoid surrounding yourself with associates who all have similar political and sociological philosophies.

Another aspect of the need for constant reappraisal of corporate goals is the ability and willingness of the CEO and his associates to measure objectively results of current corporate activities. This is obviously not possible without adequate financial controls. An accurate periodic review of the return on investment performance of all company operations is the name of the game. This, among other things, requires a realistic appraisal by the CEO and his people of the company's uses of capital employed in the business. This review should include receivables and inventories, as well as plant and equipment. Adequate financial control also requires that evaluation by the CEO and his executives of return on any investment be interpreted according to the degree of risk involved. For instance, the return on investment in a very technical business with a high obsolence factor should be much greater than in a relatively stable commodity-type business.

With the proper financial tools to work with, the CEO has to demonstrate his own willingness to respond to the facts presented. If he does, others will find it easier and more appropriate to do so. No matter how plausible a corporate endeavor may be in concept, it must, of course, show results within a reasonable length of time. Either that, or the CEO and his team will have to alter the strategic plan and admit that a mistake has been made. Here again, the chief executive must be aware of the potential pitfalls of letting his own predilections create "sacred cows." Pray for objectivity, be aware of the danger, and beware of yes-men among your associates.

Obviously, what constitutes "a reasonable length of time" can vary from a matter of months to many years, depending on the nature of the business. The effect of other variables, such as an unexpected adverse change in general economic conditions must also be measured and adjusted for. Realistically weeding out unsatisfactory operations as well as emphasizing the growing successful operations, therefore, is a vital aspect of the CEO's pattern of actions taken in implementing the strategic plan. These significant steps will be reflected in the capital allocation process.

NEED FOR ADAPTABILITY

A word of caution about the plan. Fully recognizing the benefits to be derived from corporate planning, the chief executive nevertheless should remain adaptable and exercise caution over allowing the function to become unduly institutionalized and bureaucratic. It is a mistake, of course, for an organization to cling too rigidly to a plan simply because it does exist. It is up to the CEO to take the lead in showing the organization that there is a place for rational and calculated opportunism and adaptive creativity. A company loses something if a fair sprinkling of its top people lose the instinct to pursue a new idea, a technical innovation, or an uneexpected acquisition opportunity simply because it might represent a substantial departure from the existing road map. The CEO can set a tone that can help ward off that danger.

SUMMARY

In summary, the chief executive has the responsibility of managing the investment of capital made by the stockholder. The stockholder is looking for rewards in the form of dividends and stock price appreciation in some reasonable relationship to the inherent risks of the enterprise. The management of capital assets is necessarily a long-term operation. And because it is, and because we hope that the corporation will be a permanent part of our industrial structure, the need for strategic planning becomes fairly obvious. When you pause to think about a number of important facets of the planning job, it becomes clear that the chief planner and the Chief Executive Officer really have to be one and the same person.*

---

* [Ed. Note: See the chapter by John D. Glover, "Strategic Decision-Making: Planning, Manning, Organization."]

INTEGRATION: PUTTING THINGS TOGETHER INTO LARGER WHOLES

by Bert E. Phillips
President, Clark Equipment Company

THIS CHAPTER is about corporate growth through integration, a path that has become increasingly difficult for businesses in the United States as a result of governmental intervention under the antitrust statutes. The whole subject is strewn with public policy issues, economic theory, and ideology. Issues are raised concerning the acceptable trade-offs in a particular industry between "lowest cost," large-scale production and distribution on the one hand and maintenance of the extent of "competition," as indicated by numbers of competition, ease of entry, innovation, and consumers' brand choices, on the other hand. The thoughtful chief executive will want to consider such matters as he contemplates the strategic and growth options available to him—especially expansion through integration. My purpose in this chapter is to address briefly some of the less lofty but crucial factors which a chief executive needs to take into account if and when he considers taking his company down the path of integration.

My comments mainly will be on vertical integration, both backward and forward. Horizontal integration, being fairly uncommon in today's U.S. economy, is not touched upon, although I recognize that some kinds of international growth can be viewed as a form of horizontal integration.

BACKWARD AND FORWARD INTEGRATION

My first question concerning integration of any kind is "How much money do you have?" In a world (excluding OPEC nations) that is rapidly becoming aware of the pervasive problem of capital generation, that question is more than an academic one. Naturally, if you haven't the *means* to integrate, you can't integrate. And even if a company has funds available for integration, using them for that particular purpose can preclude other, and perhaps more advantageous investments that could be made.

The goal of business strategy should be to multiply the opportunities available from application of the productive resources of the company. The question of integration can rarely be considered by itself. It must be studied in comparison to alternatives. Admittedly, there are many temptations that lead us to constantly review the integration question: scarcity of suppliers, cost, and quality, as well as fear of missing an opportunity for profit.

In its start-up and major growth phases, a business normally absorbs more money than it can generate. During such periods it does well to stay out of integration. As the business matures and becomes better established, it can begin to think of integration.

Backward Integration

Backward integration represents a decision to produce rather than to purchase materials or processes which enter into the cost of production of existing products. A popular reason, at least today, for integrating backward is to guarantee a source of supply for production. Another reason may represent an attempt to convert an internal cost center into a revenue producer. In either case, the decision to integrate backward should not be undertaken merely because the costs of production compared to the cost of buying outside show a decisive saving. One cannot ignore the fact that resources will be absorbed which can be used elsewhere, and that integration of new activities will eventually increase total fixed costs.

Substantial savings can be realized, however, as a result of increased production efficiency achieved through a steady flow of supplies of the right quality, and in adequate amounts, at the time they are needed. There is an additional benefit to be attributed to the security of knowing that the business can operate more efficiently in the face of material shortages and general economic uncertainty.

Most companies (in fact, all but a few of the largest in each industry) must recognize, however, that supplies of components often can be obtained at the lowest cost from manufacturers who can specialize in a single product line and thereby develop the volume necessary to reduce unit costs. This specialization is also likely to be associated with an expertise that is probably lacking, or is at least at a lower level in the purchasing company.

Forward Integration

Forward integration is said to be simply the extension of the business toward the market. But it often is employed as the solution to the problem of entering into new markets. Breaking into new markets usually requires the allocation of additional resources to selling, for if new products cannot be sold by an existing distribution network, then new resources may be required. And if new selling techniques must also be developed for the new channels of distribution, then substantial costs may be incurred. There may be real advantages to having the next stage "downstream" within the domain of the company. But here again, capital is required which probably has alternative possible uses.

Many businesses are constantly frustrated by the necessity to delegate their distribution function. I imagine that automobile company executives are frustrated by some of the criticism heaped on them; criticism that should properly be directed toward inadequate or poorly run dealer service. Except for the capital required, perhaps they are sometimes tempted to establish their own retail outlets. I am sure that the move would be a mistake, and I am equally sure that they know it. But be that as it may, their frustration must often make direct factory sales a temptation.

THE DECISION TO INTEGRATE

Frequently, it seems the decision to integrate backward or forward stems from an emotional base rather than good judgment. It is easier to control vital sources of supply for production if you bring them in-house. Or, if you currently purchase a component economically but cannot obtain custom specifications that are required in a given product line, then you may want to produce it internally.

Similarly, a decision to integrate forward through a dealer organization may arise from a sense of frustration with existing channels of distribution. Or, in the case of a new product, it may be better to assign it to a different dealer who will make the necessary effort to break into new markets. A problem that may arise in using an existing dealer setup is that the new product line may crowd out an existing one, so that the new business generated may be merely a trade-off for existing sales. Acquiring a dealer organization for such a purpose may be appealing. But there are also problems to think about.

Even though a company that integrates backward or forward in a sense stays in the same industry, integration often means moving into areas in which it has little or no previous experience. The company diversifies its activities. It acquires new skills, but it assumes new problems and new risks.

I believe that the decision to integrate is best preceded by a thorough analysis of the industry and the competitive market climate in which a company finds itself at a given moment in its history and in the forseeable future toward which it appears to be moving. But particular emphasis needs to be given to the analysis of the market structure. Whether or not the decision to allocate resources to new activities will be profitable for the company depends on changing supply and demand conditions in a marketplace somewhat downstream from where the company may be most familiar. The risks and uncertainties inherent in any decision regarding integration can be somewhat mitigated by a marketing-oriented audit of the company's situation.

Some Questions

Questions that might be posed in attempting to evaluate the company's strengths and weaknesses for potential growth opportunities include the following:

What is the size (and growth) of the business?

What is the size (and growth) of the industry?

What is our "right" size and growth rate?

What do we need that we do not now have in order to reach that size?

How mature is the industry in which we compete?

What is the maturity of our product line?

Are there potential new applications for these products in the markets we serve?

Are there additional markets that we should enter?

What are the financial and competitive risks we would incur?

What are our particular strengths?

Do we have a specific competitive technology, marketing expertise, or service?

Do we excel?

If not, is there a new dimension that will add to our following in the marketplace?

If we already hold a leadership position, can we defend it?

This list, which is certainly not complete, should suggest to the CEO who is considering an integration step the kinds of questions he will want to pose so far as his own company is concerned.

Thorough analysis is called for, and that requires time and effort and, perhaps, money. What is right for one company can easily be wrong for another. It usually depends on the company's size and resources as to how much it can spend in its effort at analysis. For a small burgeoning organization, obviously the ability to analyze a potential product or market is limited. Perhaps the intuitive judgments of the founder or the officers may be sufficiently reliable. But a large company with a good image and a reputation for quality, and with momentum in the marketplace—to say nothing of sizeable investments—needs extensive analysis lest it endanger all of these things by a precipitous move that fails to produce desired results.

Faced with a difficult situation, such as severe material shortages, a company may at times see no alternative but to integrate backward to protect the lifeline of its production. Thus, today, many companies are considering adding foundries because of the shortage of castings. However, if running a foundry lies outside a company's capabilities, it may still be wise to pay a premium price in the marketplace for the scarce commodity. Many companies resort to long-term purchasing arrangements rather than integrate to solve such problems. This practice is especially popular in Japanese industry.

DEVELOPMENT OF CLARK EQUIPMENT

Clark Equipment is an example of an integrated, multiproduct company which might be used to illustrate some of the points I have just presented. Over 70 years ago, we were founded as an axle and transmission supplier to the original equipment market (OEM) for trucks and heavy duty machinery. We capitalized on this basic technology, in which we had good market acceptance, to expand forward into the market as a manufacturer of industrial forklift trucks. Later, we entered into the construction machinery market, and we have expanded in that market through both internal growth and by acquisition. Although the materials handling business is distinct from construction equipment, having different customers and different distribution channels, the "core" of the product consists of the same or similar drive-train components.

We continue to refine our axle and transmission technology today, and, I am pleased to say, we have won recognition for the advances we have made in these basic components. We continue to supply the OEM market with these products in addition to providing our own internal requirements.

The Decision Not to Produce Engines

By similar logic, we discarded the option of integrating backward to manufacture engines for our product line. The financial burdens of entry into this business, as well as the fixed manufacturing and administrative costs we would take on, were major considerations. In the final analysis, we determined that, even apart from the capital investment, there was the probability that we still could not produce the wide variety of engines required for our machines in volumes and at costs that would be efficient. We believe that decision is still valid, even though we have experienced severe production problems from time to time because of capacity limitations of our primary engine suppliers. To offset future interruptions in the flow of our own production, we have sought and received commitments from alternate sources to increase their shipments to us so that we will have more flexibility.

The Timber Skidder

As a multiproduct company, Clark Equipment has some product lines that are relatively new; others are approaching maturity. An example of a new product would be our timber skidder which is actively participating in the growth of the forest products industry. That new product represents an outlet for some of our basic capabilities.

Developing Overseas

There is evidence that the lift truck is approaching maturity—at least for certain models and for certain markets. However, the potential for electric vehicle growth and the overall potential in other countries would still qualify the lift truck as a growth business.

Often when a product reaches maturity in this country, it is still a new product and in the missionary stage in overseas markets. In 1955, when we decided that we should expand overseas, we had limited funds at our disposal. In view of that limitation, the simplest way for us to go abroad was to set up licensees in each country, product by product. We obtained a disclosure fee in setting up the licensee agreement, and we often used that fee to buy an interest in the license, taking an equity interest that varied from 2 to more than 40 percent. This move represented, for us, a forward integration into new markets.

Later, as the markets developed, it became apparent that our licensing agreements were somewhat unilateral in the sense that we could not demand that the licensee grow at a pace that would match the growth in the market. We could only try to encourage him to do so. This encouragement was often expressed by our demonstrated willingness to invest more money in the operation. By these additional investments, we began to acquire larger and larger interests in the licensees until finally we acquired full ownership and began to operate them as wholly-owned subsidiaries.

MANAGEMENT PROBLEMS TO CONTEND WITH

Identifying—and then developing—the full potential of a business is psychologically difficult because it is usually opposed from within. It means breaking with old-established habits of mind. Searching for opportunity naturally exposes a company's vulnerabilities, limitations, and weaknesses, and is likely to be resented by some of its most accomplished people as a direct attack on their position, pride, and power. Therefore, it is essential to draw as many key people as possible into an analysis of the potential direction of a company, as a means of achieving consensus. This process is essential to growth and sometimes even essential to survival.

A business that is not fully integrated in the marketing function could decide to expand its channels of distribution to include a retail dealer organization. Some negative feelings on the part of "old line" company managers may be encountered because such a step will make it necessary to delegate authority and responsibility in the marketplace to a "third party," the dealer. Accordingly, it is necessary to establish controls to carefully monitor channels of distribution that will now be "in-house" to make sure that the goals you set will be accomplished. Otherwise, unfortunately, the dealers may be likely to concentrate their efforts toward areas of their own self-interest—what is easiest, and what they know best, and what may produce the most income for them—in conflict with your goals. For example, they may not allocate sufficient effort to the task of opening up new markets, which was a major reason for integrating forward in the first place.

Another major management problem encountered in integration is the risk that the autonomy of separate organizations may be diminished. This occurs because of the increased need for coordination between entities. There is much to be said for autonomy and freedom of action. The identity of people or groups of people is often lost in the layers of management put in charge of the larger integrated operation. To forestall this, many companies attempt to utilize the profit center approach. The profit center is designed to divide the organization into units that can be more easily identified.

AFTERTHOUGHTS

Apart from considerations within the company that must be analyzed prior to making a decision to integrate, it is necessary to evaluate the state of the *industry* for potential opportunities and threats. As companies grow at different rates, so do industries. In one industry, a few large firms may dominate, while another comprised of small companies may have no leaders.

It has become obvious that one of the outstanding characteristics of an industrialized economy is the dominant position in the economy as a whole occupied by a relatively small number of large firms. There is little to suggest that this trend toward concentration will diminish. The larger producer should have lower costs; frequently, this then becomes an effective barrier against the smaller firms' entry into the market.

Where there are substantial advantages of large-scale production to be obtained, the entry of smaller, usually higher-cost producers, into an industry will be possible only if the rate of expansion of the larger firms is below that necessary to answer demand. And smaller producers can still be eliminated when, and if, the larger firms do expand, especially after the initially high rate of growth of the industry starts to decline.

Large firms moving into new areas usually find a limited choice of new products which offer adequate returns. Thus, the move toward diversification often means that traditional competitors find themselves in intensified competition in new fields, as oil firms move into chemicals, steel firms into shipbuilding, soap producers into cosmetics, and so on.

Integration into international markets is a good opportunity for U.S. manufacturers to strengthen product technology, expand distribution channels, and to find new customers and applications for their products. The key to success is still management—judgment, willingness to accept political and competitive risk, and a commitment to provide the necessary financial resources to do the job.

Expanding into the market by means of integration can be a build, buy, or joint venture decision. The strategy that will work best for one company, may not work for another. We return to the original premise that integration must add to the overall profitability of the firm and enhance its competitive position.

Having spoken of expansion and integration, perhaps it may be appropriate to conclude with a few words about the opposite: divestment. More companies probably should consider the possibility of making themselves more compact—and more profitable—through getting rid of operations "upstream" or "downstream." In many cases, profitability, overall, can be improved through such a move.

Operations that do not "fit" should be abandoned. Even a profitable business should be kept only if: (a) it is found to be truly an attractive investment for the long term and promises at some point to generate cash; (b) is compatible with the overall strategy of growth; and (c) truly exploits the basic technology of the company.

There is an old saying that "Wise men do immediately what everyone else does eventually." When a company can no longer support an unprofitable or really lackluster operation, or when it identifies a part of the business that has no technological "fit" with the whole, or where there are much better possibilities in other directions, then it should make the decision to get out of it. Sometimes management delays the inevitable for a long time. But there have been cases where untold millions of dollars and good deal of grief could have been saved by biting the bullet somewhat earlier in the game.*

---

* [Ed. Note: Chapter by Albert H. Gordon, "Getting Out of a Business; When and How."]

THE CEO AS ENTREPRENEUR

by Charles D. Tandy

Chairman of the Board and Chief Executive Officer,
Tandy Corporation

I WISH that this book had been published earlier. Several of its chapters would no doubt have been helpful to me in making decisions which are now history. Take, for example, the chapters on international business. As board chairman and Chief Executive Officer of Tandy Corporation, I made the decision to go international in 1973 without benefit of these chapters. Consequently, this corporate decision, like so many others which I have had to make in the past quarter century, was not made according to the book. At least, not according to this book.

Perhaps the decisions would have been more easily arrived at, and perhaps more of them would have been correct, if they had been made according to the book. On the other hand, our corporation must have called some of the shots right, when you consider that it grew from a small wholesale leather company in 1918 to today's diversified corporation with more than 3,500 retail outlets, 20,000 full-time employees, sales of $724,488,293, and a net profit of $34,595,815 in fiscal 1974. The company operates in three major marketing areas: consumer electronics, hobby and handicrafts, and manufacturing and distribution. This growth is largely the result of an entrepreneurial spirit which I have practiced and preached since I joined the company in 1947 following service in the U.S. Navy during World War II.

I should explain that I interpret entrepreneurship broadly. In my opinion, the term applies not only to those who organize and manage a company, taking the risk involved, but also to those who acquire ailing companies and reorganize them, taking the risk involved. Tandy Corporation has practiced entrepreneurship both ways—and several times—and has the scars to prove it. I know of no better way to tell you my ideas about entrepreneurism than to preface my comments with a brief recital of my company's life and hard times.

THE ENTREPRENEURIAL SPIRIT YESTERDAY

Tandy Leather Company, genesis of the present corporation, began in Fort Worth, Texas, on a shoestring back in 1918. My father, David L. Tandy—from whom I inherited my enthusiasm for selling and merchandising—formed a partnership with Norton Hinckley to sell sole leather and other shoe repair supplies to shoe repair dealers in Texas. The firm weathered the Depression's storms, gathered strength, and established a firm base in the shoe findings business during the next 25 years.

My first contribution to the company came in the form of a letter to my father while I was on navy duty in Hawaii during World War II. I suggested to him that leathercraft might offer new possibilities for growth of the shoe findings business because leather was used in large quantities in army and navy hospital units and recreation centers. Leathercraft gave the men something useful to do; and their handiwork, in addition to being therapeutic, had genuine value.

When I returned home from the service in 1947, I obtained permission to operate the small leathercraft division which my father had formed at my suggestion. One of my early moves was the opening of the first two retail stores specializing exclusively in leathercraft. These two stores opened in 1950 in El Paso and San Antonio. I felt that if these two stores could survive, with the help of direct-mail-order sales, my formula for a leathercraft chain-store operation might be successful. The venture made a 100 percent return on investment the first year.

Our first catalog, only eight pages, was mailed in response to inquiries resulting from two-inch ads which we had placed in *Popular Science* magazine. Mail-order sales of leathercraft were a vital part of our formula.

In spite of the success of the two pilot stores, Mr. Hinckley, my father's partner, was not enthusiastic about the new leathercraft division; so, in 1950, my father and I worked out an agreement whereby we pursued the leathercraft business and Mr. Hinckley took over the shoe findings business.

From 1950 on, the successful formula of retail and mail-order stores supported by direct-mail advertising was expanded into today's chain of 236 leathercraft stores. The same basic formula has been applied to all of the specialty retailing divisions later operated by the corporation.

The do-it-yourself movement prompted by consumer goods shortages and high labor costs was gaining momentum in the early 1950s. The 15 leathercraft stores opened during the first two years were successful, and our management was gaining confidence. When a handicrafts company in East Orange, N.J., became available after it had suffered a series of financial setbacks, I seized the opportunity to buy it. American Handicrafts Company became Tandy Leather Company's first acquisition. This acquisition brought a broad line of do-it-yourself handicraft products, two established retail stores in the New York area, and useful knowledge of school and institutional markets.

We began promptly to make this sick company well and to move it forward. In 1953 we opened 16 additional retail stores, all following the basic formula of the first pilot stores.

Believing then and now that good people are as vital to an organization as good merchandise, and believing further that without proper incentives neither the people nor the company will grow, we made all of the managers of the first stores partners in the organization and cut them in on the capital investment and the profits. All of the employees in the company from file clerks up were invited to buy into the new companies as they were formed and to share in the profits.

The five-year period between 1950 and 1955 was an exciting period of growth and optimism for the Tandy organization. Sales reached $8,000,000 and earnings were $523,000—all generated from leased premises in 75 cities in the United States.

To cope with the estate and management problems created by a successful closely-held company—then owned by over 100 stockholder-managers—we chose to sell the company rather than go to a public underwriting. In 1955, therefore, we sold the company to the American Hide and Leather Company of Boston, which was listed on the New York Stock Exchange. It had been in the tannery business for some 54 years but had fallen into serious financial difficulty, its annual sales having dropped from $17 million to $9 million in recent years. Terms of the sale provided options for the stockholders of our Tandy Leather Company to buy 46 percent of the shares of American Hide and Leather Company stock at $4 per share over a four-year period.

Earnings of the Tandy organization, applied to the deficit of our new parent company, erased the losses and provided new cash flow for an aggressive diversification program which its management felt was vital to growth. Disposing of the tanneries and changing the name to General American Industries to dramatize the new management concept, the company in 1956 embarked on a diversification program by acquiring three companies wholly unrelated to the leathercraft business and the assets of Tex Tan of Yoakum, Texas, engaged in manufacture and sale of finished "western" goods such as saddles, belts, billfolds, and purses. This Tex Tan acquisition, it later developed, was the wisest decision made in 1956.

The high hopes and excitement brought about by the merger of our Tandy Leather Company changed to frustration and despair between 1955 and 1958. It became apparent that of the five divisions in General American Industries only two—Tandy and Tex Tan—were profitable. This presented me with the toughest challenge I had faced to date. It made me furious to see the hard-earned profits of the Tandy and Tex Tan groups used to plug the losses of the other divisions instead of being applied to growth and expansion as originally planned. Management of the other groups would not, or could not, pursue the profit-oriented practices of the Tandy and Tex Tan groups. Thus began a struggle for control of the parent company.

I used all of my resources to raise money to purchase the 500,000 shares of stock that were included in the original merger agreement. All of the key personnel in the Tandy and Tex Tan groups lent their support. A nip-and-tuck proxy fight was imminent. Only weeks before the annual stockholders' meeting that would decide the fate of the enterprise, I learned of the existence of a stockholder in a foreign country who controlled a very large block of stock and was not clearly committed to the incumbent management or to our group. Both factions sent emissaries to Europe to lay the facts on the table before this key stockholder.

The day of the stockholders' meeting was one of enormous strain and anxiety. Proxies were counted. The owner of the critical block of stock, in a perfect display of neutrality, had abstained from voting. Our Tandy group obtained management control of General American Industries.

In 1960, we sold the last of the unprofitable divisions. This was the first and only year in which our organization showed a loss ($267,000) and a drop in sales, both resulting from the costly divestitures.

During the "clean-up" year of 1960, our company emerged with the management team, marketing direction, and operating objectives that exist today. In 1961, the company name was changed to Tandy Corporation; the corporate headquarters were moved to Fort Worth; I became president and chairman of the board; and our company name was listed on the New York Stock Exchange.

We concentrated our efforts on expanding the Tex Tan Division, which manufactured and sold saddlery, riding equipment, and other finished leather goods, and the Tandy Leather Division. We acquired Craftool Company, manufacturer of precision leather tools, and Clarke and Clarke, Limited, a leathercraft firm in Barrie, Ontario.

By 1961, we were operating 125 stores in 105 cities of the United States and Canada. We were on our way again.

In that year, we acquired several new companies to complement our line of products, including a manufacturer of leather sport and western clothing, and a manufacturer and retailer of needlecraft items. It was now possible to use the resources of one division to develop new products for another.

In 1962, the Tandy organization advanced money to Cost Plus, a West Coast importer of decorator furnishings, gourmet foods, and unusual housewares from all over the world. The firm needed capital for expansion. We received distribution rights for the remainder of the United States and the use of the name.

Because the chain-store route had already been proved several times by Tandy Corporation as a rapid and profitable means of expansion, we established our first import store outside of California in Fort Worth, and during the following months we opened additional stores. The type of marketing used by Cost Plus—later named Pier 1 Imports —was fruitful and productive, but it required considerable continuing capital investment. By 1964, another one of our new acquisitions, Radio Shack, was beginning its vigorous expansion. The management of Tandy Corporation determined that this new acquisition offered a greater opportunity for early return on our limited capital, so we sold the Pier 1 operation to that division's executive group. Pier 1 continues to be successful today.

Our policy at Tandy has always been growth through reinvestment of profits. If an idea can't be proved effective within a reasonable period, we move on to something else.

THE ENTREPRENEURIAL SPIRIT TODAY

In 1962, I became intrigued with the potential for rapid growth in the retail electronics industry. Tandy Corporation acquired Electronic Crafts in Fort Worth as a pilot operation. The initial success of this pilot operation prompted me to seek a company in the electronics field that had the needed resources and talents for successful expansion. In 1963, I found Radio Shack in Boston, a mail-order company that had started in the 1920s by selling to ham operators and electronic buffs. Radio Shack, with nine retail stores, was in very poor operating and financial condition. It had lost $4,500,000 the year before. It owed more than $6,000,000 to a Boston bank and $2,000,000 to an insurance company. It had a net worth of minus $2,500,000.

This acquisition, more than any other in our corporate history, required me, as Chief Executive Officer, to carry out my entrepreneurial risk-taking role to the hilt—unless I've mixed a metaphor there somewhere.

When I presented the proposed acquisition to my board of directors, they were unanimously opposed to the idea. Some of them apparently thought that I had cracked up.

"Why in the world should you take on this kind of problem?" they asked. "Nobody has ever been able to make one of these electronic firms profitable enough to amount to anything."

I replied, "I believe that I can turn the situation around."

"But we don't want you to do it," they said firmly.

Here was an entrepreneur's moment of truth. I couldn't understand why all of my directors couldn't see the potential in Radio Shack that I could see. I was one director out of nine, so I couldn't outvote them. Literally with tears in my eyes, and with some emotion, I told them that I was deadly serious about acquiring Radio Shack. I pointed out that many of the inside directors had been doing what they wanted to be doing, with one of them handling the accounting, another handling this or that.

"Now, I am going to do what I want to do. If I don't get an affirmative vote on this proposed acquisition, then I will sell every share of stock that I own in our corporation and will personally acquire Radio Shack on my own hook."

I wasn't trying to run a bluff. I felt that strongly about what I could see in Radio Shack and what I could do with it. I was willing to gamble that it was something I could make into a viable, strong, and prosperous company.

When the directors realized that I was really this determined about acquiring Radio Shack, they changed their minds and voted unanimously for the acquisition.

In fiscal 1975—12 years after the acquisition—our Radio Shack Division operated 2,651 stores, did 68 percent of our corporation's $724,488,293 worth of business, and made 81 percent of total divisional income.

In those 12 years since 1963, we had made a number of major changes in the Radio Shack operation and had applied some of the merchandising techniques pioneered with Tandy Leather. Almost immediately, we reduced inventories through an aggressive direct-mail campaign to existing customers, concentrating our selling efforts on items with fast turnover and broad consumer appeal. We reduced the number of stock items from 40,000 to 2,500; at the same time, we tripled the turnover. We began requiring a 25 percent down payment and later cut out credit altogether. We insisted that buyers and merchandise men work constantly to develop new ideas for exclusive products and then buy properly so that our products would be competitive. When manufacturers in the United States were inadequate for this purpose, we developed resources abroad. We expanded retail stores rapidly. Two years after we had assumed leadership, Radio Shack was profitable and was in sound financial condition with sales approaching $20 million.

We decided to open Radio Shacks in Canada five years ago. We made profits there the second year. In 1973, we began European operations using the name Tandy International Electronics. By the end of fiscal 1975 we had more than 220 stores in Europe. We also launched Radio Shack in Australia in 1973, and had 67 stores operating there by the end of fiscal 1975.

Last year, we opened a Radio Shack either in this country or abroad at the rate of one per day, and we expect to continue this pace in the year ahead. In fact, in fiscal 1975, if you include our authorized sales centers—proprietor-owned stores in cities under 20,000 population—openings of Radio Shacks were at the rate of more than two per day.

We're going to put Radio Shack around the globe. We're going to have somebody selling our products down the Nile, down the Amazon, or wherever. We're not there yet, but that is our plan.

I think that we can do this with Radio Shack because we already manufacture more than 30 percent of our merchandise, and this percentage is steadily increasing. We intend to duplicate what we achieved with Tandy Leather—that is, to manufacture practically everything that we sell. Our motives in expanding our manufacturing activities, aside from profits, are (1) to gain the skills in design and technology required to keep us in a position of leadership; (2) to achieve product exclusivity; and (3) to reduce dependence on external suppliers.

Although Radio Shack is the fastest horse in the Tandy corporate stable, we have a score of other horses that are running quite well—plus a couple which have come up lame in the back stretch.

As the emphasis of our operations became more and more retail, rather than mail-order, we began looking for an established retail organization to merge with our expanding system. This turned out to be a full-line department store and a chain of six junior department stores in Fort Worth. We expanded the former into 3 suburban shopping centers around Forth Worth and the latter to 74 retail outlets in North Texas and Oklahoma. When we couldn't make the operation profitable after five years of expansion effort, we sold it and took our losses.

I don't believe in hanging on to operations which we can't run effectively. As many Chief Executive Officers and all football coaches have learned, many of them the hard way, you can't win 'em all.

In the late 1960s and early 1970s, we acquired no fewer than 22 companies. Many of these companies are in businesses related to one or more of our established divisions and, where feasible, we have integrated them. We have expanded some of them into chains; have merged some of them with other divisions; and have liquidated some of them.

Our latest move is a plan to separate Tandy Corporation into three publicly held companies in order to provide more intensive and distinct management leadership of the three basic and diverse businesses in which we are engaged—consumer electronics, handicrafts, and leather products. Under the plan, now awaiting the necessary approvals by regulatory agencies, Tandy Corporation will carry on the consumer electronics (Radio Shack) operations as its sole business. The plan calls for the issuance to shareholders, in the form of a tax-free dividend, of the common stock of two new companies to be drawn from the handicrafts operations and from the leather products operations of the present corporation. It will provide shareholders in the future with three clearly defined investment vehicles, each with a simplified corporate structure and business direction.

SOME OBSERVATIONS AND SUGGESTIONS

The most important element in our success is probably our people. Our executive and management people, for the most part, have been developed and promoted from within our organization. We have a motivation and career progress program which attracts and holds a particular type of individual—the type who delivers and expects to be paid for it. The program is simply this: Each profit center manager and executive is compensated with a nominal salary and a bonus formula which can yield him a generous portion of the annual profits of his unit. Nearly one out of every five of our 20,000 employees receives an annual bonus.

This program has enabled us to build a management organization of seasoned, profit-oriented people who respond to the challenge of individual progress in their personal incomes and in their careers. We have never needed employment contracts or stock option programs or retirement plans with our kind of people. We do encourage ownership of company stock through our contributory Tandy Employees Investment Plan; and today, our employees own more than 20 percent of the outstanding stock of the company and will probably own an even higher percentage in the years ahead.

We run our divisions and subsidiaries with a light corporate touch, giving the presidents and managers both authority and responsibility, pegging their bonuses to their performance. This practice identifies and encourages entrepreneurship, which is basic to our American free-enterprise system.

Our corporate president earned the post primarily by bringing the three Tandy companies for which he was responsible from a $250,000 loss on sales of $12.6 million in fiscal 1970 to a $4 million profit on sales of about $50 million in fiscal 1974.

We keep our tables of organization simple, or forget about them altogether. In my opinion, many large corporations pay too much homage to organization charts and rely on them too much. A corporation with an informal and flexible organizational setup is better able to take advantage of opportunities that come along, and can take prompt action when problems arise.

Running a corporation in today's economic climate, buffeted simultaneously by inflation and recession—and keeping the corporation profitable and growing—is a full-time job for a CEO. At the same time, all CEOs are being called upon to shoulder a large part of the growing responsibilities of corporations with respect to employees, shareholders, consumers, environmentalists, minorities, bankers, investors, the press, the community, Congress, endless government agencies, and even foreign governments. I let my associates handle quite a bit of this. Granted, some external matters you have to do yourself, simply because you're the top guy. But I never forget that the corporate woods are full of companies in trouble because the CEO was not minding the store.

It goes without saying—but I'll say it anyway—a successful entrepreneur must have the courage of his convictions.

I like the title and much of the content of a recent book on entrepreneurship by Joseph Mancuso. He titled the book *Fun and Guts*[1] —which may be overdoing things a bit—but he wanted to make the point that an entrepreneur's philosophy should be a cross between "fun and games" and "blood and guts." Mancuso claims that entrepreneurs are born, not made, and that you can spot them across a room. They will be the persons "talking about doubling sales and earnings, or attracting new capital, or a five-year growth program." They "would rather discuss raising capital than girls, rather talk of a new product, service, or marketing technique than eat." He cites energy as the one coefficient of entrepreneurial success. "You may have all of the ambition in the world, gobs of capital, a gambling man's soul, and business degrees covering the entire wall, but if you aren't virtually a human dynamo, forget it."

In my opinion, shared by Mancuso, entrepreneurs are individualistic and optimistic, and they prefer the 3-to-1 shot to the odds-on favorite or the horse listed at 20 to 1.

Some CEOs own all or a large piece of their companies. They risk their own money, and they are a very special brand of entrepreneur. We need more of them.

But some of our most important CEO entrepreneurs today are cast in the role of "professional manager." They may own a share of the company, and that share may even be significant for them in a personal financial sense; but the ownership share of these CEOs is insignificant in relation to the total ownership, which often is in public or institutional hands. These men are important in light of the vast portion of industrial enterprise which they shape. They, too, must

---

[1] Mancuso, Joseph; *Fun and Guts*; Reading, Mass.: Addison-Wesley Publishing Company; 1973.

have the courage of their convictions. Unfortunately, the list of these CEO-entrepreneurs is too short.

CONCLUSION

And, now, for some closing thoughts.

Aside from the CEO, who needs the entrepreneurial spirit? We feel that in our company, line management must be made up of entrepreneurs. Even staff managers should possess a high degree of entrepreneurship to bring creativity to their assignments and to work effectively with line management.

Can the CEO cultivate entrepreneurship in an organization? Or does entrepreneurship necessarily depend on one man? "Yes" to the first question; "no" to the second. The best way to cultivate entrepreneurship is to preach, practice, appreciate, and reward it when it is demonstrated. If the CEO is the only entrepreneur in the organization, his company is not likely to set any growth records.

Where does the board of directors fit into the entrepreneurial picture? Right in the middle. There is hardly any way that a CEO can exercise much entrepreneurism unless his directors—at least a majority of them—give him the authority and the necessary support. Ideally, most of them will be entrepreneurs themselves.

I would like to express one last thought and one hope. The thought is rather old-fashioned, but I remember that when our forefathers settled this country, nobody took them by the hand. If they had a good crop, it was theirs; if they had a bad one, it was tough. That is exactly how we try to run our company and treat our people, which is a lot different from the way most large companies are run.

My hope is that the good which the Tandy team has accomplished with its entrepreneurial efforts will be an encouraging and enlightening example to others, particularly those outside the field of business activity, whose understanding of the free-enterprise system needs to be encouraged and enlightened.

DEVELOPING THROUGH INTERNAL DIVERSIFICATION

by Werner C. Brown

President, Hercules Incorporated

> *When all the parts of a business strategy are in place, there can be no guarantee of success—only uncertainties and faith. Then, the president of a company must step forward and be counted in the face of any and all resistance. He must wholeheartedly back his team and stand by his conviction with a degree of intestinal fortitude that leaves the company no alternative but to go forward despite the usual doubting Thomases. It is a lonesome and sometimes awesome task that leads to many a sleepless night, but it is the only way I know that a sound new business opportunity can survive its turbulent ingestion period.*

THESE SENTIMENTS expressed in 1969 by Elmer F. Hinner, Hercules Incorporated's sixth board chairman, as he described his role in diversifying the company by moving it into polyolefins, summarize Hercules' management's determination to make our business a successful enterprise by tenaciously pursuing what we believe to be sound business judgments. Because new investments per se do not guarantee future earnings growth, investment decision-making is the most vital of corporate functions. This decision-making process can be aided considerably by financial evaluation of new investment proposals, but other aids also are required for top management to make the most judicious decisions that will reduce risk.

FINANCIAL YARDSTICKS FOR DIVERSIFICATION

At Hercules we use several financial yardsticks to evaluate all new investment proposals. In an industry where the rule of thumb is that one dollar of sales is generated by every dollar of investment, the most important financial yardstick is return on total investment, or on investment as total operating assets. Total operating assets consist of gross investment in plant facilities plus investment in inventories and credit through accounts receivables. Thus, we are calculating return on the fixed capital plus the working assets employed in the new investment. We eliminate the method of financing from all investment proposals, since it is a distortion to improve the return on an individual investment proposal by using the leverage of borrowed capital. Also, to assure consistent evaluation of all investment proposals, we use a theoretical depreciation rate of 7½ percent per year, although the actual rate may vary according to the class of asset. When the investment proposal is an expansion project, the investment project shows return on present investment, the return on proposed new investment, and combined return on present plus new investment.

All of our major capital expenditure projects show the forecasted rate of return on total operating assets for each year until optimum operations and sales are achieved. After the new investment has been made, our accounting system reports return on total operating assets on the actual operation. So we can quite easily compare actual financial performance with the project forecast.

HERCULES' GROWTH PERSPECTIVE

The perspective is thus: Chemistry, a science-business involving the rearrangement of molecules into an infinite number of chemical products, is unlimited in its business horizons. Within this science-business of unlimited horizons, development and growth are derived from research—research in the broadest sense: from the chemist at the bench involved in basic and applied chemical research to the MBA making careful market research analysis of allied or new ventures for the enterprise.

Growth and development within this framework are achieved through four routes:

1. Continued expansion and broadening of product lines within areas you know best. This requires constant infusions of imagination, and it requires knowing markets as well as your customer knows them.
2. "Jumping the track" into parallel business, as when research discovers something new that complements, but is a departure from, your mainline businesses.

3. Finding an opportunity to acquire another company in a parallel line of business or through buying technology in parallel businesses.
4. From nonallied fields.

In the more than 60 years of Hercules' existence in the science-business of chemistry, corporate management has found internal diversification—the art of doing more of what you know best—to be the best formula for successful, profitable growth and development.

How the maker of explosives in 1913 developed into one of the world's major producers of naval stores, cellulose products, polyester raw materials, and plastics is an almost unbroken record of management's "sticking to its knitting," yet imaginatively broadening product lines by doing more of those things it knew it could do better than anyone else. It will also become clear to the reader that where Hercules has had greatest success is in relatively sophisticated areas, ones in which it could quickly gain raw material, market, or proprietary position, and that it has lacked success in the less sophisticated businesses where anyone can easily gain know-how.

An examination of Hercules' history will illustrate the above and show the influence of management and, in particular, the Chief Executive Officer in determining basic corporate policy.

BIRTH OF A ONE-LINE COMPANY

Hercules Incorporated, born on the courthouse steps at the beginning of an era when the most promising frontiers were those of science, began operation in 1913 following a U.S. government suit against the Du Pont Company for antitrust activities in the manufacture and sale of explosives. At that time, Hercules was awarded eight black powder mills, three dynamite plants, and several patents for the manufacture of smokeless sporting powder.

Almost as soon as incorporation details were completed, Hercules' first president, Russell H. Dunham, with his management team's support, made the decision to expand facilities. A plant at Kenvil, New Jersey, was largely rebuilt and rearranged. To capitalize on the silver, copper, and coal mines of Utah and adjacent states, a new plant was built near Salt Lake City to produce dynamite, blasting powder, and related products. To supply large mining operations in Missouri, Hercules in 1914 acquired the dynamite facilities of the Independent Powder Company at Joplin. Another purchase of a black powder mill in Marlow, Tennessee, gave the company a desired foothold in the South. Even at its inception, the young company's management realized the need to diversify. Its first effort was geographical diversification, but product-line diversification would soon follow.

In recalling those early decisions to expand explosives production, President Dunham once remarked, "We were groping in the dark, working by guesses so far as building a company was concerned." Nevertheless, their efforts were encouraging, for in its first year, Hercules grossed $7.6 million and had net earnings of $1.4 million.

By 1915, World War I had made itself a factor in the business of Hercules as the company found itself called upon to take part in national defense activity. To do so, the company would expand existing production and would diversify for the first time into nitrocellulose, cordite, and acetone products allied to the explosives industry. Altogether, the company produced during the war over 100 million pounds of smokeless powder and 54 million pounds of nitrocellulose; was the country's largest producer of TNT; and was a major supplier of cordite. The latter would help Hercules' diversification and transition to peacetime activities. Cordite production requires the solvent acetone. Scarcity of acetone forced Hercules' chemists to find new sources. One came from acetic acid, made by the fermentation of alcohol. Another was from processing giant kelp. The knowledge gained by Hercules in organic chemistry through its work in producing acetone from kelp would prove of value in future diversification.

Following World War I, in an effort to keep his people employed, Dunham formed a new industrial research department whose purpose was to "locate, investigate, and report upon manufacturing propositions which Hercules may be interested in acquiring in order to use the facilities it has at hand to extend its business and increase its profits." Once organized, the department's personnel, including specialists in chemical and electrical engineering, began systematically scouting the entire United States on the trail of ideas and industries in which the company might invest.

FIRST MAJOR DIVERSIFICATION

The department decided that the naval stores (wood rosin) industry offered a promising field. So Hercules' first major outside diversification came in a field seemingly alien to its existing business.

Close examination shows that, far from being alien, it was an extension of the experience gained in the acetone episode, and, more importantly, that the richest deposits of rosin are found in the stumps of cut-over pine forests, which in those days were blasted from the ground—with Hercules' dynamite, of course.

Tenacity in pursuing what was believed to be a sound business judgment was tested quickly. One comment made around 1921 by a naval stores expert was typical of the outlook many persons had of naval stores possibilities at that time: "The development of the industry," he said, "will require very large capital expenditures, certainly without immediate return, and with little chance of a fair ultimate return unless investment in physical properties is followed by chemical research on a scale few companies are equipped to undertake."

Far from being frightened by this challenge, Hercules' management set the company solidly on the road to diversification into the naval stores business, a business they had decided had a good future, although admittedly there were a few years when some executives wondered if the millions of dollars the company poured into the diversification effort would ever be recovered.

Recalling the company's early diversification into naval stores, Charles A. Higgins, Hercules' second president, said, "We didn't get into the black on naval stores until the mid-1930s. Despite the many problems, we kept going because we didn't like to give up something we had started. We felt there was a need for naval stores and if we could just once get over the hump, we'd have it made. We got over the hump in 1928 when we learned how to take the color out of rosin-derived resins. That was the turning point in our business and Hercules has been in it ever since."

By March 1920, the company had let a contract for the construction of a plant to produce naval stores products at Hattiesburg, Mississippi. Hardly was the Hattiesburg project under way when Hercules took over the two naval stores plants of the Yaryan Rosin and Turpentine Company, one at Brunswick, Georgia, and the other at Gulfport, Mississippi. On taking over the two Yaryan plants, Hercules, one year after getting into the business, became the world's largest producer of rosin and rosin products, a position it still maintains today. Explosives had indirectly gotten Hercules into naval stores, but the key to success of the diversification was early establishment of market position.

Great as the undertaking was, the entrance into the naval stores industry was not accomplished at the expense of Hercules' main business—explosives. Along with other activities, the company was giving renewed attention to broader diversification into commercial explosives, which large-scale military activities had necessarily left neglected during the war. In broadening this branch of business, the company took a long step in June 1921, when it purchased the business of the Aetna Explosives Company. Dependent at first on the coal- and copper-mining industries, and having secured the trade of zinc and lead mines with the purchase of the Joplin plant, the company, through the Aetna purchase, gained a good portion of the trade of the iron-mining industry, thus placing the explosives branch of the company's business in a position of more perfect balance than had yet been attained.

Buoyed by broadening peacetime uses for explosives, the company looked for peacetime diversification for nitrocellulose and found it in the lacquer, plastics, and photographic film industries. Success in the business led to backward integration to establish a raw material position, and Hercules in 1926 bought the Virginia Cellulose Company at Hopewell, Virginia, a producer of the purified cotton linters from which nitrocellulose is made.

Diversification into naval stores and cellulose products would be joined much later by petrochemicals as the three most significant diversifications in Hercules history.

As converted at the Hopewell plant, cellulose is a comparatively unknown material to the layman, since it completely loses its original identity in the manufacture of hundreds of everyday products. For instance, in finished form—ready for the ultimate manufacturer of finished products—as many as one hundred different grades of cellulose pulp are turned out at Hopewell. Many of these types of cellulose are then chemically altered and eventually go into many hundreds of consumer products, ranging from minor additives for ice cream and chocolate pudding to major ingredients in billiard balls.

PINE CHEMICALS TO PAPER CHEMICALS

In seeking other new fields in which to place stockholders' investments, Hercules diversified from its rosin business by purchasing in 1931 the Paper Makers Chemical Corporation. It had been originally founded in 1900 in Easton, Pennsylvania, for the purpose of supplying chemicals to the paper industry. Rosin size was one of those chemicals.

The marriage of pine chemicals and paper chemicals gave Hercules world leadership in those areas of chemistry and led to development of technological breakthroughs in the associated areas of synthetic-rubber process chemicals and ultimately into specialty synthetic rubbers. Maintaining a necessary raw material position led Hercules scientists and managers into development work on tall oil fatty acids, and finally, hydrocarbon resins, culminating in the acquisition in 1972 of Pennsylvania Industrial Chemical Corporation.

This leads us back to the proposition previously mentioned—that investment decision-making is the most vital of corporate functions and the ultimate key to success or failure of a business enterprise.

ANOTHER YARDSTICK

When Hercules has an acquisition proposal, management uses another financial yardstick in addition to return on total operating assets. Since Hercules' stock is frequently issued to the selling stockholders, we also show the effect of this acquisition on future Hercules share earnings. This yardstick enables us to eliminate acquisition possibilities that will dilute our future share earnings excessively. If the proposed acquisition is a sizeable one in an industry having a significantly different price/earnings ratio, we will also show the anticipated effect of this acquisition on Hercules' future price/earnings ratio and market price. Also, since the depreciation rate can vary considerably, depending on the tax consequences and the nature of the business being considered, we also show the future cash flow from the acquisition, and dilutions, if any.

WORLD WAR II BRINGS EFFICIENCY

During World War II, Hercules again supplied large quantities of ordnance materials to the armed forces. The company's principal contribution, besides the production and development of chemicals for many industries, was the design and operation of government-owned plants for the manufacture of explosives.

Following the war, and based upon the experience it gained in operating the government plants, Hercules' management turned its efforts toward more efficient operation of its existing commercial plants. By the 1950s American industry faced a competitive situation that placed a premium on low-cost operations. Process improvements and projects involving more efficient operations left the company in an excellent position to meet the intense competition that was to appear in the ensuing years.

In 1953, Albert E. Forster became Hercules' third president. Far from feeling that Hercules' traditional markets were comfortably secure, Forster foresaw that they were becoming increasingly vulnerable to changing technology. What's more, the markets for many of these old-line products such as pine and paper chemicals were somewhat limited. In one of Hercules' principal products, rosin, a yellow chemical extracted from the aged stumps of southern pine trees, he discerned a very definite ceiling beyond which it would be impossible to develop new uses.

It was this simple realization, more than anything else, that was to produce the drastic corporate metamorphosis Hercules was to undergo, and that has since given birth to a whole new group of important and profitable chemicals in the Hercules sales catalog.

Forster's strategy was both direct and effective. Instead of basing his plans for growth on Hercules' traditional raw materials, pine wood and cotton cellulose, he chose the industry's fastest-growing raw materials, oil and gas.

Hercules, by tenaciously sticking to sound business judgments, had had no major business failures to this point. When the first failure came, it was to provide, ironically, a springboard into petrochemistry, the most current of the company's major diversifications.

Cellulose chemistry had led the company by the late 30s into cellulose acetate sold largely to fiber and film makers. Though Hercules management tried to establish a position in the business, it never could, and was stuck with being a "me too" in a highly competitive area. In an attempt to establish a better market position, operations emphasized plastics grades and thereby became major marketers to the plastics trade, augmenting some marketing knowledge in that trade by the earlier nitrocellulose plastics experts.

When ways of improving profitability waned and a decision seemed imminent to begin abandonment of cellulose acetate, management looked for ways to capitalize on marketing knowledge of the plastics industry.

CELLULOSE TO PETROCHEMICALS

Fortunately, a major opportunity emerged at this time. In Germany, Professor Karl Ziegler had discovered a new catalyst system for the polymerization of high-density polyethylene and polypropylene. Shortly thereafter, Farbwerke Hoechst of Germany had developed a commercial process for its manufacture. The Ziegler catalytic system, Hercules management decided, could lead to a new class of low-cost crystalline olefin thermoplastic polymers. It was precisely the type of thing for which we had been looking to replace our flagging cellulose acetate business. It was now up to management to take full advantage of our opportunities and to do so quickly. Such a break into the uncertainties of new chemistry in petrochemicals, where any position we developed would be based on a knowledge of the plastics industry and on quick action, required the severest test of courage to date for a company previously involved exclusively in explosives, naval stores, and cellulose, which had just suffered a severe setback with its cellulose acetate failure.

In 1954 a license was secured from Professor Ziegler and a technical exchange was established with Hoechst. By doing these things, Hercules quickly established a position, saving perhaps several critical years, in getting to the market-place with a salable product. In retrospect, insofar as polypropylene is concerned, these agreements were mostly hunting licenses. This is said not to deprecate the fine work that Professor Ziegler and Hoechst had done, but to indicate the enormous amount of scientific and marketing work that remained to be done.

Acquisition of a process was only the beginning. It was necessary that Hercules management commit a substantial investment to build a plant and develop markets, aimed initially at high-density polyethylene only. Major expenditures in research and development had also been committed even before our plant was under construction. Then Hercules scientists, working around the clock, discovered a completely new product, polypropylene. The vision of the market development people, plus confidence in the capability of our researchers, backed up by our management team, resulted in our sticking our collective necks out again. Before our first plant was finished, management decided to change the original intent of the plant by modifying the design and making it capable of turning out polypropylene as well as high-density polyethylene. Suddenly, Hercules had two horses in the race and felt some comfort in the realization that the odds for ultimate success were decidedly improved. Recalling these decisions, it is fair to say they represented a good example not only of management's willingness to remain flexible, but of its courage and conviction.

During those early and nonprofitable years, some of our biggest problems were internal ones. We were keenly aware that the problems of selling our capital projects to our Board of Directors were the toughest fights we faced, and this is as it should be. Management really takes its lumps during the days when a new venture is struggling to get off the ground. It takes many years to recover the costs when you are pioneering a new product, and while losses are building at a substantial rate, so too are the critics. It takes patience to withstand the mounting resistance to invest further funds in a business that has not yet begun to show a profit. Persistence, if you believe your judgment is sound, is the only answer. Persistence, of course, is a close relative of stupidity. The difference is in the soundness of your original judgment.

The story of our polypropylene development might stop here with the eventual establishment of a major profitable product and with management and the development team mutually congratulating each other for their courageous decisions. Because of our history of diversifying by taking a chemical building block and building *businesses*, not just products, management twice risked more capital to move forward into two new fields, polypropylene fiber and film.

To accommodate the former, Hercules bought the Covington, Virginia, nylon facilities of Industrial Rayon Corporation, and in six months' time converted it to polypropylene fiber, marketed under the name Herculon® olefin fiber.

Biaxially oriented film also seemed to us an attractive addition to our polypropylene venture. A license and know-how were purchased from Imperial Chemical Industries, Ltd., but both the process and the markets for this type of film had to be developed.

In both fiber and film, all the elements of new commercial development were required. Not the least of these was the same resolute devotion on the part of many of the same men who had been involved in our first decision. The training they got under fire developing the polymer certainly paid off in the development of the second-generation products.

So, within ten years from the time Hercules first heard of Ziegler's invention of organometallic catalysis, we found ourselves in the big leagues, producing major quantities of resin for the plastics industry and, at the same time, developing new markets for fiber and film.

And there were other ambitious petrochemical programs. By 1957, at the cost of over $40 million in capital outlays, Hercules was producing a number of oil-based organics such as phenol, methanol, and pentaerythritol, with a wide range of uses in plastics, paints, varnishes, and resins. For a company that in 1952 had boasted a net worth of only $78 million, this represented a tremendous effort.

Yet Hercules' ambition ran beyond merely building itself a position as a basic chemical producer. At the time of his ascension to the presidency, Forster said, "We have tended to shy away from bulk chemicals, which require heavy capital investments, where the net return on investment is often lower than in further upgraded chemicals. In any case, the best areas in basics were already overcrowded."

Instead, Forster concentrated Hercules' investment on production of primary hydrocarbon chemicals, out of which came a wide array of important intermediates. But because these building block chemicals were most efficiently produced in quantities beyond Hercules' own needs, the company had become a large commercial seller of these fundamental hydrocarbon chemicals. "This is the kind of situation," explained Forster, "where economy dictates that your plant must be bigger than any one user's needs for raw materials."

EXPLOSIVES TO ROCKETS

Forster also branched out into missile propellants. In chemical propulsion, Hercules had pioneered in the field of propulsion units for missiles and rockets since before World War II when it started work with the National Defense Research Council on rocket propellants. To the task, Hercules brought know-how based on research and experience as a manufacturer of double-base propellants since the company's beginning in 1913.

Interest in rockets during the early years of World War II demanded a high-energy propellant with larger-sized production equipment suitable for producing extruded double-base propellant grains as large as five inches in diameter. These were used in surface-to-surface rockets.

In 1958 Hercules committed itself to participate in chemical propulsion on a large scale when it successfully began development for the third-stage rocket of the ICBM Minuteman. Since Forster's decision to produce missile propellants, Hercules has produced rocket motors for such programs as Sprint, Polaris, Poseidon, and, more recently, Trident. Sales from these government contracts average about $100 million annually and provide the company with a steady and contracyclical source of revenue.

MORE PETROCHEMICAL DIVERSIFICATION

Concurrently, with entry into olefins, Hercules began development work on a product with the tongue-twisting name dimethyl terephthalate (DMT), the main ingredient in polyester fiber and film manufacture. Early technology in the production of DMT by oxidation of *p*-xylene had been licensed by Hercules in 1954.

The momentum generated by Forster was continued by Henry A. Thouron when he became president in 1963. Under his leadership, Hercules sales grew from $467 million in 1962 to $799 million in 1970. During his tenure, the investment in plants and equipment jumped 142 percent—from $344 million at the end of 1962 to $834 million at the end of 1970.

Under Thouron's direction, Hercules concentrated on three areas that he predicted would be the principal growth fields for the company: international operations, new enterprises, and dimethyl terephthalate.

Commenting on Hercules' role in world trade, Henry Thouron said: "Hercules' policy decision to organize an international department with the status of an operating department stemmed from two major factors. One was to protect our foreign markets for export sales as long as possible, and the other was to expand the profit potential inherent in Hercules technology."

When Thouron became president, Hercules had 17 plants in 11 countries. By 1971, seven years later, it had 40 plants in 18 countries.

Although Forster introduced DMT to Hercules, it was under Thouron's aegis that the company established its position as a leading international manufacturer of this polyester raw material. It was shortly after he became president that Hercules decided to build a DMT plant at Spartanburg, S.C. Subsequently, under his administration, DMT plants were built at Wilmington, N.C., at Middelburg in The Netherlands, and through joint ventures in Japan. In 1964, Hercules DMT capacity was about 180 million pounds per year; in 1975, the company expects that it will have worldwide DMT capacity in excess of 2 billion pounds per year.

By 1967, Farbwerke Hoechst of Germany, with whom Hercules had developed an association through polyolefins, decided to begin polyester fiber operations in the United States and approached Hercules about a joint venture. Thus came a diversification born of a relationship established earlier in a previous diversification.

Polyester fiber was beginning to grow, Hercules had raw material position with DMT, and movement into polyester would follow our pattern of diversification. So the joint venture was formed and a plant was built adjacent to the Spartanburg DMT plant.

Even though the time-honored elements of diversification were all in place, Hercules opted out of the polyester business within three years by selling its interest to Hoechst. That decision was based solely on the concern of top management that sufficient funds be available for the joint venture without starving capital needs in our main-line business, especially DMT. Hercules has become one of the major merchants of DMT worldwide, which requires investments that could not have been made had the company attempted the extraordinary capital investment required by major entry into polyester fibers.

OTHER DIVERSIFICATION

Thouron was also responsible for the creation of a special operating department, the New Enterprise Department. According to Thouron, when he announced the new group in 1968, "The New Enterprise Department will be responsible for leading the company into new business opportunities by commercializing new products from our own research, purchasing, or licensing technology outside the company, or by acquisition, merger, or joint venture. Although we have been expanding our normal chemical base and will continue to do so, special importance will be given to areas that move us into new areas of interest."

Since its creation, the department has led the company into such diverse activities as credit verification systems, modular housing, photorelief printing plate systems, and pharmaceuticals.

Some of these seem far removed for meeting the criterion of doing more of what we know best. Housing is an example. Yet Hercules had developed a systems approach in missile work and government contracting and believed the same techniques could be applied to factory-built homes. For a lot of reasons, however, the venture was ill-fated. We discovered early that our new ideas in housing would not sell at a profit, and we promptly sold the assets and quit the business.

The photorelief printing plate system is actually more a chemical process than a mechanical one, and is an extension of our resins business. Pharmaceuticals are closely allied with the chemical industry, and Hercules' entry into it is based on a joint venture with Montedison S.p.A. of Milan, Italy, with which we have had an association for more than two decades.

The credit verification system venture, simply put, is a diversification that breaks the established mold, being entirely outside chemistry, although based on high technology.

In May 1970, the writer became Hercules' fifth and present president. It is his belief that the function of a Chief Executive Officer is that of an "instigator" and "navigator." It is he who determines what direction the company will take and sees to it that the company stays on course.

The strategy for a company like Hercules, a strategy that must be flexible, cannot consistently be determined by committee. Sooner or later, someone has to say "Yes" or "No," or at least influence others to say "Yes" or "No," and that is the function of the Chief Executive Officer.

SETTING A CORPORATE GOAL

A common awareness of a clear goal and the clarification of corporate purpose will result in an organization of committed people. It is only in this way that a business can keep moving on a deliberately chosen path and avoid sidetracking. Although there are many alternative goals for a large corporation, the current CEO chose the relatively uncomplicated, albeit difficult, one of an annual increase of 10 percent in earnings per share of common stock.

Two things must be done to achieve this goal: (1) develop the financial capability to support the growth and (2) insure that there is an adequate flow of new investment opportunity. In addition, the CEO realized that a change was needed in the planning process as Hercules approached the billion-dollar sales level and as operations spread throughout the world.

The sheer magnitude of the numbers involved and the company's geographical diversity had rendered the "random walk" approach to strategy inadequate. The planning process had to be formalized and systematized. No longer was it possible for one man or even a committee to determine all the avenues of growth opportunities.

The goal of an annual 10 percent in earnings per share was established in 1970. Since that time, Hercules has achieved an average of nearly 20 percent compounded growth in earnings per share and earnings have improved over each corresponding quarter for 12 consecutive quarters.[1]

After first establishing the prime corporate objective, the CEO had to convince others that it could be achieved and, finally, he had to select the people to implement the project.

At the outset, the CEO outlined a four-point program that was essential to its success.

The first point of the program was to phase out marginal businesses that have no prospect of contributing to the 10 percent earnings goal. In the three years following mid-1970, Hercules sold, wrote off, leased, or otherwise disposed of $127 million in assets that weren't pulling their weight.

The second point of the program was better "total resource productivity," or the more effective utilization of assets. Our definition of productivity is the "systematic reduction of costs of total resources —manpower, capital, and purchases." In 1972, Hercules achieved a 12 percent improvement in productivity over the previous year, and 9½ percent in 1973.

The third point was the establishment of a higher threshold return of at least 10 percent on new investment and greater sales dollars per dollar of investment. To achieve the growth goals for the 70s we knew we must improve our overall rate of return on investment. Since expenditures required on projects such as pollution abatement provide little or no return and make a higher overall return much harder to achieve, sustained corporate growth can only come from the reinvestment of earnings in volume-producing investments.

Accordingly, in early 1970 Hercules established new criteria for proposed capital investment. One of the key critical statistics the company watches is the fixed investment "turnover ratio," that is, the dollars of sales per dollar of gross plant investment. Obviously, the harder we are able to work our assets, the greater our efficiencies.

Before Hercules started making large investments in polyolefins,

---

[1] As of June 1974.

fiber and film, and DMT, the turnover ratio of its commercial businesses was in the range of 1.3 to 1.5 dollars of sales to each dollar of fixed investment. At that time, Hercules' net profit as a percent of sales was 7 to 8 percent. But by the end of the 1960s, when it rapidly increased its investment in its growth products, the turnover ratio had fallen to the range of .93 to .96 dollar of sales to each dollar of fixed investment. And Hercules' net profit as a percent of sales had slipped to 6 to 7 percent.

Now the company is edging back in the right direction. In 1973 it had a turnover ratio of greater than 1 to 1 for the first time in 6 years, and the profit margin at 8 percent is the highest since 1966.

The final point in the strategy was a new business program, of which acquisition was a part.

In 1973 Hercules acquired Pennsylvania Industrial Chemical Corporation (PICCO) because it offered opportunity in a field of business parallel to that with which Hercules is familiar. PICCO produces high-molecular-weight hydrocarbon resins, and presents Hercules with the opportunity to couple our years of related experience with a fine line of rosin-based resins for specialized use in parallel markets. It provides the company with compatible technology, a solid position in raw material supply, and an opportunity to serve customer needs better.

In addition, the acquisition of Polak's Frutal Works (PFW) was completed in October 1973. The firm is a well-established producer of flavors and fragrances, with a broad spectrum of applications in worldwide markets.

In addition to securing an entry into an attractive market (flavors and fragrances markets during the past few years have grown at 10 to 15 percent annually), this acquisition complements other existing Hercules activities. It enlarges the company's role as a supplier to the food industry, and from a technical aspect encourages interaction between its expertise in gum technology and the use of flavor and fragrance compounds. Concerning cellulose gums, in 1972, the desired expansion of our base in cellulose technology led to the acquisitions of Cesalpina S.p.A., Bergamo, Italy, and A/S Kobenhavns Pektinfabrik, Copenhagen, Denmark, both leading producers of such natural gums as pectin and carrageenin, and guar and locust bean gums.

In summary, it is apparent that these four points are directed at the problem of improving our financial capability to the necessary levels to maintain a 10 percent return and at insuring a continuing flow of new investment alternatives.

The foundation for growth at Hercules must come from a sustained capital investment program. Hercules' capital expenditures between 1970 and 1973 exceeded $360 million, with the major portion devoted to the production of growth products and materials showing better than average rates of growth.

AIDS TO DECISION-MAKING

The risk and uncertainty in these investment proposals are largely related to environmental factors. There are several decision-making aids that have helped us to considerably reduce the uncertainty of long-term, large-scale investments. These decision-making aids for top management are:

1.   A risk analysis of our present and future competitive position.
2.   A long-range strategic plan.
3.   A consideration of alternative courses of action.

Risk analysis is a type of financial analysis that can be most helpful in both the preparation of an investment project and the presentation of a project to top management. In the normal project presentation, we assume the most likely sales price, sales volume, yields, conversion cost, etc., in computing the projected profitability. In a risk analysis, we assign a minimum value, a maximum value, and the most likely or probable value to each of these variable factors. Then, using a computer, we can make a large number of profitability calculations by using various combinations of variable factor values. These outputs include our usual rate of return on total operating assets as well as a year-by-year discounted cash flow analysis.

The advantages of this type of risk analysis are twofold. First, risk analysis is an excellent form of self-discipline for the operating department or division sponsoring the investment project. It forces the department to consider each variable in depth during the project preparation and focuses attention on those variables which have the greatest effect on profitability. Second, the risk analysis gives top management a yardstick with which to assess the probability of success and the risk involved in the investment proposal.

Financial yardsticks such as risk analysis are only as accurate as the assumptions underlying the input data.

The accuracy of the underlying assumptions will vary considerably depending upon whether we have control of the factors or whether the factors are beyond our control. For example, the forecast of plant investment can be made with good accuracy. Also, we can accurately forecast the operating cost—both the initial operating cost and the ultimate operating cost after process optimization. Both plant investment and operating costs are internal factors that we can control, and, therefore, can forecast with good accuracy.

By contrast, sales price and sales volume are examples of factors that are somewhat beyond our control, because they are affected by future market considerations and future actions of competitors as well as our own. These external factors—changes in market needs and unanticipated future competitive actions—cannot be predicted with the same accuracy as our own plant investment or our own operating cost. Thus, the accuracy of a project profitability forecast is essentially limited by these exogenous factors.

Another decision-aid tool is the three-year plan, which is updated and reviewed by top management annually. The elements of our company plan are the establishment of three-year goals or objectives for major products and markets, the development of tactics to achieve these goals, an action program to implement these plans, and a ten-year strategic plan.

The advantage of long-range planning for decision-making is that an individual investment proposal is considered as an integral part of the plan rather than as an isolated investment proposal. Thus, it can be considered both on its own merits and on its contribution to the plan.

The third decision-making tool is the consideration of alternative courses of action. A classic example is the make-or-buy decision when considering an investment to produce a raw material currently being purchased. If the raw material is in short supply or if a competitor has a built-in competitive advantage by virtue of his basic raw material position, the scales will be tipped to invest in the production of this raw material. If we can purchase the raw material at an attractive price, management may decide to continue a policy of purchasing and use the capital funds for a more profitable project.

Another classic example of alternative courses of action occurs when considering a foreign investment to supply overseas markets that are currently being served by exports from this country. Here, we are measuring the profitability on continued exports from this country versus the danger of losing foreign markets to competitors who win an advantage by building and producing in those markets before we do.

Another example of alternative courses of action arises when we have an acquisition proposal. Generally, we have the alternative of developing this investment opportunity internally, but internal development will usually take longer than a ready-made acquisition opportunity. Thus, we can balance off the cost of internal development with the cost of acquisition. Estimating the cost of internal development, including the delay in reaching the marketplace, can be a useful yardstick in negotiating a satisfactory acquisition price.

In summary, the use of these decision-making aids—risk analysis, long-range strategic plan, and alternative courses of action—provides top management with the insight and perspective to reduce risk and uncertainty.

CONCLUSION

Of course, corporate growth is a challenge with ever-changing parameters. Throughout its history, Hercules has frequently resorted to acquisitions and, more recently, to licensing agreements as a means of obtaining an entry into a new field. The common thread between these two sources of opportunity is Hercules' traditional strength in developing and improving upon acquired or licensed technology and diversifying internally by creating new processes and new technologies for new products.

Chemistry is a unique industry in that one development generally leads to another. We found quite early in the game that it was possible to systematize invention and innovation. Smokeless powder led to naval stores, and naval stores to cellulose. Cellulose led to petrochemistry and all the exciting horizons associated with it.

The chemical industry is unusual in another way also. Unlike most major industries, the chemical business is one of constant innovation and new product introduction. We find that today over 60 percent of our sales are of products not even invented as recently as 1950. Going back to our original explosives business in 1913, we find that today less than 4 percent of current sales are derived from that original business. The demands of mankind are practically unlimited. The products and things we can make through the magic of chemistry are also practically unlimited.

It is obvious that chemistry has provided Hercules with many opportunities—some we've lost, and some we've mastered. It is encumbent upon the Chief Executive Officer to maintain and capitalize upon the momentum generated by these opportunities and to chart a course for growth through internal and, of course, external diversification.

At Hercules, the formula used has been one of doing more of what we know best. In a science-business like chemistry, with the widest possible horizons for growth, that formula has proved successful.

THE KEY TO SOUND ACQUISITION GROWTH

by N. W. Freeman
Chairman, Tenneco Inc.

ACQUISITIONS, a key factor in the growth and expansion of many important companies in this country, should be conducted in the same precise manner that you would any vital corporate function—very carefully.

And to be effective in this area, it is not necessary for the Chief Executive Officer to be all things to all people on all proposals.

In fact, just as in other phases of business, it is impossible—and unwarranted—for him to be so.

Historically, of course, the Chief Executive Officer may not have a scientific or a technical background. Yet in all likelihood, he may well make the final decision on whether to go ahead with a new product line or install a new process or build a new plant. He may not have a legal or a financial background. But he may well make the final decision on whether to file a lawsuit or to issue debentures. His background may not be marketing, but his approval will most likely be sought on such matters as new promotional campaigns or efforts to move into new markets.

All of this is to say, simply, that a chief executive earns his keep through the exercise of his judgment across a broad spectrum of corporate functions. He carefully selects his staff. He knows how to obtain from them the information he needs. He knows how to equate conflicting opinions. He knows when and how to delegate authority, and to whom. He knows when to listen and when to talk. When to act and when to mark time. When to stand fast and when to compromise. In every instance, the key to his success is simply solid judgment.

Nothing changes when he enters the arena in search of acquisitions.

In fact, the parallels are all there. The chief executive ferrets out the information he needs and then makes the decision through the exercise of his own judgment. Although good judgment cannot be attained from reading this handbook alone, or any other book for that matter, we may safely assume in the vast majority of cases that this elusive and hard-to-define quality is already part of the make-up of the chief executive. Without it, he—or she—probably would not have risen to that present position of prominence within the organization.

What should good judgment tell him about the expansion of his business through the acquisition of other businesses?

First, it should tell him that corporate growth is an area too complex and too important to be undertaken casually or as a spur-of-the-moment task. A philosophy of growth through strategic planning is a fundamental first step. Although Tenneco has found strength in careful diversification, I would emphasize at the same time that there are numerous perils and pitfalls. You should always remember the iceberg. It's what you don't see—or can't see—that can wreck your business ship. Aimless acquisitive growth, in fact, represents not muscle but fat and potential disaster.

Second, good judgment should tell him that expert legal, financial, and tax guidance is essential during every acquisition program and should be brought to bear as early as possible.

STRATEGIC PLANNING

Just as a contractor needs a blueprint, a corporate builder needs a strategic plan to keep the growth orderly instead of helter-skelter, goal-oriented instead of aimless. The chief executive need not draft the plan himself, but his input must be present and apparent throughout. After all, this is where the buck will finally stop. Ultimately, he becomes the final authority on whether to go or not to go on an acquisition—and he had better be completely cognizant of how this move dovetails with the overall strategic plan.

A good strategic plan also provides a measure of protection against taking on a poor acquisition. Without naming names, I know we can all think of some past acquisitions that were outright mistakes and should never have been made. Many of them could have been avoided if the chief executive, in conforming to a total strategic plan, had questioned, "Where does this acquisition fit, and how does it fit? Should we be in this business, and what can we bring to the game that will help make this company perform better. Is it really our cup of tea?"

There is another advantage to a good strategic plan. In the heady atmosphere that surrounds one successful acquisition, the tendency may be to relax your standards and rush into several other less well-conceived, less well-studied acquisitions. Stick to the plan—and make them *all* conform. It's a good insurance policy.

The development of the strategic plan requires considerable soul searching on the part of the management team, but it is essential in order to provide the yardstick against which to measure a proposed acquisition.

How do you do this soul searching? Again—very carefully.

The first requirement is the establishment of the overall growth objective. How do you get there, from internal growth, that is, with what you already have? What do you need from the outside to round out that growth objective? Obviously, acquisitions made merely to force improvement in the company's earnings picture or to obtain assets with unrealistically low book values may provide short-range benefits. But in the longer run they could come back to haunt you.

Worthwhile growth objectives are many. They include: rounding out a product line; expanding a product line; filling a need for diversification in related fields; moving the company into new marketing areas; acquiring a well-established dealer organization; acquiring certain patents and licenses; obtaining increased production capacity that might otherwise take years to build. Diversification, itself, can be a worthwhile goal. But keep in mind that it should fit in some reasonable fashion within the acquiring company's areas of competence.

Guidelines must be developed to aid in deciding what growth will be generated internally as distinguished from what growth can best come through acquisition. When we evaluate a potential acquisition at Tenneco, we routinely weigh the cost of the company against what it would cost us to enter this business on our own—or how these funds could be applied elsewhere for superior results.

Also, in the development of strategy a company must ask itself what lines of business it *really* wants to be in. Now? Five years from now? Ten years from now? Can the brakes be applied on an expansion program if that should become necessary? Overall, will the heterogeneous parts of the enlarged company project an image of homogeneity? Are there some common denominators which link everything together? Does the program make good business sense—

which, of course, brings us back to the judgment factor that I am stressing.

These points are especially pertinent at Tenneco when we are considering a particular prospect. Before we get serious about any prospect, we determine how well it will fit into our present organization. Many prospects are presented to us, usually at the rate of two or three every week; but only a small percentage are actually pursued. The reason is that the great majority of prospects fail this initial test: They just don't fit our plan of what we want to be—and where we want to go.

I think it is our company's reputation as an acquirer that brings us so many unsolicited opportunities. A company that is only beginning an acquisition program will not be able to sit back and wait for prospects to come knocking on its door. Rather, part of that company's overall strategy plan should be to decide what other businesses fit its growth goals and which ones should be considered likely candidates for acquisition. Which of these might present antitrust problems or other legal difficulties? What would be the tax consequences of acquiring each prospect? The financial consequences? These questions bear out the second point I made earlier—the point that a chief executive's good judgment will tell him that expert legal, tax, and financial advice should be available to him at every phase of an acquisition program. In most instances, technical and marketing advice will also be necessary.

Tenneco does a full financial study on any proposed acquisition that survives our initial tests. Our checklist of preliminary items, then, becomes an important part of our strategy, since it often spares us this time-consuming and expensive process by establishing early in the game which prospects are unsuitable and which present promise.

A partial checklist: a determination of whether the prospect fits; an evaluation of its management team, its history and the future of the industry it serves; its position in, and relation to its labor market; its reputation in its plant communities and its attitudes toward corporate social responsibilities. Further, we attempt to determine the attitude of its people—do they regard themselves and their company as winners or losers? Finally, we look behind the scenes to establish why the company is available for acquisition. Are its people dispirited, its facilities antiquated, its products outdated, its markets diminishing? A key question always is: Why?

A certain number of negatives are to be expected, and we do not necessarily eliminate a prospect because of them. No company is perfect. It is just that we want to know all the pluses and minuses before we get into serious negotiations, and we want to know which minuses might be overcome through our methods and procedures and our input. Obviously, if the negatives continue to mount as we study the situation in its many facets, the risk grows, and the chances of getting together are minimized.

ROLE OF THE CEO

In a typical business situation, a matter requiring the chief executive's attention would most likely come to him through the normal chain of command, undergoing a refinement as various levels of the organization exert their influence and apply their expertise. The proposal would—or should—reach the CEO in a form ready for decision, one way or the other.

Not so with acquisitions, at least not as far as I am concerned. An acquisition might entail the reverse of the usual processes of corporate decision-making. As a rule, the chief executive should be involved in the matter from the beginning. Ideally, he and his counterpart at the company to be acquired reach a preliminary agreement, sealing it with a handshake or perhaps a letter of intent. Then, they step back while their respective staffs study the details.

At this point, though, I need to make a distinction. In a large multi-industry company such as Tenneco, the chief executive of a major operating subsidiary (rather than the chief executive of the parent company) might well be the one intimately involved in the negotiation of an acquisition. Two brief examples will illustrate my point. In 1970, I was actively involved, as chief executive of the parent company, in the acquisition of an agricultural management and marketing subsidiary; but in 1972, it was the chief executive of our construction and farm machinery manufacturing subsidiary who played a similar role in the acquisition of a British tractor company. Even so, no "go" signals were given until authority was received from our corporate headquarters in Houston.

I think it is well to remember that no two acquisitions are exactly alike; so be careful not to be bound by a rigid set of procedures. You always need to remain flexible.

When the two top men have made an agreement-to-agree, the negotiators strive diligently to reach a workable final agreement. But when the two chief executives do not take this important first step, the tendency is for the lower-echelon people to search for reasons why the merger should not be made. Some reasons can always be found, of course, even in the best of situations. Generally, it's easier to be negative than positive. Some people feel it is their duty to try to punch holes in the proposal. A certain amount of this is acceptable. But it should not be allowed to go too far.

In any event, I doubt that many acquisitions would ever be consummated if this initial contact and meeting of the minds between the two chief executives did not take place.

Another reason for early involvement of the chief executive of the acquiring company is simply professional courtesy. In delicate negotiations of this type, a top decision-maker should not be expected to spend his time with anyone who would not be empowered to speak with authority. If neither chief executive is participating at the outset, negotiations usually become very tedious and time consuming and probably will not be very productive.

Finally, the best acquisitions are those in which the acquirer seeks not only a company and its assets but also its management. We always look for management strength in the companies we acquire—and we want the personnel to remain after the acquisition is completed. Their participation in the negotiations helps assure this continuance—and also serves as a relief valve, for they know exactly what is going to happen.

HIGH-LEVEL ADVOCACY

The corporate system, somewhat like our government, has certain checks and balances that serve to protect a company against the possibility of grossly incorrect decisions. The chief executive should be forewarned, however, that this safeguard could falter in matters of corporate growth by acquisition.

Let me explain. Suppose the vice president of marketing wants to open a new distribution center but the vice president of finance thinks the proposal is extravagant. The chief executive, obviously not exactly a disinterested third party, can still serve as the judge in the matter. He hears the arguments and renders a decision. The decision is based on balance—and usually is correct.

But in the case of acquisitions, he may not get that balance of opinion—at least from within his own organization.

He now has to obtain his balance of information both from within and without his organization. He is also personally involved, and this could from time to time influence his objectivity. Nonetheless, through proper safeguards, he can still serve effectively as the judge in the decision-making process, provided he maintains an open mind and a full line of communications.

Sound decisions are reached through an examination of all sides of a proposition, preferably by hearing the arguments and proposals of staff people who are, in fact, advocates of a sort. And they must be sure enough of themselves, and secure enough in their own positions, to tell the chief executive all the pros and cons concerning the acquisition. In some cases, there may be a tendency to tell the boss what he wants to hear. This, of course, is a mistake and should be guarded against at all costs.

I know of one chief executive who, after he starts the wheels turning on a proposed acquisition, intentionally takes a totally negative attitude on the proposition—and in effect requires his staff to convince him that the acquisition is sound. If they are unable to do so, the proposal is rejected.

The method, of course, is not so important as the result. The chief executive should realize that if the normal system of checks and balances is not functioning because of his intimate involvement in a project, he would be well advised to set up a system which would protect both himself and his company. The key once again is to proceed very carefully.

One idea that comes to mind is a modification of the procedure used by the chief executive mentioned above. An executive need not try to shoot down his own idea. But he might do well to create an advocacy system. Without making a big point about his own involvement, the chief executive might summon knowledgeable associates who would likely have opposing views and let them thrash out the issue. Another idea might be to search the executive ranks for someone who would make a good devil's advocate. The procedure itself is relatively unimportant just as long as the job gets done right.

ONE PLUS ONE EQUALS THREE

Many of the points I have made thus far can be summarized neatly in an arithmetical monstrosity. If the union of two companies creates nothing more than the total of what existed previously, nothing much is being accomplished. One plus one must equal something greater than two. To reword the axiom from our high school geometry, the whole should be greater than the sum of its parts.

Is this really possible?

The fact is, that above and beyond the surface characteristics of the two companies—the ones that can be accurately measured and weighed against the cost of the acquisition—there should by a synergistic effect of the union, an effect that enlarges the parent company by more than what was added to it. I have seen this quality emerge at Tenneco numerous times.

The synergistic effect of a merger may defy evaluation, unlike the other effects, which usually can be measured with a high degree of accuracy. Here I have a suggestion that may be helpful.

Normally, the acquiring company expends its greatest effort deciding what it is getting from the acquisition. At some point, these considerations should be set aside. Reversing the usual line of your inquiries, you, as chief executive, should ask your staff, "What are *we* bringing to the acquisition?" Generally speaking, if the two companies in a merger negotiation each have something worthwhile to contribute to the enlarged enterprise, the acquisition begins to make more sense.

Maybe the company to be acquired has some management weaknesses that your people or your techniques and procedures can overcome. Perhaps this company needs expansion capital that your company can provide. Or certain corporate services (a computer center! a research facility! a Washington staff!) that it cannot effectively provide on its own. Some management teams, though essentially good performers, can become lethargic. A new affiliation with an aggressive parent company can be the factor that rouses them. Sometimes some cleaning up may be necessary. Ideally, the company to be acquired should accomplish this *before* the merger, reducing ill feelings toward the new corporate parent. However, this precleaning is not always possible. Sometimes a dispirited company can be rejuvenated through association with a strong family of companies.

My point is that your company, as an acquirer, must be in a position to give as well as receive. If so, and if the new company fits into your carefully prepared strategic plan, the acquisition is likely to be successful.

Another important consideration is mutual satisfaction. The final arrangements should be so satisfactory for both parties that each one is convinced of the soundness of the package. Points of contention should be eliminated as much as possible. They should not merely be bandaged. It may be necessary to surgically remove them.

Wouldn't such an attitude lead the acquirer to pay more than he has to? That could be true—but in the long run, price alone should not be the sole governing factor in effecting a favorable acquisition.

Let me cite an example. In 1967, we paid $10 million for the Drott Manufacturing Corporation, which now functions as an operating division of our J. I. Case Company. This was a very good acquisition— it fitted neatly into the strategic plan of J. I. Case, and the price tag was high enough to make the sellers happy and reasonable enough to make the prospect interesting to us. In one year alone (1973), Drott's net earnings (exclusive of federal income tax, interest expense, and outside stockholders' interest) were more than the $10 million we paid for the company.

Suppose that we had had to pay somewhat more for Drott. It would still have been a good acquisition. Certainly price is always a basic consideration. But my point is that it should not be the sole governing factor, as it may have to be in other business matters. Because most acquisitions involve publicly held companies, there is usually no great flexibility in pricing. The value of the stock is established by the market, and the acquiring company has to offer a premium above the market value in order to have its offer accepted favorably by the other company's shareholders.

Still another point worth remembering is that negotiations should not be allowed to linger. Take the time you need to decide whether a company is worth having. Once you have reached your decision, proceed with all deliberate speed to complete the acquisition. Protracted negotiations are demoralizing to a company and its staff, and such delicate matters as acquisitions have a tendency to cool off rapidly with the passage of time.

HORSE TRADING

Acquisitions, of course, are complex business matters, and usually I disdain any effort to oversimplify a complicated subject. In this case, however, I think it can be done safely. Because business is the great American endeavor, and horse trading the great American art, let's compare the two. Perhaps it is more than coincidental that parent companies are often said to possess a stable of companies.

In horse trading, both the buyer and the seller strive for the best bargain. Believe me, if you don't know horses—and I've raised quarter horses for over 20 years—you'd better get plenty of expert advice.

The real key in any horsetrade is how badly the buyer wants the horse—and how anxious a seller is to sell. Does the buyer want the mare for breeding purposes? What are the blood lines? What is the mare's history of foaling? Has she been dropping good colts?

Is the horse for personal use—for show—for competition—or for breeding? It all makes a difference. I remember once paying $11,000 for a gelding for my daughter. The price was too high, but my daughter wanted the horse—and as it turned out they made a great team, winning countless trophies and saddles in tough competition. She was happy. I was happy. And the seller certainly was happy. And I guess even the gelding was happy because he changed from a short-tempered, highly unpredictable animal into a hard-working, easy-mannered winner.

I would hope that this would be the end result of any good acquisition, whether it be a horse or a company. The dominant trait of any sensible horse trader is good judgment, and his dominant consideration is how well the proposed purchase fits into his scheme of things.

These are precisely the prevailing traits and considerations with all good acquisition-minded chief executives.

If you will indulge me one further oversimplification, a chief executive contemplating acquisitions should consider carefully the five Ps—policy, prospects, parameters, participants, and particulars.

He should have developed a policy of acquisitions, a strategic plan, and should keep it always in mind. He should know what prospects are available and how they measure up against the parameters of his acquisition policy. He should know which participants he will summon for detail work, both in the fact-finding stage and, later, in the negotiations. Regardless of whomever else he may need from time to time, he should have expert legal, financial, and tax advice always at his elbow. Finally, as the particulars of the acquisition are worked out, he should keep abreast of how the negotiations are proceeding and whether any problems are developing.

The five Ps are, if you will, the ABCs of corporate growth by acquisition.

A CASE IN POINT

In conclusion, it may interest the reader to take a brief look at the overall strategic plan of one particular company. I think it will be an effective way of emphasizing the points I have made. Since it should be a company I am totally familiar with, it must be Tenneco.

You can appreciate, of course, that there are numerous parts of the plan that would be too lengthy to discuss here, but I believe a quick overview will be sufficient.

Tenneco began in 1944 as a natural gas pipeline with a single line of 24-inch pipe stretching 1,265 miles from South Texas to West Virginia. (Construction began in 1943. The line was completed and placed in operation in 1944.) By the end of 1974, the company's natural gas transmission business consisted of four major pipeline systems and a total of 15,737 miles of pipe. I mention this fact because we stress internal growth—and experience it, too. All other factors being equal, internal growth is our preferred method of doing business.

Interstate natural gas pipelines, as you know, are closely regulated by the federal government and are a quasi-public utility, even though the great majority of them do not deal directly with the public. Thus, they are a steady source of a tremendous volume of dollars—but at a low rate of return on invested capital. We saw our pipeline operations as the bedrock upon which a diversified company could be built.

Oil and gas are so closely related (they are often discovered together) that it was quite logical for us to move into oil. We made a number of acquisitions which were to become the building blocks of an integrated oil operation. It exists today as Tenneco Oil Company.

Our expansion into chemicals was a logical step-out from both our natural gas and our oil operations. As early as 1951, we had a chemically related interest—a plant which recovers liquefiable components from pipeline gas for sale to a nearby chemical company. Four years later we bought a half interest in a butadiene plant. In 1963 we built a large petrochemical plant, and in the same year we acquired a major chemical company. Today, our chemical interests are managed by Tenneco Chemicals, Inc., which has been built by both internal growth and acquisition.

You can see the pattern. We were building our company on the discovery, production, transformation, and use of natural resources. Our acquisition of Packaging Corporation of America merely expanded this base from hydrocarbon resources to forest products. Our acquisition of Kern County Land Company, although made essentially because of its petroleum resources, also broadened our resources base to land and its use for such purposes as agriculture, real estate developments, industrial parks, and so forth.

Kern County Land Company had three manufacturing subsidiaries, and our acquisition of the parent company automatically placed us in our sixth major business area. These subsidiaries are Walker Manufacturing Company and J. I. Case Company. The third was Watkins-Johnson, an electronics company. Because this company did not "fit" our plan, we logically spun it off. In the next year, we rounded out our manufacturing interests with the acquisition of Newport News Shipbuilding and Dry Dock Company.

It is very unlikely, I think, that we will want to enter any new major business that would be totally unrelated to the businesses we are currently in. Of course, we are in a lot of businesses, so this yardstick still gives us broad room for further expansion through acquisition. Right now, our acquisition program is designed to strengthen, augment, and round out our various operations.

We still are acquisition minded!

We still have a carefully designed strategic plan for growth—both internal and external. And we are implementing it.

Perhaps you, too, should have such a plan!

PRODUCT LINE MANAGEMENT

by Edward Donley

President, Air Products and Chemicals, Inc.

MANAGING a modern corporation is among the most demanding and rewarding challenges that can still be experienced by professional people. A large business organization, encountering rapidly changing and interacting political, social, technical, and economic variables, calls upon the CEO and his line strategists and managers to use every insight available from his experience and knowledge. The psychology of customers and employees, rapid advancements in science and technology, fluid national and international politics, dramatic shifts in the social environment, and the ever-present threat of preemptive moves by competitors, all relentlessly pose both problems and opportunities for product line strategy and management.

Even today, when society is rightfully demanding greater social awareness and public contributions from corporations, the report card on management is still its economic performance. Data on stock prices, dividends, and price-earnings ratios are considered important enough to be printed by daily newspapers throughout the country. Only professional corporate managers and sports players see the results of their performance published daily in the general press. Moreover, although the results of business decisions are usually known in a relatively short period of time, the results of decisions in nonbusiness fields—in politics, education, scientific research, international diplomacy, and so forth, may not be revealed for years or for decades.

The history of man has always involved facing and being tested by challenge—in hunting, war, exploration, government, science, teaching, and many other fields. In few institutions, however, has the opportunity to make and apply judgments been subject to such a decisive test as that embodied in the profit results of a public corporation. The quality of the firm's economic performance depends, as I see it, on the management of factors of technology, finance, markets, and people, all of which are important determinants of product strategy.

DETERMINANTS OF PRODUCT STRATEGY

Technology

The technology available to the firm must be in areas where newly-developed products will fill a need that is recognized by society and that is large enough to warrant serious attention. It should be in fields where raw materials are likely to be available, and where lack of access to these materials or to technology itself can be a barrier to entry by competitors. The technology should provide a superior or unique product that will enable the firm to establish a proprietary market position. It should also provide fall-out opportunities in other fields. Above all, it should provide products that will benefit from the expertise and aspirations of the firm's people.

Here is an example of how technology opened a major new market for our company. Air Products developed proprietary know-how in cryogenics—the technology of liquid gases—as a result of manufacturing and marketing liquid oxygen and nitrogen. In the late 1950s and early 1960s, we undertook a major research and development program to determine and understand the general behavior and properties of gases at cryogenic temperatures. The work began with hydrogen and helium, as a result of the defense and space programs. This knowledge, both general and specific, of the properties of liquid gases and the perfection of the technology, then spilled over to commercial applications, especially to the liquefaction of natural gas, by which the company now helps to satisfy the need for energy in most of the developed nations of the world.

In North Africa, Southeast Asia, the Persian Gulf, and elsewhere in the world, large quantities of natural gas are available, but the principal markets cannot be reached by pipelines. The only economical way to transport the gas is as a liquid by ship. Because of the expertise of its engineers in low-temperature processing of hydrogen and other gases, Air Products was well positioned to take advantage of this opportunity by developing and building large process units to liquefy the natural gas. Moreover, it seems certain to us that this technology will enable us to participate further in the processing of residual oil and coal as hydrocarbon sources become more costly.

Technology is the most formidable barrier to entry in many industrial markets. It is thus an important strategic variable in the growth phase. A firm's technology portfolio is the total of its research, development, design, engineering, manufacturing, and marketing capabilities. Technology, properly exploited, leads to special skills, know-how, and patents. All are important barriers to entry. In the early stages of a product's life, obtaining a technological advantage is extremely important. It generally leads, as does market share dominance, to a low-cost position. In addition, it frequently leads to the discovery and exploitation of related, or completely new, markets.

High product quality is important, and will probably be a result of superior technology. Other things being equal, the higher the product quality, the higher the profitability of a business.

Finance

Product strategy can only be devised in accordance with the firm's financial goals. These include the amount of risk management is prepared to take, the balance to be struck between short-term and long-term results, the extent to which irregularity in earnings growth can be tolerated, and the dividend policy to be pursued. The degree of capital intensity of the product, the level of return on investment that is acceptable, and the length of time it is expected to take to attain it, must also be taken into account. This accounting must consider the position of the particular product as part of a portfolio which includes all of the company's other products. Weight must be given to the financial and other demands placed upon the company's resources by this whole portfolio. Finally, management must be certain that the funds required to carry a product project all the way through to completion will be available. "For which of you, desiring to build a tower, does not first sit down and count the cost, whether he has enough to complete it?" (Luke 14:28).

Air Products has shown a consistent growth in earnings over a long period of time. A key factor in this success was a financial policy that we inaugurated at the very beginning. The essence of this policy was to invest for the long term, and to minimize risk by obtaining long-term contracts from customers, with reasonable rates of return. Although today our financial strength and business diversity do not require us always to adhere to this policy, it was a must for the company when we were small, and it still offers many advantages, especially with regard to very large projects. The unusual feature of the policy was that it allowed us to obtain financing for our investments partly on the basis of the creditworthiness of our customers. By building, at incremental cost, more capacity than that required to serve the customer's anticipated requirements, we were able to provide additional incremental product to the merchant market. This approach minimized our downside risk and allowed us some upside potential through the incremental capacity. We were thus protected against the vagaries of a buyers' market and had limited benefits in a sellers' market. Over the long haul, this technique has proved very beneficial to us.

Markets

Accurate appraisals of the state of the relevant market, and the relation of the product to it, are at the heart of strategic product planning. Businessmen will, of course, always prefer markets that are growing rapidly and for which they possess a strong logistical position, outstanding applications knowledge, and extensive service capability. Because of the decisive impact of volume on unit costs where there are significant economies of scale, the company must have a substantial market share. Detailed planning for a product can begin if the state of the firm's related technology, or its marketing competence, suggests that it can achieve and maintain a dominant market position, and the other preconditions for success appear to exist.

Perhaps the experience of Air Products in the use of liquid nitrogen for food freezing will help to illustrate these ideas. In the 1960s, we had a small staff of food technologists looking at possible applications for industrial gases. When convenience foods became popular, and it appeared that consumers were willing to pay a slightly higher price for a better quality product, we were able to move rapidly to enter the market. The temperature of liquid nitrogen is minus 320°F. Because of the speed with which it freezes, it does not damage internal cell walls, and thereby provides a food product which is more palatable when thawed.

In contrast to conventional food freezing techniques, liquid nitrogen food freezers tend toward higher unit operating costs but substantially lower capital costs. They are thus particularly advantageous in economic terms for specialty product lines, which are subject to frequent changes in product mix. Using our capabilities in cryogenics, heat transfer, and machinery design, we developed a freezer which was capable of processing the food at an acceptable unit cost, at the same time meeting government standards of cleanliness. Not only was the freezer highly successful, but the market for quality frozen foods increased faster than we expected because of the rapid growth of "fast food" franchising. Our existing fleet of liquid nitrogen tank wagons, operating from a nationwide network of plants, provides reliable logistical support for the freezers.

People

The most important element in product-line planning is an adequate appreciation of the abilities and psychological dynamics of the firm's employees. No product planning and management, however well conceived, can be successful unless able people are committed to the execution of the plan. The company's commitment must call forth the dedication, determination, and elan of the men and women who are to carry it out; it must enhance their self-image and community image so that their own commitment will be sustained. Dr. Robert Mainer has expressed it well:

> Affiliation with a company that successfully manages dynamic change is almost always exhilarating to members of the organization. Planning as an ongoing activity not only represents a company's commitment to remain a vital economic entity, but it also communicates to all concerned that the organization intends to be stimulating rather than merely stimulated. It is a commitment to liveliness and a spirit of adventure. In many ways, planning is an activity that communicates a great deal about the meaning of membership in the organization and of participation in the present work of management as well as an activity aimed at insuring the future viability of the organization.[1]

Senior management must place a commanding importance on the recruiting and development of outstanding people, particularly in the professional disciplines. Abler people will produce a redundancy in product line opportunities so that management will be able to absorb

---

[1] Mainer, Robert; *The Impact of Strategic Planning on Executive Behavior;* Boston: The Boston Consulting Group, Inc.; 1968.

the company's cash flow and employ its other resources without being tempted or forced to adopt products which analysis shows to be marginal. Having enough new ideas to be able to turn down freely the least hardy brings the strength of the Darwinian mechanism to the product mix.

In addition to satisfying the overall strategic requirements of product-line planning, certain other operating aspects must be considered.

PRODUCT PLANNING OVER THE PRODUCT LIFE CYCLE

In discussing product-line planning more specifically, it will be helpful to consider the familiar concept of the product life cycle, which consists of four phases: development, growth, maturity, and decline. Inasmuch as the growth and maturity phases account for about three fourths of the life cycle, the success of a product depends largely on the soundness of the plan during these stages. But the initial phase is critical, because it is at that stage that the decision to commit the firm's resources must be made.

The Development Phase

If the firm has a well-structured research and development program, the plan may begin with the identification of a specific need, followed by an organized search for a product to satisfy it. A successful product-line planning effort should at all times be alert and searching for opportunities to acquire technology from outside sources as well as to develop it in company laboratories. The search for the product may, of course, be unsuccessful. Indeed, the product itself may prove to be technically successful, only to fail commercially because the need has been incorrectly perceived. But those are risks that management must recognize at the outset. The plan must allow for the possibility that the life of the product will end in the development phase.

Alternatively, the development phase may occur before a plan has been devised if the product is an unexpected one; that is, if it becomes available to the firm other than as a result of a deliberate development program. This could ensue from an accidental discovery, or from an unforeseen opportunity to purchase technology from an outside source. When this occurs, the development phase is relatively short and planning must begin, for all practical purposes, with the growth phase.

In either case, growth rate is a key, though elusive, strategic variable. It is difficult to estimate precisely the growth rate of a product because economic trends, technological developments, government actions, and social values often play a larger role than the company's actions in determining it. Despite this difficulty, growth rate is of such overriding importance that an intensive effort must be made to estimate it.

A common technique used in this regard is segmentation, i.e., the definition of a product/market segment. The growth rate of the particular market segment served by the product can then be carefully assessed. Some specific segments may be growing fast. For example, the use of oxygen (a commodity chemical) in foundries (a slow-growth market) has increased significantly in the last few years as a result of the changing economic and technological characteristics of the foundry industry.

The Growth Phase

The business objectives for a product in the growth phase are quite different from the objectives for a mature product. As a result, the product plan is also quite different. For a product in its growth phase, the objective should be to gain a dominant market position. For a mature product, the objective should be to convert the market position into increased profitability.

The firm must, in the growth phase, pursue a preemptive strategy, to obtain more of the market than its competitors. It is usually less expensive to do this in a growing market than in a constant one, because the company's own volume can be obtained from growth rather than from just raiding competitors' accounts. Furthermore, as long as there are economies of scale and average costs decline with increasing volume, the producer with the largest market share will have the highest gross margin. For its preemptive strategy to succeed, a firm must have adequate business capacity, including plant, capital, technology, and people. It must also have a high quality product and an effective pricing policy.

Plant capacity must be kept ahead of the market, because the firm cannot gain market share unless enough product is available.

The importance of working capital in a successful preemptive strategy is often not fully appreciated. When demand is strong, market share can be gained through faster delivery and better credit terms to customers. Working capital is somewhat discretionary, and it has been the subject of meticulous scrutiny by managers who have tried to minimize it. Commonly accepted ideas about the proper levels of accounts receivable and inventories tend to be set on the basis of experience gained from mature product lines, and are often not applicable to the growth phase. Working capital guidelines should be set so as not to inhibit rapid sales growth.

A pricing policy must also be developed that is consistent with the objective of gaining market share. This usually means reducing prices as the product matures, in order to discourage those firms with lesser market share, as well as potential competitors.

Mature and Declining Phases

A fundamental difference between the growth and maturity phases is predictability. In the later phase, the rate of change is easier to forecast, technology is fairly well established, and competitors and customers are known and stable. These circumstances, as well as the shift in objective from increasing market share to increasing profitability, dictate a change in strategy.

Plant capacity must be fully utilized, and high-cost plants replaced in order to minimize unit costs. Because it is desirable to maintain market share, capacity must be expanded at the rate at which the market grows. This is more accurately predictable in a mature market; accordingly, the firm is able to plan for and install the optimum process. Minimizing lead time for new capacity no longer has the importance it had in the growth phase. A tight rein must now be kept on working capital, and inventories and receivables carefully controlled at levels just sufficient to maintain the business.

Product technology must become more applications-oriented and must work toward increased product differentiation, while manufacturing technology aims at lowering production costs and improving product quality, which is an important tool in the mature market. Increased profits can often be realized by using quality to differentiate the product and thereby to command a premium price, especially in specialty segments of the market. Staffing should be set by the time a product reaches maturity, and thereafter it must be carefully controlled. Emphasis should be placed on finding ways to increase employee productivity.

No product plan is complete unless it includes provision for eliminating products that no longer generate adequate profits. As a product moves into the declining phase of its life cycle, management must decide when to eliminate it, and how: by simply ending production or, if the product may be of value to a firm in different circumstances, by selling it. Considerable emotion may be involved in dropping a product that has made a substantial past contribution to the firm, but failure to do so may imperil the firm's future.

PLANS REQUIRE MODIFICATION

Some of these considerations are illustrated by a plan we made at Air Products for entering the agricultural chemicals business. Plans do not, of course, always produce the results they were intended to, and sometimes do so only after considerable modification. This one experienced several false starts and underwent a number of changes; yet today agricultural chemicals are one of the significant business areas of our company.

We began by constructing an anhydrous ammonia plant at New Orleans—a logical extension of our industrial gas activities, in which we made the constituents of ammonia, which are nitrogen and hydrogen. Next, we acquired a company which had a chain of retail stores selling seed and fertilizer to farmers. Then we acquired another company, which had retail stores selling fertilizer to farmers in a different part of the country; it also operated a plant producing ammonia products (as well as various industrial chemicals). We formed a research organization, which undertook to develop new compounds, particularly pesticides and herbicides, that would give us a specialized position in the market, protected by patents and technological know-how.

As time passed, we discovered that the costs of developing these agricultural products were a good deal higher than we had expected, and that synthesizing them on a commercial scale was extremely difficult. We therefore terminated the research program. We also found that there were many problems in the retailing of agricultural products that we were not familiar with, and that the return we could expect to earn on further investments in this area was lower than we thought was acceptable. We therefore divested ourselves of these retail operations.

CONCLUSION

Planning is the disciplined application of thought and insight to the achievement of results. Product planning must throb through the lifeblood of the whole organization. It cannot be isolated in staff areas where the firm's experts in technology, finance, and marketing can safely ignore it. It requires that the professional specialist in each functional area consider himself a product planner as well as an engineer, controller, or salesman.

This attitude thrives only in those organizations where senior management, consciously and subconsciously, on a daily basis, participates in and promotes the planning process. A successful product plan will develop best where emotions are suspect and analysis is honored. Only a management that believes intrinsically in its ability to analyze and plan is most likely to shape events to serve its goals.

TURNING A COMPANY AROUND FROM REGRESSION TO GROWTH

by Herbert Roth, Jr.

President, LFE Corporation

INTRODUCTION

A TURNAROUND operation is a delicate, and very human, business procedure—delicate because conditions are poor, generally business is at a low ebb, and, similarly, morale is at a low level. When a company is in this state, it takes more than the usual business practices to revitalize it and redirect operations to a profitable vein.

There are numerous causes for the degeneration of a business to the point where a turnaround is necessary. First, for the purpose of this discussion, let us define a "turnaround." It is different from the mere implementation of an active acquisition program to bring in new and prosperous businesses on top, or in place of the existing businesses. Though hard to achieve, this can be done, especially when the company is publicly held and the stock price is healthier than the business itself. We saw numerous instances of this during the 60s when many failing companies achieved an entirely new state of health through use of their stock as part of an acquisition program. We are not talking about that when we speak of a turnaround. What we are considering as a turnaround is the redirection of the existing businesses and assets of the company within the framework of markets and product lines, utilizing the fixed assets and capital structure of the company at the time the turnaround is initiated. In other words, a true turnaround is a business operation in which the company is reorganized and redirected to achieve a higher level of performance in the same areas of endeavor, but through improved utilization of assets, facilities, and talent.

There are various reasons why company operations deteriorate to the point where a turnaround is necessary. Some of the symptoms are:

1. Deterioration of profitability.
2. Lack of growth.
3. Growth, but no profits.
4. Proliferation of new businesses while the company is unsuccessful in its existing businesses.
5. Absence of leadership at the chief executive level as evidenced by lack of planning, poor morale among the management, particularly top management, and attendant personal conflicts.
6. Lack of product leadership and failure to attain significant market position.

The most evident mark of failure that prompts action is losses, a condition that, all too often, is allowed to prevail too long. Losses in themselves are not the sole criterion, but, obviously, a continuation of losses is evidence either of poor management or, among other things, of being in the wrong markets.

SETTING THE STAGE FOR THE TURNAROUND

The single most important decision affecting the potential success of a turnaround is who should direct it. Should the existing chief executive continue, or should a new one be brought in? This is a difficult decision and one that only the board of directors can make.

Too often, the deterioration of business operations leads to uncertainty among the board of directors. There is a tendency for the board to suggest what new management actions should be taken. Unless the board is intimately familiar with the company's markets and problems, these suggestions only tend to confuse the issue. The board should focus on the primary problem and that is whether the current chief executive is the man to do the job.

It is difficult for the current CEO to lead the turnaround since the action required must result in a dramatic departure from past practices. A turnaround plan requires new ideas, and experience has shown that revitalization is most likely to succeed if new leadership is provided that represents a complete departure from the past and the associated failures. The board of one company decided to retain the chief executive and charge him with the responsibility for the turnaround. He, in turn, initiated a mass removal of the senior management and deemed that this action in itself would be sufficient to reverse the adverse trend of business. Instead, the outcome was a continuation of the existing directions and business operations without any marked change in performance. This gradually led to a rash of resignations among middle and lower management, thereby depleting the people assets at an alarming rate. In another instance, the chief executive decided to enter new markets and became involved in a radical product development program which had little hope of success within the time frame permitted by the asset structure of the corporation. Each of these examples seems to support the contention that a successful turnaround should start with a change of the Chief Executive Officer.

QUALITIES OF THE CEO IN A TURNAROUND

It is apparent from the record of successful turnarounds that the chief executive sets the pace and makes the record. One of the fundamental considerations regarding the CEO is an evaluation of his specific knowledge versus his basic capabilities. Preferably, the CEO will have a knowledge of the products and markets that the company promotes and sells into. He should have a sufficient technical understanding of the product spectrum; but the required amount of specific acquaintance with products, technology, and markets will vary with the size of the company. The smaller the company, the more involved the CEO becomes with product decisions.

The prospective CEO should not necessarily come from a competitor. In fact, it is generally advantageous not to draw from a competitor in a turnaround situation. All too often, intimate acquaintance with the past problems of the company will inhibit the free-wheeling operation that is necessary to a turnaround's success.

The CEO must have such attributes as demonstrated capability in problem solving, leadership experience, and a record of past performance. Because turnaround situations are often characterized by precarious financial circumstances, the CEO must have an understanding of financial operations and possess the ability to quickly and properly analyze them. He must also be able to promote a dialogue between himself, his lending institutions, and the trade.

The chief executive chosen to head a turnaround situation must not be an individual solely imbued with the long view. Often, a turnaround is a series of short-range, hard-hitting business operations necessary to restore enough health to the company in order to enjoy the prospects of the long view. Many of the attempted turnarounds that have failed have, in fact, done so because long-range plans were initiated that in themselves were entirely correct, but nothing was done in the short term to bring about the profitability necessary to stabilize operations and permit pursuance of longer term objectives.

IMMEDIATE ACTION—THE KEYNOTE OF A TURNAROUND PLAN

It is important that the turnaround plan provide for the immediate reversal of as many losing operations as possible. Stopping the losses is the most essential ingredient to establishing an environment for a turnaround. It will immediately enhance the morale of the employees, restore confidence among the managers, and lead toward normalization of relations with customers, the lending institutions and the trade.

There are two important operating principles that must be promoted at the outset. All management levels must understand that, if different results are to be achieved, things must be done differently! Obviously, past practice has been a failure, hence it must be altered dramatically or discontinued. Second, the management team must view the future in the light of what is vitally important to success. They must reexamine established values and practices and discern from them what should be kept, eliminating as many past practices and operations as reasonable to reduce the operations to only those that provide maximum opportunity for success. This process focuses management attention on a limited number of objectives and, at the same time, relieves the management team of many decisions, planning practices, and studies that have been sapping their strength. The management team must focus on the opportunities at the outset and plan to reduce or eliminate operations that do not fit the future plan.

Delineation of limited objectives has large payoffs. One company almost went bankrupt financing the development of a mass memory while, due to lack of financial strength, its basic product line was not being supported with the proper amount of value engineering to reduce cost and improve performance. Through the simple process of deciding which was more important, protection of the existing product base or diversification into new markets, valuable assets were conserved and financial stability was dramatically improved by dropping the new product program, channeling some funds into product enhancement, and using the residual resources conserved to improve liquidity.

In another case, the decision to reduce the total markets by half permitted more in-depth penetration of the remaining markets, as well as more rapid evolution of a product base which improved competitiveness and eliminated the dissipation of assets into marginal markets with marginal returns.

ORGANIZATIONAL CONSIDERATIONS

It is difficult to ignore the fact that failing operations are obvious manifestations of incompetent management. To some, the first reaction is to place the blame on the entire management team. This may be true in many cases and it is hard to disassociate much of the operating management from the total failure. We should remember, however, that management generally is only as good as the chief executive demands that it be. There are some corollary judgments that are pertinent. Some of the more obvious considerations revolve around the characteristics of the people in management.

It is difficult to understand how good people, if they are truly good, will continue to serve a chief executive who is leading the company downhill. Good people usually follow good people, and poor chief executives generally breed poor managers. In appraising management, therefore, the entire management team should be suspect. It may be that there are many good, aggressive people who fully recognize the deteriorating state of affairs for what it is and are awaiting the opportunity to support new leadership. There is nothing wrong with this. In fact, these are the kinds of managers who will provide a valuable pool of assets to the chief executive in a turnaround. They know the problems of the company and, above all, they know the customers, the market, and where the capabilities lie within the organization. It is not recommended, therefore, that the first step in a turnaround plan be the wholesale removal of the incumbent management team.

Precipitous action on the part of the CEO to make a great number of management changes at the outset creates additional problems. Morale can be destroyed at a time when the company can least afford it. Good people may decide to leave and, with them, the company loses trade secrets as well as good talent. The departure of some of the recognized performers usually triggers additional loss of personnel.

Contrary to popular belief, the evaluation of management and the design of a new management structure are not in themselves the most important early decisions that must be made. Too often, the CEO feels compelled to publish a new organization chart, almost on the first day of his tenure. This deprives him of the opportunity to evaluate the people and the operations. It most certainly will lead to decisions that will have to be reversed and to assignments of people who will have to be reassigned.

It would not be unusual for a CEO to wait six to nine months before arriving at a final organizational design. During that time, the early stages of the turnaround plan will have evolved and the operations will become more clearly defined.

EMPLOYEE COMMUNICATIONS

This whole area of human relations is of primary importance to the success of a turnaround, particularly among management personnel. Once the management team develops confidence in the turnaround plan, they, in turn, must take steps to communicate this feeling of confidence to all echelons. This will not be effective if it is done on a casual basis. Special meetings should be arranged with key employees, and the CEO himself must become involved and provide maximum exposure of his philosophy to as many of the employees as is physically possible. All elements of the company must be told what is happening and why. A good, forceful communication program, outlining the objectives and successes, is the best way to promote a cohesive attack on the problems that beset the company.

The human reaction to the turnaround plan is critical if the plan is to have focus. The management mentality, as well as the operations, must be turned around.

People want to know what order of priorities is intended. Is it more important to grow in size or in profits? Does the CEO want short-term profit or formulation of a long-term base? Where is the company supposed to be three or five years hence? The answers to these questions provide the momentum for the plan.

The CEO must imbue the management team and key employees with the idea that it is more important to be better than to just grow bigger. Emphasis, in the early phase of a turnaround, must be on restoration of profits and on the short view. This is not easily understood and good people have been known to resign because they felt the CEO lacked the long view. These managers must understand that there will be no long term available to them if the immediate problems are not resolved. A corollary problem relates to budgets and reduction of operations. The CEO must invoke a series of cost-cutting measures necessary to short-term health while, at the same time, he makes the management understand that business is still an investment process.

THE PLAN FOR PROGRESSION FROM REGRESSION

The critical element in a turnaround plan is timeliness of action. The operations must be improved sufficiently early to preserve as much of the operating base as possible. Continued losses deteriorate this base in every sense—financial, management, product, and technical competence.

In order to formulate a proper plan of action, an inventory of capabilities must be made. This inventory covers the critical elements that constitute the current condition of business. There should be little doubt that the financial condition, particularly cash, warrants immediate attention. The business cannot survive through the turnaround period if the financial resources are too meager to support operations through the period of change.

A detailed cash flow analysis must be prepared covering whatever period is required for the operation to move into a positive cash flow condition. The cash reserves, plus other available financial support from the equity market or lending institutions, should be fully explored and delineated. Current obligations and other financial commitments should be catalogued and defined, including any degree of latitude that can be negotiated. Not all turnaround situations originate from a serious cash shortage position, but, in any event, a period of losses must, in some way, give rise to cash problems that can undermine the turnaround plan, if not fully appreciated at the outset.

Similarly, product problems should be scrutinized, particularly undefined commitments such as product performance and warranty obligations. The very market performance that leads to regressive operations usually can be traced to some form of product problem. Only in the case of overenthusiastic expansion or diversification has this not been a cause of trouble. A complete inventory of the product line must be made to highlight fruitful areas of cost reduction, high leverage return on product improvement efforts and, equally important, aid in defining those products that should be eliminated. A harsh review of the product line can provide many additional alternatives and opportunities to the turnaround situation. Elimination of marginal products will aid cash flow through a reduction of inventory and support activities. It will aid the management in focusing on primary opportunities and, in some cases, products not appropriate for continuation might be sold off, thereby helping to achieve additional liquidity. The product line assessment and subsequent development of product strategies is the key to future success. This product line, as structured after total assessment and pruning action, will provide the bread and butter to the turnaround operations.

Along with the assessment of the product line, a thorough inventory of the customer base must be undertaken. Key customer accounts must be visited to ascertain future potential and current problems. These visits also help to provide assurances to the customers. In those cases where product lines are to be eliminated, the customer should be informed and a reasonable schedule should be worked out to permit a rational turnover. Well-defined and responsible actions by the turnaround management in these important areas of customer relations promote a positive image in the trade, as well as with the employees involved in the turnaround.

Coordination with financial institutions providing credit and other support is essential. A full and honest disclosure of the assessment of current business conditions must be made to them, preferably at the time a plan of action is being formulated. The obvious purpose of such a disclosure is to secure continued support and define the scope of such support. Keeping the financial institutions up to date on the progress of the turnaround is critical and cannot be overemphasized.

LONG VIEW IMPORTANT, BUT SHORT-TERM SUCCESS ABSOLUTELY NECESSARY

Following an assessment of the current state of operations, an immediate plan of operation, designed to restore balance to the business, must be implemented. This plan will cover a period of 6 to 12 months, and its sole objective is to achieve self-sufficiency of business operations. The test of this self-sufficiency is a net positive cash flow, as well as return to profitability. The theme of the immediate plan of action is to stop losses and this means implementation of stringent budgets evolved from the assessment of markets, product-line capabilities, and obligations. Operations must be evaluated on a month-to-month basis, not longer term. Most important, the expense trends must be reviewed and controlled toward the objective of short-term profitability. This may seem obvious, but, too often, continued high levels of expense have been justified on the basis of long-term benefit. This negates the basic tenet of the turnaround plan and, if permitted to continue, it can completely undermine the plan. The short-term view must prevail if a solid base is to be built for long-term success. Balance between the long and short terms is the most difficult judgment factor underlying the plan.

IMPLEMENTATION OF THE SHORT-TERM PLAN

Generally, a turnaround can be accomplished within one to three years. There are very few instances of success being achieved in a shorter period, and only the larger type turnaround operation should require more than three years.

During the initiation phases of the turnaround, and based on performance trends developed from actual business operations, a short-term business plan evolves. This plan is the key transitional instrument from the remedial operations to long-term stability.

The critical element of the concept of change to be introduced by the CEO is a set of well-defined goals to be achieved over a specified period of time. These goals will include those operations that will be divested, if any; and this fact must be recognized by the top management team, including those members associated with the potential divestitures.

Cutbacks in product development, marketing or engineering competence, and service support generally are necessary. Here, the CEO must be careful that, in demanding short-term profitability, he does not stifle long-term potential. Operations that will not be retained for the long term should be reduced in scope immediately and placed on as positive a footing as possible. Expenses should be cut to the bone.

Emphasis must be placed on the management of assets, primarily current assets. New programs must not be implemented too quickly if they will cause a drain on current assets. Generally, it is better to stall new products for a period of time sufficient to let the budgets take hold and the results be evidenced on the changing balance sheet.

A good financial reporting and control scheme is essential. In the spirit of cost cutting, this fact is sometimes overlooked or deemed an unnecessary near-term expense. On the contrary, such money is well spent. It provides a basis for decision-making and selection of alternate courses of action.

A small, highly specialized and hard-hitting staff is critical to the functioning of the chief executive in a turnaround. A qualified staff provides an immediate impact on the rapidity with which plans are implemented and controlled. A small staff permits direct interface between the CEO and operating managers. The CEO must not permit the staff to displace the prerogatives of line management. Staff people provide the interface, but the turnaround will succeed only if the line managers feel their responsibility and exercise their authority.

The profit objectives set by the turnaround plan must be realistic and attainable. The goals should be simple and easily understood. A turnaround plan is not an instrument for management to promulgate lofty principles of return on investment, sales, and other economic ratios. Keep in mind that a turnaround is a period of transition and many assets may be made obsolete though they do not necessarily disappear. Their cost will dilute performance for a reasonable period into the future. Instead of demanding ultimate performance, a scheme of remedial progression must be enunciated. Most successful turnarounds have been managed on the basis of interim goals. Management must determine, for example, what is the average return on investment or return on sales for comparable competitive operations and set a time frame in which to become "average." Once that is achieved, it can move on to the next objective, such as to reaching the top third of the class. In all respects, financial evaluations and the definition of goals and programs should be limited in scope and relevant to future progress.

An effective turnaround management must operate on the basis of simple and direct principles. To begin with, the market strategy should be defined to probe and compete in only those markets that are of vital importance to near-term and future success.

Product development must be aimed at enhancement of the present situation before consideration can be given to the longer term. There will be constant pressure from the marketing people to engage in extensive new product activities. These pressures must be resisted and a response limited to programs deemed essential by the chief executive.

Deployment and buildup of personnel must be reviewed and evaluated constantly.

SHORT TRANSITION FROM TURNAROUND
TO NORMAL PROGRESSION

Turnaround operations have been concluded successfully when the business demonstrates a trend of increasing profitability, but not necessarily growth. The simple test of self-sufficiency has been met. There is no specific time frame over which the business operation must continue to demonstrate profitability. This is a judgment factor based on the absence of deterioration in the underlying input of new business, a steady-state cost structure, and market acceptance. The CEO must not permit a time lag between the turnaround and assumption of new directions and dimensions.

A new business plan must be ready that incorporates a greater sense of urgency in the areas of product innovation and market operations. If the turnaround has been successful, new sources of financial support will be available and they must be utilized. If the turnaround has been managed properly and has truly been successful, a new plateau of increased profits and growth will begin to evolve. The crisis will have passed and business can proceed on an "as-usual" basis.

GETTING OUT OF ·A BUSINESS; WHEN AND HOW

by Albert H. Gordon
Chairman of the Board; Kidder, Peabody, Inc.

JOHN MURRAY FORBES, in 1828, at the age of 16, was sent to Canton, China, to represent his uncle's Boston counting house. He retired nine years later with a substantial fortune. Subsequently, he became an outstanding leader in Western railroad financing and one of the most astute entrepreneurs of his time. He doubted whether a businessman could expect to earn an average annual rate of return of more than 9 percent on his capital over a long period. In his day, such a rate of return was adequate to finance substantial capital additions, as well as to pay dividends.

When John Forbes made this comment there was no federal income tax, no Clayton Act, no Federal Reserve, no Employment Act of 1946; little, if any, pervasive inflation; and the Old Lady of Threadneedle Street maintained an orderly international money market in London. Whether we agree with John Forbes's figure or not, the return on investment (ROI) should still be the major criterion when executives consider getting out of a business. Without a sufficiently nourishing ROI, enterprises will wither and die.

ROI, AS DIVESTMENT INDICATOR

An unsatisfactory ROI should serve as an early warning signal. When it flashes, corrective action is strongly called for. Getting out of a business is one of the courses that should be considered, even though the act be traumatic. "Divestiture" is the now accepted word for "getting out." Interestingly the word has reverted from its modern dictionary description, "stripping," to its archaic meaning, "laying aside." Managements understandably are reluctant to admit mistakes, for they may hope that during the passage of time they will be corrected. Often it is painful to concede that others may make more productive use of the same assets. Like many people, they prefer the status quo in personal relations to the wrenching changes divestiture may bring to the lives of their associates.

Directors can render great service to stockholders by recommending studies of the causes of an unsatisfactory ROI. The Occidental Petroleum Corporation, a diversified company in the oil, chemical, coal, and associated businesses, sets a constructive example. It asks the heads of its major divisions to identify quarterly those segments that do not meet profitability objectives and to report on their condition at subsequent directors' meetings. Occidental's first major decision was to endeavor to eliminate its real estate venture. As a starter, it wrote off $5 million of its $106 million investment and then entered into a joint arrangement with Shapell Industries, a company with relevant expertise to dispose, through development or immediate sale, of the assets. As a second step, it sold its relatively unproductive European service stations to the French State Oil Company for $27 million, retaining for liquidation its inventory and accounts receivable.

Inasmuch as undue preoccupation with ROI can be misleading, many bases of value should be studied before one elects to dispose of a division or subsidiary. Such fundamental questions as the following should be answered: Does the business continue to meet long-range objectives? Has the parent contributed sufficient managerial advice to develop fully the subsidiary's potential? Is additional investment advisable? Sales and earnings trends, book value, quality of the assets, profit margins, and the relationship and contribution of the business to other divisions of the company should be analyzed. Figures should be obtained to show plant efficiency, competitive position, and market penetration. All of these and others should be examined in an evaluation of the business. The homework has to be done in any case because every prospective purchaser will want the same facts to help him make a decision.

ANALYSIS FOR POSSIBLE DIVESTMENT

In deciding whether to retain ownership or sell, three of the major factors to be studied are:

1.   The future likely profitability of the business and the additional investment required to increase profit margins.
2.   The price realistically obtainable.
3.   The ROI available from the reinvestment of the proceeds of sale in the business and/or in the purchase of the company's stock.

Frequently, through intensive analysis of the potentials of an operation, strategies can be developed to improve market position, correct management deficiencies, reduce unnecessary expenses, and, through investment in facilities or new product development, to increase ROI to satisfactory levels.

Important reasons for divestiture are:

1.   Unsatisfactory earnings or recurrent losses.
2.   Cash requirements for reduction of debt and/or for replacement of capital of other segments of the business.
3.   Adverse changes in competitive position.
4.   Increasing lack of compatibility between parent and subsidiary in product lines and in management.
5.   Acknowledgment by new management that diversification has become counterproductive.
6.   And at last, but not least, an attractive price.

Divestments to raise cash to reduce debt and to fund capital requirements have become increasingly frequent in the sobering 70s because of the difficulty of meeting the requirements of lending banks and the need to refinance maturing debt. An example was the sale by the Boise Cascade Co. of its wholly-owned Ebasco Services Inc., and Vernon Graphics Inc., to the Halliburton Company for $65.6 million. The sale, together with the sale of realty operations, mobile homes, on-site housing, and other engineering and construction subsidiaries, raised $370 million, all of which was used for the reduction of debt. On June 30, 1972, at the start of the divestment program, debt was $1,147 million. As of December 31, 1973, it had declined to $602 million.

The sale by Signal Oil Companies, Incorporated, on January 28, 1974 of its subsidiary, Signal Oil and Gas Company, to Burmah Oil Incorporated, for $420 million in cash, retaining a 25 percent interest in the profits of its share of the Thistlefield in the North Sea oil fields, is another example. The price, which exceeded the then market value of the stock of the parent, was obtained because of the increased value of petroleum companies as a result of the sharp rise in the price of oil. Parenthetically, the transaction illustrates the importance of timing. A major factor in the decision to sell, other than the attractive price, was the management's conviction that it could better utilize the funds in other segments of its business and in the purchase of its own stock than by putting them into its North Sea field. By cashing in, Signal reduced its long-term debt by $88 million, repurchased 12 percent of its stock (for $62,400,000), and invested temporarily in short-term securities.

The story for Burmah is a sad one. To finance the Signal purchase and to meet other commitments aggregating approximately $1 billion, it borrowed huge sums from its banks. A year later, unable to meet the covenants of the loan agreements, it had to resort to the British government for a loan guarantee of $650 million. In addition, it divested itself of its Canadian subsidiary, the Great Plains Company, for approximately $96 million to Canadian Industrial Oil and Gas Ltd. Interestingly, it turned to the former Great Plains Company president, who by then had become head of the Alberta Energy Company, a creation of the Alberta government for the purpose of investing in private companies, in order to find the buyer with the biggest purse.

Unfavorable changes in market patterns and competitive factors may induce the divestment or liquidation of a business. The sale (for stock) of General Electric Company's computer business to Honeywell, Inc., was activated by the recognition that to continue the business would require such vast amounts of capital for research, production, and leasing that the profitable operations of GE would be hampered.

Additions to product lines resulting from external factors such as the development of improved raw materials may lead to divestment. Armstrong Cork Company in 1969 sold its peripheral enterprises and phased out its original product—the application of cork—to concentrate on interior furnishings such as resilient vinyl and asbestos floor coverings, synthetic carpeting, and plastic insulating materials.

Changes in management, with the subsequent uncovering of a too-broadly diversified condition, often result in a program to identify weak segments and to weed out those with low potential. The American Machine & Foundry Co. case is not unique. Morehead Patterson, its former dynamic chief executive, built up largely by acquisitions a diverse corporate complex that manufactured specialized automatic and semiautomatic machinery for the production of cigarettes, clothing, shoes, neckties, and baked goods. In addition, AMF produced defense equipment and a pinspotter for bowling alleys. The succeeding management corrected the overdiversified condition by selling several subsidiaries and by reducing the heavy dependence on government work. It concentrated on leisure time areas, with emphasis on the pinspotter apparatus and golf equipment. For better or worse, it later acquired companies making tennis and ski equipment, sailboats, and motorboats.

PROGRAM FOR DIVESTMENT; ALTERNATIVES

As soon as a divestment program has been agreed upon, advice should be sought on the probable value of the property to be sold. Often outside consultants with specialized knowledge can estimate ranges of value. Such figures may indicate that the probable realizable price is less than that obtainable by the gradual liquidation of the business with the concurrent tax benefit resulting from the depreciation charges and any ultimate write-off of assets remaining on termination.

It is essential that the attitude of the management be ascertained. In most cases, the value is enhanced if management accompanies the assets, for most buyers know that results usually will be more satisfactory with existing management. The fact that people make up one of the most important keys to profits was lost sight of by many freewheeling purchasers in the hoped-for synergistic 60s.

In most cases, a careful screening of possible buyers will eliminate all but a limited number who have sufficient resources and interest to consummate a transaction. The Union Carbide Corporation found such a buyer for its Neisler Laboratories division. It had purchased Neisler as a marketer of the promising biological compounds it (Union Carbide) had developed. Learning that the pharmaceutical products could not be successfully distributed by a concern having, as it did, a broad range of unrelated products, it sold Neisler to Mallinckrodt Inc., for its Pharmaceutical and Science Products Group, at a substantial profit.

The screening process should exclude candidates with severe antitrust complications. It is frustrating to learn, after finding a purchaser, that Section 7 of the Clayton Act precludes a closing. Because reliance should not be placed wholly on in-house counsel on antitrust matters, the opinion of outside counsel should be sought. Illustrative of the vexations of antitrust actions is the case of the acquisition—in 1971 from Schenley Industries—by Northwest Industries, Inc., of Buckingham Corp., the exclusive U.S. distributor of Cutty Sark Scotch whisky. Although Schenley's inside and outside counsel eventually accomplished the sale, the $120 million transaction was delayed four times by the Department of Justice, even though Schenley was compelled by consent decree to dispose of Buckingham.

To facilitate a sale and to maximize price, a company should consider retaining an agent to assist it in identifying the best prospects, in approaching them, and in negotiating with them. Secrecy in the initial stages can best be insured by an agent. Such secrecy is of great importance to avoid disturbing middle management, distributors, customers, and employees. The agent can also be helpful in designing acceptable securities if payment is not to be made fully in cash. The agent may be an individual, an accounting firm, a commercial bank, or an investment banking firm. In general, banks and investment banking firms may be the best qualified because of their wide direct or indirect national and international connections. It may be more an investment banker's cup of tea than a commercial bank's because of the nature of an investment banker's business.

Regardless of the selection, outside specialists can cooperate with the in-house staff in the preparation of a package of information, including the statement analyses, comparisons, and other data regarding such items as pension plans, stock options, customer lists, manufacturing facilities, and labor contracts. A search for hidden values should be undertaken. Such values may include low-cost real estate, productive patents, written-off new product development costs, assets depreciated below their reproduction cost, and overly conservative bad debt reserves.

Sometimes the parent is the best marketer. For example, the Harris Corporation, after deciding to divest its Langston division because its product line was outside its mainstream, approached Langston's longtime English licensee, knowing that the licensee had worldwide expansion plans for its products and had the resources to pay in cash. After extended negotiations, a transaction was concluded, but only after the Langston senior manager agreed to accept an enlarged management role.

Occasionally a selling company's management may make a novel arrangement. Such was the sale by Northwest Industries, Inc., of the transportation assets of its Chicago and North Western Railway Company to a newly formed employee-owned railway company in return for the assumption of approximately $400 million of debt by the new owners.

A classic case concerns The General Tire & Rubber Company and its Galis Manufacturing Division, a maker of coal mining machinery. In 1970, General decided to divest itself of Galis because it (General) could better use its management time and the proceeds from the sale on its much larger businesses. Its investment banker, being asked to find a suitable suitor and to assist in the negotiations, sought out the FMC Corporation, a company with material handling expertise. In addition to wanting cash for the business, General insisted that the purchaser be acceptable to the Galis management. FMC met those requisites and a transaction was completed. FMC, after supplying Galis with sufficient capital to enlarge its production facilities and after providing managerial assistance, greatly improved the Galis profitability. The banking firm received incentive compensation—a percentage of the minimum acceptable price to General plus a higher percentage on the incremental amount above the minimum.

A business may be sold in a number of ways: to another company, to its management, to a group of investors, to the public through a registered public offering, partially to a joint venture, or spun off to the stockholders of the parent. A review should be made to determine the best "market." In periods of strong markets, the highest price may be realizable through a public offering. A few years ago GAC Corporation, for example, to raise capital, sold for $24 million, through a public offering, 100 percent of the stock of Equitable Savings and Loan Association—which it had acquired only two years earlier for $28,500,000.

The spin-off technique has been used primarily in cases of forced divestiture; but, under certain conditions, this method may have application in a voluntary action. A true spin-off raises no cash. It transfers ownership of a business by a company to its shareholders. Variations of the spin-off are endless. For example, a company may offer the shares of a business to be disposed of to its stockholders in exchange for its own shares. Procter & Gamble Company did this in its Department of Justice–enforced divestiture of the Clorox Company. As a starter, it sold 1.2 million shares of Clorox to the public for $33 million. Later, having established a market for Clorox stock, it exchanged the remaining 6,800,000 shares of Clorox for 1,721,000 of its own shares.

WORKING OUT A SALE TO A BUYER

After identification and selection of the most likely possible buyers, the utmost discretion should be used in making approaches. The appropriate time to approach potential buyers is of importance. In most cases, the selling company should wait until audits or interim financials have been finished, for prospective buyers will want audited statements in addition to information on the immediate outlook and on such matters as pending lawsuits and unclosed taxes.

Approaches to possible buyers can be made directly or through an intermediary so well placed as to be able to talk with the chief executive of the prospective purchaser in confidence. Such an agent can often, without revealing the identity of his principal, ascertain whether or not the possible buyer is interested in serious negotiations. If he is, a meeting should be promptly arranged to submit the material already prepared and to discuss the transaction.

The advisor and/or the financial officer of the seller should make a thorough presentation at this meeting. Because many top officers are engineers, lawyers, or marketers, and not experienced in the interpretation of financial statements, the analyses and statistics should be carefully explained.

Executives usually have had much more experience in buying companies than in selling them. It may be difficult for them to switch roles and adjust to the tactics best suited to achieve a maximum price. In the merger era of the 1960s, buyers often were more concerned with the immediate impact on earnings per share from an acquisition than with a studied appraisal of the acquired business. The stock market supported the high price-earnings ratio of the acquirer, and excessively valued common stock was widely used as payment. Today, cash is a valuable commodity and payment in it usually is a sine qua non. Bargaining at the negotiating table has become much more intense. To achieve satisfactory results, the seller, and/or his agent, must have patience and must be fully armed with all relevant facts concerning the sale, on the one hand, and the advantages to the purchaser of the contemplated acquisition on the other.

The pros and cons of dealing with prospects sequentially should be weighed. If the possible purchaser is not put under some time pressure, he may procrastinate for trading purposes or because he realizes he can attend to other matters first, without harming himself. From the seller's point of view, the longer the elapsed time, the greater the risk of rumors spreading that the company is for sale and that the buyer is hesitant—all of which might reduce the eventual price.

Sometimes, by announcing a plan to sell and by putting a business on the "auction block," favorable results may be obtained. The publicity may attract numerous potential buyers and competing bids. The "auction block" approach does not always prove to be a panacea, however, as evidenced by International Telephone & Telegraph Corporation's difficulty in selling its remaining 52 percent of Avis. A 1971 consent decree ordered ITT to sell its interest in Avis by September 24, 1974. Because of the widespread publicity of the order, ITT was forced to declare its intentions. ITT's strategy had been to sell all its Avis stock through a series of public offerings. In June of 1972, it sold 23 percent publicly, and in January 1973 an additional 25 percent. The subsequent stock market deterioration precluded further public offerings for the time being at least. ITT has discussed selling its remaining 52 percent with a number of parties. To date, in spite of the publicity, it is still in search of a buyer. The disadvantages of publicizing a proposed sale are numerous. The morale of employees can be seriously shaken, customers and suppliers may begin to do business elsewhere, and serious potential purchasers may shy away from a bidding contest.

If price is the last stumbling block, two independent financial advisors in whom both sides have confidence, one to represent the seller and the other the buyer, may be retained to study the material, to interview the officers of both companies, and to recommend price. This procedure may get the principals off the bargaining hook; it also gives some protection in the event of "stockholder suits."

Human problems should be dealt with carefully to preserve the going-concern value of the divested business. Pension plans should be reviewed and the same or better terms given by the new ownership. The transaction should be carefully explained so that the reasons for the divestment are understood. If possible, the buyer should declare his intention to keep the plant or plants in operation with existing personnel. If the sale is to a larger company with strong national (and international) business, the improved opportunities for advancement should be pointed out to the management.

ACCOUNTING, TAXES, AND ANTITRUST

Divestiture has been made more difficult by the stricter accounting rules of the Accounting Principles Board and by the more militant attitude of the Department of Justice. According to the new accounting regulation, if any company sells a subsidiary or division to another corporation, the transfer is accounted for as a "purchase" transaction. The Board's *Opinion No. 16* requires in a purchase transaction that the acquiring company's historical income statements remain unaffected by the acquisition, thereby eliminating any positive effect of a historical restatement of the combined results of the two companies. Relevant pro forma earnings data of the combined companies is required to be disclosed in a footnote. If the excess of the amount paid over book value of the assets cannot be reasonably allocated to the assets, it must be labeled "goodwill" and written off over a period not exceeding 40 years. As the amortization is not tax deductible, it is a direct charge to earnings. For prospective buyers who are earnings-per-share conscious, the existence of such "goodwill" may result in a lower offer to a seller to compensate for the amortization.

If the price paid is less than book value in a "purchase" transaction, there may be tax savings and financial reporting advantages which should be of definite value to the acquiring company. If stock is acquired, the buyer has the opportunity of using the seller's higher tax basis as a means of reducing tax liability. Also, since for financial reporting purposes the acquirer would account for the assets acquired based on their appraised value, the excess of book value over acquisition cost generally can be taken into income by the acquiring company over the average remaining life of the depreciable assets of the acquired company.

In matters concerning tax and antitrust aspects, expert legal advice should be obtained. No plan of sale should be agreed upon until the proposed terms are approved by counsel as to tax and antitrust consequences. Recent interpretations of Section 7 of the Clayton Act by the Supreme Court, and increasingly strict application of the law by the Justice Department and the Federal Trade Commission, have caused great changes in the direction of divestitures and acquisitions. As a consequence, consideration of an acquisition is often dismissed out of hand because of the likelihood of adverse action by the federal government.

CONCLUSION

It is apparent that there has been a fundamental change in the environment for sale of companies. The sellers' market of the 60s with the conglomerate buyers at the helm, is over; a buyers' market now exists. There will be more businesses for sale, but there will be fewer companies with buying interest, and less capital available for acquisitions. The decision to retain ownership or sell should be analyzed with more diligence and sharper focus than at any prior time. The successful sellers in 1974's unfavorable climate had to plan carefully and had to develop or retain outside expertise in order to accomplish divestitures on an advantageous basis. Unless and until more ebullient conditions recur, the would-be divestor will have to proceed knowledgeably and persistently. The would-be acquirer may long sit in the driver's seat.

NEW DIMENSIONS OF CORPORATE SOCIAL RESPONSIVENESS

by David B. Kiser[*]

Associate, Cambridge Research Institute

FEW CHIEF EXECUTIVE OFFICERS today are ignorant of the concept of "corporate social responsibility." Many may feel uncomfortable with it, however, inasmuch as it commonly refers to that murky realm of corporate activity—sometimes known as "doing good"—that is seemingly far removed from the conventional production of goods and services. This area of less well-defined concern has evolved over the course of many years during which the social environment in which American business operates has undergone dramatic changes. It has won the support of countless numbers of academics, intellectuals, corporate critics, and businessmen themselves. Concern with corporate social responsibility occupies a firm place, so the surveys tell us, in the expectations of many Americans for the conduct of their public corporations. And it provides a source of unending frustration for many managers because it seldom can be adequately defined or properly measured. In short, it perhaps cannot be managed; and yet it seems to be here to stay. Hence, it represents a dilemma for most of us.

The dilemma, however, is partially a semantic one. The word "responsibility" suggests an obligation and a moral duty. Indeed, this is the chief aspect of corporate social activity that has been dissected in the vast amount of literature and discussion that has been produced on the subject. However, actions fostered out of guilt or conscience are no substitute for programs developed from clearheaded management analysis. Such is the message of this chapter: Corporate social

---

[*] [Ed. Note: For a number of years, Mr. Kiser has studied the implementation of corporate social programs in a number of industries, and used the results of his studies as the basis for his doctoral dissertation at the Harvard Business School.]

activities are warranted by the clear demands of a changing environment; they produce issues and opportunities that must be reckoned with; and the resulting *business* programs *can* be managed adroitly, if the necessary administrative skills are learned. Hence the use of the term "responsiveness" in the title, rather than "responsibility."

THE CHANGING SOCIAL ENVIRONMENT

Throughout the earlier years of our country's growth, corporations were expected to achieve top efficiency and ever-increasing productivity. These goals have not changed today. What has changed is the extent to which these goals stand alone. To them has been added a relentless search for more equitably distributed income and employment, for the safeguarding of the capacities of the physical environment, and for the steady betterment of product quality and safety. This search manifests itself in such management matters as minority hiring, pollution control, consumer affairs, community relations, and corporate giving. These additional demands come at a time when most corporate presidents already find themselves burdened with inflated costs, a shrinking international comparative advantage, and an eroding natural resource base at home. Little wonder that many of them ponder inwardly how the "self-appointed" social critics could be so blind to the "real" problems facing the country!

It is only partially comforting to learn that business is not alone in its plight. The expansion of expectations which has enveloped the business community over the last decade has involved church and state as well. While the national community has searched vainly for relevant national goals, the resulting frustration has fallen on all of our goal-setting institutions, bringing with it a drastic lowering of confidence in their abilities across the board.[1] Businesses, churches, governments, hospitals, and universities have all been called upon to defend their profits, their tax-free status, and their swollen budgets; and to expand their accountability beyond their traditional missions to include some kind of "social performance" as well. But upon the private corporation, with its potential for private gain at the possible expense of the public welfare, has fallen the brunt of criticism.

It is true that the present era is not the first period in our history when corporations have been under the pressure of social change. The

---

[1] See *Public Opinion Index;* published annually by Opinion Research Corporation.

trust-busting and consumer movements of the early 1900s, the establishment of regulatory commissions in the early 1930s, and the consumer movement of the late 1930s all shared the intention of limiting or monitoring business practices. But each of these periods of zeal eventually came to an end, followed by a decade or more of flourishing business progress that was relatively unencumbered by heavy regulatory overtures or public criticism. Is it reasonable to expect the present period simply to repeat the pattern?

For several reasons, my answer to this question must be, "No." First, and most important, the societal machinery to monitor and regulate business practices is more elaborate and searching than ever. A *Fortune* article pointed this out two years ago.[2] Almost 12,000 suits were filed in federal district courts in 1972 against corporations, double the number in 1966. Of that number, environmental and fair-employment suits, which are big news items today, were just emerging; they accounted for only a little more than 10 percent of the total. But they were growing at a rate of 25 percent per year. The legal tab for the domestic cases was estimated at $1.3 billion for the 1,300 companies listed in the *Fortune* directories, or just about a million dollars apiece on average. Behind the figures were uncounted thousands of out-of-court settlements, aimed at avoiding formal litigation and gaining time for the corporation to conform to new rules and regulations.

The sources of litigation revealed even more as to the nature of this trend. Forty-four of 65 companies surveyed identified the federal government as the principal source of their legal problems. Second place, by a similar ranking, went to state and local governments. Aiding this phenomenon, of course, is the growing list of federal and state agencies whose charters include enforcement, through litigation if necessary. On the federal level, should their compliance recommendations go unheeded, the Environmental Protection Agency (EPA), the Equal Employment Opportunities Commission (EEOC), the Consumer Product Safety Commission (CPSC), and the departments enforcing the Occupational Safety and Health Act (OSHA) all have legal recourse to the courts. And understandably, the *Fortune* survey indicated that—besides antitrust and securities matters—environmentalism, fair-employment practices, and consumerism generated the most legal concern among managements. In other words, some expectations for social performance have already been institu-

---

[2] Carruth, Eleanor; "The 'Legal Explosion' Has Left Business Shell-Shocked"; *Fortune;* April 1973; p. 65.

tionalized within the levels of government that administer our laws, and within the courts who interpret them.

The driving force behind the regulatory overtures is a gathering national will that has found expression in the passage of new laws. Taking only consumerism as an example, over 50 pieces of major federal legislation are now on the books. About 30 of these laws have been passed since 1966. Within the five Congresses that have convened since that time, it is apparent that a nearly unbeatable consumerist constituency has developed. Concern for social performance by corporations is not something found only among certain individuals and groups; it has been institutionalized in the national body that makes our laws.

Of the lawsuits originating in the private sector, the *Fortune* survey revealed that most companies pointed to nonstockholding individuals as the primary source of litigation. These "activists" have been aided since 1966 by the potential embodied in the class-action suit, which allows the grouping together of a number of plaintiffs in a single lawsuit in order to resolve a number of claims at one time. Although changes in the laws governing the administration of class-action suits have made them more costly, they remain a potentially effective weapon in lawsuits against corporations because of the high damages they may entail. Activists have also shown a high degree of sophistication in recent years, not only in organizing and funding their own pressure groups, but also in using other legal avenues that are available in addition to class-action suits, such as boycotts, public hearings, lobbying, and proxy fights. They, too, have managed a degree of success in institutionalizing their concerns.

A second, more general reason why the current wave of business reform will most likely continue is that it is part of something larger. The movement for corporate social responsiveness runs parallel to similar movements for the increased use of social indicators (to measure a nation's social well-being) and technology assessment (to anticipate the social impacts of technological advances). Each has been pursued in all of the countries of Western Europe as well as in the United States. Great Britain already sports a social indicator series published regularly and is experimenting with audits of social performance by organizations, including corporations. These efforts involving Western societies aim to modify our emphasis on growth, to conserve nonrenewable resources, to expand our international—as well as our national—accounts to include other than economic performance, and to emphasize generally the improvement in the quality of our lives. All of them reflect the changing worldwide ground-rules within which business operates.

A third reason for the longevity of the current business criticism is more subtle. Stated simply, institutions that deal with the American public have reached such a level of interdependence that some cannot fail without bringing others down with them. Witness, for example, the shudders sent throughout our society by the spectre of failure by such important institutions as Penn Central and Con Edison. This state of affairs leads to something like a system-wide morality, where everybody is responsible *for* everybody else and *to* everybody else. Legal exposure brings more onus than mere legal expense, and it's easy to see why. With various media acting as watchdogs, any step which threatens the other guy's "turf" becomes grounds for a suit. And it doesn't necessarily pit noncorporation against corporation. One of the most interesting findings of the *Fortune* survey revealed that almost 1,300 *private* antitrust suits were filed in 1972; in these cases, it was often corporations suing each other for control of technologies, markets, and the like. Another observer has reasoned that product liability suits have taken off on an exponential growth track because many lawyers who made their living from liability suits involving automobile accidents were thrown out of work by no-fault insurance programs. They turned, it has been said, to product liability work because the similar themes and laws involved made the transition a natural one.

In summary, I believe that the present period of dissatisfaction with corporate social performance will not suddenly fade away. Its articulators are numerous and are fast becoming institutionalized; its threads are common to other social movements now occurring; and its beneficiaries are plentiful. Although the ups and downs of economic fortunes may moderate the trend from time to time, it seems unlikely that the search for reform will soon be terminated. If this be so, then the next question for the chief executive to face is, "What can be done about it?" To that subject I now turn.

ADAPTIVE COPING WITH CHANGE

Most successful corporations stay that way because they are capable of adapting to a radically changed environment. Old organization structures are discarded, traditional charters are abandoned, and once again the organization is set upon the task of defining a competive advantage. Whole lines of business may be shed, as though a cocoon, revealing a dynamic organism inside. New organizational forms may be invented, uniquely designed to mesh the capabilities of the organization with the exigencies of the marketplace. New financial creations may emerge to deal with tight money; bold backward integration may occur to assure supplies in time of scarce resources; and divisionalization may evolve to deal with an ever-increasing technological complexity of products and markets. Processes such as these have been occurring throughout the entire history of American business, and they continue today. Long-term success becomes almost synonymous with adaptation and transformation.

And so it is with social change. New attitudes and norms are constantly emerging and are eventually reflected in the way we organize to do useful work, in the way we treat our fellow employees, in the processes we use to reward valued behaviors and to constrain undesirable ones, in the products that we make, and in the services we offer. Conceptually, it is a small leap to extend the idea of such change to the realms of pollution control, minority hiring, or consumer dissatisfaction. Administratively, however, it may be a considerable jump!

The "right way" to handle the organizational problems posed by these issues is, of course, unknown. Unlike the other subjects in this book, success stories of corporate social responsiveness are difficult to come by, and, when encountered, difficult to generalize upon. However, it has been my experience that one does not have to have all the answers to a complex problem in order to be useful. If he can help the managers on the firing line to structure their thinking better, he can rely on their personal expertise and intimate knowledge of their own situation to enable them to find appropriate solutions.

In that spirit, listed below are some of the pitfalls I have observed in studying the implementation of corporate social programs over the last few years. If knowledge of their existence becomes more widespread, perhaps some of the more common mistakes may not be repeated in future efforts.

Implementation of social policies involves a long period of organizational learning. Research work undertaken by Robert Ackerman, Vice President, Administration and Finance, Premoid Corporation, has identified some common stages in the implementation process:[3] (*a*) The formation of a corporate policy by the chief executive; (*b*) recognition by the chief executive that the policy fails to modify manager behavior; (*c*) the appointment of a specialist to make a study of the social issue and to exhort compliance among operating managers; (*d*) the recognition again by the chief executive that little is happening, which gives rise to an informal "audit" of performance; (*e*) the acceptance of responsibility for the social program by the operating units, often as a result of a major crisis or other organizational trauma; (*f*) ultimately, the development of a regular information system that allows management to track progress over time and include it in executive evaluation. Ackerman found that such a process could easily take four, five, or six years in a large, complex corporation. Managements which have been slow to start EEOC or OSHA compliance activities and now have a shorter deadline in mind may find Ackerman's stage process informative.

Such organizational learning involves understanding the difference between learning how to do something, and learning how to get something done. Ackerman's stages really document the frustrations of a management which is faced with changing the organization's priorities, response mechanisms, and reward systems all at once. Learning how to make a safe product is far easier than learning how to insure that the organization will make a safe product, especially if profitability is jeopardized. If safety is desired, top management's intentions must be made crystal clear, and a real sense of priorities must be communicated.

"Social" issues and conventional business concerns are often inseparable. Although consumerism is often cited as the obvious example of a social issue which overlaps standard business activity because of its interrelationship with marketing, advertising, quality control, and product design, the fact is that almost all social issues require implementation through regular business operations. Equal employment can be effected only through the cooperation of every manager in the line. Pollution control cannot be adequately implemented without involving production, facilities planning, engineering, and often financial considerations. Because of this fact, the temptation to perpetuate social programs as isolated staff activities must be resisted if things are to happen. At conferences, the complaint is

---

[3] Ackerman, Robert; *Managing Corporate Responsibility*; Cambridge, Mass.: Harvard University Press; 1975.

sometimes heard that not enough chief executives are in attendance, especially when the subject matter is corporate responsibility. But if an organization is to move along with a program of implementation of social issues, it is the manager far down the line who will have problems, and it is he who should be in attendance at such conferences, not his staff or his chief executive.

It is also clear that social issues may result in improving conventional business results, although measurement is often difficult. One such example comes from the life insurance industry. For years, the life insurance rates charged to blacks were higher than those charged to whites of the same age and health. The reason given was that black mortality was higher than white mortality, and that the greater risk justified the greater fee. But in compiling such data, no one had ever examined black mortality statistics to take into account (in addition to age and health variables) education and income also, both of which are closely related to the quality of health care. When one insurance company, on what they thought were moral grounds, undertook a program to examine the possibility of eliminating the pricing differential, they found that black mortality was just the same as white mortality, if education and income were taken into account. They later succeeded in opening up a large profitable area of new business, selling life insurance to blacks at lower than prevailing rates.

Although this is an exciting example, more often than not the pursuit of a social issue will disclose to management a regular business operation which is simply in need of improvement, independent of the social issue which revealed it. Thus, trying to effect an affirmative action program may lead to improvement in the personnel function; consideration of consumer complaints may lead to improved and cheaper product service; and attempts to control pollution may lead to new processes or to the recapture of valuable byproducts.

Inseparable or not, the organization reacts to social issues quite differently from the way it reacts to conventional business concerns. Most managements tend to perceive social programs as involving nonrecoverable costs. Whether such programs do or do not, in fact, involve nonrecoverable costs, I shall leave to the accountants. But, because of this perception, and because managers are evaluated on the basis of meeting strict traditional cost and profit guidelines, tension develops around social programs, and conflict may follow.

At this point, the perceived legitimacy of the program becomes all-important. If profit center managers respect the source within the corporation from which the program suggestion has come, such as from the CEO or other top line officer, they are much more likely to consider it on its own merits. In addition, the CEO needs to give absolutely clear indications that the social program in question is to receive top priority, if that is what is desired, even at the temporary expense of conventional business concerns. If that is not done, doubt will linger among the middle managers as to the program's true importance and their own roles regarding it. Effective implementation will be delayed. (The CEO has to be sure of his own intentions, too, before he can send clear signals to the rest of his organization.)

It is also clear that social projects compete with conventional projects for scarce capital resources. To that extent, division managers and others accountable for profit must use discretion in their selection of social projects over other, waiting, conventional ones. Selection is difficult, however, because conventional projects are easily analyzed, whereas social projects are not. The former are begun in response to a clearly perceived need, such as insufficient capacity to meet sales demand, and are evaluated on a recognized standard, such as ROI or payback. For what appear to be social projects, on the other hand, there is seldom an agreed-upon standard of performance that will allow a management to compare what the firm is actually doing with what it should be doing. Here is where the judgment of the CEO and his fellow officers is most important, and most needed. To be able to measure the deviation from an adopted standard is virtually a necessity if any long-term management of a social program is to be sustained.

True implementation occurs only when line managers are required to spend time and resources on social problems as a regular part of day-to-day management. Most managers characteristically view social programs as a royal pain in the—ah—neck, even if they personally believe in the intrinsic merits which the programs may offer. It is not difficult to see why. They are simply not paid or promoted for the accomplishment of "social" goals, especially if the latter conflict with the accomplishment of business objectives. Because of this fact, they will design numerous subterfuges to protect their budgets, their bottom lines, and their careers from being dependent on the performance of a social program. Only when the program originates within the group which is to administer it are many of the headaches avoided.

Recognizing this fact, the decentralization of dealing with social issues seems to be a desirable end result, *providing* that the division managers can be inspired to act on their own initiative. Clearly, this is a major hurdle, and the CEO who attempts to begin here is bound to suffer major disappointments. Nevertheless, this is the great task facing the chief executive—to redesign the reward and control system to inspire adequate social performance without jeopardizing the handling of conventional business concerns. If successful, the CEO will have learned how to make his own organization adaptive to many kinds of change as well as social ones. This, I believe, is an extraordinarily valuable lesson, in a "profits" sense.

Seldom in the management of social issues is money the scarcest resource or the chief concern. Management time and the availability of key people are often far more important. By its nature, the corporation speaks the language of money. Revenues and costs are measures of viability; and profit is a prime measure of its performance. It is commonplace to hear a manager say, "I haven't got the money for that." Budgets are ubiquitous, and the language of budgets—filled with money terms—is the official language most widely spoken.

And yet one rarely hears a manager say, "I haven't got the *time* for that project." Managers are supposed to *make* time; they are *given* the money and the people. However, in the management of social issues, the amount of learning that must take place and the amount of attention that is called for require inordinate amounts of *time*. If time is not made available, increasing complaints will be heard about the unavailibility of "the right people" or about the "extraordinary expense" involved in social projects, when what's really lacking is the *time* to deal with the problem.

CONCLUSION

A new social environment, today, is confronting the Chief Executive Officers of American corporations. Many of its manifestations appear destined to remain on the scene during the coming years, despite temporary ups and downs. In response, management of social issues must be brought into the mainstream of the day-to-day operation of the business. To do so requires an appreciation of the complexity of the task; of the managerial learning involved; the interrelationships between social and business concerns; of the organizational resistance that arises from those interrelationships; and of the increasing importance of management time employed in the resolution of social issues.

In the mid-18th century, Voltaire wrote in his *Dictionnaire Philosophique*, "The best is the enemy of the good." So it is with corporate social responsiveness. From the corporations which handle the learning process well, we may expect a series of "good" social performances during the coming years. With their accomplishments and examples before us, we may be able to avoid getting distracted and feeling guilty by the clamor for the "best" sent up by science-fiction writers, dreamers, and those few activists who would never be satisfied with anything less.

STRATEGIC DECISION-MAKING: PLANNING, MANNING, ORGANIZATION

by John Desmond Glover

Lovett-Learned Professor of Business Administration,
Harvard Business School

There is a tide in the affairs of men,
Which, taken at the flood, leads on to fortune;
Omitted, all the voyage of their life
Is bound in shallows and in miseries.
. . . We must take the current when it serves,
Or lose our ventures.

So said Brutus, noblest Roman of them all.

STRATEGIC DECISIONS

Strategic decisions are expressions of human will. They shape the very nature of the corporation, its function in the world, what it "does for a living," and by what means. Strategic decisions result in purposeful major commitments of resources. Inevitably, these commitments run for long spans of time. Commitments are not only made. Some are refused, "omitted"; they are nonetheless fateful for that. Fortunes are made and ventures lost through strategic decisions to do or not to do, and when.

Corporate strategic decisions are of many sorts. Some represent signals to go ahead to build major structures and to equip them: a steel mill on the banks of the Delaware; a 50-story building in the eye of a metropolitan center. An airline may commit itself to buy and pay for one, a few, or a fleet of multimillion-dollar aircraft. A coal or copper company may commit millions of dollars simply to make ready a deep mine, whose estimated life may extend beyond the end of the 20th century. Some entail financial arrangements, say loans and prom-

424   *Chief Executive's Handbook*

ises to repay, that may run for a decade or more. A company may enter
with a supplier a contract that runs for 15 years, or give a franchise
that runs even longer. A chemical company may buy or sell a license
under a patent with many years to run. A company may give thousands of shares of its stock for an acquisition, or divest itself of a significant segment of its business. A company may resolve to enter a
market, in which it never has operated, with the intention of taking
over a sizeable share of that market during the next several years. To
that end, it may invest thousands or millions of dollars before the
effort gets into the black. A bank or a department store may undertake to develop one or more suburban branches which, it is hoped,
may produce a satisfactory return after "x" years into the future.
Companies undertake research and development projects that will
absorb hundreds of thousands, or millions of dollars and take years
before results may be reached.

If these decisions are premature, or too late; or too big, or too little;
the venture will be lost. So, too, if they're the wrong kind or in the
wrong place. If they're right, they lead on to fortune.

Such decisions to commit the company in major ways are sometimes—perhaps more often than not—discrete, one-time propositions.
Sometimes—I would like to think, increasingly—they are part of an
explicit, self-aware pattern of events planned and committed to take
place over a period of years. They represent major individual actions
in a schedule of steps intended to bring about a desired future state of
affairs.

STRATEGIC PLANS

A strategic plan is a pattern of past and projected decisions and
actions collectively intended to bring about a specific desired future
state of affairs. It is quantified; "priced out" on both the revenue and
outlay sides; and it is time-phased. The needed "inputs" of funds,
people, real property, ideas and other intangibles, and all the rest are
set forth with as great specificity as may be. Contingencies may be
allowed for, and points indicated where "mid-course" corrections may
possibly be made. Presently foreseen alternative courses of action that
may be, or may become feasible at those future points may also be
sketched out in greater or less detail.

Not all company strategic plans are that complete, of course. But it seems to me that the best corporate practice is moving in that direction.

The major strategic plans of the Armed Forces of the United States and our Allies in World War II—such as the Combined Bomber Offensive Plan, TORCH, HUSKY, AVALANCHE, OVERLORD, and ANVIL—were imaginative and painstakingly thorough. They stand as examples for corporations. The Germans, in contrast, never had any overall strategic plan. Even their major moves such as SEA LION for the invasion of Britain, which never came off, and BARBAROSSA for the invasion of Russia, which ended in disaster, were only incomplete sketches of beginnings, not plans for implementation and for successful endings.[1]

The moral is plain.

Plans of similar creativity, thoughtful boldness, and painstaking thoroughness of detail lay behind our astounding APOLLO program. Our national ineptitudes, irresolution, and muddlings in dealing with our "energy crisis" are an example of the absence of a strategic plan.

What's all this got to do with business? Not many businesses have developed comparable plans for themselves. Some people, both in and outside of business, question whether such plans are feasible or even desirable.

It is this writer's view that the scale and complexity; the long lead-times and the long-term commitments; and the manifold interrelationships and implications of major strategic moves of modern corporations require increasing sophistication of plans and planning. Increasingly in modern business, a "systems approach" is called for. For instance, a significant move into a new market requires people, especially managers; production facilities; reliable sources of supply for materials and components; distributors and outlets; promotion campaigns; financing; due regard for antitrust and other regulatory constraints; development of control systems; contingency plans for responses to probable countermoves of competitors—just to name some of the elements of a successful operation of the sort. And the whole plan needs to be seen and decided upon in contexts of the company's present activities, of other major alternatives available at the moment, and of foreseeable alternative opportunities likely to emerge in the future.

---

[1] See Marshall, General of the Armies George C.; *The Winning of the War in Europe and the Pacific*; New York: Simon & Schuster; 1946.

Other examples of strategic moves that call for sophisticated plans can be given: developing major new productive facilities that will embody new technologies; "going international"; opening up branches; bringing new products through the stages of research and development; adding desired new business through acquisitions; and spinning off those that are not. Some corporations are developing new logistical-distribution systems designed to reduce investments in inventories dispersed around the country or the world; to cut costs, speed deliveries; and to introduce greater flexibility into production and marketing activities. Some companies in metals, chemicals, textiles, and electronics, for instance, are integrating "backward" or "forward" to assure themselves of sources of supply and/or outlets for products.

Time was when plans for these kinds of moves could be, and were, developed and carried in the heads of gifted business leaders. But the world is now so complex and fast-moving, and strategic moves of corporations are so massive, that plans for these kinds of major commitments need to be developed systematically and explicitly.

Fortunately, ways of designing increasingly effective strategic plans are developing.

STRATEGIC PLANNING: ENVIRONMENTAL ANALYSIS

In military doctrine, strategic planning begins with an "estimate" or an "appreciation" of the situation. The whole arena of probable activities is surveyed. Courses of events are detected and projected. Threats and opportunities are identified. Then, resources on hand and procurable are inventoried and assessed. Implications and requirements of the more promising alternatives are thought through and calculated. Programs of possible action are blueprinted. Mathematical models may be designed to help figure out what all needs be done, when, and in what amounts if desired results are to be achieved. As in other human activities, not all even of the best military plans work out the way they are intended. But the process can provide useful analogs for thinking about strategic planning of corporations.

Strategic decision-making and planning for corporations logically begins with an "estimate" or an "appreciation" of the situation. In the case of business, that means the development of a reasonably complete and objective view of the "world" of the particular corporation and of, at least, the major trends in that environment that can be identified with some confidence.

Dimensions and Boundaries of the Environment

How far afield do you scan? The relevant dimensions and boundaries of the environment vary from industry to industry and from company to company. Some industries—petroleum, copper, aluminum, many textiles, for instance—can be understood only in a global context. What is happening and going to happen over distant horizons, even halfway around the world, can be of decisive moment as regards supplies, markets, competition, government intervention, and demands of organized labor.

Some industries are perhaps best understood in the setting of a national framework: furniture, most apparel, trucking, many building materials and building hardware, and communications.

For companies in some other industries, regional environments are what count most, or even the metropolitan areas in which they operate: utilities, banks, wholesaling and retailing, and much construction.

Industry Boundaries

In gaining an appreciation of the environment of the corporation, one has to consider what is the definition of the relevant "industry." Much competition now reaches across traditional boundaries of "industries": Oil, gas, and coal compete, of course. In many applications, so do various materials, metals, plastics, glass, wood. Various synthetic fibers compete among themselves and with natural fibers. Various kinds of fish and seafood compete among themselves and with meats, and even other foods. Skiing in New Hampshire to some extent competes with snorkeling in the Caribbean. A trip to Europe may even compete with a new automobile. How far to cast the analytical net is a matter of practical judgment.

Time Dimensions in Environmental Analysis and Stategic Plans

How far ahead do you scan? That depends on what is involved. The whole process of designing, building, and shaking down a new production facility may take several years; and on top of that, you will want to be sure that it will have a reasonably lengthy useful life. In that case, the whole time frame may be 10, 15, maybe even 20 years.

It may take 10 years to go from a market share of zero to a market share of 15 or 20 percent, or to develop a new distribution network. It may take a decade to build a viable business in a foreign country. An R&D project that advances the state of knowledge may take equally long. If you are selling or buying long-term credit obligations, you may be looking ahead even longer. Lead times and planning horizons of 10 years and 20 years are no longer rare in business.

The "Contents" of the Environment

"Out there," in the world of the corporation, is an environment of infinite complexity. It is surely not possible to observe, study, and forecast "everything" that may have a bearing on the company's future. But one can try to pick out what is most important and then try to collect relevant data and arrange them into some useful format.

One way of doing this is to think of, and study the total environment as a kind of system, similar to ecological systems found in nature. In this environment there are all sorts of entities important to the firm: individuals and households; other firms; suppliers, competitors, and customers—actual and potential. Concerning all of these, there are tremendous banks of available statistical and other data stretching back into the past. One can also find numerous projections of increases or decreases in numbers and of migratory movements of these entities. Then, out there, there are also government agencies, labor unions, and pressure groups that can be catalogued and their evolving positions on important matters tracked and projected.

A second component of the environment consists of the flows of all kinds of goods and services being produced and consumed. Again, there are tremendous statistical resources compiled by government, industry, and private sources that measure these flows; and there are available many efforts to project what these flows may be in future years.

A third component comprises physical elements in the environment: structures, transportation networks, resources, for instance. And concerning these, again there are lots of readily available data. To be sure, some of these are "iffy"—such as the size of American natural gas reserves. But others, such as forest resources, highway mileage, and available water resources are reasonably exact and firm.

The fourth component can be called, broadly, the "culture." That includes the laws of the land, available technology, values, attitudes, mores—all those creations of the mind that make possible and constrain the behavior of human beings and their institutions.

Studying and Projecting Environmental Trends

Some of the kinds of studies that are being made of the environment are very technical in the way they are put together. Population projections by demographers; macroeconomic projections by economists; and reserve estimates by geologists fall into this category. But grasping their significance and estimating their reliability is well within the reach of intelligent laymen. A very important point to be made and to bear in mind is that there do now exist a number of disciplines and techniques of considerable reliability and sophistication for measuring, studying, and forecasting various elements and components of a company's environment. The corporation doesn't have to invent a whole lot of wheels in these matters. Many now exist and are readily available for use.

How Good Are Forecasts of the Future, Anyway?

Decisions to make or not to make major commitments necessarily involve some ideas, however clear or fuzzy, of what the future may bring as to whether a particular commitment will turn out to be the right kind, and whether this is the right time to make it. There's no escaping the inevitability of making bets on the future, one way or another. That's clear. The question is, can we improve our odds when we do so? How?

The world as it is encountered by an individual or a single company does seem like a pretty unpredictable, chancy place. Important events—assassinations, earthquakes, inventions, for instance—often seem to come out of the blue. No one seems able to predict what the Arabs will do next. All that is true. But in all the seemingly turbulent confusion of the world as we know it, there is, just the same, considerable order and predictability. For example, although it's hard to say what may happen to a particular person, mortality tables and health and social statistics tell us with very considerable accuracy what will happen over the next several years to specified categories of people and to any number of demographic fractions of the whole population. Matters that seem chaotic for the individual have an extraordinary predictability when it comes to large numbers. There are *some* things about the future that are pretty certain.

So, although there is much present confusion and future uncertainty, and although we can't possibly know everything we should like to, there's no reason why we shouldn't make and use such reliable forecasts as we can. What are some of these?

Population Data.   People are one of the most important parts of the environment of any corporation: How many of what kind, by age, sex, occupation, education, income, ethnicity, location? How many more or less than in some time past? How many 5, 10, or 20 years hence? Where are they moving to? From? Much of this is knowable pretty accurately. And data about people are probably the biggest single category of statistics there is. Some things about people we can't be sure of: For instance, how many babies will be born next year? (Even there, we can get some pretty good estimates.) But as to other matters, we can be *very, very* sure: How many people between the ages of 20 and 30 will there be 10 years from now? That's easy. Our forecast ought to be at least 99 percent accurate. They're all here, right now. How many over 65? A little harder; we'll have to make some projections about death rates as well as projecting the process of aging of people who are here today. But morbidity and health data change in pretty regular patterns, so our forecast should be, say, 95 percent accurate.

Not only can such accurate forecasts be made at the national level, but highly usable, even if somewhat less accurate forecasts can be made for regions, states, individual metropolitan areas, and even parts of metropolitan areas.

About the work force, a highly important part of the environment of business—our people are, of course, both workers and consumers—again there is a tremendous outpouring of current data of employment, by scores of individual occupations in scores of industries, by states, counties, and cities. The Bureau of Labor Statistics, in addition to putting out raw data, also publishes a stream both of retrospective studies, that reveal past patterns and trends, and of many projections of future employment patterns.

It is now possible to forecast with useful accuracy many aspects of the human population 10 and 20 years hence down to as small an area as a political ward or individual census tract.[2]

___

[2] See, e.g., Birch, David L., et al.; *The New Haven Laboratory: A Test-Bed for Planning*; Lexington, Mass.: D. C. Heath & Company; 1974.

The Business Population.   Next, there is much we can tell about the business population: the corporations, proprietorships, and partnerships that constitute another important element of the company's environment. For many businesses, these productive entities are the market, rather than individual consumers and households. Other businesses are competitors in "output" markets where the company wants to sell, of course. Even larger numbers are competitors in "input" markets: for labor, for capital, for space, for materials and equipment. The Bureau of the Census and Internal Revenue Service, among other national sources, and many state, county, and city governments, as well as industry and business associations, publish an astounding mass of data on business firms: numbers by industry categories; asset size; location; detailed breakdowns of revenues, costs, assets, and liabilities; employment, payrolls, sales, taxes paid; values added, by industries and locations; and on and on.

Although far less is known of the demography of the business population than of the human population, a very good sense of trends can be gotten simply from tracking data over a period of time. Here, again, patterns of considerable regularity are to be seen.

Migration of business and of business activity is also important in understanding the changing and future environment of the company, along with expansion and contraction, and trends in their economics and financing. Here again, there is a great deal of order and predictability; not so much, of course, as regards a single firm, but certainly as regards categories of enterprises.

Economic Data.   Vast amounts of data are readily available as regards production, shipments, inventories, purchases, and exports and imports of scores of industries, commodity groups, and individual commodities. The national income accounts are another enormous source of data, as are financial and other economic statistics published by the Board of Governors of the Federal Reserve System and each of the 12 Federal Reserve banks.

Sometimes we get so preoccupied with current oscillations and perturbations, swings, recessions, and upsurges in such data that we lose sight of such impressive and important regularity as there is, including regular patterns of change. To be sure, it does make a difference whether some index or figure will be 5 percent or even 10 percent or 20 percent more or less next year than this. We need to think about such vagaries when scheduling purchases, production, inventories, cash flows, and other current matters. But for purposes of making *strategic* decisions according to plan, it is surely important to spot the patterns and regularities and broad sweeps of developments over time.

In that connection, the U.S. Office of Business Economics and private organizations such as the National Planning Association have developed increasingly interesting modelling techniques for estimating future levels of activities for many industries and economic sectors. Such data indicate that some aspects of the economy and certain geographical areas will be growing faster than others, and that some, despite an overall pattern of growth, will actually be declining. A number of corporations have long since developed techniques of their own for relating these kinds of projections to their own businesses for use in making strategic decisions.

Physical Features.   The physical features of the environment of the corporation, and the changes therein are now the subjects of increasing study by means of new and interesting approaches and techniques being developed by people who call themselves geographers or regional analysts. These kinds of studies look particularly promising because these elements of the company's world—highly important in themselves—have a particular steadiness, even in their changing. Three categories of such features can be mentioned: transportation networks, especially highways; buildings and other structures; and resources. Extensive bodies of statistical and other data are available concerning each of these categories.

The building up of the highway network, to take an example, has been one of the most important developments in the evolution of the environment of the corporation. It is still going on, although at a reduced rate. This buildup, especially of the interstate network, has changed spatial relationships; somewhat, in terms of miles, but drastically in terms of time and cost of movement. For one company, a new plant in the deep South East is at a smaller cost-distance from the New York region than was an older plant in western Pennsylvania. It will be some time, still, before the impact of the buildup of this network over the past 20 years works itself out. The enormous increase in highway freight movement is one index of the power of that impact. The induced migration and expansion of customers' plants, as well as those of competitors and suppliers, pose significant strategic questions for the corporation as to *where* to locate plants and distribution facilities, and perhaps more importantly, even as regards *what* to produce.

The future of that network is pretty clear: Whatever building programs are pursued over the next decade, some large percentage of the mileage that will be in place 10 years from now—say, over 90 percent —is in place right now.

As to structures of all kinds—factories, residences, offices, schools, hospitals, and all—collectively they exercise uncalculated effect upon what can be produced and consumed in the nation as a whole, in its several regions, and even in individual metropolitan areas. One can't be too sure how much construction of what kinds will be carried out in the next 20, or even 10 years. And the actual levels will, of course, affect every individual and business, directly or indirectly. But whatever may happen in this sector of the environment, certainly within the range of any reasonable probability, a large portion of the structures that will be around us some years out are already in place, now. The whole "inventory" of structures at any point in the future will be the net resultant of what is added between now and then, less what disappears. And that entire element of the environment can be estimated with a highly useable degree of accuracy as regards amounts, kinds, locations, and conditions.

As to resources, that element in the environment has already been touched upon. Aside from oil and gas, and perhaps some critical materials like uranium, we as a people, except for those directly concerned, and perhaps not even all of them—have paid relatively little attention to the buildup of resources through discovery and the like, or to their depletion through use and waste. Now, the corporation will have to pay increasing attention to these changes and their impacts. Some of these can be pretty dramatic. For example, the increases in our consumption of water have gone on to reach a point where further economic growth in large sections of the country must greatly slow down or even come to a halt. We can do much more by way of estimating our future position as to important resources and the implications of these data.

The "Culture." Finally, there is that component of the environment we can call the "culture." This term is widely used by anthropologists and sociologists who study the behavior of populations and human institutions. This component of the environment of the corporation includes our beliefs, values, and preferences; our laws; our technology. As to these elements, the most serious efforts thus far made at forecasting change are probably those relating to technology. This is such a recent development it is hard to know much as to its reliability. Suffice it to say that a number of very able people and important companies are making efforts to develop skills in that direction.

As to forecasting our beliefs, values, and preferences, we can at least be reasonably sure that changes will move us in the direction of outlooks and such of a population that is increasingly urban, white collar, educated, "liberated" from many historical constraints, and increasingly beyond the margin of bare living. These changes will manifest themselves in different life styles, purchases of different kinds of consumer goods; in housing, job preferences, and in changing senses of public priorities that will find many expressions, including future legislation.

As to our laws, we know only a little about forecasting political behavior. Beginnings have been made. The first step is to explain political behavior in the here and now, relating voting preferences and such matters to such obvious factors as age, income, sex, education level, ethnicity, occupation, nature and location of residence. Because many of these factors, individually and in combination, can be forecast with a useful degree of accuracy, it is likely that in the foreseeable future it will be possible to make useful predictions as to changes in regulatory pressures and other governmental constraints on various industries and future policies of encouragements.

In any case, we can reasonably suppose, again, that a large fraction of the American culture 10 years out, even 20—the beliefs that will then be pervasive or common, the values, and the preferences; the technology; the laws in force—are already here. We are concerned, again, in that time-span, with incremental change coming on top of much that will remain in place.

The Environment of the Future

Putting all these projections together, it is possible to arrive at sketches of future states of affairs that can have reasonably useful degrees of reliability. Far from being totally unknowable, the future cannot but be both constrained and propelled by what is already here and underway. Although the future can be *very* different, it cannot be *randomly* different from the present.

In any event, systematic efforts to arrive at disciplined, quantified, and time-phased pictures of the future at various points can give us a context against which to make strategic decisions in the here and now.

And it is precisely toward building up this kind of capacity that many leading corporations and institutions are working.

So much for the analysis and forecasting of the environment. Now for strategic planning and decision-making.

STRATEGIC DECISION-MAKING: PLANNING, DECIDING

A lively debate is going on these days as to who should do strategic planning in the corporation and as to where in the organization this should take place. In this writer's opinion, a certain amount of this debate is colored by confusions and misapprehensions as to what is involved. Perhaps these next few pages will shed some further light on the matter.

Some Basic Considerations

First basic: It is logical that diagnosis should precede therapy. A case should be argued before the jury decides. Definition of a problem should precede the solution. Purpose and objective should precede effort and action. Environmental analysis and forecasting should precede strategic decision-making. In each case, we are talking about a two-stage process. Very different intellectual qualities and exercises are involved.

One thing that is clear is that modern environmental analysis and forecasting can have an increasingly large professional and technical content. One doesn't have to be a professional economist, demographer, sociologist, political scientist, geographer, or whatnot in order to be able to use the products of these people. But using their products does require some general familiarity with the kinds of data they use, the kinds of reasoning they go through, the techniques they employ, and the reliability of their results. These are not subjects and areas in which one individual's personal, unstudied views are just as good as another's.

Second: Another thing that is equally clear. In addition to some professional preparation and aptitude, some considerable amount of time is needed to go through analyses of the kinds we have been talking about.

A *third basic:* It's one thing to work at making forecasts of things to come. These are increasingly the tasks of professionals. It's quite another to figure out what these developments and future states of affairs *mean* for the individual company. What threats to the corporation are implicit? What new opportunities will there be? Developing answers to questions like these requires more than mere grasp of what the trends are. It requires grasp of the essentials of the business. Especially, it calls for sensitivity and depth of perception, for seeing what responses may be needed or desirable. There can be no answers to questions like these without creative leaps from the observed to what might be.

Fourth: It is clear that the design of alternative programs of action for meeting these threats and opportunities also requires imagination and creativity. Especially however, does it entail knowledge of how to *do* things to get desired results. This calls for a management point of view, and it calls for knowledge of details of the business. What works? What is needed? How much time? What does it cost? What are the pros and cons of possible alternatives? This aspect of planning, to repeat, requires understanding in real depth of business and of the particular business.

These kinds of considerations are involved in *Stage I* of strategic decision-making, to which we shall turn in a moment.

A *fifth basic:* Decision-making, strategic decision-making, lies beyond all of this. It requires power of mind, greatly colored by experience, to understand and test (*a*) the quality of forecasts; (*b*) the sensitivity and depth of the efforts made to see their implications; (*c*) the creativity and soundness of the alternatives perceived; (*d*) the degree of technical and practical business competence embodied in the alternative programs offered for consideration. Strategic decision-making calls for a perspective that comprehends the entire business, not just a single division or function. It calls for horizons that reach beyond the here and the now. It calls for those ineffable qualities of "decisiveness" that people have so often tried to describe. It calls, obviously, for involvement of the person who has *power* to decide to commit or not to commit.

STRATEGIC DECISION-MAKING: PROCESS, MANNING, ORGANIZATION

We are now in position to close in on what we set out to do: to know better how and where the tides are running. How to make strategic decisions for the corporation. What kind of a craft to have. Where to go and how to get there.

EXHIBIT 1
Strategic Decision-Making: Process, Manning, Organization

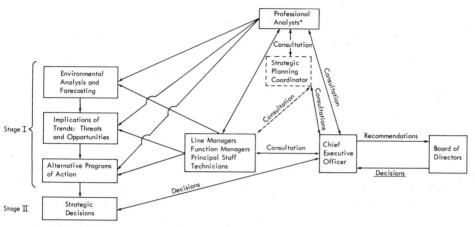

* These may be "in-house" or specially retained "outside" resource people.

It is probably true that strategic decision-making is a somewhat informal process in many companies. In some companies, in all truth, this process resembles the court of the Byzantine Empire in its decay, for intrigue, rivalry, danger to careers, maneuvering, and in the last analysis, the weight of personality, power, and irrationality. But in some companies, pretty sophisticated processes have been evolved, trying to bring order and competence to the most important of all managerial tasks.[3]

A schema of a logical strategic decision-making process is set out in Exhibit 1. This process is summarized in two "Stages," the first of which has three steps, the second of which has one. The schema also sets out ideas as to the parties involved in the several steps, their contributions, and the relationships among them.

Stage I

Environmental Analysis and Forecasting. This step has been described at considerable length. It now, as was indicated, calls for professional inputs. There are questions as to where and how to get such inputs.

---

[3] See, e.g., the chapter by Hershner Cross, "Capital Project Approval." See also Bower, Joseph L.; *The Resource Allocation Process;* Boston: Division of Research; Harvard Business School; 1965.

A large corporation can afford its own in-house professional group of environmental analysts. For a company making yearly strategic commitments having money values of, say, a hundred million dollars, prudence justifies expenditure of perhaps as much as a half-million or more trying to assure that the best possible allocations are being made. Smaller companies can make do with smaller groups, say a well-trained economist and a demographer. These people can be supplemented with such outside experts as may be useful in analyzing and projecting various elements of the environment. One thing is clear: The kinds of professional inputs needed and available for use at this step are very special.

The mission of the group, however composed, is to come up with (*a*) the best possible forecasts of trends in the principal elements of the environment; and (*b*) some ideas of their own as to what these trends imply in general terms by way of opportunities and threats. In going about their work, they need to be in consultation with the CEO, himself, as well as with key line and staff officers.

Implications of Trends: Threats and Opportunies. In addition to inputs from environmental analysts, the CEO, and other executives, this step especially calls for inputs of knowledgeable line managers, function managers, principal staff people, and technicians. This is where and when questions get dealt with on the order of, "In view of what's going on, what does it mean *for us* specifically?"

Alternative Programs of Action. At this step, questions of this order are dealt with: "In view of the implications of these developing threats and opportunities, what alternative programs of action—in detail—are available to us?" The basic inputs at this step come from the people who know the business best: line managers, function managers, principal staff people, and technicians. Here again, the CEO is called in for advice and views and, perhaps, for instruction as to ground rules with which any programs of action pursued by the company must conform.

Stage II

Strategic Decisions. Having gone through the process thus far, the management is ready for decision-making. At this stage, the CEO makes his choices among the several alternatives. He makes his recommendations to the board of directors, taking them in a general way through the several steps involved, outlining the other alternatives considered, and giving his reasons for his preferences. If and when ratified by the board, the CEO issues the appropriate instructions for carrying out the desired allocations and commitments.

"Strategic Planning Coordinator." In the schema for this process, as shown in Exhibit 1, a "Strategic Planning Coordinator" is shown in a box of dotted lines. This is to suggest that in sizeable companies having multiple and complex operations, a special staff executive is being found useful or even necessary. It is his job to see that the necessary talent, in-house or outside, is available; that the whole process takes place; that needed inputs are obtained from all concerned and taken into account; and that the CEO is presented with good documentation upon which to make up his mind and which he can draw upon in making his recommendations to the board. This executive is *not* the planner. He is an assistant to *the* planner, the person who ultimately makes the plan through his decisions: the Chief Executive Officer.[4]

Matters of Scale. The functions, processes, people, and organization sketched in Exhibit 1 can be scaled up, or down as the case may be to suit the needs of the particular company. The whole matter in a multi-billion dollar corporation will be far bigger and more complex than in a company with assets of, say, $10 million. In principle, however, these ideas have a certain general usefulness.

Strategic Planning at Divisional and Functional Levels. Much has been said and written about the virtues of "bottoms-up" planning and the like. Division managers and/or functional managers and staff sections, according to this process, each submit a "strategic" plan for his or her own activities. There are companies that follow such a procedure. Such thoughts have appeals: This sounds democratic, participative, decentralized. Such a process, it would seem, draws upon knowledge and practical experience close to "where it happens." In the lexicon of much contemporary writing about management, these are attractive ideas. And, no doubt, there is much to be said for such a process. But, it strikes me, there are shortcomings to this approach.

First, a summation of such proposals, whatever may be their individual merits, arrived at independently out of varying perspectives, representing different objectives, can only by a miracle add up to an

---

[4] See the chapter by Marvin Bower; "The Chief Executive as Chief Strategist"; and that of Alexander Calder; "Strategy and Planning: Some Personal Observations of a Chief Executive."

integrated, comprehensive, hard-hitting plan for the corporation as a whole.

Second, the aptitudes and preoccupations of operations people, indispensable to getting results, are not necessarily the same as those required for the best possible job of perceiving, measuring, and forecasting trends of the many kinds that will impact the company: demographic, economic, political, social, technological. Nor can operations people, from their vantage point, establish the fundamental policy ground rules and assumptions that must constrain and be embodied in the overall company plan. Only the CEO can do that! The particular skills of these important people down the line, it seems to me, come better into play after the environmental analyses and projections are arrived at. Their inputs are certainly needed in figuring out implications of trends and in working out alternative responses.

Third, there is the practical matter of focus and time. The attention of operating people tends to be focused on getting the job done. That's how they're measured. It's not easy to pry their attention away from that preoccupation for the amount of time that searching, sophisticated environmental analysis calls for.

Strategic Planning in Highly Diversified Companies and "Conglomerates." This is a big topic. But a few ideas may be useful. It seems to me there are two possible basic approaches, depending on whether (*a*) the company is run as a "portfolio" of companies, with only a minimum of central control through periodic allocation and commitment of capital funds; or (*b*) whether it is run as something like a whole, with many important strategy and operating decisions of divisions or subsidiaries being reviewed in a central office of the corporate CEO.

In the first instance, an approximation of a useful approach is to regard each division or subsidiary as a separate entity which is under the necessity of bargaining for capital funds from a "banker," who is the corporate Chief Executive Officer. It develops its own strategic plan along lines suggested above. The "banker"—the corporate CEO —makes his own companywide strategic plan, and grants or withholds funds to the several parts of the business accordingly.

In the second instance, an approximation of a useful approach is to think of the whole corporation as an entity that comprehends parts that are more or less different. A strategic plan can be developed for the corporation as a whole along the lines suggested, with special sections dealing with each rather different part of the business. The difference here from the "bottoms-up" approach is that the over-arching corporation plan is predicated on companywide ground rules and establishes the foundation of a common set of conclusions and premises as to trends and their general implications. These are worked through specifically for each major portion of the business. For each of these, sets of alternatives that comply with the overarching plan are worked up. Alternatives are chosen which are not only consonant with the realities of particular parts of the business but—and this is very important—with the larger realities confronted by the corporation as a whole.

CONCLUSION

Strategic decision-making in the modern corporation and the processes that lead up to it are not just "sometime" matters. They are, of fact and of necessity, continuous. The world changes. Perceptions of the future evolve and change. New demands and new alternatives come into view. New directions, new programs of action come to be indicated. Old programs get outmoded and cancelled or modified. New ones are adopted. Analysis goes on continuously. Plans are made, unmade, and new ones are put into effect. New commitments are made. It is a continuous process, just like production and marketing. To preside over this continuing process is the decisively important and distinguishing function of the Chief Executive Officer in these times.

PART IV

Directing
the
Functions
of
the
Business

PART IV-A

Development
Engineering
and
Research

THE DIRECTOR OF RESEARCH AND DEVELOPMENT

by Simon Ramo
Vice Chairman, TRW Inc.

ALL CORPORATIONS that market a *technological* product or service must conduct a *substantial* amount of research and development. Most others require a *significant* R&D effort. In all instances the CEO must: (*a*) set goals and budgets for R&D; (*b*) create the form of organization for the accomplishment of the research and development program; (*c*) choose the leadership of R&D (or decide to decentralize the responsibility to the division or product line managers); (*d*) monitor R&D progress against goals and judge the performance of the director.

This article will first discuss the functions of, and the ideal qualifications for the director of R&D. Practical compromises then will be considered. Finally, suggestions for CEO actions to enhance the performance of, guide, and judge the director of R&D will be presented.

DEFINING RESEARCH AND DEVELOPMENT

At the outset, the CEO must define R&D for his company. *Why* expenditures on research and development? The purposes could range widely—for example: very advanced research intended to form a background for superior thinking about future markets, products, potential competition, and numerous pertinent aspects of the external world; investigations on the optimum utilization of resources; development of very specific new products; improvement of manufacturing techniques. The qualifications which a competent research director must possess, the organizational pattern in which he can best carry out his duties, and the preferred handling of his necessary interfaces with other executives as well as with the CEO are all highly

447

dependent on the objectives of the program he is expected to direct.

In many large and diversified companies R&D is one of the several functions that report separately to each division or product line manager. Even under these circumstances, the CEO must be concerned with the goals of that decentralized R&D and will undoubtedly influence decisions on the timing of allocation of resources to the R&D program and its size and nature.

In companies whose products and services are technological, R&D is as key to long-term success as production and marketing. The CEO will require evidence that broad R&D decisions are satisfactory, if indeed he does not make these decisions himself. For example, critical decisions on the goals of the R&D program are often dominated by a contest between short- and long-term objectives. Choosing a modest, as against a generous, research and development program will hold down current costs and increase current profits. But it will do this at the expense of future position. The balancing process involves major risk to present and future company image and performance.

In an era of rapidly advancing technology and tough competition based in substantial part on exploiting technological leads, the CEO obviously must give high priority to selecting the goals and priorities of the R&D program, no matter how decentralized may be the implementation of the plans. If after a number of years the results of R&D are seen as inconsequential to the company's progress, it is not necessarily evidence of a lack of value in the R&D function for that company. The fault may lie instead with insufficient recognition at the CEO level of the importance of deciding upon objectives and priorities and then arranging the right organizational pattern, selecting suitable executives for direction of the research, and assigning the appropriate resources.

In summary, the CEO should define R&D for his company. He must do this before he decides on the R&D organization and the individual to direct it.

THE R&D ORGANIZATION

With the objectives of an R&D program mapped out, many organizational patterns to achieve these objectives will usually deserve consideration. The CEO must be very interested in arranging the best organizational location and interorganizational relationships for R&D. Clarity as to objectives and selection of the most competent

R&D director will achieve little in the end if organization is neglected.

A separate organization could be created to carry out the function. Or, the R&D activity could be made a part of the engineering department. Or, it could consist of several units in each of the several product divisions, if such is the pattern of the corporation. Even in a multidivisional, highly decentralized, diversified company, all or a part of the R&D might be centralized in a corporate laboratory or department. Some research aspects which are regarded as extremely advanced and exploratory, intended to move the company into new fields beyond existing product lines, might be centralized at corporate level, while R&D relating to existing product lines might be decentralized to the operating divisions.

Depending upon the organizational structure, the requirements that the R&D executives must fill will vary. Some R&D executives will need to be highly technical experts while others will be less concerned with technical matters and will occupy policy, communications, liaison, or coordinative positions. We shall discuss the functions of the directors shortly, but first, additional points regarding organization should be made.

R&D Organization for a Single Product Company

In a small, single-product-line company, it will often prove most advantageous to combine all R&D and engineering design of the product under one senior technical executive. The chief reason for this is that it is rare that the separation of responsibilities between R&D and product design can be made adequately clear. If the R&D entity develops a new product which it then transfers to engineering for final productizing for manufacture and marketing, the CEO will probably have his hands full with coordination and refereeing. Needless redesign, arguments over approaches and technical details, major differences of opinion over what is or is not ready for production, and "not invented here" problems are among the many to be expected.

In some respects the problem of separation and coordination is worse because of a basic inability to define "research and development" as distinct from "engineering design" of products. A good engineering design group, intent on ensuring the success of the existing product, must be concerned with improving it to make it cheaper, lighter, smaller, more rugged, better in performance, more reliable, or to broaden its applications or incorporate a feature which a competitor is observed to be, or might soon be, exploiting. Thus, the engineering group must include creative and inventive technical people. Inevitably this design group comes to possess what amounts to its own R&D team, which tends to be competitive with the other autonomous and separate R&D entity.

An exception to the rule of combining R&D with the engineering of existing products, if the company is small and has a narrow product base, may be justified if the CEO is, himself, a good technical professional. In effect, then, he is, in addition to being the CEO, the senior technical man of the company. Both the R&D and engineering organizations become his follow-through assistants. He does the detailed refereeing. All of the technical people in R&D, engineering, manufacturing, and marketing are then members of a single entity, which is the company, of which he is the active boss. Regardless of titles, *he* is Director of R&D, among other things.

R&D Organization in a Large, Diversified Company

In a large, multiproduct company, this question of separation of R&D and engineering arises again and again at lower levels and in each of the product line divisions. Each division manager has a problem similar to that of the CEO in the smaller, single product company. Again, he would do well to consider having a senior technical executive in charge of both R&D and engineering, or else he must take on the difficult refereeing and duplication-avoidance problem. Oftentimes, again, he can accomplish this if he is a competent technical man and actually the true director of both R&D and of engineering. But then, his operations will have to be small, and his product line narrow.

In such a diversified company, some new factors enter, however. First, there is a need at the CEO level to find ways to support all of the technical activities of the company with the least cost and the greatest opportunity for useful synergism. As a minimum, the CEO will want to organize so that there is the right amount of technological interchange, transfer of research data and ideas, and effective consulting and intelligence-gathering with regard to competitive approaches. It would appear wasteful, in general, to have a number of strong technical groups who are not in adequate communication and generate no mutual assistance and stimulation. Attempts at overcommunication and a zeal to exploit a synergism if it is, indeed, largely absent (which can be a fact if the product lines are extremely diverse) must equally be avoided. This means that at corporate level, the CEO has a need for providing judgment and leadership in this communication-support function. There is competition for corporate support for R&D among the separate divisional R&D groups. Each promises great potential results if funded. The whole program probably exceeds a proper overall corporate budget if *all* the "babies are sent to college." A corporate referee, with no motherhood biases, is needed to help the CEO allocate support.

Moreover, it is usually true that the individual scientists and engineers employed in all of the operating divisions see an advantage in their being watched over, if only in a staff capacity, by a senior executive of outstanding technical qualifications who has the ear of the CEO. This sympathetic, independent top-level leader, they feel, may comprehend their needs, hopes, and aspirations in a different and sometimes superior way from the division executives who originate their detailed objectives and operating budgets. A corporate director of research and development reporting to the CEO provides this, both in the psychological or image sense and, if he handles his task well, in a completely substantive way as well.

The CEO of the large diversified company will have additional reasons for setting up some staff R&D direction or overseeing at the CEO level. This staff will be useful in auditing and judging the quality of R&D in the decentralized divisions as distinct from the overall judgment through the p&l statement of the divisions' activities. (See "Gauging the Performance of the R&D Director" following.)

The CEO will want to explore areas of endeavor beyond those that are assigned to the various operating divisions, each of which presumably is purposely limited to very specific areas of endeavor. A centralized R&D activity of some kind is sometimes the best route for investigating new fields, often going so far as to create new products or at least embryonic versions of these. The organizational arrangement may be that, after initial explorations, the results and beginnings will be transferred to existing operating divisions whose activities are thus broadened, or into new divisions created around the new product lines.

Still another basis for a centralized corporate R&D activity is the carrying out of a broad line of research and development believed to apply generally to many divisions. For efficiency's sake, the R&D is then concentrated in one place to avoid duplication. An alternative, of course, is to place these general requirements in some one operating division's R&D unit, choosing to extend the role of that unit to include such a corporate task as the most effective or economical means of seeing that the R&D is carried out. In either way of accomplishing these more general R&D tasks to back up more than one operating division, a communications problem exists to be sure that the R&D results will impact usefully on the workings of various parts of the company. Sometimes this problem is solved by the use of a small R&D unit reporting at the corporate level which has communications and liaison as its main duty.

If virtually all R&D is decentralized to divisional operating executives below the CEO level, then, as has already been indicated, the CEO must nevertheless participate in setting objectives and allocating resources. Beyond this, the CEO will presumably oversee the R&D in only an indirect way, in the same sense that divisional marketing or manufacturing is monitored, for example. The next level of operating executive, to whom the R&D director reports directly, must be given clear instructions as to overall goals and policy, including those relating to R&D, against which that operating executive's total performance will be judged by the CEO. The specific role of R&D vis-à-vis the other decentralized functions will have to be worked out by the operating division executive so that the R&D function reporting to him is compatible with his other responsibilities.

FUNCTIONS OF THE DIRECTOR OF R&D

The previous paragraphs of this article have described a considerable variety of R&D objectives and organizational patterns for pursuing them. The job of the director of R&D will vary with these objectives and organizational approaches. The function can range from staff to line. It might involve largely liaison and communication, with little direct decision-making, at one extreme, and daily interaction, on a level of scientific or engineering detail, with a large number of technical specialists who report to him, at the other extreme. He might report to the CEO, or he might be in charge of product design in a division as well as being the R&D director of that division, or he might report to the chief designer of a division.

The CEO should see that, whatever the function is, and wherever it reports, it is *clear*. Healthy R&D in the overall company, that is, R&D consistent with the CEO-led objectives for R&D, requires that

Functions of the R&D Director

Technical:

      Propose   R&D program
      Direct   R&D program
      Select   R&D personnel
      Control   R&D expenditures
      Audit   R&D efforts
      Report   R&D progress

Communication-Liaison:

      Coordinate R&D with engineering, product design, manufacturing.
      Find company problems that R&D can solve.
      Communicate to and from external R&D community, technical societies, universities, government.
      Act as leader-counselor, representative of R&D personnel to corporate management.

Business:

      Work with marketing and general business planning to create optimum R&D program.
      Interpret to corporate management the potential benefits and impact of alternative R&D programs on the corporate goals and potentials.
      Study and contribute to overall company business plan and strategy.
      Represent company as chief scientist to business and general audiences.

---

each R&D director (by whatever title), and those with whom he must deal, all know what his function is. This would appear to be an obvious requirement for all jobs. Yet the tendency is common for the R&D function to be left vague and the job of director to be equally ill-defined. This bad practice may stem from the unjustified impression that R&D is mysterious and esoteric. It involves "searching the unknown," exploring the "unpredictable," a creative and illusive mental activity that might suffer from control and even definition. Imaginative, yet sound, professional activity is needed as well in marketing, financing, public relations—in fact, in virtually every activity in a company. R&D is different in the *substance* of the function, but not in the chances of success, if the function is poorly defined and the responsibility of its director is described too loosely.

    The following table lists functions of the director of R&D, from the most scientific and direct to the less scientific and indirect. Under some conditions of goals for R&D and organizational structure, this list would be a good description of what the job of director of R&D truly is. Under other conditions, as already noted, the list below will be too long, too all-inclusive. Under such conditions, as exemplified by the often fragmented and decentralized R&D approach, these functions will be shared amongst a number of executives, including the retention of the specific function by a divisional manager (of adequate technical background).

QUALIFICATIONS OF THE IDEAL DIRECTOR OF R&D

We shall next describe the desired characteristics for an individual who holds the job of director of R&D in a company that has such goals and organizational structure that virtually the entire list of functions just described are his direct responsibility. This is the "maximum" job and the person who is assigned to it is ideally a remarkably broad individual. Later we shall comment further on the use of a less-than-the-ideal director and on his needed qualifications if the position encompasses less than the full list of responsibilities.

The ideal director of R&D must be an individual of outstanding technical competence. He must have stature as an R&D professional both inside and outside the company. He must be sophisticated regarding business objectives, with a profit interest, and with a motivation to expand the company, using research and development as a major avenue for this expansion. The director of R&D must also be an experienced and gifted manager, a leader and motivator. He must be strong in human relations, particularly with R&D personnel, and with other R&D executives in operating divisions wherever R&D is decentralized in substantial part.

He must be a communicator on a number of levels. He must be able to articulate company policy to the highly technical personnel engaged in R&D and to comprehend readily what those people have to say to him both on technical and other matters. Equally, he must be capable of describing the needs, goals, problems, and potentials of the R&D program to the nontechnical professionals and executives in the company whose responsibilities bear on the R&D program, or whose work and thinking should be influenced by it, including the CEO.

Certain qualifications are especially basic for the position of the

senior R&D executive, whether he be the line director of a decentralized R&D effort within an operating product division, or the top
scientist of the company, reporting to the CEO with staff responsibilities only, or any hybrid combination of these. High on the list of
these qualifications are some aspects of personality.

It is important to emphasize that if certain personality negatives are
present, they should eliminate some individuals from consideration
for the position of director of R&D. Unusual sensitivity to criticism,
"prima donna" tendencies, or irrepressible and exaggerated optimism
are handicaps in any top job, of course, but certain of these personality
characteristics are particularly fatal in a director of R&D. A confirmed pessimist will surely give up too soon in pushing the frontier;
or, lacking confidence that he will find an elusive answer, will go about
his work with too little enthusiasm. It is necessary that a good R&D
man be optimistic as he attacks complex problems seeking a practical
answer which he may never find. He must possess, however, the ability
to give up on an idea to which a great deal of time and energy may
have been devoted when from the practical standpoint it should be
abandoned.

Inherent in the R&D process is a tendency to develop the "not invented here" syndrome, in which the technical staff becomes en-
amored of its own approaches. It views its ideas as superior in the
absolute sense against approaches of competitors. An individual can
go on determinedly and optimistically too long, always assuming that
he will eventually meet with success, or that his way is best. The
research director, though having grown up in an R&D environment
conducive to these habits, must shed them as he shifts to the job of
choosing or judging large-scale R&D programs.

The problem of communication between the scientist and the
businessman offers another example of a potential negative that makes
some professionals ineligible for the post of director of R&D. Competence in research and development requires patience and the ability
to work with highly detailed analytical concepts where subtle differences must be observed and dealt with. This positive requirement can
create in some R&D specialists an uncontrollable inclination toward
endlessly long and detailed written reports and oral presentations in
communicating about the prospects, needs, results, and difficulties of
R&D programs. This approach is unacceptable to non-R&D executives
who are seeking more general answers and are uninterested in the
details.

A large fraction of our top scientists are employed in academic institutions or in nonprofit or government laboratories, where such matters as showing a good return on shareholders' investment is not an issue. Freedom to search for scientific truths independent of near-term or business constraints is an accepted and necessary part of life for these scientists. Not infrequently, large corporations, seeking to enhance their image in research and also to obtain leadership possessing a broad foundation in pure science, have turned to outstanding academic researchers. Some of these individuals have shown the talent to quickly grasp the different, additional parameters of formulating and directing a research and development program in a profit-seeking corporation. Some have not. Of course, one who cannot make the change, no matter how high his stature in the scientific fraternity, will be totally unsuitable for the position of the director of R&D, from the standpoint both of the corporation and of himself.

In summary, some characteristics essential for competent, purely technical participation in R&D are not necessarily strong positive points, and may be negative points applied to *direction* of R&D in a business entity.

With the most ideal personal makeup, stature in the R&D fraternity, and successful detailed experiences in R&D, the director of R&D still will be unsuitable unless he is an experienced manager. Even a first-class R&D man will be lost without adequate managerial talents and experience, if thrust into a position involving policy, the determination of the size and scope of the R&D program, the striking of a balance between short- and long-term considerations, and the evaluation of cost-risk-benefit as applied to a particular business venture. Particularly for the most senior R&D position, either line or staff, it is desirable for the CEO to see that it is filled by an individual who has shown through intermediate steps that he is qualified in terms of business management.

An effective R&D program for a business entity involves a mixture of the practical and theoretical, of assessment and risk-taking, of business and science. The overall managerial structure somehow must include means for selection amongst the myriad alternatives for application of the R&D talent to specific advances; and this selection process must mix marketing, financial, and timing problems with the purely scientific and engineering ones. The best way for the CEO to be confident that this kind of managerial strength exists in the process is to pick the principal directors from those individuals who have demonstrated this combination of abilities in the past. An R&D director who has shown such capabilities in a small area and who shows promise of increasing breadth should be a reasonably safe candidate for higher overall R&D responsibilities, while one who has demonstrated only high personal creativity would be a gamble if suddenly thrust into the director's position.

A great difference exists in the qualifications for a director of R&D in two situations. In one, the program is closely confined to product improvements in mature and profitable technological endeavors. In the other, the objective is to strengthen the pure science base for the company's endeavors or to strike out into new areas where neither that company or any other has trod before. In the first instance, the R&D director should be particularly strong in engineering and should understand the field thoroughly as a business. In the second instance, the research director should primarily have demonstrated previous success in supervising technological breakthroughs where bold imagination is combined with a strong scientific and technological foundation. Leadership qualities must be adequately evident, but it is not so important in the second example that the R&D director have proven experience in holding a highly definable task to specific expenditures. He needs no record of success in completing projects by specific dates if what he is being asked to do is a very long-term, admittedly highly speculative advance. Neither a time nor cost estimate may be useful, then, as a managerial guide or tool because it is not known how the task is to be accomplished from the technical standpoint or even whether, indeed, it can be accomplished at all, until the research and development has passed through at least some early stages.

PRACTICAL COMPROMISES

An "ideal" director of R&D is not likely to be found very often or very easily, even granted that there are many different "ideal directors" to go with the many varying conditions of R&D objectives and organizational patterns. Usually the CEO accepts a director of R&D with shortcomings in one or another of the qualifications just described. Fortunately, practical measures can be taken to minimize the consequences of such deficiencies. Many ways are open to the CEO to obtain the equivalent of higher quality R&D results and to enhance the performance of the director.

For example, the marketing research function, though a separate activity from R&D with emphasis on investigating new market opportunities for the company, can be brought into close association with the director of R&D. A strong director of marketing research can be very helpful to the director of R&D. The marketing researcher will include in his survey of new market opportunities, not only a regular inventorying of needs which the company might hope to fill, but also a continuing assessment of what new products are possible of development through the use of the R&D organization. He will want to understand timing, cost, risk, potential proprietary positions, areas of special promise and competence, and the possibilities of breakthroughs as well as of major improvements in products or the processes for manufacturing them, particularly as compared with competitive techniques on the outside.

Capable marketing managers will press the director of R&D for information as to what is in the offing or what might be developed if properly sponsored. They know what the market demands. They will want to know the status of the technology potential of the organization, in substantial part through learning it from the director of R&D. Thus, if the director of research and development is considered less than ideal in his ability to direct R&D with an eye toward market position, the marketing and the marketing research executives may make up for most of this deficiency.

The director of R&D may be outstanding in most respects but not as strong an administrator as desired. For example, his sense of budgeting and control of size and pace of project may leave something to be desired. If so, this director of R&D might be associated with a deputy director who, though himself lacking in some aspects—for instance, he may have less than the desired personal prestige as a technical professional both inside and outside the company to be the director of R&D—might be a first-class manager. The deputy director would have to have excellent personal working relationships with the director and have the confidence of the CEO and others where administrative control and budget matters are concerned.

Supplementing the director of research with a deputy who is strong in administration and control may be especially important where the director of research is prominent in the scientific fraternity. The director then inevitably finds a substantial part of his time going into liaison with research and development leadership elsewhere in the industry or the world at large. It may be considered, with total justification, highly valuable to the company for the director of R&D to be able to use his personal reputation and position to gather in a vast amount of intelligence on what is going on in the fields that bear on the company's R&D programs and decisions for new ones. It would then be waseteful for him to attempt to be in close charge of such managerial aspects as selection of lower personnel, minor facilities expansion, many details of capital and other budgets, all items he could delegate to a strong deputy.

GAUGING THE PERFORMANCE
OF THE R&D DIRECTOR

A substantial part of the total monitoring and judging of the performance of the director of R&D is accomplished by evaluating the R&D results themselves. Here, accomplishments are compared with objectives. Certain new products were to be developed, explorations made, problems solved, scientific fundamentals clarified and interpreted to construct a technological base. If the program did not meet the expectancy of accomplishments versus time within costs, this is a warning signal to be heeded. Tangible accomplishments, if satisfactory, will count more in rating the director, at least after a substantial time, than intangible assessments of his administrative skills, communications talent, and apparent external stature.

Evaluation of tangible accomplishment is not always easy because the techniques for measurement of the success of the R&D program are adequate only up to a point. A typical project may require years before success or failure is evident. The program may appear to be achieving what was planned in every respect, yet this could merely mean that it was laid out too modestly, too expensively, or too vaguely in the first place. Failure sometimes is the result of overly ambitious goals.

Goals, plans, and budgets for an R&D program should be constantly rejudged for satisfactoriness. One criterion of whether or not an R&D plan is a practical one is whether, once implemented, it is capable of being measured. If the planner does not know *how* he will know when the project has been completed or *how* it is progressing, then the plan needs some more attention before being implemented.

The R&D program usually figures very heavily in the securing of growth for the company. For that reason, strong clues as to the value of the R&D program can often be found reasonably clearly. They lie in an assessment of the company's growth generally and an understanding of the relation to that growth of the R&D results that were intended to produce growth.

Mature products will decay in volume and profitability in time as they are replaced by newer products. Market studies will disclose the potential of the continuing mature products and the expected contributions of the new ones. The R&D program may be intended to cover the enhancement of mature products, extending them into new fields and improving them so that they will live and continue to grow. It may also be intended to develop new product areas. The success of the R&D program as it progresses over the years can be judged against the continuing estimates of the company's future obtained from market and profit projections. If the estimates disclose that the goals of market and profit growth are apparently not being met, it may be because the R&D program is not well directed. It may also be because it was too modest or lacking in the proper goals in the first place.

Gauging the skill of the director of R&D by observing only the changing estimates of the future for the company is not justified, because there is no one-on-one relationship. Separation of the impact of the decisions made by the R&D director from that of the decisions of the CEO with regard to the R&D program is difficult. Yet these separations and interrelationships must be attempted if the director of R&D is to be gauged as to his effectiveness.

In addition to absolute evaluation of the director of R&D by performance against company plans and objectives, a relative reading is important and should be made periodically. This is against the apparent R&D accomplishments of other similar companies tackling the same kind of technologies and markets. Do others seem to be progressing more in R&D results, perhaps getting more useful results per dollar of expenditure? Is the company being bested by competitors who are bringing out new and improved products more rapidly? Such comparisons cannot be helpful if made too casually. A competitor might have twice as large a program, be getting only a little more for it, and thus be rated lower as to accomplishment per dollar expended in research and development. Yet that competitive company's program may be superior in that the "expensive little additional accomplishment" was well worth the very high increment of expenditure. Perhaps the R&D Director is too conservative and too modest in his requests for an adequate budget. Perhaps the competitor who mounts a much larger program comes closer to meeting the potentials.

It is difficult to compare the R&D projects of two companies, even if they appear to be very similar on the surface. The expenditures for R&D of one company may be largely to improve the existing product line and to extend the time during which it can contribute to profits, while a competitive company may decide to put emphasis, instead, on longer-range developments that will lead to entirely new things. It may take years to find out which was the best choice. Furthermore, the choice might not have been equally available to both. For example, the very new items using up the research and development budget in the second company may have been the result of a specific invention made there. They should be credited with having created, presumably, the environment for inventive work by the R&D staff. In this, they clearly have led the first company. What is more important, even, is that the first company, without the invention, does not have the same choice.

There is, of course, a long list of almost routine, mechanical checks that the CEO should make as regards the R&D program and the R&D director. How many patents are being applied for? Is there evidence that the director of research has the prominence he needs in the scientific fraternity? Are the leading scientists and engineers receiving their share of awards by their peers? What is the record of articles and books published? Elevation to the academies of science and engineering? Success in recruiting the brightest young scientists and engineers as compared with competitors, or as judged by basic common sense?

How is the director of research evaluated by other executives with whom he must deal? Is he providing for a strength of organization beneath him? When required to do so, can he bring forth the necessary deputies to present progress reports and budget requests to support him, as one might expect in a large operation?

There are other indicators that may help the CEO gauge his director of R&D. For instance, almost certainly a group of key issues will develop in the R&D program on which the director of R&D must take some strong stands. As matters turn out, did he pick the right side to come down on? How did he reason out his position?

There are other indicators to be found in the director's personal decisions or recommendations: Specific accomplishments to be sought versus time. Projects selected from among the many possibilities. (This is always difficult, because there are competing alternatives for using manpower and money!) His evaluations of serious competitive challenges and his counter programs to defend the company's technological position.

Keeping these closely in mind and observing actual history is perhaps the most important tool available to the CEO for gauging the effectiveness of the R&D director.

SETTING RESEARCH AND DEVELOPMENT STRATEGY

by Robert E. McDonald

President and Chief Operating Officer,
Sperry Rand Corporation

THE WORDS "research and development" are the poles of a spectrum ranging from basic research to product modifications. Although the federal government has done much to standardize definitions, the situation in the private sector is not as clear. In industry, one firm's "research" is often another firm's "development." Because the spectrum is so broad and the definitions used in industry so varied, I have found it useful to unify R&D as "technology," and so have directed my remarks here toward setting "technology strategy." As I see it, the "technology strategy" involves all the technical efforts of the firm, regardless of where they lie on the spectrum. The chief executive's view must span the entire spectrum of technological activity and he must deal with the overall strategy rather than its parts. Speaking of "technology strategy" is a constant reminder of the broad viewpoint required.

My comments draw upon my experience with Sperry Rand Corporation, but I believe that the same general principles apply in all firms. Sperry Rand is a multidivision firm operating in several industries and many countries. Our technology strategy is the sum of strategies developed and implemented in the divisions augmented by a central research laboratory which reports at the corporate level. Our strategy is complex, but I suspect that its basic elements also exist in single-division, single-industry companies. In smaller firms, the spectrum of technology may not be as broad and one end may be favored over the other, but the Chief Executive Officer must still see it as a whole and he must see the total spectrum in place as part of overall corporate business strategy. The technology strategy cannot exist alone.

I see three elements in the process of setting technology strategy. The strategy must be formulated, it must be implemented, and it must be evaluated to maintain its relevance and effectiveness. As I address these elements I will first cover some of the alternate roles the "technology organization" can play in a firm. Next I will review some of the ways the overall technology strategy can be implemented. Finally, I will point out some of the "signals" I have found to be useful indicators that a change of strategy may be needed.

FORMULATING THE TECHNOLOGY STRATEGY

At Sperry Rand we have devised a system of plans that permits us to consider separately the actions which are needed for short- and long-term results. Each year, the divisions prepare plans dealing with the immediate future and plans which look ahead five years. Over time, the five-year plans lead to one-year plans and to measurable results. The divisional strategic plans are reviewed at the corporate level and, once approved, become a set of business development plans conforming with the corporation's overall strategy. Except for a small number of technical initiatives emanating from the president's office, the total corporate technology requirement stems from these approved divisional plans. In general, the major portion of the overall technology requirement is met within the divisions, but they may choose to assign longer range elements to a central research laboratory funded directly by the corporation.

It is the responsibility of the executive office to create the environment within which the divisions can plan and execute their plans. As we view it, this includes working with the divisions in setting goals and seeing that the technical plans required to meet those goals are realistic and achievable. Toward this end, we maintain a small corporate staff which includes technical talent capable of evaluating the realism of divisional technical goals and progress toward them.

Alternate Strategic Roles for the Technology Organization

Our technology strategy generally includes some measure of effort near each end of the technology spectrum. Some programs have a long-term outlook while others have a close-in horizon and are directed toward specific ends. But the sum total of all the effort must lead to value for the firm. This requirement essentially rules out what is commonly called "basic research" (research aimed at the creation of new knowledge) and keeps the emphasis toward applied research.

Although at first glance a constraint against basic research may seem severe, there are in fact a wide variety of roles for technology. Product diversification (the creation of new products in planned business areas) has, historically, been considered the most important role, but portions of the technology investment can be devoted to other areas as well. Part of the investment, for example, can be directed toward general increases in productivity, improvement and substitution of materials, response to environmental issues, or counters to regulatory constraints. A conscious recognition of the diversity of roles is important because their very diversity dictates that distinctly separate groups should bear responsibility for execution. For example, the assignments for new product development and innovative enhancements of ongoing products generally will be made to different groups, if for no other reason than the differing time horizons.

It is interesting to compare the characteristics deriving from two missions that are often thought of as one but which are, in fact, quite different—product diversification and product improvement. True diversification implies new products serving new customers in new markets. While many firms have "diversification" as a constant mission, more resources are usually devoted toward developing new products for untapped customers in familiar markets. In both cases, the relevant time horizon is distant. Projects started today are not expected to result in profits for five years or more and there is a risk that the product will not succeed in the marketplace. Scheduling is rather loose and there is high "infant mortality." The technical staff must be highly creative, "research oriented," and must approach problems at fundamental levels.

Product improvement, on the other hand, implies new features for existing products. Product improvements have a short time horizon, seldom more than one year. Quick reaction is important, because projects often are initiated in response to competition. The staff must be weighted more toward engineering than research. It must be very familiar with the product line and closely coupled to the market.

The differences in staff characteristics and outlook which derive from the diversification and improvement missions are vital considerations in formulating technology strategy. Most firms with a history of internal growth have adequate staffs oriented toward product improvement. But if a new mission of diversification is to be added, the existing structure must be reviewed. If the two missions are to coexist, completely separate organizations may be desirable.

IMPLEMENTING THE STRATEGY

Although most of the actions involved in implementing technical strategy are the responsibility of divisional management, they derive from the overall direction set by the chief executive. As I see it, the CEO must provide the structure and funding necessary to execute the technical strategy, he must keep the technical effort channeled in the direction of greatest value to the firm, and he must maintain a climate that maximizes the creative output of the technical organization. We have found reviews by executive office staff people to be a simple and effective way to monitor the direction of divisional programs. But the problem of ensuring the favorable climate needed for creativity is not so easily solved. The CEO influences the climate in many ways. For example, his choice of staff people can be a positive or negative influence depending on how they are perceived by the technical organization. The staff must be recognized as technically competent. If they are not seen as competent, they pose communication barriers and project the impression that top management does not recognize the importance of technology. Another example is the chief executive's attitude toward stability of research funding. If the technical organization feels its funding to be volatile, creativity gives way to frustration.

The basic structural decision facing the chief executive is whether to centralize or decentralize the technical organization. At Sperry Rand we have established a mixed structure which includes a corporate-funded central research center which focuses on long-range effort while the divisions focus on technology with more immediate market impact. We leave the actual separation of effort to be negotiated between the divisions and the central facility. By removing the executive presence, this approach keeps the burden of meeting commitments squarely on the divisions. It also ensures that the central facility is used to the greatest benefit of the business, and, by keeping the divisions directly involved, facilitates the hand-off of new technology. For its part, the research center must make itself relevant and valuable in order to attract requests from the divisions. The divisions, on the other hand, must convince the center that their requests are truly related to business plans.

In Sperry Rand, funding of the technical program derives from divisional business plans reviewed and approved by the corporate office. Once approval has been given, the divisions have a clear idea of the total funding available to generate the technology needed to support both short- and long-term plans. During preparation of the plans, the divisions have analyzed their strengths, weaknesses, and relationship to competition. With this background they are in a position to allocate the available funds in the way they feel will be most effective. This approach further places responsibility for performance at the divisional level.

A method for monitoring divisional progress in technical effort is important. The magnitude of the monitoring problem necessarily varies with the technical makeup of each firm's business and with the chief executive's personal management style. For example, a firm with a highly diversified product line and a widespread organization faces a more complex monitoring task than a single-business firm. The CEO contributes to the magnitude of the task by his own preferences for level of detail and personal involvement. At Sperry Rand, we conduct periodic reviews of major technical programs using a small, technically trained staff from corporate headquarters. The results of these analyses are further evaluated during quarterly sessions, conducted by corporate executives, which review each division's total performance. Members of the corporate technical staff are alert to signs that technical problems large enough to influence performance may be in the offing. They see that the balance of the funding investment is not dangerously skewed toward the short or long term, and they are alert to the implications of policies that might impact the creative output of the total technical program. We have also found that this approach pays dividends in exposing and bringing together similar technical interests among the divisions.

Implementation Alternatives

Success in meeting the goals established during strategy formulation depends on the effectiveness of the technology organization as well as the level of funding. Periodically, the organization should be reviewed to see whether its structure contributes to or hinders accomplishment and to see whether it is, in fact, strong enough to meet the firm's needs or whether outside support should be sought from government or other sources.

The balance of effort between centralized and divisional research organizations is a perennial topic of discussion on organizing for technology. In a multidivision company this debate calls for a policy decision on the degree of dependence that will be placed on the central or corporate laboratory as opposed to the divisions' technical staffs. Centralizing the technical effort should bring economies of scale. Duplication of facilities should be minimized. Specialists need not be duplicated, and layers of management can be pared down. Experience has shown that the interaction of highly trained staff members with outside technical colleagues can unlock great creativity. But it is clear that a centralized group cannot be close to all markets served by the firm. Distance from the marketplace is probably the most serious weakness of a centralized technology organization. Lacking the immediate feedback and pressures of the marketplace, centralized groups eventually find it difficult to focus on the near-term solutions that ultimately are necessary for day-to-day profitable operation. Specialists in centralized organizations tend to develop along technical rather than product directions.

In many ways, divisional product-line technology organizations are a mirror image of the centralized organizations. Coupled to the marketplace, they are goal-oriented and have distinct product orientations. Short-term solutions are expected and delivered. But this short-term orientation can endanger the future. When fluctuating business conditions demand budget adjustments, longer range technology effort is frequently sacrificed.

We are not certain that we have found "the answer" at Sperry Rand but our approach works well in our context. We assign the divisions primary responsibility for generating the technology needed to meet planning goals. Their effort is augmented by the central research laboratory whose charter calls for it to focus on technology with a longer time horizon. By this mixture we recognize the differing loyalties and outlooks that are natural in divisional and centralized organizations and hope to capitalize on them rather than be burdened by them. Corporate funding of the central facility, which represents only a small fraction of our total technology effort, provides the stability needed for a long-range outlook and permits us what is in effect a "wild card" that may be called up when needed.

Sperry Rand looks mainly to its own organization to meet its requirements for technology. The particular merit of being self-sufficient is, of course, the resulting proprietary position. There is also merit, however, in a willingness to consider outside sources when appropriate. Some firms are more open to outside ideas than others, and the tradition seems to vary with the industry involved. Pharmaceutical and chemical firms, for example, have a long history of in-licensing while electronic firms seem to prefer to "do it themselves." It is technological conceit to assume that the in-house staff is omnipotent; shortcomings should be faced realistically. The climate ought to encourage technical management to feel free to admit shortcomings and to take positive action by contracting for work to be done outside or by locating the needed technology in already-developed form. The CEO can work toward developing such a climate by his own actions and his direction of others during, for example, goal setting, funding decisions, and performance reviews.

One outside relationship we have found helpful is the use of government funding in long-range high technology areas. It is important to differentiate here between the solicitation of government research as a primary business element and the use of government contracts to assist in developing a new technology. Many firms have built a substantial business performing research under contract to the government. In a firm whose business includes a major fraction of commercial business, especially in areas with a high technology content, performance of selected government contracts can be used to develop advanced technology for future products.

Use of government contracts to assist in bearing the load of developing a new technology is not without its own dangers. Whenever a firm takes a government contract, it must be prepared for some dilution of proprietary rights. Further, the danger always exists that contracts will come to be seen as an end rather than a means and allowed to dominate the total technology program. Government assistance has the greatest value if it is carefully constrained to technologies already of interest to the corporation. The important point here is that it is necessary to have a stated policy on what areas of technology will be solicited and the total volume of support that will be taken.

Funding the Technology Effort

Another frequently debated topic is how much to budget for technology. Again there are no clear-cut answers. Whatever method is used, it must provide for effort adequate to maintain or improve the firm's competitive position and meet the "planning gap" seen in the future. Further, it must not lead the company to spend more than it can "afford" or generate more technology than can be absorbed. Finally, it must provide the stability and continuity needed to maintain a healthy creative organization and to carry out programs with long-range horizons.

A good starting point to the funding question is the decision on how much technology is "needed." Technology is expected to supply the products needed to meet the "planning gap" at some point in the future—the gap between desired growth and that foreseen from existing products. But it is not clear just how many dollars will buy how much new technology. Here, heavy reliance must be made on the experience of technical managers who are familiar with past patterns of research productivity. In some industries, the research-to-product cycle is quite regular and can be simulated on a computer. It is also appropriate to look at the investment pattern of successful firms in the industry and at how rapidly technology is changing. The latter point is especially pertinent in these times of change when technologically dormant industries may be overturned by the sudden infusion of new technology, making "catch up" spending or acquisition of outside technology appropriate and necessary.

The matter of how much technology the firm can "afford" has both financial and organizational aspects. Certainly, the firm's financial circumstances must be considered . . . its history, its expectations, its margins and forecast of revenues. But the need for stability in funding levels must also be given explicit recognition. Technical programs with a long time horizon require a similarly long budgeting horizon. And equally important is the need to maintain a stable working environment to ensure creativity and continuity of staff. The funding level should not be set so high that minor changes in company fortunes force large swings in the technology investment. The level should be sustainable so that staff creativity is fully realized and the inefficiencies of starting and stopping programs are held to a minimum. There is an analogy here to the stability that is desirable in dividends to shareholders. If a fair degree of stability cannot be maintained, the budget is more than the firm can "afford."

It is possible to establish guidelines to aid in making the funding decision. Setting the technology budget as a percent of sales revenue is perhaps the most widely used approach. It is easy to conceive and implement and can be at least roughly compared with published statistics on other firms. Its major drawback is that it lacks a measure of stability and thus must be modified to lessen the impact of fluctuations in revenue. Budgets set as a percent of revenues are not truly related to the tasks which ought to be done but, used with common sense, their advantages seem to prevail.

At least three other guidelines exist, and have particular merits, but their additional complexity does not seem to justify them over the percent of revenue method. One method attempts to match competitors' outlays, either in dollars or as a percent of revenues. In another, the revenue growth rate target set by management is automatically applied to the technology budget. In the third method, proposed projects are reviewed individually and an attempt is made to estimate total costs to commercialization. These expenditures are then related to profits forecast for the new product and the return on investment is calculated. The technology program is assembled from those projects meeting ROI standards.

With the overall funding level established, the type and degree of control exercised over individual projects must be tailored to make the total effort most effective. Just as differing staff characteristics descend from the differing time horizons of research and product development, requirements for project control also differ. Shorter term "product development" effort should be tightly controlled, and an appropriate system of reporting should be instituted toward that end. The problem with longer range research, however, is more one of channeling than control. Immediate results should not be expected and reviews should be scheduled fairly far apart. Milestones indicating progress need not be numerous, but should represent critical turning points in the program. A control mechanism we use at our corporate research center is to require the "client" division to supply a monitor for each project. He provides the liaison to make certain that the project schedule and direction continue at all times to be consistent with divisional business plans.

The technology effort can and should be planned. Projects must be chosen with an eye toward value and controlled to make certain that value will be realized. By its very nature, though, research involves a measure of risk taking. Not all projects will turn out as planned and not all which do will be exploited. To some extent, especially in longer range technical efforts, one must "expect the unexpected" and hope it will take the form of serendipity. It is best not to schedule the longer range effort so tightly that the happy accident that is serendipity simply cannot happen. Some guideline should be established for exploratory work not clearly related to identifiable divisional plans. While technology can and should be planned and scheduled, careful choice of procedures will maintain the environment needed to capitalize on a creative staff.

EVALUATING THE TECHNOLOGY STRATEGY: TIME FOR A CHANGE?

The chief executive must evaluate his firm's strategy against the background of changing external events. Changes in technology, trends in the economy and world society, actions by government and competition are examples. He must be sensitive to the effects of these changes and must see that his firm's technology strategy is consistent with them. Meeting this responsibility requires that he establish an appropriately strong technology organization, maintain clear communication channels to it, and be ready to change it as required to keep the strategy effective over time.

The technology strategy, however sound, cannot be effective if the organization behind it is weak. The technology organization, in our case the sum of the divisions and the research center, must have the necessary mix of talents and outlooks. With changes in society and the nature of business, the "right" mix of talents changes. Let me give two examples. The trend toward digital technology, reflected in the growth of our Univac computer division, led us to establish a special digital group at our central research facility. And in response to the world need for more efficient harvesting equipment we have added capability to introduce electronic systems in farm machinery sold by our New Holland division. While the divisions are charged to develop their own organizations in consonance with their plans, overall responsibility for strength and direction remains at the top.

Clear communication channels are perhaps the most vital tool in evaluating technology strategy. Good upward channels and means to monitor them must be established. Elements of divisional technical strategy which strongly determine business results must be allowed to surface. The CEO must develop the familiarity necessary to evaluate divisional management, and divisional management must feel free to discuss major strategic decisions. Certainly, management style has much to do with establishing clear communication channels. Our approach includes the use of a small staff of competent people to maintain close review of divisional technical programs. This staff provides visibility into divisional activities, monitors the external environment for warning signs, and serves as a cross pollinator of technology across divisional lines. I have found, incidentally, that successful use of staff people in these roles depends not only on competency but also on their acceptability, as individuals, to the divisions. A mix of technical competency and human relations skills is required.

External factors occasionally overtake even the most carefully laid plans and the executive office must be ready to perform major surgery to set things right. New technologies may loom as threats from unwatched quarters or other market forces may indicate that major elements of the overall technology strategy must be altered. The proper response may be acquisition of a new base, sale of a division, or merger of two divisions. For example, we recently changed our market posture and technical direction with two moves. Acquiring the customer base of the RCA computer operation added to Univac's revenue stream and brought in new ideas in technology as well. In 1974, the merger of our Remington division into Univac recognized the growing sophistication of office equipment typified by typewriters with editing capability and accounting machines with computing power. Remington equipment will benefit from Univac's more highly developed technical organization. Decisions of this sort must rest with the chief executive. He must establish a strong technical organization, communicate freely with it, and, finally, be ready to take strong, positive action to redirect it when necessary.

Signals of Change

Technology strategy must be viewed as a relatively long-term commitment. It cannot simply be established and set aside to be forgotten. The CEO must have a mechanism for monitoring signals which indicate that technology strategy should be called up for review. When evaluating divisional strategic plans, or, less formally, monitoring the ongoing business environment, certain key signals bring to question the appropriateness of the firm's technology strategy. Many of these signals are equally applicable to evaluation of a firm's business plan, but I have found a small group of them especially appropriate in the context of technology. Shifts in the firm's business strategy or its market environment, the appearance of new technology, or competitors' actions all may signal the need for change.

The business environment provides leading indicators of change required in the corporate technology program. Often the subtlest indicators prove of greatest value as leading indicators while the more conspicuous signals require a rapid, tactical response. In consumer markets, slow changes in demographic factors can be forecast. In industrial markets, long-range forecasts of business growth can be translated into requirements for technology to produce new products. For example, energy requirement forecasts can be translated into forecasts of tanker construction and then into requirements for navigation equipment. The important common element of these indicators is time. The time horizon must go beyond the firm's needs for the products of tomorrow. It must consider the time required to build a base of new technology and convert it into the products required five or more years in the future.

By contrast, the more direct indicators of change require a response at the short-term, "development" end of the technology spectrum. The structure of the overall technology program must provide for the rapid response necessary to meet effectively the dislocations caused by suddenly imposed regulations or uncontrollables such as the "energy crisis" of 1973. Certainly, best efforts must always be made to forecast even the uncontrollables. But, as a minimum response, the overall technology program should be structured so that some degree of short-term dislocation can be tolerated without permanently disrupting the effort planned for the longer term.

It is also appropriate to look to the corporation's annual strategic planning function for signals indicating change in technology strategy. Certainly, changes in the expected financial outlook for the corporation may require changes in the technology program. But plans to enter new markets or more ambitious growth-rate goals should also be considered. Divisional growth plans, for example, should be reviewed to see that they are, in fact, backed up by appropriate commitments to produce the necessary technology.

Yet another indicator is the firm's expectations for its divisions or other major units of its business portfolio. While a single-division, single-product firm need only concern itself with the absolute level and directional emphasis of its program, a multidivision or multi-product firm should also consider how the technology investment is balanced among the major elements of its business. The reader may wish to refer to later texts on strategic planning for a detailed discussion but, in brief, the approach is to allocate resources to the business areas which hold the greatest potential for growth and which provide the greatest available market. Resources should be withdrawn from elements of the business serving declining markets and maintained at a continuity level in areas serving mature, but profitable, markets. The cash made available by withdrawals and that generated by the mature businesses is invested in the growth elements of the firm's portfolio. We find this concept very valuable. High-technology growth businesses, such as our Univac division, require a large and continuing investment during early market stages. Our planning system recognizes the balancing concept and we see that it is taught at our internal management development seminars.

Balancing the resource allocation can be a powerful tool for optimizing the effectiveness of the overall technology program, but proper use of it demands a realistic assessment of the growth prospects for each major element in the portfolio. It is often difficult to look beyond the resource demands voiced by line managers, yet this must be done if growth is to be managed and planned instead of allowed to happen or merely be desired. When a change in growth outlook is perceived, the technology strategy must be called to review. Line managers justify their requests with short-term arguments. The CEO must take a longer view. He must recognize when growth prospects in one element have truly leveled and he should shift his strategy to maintain technology at a continuity level there while force-feeding the technology base of elements in early market stages.

It would appear that technology itself should provide the most direct signals of needed change. They do exist but they are often the most difficult to see. Changes occurring within the firm's own industry are the clearest to see and are those most often heeded. On the other hand, changes outside the firm's industry often go unnoticed even though they can carry the most serious implications. Monitoring technological change within the firm's industry is the responsibility of divisional top management. Generally speaking, a formal monitoring program seems unnecessary, but some arrangements should be made to take notice of factors such as the introduction of new technology, however small, by competitors, vendor suggestions, and trends in customer requirements that can be met with new technological solutions.

A constant danger in focusing on one's own industry is that the most revolutionary changes in technology often occur outside. Unless unusual sensitivity is maintained, threats or opportunities resulting from technological changes outside the firm's industry are met with reaction rather than consideration. Industry abounds with examples of disruption and opportunity arising unnoticed. Perhaps one of the most dramatic examples of recent times is the explosive growth of the consumer market for electronic calculators, and the decline in the office market for electromechanical models, arising from the development of low-cost integrated circuits.

Actions of competitors would seem to be the obvious place to look for warning signals indicating a needed change in technology strategy. A competitor's actions cannot be ignored. But when one considers the gestation time required to introduce a new product with advanced technology, it is apparent that truly strategic responses are not possible to competitors' product announcements. Immediate, tactical responses are necessary, and such actions are correctly charged to line management.

Competitive actions should be monitored for strategic implications in at least three areas. First, the competitor's rate of new product introductions is an important indicator of the effectiveness of his technology investment. While the introduction of any one new product must be met in the marketplace, the competitor's longer range plans are often telegraphed by a change from his traditional rate of new product introductions. Given an increased rate of product introductions, it may be possible to predict the time required for a complete turnover of the competitor's line or to estimate his planned aggressiveness in seeking increased market share. Because the observations are to establish a trend over time, a strategic shift in technology strategy may be possible.

Two other fruitful areas to monitor are changes in the absolute level and the direction of emphasis of the competitor's technology investment. Both factors are, of course, difficult to monitor, but used with judgment, observations can be a useful guide in developing a strategic response. Many firms publish their R&D figures, but differences in definition and a lack of breakdown by product area make direct comparisons difficult and possibly misleading. A great deal of care must be exercised in basing judgments on published figures.

Your own technical staff, particularly technologists operating at the "research" end of the spectrum, are probably the most valuable point for monitoring the emphasis of the competitor's technology investment. Their readings of scientific journals, attendance at society meetings, and readings of patent announcements provide an indicator of new directions by competitors well in advance of new product introduction. These points of contact should be encouraged and means established to integrate, evaluate, and exploit this intelligence.

The chief executive cannot be in constant touch with all points of his business, nor can he scan all the possible warning signs. But he must develop a sensitivity to their existence and see that a proper mechanism for observing the signs and analyzing their meaning is created. And finally, he must see that the technology strategy is properly directed as the signals of change are seen over time.

ALLOCATION OF DEVELOPMENT RESOURCES IN MAJOR DIRECTIONS

by Jesse Werner

Chairman and President, GAF Corporation

ESTABLISHING THE BOUNDARY BETWEEN RESEARCH AND DEVELOPMENT

THE CHIEF EXECUTIVE OFFICER particularly in a technically based business, must maintain a deep personal responsibility for, and commitment to research and development. He must involve himself both with the input into R&D and the results obtained therefrom.

Although the phrase research and development is usually mentioned in one breath, almost as if it were one word, it actually combines two distinct concepts. If one agrees that research is the first stage in which a vast input of technical and business information and skills are brought to bear in order to solve a specific problem in the laboratory, then by contrast, development is the sum total of activities involved in turning the solution of the problem into a commercial reality.

Within the constraints imposed by the necessity of making a profit, research must be free-form to a substantial extent and must be encouraged to continue in that vein. This is obviously the case in fundamental research; but the same is also true, albeit in a more limited way, of applied research and application research. Because research often attempts to answer questions which may not have answers and where the only feasible way to obtain rational answers is to modify the questions, a spirit of free inquiry must be maintained. Moreover, timetables must be somewhat flexible. Not only is there no guarantee that results will ever be obtained, but initial results will often determine whether to expand or contract the areas of further work to be covered.

478

To the trained scientist, whose natural home is the laboratory, the fun of the search tends to be a more important priority than eventual commercial potential. The chief executive must make certain that research management has sufficient managerial and business skills to know when a research project should either be terminated or moved to the next stage and become a development project.

Obviously, there is no way to automate that decision. However, if the company has a strong development organization ready and anxious to take over a research project when the time is right, the job is made considerably easier.

COORDINATION OF DEVELOPMENT

We have defined development as the sum total of activities required to turn a positive research result into a commercial reality. This may mean that a piece of research involving perhaps not more than a few ounces of product is to be evaluated for multimillion-pound production and sale.

In the chemical industry, particularly since World War II, the concept has evolved that the best way to move new products from the laboratory through the pilot plant to substantial commercial volume is by assigning the overall responsibility to a special group which is not part of research, production, or marketing but which works closely with all three. This commercial development group is the key to successful development.

While the technical organization is working on product and process development, the commercial development group is acting as the business focus of the project.

An appreciable part of my own industrial career was spent in commercial development and I can therefore speak with first-hand knowledge of the importance of this function in pushing forward a project on a coordinated basis. I can also speak of the importance the chief executive of the company had for me in this area. I was running what could only be considered a small independent business using the services and resources of a large organization. Obviously, my demands on the organization for help for products with only potential commercial viability were often looked on by busy operations managers as something close to impositions. The interest and help which I received from the chief executive in dealing with my problems were undoubtedly the key factors in reaching eventual success.

The first part of commercial development work is bringing together the known facts about the product and its potential applications. This should include running some high spot economics (to determine both operating and capital costs), setting up a timetable, and finally analyzing the skills, whether new or in-house, that will have to be brought to bear on the project in order to achieve success.

The first plan, however rough it may seem to be in the face of what is likely to be a considerable body of unknowns, will, if done by experts, give a very good feel of the practicality of a project. That practicality is basically based on a cost versus chance of success analysis. This will, of course, be shaded by the chief executive's outlook and philosophy. If, for example, he shies away from basically new technology or the building up of entirely new market concepts, then no matter how attractive a new project may be, it will be felt that it is really outside the scope of the company. In all cases, the question to be decided is whether the potential profits are likely to be worth the effort that will have to be expended to bring the project to fruition.

MARKET RESEARCH AND MARKET DEVELOPMENT

In the commercialization of new products, market research and market development are two coordinated functions that go hand in hand. The market research function is responsible for evaluating the potential size of the market for new products or services and as much additional information as can practically be obtained. This includes the nature of competitive products, who the potential customers are, and what their needs are in terms of price, quality and service. Equally important is the establishing of the longer-term industry and product use trends and their effect on the future potential of the new products.

Market development is that segment of the activity aimed at actually establishing new markets for the new product when the market research and economic evaluation analysis have indicated the possibility of a profitable new field. The market development specialist is, therefore, the key man in making his organization help his new product come to commercial birth.

Internally, he must persuade his research organization to continue its interest in the new product after the first research stage has been successfully completed. The embryo product needs application studies, analytical research, and product improvement. The market development specialist must also be able to work with the pilot plant and production people so that increasing development quantities of materials are available as customer requirements grow. Contacts with the marketing organization, which will take over the new product, must be maintained with emphasis on pricing policies and customer coordination. The other staff departments, patents, legal, advertising and promotion, must be consulted and their help secured as necessary.

However, the market development specialist's even more important function is to work with potential customers. He must persuade them to spend valuable time and money in evaluating a product which may be in a far-from-finished stage and which indeed may never become a commercial reality. He must obtain their technical respect and their trust so that they will share with him the results they obtain in their own work. He must have this input to keep on modifying the product and the project.

A combination of patience, tact, and thorough technical knowledge is required along with a grim determination that no obstacle will be allowed to defeat the project.

PRODUCT DEVELOPMENT AND PROCESS DEVELOPMENT

While the members of the commercial development group are performing their varied functions, the result of their input is being made available to the research, engineering, and production functions. The key effort by these functions at this stage is the development of the product in the form required by market demand and at the same time, the development of a process which makes this product economically practical to sell.

Here, R&D management must show qualities appreciably different from those which activate research. Although the technical skills required of the participants in this effort are every bit as high as in the research portion of the activity, goals are now more tightly defined and timetables are more rigid. The ability to respond intelligently to the customer input provided by commercial development is essential. However, development is a continuing dialogue, and the laboratory personnel must make a continuing set of suggestions back to the market development specialist and through him to the potential customers. Demands which cannot be met must be recognized and product applications adjusted accordingly. This is just as important a technical input, because an enormous amount of time and money can be spent in trying to achieve aims which are not commercially feasible.

Equally important is the manufacturing aspect of this program. As a first step, the market development effort needs product at least in small quantities. The pilot plant must, therefore, develop techniques for providing sample requirements. Although the material will obviously be extremely expensive on a cost per pound basis, here the most important requirement is providing sufficient material in something approximating the ultimate commercial specifications.

At the same time, the process engineering group will be working with the laboratory personnel on the development of the commercial process. Here the variables to be balanced are the projected size of the first commercial installation; the expected sale price of the commercial product; the availability of technology and equipment within the company; and, very importantly in recent times, the availability and price of possible starting materials.

As requests come in for new pilot plant equipment and for the hiring of technical personnel with new skills, the Chief Executive Officer should participate in these decisions, in order to keep the overall project in focus and on track. It is very easy to wake up and find that, in rather small chunks, a formidable project has been assembled with hundreds of thousands of dollars of equipment and a respectable cadre of people, all of whom are answering a series of piecemeal requirements which do not add up to an economically viable project. The end product of this sort of expenditure is not only a severe operating cost which will have no ultimate benefit for the P&L statement, but a possible write-off of equipment which has no further use to the company when the project is terminated. If such a folly develops, it will be the responsibility of the chief executive. He must see that it does not happen.

GENERAL DEVELOPMENT

There is a third aspect to commercial development, and this is usually denominated general development. It is concerned with planning, screening for acquisitions and mergers, joint ventures, acquisition of outside technology, and the like. We have found that even a small group of technically trained people with an interest in, and feel for, business, economics, and finance can make very meaningful contributions in: (1) short- and long-range planning; (2) economic evaluation of new and old projects; (3) study and negotiation of possible acquisitions, joint ventures, and mergers; (4) commercial intelligence both domestic and foreign; (5) technical assistance in patent and know-how licensing; and (6) the nucleus of an internal management consulting service.

INTERRELATION OF RESEARCH AND COMMERCIAL DEVELOPMENT

A well organized and properly functioning commercial development group or department can be of immeasurable help in assessing research projects at all the stages from inception to completion. Market research can help to evaluate customer needs, size of potential market, competitive products, and related aspects. Market development can help to project the ease of market introduction. General development can provide economic evaluation, overall technical assessment, and advice as to whether outside technical help should be sought.

Obviously, these sorts of disciplined analyses can be crucial in "selling" or explaining new research programs to top management or in deciding when to cut them off. They can also help research management as well as top management in the allocation of dollars and manpower among competing research projects; in the assessment of technical as well as market risk before commitment to a research idea; and in deciding whether technology or research talent should be purchased on the outside.

Top management, and especially the Chief Executive Officer, should not be deprived of the type of advice and help that can be given by such a group.

A DEVELOPMENT CASE HISTORY

The story of the commercialization by GAF Corporation of the PVP (polyvinylpyrrolidone) family of high-pressure acetylene chemicals represents a classical example of what commercial development is all about. It also points out why this function is so essential to technically based companies, if they are to grow and prosper. As briefly as is possible, I shall try to reconstruct the technical and business background of this project, and describe what coordinated development efforts were involved that made the eventual marketing success possible.

The story begins, as it must, in the laboratory of a truly creative research chemist. In the late 1920s, Dr. J. Walter Reppe, working in the laboratories of I. G. Farben in Germany, found the first clues to the technique which permitted him to carry out entirely new syntheses using acetylene under pressure.

After about ten years of work, he had discovered four new types of reactions. From each of these reactions, he had synthesized a host of new and old chemicals. In addition, he had developed potentially economical methods of manufacture for a great many of these chemicals.

GAF Research

Shortly before World War II, the management of GAF became aware of this work being carried out by its then parent company. Laboratory work was started in this country but World War II brought to an end any possibility of a broad development program at that time.

After the war, a research and development program was started up again at our central research laboratory. Because GAF no longer had any technical contacts with the German "I.G.," it was necessary for us to develop all of our process and product know-how on our own. A large pilot plant was later erected, and it was placed in operation in 1949.

During this period, GAF carried out extensive work on three of the four Reppe reactions. Literally hundreds of compounds were synthesized, many more than could possibly be evaluated in our application research program. Although all of this work was absolutely essential to develop the technical familiarity which must be the base of such a venture into truly new fields, it could never in itself result in commercial sales and profits.

Initial Market Development

The clues of how to achieve this on the marketing side were rather limited and in some ways misleading. The work in Germany had led to the limited commercialization of a few products from one series. In addition, a few important uses had developed for another, called the PVP series. One involved PVP (polyvinylpyrrolidone), itself. This physiologically inert white powder, dissolved in isotonic salt solution, was given during the war years to many, many thousands of people in Germany as a substitute for blood plasma in the treatment of shock.

The synthesis of PVP involves the step-wise production of five chemicals; each of these products was then absolutely unknown to American industry. Further, each of these chemicals is a unique product capable of undergoing many reactions and becoming the progenitor of innumerable new chemicals on its own.

Once the research and development work had progressed to the point where at least sample amounts of these products could be made available, a rudimentary market development program was also started. On the basis of the German experience, two obvious avenues were explored. One was to endeavor to find a large-volume use for one of the chemical intermediates (called butanediol) in some polymer application, and the other was to establish PVP in the United States as a synthetic blood volume expander. In retrospect, it is evident that we could not have chosen two more discouraging paths.

Butanediol was indeed tested by synthetic fiber producers interested in new types of polymers and some samples of cloth were actually produced. As we learned by hard experience, it is a long road from making a sample to the decision to invest the many millions of dollars required to introduce a new fiber.

Our shocks in that area, however, were as nothing compared to the rude experience that awaited us when we found out what was required to have a new synthetic chemical accepted as a blood plasma replacement in the United States.

We plunged enthusiastically into a costly biological and chemical testing program and worked with all the governmental agencies concerned. They encouraged us to continue to spend our money and talked in terms of fantastic volumes. I can only say that time passed, the physiological inertness of PVP and its interesting detoxifying qualities were established by many dedicated investigators, but no New Drug Applications clearances were issued by the Food and Drug Administration.

Program Reappraisal

At the low point in our efforts to have PVP accepted as a blood volume expander, the then chief executive of GAF realized that the company had spent a good many millions of dollars and learned a great deal about a large number of new products but that, unfortunately, the gap between the great chemical interest .they evoked and their profitable commercial acceptance seemed as wide as ever. After a period of agonizing reappraisal, he insisted that a major, sophisticated, and expensive market development effort was the only answer if we were ever to achieve the commercial acceptance that products with such fascinating structures and properties ought to have.

In 1952, it became my assignment, as a new director of commercial development, to put together the programs and manpower, and to direct the effort necessary to achieve this goal. It seemed apparent that, if there were to be any chance of success on the project, we would have to concentrate all of our efforts on only one of the Reppe syntheses, and not on all three as heretofore. After weighing all of the factors, we decided to concentrate on the PVP family. Our decision can be explained in part by noting that although we realized the difficulties involved in simultaneously launching the market development of PVP plus the five other chemical intermediates—each with absolutely different application and industry potentials—the fact that they were related intermediates meant that as each one grew it would help to insure the economic viability of the others. Another factor which entered into our considerations was the fact that all these products were obvious starting points for additional reactions which could be carried out in our existing plant equipment. More important, we had by then learned a great deal about the interesting properties of these materials, and particularly about the properties of our water-soluble polymer, PVP.

Stepped-Up Market Development

Once this basic goal had been set, the next step was to decide how the market development would be carried out. Serendipity having failed, and no large-volume, high-price use having been dropped on our doorstep, we turned to the opposite approach. The new program assumed that if samples of these unusual products could be put in the hands of a sufficient number of industrial chemists, and if they could be motivated to work with them in their own research efforts, industrial acceptance would have to follow for many, probably smaller, applications.

Therefore, the next job was bringing together a team of market development people who would be able to carry out the field work and the intracompany activities that were required. I may say that I was exceedingly fortunate to have a group of excellent people, all technically trained and marketing oriented, who shared my enthusiasm about these products, and who were willing to work tirelessly, singlemindedly, and most effectively on our program.

The six products, which were different in applications potential, were split into groups and each group was assigned to a separate team of market development engineers. Each product was then considered carefully on the basis of all the information already developed in our own laboratories. This was used to prepare preliminary data sheets and to decide on the customer calls where personal contacts might elicit the most favorable response.

Obviously, when dealing with entirely new products it is impossible for any one group to imagine all the places where the product should be tested. Therefore, the schedule of personal visits to research laboratories was supplemented by advertising and direct mail campaigns. This allowed us to introduce the products and display our rather limited stock of knowledge about their possible applications in the most intriguing manner we could muster.

Our program brought forth an immediate flood of inquiries and requests for samples. Then came the long, patient work of encouraging these potential customers actually to use the samples in their research programs. Even more important, we were able to persuade these prospects to confide in us about their activities so that we could bring our company's skill to bear in helping them solve their problems by the use of our products.

Problems Encountered

In these early development stages, there seemed to be a universal conspiracy to plague each product with every possible problem simultaneously. First of all, the potential customers were being asked to spend their R&D funds on testing products of unproven qualities and which might never be commercially available even though uses should be developed for them. Furthermore, at that stage they were rather expensive, and potential customers had to rely on assurances that when commercially available, the prices would be more in line with their requirements.

Then, when any customer demand did develop, the supply problem immediately became acute. The pilot plant installation was intended primarily for process development and sampling. Manufacturing products in sufficient volume to satisfy sales requirements was an unreasonable additional demand, so far as our process engineers were concerned.

From the overall management point of view, one of the really sore subjects was the pricing of the new products. A pilot plant which was simultaneously a semiworks and a process development unit did not give respectable manufacturing costs, and customers could not be expected to pay prices set on the basis of these costs. Future prices from a full-scale commercial unit were only a remote promise at this time. Our initial development prices were so high that many people refused to consider the products at all. This was quite a problem for a few months. It was finally settled when our Commercial Development Department obtained complete control over prices, which were to be set as close to the eventual commercial prices as possible, with the proviso that no out-of-pocket losses were to be incurred on the pilot plant production. I must say parenthetically that we had to make some exceptions to this rule as time went on.

Commercialization

With this problem solved, and development prices sharply reduced, our program went into high gear. Working almost feverishly, we called on a large number of potential customers all over the country and flooded most of the others with letters and technical bulletins, ads, magazine articles, talks at technical societies, and even general seminars at many of the larger companies. All of the field information was brought back and evaluated to guide the efforts of laboratory research and the manufacturing units. More complete data sheets and bulletins were written, more sharply defined ads were prepared, prices were adjusted to fit market needs, grades of product were clarified, and gradually the most important problem evolved: When to build a large plant?

During all of this, the Chief Executive Officer of the company remained intimately involved. He set the tenor, helped me open doors, asked me to give periodic reports to the board of directors and, by example, established a level of unparalleled enthusiasm for the project Without his interest and support, results would not have been the same.

The more customers we found and the more interested they became, the more they wanted to know when commercial prices and volumes would be available. If the program was to preserve its momentum, a decision to build a commercial plant now had to be made by the GAF management and board. By the beginning of 1954, the results obtained by market development were sufficiently promising to convince the board to allocate six million dollars to the construction of the first United States plant for the manufacture of high-pressure acetylene derivatives at Calvert City, Kentucky.

The plant went on stream early in 1956; and the period between authorization and commercial availability was an exceedingly difficult one, because customer use had to be maintained and increased in the face of rather limited supplies. Just how we did this almost defies explanation; but I might add that by 1955, we had reached our first million dollars of sales.

What actual or possible uses had we developed for our products by 1956? Certainly many that no one could have predicted when we started our push.

PVP itself had found its first big success as the film-forming ingredient in the aerosol hair sprays then beginning to achieve their initial popularity. Once it was accepted in the cosmetic field, additional cosmetic uses followed in lotions, rinses, shaving lathers, and other related applications.

Our long years of effort on PVP as a blood volume expander were not really wasted, because the pharmacological information accumulated gave it a place as a tablet binder, drug vehicle, and detoxifier. The unexpected complex compound it forms with iodine made possible a new type of water-soluble, nonstinging iodine disinfectant which has been the basis of a series of ethical and proprietary products under the Isodine and Betadine trademarks.

PVP was also established as a fiber additive, a dye stripping agent, a protective colloid in printing pastes, and as a complexer to reduce "chill haze" in beer and other beverages.

Other products in the family were being used as powerful solvents for resins which presented solubility problems and other chemicals, as well as in gas separation. Still others found such diverse uses as corrosion inhibitors, additives in electroplating solutions, essential components in polymer synthesis, and as intermediates for pharmaceuticals and agricultural chemicals.

In Retrospect

From an overall point of view, we developed a myriad of specialty applications, all requiring a technical sales skill and a willingness to give customer service which happened to fit in amazingly well with the overall pattern of our well-established specialty chemical sales effort.

We are a company which began in dyestuff manufacture and which therefore is accustomed to making relatively small volumes of complex products by multistep synthesis. We are used to providing customer service at a high technical level. Furthermore, we have extensive experience with difficult and potentially dangerous reactions carried out on a commercial scale. Without all this background, I doubt if any management could have had the necessary faith and understanding while we were going through our PVP family growing pains.

I have not stressed the difficulties connected with developing and then scaling up a multistep process involving such potentially dangerous reaction conditions, and where each step must work effectively if the final product is to be obtained at desired volume and cost. The starting up of the first plant (we now have two) brought its inevitable share of problems. To solve them took all of the attention we could muster for quite a period of time.

I have also not mentioned the total investment in this program. By the time it was a success, GAF had invested over $30 million in research, engineering, pilot plant, commercial plant, applications research, and market development.

The field or high pressure acetylene chemistry began because a laboratory chemist approached his research with courage, self-confidence and thorough technical skill. Perhaps it's not strange that the same qualities were required for the development phase, and the sales process continues the same demands.

Two Morals

I would like to draw only two morals from this story. The first is simply that we would not have developed a profitable and substantial business in this field if we had not had a position in the councils of the company and the complete and thorough backing of all of top management, especially the Chief Executive Officer.

A complicated development program of this type cannot be left solely to a Commercial Development Department to sink or swim. It must be a completely coordinated effort of the entire company, spearheaded by the Commercial Development Department, but carried out in an atmosphere of understanding unity of purpose. Otherwise, the time and money had better be spent on something else.

The second moral is that when you really believe in a project, do not be detracted by skeptics. They only serve one purpose—to make the optimists perform.

THE INPUT INTO DEVELOPMENT BY THE CHIEF EXECUTIVE

The entire subject of development is so ill-defined in many executives' minds that I have felt it necessary to explain in the previous sections exactly what its components are and how it differs from research. I have also felt it necessary to give a concrete case history of a development project to help clarify the subject matter. It is obvious from the previous discussion that both research and development in the technically based company are aimed at growth. It goes without saying that one of the key jobs of the chief executive in any corporation is not only to plan for profitable growth, but also to keep within his purview the actions necessary for making that growth come about.

I believe that the chief executive must, first of all, participate in the planning by which the line and staff people jointly formulate the overall areas of research needs for the corporation. He should then continue his interest in the progress being made during the research phase. However, it is the nature of large organizations that inertia will continue projects in the research stage too long unless decisions are pressed for. No one can do this more effectively and incisively than the chief executive. The balance between patience in letting research do its work without pressure and impatience in getting projects to a commercial conclusion is one that must be recognized. There is no easy solution that I know except the integration of all the knowledge of technology, marketing, finance, and people which the chief executive has built up over the years.

Once the decision point has been reached and the planning has begun on the major development project, then the participation of the chief executive becomes essential. His drive and enthusiasm for the project are a necessary part in assuring that it will have a chance of success. His input on the analysis of the path to be followed is also critical, because he should have the best long-range grasp of what projects the corporation will be engaged in, what problems the corporation will be facing, and how each new project will integrate into the existing network of such activities.

Once a practical plan has been agreed on, the Chief Executive Officer must keep his interest focused on the results. Like the laboratory people, who enjoy researching a project to death, development people are very reluctant to admit defeat. They will continue spending corporate time and funds in what sometimes turns out, eventually to be an exercise in futility. Once again, there is a continual conflict between patience and impatience which the chief executive must integrate. No development project can be expected to go smoothly. Obstacles, delays, crises, disappointments, and frustrations are inevitable parts of any journey into the unknown—which is what a development project is. However, at some point it may be necessary to recognize that there is no way to reach the goal over which so many people have spent so much blood, sweat, and tears. Unfortunately, the perspective of the chief executive makes him the person best suited in the organization to decide when an obstacle can be overcome as against when it must be recognized as fatal to the project.

No corporation, however large, can explore everything that seems potentially attractive as a possible growth area. Even a project as relatively modest as the one I described, in which we brought a limited set of chemicals to the commercial stage, cost my company some $30 million before it began earning its way. The investment was worthwhile because the company recognized that if we were successful, we would have a unique series of products with long-term viability and appreciable profit potential. That has indeed been the case for GAF's PVP family of chemicals; but the columns of *The Wall Street Journal* are strewn with stories of companies announcing the closing out of projects which started out with equally high expectations and which ended in smaller or larger writeoffs.

It is my firm belief that the tools for keeping such disasters to a minimum exist in the kind of sophisticated commercial development activity which I have outlined. It is also my firm belief that the chief executive must insist that the corporation use these disciplined tools and not allow the organization to fall into the traps of short cuts, or assumptions, or overenthusiasm which can lead to expensive misadventures.

Although I put it last in this discussion, the chief executive's most important job in the development area is the selection of the key management people who will have the day-to-day responsibility for the project. As in all other areas of a business, people are the unique ingredient. In the case of development, the normal requirements of intelligence, honesty, and common sense are not enough. People must be found who will bring high-level business creativity and a crusading spirit to their work. Their selection and motivation by the Chief Executive Officer are essential.

PRODUCT ENGINEERING

by James W. Wilcock

President, Joy Manufacturing Company

UNLESS the Chief Executive Officer has an engineering degree and has climbed the corporate ladder through the engineering function, he is usually neither comfortable with nor close to the product engineering activity. This quite naturally leads to his being extremely dependent upon his vice president of engineering for the satisfactory performance of the engineering department.

Whether your company is small, permitting you to communicate daily with the head of engineering, or large and requiring scheduled staff conferences on engineering problems, is not significant. For our purposes, we want to examine the nature of the engineering beast to remove any mystique that may exist and to understand its importance today in the overall corporate structure.

After all, *you* are responsible for the satisfactory performance of your company, and to be unable to critically analyze, measure, and evaluate the engineering function is both dangerous and unnecessary. If your background has been predominantly marketing, financial, or manufacturing, you will have individual prejudices to overcome. After all, what marketing man has not said, "If engineering would only design a product we could sell!" Or what financial man has not torn his hair trying to understand why it takes 3,000 man-hours to draft a new design of product. And manufacturing *always* feels tolerances are too tight and costly methods are being spawned by poor design.

THE PRODUCT ENGINEERING FUNCTION

Let's forget these emotions and objectively examine a definition of the function.

494

Product engineering has the sole responsibility to produce the specifications, designs, and manufacturing instructions (drawings) for the company's products, both current and newly-developed.

In fulfilling its mission it employs information supplied by the marketing group and thus provides the company with its *most basic need:* the design of products to sell that will return a profit.

Execution of its responsibilities encompasses many considerations having major financial, legal, manufacturing, and sales impacts on the company. The function must therefore be carefully managed and measured to insure the maximum contribution and minimum number of negative results.

This is a broad definition and attempts to straddle the requirements of two categories of business: those producing standardized, catalog-type products and those producing custom products. I am sure you can recognize the differences in the approach to designing a toilet seat as compared to a turbogenerator. Space prohibits a critical review of all the differences so it is necessary to concentrate on those aspects that are more common to both.

Some of the major objectives in *all* engineering departments include design simplification to minimize cost; innovation to enhance the product's market appeal; compliance with various laws pertaining to safety, noise reduction, and consumer protection; and performance to meet guarantees and warranties, express or implied.

Some of the minor, or secondary, responsibilities include constant product cost improvement through redesign, continuing standardization of product components, and assistance to marketing and manufacturing.

Along with these duties there is constant cooperation required with the R&D group, field service, purchasing, and the legal department.

THE MANAGER OF ENGINEERING

Let us analyze the man who is responsible for this function at the operating level, a "chief engineer," "director of engineering," or whatever title you use. He certainly must be an engineer himself and he must have outstanding administrative ability as well as technical savvy. Recognizing the interests of the other key functional managers with whom he must work, he must be able to communicate well, understand product requirements from many aspects, and *understand cost and expense* in the company's P&L statement. The latter is often difficult for many engineering managers.

The expense involved in his own function, as it is allocated to the individual engineering of products, is generally understood. But he must also understand the follow-on costs and expenses related to manufacturing, selling, promotion, distribution, shipping, field service, and warranty. These are often not properly related to the needed engineering design quality that can affect these subsequent charges.

Too many engineering managers are purists to the extent that they know better than the customer what the customer wants. Proposed specifications from marketing are deemed constraints rather than facts. Overengineering is a common trait: Material too heavy, safety factors excessively great, better-than-required types of materials, and too costly an appearance show up in many products. Westinghouse utilized the single practice of weighing their appliances and comparing gross weights to those of competitive products. Overengineering sometimes showed up, and when it did, this led to cost reduction redesigns.

The engineering manager must be carefully selected and constantly evaluated. As in all other functions, you want a well-balanced, common-sense executive. Beware the genius! Design your own accountability system to be used for this individual, but be sure you include *all* the facets of his activity and have frequent reviews of measurable objectives that were agreed upon in advance. Make sure he is not a frustrated director of R&D as nearly every engineer has a bit of the "I could invent it better" trait, plus too often a dash of the NIH factor, i.e., opposition to any idea because it was "not invented here."

The overhead costs of engineering are fairly easily measured, but it is next to impossible to measure real productivity. So your engineering department has to have more than the usual accounting controls. And that means that your engineering manager must have a high degree of personal administrative ability in order to achieve an output that meets your internal economic requirements.

Engineering turnover and rising costs must be ably managed. In one large U.S. company, engineering expense increased five-fold in eight years and turnover was 10 percent. Most of the quits were among employees with four to six years of service, just when their value was becoming important.

This sort of danger suggests the desirability of a periodic analysis of your own situation with regard to—

1. Increased expense over a period of time.
2. Change in number of employees versus increase in total sales.
3. Cost to hire and train in this function.
4. Turnover and reasons (use exit interviews!).

DEPARTMENT STRUCTURE

Depending upon company size, departmental organization structures vary widely. There is no standard to follow except to determine the functional activities in each case. In many companies the engineering manager has the following executives reporting to him:

1. Chief design engineer—supervises group responsible for new product engineering design details.
2. Chief draftsman—supervises group who makes initial drawings of new products and revisions of existing drawings. Subsequently produces drawings for manufacturing use.
3. Standard development manager—responsible for making design changes of existing products to adapt the product to the customer's requirements.

Where the size of the department dictates, section supervisors are used in the above activities to decentralize control and supervision. Size may also dictate having a propositions manager directing the engineering input required in quotations on complex equipment.

When a company does not have a separate R&D department, it is common to incorporate an advance development or long-range development group in the engineering department. This is under a separate manager reporting to the engineering manager, and he also supervises the model shop, laboratory, testing, and similar development-type work.

THE COST OF THE ENGINEERING FUNCTION

What should all this cost the company? No two companies see this the same way, but usually, if they compete generally in the same markets they are likely to have similar expense ratios. The following guidelines are offered as to expense ratios one can expect, first, in the case of a custom-products business and, second, in a catalog-type of business. The guidelines show the approximate expected cost ratios as percentages of sales for three different scales of operation.

		Total Sales	
1. Custom Products	$25,000	$50,000	$500,000
Activity:			
Design and custom development..........	3.2%	3.3%	2.0
Drafting and reproduction..............	.7	.8	.6
Testing...............................	.2	.4	.3
Complaint expense.....................	1.2	1.0	1.0
Propositions..........................	.2	.2	.1
Total..........................	5.5%	5.7%	4.0%

		Total Sales	
2. Catalog Products	$30,000	$65,000	$600,000
Activity:			
Design and custom development..........	1.4%	1.7%	.85%
Drafting and reproduction..............	.8	.9	.50
Testing...............................	.5	.4	.25
Complaint expense.....................	.8	.8	.40
Total..........................	3.5%	3.8%	2.00%

The foregoing figures merely offer a general idea of the costs of these activities as percentages of sales in order to provide comparison with expense ratios for sales, advertising, G&A, and other functions. Actual dollars can be large amounts; and this, again, stresses the need for managerial accountability and carefully-established objectives. You can never stop asking, "Do we spend more than we receive?" You can also count on the fact that you will never be sure, but diligent review will increase your chances.

PRIMARY PRODUCT DESIGN RESPONSIBILITIES

To better evaluate the function, it is important for the CEO to understand the major responsibilities for which his company is paying. Rather than describe these, I would prefer to point out facts of which to be aware.

Application Engineering

The products of many companies require modification to adapt to a variety of applications. Remembering that the basic product already exists, i.e., has been developed, tooled, cataloged, and previously sold, you should be alert to the following problems:

1. The sales organization may not have procured an accurate estimate of engineering design modification time required when it quoted the customer. This may have helped secure the order through a lower price. And a lower profit!
2. Whether this was so or not, engineering often spends more time than needed to make changes and thus reduces profitability.
3. Many studies reveal engineering does more than necessary because of poor information from marketing.
4. Changes *can* require new tooling and this is often overlooked as a cost factor in the quotation.
5. Changes made can create new safety problems or diminish the design safety originally included.
6. Extensive changes can cause warranty problems because modified products are rarely tested as is a new product. Retrofit costs can further erode profit.

Advice. Enforce maximum consultation between sales and engineering when estimating the costs for quotations. Then, use a project system to insure that modifications are made on a budget basis related to the amount of cost built into the quotation. Review the extent of modifications to see if testing is needed to protect warranties.

Modification of Existing Product Lines

Competition and changes in market needs and in regulatory legislation require that existing products be under constant review for improvement. Observe the following suggestions.

1. Marketing must continuously watch for sales declines by product line and determine the reasons.
2. Together with marketing, engineering should determine if a product modification can be successful and less costly than a new development. That is the trade-off—change versus total redesign. It is the story of the new cover for a book that has not sold well. Like

the book, a sexier product color, minor improvements, or a redo of overall appearance may do the job.

3. New laws will require modifications to improve product safety and reduce the well-known product liability. (More on this in following pages.)

Advice. Product modifications can be inexpensive and produce more sales, but any such effort should be carefully evaluated to insure, on one hand, that *modification* is not being done when a new *product* design is needed. Conversely, it may be clear that a new product is needed, but modification is selected because it is faster and cheaper. Facts are needed from marketing, not opinions.

Extension of Product Lines

To fend off the common sales cry, "If only we had another size, we could sell a zillion more!" you must consider extending the scope of current product lines.

1. Marketing input must be very carefully evaluated to make sure you get enough sales of a new size to cover costs. Any product having a number of sizes or capacities sells on a bell-shaped curve (this is an application of Pareto's Law).* Certain sizes and capacities in the middle range will probably sell the most; the smallest and largest of the sizes will probably sell the least. Plots of existing sales by product model can assist when estimating the demand for a new model.

2. Be sure to include in the cost projections all the related factors of tooling, cataloging, and general support. They are often hidden, but they are there. In effect, you are adding to the total investment in the product line, making it more costly to obsolete it in the future with new developments.

Advice. Be sure of your return on investment.

Maintenance of Product Lines

Many companies use the product manager concept to keep track of certain product categories. It is his specific job to keep his product

---

* [Ed. Note: Vilfredo Pareto was an Italian economist, sociologist, political theorist *and* a practicing engineer! An application of one of his ideas would run something to the effect that 20 percent of the number of a firm's products will account for something like 80 percent of its sales.]

lines under review, and to propose changes that may reduce cost and enhance sales. Keeping the product up to date is the goal, and one way of doing this is by switching to other makes of purchased components and by substituting new materials for old. Engineering can offer assistance through their knowledge of new materials and other components.

Health and Safety Requirements

We already have the Occupational Safety and Health Act, the Mine Safety Act, the Clean Air Act, and the Clean Water Act on hand. The latest is the Consumer Product Safety Act. All these legislative requirements portend enormous product changes and millions of dollars of cost for manufacturers. Depending on the nature of your products, it is imperative that you assign certain individuals the responsibility of knowing all there is to know about these acts as they apply to your requirements. Legislation is not necessarily prepared by experts; interpretation by any one person alone is difficult and may lead to trouble.

Advice. A team made up of people from the engineering, manufacturing, and legal departments can operate as the council within your company to review and assure compliance with these laws. Because product design is the starting point, engineering has a major responsibility.

Repair and Service

Quality of design and close attention to ease of repair can make your product more attractive to customers. The less repair and service, the happier everyone is; but beyond this, products out of service for long periods and requiring costly repair bills will ultimately affect your sales. I have a well-known make of lawn tractor that requires three hours of direct labor time just to replace the rubber drive-belt. My second one won't be the same make!

Advice. Track your customer service costs in fulfilling warranties and dig out the facts about ease of service. Distributors, repair centers, and customers will all be glad to tell you about your products' score in this regard. Most problems can be traced to poor engineering design.

SECONDARY DESIGN RESPONSIBILITIES

Product Cost Improvement

This function used to be somewhat desultory and subject to lip service. In our company, it is headed by a vice president, Mr. Arthur Mudge. He has produced an outstanding book that details all that cannot be written here about "value engineering."[1]

The rate of external economic changes and continuing internal cost increases are so great today, that *not* to employ product cost improvement techniques is unthinkable. Unless you can raise prices to cover all increased costs, what other tactic can be employed except cost improvement? Mr. Mudge explains in his book how we have formalized our approach, how we audit results, and how we motivate our people. Again, engineering is involved heavily in all this work. It is a state of mind, a way of life; and to succeed, it *must* have the total commitment and direct involvement of the top corporate executive.

In addition to product cost improvement through redesign we have formal programs in purchasing and overall expense reduction. I have awarded plaques to five secretaries in one division who individually created savings of $10,000 each!

Advice. Get personally involved.

Standardization

Concluding the secondary responsibilities, I must mention the need for constant effort for standardization of product designs. All engineers seem prone to select hardware and other components that are not presently in use and thus compound the purchasing, inventory, and cost factors. Standards books are either out of date or not used enough. A review of new and modified product designs by a standards engineer can save thousands of dollars and also be a cost improvement. In one division, we once mounted on a wall, in graduated order, every screw and bolt in current use. There were hundreds, and the differences among many were in very small fractions. "Purification" eliminated 45 percent of the different varieties, and saved thousands of dollars.

---

[1] Mudge, Arthur E.; *Value Engineering: A Systematic Approach*; New York: McGraw-Hill; 1971.

COLLATERAL ENGINEERING RESPONSIBILITIES

You must recognize the need for, and the value of having constant consultative contact between engineering and other functions. It dilutes the main job of engineering personnel, but it cannot be otherwise.

With Marketing

The required information for new products and redesign of current products should come from customers via marketing. This input establishes specification guides, cost targets, appearance factors, performance, and a host of other factors. A true spirit of cooperation must exist between marketing and engineering, or you are in trouble.

Under the right circumstances, engineering can be extremely helpful in advising marketing as to the practicality of doing what is requested, because marketing people are sometimes as emotional as engineers are subjective. Your presence in some of these reviews can induce an equally objective performance by both departments.

With Manufacturing

Inasmuch as manufacturing has to produce the product to an engineering design, there will always be a need for consultation between these two groups. Beyond this, however, a great deal of value can be derived from a good working relationship. Together, these two functions can improve methods, tooling, processes, and manufacturing cycle time, and generally reduce costs. A feeling of solid, mutual respect needs to exist between the engineering and manufacturing managers if your company is to prosper. Neither can feel that the other complicates his job, because, really, each must complement the other. Equally innovative managers of the two functions can have a blissful relationship that is second to marriage, and if you also have good sales people, this harmony can enable you to be the dominant factor in your markets.

With Field Service

Service and repair personnel are the best suited to witness product deficiencies in the field. Without a feedback system from them to engineering, problems can continue. The proper system employs detailed field reports prepared by servicemen on repetitive problems, and regular meetings with engineering and manufacturing to discuss the problems and institute action plans to correct them.

Many corporate chiefs are not aware of any service problems until they receive letters of bitter complaint, and only then are investigations started. Brief monthly summary reports are helpful to keep the president informed because little complaints today have a habit of growing into large litigations. With product liability suits becoming a popular indoor sport, this entire area cannot be left to subordinates as in the past.

With R&D

The "R&D" function is treated separately in this *Handbook*,* but I would like to add that the development section of "R&D" has to have an interlocking relationship with product engineering. This latter group should provide good practical inputs to new developments, as it is likely to have a better background and experience in this regard. Pride of authorship can be a problem in some companies; but any such "relationship difficulties" reflect the personalities of the respective managers. These intergroup and interpersonal relationships must be watched by the top management.

EXPENSE CONTROL

Expense is a function of the number of people involved, the qualities of each individual *and* the proper assignment, or the round-peg, round-hole philosophy.

Adding clerical people for routine functions can increase the head count, but if engineers are freed to do more highly-skilled work, the result may be positive. Lab technicians can relieve engineers in routine testing, as is done in hospitals.

Careful appraisal of individuals can result in reassignment with notable increases in productive output and happier employees. Salary administration and performance review is a form of control, as it relates to what you are getting for what you are paying.

---

* [Ed. Note: See the chapter by Robert McDonald entitled, "Setting Research and Development Strategy," and also the one by Jesse Werner, "Allocation of Development Resources in Major Directions."]

An analysis every few years can provide an insight into the departmental operation: the work load; division of load between personnel and sections; productivity, and how work is being done; and the time and cost required to complete jobs.

After a thorough understanding is obtained, new objectives can be established, budgets redrawn, and review held with section supervisors to get their agreement as to the feasibility of the new objectives.

Following this, the suggestions of the exempt or nonunion department personnel can be requested in order to improve department performance. These suggestions, when implemented, can be valuable, and any subsequent reductions in force are better accepted. (The reduction is not tagged solely as a management action.)

Changes in drafting practice, use of sketches for models, and other simplification can reduce drafting requirements.

Basically, the engineering manager has one tool—the available engineering man-hours. Improvement of quality and/or reduction of quantity reduces expense. Use of a drafting "pool" under a chief draftsman can be weighed against assigning draftsmen to specific sections.

This and other organizational arrangements can prove to work better or worse. You have to try them.

If each section of an engineering department can have fairly equal work loads, it becomes easier to compare hourly work loads with output and thus identify those who are slower. Further investigation will show why, and then action can be taken.

PRODUCT LIABILITY

Of all the reasons why the chief executive should have an interest in the product engineering function, none is so important as that of product liability!

Tomorrow may be the day *your* company is sued for millions of dollars for compensatory, or even punitive, damages resulting from an allegedly defective product. There were 50,000 such suits in 1963; 500,000 in 1970; and by 1975, estimates run to 1 million suits a year. Judgments have also risen: They doubled in the years 1969, 1970, and 1971 compared to the previous three years.

Product design has become a prime target area in which to probe for alleged product defects. Engineering judgments using expertise based on state-of-the-art knowledge suddenly become suspect when reexamined and magnified by self-proclaimed experts hot on the trail of a favorable judgment and a hefty award. This approach may seem unfair, but after all, every product is born on a drawing board and usually in product engineering departments. A new twist and added burden must be recognized in the fact that many hazards that everyone once took for granted are no longer acceptable.

You, as the corporate head of your company, must recognize, understand, and act on those things related to insuring safety for the users of your products. Today's liabilities are already becoming a factor of cost and pricing and must be held to a minimum.

I urge you to be sure that in your company the following steps have been taken:

1. Adoption of a corporate policy on product safety which *clearly* assigns and fixes responsibilities.
2. Screening of products through a *thorough* design review for hazards of all kinds.
3. Insuring that applications of existing and pending codes and standards have been *carefully* checked.
4. Establishment of record keeping and preservation of efforts related to product safety.
5. Careful reviews, where hazards are unavoidable, of the warnings provided by your company in placards, labels, and manuals.

The total organization must become more safety conscious to insure compliance with the law. One thing is certain—the product engineer, more than ever before, is the pivotal element in the process that takes a product from conception to sale on the market.

PERSONNEL

To discuss people, their selection, supervision, training, and motivation in this last section is a seeming denial of the fact that their importance ranks first. I have chosen to do so on the theory that the last subject read is often the longest retained.

Second Level of Management in Engineering

This is often a group of section managers with very carefully delineated responsibilities. They execute their duties in product engineering with some degree of isolation from the other managers in the department. Engineering, at many levels, is a specialized occupation. This was personified among the engineers at Huntsville, Alabama, working on the space project: Men with several university degrees concentrated on miniscule segments of a spacecraft to such an extent that when their particular activities were eliminated they could find no similar employment in industry. No one had need of their highly-developed and focused specialties.

Care must be taken in a company to see that, through rotation or new assignment, second-level men acquire the skill to back up the engineering manager. Specialization can lead to a reduction in challenge, then to loss of interest, and then to stagnation or resignation. Turnover and loss of a man's knowledge about your products is extremely costly. Keep them growing.

Managing Technical Personnel

The chief executive can play a real role in this area by recognizing the climate in which technical personnel work. Too often credit for the success of a product is given to sales, and not enough to engineering. Patent disclosures, cost improvement, and technological innovation are only a few of the activities that can be singled out for recognition.

This can be used as a form of motivation by the CEO to underscore his interest in, and appreciation of the work done in engineering. I recognize that today engineers are not a forgotten race, but I rarely see them receive the same acclaim that is often given to sales for increasing volume or to manufacturing for "getting it out the back door."

Training

The introduction of a new person to an engineering department, and the degree of training provided, varies with the experience of the new employee. Younger engineers would profit from spending several months each with sales and manufacturing, and from going into the field with service people. The personality of the company, its presence within its markets, and the quality of its products, as seen first-hand, provide a good background for the new engineer when he starts to undergo training within the engineering department. He must certainly appreciate the interaction required between functions, and he should be indoctrinated with the understanding that *through* product engineering passes all the information that can be transformed into the successful products needed by any growing and profitable enterprise.

PART IV-B
Production

THE DIRECTOR OF MANUFACTURING: A CAREFUL LOOK AT LEADERSHIP

by Richard F. Cole
President, Cryogenic Technology, inc.

WHAT SHOULD the Chief Executive Officer look for when he attempts to evaluate the manufacturing operation? After examining the essential, short-range, results-oriented questions of cost, schedule, and quality, he must then thoughtfully appraise the ultimate question: the quality of manufacturing leadership.

For the long term, the CEO must view the performance of his manufacturing manager as a key to the company's achieving adequate return on capital used. To succeed both in the long and short term, the manufacturing manager must possess a balanced combination of intellect, stamina, high standards of performance, and creativity.

A major purpose of this chapter is to help the CEO who may know little at first hand about manufacturing to understand his manufacturing executive somewhat better. The CEO must be able to communicate with him effectively and be able to assess his competence. Another purpose is to help the nonmanufacturer to understand a bit better just what a factory is and to grasp the fact that it is a system with many interacting parts and important interrelationships with other parts of the business. In order to evaluate manufacturing leadership effectively, the CEO will first need a basic appreciation of the manufacturing task. This discussion therefore should begin with the plant or factory where production takes place.

THE FACTORY AS A SYSTEM

Although everyone knows that a factory is a place where things are made, few appreciate the complexity of a factory and the multitude of factors that must work together to achieve results. A factory has machines and equipment of various kinds; there are people doing things, operating equipment, moving materials and parts, working; other material is standing ready to be put into the productive process; there is work progressing through the plant; there is inventory of what has been made. Some factory systems are highly specialized and can make only one product, sometimes only one grade of that product. Some are very versatile, and are capable of manufacturing wide ranges of outputs made out of many different materials. Most, probably, are in between. Some are larger and involve far more complex process and products than others. But a very important fact to grasp is that the factory is a system of many interacting and interrelated parts.

People are sometimes helped to understand the notion of "factory system" if they can think of it as a mobile. One such "mobile" is represented in Exhibit 1. Like all mobiles, it moves in response to impact: lift up here, push down there, rotate it this way, push it. Change it in any way, and it is likely to move in many different directions at once. It can assume many shapes, but it is always the same mobile made up of the same interrelated and interacting component parts.

In the illustration, each key element of the factory system is free to move in relation to the others, yet is so situated as to affect some of the others as a result of its movement. At any time, most elements are in motion. Some are going up in effectiveness, others down, and others are seemingly still; but there is always potential interaction. Both the CEO and his manufacturing manager need to share an awareness as to where the movement is in the factory system. What is sensitive, when; where to look and what to do when costs go up, or inventory soars, or output falls.

This mobile suggests many of the trends or interrelationships and interactions you may find in a plant. And it suggests many of the trade-offs it is possible to make in designing a plant that is intended to produce any given output.

This mobile also suggests some of the variables, interrelationships and interactions which the manufacturing executive must understand, work with, and explain to others: the CEO, the financial officer, the marketing manager, the research and engineering people, and to directors when need be.

Beginning at the top of the mobile represented in Exhibit 1, the obvious point is symbolized clearly that the effectiveness of factory operations impacts directly on profits.

EXHIBIT 1
The Factory as a System

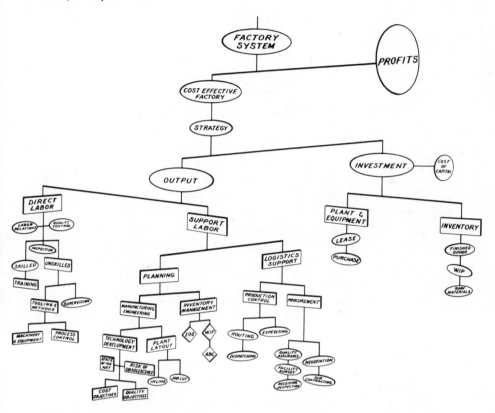

Then we encounter a question of basic strategy: What kind of a plant? Job-shop? Continuous flow? Capital-intensive? Labor-intensive? Sometimes the range of choices at this point is constrained by technological factors. But there are generally a few alternatives as to how much to automate or how much to rely on labor. Partly, of course, it is a question of relative costs. But there are other considerations that also can be very important, such as flexibility and versatility of the system in response to schedule fluctuations, to product mix, to variations in available raw materials, and to quality control. And then there are questions as to what kind of labor, skilled or unskilled, and possible investment trade-offs between plant and inventory.

With inventory flexibility, one can build a smaller plant and run it at maximum efficiency. On the other hand, with the ultimate plant, one can minimize inventory. Usually, good strategy involves balancing these considerations in an effort to get an overall optimum. And, of course, inventory represents major points of linkage between the factory and its suppliers and customers.

Of the many interrelationships and trade-offs within the factory system suggested by this mobile, look at just a few more. First, interaction between direct labor and support labor. Good staff work, scheduling, and engineering are likely to build up the size and cost of support labor; but all this can make the direct labor much more efficient, and very often avoid fluctuations in work force as well as insuring timely high quality production.

A very modern "out-in-front" plant, with special equipment, may run at lower cost. But sometimes the very newness of such a plant may entail risks of obsolescence not raised by a more traditional plant. Specialization may have cost and technical advantages; but more general-purpose equipment may provide greater flexibility and pose fewer training and maintenance problems, and perhaps be more useful for a longer period of time.

Sometimes skilled and less skilled or even unskilled labor have some interchangeability. Relative production costs are only one consideration in deciding among them. Other factors include availability, labor and possible union relations, and turnover. Less skilled labor can be upgraded through more training and supervision, special tooling, and more automatic controls.

Once the CEO is able to appreciate and understand the complexity of the factory system, the task of assessing the quality of manufacturing leadership will become both manageable and constructive.

WHAT THE MANUFACTURING EXECUTIVE NEEDS TO KNOW AND TO DO

The manufacturing manager must view himself and the factory as vital to shaping the ultimate success of the firm. Therefore, the production operation must be managed with full recognition of its vital role within the firm and of the probable requirement for change. The factory must work both in response to, and in anticipation of market needs. Today's environment is one of changing technology, changing consumer preferences, sporadic materials shortages, rising labor costs, and, with few exceptions, very tough competition. In this atmosphere, the manufacturing manager has the singular opportunity to set his firm apart and differentiate it from the competition. The man who can optimize the factory to meet today's needs, and has the mechanisms at readiness to change emphasis, to adapt, or excel in an extra dimension of performance, can provide his company with a fresh competitive edge.

The manufacturing manager must devote a reasonable portion of his concern to change. However, he must anticipate change and not just react to it. Change can come from a variety of sources and it can be subtle or dramatic: shifting markets that can influence product mix; declining or increasing sales patterns affecting volume; requirements for shortened response time in the manufacturing process; difficulties with materials suppliers or subcontractors; "Murphy's Law" problems with products within or outside manufacturing control. In virtually every deliberate decision, whether to increase or lay off staff, to add or dispose of machinery, plant, or inventory, he must question the adaptability of his decision to further change.

Adaptability is created first in an awareness of the marketing, engineering, and financial pressures or incentives that form the strategy of the firm; and second, through an appreciation of the business environment in which he must run the factory. What are the trends in labor costs? What is the level of productivity within his work force? What is the availability of skilled labor? What are the near- and long-term ramifications of energy problems? Attention to questions such as these will constitute a personal early warning system that can be put to work every day but which will be particularly useful in time of stress or of change.

The man who leads the manufacturing operation must be visible in other functional areas of the company. If he is generally regarded by his peers as "out there," in the factory, or on the "other side of the wall," it won't be long before the firm is in trouble. The manufacturing operation will have failed to anticipate change and will be forced too many times only to react.

Finally, the manufacturing manager must feel that the financial success of the firm is largely a function of the manufacturing operation. In conditions of chronic shortage of capital, or where return on assets or on capital used is the primary measure of financial performance, it is easy to see that the focus belongs on the capital committed to the manufacturing operation. The management of inventory, and choices with respect to machinery and equipment can determine, for example, the extent to which a company becomes capital-intensive.

To the extent that internal operations contribute to the financial strategy of the firm, the manufacturing manager, in his judicious use of the precious capital resource, must play a key part. He needs to know and to feel in a visceral sense where capital comes from, how much it costs; and he must measure everything he does with the feeling that he, more than any other man in the firm, can impact the return on capital in the near term.

The manufacturing manager must be unusually skilled in interpersonal relations and communications. The manufacturing manager, by his own style, can contribute to productivity, to morale, to quality, and to lowering the overall cost of doing business more directly than can any single other person in the firm.

The manufacturing manager must be a communicator. He must think well on his feet. He must be able to give comprehensive answers to either complex or sometimes oversimplified questions. He can be expected to know his operation well and to be able to talk with clarity about it. If a particular subject or problem is really too complex for ad hoc discussion, he must be prepared to explain why. The key word is *explain*. To explain is to instruct; to instruct is to help others gain an understanding they will generally appreciate. With new added insight, they will become easier to work with. A man who can think and respond well extemporaneously, unmistakably conveys the fact that he has a grasp of his subject, and further, that he can be counted upon for straight answers and for help. This ability is vital to the establishment of effective peer group relationships and to the building of a management team that can work well today and in the future.

There is no one best way of making the many decisions that go into designing, adapting, and running a plant. And no one person, working by himself, is going to be able to come up with the one best answer that takes into account all the many factors that are important in their own ways in any particular set of circumstances. The manufacturing executive must, however, take the lead in such matters. But it is an absolute must that he be able to work with everyone else on the management team to get their ideas as to what is important from their point of view; and, of course, he has to be able to work smoothly with the CEO.

Simply to recognize all the possible interrelationships and interactions in even a relatively simple factory system calls for both training and experience. Some of these matters are hard to learn on the job. Some are impossible to learn from books. A good manufacturing executive understands well the commonly recognized topics and also the imponderables that go into his job. And he knows that marketing, community relations, financial, and engineering considerations must find their way into his straightforward particular objectives.

The most important facet of the manufacturing manager's personal style is revealed in his one-on-one relationships. If he can honestly convey to all a legitimate sense of concern for the quality of effort, for the importance of the job, and, although somewhat impractical, the sense that no problem is too small for his attention, a number of predictable and desirable reactions should occur. The idea of a committed and involved management will pervade the shop. The stage is then set for people to work with a heightened sense of recognition and a better understanding of where they fit. This requires creating an environment where a community of interest is more binding than the organization chart. It can actually result in stronger middle management and first-line supervision. The CEO himself must support the concept of personal involvement of management in the factory. He should show concern with the human aspects of factory operation. This is easy in a small firm but becomes increasingly difficult with size. Nevertheless, the objective is worthwhile, and he should make every effort to be in touch. In addition, the way the factory staff and manufacturing support personnel feel about their company can help shape the image of the firm in its community. The majority of a firm's employees probably work in the factory, and to that extent, represent a conduit for the establishment of public opinion about the firm.

The manufacturing manager needs specific know-how. A really good manufacturing manager has the interrelationships within his plant clearly in mind at all times. He should know where the strengths are and where trouble could most likely show up. The factory, for him, should be an orchestration of individual elements and of units or groups of common elements all functioning in harmony with a manufacturing plan and strategy. He should be acquainted with every element and its potential, and he should be specifically proficient in dealing with those elements that constitute the core of the manufacturing strategy. If, for example, the plant must operate on a continuous-flow, high-production-line concept, skills in tooling and computer control would be far more vital than in a job-shop, limited-production environment where project management, scheduling, and quality control may need to prevail.

The CEO needs to know, in a general sense, what are the critical paths in the factory. He needs to visualize the "mobile" of the plant, and to know which elements have the greatest leveraging effect on others. All the elements interact; but some can whipsaw the whole company. For example, if the company is counting on rapid delivery response to be competitive, the inventory of finished goods will always be critical. If the strategy is based on quick response to many requests for special variations in standard products, then the work-in-process inventory level would be more critical. On the other side of the mobile, if costs are decisive, then the focus belongs on the balance of labor and tooling to achieve optimum low cost. The manufacturing executive should be able to make all this clear and to explain simply what's involved in problems and decisions.

The CEO, in looking at his top man in manufacturing, must be able to find competence in the principal disciplines required to succeed. In addition, the CEO should be comfortable with the breadth of thinking and the ability of his manufacturing manager to know, based on insight, intuition, and understanding of fundamentals, where the risks are. With this degree of acuity, he can adapt the formal system of control to be most effective. In terms of data, certain measures of output based on quality and volume and variable cost can then be easily defined. Too often, data produced for control purposes are too late, too cumbersome, and too unfocused to be really useful. A keen-minded manufacturing man knows what is really critical . . . what is fixed, what is variable, what is controllable, and what isn't. And he makes certain that the data he receives are adequate and timely for their specific purpose, short- or long-range.

EVALUATING THE MANUFACTURING EXECUTIVE

The best way for a CEO to look at the manufacturing operation is to look at results. The CEO can simply describe the job of the manufacturing manager as requiring the successful integration of the tangible and intangible assets to produce both short- and long-range results which can be expressed in terms of costs, schedules, quality, and return on assets used. These items are easily defined as factory cost targets, monthly shipments, inventory levels, reject rates, warranty experience, and customer complaints. The CEO need only determine current performance, vis-à-vis targets or contractual obligations, to begin measuring results in key areas.

It is more subtle and requires more awareness of risk to set new goals or to establish rates of change or targets for improvement. The process here should be bilateral and should involve both the CEO and the manufacturing manager, and should take into account the needs of the firm in the broadest sense. The answer to the question, "What's important?" sets the emphasis in manufacturing for months and years ahead. It should determine the components of the mobile that are strengthened and those that are deemphasized. The CEO and the manufacturing manager together must continually reexamine assumptions about technology, about control, and about employee relations, always expecting to find areas to improve, to redirect, to eliminate . . . all changes ultimately meant to make the factory more effective.

SUMMARY

In summary, the Chief Executive Officer, in assessing the underlying strength of manufacturing leadership, needs only to look at relatively few key indicators. But he should look carefully.

1. Does the manufacturing manager have a good appreciation of the role of manufacturing in the firm's total strategy?

2. Is the manufacturing manager sensitive to the pressures of business in the broadest sense, and can he be considered adaptive in his approach to the future?

3. Is the manufacturing manager unusually skilled in communications, and is he skilled at interpersonal relations?

4. Does the manufacturing manager have the right technical or professional skills? Does he fully appreciate the factory system, and do his special talents match the unique needs of his plant?

5. Have the manufacturing manager and the CEO, together, developed a basis for looking at results and, further, a basis for establishing and reestablishing goals for the future?

6. Does the manufacturing manager usually meet his commitments?

If these questions can be answered affirmatively, the CEO can rest easily.

MANUFACTURING PRODUCTIVITY

by Gerald B. Mitchell
President, Dana Corporation

PRODUCTIVITY can best be defined as *output*–per man–per hour–per dollar of investment. This chapter outlines some of my thoughts as to the need and the method of both achieving and holding productivity improvements. I do not attempt to deal with some important aspects of this problem such as personal motivation and incentive systems but primarily with a philosophy of management which I believe creates a favorable climate for improved productivity in many areas of the company.

The chapter is divided into the following six segments:

1. The Need.
2. The Organization.
3. The Computer.
4. The Controller.
5. The New Investment in Automation.
6. The Maximum.

Where possible, I have attempted to define a function rather than use the more common job titles because of the wide discrepancy in job content within these various functions.

THE NEED

The marketplace determines the selling price of a product. Any company or manufacturing concern striving to sell its product is faced with the problem of arriving at and maintaining a competitive, profitable price for that product.

Some companies depend on controllers, costing, or estimating to determine the cost and margin of profit and so the selling price of their product. But unless you completely dominate the market you usually can't do that. So you must, then, have sufficient productivity gains to remain competitive and to enable you to be flexible and profitable in the marketplace.

When you make an investment in a plant or facility, you must have determined what return you expect on this money. If you are to use shareholders' money, or your own money, you must make a return that is better than what the money would earn from banks or bonds—and it has to be sufficiently better to warrant the risk. Therefore, it is one of the responsibilities of management to determine what the return on each dollar of investment should be to warrant the risk involved and to be reasonably confident that this return will continue for a sustained period of time.

The one thing we can't control is what the market is willing to pay for our product. Therefore, the only way we are going to have any security for our investment is to have a constant improvement in productivity. If we have that, then we should, in a general sense, be able to improve our profit margin and our return on investment with the minimum of risk.

If your company is providing products to a growing market, then, on a frequent basis, you must constantly judge whether or not you should make a further investment in facilities. Should you increase the size of the plant? Add more equipment? Certainly, the life's blood of any business is to grow, but if you have not been able to maintain a productivity improvement program, you will find that in a very short while you can no longer justify further investment. And once you have reached that position—although you might still exist for a period of time—you are finished.

For the purpose of this article, I am assuming that the company can maintain or improve its competitive position in other related functions such as product engineering, marketing, and so on. Assuming that all of these things are being maintained at a satisfactory level, only through improved productivity do you have the assurance of a healthy and secure company—one which offers security to your shareholders and, very importantly, to the people within your company. There is no other security.

Once you have determined what your return on investment should be, it is absolutely essential that all of the people of your company, or plant, know why it is necessary.

The first problem I find in most companies is the belief that they don't have to communicate this necessary return on investment to all of the people of the company. With some, it may be a feeling that they don't have to justify themselves to their people. Or it may be a fear (or reticence) to commit themselves publicly. But if you, in management, don't communicate this to your people—and explain it—you immediately run into the first major roadblock of achieving productivity—a lack of cooperation of your people in achieving your objective. They have to know the goal if they are to achieve and maintain it.

THE ORGANIZATION

This is a difficult area to talk about with many people. I suppose this is so because you begin to hammer at a philosophy of management and how to motivate people, to inspire them—to generate loyalty—to reduce friction. My view of this is that you must be able to communicate to all of your people, very clearly, your company's goals and objectives. In communicating these goals you have set, you expect to make everyone accountable for some portion of them. Some companies mask or confuse these goals or objectives with the result that the individual—be it the foreman, superintendent, plant manager, or controller—does not have a clear and specific responsibility for which he—and he alone—will be held accountable.

If you look at a "typical" secondary manufacturing operation which carries a high investment of equipment, plant, and inventory, I think you will generally find that its organizational concept goes back to World War II, when it was structured to work with various government bodies, and from that point has changed little other than to "match" the customers' organizations.

At that time, we began to have within the organizational structure of industry such titles as "purchasing agent," "production control," "tool engineering," "master mechanic," "chief metallurgist," to name a few. In my view, this is a major roadblock to increasing productivity. Let us say that you hold your plant manager responsible for a 15 percent return on investment. If he sits down to look at those factors —or functions—which control his ability to achieve that return on investment, he will oftentimes be sitting with his superintendent, and —by whatever title you may use—the head of "production control," "purchasing," "sales," "quality control," "tool engineering and repair," "plant maintenance," and so on—and they will be functionally responsible for things relative to his cost of sales: scrap, expense items, cutting oils, steel, labor contract, and so on. Of all the men sitting there with the plant manager, only one really controls productivity and is goal-oriented: the superintendent!

In the organizational structure, you will generally find that such functions as sales, purchasing, and production control generally do not report to the superintendent. Instead, they report to someone above the level of the plant manager in the organization. It is the plant manager who carries the brunt of your investment, yet his is but one voice in this group of six or seven people. And you will find that you cannot clearly say to him, "Mr. Plant Manager, you are responsible for a 15 percent return on investment." Because he probably didn't negotiate his labor contract. That was an industrial relations function. He didn't buy the steel. The purchasing people did that. He didn't set the production schedule. That was done by "sales." He didn't schedule the plant. The production control people did that.

And yet, at this point, your plant manager is the man who must generate the productivity increases and be responsible for attaining this goal, this objective, this return on investment of yours!

People in functional positions tend to be judged relative to standards that they, themselves, set. For example, a man buying steel can argue and bargain and be as expert at buying steel as anyone, anywhere. He endeavors to buy at what he thinks is the lowest possible price. His problem is always to justify his purchasing expertise to management.

But there is only one criterion for good purchasing, and that is that the material you are buying is "laid in" to that facility and at a cost and in a manner that is agreeable to—and accepted by—the man who is responsible for your return on investment.

My point is that when you organize for productivity, you must take all of those functions which are a part of productivity (purchasing, scheduling, maintenance, tooling, and so on) and put them within that structure. If necessary, you must take your facility and subdivide it into areas and place these functions into those areas, and not permit them to grow into staff organizations that report higher up in the company.

And if you do not accept this as being required—and organize to do this—then you are putting an obstacle in the path of achieving productivity.

Observe what happens when government control reaches into an industry and exerts an influence in one of these functions. Such industries generally become poor investments, do not have productivity increases, and staff functions become so expensive as to be ridiculous.

I also believe that when all of the indirect functions are permitted to group together, separate from your major investment, you will get an increase in indirect cost, because the indirect function is not judged on the basis of what you can afford.

You will find that in a little while the indirect function—purchasing, maintenance, tooling, metallurgy, or whatever—will begin to institute procedures and forms and paperwork to achieve an end that is the purpose of that department *but not primarily dedicated to your return on investment.*

Any indirect function is acceptable only if it is within the structure of cost that you have determined you can afford! If it is not within that structure, then it doesn't matter what the function is; it must be done away with.

People who comprise the first level of employment in a company—machine operators, sweepers, toolmakers, salesmen, and the like—are for the most part directly job related and generally perform a necessary function. You can look at these functions and say "I don't need to do this or that," and reduce it, if necessary. At this first level of employment you can pretty clearly determine whether or not a specific job—or function—is required and determine the necessary level of employment.

Any company organization should always be judged on the basis of what a man can supervise. For example, if a man is supervising skilled workers such as toolmakers, he should be able to supervise 30–40 people. If a man is supervising assembly line production workers, he should be able to supervise 60 people. In the case of fairly complex, costly equipment such as big presses or automated equipment, because of the sheer size of the equipment and floor space required he may be able to supervise only 25 people.

But the point is that you should first consider how many people a man can supervise, not what the function is that he is supervising.

A test most companies usually fail is manpower per supervisor. You will find that they probably have a quality control supervisor supervising 6 people, for example, and because it's a specific function, they haven't recognized the fact that he should be supervising 25 people! Maybe he should be supervising some sweepers, or a shipping dock, because he has the ability to supervise a greater number than 6.

At the second level of management, you will find a wide difference of opinion as to what—or how many—this level of supervision can supervise. Some will say 6 . . . some will say 15 . . . so let's assume that it could be 10 people.

Then move up to the next level and say that at this level a man can supervise 6 or 8. Then you will come to the fourth level . . . and I think the president of a company should really have no more than 6 or 7 people reporting to him.

Therefore, in your secondary manufacturing organization, if you need 1,000 people performing first-level functions, you should have approximately 33 people at first-line supervision, only 3 people at the second level, and then 1. And your total employment should be 1,037 people! It doesn't matter *what* the functions are. Those are all you need for effective supervision. Don't compromise.

Destroy any myth that engineers should supervise only engineers and salesmen should supervise only salesmen and production people only production workers. You should always be prepared to subject the function to the test of what a supervisor can supervise, and this will lead you to a great reduction of indirect costs and unnecessary paperwork, and a manager will be more of a generalist.

I also believe that to achieve increased productivity all possible indirect functions must be placed under the production responsibility within the plant. The only functions that I would separate from that approach would be those things that are generally determined to be corporate functions—taxes, financing, shareholder relations—things that you cannot put within the plants and which, really, have relatively little impact on productivity.

What you are coming to, then, is a subdivision of your manufacturing operation into smaller segments (which may still be quite large, i.e., 400–500 people) with the person responsible for that group, and the product it turns out, also being responsible for all of the functions related to getting the product out. And his communication chain to inform all of his people is much shorter, more direct, and more efficient.

And because I've seen it, firsthand, I know that you will defeat your goal of improving productivity when a schedule is written in one part or segment of a plant and imposed on another group. Because it is *not their* schedule, they do not identify with it. They didn't participate in establishing it. If they can't see the people who make up their schedule—and *know* them—then they can't identify with them.

When purchasing is something remote that occurs in the "corporate office," then nothing you buy is ever really acceptable, on a continuing basis, to that group out in the plant. But if they buy it, they will make it work. They will recognize that it is part of their responsibility. If they can identify all of the people, visually, then they will identify with the group and will accept accountability.

You may design machine tools in a tool design shop 15 miles away from the plant. Don't be surprised if your people "prove" to you that they are no good; they are not *their* tools.

I'm not saying that they *can* design them—but you will have better productivity if they have a chance to approve them, even in layout form, and if they know it is their responsibility to give them the OK. It would be better if the guy who did the drawing actually sat in a glass-enclosed office out in the middle of the area because then he would be "one of them" and the tools would be *"their* tools."

One of the benefits of an organization of this type, where responsibility and accountability are tied to production, is that over a period of time, as you demonstrate to all of the people, repeatedly, that you do value their opinion, that your goals and objectives are reasonable, that you are concerned about their security, they will very gradually shift their allegiance and begin to identify with the group.

We have done it with some of the most "difficult" plants in our company: plants where the people have moved toward unionism and encouraged unionism primarily for security motives. So many things were not within their control—were not explained to them—and the only course left open to them to have a voice and a feeling of security was for someone—a union—to protect them. It is extremely hard to achieve a good climate for improving productivity where you encourage a three-party system—management, employee, and union.

The more the related functions become exposed to the people who run your machines and perform the functions within a smaller and more-direct area, the less there is a need for third-party intervention. And more clearly, day by day, you get an understanding that the only real security is an improvement in productivity that puts you at an advantage competitively, in the marketplace.

The average working man does understand this, very readily.

One of the worst things you can do, in my view, is to have any form of "master contract" that results in impersonal people, at some distance, determining what is good for another group without being involved with them or with their own unique problems.

Any form of nationalized, countrywide, industrywide negotiated labor contract will hamper productivity.

But if you try putting in all of the related functions so that they must stand the test of each person's scrutiny and acceptance, then you begin to defeat the need for the third party—and then the second party—and eventually, you become one group trying, together, to achieve better productivity.

And whether a person is union or nonunion is of no importance whatsoever! They must simply feel that they are involved, that they have a voice in what you are doing, and an opportunity to share in the benefits.

I'm not saying that all of this is easy. In most instances it requires a tremendous change in attitude. But, considering the alternative, it is, most emphatically, worth whatever effort it takes to achieve.

THE COMPUTER

In my view, the computer, and the generally-accepted practices of conformity that creep into a computer-oriented company, are detrimental to achieving productivity gains. In saying that, I don't want to convey the idea that there is no use for the computer, because I think that it has very real and important uses within any company and can save considerable dollars in expense. Certainly, a computer is the only way to take complex assemblies of different products and "explode" them to determine the individual requirement by part, or by number, or by specific operation. For such purposes, the computer should be used. It can do a superb job on things in your accounting area, such as payroll, payables, and receivables.

The risk of the computer and the most common sickness that accompanies its use is that computers tend to become an activity within a company that ultimately results in a department or function identified as "computer control" or "computer center," and therein lies a problem. Such a centralized body will immediately define or specify computer programs, times, and schedules, and force conformity. Profit centers such as plants or warehouses should have the right and responsibility to buy or create their own computer programs, the existence of which should be justified only by that particular profit center.

We talked in the Organization section about the need to have the scheduling and purchasing functions as part of an area or profit center, and having them within the area or profit center for identity of the people within the area. Let's take that a step farther and look at the average company that controls its inventory and scheduling through a computer. You will find that normally the computer is, in some fashion, connected to customers' output through some sort of mechanism such as an order drawer. And this procedure generally carries with it a belief that if you are constantly feeding in the order position, manufacturing, and shipping reports, you will constantly have a fix on what production you should be running and the inventory level of the company.

My experience with some 50 plants and facilities of our company is that 85 percent of the input from our customers is either false or equalizing! (By "equalizing," I mean that, over a short period of time, the "plus" and "minus" offset each other and are meaningless.) Thus, 85 percent of that paper you are processing does absolutely nothing beneficial.

One of the favorite statements of computer people is, "If you put garbage in, you get garbage out." If you put mistakes into a computer, it isn't smart enough to correct them—it doesn't have a brain—it turns them out in the same fashion. There are *always* mistakes in a computer where scheduling and inventory control are concerned. If you have 1,000 men on the floor of a plant taking a physical inventory, and they "weigh count" it—and then "hand count" it—and you do it three times, you will still have at least 5 percent error in your count. And if you are feeding these data into your system of orders which is then fed into your computer, you are automatically feeding a 5 percent error into the figures that are coming out in your consolidation. In addition, some of the errors will "plus" the situation and others will "minus" it—so that a large portion of your input just offsets itself and comes out meaning nothing.

So you have done all of that for no beneficial purpose. You must stop the customers' paperwork at your shipping dock and never permit it to go beyond that point! You must always run your plant against your own internal master plan or annualized form of scheduling.

And never permit the customers' multitude of costly, useless paperwork to creep into your production control system through the computer under the guise of being a benefit, because it is never beneficial! It is always an increased expense. And this is an area where a company can very quickly achieve a productivity gain.

The second problem with a computer is the belief that conformity is, in some way, beneficial. Conformity—particularly in the areas of cost control—is the enemy of productivity increase! Some companies turn out masses of data every month on inventory, indirect labor, and so on, in a standard fashion for all of their plants because someone, at some time, let one of these elements get out of hand, or couldn't account for it, or something of that sort. In other words, 85 percent of all paperwork is to protect yourself. And thus, you create a monster in the form of all this data that no one can read anyway. The only time you read it is after you obviously know that things are out of control to begin with. So through this conformity, you have the expense of the computer and the paper and the people to analyze and read—and they can't do anything about the problem anyway! The person who can really control this problem is the one who is actually spending the money within the area, the one who is performing the production operation. Capable, superior, first-line supervisors, who daily have the problem of producing a product on time, at the right cost, can rarely look at more than four or five items and make a significant improvement in them. If a man has a problem of high scrap cost, he can work on that. If he has high cost of labor, he can work on that. If his changeover time is too high, he can work on that. But there is no foreman in this world who can work on 89 different items of cost or expense as generated by a computer. One, he isn't going to look at it; two, he hasn't got time to look at it; and three, if you ask about it he will give you some sort of fictitious generalization which is a waste of time. You are better to identify the four or five most meaningful items within an area and to work on those—and to ignore the others, as only a generalization.

In this way, you can achieve a productivity increase—and you destroy this terrible risk of conformity, of justification through conformity, which adds nothing but expense.

THE CONTROLLER

Seemingly, cost control automatically follows the computer in most companies. Generally speaking, the function of the company controller has been moved from the plant to the central office. And here we find two things being done which I think are mysterious, detrimental, and without logic. We find that the controller is involved in the financial end of the company—and he has nothing to do with corporate finance! As a matter of fact there is every reason to keep him as divorced as possible from corporate finance because he begins to get into the problems of liquidity and cash flow—and he begins to view things such as inventory levels and so on as part of his function with corporate finance. While inventory and processing have an impact on corporate finance, they are a function of *productivity* and they are vital to earning a decent return on your investment. And if they get distorted by corporate finance, then you *really* have a problem!

In most companies, the function of cost control is the responsibility of a group headed by the corporate controller, with all other controllers at various levels reporting to him. In our company, we have totally dismembered this organization, although we do recognize that there is constant communication and flow of information among the controllers of the company. This involvement is not the adding up of numbers nor the keeping of things in order in a uniform manner. Rather, we view it as creating a climate of responsibility for the controller which requires him to intrude, constructively, into those management areas from which he is normally excluded.

The controller should never report above the level at which you have defined accountability for a given area. He should never be controlled in this responsibility by any overriding rule of conformity. To put it another way, if a plant manager represents the overall profit center, and within the plant you have six areas which are, themselves, profit centers within that overall profit center, then each area should have a controller. And each of those controllers should report to, and be responsible to, the head of that area. And the controller of the whole facility should report to the plant manager (or whatever you choose to call him) and not to the corporate office or to any central body. He should never be forced to conform to the whims of any central body—and he must never be split, in any way, regarding where, or what, his accountability is. The accountant, without understanding all of the facts, must encourage other members of management in this area to make decisions, clearly indicating that he is in agreement with the decisions. Sophistication in the area of cost control is simplicity and the controller must strive for simplicity.

THE NEW INVESTMENT IN AUTOMATION

If you can accept the fact that the controller, and cost control as a function, must report only to the head of the profit center, then you begin to create an organization, or climate, within which you can take a different approach to the mechanization or automation of your facility. In any facility, as your volume climbs and you reach the limits of your existing capacity, or can see by demand that you will exceed existing capacity of your facility, you immediately become involved in the calculation or the estimating of what your new capital equipment and tooling should be, what it should look like, and what it can produce. And, as a general statement, what you are striving for at this time is an increased output with a reduced labor content. In our company, we always try to recognize that in every facility we create we must absorb its cost through some form of applied burden. So that as facilities become bigger and the volume becomes greater, we find that, automatically, we have a greater portion of relatively fixed burden and a smaller portion of labor in the cost of generating each sales dollar. We also recognize that this approach has led to the demise of more companies than almost any other single area of management.

Rapidly growing companies, with greater demand for equipment and facilities, generally get into much more difficulty in controlling their labor and burden costs than do smaller companies that are run in a much more intimate manner by a closely-knit group of people. The principle reason for this is that unless you happen to have a unique market, as your capacity grows and your output grows, you are usually much more susceptible to changes in the market, or demand for your product. The facility or company whose product is required in low volume and is made with high labor and low burden, can rapidly adjust to cope with changes in demand without big impacts on profits, or margin, or productivity gains. But the facility that becomes more highly automated, with a higher percentage of relatively fixed burden in its costs, becomes much more vulnerable—and, on the down side, finds that what it thought was productivity gain has turned out to be a disaster, that it very rapidly moves into a loss position. So in looking at mechanizing, automating, or increasing your capacity, when you have the controller as a function within the profit center, he should always generate and know a number or a percentage—relative to your conservative forecast of sales dollars—that he will permit the plant manager to spend on plant, property, and equipment. And he will protect you against investing too many dollars in capacity. He should be forcing—constantly forcing—the balance of the people in that profit center to spend only as much money as he recommends! As an example, if a secondary industry machining facility with gear cutting, turning, heat-treating, and so on, were to permit the book value of its plant, property, and equipment to rise to 60 percent of its sales volume, any productivity gains, in my opinion, would prove to be completely worthless. The facility has no downside protection. It would be looking at figures that were utterly meaningless. But if it can consistently handle swings of 10–15 percent in demand and hold its plant, property, and equipment to an average figure like 40 percent of sales volume, it will have productivity gains that are honest and meaningful. Because you know that it has some form of downside protection. And you know that the controller, because of his intimate knowledge of their costs, has been influencing each area, each profit center, to make outside purchases—or has forced them into some direction other than putting in plant, property, and equipment.

Again, you are not preaching conformity here—you are dealing with the everyday problems as they occur. Many times you will find that if you leave it up to a tooling group or a processing group, they will "prove" to you that you can make something for 10 cents, that would cost 12 cents to buy. But if in making it for 10 cents you have to raise the value of your plant, property, and equipment to 60–65 percent of your sales volume, then ignore the 10 cents, because that 2 cents difference is not a productivity gain for the brief period that you get it, or for any period of time—because you are leaving yourself open to the risk of a downturn, at which point those pieces will no longer be costing you 10 cents. Because of the high burden, those pieces may be costing you 15 or 16 cents, and you would have been better off buying them at 12 cents all along, knowing that make-or-buy decisions are not based purely on the estimated cost of internal manufacture versus outside purchase, but on those costs plus the judgment of value of required plant, property, and equipment as a percentage of your sales volume. It must be clearly understood that you must always put these three elements into your calculations, and you cannot put them in unless the controller is an integral part of that area or profit center. Therefore, I never worry particularly about automation or mechanization where it is treated in this fashion, because I believe, then, that it will be controlled. When it is handled by a separate activity or function-oriented engineering department, it is nothing but trouble and ultimately will cost additional expense. And rather than creating productivity *gains*, in the main it will probably *lose* your productivity gains.

THE MAXIMUM

We have talked of the production control function, about controlling the customer influence, and about the risk of conformity through use of the computer. In trying to achieve maximum productivity I find you must start on the production line. When I visit a plant and I walk up to a line foreman, the first question I always ask him in some form is, "What is your controlling operation?" And I'm happy to say that in our company now, eight out of ten of them can tell me what the controlling operation is. But I can go back five or six years and then it was exactly the opposite! Maybe one or two of them could tell me, but 80 percent of them couldn't.

The line foreman must know his controlling operation, because that, then, controls every other operation in the plant. And that's the one he need worry about. There is little sense in running one machine for four hours at some advanced rate when other operations require 12 hours. The cost of the one standing idle defeats any productivity gain. And to spend any money for improved processing in one area when you can't match it across the whole plant is just a waste of time. What you are really looking for in getting maximum productivity is also a *balanced* productivity with the lowest asset-to-sales ratio possible. Therefore, your production men and your controller within a profit center must know your controlling operation. And there is a second thing that they must know, automatically—and that is the guideline to operate the controlling function or the controlling operation. They must know what they have to do to maximize productivity. The best way I can describe this is to give you an example. In one of our press plants—with as many as 100 presses in a department—we would calculate our annualized demand for stampings and break it down into monthly requirements of stampings. So, let's assume that our plant with 100 presses must produce 10,000 individual part numbers and that these parts each average seven separate operations. For scheduling purposes we are then considering 70,000 different parts (10,000 individual numbers × 7 different operations each = 70,000 different parts). There is no point in just knowing part numbers—you must know how many part numbers and how many production operations have to be done to complete them. And that tells you the first answer. The second step is to set aside that number of parts required, and the controller and the people within that area now have to start looking for maximum productivity, and you have to ask yourself some questions. In the area of a press, you have to ask yourself, "How long does it take for the average setup on that press?" "How long to tear out one die and put in another?" (This applies on a lathe, milling machine, or anything else.) If it takes two hours to accomplish this, and you are charging your press off in the burden rate at so many productive hours in a month, then to achieve a productivity gain you must run the press more hours. So you can very quickly determine how many setups you can permit a day. Let's say you decide that you can set up a press once a day in two hours' time and that, normally, the press has to be down two hours a day for adjustment, repairs, or whatever. That's 4 hours a day—so you are left with 20 hours that the press can run. You may also have some other calculations, such as lunch time and things like that, but let's not complicate it.

We now have established the two most important considerations in scheduling our press department.

1. We have 10,000 part numbers requiring an average of seven operations each or effectively 70,000 distinct parts.
2. We have 100 presses and we must limit setups to 2 hours per press per day and service time to 2 hours per press per day to achieve maximum productivity.

We now can schedule our press department because we can determine the basic schedule.

Using a 20-day work month we know:

1. We can run on the average 100 different parts per day for maximum productivity.
2. We can run 2,000 different parts per month for maximum productivity.

Now you can look at your customer or assembly department requirements and attempt to make them conform to your production plan: 2,000 setups maximum; 40,000 productive hours minimum.

It is apparent that if 2,000 setups per month or 24,000 setups per year are desirable, and you require 70,000 individual operations, then you need to apply a good deal of management judgment. You are striving to achieve maximum labor productivity and maximum utilization of your investment and you're faced with some important make-or-buy decisions. These decisions must be reached by involving your controller, and the most important thing you have accomplished through organization and philosophy is to place the total accountability for inventory, plant, property, and equipment within a clearly defined area with one group of people and ultimately one person responsible.

CONCLUSION

Productivity gains are hard to acquire and even harder to retain. My approach as chief operating officer is to follow a four-step plan with relentless determination:

1. Review management philosophy.
2. Be goal oriented. Subordinate all functions to goals or objectives.
3. Test your Organization Chart. Never be satisfied with the number of indirect or nonproduction people. I firmly believe that the number of indirect people should always be less than the number of direct people by a ratio of approximately .7–1 or .8–1, and if after working with the plant management for a reasonable period of time this is not attained, then you have the wrong plant manager.
4. Communicate—communicate—communicate all goals and objectives!

MANUFACTURING OUTSIDE OF THE U.S.A.

by William Blackie

Senior Partner, Lehman Brothers;
Chairman (Retired), Caterpillar Tractor Co.

SOME PRELIMINARY THOUGHTS

The ideas expressed here—as the title of the chapter indicates—are confined to (or inhibited by) the case of a manufacturing enterprise. Concerns engaged, for example, in the extractive or natural resource industries are limited in their foreign investment policies by the nature and location of their raw materials: mineral ores, crude oil, timber, et cetera; while service industries such as banking and insurance are generally faced with regulatory conditions which are not common or applicable to manufacturing enterprises. Organizations which confine their activities solely to trading also are affected by different considerations; and in their case, the major assets generally consist of fairly liquid accounts receivable and, possibly (but not necessarily), inventories. Their risks in foreign investment are, accordingly, relatively less than those undertaken by a concern acquiring "fixed" land, buildings, machinery, and equipment in the establishment of a foreign manufacturing facility.

Lest it be overlooked, let it also be understood that once a "foreign" investor has established substantial investment in the development of an effective work force, the investor has not only created a valuable asset but has also accepted (or incurred) responsibility for commensurate influence (good or bad) upon the very human aspirations and satisfactions of its dependent employees.

Incidentally, the word "foreign" is used here only for lack of a more suitable single word—although "overseas" used loosely might serve the purpose. To the true multinational concern, nothing is foreign.

536

In the ordinary course of business, the unit of enterprise (here-after referred to as a corporation) is, from time to time, prompted into action by a desire for aggressive seizure of new profit-seeking opportunity or by a defensive need to protect its already vested inter-ests against loss or encroachment. Either condition may arise where-ever the corporation has already established itself in business or has developed a market for its product. But, as a general rule—and "other things being equal"—most business enterprises incorporated in a particular "home" country and obtaining all or a significant propor-tion of their capital from citizens of that country would prefer to confine their major capital investments to that country. By doing so, they would avoid exposure to the hazards of conducting business under conditions with which they are likely to be unfamiliar. These would include the laws, rules, practices, and language of a foreign country, foreign exchange losses, and, in certain extreme instances, expropriation by an ungracious host country government.

But such corporations would also forgo such business as could not be obtained or retained solely by exports from the home country. The advantages or disadvantages of one course of action (or inaction) versus another have, accordingly, to be weighed in a trade-off among the available alternatives.

LICENSING—AN ALTERNATIVE

One of these alternatives might be to grant a license to an inde-pendent foreign concern to manufacture the product. The basic value in such a license would generally lie in all or any of patents, trade-marks, "know-how," or access to an already established distribution system. The consideration upon which the license fee is most likely to be based may be presumed to rest upon the separate party's ap-praisal of the profit-earning opportunity granted to the licensee and surrendered by the licensor. On the surface, it would appear to be a relatively simple way for the licensor to obtain income at minimum risk. Practice, however, indicates that it is not without its own haz-ards.

If the profit-earning opportunity is limited or doubtful, this will be reflected in a fee which is commensurately low, as well as of uncertain longevity. More important: If the opportunity is favorable, the licen-sor may live to regret surrendering it to a licensee which, if appropri-ately selected and tutored, could develop the capacity to become a strong competitor—as a licensee or as an independent—and at home as well as abroad.

In a number of instances, the success of a licensee has led to its ultimate acquisition by the licensor. Such success, however, must be presumed to increase the cost of the acquisition. To some extent, this means that earlier fees taken into income from the license are offset by cost capitalized in the acquisition. The more important problems, however, can arise when an overly successful licensee cannot be acquired.

In any event, licensing (other than in a context mentioned later) is outside the direct scope of this writing.

MANUFACTURE

The major alternative to a licensing arrangement is a do-it-yourself direct investment in foreign manufacture. Resolution then calls for decisions as to "where" and "what"—with the two usually mutually dependent.

As to "where," there seems to be some evidence to suggest that the old term "political economy" is still more apt than any modern notion that economics is a relatively pure science divorced from political influences. Frequently the two go hand-in-hand, and each may have to be considered in the light of the other. Furthermore, experience would seem to suggest that "businessmen" be wary about the opinions of economists or other advisers who may be unduly influenced by "statistics."

Thus, for example: Brazil. In all respects, its earlier economic record dictated against ingoing foreign investment—and at certain times the political conditions were even more inhibiting. Inflation was—as Damon Runyon might have said—"More than somewhat," and population growth was operating to retard increase in "per capita" gains. But in most countries, the customer for the product of foreign investment is to be found primarily in that portion of the population which can afford to pay the price, and a relatively small portion of a high population can provide a market as good as or better than a relatively large portion of a less populated country. Per capita averages can be particularly misleading, and the "evidence" of purported mathematical truth is seldom as informationally helpful as such visible or tangible indicators as building construction, the rise

in land use values, or the (positively dangerous) growth in automobile population in a city like São Paulo.

The one best way for a business decision-maker to form judgment
about investment in a foreign country is to go there himself.

WHERE?

Most countries desire to have the benefits to be derived from new
investment, but not always are they completely willing to receive
incoming foreign capital on terms that would be considered wholly
desirable by a prospective foreign investor. In the selection of a country for the placement of new direct investment, the considerations
would accordingly include such factors as the character of the government, as evidenced by its past behavior; its attitude toward foreign
investment; its policies regarding taxation, repatriation of capital, and
the payment of dividends; its position on imports and exports; and
the status of its currency in free market exchanges.

In this general connection, one relatively recent development
might call for increasing consideration. In the beginning, foreign
countries frequently welcome or even press for foreign investment in
indigenous production as a means of substitution for imports and,
among the other benefits, as a means of conserving foreign exchange.
In the course of time, however, it is not unusual to find import substitution being supplemented by—or even subordinated to—pressure
for export expansion. This not only increases the other benefits to the
host country of domestic manufacturing, but also increases foreign
exchange income. But the switch from import substitution to export
expansion—from exchange saving to exchange earning—can have
varying impact according to the circumstances of each particular case.
It is mentioned, therefore, only to alert the reader to a fairly general
expectation which may raise complications but, in many instances,
may also be turned to advantage.

It might also be worth passing notice here that, in several countries,
the desire for exports and foreign exchange earning has recently been
given such importance that satisfaction of it will be accepted as a
consideration for granting greater leniency to foreign-controlled corporations in such matters as imports, local content, and ownership.

If the more political problems of country selection can be overcome or accepted, the economic aspects will call for collateral con-

sideration. There are, however, few, if any, means for estimating long-term economic trends; and, even if there were, they could easily be overturned by political events which frequently defy forecasting or rationalization. Such risks are generally inherent in profit-seeking enterprise; and, if they seem greater abroad than at home, this may be only an indication that the familiarity which arises from experience can produce a capability to cope with change—abroad as well as at home.

Among the more important elements in the context of a national economy will be its relative price levels. This tends to focus attention on wage rates because they can have such an influence upon costs and cost-price relationships. Within the host country, there will generally tend to be some rough equalization which should, at least, permit of effective competition against local production or, possibly, imports from third countries. Outside of the host country—in international exports—the competitive equation would encompass both domestic prices and foreign exchange cross-rates. These are variables which change from time to time and in relationships which may become more or less favorable.

Another element is deliberately introduced by certain host countries when they offer special tax incentives or grant "tax holidays" in order to attract foreign investment. The temptation to be influenced by such concessions can be substantial; but the inducement is designed to have the investment placed where it would serve the interests of the host country, and these will not always coincide with the best long-term interests of the investor. Care is, therefore, necessary: first, to weigh the short-term benefits of being in the "wrong" place against the long-term advantages of being in a more suitable location; and, then—if a tax incentive would be otherwise acceptable—to ensure that it is not wiped out because, in the absence of a tax-sparing treaty, the full home country tax rate is applied to all income earned abroad.

INDUSTRIAL RELATIONS

In certain countries, the manner and condition of employee representation may require particular consideration, but—as indicated by the record—seldom to the point of being a prohibitive factor. Labor-union power and practice vary from country to country, as well as from time to time, and there can be neither assurance nor conviction that any state of industrial relations—favorable or unfavorable (according to the judgment of the employer)—will continue indefinitely.

In some respects, differences in freedom to discharge managerial responsibilities may weigh more heavily than other aspects of employee relations. The responsibilities involved in any question of abridgment should, however, be only those significantly relevant to performance—to the achievement of worthwhile long-term results. This means that they should be divorced from those elements of pride and prejudice which are too frequently deemed to be management "rights" or "prerogatives."

This is a matter which could be of some growing significance in a number of countries that have adopted laws requiring the placement of employee representatives on boards of directors or supervisory management councils. So far, these seem to have produced no particular difficulties, but it is not easy to determine whether this is a result of compliance or of adroit circumvention. Obviously, the situation involves conflict of interest on the part of the employee representatives. Where there is collective bargaining on employee relations, it is not possible for nonmanagement employees to discharge faithfully all of the responsibilities of both a corporation representative and a labor-union representative.

The future of the movement remains to be seen—and carefully watched. It has reached its most advanced state in West Germany, where nonexecutive supervisory boards in coal, iron, and steel corporations are already composed of an equal number of representatives of labor and capital with an independent chairman. Unions are now pressing for extension of the system to most of German industry, and similar proposals have emerged from Britain's Trades Union Congress.

Another development which might be worth observation is the emergence of an attempted internationalization of labor-union power —said to be a countervailing response to the internationalization of production. Among its other claims is one to the effect that, although the operations of multinational corporations should be domestically regulated, they should also be internationally "organized" by labor on the grounds that they are free to play a unit in one country against a similar unit elsewhere, or even to emigrate—all to the detriment of unionized employees. The latter idea—emigration—is, of course, usually far-fetched. The investment involved in a manufacturing operation is generally financially illiquid as well as physically immobile.

And no prudent business corporation would lightly ignore the fact that an established work force is an asset—with both great value and formidable political significance.

But attacks on the multinational corporation can hardly be ignored. They come from within both the home country and the host country. At home, it is claimed by some politically-supported labor-union leaders that foreign investment is an "export of jobs"—reducing the volume of, and opportunity for domestic employment. Relying upon isolated minority cases and disregarding the preponderance of evidence to refute their claims, these proponents seek to have restrictions, controls, and a ponderous reporting system imposed upon foreign direct investment.

Within any country, there is almost certain to be some element which resents (usually more than it resists) incoming foreign investment. Among other lesser evils, it is claimed that multinational corporations have too much power which they could use to affect, adversely, the economy of a country and the condition of its employed citizens. Illustrations are untypically few and exaggerated; but concerns that rest more on fears than on facts can have an elastic combination of emotional and political appeal. These will seldom prompt sheer prohibition of incoming investment; but they can lead to the imposition of conditions which may or may not be acceptable. Caveat investor!

WHAT TO MAKE?

The basis for selection of those items to be made abroad will vary with the circumstances peculiar to each particular case. Here, the reader should perhaps be reminded that the thoughts being expressed come primarily from one identified with the manufacture of heavy-duty construction machinery. For that purpose, a major prerequisite would be the capacity of a country to provide the basic materials, the ancillary supplies, and the work skills required to manufacture the product, as well as to do so, of course, on the basis of a cost-price relationship which would permit the enterprise to be economically feasible.

By their nature, some goods permit of a wide range of international selection for a manufacturing base; but for products such as engine-powered machinery, where reliability and high precision are compounded into quality and value, there are few countries which meet the requirements. Steel would obviously be a basic necessity, and no major manufacturer-marketer could be so self-supporting that it would not need reliable indigenous sources of supply of the forgings, castings, bearings, pistons, ignition systems, and a host of other items which go into the operating assembly of a complete machine.

In general, the items selected for manufacture in a particular host country would be those which could not only be made there, but which could also be expected to find a ready market within that same country and, preferably, also in others within competitive reach of it. Thus, for example—and for many products—Great Britain and Japan can provide both a worthwhile domestic market and a very viable base for exports. In modified contrast, Belgium could generally provide only a limited national market for many products; but as a member of the European Community—free to import production materials and supplies and to export finished product within the broader economic union—Belgium can be an excellent base for European operations.

Within the limits of "what can be made" in a particular country, there will generally be some room for related decisions as to parts or components. These decisions will be based on a selection among the alternative means of putting together the complete finished product: (1) make or (2) buy (locally); or (3) import. Other things being equal, "least-cost" analysis might be expected to provide the logical answer. But other things are seldom equal—anywhere; and, especially in foreign operations, the logic of industrial analysis is frequently obliged to bow to the art of the expedient.

In this respect, several countries pose a conflict between objectives. On the one hand, they wish to maximize the local content in a manufactured product while, on the other, they wish to maximize exports. But if the justification for importation of parts or components were to lie in least-cost, then substitution of a higher cost local product would operate to raise the price for export (as well as domestic) sales. This could be expected to reduce international competitiveness—not excluding that against the same product being sold from related sources in other countries.

A somewhat similar problem can arise when, in the absence of ability to obtain locally items identical with those in the home-country product, the newcomer is pressed to "make the best of what is available." Within the host country, this might not always be unduly harmful, but in export competition there is likely to be a general predisposition to favor an established original over the parvenu "substitute."

OWNERSHIP: WHOLE OR PARTIAL

Having selected both the host country for the investment and the products to be made within it, there remains a question of whether to "go it alone," with 100 percent ownership, or to permit and solicit equity participation by host-country interests. Each alternative has its advantages and disadvantages, according to the particular circumstances of each separate case, and no broad generalizations are properly applicable.

Natural resource enterprises may feel particularly justified in having local investment participation in mines or oil fields; and some of those who do so can certainly claim that, although it does not prevent expropriation (as had been hoped), shared ownership does, at least, reduce what otherwise might have been a larger loss on "nationalization." In several countries, unfamiliar local customs, language difficulty, and government policy may offer no alternative to some form of joint ownership. In such event, there may then be a choice among having the foreign portion of the equity in the hands of (1) the host country government; or of (2) some strong, already-established partner (as in a so-called joint venture); or of (3) the general public—sometimes to avoid risks in the other two more powerful alternatives.

The cause of "local participation" has been extolled in many writings—with supporting arguments which are often more theoretical than empirical. Where, in the absence of better reasons, local participation is claimed to be justified on the grounds of international industrial "diplomacy," that may be as good as any.

There can, however, be valid grounds for favoring 100 percent ownership of voluntarily created foreign subsidiaries, not the least of which is freedom to control affairs without any need for participation by others who are less qualified to enter into the decision-making and management processes. Divided ownership can, furthermore, introduce conflicts of interest on such matters as marketing, transfer pricing (involving profit placement), the selection or promotion of management personnel, dividend policy, and others.

When the interdependence among related units calls for inter-company transfers of goods or services, there must almost inevitably arise some possibility or degree of conflict of interest. There will seldom, if ever, be any such thing as a pure absolute for the determination of fair value in all kinds of intercompany transactions; and to whatever extent prices, fees, and other debits or credits depart from an unattainable arm's length objectivity, one party or the other is going to gain or lose. Any resulting dissatisfaction obviously raises the possibility that contention may weaken cooperation.

Conflict of interest could also be reflected in the use of influence —as in the direction of orders from independent customers toward one source of supply rather than another. Where the effect is only a redistribution of business within one total family, this may be of limited consequence. But when outside interests are involved, there obviously is a danger of having one set of interests gain at the expense of another. Some proponents of participative ventures in international trade meet this contingency with a predetermined plan of marketing —one in which territories are assigned or restricted. Increasingly, however, "market sharing" is being prohibited or at least frowned upon by the antitrust notions of a growing number of countries. And it can be claimed that if the basic tenets of free competitive private enterprise are really "principles," then their application should be— and should be made—universal.

One legal opinion expressed on this matter of conflicting interests also pointed out that:

> A variety of serious problems arises where the parent is an actual or potential competitor of the subsidiary joint venture, while at the same time it has representatives on the board of directors of the venture. . . . These representatives necessarily will acquire information of competitive value which would enable the parent to compete more effectively against the joint venture. Its representatives will be confronted with decisions concerning prices, capital expansion, proposed transactions, etc., where conflicts of interest are unavoidable. While as a matter of law any member on the board of directors of a corporation is required to vote solely for the best interests of that corporation, a representative on the board of a joint venture corporation whose salary is paid by a parent company, or whose future business career depends upon that parent, might be tempted to favor the best interests of the parent when these are in conflict with those of the joint venture subsidiary.

In these remarks, no special recognition has been given to the *degree* of ownership in a subsidiary when it is less than 100 percent owned. This is the reflection of opinion that whenever there is *any* other interest in a subsidiary—even though it be only a small minority position—the exercise of "force majeure" through the legal power offered by majority shareholding will generally be imprudent. Where one corporation owns more than 50 percent but less than all of the shares of another corporation (foreign or domestic), it acquires a fiduciary obligation to deal fairly with minority shareholders and not abuse its power. And if joint participation in an enterprise is meant to be something more than a mere marriage of investment convenience, the overruling of minority interests by majority holders will not be likely to promote the most effective working partnership.

Among the benefits claimed for joint participation, there are many which are no less available through whole ownership. One of these is the transmission of technical and managerial know-how into the host country's industrial community—through the subsidiary conduit. But, surely, this is a matter which is only one of *time*. In general, the responsibility for managing a new subsidiary rests initially with those who are responsible for its creation. To whatever extent the host country can provide the quality and quantity of the skills necessary for the enterprise, they should and usually will be sought. But most frequently, it will be found that the most effective way in which policies, practices, and the refinements of managing and processing can be conveyed to and instilled in a new organization is through *people* who are already experienced in the requirements. Written instructions, procedures, and blueprints will not do the job. The basic need is *understanding*, and this can generally be best brought about in the ordinary course of transfusion through the osmotic processes of man-to-man communication while working together.

In any event, it would seem advisable to require that, without regard to the degree of ownership, a foreign affiliate which is granted the right to manufacture and sell a parent company's proprietary products do so only under the terms of an appropriate controlling license. This may involve patents, trademarks and access to an established distribution system, but the most valuable assets in a transfer might well be "know-how" and goodwill. For such values, there certainly should be commensurate consideration—usually in the form of a fee related to performance and preferably determined on the same basis as it would be in a similar arm's-length transaction with a wholly independent concern.

This latter requirement would seem to be a matter of both good industrial discipline and international prudence. Children who are indulged by overweaning paternalism often lose a sense of obligation and accountability. And governments which in times of financial stringency may be prone to introduce exchange controls or otherwise restrict dividend payments will nevertheless usually be more willing to permit the payment of creditor obligations represented by contractual liabilities.

Before leaving this matter, it might also be worth expressing a thought that, among the justifications for local equity participation, the desire for external capital contribution merely as a means of reducing internal contribution would seldom provide a sound basis for a wholly satisfactory capitalization. Of all the contributions going into the making of a worthwhile "controlled" foreign investment, money should be a relatively minor element—not so much in amount, as in its capacity to help make the enterprise viable. If the venture appears to be really worthwhile, capital should be forthcoming; but in case of doubt, the last thing a foreign investor should contemplate is any idea that local participation in ownership would be an appropriate means of having host country investors share losses.

HOST COUNTRY BENEFIT

Nothing said here should be regarded as contradicting the fundamental fact that, in order to have and to hold the right to work with the consent of any country under its laws, the results of the enterprise should be beneficial for the host country as well as the investor. Over the long term, the return to the investor should be dividends; to the country, it should encompass a compounding of many worthwhile benefits.

Too frequently, however, dividends paid to foreign shareholders are claimed to be an unwarranted withdrawal of national resources, and sometimes they are described as piratical seizures of wealth derived from the exploitation of the country and its people. In this sense, "exploitation" is used to connote something evil—a selfish utilization—ignoring the fact that an exploit, even a business one, is frequently a heroic accomplishment and that exploitation means turning something to practical account.

Profit, these detractors would apparently consider as a penalty first exacted by the seller from the buyer—and then extracted by the investor from the country in which it was earned. They ignore or fail to appreciate that real profit is a complete addition to the sum total of national wealth—something *created* which would not otherwise have been brought into being. They do not seem to understand the difference between real capital formation and zero-sum transfer income—as in, say, gambling. They treat profit more in terms of money rather than as a rough monetary measure of the contribution to national wealth and human welfare. And although they should know that dividends can come only from profit, they nevertheless ignore the fact that after the distribution of dividends, there always remains a residual net addition to the accumulation of capital employed in the business and in the country.

None of the benefits created and conveyed by multinational enterprise are the exclusive result of any one form of international investment. They can all be derived from any successfully constructive enterprise and without regard to the composition of its ownership. The test should, as always, be "appropriateness for the purpose," with the purpose being that established primarily by the promoting investor (otherwise, why the initiative?), and appropriateness being a matter which encompasses all the pertinent internal and external aspects of each particular case.

KNOW-HOW TRANSFER

Having resolved the questions of investment location, product selection, and equity ownership, the time comes for "doing business." If the foregoing measures have been taken soundly in a manner wholly appropriate for all the circumstances of the particular case, then operation in terms of employing, buying, making, and selling will, as a rule, conform much more closely to established practice within the parent company and its home country than is generally assumed or admitted. This will be especially true if the products, processes, and procedures of the parent can be carried into the foreign operations.

Thus, for example, in the machinery business, which is a major part of the metalworking industry, the means of casting, forging, forming, and heat-treating iron or steel, or otherwise giving the basic constituent materials the desired physical and chemical characteristics, are almost universally the same or similar. Machine tools, jigs and fixtures, dies, and patterns can usually be imported, purchased, or made, and then successfully employed in any country where the related capital investment is justified. In such event, it can be readily possible not only to employ the same "standard operational procedures" which have been proved successful at home or elsewhere, but also to adopt the same work standards for output per unit of time or time per unit of output.

As mentioned earlier, the most effective way in which established successful practices may be conveyed from an older experienced organization into a new offshoot from it is through *people* who are already experienced in the requirements. This involves an international transfer of residence not only of the employee but also of his family—usually including a wife. Much has been written on the "culture shock" which can occur as a result of such a transfer. For this and other reasons, there has properly been a need for especially careful selection of those who would represent the parent abroad and carry into the new venture, as well as the new country, their skills and their behavioral mores. The skills, of course, are basic but not necessarily the most important; enthusiasm for the adventure can be more stimulatingly helpful than technical proficiency.

Where there is a language difference, an ability to use that of the host country naturally offers many advantages both inside and outside of business. If time permits, the learning process should begin *before* the transfer—and should preferably include the wife. She, indeed, is the more likely to encounter difficulties in the ordinary course of maintaining a household and her ability to adapt to the new mode of living can be important for the peace of mind of the new business "expatriate." He will frequently be inclined to devote even more attention than usual to his work—just at a time when his family most needs his help, understanding, and company.

Properly handled, the transnational transfer can be a great adventure—full of new interests in people and places, in history and geography, and in the comparisons and contrasts which make travel a broadening educational experience. Realization of the benefits should not, however, be taken for granted lest the early disappointments and difficulties dull the later pleasures and opportunities. Where there is not an already established nucleus of fellow employees —with families—the situation deserves close headquarters attention.

These and other considerations seem, in a number of instances, to have suggested that the industrial missionaries selected for transfer should be younger rather than older even though this were to involve some deficiency of desirable experience. And there also has been some idea that new foreign experience provides an excellent training ground for emergent managers. It does; but the purpose of foreign investment is not the development of parent company embryos. The training required is that of the employed nationals who will constitute the basic work force of the new enterprise. On them will depend the success of the venture, and it could be folly to jeopardize that goal by starting off with anything less than a transfer of wholly adequate experience by the most qualified representatives available.

It might be well to note also that the bringing of a foreign operation into fruition will probably demand on the part of its pioneer executives more versatility and entrepreneurial flair than is required, desired, or permitted in the running of a mature home-country establishment.

As to the local national employees: It is too generally assumed that differences among the peoples of different countries are more significant—and therefore present more difficulties—than their similarities. There are, of course, differences arising from all or any of whatever elements enter into the creation of a so-called national character—race, religion, tradition, education, and stage of development as well as the influences of history, climate, language, political ideology, and even dietary habits. But the similarities among people are, for the purpose under consideration, more general and, as a rule, more usefully important than the differences. And none of the differences is likely to prove insuperable. Business managers who can adjust and adapt to the changing conditions of changing times should have no great difficulty in achieving an accommodation which would continue to recognize that the hopes and aspirations of people born of parents and reared in families are substantially similar all over the industrialized world.

ORGANIZATION

Once a business concern of size graduates into international operations, there is a call to reexamine the form of its total organization structure. The essential requirement is not necessarily change. It is, rather, a redetermination of purpose and direction accompanied by an understanding among those key officials without whose cooperation no form of organization can be wholly effective.

Organization is primarily an instrument for the purposes of control—to be modified and adapted according to the changing conditions of the changing times. It can be formed in a variety of permutations and combinations; but, in the course of pragmatic time, two basic structures have emerged: one a divisionalization separating domestic from foreign business; the other a unified consolidation without such a distinction. In the former arrangement, the section devoted to foreign operations has been frequently identified as "international," but this practice is gradually giving way to a recognition that the latter arrangement is more truly international—being world-wide in its scope.

Each of the two basic forms has its advantages and disadvantages, but in recent times the trend is toward the more unified consolidation. The thinking seems to be to the effect that if a corporation is truly multinational in its operations and aspirations—that is, *globally* oriented—then a division between the affairs in one (home) country and those in all other countries presents some conflict with the concept.

To be sure, divisionalization offers greater opportunity for a higher degree of (narrower) specialization—if that is necessary or desired. But it also inhibits the transfer of people between the divisions and thereby tends to operate against having—within the total organization—the right man in the right place at the right time. It can also produce a spirit of rivalry which could be more divisive than constructive. And the existence of two divisions tends to prompt the creation of two general staffs—which is one more than would usually be necessary under a unified consolidation.

In earlier times, the international division was frequently a sort of stepchild operation—appended to the apron strings of an indulgent parent. Those employed in it often remained in it for all their working lives, and few of them moved into the very upper echelons of overall administration. In more recent times, this condition has been giving way to one in which those having international experience—working and living abroad—are finding or earning more favor in top executive selection and promotion. The change is undoubtedly a reflection of the fact that international trade and investment have assumed greater proportions and are producing more significant results. This, in turn, has dictated that more of those in the top command have both domestic and international experience; and this can be more readily obtained within a consolidated unity than under the divisional form of organization.

Within the total structure, whether divisionalized or consolidated, there may, of course, be such subdivisions as would be appropriate to give separate jurisdiction and responsibility according to, say, manufacturing or marketing, type of product, or geographical area.

In any organization composed of a number of units operating in a number of different locations—especially if both at home and abroad —there will generally be a need for some kind of central or general staff. This need not, however, induce any hair-splitting definition about whether the administration or management is "centralized" or "decentralized." With few exceptions, an organization of any size has to have within it elements of both forms. Certainly the main thrust of direction and related basic policies must come from the highest and, therefore, top or central authority. That being so, the responsibility for control also is vested in that authority. But in line operations where policies are resolved into practice, there should be ample scope for such a decentralization of *functional* responsibility as would permit those closest to, and best informed about, localized realities to discharge *their* responsibilities in whatever manner they deem to be most appropriate in the particular circumstances. This freedom of adaptation to localized conditions should not, however, be so loose as to preclude, at least, parallel review by a central source of companywide experience and communication.

Thus, in successful practice at Caterpillar Tractor Co., the rule is that those in charge of establishing a new unit—be it a domestic plant or a foreign subsidiary—are free, by a sort of common law, to adopt those practices which have become standard practice elsewhere in the organization. But if, *for any reason,* there is a desire to introduce some new procedure, then it is to be reviewed with the applicable staff section. The purpose of this is twofold: one, to consider whether there is any prior experience having a bearing on the new proposal; the other, if the proposal would introduce improvement, to have it disseminated wherever else applicable throughout the entire organization.

Where there is a central staff, it is commonly assumed that there will inevitably be a certain amount of friction between it and those in line operations. To the "doers" on the line, staff representatives are fictionalized as irresponsible "overhead" espousing impractical or inapplicable theories from the ethereal heights of an "ivory tower." If, however, any shades of such a feeling were to exist, the cause would probably be found to lie not in the assignment of duties, but, rather, in the placement of responsibilities. The solution—again as tried and proved at Caterpillar Tractor—is to provide that, throughout the whole management organization, there shall be *no one* without designated responsibility.

Thus, for illustration, in a manufacturing plant or subsidiary, responsibility for performance of the unit rests with its line manager. The staff official assigned companywide responsibility for, say, manufacturing (as a separate function) is charged with responsibility for auditing the procedures and practices employed in unit operations with a view to determining—at least, in his opinion—whether they are the best believed to be available. If the two officials agree—as evidenced by the continuance of existing practice or by adoption of a change—there is a harmonious disposition of the matter. If they disagree, they are not empowered to compromise. The matter is then to be carried by each official to his next higher level of authority and, if necessary, beyond that until resolution is decreed by that level of authority which is beyond divisional status.

The essence of the arrangement is that *each* of the line and staff officials is held responsible—but *severally*, not jointly. Thus, there is preserved a principle that for everything done, some *one* is responsible—without any excuse of "sharing" or the conflicting obfuscation of "buck-passing."

CONCLUSION

In business there is no greater accomplishment and therefore no greater pleasure than that to be found in the *creation* of goods and services and an organization of people finding useful employment in their manufacture and marketing. This is sometimes obscure to the man who extends the limbs of an already well-established tree; but to the man who participates in the planting of a new and thriving tree there is a stronger personal identification that provides a more intimate source of satisfaction. And, more than anything else, that is what the good business manager seeks—satisfaction in accomplishment. It can be gained (or lost) anywhere in the world, but is most likely to be found in the pioneering stages of new ventures. Among these, few offer more opportunities than the offshoot of a progressive parent extending the scope of its social as well as its economic affairs into lands that once were "foreign."

PLANNING FOR PLANT:
HOW BIG, WHEN, WHERE, AND
HOW TO FINANCE

by Gordon R. Corey
Vice Chairman, Commonwealth Edison Company

PLANT INVESTMENT decision-making is similar to portfolio management, although more precise data are generally available to the plant manager. On the other hand, the portfolio manager can sell his mistakes while plant investment is for keeps.

Major plant investment decisions often affect the future course of the enterprise, and so must wait upon policy or strategic decisions as to such matters as market expansion or withdrawal. On the other hand, many plant decisions are fairly routine and can be made by simply comparing the estimated cost of replacement with that of continued maintenance.

Broadly speaking, all plant decisions should be based upon their projected economic effect. Good decisions pay off; bad decisions cause bankruptcy.[1]

This paper will concentrate on those approaches which will provide a sound basis for decision-making although, regrettably, they cannot ensure against mistakes. We shall discuss, first, a number of acceptable approaches to long-range forecasting; second, conventional techniques of economic analysis; third, some rules-of-thumb which may be useful; fourth, the effects of chronic inflation; and fifth, methods of financing plant expansion.

---

[1] No manager can voluntarily undertake to authorize expenditures which are non-productive from the viewpoint of the firm. Consequently, if desired social welfare objectives like environmental cleanup are to be achieved through the market system, it is mandatory that their costs be "internalized" by *law*, which is to say, made real for the firm by regulation or taxation.

LONG-RANGE FORECASTING

Long-range forecasting is always risky. Business executives who authorize major plant investment programs, relying upon such forecasts, must have intuitive feelings for the direction of social change. What will the social climate be 10 or 20 years from now? What tax and regulatory environment will obtain? What will be the market demand? What the environmental requirements? What new social concerns will arise? Will adequate supplies of fuel and raw materials be available?

Difficult or not, long-range forecasts must be settled upon before making plans for long-lived plant expansion—or contraction.*

Careful market research is essential of course, including research as to the future availability of essential fuel and supplies—as well as future demand for the product. Ten years ago, who would have expected the worldwide oil shortage to come so soon? And now who can say when other critical supplies will be embargoed?

Broad consultation is essential—with outsiders; and with youngsters.

The use of young ideas is especially important, if a sharp shift in techniques or markets is being considered—or resisted. Success in these cases will depend upon changes in the total market, plus what competitors will do. Thus it is essential to consult the younger executives who are most likely to be most alert to social change and to the advisability of switching fields—although the older hands can remind us that change has occurred before and that new approaches, too, may be only passing fancies.

In any case, it is only after basic policy or strategic analyses and projections indicate the general desirability of investing in plant that the kinds of matters I am going to discuss here come into play. And these matters need always be contemplated and dealt with in light of those broad policy or strategic considerations. The kinds of things I shall touch upon throw light upon such questions as to whether, specifically and concretely, a plant investment is presently desirable and feasible from an economic point of view; some general thoughts gleaned from experience; the possible impact of inflation; and methods of financing.

---

* [Ed. Note: See the chapter by J. D. Glover, "Strategic Decision-Making: Planning, Manning, Organization."]

TECHNIQUES OF ECONOMIC ANALYSIS

Although no predictions can be precise, of course, the analysis of future cost (*sans* inflation) is likely to be more reliable than the prediction of future markets. Executives whose backgrounds lie outside the engineering and accounting areas should recognize this—that cost analysis techniques are well developed and reliable, although the assumptions upon which they are based must always be examined critically.

The following discussion reviews the most common techniques of economic analysis but avoids a detailed description of each. I shall not go into the arithmetic of these analyses; there are textbooks that do that. What is emphasized here is not how to *analyze* the data, but how to *use* the results. Presumably your people will provide you with valid analyses. Your problem is to avoid pitfalls by appropriate testing, checking, and questioning.

Discounted Cash Flow

The most widely accepted technique for analyzing the economic consequences of alternative plant expansion or retirement programs is known as "discounted cash flow" (or DCF), a phrase which applies to a generalized system for analyzing cash flows.[2]

A frequent objective of DCF analysis is to determine which pro-

---

[2] The customary DCF procedure is to relate a stream of expenditures, "I," to a stream of revenues, "R," using something like the following general formula:

$$\sum_{n=0}^{N} I_n \left(\frac{1}{1+r}\right)^n = \sum_{n=0}^{N} R_n \left(\frac{1}{1+r}\right)^n$$

In the above formula, $\left(\frac{1}{1+r}\right)^n$ is the present value discount factor; r, the annual return or discount rate; n, the time lapse in years before each expenditure or recovery occurs; and N, the project life in years or the pay-back period. The equation can be solved for the rate of return (r); for the pay-back period (N); or for the present value of the revenue requirements, which is represented by the entire right side of the equation.

In words, this equation, which may look a little forbidding to the nonmathematician, means simply the following:

a.   The sum of the several annual Investments, I's, to be made in future periods (the stream of expenditures) between *now* ($n = 0$) and the end of the project life or pay-back period, N, expressed as a number of years—each investment being discounted by an assumed rate of return, r, for the number of periods (years), n, before it is to be made, is equal to:

b.   The sum of the several annual Revenues, R's, to be received in future periods (the stream of revenues) between now ($n = 0$) and the end of the project life or pay-back period, N, expressed as a number of years—the Revenue of each year (R) gram will provide the highest rate of return on an investment, but this is by no means an essential DCF characteristic. As a matter of fact, ". . . the phrase 'discounted cash flow' is properly applied to any calculation to find the present worth of [future] cash flow whether or not the calculation is used in computing the rate of return." [3]

There are several different DCF approaches, as follows.

(*a*) *The Rate of Return Test.* A common approach to plant investment decision-making is to determine the *annual rate of return* that may be expected from an investment. A program or investment is then recommended if its indicated rate of return meets minimum standards; or, if several programs are under consideration, it indicates the program which provides the highest rate of all programs considered.

Most businesses other than regulated utilities have considerable latitude as to the areas in which they can invest their funds. For these, it is generally desirable to maximize the rate of return. *In fact, the rate of return test is normally preferred where funds are limited and the firm free to expand or not.*

However, the rate of return objective should not be pursued blindly. It can be misleading if there is a sharp difference in magnitude between mutually exclusive programs, or programs that are not really comparable. For example, the possible investment of $10 for an annual benefit of $100 would produce a return of 1,000 percent per year. But, if the alternative course of action would be to invest $1 million for an annual return of, say, $300,000 or 30 percent, it could well be the preferred course of action, provided the million dollars were available.

Another shortcoming of the rate of return approach is that it assumes that the funds recovered can be promptly reinvested in equally attractive projects. For example, a 25 percent return would at first blush appear to be better than a 15 percent return. But, if the 25

---

being discounted by the rate of return, r, for the number of years, n, before it is to be received.

If the other factors are known or assumed, the value of any one of the variables can be determined.

[3] Grant, Eugene L. and Ireson, W. Grant; *Principles of Engineering Economy;* 5th edition; New York: The Ronald Press; 1970; pp. 115–16. To summarize the views expressed by Grant and Ireson, "discounted cash flow" and related procedures comprise a general group of computational techniques rather than methods of interpretation. And the question as to what the final decision should turn upon—rate of return, present value, or something else—is generally unresolved by the mere adoption of the DCF approach.

percent return applies to a relatively short-lived program, while the 15 percent return applies to a long-lived program, the latter would probably be preferred if reinvestment opportunities were limited.

(*b*) *The Pay-Back Test.* Another common approach is to determine the time required to recover an investment. A program is then recommended if its pay-back time is acceptable; or, if several programs are under consideration, the program with the fastest pay-back will ordinarily be recommended.

The most common approach is to compute the pay-back period *without* interest. It is often said, "We can get our money back in X years"—meaning that the program will produce enough benefits in X years to recover the investment, without considering interest, return on investment, or related income taxes. This is the quick-and-dirty approach commonly used to justify an obviously acceptable rapid-recovery program where interest and income tax considerations are nominal.

On the other hand, where the choice is close, it is wrong to ignore the cost of money. Under these conditions, a sophisticated pay-back or "recovery period" computation will consider money costs by following accepted DCF procedures. When this is done—where the recovery period represents the time needed to recover the investment *with interest*—the pay-back test will give essentially the same answer as the rate of return approach; and it will have the same infirmities: A miniscule program shown to have a very short recovery time may not, in fact, be nearly so attractive as a larger program with a longer (though still acceptable) pay-back period.

As to choosing between the rate of return and pay-back approaches, the latter has one advantage. It obviates the need to make a precise determination of the projected useful life of the new facility—except for tax purposes.

On the other hand, a special warning applies to the pay-back approach. If some of the programs under consideration involve significant cash flows *after* their initial pay-back periods, these must not be overlooked if one is to avoid favoring short-sighted, temporizing solutions.[4]

---

[4] For example, if one program involves an expenditure of $1 million to modernize plant, while under another program only $100,000 would be spent for the time being, with the major expenditure postponed for, say, 10 years, then we cannot be satisfied with the conclusion that the second alternative is better simply because the $100,000 would be paid back soon—say in 7 years. To get a valid answer, we must look well beyond

(c) *The Present-Value Tests.*   In general, these approaches concentrate on *relative dollar values* to be obtained from investment alternatives (appropriately discounted for time) rather than *rates* of return or pay-back *periods.*

There are many variations of the present-value approach. They bear such varied labels as "profitability index," the "investor's method," the "revenue requirements" approach, and the "level premium carrying charge" approach.[5]

The present-value approach (in common with the sophisticated form of pay-back test) requires that an appropriate present-value discount rate be selected (or *assumed*) in advance, for purposes of calculation, whereas the rate of return approach in effect *solves* for the discount rate that is implicit in the income to be derived from an investment. In this respect, the present value approach presents an added difficulty.[6]

On the other hand, the present-value test avoids the problem of evaluating reinvestment opportunities for funds recovered (a problem which may arise under the rate-of-return approach), because the minimum acceptable rate of return established for the present-value test normally represents either the return available elsewhere or the "rate of disadvantage" (a rate equivalent to the marginal cost of new money *less* the federal income tax saving on the interest component of that cost) which can be avoided by not going forward with the project under consideration.

A more important difficulty with the present-value test arises from its assumption of the unrestricted availability of funds, and the corollary assumption that the present-value discount rate reflects the full cost of providing such funds. It is unrealistic, however, to assume unlimited availability of funds, especially when capital markets are in disarray and capital funds in short supply.

---

the ten-year scheduled time for the major investment outlay contemplated under the second plan.

[5] For a detailed description of a typical approach, see the manual put out by Commonwealth Edison Co.; entitled *Engineering Economics*; copyrighted 1963. There have been frequent revisions of this manual; the latest is 1975.

[6] As a matter of top management judgment, of course, one need not try to be too precise about either the present-value discount rate or acceptable rate-of-return objectives. Capital markets are so volatile that money-cost estimates for the duration of a long-lived plant investment are at best an exercise of judgment. Many firms make little pretense at precision in this area. They simply establish rough overall rate-of-return objectives of 20 percent or 25 percent a year and let it go at that. There is much to be said for this approach.

The present-value approach is generally preferred for public utilities, which are not free to choose not *to expand, if expansion is called for by the marketplace.* Public utilities are legally required to provide adequate service at minimum rates. The present-value test, which seeks to minimize future revenue requirements, is consistent with that requirement, whereas the rate-of-return or pay-back approach would be inappropriate for these companies. However, when the availability of capital funds is sharply restricted, we at Commonwealth Edison deliberately bias the cost of money assumption upward, reflecting the need to penalize the more capital-intensive alternatives.

(d) **The Cost-per-Unit-of-Output Test.** Frequently, the results of economic analyses are expressed in terms of the relative cost per unit of output—per kilowatt-hour; per barrel of gasoline, intermediate distillates, and residual oil; per ton of finished steel; per razor blade or match box; or merely per standard unit of production. Unit cost comparisons have one of the infirmities common to the rate-of-return and pay-back tests. If there is a sharp difference in size of one investment program versus another, the reported costs may not be strictly comparable. Also, in common with the present-value test, unit cost comparisons normally assume unrestricted availability of funds, with money costs established at some predetermined acceptable level and allocated over the anticipated output. However, these unit cost methods nevertheless have considerable usefulness because the comparisons are presented in terms which all levels of management can readily relate to.

GUIDELINES FOR EXECUTIVE DECISION-MAKING— SOME RULES-OF-THUMB

Once the economic effects of several plant programs have been analyzed and reported on, the final decision is up to the boss—and will depend on his ability to evaluate the recommendations and to question wisely.

Executive decision-making often follows an array of unconsciously accumulated rules-of-thumb. Here are a few which may be useful:

Get good tax advice. Tax effects often tip the scale. Attention should therefore be paid to all taxes, especially to income tax provisions related to plant investment—investment credits, accelerated depreciation, guideline and ADR lives and the deductibility of overheads.* The technical analysis should not be left to mathematicians and engineers alone. Competent tax advice must be brought to bear on every significant investment decision.

Evaluate the risks carefully. Differences in degree of risk can far outweigh the seemingly precise differences in predicted costs or benefits. Consequently, the riskiness of each alternative course of action must be examined and weighed. Is the program likely to work as planned? Will it work at all?

Insist upon a straightforward analysis of cost differentials. Most economic comparisons are made by adding up the consequences of one course of action and comparing them with the consequences of doing something else. The proof of the answer should lie in a ready demonstration of the factors contributing to the aggregate cost differentials. Can the differences in cost be readily explained in terms of major causes? Are the causative factors equally valid? Have we overlooked anything which might significantly affect the answer?

Test each answer by taking a different tack. Analysis of cost differentials is one way of approaching the problem from a different angle. But it is not enough. A whole new look may be needed before reaching a final decision. For example:

a. If the initial analysis tried to minimize pay-back time, an alternative attempt might be made to minimize revenue requirements.

b. If the initial approach was based upon a 20- or 30-year life-of-plant analysis, an appropriate alternative might be to analyze cash flow and carrying charges for an initial period of 5 or 10 years. Will the relative attractiveness of one investment program over another change if the early years, only, are considered? If so, why? What significant events are likely to occur after 10 years? Is their likelihood strong or uncertain?

c. If the initial analysis was based upon a comprehensive array of all cost effects throughout the firm, it may be well to examine only those costs which may be affected directly by the proposed programs, to set aside peripheral events and concentrate on the direct consequences of the programs in question.

Do not underestimate the ongoing cost of maintaining an antiquated facility. If there is a close question between installing a new

---

* [Ed. Note: ADR ("Asset Depreciation Range") refers to regulations of the Internal Revenue Service which allow reductions or increases in asset class life for tax purposes. See the chapter by Phillip Lifschultz, "Tax Management, Taxes, and the Company."]

facility and continuing to maintain an old one, it should ordinarily be decided in favor of the new. This is because the full cost of continued maintenance is rarely anticipated. Costly fix-ups are the rule rather than the exception; these can be dictated by unexpected breakdowns or unexpected government action, for example.

Similarly, do not underestimate the cost of premature obsolescence. The useful life of a proposed facility usually turns out to be different from what was predicted. However, the time-value of money being what it is, mistakes on the short side tend to be more significant cost-wise than those on the long side. The chance of loss is greater than that of gain. This should be reflected in the calculations, by deliberately understating the life expectancy of the new facility or, better yet, by making a separate cash flow analysis for the early years—as suggested under *b* above. Considerable weight should be given to such short-life analysis.

Make full use of computer modelling. Large-scale computers provide an enormously effective tool for reviewing the effect of a large number of cost and revenue variables. They should be used at the outset of the study to help narrow the range of choices, and from time to time throughout the study to verify the conclusions.

But complex computer models should be used wisely. Complex mathematical models tend to compound estimating errors. If input assumptions are not readily understood, their significance may be lost and wrong decisions made.

Let us suppose that there is a plant siting problem with numerous possibilities. A computer model may be developed to narrow the list. However, the cumulative effect of dozens (even hundreds) of small errors embedded in the vast array of input data may result in excluding some likely possibilities. The errors, themselves, may never see the light of day unless all significant input assumptions are fully reviewed, discussed, and understood by top management.

In addition (and some of my younger associates dispute this), the completed comparisons should be tested for reasonableness by manual calculation, without resort to the computer, perhaps by an entirely separate team using nothing more sophisticated than a worksheet and a small hand-calculator. *If cost differentials cannot be explained rationally in simple arithmetic, better go back to the model. Something may be wrong.*

Beware of broad overall comparisons; follow a step-by-step approach. It is illogical, of course, to examine a single facet of a complex decision in a vacuum. Nevertheless, most complex decisions are made piecemeal—one step at a time. Rather than starting right out to compare one elaborate program with another that is equally elaborate but quite different—rather than that, try to analyze the effect of an array of small shifts in just one of these programs. Find out what such shifts will do to the figures. In that way, try to find out what is going on, what little quirks analysts may have built into their models. In this way, your own understanding will be improved and the decision-making problem perhaps simplified by carefully narrowing down and centering in on a single "best choice."

Beware of broad overall decisions made in one fell swoop.

Use the computer to verify the final decision. At the very end of the decision-making process, it is wise to turn again to the computer for a final comparison run. If something looks phony at that stage, all aspects of the matter should be reexamined. There should be no reluctance to change, even this late in the game, because unwillingness to admit error is fatal to long-run business survival. In short, *the computer model should be used to check and validate the final executive decision!*

Beware of large meetings. Complex data simply cannot be carefully evaluated in concert with the many conflicting irrelevancies of a large meeting. The problems and concepts are too complex for accurate communication under these circumstances. How many times have I left such a meeting, in which I had asked a question and received an answer, which I thought I had understood, only to find later that I had misunderstood the response, due to interruptions and cross-fire, or merely due to my own reluctance to occupy everyone's time in a detailed pursuit of the truth.

THE EFFECT OF CHRONIC INFLATION

Some of the best decisions in history appear to have been based solely on intuition. Contrariwise, several notoriously bad decisions were made with the benefit of the most sophisticated techniques of market research and economic analysis.

This chapter has made a few suggestions for avoiding disaster. Yet the future is uncertain, and the chances of being wrong seem greater than ever. Today, extrapolation of the past seems less and less likely to provide a reliable basis for predicting the future. Society is changing. New costs imposed by law appear almost daily. And the possibility of social instability can also throw a monkey wrench into our future calculations.

In particular, a high rate of future inflation can have a significant effect upon conventional plant investment decision-making.

Even during the mild inflation years of the 1950s and 60s, there were many, many cases of marginal plant expansion being bailed out by subsequent inflation. Today the situation is more complex because the inflation rate is higher. If market prices rise sharply in response to higher plant replacement costs, an investment which appears submarginal today may well prove very profitable indeed in the future. On the other hand, runaway inflation can have disastrous effects upon capital formation; and if interest rates go out the window, a marginal investment requiring undue borrowing may result in bankruptcy.

With capital in short supply, many firms have no other choice but to bias their decision-making against the early-replacement or capital-intensive alternatives. More fortunate businesses may, however, feel free to accelerate their construction programs to avoid future escalation. For these firms, the following comments may have some relevance.

a.   Time is money. The businessman who invests too early, merely to avoid inflation, could go broke. The high interest rates generated by the very inflation he anticipates could prove his undoing.

b.   The tendency of conventional economic analysis to evaluate investment proposals in terms of going interest rates can lead to short-sighted decisions in times when interest rates are high, reflecting the anticipation of significant future inflation. Under these conditions, conventional DCF (discounted cash flow) approaches may repeatedly suggest waiting just one more year, whereas one more year inevitably brings still higher construction costs and, as time goes by, the firm may be forced out of business by more daring competitors.

c.   To correct this, estimates of future construction cost inflation should be reflected in at least one set of the DCF computations. Alternatively, the carrying charge and discount rate assumptions might be reduced somewhat to eliminate part or all of the inflation component.

A Concluding Thought about Inflation

Where conventional analysis, with little consideration of inflation, clearly indicates one course of action to be preferable, there is much to be said for following that course, because predictions of future inflation and interest rates are at best uncertain. On the other hand, where a plant investment decision is close—and particularly if it seems to be only a matter of when, not whether—then the decision should probably be made in favor of prompt expansion, provided the funds needed can be obtained without undue risk.

FINANCING

The ideal way to pay for a proposed plant expansion program, in these days of tight money, is what one large Chicago savings institution calls the "Bohemian easy payment plan": Pay in cash, internally generated cash. Don't borrow; don't sell stock; don't lease; and don't enter into joint ventures. Simply follow a sufficiently conservative policy so that there will always be enough *cash* on hand to do the trick. Such a policy is probably overly cautious.

Today, business practices are not as frugal as they used to be. Current operations are not generating the funds needed for plant expansion. Firms are looking more and more to the outside money markets for capital funds.*

The chances are that a major plant project will have to be financed with outside funds. If so, how? Through the sale of debt or equity? Or through a hybrid approach like lease financing? If debt, should it be short, intermediate, or long?

Debt

Conventional wisdom is that long-lived plant ought to be financed with long-lived obligations; that equipment like machine tools and trucks can appropriately be leased or financed with intermediate-term debt; and that seasonal inventories and receivables may appropriately be covered by commercial paper or bank loans. There are many exceptions, however. For example, when interest rates are high, but there are prospects that they may decline, and that it may be possible to refund debts reasonably soon, taking advantage of lower rates, it may be wise to finance a modest portion of even long-lived plant investments with intermediate or short-term debt so as to avoid the substantial call premiums involved in refunding long-term debt before its maturity.

---

* [Ed. Note: See the chapter by Eli Shapiro and Barbara Negri Opper, "Changing Structure of the Financial Markets."]

Equity

Financing options involving equity are of many kinds. They range from common stock and common stock warrants, which may be sold for cash to existing stockholders (perhaps with rights, or under a dividend reinvestment plan), to employees, or to the public, or issued in exchange for property; to convertible preferred stock or convertible debt; to straight preferred stock and subordinated preferred or preference stock of one kind or another; to a whole array of special instruments like participation certificates, partnership shares, oil payments, mortgages with equity "kickers," etc. The list is almost unlimited.

This is not a textbook on finance. Nor is it intended to specify how to finance a particular plant expansion or modernization project. Nevertheless, here are a half dozen specific suggestions:

First, if outside funds must be obtained, it is safer to use common stock than preferred, and safer to use preferred than debt.

Second, debt money is cheaper, of course, interest being deductible because of income taxes. Beyond that, however, there is little to be said for the old hypothesis that debt is cheaper per se than stock and that capital-intensive businesses should therefore carry a high debt ratio. There is certainly an optimum debt-equity structure for a stable enterprise—and too much debt can be very expensive!

Third, consistency is of first importance in establishing fiscal policy. The financing for one project should ordinarily be similar to that for earlier projects unless there are good reasons to change. Fiscal policy is established for the long pull and should not be varied sharply for temporary overnight benefits if a firm desires to maintain market stability for its securities.[7]

Fourth, the straightforward sale of a debt or equity security is generally to be preferred over indirect approaches. It is usually better to sell stock directly than to do so through warrants or convertible securities, unless the firm needs to issue equity (common or preferred) now, but expects to be in a significantly better position to do so later on. In the latter case, it may well make sense to use an option-type security in order to delay the ultimate issuance of the stock in question.

Fifth, a simple option to purchase stock (a warrant) can generally

---

[7] This is not to argue against innovation and imagination; merely to suggest that change should be made only when there is good reason for doing so.

command a higher price, provided it can be traded separately, than if it is embodied in the terms of a convertible security.

Sixth, off-beat financing—leases, leasebacks, bankable "take-or-pay" purchase agreements, oil and mineral payments—have their place, but they should not ordinarily be relied upon as the primary financing vehicle for a large new plant facility.

Financing problems are many and varied and require expert advice. Above all, wise counsel should be obtained before embarking upon a large financing program.

SUMMARY

Good decision-making depends upon the intelligent use of the full range of analytical tools, plus a substantial degree of intuition. All business is a gamble, but it should be at least an educated gamble. The plan settled upon should ordinarily provide hedges against the more obvious risks. We at Commonwealth hedge our bets, for example, by trying to diversify our sources of fuel supply.

Executives must be quick to admit mistakes and be eager for criticism. Significant decisions should be fully accepted by the entire management team—a condition most easily met if all have participated in the decision-making process. Everyone on the team should recognize that the authorized plan has been carefully arrived at, and agree that it must be made to work!

PART IV-C
Marketing

THE TOP MARKETING EXECUTIVE

by Gerald A. Simon
Managing Director, Cambridge Research Institute*

As EVERY entrepreneur knows, corporate survival is utterly dependent upon the ability to serve markets, and it is maintained by the continuing ability to compete effectively in markets. That being the case, the marketing activity that goes on in private enterprises deserves the most thoughtful consideration by chief executives. Although this has always been the case, it is all the more true today. Our markets for both products and services often exhibit rapid and dramatic changes stemming from changes in tastes, increased government regulation, rising or falling cost structures, and new sources of competition. As technology becomes more complex and as new products continue to proliferate, such changes are bound to intensify.

One has only to think back over the past year or two to come up with a few examples of this dramatic change. In the electronic calculator business, technological efficiencies and their resultant downward effects on product costs and, consequently, upon prices, turned a fantastic growth business for dozens of companies into a lethal shakeout which only a handful of integrated producers survived. In several resource industries, most notably in the case of oil, cartel pricing almost overnight drove prices up and, in their market places, changed demand levels, customer mixes and competitive practices. There even came about secondary change effects in the markets served by the customers of those industries who use those materials in their own products and processes. Dozens of other companies experienced many of the same effects simply in consequence of the general serious inflation affecting the prices of both agricultural and industrial commodities.

Only for the most obdurately production-oriented companies is

* The author was aided in preparation of this chapter by John D. Glover, Lovett-Learned Professor of Business Administration, Harvard Business School, and by David Kiser, Associate, Cambridge Research Institute.

there any doubt that marketing matters are important enough to warrant a lot of attention from the Chief Executive Officer. Indeed, marketing is an important subdivision of the corporation's overall strategy, and as such must be a matter of the CEO's continuing pre-occupation with that overall strategy. Marketing strategy, inevitably, is interwoven with such overall considerations as whether the business is to be managed for profits or for growth, whether the product line is to be innovative or follower-oriented, and with the way in which the firm organizes itself to do business. Marketing, of course, is not alone in being of vital importance. So also are research, finance, production, and control, all of which also compete for the chief executive's attention. But it is in marketing where the company's effectiveness or weakness is likely to be most perceptible and likely to show up first.

As in other functions of the business, however, the CEO must work through others when it comes to marketing. And that means he cannot avoid the need for delegating the responsibility for much of the marketing job to somebody else. If he is an old marketing hand, himself, he will understand that job very well—perhaps better than the present marketing chief. (He may, in fact, be tempted to meddle too much, for that very reason.) If he is not, the job of marketing may strike him as somewhat mysterious, and he may overdelegate. A way of conceiving of the marketing task may make the job seem far less mysterious and may help him to understand better not only the job, but the person who is doing it. And it may help him to evaluate how well that job is being done.

DIVISION OF LABOR: THE CEO AND HIS TOP MARKETING EXECUTIVE

In firms large enough that the chief executive recognizes that he cannot handle the job himself no matter what his background and interests and, therefore, has a top marketing executive on his team, the relationship between the two is apt to be a close and personal one. The two executives are likely to adapt to each other's strengths and weaknesses as they work together to manage the marketing effort. Where such a relationship exists and is operating smoothly, it should, by all means, be allowed to continue. No formal description of duties or mechanical separation of roles could hope to improve very much, if at all, on the effectiveness of a comfortable relationship.

In the very largest firms, however, such a *personal* working relationship may be much less needed as well as more difficult to achieve. Here it really is necessary that the chief executive and the top marketing executive make clear what each is to expect from the other. It is no less important that other members of the management team also understand that relationship. Because the principal concern of the chief executive (corporate strategy) and the principal concern of the marketing executive (marketing strategy) need to fit together compatibly, and because there may well be some overlap between them, it becomes especially important to avoid duplication of effort between the two executives. From a human and personal standpoint they, and others, will find it highly useful to delineate with care a meaningful "sphere of influence" or territoriality for each of them that makes sense and is comfortable to both. The skill with which the Chief Executive Officer structures and evaluates the top marketing executive's job can play a major part in determining the extent to which the marketing activity is consistent with other corporate objectives. When the functional and overall strategies of the firm are logically consistent, the CEO has come a long way toward setting the course of the firm in the near term. A clear definition can also help give the top marketing person a well defined charter and mandate, within which he can release his full energy and capabilities.

In my experience, a chief executive simply cannot evaluate a top-level marketing executive—as a *marketing* leader—without also assessing the marketing strategy of the firm. Of course, there are some general assessments of any executive which can be made independently of his tasks: how well he performs against measurable objectives; how well he sees beyond the details of his job to understand the fundamentals of the business; how well he leads and motivates his subordinates; and how well he provides himself with sufficient information to make good judgments and to anticipate changes in his area of responsibility. But for assessing the top marketing executive, these are not enough. The CEO needs to be able to judge also whether the substance of the marketing activity of the firm is reasonable and makes sense. Only in that context can he then evaluate the ability of his top marketing executive to formulate and implement specific aspects of the overall marketing strategy, to change them when necessary, and to allocate resources properly among them.

To assist the Chief Executive Officer in this task, I have identified a number of analytical frameworks I have found useful in testing the marketing strategy of the firm.[1] Some of these will no doubt be familiar to the reader. Others may seem familiar, even if they are used in a different way. These simple frameworks can be helpful to the CEO not only in thinking about his firm and its strategy, but also as he works to enhance the depth of his understanding of his top marketing executive. These are the frameworks I have in mind, and which I shall take up in the rest of this chapter:

1. The marketing mix;
2. The industry anatomy;
3. The product/customer mix; and
4. The marketplace characteristics.

THE MARKETING MIX

The various marketing activities of the firm, taken in combination, are collectively known as the "marketing mix." They are an interrelated "bundle," so to speak, that collectively make up the company's marketing effort. The mix includes: product, pricing, promotion, personal selling, channels of distribution, and branding. For an individual firm, a description of the particular nature of each of these activities, and of the roles and relative emphasis in the overall assigned to each, constitutes a description of the firm's marketing strategy. Moreover, each of the separate elements of the mix interact strongly with the others. They are a group and are best thought of as a *system* of interacting components.* The several components are not only interrelated and present important trade-off alternatives among themselves, but within each of them, as I shall point out, there are also likely to be important alternatives—as among different possible price structures. One of the great areas of skill and artistry in business is the selection of the particular elements within each of the components of the marketing mix and the balancing and harmonizing of the components of the overall mix.

---

[1] Although the discussion of marketing in this chapter is couched in the language of business and is placed in the context of the corporation, many of us recognize there are aspects of marketing that—with appropriate translation—are applicable to other kinds of organizations and institutions as well. I have in mind organizations in government, education, health care, religion, or other "nonbusiness" areas. In fact, the application of marketing concepts, analytic approaches, and skills to these areas of endeavor is an activity of growing importance in our increasingly service-oriented society.

* [Ed. Note: See, by way of a parallel, the chapter by Richard F. Cole, "The Director of Manufacturing: A Careful Look at Leadership."]

Product.   The marketing mix starts with the product itself. What *is* the product? What are all the dimensions and facets: purpose, features, performance characteristics, chemical and physical specifications, color, style, packaging, warranty, after-service, product *line* (as in various price ranges)? The design of a product, in all its dimensions, that will meet customers' needs and *sell* in a competitive market place is, perhaps, the key component in a successful marketing mix. But it is not the only important component. No matter what Emerson said about better mousetraps, the best mousetrap in the world won't get anywhere without support from the other components in the marketing mix.

Pricing.   Pricing has to do not only with the unit price, itself, of the product or service, but also with discount structures, terms of payment, and the use of credit, all of which are also part of the pricing structure. These other elements of pricing can be tremendously effective competitive tools, or they can confuse transactions unnecessarily. Of course, the firm's prices and pricing take into account unit costs, cost-volume relationships, competitive prices, and the intrinsic value of the product or service to the buyer.

Promotion.   Promotion includes all of the impersonal modes of communicating messages to users and middlemen regarding products and services offered: media advertising, direct mail, in-store point-of-purchase promotion, sales literature and catalogues, exhibits at trade fairs and conventions, and the like. Individual "promotions," as distinct from the whole effort of promotion, are specific programs of limited duration in which special product or service offerings are made. Such "promotions" often involve a reduced price or an offering of a combination of products or services at a total price less than the sum of the individual prices of the separate elements. They are best conceived and carried out as parts of a larger, encompassing effort, rather than as isolated or sporadic efforts.

Personal Selling.   This denotes the particular kind of personal selling activity involved in sales transactions. For some kinds of products or services "personal selling" may be no more than a simple annual sales call by telephone to replenish an inventory of thousands of units of an industrial component. Or, personal selling may mean frequent calls on various executives of a customer organization to sell a big ticket commercial item. Or it may mean door-to-door calls to sell brushes, cosmetics, or vacuum cleaners; or calls by a manufacturer's sales force on brokers, wholesalers, or retailers.

Channels of Distribution. Channels of distribution have to do with the movement and transfer of goods and services from producer to ultimate user. Channels include wholesalers and retailers, of course, but there are many other means of moving products along: brokers, commission merchants, mill-supply houses, direct selling, and so on. As in other components of the marketing mix, companies have alternatives as to the channels they use. A producer of hand tools may decide to utilize mill-supply houses rather than selling direct to manufacturing plants. A producer of consumer packaged goods may elect to sell to small retailers by means of mail order rather than through a direct sales force, or through independent representatives. Matters of warehousing, transfers of legal title to goods, and overall logistics of distribution come under the general heading of channels of distribution.

Branding. Branding has to do with the identification of goods and services as to their corporate origin or their familial relationship with other goods and services of similar origin. There are manufacturers' brands ("Ivory Soap," of Procter & Gamble) and retailers' brands ("Ann Page," of A&P Stores). There are family brands where a whole product line is identified by a simple name ("Chevrolet"); and there are brands devoted solely to a single product ("Coca-Cola"). There are well recognized brands in the field of producers' goods ("Caterpillar" tractors). And, there are unbranded goods, most of them fungible in nature, such as wheat and other grains, electrolytic copper, and basic chemicals such as sulfuric acid. What brands to use, if any, and how to use them is one of the areas of marketing in which intuition and experience seem to count very heavily.

Trade-Offs within Components of the Marketing Mix

As I suggested, within each of the components of the marketing mix—product, price, promotion personal selling, channels, branding—there are usually a number of alternatives. One of the jobs of marketing management is to see which of the possible elements are included within each of these components and how they are interrelated, and to select the "best" packages of elements in each of the components.

Consider the product itself. More performance or more style? Simpler design or more range of choices? Or in promotion: More media advertising or more exhibits in trade shows and conventions, or more direct mail? Higher unit price and steeper quantity discounts or the other way around? Lower discounts or more favorable credit terms? A low cost, less productive channel—manufacturer's agents working on commission, perhaps—or a higher cost, more productive one—maybe direct selling by a technically trained sales force.

Working through all these possible alternative trade-offs among the several elements within each of the components of the marketing mix, and then putting them all together—that is the name of the game in the design of marketing strategy.

The Mix as Part of a Strategic System

These components of the marketing mix are in fact, and are best thought of as interrelated parts of a coherent system. Among these components there are *interdependencies* and *tradeoffs*. A good example of interdependency can be seen in the case of a company in the business of selling consumer products door-to-door. They have one of the hottest mixes I've ever come across. Their top quality product is sold through demonstrations to the consumer in the home. Because of the attention the product generates, it commands a premium price. The door-to-door selling, combined with the premium price, avoids the expense of selling through middlemen and generates a much higher than average operating margin for the firm. But because the direct sales force is the key to sales generation, much of the higher margin goes to them in the form of healthy sales commissions. These tend to induce the salesmen to stay with the firm, and this tends to reduce training and recruiting costs, and to maintain a high quality of salesmanship in the sales people. The company handles its own logistics, factory to user. The mix hangs together beautifully. As a result, the firm is immensely successful. Clearly, no one component of this mix should be altered without the most careful attention being given to the possible impact of that change on each and all of the other components.

The same company provides an illustration that there are significant tradeoffs between components of the mix. Because the components interact in a web of interrelationships, one must constantly bear in mind possible interactions: If you "push in here," it will "come out there"! For example, some years ago, the management of the firm experimented for the first time with the use of consumer advertising in national magazines. It was thought that the higher advertising costs would be more than balanced off by reduced selling costs. That was the tradeoff the management was thinking of. If, indeed, the time taken by salesmen in acquainting consumers with the product could be reduced, the productivity of personal selling would be increased; the sales force would perceive, and be motivated by greater company support, and attrition of valuable members of the sales force would be reduced. Because the experiment was conceived with tradeoffs in mind between the components of the company's mix, it made sense to try it. (The effort did reduce personal selling time, incidentally.)

The important thing to recognize is that a marketing mix must be tailored to the particular circumstances of a specific firm. It is not good enough to pattern one firm's mix after another's in the same industry, or after that of a firm in a different industry but with similar market share. Each firm's situation needs to be examined individually and specifically.

At the same time, there probably is no one perfect mix—no one, simple optimizing answer for a firm. Almost always there are alternate mixes which, conceivably, could be used to achieve the same strategic objectives. And, anyway, an appropriate mix today can soon become inappropriate as market conditions change.

Management of the Marketing Mix

It is the responsibility of the top marketing officer to formulate, propose, and develop the marketing mix. The top marketing officer should also assume leadership as to the development, provision, and application of key information which will enable the chief executive to assess objectively the mix and the calibre of the marketing people who are working under the mix.

On his part, the Chief Executive Officer should know what the mix is, and why; what the alternatives were and why the various choices were made as they were. He should see how the marketing strategy fits in with overall strategy. And, he should either support the marketing strategy or see that it is changed. The CEO is a central participant, if not (along with the board of directors) the final authority over policy decisions affecting the mix. If he does not agree he should not blindly force his own judgment upon the marketing executive, but should discuss his reasoning, perhaps with the assistance of others, until a consensus can be reached. If the difference can be settled by facts which are missing, such should be acquired. If it is a question of judgment, it should be so recognized and a clear decision reached as to whose judgment is to be relied upon and why. Eventually, the emerging mix should stand the tests of tough factual analysis, internal consistency, timeliness, and relevance in the light of market realities.

The chief executive will also insure that the top marketing executive has the final say over the kinds of internal information he needs and gets in order to develop the mix, rather than letting a controller make this judgment. The latter may not know, understand, or be concerned with what marketing people need. He may tend to provide information which is accounting and cost-oriented, when what is needed for marketing decisions and performance assessment is information much more oriented to the economics of decision-making.

Only recently a railroad faced this very problem. A marketer needed information on the *incremental* contributions to overhead and to profit per ton-mile for various commodities and types of equipment in order to design the basis for a new, more profitable rail service. All the information he could get from the numbers people, however, were profit data based upon railroad system *averages* which reflected fully allocated overhead costs and which were designed primarily for accounting, regulatory reporting, and cost control purposes. In another case, a well-known consumer products firm moved to a decentralized management of sales and profits by product line, but neglected to provide the product managers with data reflecting the per-unit marketing margin over variable costs. Once these problems were relieved, the marketing executives, and the marketing strategy became increasingly more effective.

THE INDUSTRY ANATOMY

A second framework for viewing the top marketing job is that of "industry anatomy." By this term, I refer to the structure of activities in which the industry is engaged, all the way from basic inputs through all forms of processing and transportation, storage, and distribution to the point where products are turned over to customers or users. This anatomy or structure includes all the organizational forms established for carrying them out, and the relationships which are maintained between the various entities and sectors of the industry. For example, establishments within an industry will differ according to various characteristics, such as the functions they perform, their ownership, size, and location. Between the establishments there is a flow of outputs from some that are inputs for others. These flows take the form of products and services. Flowing back, in the other direction, are streams of monetary payments and receipts. In each establishment, one or more conversions take place: goods are physically modified, costs are incurred, and value is added through labor and mechanized equipment.

All of these elements in the "anatomy" of practically all of our industries are changing over time. Systematic identification and projection of patterns of change, which are observable in every industry, can be immensely important to a chief executive and his top marketing executive for several reasons.

First of all, understanding the anatomy of industry, and its dynamics, is an important step in reaching a deepened understanding of "what business" a firm is really in. A particular product is often merely a specific manifestation of a means of meeting a generic need. Is a steel company in the business of selling *steel* or providing building and fabricating materials? Are its competitors primarily other steel companies—or producers of cement, glass, or aluminum and plastics? How should the managers be thinking about the company, its customers, and its competitors? Issues of business definition such as these are largely a function of the dynamics of *needs of customers*, *markets* and *competition* among those offering means for satisfying those needs. These are aspects of industry anatomy which a top marketing executive needs to understand fully. Seeing and thinking about a company in the context of a dynamic anatomy of an industry defined in functional rather than traditional terms can be a major step in rethinking its own definition and reformulating its strategy more effectively in tune with changing realities.

Second, most company marketing departments are skilled in collecting, organizing, and making available external information that is useful in policy formulation for the firm. Industry anatomy represents an extension of the marketing department's historical role as the provider of marketing research. Responsibility for describing and analyzing industry anatomy deserves explicit assignment within the company, to insure that adequate analysis of the business environment is undertaken as a prelude to strategic planning. If there is a strong market research interest and capability in the company, a very good place in the organization for this kind of work may be in the marketing department.[2]

Third, much as knowledge of human anatomy increases our understanding of the processes which occur inside the human body, so study of industry anatomy can augment an appreciation of the dynamics of the processes that go on in an industry. For example, it is often meaningful to attempt to predict what kinds of changes will occur in an industry after a major competitive or technological shift has taken place. A major new entrant into an industry, a significant product innovation, or a takeover of an important market share where the impact of the change is likely to be felt across the entire industry as well as by some individual firm, are matters well worth understanding in as much depth as possible. Figuring out what the consequences may be is a lot easier if one has well mapped out the anatomy of the industry and has determined what the principal dynamics are and how they work.

Finally, a knowledge of industry anatomy is of tremendous value in designing the marketing mix. The numbers and natures of the firm's suppliers, competitors, distributors, and customers need very much to be clearly understood when decisions are to be made as to product design, pricing, promotion, channels, and the other components of the marketing mix. Even in such a down-to-earth matter as location of warehousing points, decisions are likely to be effective in proportion as they take into account not only the firm's own transportation costs, but, perhaps even more important, the location of plants and warehouses of competitors, innovations in packaging and production scheduling and, especially, changing needs of customers. In this way, the facts of industry anatomy become major inputs to the decisions which produce an effective marketing strategy.

The Chief Executive Officer inevitably has ultimate responsibility in the resolution of the kinds of issues which come to surface through careful study of industry anatomy. For, not only are the issues major ones for marketing, but for other functions of the business as well, including plant design and location, plant expansion, acquisitions, to name but a few. *The top marketing executive can make a major contribution to strategy formulation by taking the lead in gathering information, producing analyses, and drawing implications from the detailed picture of a changing industry anatomy,* just as he does in

---

[2] See the chapter by J. D. Glover, "Strategic Decision-Making: Planning, Manning, Organization."

connection with developing a well integrated and targeted marketing mix.

THE PRODUCT/CUSTOMER MIX

A third useful analytical framework for viewing the top marketing executive's job in the context of marketing strategy is the product/customer mix. By this term, I mean the fraction of unit sales, dollar sales, and profits for each product which is accounted for by each customer. The concept is handy for many purposes. Knowing what are the bread and butter products in the whole line, and which specific customers are important to profits, and watching the trends therein can help the firm identify its own major strengths and weaknesses. Discovering that a particular product is relatively high in unit sales but relatively low in profits may be a signal for product-line changes. It may suggest deletion of the product, new product development, simplification of the product line, or repricing. If some customers produce lots of servicing requirements, or even substantial sales volumes but do not contribute in proportion to profits, questions arise as to the effectiveness of the company's selling efforts, or even the merits of its products.

In diversified companies, it is especially useful to keep an eye on how the different parts of the business contribute to sales and profits. A recent story in *Business Week* told of how Dart Industries, a company with sales of $1.2 billion, had reached a point where the firm's Tupperware line of interlocking plastic bowls and cannisters accounted for 26 percent of sales, but 50 percent of net income.[3] The story went on, because of the disparity of the two figures, to raise important questions as to whether other areas of Dart were deficient or marginal operations, and what should be done about them.

Where customer groups or market segments are identified as low contributors to company profitability, it does not, of course, automatically follow that they should be lopped off. By the nature of things, there is almost always an uneven distribution of sales and profits among products and customers. A large fraction of sales is often accounted for by a small number of items in a product line. This phenomenon is sometimes referred to as the "Pareto's Curve" effect. Concentrations of 80 percent of a firm's profits derived from 20

[3] *Business Week*, May 5, 1975, pp. 63–64.

percent of its customers are not altogether unusual.[4] Such a concentration may or may not be cause for alarm; it could be a normal condition for a particular industry or market segment. But it does call for the most searching marketing thought as to its implications.

The top marketing officer is not the only one interested in knowing about the product/customer mix. (So, also, is the financial officer, among others.) But, the ball falls in his court. The CEO will recognize this and make it *the responsibility of the top marketing officer to provide timely information and analysis of the product/customer mix*. It is not easy to come up with an effective marketing strategy in the absence of such information and analyses.

THE MARKETPLACE CHARACTERISTICS

The marketplace is a fourth analytical framework for viewing the top marketing job. The marketplace is where your customers are, or your hoped-for customers. Sometimes it is also where your customers' customers are, if you need to take them into account, as you may if your product is a key input for your customer. Customers are the object of every marketing mix. They are the "bottom line" of every industry structure. They figure in the product/customer mix. The marketplace is where purchase decisions are made.

Understanding the marketplace is understanding:

Who and where the customers are; are they migrating, perhaps?

When, where, and how they buy.

Why they buy or don't buy.

What are the major influences on their buying?

Who the competitors are.

How they compete and why.

What trends are apparent in product styles and performance, prices, warranties, and so on.

These are the facts of the marketplace.

Customers are *people*—whether they are housewives shopping in a supermarket, or corporate chief executives or purchasing agents, or executives in nonprofit or governmental institutions. And, obviously, firms strive to know as much about them as possible.

---

[4] See the chapter by James W. Wilcock, "Product Engineering."

It is axiomatic that successful marketing strategies are based on a factual understanding of the marketplace. Much like aerial photo reconaissance, periodic statistical and qualitative "pictures" of the marketplace are employed to identify customers, competitors, changing behavior patterns, and other important elements of that important economic and business arena. The purpose of this periodic reconaissance, of course, is to get as firm data as one can for use in the design of components and elements in the marketing mix, including the design of product offerings and of promotional messages to fit the specific emerging circumstances.

Providing market facts and understanding of changes in marketplaces are, of course, the traditional province of marketing research departments. Recent developments in these kinds of activities include various mathematical modeling approaches, such as of consumer brand choice decisions. Models are being developed of demographic and business trends in metropolitan areas. Fundamental trends in the social, economic, political, and technological environment and their effects on consumers and companies are being examined as a basis for anticipating what the future marketplace will be like and where! Models offering promise of predictive value have already been developed and are being refined and improved still further.

The determination of just what kinds of market facts a firm should have is one of the things a CEO expects from a top marketing officer. In the event of a marketing failure, such as a withdrawal of a new product from the marketplace, a CEO can ask about the adequacy of the market facts that were the basis for the plans that were drawn up to develop and introduce the product. The particular array of data useful in portraying a marketplace will, of course, depend upon the particular circumstances of the firm, its products, and available analytical and projective techniques. This is an area where creativity and technical skill in the top marketing executive will make a world of difference.

PUTTING IT ALL TOGETHER

These four frameworks can help a chief executive think more effectively about his firm's marketing activity and to examine it more comprehensively than perhaps he could without some such conceptual apparatus. With this apparatus, he not only will have tools useful in evaluating the company's marketing strategy, but he will also have a structure for examining and evaluating the performance of his top marketing officer. They will help him make this analysis and evaluation, not in just a general overall and not very well focussed way, but specifically, area by area—one after another—over the range of the whole marketing job.

We have seen that the marketing mix of a firm is the basic expression of its marketing strategy. And this, of course, is a major component of the overall corporate strategy. Evaluating the performance of the top marketing executive, which is a major responsibility of any CEO, is not merely a matter of looking at the bottom line. Even a "fat" figure may represent mediocre performance in a great growth situation. If the CEO can understand how those results came about, area by area, he can do a far more perceptive job of evaluation. Not only that: He may be of more help to the top marketer even if he—or she—is not an old marketing hand himself.

Using these kinds of frameworks can help the CEO not only to understand and to evaluate knowingly the performance of the top marketer and the marketing arm of the firm as a whole, it should help him gauge the capacity of the whole management team to capitalize on opportunities and to adapt to change.

Finally, using this kind of a conceptual apparatus to think about the firm may help the CEO to see more clearly his own role in, and contribution to, management's strategic decision-making. To the extent that the CEO enhances his own understanding of these important aspects of the business, he will also gain in his understanding of his own capacity for guiding the destiny of the firm.

THE MARKETING MIX

by Richard L. Gelb

President, Bristol-Myers Company

THIS CHAPTER will be written from the point of view of the CEO of a diversified, multiproduct, consumer package goods company operating on a relatively highly decentralized divisional basis. Inherent in this type of organizational structure is the fact that the traditional elements of the marketing mix are basically managed at the divisional level by the marketing managers who are closely supervised by their divisional presidents. The divisional marketing decisions run the gamut from the development of a new product, the extension of an existing brand into a related category, product formula changes, packaging changes, and advertising copy decisions, to changes in product pricing and consumer promotions. Decisions must be made on whether selling effort should be placed against the consumer or against the wholesaler or retail outlet. Research departments must be managed intelligently and productively. Test markets for new products must be organized and national plans formulated. These, plus other variables must all be faced by the marketing executive, and in a company that has perhaps 100 different brands it is quite clear that the CEO cannot and should not be involved other than on an exception basis. A CEO who has himself come up the marketing route has to be particularly careful that he does not get himself overinvolved in marketing decisions that can be made at a lower level.

However, even though the CEO does not get involved in the traditional marketing problems, he will find himself actively engaged in the constantly changing world of marketing policy. This statement presumes that the CEO sees his company striving for certain goals and standing for certain things. It presumes that the CEO believes his company should be more than a purely financial holding company and that divisional objectives may at times have to be sacrificed for corporate objectives. The CEO who sees his role as that of a strategist, utilizing his company's strengths and strengthening his company's weaknesses can, and should be engaged in a wide variety of policy decisions in the marketing area. However, those are not the decisions of the marketing specialist, but rather the marketing decisions of a well-informed generalist who knows where he wants his company to go.

For example, the CEO must determine what consumer markets he wants his company to be in. Having made the decision, he must determine whether to achieve a position in that category by acquisition or by internal expansion. If by acquisition, he must select the proper candidate; and if successful in acquisition, he must decide where in the organization the new company will go: Should it fold into an existing division or group, or should it become a new entity reporting directly to corporate headquarters? On the other hand, if internal growth into the new category is indicated, then which division has the best credentials to do the job, and are they prepared to do it? An effective CEO will find that he spends a great deal of his time negotiating with his divisional presidents in order to achieve his goals, and very little time will be spent issuing direct orders. I might add that, even though an organization may appear to have a military structure and even though military terms like divisions, lieutenants, and the like may be used, I have found that, at least in our company, the resemblance ends there. Although the CEO has the ultimate power to issue a direct order, if he has to issue very many, then his company is probably in trouble.

The CEO may also have to make basic decisions as to what general marketing areas his divisions should stick to. What happens if he learns that three divisions have each decided to enter the mouthwash business? Does he let each one go its own way and see how it works out or does he say "We have limited time and limited money and I think the Y division is best equipped, so I'll let them go ahead."

Another basic marketing decision is what the relationship of sales and profits should be. Should sales be the prime goal, with the assumption that profits will follow? Or should sales be sacrificed if they cannot produce the required corporate return? The CEO must decide on the levels of profitability he expects his company to achieve. He must also assign his divisions realistic goals that reflect their capabilities in the marketplace and that also reflect corporate goals.

The CEO may often be faced with this type of marketing decision: His company's profit goal is a 15 percent increase over the previous year. One division has a runaway best-selling product that would become even bigger if the division were to be relieved of its profit objective so it could spend more marketing dollars against the brand. Should the CEO give this division profit relief? If so, should he do it, and lower the corporate profit goals for this year in anticipation of a larger reward in the future? If he is not willing to do that, can he realistically turn to the other divisions and ask them to raise their profit objectives? And if so, what will be the long- and short-term impact of that action?

As times change, basic marketing principles can change. For example, years ago it was rather commonplace for a company to develop a new brand and spend so heavily in the first and second years of its life that this investment might not be fully recouped for five years. Today, although this approach may be sound for a high-technology product breakthrough with a fairly high degree of fixed investment needed, it may be totally improper for a more run-of-the-mill new product based on a minor formula change in a market with high accessibility and great ease of entry for competition. The CEO must be alert to this type of change and may often have to be the one to implement it.

Although I indicated earlier that traditional marketing decisions must be delegated, I expect our divisional people to keep me posted on certain types of basic information. I am interested in sales of our major brands, not just in absolute numbers, but in relation to the growth of the market and our share position within that market. In these days of high inflation, it's particularly important to keep track of your unit sales as well as dollar sales. For example, I am particularly interested in any new success achieved by a competitive brand that's doing well in any of the major product categories we're active in. And I want to know what the concerned division is planning to do about it. Is new technology involved and, if so, can we match it? Is, perhaps, a change in marketing strategy called for?

Advertising copy is a "fun" area of our business. Everybody is a born copywriter. The CEO must take special pains to stay away from that temptation. However, I believe the CEO does have a role to play in deciding whether any of the brand advertising may be in conflict with government regulations, existing advertising codes, or his own feelings of what is proper and in good taste.

If the CEO sees any company advertising that basically offends him, then, I believe, he should step in and do something about it. Today, particularly, a great deal of advertising is under fire from government and from the consumer movement, and very often the CEO is the only person who can make a fundamental decision. For example, in past years there was great pressure to take children's vitamin advertising out of children's TV programming. Although a very strong case could be made as to why children's vitamin advertising should be left on the air, it was taken off, and that was a decision only the CEO could make. The divisional executives charged with sales and profit performance knew that such a decision would seriously hurt their business; but they were not really charged with the responsibility of determining the impact that a "leave-it-on-television decision" would have on the corporation. However, the CEO did have to weigh governmental and consumer attitudes toward his company and make a decision which in effect said, "I'll relieve you of your profit responsibility, because I believe the total corporation can be hurt unless we remove this advertising from the air."

This type of decision has become, and will become more frequent in the future. As it arises, the CEO will always be involved, and not only as it affects advertising, but in all parts of the company's business.

For example, if the use of packaging material comes under question, what should the corporate posture be? Ten years ago, you could probably have said, "It will all blow over. Let's do nothing." Today, the chances are it won't go away. But what should you do? Wait and see? Start using different materials? Let each division go its own way? Or communicate a corporate policy which says, "We will, as a company, move out of this material as quickly as we can." Only the CEO can set the definitive corporate policy.

During the past ten years, the pressures on business have changed drastically. The rise of a strong and vocal consumer activist movement, tighter government regulations, and the growing concern for a cleaner and healthier environment, have all become major components for the CEO to incorporate into his marketing mix.

I believe the companies that perform well in this changing marketing environment will be those which recognize the opportunities implicit in change rather than those which concentrate solely on the obstacles which change presents. To the chief executive falls the responsibility to see that his company recognizes the profound social changes which are taking place around it and that it meets the new needs which arise from those changes.

CLEARING THE HURDLES OF NEW PRODUCT INTRODUCTION

by John M. Fox
President, H. P. Hood Inc.

THE PROFITABLE life span of many, if not most of the items in a company's line of products is becoming shorter and shorter in duration. There was a time when management could rest comfortably for years on a product that had attained satisfactory user acceptance, that had developed adequate sales volume to assure low-cost production, and for which improvements in product performance, packaging innovation, labelling modernization, and the like had not been neglected. Such is no longer the case.

There are exceptions, of course. Coca-Cola rolls merrily along. Wrigley's gum and Campbell's tomato soup are nearly unchallenged in their respective predominance in the consumer's minds. For the most part, however, the stiffening competitive forces coupled with the technological advances that exist in our present-day business environment make it imperative that a constant stream of new and innovative product concepts emerge from our corporate labs and development departments to replace the items that will wear out and fall by the wayside. "Product fatigue" at an increasingly early stage is becoming more and more the standard of behavior in industry today.

Therefore, this chapter will attempt to deal with the need for new product conception and the role of the chief executive in this extremely vital corporate activity.

SOME ASSUMPTIONS

There are a number of important assumptions that must be established in treating the subject of new product introduction.

Of prime importance is the "attitude" of the board of directors, the

CEO, and the top management team. A determination must be made as to whether the company needs to be, wants to be, and can afford to be a "growth" company. In spite of pious statements by most managements that the strategy of growth is paramount in their planning, there are indeed some firms that don't have the human or financial resources to mount an effective new product development program. Instances abound where a strategy of "fast following" is not only the prudent, but also the practical course to follow.

Internal or "organic" growth is both glamorous and desirable, particularly in the eyes of the investment community. Witness the relatively high P/E's that the Polaroids, the Xeroxes, the 3Ms and the IBMs traditionally command. Growth from within requires, however, unique strengths in the departments of research and marketing, not to mention the balance sheet. I shall treat these areas in more detail later.

In dealing with the subject of new products, a definition is required. Our meaning of the phrase encompasses a truly new item such as the Xerox copier; a truly new business such as the solid state transistor industry developed by Bell Labs; a truly new service such as the financial service innovations launched by Bank of America; or a truly new system of manufacturing or distribution as exemplified by Henry Ford's mass production line; or Clarence Saunders's invention of the supermarket.

What I do *not* mean to deal with here is a "me too" item or service, a style change, a new logo, a new package design, a minor product formulation improvement or a "sensational" new flavor of a traditional product. Such innovations, if they can be called that, are important but they do not represent the thrust of this author's opinion about new product development.

PREREQUISITES FOR SUCCESSFUL NEW PRODUCT PROGRAMS

It is my conviction that there are a couple of key prerequisites that a company must possess if it aspires to success in the tricky field of real product innovation.

The number one prerequisite is that the company must be "innovation oriented." This sounds obvious and simple, but it's not. To be "innovation oriented," the top management must really believe in, and truly understand innovation. They must encourage it at all levels and support it at the top. It is the antithesis of "care-taking." It implies unusual combinations of courage and judgment at the highest level of management. To be "innovation oriented," a company must have a management that is not only capable of accepting change but knows the secret of encouraging it and rewarding it.

Innovation must be managed quite differently from the routine operations of the business. Not only must the planning and direction be more skillful and sensitive, but the measurement and accounting must be done quite differently than in the rest of the business.

The planning or strategic aspect of an innovative business starts out with the assumption that the present product lines are on the way out and must definitely be replaced. This is quite different from the governing strategy of the ongoing business which is to strengthen and optimize the product lines that already exist.

Similarly, the accounting conventions for an innovative business concept must be quite different from those employed in an ongoing element of a company. The latter requires mental exercises involving alternatives that *minimize* investment and maximize early results. The management of innovation requires different goals and different judgments. The odds of final success become the decision criterion. If the odds look good, it becomes paramount that the best, and not the cheapest route be sought, and that the ablest, not just the adequate people be devoted to the project.

The company must be structured for innovation. It is not realistic to expect that an organizational structure designed to manage ongoing businesses can at the same time ride herd on the totally different set of circumstances that pertain to creating the new businesses and the new products of the future. Each task is a big and important one—each requires special talents and special dedications. Rarely do they mix well. The truly successful "innovation factories" such as Du Pont, the 3Ms, or the World War II Manhattan Project realized this truth and set up their creative units outside of the daily breadwinners, in the case of the above companies, and outside of the existing academic and governmental structure in the case of General Groves's vehicle that created the atom bomb.

There must exist within the company a "risk tolerance" and accompanying iron nerves to take the high failure rate that is inevitable. It is estimated that only one or two out of ten projects really make it—the balance fail with varying degrees of monetary and mental pain.

For example, there have been any number of attempts to bring a successful freeze-dried food product to market. The writer himself has been involved in "white hopes" for a freeze-dried orange juice and a line of freeze-dried salad ingredients. Both ventures went down in flames. Finally, after nearly 20 years of promise and failure, a successful freeze-dried coffee saw the light of day and has now taken its place as an important item on the grocery store shelves.

As another prerequisite for a company which intends to launch successful new products is the existence of a strong entrepreneurial streak in the top management generally, but in the CEO particularly. This instinct is much more the key to successful product creation than administrative aptitude. I subscribe to Peter Drucker's premise that the two basic entrepreneurial functions of any business are marketing and innovation. In Drucker's opinion, these functions alone produce results—all the rest are "costs."

The day of the individual entrepreneurs is not completely gone, but they are becoming mighty scarce. However, this important source of new concepts has been largely replaced by the corporate entity, and the latter must learn how to behave in a fashion similar to the Firestones and Edisons of yesterday.

The key characteristic of the entrepreneur is the ability and propensity to turn his back on the traditional, the tried, and the established production or system and to embrace wholeheartedly the new and different. He is not only prepared to, but relishes in sloughing off the known. The entrepreneur, be he a man or a company, creates the tomorrow.

For many companies, the acceptance of the idea that the firm's business tomorrow will be different, perhaps vastly different, from what it is today comes hard. But come it must, that acceptance, philosophically and with conviction, or the necessary drive for change will be lacking.

THE MODUS OPERANDI OF NEW PRODUCT INTRODUCTION

The Search

Where do the ideas for new products come from? The simple answer is, "Find a need and then fill it." Unfortunately, like most simplistic solutions to complex problems, you quickly come a cropper with this one when you ask the obvious questions: What determines there is a need that is unfilled? Or where do you look for needs that can be filled profitably? Or how do you make certain that the needs that are out there waiting to be filled won't be overlooked by your people? These are difficult questions to treat with. The key thing is to keep the minds and the channels open in those areas in the company from which you expect new product performance. The most important mind and channel to be kept open is that of the CEO.

New product ideas and concepts come from everywhere. From within the company, one of the richest sources is the ranks of the junior executives. They are usually energetic and ambitious. They for the most part are better educated and are, in fact, brighter than most of us were at their age. But mostly they haven't been around long enough to know all the reasons why something can't be done or why some product won't ever sell.

Our sales departments are a most logical source of creative ideas. These people are in close contact with the trade and are, or should be very aware of the wants and needs of the customers or clients.

Not to be overlooked, however, are the ideas that come from outside the organization. It is in this area that the CEO must be vigilant to spot the "N.I.H." syndrome. N.I.H. stands for "Not Invented Here," and it is far too prevalent in many organizations. There is a natural tendency for our people to look down their highly-trained noses at anything coming from "outsiders" that bears on the industry or business we are in.

The role of the CEO and/or top management in this early stage is very important. Almost without exception, new ideas are "impractical" at the conception. Someone at the top must have the vision and above all patience to convert these "hare-brained" schemes into reality. It takes skill and real brainpower to organize the wildest ideas into a realm of feasibility.

The Screening

With any sizeable organization there will be, and should be a substantial number of new concepts for products or services flowing into the company constantly. To deal with this flow in an orderly fashion, careful thought by the top management must be given to the overall corporate strategy. From this will emerge the company's unique screening criteria.

Some of the considerations that should be included in the development of these criteria are:

a.   The degree of "fit" with existing facilities and/or skills.
b.   The technical feasibility as it pertains to the company and its resources.
c.   The legal and patent aspects of the concept.
d.   Potential size of market; rate of growth; market share targets; the competitive outlook now and for the future; and distribution requirements.
e.   Financial criteria involving pay-out times, ROI, cash flow estimates, and other elements of risk.

A written checklist is essential, not as a final determinant but as a useful device to rank the relative merits of a series of opportunities.

Wherever possible it is very desirable to find a "sponsor" for the project within a going division. However, the lack of enthusiasm on the part of a logical profit-center sponsor should not "screen out" a likely candidate.

Some companies are beginning to use computer models to assist in the screening process. The writer has not had any personal experience with the idea, so I can only surmise that the cost of building the model and keeping it current could be high; and I suspect that until computers are developed with "judgment," the machine will not replace a thoughtful, experienced executive.

The role of the CEO at this stage is one of deep involvement in the determination of strategy, concern over the completeness and consistencies of the criteria, and the encouragement of, but not dependency on sponsorship.

The Concept

A relatively new idea in the innovation procedure is that of concept-testing. The basic scheme is to try out the product or service conceptually before a panel of people representing a cross section of potential customers. This "jury method" is helpful in that it forces the innovator to define precisely what he is innovating and why, and to describe the desirable features of his innovation rather precisely. It has the further rather obvious feature of affirming or negating cheaply, quickly, and relatively securely from competitive knowledge, the existence of a need to be filled.

Useful as the concept-testing procedure undoubtedly is, care must be exercised in the interpretation made of the "jury's" response. Too much can be read from it, and enthusiasm does not always bode a great winner. However, a largely negative reaction should not be ignored.

Some of the elements of a new product idea that cannot be determined fully in advance are:

a.   The very important taste factor in food.
b.   The "product-fatigue" factor—the new item that loses its novel appeal too quickly.
c.   The subtle hurdles of timing and trends that spell doom for a new product. Don't forget, the Edsel was concept-tested to a fare-thee-well before it was introduced.

The role of the CEO at this early stage is primarily one of encouragement and support. Many new product ideas get shot down in the concept phase—and should be. Because of this high level of mortality, the boss must be particularly lavish with his optimism and his praise to keep the troops from taking a "what's-the-use" attitude.

The Invention

Next comes the actual creation of the product from the idea or concept stage. Here the research organization takes over. A most important element at this point is a truly honest assessment of the capabilities, both human and physical, that are available in-house. The natural tendency of many technical people to reach beyond their skills, and thus to assume research responsibility upon which they really can't deliver, must be guarded against. Sometimes the research role is best done if farmed out—but that's often a hard pill for the company R&D director to swallow.

Before a single test-tube is filled or a microscope focused, the project budget must be developed. Budgetary discipline comes hard for the scientific fraternity, but here the CEO must truly lay down the law with definitive written policies covering the practice. Otherwise, you'll be amazed at the magnitude of the financial rat-hole that can result. The budget should spell out the timing of the expenditures as precisely as practical, and progress reviews should be set up to coincide with this schedule.

The review stage will require a high level of managerial judgment.

For it's here that the ever-optimistic researcher will request the extra funds to reach the goal which will quite often be "just around the corner." And the trouble is that every now and then it is. It must be constantly kept in mind that research cannot be programmed like a computer, and allowances must be made for delays and setbacks that can never be fully anticipated. However, at some point a "loser" must be recognized, and in spite of the inevitable reassurances that the "corner" is nearby, the unsuccessful search must be turned off.

As the new product begins to emerge, when it does, at a fairly early stage it should be exposed to tests by a small focus group of typical users. This prototype testing may be required over and over as flaws are exposed and the item sent back for correction. These first focus groups are quite often in-house employees whose regular function may have nothing whatsoever to do with product research. For instance, at Procter & Gamble, one of the most thorough and careful new product innovators in the world, I understand they have a Hair Care Evaluation Center where female employees are currently having half their hair washed with a new shampoo P&G is developing, and the other half with their regular brand as a control. They even have in-house breath and armpit sniffers to test their new mouthwash and deodorant entries.

At this so-called "invention" stage, the CEO's role is a combination of disciplinarian and cheerleader. The hard ground rules of the financial guidelines must be laid down and monitored, but words and acts of encouragement and support are equally essential. Good innovators are quite often highly emotional individuals. As such, their moods tend to cycle more violently than the rest of us. The CEO can and should be watchful for the periods of discouragement and frustration that will occur with his inventing cadre. A few words of praise and overt signs of interest on his part will have great positive impact on the morale of these key people.

The Market Test

After the new product has cleared the hurdles of the focus group, in-house and/or outside, the standard tool next employed is the market test. This step is particularly pertinent in the world of consumer goods and is considered absolutely essential with food introductions. Its use unfortunately does not apply to many new products where surprise and style are keys to success. And, for tooling and marketing reasons, I presume, a new generation of computers or a new design of a kitchen stove combining a microwave oven with a regular one could not be market tested in the food industry fashion.

However, where so much financial investment in advertising, distribution, and placement costs, and inventory build-up is involved, the usual and accepted procedure is to take the product to three of four carefully delineated geographic market areas for the acid test—to find out if the ultimate consumer agrees with your innovators.

In addition to learning whether you do indeed have a product for which there will be a *repeating* market, many other important marketing and distribution options are available for comparison. Advertising strategies and weight are important items that can be compared. Pricing and competitive positioning can be checked for effect on sales. Volume potential indications usually emerge although there may be some surprises here, as I will describe later. Alternative distribution systems are sometimes compared. Obviously all of the above cannot be tested at the same time—the analysis of the results would be meaningless if multiple variables were involved.

The length of the testing period is another critical factor which requires careful thought and good judgment. Too lengthy a period will give your competitors time to copy and preempt some important marketing areas. Too short a test period can cause a disaster if early consumer purchasing is distorted by atypical circumstances.

The latter situation obtained in a famous market test for a line of frozen baby food. In this case, the test was of such interest to potential competitors that a high percentage of the initial buyers were competitor representatives who were sending samples home to their respective labs for analysis!

A new product concept with which I was once involved nearly came a cropper because of shelf-life problems. We had developed an excellent and initially well-received line of freeze-dried salad ingredients. These were foil-envelope-packed ham, shrimp, tuna fish, chicken, and egg salad mixes. The product, when simply mixed at home with mayonnaise, could be used on lettuce as a salad or between bread as a sandwich. The initial test-market response was just short of spectacular. The advertising was compelling and the early housewives who bought and were interviewed were enthusiastic. It looked like we had a real winner!

Fortunately, we decided to extend the test beyond the initial three-month period to test some pricing alternatives. Abruptly the sales of the product dried up. And equally abruptly the consumer complaints began to pour in. It turned out that the shelf-life of the mixes went to pot after three to four months and a large percentage of packages with this amount of age were literally inedible. We beat a hasty retreat.

At this stage of the procedure, the CEO's role is primarily one of being sure his marketing technicians are objective; and he has to be particularly careful that the advertising agency boys, who play a big role in this exercise, are not being overly optimistic at best, and self-serving at worst.

The Roll-Out

The final step that requires managerial monitoring is the product roll-out. This is basically a matter of thoughtful planning and a careful matching of manufacturing capability with financial strength. Pay-back requirements vary widely from company to company. Corporate "war chests" for this type of activity often dictate the speed at which a new product is introduced in ever-widening national and eventually international markets. Here again, the expected competitor response must be factored in. It is a fairly dependable truth that in the food industry, the first one into a new market with a new product has at least a three to one edge on the second man in. In other words, the follower will pay at least $3.00 for every dollar the pioneer has spent to open the market for his new item. Sometimes a major market share in a given area will be established by the innovator who can never be really dislodged.

For organizations that have not had experience in marketing on a national, let alone international, scale, this phase of the project can present a multitude of pitfalls and booby traps. Differences in markets can present some unpleasant surprises. Trade elements don't all react alike by any means. New York City is a vastly different food market from Boston or L.A. Different in store type; different in physical distribution problems; different in the ethnic makeup of the population; different in taste habits and preferences.

Adequate and knowledgeable sales people must be in place to implement the programs developed by the market planners. The introductory programs themselves must be flexible and not rigid. The roll-out stage can be terribly expensive if not handled carefully. It can be a disaster if the product fails to make the grade and is discontinued, generally after initial placement. Rarely does the marketplace forgive and allow a second try for an item that has "bombed" on the initial go-round.

In this the final and climactic phase of a new product's introduction, the CEO is pretty much in the hands of the professionals. The details to be monitored are myriad. The need for vigilance and on-the-scene inspection are beyond the scope of a single person to stay in touch with, much less be on top of. So the CEO had better be sure that his marketing "pros" know what they are doing, are sure-footed, and are getting their inputs first-hand in the marketplaces that are being opened. He should expect a heavy dose of travel expense and often some domestic disaccommodation for his marketing staff members.

CONCLUSION

As I read back through this treatise, I note that the main thrust of my opinions seems to relate to the introduction of new items in the food arena. For this I apologize to those whose new product objectives and problems may be quite different from what mine have been. It does strike me, however, that many of the fundamentals that are required for a company to succeed in the field of innovation are basic to all enterprises. And perhaps the most basic is the attitude of the Chief Executive Officer himself. His interest and support are essential to the proper climate. His patience and courage will be constantly tested. His leadership will usually determine whether his company will be judged to be just another place to work and to invest in, or a truly exciting and rewarding career and financial opportunity.

REEVALUATING YOUR DISTRIBUTION STRATEGY

by Michael L. Sanyour

Executive Vice President, Science Management Corporation;
Former President, Subaru of America, Inc.

ONE OF THE unique advantages an executive can have in gauging the effectiveness of a company's distribution strategy is to examine it with fresh eyes. It's a natural advantage that comes to any chief executive who steps into a new company, and one that I enjoyed on joining Subaru of America. My prior years at Volkswagen, which had a distribution strategy that had been shaped over a period of 20 years, helped to provide me with a perspective on where Subaru was and where it might go.

Although the examples of Subaru and Volkswagen might appear to cover a limited area, there are basic factors in distribution common to all products. A comparison of their distribution policies, and how they evolved, offers a good example of how different practices can be successful if they reflect a response to changes in the market and the capabilities of the parent company.

Like many companies entering a new market, Volkswagen at first relied on independent distributors but later decided to alter its distribution policy; it now controls most of that distribution through a consolidated network of regional offices rather than independent entrepreneurs (who are relied upon at retail). Subaru began its entry into the American market by relying almost totally on direct distribution to retail dealers, but now operates through a network of independent distributors. Obviously, even with the same type of product in the same industry, there is no single answer as to which distribution strategy is best. The real question is then, "What is the best distribution strategy to meet your needs?"

Before this question can be answered, it is essential that the chief executive know exactly where he stands in terms of marketing effec-

601

tiveness, the existing point in the life cycle of a product, and which are the most important objectives from both a short- and a long-range viewpoint. Is quick entry into a market more important than a higher net profit? Is higher turnover more important to maintaining production capacity than maximizing your return on investment?

DIRECT VERSUS INDEPENDENT DISTRIBUTION

The Volkswagen shift in emphasis from independent to direct distribution is in keeping with the history of American and imported automotive products. Perhaps the most significant reasons for this change in distribution strategy, applicable to many industries, are: (1) independent distributors may wish to capitalize on their investment and hard work, or may face estate problems; (2) declining margins due to competitive pressures; and (3) distributor activity may become stultified over a long period of time, as the distributor becomes larger and more affluent, particularly if no effective plan has been developed to provide for second-generation professional management.

In the first two situations, a manufacturer may have little choice other than to assume responsibility for the regional distributor functions if he is in a mature market and therefore, he may be unable to locate individuals with the combination of financing and entrepreneurial spirit needed to carry out corporate goals. But even if such choices are available, there are substantial advantages of control and overall cost rationalization in vertical integration. This is especially true in the case of "big ticket" items funneled through a single-line, independent distribution organization that serves multiple retail organizations.

In the third case, to guard against declining performance, it is essential to provide for renewal of management as distributor operations become big business. The dangers here can be kept within limits. But when a change is required, one possibility is absorption of the distributor into the parent company for cash or stock or some combination of each, or debentures, etc. The noncash approach provides distributor owners with a continuing financial interest in the total corporation and may also provide a means for solving inherent problems of management succession. In any event, the chief executive who concentrates on "his end" of the business in production and filling the pipe line, while putting most of the burden for end-user sales on his distributors, is sailing in shallow waters.

But these are not the only factors involved in direct versus independent distribution. Within each market territory, a chief executive must have full information on which to judge performance. Sales volume, market potential, share of market, and competitive activity in all segments of a territory must be known and acted upon. And, though a manufacturer may have a uniform distributor agreement, it is impossible to gauge distributor effectiveness on a single scale of performance.

The present distribution pattern developed at Subaru is one example which points up the many variables to be considered in achieving profitable market penetration. We built into our system the necessary controls to gauge effectiveness, determine areas where extra support is needed, and provide the feedback necessary for effective management.

If the initial policy of direct distribution had been maintained, it was obvious that the resources of the company would not have been sufficient to achieve rapid market penetration on a nationwide basis. In a highly competitive market like the automotive business, the complexities of dealer development, sales and service training, the need for almost instantaneous nationwide availability of parts, and the depth of management to support such an operation—coupled with the need for intensive advertising and promotion—would have strained the company beyond its available resources.

Independent distributors became an almost obvious choice in order to gain leverage. Because of the nature of our product it was essential to secure single-line, exclusive distributors. This is in contrast to certain industrial and consumer products which may fit well into an existing multiple-line distributorship or into a manufacturers' representative type of distribution structure.

In 1970, Subaru, as a newcomer, was probably the least known automobile in the United States. After four years, having 14 independent distributors and over 500 dealers nationwide, Subaru entered the "top ten" among imports. In those years, unit sales rose from 5,000 to 14,000 to 24,000 to over 37,000. And with greater product availability the company expects continued growth. Distributors have consistently upgraded their operations with added staff and field personnel as well as larger facilities—a trend expected to continue.

How this was achieved is a tribute to the many people involved and to an outstanding product line in the subcompact automotive market. An understanding of how our distributor network was developed and of the continuing evaluation of performance may prove helpful to the chief executive interested in reviewing his current distribution strategy.

SELECTING DISTRIBUTORS—TURNING DECISION INTO ACTION

There are numerous products in the "considered purchase" category which require a substantial investment at every level—from buyer through manufacturer. And, of course, at each level the investment required increases, so that a distributor's investment will usually be second only to that of the original supplier. Subaru operates with 14 distributors through the United States and Puerto Rico—a number dictated by the market potential for the product, a distributor's ability to effectively cover his territory, the distributor investment required, and the profit potential for both Subaru and distributor. These are the primary considerations in determining the number and location of distributors required to achieve corporate goals. This "magic number" must be determined by each company's needs and type of product. Generally, the number of distributors will vary inversely with the size of the investment the particular product requires. Furniture, appliances, medical and dental equipment, and machine tools, for example, will require varying distribution patterns.

The smaller the number of distributors needed to secure and increase market penetration, the more crucial their selection becomes to the chief executive.

Because we were faced with the need to establish new, single-line distributorships with substantial capital requirements, our early efforts were concentrated on groups and individuals with strong financial backing. We soon found, however, that this criterion was of less importance than others. Money is more freely available than knowledge, drive, and talent. As a result, we decided to seek out those who had these qualities *as they applied to our product.* This is a significant point for every chief executive to consider when establishing or reevaluating a distributor organization.

In some cases, financial backing was downgraded as a consideration to the point where Subaru spoon-fed its product to the distributor in order to minimize his capital outlay and to enable him to direct his money and efforts to building a strong dealer organization. This same approach was recommended to distributors in their own dealer-development programs. For example, to foster an increase of exclusive dealers—those who sell only Subaru—the capital usually required for a franchise is, instead, utilized to finance adequate inventory, parts and service, and training. As a result, approximately 40 percent of our 500 dealers were exclusives at the end of 1973 and the percentage has continued to grow. Obviously, an exclusive dealer will devote more effort to a single product line than a dealer with two or even more lines. Sales reports consistently show the exclusive dealer nearer to the top in unit sales per outlet.

DISTRIBUTOR MANAGEMENT

Traditionally, automobile companies divide distribution management functions into three areas—sales, parts, and service. Sales usually gets the most attention. For an imported automobile, or any product for which a national parts and service capability does not already exist, this can be a costly error. Organizing distributor management as a single, integrated entity is one way to assure equal attention to all three areas; and that is the course we chose. If good service and fast parts availability are not provided, the chances for sustained sales growth are slim. This is especially true with automobiles; but it also applies to any complex product that requires more than routine servicing.

The coordination of Subaru distributor management funnels through a key operating executive, the "manager of distributor development." Reporting to that executive are regional distributor-development managers who maintain constant contact with distributors and dealers to assure that corporate and regional programs are carried out. They are also responsible to see that regional problems and inputs are fed back to the corporation.

With a direct, coordinated channel of management from Subaru to distributor to dealer, the company is in a much better position to maintain an orderly market. In a reversal from the usual practice of loading distributors and dealers to force sales, we try to maintain a balance so that distributors are always asking for more product. At Subaru, the product is the "carrot" rather than the "stick." By setting each distributor's sales objective at an attainable level to serve as an inducement rather than a demand, the idea is to keep the competitive drive and growth orientation of distributors at high levels. The ideal to strive for is to have every distributor and dealer with just one less unit than can be sold; but at the same time, to have effective inventory at all levels so that sales are not lost for want of available choices for the customer and so that everyone feels sufficient inventory pressure to keep working hard.

ESTABLISHING OBJECTIVES

Each year, overall objectives are established for distributors on the basis of a number of factors related to a careful assessment of each distributor's capabilities in all areas. The starting point is an initial unit sales figure determined by the distributor's previous rate of sale compared to corporate sales. This figure is then adjusted on the basis of dealer development plans, facilities, staffing, sales and service training programs, etc. A mutually agreeable figure is then arrived at which may be higher or lower than the initial unit sales objective.

It is in a company's best interests if a higher goal can be set, given sufficient product availability. Meeting that goal will usually entail increased support from the manufacturer. For example, certain areas are considered "bellwether" markets for imported automobiles, just as acceptance for a new product in a specific industry might be essential to its success in others. Concerted efforts in the form of heavier promotion and additional help from regional distributor-development personnel can be provided to support distributors and their dealer organizations in these particular markets to achieve greater penetration. These efforts naturally involve a trade-off elsewhere; in our case, entry into large metropolitan markets was deferred until a beachhead had been established in secondary markets.

To protect a distributor on the down side, there is a floor established which is based on the cost of doing business, and when availability is tight product must be rationed to help assure each distributor of profitable operations.

TRACKING DISTRIBUTOR PERFORMANCE

Regional representatives work constantly and directly with distributors in the areas of dealer development, sales, parts, service, training, and customer service. As a result, they are constantly attuned to what is happening in each market. On a corporate level, a monthly financial report is analyzed to gauge the effectiveness of management in all areas of operation as well as profitability. On a more frequent basis, ten-day sales reports detailing unit sales by territory and by model provide a continuing picture of distributor activity. And, at times, even daily reports are required to keep an eye on critical situations.

The frequency and type of reports required from channels of distribution will vary from industry to industry. Inventory requirements and production lead time are certainly two major factors to be considered, but buying habits and patterns also play an important role. Machine tool buyers are accustomed to long delivery schedules; on the other hand, lack of almost immediate availability will mean a lost sale for most automotive products.

Given the interrelation of Subaru, its distributors, their dealers, and the consumer, it is essential for product planning to have a constant awareness of short-term needs as well as longer-range trends. Because there is typically a four-month minimum lead time between order and receipt of cars at our ports of entry, distributors are required to place firm orders three months in advance of the receipt of the cars. This leaves the company somewhat extended but, on balance, tends to lessen Subaru's risk as an importer. This, in turn, provides a basis for Subaru to make longer-term firm commitments to the manufacturer, Fuji Heavy Industries, Ltd.

Also required is a monthly inventory report which permits analysis of a distributor's ability to supply dealers. A monthly dealer development report keeps the company abreast of the regional distributor's plans for the addition or termination of dealers. Of course, it is most important that Subaru retain the right of final approval of new dealers, rather than abdicating this responsibility to its distributors.

AIDING DISTRIBUTORS IN DEVELOPING A MARKET

The supplier-distributor relation should be a mutually protective one. Because our joint goal is to get cars on the road in the hands of owners, not backed up in the pipeline, we encourage each distributor to follow the same basic principles that guide our operations. This is one area where the chief executive should avoid falling into the trap of ranking distributors solely on their own performance. Without guidance, motivation, and assistance, a distributor organization cannot be expected to function effectively. Nor can individual distributors, by themselves, afford the cost of developing much-needed programs such as those for training, service, advertising and public relations, etc. Just as we recognized the need for fully committed distributors to gain leverage for Subaru, our initial efforts were devoted to having distributors sign up personally-managed dealers in smaller towns. Because of Subaru's newness in the imported car market, it was also essential to sign dealers with a good service reputation. This enabled us to utilize the status of the dealer to help establish the reputation of the product—an established principle of effective retailing.

This approach is a sharp contrast to that of manufacturers both within and outside the automotive industry who choose to enter markets through large volume outlets. We did not take this approach for various reasons. First of all, with exclusive dealers, it leads to a high, fixed-cost factor at retail. This is likely to lead to pressure on the manufacturer to make major concessions or deals. Secondly, that approach leaves little flexibility for coping with cyclical swings. Similarly, we didn't seek out the multiple-franchise "chain" operator, the "mass outlet," and the "system houses" which may tend to offer only marginal support in developing a quality image for a product and may also tend to be short on service. Consequently, such outlets may present disciplinary problems for the company that wants to set a good tone in the marketplace and maintain a pervasive influence throughout the channels of distribution. The consumer electronics industry is a good example of the pitfall of securing volume at the expense of establishing a strong consumer franchise. Often, this has led to an eventual decline in profit and/or volume as private labels entered the picture and as national brands have been used as price footballs.

How our dealer development strategy paid off is shown by the fact that the company can now sustain the effort to support distributors in focusing on metropolitan areas. With enough product on the road to establish a presence, consumer acceptance, and a developing organization, Subaru is now able to begin the penetration of major metro markets on its own terms. This would have been impossible in earlier days.

To support this effort, Subaru has undertaken increased advertising and promotion programs in selected markets to help insure the success of regional and local efforts. This naturally required an intimate knowledge of particular markets. What works in Los Angeles, for example, requires extensive modification for New York City. One has a widely dispersed population which necessitates a promotion media mix and a message different from that of the higher-population-density city.

We developed a cooperative advertising relationship with our distributors and dealers which works to mutual benefit in providing coordination between regional and local advertising and with the national umbrella advertising programs. It became possible to maintain a unified advertising program; each distributor and dealer benefited from professional help which might otherwise not have been available because of the size of the individual advertising budget. Although it is common practice to provide channels of distribution with advertising and sales promotion materials, much of what is done by some companies is wasted because of failure to get effective regional and local support. Too often, such programs are designed without the flexibility required to meet varied needs of different markets.

Product development also plays an important role in distribution strategy and market development. For example, Subaru did not have an automatic transmission in the line when our distributor and dealer organization was initially developed. And the product line was kept simple with only three models with very few options and a limited color range for the first three years. Then we phased in additional models, options, etc., as seemed warranted by increasing volume and market requirements.

To sum up, the basic philosophy in aiding distributors is to assess what is the most practical way to get a foothold in a market and then to concentrate on expanding penetration in it.

REEVALUATION OF DISTRIBUTOR POLICY IS A CONTINUING PROCESS

The chief executive should establish procedures that enable a continuing examination of distribution strategy to make certain that it is in support of overall corporate objectives. A program to modify or alter distribution policy should not be a process undertaken only because of crisis circumstances or as a result of change in management that brings new eyes to a situation.

For Subaru, it is essential to try to achieve balanced distribution across the country from ten ports of entry. However, it is not always possible to secure adequate shipping capacity to all ports. As a result, at times it is necessary to supply a distributor from a distant port which involves more expensive overland shipping. Because Subaru pricing is based on port-of-entry, it's obvious that this added cost must be taken into consideration so that uniform pricing to distributor regions can be maintained over time.

Every chief executive faces similar problems of maintaining a distribution-cost equilibrium. If distribution cost is not given consideration equal to all other costs, major markets can be lost because of an inability to offer competitive pricing. Only through a continuing analysis of distribution strategy is it possible to determine reasonably when and how to undertake such major steps as opening a new manufacturing or assembly plant to feed a given area, or changing the basic terms of doing business.

Just as you constantly look at your product line to see how it can be improved upon, and maintain tight cost control to determine how to effect economies in manufacturing, you should apply the same critical standards to channels of distribution and their effectiveness. What was acceptable last year should not be automatically considered acceptable for the next year. It is essential to keep escalating your sights. Being a tough taskmaster, seeking constant improvement in performance from distributor channels, can have as much of an effect on your bottom line as a major investment to help achieve production economies.

Distribution is not a science nor can it be evaluated and quantified as clearly as quality control, for example. It is much harder to gauge and therefore requires a personal situational analysis on an almost day-by-day basis. New demands on companies imposed by the energy crisis provide good examples of why there is a need for constant monitoring. Many of the companies affected by it were forced into an immediate reevaluation of distribution strategy, and they found serious deficiencies in their procedures not the least of which was a lack of important information needed to make sound decisions. In Subaru's own case, there has as yet been no need for fundamental changes, but the resulting higher costs of distribution have had to be weighed and adjustments made.

Because distribution accounts for an increasingly higher percentage of the ultimate cost of a product to the consumer, there can be no doubt that it will demand increasing attention from the chief executive.

If the author may close on a personal note, I would like to say that the writing of this article has in and of itself been a valuable educational experience. The profound changes in the automobile market, especially during 1973 and 1974, and the domestic and international developments that have impacted on Subaru's business really kept the subject of distribution channels and strategy very much in the forefront of priority subjects that have demanded attention on a daily basis. And although nothing is ever set in concrete, it seems that, thus far, Subaru has developed a basic approach that works reasonably well in good times and tough times. And that, in the final analysis is, perhaps, the best test of all.

WHAT THE CHIEF EXECUTIVE NEEDS TO KNOW ABOUT MARKET RESEARCH

by Samuel G. Barton

President; Webber, Barton, Jolitz, Shaw, Inc.

THE CHIEF EXECUTIVE OFFICER is periodically faced with problems as to which of the company's existing products or services should be given the "green light" or "yellow light" or "red light" as far as reinvestment or promotional expansion is concerned. These problems are related, not only to the characteristics of the company's products, but also to the characteristics of the expected market and those of specific products or services of competitors. The chief executive should look to the market research department for guidance and assistance on these problems, and written reports and recommendations should be available to him even though the market research department may be assigned to report administratively to the company's marketing management. Firsthand access to the essential market statistics and the interpretation and gut feel of the market research staff can be useful in his individual appraisal of the feasibility and risk of the company's pending marketing plans.

Similar problems needing the direct assistance of the market research director or his staff include the future market appraisal for possible products in the research or development stage or those being marketed by a company which might be acquired. On the other hand, market evaluation is needed by the top officer in considering which existing or newly acquired products or services in the line should be milked, spun off, or abandoned.

Clearly, personal probes of the judgment of staff people in market research pose for the top executive the same cautions of protocol and finesse that he is familiar with in his other business relations and he will likely need his best skills in constructing his own assessment of the company's assumptions and marketing plans so as neither to stifle the marketing director nor muffle the researcher's opinions. The market research person does often have some expectancy of risk, and this may be worth sensing from the experienced staff person as it is never explicit in the survey report.

Market research represents a many-faceted field because it is called upon to serve many levels and departments of the corporation. Accordingly, it is not a simple matter to appraise the performance of the market research function. If the research director reports directly to the corporate top executive, appraisal of the man is direct. "Does he understand my needs? Is he as helpful to me as I can reasonably expect? Do I have confidence in him?" But when the market research department or market research is looked at as a function which serves the needs of the many operating levels or departments, the appraisal is more difficult and more complex. In the opinions of various departmental or functional heads, the company's market research staff may be servicing the new product conceptualization or package design function very well but may be far below the level of competence of the competitors' departments in reporting marketing conditions, in testing new products, or in providing selling or advertising aids. Such a complex appraisal of market research competence can be accomplished by delegation through the organization structure or can be professionally made by consulting firms who are familiar with the performance of many companies. Such appraisal can be executed by consultants with very broad interindustry expertise or by firms specializing within an industry. Both approaches have benefit and in either case should involve the cooperation of the company's several line and staff departments; the Chief Executive Officer should also participate in order that his personal needs and views be represented.

A characteristic of a successful market research function is that it is able to adapt to the changing needs of the executive and operating people, to the changing conditions and structure of the market, and to the emergence of new services and technologies in research. A second indicator or characteristic of a good market research function is evidenced by the degree of respect with which the research people are regarded by other line and staff departments. In some companies, people destined for or taken from the sales or marketing departments are given temporary assignments in the market research department. If they end up respecting research people and being appreciative of this experience, it likely indicates a good market research function.

A third indicator is the quality of the professional people the department is able to attract. This is likely to be associated in part with the company's reputation in market and operations research circles and, in turn, is a reflection of the people currently and previously manning the research director's job.

To do his job, the top executive needs certain data reported routinely, certain data reported as exceptional conditions are noted, and other information reported at his specific request. In specifying the information he regards important in the exception reporting system and in requesting new information, he will do well to spend sufficient time with the market research director and his supporting staff so that misinterpretation and omission of relevant specifics are minimized. Such interface is essential on requests originating in the chief executive office. Close communication with the CEO is also advisable, either with the research director alone or in conjunction with the divisional or staff director, when assessment of inconclusive market data is to be made prior to and as a basis for a major operating policy decision. The frequency of the interface with the research director or his staff will depend primarily on the CEO's personal judgment and assessment of his own needs; and this will be affected by the organizational structure which he inherits and the degree of urgency of change.

THE MARKET RESEARCH BAILIWICK AND EXPERTISE

Market research as a title may include a variety of functions depending on the industry and the traditional organization of the particular company. In an industrial or manufacturer's goods company, many market research functions may be performed by the technically trained sales staff or sales engineers. In some retailing chains, some of the work may be done by the architectural firm or by the store planning staff. In any company, the responsibility of interpretation of an important market appraisal rests with the chief executive or his deputy. In every company, there is implicitly a list of market research functions to be performed by someone if not by a formally assigned department. These functions or activities are likely to include:

1. Collection and accessible storage of external (market) data and reports relevant to the company's current products or services and to its possible new ventures.

2. Identification of problems or market opportunities relevant to the company's products or services with respect to prices, packaging, distribution or selling methods, and promotional or advertising activities.

3. Analysis of internal (accounting) data and external data from the viewpoint of the company's marketing plans and sales objectives. Analysis requires the accumulation of experience on the variability or expected fluctuation of the data by time periods.

4. Informal or judgmental recommendations to marketing or general management that reflect the researcher's sensitivity to risk.

5. Design, supervision, and analysis of marketing tests. Analysis includes the recommendation as to whether the test should be extended, broadened, or curtailed. (Curtailment might be advised because the test is conclusive or because it will likely be inconclusive, even if extended, or because new competitive activities effectively make test results irrelevant.)

6. Estimation of the benefit/cost of new or different market tests or market research. Once a major decision is made, there may be many alternative methods of implementation. Some of these may be entirely creative or judgmental, while others may wisely be handled as matters which can usefully be tested by using one marketing technique or product version in some regions and using an alternative in others. Designs of large-scale ongoing tests require that they be feasible to administer and that the sales department not be too deeply prejudiced as to the outcome.

7. An important and often overlooked function is the careful documentation of test or experimental marketing results in order to facilitate future comparisons. Given some possibility of staff turnover, a new marketing director, a market research director or the president's assistant should be able to retrieve the company's body of experience. In general, good documentation of test results exists in a company only when the Chief Executive Officer insists upon it as a standard procedure.

8. A particular function of an experienced market research director is his provision of assistance to general management people in the specification of recognition characteristics with respect to exceptional or noteworthy sales or marketing conditions and events. This may be important help to the Chief Executive Officer in describing his information needs to information system technicians.

9. Assistance to the sales or sales promotion departments in the

documentation of performance results which may also serve as selling aids. For some companies, such documentation may be critical to the support of the sales staff. The market research director may carry out an important function by knowing the various classes of significant problems of the company's customers and being alert to the appearance of cases where the company's products or services facilitated a customer problem solution.

There no doubt are many more functions which could be listed and many may have been traditionally established in the individual company. Certainly when the new Chief Executive Officer takes charge, he can modify these to suit his needs—once he has time to turn to the market research department organization and functions.

DEPARTMENT ORGANIZATION

Looking at various companies, we can find examples of several different market research department or staff organization structures. We must conclude that the ideal organization is the one which best fits the particular corporation and its particular short- and longer-term plans and objectives.

The kind of organization seen most often is the simplest: the single central market research department. The advantage of such organization is that it provides for efficient administration of extensive data collection facilities and the sharing of costs of highly specialized technicians used periodically by divisional or product management people. The facilities may, for example, include a centralized national telephone survey facility, or a staff of clerks measuring the advertising expenditures of various products or digesting the field observational reports of the corporate sales staff. Specialized technicians may include a mathematical statistician, an experimental design specialist, a psychologist, or a person with scientific training in the particular field of manufacture or processing. Accordingly, such a central department is a good arrangement for providing technical training to market research people, but it is not so good an arrangement for training them in marketing or administration of the company. This is less true if the organization plan assigns an individual assistant market research director to the dedicated service of an individual divisional or product group marketing manager. Under such a plan, the research person learns more about marketing and what information is important to the individual executive. In turn, the communication problem for the marketing executive is reduced in comparison to going through a departmental hierarchy.

Some larger companies have opted for several separate market research departments with one assigned to each product division. This overcomes some of the disadvantages cited for the central department and gives the maximum freedom to divisional management to organize and utilize a complement of market research people as best suits their individual needs. This sort of divisional organization may be observed in most conglomerates, but it is not uncommon among some larger companies with a diversified set of products within the same industry. This makes good sense, especially where the divisions tend to use different primary distribution channels or where the division's products require different transportation or warehousing facilities.

Some of the largest companies use both a corporate central research department and divisional market research departments. Although some advantages, such as centrally coordinated buying of syndicated research services, are obvious, other advantages may be the provision of specialized talents and training facilities. Above all, such organization can provide for specialized consultation with the chief executive or with the corporate development officer and provides an important alternate career path for the dedicated staff research man.

Most of the foregoing remarks are addressed to the organization of a multiple-person department; and they are based on the assumption that the company need is for the "manufacture" of various market research field studies, including data collection, processing, and report writing. An alternative view of the work of market research is that of a consultative, interpretive, and buying function. Some companies, especially perhaps in times of transition, have elected to assign individual market research or quantitative specialists as full-time assistants to the several top corporate executives concerned with marketing, including the Chief Executive Officer. The attachment of a market research specialist to the chief executive's research staff may be particularly helpful when the top man is new to the corporation or when he has moved into the top executive post from a background other than in marketing.

MAKE OR BUY RESEARCH

To some extent, most companies or corporate divisions have various make or buy decision options with respect to external market data. In the organization plan of assigning to executives individual research assistants, the market research studies are in effect purchased. They are purchased from an outside organization or possibly from a central corporate research department. One of the advantages of buying market research services or studies is that the internal staff is left free to analyze and interpret results or to retrieve and abstract data in the best form for absorption by the appropriate corporate officer. In some instances where the data needed are concerned with distribution requirements, or market potentials and market shares, syndicated measurement services may be available which provide a large quantity of data per dollar of cost.

In some fields, such as most consumer goods industries, several data sources are required. Characteristically, these industries distribute through several wholesaling networks and through several types of retail or institutional channels. To estimate industry volumes through each of the several marketing systems or channels requires collection of data from many sources. Some syndicated services may be offered which, in effect, distribute the cost of data collection, processing, and publication among several clients or subscribers. Typically, the several syndicated or standardized report services overlap in some respects while leaving some (possibly important) gaps in their coverage of the market.

In certain fields, such as the grocery products industry, an important contribution of the market research person or staff is the integration of these multiple data sources including the company's own shipments records and sales activities reports. The purpose of such integration is to utilize the best features of each of the syndicated special and company services so as to yield a single best estimate of current and expected market conditions and the sales associated with such market conditions. The market research director with the help of the top corporate officers and a team of information system specialists can contribute much to bringing up on line a marketing information system that will be much more helpful to the Chief Executive Officer than the typical uncoordinated set of market measurements used until recently by most companies.

The importance of an official single best estimate for all the corporation's statistics can be well appreciated at budget times when division and product managers are willing to use any evidence available for getting a bigger share of the corporate marketing funds.

PEOPLE IN MARKET RESEARCH

Like divisional or product managers, market research people have their own peculiarities. Some of these peculiarities are associated with the constraints of the organization but some are associated with the complexity of the job and perhaps with the fear of making an error. Because the purpose of marketing research is to keep the company from making errors, a sincere market researcher believes that a good market researcher is logical, should strive for zero error, and recognizes the need for a hedge. Some have little balance or perspective about this.

The very diverse nature of the several functions grouped under market research calls for several different types of people: some creative, some disciplined, some qualitatively oriented, and some quantitative. They may be required to contribute to or to criticize the color of an advertisement, the attractiveness of a package, the clarity of a technical specification, or the relative validity of two information sources. No one person can be best at all these things. In a corporation of some size there is a good argument in favor of a department of several people, each able to reinforce the others in some creative or technical respect. One problem, of course, is to find the person who can administer such an odd and diverse collection. The probabilities are that the market research director who is a good department administrator is not likely also to be the best adviser and consultant for the top corporate officer.

There are without question individual market research directors whose orientation or focus is on running a large operation with several functions reporting to them. The objective of such a person may be to gain fame or prestige within the market research field or eventually to take over an even larger administrative assignment in the company. He is likely company-loyal and not likely to make any unqualified recommendations to line officers. In some companies, this sort of big-department operator will find good reasons for making whatever research he can (rather than buying) and will undertake to have the sales staff collect data, maintain a panel of customers, and a company-dedicated testing facility. His visible bias may be to reduce marketing risk to zero or otherwise avoid for his department any responsibility for a wrong marketing decision.

Another identifiable type is in many ways almost an opposite. He may have been shifted from some other part of the company into an apparently permanent post of market research director. He functions as a purchasing agent, buying what is needed and available; he likes good hours, security, and a retirement program. He, too, is no adviser and no risk-taker.

A third type, certainly more rare, is the marketing-executive-oriented man gaining the necessary experience in marketing research on the way to his goal of a top marketing job. He is most likely to end up in another company, but he may return if the price is right; his credentials will be well rounded and good.

Maybe the rarest market researcher is the company-ambitious type. He is really company-loyal, and is hoping he is on his way to becoming a top officer (maybe Chief Executive Officer) in this company. One or two have made it in several industries, including William B. Murphy of Campbell Soup and Dr. Frank Stanton of Columbia Broadcasting; and there are other outstanding successes. Most market researchers are never asked what their long-range plans or ambitions are, and it might be a good practice for some chief executives to make such inquiry.

Some companies, as a regular plan, practice a system of job rotation as between the market research department and the other staff and line departments. This is facilitated where the operation is large enough to have a multiple person department. It may be that more or less permanent market research staff people are assigned to half or two thirds of the posts and the remaining positions are filled with sales people, product managers, operation researchers, or laboratory research people on some rotating basis. Similarly, some manufacturers start out their market research people by having them work six months or more in a selling job as part of the regular line operation.

Some of the benefits of intermittently exposing market research people to the day-to-day firing line problems of the salesman include the awareness they gather of the salesman's communication load, his customer call load, and some awareness of the problems of the customer. If the market research director is not a one-man staff assistant to the marketing vice president, it could be helpful periodically to assign him for a month or two to work as a right hand man. Such exposure can improve the communication process and assist in making explicit the kinds of market conditions or changes that are currently important to the top officers.

Similarly, there may be benefits of periods of intensive and extended exposure to the working problems of the agency creating the company's advertising and the company's own promotion planning, advertising, and product management people. Certainly, product management people have no exclusive knowledge of marketing strategy and market research people do not have a complete understanding of what information is both good for the product manager and good for the company. This is all part of the internal training program. Some external training and exposure can be of assistance if market research people are most effectively to be helpful as the corporation's eyes and ears. Ideas can come from the marketing and research activities of similar companies in other countries. Other good meeting grounds are the seminars and courses in operation research in marketing as offered by Massachusetts Institute of Technology and other advanced business and technical administration schools. Such exposure and exposure to some commercial organizations' technical seminars help the market research man to understand formalized model building and to interface between the top executive's need and the corporate information system.

SOME INTERFACING PROBLEMS

Whatever organization structure exists, there will be operating problems of coordination and special demands on the market research department if the corporation is to make good use of the marketing research staff at the operating level. Some of the most visible problems are related to the development of a new product or service and then the transition of this fragile creation from the laboratory or test market stage into the hard-nosed day-to-day business of the corporate sales department. In this creation of a sensible new product (from a marketing viewpoint) and the subsequent big shift of gears into the medium of regular marketing operations, the market research departments of some companies have been a considerable help.* Although the R&D director may be in charge of new product development and testing, up to some point, and the marketing or sales department in full charge after some point, the Chief Executive Officer is in charge

---

* [Ed. Note: See the chapter by John Fox, "Clearing the Hurdles of New Product Introduction."]

(ex officio) of the transition. In some companies, the market research director or his task force assignee may be used as the liaison or the coordinator between the R&D staff and the regular organization.

Test marketing operations may be controlled by the R&D department, by the regular marketing or sales department, or by the market research team. In this case, the department not only manages the test but facilitates the transfer of responsibility for ultimate national marketing. Thereafter, the market research department will likely assist both in the preparation of product performance documentation and also in the presentation of such findings to the manufacturer's customers. Clearly such responsibilities are not to be administered by either the tyro in research or by the new man in the company. A good balance of training and company experience is likely essential for such an important interface or transition.

APPRAISAL OF MERGER OR ACQUISITION POSSIBILITIES

A final function of market research for the Chief Executive Officer, which should be touched on, is related to the evaluation of future marketing for the products of other companies. These may be considered individually or as necessary components of the corporate package. Some of the contributions the market research specialist can make which are possibly different from those of the accountant or production man are:

1. Definition and measurement of the various market segments in which a particular product is competing.
2. Estimation of rate of development of new customers by product.
3. Estimation of repeat volume of business from old customers.
4. Forecast of changes in the future dimensions of salient market segments.
5. Degree of complementarity or competition between specific products and the company's existing products.
6. New channels of distribution opened by the products under consideration.
7. Degree of competition with the company's products for existing distribution channels.
8. Estimation of relative brand loyalty of customers.

In addition to these few points, market research personnel can likely be usefully assigned to verifying or validating any possible critical claims or assumptions with respect to market shares, distribution, relative prices and inventories, and with respect to customer buying histories, loyalty, and future buying intentions.

It is worth noting that, when the corporation considers revising or spinning off an existing product, the market research staff can be of assistance in appraising the alternatives, as proposed above; and in addition, it should be able to provide the necessary market performance documentation in the case where a prospective buyer is sought.

THE IMPACT OF CHANGING TASTES AND STYLES

by Peter G. Scotese

President and Vice Chairman, Springs Mills, Inc.

RECOGNIZING and making the most of his company's exposure to opportunity are at least as important as any other responsibilities the chief executive must face. As the investor of shareholders' funds, he must analytically seek out and aggressively pursue those risk opportunities which offer the greatest potential for return on investment. He must be both trustee and entrepreneur, with ability and total commitment to steer his company consistently on the courses dictated by its operating and social environments.

The accelerating rate of change in our individual companies, industries, and total environment makes successful management increasingly difficult and complex. Yet this same force offers opportunity to those managers intelligent and imaginative enough to discern the leading edge of change and capitalize on it.

Some of the rewards of sensitivity and responsiveness to change are obvious—increased profitability, competitive stature, and attractiveness to capital and human resources. What often are not so obvious are the penalties a company pays for failing to recognize and deal with change. In many cases, the cost is not simply poor return or loss of a notch in the competitive standings; sometimes it is loss of market, or product, or even liquidation of the enterprise.

So the competent chief executive of today has no choice. He must accurately anticipate and interpret the forces of change, and translate these into programs that are completely responsive to them. This is his personal responsibility and he must develop to the utmost his ability to accept it. But, of course, the chief executive isn't a one-man gang, so he must also create a climate that encourages that same sensitivity to change among his key people.

The changes being discussed in this chapter are the nonquantifiable changes in overall environment which might be characterized as cultural changes. Some of these are prompted by, or interact with, physical or technological changes which are quantifiable, but we are concerned here with trends and movements in our cultural patterns which bear heavily upon marketing policies and strategies and, in turn, upon overall corporate policy.

For convenience we will designate these as changes in *tastes* and *styles:* forces which govern life styles, buying habits, and consumer preferences as to form and functionality of the goods and services they buy.

Many companies, these days, do a pretty good job of keeping up with *technological* change. Some, of course, have had real records of leadership. And even though some companies have, in fact, fallen behind, almost all executives do seem to recognize the decisive impact of changes in technology. What seems to be less widely appreciated is the importance of change in *tastes* and in *"style."*

POSITIVE AND NEGATIVE REACTIONS TO CHANGE

America has undergone radical changes in tastes and life styles in recent years. These have had an enormous impact on business. Many businesses have either misread or ignored the signals that change was coming. Examples abound.

Major retailers in groceries and soft goods didn't read the economy, and underestimated the appeal of so-called discount operations. They didn't sense the changes in consumer shopping patterns.

Auto makers were caught with huge, costly inventories of big cars, despite signals being transmitted by years of increasing imports of small cars. For the most part, they recognized too late the impact that changing consumer tastes, influenced by operating costs, inflation, the looming gasoline shortage, and urban congestion, were having on the demand for smaller, more economical vehicles.

Many textile and apparel companies continued to look to Paris for fashion direction, even after their younger, more independent, more affluent consumers had served notice that they—not the couture designers—were going to call the fashion shots. Many manufacturers failed to note that much apparel styling was created "from below." For instance, the denim trend.

Those companies, many with large financial resources, who were unable to read and respond to change, had disastrous results. It has also happened in other industries. Packard, Hudson, and Pierce Arrow are examples of companies which encountered the same fate through inability to meet customer wants in styling. Ford almost went the same route to oblivion with the Model T.

Many companies have read the tea leaves correctly and have prospered—the persistence of American Motors and Avis, and the innovativeness of C.I.T., are prime illustrations. Such single-product companies as Tampax and Wrigley have adapted and withstood the demands of changing times so far. So have relatively new growth industries: the fast-food and convenience store chains, like McDonald's and "7–11" stores; hospital and health care suppliers, like Baxter Laboratories; and the more aggressive banking institutions, such as First National City Bank.

Of course, changes in tastes and styles are decisive in the author's industries—textiles, apparel, and frozen foods. But these kinds of change have their impact in many other areas as well: other foods, home furnishings, leisure products of all sorts, even financial services for the individual. In short, in all consumer goods and services. But changes in taste and style make themselves felt decisively in business and industrial fields as well: in office equipment and furnishings; in industrial trucks and earth moving equipment; and in machine tools. Successful companies in all of these fields have appreciated the importance of color; simplicity and functionality of design; ease of use and operation; the aesthetic as well as the technical importance of *precision*; the saving of physical effort; and the saving of time. Even in such areas as basic metals, changing tastes and styles have made themselves felt in the increasing demand for lightness combined with strength, and ability to develop resistant as well as attractive finishes.

In a mobile, technological society based more and more on instant mass communications, change happens rapidly. By the time it happens, it may be too late for a corporation to do something about it in a significant way.

An example of how an appraisal of changing tastes and styles in a community influenced the development of a company's overall business strategy is given below. It is taken from the author's personal experience.

The Boston Store in Milwaukee, the city's then second largest department store, was lagging substantially behind its major competitor in the early 1960s, at a time when a management change was made. An analysis of the local retailing situation and of the Boston Store's posture in the community, as well as an appraisal of people making up the community, indicated that:

1. The city was "over-stored" in relation to population, buying power and growth rate, particularly in basement and discount price lines.
2. The city's downtown area was uninteresting, as were its shopping facilities.
3. Downtown parking was inadequate. Large open mall-type shopping centers with parking were relatively close to the downtown area.
4. Milwaukeans, compared to residents of other cities of comparable size, were somewhat behind the times in home and apparel fashions taste levels.
5. Much of the Boston Store's merchandise was offered in basement and budget price lines.

Sensing that Milwaukeans were ready for a step up in their fashion sophistication and response to a changing downtown shopping atmosphere, the Boston Store's strategy called for the following programs:

1. Introduction of "excitement" in the downtown store through continual special events. One such event was an Italian Import Fair which included a bronze reproduction of Michelangelo's *Pieta* at a time the original was being much publicized throughout the United States.
2. Building of an up-to-date parking facility for the downtown store with convenient entry into the store.
3. Sharp step-up in higher fashion offerings from budget to moderate price brackets in both apparel and home furnishings.
4. Flanking of the city on three sides with modern enclosed mall multilevel shopping centers, inviting major competition to participate.

This strategy resulted from perception that Milwaukeans had been underestimated as to their potential taste levels; that changes were taking place in these taste levels; and that these consumers would respond to fashion leadership and convenient shopping in well designed centers. Further, that Milwaukeans were ready for the more sophisticated excitement of special promotions, tailored to the arts, sports, events in other countries, etc. They did respond—overwhelmingly. By the end of the 1960s the Boston Store had achieved substantial increases in sales volume, profits, and fashion dominance in the community.

PERCEIVING AND MANAGING CHANGE

It is the chief executive's job to understand the changing environment and its impact on his business. This is difficult to accomplish. It requires a great deal of the man or woman at the top: intelligence, intuition, imagination, sensitivity, awareness, judgment, and flexibility. Most importantly, it requires an objective detachment from the business which permits the chief executive, intellectually and emotionally, to gain perspective on the critical issues that underlie social, economic, and political realities. He or she must extrapolate these personal traits into the character of the organization.

How does the chief executive go about it? How does he use his and his organization's talents to minimize the negative impact of changing tastes and styles, and to maximize his company's exposure to opportunities which change provides? Many considerations are involved, but I would like to describe three areas which I feel are especially important:

1. Environmental sensitivity.
2. Judgment and intuition.
3. Organizational flexibility.

Environmental Sensitivity

The consumer is constantly telling business what she wants, and what she will want. She does this in a variety of ways, often without realizing what she's saying. The successful executive learns to listen, and to translate. The consumer may not *say* she wants no-iron sheets; but she may say she wants more leisure time or intensely dislikes ironing. In fact, she did say this, and it precipitated a fundamental change in textiles from all-cotton fabrics to blended fabrics of cotton and man-made fibers. Many companies missed the signals, and were late in joining the trend to no-iron blends.

The consumer may not say she wants more style and color in her home; but she may demonstrate a heightened interest in the arts which eventually leads to her satisfying this want.

Wars, revolutions, world events, personalities, art, and new technology influence fashion; and fashion influences home decoration. Today's trend to casual living has elevated a work clothing fabric like denim to a status symbol here and abroad. Casual life styles and casual fashion are also resulting in casual home decoration—the designs and colors of apparel and home fashions are blending.

To the sensitive, imaginative chief executive, there are many signals that *change* is in the making. In order to hear the signals, he must be attuned to what is going on in the world where his ultimate customers live. By what means does he receive these signals?

More than ever, *the visual arts* offer particularly vital insight into what people are thinking and doing. The fine arts, especially, are often trial balloons of trends in the making. They generally represent the leading edge of response to currents of thought and expression.

Many chief executives are involved in art through their personal collections, and through their companies' sponsorship of art exhibits, collections, and competitions. They consider art a window on the incoming environment. Perhaps of more significance is that an interest in the arts, in itself, can improve perceptions and heighten sensitivity to trends in public preferences for form and color. An appreciation of art develops an attitude and a taste level that spills over into everything one does. Art is color, shape, texture, design, line, space. Art interest can develop a seventh sense. One becomes a more visual person and has the ability to refine one's senses. The physical eye and, more importantly, the mind's eye become exercised. It is this awareness and appreciation that sharpens one's perception about all things going on in the world's environment.

Extensive reading is another must for understanding our environment. One company president, already heavily involved in art, also subscribes to, and reads some 44 different magazines, periodicals, and newspapers. Many of them are specialized and esoteric. Even leafing through this collection of material takes time. Reading key items really takes a lot of his time. But this man feels his reading over a broad spectrum provides an invaluable feel for his company's environment.

Exposure to the visual arts is an important segment of this reading spectrum. Included are such publications as *Apollo, Artform, National Sculpture Review, Architectural Digest, Art International,*

Connoisseur, Arts in Society, The Art Gallery, and the newsletters of the Southeby-Parke-Bernet Gallery, Metropolitan Museum of Art, Museum of Modern Art, and the Guggenheim Museum.

Maintaining contact with the changing life styles and mores of contemporary society is given an assist by a diverse group of periodicals: *Town and Country, Fortune, Time, Realities in America, People,* and (of course) *Playboy,* and *Penthouse.*

This man's reading in the area of management practice includes the *Harvard Business Review, Dun's, Sales Management,* and bulletins and reports of the American Management Associations and of the National Industrial Conference Board.

News of activities and change in his own industry, in addition to word received through personal contacts, gets to him via three daily trade papers and three monthly magazines devoted to process technology and new product developments. For more general business news he sees the *New York Times,* the *Wall Street Journal,* and *Business Week.*

More general reading by this man includes *National Geographic, Horizon, Smithsonian.* And, not so incidentally, he has for years perused the semiannual mail order catalogues of Sears, Roebuck and Montgomery Ward, two of the finest reflectors of consumer tastes in the medium-priced mass markets. *Consumer Reports* is thumbed through periodically to see what product performance standards are being brought to the consumer's attention.

Suppliers, customers, and consulting groups have market intelligence that can be very useful. Developing close personal relationship and dialogue with key people within these organizations, the chief executive can sell them on his own company's plans, and can learn what they are expecting in the marketplace by way of changes in tastes and style. In particular, the major national retail chains and mail order houses are meaningful sources of information and viewpoints on the future of certain products and markets.

Consumer organizations publish material that could have an impact on particular markets, and the chief executive should be aware of what they are saying.

Through these sources, he is likely to pick up signals that tell him, for instance, that customers are increasingly interested in safety—as in children's clothing and household electrical equipment; or in ease of maintenance, as in modular construction of appliances.

Other media can also provide environmental signals. What are they saying on the talk shows? What's the big event on Broadway or in Hollywood? What's the trend in pop music, or in television entertainment? What fads or personalities are the news media featuring? The chief executive, living a different life style from that of most of the consumers who use his products, must be sure that his sensitivity to the life styles of others is not lost. These "other" media can help keep him in touch.

Contact with executives of other companies, particularly those in different industries will build perspective. This can take various forms: business association activities, social relationships, community projects, or so-called outside seats on boards of directors. This cross-fertilization of ideas can foster greater receptivity to the unusual or nontraditional. It builds important objectivity into the manager's judgment. He learns that other points of view exist besides his or his company's.

In what I have been saying, I have been referring to the non-formalized avenues for perception of change available to management personnel at all levels in their day-to-day business and personal activities. In addition, there are the many techniques for marketing investigation which are known to modern managers.

Consumer and market research into buying habits, brand preferences, purchase stimuli, demographics, and the like are important. Such research can be generated in-house, through specialized research organizations, or both. A range of techniques—and cost—are available: group focus interviews, point-of-purchase surveys, continuing panel surveys, "piggy-back" questionnaires. The data thus obtained are a valuable tool in the corporation's early warning system and marketing planning. However, these techniques are complementary to, but not a substitute for the manager's own perceptions in evaluating changes in tastes and styles.

Judgment and Intuition

Despite the use of proven market research methods, plus doses of game theory, probability theory, decision theory, and/or other sophisticated tools, along with advanced computer technology, there are no absolutes or guarantees in attempting to anticipate changes in taste and style. Often the ultimate decision boils down to the sum of the decision-maker's experience—his knowledge of the environment and his intuitive feel for change.

Most major decisions don't happen in a lightning stroke; they evolve over a period of time as more and more inputs are made available. Soon a decision takes form, and no other alternative seems as good.

Much of this depends on the quality of the chief executive's environmental assumptions—what he has concluded from his internal and external observations. He must ask himself such questions as: Have I evaluated the numbers properly? What's the dollar value of the risk if everything goes wrong? What effect can government have on this market? How will consumers really react to this? Can I delay the changeover? Is it fad or fundamental?

For example, a bath towel manufacturer can't simply decide to make bath towels. He has to decide if he'll make traditional woven towels, or the more complex Jacquard woven towels, or both, and in what proportion. He has to decide whether they'll be all cotton, or blended with man-made fibers, and in what proportion. He has to decide whether to take a branded or unbranded route to market, or both, and in what proportions. He has to decide what parts of the market to shoot for, and what distribution patterns are most profitable. He has to decide whether the high risks involved in raw material purchasing, single product machinery, and the share of market dominance by a competitor will permit profit rewards commensurate to the risk factors involved. There are other environmental pressures to be considered at each of these points of decision.

This is the subjective part of corporate management's effort to maximize the impact of change. It's an important and often maligned part in our technocratic age.

But it's why we have managers instead of machines at the head of business corporations and that is why today's successful managers have to have a subjective streak that tracks well the changes of tastes and style.

Another reason is the complexity of modern society, which requires innovative problem-solving for which there is little specific precedent. Because of today's rate of change, looking backward at historical judgments is no longer the highly useful tool it once was in estimating present or future directions.

The chief executive has to recognize the role of judgment and intuition in the management process. He must sharpen his skills of evaluation to the point that he has confidence in them, and knows when and to what degree to use them. They are indispensable tools in the management of change.

Organizational Flexibility

Perceiving change, sensing its directions, making use of applicable analytical techniques, exercising intuition and good judgment in devising appropriate strategies for coping with change—all these steps can be adequate in a small company. In a large enterprise, an additional factor must receive the chief executive's attention. That is, he must be sure his organization is highly flexible. Many of the negative responses to change which have brought companies to their demise, a few instances of which were cited earlier in this chapter, could very possibly have occurred because of failure of the organization to take action even when change was recognized.

The chief executive must recognize the degree of flexibility his organization has. Generally speaking, the larger the company, the less desirable it is to pursue short-term fads. It simply costs too much. The larger companies generally attune themselves to the more basic fundamental changes in tastes and styles, and let the smaller specialty companies have the platform shoes, mini-skirts, and hula hoops.

You don't have to be first in recognizing new product opportunities or introducing new products. Flexible companies such as Johnson & Johnson have frequently been successful as "Number Two" in many instances of new product introduction because of their unusual marketing strengths. They are confident that their flexibility and marketing capability will allow them to take advantage of new products introduced and initially promoted by others.

How the chief executive maintains flexibility within his organization is a separate subject in itself. It depends a great deal on good leadership at the top and through the ranks of middle management. It certainly involves good communications in all directions. Already mentioned is the chief executive's responsibility for helping his aides to develop their own sensitivities to changes in taste and style and their own "marketing" orientation.

The formal planning function, now common to most large companies, and covering both short-term and long-range planning, provides an excellent means for the chief executive to use in promoting and monitoring the flexibility of his operating and staff departments. All planning should start with the question, "What kind of environment will we be operating in during the planning period to be embraced?" This means, among other things, the marketing environment; in turn, it has to include a consideration of changes in tastes and styles.

The Chief Executive Officer, whether or not he personally participates in the formal planning process or merely reviews and passes upon the plans submitted, can and should insist that the questions regarding market environment have been thoroughly considered. Further, he should be sure that alternative strategies for dealing with indicated changes have been dealt with in depth, and specific actions have been recommended as part of the plan. In a very large organization the formal planning process is perhaps the only way a Chief Executive Officer can be sure that his team has recognized change, is prepared to deal with it, and has formulated concrete action plans to that end.

So important is flexibility in an organization that instances can be cited wherein a major company objective in establishing capital expenditure policy is that of flexibility. For example, one company recently had a new product line under consideration. The minimum investment to move from pilot to full-scale production was $30 million in plant and equipment. The product line had to sell in volume to produce an acceptable return; if it didn't the plant had no alternative use. The company turned it down. The president felt strongly that single-product equipment in a field subject to rapid changes in tastes and style presented too great a risk of quick obsolescence, and that the company couldn't afford that risk.

On the other hand, the same company has invested much more than $40 million to enter the circular doubleknit business. The divisional executives were pushing the project primarily on the basis of product washability, no-iron features, and relatively low labor content. These are highly desirable factors.

But the president was really sold for a different reason: flexibility. This highly productive machinery could make various patterns and weights of doubleknit fabrics with a minimum of downtime. Most importantly, they could cut the lead time between product idea and finished, delivered product from months to weeks, when compared with conventional weaving processes. That adaptability to changes in the marketplace was an important factor in the decision-making process. Time and events have yet to prove the rightness of this decision.

It's important to understand that fundamental technological change, and changing tastes and styles sometimes go hand in hand, as previously mentioned. For example, the housewife's cry for freedom from the ironing board couldn't be met until textile industry technology came up with an acceptable durable press finish. When that happened, a major industry upheaval took place as some people in the industry clearly foresaw. It cost billions of dollars in new plant and equipment, and it spelled doom for the all-cotton shirt and the all-cotton sheet.

SUMMARY AND CONCLUSION

A few current trends in life styles and tastes are listed for consideration. The author believes these to be either already operative or shortly to become very evident. What impacts will they have on your business?

1. Reversal in standard-of-living objectives—to less materialism.
2. More unisex.
3. Increased simplicity and casualness in dress and home furnishings.
4. Greater appreciation of the natural environment (by other than just conservationists).
5. Greater influence of the young—they will set many patterns and standards.

In anticipating and taking advantage of change, the chief executive must be sure to embrace in his perceptions those nonquantifiable changes in environment which can be characterized as changes in *tastes* and *styles*. He must develop the sensitivities of his staff to such changes and make certain the organization has sufficient flexibility to handle rapid change.

In dealing with change, the chief executive will apply his own judgment and intuition in addition to employing the many formal management tools available to him. He will monitor the organization's handling of change via the short- and long-range plans submitted for his approval on a periodic basis.

The competitive edge in the 1970s will go to the imaginative, environmentally sensitive, flexible corporation. The same characteristics must first apply to the Chief Executive Officer. He has to set the example. He has to make things happen.

The primary challenge of the contemporary chief executive is to see that change becomes his partner, and not his executioner.

TRADE REGULATION AND MARKETING

by William R. Tincher
Chairman and President, Purex Corporation

OTHER CHAPTERS in this section on marketing delineate sound organizational and operational steps to success in marketing. Unfortunately, success in those objectives is not the end of the marketing study because the proposed marketing strategy may violate the nation's antitrust and trade regulation laws.

These federal laws are baffling and frustrating to many businessmen, understood by few businessmen, and cussed by most businessmen at some time.[1] Like all laws and regulations, they are restraints and limitations on otherwise unfettered conduct. Most businessmen today recognize that some restraint and limitation is needed but the debate rages on the question of how much is needed. The problem is complicated in this country due to our emphasis on freedom of action in the marketplace and on separation of government and business.

The threshhold problem most marketing people have with trade regulation is twofold: (1) it prohibits that conduct which would be the most successful in the marketplace and (2) it does not appear to be sound on strictly economic grounds in many applications. Both beliefs are correct; and yet, I submit, we still need our national trade regulation laws.

A BIT OF USEFUL HISTORY

A brief history of why we have trade regulation is useful to address the above two points and to better understand specific trade regulation laws.

---

[1] Many states also have modified forms of antitrust and trade regulation laws. As a general rule, compliance with the federal laws obviates any state problems as most of them are based on the federal laws and are generally aimed at those businesses that may avoid federal coverage by their smallness or local nature.

From our independence and until a decade after the Civil War, we were a nation catching up with the industrial revolution of Europe. We were occupying the continent, ever expanding westward. The times were challenging; there was need for quick intra- and inter-industry cooperation; the economic growth in sight was unlimited. In short, except for an occasional panic, such as in 1837, there was, generally speaking, plenty of business for everyone.

Then, in the 1870s and 1880s, as the boundaries of the continent had been reached, and the space between settled and tied together, visible ceilings on growth began to appear. By then, great combines of enterprises which had joined together, of necessity, to meet the need for western expansion began to concentrate their strength in the older parts of the nation also. This strength, needed earlier for expansion of the nation, began to hurt smaller and independent concerns.

Simultaneously, two other movements rapidly gained momentum. Beginning in the Midwest, the great Populist political movement arose. For almost one hundred years the national Congress had been controlled by the eastern and southern states. In the 1870s and 1880s, the Populist movement, born in the middle states, began to assert itself. It needed an issue. Abuses by the gigantic combines and trusts furnished the issue. (Practically all of the nation's trade regulation laws mentioned hereafter had midwestern and western congressmen and senators as authors, and it is to be remembered that as early as the late 1850s the Republican party was born in Ripon, Wisconsin, as the liberal party of the day.) The second movement was in the large eastern cities—the rising attack against laissez-faire free enterprise, as another import from Europe, the emerging dogma of Marxism, began to be heard.

So, by the 1880s two facts stood out. American business was heavily concentrated in combines and trusts which hurt the smaller competition; and a new breed of politician, then as now in the 1970s, was eager to point out and capitalize on the obvious abuses.[2]

This concentration of sheer economic power, and resultant competitive abuses, thus brought in the late 1880s the first federal regulatory administrative body, the Interstate Commerce Commission—

---

[2] In all fairness to the reader, it should be pointed out that the author is an economic, political, and social conservative (and proud of that); but he also believes that business has been its own worst enemy and has brought on all the trade regulation laws by its own abuses. The only exception, he thinks, is the relatively recent so-called "fair packaging laws" which were unnecessary.

an attempt to regulate what even then was a mess in our railroad system. Then, in 1890 the Sherman-Antitrust Act was passed—the first real trade regulation law.

This law was an attempt to bring about the dissolution of the combines and the trusts—especially where large producers and railroads, in combine, froze out smaller producers. The law was ambiguous and largely unsuccessful and the few victories for the government took forever in litigation. The law aimed at monopolies and attempts to monopolize; but these were difficult for the government to establish, and for the courts, then far more conservative than the Populist movement, to interpret.

By Woodrow Wilson's presidency beginning in 1912, the nation was ready for more definitive trade regulation laws, even though by then the Sherman Act test of "reasonable probability" of monopolization had finally been initiated by the courts. The Clayton Act, and then the Federal Trade Commission Act, both in 1914, made a new ball game.

The Clayton Act outlawed certain *specific* acts in contrast to the earlier Sherman Act's broad and undefined "monopoly" theories. Outlawed, if the new and easier "may be" and "tendency to" monopoly tests were present, were tying agreements (if you want my Scotch, you have to buy my rum also), and certain exclusive dealing agreements, acquisitions, and interlocking business directorates.

The Federal Trade Commission Act took a completely different approach. Congress decided it was useless to list, say, 179 forbidden business practices because the business community would then conceive of practices numbered 180 and higher which would not be specifically outlawed. The Congress, therefore, in the FTC Act outlawed, on an undefined basis, all "unfair" methods of competition including false and misleading advertising; and an amendment in 1938 outlawed unfair or deceptive acts or practices in commerce. This broad mandate left the new FTC, as a quasi-judicial authority, to determine what was illegal.

The final mosaic of major trade regulation came in the Robinson-Patnam Act in the mid-30s amending the Clayton Act. This act prohibited certain price discrimination which would injure competition. Then, in 1950, the Celler-Kefauver amendment closed loopholes in Section 7 of the Clayton Act which had prevented the outlawing of most challenged acquisitions and mergers.

This brief background is presented to answer the two objections to trade regulation noted earlier. First, without any trade regulation laws certain marketing approaches were *too* successful. They literally destroyed competition—not by skill or brilliance, but by sheer, brute economic power. It was not a fair fight, and the American public said "stop." Second, the history explains why trade regulation laws are not "sound," in some cases, on strictly economic grounds. It is because they are far broader than economics—they embrace the nation's political and social policies. The nation, through its Congress, has decided that there have to be some ground rules regulating our otherwise free enterprise system.

Unfortunately, and especially in recent years, political demagogues have seized upon business abuses to pass laws far more strict than needed to curb the exposed abuses. Knowing this, business should be forewarned not to abuse the free enterprise system. But, as is true in practically all areas of law, the many have to pay for the transgressions of the few.

I do not ask you to agree with trade regulation or even to like it. I do suggest you understand the reasons as to why we have it. Today's chief executive has to live with trade regulation whether or not he likes it. His approval of marketing plans is ignorance compounded if he does not consider trade regulation implications in arriving at those plans.

FALSE AND MISLEADING ADVERTISING

The most common potential clash between marketing and trade regulation occurs in the field of advertising—which includes labels, brochures, and point-of-sale material as well as representations made in the media. Until the FTC Act of 1914, there was chaos in the nation's advertising—such chaotic abuse that the now humorous "snake oil" medicines, then offered to cure *all* ailments, were standard fare.[3]

In the intervening 61 years, the test for legal advertising has not changed its major premise. The test is—is it truthful? This is basically an easy black or white decision compared to the "grey" areas of most trade regulation. There have been several important refinements over the years from court interpretations of the FTC Act.

First, the courts early established the doctrine of "failure to reveal"

---

[3] By then, "snake oil" medicine advertising had reached a zenith and *any* claim was possible without reference to truth or accuracy.

(the forerunner of much SEC restriction). This doctrine held that advertising was false and/or misleading, even though the ad copy was literally true, if a material fact was omitted which would negate. or modify the advertising claim. To a chief executive who knows his products and what they can and cannot do, this doctrine is not too severe a test.

Another early interpretation by the courts was the "puffery" doctrine. This ruling allowed hyperbole and product bragging which was not 100 percent scientifically accurate but which was so close to truth, or was used in such close context with completely truthful ad copy, that the "puffery" for the product was considered unlikely to deceive the purchaser. Now, however, the puffery doctrine is not so available as a defense. This tightening of the puffery defense "loophole" has come about basically because advertisers have gone from the simple puffery common at the time of the early puffery decision, to the comparative, and then to the superlative puffery claim (i.e., from "good" to "better" to "best"). Currently, the FTC's attitude is that all but the most innocuous puffery must be capable of direct proof.

With the advent of television and the fantastic post–World War II growth of advertising, the business community itself has taken firm steps to assure honest advertising. The National Better Business Bureau is very active in self-policing of ads and business practices. The National Advertising Review Board, whose members come largely from large advertisers, takes an active role in encouraging truthful advertising, especially in TV ads. It is in this area of trade regulation that state attorneys general and local district attorneys have been most active. (Since 1945 the most blatantly false and misleading ads have been local in nature.)

In most cases, the CEO can determine the truthfulness of his company's proposed ads. I recommend that he get involved before they get before the public (1) because challenged ads can be very costly and embarrassing; and (2) because he learns a great deal about his marketing, his competition, and his marketplace by doing so.

Even in this most black-or-white area of trade regulation, the CEO will encounter borderline choices. His own brand managers or other house marketers and his outside advertising agency probably will encourage him to take a risk (called "brinkmanship" at the FTC). His house and/or outside lawyers will probably advise him not to take the risk. Who will play the role of Solomon? I recommend that the CEO make the decision. He, alone, has the overall view; he alone can evaluate the harm to the entire company if one ad is challenged—

for some companies the publicity harm from one challenged ad can tarnish the reputation of the entire company. In this deliberation, I can only advise him that the risk is seldom worth the potential gain.

Incidentally, this decision-making role by the CEO will occur also in the more serious and "greyer" areas of trade regulation. If somebody in the company is going to take trade regulation risks, it should be the CEO. If he allows subordinates to make these decisions, they will usually be more inclined to take small risks at first and then much greater risks. Subordinates can ruin a CEO, especially in trade regulation.

The newest wrinkle in advertising is direct head-to-head slugging, naming your competitor or his brand directly in your ad. This practice was almost unknown nine years ago and the networks, especially, strongly resist it. Here the advertiser has to be 100 percent truthful because the competitor will come charging back—in his ads, and with his lawyers in private lawsuits, and the FTC will be especially interested.

False and/or misleading advertising is of short range and short sighted value to the advertiser and competitively harmful to legitimate advertisers. It almost always can be avoided, especially if the CEO, or someone reporting directly to him in very large companies, makes the final decision.

OTHER DECEPTIVE ACTS AND PRACTICES AND UNFAIR METHODS OF COMPETITION

Congress has never given a federal regulatory agency a broader and less defined mandate than the FTC Act. Because specific practices are not outlawed, the Commissioners themselves can examine each new business practice to determine if it is unfair or deceptive.

Occasionally, the Commission will use this power (Section 5, FTC Act) to challenge rather hard-core antitrust practices which may not be reachable under the Sherman Act for narrow, technical reasons. Usually, however, the practices challenged are more in the areas of fraud, disparagement, or deceit than in the conspiratorial, monopolization, or discrimination area. Sometimes the challenged business practices are used in conjunction with false or misleading advertising although this is not a requirement.

Activities of door-to-door salesmen and offers of riches by mail are the most common. Again, as in false and misleading advertising, a test of simple honesty—moral and legal—can be made before a new practice is approved and then brings forth an FTC complaint. As might be expected, this type of trade regulation is the one in which state authorities and the consumer movement are most active.

As CEO, you should know that your company's representatives, whether they be door-to-door salesmen, retail salesmen, brand managers, engineers, or people in any other function, cannot:

a. Inaccurately disparage your competitor or his product.
b. Damage or destroy competitive merchandise.
c. Make promises which will not be honored.
d. Represent themselves or your company to be something they or your company are not.
e. Inaccurately claim affiliation, sponsorship, or participation with any other person or organization when such is not the case (especially if the organization is a governmental unit).
f. Take advantage of infirmities or handicaps or age (old or young).
g. Exaggerate fears, shortages, or catastrophes to achieve business.
h. Represent profit or earnings potential when your company's records show the potential gain is unlikely or only theoretically possible or mathematically unlikely.
i. Contend the listener has won or will win a prize or price reduction or contest unless it is an unqualified fact and, even then, the practice will be challenged if it is just a device to switch the customer to more expensive merchandise or to expend large sums of money subsequently.
j. Obtain large orders by indicating at first contact that only a small order is required.
k. Claim to offer degrees, awards, licenses, or jobs your company is not qualified to offer.
l. Take orders for inexpensive merchandise or services and then claim that only more expensive goods or services are available or adequate.
m. Send unsolicited merchandise and insist on payment.

This lengthy list is only a small fraction of acts and practices the FTC has found to be unfair and deceptive. They are unfair to honest competitors; they are deceptive to customers. The prevalent theme in all these cases is obvious—fraud, both legal and moral. Fraud, like the previously discussed false advertising, is relatively easy for the CEO to determine as he reviews proposed business practices. The test actually is more a question of common sense overcoming greed than it is a legal test—although a CEO should have experienced legal advice as he says yes or no to a proposed marketing method.

THE CLAYTON, ROBINSON-PATMAN, AND SHERMAN ACTS

These laws are far more complex and difficult to understand than the FTC Act. The CEO, therefore, cannot evaluate potential violations of these acts as he can most FTC Act problems as discussed earlier. Expert and experienced legal advice to evaluate compliance with or potential violation of these laws is essential and that advice must be taken very seriously.

Some transgressions of these acts can result in criminal charges and jail sentences, in treble damage lawsuits by governments (local, state and federal), customers, or competitors. Brinkmanship in these trade regulation laws is not risking the "slap on the wrists" of the ordinary FTC order; it is a major risk and exposure. This fact makes even more compelling the necessity of final CEO approval of marketing plans which might violate these acts. Subordinates are too prone to take unreasonable antitrust risks for which the CEO can be held responsible.

This risk historically was limited, because the Antitrust Division of the Justice Department and the FTC (which share concurrent jurisdiction in some antitrust enforcement and which enforce certain laws separately) were limited in funds and personnel; this limited the chances of antitrust violators being prosecuted. In recent years, however, their appropriations and complement of staff have increased dramatically.

Also significant to the CEO is the danger of antitrust violations causing private antitrust suits against his company. In 1946, only 68 such suits were filed; in the last two fiscal years almost 2,500 companies sued other companies alleging antitrust violations that damaged the plaintiffs. In the same period, the federal government filed only 108 antitrust lawsuits. The government usually only fines guilty companies, or orders them to "cease and desist" or orders divestiture as the case may be. Successful private plaintiffs collect *treble* damages.

The Robinson-Patman Act

A large proportion of the private and government antitrust actions involve price discrimination. By the mid-1930s, two curves had crossed on the business graph, especially in retail and wholesale trade—bigger sellers and bigger buyers. Production line techniques introduced decades earlier by Henry Ford had improved to the point where economies of scale were astounding. In many industries, the 1,000th unit produced, because of fixed cost and various economies of scale, produced far more profit per unit than the 100th or even the 900th. Simultaneously, because grocery chains were replacing "Mom and Pop" stores, and this chain movement was spreading in drug and other retail outlets, the voice of the proprietor became less and less important in recommending the brand to be purchased, as advertising or "preselling" became more powerful. Market share became far more important than in the past and huge national sales forces were pushing their companies' products more aggressively than former distribution methods had.

This chain of events led big sellers to offer their competing customers prices individually arrived at, based largely on the size of the purchase. Thus, the small customer or chain which could not use as many units as its bigger competitor was charged far more per unit than its bigger competitor. Also, small sellers which did not enjoy the economies of scale benefits because of their smaller production, or could not advertise heavily or did not have a powerful and aggressive sales force, found that the special prices offered by their larger competitors to their larger customers also had an effect beyond the immediate lost sale. That effect was that the large customer bought so many units at one time at such a lower price per unit that his needs for subsequent purchases for weeks or months were satisfied, and the small producer was foreclosed and lost his market share.

These abuses led to the Robinson-Patman Act in 1936, which prohibits price discrimination by a seller to its competing customers. This law is complex and, by FTC and court interpretations, has changed direction in some respects over the years. In general, sellers must charge *competing* customers the same price, although *genuine* cost savings to the seller because of a particular buyer's purchasing habits or quantities can be passed on to that buyer. Likewise, a "good faith" meeting of a competitive price is generally allowed; but this means to "meet and not to beat" the competitive offering and not to sell below cost.

These two exceptions are confusing and complex. They are deeply based in accounting theories and the FTC's accountants many times do not agree with a defendant's ("respondent's") accountants. (Accounting, it must be remembered, is in some applications more an art than a science, and there are different schools of thought within the accounting profession.) Quantity discounts are permissible if based on genuine economic savings to the seller that derive directly from the quantity purchased. The most common of these is the much smaller cost per unit for freight if the buyer orders a carload (rail or truck) rather than a fraction of a carload of the seller's merchandise. This, of course, benefits the multiple product producer of goods going to the same customer, because customers ordering several items are more likely to fill a car with the order than those ordering only one product from a seller.

Although the accounting problems can be a nightmare, the thrust of the law is that competing customers should pay the same price unless the sheer size of a customer's order causes genuine direct and measurable economic benefits which—but only to that exact extent of savings—may be passed on to that customer via a lower price. Thus, some price "discrimination" is allowable and is commonplace, but it is minor compared to the arbitrary and massive price discriminations that were common before the act was passed. Actually, the law causes most economies of scale by the large seller to be passed on to all customers rather than to only a few favored large buyers. Guidance for the CEO on pricing must come from his lawyers and his accountants.

The act also outlaws geographical price discrimination—selling your product at lower prices in one area than in others—if your competitors in the lower-priced (usually a small or local) area may be damaged. The theory involved here is the "deep pocket" theory—that a large and powerful (usually a national) seller will cut its prices in a small area to hurt competition with the idea that its reduced income in the small area will be made up or subsidized by its sales outside the small area. The practice is especially harmful to a local or regional competitor who is adversely affected in his entire sales universe while the price cutter's lower prices affect it in only a small part of its much larger sales universe. The local congressman becomes especially incensed at this practice when his constituent businessmen complain (and that is the first place many businessmen, especially small ones, take their antitrust complaints) and the congressman demands FTC action. The FTC, as an independent regulatory agency, is a creature of the Congress and not of the executive branch. It is not unimportant that FTC appropriations come from Congress.

Although the particular circumstances are not delineated in the statute as a defense, the FTC usually does not proceed in geographical price discriminations if only a *limited* introduction of a new product is involved, whether by the larger or the local concerns, and if a new competitive structure is being created. After the limited introductory period, and from the beginning if new products are not involved, geographical price discrimination is dangerous from a legal point of view. The degree of difference in the price between the target area and the other areas is important. If the difference merely reflects freight differences, there usually is no problem.

In all Robinson-Patman problems, including cost justification, selling below cost creates an extremely heavy legal burden for a seller to overcome. The appearance of predatory behavior in many cases overcomes all accounting defenses. Absent a new product introduction, as to which there are different theories of what "cost" is (and the FTC really does have some understanding of the need for, and problems of new product introduction), selling below "cost", even if to competing customers, is considered so predatory that the Sherman Act (attempt to monopolize) as well as the Robinson-Patman Act may be a real danger to the seller.

The Robinson-Patman Act takes cognizance that price discrimination also can occur indirectly. To prevent this, the act requires that advertising and promotional allowances to a seller's competing customers must be offered on a "proportionally equal" basis. This language recognizes that competing customers advertise and promote differently and that a seller cannot give to every competing customer exactly the same allowances for these services which benefit his product. Thus, he can, in the grocery trade for example, help underwrite both the large chain's newspaper ad and the handbill of the small "Mom and Pop" store which cannot afford more expensive advertising. In exercising this flexibility, however, the seller cannot arbitrarily allow some customers more monies (or free goods or whatever) than smaller ones on a *per-unit-purchased* basis. Promotional programs, thus, can be tailored for classes of customers within the larger group of all competing customers, but must be carefully done on a proportionally equal basis.

If he grants such allowances (and practically all sellers do, at least sporadically), the seller must set up on paper a compliance program to prove, later, that the customer actually performed the promotional service for which the seller paid him (otherwise the nonperformer simply received a price discrimination). To meet the legal test, most sellers require a performance certificate and proof of the performance (copies of the ad, pictures or lists of the stores featuring the special displays, etc.). Unfortunately, the enforcement of the proof of performance must usually be left to sales personnel who dislike fussing at the customer for the proof. Like any other type of legal evidence, however, contemporary documents are much better than proof that was re-created later.

The act also requires brokerage payments to be genuine, because, if they are not, the buyer probably receives a discriminatory price. The broker must be independent, perform an actual, useful service, and must not be a sham set up by either party.

Finally, the act believes it is as bad to receive as to give discriminatory prices; accordingly, one of its sections can be used, in addition to proceeding against the seller, to proceed against a buyer who induces, compels, or otherwise receives an illegal pricing advantage not received by his competitors who buy from the same seller.

The interpretation of the law exempts *genuine* sales of obsolete and "off spec" goods and sales to the government (which does not mind receiving lower prices!).

The objective of the act is quite clear, to prevent price favoritism, direct or indirect—to selected competing customers. After almost four decades, how to comply is still very confusing and changing. The antitrust bar is usually vociferously critical of the act. The criticism goes to legal ambivalence and to accounting disputes, however. To most of us in the business community, this act is a security blanket. It means that we can plan our marketing on a fairly reasonable and long-range basis, knowing that the most affluent and the most aggressive of our competitors—whether we are sellers or buyers—legally cannot quickly and devastatingly depress our sales by giving or receiving massive discriminatory prices.

The Remainder of the Clayton Act

The Robinson-Patman amendment to the Clayton Act is the most common pitfall of marketing problems. The Clayton Act also outlaws tie-in sales wherein a seller requires a buyer to buy a less desirable or less needed product in order to buy a more needed or more desirable product. The objective is to protect the one-product, or small concern against the multiple-product, or much larger concern. This prohibits direct full-line forcing by the multiple-product company.

The most difficult interpretation usually occurs when a seller maintains that, because it has to warrant the untied product, it should have the right to require the purchase of the tie-in product, if the two products are used together, to assure proper functioning and quality (for example, if the untied product is a machine using chemicals, the tie-in chemical product is used in performing its task). This is about the only good defense to forced tie-in sales and it is good only if products competitive with the tie-in product actually will not perform satisfactorily in, or with the seller's untied product. This does not occur often.

The law also prohibits various attempts at exclusive dealing such as requiring your customer or your franchisee to handle only your products, or giving your customer or franchisee exclusive territories. Although marketing is involved in these decisions, the main question is how to distribute, rather than how to market per se. Therefore, this article will not go into that hornet's nest except to note that this is a volatile and changing area of the law. Rights and duties of exclusivity that were unchallenged in the past are now being challenged—not only by the government, but by the customers and franchisees themselves in private antitrust actions (car dealers against car manufacturers, fast-food franchisees against fast-food franchisors). In today's climate of consumer and small-company champions (mostly self-appointed) and stepped up government action against bigness and market foreclosures, the very words involved—exclusive, sole dealer, territorial rights, purchase requirements, quotas, termination penalties, etc.—are sufficient warning to the CEO not to proceed in these activities without competent antitrust advice. The tremendous recent growth of the service industry and of franchising has focused attention and action on all distribution techniques involving exclusive arrangements. Indeed, a very recent Supreme Court ruling should cause all CEOs to review existing exclusive arrangements.

A seldom-used section of the Clayton Act forbids interlocking directorates of individuals. The original target was competitors sitting on each other's boards of directors. Recent threats of the use of this section have caused directors to resign from boards where a vertical relation exists (i.e., a seller being on a buyer's board or vice versa, or both, or even where the vertical arrangement was only potential and not actual). There is not yet a definitive court ruling stretching the section's coverage that far, and the practice is quite common. In the vertical cases involving the "jawboning" resulting in subsequent resignations, the individuals involved probably did not desire the publicity and, in most of them, one, or both, of the companies involved was already in the government's or the public's spotlight of disfavor for various reasons and did not want the further publicity of formal charges. This new application is, of course, diametrically contrary to the increasing trend of American concerns to have more "outside" directors and to the shortage of good, qualified outside directors.

The last pertinent section of the Clayton Act is Section 7, the antimerger law. The amendment of this section in 1950 eliminated several key loopholes which, from the government's viewpoint, had made the law ineffective. The legislative history made quite clear that the amended law applied to vertical and conglomerate, as well as horizontal acquisitions, and even to limited geographic areas ("in any section of the country") larger only than a small village. The government's attention in the 60s swung from the price fixing cases of the late 50s and early 60s ("the desire to conspire") to the tremendous number of acquisitions and mergers in the 60s ("the urge to merge").

From a marketing view, antimerger law is the most difficult of the antitrust laws to understand because the factors that make an acquisition most valuable and economically sound are the very same factors that make it, from a legal view, most violative of law. Synergism, efficiencies, elimination of duplicative and/or overlapping costs, functions, or services, increased competitive strength, better market share and/or market rank, larger advertising discounts, enlarged or consolidated sales forces or elimination of brokers, reduced sales costs per unit, increased distribution, reduced out-of-stocks, adding to or complementing a line of related products, and many other benefits, can accrue to the acquiring company and add immeasurably to its marketing strength. The paradox is, however, that these acquired advantages are also large factors in a governmental decision to challenge and declare an acquisition illegal. The government rationale is that new strengths flowing from an acquisition must, of necessity, cause offsetting new weaknesses in the remaining competition (usually in the acquired's "line of commerce").

This is by far the most complicated, controversial, and time-consuming—and probably most expensive—of all antitrust actions. There are scores of tests and relevant factors intertwined in determining legality; the study is economic more than legal; the relevant industries and their members involved are studied, dissected, and compared, as well as the acquirer and the acquired; and the relationship and importance of all these factors is argued and theorized. The study of the involved companies and industries covers every function of management, especially marketing. All of this vast record is used, not to determine a relatively easy question—*has* competition been injured by the acquisition—but to answer the statute's test which is a far more difficult guessing game: *Will* competition in the *future* be sufficiently damaged ("may be substantially to lessen competition, or to tend to create a monopoly")?

For all of these reasons, it is impossible to guide the CEO in these pages on how to determine, himself, whether a proposed acquisition would be challenged and, if so, the odds on the success of the challenge. However, several suggestions can be useful in any acquisition situation, as follows.

1.   You need the advice of an experienced merger attorney; there is no alternative.

2.   You, and perhaps your lawyer, have to evaluate the proposed acquisition from the view of what the law is, and not what you think the law should be. This may sound funny, but this law, more so than any antitrust law, is predicated on congressional embodiment of national social, political, and economic *attitudes* rather than on objective realities of sound economics or sound business approaches. Thus, for example, the argument which occurs naturally to a CEO that A acquiring B will make a more efficient and economically viable survivor and that this fact, therefore, logically, should validate the acquisition, is actually contrary to the controlling decisions. The greater the efficiency or economic strength achieved by an acquisition, the greater also is the legal risk.

3.   In horizontal cases (acquiring your competitor) and in vertical cases (acquiring your supplier or your customer) even *very* small market shares can be challenged successfully.

4.   In all situations, the concentration within the relevant product and geographic markets is a key factor, and acquisitions in highly concentrated industries are more likely to be challenged than where there is a lack of concentration.

5.   Acquiring "to be more competitive with the industry leader(s)" generally is not a valid defense if enough other factors are against the acquisition.

6.   A defense that the challenged acquisition occurred because of

other acquisitions by competitors will also fail if enough other adverse factors are shown by the government.

7.   Ease of entry by prospective entrants is a key test. The more difficult and costly entry is, the weaker the defense of an acquisition in that industry is.

8.   The *probability* that the acquirer would or might have entered the acquired's industry by internal means if the acquisition had not occurred is a key test. The more likely that probability, the weaker the acquisition defense is.

9.   The marketing clout, image, and history of both the acquirer and the acquired, and of their remaining competitors, is a key test. This will be studied in a context of change (if any) in the competitive viability of the relevant competition.

10.   Intent is not a required test for the government, although evidence of predatory, aggressive, or ruthless competitive history by the involved parties is evidence relating to the ultimate conclusionary question of what will happen after the acquisition. In that connection, the old Sherman Act test has been adopted that mere *possession* of power (as a result of the challenged acquisition) is the test and not an objective showing that the power will be used nor a subjective contention that it will not be used.

This frightening array of legal tests must be considered in the proper frame of reference by the CEO. Thousands of acquisitions have occurred since the law was amended in 1950. Only a relatively few of these have been challenged—many involving hundreds of millions of dollars have not even been challenged.

The name of the game in American business is growth, which comes either from internal efforts or external techniques—largely acquisitions. Internal growth usually means growth of new products that, at least, will offset the decline of old products which are on the downside of the maturity curve. Unfortunately, about 85 percent of new consumer products introduced do fail and the failures are costly. Although the figure is not easily determined, a large percentage of new industrial products also fail. Avoiding these costly failures and also gaining valuable time by acquiring products which have survived this entry test and offer an instant and established franchise, and which may help the acquirer in other aspects as well, is the benefit the CEO must weigh against the antitrust risk of the acquisition (*a*) being challenged and (*b*) being successfully challenged. The task is not easy, but the rewards can be quick, substantial, and long lasting or, as the 70s have shown, disastrous as well. For the CEO to play in this expensive and complicated game without competent *merger* attorneys is, in today's world, unthinkable.

The Sherman Act

This grandaddy of the trade regulation laws is potentially the most dangerous of all of them for the CEO, because violators are subject to heavy penalties, possible jail sentences, and a far greater degree of public scorn than other types of antitrust violations. The overall objective of the act is to prevent restraints of trade, attempts to monopolize, or actual monopolies—whether by singular means or in combines or conspiracies with others.

Marketing people are the ones most likely to cause Sherman Act violations and, generally speaking, they are more prone to live dangerously (antitrust "brinkmanship") than are CEOs. It is incumbent on the CEO to set up some sort of legal review of proposed marketing actions to prevent antitrust problems, especially Sherman Act situations.

The law is far too voluminous to review here. Once again, certain major tests should be familiar to the CEO as an early warning system so that he will at least know to call in his lawyers.

a. Competitors (two or any other number) cannot get together and fix or determine prices, bids, terms, and conditions of sales, the makeup or quality of products, dates of price changes, who will or will not sell to certain customers or in certain areas or at certain times, boycott suppliers, customers, or competitors or decide upon any course of joint action directed against any other business concern or group.

b. Competitors cannot directly accomplish any of the forbidden practices mentioned in paragraph *a* above or indirectly through intermediaries, other third persons, or trade associations. A special body of trade association antitrust law has developed to prevent illegal conspiring, or collusion among competitors. Trade association memberships are usually held by marketing executives. The CEO should require his representatives in trade associations to meet with the company's lawyers in order to learn of the pitfalls and danger signs and limitations on trade association activities. There are many valuable things a trade association can do; there are some activities it cannot do because of antitrust and, especially, the Sherman Act. The CEO's trade association representatives should know the difference.

c. A company can also violate the Sherman Act all by itself. Marketing activities which would not concern the government if done by a weak competitor can be considered overly aggressive, predatory, or an attempt to monopolize if done in certain factual and competitive settings by a major competitor. It is comparable to the average citizen swinging his fists around compared to the professional prizefighter swinging *his* fists. In the latter cases, the fists are, so to say, "lethal weapons" from a legal point of view. Marketing power and size carries a heavier Sherman Act potential liability.

d. The government antitrusters are cynical and suspicious (and with lots of reason to be so, unfortunately). They believe conspiracy, even industrywide, can be achieved—especially to fix prices—without actual meetings or agreements. Thus, such exotic antitrust theories as "conscious parallelism" and "administered prices" are advanced to allege conspiracy and collusion when no overt and direct proof can be found of nonunilateral action.

e. The best advice is to make all your business decisions, especially marketing ones, completely unilaterally. A few idle remarks, a casual meeting, even an exchange of season's greetings have been used as code words for conspiracies in the past. What the businessman knows to be innocuous at the time can appear damning at a later date. Where intent and subjective evaluation is involved, as here, the total can be, and even more often appears to be, greater than the sum of the parts.

CONCLUSION

Entire books have been written on single minor antitrust terms or tests. Giant multiple-volume sets of guides with regular supplements are required to keep even the most experienced and sophisticated trade-regulation lawyer up to date. Obviously, neither the CEO nor his marketing people can be expected to (nor should they) become experts in this field. For the same reason, this article can only lightly touch upon the subject and serve as a background sufficient to describe danger areas. Even this limited undertaking must contain the caveat that the general statements are subject to exceptions, modifications, practicalities, and changing decisions. Also, one company can do with legal impunity that which hangs another company because of even minor differences in the competitive situation, the workload of, or the political pressure brought upon, the enforcement agencies, and other prevailing public attitudes. The objective in this article is simply to warn the CEO of the overall nature of trade regulation so that he can recognize symptoms and know when to see the doctor—his trade-regulation lawyer.

PART IV-D
Finance

THE CHIEF FINANCIAL OFFICER: WHAT TO LOOK FOR, HOW TO GET TOP PERFORMANCE

by Robert Anderson
President and Chief Executive Officer, Rockwell International

As LATE as the 1960s the Chief Financial Officer (CFO) in many manufacturing companies might as well have been titled CBC—"Chief Bean Counter."

Essentially, the Chief Financial Officer was the record keeper of the company's past performance and condition. If he did have an influence on current and future business, it was in a passive and negative mode. He could show you where things went wrong or right, and if you were lucky, he could tell you why. But he probably couldn't tell you how to do it better next time, and he certainly wasn't expected to suggest wholly new avenues for making more money than before.

In short, top management's view of him and his staff was strongly tinged with the Dickensian image of Bob Cratchit, eyeshade and all, who sat on a high stool marking a ledger sheet with a quill pen.

If the Chief Financial Officer was also the Treasurer, then he had an additional role—that of cultivating the company's banker.

So in choosing a CFO, the CEO tended to look for the best accountant on the staff and perhaps also one who had the personal "moxie" to get a sizable loan with a phone call.

All of this began changing in the late 1960s—faster with some industries and companies than others. At that time management began to recognize several new factors in the business world.

NEW FACTORS

Some of the new factors recognized by management were:

1. Fiscal considerations—taxes; depreciation and appreciation; interest; insurance; receivables and payables; government reporting and

bookkeeping requirements—had become more complex and far more important to the company's P&L results. In some cases, they had become more important than the company's competitive performance in the marketplace.

2. Operating factors—materials purchasing; make-or-buy decisions; capital expenditures; inventories; pricing; labor contracts; pensions and other benefits—were all recognized as being primarily financial matters. They needed to be influenced by a financial function capable of quantifying and evaluating a vast pattern of alternative trade-offs.

3. A growing array of government requirements—consumer; safety; environmental—were now of such magnitude that they impacted heavily on financial results, and their effects had to be measured and factored into the total picture.

4. Because outside financing had become particularly important as a source of capital, the CFO in the role of Treasurer had to be an expert in the money market. No longer content to maintain a close relationship with one or two banks, he had to understand and be able to choose among a wide range of capital sources for various purposes and time periods.*

5. Diversification was seen as an important means of improving company security and stability; mergers and acquisitions were recognized as the best way to accomplish this in the shortest time. This brought a new need for outside capital, and the CFO had to become an expert in high finance.

6. New data handling capabilities (in the form of computers and computer programming) were now available to provide more penetrating and timely visibility of operations. This meant that the CFO was no longer just an historian; instead of giving you last year's or last quarter's results, he could give a monthly or even weekly status, and even an almost instant report on a key factor if it were really needed. Moreover, he could give you new and more telling measurements of performance by a division, a product line, or even an individual executive. All of this enabled the Chief Executive Officer and his line officers to react to bad news—or good news—on a timely basis.

7. Corporate planning could and should be depicted in quantitative terms, and hence it often fell into the province of the CFO. In

---

* [Ed. Note: See the chapter by Eli Shapiro and Barbara Negri Opper, "Changing Structure of the Financial Markets."]

fact, among corporate officers he was often in the best position to contribute an evaluation of certain crucial outside conditions—the worldwide financial and economic environment—within which the company must operate. He could warn of dangers and, more important, he could identify profit opportunities.

ROLES

As these new business considerations came to be understood by top management, the CFO took on much broader responsibilities and authority. He moved from a passive to an active role in corporatewide management—a role in many cases subordinate only to the President and the Chairman.

He became the Chief Executive Officer's main source of hard information about operations throughout the company—not just their past performance, but their current position relative to plans and budget and, most important, their future prospects.

The new roles for the Chief Financial Officer have certainly affected the type of capabilities to look for in choosing him. Accounting skills are still basic, of course, but virtuosity in these skills can be hired as part of the financial staff. What really counts for the CFO is to know how to use the results of these skills in the larger direction of the company—in promoting cost-effective operations and especially in flagging out areas promising the best return on company resources.

So, far from being a topnotch numbers man, he needs to be what might be called the "compleat man."

This does not really start with being a strategist or planner, though these are essential, but with being a philosopher. For the CFO should share with the CEO the task of formulating and reviewing the company's goals, to which strategy and planning then become tributary. And he needs to conduct his planning in the full awareness of the worldwide social, political, and economic environment that will affect both the direction and the feasibility of those plans. He must be so attuned to the present that he can do as well as anyone else in predicting the future.

The CFO must instill in the organization the necessity for profit planning and effective cost controls. The profit plan serves as a road map indicating how the company will reach its goals and as a benchmark to measure periodically the company's progress. Cost controls provide a vehicle to monitor performance in controlling every significant element of cost by comparing actual results with plans and forecasts and by determining the factors responsible for variances. This information allows management to take corrective action promptly.

Without these two fundamental financial planning tools, a company is like a ship sailing uncharted waters without the aid of navigation equipment.

ORGANIZATIONAL RELATIONS

The CFO should have other sensitivities that are outside the tradition of the Chief Bean Counter.

Probably the foremost of these ingredients is a strong dose of human *simpatico*. He needs to be expressive and persuasive in putting forth his own ideas, and he needs to be sensitive to the underlying needs, desires, and motivations of others—the CEO, the operational heads whose business he must monitor and to a degree influence, and his own staff members whom he must recruit and inspire.

Vis-à-vis the CEO, he needs to have a close comfortable working relationship—not necessarily in a social sense, though that helps, but certainly in an intellectual sense. The two should understand each other to the degree that they can predict each other's reaction to a particular business situation. This doesn't mean that the CFO should be programmed to agree with the CEO on every proposed solution— this would destroy his usefulness. But he and the CEO should have the same general set of values and objectives as far as the company is concerned. Thus they can bounce ideas back and forth within the same frame of reference, leading, let us hope, to a decision that is agreed upon because it is the product of logic.

In his relationship with the heads of line operations, the CFO has to maintain a personal rapport that invites cooperation. But more than this, he has to maintain a high level of credibility in his knowledge of their work. He should be so sensitive to their special problems that, in an Operations Committee meeting, he can blow the whistle on a general manager's plan and still retain the manager's respect and confidence. He should be able to say, "That won't work," and prove it.

Regarding his own staff, the CFO should be a superb picker and developer of people. For no matter how brilliant, he cannot cover his many responsibilities by himself nor even make all the necessary evaluations and judgments himself. To provide all the contributions to corporate management of which the financial function is capable in today's environment, the CFO needs not only a headquarters staff but also echelons of financial people who serve in a controller's role at the operations level. These may have either a solid-line or a dotted-line relationship to the CFO, but their function is to give fiscal control and direction to the line operations at the level where the operating decisions are made.

To fill these posts, the CFO needs to recognize talented people who, like himself, understand how data can be used as a vital tool in guiding the commitment of resources. He needs to see that they are exposed to the other major functions of the business—marketing, engineering, purchasing, and the like—so that their inputs to the system will be realistic. And he needs to inspire them with the importance of their function to the security and success of the business.

PROFIT IMPROVEMENT

However, above all, the CFO in today's business world must be sensitive to the dynamics that determine profits. And if he is using the data-generating tools available to him, he has at his disposal a network of information sources that can turn up such profit-improvement possibilities.

He can show the CEO the total costs of employing capital, acquired either internally or externally, and what kind of ROI should be achieved to justify any given project.

He can put the calipers on any particular risk under consideration, so that top management's decision will be based not on seat-of-the-pants "feel," but on a quantified estimate of the chance of success.

He can approach any given business problem and, by changing the variables in the equation, come up with alternative eventualities that could be expected under changing conditions.

With such a capability the CFO can tackle such questions as:

Do new conditions in the domestic or international markets warrant investing in a new product line, a new subsidiary, or a new market?

What would be the company's financial exposure if it were to win a life-cycle government procurement contract involving fixed price elements, considering the technical advancement required and the anticipated inflation during the contract period?

What ROI could be anticipated in a future time frame from a specific acquisition, in view of the need for a large infusion of resources to strengthen the company's technical, marketing, or other capabilities?

Regarding sublevel performance by a particular division, what steps must be taken to bring it up to company standards, and how do the chances of accomplishing this compare with the possible advantages of selling the operation and channeling the same company resources in another and possibly more profitable direction?

In determining whether to buy or lease a major facility or a string of outlets, how is the decision affected by the anticipated rate of property appreciation in this time of inflation?

It should be noted that these kinds of questions in which the CFO should play a major role run the whole gamut of company operations. Whereas the CFO used to be the main determinant for only the liabilities side of the balance sheet, he has assumed this role for the assets side, and he has also become a prime factor affecting the numbers that appear on the income statement.

He has, or should have, an organization and an accounting system running throughout the company that provides timely and trustworthy data—not only on financial performance but also on operating activities and executive performance.

As these data are analyzed, he can then provide the refined information on which a decision may be made, and can even offer quantified arguments for a whole range of solutions to maximize performance and profit.

From this it may be seen that the CFO's function can no longer be considered a staff function which simply serves the line operation. Since it has become a prime mover in the determination of profit throughout the organization, it has itself become a special kind of line operation. The CFO must hang up the eye shade of the bean counter and visualize himself as wearing the hard hat of the doer and the maker (money maker, if you will). And the CEO must find and choose a CFO who accepts this responsibility and thinks of himself in this role.

PERFORMANCE OF THE CFO

Having chosen his CFO, the CEO must determine how to get top performance. But in large part this has already been answered in making the right choice.

Let us assume that the modern incentives for corporate executives are well used in this case, and that another normal requirement for high morale is fully met—that of matching assigned responsibilities with the appropriate authority to carry them out.*

Then it seems to me that, if you have chosen a CFO who understands the major role expected of him, who knows how to carry it out, and who is exhilarated by tangible results of his work in terms of company profits, you will get top performance.

The one additional ingredient for this kind of success is the CEO's personal, highly visible support for the CFO and the work of his staff. In his role in today's management, the CFO enters boldly where he scarcely dared tread a few years ago. He and his staff inject themselves into the very business of the line operations, in effect looking over the shoulders of the division presidents, in many cases suggesting what they should or should not do, and in turn reporting on their performance to the CEO. This is a situation made to order for resentment and bad feeling if it is not well handled.

It is up to the CEO to make it clear to the line officers from the beginning that this charter for the financial function is part and parcel of his way of doing business. It is not a peripheral activity or an experiment. In operations committee meetings and in other personal encounters, he needs to demonstrate that he relies highly on the inputs of the financial function, that he places great value on the judgments of the CFO, that the financial activity is in fact an extension of his own managerial arm, and that it is essential in maintaining the company's success against its competitors.

If he does this, and if the CFO is as good at maintaining personal rapport as we have already described, then the CEO will get top performance from his financial function, and he will go a long way toward winning top performance for the company.

---

* [Ed. Note: See the chapters by Milton L. Rock, "Managing Executive Compensation" and by Donald S. MacNaughton, "Basic Organization Structure."]

FINANCIAL STRUCTURE: BASIC BUILDING BLOCKS

by George H. Dixon

Chairman and President, First National Bank of Minneapolis

and John Schreiner

Chairman, Department of Finance, University of Minnesota

INTRODUCTION

THIS CHAPTER is written for the benefit of Chief Executive Officers who have moved to the executive suite without having had significant experience in matters of financial policy and strategy. This chapter's purpose is to provide you, the chief executive, with a beginning and, we hope, useful framework with which to consider how best to build and maintain an optimal financial structure for your company.

Let's begin with some straightforward wisdom and advice:

DO make up your mind whether, financially speaking, you prefer to "eat well" or to "sleep well"—whether you favor a financial structure which is relatively speculative or one which is relatively conservative. Where your company should lie on the "eat well/ sleep well" continuum depends on the nature of the business and on the style of the management.

DO remember that most of the time, confidence in a company's financial structure is greater if it falls within the spectrum of financial structures of similarly situated businesses.

DO remember the three tenets of good financial management— simplicity, flexibility, and safety. Somewhere, sometime, your business will surely be confronted with significant unplanned and unforeseen adversity. This is when you'll understand and appreciate having lived by them (or regret mightily your failure to have done so).

Financial structure can be thought of as a set of building blocks

664

which define the relationships between a business's investors and that business's assets. Every businessman knows, for example, that the basic building block, the foundation of every financial structure, is common stock. All other financing forms are related to and build upon this base in a pyramid-like fashion, as illustrated in Exhibit 1. These financing forms include (in decreasing order of maturity and risk): preferred stock, bonds, leases, and current liabilities, each of which has many varieties. All of these bear less risk than common stock and all receive a limited reward. These building blocks introduce leverage into the financial structure and, at the same time, permit potential investors to choose among securities of various risk-reward classes.

EXHIBIT 1
Financial Structure (a pyramid of building blocks)

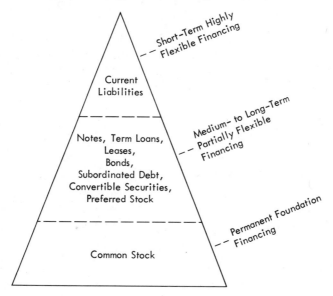

Financial structure is not necessarily static; it can, and perhaps should, shift over time as a result of various internal and external forces. The significant internal forces are the business's funds flows and its asset-mix requirements. Funds in-flows are generated from operations and from the acquisition of new outside capital. Out-flows result from acquisition of all kinds of assets, from payments to creditors, and from distributions to stockholders.

Externally, you are concerned with the availability of capital. This depends upon your company's attractiveness as an investment alternative and upon the general availability of capital in the capital markets in the building-block forms which you can use. An ideal financial structure consists of that simplest set of financial building blocks which, on the one hand, caters to investor preferences and, on the other hand, provides funds to your business at reasonable cost. Building a financial structure is a process of "mediating" between the needs of investors and the needs of the business.

The mediation process by which financial building blocks are constructed with some relationship to assets is expressed in the diagrammatic balance sheet, Exhibit 2. The blocks on the left represent asset categories. These appear in order of their liquidity, beginning with cash and followed by accounts receivable, inventory, fixed assets, and other assets. The first three of these constitute "current assets," which, by definition, are expected to be converted into cash within a year.

The building blocks on the right represent debt and ownership. These traditionally appear in published financial statements in order of "seniority" and/or length of maturity. Seniority means priority of claims on earnings or, in the event of liquidation, priority of claims on assets. Maturity is simply the due date for repayment. Assets are always funded by the sum of current liabilities, long-term liabilities, and ownership capital.

The simplest capital structure consists of two financial building blocks—common stock and current liabilities. This conservative structural form is appealing from many standpoints and is, in fact, used by many firms, including some that are large and well known. It is the most stable, the least risky, and normally the most flexible of financial structures. The stockholders carry all of the risks and receive all of the available rewards of the business.

More often than not, however, a simple two-building-block structure fulfills neither the goal of the business manager to increase profits, nor the preference of some investors to lend fixed amounts for a specified period rather than invest permanently in common stocks.

Many managements make use of "leverage," that is, strive to increase long-run average profits for common stockholders by borrowing money and then attempting to employ it at a net profit over its cost. The gain, or leverage, comes—if it does—from paying an interest rate lower than the rate of earnings realized on the total capital invested in the business. Leverage may increase profits, but it also increases the volatility of earnings and the riskiness of the business. Leverage be-

EXHIBIT 2
Balance Sheet (in building block form)

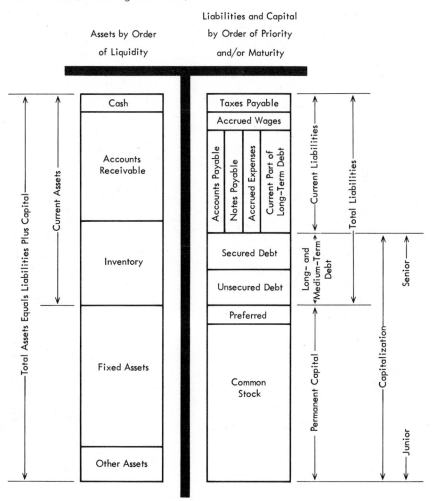

comes negative when the rate of return earned is less than the interest rate that has to be paid on the borrowed money. So if leverage is to be used, it should first be thoroughly understood.

    DO remember that leverage works in two directions—its desirable effects in good times must be weighed against its undesirable effects when operating earnings are down.

    DO remember that the corporate wrecks which lie on the shoals of pyramided debt, or excessive leverage, are legion.

Let's look next in some detail at the individual financial building blocks and then return to the matter of leverage and to other considerations in financial structure decision-making.

COMMON STOCK

Basic Building Block

As has been explained, common stock, the corporation's most junior security, is the basic building block of its financial structure. There may or may not be preferred stock, bonds, or leases, but every corporation has common stock.

Common stockholders are the recipients of all income and of all liquidating value—if any—which remain after the claims of employees, governments, trade creditors, and of senior securities holders have been met. Often called the residual security, common stock has no fixed claim, rather simply stands last in line and receives whatever is left—much, little, or nothing.

Voting Power

In addition to their residual rights to earnings and assets, common stockholders usually have all, or nearly all, of the voting power to elect the corporation's directors. The typical exception is that preferred stockholders usually receive partial voting rights when a specified number of preferred dividend payments have been omitted.

Two Initial Decisions

In preparation for the initial issue of common stock, two significant decisions must be made—whether voting for directors shall be cumulative or noncumulative, and whether existing stockholders are to have preemptive subscription rights in subsequent stock offerings.

Cumulative Voting

Under cumulative voting, each share of stock has votes equal to the number of directors to be elected. A stockholder can concentrate his votes in behalf of one or a small number of directors (to the exclusion of others) in the hope of their gaining representation on the board.

Under this procedure, a minority group has the power to elect a given number of directors if the number of shares which it owns is greater than:

$$\frac{d\,N}{D+1}$$

where:

d = number of minority directors sought
N = total number of shares to be voted
D = total number of directors to be elected

If, for example, a total of 1,000 shares outstanding are to be voted for 10 directorships under cumulative voting, a minority faction with at least 91 shares ($1,000 \div 11 = 90.9$), has the power to elect one director; and it can elect two directors if it has at least 182 shares ($2 \times 1,000 \div 11 = 181.8$).

Cumulative voting is appealing to the democratically minded because it offers an opportunity for various stockholder groups to achieve board representation, somewhat like a legislature. And in various family and merger situations, cumulative voting can be used to assure minority interests of *some* representation on the board. In the absence of this provision, a majority stock interest has the power to elect the whole membership of the board. A factioned board, however, may operate in an adversary atmosphere, making management difficult and the best interest of the corporation harder to identify and serve.

Noncumulative Voting

It is most often felt that a board can give more stable and effective leadership if it operates in a harmonious atmosphere, like a united administration rather than a legislature. This is most likely to happen when the directors are elected under noncumulative voting (also known as "majority role voting").

In this instance, a stockholder has one vote for each share held, and casts his votes for a given *slate* of directors. The holders of a majority of shares (even as few as 51 percent), elect their preferred slate, i.e., elect all of the directors who then carry full responsibility for the conduct of the corporation's affairs.

Preemptive Rights

Rights are sometimes issued to existing stockholders when a new issue of common stock is to be sold. The holder of a specified number of rights can purchase a new share of stock for a stated price which is a little lower (generally 10 percent to 20 percent lower) than the current market price. Stockholders so desiring can maintain their proportional share of total common stock by exercising the rights and buying a fraction of the newly offered shares equal to the fraction of total shares which they presently hold.

In practice, however, and especially where the shares are widely held, most stockholders have little concern over a negligible reduction in their minority proportion of ownership. Also, they may lack either desire or funds to buy new shares. Further, a large shareholder (example: a mutual fund) who chooses not to exercise his rights may endanger the offering. And, an agreement to issue rights can be troublesome when shares are to be issued in connection with an acquisition. Unless externally required, such as by law in the state of incorporation, there is usually little point in requiring that rights be issued.

Internal Common Stock Financing

Additions to equity capital can be achieved both externally—via sale of additional shares—and internally via retained earnings. Retained earnings have been the most significant source of long-term financing for American corporations in recent years, representing about 75 percent of the total. This approximate proportion is likely to continue in the foreseeable future for a variety of reasons including, especially, the high cost of equity capital in the capital markets.

Retained earnings as a financing source are dependent on corporate profitability and on dividend policy. Generally speaking, stockholders have been willing to have a fairly substantial proportion of earnings retained for reinvestment in the business. Their incentive for doing so is potential growth in share price. Assuming that the business can earn a reasonable return on additional retained earnings, there are basic efficiencies in such internal financing—one round of taxation is avoided, and shareholders' reward, if and when realized by sale of their stock, is taxed at the more favorable capital gains rate.

Dividend Policy. Dividend policy is a complex matter. It is a challenge to design a dividend policy which reasonably satisfies the competing cash needs of the stockholders—and potential stockholders—and of the business.

As a general rule, dividend payout ratios should be inversely related to the profitability of the corporation's investment opportunities. The more profitable those opportunities appear to be, the less should be paid out in dividends and *vice versa:* the less profitable, the higher should be the payout ratio. A firm with highly profitable growth opportunities that require major amounts of capital to exploit, might decide to reinvest all earnings and pay no dividends. In practice, many publicly-owned corporations in this situation pay, instead, a small token dividend, recognizing that dividend checks are a useful mode of communication with shareholders. Also, a long unbroken dividend payment record is highly esteemed in the investment community.

The directors of cyclical companies must decide whether or not to pay cyclical dividends. Most boards of such companies endeavor to reduce or eliminate dividend volatility by voting increases only when it appears that the new rate can be sustained for the reasonably long term and even in the face of cyclical downturns in earnings.

Dividend reductions are particularly painful and should be avoided if at all possible. When a dividend cut becomes necessary, it is usually best that the reduction be decisive, that is, borne in one jump, in one shock, rather than by having successive smaller reductions over several quarters.

Going Public

The first time common shares are sold to the public is the event known as "going public." Many chief executives find this to be a profound, traumatic experience. A private company which has always "done what it pleased, answering to nobody," becomes overnight a public company with outside stockholders to court. Stockholder reports, annual meetings, relationships with the Securities and Exchange Commission, perhaps also with a stock exchange, and critical inquiries of security analysts become a regular way of life. Detailed financial data including sales volume, profit margins, operating results by product lines, and even the chief executive's salary, are transformed from being "closely guarded" to "widely disseminated."

In spite of all the shocks of change, most chief executives survive going public and, in retrospect, agree that the bark is worse than the bite. There are a number of advantages to becoming a publicly-owned company. First, are the key reasons for taking the plunge—to gain access to capital for expansion, to assist major stockholders in estate planning, and to assist in diversifying family investments. Second, there is a useful discipline and a larger sense of responsibility that comes with public ownership. Strategy and risk-taking may, for example, be tempered to accommodate the perceived preferences of the new, outside shareholders. Third, a public company often has a relatively better chance of competing for executive and employee talent.

There is, of course, another side of the coin. Major disadvantages of public ownership are: the time and administrative costs of preparing a myriad of regulatory agency reports; the added risks of stockholder suits, tender offers and takeover attempts; stock trading restrictions on corporate insiders; and a tendency of some managers to become overly "stock price conscious" and oriented to the short term.

External Common Stock Financing

Once a corporation is public, the sale of additional common shares can be an important new financing alternative, to be considered along with bonds, leases, and short-term borrowing arrangements.

The principal advantages of selling stock are: Permanent capital is obtained; the equity base is widened; and the potential for future debt financing is increased.

The principal disadvantages are: Equity financing is usually the most expensive alternative; new shareholders are, in effect, new partners with whom the success of the business must be shared; and control by existing blocks of stock is diluted.

BONDS AND PREFERRED STOCK

Bonds and preferred stock are financial building blocks which rise upon the foundation of common stock. These forms of capital usually provide funds at lower cost than that of common stock. On the other hand, they introduce leverage into the financial structure and thereby increase both the possibility of gain to, and the risk borne by the common stockholders of the business.

Bonds are often referred to as senior securities because they have prior claim on the corporation's earnings and, in the event of liquidation, on its assets. Interest and principal due on debt (and, to a lesser degree, dividends on preferred stock) must usually be paid whether or not earned. In return for this senior claim, holders of such securities agree to receive a fixed predetermined rate of return.

The common stockholder's reward for standing junior to other securities is the expectation that the capital provided by senior securities will earn more than it costs and that the excess earnings will increase earnings per share of common stock and eventually boost common dividends and the stock price.

Let it be said again that chief executives who would use leverage must understand that, just as it can enhance owner investment values more rapidly, so also can it depreciate them more quickly. Earnings per share may average somewhat higher, but they will surely be more volatile.

Preferred Stock

Preferred stock is a hybrid security which has some of the features of bonds (debt) and other features of common stock (equity), as shown below:

	Preferred Features Similar to	
	Common Stock	*Bonds*
Usually permanent capital	X	
Income paid as dividends, not interest	X	
Ownership, not debt	X	
Issued in shares	X	
Income payments by declaration of directors, not contractual obligations	X	
Income payments not tax deductible by issuer	X	
Claim on assets senior to common stock		X
Upper limit on income received		X
Creates leverage		X

From the standpoint of an operating business in a good state of health, the similarities of preferred stock to common stock are mostly legalistic and of relatively minor significance. For example, although payment of preferred dividends is at directors' discretion (unlike bond interest which is a contractual obligation), preferred dividends are automatically secure if a regular common dividend is being paid.

If the business is not proceeding successfully and/or if there is no regular common dividend, then the distinctions between common and preferred must be carefully considered.

With the exception of a few industries such as public utilities (where a preferred issue may expand total financing capacity), preferred stock is a seldom-used security these days. For issuers, preferred has most of the features of debt, but its dividends are not a tax-deductible expense to the corporation as is bond interest. For investors, preferred stock has ownership risks, but the available reward is limited. For this reason, the nominal dividend of a preferred stock is generally higher than interest rates on bonds issued at about the same time. Most corporations have largely replaced preferred stocks with subordinated debentures.

Bonds

A bond is a corporation's promise to pay a specified amount on a specified maturity date, usually in ten to twenty or more years. The typical denomination is $1,000; standard practice is for interest payments to be made semiannually.

The Private Offering. Bond issues are either privately placed with a single lender, such as an insurance company or pension fund, or are issued publicly to many lenders. Smaller companies are more likely to arrange a private placement. Large private lenders can often meet the full financing needs of the smaller firm and still maintain diversification of their investments. The interest cost of a private placement is typically slightly higher than for a public offering. Moreover, the covenants and restrictions placed on the borrower are generally tighter and more extensive than with a public offering. But these disadvantages are offset by having only one party with whom to negotiate a needed change in restrictions and by avoiding the time and costs of a public underwriting of debt.

The Public Issue. A public bond issue is negotiated with an investment banker who usually underwrites it, that is, guarantees that the bonds will be sold in the principal amount and at the price and other terms which have been mutually agreed on with the company. With numerous bondholders in prospect, a detailed agreement, the indenture, is drawn which provides for a trustee (usually a bank) to represent the bondholders as a group.

Bonds may be either secured (mortgage bonds) or unsecured

(debenture bonds, or simply "debentures"). In the first case, a mortgage instrument describes property on which, through it, the bondholders have a lien. In the second instance, the bonds are backed by the issuer's general credit standing. A frequent indenture covenant in debenture issues is that none of the issuer's assets not already mortgaged shall be mortgaged to other parties.

Principal Terms in Bond Issues. Some of the terms commonly associated with bonds, together with their meanings, are given below.

Par value. The face amount of the bond and the amount of principal to be repaid.

Term. The length of time until maturity, when the principal is due.

Coupon rate. The percentage annual interest rate or cost of the bonds, assuming issuance at 100 percent of par value. The dollar amount of annual interest is the product of coupon rate and par value. Typically, half of this amount is paid every six months. Upon surrender of the bond on the maturity date, the final interest payment and the principal (par value) are paid.

Amortization. Some partial repayments of a bond issue are normally required prior to ultimate maturity of the issue. The borrower accomplishes this either by making payments into a sinking fund, the proceeds of which are used to retire individual bonds drawn by lot, or by buying back its own bonds in the open market. The latter alternative is particularly desirable when the bonds are trading at discount prices. A device commonly used in municipal issues is "serial maturity," according to which certain bonds in specified principal amounts become payable on certain dates spread over a period of years prior to some final date upon which the last bonds of the issue are retired.

Subordination. A bond issue may be subordinated to other bond issues and/or to other debt. There are various kinds of subordination, but the usual meaning is that interest and principal payment obligations must first be made to senior creditors. Subordinated debentures are similar to, and are frequently issued in lieu of preferred stock because of the advantage of interest payment tax deductibility.

Covenants. Bond indentures typically set forth a wide variety of restrictions upon the borrower, such as maximum dividend payments, minimum working capital, maximum capital expenditures, maximum officers' salaries, and prohibition on the pledging of assets.

Bond Yield. Bond yield is the overall annual percentage return to the investor. This includes return from interest payments as well as from capital gain or loss at maturity. Bonds are usually issued at or near their par value. A bond selling at 100 percent of its par value (i.e., "at 100"), yields the specified coupon rate. As a bond's selling price increases, yield decreases, and vice versa. Precise yields to maturity are found in commonly available yield books, and approximate yields can be computed with a simple formula.

Bond Ratings.   Publicly issued bonds are generally rated by one or more bond rating firms, the most prominent of which are Moody's and Standard & Poor's.

SPECIALIZED FINANCIAL BUILDING BLOCKS

In this section, less traditional, more unusual financial building blocks are considered—convertible securities, warrants, leases, and industrial revenue bonds. Although these are considered by some to be somewhat strange and unfamiliar devices, they do represent important innovations which the chief executive should understand and be able to analyze. Such analysis involves many considerations, some of which can be evaluated only subjectively.

Here are some good rules of thumb relating to such financial devices as these.

DON'T use specialized financial building blocks without a compelling reason.

DO make an even more careful analysis than usual when considering the use of these financing methods.

DO consider the nonfinancial costs of using less orthodox financing techniques, in addition to their perceived benefits.

Convertible Securities

In practice, "convertible" means convertible into common stock. Almost all convertible issues are either convertible subordinated debentures or convertible preferred stock. Attention here will be on the former because preferred stock is seldom issued these days. (Most of the relatively few convertible preferred issues of the past decade have been portions of fairly complicated merger packages.)

Convertible subordinated debentures differ mainly in two ways from ordinary subordinated debentures. First, through the convertible feature, the holder is given the option of exchanging the debenture for a given number of shares of common stock. Second, the buyer pays a small premium for this option and accepts a correspondingly slightly lower yield. There is always also a "call" feature, whereby at a stated price the company can "call" in, or reacquire, the debentures.

The market value of a convertible debenture depends on the value of a comparable nonconvertible debenture and on the value of the shares into which it is convertible. A debenture's value is the greater of these two underlying values plus a small premium.

Why convertibles? The issuing company, in effect, has the opportunity to sell common equity at a premium and, in the meantime, is able to borrow at a lower than market rate. The investors have the advantages (1) of downside protection inherent in the senior status of a debenture as compared to stock and (2) of upside appreciation potential if the market price of the common rises sufficiently. Both parties enjoy substantial benefits.

Convertible debentures were popular in the 1960s for the foregoing reasons. In 1969, however, the Accounting Principles Board reduced their attractiveness by decreeing, in *APB Opinion No. 15*, that in many instances, publicly reported *primary* earnings per share must be computed as if conversion had taken place. Since then, there has been a considerable trend away from the use of convertibles.

Off-Balance Sheet Financing—Warrants

A warrant is a document giving its holder the right to buy a share of common stock at a stated price. As the stock's market price declines toward the stated price or below it, warrant value approaches zero. But as the market price rises above the stated price, warrant value increases rapidly.

Warrants are occasionally issued as "sweeteners" in bond offerings. Bondholders are thereby able to share in the good life of common stock price increases while escaping a penalty for price decreases.

As a financial building block, warrants are an uncertain quantity. If and when exercised, they may provide substantial equity financing; until then, they are, for the most part, only a speculative investment opportunity for their holders.

Off-Balance Sheet Financing—Leasing

A lease is a medium- to long-term rental obligation. Leasing has been a popular financing method for several decades in the railroad and office equipment industries. More recently, leasing has mushroomed in volume and in the varieties of equipment thus financed.[1] What is its lure?

Until recent years, a major advantage of leasing was that lease payment obligations appeared as a balance sheet footnote rather than as a liability. It was felt that few credit analysts read such footnotes, and that fewer still knew how to interpret them. Leasing was a convenient and flexible financing vehicle which, as matters worked out, often represented an increase in a company's financing capacity.

Awareness of the contractual, hence debt-like, or obligation nature of lease payments has slowly but steadily developed. Most accounting authorities agree that many types of leases should be capitalized, but there is disagreement over details. The senior partner of a major national accounting firm recently cited the accounting treatment of leases as one of the three most critical issues facing the accounting profession.

Another key advantage of leasing has been the tax deductibility of lease payments as a business expense. The Internal Revenue Service has attacked this practice in instances where a purchase option of nominal amount is negotiated in advance. In any event, current liberal depreciation allowances and the investment tax credit reduce this potential advantage substantially.

Leasing may be advantageous under one or more of the following circumstances:

1. 100 percent financing is desired.
2. The period of equipment use is less than its minimum depreciable life.
3. Current lenders or corporate policies restrict capital acquisitions but not operating expenditures for leases.
4. The equipment user cannot take advantage of an available invest-

---

[1] A number of varieties of leasing have also developed. This discussion considers *finance* leasing, where the arrangement is merely a financing method. Under an *operating* lease, the lessor may furnish nonfinancing services to the lessee, notably maintenance. *Leverage* leasing is a sophisticated form of finance leasing often used in large transactions such as for locomotives, jet airplanes, and oil tankers.

ment tax credit (for example: user's tax liability is low because of loss operations).

5. The lease includes use of land which is not depreciable.
6. The time is inappropriate for selling new securities.

Off-Balance Sheet Financing—Industrial Revenue Bonds

Firms which are building or expanding a plant, or investing in machinery, pollution control equipment, etc., may find advantageous financing through industrial revenue bonds. (These are also known as industrial aid bonds and industrial development bonds.)

Industrial revenue bonds are not issued by the firm, itself, but rather by a local government unit which buys facilities specified by the firm. The facilities are then leased to the firm by the government unit. Lease payments are the source of the government unit's interest and amortization payments to the bondholders. The key advantage is that the cost of such bonds is the relatively low interest rate of tax-exempt municipal securities. This advantage basically accrues to the firm. Usually the company is an important employer in the local community and benefits to it accrue indirectly to the community.

Aggregate industrial development bond financing grew dramatically until 1968, when Congress determined that such financing in behalf of a given firm could not, in most instances, exceed $5 million. Since 1968, this activity has again grown rapidly, but from a much reduced level resulting from the $5 million limit.

SHORT- AND INTERMEDIATE-TERM CAPITAL

Although this chapter is mainly concerned with long-term and permanent forms of capital which constitute a firm's capitalization, shorter-term forms of capital can have the near-equivalent effect of longer-term forms through the practice of continuous refinancing.

Bank Loans

For most firms of all sizes, banks are the common and sometimes the only available source of short-term funds. The short-term unsecured loan is the banker's classic ware. In the last 25 years, however, bankers have steadily broadened their offerings, notably into intermediate-term loans due in 3 to 8 years (universally referred to simply as "term loans").

For term loans, bankers carefully analyze multiyear cash flow potential in order to judge loan amortization capability. A loan agreement containing numerous restrictive covenants is typically required in order to provide protection to the lender against the unforseen over the amortization period.

Commercial Financing

Small and medium-size businesses may wish to consider commercial financing, which is short-term lending secured by accounts receivable and inventory. This financing form is offered by commercial financing firms and, as a specialty service, by some banks. Commercial financing is an attractive financing method for businesses with high growth potential and/or under capitalization. Secured lending typically makes possible larger borrowings, for given financial statement ratios, than are available through traditional bank borrowing.

Such loans are particularly flexible. As an example, cyclical firms need larger loans as receivables and inventory increase. The needed funds may be available in this fashion because loan limits rise in parallel with growth in collateral values.

Another feature of flexibility is that loan level is adjustable on a daily basis. This permits the financial manager to plan cash requirements very closely. The result may be a partial offset to the higher interest rates required under commercial financing in order to process the continuous turnover of collateral and to compensate for the somewhat greater risk.

Commercial Paper

Major manufacturing companies, their finance subsidiaries, and large finance companies often raise significant portions of their borrowing needs through the sale of "commercial paper," which is short-term unsecured debt having a maturity of up to 270 days. Commercial paper is typically sold in amounts and maturities to meet the individual buyer's needs. Buyers may be individuals or institutions interested in investing temporarily excess funds, usually in the range of $10,000 to $1 million.

FINANCIAL STRUCTURE DECISION-MAKING

In identifying your company's financial structure problem, and in analyzing alternative solutions, there are some basic considerations you will want to talk over with your financial officer or adviser. They are interrelated. You can think of them as a set of mental benchmarks which you need to understand clearly, approve, and insofar as possible, feel comfortable with, as you move to make your decision.

Amount of Leverage

Will you serve your corporation best by assembling building blocks which represent the "eat well" or the "sleep well" philosophy? Leverage lies at the root of every financial structure decision. How "top-heavy," or "bottom-heavy," shall the financial building blocks be stacked?

Two leverage measures are widely used by financial analysts—"debt-to-equity ratio" and "debt-to-capitalization ratio." ("Debt," for the purpose of calculating these ratios, usually excludes current liabilities.) For most purposes, we prefer the second ratio, "debt to capitalization," because it indicates the proportion of *total* capitalization that is financed by debt.

High leverage or "top-heaviness" is usually tolerable for firms such as utilities and finance companies, which have liquid, stable assets and/or smooth, stable operating income. Relatively high leverage may also be acceptable if management is willing to endure the implied risk and if the shareholders understand its implications. In contrast, low leverage is preferable for firms in volatile industries, such as many kinds of manufacturing, or for firms having conservative managements. This is illustrated in diagrammatical form in Exhibit 3.

Some advice:

DO match liquidity structure and maturities of financial building blocks with similar characteristics of assets. In other words—

DON'T construct the right side of the balance sheet without regard for the characteristics of the assets on the left side and for the volatility of the income stream.

EXHIBIT 3
The Relationship of Assets and Income Stability to Financial Structure

An Asset/Income Structure Built Like This:	Is Generally Matched with a Financial Structure Built Like This:	Examples

1.

(very liquid and/or stable)

"Stable"

(high leverage)

"Top Heavy"

Utilities,
Finance
Companies

2.

(illiquid and/or volatile)

"Top Heavy"

(low leverage)

"Stable"

Manufacturers of
Capital Goods,
Fashion Articles

Rainy-Day Protection

Will you have an adequate flow of funds to make interest, principal, and dividend payments? In the final analysis, your job as chief executive is to preserve the enterprise, to keep it from going under. Everything depends on your ability to keep funds flowing—in bad times as well as good. This means generating a cash stream sufficient to pay the operating bills, to make the interest and principal payments on debt and lease payments, all when they're due, and also, let us hope, at least some minimum of common stock dividends—*comfortably.*

Banks, investment bankers, and institutional lenders such as insurance companies attempt to judge a business's ability to generate the required cash stream by the use of debt service coverage ratios. These ratios typically use for the numerator, the sum of pretax income, interest expense, depreciation, and other noncash expenses. The denominator is the sum of interest expense, rental payments on leases, and the pretax cost of debt amortization. (The denominator sometimes also includes the pretax cost of preferred dividends and of an assumed common dividend.)

Ratios like this are calculated historically, and are projected prospectively under various possible financial structure alternatives to aid lenders and borrowers in determining which structure is mutually the most desirable. Lenders may have developed standards commonly used for your industry as a further aid in their analysis of the quality and acceptability of your financial structure and of the specific debt instrument you are contemplating.

The fact that lenders usually seek debt service coverage of four or more times is their way of gauging your ability to withstand business adversity.

Such rough and ready measures are, though, no substitute for a careful internal analysis of the continuity of funds flows in the event of severe (but less than catastrophic) adversity. Such analysis is also useful to parties on both sides when considering leverage level and when negotiating specific loan covenants. It should include computation of the decreasing levels of earnings before interest and taxes (EBIT) at which it would become necessary, in turn: to reduce the common dividend; to suspend the common dividend; to suspend the preferred dividend; to suspend principal payments on debt; and to suspend interest payments on debt.

Also, care should be taken in determining at what point, following a given suspension, fixed-income security holders gain extra voting or other rights. What do you and your advisors estimate would be the likely practical effect of this action—in routine matters? In strategic decisions where there may be strong divergent feelings? (If you, the reader, are basically a marketing executive, when you are estimating possibilities, consider cutting 20 percent from the levels of volume and profit you feel *sure* of. Why? Because the marketing executive is optimistic by nature, whereas the best financial management generally leans toward the "conservative" side when projecting into the future.)

You can't run your finances as if tomorrow will be doomsday, but you can and should have some sizeable cushions—margins of safety—for unexpected, unanticipated crises, which will surely develop sooner or later.

Loan Restrictions and Operating Flexibility

When thinking about the financial structure, remember that almost all term borrowing entails accepting restrictions. These restrictions are generally set forth in the loan agreement or indenture. Such restrictive covenants require the borrower to do certain things and to live by certain rules. Covenants usually cover a wide variety of matters, most of which are determined by negotiation.

You will want to be sure that the covenants to which you agree leave you with sufficient operating flexibility. For example, consider carefully the portion of retained earnings restricted from dividend payments. Keep in mind that there is a trade-off between the cost of debt and management's freedom to operate. Obviously, your goal is to achieve a balance—the most freedom at the least cost.

Cost of Financing

A major goal for management is to seek a financial structure providing the lowest average cost of capital. This can't be measured precisely, but it can be estimated by weighting the cost of each category of capitalization by its dollar value.

Financial Structure Simplicity

Conservative financial management usually favors a simple financial structure; the *most* conservative structure being a capitalization consisting only of common stock. Aggressive financial management is inclined to take advantage of every opportunity to utilize leverage by borrowing. Such management is willing to endure the rigors of a complex financial structure, which may entail several classes of debt and stock. Its goal is to reduce average cost of capital to the very minimum by catering to several specialized investor classes.

Advice: Whether you are conservative or aggressive in the use of leverage, keep your financial structure just as simple as possible. A complicated web begets problems which, at the very least, are overly time-consuming.

Timing

A lot of management effort is devoted to forecasting the course of interest rates and stock prices in order to obtain the most favorable capital costs. But good timing decisions are usually as much a matter of luck as of skill. Although there is merit in attempting to forecast optimum timing, there is, unfortunately, little assurance that this will produce a lower average cost of capital over the longer run as compared to the alternative of simply paying the market price when financing is needed.

Control

Changes in financial structure may affect control of the firm. The sale of equity reduces the ownership proportions of current stockholders, whereas the sale of debt does not. (The important matter of cumulative versus noncumulative voting was discussed earlier in this chapter.)

The matter of control is often of great and sensitive importance in decisions on the financing of acquisitions. The small company being acquired may have concentrated ownership whereas the acquiring company does not. After such a merger, the acquired company's owners may be among the largest shareholders in the combined firm.

General Conformity

There is wisdom in the saying:

> *Be not the first by whom the new is tried*
> *Nor yet the last to lay the old aside.*

It is usually a good idea to conform reasonably with the characteristics and traditions of business generally and of your industry in particular. The firm which deviates significantly from such norms is likely to experience reduced acceptability and respectability in the capital markets. The maverick must endlessly explain and defend. Aggressive managements tend to accept this burden; conservative managements try to avoid it.

SOME THOUGHTS ON FINANCIAL STRATEGY

A business seeking capital competes with other capital seekers for a portion of the aggregate supply of available savers' funds. What does this mean to the chief executive eager to create and maintain an effective financial structure? In essence, it means that he must be competitive in the capital markets in much the same way that he strives for competitiveness in the markets for the product or service his business sells. In capital markets, as in product markets, powerful, dynamic forces of supply and demand determine the prices and terms on which business is transacted, and these shift constantly with changing conditions.

Firms should attempt to package their securities by matching management's preferences with those of chosen classes of investors. An ideal time to sell convertible debentures, for instance, is when they are popular and investors are clamoring to buy them. Again, this process of trying to respond to developments in the capital markets closely parallels the manner in which most businesses attempt to structure their product categories in order to meet the needs of various classes of customers.

The Investment Banker

Advice on all these matters pertaining to conditions in the capital markets, and recommendations on how best to respond are services provided by investment bankers. Primarily because the sale of securities is a major but fairly rare event, investment banking is almost universally retained as needed rather than established as an in-house function. The relationship between investment banker and management is usually of a long-term nature, both by tradition and in order for the necessary mutual trust and understanding to develop. The chief executive who is forever "itchy" to find a "still better" investment banker or who in fact makes frequent switches, may become known as a "shopper" and end up with no satisfactory relationship.

Financial Strategy

Corporate financial strategy implies the existence of a long-term corporate objective which financial strategy assists in implementing. This objective, for example, may be to grow from a small company to a big one, or to prune stale products and concentrate on promising new ones, or to become more vertically integrated.

It should always be remembered that capitalization is not adjusted smoothly over time. Retained earnings grow and long-term debt declines as profits are made and debt is retired, respectively. But major adjustments must be made from time to time, as by the sale of new securities. Financial strategy must take into account how often it is useful or wise to adjust the financial structure—how often to "go to the well." Each financing transaction is costly in money, time, and nerves. Strategy must balance the need to limit debt ratio ranges with the need to increase the size and reduce the frequency of major financing transactions.

Strategy must work around obstacles such as periods of weak market conditions. When interest rate declines are anticipated, short-term financing may need to substitute temporarily for bonds. If equity markets are weak, it may be necessary to substitute a bond issue, giving attention to favorable call privileges by which to refund the issue later when equity can be sold more favorably.

A balance sheet, as such, is static—a snapshot of the asset and financial structure at a given moment. But balance sheets shift over time in a complex, dynamic process. The chief executive can't ever "go to sleep" as far as financial structure is concerned and assume that matters will stay on course by themselves.

EXAMPLES

How do firms actually structure their finances? What strategies do they employ to accomplish their corporate objectives? It is hoped that the following four mini-cases will suggest useful applications of the principles suggested in this chapter.

Du Pont—Conservative Financial Structure

E. I. Du Pont de Nemours is a low-leverage firm. Its long-term debt, all of which happens to be foreign, is only 6 percent of capitalization. Du Pont has had no major long-term domestic debt since the early 1920s.*

Litton Industries—Aggressive Financial Structure

Litton was founded in 1953, with an ambitious plan to grow swiftly in the churning, burgeoning electronics industry. The initial capitalization was as follows:

Bonds	82%
Convertible preferred	17%
Common	1%

Talk about high leverage! With such leverage, of course, as things go well, the common shareholders reap handsomely. This they did. The stock rose from 1¼ almost steadily to 120⅜ in 1967. When leveraged firms do poorly, the common shareholders suffer. This, too, has hap-

---

* [Ed. Note: Du Pont floated a long-term domestic debt issue in late 1974, raising long-term debt to 16 percent of capitalization.]

pened to Litton. Following 1967, Litton stock dropped from its high of 120⅜ to 2⅞; as of January 1975, the stock was selling for about $4.[2] Although Litton's common is now 40 percent of assets, leverage still is high for a major industrial firm.

Strategy for Maintaining Control

One firm with shares traded over-the-counter, apparently foresaw long in advance the possibility of an unfavorable shift in voting power among the principal owners of common and made interesting provisions to avoid it. The entire preferred issue (accounting for 1 percent of capitalization, each preferred share being entitled to an unusually high 80 votes) is owned by the firm's chairman. The multiple voting right of any such preferred shares will reduce automatically to a more normal one vote per share when sold out of the hands of the initial holder or his family. Further, the multiple voting rights of all preferred shareholders will reduce, to one vote per share when the present chairman and his family no longer own a majority of the preferred stock. With the multiple voting rights provision effective, preferred shareholders have 35 percent of total votes. If and when all of the preferred stock becomes votable at one vote per share, preferred shareholders will have less than 1 percent of total votes!

The Family Firm—Strategy for Ownership Succession

Privately-held companies are often threatened by instability of management and ownership.

In a commonly found situation, a firm's owner-founder approaches retirement and seeks alternative ways to provide for management and ownership continuity. His sons have grown up in the business, are assuming increasing responsibility, and are eager and able to take on overall management upon the father's retirement. His daughters have pursued independent interests and look upon the firm strictly as a potential inheritance.

Often, fathers simply will proportions (perhaps equal) of the firm's stock to each surviving child. But considerable conflict can then arise. The managing sons may be eager to expand operations and hence inclined to reinvest a high proportion of earnings and pay low divi-

---

[2] These prices have been adjusted for stock splits but not for the 2½ percent stock dividends declared annually since 1959. Litton has never paid a cash dividend.

dends. The daughters, on the other hand, may have more immediate personal financial interests and participate neither in the management nor have a sense of commitment to business expansion, low current dividends, and the possibility of higher ones in the future.

A creative solution is found in an agreement providing that upon the death of the founder-owner, the company shall be recapitalized from all common stock to a combination of preferred and common. The founder's will provides that the daughters receive preferred stock and the sons common stock.

(In one actual instance, provision was also made for the orderly retirement of the preferred. It is callable by the company at any time; however, if is not called within five years, any preferred stockholder then has the right to require the company to purchase his preferred stock at any time thereafter, up to 7 percent of his initial holding per year.)

The resulting leveraged capitalization meets the different and partially competing needs of owners active in the management and of those not active. The former have a personal incentive to operate and expand the business, supplying much of the needed financing through retained earnings. The latter have current income together with provision for eventual liquidation of their holdings for cash.

This "strategy" has truly "mediated" a potential family dispute!

WHAT TO EXPECT FROM YOUR BANKERS

by Jesse Philips

Chairman and Chief Executive Officer, Philips Industries, Inc.

INTRODUCTION

A NUMBER of years ago, when our company had reached the legal lending limit of our local bank, the president of the bank suggested that we open a credit line with one of the large New York banks of which our local bank was a correspondent. The million-dollar added line which we needed was approved shortly, but it was suggested that I go to New York to meet the officers of the New York bank. Shortly after the introductions, the young New York bank vice president said to me, "I have looked over a number of your balance sheets and I notice that from time to time you invest your excess cash in short-term securities. We think that since you use your bank, you should have those funds in your commercial account for the benefit of the bank."

I was very surprised at this attitude, to say the least. I replied, "I know you expect our company to run its manufacturing operations efficiently. In fact, I doubt that you would want to loan us any money if you were not confident that we were efficient operators. So, why do you even suggest that we run our money management less efficiently than the rest of our business?" I was taught by J. Franklin Ebersole at Harvard Business School that the goal in money management was to end every day with a zero cash balance. The advice I received from this New York banker was certainly not what I expected from our bankers.

As we all know, there are many different kinds of bankers and banks. In this chapter we will discuss two of the more important types: commercial bankers and investment bankers. You may use one or more of these institutions in different ways depending upon the needs, the size, and the stage of development of your company, and the nature of the different money markets at the time of need. We shall discuss in this chapter what the roles of these bankers are and what should be your relationship with them. Let's begin by looking at the commercial bankers.

COMMERCIAL BANKERS

The Lead Banker

There used to be a time when a company's relationship with a commercial bank was very stereotyped. The company merely deposited its funds, drew checks, and occasionally borrowed for seasonal needs. That day is gone. Today, most companies have, or should have, a very intimate relationship with their commercial bank. This bank is known as the "lead bank." You should know the top officers of this bank—not only one individual but several, because, when one retires, you do not wish to be dealing with strangers. They should know as much about your company as do your directors. I do not believe any bankers should actually be on the board of directors of the company, because this may lead to the company banking business being a captive of the banker on the board. Also, I don't think it adds anything because you can secure the same advice and use the same intimate relationship without his being on the board.

However, I believe it is paramount that you keep your banker informed—not only when you are in trouble or when you need money. The best time to see your banker is when you don't need anything except his advice and counsel. Make it a point to see him, say, quarterly or when you foresee a change in conditions. Keep him up to date and educate him about your company and industry. I remember one such meeting with our banker who, in reviewing our financial report, expressed concern that our credit losses were over 5 percent. I pointed out, "Our selling price takes those losses into account and we still show a very acceptable profit. So, why should you care about the percentage loss?" Thus, I educated him about the peculiarities of our industry.

What you get from your lead banker depends upon what kind of a relationship you establish. He can be your chief business adviser and counselor. When we were small and growing, our loans were out of proportion to our net worth and he was virtually our partner as well as quasi-financial officer. When your company is large enough to employ a financial vice president, your lead banker is the one to whom you might go to evaluate the suggestions of your financial vice president when you want an outside opinion. It is at your lead bank that you keep your personal checking account, your will, and trusts. Of course, here is where your company keeps its key commercial accounts, has its most activity, and largest cash balance. Specifically, the relationship which you might have with the lead bank might include the following.

Loans

Seasonal Loans. Of course, your first stop when you need seasonal funds is your lead bank. You hope to have an open unsecured line at the best competitive rate. On the other hand, you can't expect to get somthing for nothing or on terms that are not realistic. I have gone the full gamut with one bank. The first loan to me for a new company was for a limited dollar amount backed by my life insurance, personal endorsement, and a pledge of the accounts receivable of the company at a high interest rate. As the company's financial strength increased, the bank first released the life insurance, then the personal endorsement, and finally the accounts receivable. The interest rate was reduced and we ended up with an open line at prime rate. The day of the smug, independent banker who is doing you a favor by loaning you money is gone. I once had a banker tell me, "Our bank does 54 percent of the clearing house volume and therefore, we are entitled to 54 percent of your business." Of course, that attitude did not do much for that bank. These days you will find that your banker tries to earn your business by the service he renders. Of course, he expects fair treatment in return. That "fair" treatment should be given even when money is plentiful if you expect any favors when money is tight.

When you are asking for a seasonal loan, come prepared with your best reasonable financial projections. Do not make any statements or claims that you cannot substantiate. Do not "blue sky." I usually make it a point to say I will repay the loan a month or so later than I expect to do so. This gives me a little cushion for safety. Nothing inspires confidence in a banker more than having your projections come out better than you outlined. Also, make your plans in such a fashion that all your loans with your lead banker are fully paid each year for at least 30 or 60 days. This way you are indicating to your banker that you are not using him for permanent working capital.

Should your business develop in such a fashion that you need more funds or more time to repay your loans, go to see your banker immediately. Do not wait until he calls you. Explain your situation and show him how and when you plan to work out of the bank.

Banking usually is a competitive business, so you can negotiate on the rates and the type of loan (secured or unsecured). However, the banker has to make his profit, so do not be unreasonable. The bank will expect you to keep a compensating balance. Today, 10 percent when the line is not used, and 20 percent when it is used, is considered normal. Perhaps you can do better.

As your business grows, you may find that you need more money than the legal lending limit of your lead banker. This should be no problem. You may well find that your banker will make arrangements for you to secure the excess from the banker's correspondent bank, which may be a major city bank.

Term Loans. At one point in your company's growth, you may find that you need funds for more than seasonal needs. You may want to open a new outlet or plant and do not have the necessary working capital. Yet, you believe that if you borrow the money, you will be able to pay it back within five years. This is the typical case for a five-year term loan. Normally, commercial banks do not like to make loans for more than five years. In this situation, your banker will work out an arrangement for you to make reasonable payments and pay out the loan over a five-year period. You can expect that the interest rates will be somewhat more than you pay for a seasonal loan.

Mortgage or Long-Term Loans. Perhaps at some point you will need long-term funds for more than five years. Here, too, your first stop should be your lead banker. After reviewing your projected cash flow, you may find you need a term-loan or a 15-year loan. Your banker may agree to take the first five-year payment himself and you may then turn to your investment banker to make arrangements for the balance of the loan to be placed with an insurance company, a pension fund, or with others. Or, where tangible assets such as real property are involved, your banker may be able to execute a mortgage instrument and handle the entire transaction.

Help Handle Funds

Collections. In addition to loaning you money, your lead banker will help you in many other ways. One of these is to help speed up the collection of funds from your customers. Especially today, with high interest rates, the sooner you can get your money collected and deposited to your account, the sooner you can use your money and have it work for you. For example, if one of our customers in California writes a check to us drawn on his California bank, and then mails it to us in Dayton, several days may elapse until we receive the check in the mail. By the time we deposit the check in Dayton and our bank processes it through normal channels to have it clear the California bank, another week may have elapsed. Thus, it may be a week or ten days before we are able to use the payment our customer made to us. To eliminate this delay, we made arrangements with a California bank for a "lock box." We informed all our West Coast customers to mail their payments to our California "lock box." The California bank, once it receives the payments, wires our lead bank the funds on the bank wire. Thus, many times we have the use of the funds almost the same day that our customer mails his check. The saving that we are able to make in interest expense is substantial. We have such a "lock box" not only in California, but in all major cities where we can collect substantial funds.

Investment. Your lead bank may also help you invest your excess funds. Many times it is possible to invest your funds for as short a time as one day. One person should be given the specific responsibility to see that any excess funds are always invested. There is almost no easier way to increase your profits when you have such funds. We always try to pay off our loans on a Friday and to borrow funds on a Monday. There is little point in paying interest on money for Saturday and Sunday when you are not using such funds.

Also, you may gain by paying attention to your float. Through a brief study, you may be able to figure out an amount that you always have in float. Then you can use this amount to help increase your profits.

Your lead banker or your investment banker, if he deals in money market securities, will help you invest those excess funds. Perhaps the bank may need the funds and borrow them from you via their certificates of deposit. Perhaps it will advise you to buy commercial paper or U.S. government certificates. The relative desirability of these different forms of investment changes from day to day. Your bank, however, should be in a position to advise you as to the best buy.

Local Community Relations

Another area in which your banker can help is with your local public relations. He probably knows the proper civic officials, the police, the labor leaders, etc. Should you need help, he can probably advise you and introduce you to the proper people. If you are looking for a plant site or a new office building, he may be able to help with the arrangements.

Registrar or Transfer Agent

Once your company has gone public, you will find that your local bank can well act as registrar or transfer agent for your stock. If you are listed on the New York or American stock exchange, you will probably want a New York bank to perform those functions. However, it is a help to also have your local bank serve in a dual capacity. The local bank, being much smaller, can probably give you much faster service when you need it. Also, their rates are apt to be lower than those of a New York bank.

Trust Department Service

Do not neglect the trust department of your local bank. It can act as manager or custodian of your profit sharing or pension funds. It can act as escrow agents in various transactions. Also, it may have a real estate department which can help you as well. You may find that, from time to time, they can bring business opportunities or possible mergers to your attention.

International Banking

Should you be interested in doing business outside of the United States, your lead bank probably has many foreign connections through its correspondent banks. They probably can arrange contacts to get you started. In addition, of course, they will handle all the foreign exchange transfers and mass of detail which you may find difficult in this new area.

Executive Help

From time to time, your executives and staff are apt to come to you with their personal financial problems. You may be able to help them by making a quick phone call to your lead banker, who can then work with them on solving their financial problems. At one time, over 20 of our executives had loans at the bank to provide funds to purchase company stock via stock options or outright purchases.

COMMERCIAL BANKS OTHER THAN LEAD BANK

In many situations, you may find it advisable to do business with additional banks other than your lead bank. Our company has relations with over 40 banks. We use a bank in every city where we have a plant or warehouse. Most of them have a payroll account against which we draw checks. This makes it easier for our employees to cash their payroll checks. In most cases, we try to establish a local rapport through the bank. We usually establish an open credit line and use it even if the legal limit of the bank is small in relation to our overall needs. In many cases, these small local banks are not as quick to raise their interest rates as the larger city banks. Also, they are not as strict in demanding compensating balances. There also may be some advantage in not putting all your eggs in one basket. In some small towns, as a result, we are the most important customer of the bank. We usually find the bank very helpful in community relations. When we have a problem, often the first person we call is the president of the bank. We also try to establish a good enough rapport that the president will phone us if there is a problem involving any of our local personnel. Not too long ago, we almost lost a good manager because he was playing too much poker at high stakes at the local club. The bank president gave us the facts and we were able to save a good plant manager.

Thus, in summary, to a large extent what you can expect from your commercial bankers depends upon what you want to expect.

INVESTMENT BANKERS

When and how you choose your investment banker (or, perhaps, how he chooses you) is more complex. You may use several investment bankers, depending upon the conditions and needs of the company at a given time.

Let us assume that your company is going public for the first time, and trace its use of investment bankers as the company grows and increases in size and scope.

When to Go Public

Needs of Company. There comes a time when a company can no longer finance its growth through temporary commercial bank borrowing plus internally generated funds. Then, the owners have to face the question of where to get additional funds. The investment banker can be of great help. He knows the sources of long-term money and their relative costs. He can also help with complex negotiations over covenants and terms. After exploring all the options, such as mortgages, private placements, and long-term loans, the owners may decide that, perhaps, selling stock to the public is their best option.

Needs of the Owners. Another case in which a company may decide to go public might be because of the personal needs of the owners. The company may have adequate financial resources, but the owners may need liquidity for personal reasons. An estate tax problem, a desire for liquidity (e.g., cash), a need to attract executive talent through stock options, or other personal reasons may prompt the owners of a company to want to go public.

Input of Money Market. Against the financial needs of the company, one has to weigh the mood of the money market in order to determine an appropriate financial strategy. In the first half of 1974, it was almost economically impossible for most companies to raise equity capital by issuing stock. Interest rates were so high that there were few buyers for common stock. Your investment banker will, of course, help you pick the right time to go public. The history of the company and the industry of which it is a part is an important factor in helping make this decision.

Intrastate versus Interstate Investment Bankers

What sort of an investment banker should you choose? There are a few large investment bankers who will not take on a company unless it has sales in excess of $25 million and after-tax profits of over $1 million. Thus, if the company is small, many investment bankers are automatically excluded. On the other hand, the company may feel lost with such a large banking firm and consider the relationship too impersonal.

Intrastate Investment Bankers. There are, however, a number of excellent smaller firms, many of which specialize their business within one state. True, these firms may also take part in national offerings, but their strength is concentrated within their own home states. These firms are intrastate investment bankers. A smaller company may find that an intrastate banker is the best or only alternative. Yet, there are a number of advantages in having your first public offering intrastate.

First, it is quite possible that you will not have to file an S.E.C. registration. Thus, the costs of registration, printing, accounting, and legal fees are substantially reduced. Also, if the number of shares being offered is small, the intrastate firm may be able to make a better "after-market" by concentrating the shares in a limited area. Although selling the initial offering is important, making a market for the shares after the shares are once sold (the after-market) is, perhaps, even more important. On the first offering, a company is apt to sell less than 20 percent of its equity. If there is no activity in the stock after it is first traded, the company may have difficulty with future offerings.

In choosing your intrastate banker, you will want to consider what sort of contacts it has throughout your state. How many offices does it have and how strong is its selling organization? You want to know how widely it will place your stock and how many shareholders it will secure. In fact, you may want to restrict the number of shares sold to any one holder. You want to know how many shares the banker will be willing to carry in inventory in order to make a market in your stock. How many other investment bankers will be included in the underwriting group and how many of these will make an active market in your stock?

Then, of course, you want to know how much the investment banker is going to charge you for the underwriting and sale. You want to know whether he guarantees to take all the shares offered or whether his proposal is a "best efforts" deal in which he only buys from you the amount of shares he is able to sell.

The big disadvantage of an intrastate underwriting is that, should you decide at a later date to go "interstate," you may have to re-register all the intrastate shares, thus duplicating the expense. However, the advantages of the intrastate offering at the time it was needed may more than compensate for the additional expense.

Interstate Investment Bankers.   There may come a time when the company feels that it should go to the regional or national markets for its financing. Perhaps a large secondary offering is contemplated. You could use the same intrastate firm that you have used. However, perhaps you feel that you need a larger national investment banker with more selling power and more prestige. Selecting such an investment banker has many ramifications. The national investment bankers, by tradition, are unofficially ranked as "major bracket," "sub-major bracket," or "regional bracket" companies. This bracket rating system indicates the bracket position in which the investment banker will be listed in the "tombstone" advertisement of your offering. It also generally indicates the firm's prestige position in the investment banking industry. The managing underwriter, of course, will be listed at the top. Then, the others in the underwriting group will take their traditional groupings. If you feel strongly that your intrastate banker has done an outstanding job for you, perhaps you can break tradition and insist that he be either comanager of the underwriting or be placed in a higher bracket than he would be under traditional procedures.

We still haven't explored the question of how you choose your investment banker who will be the manager of your underwriting. The prestige and contacts of the underwriter are very important because this, to a large extent, may determine what sort of an underwriting group can be put together. The quality of the group is very apt to determine the initial success of your underwriting as well as the activity of the after-market in your stock. In making your selection, you will want to consider the personality and ability of the individual in the firm who will handle your account. Your success may well depend upon him.

We had a number of investment bankers call on us long before we went public. One young man kept calling every month. We were much too small an account for his company, but he called every month and many times offered us helpful advice with our financial problems. He kept telling me, "I know you are too small a company for us, but on the other hand, I can't expect to walk into a company when they are the right size and expect them to come with us. I have confidence that you will grow and, perhaps, someday you will be big enough to consider us. So, if you don't mind, I will keep dropping in to see you when I am in the area."

The day did arrive when we needed a major investment banker. It was an easy decision for us to choose the firm of the young man who had been calling on us for three years. The help he had given us over the years had proven to us his competence, reliability, and compatibility. In addition, he represented one of the top ten investment banking firms, one that was gaining in status and strength.

There are a number of other factors you may wish to consider in choosing your investment banker. His ability to place large blocks of your stock with institutions, funds, etc. may be very necessary to some underwritings. A knowledge of your industry could be very helpful. An underwriter may be known for his knowledge and contacts in a specific industry, for example, oil, or aircraft, or retailing, etc. Perhaps, the international capabilities of the banker may be a factor. Certain bankers are known for their knowledge and contacts in financing abroad.

Of course, the price the investment banker charges you is another factor. Usually this price is subject to negotiation. However, the prices which were charged for recent underwritings will help set the level for the negotiations. This information is readily available. How and where you receive the cash proceeds of your underwriting can save you some money. It might be advisable to have the closing in New Jersey rather than in New York in order to save the New York tax. You may want to have the funds sent by wire to the locations where you have made arrangements for their immediate use so that you do not lose the interest for several days.

What to Expect from Your Investment Banker

As with your commercial banker, you should have a strong personal relationship with your investment banker. He is the "expert" in financial matters. You probably will seek his advice as to when and the best way to raise needed funds. He should advise you as to whether you should sell common stock, preferred, bonds, or perhaps have a private placement, or perhaps the many other possible alternatives. In addition, he will be knowledgeable on the length of maturity, the interest rate, and other provisions of your agreement.

Your investment banker is not restricted merely to helping you raise money. He can be a source of leads and help in regard to acquisitions and expansion possibilities. He will also have some opinion as to your dividend policy and stock splits. For example, our banker had us defer any stock split until we were in a position to split four for one which gave us enough shares to qualify for listing on the American Stock Exchange. He arranged for our listing. Eventually, we moved over to the New York Stock Exchange, also with his help. He also informed the exchange and certain of its specialists about our company so that, as a result, we were assigned a specialist well equipped to make a market in our stock.

Of course, you want to generate interest in your stock. In this regard, it is important to get the proper information to the proper people at the proper time. Your banker probably has contacts with the news media, the security analysts, and the institutions. Special luncheon meetings, to which these people are invited, are a great help.

There are many other ways in which your investment banker can help. He may help in recruiting your key financial executives. Also, he may help your key executives with their estate planning, investments, and tax shelters. Regular policy meetings of the key company management group and the investment bankers can be very helpful. A scheduled six-months review to discuss the overall plan, interest rates, and financing might be done on a regular basis. A quarterly meeting to review operating results and problems can help keep everyone informed.

Using Other Investment Bankers

Certain investment bankers have, over the years, established a reputation as being specialists in certain areas. As a result, they are able to make a better market in such areas. For example, if you wish to buy or sell commercial paper, there are three or four investment bankers who are outstanding in this. If you wish to deal in government securities, there are outstanding firms in that area. The same is true of sales and lease-back situations. Also, if you are contemplating revenue bond financing you may wish to deal with the firm which specializes in this area. It is not difficult to find out who the best specialist is in a particular field. You may want to check with the specialist in addition to consulting your regular investment banker.

SUMMARY

As we have seen, the role of both your commercial bankers and your investment banker has many facets with an infinite number of hues and shadings. "What can you expect from your banker?" The answer could be, "A lot" or the answer could be, "Very little." To a very large degree, it depends upon you. It is very much like love. In order to be loved, you have to love in return. Thus, what you get from your banker depends upon what you are willing to put into the relationship. It is my belief that the relationship is very worthwhile, stimulating, and enjoyable. Now, it is up to you to supply your own answer as to what you can expect from your banker.

FINANCIAL VULNERABILITY: THE POTENTIAL UNAVAILABILITY OF FUNDS WHEN NEEDED

by Samuel H. Woolley

Chairman (Retired), The Bank of New York

THE BALANCING of the flow of funds (cash coming in and cash going out) in a business enterprise is fundamental to its viability. Managing these flows to assure a proper balance is an underlying requirement of successful business management. This management entails anticipating and adjusting the increases and decreases of these flows that are caused by such changes as fluctuating sales, money availability, or increasing costs—thus maintaining your financial liquidity. Such a balance will minimize your financial vulnerability and maximize your marketing and production flexibility.

The principles of financial management discussed below are applicable to businesses of all sizes. Larger companies, of course, have internal staff capabilities in this area and are constantly monitoring their operations. Accordingly, my remarks here are addressed primarily to the chief executives of smaller companies where the need for sound financial management is every bit as great, but where often the internal staff support is limited and a considerable burden inevitably falls on the chief executive.

FINANCIAL VULNERABILITY—WHAT IS IT?

A few years ago, one of our officers was asked to meet with executives of a company having serious financial problems which they thought could be remedied by additional borrowings. They hoped that because of this officer's knowledge of their industry, he would be able to find a way to justify an increase in their already debt-heavy position.

702

The company had exceeded their established bank credit limits and the situation had deteriorated to the point where they were forced to further increase their borrowings on an emergency basis to meet their payroll. Their regular bank was understandably reluctant to continue that type of support.

A review of the situation confirmed that the company was already borrowing more than they could properly maintain in view of the uncertain sales trend and questionable profitability that had developed. In the circumstances, the company was substantially under-capitalized. The equity in the company was too small in relation to their sales volume, and excessive borrowings and other liabilities were necessary to support operations. However, the company simply couldn't sell additional shares at that time because of a weak equity market (both the stock market generally and the company's shares were declining), compounded by their internal problems.

The basic question was how did the company get to this point and, having gotten there, what could be done to get it on a stronger financial footing. Further research revealed a number of factors.

The president of the company was an outstanding design engineer with a number of brilliant developments to his credit. However, a walk through the plant revealed over a year's supply of expensive castings piled in various locations including a hallway. The president explained, with a touch of pride, that they had been purchased at a bargain price. Unfortunately, this tied up a large amount of cash which was urgently needed in their day-to-day operations.

Because of this cash shortage, the company got behind—past due—in their payments to trade creditors, particularly to one who supplied a few inexpensive but critical components. The components supplier, in turn, placed the company on a C.O.D. basis, which completely disrupted deliveries. As a result, these components were not in stock when needed, work in process stopped at the bottleneck, and shipments to customers were interrupted. This delayed sales and compounded the cash shortage.

Other examples of an earlier lack of planning and control could be seen in the company's operations. However, a few steps had been taken to remedy some of the problems. For instance, a manager with financial control experience had been hired. But the basic decisions were still being made by the engineer-president who, not incidentally, was the largest single shareholder.

The ingenuity and determination of the president during that period to find ways to continue the operation—often on a day-to-day, hand-to-mouth basis—were impressive. He managed to continue to operate the company on that basis for a number of months.

This is an example, in the extreme, of some of the causes and effects of financial vulnerability and how it can lead to trouble if it is not recognized and properly handled.

The Nature of Financial Vulnerability

A company is financially vulnerable if it is in a position where the availability of funds, when needed, is limited. It becomes ultimately a matter of cash availability. Yet, financial vulnerability is not an absolute; it is a matter of degree.

Every company has some degree of financial vulnerability. It is a fact of business life. The skill lies in managing your company so as to minimize vulnerability while achieving optimum results. This is accomplished by looking ahead to determine your future financial requirements under various operating plans, and then being sure that the necessary financing is in place to cover the least favorable condition, before going forward. In this respect, your financial structure (the interrelationships between assets, liabilities, and equity) should be determined by your operating and marketing needs. To minimize vulnerability, your financial structure should provide sufficient flexibility to allow you to adjust to changing needs. Conversely, vulnerability increases as flexibility decreases.

External Factors

Your degree of vulnerability is also influenced by such general factors as economic growth and expansion, inflation, shortages, general money market conditions, and money availability, as well as the nature of your industry. The size of your company is not as important in this respect as its structure, including its degree of integration, product diversification, and the volatility of its markets.

Additional factors are time and change. Since a business operation is dynamic, the significance of changing circumstances over a period of time is important to recognize and prepare for. Thus, a course of action which could be perfectly rational over the short term might be improper over the longer term as circumstances (such as conditions in your market, availability of supplies, or inflationary trends) change.

It is evident that such external influences need to be recognized and adjusted to since they cannot be controlled by an individual company.

An example of this is the growing number of attempts by suppliers to renegotiate old fixed-price contracts because of rapidly increasing price levels. If this trend continues, price provisions pegged to an index reflecting changing price levels could become common for long-term contracts. In some cases, even current orders are being based on a forward price—generally at delivery—rather than on prices in effect at the time the order is placed. Although this may be an extreme example, it does help to illustrate the point that as the environment changes and as attitudes concerning it change, the practices of both customers and suppliers are in fact being modified.

Internal Factors

There are also some internal influences bearing on vulnerability which often are not so obvious. These usually arise as a result of not being aware of potential problems until they become serious. Such unawareness may be caused by preoccupation with other problems, enthusiasm, frustration, or complacency. Because these internal causes can be controlled, it is particularly important to be aware of their possibility and to maintain a sense of perspective in order to avoid being surprised.

Financial vulnerability also is affected by leverage and staying power. Leverage—both operating and financial—is created by high "fixed" costs (charges which do not vary with sales volume) and results in providing the probability of disproportionate gain or loss as a result of incremental change. It is important to understand how your particular type of leverage influences your results—both good and bad—under varying circumstances. This is an area where good outside advice can be of particular value.

Staying power involves the interrelationship of cash requirements and cash generation in a company. It centers around the question of how long you can operate effectively under adverse circumstances. If your operations are run with a very close correlation in timing and amount between cash generation and cash requirements (cash flow), a relatively small variation in either could result in a large variation in cash availability.

Cash flow has three components: (*a*) funds from operations; (*b*) changes in working capital; and (*c*) changes in noncurrent assets, liabilities, and equity. Funds from operations consist of the company's net income plus such noncash charges as depreciation, amortization, and deferred taxes. Usually, unless there is an operating loss, funds from operations are a generator of working capital.

Working capital consists of total current assets minus total current liabilities. It is an expression of the net working assets in a business and when it increases it is a user of funds. The major components of working capital, other than cash, are accounts receivable and inventory on the asset side and accounts payable and accrued expenses on the liability side. These are the accounts that most directly interrelate with the current operations of a company. Thus, increased sales usually will generate increased receivables and will require a higher level of inventory which in turn will generate higher payables. It is this direct interrelationship between sales and working capital which primarily influences your operating funds requirements and which needs to be understood and monitored.

In addition, changes in noncurrent assets and liabilities and in equity also affect cash flow. For instance, an increase in property, plant, and equipment (usually the major noncurrent asset) uses funds and an increase in long-term debt provides funds—as does an increase in equity. Good practice dictates that funds needed for increasing noncurrent assets should be provided by long-term debt or equity rather than by short-term sources such as bank loans.

Because the degree of vulnerability of your company is based in part on the combination of potential profitability of your operations and the correct level or mix in your working assets, a cash budget to monitor these elements should be prepared as part of your overall operating budget. Thus, while the operating budget will pertain to the company's overall sales and production costs and will serve as a profit planning tool, the cash budget or cash flow forecast will show the level of working assets needed to support the operating budget and will highlight the timing of cash movements as well as the amounts and interrelationships of the accounts. It is in this way that you can have a tangible means of both monitoring and controlling your cash flow.

Finally, it is essential to recognize and honor the fundamental point that a company's financial structure is the servant of its operational and marketing needs. A company's financial structure (and its accounting) is a means to an end.

If you manage your company with its operational and marketing needs foremost in mind and plan its financial structure around these needs, you will be taking a major step in controlling your financial vulnerability.

HOW TO GET INTO TROUBLE

Nobody sets out to get into trouble. More to the point, the possibility of getting into trouble is not often considered seriously. Therefore, the most common underlying ingredient in getting into trouble is a lack of sensitivity to what is going on. This can take the form of unawareness of the possibility of problems arising—a lack of alertness—or even a sense of complacency if things are going well.

Conditions and events which most frequently lead to trouble (financial vulnerability) more often are self-generated rather than external. This is important to recognize, however uncomfortable it may be. In the majority of cases, companies which have gotten into trouble have done so as a result of their actions and decisions, including ignoring danger signals such as disproportionate changes in receivables, inventories, or payables in relation to sales, rather than as a result of things that have been done to them.

"How to get into trouble" involves a multitude of sins. The following four are common to practically any situation.

Lack of Good Analysis and Planning

Sometimes we hear a manager say that he cannot do a good job of planning because his company or industry is too volatile or there are too many uncertainties or he doesn't have time. Frequently, because of such arguments, no planning at all is done.

Postponing or ignoring the need for analysis and planning, including financial planning, can substantially increase your vulnerability. It is analogous to setting out on a trip to an unfamiliar area without a map or provision for accommodations—except that in the case of running a business, such lack of planning can result in more serious trouble than just losing your way temporarily or being inconvenienced.

In this respect, one question that should be asked periodically about any business, and particularly one that is in trouble, is whether it is in fact viable in its present form. Is there a market for the product at a price that will permit sufficient profitability? Is sufficient capital available to allow the company to be adequately financed? If such questions are not thoroughly explored and definitively answered, you run the risk of serious trouble.

This is illustrated by a thinly capitalized company that was starting a new venture—a service. They were deliberately underpricing their competition in an effort to build their customer base as rapidly as possible. Their reasoning was that the resulting increased sales would rapidly lead to profitability and relieve their constant need for additional funds. Unfortunately, the profits did not develop. As a last resort, they sought outside advice.

An analysis revealed that the company was so underpricing its service that they were losing money on each additional sale. Costs which they thought were fixed actually turned out to be variable, which meant that the company had much less operating leverage than they thought. The obvious solution was to raise the price; however, they concluded that they would not be competitive at a higher price. The next day the decision was made to discontinue the venture.

The management of that company thought they had a capital and sales volume problem. Actually, they had a cost-price problem in a market where their only competitive advantage was price. Getting good outside advice at the outset—since they lacked adequate internal analysis and planning—could have avoided the entire problem.

Improper Management Priorities

It is important to establish early your objectives for your company together with your priorities for achieving them. This is particularly true in differentiating between long-term and short-term strategies. Guard against a short-term expediency at the expense of compromising a long-term objective. For instance, interrupting a research project might improve earnings in the current year but could seriously compromise the longer-term future of the company.

A common problem, especially in small companies, is the need for close attention to day-to-day operations by the chief executive. If this need develops into a preoccupation with day-to-day activities, you run the risk of losing sight of the larger picture, particularly as it relates to cash requirements. The danger is that you become so busy moving goods through the plant and out the door that financial problems don't get proper attention early enough.

Uncontrolled Growth

It is important to control your growth consciously. This involves monitoring the profitability of *incremental* sales as well as making sure that there is adequate provision for their necessary capital support, including both plant and working capital. If you are not conscious of the working capital requirements of your incremental sales, particularly as regards necessary increases in receivables, inventories, and payables, you take the risk of running out of cash at the wrong time.

During a period of growth, the total impact of increasing operating costs and working capital requirements tends to be obscured and this can lead to a false sense of security. In any expansion plan, after the analysis and the projections are completed, be sure that the necessary financing is in place before going forward. Simply assuming that the necessary financing will be available without specifically providing for it, especially if everything is going well, can result in no financing when it's needed.

During periods of rapid inflation, the increasing prices sometimes are confused with growth—especially during the earlier phases. Thus, during inflationary periods, you need to be aware of unit production and unit sales as well as the dollar figures. It is also important to recognize the impact of your inventory valuation methods on your cost of goods sold and thus on your indicated profitability. Earnings resulting from "inventory profit," particularly if you are transferring inventory to cost of goods sold on a Fifo (first in, first out) basis, can be misleading. From a cash flow standpoint, you are reporting earnings based on historically lower costs while you are replacing those lower-cost inventories with inventories purchased at higher current prices. Furthermore, you are paying taxes on those higher earnings. Thus, your actual liquidity can be substantially less favorable than your indicated earnings would imply.

Materials shortages will further compound these trends and can lead to compromises in purchasing practices and an erosion of cost control. As a result, inventories are more likely to get out of control during such a period. It is therefore important to watch the interrelationships between accounts receivable, inventories, cost of goods sold, and payables—in units and dollars—during any period of rapid growth and especially so if it is accompanied by substantial price increases or materials shortages. Conversely, a period of deflation would present equally difficult problems which need to be anticipated.

Increased size is of little value unless it is accompanied by increased profitability. Unfortunately, one does not automatically follow the other. This has been particularly evident in some attempts to grow by acquisition.

In analyzing a proposed acquisition, it is important to understand its longer-term capital implications as well as the purchase price and terms. Be sure you understand how much additional capital will be required to support or create the results for which you are making the acquisition. Add the additional capital requirements to your purchase price to determine the total investment on which you will need to earn a return.

In short, growth for growth's sake can be dangerous. Underlying capital needs resulting from growth can be large. If these needs are not recognized at the outset, they can come as a rude and expensive surprise when they do surface.

Unwise Leverage

"Buy now, pay later" has gotten many an unwary individual—and company—in financial trouble. We've already discussed the dangers of assuming that additional credit will always be available whenever needed. However, from an operating standpoint, even if the credit is available, there is danger of unwisely leveraging your company by borrowing more than you can safely support. This can generate such large interest charges and amortization payments that an interruption in profitability or cash generation could seriously impair your ability to maintain the payment schedules.

In this respect, it is also important in planning your capital structure to finance your long-term assets with long-term liabilities and equity. Specifically, avoid financing long-term assets with short-term borrowings. There is a tendency to assume that things will always go up and that you can count on continuing growth to bail you out. This is not a valid assumption.

Leverage is often thought of as strictly financial, i.e., the use of borrowed money as part of the capitalization of a company. However, there is also operating leverage, which takes the form of fixed operating costs such as those resulting from large plant and equipment requirements—as in the steel industry.

A particularly subtle form of adverse operating leverage occurs when costs which were viewed as variable on the way up, such as production- or sales-related support activities, turn out to be not so variable on the way down. This was dramatized during the recession of 1970 when many companies experienced a leveling or a decline in sales for the first time in many years. Most found that they could not reduce their costs proportionately. This resulted in some surprisingly large earnings declines. Thus, leverage is a two-edged sword.

Financial planning, coupled with effective financial analysis, is indispensable to effective management. Regardless of the maturity of a company, business and economic uncertainties emphasize the need for better analysis and planning.

At The Bank of New York, we were so convinced of this growing need for better financial analysis and planning that several years ago we established a separate Corporate Financial Services Department which specializes in assisting companies in these areas.

HOW TO GET OUT OF TROUBLE

The best solution to a problem is to avoid it. However, if you find yourself in financial trouble or believe that you are getting into it, it is important to begin corrective action immediately. Good outside advice can be especially valuable under such circumstances, and both your banker and your accountant can provide such advice along with useful objectivity. The sooner you start, the easier it will be. The following steps have evolved from experience, and they work.

Identify the Problem

The first step is to recognize that you have a problem or that you may have one. The earlier you catch it, the better. A disciplined internal program of monitoring your progress, particularly as it relates to your working capital and sales, will help to detect potential problems while they are still manageable. This can best be done by preparing periodic financial statements and comparing these actual results with your earlier projections. By thus identifying variances, you can initiate necessary corrections.

It is essential, however, to identify specifically what the problem is and how it developed. For instance, not having enough money usually is not the problem; it's the symptom. Your job is to find out why you don't have enough money.

Develop an Operating Strategy

Once the basic problem has been identified, the next step is to generate an operating strategy for correcting it and avoiding its repetition. This involves laying out specific steps to be taken, including a timetable. Thorough analysis and planning are a must, followed by the specific implementation of the planned solution. You cannot just assume that everything will work out. If you are already in trouble, you need to consciously get out of it and this requires decisive action.

Develop a Financial Strategy

A financial strategy will be needed to support your operating strategy. It should incorporate financial projections including probable working capital and invested capital requirements and alternative ways of financing them. This will help to assure that the financial structure of the company will effectively support the operating requirements.

Projected income statements are not enough. Projected balance sheets and sources and uses of funds statements are necessary to correlate the interrelationships of the financial plan. A projection of key ratios, such as debt to equity, return on equity, return on sales, return on incremental sales, and incremental working capital requirements, also helps in further evaluating the implications of a plan. Other valuable analytical aids are projected "common size" income statements (costs shown as a percentage of sales) and "common size" balance sheets (assets and liabilities as a percentage of total assets), percentage change income statements and balance sheets, and balance sheet items shown as a percentage of sales. These aids will help you to analyze projected trends and uncover possible inconsistencies in your projections. You can easily prepare these projected statements by using computer programs already designed for this purpose.

This is also the time to consciously consider alternative operating and financial strategies—especially different sales projections and financing options—including the possibility of adverse results. Such projections should include provision for adequate working capital— with particular attention to levels of receivables, inventories and payables—to support the various sales levels. Objective evaluation of possibilities and alternatives at this point can help to avoid surprises later.

As an example of this, in late 1969 we noted that in line with the general economic climate, most of our customers were projecting increasing sales and were concerned about their ability to finance the continuing growth which they seemed to be taking for granted. We felt that as part of the planning process it was important to explore the potential financial impact on those companies of reduced growth rates or even declines in sales.

As it happened, during that year the economy experienced the first significant slowdown in many years. Those companies that had responded to the recommendation that a possible slowdown be considered and had anticipated its financial impact, found it much easier to adapt to that situation when it did occur.

Few things are less welcome in business and in banking than a surprise—particularly an unpleasant one. The advantage of financial planning which enables you to experiment with and evaluate alternatives, is that it allows you to anticipate potential problems and in this way reduce the likelihood of surprises. This helps you to manage rather than react, and thus effectively regulate your growth and your financial structure.

Monitor and Adjust

The final step in getting out of trouble after you have identified your problem and adopted the appropriate operating and financial strategies is to monitor your progress and make adjustments as needed. This again involves preparing periodic statements for comparison with your plan, to serve as a basis for adjustment. This concept of on-line feedback and adjustment is well accepted in manufacturing and processing systems. It is equally valuable in the management and planning area. Thus, a specific methodology should be established which would require a continuing reevaluation of your progress on a systematic basis.

This chapter began with a story about a company in financial difficulty which managed to survive for many months in spite of serious problems. In time, the equity market became more favorable, and the company was able to sell additional shares to the public. The proceeds were sufficient to allow them to repay their creditors and still have a comfortable financial cushion. Having decided that they should diversify into new areas, they made a few acquisitions and also started an internal product development program. For the first time in several years, the president felt he could relax, but that proved to be a false sense of security. Within two years of the sale of the shares, the company had filed for bankruptcy.

It is ironic that in great adversity they managed to keep the company alive; but, when the pressure was off, the ingenuity of desperation was not replaced with careful planning and a well-thought-out operating and financial strategy. Rather, they fell into the trap of the fashion of the moment which included some unwise acquisitions and diversification in areas foreign to their historical capabilities. By the time they realized they had gone too far, it was too late.

Part of your job as a manager is to recognize that financial vulnerability is a fact of business life and so to manage your company that you are not surprised by it. You can maximize your effectiveness by practicing three elements of good management: self-knowledge, planning with flexibility, and follow-up.

If you know yourself, which includes knowing the strengths and weaknesses of your company; if you stick to the fundamentals and recognize the need to maintain flexibility in your planning; and if you then monitor your progress and make adjustments as necessary, you will find that you can keep your financial vulnerability well under control.

CHANGING STRUCTURE OF THE FINANCIAL MARKETS

by Eli Shapiro

Chairman, Finance Committee, and Director,
The Travelers Insurance Companies

and Barbara Negri Opper

Financial Economist, The Travelers Insurance Companies

MANY OF TODAY's chief executives have grown up professionally knowing comparatively little about the money markets—what they are, how they work, and what their importance is for the corporation. This is largely attributable to the fact that up until about 1966, money was available for corporate purposes in relatively stable abundance and at relatively low cost. These were also years of comparative corporate prosperity. Because financing considerations were not a challenge in that earlier era, corporate money matters didn't generally require the attention of the then-younger marketing and production and staff executives who are now chief executives.

All that is past! When well-known companies with excellent credit ratings have to calculate carefully the timing, maturity, and structure of new borrowings—and when the returns on assets do not provide the same once-wide margin above financing costs, as is true of many industries—it is not surprising that Chief Executive Officers have had to pay close attention to financial considerations. It is now imperative that they have some knowledge of changes and developments in sources of funds available to their companies, of changing financial practices, and of the consequences of these trends for their businesses.

This chapter is an effort to hit a few high points as to what the Chief Executive Officer "should know."

The management of current assets and liabilities by corporate businesses has shifted since the credit cycles that began in 1966. The general operating behavior exhibited by corporations prior to 1966

715

indicated that they regarded those portions of their balance sheets more or less as necessary adjuncts to the process of conducting their "real" business. It was the frequency and severity of the post-1966 credit cycles that apparently inspired in corporations—all business, for that matter—a more aggressive and ingenious management of their financial assets and liabilities.

The credit cycles that began in 1966 were characterized by a volatility in interest rates—both in their levels and in their term-structure relationships[1]—and in the availability per se of credit that was far greater than anything businesses had had to face during the earlier part of the postwar period. At the same time, the growth in retained earnings, which had provided an important source of investment capital, also slowed. Those conditions increased the opportunity costs of misforecasts and unpreparedness, enhanced the value of internally-generated funds as a source of capital, and placed added value upon the inventiveness of financial managers in their quest for investable funds.

We shall examine the sources of funds used by businesses, with special emphasis on the change in financing patterns that resulted from the more volatile credit market conditions that generally prevailed between 1966 and 1973. The focus will be upon the kinds of instruments used to raise capital and the nature of the suppliers of external capital.

SOURCES OF CORPORATE FUNDS

There are two basic sources of funds invested by businesses. One is internal; this consists of retained earnings and depreciation allow-

---

[1] "Term structure" is the phrase used to describe the relationship between yield and maturity on debt instruments. The term-structure relationship is thought to be governed by two kinds of considerations. One is liquidity, which generally can be characterized as follows: For any given borrower (i.e., credit quality being equal) a lender accepts more risk the longer the time-lapse to maturity. The second consideration is expectations of future interest rates, specifically as they affect borrowers' and lenders' willingness to participate in the longer or shorter segments of the debt markets.

Under "normal" economic and credit conditions, these two considerations work together and produce a sequence of interest rates that, when all else is held constant, shows an increase in rates as the maturity of the debt is lengthened. When economic and credit conditions are unsettled, however, the expectations element becomes overwhelming. Liquidity considerations to the contrary, the sequence of interest rates then can show a flat, or even declining, pattern as maturities progress from short to long. The term structure is said to have "shifted" when the relationship of interest rates with respect to term to maturity has changed.

ances. The other, of course, is external: funds borrowed in the long- or short-term debt markets and funds raised by selling new equity shares.

Internal Sources of Corporate Finance

During each year of the entire postwar period through 1973, the largest source of funds for financing corporate capital expenditures and acquisition of financial assets was generated internally. During that time, internally-generated flows of funds from business corporations—retained earnings and depreciation allowances, mostly—furnished from just above 50 percent to over 90 percent of total annual corporate financing requirements.

In the early part of the postwar period, retained earnings were a crucial source of finance. Their relative importance faded, however, with the steady cumulation of depreciation allowances. These non-cash charges against reported profits have been a source of cyclically stable investment funds. Reflecting the enormous investment in plant and equipment that took place during the whole postwar period, annual capital consumption allowances grew steadily from just below $5 billion in 1946 to nearly $70 billion in 1973. Their recent relative importance has been magnified, moreover, by the lack of growth in retained earnings since 1965.

The averages of annual amounts shown in Table 1 provide a perspective on the sources and uses of business funds between 1952 and 1973. These flows are presented both in billions of dollars and as percentages of total sources and uses of funds.

As Table 1 shows, the dollar growth in depreciation has been strong throughout the postwar period. Because these allowances are based upon the size of the capital stock already in existence, they are not responsive to current business or financial conditions (except insofar as income tax policies might change to reflect those conditions). These allowances are therefore a vital base to any corporation's total supply of funds available, inasmuch as their volume in any given corporation tends to be fairly stable from year to year and is therefore readily and accurately predictable. At a time of strong credit market fluctuations, that feature is of considerable significance in financial planning.

The relative importance of depreciation allowances as a source of business capital is shown in the right-hand columns of Table 1. It will be seen that those allowances have varied little as a percentage of total sources, ranging from about 45 to 50 percent during the entire post-war period through 1973. Thus, despite all the innovation and emphasis on financial management, this relatively mundane source of investable funds remains the largest and by far most stable component of funds available for business acquisition of assets.

Part of the need for financial innovation between 1966 and 1973 can be seen in the lackluster performance of the other component of internal funds, which, of course, is retained earnings. The use of annual averages over periods of years in Table 1 obscures annual and cyclical variability in this component. Nevertheless, the basic downtrend in retained earnings is validly presented in the Table.

The derivation of retained earnings is presented in Table 2, where it can be seen that the growth patterns of profits both before and after taxes have been considerably stronger than that for retained earnings. Part of the lack of growth of retained earnings between the early 1950s and the early 1960s stemmed from higher dividend pay-out ratios. But in the decade ending in the early 1970s, there was little further change in the share of profits before tax paid out as dividends. The major factor inhibiting growth of retained earnings in the early 1970s has been inflation; this is clearly reflected in the size of inventory valuation allowances. Those adjustments attempt to reflect that part of profits which is illusory. These are temporary, and will disappear as soon as existing inventories are replaced at the new higher level of prices.[2]

Taken together, these two components of internally-generated funds have provided an important mainstay for corporate funds. Nevertheless, the more interesting story of the 1966 to 1973 period revolves around the raising of capital from sources outside of the company, for it is there that the efforts to counterbalance the shortfalls in retained earnings produced innovation.

External Sources of Corporate Funds

The need for greater reliance on external finance during the 1966 to 1973 period arose because internally-generated funds grew more

---

[2] Although profits resulting from the sale of inventories from pre-inflation supplies may be illusory, they nevertheless are taxed like any other source of income. The shift in inventory valuation accounting from Fifo to Lifo will, in an inflationary period, reduce both these illusory profits and the associated income tax liability.

TABLE 1
Nonfinancial Corporate Businesses, Sources, and Uses of Funds (annual averages)

	Billions of Dollars					Percentages				
	1952–55	1956–60	1961–65	1966–70	1971–73	1952–55	1956–60	1961–65	1966–70	1971–73
All Sources	**31.2**	**42.6**	**61.5**	**92.6**	**135.8**	**100.0**	**100.0**	**100.0**	**100.0**	**100.0**
Internal	**23.7**	**31.7**	**45.7**	**60.9**	**77.1**	**76.0**	**74.4**	**74.3**	**65.8**	**56.8**
Retained earnings	9.8	10.3	15.0	15.3	14.4	31.4	23.9	24.4	16.5	10.6
Depreciation	13.9	21.4	30.7	45.6	62.7	44.6	50.2	49.9	49.2	46.2
External	**7.5**	**10.9**	**15.8**	**31.7**	**58.7**	**24.0**	**25.6**	**25.7**	**34.2**	**43.3**
Equity	1.8	2.0	.7	2.5	9.9	5.8	4.7	1.1	2.7	7.3
Debt	**6.0**	**10.0**	**13.8**	**30.4**	**46.5**	**19.2**	**23.5**	**22.4**	**32.8**	**34.2**
Mortgages	1.3	2.3	4.2	4.8	14.4	4.2	5.4	6.8	5.2	10.6
Bonds	3.6	4.4	4.5	13.9	13.4	11.5	10.3	7.3	15.0	9.9
Tax exempt bonds	—	—	—	—	.8	—	—	—	—	.6
Short-term	1.1	3.3	5.1	11.7	17.9	3.5	7.7	8.5	12.6	13.2
Profits tax liabilities	-.5	-1.3	1.2	-1.7	1.4	-1.6	-3.1	2.1	-1.8	1.0
Miscellaneous	.2	.2	.1	.5	.9	.6	.5	.2	.5	.7
All uses	**31.2**	**42.6**	**61.5**	**92.6**	**135.8**	**100.0**	**100.0**	**100.0**	**100.0**	**100.0**
Capital expenditures	**25.4**	**34.5**	**47.8**	**78.1**	**103.7**	**81.4**	**81.0**	**77.7**	**84.3**	**76.4**
Plant and equipment	23.2	31.4	40.8	67.7	89.2	74.4	73.7	66.3	73.1	65.7
Residential construction	.7	1.1	2.2	2.3	5.3	2.2	2.6	3.6	2.5	3.9
Inventories	1.5	2.0	4.9	8.1	9.2	4.8	4.7	8.0	8.7	6.8
Net financial assets	**5.8**	**8.1**	**13.7**	**14.5**	**32.1**	**18.6**	**19.0**	**22.3**	**15.7**	**23.6**
Liquid assets	1.9	-.2	3.1	2.2	7.2	6.1	-.5	5.0	2.4	5.3
Net trade credit	1.1	1.6	1.7	1.7	5.6	3.5	3.8	2.8	1.8	4.1
Miscellaneous*	2.8	6.7	8.9	10.6	19.3	9.0	15.7	14.5	11.4	14.2
Capital expenditures as percent of gross internal finance	107.5	108.9	104.3	128.4	134.0					

* Includes discrepancy.
Source: *Flow of Funds*; Board of Governors of the Federal Reserve System.

TABLE 2
Nonfinancial Business Retained Earnings (annual averages)

	Billions of Dollars					Percentages				
	1952–55	1956–60	1961–65	1966–70	1971–73	1952–55	1956–60	1961–65	1966–70	1971–73
Profits before tax............	35.6	39.7	51.1	66.6	78.1	100.0	100.0	100.0	100.0	100.0
Profit tax accruals...........	−17.9	−19.0	−23.0	−30.7	−34.5	−50.3	−47.9	−45.0	−46.1	−44.2
Net dividends paid..........	− 8.3	−10.6	−14.1	−19.7	−22.0	−23.3	−26.7	−27.6	−29.6	−28.2
Inventory valuation adjustment................	.5	− 1.0	.5	− 3.2	− 9.8	− 1.4	− 2.5	− 1.0	− 4.8	−12.5
Plus: Foreign branch profits............	.9	1.1	1.5	2.2	2.6	2.5	2.8	2.9	3.3	3.3
Equals: Retained earnings...............	9.8	10.2	15.0	15.2	14.4	27.5	25.7	29.4	22.8	18.4

Source: *Flow of Funds*; Board of Governors of the Federal Reserve System.

slowly than capital expenditures. That ratio, shown as the bottom line of Table 1, on the right, indicates that by the early 1970s, the equivalent of about one third of capital expenditures (and, of course, of all financial asset acquisitions) was financed by funds raised from sources outside of the corporations, whereas in the years 1952–55 less than 8 percent was so financed.

The years 1966 to 1973 were characterized by strong fluctuations in overall credit availability, shifts in loanable funds among various lender groups, large changes in yield term-structure relationships, and large fluctuations in yield relationships among types of instruments and among quality levels within categories of financial instruments. The unusual width of those fluctuations was probably associated with both the cause and the effect of a new-found activism on the part of corporate finance officers as they moved among the markets for different kinds of money, according to their own expectations and relative cost calculations.

For example, although businesses sought the least costly forms of external capital, the measure of cost was not necessarily made in just the simple terms of contemporaneous cost. One other factor taken into account as a constraint was the relationship of total debt to total assets. That constraint was particularly important after the long postwar trend among all corporations to reduce their total equity-to-asset ratio. This increase in leverage appears to have been a conscious business goal that took place in an economic environment deemed stable enough to merit the additional risk of a heavy debt-to-asset ratio.

Still another constraint was expectations. Corporate finance officers acted upon their interest rate forecasts by shifting to and from short- and long-term debt in their efforts to minimize the total interest cost of borrowed funds for a given project. This kind of shifting generally took the form of borrowing at short term when long-term interest rates were perceived to be at a peak, and then replacing those short-term loans with long-term debt after long-term interest rates fell.

A final constraint was credit availability in general and the shifts in availability among different sources of credit. In those years of periodic "disintermediation"—the wholesale shifting of the public's funds from depositary intermediaries to direct investments in capital market instruments—there were shortages in certain of the kinds of credit in which these institutions dominated.

An example of the multiple factors that entered into business financing choices can be seen by examining the patterns of increase of long-term debt relative to equity during the 1965 to 1973 period. Between 1965 and 1969, only $4 billion out of the $141 billion total in net external finance raised by nonfinancial corporate businesses—less than 3 percent—came from net new equity issues.

During that same time, the real cost of issuing equity—relative to both its subsequent value and to its previous highs—remained on a fairly low plateau. There was, of course, logic behind the seemingly contradictory behavior of a relatively small volume of equity issues being sold at a time of low relative costs of issuing common stock. That behavior did not imply that firms based their external financing decisions upon factors other than relative cost. But it did demonstrate the multiple facets of the measurement of relative cost, some of which relate more to future than to contemporaneous costs. One, for example, is the earnings-per-share performance that would be necessary to maintain a market valuation for the firm: The 1965 to 1970 period was one of declining earnings for business corporations; for manufacturers, operating ratios to sales peaked at 9.26 percent in 1966, and declined from there to hit a low of 6.99 percent in 1970. If corporate financial officers were at all accurate in forecasting those declines—which seems safe to assume in general—an increase in the number of outstanding equity shares would have exacerbated the downward stock price pressure exerted by falling earnings.

Another factor that was operating was the increase in the long-term debt component of the capital structure of business firms. To be sure, part of the increasing long-term debt portion was a direct result of the relative cost-earnings projections discussed just above. But an important part also arose from the direct endeavor to maximize return on net worth by gaining some leverage through judiciously increasing the amount of total assets in relation to equity capital.

Financing of Capital Assets

There are three principal ways of financing capital assets: mortgage loans; general debt obligations; and, more popular in recent years than before, leasing. For companies whose credit is not well established or has become weakened, mortgage financing may be the best, or even only, means of finding necessary borrowed funds. For many companies, financing through general obligations was preferable to borrowing via a mortgage, even though the nominal interest rates on the two forms of loans have remained quite similar.[3] For one thing, general obligations may make it possible to finance the whole cost of the assets in question whereas in the case of mortgage financing, the borrower usually is required to tie up a significant fraction of the cost as an equity cushion for the mortgage. Moreover, it is often true that a general obligation that pledges the full faith and credit of a financially sound company may actually carry a lower interest rate. It is not surprising, therefore, that mortgage finance was a significant source of long-term credit only for certain industries that had used up their borrowing capacity—such as utilities in the early 1970s—and for firms that, regardless of their industry, were unable to attract the less expensive forms of long-term credit.

More recently, leasing has become quite widespread as a means of financing capital assets. In contrast to a traditional mortgage, leasing provides a means of financing the total cost of the asset or assets in question. Structured with third-party ownership, moreover, the lease does not show up as debt on the balance sheet, although lease payments may be mentioned in a footnote. This method of accounting helps preserve borrowing capacity for the lessee. The cost of the lease provides an accurate measure of the full cost of the asset to the corporation including interest, depreciation, taxes, etcetera. Usually, the interest rate implicit in the lease payment is higher than the interest of a general debt instrument. For a creditworthy corporation, however, the lease interest rate is usually considerably lower than a pure mortgage interest rate. For all of these reasons, leasing became an increasingly common means whereby many of the nation's most credit-worthy corporations financed their property expansion needs during the 1960s and 1970s.

Another important factor in the choice between bonds and mortgages, during the past decade, was a great shift in the years 1965–1973 in the availability of funds among various sources. During this volatile period in the credit markets, there were occasions when traditional mortgage-lenders were experiencing great shortfalls in loanable funds. This came about as the public—never very important in the market for mortgage financing by business—sought to participate directly in capital markets, bypassing the mortgage lenders. At other times, as during 1973, commercial banks—traditionally active in the business mortgage market—had ample loanable funds. In that year,

---

[3] Specifically, the nominal rates on Baa-quality private placement commitments have remained similar to nominal rates on large income-property mortgage commitments.

businesses financed an unusually large portion of their need for external capital through mortgage loans from banks. At other times, when mortgage money was tight and interest rates rose, downpayment requirements also increased. Thus, the equity fraction of the financing requirement of the borrower also rose, adding another element to the cost of financing.

SHORT-TERM CAPITAL

The most striking developments in business finance over the decade from the early 1960s to the early 1970s have occurred in the short-term market. Innovation in this segment of the market took place not just in the development of new instruments, though that certainly occurred; innovation took place also in the more basic sense of the institutions acting as suppliers and users of funds.

Prior to 1966, business corporations—as we mentioned—behaved as though they viewed their liquid assets more or less as one of the necessities of an ongoing business. During the entire pre-1966 period back to 1946, the annual net changes in their liquid assets fluctuated relatively narrowly between plus and minus $5 billion. But in certain years between 1966 and 1973, nonfinancial businesses increased their holdings of these instruments by increments on the order of $10 to $20 billion.

At the same time, business corporations issued short-term liabilities in vastly increased amounts. Commercial paper, which is the negotiable short-term promissary notes of corporations, became extremely important. It burgeoned in volume from $9 billion outstanding in 1965 to $43 billion by the end of 1973. For nonfinancial corporations alone, there was $10 billion in commercial paper outstanding at the end of 1973. And annual changes in short-term debt of nonfinancial corporations, which had never exceeded $6 billion in the postwar period prior to 1965, occasionally reached $36 billion per year in some years between 1964 and 1973.

The sharper fluctuations in the interest rate cycle, and the periodic shift toward a downward slope in the term-structure of interest rates—according to which longer-term loans carried relatively lower rates than short-term loans—no doubt played an important role in the vast increase in the participation of nonfinancial corporations on both sides of the short-term lending market.

As can be seen in Exhibit 1, in January 1972 we experienced an

EXHIBIT 1
Term Structure of Interest Rates,
U.S. Government Securities

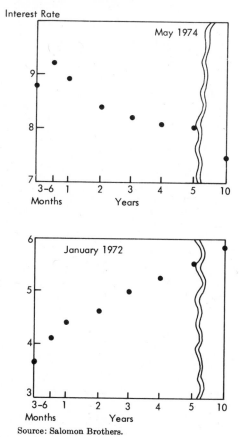

Source: Salomon Brothers.

upward-sloping yield curve. Thus, interest rates in the short-term market were much lower than interest rates in either the intermediate or long-term debt markets. By contrast, in May 1974 we observed a downward-sloping yield curve with short-term interest rates substantially higher than rates in both the intermediate and long-term debt markets.

The new higher level of short-term yields in general, even aside from their record cyclical peaks, was an inducement to these corporations to increase their holdings of interest-bearing short-term assets. And the sharpness of the credit cycles in the years 1966–1973 brought a premium to the businessmen who were able to forecast accurately the peaks and troughs of long-term interest rates. It is quite apparent that many corporations hedged on the interest rate cycles by financing their debt requirements at short-term when rates were high, in anticipation of funding those loans at long-term when interest rates receded from their cyclical peaks.

So, as can be inferred from Exhibit 1, there has been a parallelism between the acquisitions by companies of short-term, liquid assets and their issuance of short-term debt, both of which have moved with the general pattern of short-term interest rates.[4] What this has meant is that, to an unprecedented extent, business corporations have, in effect, functioned as financial institutions.

As the volume of funds increased in the short-term markets, so too did the variety of instruments, their issuers, and their purchasers. A couple of interesting and important examples are given by the growth of certificates of deposit and commercial paper. Certificates of deposit issued by commercial banks grew from literally zero in 1959 to about $65 billion outstanding by the end of 1973.

The growth in the use of short-term borrowings of business over the past 20 years or so has been a major development in the money markets. The lion's share of these credits has come directly from commercial banks. Commercial paper issued by corporations, another important source, has been a distant second on the supply side of short-term capital for business. Table 3 shows the growth in sources of short-term capital for business. The preponderant importance of bank loans to business is clearly shown.

TABLE 3

Nonfinancial Business Corporations, Instruments Used to Raise Short-Term Capital (amounts outstanding at year end, billions of dollars)

	1952	*1960*	*1965*	*1970*	*1973*
Bank Loans*	22.8	37.7	60.1	102.6	151.2
Short-term (estimated)	n.a.	n.a.	n.a.	61.5	95.2
Other Loans	3.0	7.6	10.5	26.3	31.7
Finance company loans	1.8	5.6	7.6	13.7	20.2
U.S. government loans	.7	.9	1.7	2.1	1.8
Acceptances	.2	.4	.4	1.5	2.5
Dealer-placed commercial paper	.3	.8	.8	9.0	7.2

* Includes loans maturing in one year or more. The amount in short maturities is estimated from proportions for a sample of banks accounting for 70 percent of all commerical and industrial loans.
Source: *Flow of Funds;* Federal Reserve Board.

---

[4] The one major exception to this pattern occurred in 1970, when the bankruptcy of Penn Central—and the resulting losses on the part of holders of its commercial paper—led to a severe contraction in volume that year, despite the high interest rates.

The rising importance of short-term credits to business from commercial banks resulted from a number of forces and developments that need not be gone into here. Important to any of these considerations, however, were efforts by banks, in times of uncertainty, to maintain liquidity against risk of possible large outflows of deposits by emphasizing shorter-term loans. Moreover, when banks expected interest rates to rise, they were, naturally, inclined to either emphasize shorter-term loans or use on longer-term loans interest rates that were tied to their prime rate. The prime rate itself changed, in the early 1970s, from being an administered rate to a market-determined rate tied by formula to current yields in the commercial paper market.

In addition to the direct importance of commercial banks as sources of short-term credit for business, they have indirect importance as well. For example, acceptances, which are used primarily in international trade, represent unconditional guarantees by a bank of sellers' receivables. These instruments, by interposing a prime bank guarantor, facilitate trade between foreign firms and unknown, or less-than-prime, U.S. business firms. As another example, commercial banks also serve an important function in the commercial paper market, a market which grew from insignificance in the 1960s to critical importance by the end of that decade.[5] Banks are the source of contingency lines of credit—stand-by agreements that would provide funds to repay commercial paper holders in the event maturing issues could not be renewed. These agreements provide another layer of security to purchasers of commercial paper and thereby, theoretically at least, help keep down the borrower's interest cost. Banks also serve an agency function in the market; they issue the notes, hold them for safekeeping, and facilitate payments.

LONGER-TERM CAPITAL—DEBT AND EQUITY

In addition to supplying short-term capital to business, the financial intermediaries have been major suppliers of longer-term debt and equity as well. Between 1960 and 1973, financial institutions supplied

---

[5] "Commercial paper" is unsecured notes of indebtedness of corporations. The notes typically are short-term, ranging from maturities of one day to as long as 270 days. They are usually issued in bearer form and in large minimum denominations. Issuers are restricted to the largest and most credit-worthy corporations. There are two types of commercial paper: (*a*) dealer-placed, which is generally paper issued by nonfinancial corporations; and (*b*) directly placed or finance company paper, which is generally issued by sales- and consumer-finance companies.

95 percent of the longer-term debt and equity raised by corporations.

Individuals acting on their own behalf have supplied a decreasing portion of total business funds, but have shown considerable sensitivity to relative yields between direct investment in business corporations and "intermediated" investment through financial institutions. This was observed in the behavior of individual investors during the 1960s and early 1970s. The phenomenon of "disintermediation"—a word coined in 1966, as individuals withdrew deposits en masse to take advantage of higher yields available from direct investment in government and corporate debt—was a real or impending force throughout the period of activist monetary policy that began in 1966 and extended through 1973. With respect to individuals' acquisitions of fixed-dollar obligations, the story really began about 1958, when banks, savings and loan institutions, and savings banks were all aggressively competing for funds and offered yields far more attractive than available from short- and intermediate-term market instruments. As a result, households, on an overall net basis, disinvested out of direct holdings of corporate fixed-dollar issues and channeled those funds through the intermediaries. During the 1960s, households maintained their steady net selling of directly-held corporate equities—stocks—a process that has persisted in each of the subsequent years through 1973. The acquisitions by individuals and households of investment company shares have not counterbalanced that disinvestment since the early 1960s.

One principal source of corporation long-term and equity capital has become pension funds. These funds have expanded from their position in the immediate postwar years. As can be seen in Table 4, in the first postwar decade, uninsured pension funds alone provided an average of 18 percent of long-term corporate capital raised externally.[6] They have been providing since then about one third of the externally-raised longer-term capital of corporations. Moreover, the volume of funds flowing through the pension medium has been cyclically stable and growing—two attributes that took on great significance during the hectic credit markets between 1965 and 1973. Much of this pension money, of course, flowed from corporate business at the outset, as the growth in fringe benefits accelerated during the postwar era.

Life insurance companies have traditionally been important suppliers of long-term credit to businesses. Corporate bonds and mort-

---

[6] Unfortunately, data for the insured pension funds cannot be segregated in the asset acquisitions of life insurance companies.

TABLE 4

Noninsured Pension Funds as a Source of Business Capital

	Average Annual Net Increases in Corporate Long-Term Debt and Equities Acquired by:		
	Noninsured Pension Funds	Life Insurance (includes insured pensions)	All Financial Institutions
Billions of dollars:			
1946–1955............................	1.0	2.7	4.9
1956–1965............................	3.4	2.7	11.1
1966–1973............................	6.4	6.1	29.0
As percent of total corporate debt and equity:			
1946–1955............................	17.9	48.2	87.5
1956–1965............................	34.7	27.6	113.3
1966–1973............................	24.1	22.9	109.0

Source: *Flow of Funds;* Federal Reserve Board.

gages are the dominant assets, by far, of the life insurance industry. More important, the life insurance industry has played a special role in corporate finance by acquiring private placements—corporate debt issued directly to one institution or a small group of lenders rather than floated in the open market through underwriters. The especial significance of direct placement lies in the fact that this form is basically the only way in which small, unknown, or less credit-worthy firms can issue long-term debt.

Fire and casualty insurers also have traditionally acquired long-term corporate debt; but, in their case, the issues acquired are nearly always publicly offered bonds of large corporations. The volume of fire and casualty acquisitions was generally small until the 1966–1973 period, and it tends to be quite sensitive to relative yields on the many other instruments available to these diversified investors.

Mutual savings banks and commercial banks—depositary institutions which are empowered to invest in corporate issues—have in the past been rather cyclically volatile sources of long-term debt and equity capital for businesses. A good part of that instability, of course, stems from the fluctuations that have beset them in their own attempts to attract funds since 1965. Another source of instability with respect to their acquisitions of corporate bonds and equities has been their own internal allocations among asset choices. Mutual savings banks, up until about 1965, had traditionally been mortgage lenders; but thereafter the money markets saw a deterioration in the relative yield attractiveness of single-family home mortgages, and as a consequence, mutual savings banks shifted strongly to the corporate bond market, nearly tripling their holdings of those instruments between 1965 and 1973. Their choices among assets—basically single-family home mortgages, commercial and multifamily mortgages, and corporate bonds and equities—seem to be governed by relative yields, given certain minimum levels of activity.

Commercial banks became important as sources of funds for corporate bonds in 1967, and since then their activity in this market has fluctuated considerably. The importance of commercial banks as total suppliers of external funds to corporations was developed earlier. Although they have not been dominant long-term lenders to corporations by way of corporate bonds, commercial banks are crucial to the short-term markets in which corporations raise funds, and they have at times, between 1966 and 1973, been extremely important lenders in the intermediate-term area and by way of mortgage loans extended to corporations.

CONCLUSION

The amplitude of interest rate variations and the shifts in the volume of available funds during the 1966 to 1973 period forced corporations to manage more actively their financial assets and liabilities. In particular, they became much more active and sophisticated in the short-term markets. Nonfinancial corporations very strongly acted out their interest rate forecasts by shifting from long- to short-term loans when rates were expected to fall. They increased greatly their short-term assets at those times, also, by taking advantage of inconsistencies among short-term interest rates. In the whole process, they acted at times very much like financial institutions.

Most of the innovation as to financial instruments and practices during those years took place in the short-term markets. And because commercial banks are the dominant financial institutions in the short-term markets, either as sources of funds or as functionaries, buyers, and holders of obligations, the banks played a vastly enlarged role in corporate finance during that period.*

---

* [Ed. Note: Readers interested in further discussion of financial "building blocks" are referred to the chapter by George Dixon and John Schreiner, "The Financial Structure: Basic Building Blocks."]

CAPITAL PROJECT APPROVAL

by Hershner Cross

Senior Vice President, General Electric Company

AMONG THE many responsibilities of general management, approval of capital projects must rank among the more challenging. The process of committing resources to an enterprise involves many dimensions of decision-making and many diverse interests, concerns, sponsors, opponents, and sources of input.

ROLE OF THE CAPITAL BUDGET

Many companies have found it useful to approach the task of approving capital investments on a two-phase basis. The first phase consists of preparing an annual capital budget which will include an identification of a number of specifically known projects and a further provision for projects to be considered during the course of the year. The purposes to be served by this capital budget would include assurance that it is acceptable as part of the financial plan of the company, with sufficient provision for funding, and to provide for the cost and expenses associated with capital investment projects. It permits the company management to assure itself that the principal investment plans for the year are generally in accord with the strategic thrust of the business, and to provide appropriate balance in the allocation of funds to the divisions or individual businesses of the company.

CASE–BY–CASE REVIEW

The second phase followed by many companies is a case-by-case review of individual capital investment proposals arising during the year, regardless of whether they have been included in the overall capital budget or not. The purposes to be served by this case-by-case review include: the individual evaluation of each proposal as it is brought through the planning stage, to assure that it receives necessary technical, economic, and operating inputs and reviews before referral to higher management; and to permit a "second look" before money is actually appropriated so that significant changes in the economy, the state of the company, or of the individual business proposing the appropriation can be considered.

It is our purpose here to explore the case-by-case evaluation of capital projects. They involve many more considerations than the capital budgeting process, even though many of the same concerns will be reflected in executive thinking at the time the capital budget is prepared.

A PROCESS, NOT AN EVENT

As most executives quickly discover, approval of capital investments is not an event, but a complex management process. Even though final approval of important appropriations is reserved for the general management or chief executive level, the act of approving, disapproving, or sending back for further information is most frequently only the "tip of an iceberg." The proposal is usually the culmination of weeks or months of intensive analysis, computation, discussion, persuasion, convincing, and recycling.

Much has been written about capital investment evaluation, often centering on techniques for economic appraisal such as return on investment, pay-back period, or discounted cash flow; or on criteria for evaluating the results, such as against the cost of money, or average return on investment for the company; or on techniques for reducing risk on assumptions, such as the use of risk analysis or modeling. These approaches all have real merit, especially for individuals charged with economic analysis of the proposals. Clearly they are of great value to the management of small organizations which are closely involved in all aspects of the business.

But for the larger companies, the capital investment project is generally worked up by the proposing lower levels of the organization utilizing most known techniques to reinforce the logic and attractiveness of the proposition. In many instances, lower organization levels will have already turned down proposals that lack economic appeal except in special instances, such as those involving safety, health, etc.

However, the chief executive must realize the rapidity with which the organization learns the height of the qualifying "hurdles" and how to make and support proposals that will clear them.

It therefore becomes the role of the chief executive to determine whether to commit actual company funds, or whether in spite of the seeming attractiveness of a proposal, there are other corporate considerations dictating its rejection. To do this most effectively requires an understanding of major issues involved, whether they be economic, organizational, environmental, or other. It is our purpose here to suggest some of the sequential considerations in the evaluation of capital appropriations that the experience of numerous operating executives suggest are most important in this process.

The considerations to be discussed can include only some of the more significant and generic. Obviously, specific industries and individual companies involve many different issues unique to their circumstances.

At the outset, it is important to consider the *category* or purpose of the capital investment being presented. Although there are many possible classifications, three principal categories seem to stand out because they have inherently different implications for management:

1. *Social investments*—involving mandated legal or environmental requirements (such as OSHA or EPA) or discretionary investments (such as to improve working conditions or appearance of a facility).
2. *Cost improvement investments.*
3. *Capacity expansion investments* for existing or new products.

SOCIAL INVESTMENTS

Generally, social investment projects involve such requirements as antipollution equipment, noise reduction, or safety measures. They often constitute only a small percentage of the appropriations being considered by an organization (even with the new pressures of OSHA and EPA) even though they may be of real importance to the reputation and image of the company. In some companies, they may constitute less than 5 percent of the total number of projects, and, except for special industries with heavy pollution problems, are often less than 5 percent of the investment dollars, but the management considerations are somewhat unique. (It should be noted that these are individual projects; in addition, most new facilities investments carry a significant allowance to meet environmental requirements.)

Perhaps the first executive decision must be whether to accept the requirement, or whether to appeal it further; considering the "do-ability" of the fix, the image of the company as a good corporate citizen, and its standing in its community, and the costs versus demonstrable results to be achieved. In addition, the executive should consider pending changes in the law which could negate the fix or require a different or additional thrust. Unfortunately compliance with certain environmental regulations can be like trying to hit a moving target.

A second key determination is whether a slightly less stringent standard might be achievable at substantially less cost; for example, whether meeting a requirement of 98 percent versus 100 percent might cost half as much, and whether this might be saleable to the requiring authorities.

A third consideration is whether the rest of the specific industry will be confronted with similar cost increases, and whether the market will absorb such added costs. In some instances, the added costs could force the market to turn to other products, and the entire industry might find itself obsoleted.

More frequently the problem will be less drastic. The principal considerations will involve first, the timing of the requirement to be met, and whether the appeals process may afford additional time for consideration of alternatives, if necessary.

The likelihood of success with the new proposed change in equipment, process, or methods is a significant issue, as well as the completion of the change in sufficient time to meet the required regulations.

If the project involves a *discretionary* proposal to improve facilities, executive concern will center on whether it is needed to stay competitive, or what benefit is really anticipated, usually in the form of employee relations or community satisfaction and support. For example, a new cafeteria might be proposed to enable more competitive recruiting and retention of needed employees; or actions to improve working conditions which could be perceived by employees as a step by management which might be returned through dedication to greater productivity. The likelihood of such reciprocal benefits is about the only business consideration available on such projects.

However, if such requests are numerous, it could be taken as a signal that either the management is not taking sufficient interest in basic facility conditions; or that possibly employees are not sufficiently involved in the main business thrust of the company and are indulging too much in peripheral concerns.

COST IMPROVEMENT INVESTMENTS

The second category of investment involves appropriations for cost improvements. These often comprise a substantial percentage of capital projects, and in some companies may constitute 20 to 30 percent of all proposals submitted both in numbers and dollars.

Such projects typically include changing a factory layout, modernizing equipment, installing a new process, all with the objective of reduction in the cost levels presently being attained through existing equipment and methods.

Although there may be elements of environment, safety, etc., to be considered as well, the major thrust is on economy to be achieved over an acceptable period of time.

Perhaps the most pressing consideration of the executive will be the size of the required commitment of funds relative to the business and its resources, and the time of pay back. Here his concern must center on the maturity of the product, the prospects for continued existence of the market, the anticipated life of the design, process or manufacturing method to be employed, the potential trap of inflexibility if demand should decline, etc.

But for the most part, cost improvement projects are based on fairly hard data and facts against which to evaluate alternative approaches. They do not characteristically involve many new variables (such as new markets, new applications, new products and the like). It has been said that cost reduction appropriations are usually the best kind for new executives to tackle because the ratio of hard fact to assumptions and hope is relatively high.

CAPACITY INVESTMENTS

These capital projects present the most complex conditions, and could be described as essentially entrepreneurial in nature. In some companies, the capacity investments constitute about half of all capital projects in number and value, and therefore set the entire tone for the process of appropriation consideration and approval. They frequently involve adding capacity, providing facilities and equipment for new products, establishing a geographic plant or ware-house, etc. It is with this kind of capital investment that the chief executive has to exercise the greatest care and the best judgment possible.

This type of capital investment, which might be thought of typically as a major capacity expansion, involves not only many of the considerations of the two simpler types of investments, but also a host of other issues with which the management must cope. It is with such projects as these that the chief executive is clearly aware of the two distinct aspects of the appropriation review process: the technical, economic, and operating inputs; and the determination of which proposals should be approved for investment.

It is at this point that he may discover several fundamentals that appear associated with the entire process of capital investment approval:

1. A highly critical role for the chief executive is the "vetting" of assumptions made by the projects' proposers and sponsors. Most of the quantifiable economic analyses will have been done by specialists, but the executive must decide:
    a. Whether the assumptions are realistic in the light of his experience and knowledge. (He will recognize the tendency of subordinates to project optimistic market needs which escalate pressure to add capacity.)
    b. Whether he is satisfied with the less economically assessable needs of the project, such as better quality or service.
    c. Whether the entire business will be better off for the project regardless of the merits or shortcomings of the specific proposal.
2. He can do little to influence an appropriation once it has reached his level short of:
    a. Approving.
    b. Rejecting.
    c. "Recycling" for new inputs, analyses and information.
3. To avoid having to reject half-baked proposals, he must assure that the business has in place a systematic process for subjecting proposals to expert inputs, operational reviews, and checks and balances at sufficiently low organizational levels to preclude hard positions from being taken.
4. The initiators of capacity investment proposals are frequently

functional managers whose primary concern is getting out more products. The chief executive must examine the impact on the company; namely, the likely effect of the project on the company income and its balance sheet.

5. The processes for capital investment evaluation and approval are closely related to the company's infrastructure and management system: objectives and goals, drives and incentives, measurements and rewards.

These systems can turn on or turn off capital investment requests and influence their number, size, riskiness, profitability, and likelihood of success.

MAJOR SEQUENTIAL CONSIDERATIONS

With these fundamental points in mind, some of the major sequential considerations are as follows.

Consonance with Strategic Plan

Although practices vary widely among businesses with regard to the formalization of their strategic plans, the chief executive (as perhaps the principal architect of the strategy for the business) will be fully aware of its basic thrust and direction. He will be vitally concerned whether the proposed capital project supports the strategy totally, in part, not at all, or in fact may be in conflict with it.

Major conflicts between established strategy and proposed capital projects are usually obvious. For example, the request for adding capacity to a line which has been selected to reduce growth and generate cash; or a make-versus-buy manufacturing project when the business strategy is to go for lower fixed costs and higher flexibility.

But it appears much easier to miss some of the less obvious conflicts which unobtrusively influence organization thinking away from the desired strategic direction. For example, when a new facility produces such low costs that the organization seizes on the opportunity to penetrate low end markets—even though the management is driving for higher quality image and a different market segment to serve.

Furthermore, the very existence of physical facilities already in place imparts a heavy bias to employee views of the possible courses available for business strategy. This can and does exert a powerful impact on the general management who understandably would prefer to follow a strategy that will build on employee perceptions and not find itself going "against the grain" of organizational culture. For example, with a strong tradition of quality manufacture in a community of high skills, a business would have a difficult task in reorienting its thinking to offshore sourcing which conceivably could be critical to survival. And every dollar invested in improving the cost performance of existing facilities (a natural action under the circumstances) makes the problem more difficult. In such a case, the strategic courses open to management may be seriously curtailed.

Clearly the compatibility between capital investment projects and the strategy of the business should be a first and foremost concern of the chief executive.

Economic Attractiveness

In a multiline business or a multibusiness corporation, a necessary early step should be the determination of the relative importance of the specific product line to the company, its specific mission (such as growth versus cash generation), and the priority accorded to investment for it. The importance of decisions on these questions can be readily appreciated by recognizing that management will tolerate much longer payout times in a growing business than in a mature cash generator. Almost identical projects for two different product lines in the same business may understandably be accorded quite different treatment, owing to the variation in importance, nature, and role of the two lines in the strategic plan of the business.

A second necessary step would entail an examination of the intrinsic economic appeal of the propositions being considered. In order to protect itself from the impact of day-to-day swings in economic climate, personal biases, and varying degrees of familiarity of general management with the specific businesses involved, most companies rely on certain basic criteria for evaluating economic attractiveness. For example, the time required for pay back; or, the return on investment for the specific project. Each of these criteria has its advocates and opponents resulting from historic usage, applicability to specific businesses, or even personal preferences of individual management.

At this point, it would seem obvious that:

1. The chief executive must usually look beyond the economic return on a specific appropriation and think of the impact on the entire business; and

2. He should also recognize that there will be numerous occasions where the economic analysis carries a relatively lower significance than other specific concerns or results to be obtained. For example, replacement of a burnt-out boiler is tough to justify economically, except to keep the plant operating! Or where the management wishes to protect existing company interests with an apparent noneconomic step, such as integrating into a raw material to protect source or quality of supply. Or where management wishes to change the strategic thrust of the business, such as to enter international markets. Or wishes to support longer-term interests such as providing capital equipment to facilitate research and development, or employee education.

An additional challenge to the importance of the economic analysis lies in the significance of the potential commitment of other company resources, such as scarce skills and talents. Even though an individual proposition may seem to meet all existing economic criteria, the implication for tieing up key people and organizations to get it done may be an important offsetting factor. In some companies, the manpower commitment becomes of significance equal to the economic consideration.

Although much has been written about the varying advantages of such tools for economic evaluation as return on investment or discounted cash flow, most of them appear as necessary but insufficient tools to use. In many cases they are based on varying assumptions as to what investment is involved, such as average investment, closing investment, etc. Discounted cash flow is widely employed as a good measure of the time value of the money invested. But it appears less useful in long-term projects which must count on residual values, since the accuracy of such determinations gets questionable over time. Discounted cash flow does not measure risk, in that it may give equal value to two proposals with widely differing payout periods, and hence, differing risks.

The cost of money is, of course, factored into the economic evaluations regardless of the tools employed. But the cost of money has additional significance for the chief executive that cannot be ignored. The prospect of change in the cost of money can influence a decision to delay or advance the timing of a project or even eliminate it from consideration entirely. But of even greater concern is the possible impact that raising the funds required to meet the appropriation may have on the capital structure of the business. Although determining the "bankability" of a proposal may be the province of the chief financial officer of the business, the effect on credit lines, need for additional equity, impact on dividend policy, or need for long-term debt are all of vital concern to the chief executive. As a result, even though a specific proposition may meet and pass with flying colors all the necessary other criteria and considerations, the impact of the proposal on the company's balance sheet and its capital structure may be of sufficient significance to warrant its postponement or outright rejection. This is perhaps one of the outstanding examples of where the economic evaluation of a proposal alone is not sufficient in the light of the impact on the total company.

Realism of Underlying Assumptions

The third area of major consideration involves the realism of underlying assumptions and estimates.

Of all the areas of assumptions which usually have to be made in projecting the results of a capital investment, the market forecast seems to win the honors for the "least likely to come through." The very nature of market dynamics makes this area difficult to forecast successfully. Volume and price forecasts have high mortality rates. Management has every reason to have reservations about assumptions on these critical factors and to scrutinize them carefully.

A second area which holds high risks is the technical sector. This concerns the technology and producibility of the materials and products, changes in design, processes and equipment to be used, automated approaches, and so on. Additionally, there is the question as to the assumption about the technical competitiveness of the product and if and when it may become obsolete.

A third area of assumptions is the economy, its stability and future prospects. Since the management of the business is engaged daily in developing viewpoints on the economic outlook, this imposes no new additional burden; but the investing of large capital funds based on specific economic assumptions confronts the chief executive with the moment of truth.

Other areas on which assumptions or estimates have varying effects would include: the labor force, its availability, productivity, skills, community pay rates, etc.

A further area would be the community itself and its characteristics with respect to services, utilities, equitable taxes, zoning, acceptance of newcomers, local business attitudes toward expansion, availability of housing, the minority situation, transportation and traffic, etc. Although much hard data is available for many of these elements, reliability of estimates must be taken fully into account.

Capability of Organization

Although sequentially this consideration appears fourth on the list, it is, in many instances, the decisive factor in the chief executive's conclusion.

Young, energetic, and enthusiastic teams have a way of over-optimistically committing themselves and their resources. For example, a capital project may be proposed which would involve a combination of new product, new process, new plant, new people. Success in pulling off a project of "everything new" is not a usual occurrence. Clearly the scope of the proposed project is an important factor in considering its "do-ability," and immature teams often propose undigestible projects.

Next is the background, experience, and performance of the team undertaking the project. The proven track record of the sponsoring organization in successfully bringing through capital investments is possibly the most important tool available to the executive. It can give him real confidence in the probability of success, and frequently can tip the scales of decision when other factors appear about in balance. A top team may be entrusted with *relatively* risky propositions which might otherwise be rejected.

Generally, the more borderline a proposal is with respect to its inherent attractiveness, the more weight will be given to the track record of the team. In cases involving new products, new processes, or new markets, many executives will approve only if time-tested organizations are responsible for the implementation.

It would be difficult to overstate the importance seen by executives in the proven "track record" of the organization sponsoring the proposal and responsible for its execution.

Flexibility

A fifth major consideration is the degree to which flexibility has been built into the proposal.

To protect against downside risk, consideration should be given to the ability to slow down the project, possibly reduce it in scope as circumstances dictate, or even to cancel it out entirely. The ability to adjust the project downward can be an important insurance factor to consider.

At the same time, a serious look should be taken at how it copes with upside risk, if expansion should be required, and what means for this have been provided in the proposition.

Judgment and Intuition

A sixth consideration involves the personal judgment, personal feeling, or intuition of the executive. This is an important characteristic not to be underestimated, for in an experienced manager it can represent the optimization of a great many additional and often unexpressed factors. The availability of high-speed computer capability enables so many variables to be reduced to fixed values that personal judgment and feeling can be reserved for those relatively few for which quantification does not appear possible. Taken as the last consideration after carefully weighing the rest, the judgment of the manager may be of highest importance.

Most executives resist the use of intuition in situations where the lessons of previous experience are available. This appears especially valid in businesses with well-beaten tracks. However, in situations where little or no existing experience is available, the executive has few options other than to use the judgment of others and himself, and his own intuitive instincts.

CONCLUSIONS

The process of approving capital investment projects involves most of the talents and skills required of an executive.

The most difficult projects are those requiring large commitments for businesses with relatively low returns, or substantial investments in new undertakings. The easiest, quite obviously, are those requiring relatively modest investments in higher return businesses with experienced teams in place.

Contrary to conventional wisdom, economic analyses of a project are often of less importance to the CEO than other factors, such as the impact on the entire business or the track record of the team responsible for the execution.

The chief executive needs to appreciate the heavy interrelationships of the process with the management systems of the business. He should assure the existence of a strongly established procedure for operational, functional, and economic inputs at sufficiently early stages to avoid premature commitments or locked-in positions.

He will find that among the most important overall considerations are conformity with the strategic plan of the business, economic attractiveness, realism of underlying assumptions, capability of the organization, flexibility in the project, and his own personal judgment.

Finally, he will recognize that individual appropriations cannot be looked at in isolated form. The entire company has strategic concerns, growth objectives, return on investment targets, and the like. Therefore, the chief executive must look at each appropriation in the context of the interests of the entire business.

TAX MANAGEMENT, TAXES, AND THE COMPANY

by Phillip Lifschultz
Vice President—Taxes, Montgomery Ward

BESIDES creating jobs, goods, and services, business organizations and their employees provide directly over one half the revenues used to fund government and government benefits. Business's stake in taxation is important. With better understanding of the tax system and his company's relationship to it, the CEO can more effectively control this significant and increasing cost of doing business.

Knowledge and understanding of related tax implications are indispensable to sound business decisions. Whether routine or unusual, any transaction will likely be affected by one or more kinds of tax, and the consequences may present either problems or opportunities. How profitable a company's operations are will depend in part on how well its taxes are managed.

Some think that the function of a tax department is relatively mechanical—involving merely the transfer of numbers from accounting statements to tax return forms and computing the tax according to a defined procedure or formula. But even the simplest business environment involves alternatives that could cost the enterprise more or less tax. I assume the obvious, that every CEO wishes to minimize his company's tax liabilities, and that he would insist that this be accomplished legally and without distorting business objectives.

Companies that approach the function positively will fare better than those which merely accept the tax department as necessary. Any activity that saves expense adds to earnings. Because of the leveraging impact of the cost of tax competence on profit, one of the most relatively productive expenditures in the company budget could be the tax function. If the company is large enough to organize all principal administrative activities into separate departments, then it is probably

744

large enough to have a separate tax department. A good tax department should pay for itself annually several times over in lawful tax benefits.

Although an effective tax function may be essential in many situations, there are circumstances where it may be an unaffordable luxury. The work in these instances of the smaller company would generally fall into the financial, legal, or control areas, and outside counsel would be relied on for the unusual, nonrecurring tax problems that may arise. The first part of this chapter deals with administering the function. Although it may not apply directly to the smaller company without a separate tax function it may nevertheless be useful for future reference to the CEO of an expanding organization.

Effective tax administration requires knowledge of the company's activities and plans as well as specialized technical competence in each of the various areas of taxation.

ADMINISTRATION

Structure

The best organizational structure for the tax function is one built around the people possessing those attributes required to satisfy the functional objectives of the company. It should be flat, reflecting an emphasis on functional responsibilities rather than administrative relationships. Communications will be considerably more dynamic in such an environment with resulting productivity enhancement.

Because the knowledge and abilities required for each tax function are different, combining tax functions should be avoided if feasible. Property taxes, for example, are unlike income taxes—they each require different skills, training, temperament, and its own particular aspect of the company's facts. The various principal taxes are: federal income; state income and franchise; property (ad valorem); payroll and unemployment; sales and use (consumption); excise; and other specialized industry taxes and licenses. When the level of activity is sufficient, each of these functions generally will be the responsibility of a separate person or group. Where for lack of sufficient activity, combinations are necessary, the functions tend to be grouped and divided between federal taxes on the one hand and state and local taxes on the other. This may vary depending on specialized industry requirements.

The tax department structure must meet the company's needs. Because of geographical dispersion of facilities and accounting, a decentralized organization might better suit requirements of state and local taxes than would a centralized organization.

Qualifications of the Tax Director

Accounting and law are both involved in tax management. The C.P.A. certificate and a law degree provide the foremost academic credentials. A successful background in a professional accounting or law firm is most helpful, not only for the variety and complexity of technical experiences but also for the proven ability to relate effectively to top management. If the tax director has enjoyed his clients' trust and confidence, chances are he will perform well as part of your management. This writer believes the tax director's principal experience should be with the federal income tax. It is the most complex tax, and generally involves the greatest burden to the company. Exceptions exist in certain specialized industries.

The tax professional should possess a strong sense of commitment, be an effective communicator and adversary—for much of the work involves controversy—an effective manager, management team member, and a student. Because the tax field is complex and dynamic, past performance is no assurance for the future. He must be willing to continue to learn and be able to stimulate that attitude in others who report to him.

Reporting and Title

The different possibilities of reporting levels and relationships of the tax function are perhaps greater than for most corporate activities, because the tax function has developed generally as a part of one of three separate staff activities—law, accounting, or finance, and only recently has it become a separate staff activity in its own right. Reporting possibilities are to the financial vice president, treasurer, general counsel, or controller. Any one of these can work well. The CEO may, however, want to have the tax manager report to him, because some of the most dramatic undertakings the company may engage in will involve important tax considerations. Firsthand interaction with the CEO could enhance the success of a venture.

An incorrect reporting relationship may subject a professional tax man's creative abilities to undesirable limitations, and you may never know what opportunities your company will have missed. If your tax manager does not make significant contributions to corporate decisions, chances are you have the wrong man in the job, he is reporting at the wrong level, or communications are inadequate.

The head of the tax function is generally called tax director, tax counsel, tax manager, or a variation of one of these. He may be a vice president, assistant vice president, assistant treasurer, assistant controller or assistant counsel, as well.

Staffing

How much can you afford or, more significantly, how much can you not afford? Staff adequately! Otherwise, you may reduce your best talent to clerks filing against deadlines. Overstaffing is equally undesirable. In any case, it has been this writer's experience that fewer and more highly compensated professional personnel backed by adequate numbers of clerical and statistical personnel operate more effectively than a greater number of lower-cost semiprofessional personnel.

In staffing the tax department, it should be kept in mind that the corporation will be drawing from, and competing with large accounting and law firms for talent. Factors important to the tax professional are compensation (of course!), the challenge of job content to his wit and intellect, and such fringes as status in the organization, and the caliber of people and events that will involve him. The real professional needs to communicate, and channels must be open for him to achieve best results.

The administrative head of any function generally has some discretion in selecting those who will work with him. It may be desirable in the case of the tax function for the immediate superior to at least counsel with the tax manager in filling key positions in the tax organization. This could provide both better back-up and help in avoiding cultural sterility.

Budget

The major appropriation in the tax department budget will be for personal services. It may be difficult for a personnel department to recognize higher compensation levels for a group whose productivity is almost impossible to measure against the usual standards, but there are factors that favor such recognition in respect to the tax function as well as in other areas where the company is competing with independent professional firms for the best talent. I am assuming that your company is relatively complex and that activities and projects depart from ordinary routine more than infrequently. If in-house competence is lacking, then greater reliance must be placed on outside tax counsel.

Outside professional services may require a sizable portion of the budget. Often, the amount cannot be predicted because of the uncertainty of government challenges leading to litigation. Also, unanticipated corporate activity involving tax considerations may arise after the budget is prepared. These items are nonrecurring and are thus difficult to provide for adequately in the budget.

Travel may be necessary in connection with audit appeals, rulings, and other matters that require meetings with governmental personnel at the federal, state, and local levels. Also, property tax renditions for large facilities are better done face-to-face with the local assessing authority after a visit by your property tax representative to the facility to learn about any factors bearing on the assessment of inventories, equipment, or buildings.

Periodic visits to company facilities often turn up valuable tax-related information. Occasional attendance at tax conferences or industry meetings on tax topics will provide informational inputs that can return the cost of the attendance many times over. I have yet to come away from such a meeting without some new information or idea.

Other areas in the budget are generally minor. One worth noting is tax publications. Tax services and periodicals are the lifeblood of the tax profession. Changes in laws and regulations, new rulings, and court decisions proliferate in the tax field. An effective tax professional must keep pace with the flow of information.

Outside Counsel

The company may look to its outside attorneys, C.P.A. firm, or other competent tax specialists for tax counseling. Use of outside tax counsel is indicated when management requires an opinion respecting the tax consequences of some contemplated transaction that would have a significant impact on the corporation, and the independence of counsel rendering the opinion is important in the circumstances. Outside legal counsel is generally needed when it becomes apparent that a tax controversy ultimately will be litigated. In such cases, legal counsel should be brought in at an early stage in the administrative process. Also, there may arise situations where highly specialized and experienced competence is required in a particular area, and time or manpower limitations won't permit in-house counsel to do the job as well and quickly as necessary. A first-class tax manager will be sensitive to these needs and would be the first to recommend use of outside counsel. On the other hand, if outside counsel is too readily relied upon, you may have some needed correction to make internally.

THE TAX FUNCTION

Compliance

The sine qua non of tax work is filing returns. Although it is the basic element, it is neither the beginning nor the end of the process. Although, perhaps, the least dramatic aspect of the work, it may be the most important. A strong compliance function is essential to satisfy legal requirements for timely, accurate, and complete returns. The presentation of the company's information in order to determine its tax obligation must truthfully disclose all material facts. The presentation also should be supportive of the company's interpretation of how certain transactions should be treated for tax purposes. Generally those responsible for compliance are responsible also for accounting for taxes and working with government auditors reviewing the returns.

Compliance may be the only tax function in some companies. Although a strong compliance group is essential, a failure to round it out with an effective research and planning function would be like having a ball team with a great defense and no offense. Balance is necessary for top performance.

Research and Planning

For best results the tax process should begin with the research and planning function. It requires a person with an understanding of both accounting and law, an in-depth knowledge of technical resources and company facts, and an ability to relate effectively with the operating and financial management of the company. It is in the company's interest, of course, that the tax person be informed early in the decision-making process regarding major moves. If he is the right person, he will be sensitive to matters beyond narrow tax considerations. He will understand financial and accounting aspects of the matter and possible impacts of government policy or regulations. If he is the right person, he can make his knowledge and observations understandable to other executives. If he is the right person, and if he is brought into projects in their early stages, he can make positive and creative suggestions while they are still timely, as well as point out pitfalls and problems.

Audits, Appeal, and Litigation

The tax laws do not cover all possible fact situations, nor are they always subject to precise application. Controversies arise occasionally, beginning with an audit of the return.

The audit is an important phase of tax work. Most issues raised by auditors can be and generally are settled at that level. Issues may involve questions of fact or law, or both. The audit may be made by one person or a team, depending upon the size and complexity of your company. It may take only a few weeks or it can extend beyond a year.

It must be remembered that an audit is an adversary procedure. For effective administration and control, questions and replies should be in writing. This prevents misunderstanding and in the long run will save time. It is usually wise to channel all communication through one company representative, and he should be present any time the auditor is interrogating other officials of the company. Remember, you won't win all the issues. If your tax man is aggressive, he will reach for every justifiable tax benefit. If the auditors make no adjustments, either your tax department may be too conservative and your company is overpaying its taxes, or else you have the world's best tax department.

If adjustments are made by an auditor and you disagree, your company can appeal administratively before going to court. In the case of a federal tax issue, a district conference may be all that is needed to resolve the issue; but, if necessary, further appeal may be taken at the regional appellate level. Beyond that, you may go to the tax court, and if you lose there you may seek further judicial review before paying the deficiency. Most states permit payment of an asserted deficiency, then filing of a claim for refund, and upon disallowance, suing on the claim. The choice of procedure and forum involve tactical considerations that require highly skilled professional knowledge and judgment.

In considering litigation, you should recognize that the government's resources are generally greater than those of a taxpayer, and in many cases the issue may involve a great deal more revenue to the government than the amount of tax involved in your particular case. Consequently, be prepared for a tough and costly process; but if the value of winning (generally the amount of tax and interest involved factored by the risk of losing) sufficiently exceeds the estimated cost, go ahead. Above all, don't do a halfway job. Many good cases have been lost because of inadequate representation.

At various stages of a tax case, the possibility of a compromise may come up which is advantageous to both the taxpayer and the government. In some cases, the examining auditor may feel the issue is beyond his authority to compromise, and in other cases an administrative policy concerning certain unsettled issues is to litigate. But in any case where settlement is possible it should be explored taking into account the expense and risk of litigation.

Rulings

In some situations, the taxpayer may want an advance ruling from the Internal Revenue Service on the tax implications of a contemplated transaction. There are some situations in which a ruling will not be issued; and in some cases, submitting a request for a ruling may not be advisable. A favorable ruling based upon a complete and accurate representation of facts before the transaction is of great value in removing tax uncertainty. It can often mean the difference between go and no go if the economics of the tax consequence variation is great enough.

Ruling procedures at the state level are varied and generally less formal. Rulings by state tax officials often are not published.

Some federal rulings of particular significance are published (without identifying the taxpayer making the request). This provides guidance to other taxpayers and Internal Revenue Service personnel in similar situations. Although published rulings are revocable, you can generally rely upon them until revoked or modified as representing how the government would interpret the law in a given situation.

Akin to the advance ruling is a procedure employed by the Internal Revenue Service when an examining agent requests guidance from the national office on how to treat a significant transaction that he may question in the course of an audit. In some cases, additional time and expense can be avoided by this procedure which is called Request for Technical Advice. Although this is an internal governmental procedure, the taxpayer has the right to participate in the process and should.

Legislation, Regulations, and Rules

The source of tax "law" is the statutes enacted by legislative bodies. Tax statutes are organized into a comprehensive code which expresses the fundamental scheme of taxation—that is, who or what is to be taxed; the tax base and how it is measured; when the tax is to apply and be paid; jurisdictional limits, if any, of the tax; and how the tax system is intended to operate administratively.

The administrative body designated to enforce the law and collect the tax publishes general interpretations of the statutes in the form of regulations or rules. These carry the force of law if they are within the scope of the statute. Because these interpretations must of necessity be more detailed and contain examples of how the code is to apply, they sometimes go beyond the scope of the code and are therefore subject to challenge in the courts.

As mentioned earlier, rulings covering specific or limited fact situations not covered in the regulations or rules, and announcements explaining procedures, may be published from time to time. Also, tax treaties between nations and related regulations represent another significant portion of the body of tax law applicable where international activities are involved. All the foregoing plus numerous published decisions of courts and appeals boards constitute the tax "law."

Considerable additional unofficial commentary is published in tax services and periodicals. There is no substitute for the tax man who has a general knowledge of what is available as research resources and who knows how to find his way through the complex maze of subject matter. It can happen that, after thorough research taking many hours, the conclusion is reached that there is no law covering a particular set of facts. Where no answer is the answer, then the highest form of the art through the exercise of professional judgment must be applied in an attempt to ascertain what the answer would probably be. Remember, experts can and often do disagree.

TAXES AND THE COMPANY

Of course, the CEO is not likely to understand all the ins-and-outs of taxes, but there are a few basic concepts that he will find helpful. There follow some of these.

The tax obligations that your company assumes in conducting its business are reflected in the economics of each transaction. Every expenditure carries an implicit federal income tax recovery of 48 percent currently, and in addition, state and local income taxes may increase the recovery rate. Tax recovery or benefit may be received within the current year of the expenditure, or it may be delayed for an ascertainable term, or indefinitely. Because a delay in the recovery will cost the company interest (either through a reduction in currently available funds for investment in the business or increased debt), the value of the future tax benefit or, alternatively, the after-tax cost of the expenditure should be measured in current dollars. The tax cost implicit in an income-producing transaction decreases as the term over which the tax must be paid increases. Tax deferral opportunities should be utilized whenever possible (especially when borrowing costs are high!) like any other legitimate tax saving.

For example, your company may be operating a facility that is no longer adequate for your needs. Its value exceeds your adjusted tax cost. You could sell it at a gain, pay tax on the gain, and reinvest the remaining proceeds in a new facility. Or you could trade your existing property for one that meets your requirements and *postpone* legitimately the payment of tax on the excess value of the new facility over the tax basis of the old. The new facility acquires the tax basis of the old (adjusted for any additional consideration paid or any partial gain recognized if you receive any additional consideration), thus resulting in deferring the gain and related tax.

Impacts of Taxes on Decisions

Tax effects will influence reported earnings through either the tax burden or interest expense. Tax effects and their timing will also affect comparative present value results of financial projections. Consequently, decisions on whether to invest or spend are influenced by tax considerations.

The tax bias in our federal tax system generally favors expenditures which may be expensed currently rather than be treated as long-term capital investment. It also generally favors debt over equity financing. Notwithstanding the general bias, each individual situation should be computed to ascertain both the earnings and financial effects. But the bias does tend to promote a misallocation of resources and is a deterrent to capital formation. Capital recovery incentives such as the investment tax credit and accelerated depreciation reduce somewhat the adverse impact of the anti-capital tax bias.

There are instances when the tax result may not be certain. In such a case, all the possible tax results should be factored by a probability analysis. In complex situations where factual variables are controllable, and tax results and risk probabilities are multiple, the computer could be of great help in decision-making. Reorganizations, for example, frequently provide such complexity.

EFFECT ON EARNINGS

Book versus Tax Accounting

Book accounting has its own logic. Compared with tax accounting, book accounting is generally both economically realistic and conservative in respect to results as to income. It is subject to a body of principles generally recognized in the accounting profession. It is also subject to rules of regulatory agencies. The businessman usually learns to think in terms of earnings and financial position in accordance with general accounting concepts. But, he pays his corporate taxes on the basis of tax accounting, which is different. Because it is based upon revenue objectives, its bias is often opposite, accelerating the recognition of income and delaying the recognition of expenses to favor the revenue. So called *tax-effect* accounting is designed to bridge the gap.

Timing Differences

Some transactions are reported on a tax return for a subsequent year. The tax payables or receivables related to those transactions will be carried on the balance sheet in a deferred status until the year in which they are either paid or realized. As a result, the income statement will reflect the tax expense attributable to operations of the year regardless of when the actual tax may be due or the benefit realized.

FINANCIAL EFFECTS

Capital Recovery

As compared to other free industrial nations, the United States limits more severely the formation and growth of capital through its tax policy. Consequently, the managers of U.S. businesses that depend on capital must carefully allocate resources to achieve their most effective use. The amount and the timing of tax will affect materially the recovery and profitability of capital transactions.

The amount of tax effect of a particular transaction may be uncertain. In computing a present value after tax cost or rate of return, therefore, the financial analyst should consider the probabilities of tax consequences of each alternative. This ordinarily requires professional tax judgment that should be neither overly cautious nor unduly optimistic.

Computing Tax Effects on Present Values of Future Income

Although, in general, it may seem trifling to discuss the interest factor to be used in determining the present value after tax result of a proposed transaction, the tax factor in such a determination can influence the decision. A taxpaying company which borrows part of its capital and therefore pays interest on its debt deducts that interest in its tax return and receives a tax benefit for that interest cost. Consequently, the actual interest cost is really an after-tax cost. Assuming an effective income tax rate of 50 percent, the difference between a pretax 8 percent borrowing cost and its effective after-tax rate of 4 percent can make a material difference in the present value of a capital recovery measured over a period of years. The CEO, as decision maker, should insist upon a realistic analysis not only of the tax effect of a transaction but also of the value of that transaction in present dollars determined by using an after-tax discount rate.

Acquisitions and Dispositions

Taxes play an important role in acquiring and disposing of businesses. A transfer may be taxable, partially taxable, or nontaxable. Tax on taxable transfers may be either deferred or currently payable. A tax previously deferred by the business being sold or acquired may become currently payable, or a previously realized tax benefit of that business may be forfeited upon the transfer of assets. Unrealized tax benefits of losses or credit carryovers may either become more readily realizable or may be lost altogether. Acquisition cost may be either recoverable for tax purposes or nondeductible. Favorable tax treatment of qualified employee profit-sharing, stock bonus or pension plans can be jeopardized as well as can unexercised qualified stock options. This is not intended as a checklist of tax points to consider in acquisition and disposition transactions. It does represent, however, some of the more obvious tax implications that may make a profound difference in the results of buying and selling businesses.

Experienced managers responsible for acquisitions and dispositions will generally have tax counsel brought in at initial stages in order to avoid possible false starts and unnecessary work in the negotiations. It is not uncommon for deals to fail for lack of timely and creative tax thinking.

On the other hand, an otherwise unattractive acquisition or disposition can be improved to an ultimately successful completion with appropriate tax input. If any area of activity can showcase a dramatic benefit from outstanding tax participation, it is this area of acquisition and disposition of businesses. If your company is a corporate swinger, be sure to have the best tax talent available—and use it.

COMPENSATION AND TAX INCENTIVES

A subject of importance in any corporate organization is how key people are compensated. Current salary and bonus, deferred compensation and bonus, profit sharing and retirement benefits, insurance and equity incentives all involve tax considerations. A balanced package is generally sought in which maximum after-tax benefits can be provided the employee for current income coupled with an opportunity to build a retirement fund.

An effective plan should result in the present value of the corporate outlay after tax being *less* than the present value after tax amount ultimately retained by the participant. Tax bracket differences and timing are material factors in measuring the cost-benefit relationship. The benefits of an expensive supplemental compensation or incentive plan should not be eroded by excessive tax cost to the participant. Although at one time it was relatively easy to generalize on the tax treatment to be accorded a given plan, this is no longer so. Changes in the Internal Revenue Code in the last several years have created a need for special analysis for each situation. Use of a competent tax counsellor is more important today than ever before in the area of supplemental or incentive executive compensation.

CONCLUDING OVERVIEW

Before this chapter is closed, a few words on tax philosophy may be appropriate. When faced with a choice involving whether to support or resist a change in tax law that would affect the amount of tax a particular company pays, it may be prudent for the CEO to look beyond the immediate first-level impact on the company to the impact *on the community as a whole.* Tax policy is an integral factor in fiscal and economic policy. If a shift in tax incidence spurs economic activity, it may mean increases in sales and profits. Even though the direct first-level effect of the shift might adversely affect your company, the indirect, "ripple" effect could very well return the first level incremental tax cost many times through increased profit. The growth of a company depends on growth in the economy and in its markets. When tax policy contributes to that growth, a healthy situation is produced, and the company should enjoy its share of the benefit.

The CEO, through his broad perspective and influence as an opinion maker, should assume a greater role in attempting to influence tax policy. Too frequently, the role has been played with a narrow, parochial view proceeding from misleading appearances. Today's dynamic economic environment demands a broader perspective and deeper involvement from our business leaders if our economy is to maintain its competitive position in the world industrial community.

CORPORATE INSURANCE AND RISK MANAGEMENT

by T. F. Willers

Former Chairman and Chief Executive Officer,
Champion International, Inc.

PERHAPS the most useful treatment of the subject of risk and insurance management for the chief executive is from the point of view of the hypothetical company executive who has assumed the leadership of a medium-to-large corporation and whose first concern is to learn the new company from the ground up. He will normally find many differences in organization and management methods from the company with which he previously was associated. We will assume that he has carried high executive responsibilities, has above average experience in business management, and has a capacity for quick perception.

TWO CATEGORIES OF RISK

In his accountability to the company's board of directors and stockholders, he must satisfy himself that the stockholders' interests are protected against loss. This dictates prudence in dealing with exposure to losses arising from either of the two general categories of risks. On the one hand, a company can suffer a loss in consequence of a "business risk" or, that is to say, a "calculated risk," taken with forethought as a management decision in the course of doing business. On the other hand, it can suffer an "accidental loss" from a specific, unforeseeable cause which is fortuitous and may be beyond the company's control. The frequency with which such "accidental losses" will occur can, however, be predicted if the risk is spread broadly throughout the company's operations and if adequate records have been kept of its loss experience. I find it helpful to distinguish between "business risks" involving possible profit, and so-called "insurable risks," normally involving only a possible loss.

758

The various measures which can be adopted for protecting a company against loss from risks of either of these two broad categories are similarly divided, in modern business practice, into two distinct kinds. First, a company may "self-assume" a risk against which it is either not possible or not in the company's best interests to provide protection otherwise. Second, a company may "transfer" losses arising from insurable risks by purchasing insurance from an outside insurer.

A simplistic answer to the question as to which of these two methods to adopt for each of the two categories of risks might be to self-assume business risks; and buy insurance against accidental losses.

Although this first approximation of an answer applies in a very general way, it has many exceptions. I shall discuss in a moment some guidelines I have found useful in dealing with these exceptions. Exposure to business risks and accidental losses will be examined in sufficient depth only to formulate: (*a*) a chief executive's risk-management philosophy; (*b*) the formalized statement of company risk-management policies which stem directly from it; and (*c*) appropriate companywide procedures to carry them out. I shall also suggest a quick method for determining the adequacy of the existing risk-management program in the company of which the new chief executive has recently assumed leadership.

BUSINESS RISKS AND UNINSURABLE RISKS

Business risks can be treated rather summarily for, by their very nature, they are taken as a matter of volition on the part of management, the thoroughness of whose research and the soundness of whose business judgment as to what constitutes a "good risk" are probably the best, and frequently are the only insurance against a venture "going sour." For, although it is probably true theoretically that one can insure against anything for a price, it would certainly not necessarily be good business to do so.

An important caveat: Unqualified acceptance of the philosophy of self-assumption of all business risks as have been defined can nourish a false sense of security. For example, an aggressive management, in its efforts to expand its present business and move into new markets, may find itself—and historical examples are legion—with an overextended acquisition program. Inherent in the aphorism "you can't win 'em all" and in the accepted practice of relying on the ones that "pay out" to cover your losses on the rare one that doesn't, lies the risk that circumstances beyond management's control could cause *several* of them to go sour at once. Concurrent write-offs necessitated by unanticipated loss of market, political instability, vagaries of fiscal and monetary policy, and a host of other hazards of doing business, although in consonance with the sound principle of "cutting your losses early," together can amount to enough money to cause excessive impairment of a company's financial position.

A first principle of risk-management philosophy, therefore, is never to exceed the total dollar limit of business risks that the company can afford to self-assume each year without unacceptably impairing its liquidity. If this dollar limit, once determined, has already been reached or exceeded, then look out! For you probably should not have joined the company in the first place!

When such a situation is found to exist, it is probably time to consider "risk management" in its broadest sense, as embracing such extraordinary measures as a moratorium on acquisitions, a sharp reduction in capital expenditures, the institution of an aggressive cost reduction program, the conversion into cash of working capital tied up in inventories and accounts receivable, and, in a word, a program of general retrenchment.

In the normal case, the company's self-assumption of its business risk exposures will have been kept within bounds. The likelihood of several disappointing ventures coinciding will be minimal, and unacceptable erosion of the company's financial position thereby is not a threat. The informed chief executive, recognizing that self-assumption does not necessarily mean "noninsurance," nevertheless should provide himself with a breakdown of the exposure which is self-assumed. The various methods of self-assumption include deductible provisions for insured risks; the disappearing deductible; retrospective rating in the case of casualty coverages; self-insurance or setting aside reserves against large identifiable exposures; the formation of captive insurance companies, frequently established offshore; and lastly "noninsurance." Such a breakdown will permit him at a glance to determine the dollar value of the *total* risk against which the company is "noninsured."

A Risk-Management Philosophy

With this information at hand, the chief executive is in a position to consider in toto his risk-management philosophy which might well take the form of a written statement as a broad guideline to company policy. A workable philosophy might be stated thus: (*a*) to *assume* losses which present little catastrophe exposure because of their size or the spread of risk and which therefore would not cause excessive impairment of the financial position of the company; and (*b*) to *protect against* those losses not assumed through the buying of adequate and appropriate insurance coverage. Risk-management philosophy will vary by company and with the experience, judgment, and management style of its chief executive. Once determined, however, it should be preserved carefully if only for the chief executive's personal reference to insure consistency of company policy.

Noninsurable Risks

Having thus codified his risk-management philosophy and assured himself of the adequacy of the company's program to manage business risks, the chief executive might well check the availability of insurance coverage before examining in depth the management of insurable risks. From a practical viewpoint, insurance today either is not available or is economically prohibitive for such risks as non-accidental pollution; destruction of standing timber; spoilage, generally; failure of financial depositories; loss of market; war damage; wear and tear; strikes; product performance; inventory shortage, generally; cancellation of export or import licenses; disclosure of trade secrets; and obsolescence.

It is fairly safe to assume that a willing and competent insurer can be found to provide coverage, at a price, for all other risks to which a company is likely to be exposed. These can be considered insurable risks in the strict sense: risks for which insurance can be purchased in the market.

RISK ANALYSIS

With this brief review of business risks and risks which are not practicably insurable, we are now in a position to consider a workable program to manage insurable risks. The first step in such a program is "risk analysis." In performing such an analysis, the chief executive must determine whether, and to what extent there exists in the company a catalogue, by location, of the company's exposure to the several types of accidental losses. The completeness of such a catalogue will, in itself, give him an indication of the effectiveness of the company's risk-management program and of the risk manager himself if, in fact, there is one.

Checklist for Insurable Risks

A useful checklist as to the completeness of such a catalogue could include, but would not be limited, to the following questions:

Has an insurance policy register been prepared, and is there a record of loss experience by type, covering the past several years?

Do the legal department and risk-management personnel review periodically deviations from the standard printed forms for sales agreements, purchase orders, construction and lease contracts and the like, in order to identify risks inherent in departures from "boiler plate"?

Have the values of the company's fee-held lands, including timberlands, been established?

Have the book values and actual cash values (replacement costs less physical depreciation) been established for all company-owned real property, and does the listing include type of construction, existence of sprinkler systems, fire hydrants, pumps, fire extinguishers and other loss-prevention equipment?

Are current valuations made of company-owned personal property, including raw materials, work in process, and finished goods?

Are regular boiler and machinery inspections made showing alternate sources of power available in the event of a breakdown?

Has the company's exposure to business interruption from boiler and machinery breakdown and from fire, flood, earthquake, collapse, windstorm, and other hazards, been evaluated for both loss of profits and direct damage?

Additions to the Checklist

Additional items which should be considered in the chief executive's risk analysis checklist could include:

Have the leases for all company-leased properties been reviewed as to responsibility for insurance coverage?

Are there abatement provisions in the event of serious loss, and has a waiver of subrogation been requested in cases where the lessor carries the insurance?

Have exposures to loss of cash, securities, payroll, and checks in the hands of bank messengers been evaluated at all company locations?

Are alternate EDP facilities available, and have duplicate data banks been stored at off-site locations against possible losses from disruption or destruction of records?

Have heavy extra-expense exposures at laboratories, testing facilities and the like been analyzed?

Is there a product-testing program, with emphasis on the elimination of past product liability losses?

Have the values of incoming and outgoing shipments at principal company locations, and the responsibility for sales and purchase contracts for these shipments been established?

Have the values of company-owned aircraft and watercraft been determined; or, if leased, has the nonownership exposure of such leased equipment been evaluated?

WHAT SHOULD BE INSURED

By the time the chief executive has gone through, if only in summary form, the steps of proper risk analysis inherent in such a checklist, overwhelming as it may appear, he will have obtained a fair knowledge of the effectiveness of the company's risk-management program and will now be in a position to formulate his own views as to what should and what should not be insured. This is, of course, the crux of the problem, the answer to which will govern the company's formalized statement of its risk-management policy, the procedures to be followed under that policy, and the organization required to carry out the company's risk-management program. The chief executive should now ask himself, and answer the question, "Of all the complex and interrelated insurable risks to which the company is exposed in its various locations, which of these should I, as the Chief Executive Officer, insist be insured?"

Standard Forms of Coverage

To answer this question, he will find it useful to review the forms of coverage available to offset the risks identified in the risk analysis. Principal among these are standard coverages of:

Physical Damage. Damage to company-owned or leased property from various perils has three general types of coverage: fire and extended coverage; boiler and machinery policies; and coverage of the so-called unusual losses from earthquake, flood, or collapse collectively termed "Difference in Condition." The omission of any one of these three leaves a potentially serious exposure uninsured.

One can cover these risks at replacement value or at actual cash value of replacement cost less physical depreciation. In these times of inflationary construction costs, I prefer to cover the full replacement value, taking perhaps a front-end, known deductible rather than to self-insure the major part of full replacement cost of a valuable property with heavy physical depreciation. Blanket protection policies for such risks deserve careful consideration.

Business Interruption. One can insure against the loss of profits and the continuing expense resulting from damage to an installation, particularly a manufacturing unit, from any of the foregoing perils. Alternatively, "Extra Expense Coverage" is available in some cases and may be preferable.

Casualty. Casualty or third-party liability coverage is available in many forms including: Public Liability; Products Liability; Automobile Liability; Aircraft Liability; Advertisers Liability; Host Liquor Liability; Employers Liability; and Employee Benefit Liability. In addition, Blanket Excess Umbrella Liability is available to cover losses in excess of the normal policy limits of any of the foregoing as well as any liabilities not otherwise insured. Such policies are normally subject to agree deductible provisions.

Directors and Officers Liability. This covers the company's liability to reimburse them for loss as well as the individual directors' and officers' insurable but not reimbursable liability.

Crime Coverage. Employee Dishonesty, Depositor's Forgery, and Theft Inside or Outside Premises are available to cover this type of risk.

Workmen's Compensation. This is available to cover the employer's liability to provide benefits prescribed by statute of any of the 50 states or Puerto Rico.

Other Coverages. Additional coverages including Surety; Guarantee and Timber Bonds; Ocean Marine; Electronic Data Processing; Destruction of Records; Travel Accident; Kidnap and Ransom; and many forms of Employee Benefit Coverage are available.

To Buy Insurance or to Self-Insure

With such an impressive array of merchandise for sale in the insurance market, a company shopping list should be prepared with prudence. Basically, *only those risks which could cause excessive impairment of corporate assets or earnings need be insured.* However, it is frequently economical to buy a policy for other reasons. Many insurers provide, as part and parcel of a standard policy, essential services which may prove, on analysis, to be more expensive if provided otherwise.

Good examples are the services provided in conjunction with the standard boiler and machinery coverage; the cost of these services represents probably 50 percent of the total premium. Although this may seem high, it is frequently found to be less than the cost of hiring and training company employees for these highly skilled tasks or, alternatively, of retaining one of the few available qualified service contractors. In either alternative, the cost could run well in excess of 50 percent of the annual premium of the boiler and machinery policy. Moreover, you can be sure the services will be performed effectively by qualified insurer personnel, because in the case of inspection services, for example, the insurer is representing his own interests. Loss prevention services provided by Workmen's Compensation carriers are other examples.

Whenever it is more economical to do so, however, a company should self-assume such risks through self-insuring or one of the other options. To pay the insurer's overhead to do something you can do as well yourself makes little sense.

Self-Insurance Possibilities. What are some of the areas in which self-insurance can be more economical than purchased coverage? Depending on the size of the company and the spread of risk, an example or two will best serve to answer the question. Plate glass insurance for most companies should be self-insured because the cost of repair is a manageable part of most companies' maintenance budgets. Collision insurance of company-owned or leased vehicles, with a good spread of risk and a reasonably large fleet, should not be purchased because the risk of loss bears a manageable limit and you avoid paying a carrier for settling claims which can be handled in-house at less expense. A large number of trucks concentrated in a single garage, however, can entail a risk considerably larger than it would be advisable to self-insure. Special coverage for such situations can be written and should be considered as an exception to the rule. A good spread of office or warehouse locations in which the individual values are not excessive should probably be self-insured. A comparison of the loss experience with the premiums for various levels of deductible coverage charged by a reputable all-risk carrier may well indicate the fallacy of purchased coverage. A corporate reserve to cover small elements of the company, each unable by itself to bear the loss of a facility, should be considered. In areas such as Workmen's Compensation, where benefits are statutory, self-insurance is permissible in most states and its desirability should be compared to purchased coverage.

The foregoing examples are illustrative of the factors which a chief executive must take into account in determining what should and what should not be insured. He should not attempt to issue detailed instructions as to each individual insurable risk; rather, through discussions with his risk-management people, he should formulate sufficiently broad policy statements which, when published, will provide guidance in the day-to-day matter of risk management.

A "Risk-Marketing" Policy for Buying Insurance

After one has gone through the steps of proper risk analysis and determined what should be insured, it is most important to develop a "risk-marketing" policy and the procedures for implementing it. The policy itself can be copied verbatim from that of the company's purchasing department; buying insurance is governed by the same principle as in buying in any competitive market: *to get the most value at the least cost.*

There are important substantive as well as economic advantages in having uniformly broad protection of similar loss exposures. These advantages and the most favorable terms can be achieved only by full utilization of the company's combined purchasing power in the insurance market. The obvious goal to be achieved could be stated simply as follows: *to consolidate the company's insurance program into as few policies with as few insurers as possible.* Or, more precisely: first, to consolidate the insurance of all divisions and subsidiaries, covering the same or similar loss exposures under blanket policies to the extent practical considerations will allow; second, to procure all related classes of insurance from or through one insurer, underwriting group, or syndicate; and, third, to make judicious use of all segments of the competitive insurance market by well-timed and restricted exploration of qualified alternate sources of insurance, either through direct writers or carefully selected brokers.

Having determined a logical objective for his company's insurance program, the chief executive should review the risk manager's procedures for consistency with this objective. In a larger company, these will normally be codified and published. In essence, they may take the following form:

Soliciting Competitive Proposals. When competitive proposals are solicited for the purpose of consolidating the insurance of two or more of the corporation's divisions or subsidiaries, brokers who, in the past, have provided satisfactory services in handling parts of the now-proposed consolidation and are considered qualified to service the combined account, should each be given an opportunity to submit a proposal. Others invited to compete should be limited to brokers and direct insurers qualified and of record for the type of insurance to be consolidated.

When solicitation of competitive proposals is deemed necessary for purposes other than consolidation, one or two qualified sources other than the broker or insurer currently handling the account should be invited to compete.

Competitive proposals should be required to conform to specifications drawn by the risk-management or insurance department as a condition precedent to consideration of any alternate proposal an invitee may wish to offer. In order to avoid the adverse consequences of indiscriminate "shopping" of the corporation's insurance in the market, those invited to submit proposals should not exceed three carefully chosen brokers, underwriting groups, or syndicates in addition to a single qualified direct writing insurer.

Award should be made to the lowest qualified bidder purporting to meet the specifications. Conflicts in the selection of insurers should be resolved in a fair and equitable manner with the broker of record given precedence in case of doubt. Merits of the proposals should be evaluated on their overall value to the company including the scope of coverage, engineering inspection and collateral services offered, and the financial position and management reputation of the broker or insurer, with premium cost being an important but not dominant consideration. The value to the company of a well-established, satisfactory service relationship with an insurer who has contributed to good loss control should not be discounted.

Use of Consultants. A published statement of procedures for dealing in the insurance market should give the chief executive confidence. Nevertheless, the services of an independent insurance consultant might also be retained from time to time. Qualified firms are available to assure that corporate procedures and the insurance protection they generate reflect practices which are generally regarded as sound and that the cost is reasonable in the light of current market conditions. Consultants may also be found useful in preparing bid specifications and in evaluating competitive proposals.

EVALUATING THE RISK-MANAGEMENT PROGRAM

Most of us will find it useful at this point to make a few notes summarizing our impressions of the company's risk-management program from what we have seen thus far. These notes may take the form of questions the chief executive poses to himself followed by his own answers, something like:

Q. Is there an existing risk-management program? A. Yes.

Q. A risk-management department? A. Yes.

Q. Does the manager report directly to the chief financial officer? A. No, to the Vice President—Finance Services who, in turn, reports to the Senior Vice President—Finance.

Q. Has a clear distinction been made between losses from business risks and accidental losses? A. No; a clear distinction is not always possible.

Q. Is there a published risk-management policy conforming to my own risk-management philosophy? A. Yes, in general; but I would want to suggest some revisions to reduce the company's noninsured exposure in those risks we currently self-assume.

Q. Am I satisfied from my cursory risk analysis that there are no major hidden risks remaining undisclosed which have not been evaluated and which could give me an unpleasant surprise? A. I don't know; the property records seemed reasonably complete, but insufficient attention has been given to loopholes in our construction contracts which our loss experience indicates have given rise to costly claims in the past.

Q. Does the company's insurance register indicate that we have a clear idea of what to insure? A. Yes, generally; however, I think we are carrying insurance on too many small, widely spread risks which we should probably self-insure.

Q. Is there an ongoing program to consolidate insurance carried by recently acquired subsidiaries with the corporate coverage under a single insurer for like risks? A. Yes.

Q. Does the risk manager shop around excessively in the insurance market? A. No, he is generally fair, equitable, and prudent in his dealings with brokers and direct insurers.

Q. From what I have seen, am I satisfied that the company is not exposed to uninsured risks that could excessively impair its assets or profits and consequently the shareholders' interest? A. Not altogether; I am concerned about the political situation in Lucitasia, where our company has extensive capital investments and for which we have not set aside reserves to cover write-offs in case of expropriation or destruction through civil disorder; there may be others. This should be carefully examined by senior management.

"LOSS CONTROL" IS "COST CONTROL"

Every chief executive will have different answers to his own self-imposed questions. However, should his initial reactions be as favorable as those of our hypothetical chief executive above, he can feel justifiable satisfaction with the adequacy of the company's risk- and insurance-management program per se. However, as an experienced business manager, he will realize at once that this is not the whole story inasmuch as the program could be seriously and adversely affected by deficiencies in the company's companion program for "loss control."

Risk management is, by its very nature, a "cost control" program and the key to cost control is loss control. The importance of a good loss prevention program cannot be overemphasized. Moreover, the Occupational Safety and Health Act of 1971 makes such a program mandatory. Here, the chief executive is himself the crucial element, for without his constant personal attention, the best loss prevention program may fall apart. He must keep it in the forefront with his senior executives who, in turn, must sell and support it all the way down the line to each employee.

In examining the effectiveness of the company's loss control or loss prevention program, let us review briefly some of the elements it should contain.

A Separate Organization for Loss Prevention

In the first place, the administration of a company's loss prevention program normally will be organizationally separate from the risk-management department and indeed from the jurisdiction of the chief financial officer. Most companies today place it in the employee relations department in view of its impact on employee safety and benefit compensation. Whatever the organizational arrangement, there must be close and continuing communication between the staff elements charged with risk management and loss prevention. At every operating location, a designated employee should be specifically responsible for the safety function.

Operating management's awareness of the direct bearing of losses on operating profits can be emphasized by assigning losses back to the profit center in which the loss occurred. Recommendations from insurance companies and government agency inspection reports should be acted upon promptly. Regardless of the frequency of inspection of operations by outside agencies, statutory or otherwise, *there is no substitute for an effective in-house prevention program.* Operating units with good loss prevention records should be appropriately recognized. All plans for acquisition and major construction should be reviewed by a competent safety engineer.

Preventing Losses from Product Liability, Warranties, etc.   In approved standard contracts, leases, warranties, and the like, it is well to assure that the company does not take on the liabilities of others. For many companies, "product liability" constitutes a serious exposure; consequently a product labeling committee should not be considered a luxury but rather essential to protect against the consequence of product liability claims.

These are only a few of the many areas of loss prevention and risk abatement which merit attention. Much has been published by the National Safety Council and others which provides a deeper insight into current practices. As a minimum, every chief executive should be conversant with his company's accident frequency and severity rates, and know how its accident index is determined and how it compares with the index for his industry.

CHOOSING A GOOD INSURANCE AGENT

I have been asked from time to time how one tells an insurance executive who is knowledgeable and effective from one who is not.

For one thing, there are various formal degrees held by members of this profession. The Certified Life Underwriter, the Chartered Property and Casualty Underwriter and, recently, the Diploma in Risk Management are among them. However, in the long run there is no substitute for the executive's track record. Within any company, the manager who continues past practices with few innovations is merely an insurance buyer, not a risk manager.

An executive who can answer affirmatively questions such as these is certainly on the right road to becoming an effective member of your management team: Has an analysis been made of all risks to which the company is exposed, together with sound recommendations to management on these exposures? Are the advantages of deductibles and self-insurance as opposed to renewing commercial policies under continuous review? Are adequate statistical data on loss experience available to document the desirability of changes in the program? Are the services of your brokers, agents, and direct insurers evaluated regularly with recommendations for changes, when indicated? Does your risk manager communicate effectively with line management, and has an understandable risk-management manual been provided for their use? And, finally, is line management generally satisfied with the manner in which claims have been adjusted?

CONCLUSION

Each chief executive is accountable to the board of directors and shareholders for the risks he either creates or condones. The ones he hasn't thought about may be the closest to him. For instance, although he would be quick to acknowledge the company's people as its greatest asset, from his management team all the way down the line, has he ever thought to find out which type of automobile accident causes the highest lost-time injury frequency rate, and done something about it? Most of us, as a matter of course, would forbid the senior members of our management to fly together commercially or in the company plane if we knew they planned to do so. Yet, how many companies have strictly-enforced policies to prohibit exposure to such an irreplaceable loss?

Risk management is a cost-control program which involves large corporate expenditures. It merits the close, personal, and continuing attention of every Chief Executive Officer.

PART IV-E

Management
Information
and
Control

THE TOP EXECUTIVE FOR MANAGEMENT INFORMATION AND CONTROL: WHAT TO LOOK FOR, HOW TO GET TOP PERFORMANCE

by E. Burke Giblin

Chairman and Chief Executive Officer, Warner-Lambert Company

THE CHIEF EXECUTIVE clearly has the ultimate responsibility for decision-making or the failure to make key decisions. He must have adequate information on which to base his judgments. For this he depends to a great extent on the control and financial organization of the company to insure that his plans and the plans of others to whom he has delegated major responsibilities are properly measured and evaluated in terms of their profit impact on the business, both short-term and long-term. Obviously, once actions have been taken, he is also dependent on his control and financial organization to translate correctly the results into financial statements based on accepted accounting principles.

One of the major sources of business communication to the community at large over the years has been financial reporting through the medium of published quarterly and annual reports. These are clearly no longer adequate, alone, to explain business activities because growth in sales and profit, alone, is not now generally considered a full measure of corporate performance. In fact, substantial growth in sales and profit may, indeed, attract as many questions as failure to grow attracted in the past, although the present-day questions are directed more toward the impact of the growth on society.

This brings into focus the limitation of accounting fully to explain business operations; this stems from the fact that figures can't talk and, as business activities become ever more complex, words are needed to support the figures. This limitation affects how the CEO deals with the various public or external audiences for financial data about his company; it also has to do with the use of information within the organization for various purposes relating to decision-making and planning.

ACCOUNTING LIMITATIONS

One fact that must be recognized by all users of financial figures is that accounting is far from an exact science, if indeed it can be called a science at all. It is doubtful that any two accountants, or accounting firms, given the same business operations to audit or for which to set up books of account and information systems, would devise identical systems. Nor would the results of operations as shown by them be completely the same. Why? Because many judgments in the interpretation of facts and figures must be made.

Most of the accounting principles we have today were set up to serve the purposes of creditors, bankers, and investors, not to mention the Internal Revenue Service. Such "outside" parties are interested mostly in the state of the business as of a given time. Conservatism has been the watchword measured almost against the golden rule of "how much is the business worth in liquidation?" In no way do I criticize this, because there must be a measuring point in time for tax purposes and for the evaluation of the progress of the business from period to period. It is simply to indicate that, important as they are, many financial statements required for these purposes are of little value to the chief executive in his current decision-making. They are historical by the time he sees them in quarterly reports and annual reports.

There are, then, two prime limitations which the CEO must keep in mind. First, the lack of appropriate precision, if not—as is often the case—relevance for purposes of operating decision-making. Second, the historical character of accounting reports.

Some recent examples of the latter relate to hedging in foreign exchange transactions and commodities, profits in inventory during periods of rapidly rising prices and costs, and the replacement cost method of accounting for inventories (Lifo).

As to the former, there are many activities—including allocating costs for research and development, accounting for new product introduction costs, and allocating costs for pricing and price justification—that are subject to variation in the methods used and in the judgments and interpretations of accounting terminology. How these matters are handled affects a company's profits and its relations with its stockholders and potential investors. This handling also affects the public acceptance of the company as a socially responsible or irresponsible business organization. Over the years not enough concern was paid to the latter, so that accounting systems and terminology were set up to meet the needs more of investors, creditors, and taxing authorities than to explain fully the operations of the company as a continuing operation. Business executives must either understand these limitations themselves or have the quality of control officers who can help them and others to recognize these pitfalls.

To give a specific example of how accounting without *conceptual* understanding of what, concretely, lies behind the numbers can mislead, I will cite an example from my own managerial experience. Earlier in my career, I was sent to manage a large division of another company which was engaged in selling bulk products based on an imported commodity that represented the major cost of the end product. The division had suffered significant losses and it was believed by the home office that local management was speculating in the commodity because the books indicated a large sum lost on a short position. The division manager had been replaced. Incidentally, he had been sent there only a short time earlier from another division where he had an excellent record as a manager. Subsequently, it became apparent that the home office, including the auditor and chief financial officer of the corporation, were "literal accountants" with no conceptual understanding of the business or of what was really involved.

The facts were simply that, because of rumors of a short crop, the division had felt forced to buy its required inventory earlier and at higher prices than in the prior year. Division purchasing people were uneasy and concerned that the crop, which was harvested in different countries at different times, might, in fact, turn out to be larger than they anticipated. They knew that rumors of shortages were often put out by producers to push prices up. The crop also came from numerous "developing" nations; accordingly, it was difficult to evaluate its size until the crop season was well along. To protect itself the company had two possibilities. One was to book forward sales at a fixed price to customers who would buy at that time. The other was to hedge the unsold commodity (i.e., keep it at market price) until customers were subsequently willing to buy at the then current market price. By hedging, which is to say, selling contracts on an exchange for future delivery, the company was able, at the same time, to secure an adequate supply of the commodity, protect its conversion profit, and risk of substantial commodity loss which might bankrupt it. (It should be recognized that by the same token, hedging also eliminated the opportunity for substantial inventory profits if the price moved even higher.)

In this case, the company booked all the forward sales it could and then hedged its unsold inventory and commitments to purchase by selling forward contracts for the unsold amount, intending to lift or buy back the hedges as customers bought the inventory at the then current prices. If the market prices went down, the company, of course, had to base its selling price on the then lower current market which would be less than the inventory price. But what it lost there, it made up when it bought back forward contracts at lower prices than they had been sold at. The gain or loss on inventory was offset by the gain or loss on the hedge so that the division realized its normal margin as a converter without running the risk of commodity market fluctuation.

Well, here's how accounting handled the transactions when the hedges were sold: An account was set up on the books—"gain or loss on short position"—and the position was valued monthly against market. In the marketplace, the price of the commodity continued to rise as widespread concern about a short crop increased. Some customers were willing to buy; but most held back, so the division continued to have a major portion of its inventory hedged. As the market rose so did the loss in the short account continue to increase. By year end, the loss on the short position had increased to $5 million dollars. Because there was no offsetting account to show the increase in inventory value (such as unrealized gain in inventory value) that was taking place at the same time and for the same reason, there was nothing to do for the closing except to include the loss in the profit and loss statement. Meanwhile, at corporate headquarters, news of this loss on a "short" position was brought to the chairman of the board who was understandably furious about "speculation," because he didn't understand the limitation of the accounting to express the true nature of a hedge, nor did his financial advisors. The net result was that the division management was replaced, but not before they had been instructed to "get out of the short position" (the words "short position" still frighten managements, stockholders, and the public, dating back no doubt to stock market operators).

Getting out of the short position was done with a realized loss of $5 million dollars. Corporate management then relaxed with a sense of security, feeling that they had ended a speculative position. In reality, of course, they had *entered into* a speculative position. The major portion of the division's inventory was now uncovered by forward sales contracts or hedges and was now subject to market fluctuations. Unfortunately for the company, after a period of time it became apparent that the crop was, indeed, larger than first thought, the market price of the commodity dropped below the price the division had paid for it, and the inventory had to be sold to customers at the best price obtainable. An operating loss was suffered in addition to the loss that had been suffered by closing out the "short" position before the inventory was sold to customers.

The literal accountants were unable to think in concepts appropriate to the facts of what was actually happening. They were, of course, affected by the "conservatism" of accounting that is quick to recognize potential losses but quails at the thought of valuing the unsold inventory at current market, which would have offset the loss; this they could properly have done because of the hedging. Subsequently the problem was resolved by setting up a "gain or loss on unsold inventory account" to offset the short position lost account and everyone was happy—even the public accountants.

In my more recent experience, I observed that many businessmen in late 1973 were lulled by inventory profits; neither they nor their financial men recognized how fast the replacement costs of everything they were using was going up in price as item after item was price decontrolled. If their company was still under price control, their only other choice was to take severe steps promptly to reduce other costs in every area of the business. The accounting records could not keep up with the unusual speed at which costs were increasing. Many monthly statements were based on a standard cost which had been predicted at the beginning of the year, prior six months, or quarter; and the variations were not reported until quarter end. This must have created some awful shocks. Very substantial variations came in at quarter end. What is being pointed out is that to protect a business and its management there must be *conceptual financial leadership* which can anticipate what is going to happen in unusual periods, and can inform management so action can be taken, such as in pricing and cost reduction.

This leadership should be sought in control or financial officers. The lag between recognition of a problem and the time action can be taken in pricing or to affect a cost reduction is considerable—often as long as six months. In the meantime, profits and profit margins can be badly squeezed. Even though responsibility for pricing generally lies with marketing management, control or financial officers should assist in the process because of the overview they can bring to the problem. Marketing management may be reluctant to face the need to raise prices because they are concerned, as they should be, with market growth and competition's share of market, and are likely to feel strongly that if a product line is growing any price change may have a ruinous effect. Alternatively, for products with a heavy seasonal aspect, there may be little gained in raising a price after the customers have committed for their usual seasonal inventory buildup. There is also the possibility that a trade promotion has been announced which often requires 60 days advance notice and an attempt to increase prices would interfere with the promotion. Whatever the case, controllers and marketers together should develop the solution.

I don't want to get diverted into pricing; my point, here, is to illustrate the difference between *conceptual*, management-oriented accounting and *literal* reporting-oriented accounting.

Granted that there is a need for what I have called literal accounting, what else does the chief executive need from his controllorship organization and from his own business knowledge?

CONCEPTUAL ACCOUNTING

First of all, by the time a man reaches the position of chief executive he should thoroughly understand his business so that he can *conceptualize* the probable financial results of profit plans and forecasts in at least order-of-magnitude terms. (Incidentally, it seems to me that much decision-making really only requires order-of-magnitude information, although considerable time and money is too often spent in developing detailed and seemingly very precise information which is never used or needed. I'm inclined to think that if the decision on a plan is very close, the plan should probably be rejected.) If an executive knows his business and can think conceptually about it, he should not be surprised by the results of operations as they are subsequently reported and presented to him. They should, in fact, confirm his judgments and those of his associates. If they do not, then something is clearly wrong; perhaps a plan has not been followed, or it may turn out that the figures are, in fact, wrong; that something was accrued or not accrued; that some judgment in the accounting area was wrong or not properly timed; et cetera. Here, I am also assuming that each key member of his staff is charged with the responsibility to inform him promptly of any changes in plans or looming problems that would make plan accomplishment doubtful. This use of accounting for operating decisions I call *conceptual accounting.*

Few chief executives, if any, can gain this perspective of a business without a chief "control" officer, who can think conceptually about the business and help him extensively in the use of control information.

The Chief Officer for Control

I am totally unconvinced of the notion that the chief financial officer should be responsible for both information *and* the treasury function, particularly in the case of companies with large foreign operations. I believe that both—which is to say, two—officers are needed. Otherwise, the CEO loses out in the contact with the kind of expertise he needs in each of the two fields.

Let's assume that the chief executive is leading a company of at least medium size and with a fully or at least reasonably sophisticated planning and accounting system; if so, he has available to him most, if not all, financial *information* needed to make his judgments. What we are now concerned with is the quality of the senior controllership or financial *people* he needs close to him. In a large decentralized organization, one needs to be sure of the quality of the people his key profit-center heads have around them. If we go back to the distinction between literal accounting and the conceptual accounting that is needed for operating purposes, it is readily apparent that the young person trained in college or business school is most likely to be exposed to the former first and, indeed, his early jobs in either public or private accounting tend to stress this. Possibly this sort of accounting is likely to be his major activity for the first ten years or more of his business career.

How then does this Chief Executive Officer identify and find the kind of control officer that he needs to help him with conceptual accounting? It seems that there is a relatively small but growing percentage of men who are attracted to accounting who at some point in their career gain the ability to conceptualize figures into business activities. They can, within the literal rules of accounting, visualize human beings engaged in work of various kinds, in production or service activities, using materials or talents at various locations and under varying conditions in many different countries, and providing goods or services for the use of others. As they deal with the figures these broader people become sensitive to these operations and gain intuitive ability in identifying either errors or limitations in accounting science which do not, from a management point of view, properly set forth the true cost or profit of a business activity.

The controller needs to be imaginative and able to think conceptually along with you as a key member of the decision-making team. He cannot be a literal accountant, only, in the sense that a literal accountant deals just with figures. The conceptual accountant sees in the figures the operations of the business. Each account portrays to him an activity of the business; raw materials being purchased, moved to locations to be processed; men and machines in action; men engaged in marketing, research, selling, and management. If the controller can view the business in this fashion, he will sense when something is wrong or where there is a potential opportunity. For this kind of man, the term controller is a misnomer; he might better be termed a "growther"—one who seeks not to limit the business, but rather to find, through the figures, new opportunities for growth. He can anticipate, and he must have the same feel about the business as the key operating executives, so that he and they as a team do not let problems or opportunities go unnoticed.

He also can advise management of the kind of interpretation, description, and explanations that should be made with, or in advance of, the release of figures. One important thing that must be emphasized is that the controller should have a highly developed sense of integrity so that he never permits a conceptual approach to the understanding of business transactions to be used as an excuse for releasing possibly misleading accounting information to the public. There are, of course, as I said, many interpretations of the proper recording of transactions, both in relation to how they are shown, and as to timing and explanation, but each choice should be based on the way which most clearly portrays the true situation.

Although the operations of a business do require interpretation and decisions to try to insure that the true situation is shown, this fact should never be permitted to allow the selection of alternate methods of accounting which would result in misleading reports. It is an absolute requirement for the chief control officer or controller to recognize this as his unavoidable responsibility. In doing so, he can be helped and supported, if necessary, by the public accountants doing the audit work.

Reporting to the controller, however, there must be a highly qualified accountant who is thoroughly conversant and knowledgeable in accounting rules and procedures. Some organizations have made the mistake of having an organization led only by analysts, profit planners, et cetera, all of whom are, of course, needed. These companies forget about the solidly knowledgeable accountant who knows the rules and systems thoroughly, and who can assure management that the financial information collected is accurate and timely. He and his group are the solid base of the financial departments and should not be overlooked or unrewarded. This is not to say that the traits of conceptual understanding of figures and fundamental accounting ability are not necessarily found in the same person. In many cases they are not. But both abilities are needed within a topflight control group.

CONCLUSION

I hope that this discussion has served to bring clearly into perspective some of the limitations of accounting and hope it also brought out the difference between the objectives and point of view of management, who must view the business from the standpoint of a continuing operation, and of those who are most interested in certification. This latter, which is akin to a guarantee, that assets and income are as stated even conservatively so for purposes of credit analysis of the company, for assessment of taxes, and for the purposes of the investing public. Out of this mixture of needs, there has evolved and is still evolving a set of rules and procedures which have many limitations from an operating point of view. Accordingly, every chief executive has to have at his right hand talented financial men who can understand business concepts as well as literal accounting rules and interpretations.

I am well aware that, in pointing out the limitations to the operating manager of a literal accountant versus the conceptual accountant, I have left open an opportunity for some to say that certain businessmen have used the newer concepts to report operating results that actually were misleading to creditors and investors. The comment is justified. As a result, there is today a cry for more and more information, more breakdowns of figures, more detail on almost every element of a business—to the extent that the businessman feels overwhelmed with reporting requirements which are extremely costly and of questionable value for broad public use. This demand for complete and total accuracy has also affected the public accounting profession and has involved them in many suits. As a result, they also are attempting to respond with still more rules which, let us hope, will be acceptable both to business, from a practical viewpoint, and to those who are demanding massive reports and tighter rules.

The issue, to be sure, can be argued from both sides. But it is my opinion that figures will always have the limitation that they can't talk and interpret what they really and fully represent. Yet once written down, they give an appearance of being complete and "correct" and requiring no interpretation. Because this is not so, more and more figures provided to the public will not, of themselves, eliminate misunderstanding or fraud. More information, in addition to being costly and cumbersome, may also serve to confuse. The answer, at least in part, seems to me to require better interpretation by management of their operations and greater integrity on the part of some who achieve leadership positions.

WHAT DOES TOP MANAGEMENT NEED TO KNOW IN ORDER TO BE IN CONTROL?

by Lynn Townsend
Chairman and Chief Executive Officer, Chrysler Corporation

INTRODUCTION

BACK YEARS AGO the information—internal and external—needed by the Chief Executive Officer in order to be in *real* control was much less extensive and far less varied than is true today. Today, the information *needed*—and the information available—has proliferated. Business is more complex. The world is more complex. Computerized information systems, internally, and sources of statistical and other kinds of information are all generating far more information than ever before. The top-level information-management job, these days, has to be as much concerned with *selection* as with information *generation.* The Chief Executive Officer needs to limit the amount and type of information coming to him and to see that his associates do likewise so that they have what they *really* need without being overwhelmed by a flow of information they can't cope with.

NEED FOR SELECTION AND FOCUS

The activities and interests of a Chief Executive Officer will naturally vary from company to company and individual to individual. His primary function, however, must be to determine the long-range objectives of his company, to determine the optimum corporate structure consistent with meeting the objectives, and to revise or reaffirm those objectives according to what he sees in the present and out ahead.

While it may be true that "a businessman's judgment is no better than his information," it is also true, particularly in the larger organizations, that the CEO must resist the natural temptation to demand or accept *too much* information.

This is especially true when products are diversified and operations are multinational.

Obviously, any sizeable organization generates a staggering number of problems and decisions that must be dealt with on a day-to-day basis. The CEO, if he hopes to be effective, must delegate the job of interpreting and dealing with this input to a carefully chosen and competent operating staff, and concentrate on the *long term*.

"MANAGEMENT BY EXCEPTION"

At the same time, the CEO has to be alert to any deviation from the company plan as soon as it becomes apparent, and to concur in the steps taken to bring operations back in line. Toward this end, I receive daily reports from the operating staff on what I believe to be key indicators—figures on incoming orders, industry and company sales, our production reports, and a statement on cash and securities. These data are roughly equivalent to the "pulse" of the corporation, and provide enough symptoms to diagnose potentially unhealthy trends.

Guiding the growth of a corporation by correcting exceptions to an established norm as soon as they appear is a long-accepted practice. But in recent years, the factors we once considered to be relatively constant no longer meet the definition.

NEED FOR PROJECTIONS

The basic business practices of design, engineering, production, and distribution—the fundamentals of a manufacturing business—have been greatly complicated by the fact that circumstances change so rapidly we often find that what was true back in the design stage may well be no longer true by the time we reach the final stages. Specifically, projected costs and availability of materials, and consumer trends resulting from factors outside any individual business operation are changing at an accelerated rate, and the amount of information required to keep current with these changes is taking more and more of management's attention.

NEED FOR STRONG TEAM

This increase in the flow of information tends to draw the CEO more deeply into the operational phase than he really ought to be. If he has a sound personal knowledge of the capabilities and potential of his top staff, he can realign or expand responsibilities in critical areas in such a way that most information flowing to him concerns what has been done about problem solving rather than what problems are in need of solutions. This presumes that he has taken the steps necessary to build the breadth and depth of executive talent available to him, so that operations stay within the lines of the objective, and so that only the information affecting the objective itself is brought to his attention.

In short, just as it is essential for the CEO to discriminate in the kind of information he needs, it is equally important to have developed a staff that is as reliable and perceptive as possible in its reporting.

Attaining and maintaining this kind of control over the basic—not simple, but fundamental—elements of doing business, staying in business, and sustaining growth, have become more and more demanding on the time and energies of the CEO.

PROBLEMS OF MAINTAINING GROWTH

Sustained growth, as a case in point, is a major objective of the CEO. Yet in corporate America today, particularly in the basic industries, there is a critical shortage of the equity capital needed not only to grow, but simply to stay healthy. Much of the industrial plant in this country is old, while much of that of our overseas competition is comparatively new. If basic industry in the United States is going to survive in the face of that competition, it is imperative that outmoded, inefficient plant and equipment be replaced with the latest technology, and very soon.

Yet the executive officers of corporate America find themselves fighting for the right to a fair profit, and combating the lack of understanding of the function of profit in a free society and an ignorance of the relationship between capital formation and new job formation. The CEO needs a constant reading of the availability and cost of basic resources—materials, parts, capital, and personnel. But even if the CEO is successful in these basic efforts, it will be only half enough of what is required for that primary objective, to plan and attain practical long-term goals.

NEEDS FOR EXTERNAL INFORMATION

A great proportion of the major concerns of today's CEO are not directly related to parts, production, and profits at all. But he has to be aware of them, and ahead of them, if he is to succeed in the long run. He has to recognize, anticipate, and cope with the effect on his business of, for just some examples, organized labor, Wall Street analysts, consumer groups, environmentalists, institutional investors, federal and state regulations, Congress, federal agencies, bankers, and the buying public.

These "outside the business" considerations have proliferated in recent years to the point that it is estimated the typical CEO is now spending about 40 percent of his time on external matters. Here again the executive officer, if he is to remain effective, limits his flow of information to the essentials and depends on members of his staff to assimilate and distill the pertinent data.

At my company, the top officers are provided a twice-daily summary of current relevant developments, compiled by an in-house News Center drawing upon the resources of the major wires, radio and television networks, periodicals, and daily publications. As in most large companies today, we have assigned the continuing task of staying current in the nonoperational aspects of business to an appropriate group of individuals within the company. Our Public Responsibility Committee, made up of members of the board of directors, and our Office of Corporate Responsibility, headed by a corporate vice president, keep top management abreast of developments and trends in such areas as consumer affairs, equal opportunity, energy conservation, and environmental, governmental, and safety activities.

WORKING WITH GOVERNMENT

As government increases its direct participation in matters previously considered the sole province of business itself, top management finds it useful, and often necessary, to join in meetings with government agencies, accept assignments in government programs, and to offer advice or testimony to congressional committees. In one recent week, executives from my company, including myself, made seven separate appearances before congressional committees alone.

No one man could hope to familiarize himself with the intricacies of the myriad regulations and regulators now confronting business, and again the CEO must rely heavily on his staff to provide the cogent highlights of developments that could help shape his decisions for action against the future.

WORKING WITH COMMUNITY AND OTHER ORGANIZATIONS

In addition to coping with outside influences that exert themselves on his company's operations, today's corporate officer finds himself voluntarily involved in a growing number of activities that were previously regarded as being outside the province of business. American businessmen are in the vanguard across the country in programs and projects dedicated to increasing employment among the chronically unemployable, restructuring our urban centers, rehabilitating society's drop-outs, and confronting a wide variety of social ills.

In recent years, officers of my company have headed such groups as the National Alliance of Businessmen, and have served on the local equivalent of the Urban Coalition, Detroit Renaissance, the President's Export Council, and the Business Council. Others serve on the boards of major hospitals, colleges, and cultural organizations. As the business community becomes more and more incorporated into the social and political communities, it becomes more and more important for management to be aware of, and to help shape, the trends and ambitions of those communities.

INFORMATION FROM ABROAD

At the same time, as the number of truly multinational companies continues to grow, the CEOs of these companies require a new flow of information about the economic, political, and social developments in those countries. They are required to identify the same potential obstacles and opportunities abroad as at home, and to make the same type of adjustments to them.

It might be argued, then, that in a time of growing interaction and interdependence among the nations of the world, given the vast number of multinational companies doing business in those nations, and the even greater number of peripheral businesses dependent on the fortunes of those companies, everything that happens, everywhere, has the potential of affecting the corporate future. Although that is probably true to some degree, it would be foolish, and futile, to argue that the effective CEO has to keep himself fully informed about *every* new trend, *every* progress and *every* reversal. He needs to be attentive to the *key* performance figures provided by the operating staff, and to the constant changes in supply and expense of the critical resources as they affect the near and long-term prospects for his organization.

SUMMARY

The successful chief executive is obligated to develop and perfect a sense of priorities, and a talent for sifting from the huge store of facts available to him those which are valid indicators of what *new* action his company should take, what current programs should be accelerated or phased out, and whether the course he has charted is going to bring his company to an intersection of growth and strength in the years ahead. He needs to do more than look at the facts. He needs to use today's facts as a solid platform from which he can search the horizon of his company's future.

PROFIT PLANNING AND BUDGETING

by Gaylord Freeman

Chairman of the Board, First Chicago Corporation/
The First National Bank of Chicago

INTRODUCTION

IT IS PERHAPS ironic that a banker should be asked to contribute to a publication on the subject of profit planning. For years we, as lenders of funds, required vast, sophisticated planning and control systems for potential borrowers and yet, as an industry, we had done virtually nothing in the field ourselves. After we "got religion" and moved into the functions of planning and control, we utilized tools which industrialists had pioneered and developed. We then merely adapted them to our environment, rather than trying to "reinvent the wheel."

However, despite the disclaimers above, I believe we were reasonably apt students and proved to be effective in making these techniques work for us. So, although we were late starters, I believe we can speak with some practical experience.

My assigned purpose is not to provide a text on accounting/budgeting theory or a "how-to-do-it" approach to profit planning. There are many excellent papers which cover those subjects with far greater expertise than we can muster. I would merely like to discuss some of the uses and potential limitations of planning tools and consider the role the Chief Executive Officer (CEO) needs to play in the process. In order to avoid any confusion on semantics, inasmuch as we are dealing with a fairly technical subject, it may be desirable at the outset to define two basic terms: "profit planning" and profit centers."

In the context of this discussion, the technical term profit planning —as we use it—describes an annual income and expense budgeting process. We also have related support functions, such as a qualitative planning of objectives (e.g., share-of-market statistics, employee efficiency, new product development, etc.); there is also a cost accounting

791

system to facilitate orderly transfer pricing of services between profit centers. In summary, our profit planning develops a formal annual operating plan (both financial and qualitative) for all of the responsibility centers (organizational units) within our corporation. However, we view the profit planning as much more than a mechanical process. In our planning, we strive to look into the future, not merely to forecast what will happen, but to specify what we think we can *make* happen. We attempt to define those internal and external conditions that will have an impact upon us and then we select the courses of action that, we believe, will allow us to take maximum advantage of these conditions, whether or not they are controllable.

The profit centers are defined as those organizational units which will implement these plans and will produce revenue as well as expenses. By way of additional criteria, they also have an element of control over that revenue, in terms of pricing, marketing, and the resultant volume. Those areas of the corporation which do not have this revenue responsibility, but which do expend funds for the benefit of other areas of the bank (e.g., data processing groups, personnel division), we treat as service centers. These areas plan their expenses, and their qualitative objectives; and then, through the cost accounting mechanism, their services (i.e., hours of computer time, number of personnel employed) are charged to the appropriate areas of the bank. Thus, all organizational units are designated as either profit centers or as service centers, and their performance as to both expense and income (or intracompany charges) is evaluated accordingly.

BACKGROUND OF PLANNING—FIRST CHICAGO CORPORATION/THE FIRST NATIONAL BANK OF CHICAGO

Two major historical characteristics are relevant as background:

1. Operations were very centralized in a single (Chicago) setting. (Illinois law prohibited branch banking.)
2. We had developed an extremely strong capital position, but had placed relatively little emphasis on earnings.

Both situations were appropriate in their time; however, as we expanded domestically and internationally, it became apparent that we needed more decentralized decision making combined with a greater profit awareness. The time for a modern profit center-based planning and control system had arrived. Our implementation sequence was as follows:

1. We acquired professional profit planning personnel; this from manufacturing and consulting firms.

2. Next, the responsibility centers were defined. All planning units were assigned to one of eight major departments (six profit centers, two service centers).

3. After the approval of the initial profit plan, we initiated quarterly profit center reports. The first year's reporting started building a profit awareness through all levels of organization.

4. In the second year, reports were accelerated to a monthly cycle. At the same time, we began reviewing the results of the departments, one at a time, with each of the eight department heads individually. We did it this way in order to demonstrate to them the importance we attached to the planning exercise.

5. The final step was the establishment of meetings to review actual results versus the profit plan. These meetings are conducted every month and are attended by all of the department heads, the comptroller, and myself. In addition, every quarter, each profit center head reports to the board of directors. This both informs the board and impresses upon the department heads the importance of both the planning and performance dimensions of the profit planning activities.

After the successful implementation of the above short-range plan, we expanded the planning to include an annual corporation-wide, long-range (five-year) cycle. In 1975, we are presently in the seventh year of profit planning and the fourth year of long-range planning. Between the two exercises there is a heavy commitment of approximately 15 of our senior officers. In addition to the time cited above for the monthly and quarterly review of the actual results versus plan, we spend an additional six days physically off-site. Once a year, we spend three days reviewing and approving both the profit plan and the long-range plan.

I should say that the long-range plan is updated during the second quarter of each year. The annual profit plan is prepared during the period from the first of September to the beginning of December and is presented to the board of directors in January.

The amount of executive time we have been willing to invest, I believe, has clearly demonstrated to all of our personnel the value we attach to planning.

KEY SUCCESS FACTORS

With the above as background, I would like to discuss some of the key areas to consider in installing and administering a planning system. Of all these factors, the most important one is senior management involvement. (This is particularly true regarding the time of the CEO.) Several activities are required:

1. The CEO's physical presence and active participation in the plan approval and review process is absolutely essential. The monthly sessions provide an ideal occasion to discuss remedial/exploitive action in light of problems/opportunities.

2. The careful analysis of the proposed plans during the review process, of both the short- and long-range plans, provides an excellent opportunity to satisfy yourself, as CEO, that future alternatives are thoroughly considered and understood.

It is also important that you, yourself, take the time to review and accept (or revise) the basic economic/accounting assumptions in the system. The knowledge you gain from this is also necessary for a related task, namely, constantly evaluating whether the system causes people at all organizational levels to act in accordance with the corporation's objectives.

In addition, you should remain reasonably flexible as to format, method of presentation, etc., as long as your chief financial officer is satisfied that results are consistent and comparable. This can become very important in terms of corporate acquisitions or very specialized *de novo* activities. (It is frequently helpful in activities which differ substantially from your principal business, to allow formats which are meaningful in that particular business—e.g., we experienced this with the consulting firm acquired by our holding company.)

Over and above being knowledgeably involved and flexible, I encourage you to resist the temptation to *dictate* the plan. Frequently in the early stages of profit planning, the initially-submitted plan may not be acceptable. In that instance, the plan (or portions thereof) will need to be resubmitted; however, there has to be a meeting of the minds so that the plan remains "theirs" (the profit center heads) rather than "yours." It is a fine line between ensuring that the overall profit plan provides an acceptable return and, at the same time, still retains a sense of commitment on the part of the profit center heads. The renegotiating iterations described above have enabled us to maintain this balance. However, before leaving this topic, I should point out that others deal differently with this problem.

An alternative approach used by some companies is to accept completely the profit plans submitted by each center and, in the consolidation, to add a lump sum (plus or minus) which the Chief Executive Officer believes to result in a more realistic overall performance. This permits the bottom line to appear realistic to the chief executive without disturbing the individual plans of each of the department heads.

The crucial factor, under any approach, is the maintenance of a high level of commitment to the plan. This difficult task can only be dealt with by you as CEO.

POTENTIAL PROBLEMS

In addition to the commitment question, there are other people-related problems you may need to resolve. For example:

1. Short-range profit pressure may tempt the profit center head to be myopic as to the long-range impact of certain actions. You must be alert to this potential trade-off. For example, the costs of successor management development can penalize near-term earnings, and, for that reason, may get short-changed.

2. Similarly, you don't want the profit plans (budgets) to be overly restrictive if the manager has a good reason for his variance from plan. Therefore, the whole concept of "explainable" variances should be allowed. The profit center head should be able to exceed his expense budget, if the "bottom-line" impact is positive. This may require explanation on his part, because the overexpenditure may occur in an accounting period prior to the anticipated benefits. The burden of advanced notice has to be on the profit center heads (clearly you don't want surprises); but if they are to be entrepreneurs, this approach must be available to them.

It is also important to be alert to the continuing effectiveness of your various planning activities. For example, we found it was necessary to change our basic review procedure. Initially, I reviewed results "one-on-one" with each profit center head with the comptroller and the manager of profit planning also in attendance. This caused two problems: This arrangement did seem to generate something like a "Star Chamber," repressive atmosphere and, upon occasion, led to attempts to "blame the other guy," (i.e., the head of some other department). We moved away from this approach to one wherein *all* profit center heads are present for each other's reviews. This modification has been very effective in sharpening the presentations and obtaining the ideas and judgments of the entire management team. It illustrates the desirability of a continuing appraisal of the entire process.

The plan is not an end itself. In addition to reviewing results versus the plan, you should also reevaluate the entire process on an ongoing basis. Is it continuing to be a viable method for you, as the CEO, to understand, motivate and control your business at all organizational levels?

SUMMARY

We are in our seventh year (1975) of profit planning and are convinced it has materially aided us to increase our profit awareness and improvement. The system has enabled us to prepare formal (i.e., written) plans to achieve specified goals and then measure, on an interim basis, the actual results against those goals.

Of all of the key factors in making the plan a success, none is more important than your own knowledgeable, interested involvement as CEO. This is true during both the approval and review processes.

Finally, inasmuch as people are the most important asset (particularly in the banking industry where they really are our only asset), you can never cease verifying that the planning system is not only understood by the key people but treats them equitably. If the system does not do this, it will be very difficult to consistently motivate them to act in the stockholders' best interest. On the other hand, if your system enables their goals to be the same as those of the stockholders. profit planning will more than pay its way.

THE IMPLEMENTATION OF LONG-RANGE PLANS

by William M. Ellinghaus

President, New York Telephone Company

and William G. Sharwell

Executive Vice President, Operations, New York Telephone Company

EVERY Chief Executive Officer knows, or comes eventually to know, that it takes more than a great idea to produce great results. Between the birth of an idea and the success of an operation lies a vast gap to be bridged. Tasks must be identified and scheduled, resources must be acquired and allocated, plant must be built, manpower must be developed, all in an orderly and controlled fashion. In this chapter, we shall call this set of activities, aimed at insuring an orderly progression from the idea stage of planning to the initiation of successful operations, *implementation*.

The CEO has a direct stake in implementing many long-range plans, whether they are thought of as strategic, transformational, tactical, or operational. Organizations that attempt to leap from grand ideas straight into operations, without careful consideration of the implementation problems, can find themselves quickly enmeshed in a multiplying series of problems—from deteriorating product quality and service, to cost overruns, declining productivity, shrinking profits, and customer and shareholder dissatisfaction. Eventually, all of these problems can wind up on the desk of the CEO, demanding his time, his energy, and in the end more resources than he originally intended to give to these matters. Because he must deal with implementation problems sooner or later, it is of course best that he cope with them when he chooses to, and not when the problems come knocking at his door.

This need to manage the implementation process, though always

797

present, comes at a time when the business environment poses more challenges to business than ever before. (Consider, for example, inflation, consumerism, energy and resource shortages, government regulation, and the declining birth rate, to name a few.) In the face of these burdens which often require a rethinking of assumptions, the CEO may be kept from spending enough time on seeing that painstakingly developed business ideas eventually become successful ongoing operations.

Given these tremendous demands on today's CEO, how can he be sure he is devoting the right amount of attention to the implementation of plans? What tasks actually are involved? What methods and techniques can a CEO rely on to stay in touch with the more essential elements of implementation without becoming overly involved in the process? Based on our combined experiences in the telephone business, we hope to offer some practical observations on these questions in the remainder of this chapter.

KEY ASPECTS OF IMPLEMENTATION

Successful implementation of plans demands careful administration of several activities:

1. Each important task necessary for fulfilling plan objectives must be clearly identified and recognized by all concerned.
2. Responsibility for completing each task should be precisely assigned to qualified individuals or specific, capable groups.
3. A sequence of tasks sensibly scheduled for efficient completion must be developed and followed.
4. All the essential resources (financial, manpower, and material) for achieving planned objectives must be accumulated; those needed for each task must be allocated to it.
5. Procedures for supervising and coordinating the completion of the task must be clearly provided; formal reporting relationships must be designed and made known to all concerned.
6. For large tasks, it may be necessary to restructure the organization so as to create more efficient division of labor, more highly motivated employees, or better utilization of resources.
7. If the plan calls for activities which are radically new, a change in the approach to incentives may be required and certainly should be considered.

Activities such as these are familiar to every manager. However, in the rush to meet deadlines, some aspects of implementation which make the difference between success and failure are often overlooked by busy managers. These overlooked aspects can include such factors as an appreciation of the interdependency of plan formulation and plan implementation; the use of feedback; the importance of learning time; and the realization that organizational structure and process must be consistent with the objectives sought in long-range plans. Each of these ideas is discussed below.

Between Plan and Operation

The implementation stage of planning can be viewed as a sequence of tasks, or more aptly a *cycle* of tasks, with the links in the implementation chain overlapping and influencing each other. A CEO who feels his time should be devoted exclusively or even mainly to defining where his firm *should* be going therefore makes a serious conceptual mistake. No strategy stands alone. No operating process stands alone. Every stage of planning is dynamically interlinked.

As an illustration, consider the case of an entrepreneur starting a new business, say, the production of a new kind of hi-fi speaker. He begins with an idea, perhaps a technical breakthrough, that leads to the recognition of a new perceived need in the marketplace. He adopts a long-range plan to introduce his product into the marketplace and to capture a respectable share of the hi-fi speaker market in five years. He determines how many speakers he may reasonably expect to sell during the introductory year, to whom, at what price, and at what cost to him. He must arrange for their production. He must convince distributors to stock and push them. He must train people to assemble them in the most efficient manner. And he must keep a close watch on his available cash. All of these things he builds into his long-range plan, and slowly he develops it as a statement of his assumptions and his aspirations.

Throughout this process he must stay abreast of his competition and continually test the viability of his plan. Perhaps his specifications will need to be altered following the adoption of a new industry standard. Or perhaps a larger market niche is available in another price category because Brand X recently discontinued operations. Maybe Brand Y has discovered the same breakthrough he has identified. Should he speed up introduction or wait for clarification of his patent protection? Over and over, he makes such judgments, first altering his implementation to fit his objectives, then adjusting his objectives to reflect the scope of what is possible within the administrative point of view. Eventually, concept and plan evolve into an internally consistent statement of ends and assumptions, with steps for achieving those ends clearly spelled out and with major go/no-go decisions identified, all in a conscious, well-timed pattern of do-able activities.

Each of the elements of implementation can influence the prior goal or the succeeding operation. In that sense, the implementation of a long-range plan is very much like the fabled two faces of Janus, one looking forward, the other looking backward. The forward-backward look serves as a check on the soundness of strategy or tactics and on the quality of operations. What's more, the process is ongoing—stretching forward into the time period when operations are in full swing, and backward in time, to the stage of idea generation.

The Use of Feedback

A plan that assumes that the march from goals to operations is inexorable, with no room for adjustment once past certain landmarks, is asking for trouble. Few, if any achievements are accomplished with single-shot accuracy. Realistically, most goals are achieved through a process that can be termed "management by successive approximations." Whether the goal is landing astronauts on the moon, marching a football team down the field for a touchdown, or completing a successful business strategy, the gap between ideas and performance must be filled with up-to-date information on the results of actions taken by the organization and on reactions of the environment. This information is *feedback*.

To understand the importance of feedback, consider an attempt to drive your car down the highway at a constant speed of 40 mph. Without feedback information from your speedometer or tachometer, it would be very difficult to carry out such a task. But with such information, the accomplishment of the goal within certain limits is practically guaranteed. In other words, *feedback allows you to control system error.* The more thorough the feedback, the more thorough the control over the error. In business, the better the feedback, the less waste that goes unnoticed, whether in finished inventory, raw materials, cash flow, resource waste, lost sales or whatever. Without feedback, there can be no confident implementation of plans. In fact, in these days and times, without feedback there can be no confident management at all.

For the hi-fi entrepreneur, for example, feedback is absolutely necessary for monitoring the start-up of his business. New-order rates, inventory buildup, speaker assembly time, and cash flow figures are just some of the data he must have in order to know if his business is viable. They tell him when adjustments are needed, and where, and will continue to measure the pulse of his business whenever necessary.

The Importance of Allowing for Learning Time

The time factor becomes especially critical when feedback information is used in getting back on course toward completion of planned goals. If our hi-fi entrepreneur's routine operations are being controlled by feedback, for example, he will no doubt know what needs to be done to speed up the assembly of speaker sets necessary to fulfill his production goals. Such "management by exception" is ideally suited for day-to-day activities. But if new activities such as new product development or installing a data-processing system are undertaken, the proper use of feedback cannot be expected until those responsible for monitoring the operation have learned what kinds of feedback can be designed and how to use them to modify results.

This appreciation of learning time often is ignored or omitted from long-range plans by planners and managers. It often is mistakenly assumed that "course corrections" are instantaneous. In reality, of course, it often takes years for the new endeavors sketched out in long-term plans to reach operating status.

Making Use of Organizational Structure and Process

The structure and process of an organization should always be scrutinized to be sure they serve the long-range purposes of the business. Business abounds with organizational forms that are grounded in company history, industry traditions, personal whims, or textbook solutions, even though such forms no longer match the new expectations of the company leaders. Unfortunately, the organization structure—the design and placement of functions—also is the most difficult to deal with, for it is usually a "given" that the CEO is supposed to work his way around. Yet despite the difficulties and organizational trauma that accompany a change of structure, the possibility of that change is always implicit in the CEO's considerations.

When plans call for transformational change—that is, when they call for something considerably more than simple linear change—the need for structural change often is inescapable. Once the planning engine has been tuned to fit changing environmental conditions, little can be done further to improve performance without a new design. Here the organizational and behavioral processes of modern administration—compensation, budgeting, promotion, performance measurement, and the extent of executive supervision, to name a few —can provide leverage to facilitate change. Every CEO has to ask two questions in this regard of every plan: "Is my organization designed to deliver what the plan asks for?" and, if not, "Are the organizational changes required the kind we want to make?" If not, the plan should certainly be altered; if so, the processes above should be modified to serve the purposes of the plan.

PUTTING IT ALL TOGETHER IN THE TELEPHONE BUSINESS

Implementation of long-term plans in the telephone business is an enormous undertaking, and it is not an exaggeration to say that the development of a large-scale project management capability to handle it has been the secret of success in the industry. Each day millions of messages go through the telephone system—from people or computers; by voice, data, TV, radio; by cable, satellites, and by microwave. While all this is happening, telephones are connected and disconnected, plant and facilities are replaced, new and modern equipment and facilities are installed.

To achieve this ongoing expansion, replacement, and rearrangement of communication facilities, a telephone company uses a long-range plan called the construction program. It is a statement of the company's plans covering a three year period, the current year and two years following. During this period the construction program is continually being remolded as the result of tactical shifts, whether from internal decisions such as putting all new subscriber cable underground, or from environmental changes, such as rapid economic growth in a previously stagnant area, which calls for a build up of communication facilities.

As a long-range plan, the construction program serves telephone managers in several ways. First of all, they can use it as a summation of dollars and materials needed to add, rearrange, or replace telephone plant. The program includes expenditures for telephone instruments (including the cost of labor to install telephones), for subscriber cable, central offices, for trunks (or the paths carrying calls between central offices), for land and buildings, for outside plant (telephone poles and conduit), and for general equipment (that is, tools, motor vehicles, offices, machines). Secondly, the construction program can be used as a means for determining how the company sets priorities for its capital resources among such objectives as expansion, modernization, plant replacements and rearrangements. Third, the construction plan is of critical importance to the CEO in crystallizing financial strategy, for it helps set the order of magnitude for new capital requirements. New York Telephone spends about $900 million annually in capital construction, and the Bell System spends about $8 billion. Such expenditures clearly require extensive advance planning, careful studies of strategic priorities and organizational alternatives, and studious monitoring of feedback to insure proper results. Let's see how part of such a plan might be implemented.

The Cutover of a Switching Center

Let's suppose a telephone company's studies indicate that a cluster of central offices within a major city like New York are beginning to reach the point where they must be expanded. Options abound. Each office might be expanded through a series of small additions; or one might undergo major expansion, and the lines from the other offices might be connected to the newly expanded office.

Let's assume, however, that the growth prospects remain strong, and the need is established for an entirely new building to serve the area. Then a series of Janus-like decisions, half strategic and half administrative, must be made. How much growth should the new center be prepared to handle? Should the new building be exclusively a switching center, or should it also have administrative office space? Are the criteria of "adequate capacity" likely to change? What existing customers will be served by the new exchange? Will the center be woven into the existing network of local and long distance trunks and switching centers of the network? How should the switching equipment itself be selected and designed to fit the calling characteristics of the area's customers? Should it offer operating savings or new services? And so on.

These decisions are made at a variety of levels in the organization. From field engineers to the board of directors, criteria for performance across a wide gamut of dimensions are built into the construction program, with broader financial and social objectives incorporated into the plan as it nears approval. Finally, the plan is approved, and work begins.

The interrelationship between concept and plan continues as work proceeds. As we have said, it is a rare plan that does not need some amendment somewhere along the line. Circumstances change or fail to materialize as expected, or some hidden flaw inevitably comes to light as events unfold. Although the CEO cannot keep track of every part of the evolving operation, he must, however, shepherd and evaluate the overall picture.

The Importance of Learning

It is not enough simply to check the progress of the "plan." Everything may be going according to schedule, but conditions may have shifted. An unexpected slackening in demand may force the CEO of a telephone operating company to switch funds from expansion projects to modernization of existing facilities. Strained earnings may call for a deferral of certain projects in order to curb growth in capital investment. Or plans for additional facilities in one locality may have to be dropped because a federal housing project did not come through, although overall construction program spending may have to be boosted in order to meet generally rising demand. It is during this phase of implementation that knowing what to do is crucial. If the particular problems experienced have never been seen before, even the best of managers will have to learn how to cope with the new changes, and the plan will be delayed accordingly.

This chain of events, of decisions interlocking with other decisions, may extend over a period of two or three years. Strikes, material shortages, acts of God and man, and new data, all will come to the surface during the process. They will call for rethinking, changes, and new decisions. To make sure all systems are "go," progress and results will need to be checked throughout, often by specialists, sometimes by the CEO. Finally, the new equipment is installed, tested, and put quickly into operation so that customers' telephone service remains virtually uninterrupted.

Feedback

The cutover of a major switching center, where thousands of telephone customers are severed from one central office building and connected to another, commands a lot of monitoring especially in the initial hours after cutover. As with a patient fresh out of surgery, all life signs must be checked. To this end, the telephone companies produce data on switching times, switching accuracy, and load-handling capabilities. Then, as time passes without incident, the intensive monitoring becomes absorbed by the normal routine of service monitoring which keeps track of dial-tone waiting periods, delays in providing directory assistance, and many other parameters.

Certainly no telephone operating company CEO can personally administer every major decision. With the construction program, however, he is constantly monitoring *the results* of major decisions. He gets the feedback through an elaborate array of technical indicators as to how the new facilities are performing; he gets it in the volume and nature of complaints to him, to his management, to the regulators. With the continuous, iterative nature of the construction program, today's feedback helps reshape operations plans and strategies for tomorrow.

Amending Structure and Process—The CEO's Principal Role

Ideally, construction programs are initiated in the field and reviewed up the chain of command, with the details having been handled at lower organizational levels and checked against standards the CEO is well acquainted with. However, if proposed programs are ignoring current business imperatives, draining away too many expense dollars, continually missing targets, or whatever, it's the CEO's job to redesign the implementation system to better serve the organizational goals. For example, suppose key capacity needs are not being recognized soon enough. The CEO can improve that by pushing the responsibility for staying abreast of capacity needs and forecasts down to an organizational level that understands the problem— and then gaining a personal commitment from those at that level for the plan they come up with. If competitive conditions are changing rapidly, criteria for expansion, investment, and modernization can also be changed from time to time to fit better with external demands. And if follow-up is a problem, meeting planned performance goals can be made a major factor in determining compensation.

Through the use of such techniques, the CEO succeeds in managing the implementation of long-range plans through the efforts of others. To be sure, urgency or scale of operations may often dictate that he step in himself from time to time, perhaps occasionally running the whole show. But by training *the organization* to respond to new criteria for success, changing resource constraints, new feedback, and new learning, the CEO goes far toward insuring organizational adaptability and stacking the cards in favor of meeting implementation goals on time.

SUMMARY

In conclusion, implementation of long-term plans is a central part of business management. It allows for the successful translation of existing objectives into viable ongoing operations. It demands much on the part of the CEO—the identification and assignment of key tasks, decisions as to the division of labor, a clear understanding and use of feedback, an appreciation of the time required by people and organizations to learn, the measurement of performance in a way that inspires goal-directed activities, and dynamic personal leadership, as well. What's more, effective implementation structures our aspirations and our desires in such a way as to make them attainable—and that is one of the great satisfactions available to the Chief Executive Officer.

AUDITING

by Joseph B. Hall
Chairman of the Board (Retired), The Kroger Company

AUDITING, broadly defined, is an important function of corporate management. This opinion is based on 19 years as Chief Executive Officer of a retail chain with annual sales of over two billion dollars and many years as a director of ten corporations, both large and small. This chapter covers both internal and independent (outside) auditing, the latter including a discussion of the audit committee of the board of directors.

Auditing, in a narrow sense, is an official examination and verification of accounts and records, especially financial records. Internal audits are conducted by company personnel who should be independent of the operations they are auditing. Annual and external audits of the company's financial statements are made by outside accountants and auditors who are independent of the company and its management.

There has developed a more general use of the term "auditing" which covers functions that might be termed "management control" such as checks on procedures, verification of agreement with accounting principles, authorization for action taken and conflicts of interest. Special investigations can be included also.

THE INTERNAL AUDIT

A good description of the internal auditing function is included in a Policy Statement of Tenneco, Inc., on auditing:

> Internal Auditing is an independent management control and appraisal activity established within Tenneco and its subsidiary companies for the review of accounting, financial and other operations of the companies as a service to management. The Internal Audit ac-

tivities of Tenneco Inc. are under the direction of the Director of Internal Audit, reporting to the Executive Vice President of Finance. The responsibility for Internal Audit function for the major operating divisions of Tenneco Inc. lies with the management of each division. The Director of Internal Audit has the functional responsibility to see that the Internal Audit program of each of the operating divisions is adequate and is carried out in a professional manner.

The objectives of the internal audit may vary from company to company. One of the principal objectives is to check on the reliability of the accounting and reporting system and verify the accuracy of the figures and the existence of assets. The internal audit should determine the adequacy of the system of control, the safeguards for maintenance of assets and prevention of fraud. It should investigate compliance with company policies and procedures. It should report findings to management and, where necessary, recommend corrective action.

Special investigations can be made by the internal auditing staff since they visit the various operations and present a viewpoint distinct from the operating management. The internal auditing staff becomes an extension of "the eyes and ears" of management.

Years ago as branch manager (now called Division Vice President) of the St. Louis Division of The Kroger Company, I made effective use of store auditors. In addition to their financial and inventory audits, they would report on store conditions as well as any unusual situations which they observed. When I was president, the chief auditor furnished to me copies of the division audits with a memorandum pointing out conditions which required attention. These reports had been reviewed with the division managers and often would include an explanation and action the division manager proposed to take.

The internal audit can investigate compliance with the rules of regulatory agencies. It can check on conflict of interests. On the other hand, some companies prefer to handle these matters through the legal department, but there should be an annual review. The internal audit can serve as a training ground for personnel as well as help in the evaluation of personnel performance.

The CEO should determine the objectives of the company's internal audit department. This should be done in consultation with his financial officer. The CEO should then ascertain that the director of internal audit is fully qualified for the position. The auditors within the department should have some business and accounting background. The training on the job can be supplemented by evening accounting college courses with the end objective of passing the C.P.A. examination. In larger companies the supervising auditors should have qualified as C.P.A.s. It is the responsibility of the director of internal audit to develop a capable auditing staff.

The scope of the internal audit should be determined each year by the director of internal audit in consultation with the CEO and the financial officer. The proposed program should be discussed with the outside auditors for any suggestions they may make and then submitted to the CEO for final approval. It is possible, in many instances, for the outside auditors to reduce the scope of their work because of the effective internal control brought about by the internal audit activity.

Appendix A presents a summary of the scope of the internal audit work at the Goodyear Tire & Rubber Company as it was set forth a few years ago. The indication of the several types of audit is particularly noteworthy. Goodyear, of course, is a large corporation with many divisions both nationally and internationally. This statement portrays the extensiveness of the internal audit.

The CEO should review the internal audit reports with the director of audits. Frequently, he delegates this responsibility to the chief financial officer. If this is done, the CEO should review the summary of the audits with the financial officer and discuss with him any unusual situation or conditions that require correction. At least annually, the CEO should meet privately with the director of audits to review the activities of his department. Where internal auditors are used for special nonaccounting investigations, the findings should be brought to the attention of the CEO to determine the action that should be taken. Even though the responsibility for audit reviews is delegated to the financial officer, it still is the responsibility of the CEO to see that organizational standards and procedures are sound and that the audits are properly carried out.

It is becoming generally accepted that the director of internal audit should report either directly to the CEO or to the chief financial officer. The director should be independent of all operational responsibilities inasmuch as he and his staff are checking on the operations of all other units in the company. The director of internal audit should work closely with the company's outside auditors. He should look to them for suggestions and advice. The outside auditors are in touch, at all times, with changes in government regulations and changes in accounting principles—those which have been approved, as well as those contemplated. A close relationship between the inside auditors and the outside auditors can lead to lower overall auditing costs.

THE INDEPENDENT AUDIT

Accounting is a developing profession. Changes are being made continuously due to the requirements of the Internal Revenue Service, the Securities and Exchange Commission, and the New York Stock Exchange. The responsibility of outside auditors has been broadened as a result of suits against companies, directors, and their outside auditors. It is not the purpose of this chapter to discuss the subject in detail. I refer the reader to "Corporations and Their Outside Auditors," published by the Conference Board.[1] This booklet is an excellent 212-page summary of "the relationship of a certified public accountant to his client."

The changes that are taking place in the field of accounting and auditing emphasize the importance of selecting a capable certified public accounting firm. The size and complexity of the company play an important part in the choice of the C.P.A. firm. The reputation of the auditing firm is all important. Geographic diversity is advantageous to large concerns. Multinationals employ those C.P.A. firms that have offices in the countries where they have manufacturing and major distribution facilities. Some C.P.A. firms specialize in particular fields, which makes their selection desirable for companies operating in these fields. Knowledge of the clients' business and industry is an asset. It is important that C.P.A. partners be available for consultation.

The question frequently is asked, "Who selects the outside auditor —the management, the directors, or the stockholders?" Because the stockholders rely on the certification of the financial statements by the outside auditors, there is a growing tendency for the outside auditors to be acted on by the stockholders at the annual meeting. A choice is not offered, but the recommendation of management, as approved by the directors, is submitted in the proxy statement. Where there is an audit committee of the board, their recommendation usually is submitted to the full board for approval.

---

[1] The Conference Board, Inc.; Report No. 544; 845 Third Avenue, New York, N.Y. 10022; 1972.

Usually the relationship between the company and the independent auditing firm continues over many years. Where differences occur, they can be resolved, in most cases, through consultation. Sometimes there is a conflict of personalities that may require a change in the engagement partner assigned to the company. Rotation of personnel of outside auditing firms is often arranged in order to bring in a fresh viewpoint. This is desirable for both the auditing firm and the client.

Changes are seldom made in a company's outside auditing firm. Sometimes when the geographic extension of the company's operations occur, the services of larger auditing firms may be required. Mergers may lead to the elimination of one of the firms being used. Companies subject to SEC reporting requirements must furnish the SEC with an explanation of the reasons for changing outside auditors.

When the outside auditing firm has been selected, discussions should be held with the director of internal audit and the CEO or financial officer to determine the scope of the outside audit. The outside auditing firm should submit its recommendation for review with management and the board before the work is begun. Its program should include estimated fees, usually submitted on a per diem basis for men assigned to the audit, with an estimated number of man-hours or man-days involved. A typical proposal for a larger company is shown in Appendix B. This proposal covers the audit coverage for the last visit, the program for the current year, the participation by the internal auditors, and the estimated fees.

Situations may arise during the audit which will require discussions between the outside auditing firm and management. When the audit has been completed, the audit results should be reviewed with the CEO and/or chief financial officer. The financial statements prepared by the company are then submitted to the outside auditors for certification. A representative of the outside auditing firm should meet with the full board, unless there is an audit committee of the board; and perhaps even then. This provides an opportunity for board members to review the results of the audit with the outside auditors and secure their comments on the company's controls. Questions can be asked concerning the financial statements and footnotes in the annual report which will be certified by the outside auditors.

In addition to the regular audit, special assignments may be given to the outside auditors for such matters as SEC reports, mergers, and special tax and other reports.

THE AUDIT COMMITTEE OF THE BOARD
OF DIRECTORS

Audit committees of the board of directors have been in existence for many years in some companies, but until more recent years, they have been the exception rather than the rule. In 1967, the Executive Committee of The American Institute of Certified Public Accountants recommended that publicly-owned corporations appoint committees composed of outside directors to nominate the independent auditors of the corporation and to discuss the auditors' work with them. The Securities and Exchange Commission and the New York Stock Exchange recommend similar action. This has accelerated the establishment of audit committees of the board in many companies.

Audit committees, composed of outside directors, preferably with financial experience, can be a constructive force in the overall review of internal control and financial structure and give added assurances of the reliability of corporate financial statements to stockholders, customers, creditors, analysts, and regulating agencies. Typically an audit committee, consisting of three to five members, is appointed by, and reports to the full board of directors. Usually the members are recommended by the CEO. The ultimate responsibility for approval of financial statements rests with the entire board. The committee, however, can take the necessary time to meet with the outside auditors and management to review the scope of the audit in advance, discuss any problems that develop during the audit, review the C.P.A.'s management letter, the financial statements, and proposed certification upon completion of the audit, and recommend to the board the acceptance of the statement and figures for publication in the annual report.

The audit committee should meet privately with representatives of the auditing firm to assure themselves of the cooperation of management and that no restrictions were placed on the scope of the examination or implementation. They should review with the outside auditors the officers' expense accounts. They should meet also with the company's financial officer and internal auditor to review the adequacy of the internal audit program; also to discuss the appointment of the independent auditor and basis for fees.

The number of meetings of the audit committee depends on the problems that develop. There should be a meeting of the committee to review the management letter discussing internal controls and the scope of the audit for the coming year and the per diem fees and estimated costs. There should be a meeting upon completion of the audit to review the findings and proposed certification. They should meet with the auditors where any unresolved differences with management exist. There will be meetings to discuss with the outside auditors any investigation which is to be made by them.

Much has been written about the audit committee in recent years. The CEO should recognize the usefulness of such a group. The appointment of such a committee depends on the size and complexity of the company. Appendixes C, D, and E contain additional information regarding audit committees. In Appendix F reference is made to several excellent discussions of the responsibilities and operation of audit committees.

SUMMARY

The complexity of business, the increase in government and stock exchange regulations, and the many legal actions against public corporations, their officers and directors, have emphasized the importance of proper auditing, both internal and external. The CEO is responsible for the financial statements of the company. It is the responsibility of the auditing function to assure the CEO, the stockholders, government regulatory agencies, and all other users of the correctness of the financial statements.

APPENDIX A

Summary of the scope of internal audit at The Goodyear Tire & Rubber Co. (1968):

1. Corporate Home Office

a. Financial audits: Corporate general ledger accounts are examined for accuracy, appropriate supporting detail, verification of underlying assets, etc.

b. Functional audits: The operations of various departments are audited and, where applicable, their financial records are verified to the general ledger. The principal functions audited are·

Purchasing
Receiving
Accounts Payable
Traffic Dept. (claims)
Payroll (hourly and salary)
Billing
Accounts Receivable
Finished Stock Controls
Hospitalization Insurance

Workmen's Compensation Dept.
Returned Goods
Salvage, Scrap and Surplus
    Equipment
Employee Organizations
    (company-sponsored)
Hospital
Garage Operations (automobile
    pool and employee parking)
Airplane Operations
    (executive fleet)

2. Factory Accounting (Principally Cost Accounting and Property Records)

The principal areas covered, which applies to all plant locations, are:

a. Materials and Supplies—Inventory and Control Accounts.

b. Factory Ledger Accounts, which control raw materials, stores, work in process, distribution of overheads, etc.

c. New Work Orders, which control construction work in progress.

d. Property Accounts.

3. Field Operations (Wholesale and Retail Distribution and Marketing)

a. Warehouses, company-operated and public:

Cash
Hourly Payroll
Receiving
Stock Records

Physical Inventory
Shipping Documents and Procedures
Security

b. Retail Stores:

Cash
Billing
Accounts Receivable
Credit Extension and
    Collection Activity

Stock Records
Physical Inventory
Security
Housekeeping

c.   Field Accounting Offices (Zone Accounting):
These are highly mechanized regional accounting offices servicing both retail store and wholesale operations.

Cash	Consigned Merchandise
Billing	Controls
Accounts Receivable	Accounting Summary Controls
Credit Extension and	Internal Control Over
Collection Procedures	Documents
Accounts Payable	Assignment of Functions

d.   Employee Defalcations:
Auditors investigate the circumstances, develop evidence and report their findings.

e.   Acquisition from and sale to independent dealers of retail stores. Field Auditors supervise consummation of these transactions in cooperation with field management.

4. Subsidiary Companies

All domestic subsidiary companies except Kelly are audited by Akron staff personnel. The programs encompass the general scope of accounts and functions as outlined in Items 1, 2, and 3 above.

5.   Suppliers' Charges under Contracts (Time and Material or Cost Type) and Suppliers' Claims under Termination of Government Contracts

All payments to these vendors are audited as appropriate to determine correctness and conformity to contract.

APPENDIX B

Proposed Scope of an Examination of Financial Statements

To the Audit Committee of the Board of
Directors of *Mixon International, Inc.**

We are pleased to submit this proposal of the scope of our examination of the consolidated financial statements of *Mixon International, Inc.* and subsidiaries for the year ending December 31, 1973. Our ex-

---

* *Mixon International, Inc.,* is a pseudonym for a large U.S. corporation.

amination will be made in accordance with generally accepted auditing standards, and accordingly will include such tests of the accounting records and such other auditing procedures as we consider necessary to enable us to express an opinion on the consolidated financial statements of the Company as well as the financial statements of certain subsidiary companies which, for various reasons, are to be examined and reported upon individually.

As in prior years, our examination will be based on selected test checks of recorded transactions. The primary purpose of these checks is to test procedures and systems of internal control, rather than the detection of irregularities. The Company's principal reliance for the detection of irregularities will necessarily be placed upon internal audit and control measures, since the extent of the activities and the large volume of transactions make it impracticable to have a detailed audit of the transactions made by us. Any irregularities which might come to our attention during the course of the examination will, of course, be reported to you.

This engagement will be under the direction of our New York office and will utilize the resources of our personnel and offices throughout the world.

The scope of our audit of domestic operations will include substantial work within each of the Company's major lines of business and the corporate headquarters and computer center, as set forth in the attached schedule of domestic audit coverage. Our charges for this work will be made at our regular per diem rates, which we now estimate will approximate $285,000, plus out-of-pocket expenses. This estimate does not contemplate acquisitions or possible legal requirements for additional work, such as special reports for the Cost of Living Council or other regulatory agencies. This estimate reflects extensive participation by the internal audit group. This participation is already in the planning and coordinating stages.

As in the past, separate arrangements are being made for the examinations of the financial statements of Canadian and overseas subsidiaries, as set forth in the attached schedule. Our estimated charges for the 1973 Canadian and overseas audits are approximately $185,-000, plus out-of-pocket expenses. The requirements and related scopes of all Canadian and overseas audits are currently being reviewed by our New York office.

At your convenience, we shall be pleased to answer any questions you may have relating to the matters contained herein.

Mixon International, Inc.

DOMESTIC AUDIT COVERAGE

	Year of Last Visit		1973		
	Limited Review	Full Audit	Limited Review	Full Audit	Internal Auditors Participation
Corporate Headquarters and Computer Center	—	72	—	X	X
Chemical and Allied Products Co.:					
Jamison Mfg. Division					
Headquarters	—	72	—	X	X
Columbus Plant	72	—	—	X	X
Gainesville Plant	72	—	X	—	X
Huntsville Plant	—	72	X	—	X
New Brunswick Plant	72	—	X	—	X
Waco Plant	70	—	X	—	X
Dyestuffs Division	72	—	X	—	X
Packaging Division	72	—	X	—	X
Distribution Division	—	72	—	X	X
Printing Ink Division	72	—	—	—	—
Kaolin Mining Division	71	—	—	—	—
Plumbing and Hardware Company:					
Industrial Division					
Headquarters	—	72	—	X	X
Distribution Operations	—	72	—	X	X
Manufacturing Operations					
Bonnerville	68	—	X	—	X
Canton	—	—	X	—	—
Cincinnati	70	—	—	—	—
Kutztown	72	—	—	—	—
Monks Corner	69	—	X	—	X
Pittsburgh	71	—	—	—	—
San Diego	68	—	—	—	—
Seattle	71	—	—	—	—
Syracuse	72	—	—	—	—
Vernon	—	72	X	—	X
Consumer Products Division					
Burns Hardware	72	—	—	—	—
Engineered Products	69	—	—	—	—
Albany Supply	69	—	—	—	—
Allen Gordon	71	—	—	—	—
Plumbing Products	68	—	X	—	—
Smythes Consolidated Industries, Inc.	72	—	—	—	—
Paul Plumbing	68	—	X	—	X
Biddle & Battle	—	72	—	X	—

Mixon International, Inc. (continued)

FULL AUDITS OF CANADIAN AND OVERSEAS OPERATIONS*

	1972	1973
Mixon Chemicals, S.A.	X	X
Mixon Chemicals, Ltd.	X	X
Mixon Chemicals, A.B.	X	X
Mixon Industries, S.A.	X	X
Hunt, S.A. (Consolidated)	X	X
Mixon Industries, Ltd.	†	†
Smythes Subsidiaries		
Smythes Co. Pty., Ltd.	X	X
Smythes Supply, Ltd. (New Zealand)	†	†
Smythes Supply, Ltd. (England)	X	X
Smythes Co., N.V.	X	X
Smythes Co., Canada, Ltd.	X	X
Smythes Supply, A.B.	X	‡
Smythes Supply, A.G.	X	X
Schneider GmbH	X	X
Salas, S.A.	X	X
Burns Hardware		
Brussels Branch	X	X
Burns International, S.A.	X	X
Mixon International of Japan	X	X
Mixon of Canada Limited	X	X

* Most of these audits are required by local statutes or because of minority interests in some of the companies.
† Audited by other public accounting firm.
‡ Inactive operation.

APPENDIX C

Audit Committee Responsibilities*

1. To provide the instrumentality for direct contact between an independent committee of Directors and the independent accountants for discussing any subject either group considers appropriate.
2. To ascertain whether the independent accountants have any recommendations for the Directors as distinguished from recommendations which they consider are more appropriately made to the management.
3. To review and agree on the scope of the independent accountants audit activity.
4. To be apprised by the independent accountants of the nature and adequacy of the company's basic accounting system and methods.
5. To receive each year, together with the Chairman of the Board and the principal accounting officer, the independent account-

* Source: A large U.S. corporation.

ant's annual internal control letter (sometimes referred to as "Management Letter") and any recommendations made by it to the management in regard to accounting procedures and policies and to follow up as necessary on subsequent management action on any such recommendations.

6. To meet privately with the principal accounting officer of the Corporation whenever the Committee so wishes.

7. To be apprised by the independent accountants of the nature, if any, and effectiveness of the Company's internal audit activities.

8. To recommend to the Board the selection of the independent accountant for the ensuing year.

9. To review the financial statements which are the subject of the independent accountant's certification (preferably in advance of certification, but if this is not feasible without delaying issuance of the report, such review would occur thereafter).

10. With respect to accounting policies and/or accounting practices pursuant to APB 22, the Committee will periodically identify such items applicable to the Company, determine whether or not they will be reported to the stockholders, and if so in what format; but it will not involve itself in the determination of such Accounting Policies or Accounting Practices unless there is a major area of disagreement between the management and the auditors in which event the Committee will resolve the issue. Both the management and the auditors would be requested to advise the Committee of any such disagreement.

11. To request the auditors to advise it with respect to any unusual expense reimbursements to the officers.

12. To instruct the auditors to communicate directly with the Committee on any matter which, in their judgment, the auditors have not satisfactorily resolved with the management.

13. To make a report of its activities to the full Board at least once a year and to report at any meeting of the Board when the Committee feels it has timely and significant information.

APPENDIX D

Some Questions for the Auditors*

Listed below are some of the many questions which might be asked by members of the audit committee:

* Source: *The Audit Committee*; a handbook published by McDonald, Currie & Co. and Coopers & Lybrand; p. 11.

Are there any matters which you wish to bring to our attention?

Does your firm audit the accounts of all the subsidiaries?

What steps did you take regarding the accounts of subsidiaries not audited by you?

Are all divisions and branches of the company visited by you in the year or do you rotate your visits year by year?

To what extent have you relied upon the work carried out by the Internal Audit Department?

Did you receive full cooperation from officials of the company?

Were there any deviations from the requirements of the company's letters patent, bylaws, and directors' resolutions?

Did you become aware of any conflicts of interest with regard to directors, officers, or other employees?

Have covenants given to lenders been complied with?

Are there any changes in the methods of accounting for: inventories; depreciation; goodwill; deferred expenses; deferred income?

Have all significant commitments and contingent liabilities been noted on the financial statements?

Does the method of taking up income generally conform to that of the industry? This is a loaded question, since practices differ among industries such as insurance, real estate, contracting, and mining.

The types of possible questions are of course infinite but will generally concern the scope of the audit; the financial statements; and the system of internal control.

APPENDIX E

Agenda of First Audit Committee Meeting, Atlantic, Inc.*

1. Review extent of services performed for Atlantic, Inc. by the auditor.
   a. Certification of year-end statements.
   b. Other

---

* Atlantic, Inc., is a pseudonym for a large U.S. corporation.

2. Review the auditor's billing to Atlantic, Inc. for 1971 and 1972 for:

   a. Certification of year-end statements.

   b. Other.

3. Review extent of audit adjustments for year ending December 1971 and 1972.

4. Examine adequacy of Atlantic, Inc.'s basic accounting system and methods.

5. Ask the auditor's views regarding the efficiency of the company's accounting operation (as contrasted to the reliability of the financial statements produced from it).

6. Review scope of audit for 1973.

7. Review capital expenditure control procedures.

8. Verify adequacy of computer system controls.

9. Review Atlantic, Inc.'s internal audit activity.

10. Review the auditor's internal control letter dated 1/31/73.

11. Review Woodward's internal control comments of May 22, 1973, regarding H. & R., Inc.

12. Review recent Accounting Principles Board rulings and impending Financial Accounting Standards Board policy changes which might have a significant effect on Atlantic, Inc.

13. Review *APB Ruling #22* for its future effects, if any, on Atlantic, Inc.

14. Ascertain extent to which Atlantic, Inc. accounting is manualized.

15. Discuss time of appointment of independent accountants for 1974 (review this in relationship to stockholder action thereon).

16. Review any other matters relating to the committee assigned responsibility from the Board.

APPENDIX F

Auditing Bibliography

New York Stock Exchange, Inc.; *Recommendations and Comments on Financial Reporting to Shareholders and Related Matters.*

The Audit Committee and the Board of Directors; Arthur Andersen & Co.; 1972.

The Audit Committee; McDonald, Currie & Co.; Coopers & Lybrand.

American Institute of Certified Public Accountants; A *Statement on Audit Committees of Boards of Directors*; 1967.

Corporations and Their Outside Auditors; Conference Board Report No. 544; 1972.

Mautz, R. K.; and Neumann, F. L.; "The Effective Corporate Audit Committee"; *Harvard Business Review*; November–December 1970.

PART IV-F

International Business

INTERNATIONALIZATION OF BUSINESS MANAGEMENT: ITS POSSIBILITIES AND PROBLEMS

by Yoshizo Ikeda
President, Mitsui & Co., Ltd.

INTRODUCTION—ENVIRONMENTAL CHANGES AFFECTING BUSINESS MANAGEMENTS

DEFINING MANAGEMENT as "an entity embodying systematic leadership to cope with changing circumstances," I must first deal with my perception of those environmental changes which affect business managements.

The capitalist economy, the very system whose maturity and progress we strive for, has faced many crises since the Industrial Revolution, the period during which capitalism was firmly established; but thanks to the efforts of the disciples of capitalism, each crisis has been overcome. What we must do now is to perceive distinctly the nature of current change with a cool and dispassionate historical perspective and a strong faith in the possibility of an ideal society for humanity; and we must grope for appropriate measures to advance this ideal.

The nature of current change, conceived of in terms consistent with modern economic theory, can be expressed under the headings of the following four problems with which we are confronted. And, when we consider how closely these problems are interrelated, we shall clearly perceive why this age is termed an era of crisis.

International Cooperation

The first problem is the disturbance in the systems for international cooperation. These systems, with The International Monetary Fund (IMF) and The General Agreement on Tariffs and Trade (GATT) as their main axes, have supported the phenomenal economic growth that has taken place since the end of World War II. However, they are now exposed to very severe stresses owing to a shift in the balance of power among the advanced industrial countries and to the emergence of the problem as to how to adjust the interests of developing countries with those of the industrial countries.

However, it must be pointed out that, rather paradoxically, this problem, which suggests the resurgence of nationalism, has been caused by the success rather than the failure of international cooperation. To wit, existing systems of international cooperation in their advanced stages, have established a structure of interdependence; in turn, this has given rise to an "allergic" reaction against interdependence. One consequence is that a small "ripple" of nationalism in one country, or in one region, can spread by way of a chain reaction all over the world.

We, of course, are convinced that only international cooperation can lead mankind toward peace and stability; but it seems probable that, from now on, most countries will try to formulate their own international policies by groping concurrently for both independence and cooperation until a reasonable degree of interdependence is established.

Economic Growth

The second problem is the revelation of "blights" caused by economic growth. As human vision becomes narrower in proportion to the speed at which a man travels, speedy economic growth has left many unattended areas of concern. For example, we are faced with environmental destruction, spiralling inflation, resource and energy problems, and the spiritual devastation accompanying materialistic civilization. Never before has the question "opulence for what?" been asked with such insistence.

Equitable Distribution

Third, there is the intensifying problem of "equitable distribution" of wealth. With economic growth, democratic equality has been established as a social value, but, on the other hand, as inflation has progressed, the disparity in distribution between owners of real assets, such as land or securities, and those without them has become wider. This has stimulated greater concern among both the haves and the have-nots in regard to distribution.

As it has become evident that economic growth will be restricted by factors such as resources and environment, "the baking of a bigger pie," which hitherto was thought to be the best solution for the distribution problem, is fast becoming inoperative.

Thus, the distribution problem is expected to assume greater importance hereafter. From another point of view, it is another version of the developed versus developing nations problem.

Large-Scale Enterprise

Fourth, there is the problem of justifying the operations of big enterprises. In the 1950s and 1960s, big enterprises claimed that, despite the tendency toward oligopoly, they were the ones who bore the burden of economic progress by fierce competition based on technological as well as managerial innovations. By way of verifying their assertion, they sought to appease the people's antipathy toward big enterprise. But in recent years, the position of big enterprises has been questioned in the light of factors such as: (1) the stagnation in economic growth which some believe had been promoted by big enterprise; (2) the problem of administered prices in the face of spiralling inflation; (3) fewer achievements in technological progress; and (4) labor's growing dissatisfaction with the organized and standardized work of big enterprise.

Obviously, international and national measures should be meticulously formulated to cope with these four problems of modern capitalistic economy. But, I believe that it is of greater importance for the managements of enterprises to consider measures on their own initiative. That enterprises played the major role in promoting postwar economic growth is the very reason why the managements of enterprises should seek to function innovatively and effectively in the solution of the contemporary crisis.

Now is the time for us to remember that the ideal of "calling" that is involved in professionalism implies that we should cherish diligence, progressiveness, fortitude, frugality, and saving—all of which formed the guiding spirit in the early stage of capitalism. We should strive to reconstruct the spirit of enterprise to challenge contemporary problems through "promotion of new projects," "fulfillment of corporate responsibilities toward society," and "renovation of intraenterprise systems."

Being concerned with social issues, and searching for industrial solutions to contemporary problems should underly the philosophy of business management today.

INTERNATIONALIZATION OF BUSINESS MANAGEMENT AND ATTENDANT PROBLEMS

With the foregoing changes in the environment of the corporation in mind, let us now proceed to our main subject, internationalization of business management.

Problems in International Business Activities

International business activities of the so-called multinational corporations are being subjected to various criticisms. These criticisms may be classified largely into three categories. One is the criticism heard in the home country against the adverse effect that such activities may have on the balance of payments and job opportunities at home. Another is the criticism raised in the host country due to apprehensions over economic domination, misgivings about repatriation of proceeds, and conflict with domestic economic policy and business management practices. Third, from an international angle, critics point out the danger of monetary instability being created by short-term capital movements, and warn against international monopoly and labor problems. Each of these criticisms touches on crucial issues. The investigations of the actual situation now being conducted by the United Nations, OECD, and other international bodies deserve attention.

The Positive Role of International Business Activities

Notwithstanding these criticisms, I must stress the positive role that can be played by multinational business activities. In addition to the benefits to be gained by the enterprise involved, such as the diversification of the sources of funds and labor, and dispersion of business risks, there are general positive benefits deriving from such business activities, in that they ensure efficient distribution of resources and help disseminate and exchange new technology throughout the world. For the host country, global business activities contribute to increasing job opportunities and enhancing living standards; for the home country, they promote export and, through repatriation of proceeds, improve the balance of payments.

In short, multinational corporations have many-sided roles to play. Basically, they can serve as standard-bearers of globalism in the true sense, realizing profits across national borders. I am convinced that sound international business activities can, eventually, induce solidarity among the world's nations, not only in the economic arena but in political and cultural fields as well.

INTERNATIONALIZATION OF JAPANESE BUSINESS MANAGEMENT

If the balance of private overseas investment is any indication of the degree of internationalization of Japanese enterprise, one may say that the tendency toward internationalization has increased markedly since the beginning of the 1970s. Specifically, these investments, which had stood at $6,800 million on March 31, 1973, exceeded $10,000 million on March 31, 1974. The last figure ranks Japanese enterprises side by side with West German ones, following those of the U.S. and Britain.

Mitsui, by March 31, 1974, had invested abroad a total of $660 million, the largest overseas investment made by any Japanese corporation.

Problems

As is customary with any undertaking involving a huge quantity, quality always comes into question. The enormous growth of overseas investment by Japanese enterprises has made them keenly aware of the difficulty of international business activities.

The first and foremost problem encountered by Japanese enterprises in their internationalization efforts concerns the culture gap. Being an insular nation which has only a short history as a member of the international community of nations, the Japanese find it extremely difficult to carry on international business management, overcoming the differences in language, customs, and mores.

A second problem is the immaturity of management resources.

Overseas advancement of Japanese enterprises has been said to feature low technical standards and small-scale operations, and to be directed toward developing countries. One reason for this can be said to be the lack of management resources, ranging from knowledge of, and experience in business management and operation to qualified personnel, adequate funds, information, and technology.

A third problem is the lack of comprehensive planning. Overseas investments by Japanese enterprises gained momentum since the beginning of the 1970s owing mainly to uneasiness over the export price competition triggered by the upward revaluation of the yen and the growing interest in resource development. As more and more Japanese companies advanced abroad, they tended to converge in certain chosen areas and to be engaged in limited lines of business, without giving much thought to long-term objectives or profitability, or to comprehensive management strategy.

We must seriously search our souls in regard to the stated problems in planning for future business activities abroad. One indication of this soul-searching is the "Guidelines for Investment Activities in Developing Countries" published jointly by Japan's five leading economic organizations in June 1973.

Possibilities

In spite of such shortcomings, however, Japanese business activities abroad have displayed merits worth noting.

Whereas the "U.S.-type" overseas investment has been predicated upon the drive of big corporations for a larger share of the world market, the Japanese counterpart has aimed at transplanting labor-intensive industries into developing countries, thereby contributing to a reorganization of trade between the developed and developing countries, and has been compatible with the interests of host countries in that Japanese parent firms have merely sought a minority ownership in overseas subsidiaries. In this respect, some economists give the Japanese investment activities abroad high marks. Apart from such macroeconomic evaluation, I believe there is much room for Japanese enterprise to contribute to international economic activities, giving full play to what is known as the Japanese system of business management. For instance, the "circular system" of decision-making (in which drafts are circulated among executives for approval) and the seniority rule and life employment system are plus factors in that they enhance the employee's sense of participation in management. Successful internationalization of Japanese corporations depends on how far this Japanese-style management system can be reconciled with functionalism which stresses efficiency and justice.*

In conducting their business, Mitsui's overseas offices endeavor to conform to local laws and regulations as well as commercial practices. Also, in an effort to tighten relations with local communities, we try to incorporate our overseas offices under local laws, so that powers and responsibilities may be decentralized. In parallel with this assimilation effort, we constantly strive for further refinement of the Japanese-style management system.

I earnestly hope that Mitsui will grow into an international affiliation of locally incorporated firms, and that some day the company's officers and executives of different nationalities will sit together at the conference table to discuss Mitsui's overall business policies.

Role of the General Trading Firm

Let me now touch on the role that has been and is expected to be played by a general trading firm like Mitsui in the internationalization of Japanese business management.

Internationalization of Japanese business management cannot be discussed, it is said, without discussing the activities of general trading firms. Indeed, they have played a significant role in this field. This is obvious from the fact that the 10 leading trading firms account for more than 20 percent of the country's total overseas investments. But what is more important is the function of these firms. With their long overseas experience, great market development capabilities, and extensive information networks, all built up through their worldwide trading activities over the years, they have been called upon to play the function of organizers for overseas advances of other Japanese corporations which do not have a sufficient accumulation of management resources.

More specifically, many overseas undertakings have taken the form of joint ventures between general trading firms and manufacturers. In this way, the manufacturer has been able to minimize his risk in operating in faraway foreign lands beyond the reach of his own government's power, while the general trading firm has been able to carry

---

* [Ed. Note: See the chapter by Michael Yoshino, "Decision-Making in Large Japanese Corporations."]

on direct overseas production and sales as a new trend in international business activities.

In the years ahead, too, general trading firms are expected to play major roles in the internationalization of Japanese business management. In doing so, I believe the managements of general trading firms should place the greatest emphasis on information and technical capabilities.

In predicting and meeting the rapid changes in the world situation, particularly in the business climate, information is essential. Again, in keeping up with the advances in industrial technology, technical capabilities are indispensable. To meet the former needs, we have a Mitsui Global On-line System which consists of communication lines with a total length of 380,000 kilometers and large-size computers linked to them, to gather, transmit, receive, and process all sorts of information. To keep ourselves abreast of the latest technological developments, we have competent engineers who are specialists in their respective fields.

QUALIFICATIONS FOR INTERNATIONAL BUSINESS MANAGERS

Let me sum up my discussion by presenting my views on the qualifications for the manager of a world enterprise.

Whether or not the corporation involved operates on an international scale, the first and foremost requirement for a business manager is, I believe, that he have a management philosophy of his own. I do not mean that he should follow a simple established doctrine. It may be more appropriate to call it a process of sincere thinking. Through such a process, it is of crucial importance to consider seriously the objective of corporate activities and the motivation of employees. I have set myself the task of studying the possibility of reorienting corporate activity from the present material production to "spiritual production." If the values we have sought heretofore through modernization are prosperity, peace, and freedom, then the values we should strive for henceforth are—in addition to these three—quality of life, social justice, and the common weal. A corporation is no longer allowed to remain content with simply creating material desires in the consumer and supplying goods or services to satisfy them. It should go a step further and achieve harmony between spiritual production and material production.

A second requisite is the accumulation of international experience. "International experience" as used here does not mean simply many years of living abroad. It means a broadened mind and perspective that enables one to put oneself in the position of someone with a vastly different cultural and social background; in short it means empathy. Without acquiring such an attitude, it would be impossible to carry on productive international communication, no matter how much one excels in linguistic ability.

A third qualification is specialized knowledge. This depends, to an extent, upon on-the-job training, but to a greater extent, upon one's will and effort to improve oneself. Time and again, I have personally experienced the great convincing power of a man who is sure of his knowledge and principles.

CONCLUDING REMARKS

International business management, admittedly, is no easy task. But I firmly believe that it is a task well worth devoting all one's energies to.

I enjoy oil painting in my leisure. And I feel matchless pleasure in the mental strain I experience as I face the canvas which signifies limitless possibilities and put all my creative power into it. Business management, in my opinion, does not differ in essence from the world of artistic expression—both afford one an opportunity to give full play to one's intellectual creativity on a high plane.

STRUCTURING OWNERSHIP AND FINANCIAL RELATIONSHIPS IN THE INTERNATIONAL EFFORT

by Tom Lilley
Former Director, Export-Import Bank

STRUCTURING any kind of international operation is not an activity that fits into neat patterns and pigeonholes. Structure depends on the kind of business and kind of country—the ownership of what business, where. The variations can be infinite.

If one had to pick a general approach, it might be along these lines:

1. Don't expect to carry out a single global program in world markets.
2. Instead, start with a country or group of countries. Determine if you want to try to be in that market. If so, what is likely to be the most profitable way to do so in the short and in the long run?
3. Ownership patterns and financial relationships will simply be a part of this process of determining what to do, where, and how.
4. For most industries, expect significant variations between countries—and, for multiproduct companies, variations for different product lines.

In discussing some of the more frequent variations in ownership and financing patterns, I shall: (1) Outline some of the patterns used in bringing a manufactured product into a new market (typically a prospering but still developing nation); (2) consider variations for different types of businesses—service businesses, franchised products, extractive industries; and (3) then consider variations among nations, including both the very poor and the well-to-do developed nations.

MINIMUM INVESTMENT PATTERNS

First, let's take a look at a few relatively easy ways to enter a new market, which occasionally are available for some industries in some countries. These patterns have the decided attraction of involving little money and usually less initial management effort than alternatives. But they are available if—and only if—competition and host government policy make such patterns possible.

Zero Investment Approach: Distributor—Dealer

By most standards, the easiest way to enter a market is to pick one or a few local dealers or distributors to handle your business there. It is a zero-ownership, zero-investment approach (unless consignment stocks are involved). If competitive and governmental circumstances make this approach possible, you may have a chance for a sizeable profit on a near-zero investment. And later the arrangement may evolve into dealer assembly and/or dealer procurement of local components.

You may lose out, of course, to a competitor who puts more direct effort or money into reaching the market. And—a *warning*—once you have appointed distributors, you may be locked in and be faced with a difficult "buy out" problem, if you want to change your operating pattern at some later date.

Zero Investment Approach: Licensing, Royalties, Sale of Know-How

On occasion, licensing, royalty arrangements, or sale of know-how to a local existing company can be useful and desirable, if your company is short of cash or finds a high profit offer for certain products or processes in certain countries. It is an approach that promises maximum use of local know-how with little or no capital at risk.

The penalties of being wrong, however, can be severe. If the local licensee falls down on the job, now or later, it may not be easy to negotiate a divorce; or you may then want to enter the market directly and be blocked. In a word, there is a risk of making a short-run gain at the expense of control over the long-run future.

Low Investment Approach

The next step up from a zero-investment approach is a "start off easy" investment of your own—for example, a sales company (with some investment in inventory of finished goods and/or parts) or a simple assembly operation.

If feasible at all, this may be a convenient first step, a good "jumping off place" for future expansion of activities. You can often—not always—obtain 100 percent ownership or at least control with little investment and be in a position to expand further, when circumstances warrant. Compared to zero-investment, this approach is likely to call for more negotiating time, more money, and more management effort. It may or may not yield a better initial profit, but it probably will give you more flexibility and control over your future.

MAJOR INVESTMENTS

At some stage of development, any of the "minimum investment" approaches we have discussed may not be enough. The host government, particularly in larger developing nations, may press for large-scale industrialization. Or moves by local or international competitors may make it essential to make a major new investment in a country, involving sizeable manufacturing facilities and the build-up of a complete local corporate organization. Or your company may make such a move on its own initiative to gain a competitive advantage and maximize long-run profits. In any event, the structuring of such a new investment requires a series of decisions on ownership and financial relationships. I shall summarize some observations about ownership and suggest some of the relationship issues which should be considered before negotiations for a major investment are completed.

Some Points concerning Ownership

Regardless of the pros and cons of different percentages of ownership from the outside investor's point of view, it must be recognized that in many developing countries 100 percent ownership, and at times even control by outside investors is not possible. Plenty of important exceptions exist, but 100 percent ownership is not the "wave of the future." In some cases, nations insist on local private partners or, in others, government partners (through national development banks or other kinds of government agencies). In yet other cases, existing competition may make 100 percent ownership difficult or impossible.

Subject to these overriding facts of life, let's consider some points which might be considered in making ownership decisions:

1. In many instances, it is worthwhile to consider buying into or buying out an existing company, as an alternative to a totally new investment on your own. No generalization can cover all the circumstances involved, but this possibility should be on one's checklist of choices to be considered. In spite of the obvious disadvantages likely to be encountered, this approach may be, in a few cases, the only way to invest in a country and, in other cases, the least painful way.

2. Typically, it seems worthwhile to seek at least control of a major new investment in a country—control of key decisions "here and now," and key decisions for the future. It is important for your staff to get legal advice on the consequences, in the country involved, of ownership of 51 percent or 76 percent or other specific percentages of ownership. In some countries, ownerships of less than 50 percent will suffice for your needs; in others, 51 percent will do; and in yet others, 76 percent or some other percentage may give the owner important additional rights.

3. In some cases, 100 percent ownership is possible and desirable; 100 percent or near 100 percent ownership is especially important for a subsidiary which will sell to or buy from subsidiaries in a number of other countries. Otherwise, there are potential conflicts of interest with minority shareholders in making decisions that are in the interest of the whole network of companies. Under such circumstances, even the wisdom of Solomon may not avoid questions and clashes about intercompany prices, contractual relationships, et al.

4. In negotiations about ownership and financial arrangements, use the advice *both* of informed citizens of the host country and men from your own headquarters. The local citizens have an essential input regarding local conditions; but, on some sensitive issues, would and should represent the interests of their country rather than your company. Your own men know your interests but may be uninformed or naive on some local issues. Highly desirable is a dialogue and, one should hope, genuine communication and understanding on both sides.

Some Points to Be Considered in Negotiations

In negotiating with governments and/or local partners, some of the points to be considered before a deal is concluded include the following:

1. First, on technical matters: Decisions on such issues as plant location, the extent of local make and local buy content versus import content (both now and for several years ahead), and the question of who will have the right to decide which kinds of components are to be sourced locally and which are to be imported.

2. Procurement and marketing decisions, including approaches to pricing, particularly if the local partners or their associates have a stake in local component manufacture or in distribution.

3. The mix of management personnel between local versus imported people, during both the construction and break-in period, and guidelines for the longer term.

4. The financing plan, including the proportions of debt and equity. (Typically a high debt/equity ratio is likely to be desirable; and consideration should be given to some company investment in the form of subordinated debt instead of equity.)

5. Plans related to future cash flows from subsidiary to parent, covering such variables as repayment of local versus external debt, subordinated debt, and dividends; and, in a related area, provisions for controls and auditing.

6. Management fees, technical, and other fees to be paid by subsidiary to parent. (Although the maximizing of fees is usually desirable, such fees must make sense when examined by local partners or by local government authorities.)

One final suggestion: Be willing, if the going gets tough, to say "No" in negotiating a deal on a major new international investment. You do need real bargaining power in negotiations with local partners or governments. And, unless circumstances are most unusual, you do *not* have to be in business everywhere (in spite of enthusiasms of local nationals and your own international organization). You may find it better to have significant ownership of some profitable companies in not unfriendly countries, rather than a scattered stake throughout the world.

VARIATIONS IN TYPES OF INDUSTRIES

So far, we have talked about an unspecified manufactured product and problems associating with bringing such a product into a developing-country market. Clearly, there is a great variety in products and combinations of products. I shall cite just a few extreme variations, to illustrate how such variations may affect ownership and financing patterns.

Service- and Franchise-Type Industries

At one extreme, are the service industries: the sale of engineering services or various other kinds of consulting services. Large-scale investments in brick and mortar are simply not a part of such businesses. In a few of the larger, more sophisticated developing countries, build-up of a local organization or affiliation with an existing one may be desirable. But in the typical case, services are exported to a developing country, without major investment implications.

Another variation in type of product is, for example, cola or other soft drink bottling. In such a case, where the parent company has a pattern in its home market of franchising independent local bottlers, it can follow a similar pattern overseas. Ownership of the overseas bottler would typically be zero or near-zero and the contractual relationships could be modelled, with variations, on the home market pattern. Either at home or overseas, there is a neatness about this type of company-to-franchise-holder relationship.

The typical pattern for financing hotels represents another variation. The hotel chain usually obtains a management contract and perhaps some ownership, but the major capital investment typically comes from other sources, inside and outside the host country. The hotel chain sells its services to the local hotel and often "puts the deal together," using whatever sources of capital it can find.

In each of these special cases, ownership by a parent company is usually not a primary issue. The nature of the payments for services and goods and the contractual relationships involved follow in considerable measure the structure developed in the United States and Europe. Certainly, competition in these industries can be intense, and negotiations associated with new ventures in new markets equally intense. But the pattern of financial relationships usually is parallel to that used in home markets, which in turn was dictated by the nature of the product or service itself.

Other Extreme: Extractive Industries

At the other extreme, away from service-type industries, one could cite the extractive industries, such as mining and petroleum. In these industries, involving removal of natural resources from one country for sale in world markets, the amounts of capital involved typically are large, the payout period long, and the political sensitivities very real. Clearly, negotiations for agreements before going in, in as explicit terms as possible, are even more important than for other products—including agreements as to who will pay whom what over the period of amortization of investment, who will have first claim on hard currency proceeds of sale of the products, and how disputes will be adjudicated.

One aspect is worth a comment: Most people would agree that, it is better, where possible, to have a multinational enterprise, through which the outside investment in the host nation is made by parties from several different countries. For example, in contrast to a U.S.-owned international investment, a venture having ownership and loan capital from several sources—such as the United States, Europe, and Japan—is likely to be less sensitive politically and probably advantageous in the long pull.

One can only add that regardless of the financial structures or understandings, history suggests that there are no foolproof answers to all the problems inherent in extractive ventures.

VARIATIONS AMONG NATIONS

The pattern of international investments must adapt to extreme variations among different nations as well as extreme variations in types of industries. I shall highlight briefly some of the kinds of variations among developing nations, and then suggest some of the ways the sophisticated developed nations differ from the less developed countries.

Variations among "LDCs"

Well over 100 nations are classified as Less Developed Countries—LDCs—simply for lack of a better "catch-all" phrase. These nations certainly differ among themselves in every conceivable way, including, but not limited to:

—Historical background, and the sense of values related to that history—for example, India as compared to Peru, or both of them compared to some of the newer African nations.
—Political systems, which run the spectrum from military governments, to one-party rule of the left and center, to governments elected from among multiple parties.
—Size, which runs from 600 million people in India to a couple of million in some of the African countries, or even less, as in the case of some of the Carribbean countries.
—Wealth, in terms of per capita income and rate of economic growth, varying, for example, from a relatively sophisticated Mexican economy to nations barely sustained by a one-cash-crop agricultural economy.
—Attitudes toward outside investment, varying, in the early 1970s, from the welcoming attitude of a Brazil or Iran to attitudes of downright hostility.

And some of these factors can change radically, between one year, or one decade, and the next in a single country. No purpose can be served here by trying to categorize the nations of the earth. Let it only be said that in determining which markets to enter, and how to go about negotiating ownership and other financial arrangements, staff time should be spent on becoming acquainted with the history, politics, and attitudes of different nations as well as their statistics. At some point in the selection and negotiation process, one should seek to absorb wisdom in these matters from many sources, including, for example, knowledgeable insiders, other multinational companies which have had experience in the countries involved, and U.S.-based analysts, including your own.

The communist-bloc countries represent a special case, where new patterns are just emerging and background knowledge as well as statistics are often not readily available. Moreover, in these countries, new kinds of questions became crucial. For example, what is the concept of "ownership" under the commercial codes of different countries? What kind of sale-of-know-how deals can be arranged? What are your legal rights if your know-how is transferred to a third partner in another country? Clearly, before financial relationships are negotiated in these countries, specialized briefing from private and governmental sources is needed, in order to determine for your industry or product, how practices in different bloc countries differ from each other and from the patterns used in the Western world.

Variations for Developed Nations

Up to this point, we have concentrated on approaches to investment in the LDCs. For most international companies, however, the dollar value of their investment is substantially larger in the developed nations of Europe, Canada and, on occasion, Japan than in the LDCs. Some of the ways in which developed "rich-country" investment may differ from investment in the LDC areas are:

1. For most products, a viable industry already exists in the developed nations to a far greater degree than in the LDCs. A company exploring new markets typically will find tough competitors either locally-controlled or controlled by other multinational companies. Of necessity, the newcomer must give serious consideration to the possibility of "buying into" or "buying out" an existing company, as well as the possibility of starting up a new enterprise. How to do it? In many of the developed countries, the choices available and the kinds of staff work needed are very similar to those met in seeking to enter a new market or increasing one's share in a market in the United States. Such melding of points-of-view and practices may become even greater if the trend continues for direct investment in the United States by Europeans, Japanese, and others—the so-called direct "reverse investment" flow.

2. However great the similarities are, the specialized legal aspects of venturing into a new country are worth noting. Even though the business decisions may be identical to those in Illinois, the legal system of the new country can be quite different and potentially important with regard to mergers, acquisitions, or new ventures. Hiring well-qualified local counsel is usually a must.

3. Then the point must be made that there can be wide variations among developed countries, which require wide variations in approach. For example, investment in non-European countries may represent a more difficult problem than investment in most European countries, with differences in attitude toward outside investment, in government participation in decisions, and in the need for mutual understanding of historical and cultural differences. Or, the attitude

of Canada toward 100 percent ownership and other aspects of outside investment can be very different from that of some other countries. Even among the European nations, marked differences exist in the kinds of pressures that can be exerted by governments and existing industries to foster or to block individual deals.

4. Finally, for some industries, the potential for a Europe-wide market exists, covering the European Economic Community countries and possibly others. Today, there are no easy means of creating a "European company"; and mergers and alliances across national borders have often encountered serious problems. In certain instances, however, where the economics of scale are crucial, a multinational company may find it very advantageous to treat Europe as a single market. Under these circumstances, it can adapt a management structure capable of making Europe-wide decisions, even though the corporate structure involves separate companies in each country. Such a process is eased if the key companies are near-100 percent owned by a parent company, so that conflicts of interest with minority shareholders in different countries is minimized. For many, probably most companies, now may not be the time to go "Europe-wide." But, in moves that are made now, it would seem wise to keep that possibility in mind for the future.

IN CLOSING

What I have expressed is some preference for:

1. Moving gradually into a new market, starting with initial zero-investment or low investment approaches—where possible.
2. Obtaining control when investments are made and, on occasion, seeking 100 percent ownership, where possible.
3. Negotiating explicit arrangements with governments and/or local partners on a series of financial and operating points before making a major international investment.

The problem with any such generalizations, however, is that the variations in practice are likely to be greater than any uniformity. Hence, I offer these suggestions:

1. Regarding ownership, do not start with a global conclusion to be applied in West Germany, Japan, Brazil, and India. Get realistic advice and make your decision in the light of the governmental and competitive facts of life.

2. Be prepared to be selective, choosing those countries which seem best as markets and deciding how best to reach each of those particular markets profitably.

3. Be prepared to say "No," in negotiations and "for real." It may be better in money terms and in management effort to have a smaller network of *good* companies than a "mixed bag" scattered around the world.

CONTROL VERSUS AUTONOMY OF OVERSEAS OPERATIONS

by Richard C. Gerstenberg
Chairman of the Board (Retired), General Motors Corporation

BECAUSE the business environments of foreign countries are not mere extensions of the U.S. domestic environment, coordinating the operations of foreign subsidiaries becomes a far more complex proposition than coordinating those of a domestic subsidiary or division. In contrast to the general homogeneity of the U.S. domestic business environment, each foreign operation is a function of many local factors often peculiar to the particular country or region. Therefore, achieving success in each foreign country requires that the local operation adapt to such local factors as: political orientation, state of economic development, legal and tax systems, and cultural heritage. These factors, in addition to differences in language and in the skill and availability of local management and labor, create a unique environment in which the overseas subsidiary must operate.

If an overseas subsidiary is to be a viable business organization, it must adapt to the demands of its local environment, or marketplace; therefore, parent-company control must be sufficiently flexible to permit the overseas subsidiary a greater degree of latitude, or autonomy, than a domestic subsidiary would ordinarily have in order to determine, or at least recommend personnel, product, sales, marketing, manufacturing and other local programs. Such flexibility may also require in the case of overseas subsidiaries more particularized central staff *support*, in contrast to the performance by central staffs, of functions carried on uniformly for numbers of U.S. divisions or subsidiaries. In General Motors this added flexibility is facilitated by the corporation's long-established worldwide operating policy of decentralized operations with coordinated policy control.

DEVELOPMENT OF GM'S OPERATING POLICY

This operating policy, which is said to have had some influence on the organization of other large-scale industrial enterprises in the United States and abroad, was developed and initiated in the 1920s at a time when General Motors faced a number of operating and organizational problems created by the rapid expansion of the corporation after World War I. The solution of these problems was in major part the result of the management genius of Alfred P. Sloan, Jr., who retired as chairman of the board of GM in 1956.* According to Mr. Sloan, these organizational problems arose to a very significant degree because the various divisions of the company were being operated on such an uncoordinated, or completely decentralized basis that the corporate level management had little control over the operation of the business. At the time, there was a great deal of duplication of facilities among the divisions because capital spending was a divisional matter; there was a severe shortage of cash because there was no central cash control program; there were excessive raw and semifinished material inventories because these purchases by the divisions were uncontrolled; and levels of inventories of finished vehicles were erratic because production schedules were determined by each division independently.

In the early 1920s it became clear that the implementation of coordinated policy control was necessary. In 1922 a well-defined capital appropriation procedure was established requiring corporate approval of all capital expenditures. Shortly before this Mr. Sloan had noted that the corporation lacked any realistic basis on which to allocate investment funds among the divisions because there was no objective standard of measurement of the relative performance or contribution to the corporation by each division. In Mr. Sloan's words, ". . . it was irrational for the general officers of the corporation not to know where to place the money to best advantage."[1] To fill this gap, at Mr. Sloan's suggestion the corporation established return on investment as the tool for evaluating the performance of each division or unit, thus constituting each division or subsidiary as what would today be called a "profit center." To lessen the impact

---

* [Ed. Note: See the chapter by Alfred D. Chandler, Jr., "The Chief Executive's Office in Historical Perspective."]

[1] Sloan, Alfred P., Jr.; *My Years with General Motors*; New York: Doubleday & Company, Inc.; 1964; p. 48.

of the cash shortage problems, GM established a consolidated cash control system in 1922 which put the corporate financial staff in control of all cash disbursements. Control over divisional inventories was effected by the issuance of a set of policies and procedures to be followed by each division. In essence, each division was permitted to purchase inventories of parts and components equal to requirements for a specific production period, and by this means inventories were limited by production estimates. Finished vehicle inventories were controlled by coordinating all divisional production schedules at the corporate level. These are but a few of the more important examples of the beginning of what was to become the basis for coordinated policy control within General Motors.

The procedures for implementing GM's basic operating policy of decentralization together with coordinated policy control have been modified over the years, particularly as they apply to the control of overseas subsidiaries, but we have maintained this basic operating policy corporation-wide. In the balance of this chapter I shall describe the modifications to the basic policy and some of the control techniques which we have found useful with respect to the activities of our overseas subsidiaries. (I should point out that the development of the Canadian automotive industry has so closely paralleled that of the United States, that General Motors' Canadian subsidiaries have not traditionally been considered part of our "overseas" operations.)

GM'S OVERSEAS ACTIVITIES

To provide perspective on the formation of our operating policy, some background on the development of GM's overseas operations will be helpful:

After General Motors was formed in 1908, its divisions initially participated in overseas areas by exporting fully-assembled vehicles through dealers and direct sales representatives. General Motors' exporting activities became coordinated in 1911, when the General Motors Export Company was formed to provide an overseas distribution framework for the individual U.S. automotive manufacturing operations. GM distributed its products overseas only in this way until the early 1920s. When the effects of rising personal incomes overseas, as well as the economics of shipping unassembled vehicles for assembly near the customer, made exporting fully-assembled vehicles less competitive, the corporation established assembly facilities in 15 overseas countries between 1923 and 1928. Thus, the origin of General Motors as an international corporation can be traced back to our establishment of these early overseas assembly facilities.

Although the assembly of cars overseas required a smaller investment in management resources than would have been necessary for fully-integrated manufacturing facilities, the establishment of these overseas assembly plants furnished an opportunity for GM to evaluate its basic operating structure and organizational philosophy on a worldwide basis.

In the mid-1920s, in response to high vehicle operating costs, short distances to be traveled, and local tax systems which discriminated against larger cars, Europeans began to demand cars of smaller size and lower horsepower than GM was designing and manufacturing in the United States or Canada. During the latter half of the Twenties, GM established two European manufacturing subsidiaries, Adam Opel AG in Germany and Vauxhall Motors Limited in England. The establishment and operation of these overseas manufacturing subsidiaries was facilitated by the favorable experience acquired by operating the overseas assembly subsidiaries during the early 1920s.

Over the ensuing years, additional manufacturing operations were established in overseas countries; by 1970, we had wholly-owned manufacturing operations for the production of vehicles and other products in 13 overseas countries, including many of the larger, more developed countries of the world. The number of wholly-owned vehicle assembly operations had decreased to eight.

In the following paragraphs I shall discuss GM's policies and procedures regarding our wholly-owned overseas operations, which I shall refer to as subsidiaries.

OPERATING OVERSEAS SUBSIDIARIES

As I have said, the organization principle of decentralized operations with coordinated policy control applies to both domestic and overseas operations. But the objective of creating an organization that will grant to its local units the flexibility or autonomy necessary to adapt to local circumstances is especially important in operating overseas subsidiaries.

I should mention that, when we establish an operation in another country, we do so with the intention of being a good corporate citizen of that country and with the philosophy that we are a guest of that country. This "guest philosophy" is a cornerstone of General

Motors operating policy. In line with this policy, each General Motors subsidiary is expected to contribute in its area of competence to the broad spectrum of national goals of the host country. The subsidiary is subject to the host country's laws, and—of equal significance—it is committed to respect the customs, cultures, and traditions of that country. When General Motors Corporation does not agree with some of these laws and customs, it tries to work within the system as a positive force for progressive change and to serve the local residents of the country by developing business opportunities in that country and discharging GM's responsibilities to all of those affected by our business.

It should be noted that, as a U.S.-based multinational corporation, General Motors has occasionally been faced with conflicts between the laws and policies of the United States and those of the particular host countries where we operate subsidiaries. These situations, which are not unique to General Motors, demonstrate the fact that we do not exist with a supranational and unregulated status but rather that as a multinational firm we must accommodate our operations to the diverse and sometimes inconsistent national regulatory standards which frequently have extraterritorial impact.

Because of the more varied environments in which overseas subsidiaries compete, it becomes less feasible for the Chief Executive Officer and other top corporate management to establish the day-to-day operating procedures for each overseas subsidiary. Therefore, we believe that overseas subsidiaries must necessarily be permitted a greater degree of autonomy than their domestic counterparts. This point was summarized by Frederic G. Donner, former chairman of the board of General Motors:

> The concept of decentralized operations and responsibilities with coordinated policy control has proved to be particularly important in our overseas operations. On the one hand, our manufacturing and assembly facilities are bound together on a continuing, almost daily, basis by the economics of producing, assembling and distributing vehicles. The closely interrelated activities must be coordinated within a unifying policy framework to achieve maximum efficiency. On the other hand, each overseas plant manager must adapt his operation to the legal and market requirements of the national economy he serves. These requirements demand the flexibility of decentralization.[2]

_____

[2] Donner, Frederic G.; *The World-Wide Industrial Enterprise*; New York: McGraw-Hill; 1967; pp. 32, 33.

The goal of GM's operating principle has also been summarized by Mr. Donner:

> . . . to create an organization that can adjust to different and changing circumstances. This is intended to give a maximum of freedom and incentive and, at the same time, to realize the efficiencies and the economies inherent in a closely coordinated operation.[3]

At GM the CEO and other top corporate management formulate policies applicable to the business as a whole and these policies are administered by the use of centralized staff functions. For this purpose, the responsibilities of the central staffs have been expanded beyond traditional advisory functions to include policy coordination. Line executives at GM are given full operating responsibility and authority within the established policy limits, thus providing the necessary flexibility for the local operations to adapt to local legal and marketing requirements.

The highest line manager, or chief executive, at each of General Motors' overseas subsidiaries is called the managing director, or manager, depending on the legal structure of the subsidiary. Because the overall policies which we establish at the corporate level serve only as guides within which they must operate, chief executives of overseas subsidiaries generally have more autonomy in the day-to-day operation of their subsidiaries than do the managers of domestic divisions. For this reason, when selecting the chief executives as well as the chief financial officers for our overseas subsidiaries, we must consider factors over and above those pertinent to selecting their domestic counterparts.

Each of our overseas subsidiaries is staffed with local hourly and salaried employees except when local personnel with specific technical or managerial skills are not available. To help provide indigenous personnel with the many technical and managerial skills required to operate a vehicle assembly or manufacturing subsidiary, General Motors Institute conducts a regular two-year program specially designed for employees of GM's overseas subsidiaries to provide them with the skills necessary to advance to higher levels of responsibility at their local operations.

At the beginning of 1975, of GM's total overseas employment of some 187,000 hourly and salaried personnel, only some 480 were "International Service Personnel" (ISP), of whom about 407 were of U.S. origin and 73 were nationals of other countries. However, I

---

[3] Ibid.; pp. 29, 30.

should point out that in many cases these ISPs hold the more responsible positions, generally including those of the chief executives and chief financial officers of major overseas subsidiaries. These ISPs are assigned from the United States (but are not necessarily U.S. nationals) because local employees have not generally been available who have had extensive experience with General Motors. This includes divisional central office staff experience as well as service at other overseas locations, both of which provide training and experience which are considered desirable for these positions.

In addition, we achieve an added degree of coordination and financial control by the dual responsibilities with which the chief financial officer of each overseas subsidiary is charged. The treasurer or finance manager of each of our overseas subsidiaries is responsible to his local Chief Executive Officer on matters that pertain to the day-to-day operation of the subsidiary's business. However, on matters of divisional or corporate financial operating policy, he is responsible to the finance manager of the Overseas Operations Division who, in turn, is responsible to the comptroller of the corporation. Organizationally, this dual status provides an underlying structure which ties the various overseas subsidiaries together within the Overseas Operations Division, just as the corresponding dual status of the divisional comptrollers and finance managers ties the U.S., Canadian, and Overseas Operations divisions of the corporation together.

At GM we define the responsibilities of each overseas chief executive in terms of a geographical area. Depending on the size and/or interrelationships of their operations, they report directly, or through regional managers, to an area general director whose responsibilities are also defined geographically. There are four such general directors —one each for Europe, for Latin America, for the Mid-East and Africa, and for Australia, New Zealand, and East Asia. In recognition of the need for flexibility overseas, these general directors are located in their areas of responsibility, or in the most favorable location for travel and communication with their areas, in order to provide another level of decision-making geographically close to the particular local conditions which we must consider.

OVERSEAS POLICY FORMULATION

Formulation of corporate policy relating specifically to overseas activities is initiated by the Overseas Policy Group. This group, formed in 1936 as an arm of the corporation's Executive Committee of the Board of Directors, has the responsibility for making overseas policy recommendations to the Executive Committee. Its membership includes all members of the Executive Committee (which consists of the chairman (CEO), the president, the two vice chairmen, and four executive vice presidents), the top executives of the Overseas Operations Division, and other top corporate officers. The group acts as an advisory body and preliminary screening group whose views are sought by the management of the Overseas Operations Division on major policy matters. These include the establishment of new operations, capacity expansion programs, and other capital expenditures requiring corporation approval. These are generally reviewed by the Overseas Policy Group prior to their being submitted to the corporation's Executive Committee for approval from an operating point of view and, if required, to the Finance Committee for policy and appropriation approvals.

To provide guidance and assistance to the management of the Overseas Operations Division and the executive vice president in charge of overseas operations in the development of policy proposals to the CEO and the Overseas Policy Group, and in the recognition of the communications problems inherent in worldwide operations, two overseas advisory committees have been established. The Overseas Administration Committee, formed in early 1970, includes the top 18 corporate, divisional, and major overseas subsidiary executives responsible for overseas activities. This committee meets on a quarterly basis and serves basically as a forum for group discussion of the current or contemplated activities or problems relating to GM's overseas operations. The general manager of the Overseas Operations Division serves as chairman of this committee. The meeting location is generally alternated between New York or Detroit and one of the principal overseas areas in which the corporation has facilities; host-area managing directors participate in each meeting.

The other committee, the Overseas Executive Committee, consists of the top eleven corporate and divisional executives responsible for overseas activities. This committee, which meets monthly (with some of the members participating from their offices overseas via an international telephone conference call) is responsible to the executive vice president in charge of overseas operations for making recommendations to him with respect to divisional financial matters, projects for capital expenditures, pricing policies, personnel matters, and divisional operating policies. This committee is chaired by the executive vice president and is also responsible for ensuring that all overseas subsidiaries operate under the same policy guidelines.

Both the Overseas Executive and Overseas Administration Committees provide forums for regular discussion and communication of corporation and divisional policies by the staff and line executives responsible for GM's overseas activities.

Another group has recently been established to provide additional insight and advice to GM management in the formulation of policies related to the Corporation's European operations. Called the European Advisory Council, it currently has ten members, including seven prominent European business and professional leaders and three GM executives. The Council, which meets quarterly, reports directly to the chairman and CEO of GM who participates in Council activities as an ex-officio member.

The Council provides advice on European social, economic, governmental, and industrial developments. It assists us in formulating operating policies for our local subsidiaries. This enables us to operate more effectively in Europe as well as to maintain our standing as a good corporate citizen throughout Europe.

COORDINATION THROUGH CENTRAL OFFICE STAFFS

As noted earlier, under our organizational structure, corporate central office staff responsibilities include both policy coordination within their defined area of responsibilities and the traditional advisory functions. Reflecting the complexity of operating overseas subsidiaries, including such considerations as the wide variety of local government regulations, labor practices, and supplier capabilities, the Overseas Operations Division has its own divisional central office staffs which work closely with, and supplement the corporation's central office staffs. Through liaison with these corporation central office staffs, the overseas divisional staffs assure coordination and continuity of policy between General Motors' North American and overseas operations.

REVISION OF GM'S OWNERSHIP POLICY RELATED TO OVERSEAS OPERATIONS

In the foregoing discussion of GM's overseas operations I have considered only General Motors' policies applicable to the activities of our wholly-owned subsidiaries. Prior to 1971, the wholly-owned subsidiary was the only form of business organization which we utilized overseas, whether for assembly, manufacturing, or sales operations. However, in response to changing worldwide conditions, we revised GM's long-standing 100 percent ownership policy so as to permit GM participation in partially-owned operations.

During the 1960s, some of the fastest growth in the motor vehicle business occurred in those countries in which we did not then have vehicle assembly or manufacturing operations. From 1960 to 1969, vehicle sales of all manufacturers in the countries where GM was represented only through sales activities grew from 34 percent of the total overseas Free World sales to 52 percent of such total sales. Reflecting pressures on their foreign exchange reserves and a tendency toward economic nationalism, many countries implemented tariff and quota barriers, and introduced "local content" regulations which limited the potential of vehicle importation programs. Furthermore, in order to improve the viability of these local content regulations, "deproliferation" of the motor vehicle industry was often sought through the authorization of only a limited number of manufacturers and models for local production and sale. Because of such national policies and measures, continued GM participation in these countries with the faster growing motor vehicle industries could be maintained only through establishment of local assembly and/or manufacturing operations. Furthermore, because many of these developing countries required local equity participation in certain local business enterprises, often including the automotive industry, our direct participation in the motor vehicle industries in these countries necessitated relaxation of our policy of complete ownership.

In late 1969, a review of our foreign ownership policy resulted in a modification of that policy, which was approved by the Finance Committee, leaving the way open for partial ownership if required by local conditions. Although this deviation permits us to acquire less than complete ownership of other companies or to establish new operations in which we do not have all the equity, the corporation still prefers to have 100 percent of the equity of the firms in which we invest. When complete ownership is not possible or considered feasible from a practical point of view, we generally negotiate the largest percentage of equity participation that we can obtain from the partners or that might be permitted by the local government.

Since the policy revision in late 1969, we have entered into seven partial equity affiliations. In 1971, we acquired a 34.2 percent interest in Isuzu Motors in Japan. Since then we have established GM Allison Japan (50 percent owned); GM Korea (50 percent owned); GM Philippines (60 percent owned); GM Iran (45 percent owned); GM Saudi Arabia (60 percent owned); and have acquired a 60 percent interest in Bangchan General Assembly Co. in Thailand. (It should be noted that the corporation has also established six new wholly-owned subsidiaries during the same period: in Malaysia, The Philippines, Thailand, Zaire, and two in Brazil.) It should also be noted that we declined invitations to submit proposals to participate in the automotive industries of certain countries whose economic and political environments were considered too unstable or whose regulation of the automotive industry was considered too restrictive.

Although I do not generally consider partially-owned operations as the optimal means of establishing facilities in developing countries, local laws or other conditions may make such operations the only means of gaining representation in certain countries. Even though our experience with participation in the management and coordination of operations with less than full ownership has been relatively short, I am confident that the corporation has adjusted to this new mode of operation in a way that benefits the host country as well as General Motors.

CONCLUSION

General Motors' long-standing operating policy of decentralized operations with coordinated policy control is ideally suited to the operation of our overseas subsidiaries which are of necessity organized on a decentralized basis because of the more diverse and complex environment in which they operate. A well-defined line management operates the decentralized units within the framework of policies established by the CEO and the corporation policy groups or committees and coordinated by the various central office staffs. This reflects the premise that a group can make policy but only individuals can implement it.

Although our experience to date with this operating policy has been primarily related to wholly-owned subsidiaries, I believe that the modified application of these basic principles to partially-owned operations appears to be working successfully.

General Motors' individual overseas activities have long been tailored to meet the needs of each country in which we or our affiliates operate; this is even more the case, now, with our revised ownership policy. General Motors' technique of policy coordination that stresses an efficient communications system and a high degree of management teamwork permits it to remain a well-coordinated worldwide industrial organization.

CROSS-CULTURAL PROBLEMS IN INTERNATIONAL BUSINESS MANAGEMENT

by Enrico Bignami

Managing Director and Vice Chairman (Retired),
Nestlé Alimentana, S.A. (Switzerland)

GENERAL REMARKS

THE WORLD is shrinking. This idea is accepted today as commonplace. One is aware of the part played in this process by improved communications, the growing use of certain key languages, international trade, and, unfortunately, wars. The regional political and economic organizations which are being formed strengthen the world's present tendency toward uniformity, and it is apparent that, slowly but surely, a certain universal outlook is gaining acceptance.

But there is still a long way to go. Nationalisms and particularisms are deeprooted and enduring, be they the aspirations of the people of the Third World or the resurgence—particularly striking at a time of international crisis—of deeply imbedded nationalistic feelings on the Old Continent; feelings whose importance certain economic circles tend to underestimate. This is demonstrated, for example, by the extreme difficulty the members of the European Economic Community have in delineating the framework of a common policy.

It is once again in the business world (is this a good thing?) that universality is taking the most rapid strides, and to such a degree that it is sometimes "dangerously" ahead compared with politicians and ideologists. But here again, the importance of the large cultural and ideological differences separating different peoples must not be overlooked; the only way successfully to wipe out these divisions is precisely through the understanding of others. It is immediately obvious that the only possible approach to cross-cultural problems is an essentially pragmatic one; it is equally obvious that every international manager can and must know the political and social spheres in which he is moving, and keep himself informed regarding the evolution of international relations in the world in general, and in those areas in which he is operating in particular. This is self-evident and beyond the scope of this paper.

As far as cross-cultural relations and problems are more specifically concerned, things are not so simple. There is neither a theory on the subject nor a plan of action suited to such and such a section of the business community or a certain type of country without there being a strong risk of error. However, if some basic criteria were needed to govern the ideal behavior of an international manager in the face of cross-cultural problems, I would choose these two.

1. Above all, be prepared to understand everything in order to like everything ("tout comprendre pour tout aimer," as Guyau put it). In effect, having a propensity for *liking* is of a greater importance than merely possessing specific pieces of knowledge—or, at least, the latter is of no use without the former.
2. Avoid becoming completely absorbed into another's culture or risk destroying your own roots; retain your own identity whilst welcoming the enrichment that is inherent in all relationships. It is, of course, true that really to understand someone inevitably implies acceptance that one will come out changed oneself.

It is apparent that these two basic requirements are likely to be in constant opposition to each other, and it is easy to imagine that maintaining a lasting balance between them requires a constant exercise of will and curiosity. It is not, therefore, a question of finding a magic formula once and for all, but to preserve at any cost a certain mental attitude and always to be prepared to reexamine the chosen line of action. This is the most important. The small number of problems—out of so many—that will be examined here serve only to illustrate these two principles, and in each case finesse is more important than geometric symmetry.

COLLECTIVE ATTITUDES

The notion of "collective attitudes," as with that of national characterics in a slightly wider sense, is rather vague, which is why I am referring to it. For it is clear that, on the one hand, such attitudes do exist and the international manager must take this into account. It is also clear, on the other, that many persons' understanding of other peoples can be frighteningly simplistic and in certain circumstances can lead to grievous errors. In this context, we shall never be able to emphasize sufficiently how extremely important it is to be on one's guard against the dictums which are rife in this area, such as: the Germans are disciplined and have a gift for organizing; the French are Cartesian; the Italians are Don Juans; the Spanish, proud; the Greeks, crafty; Americans think only of business; the Japanese are inscrutable. These are drawing-room clichés which have absolutely no operational utility and which are like certain children's coloured prints showing, for example, the Swiss milking his cow and, in the evening, mending watches by the chimney. Prejudices and folklore often go together.

On the other hand, each people has its own character, which is all the more difficult to define, in that they often do not follow geopolitical boundaries.

Thus, an inhabitant of Milan is likely to be more like someone from Lyon than his Sicilian compatriot. In the same way, a Provençal will probably find more in common with a Tuscan than with his fellow citizen from Lille, who, in turn, will be closer in certain ways to someone from Zurich than to a Marseillais. A different sort of example is that of French-speaking Switzerland: Although this part of that country is strongly influenced by intercourse with its Germanic compatriot, cultural snobbery will often make it try to imitate the way in which it thinks (frequently mistakenly) Parisians behave. At other times, however, the reaction is totally different: because of the close proximity to its large neighbor, it seems openly to reject the Gallic influence in order to be able to stress the distinct identity of the small group to which it is conscious of belonging. This is why, with the Protestant influence helping, the English feel at home in Geneva and find that they have things in common with the French-Swiss that they do not have with either the French themselves or with the Germans. The point of this small example is to show how very difficult it is to generalize, even for a tiny country like Switzerland.

When attempting to lay down guidelines in the field of collective attitudes, it is therefore necessary to proceed with extreme caution.

Generally, the American businessman divides the world into five large areas: Europe, Asia, the Near East, Black Africa, and Latin America. These should, of course, be cultural rather than geographic divisions. Thus the South African, Australian, and Canadian are

Westerners ("European") but transplanted, immersed in different surroundings and circumstances and, like the American, marked by the adventurous and pioneer spirit of the first immigrants. Generally speaking, it is the Anglo-Saxon tradition and spirit which provide the drive of the new European stocks coming to those countries.

By force of circumstances, patriotism in America is much greater than the initial national feeling of the many immigrant ethnic groups, and it does no harm to remind Americans of the strength of the different nationalisms which continue to affect relations between Europeans. For the time being, one can say that the nation state— a preeminently European invention—remains an essential (if not all-powerful) factor on the European scene and one which in most European countries results in a certain narrowness of outlook, most evident in state administration. Interestingly enough, this kind of "national jealousy" is sometimes more apparent between small states than between small and large, where the competition problem between cultures takes a different aspect. These are basically political obstacles but which, in turn, engender habits—a cultural trait— which the Europeans find it difficult to lose, even when some of these obstacles have been removed. Moreover, as has been seen, one must be wary of attributing too much to "national characteristics" because cultural problems do transcend borders.

Rather than examine each country separately, it might be more useful to look at what could be termed two important cultural traditions (or tendencies) of Western Europe (leaving aside the Eastern European socialist countries for the moment): on the one hand the Nordic (Scandinavian, German, Flemish, etc.) and Anglo-Saxon temperament and, on the other hand, the Latin temperament. Nordics and Anglo-Saxons have, more often than not, a very "matter-of-fact" approach to reality, which is an asset in business. One could perhaps mention in passing that one does not always find in Germany the flexibility which is common to the Anglo-Saxon and, with some nuances of difference, to the Scandinavian. However, for each group, it is the concrete, technical aspects of business relations which are far and away more important than any other considerations, particularly emotional ones.

For the Latins, on the other hand, friendship outside business can sometimes be a determining factor. However, one must not be so naive as to suppose that the emotional aspect automatically outweighs all others for the Southern peoples. Although it may be said that emotions can play a larger rôle in the South than in the North, this generalization must be tempered, and not only by the differences between the peoples themselves. (The Italian, for example, is likely to be more spontaneous than the Spaniard who is more self-controlled.) What is perhaps more important in this respect is the *class* rather than the nationality of person with which one is dealing.

It has been recognized that the further down the social scale one goes, the more marked are the basic cultural characteristics of the people composing that society. Thus, in nearly every European country, business circles tend towards greater uniformity every day; but the cultural question regains all its importance when attacking, for example, the problems of labour, or when dealing with civil servants, especially those in the middle or lower grades. It is interesting to note that, in an individual person, class (or cultural) "reflexes" are likely to be much stronger in certain areas than others. This also implies that the businessman must know exactly what he wants to give to, and receive from his counterpart, what he is prepared to adapt to, and what he wants to change in the society in which he is operating.

We have not yet considered the Soviet Union and the socialist countries of Europe. Purposely. In effect, it is useless to wish to isolate and examine the predominant cultural elements of these societies without extensive study of the ideological and political factors which have radically changed them, and which, especially, render by definition the Western businessman an adversary of the socialist system. In any case, the man who possesses an accurate and extensive knowledge of the principles of and way of life under state capitalism is likely to be well thought of in the socialist world.

Reservations in setting down certain generalizations on cultural attitudes increase the further away from the "Old Continent" we go toward the East, and with them, the difficulties of being able really to understand another person.

The Arab civilization and Europe share the Mediterranean and perhaps more today than ever before this forms a very strong link between them. There is no doubt whatsoever that the European understands the Arab better than an American can. For centuries the Christians of Europe and the Arabs of the Near East have been, and remain, in close contact. But while the Christian religion has perhaps lost some ground in Europe (especially in the North), Islam has retained a relatively greater strength in the Arab world. This element is essential to the understanding of the Near East and North Africa.

The discord which never seems to fail to arise between Arab states at a political level should not be allowed to deceive. It is a region that is humanly and socially united by a deep-rooted culture and whose civilization is markedly different from every other one. The short period of European domination only touched the surface.

Black Africa is a different case, but to date, Europe has also had privileged dealings with it. To a large extent, cultural unity is still a thing of the future. Colonialism—however debatable and debated it be—undoubtedly introduced some unifying factors, but in so doing, it divided the continent into two principal distinct cultural groups. Over and above the purely linguistic question, the two almost opposed systems of administration (the English and the French) imprinted on the numerous and diverse peoples of the black continent two different mentalities. The businessman is well advised to bear this in mind. And also, in whichever African country he is operating, he should carefully study the overlapping and cultural characteristics contained within national borders, further segmenting the people. For, if Africa lacks a global cultural unity, its different cultures play an all important role at the local and regional levels. It is impossible to understand anything about an African country, or to attempt to undertake anything there, if an effort has not been made to know the main peoples composing it and the relations between them.

As far as the huge and diverse continent of Asia is concerned, suffice it to say here that the further one goes from base (if I may say so), the more important it is to beware of the temptations of one's own culture. With the Oriental world more than any other, what is evident to us may not be for someone else, even if the other person appears to have the same standards as ourselves. Thus, the Japanese could after all appear to be similar to us at least as far as business is concerned. In practice, however, it is not always easy to get them to understand our point of view, and vice versa. And from this, springs the need sometimes to allow our bargaining partners the time to digest our propositions rather than trying—in vain—to rush a decision. Business is not jujitsu.

In Asia, more than anywhere else it is dangerous, for a westerner, to show that he is trying to put himself in his bargaining partner's shoes in emphasizing, for example, the advantage that might accrue to the latter in concluding this or that agreement, or in inserting this or that clause. Such an attitude often awakens suspicion.

In the course of the last decades, Latin America has drawn considerably closer to the Americans and further away from the Europeans. Undoubtedly, some of the typically Latin characteristics also apply to the southern peoples of the Latin American continent. Following certain developments on the ethnic plane, and because of the physical environment, the problems are often transferred into forms of keen nationalism which carry a certain emotional charge. In the field of cross-cultural problems, however, the essential cannot be drawn from an instruction manual.

To know others, both persons and peoples, is therefore first and foremost a question of having an open mind. Book knowledge—as long as the books are good ones and well digested—can undoubtedly provide a good starting point. In particular, it is vital to possess a clear idea as to the geography and history of the areas in which one is operating; and also, of course, as to psychological characteristics. From there on, the most important factor is actual contact with the milieu. The international manager must sincerely try to approach it without prejudice and live fully in it. Unfortunately, many executives look upon their stays abroad as a kind of temporary penal servitude. There is nothing worse. Many a promising career has been shattered on that stumbling block. It is the duty of those with overall responsibility for running a business to remove from foreign branches those imported members of staff (managers, technicians, experts, etc.) who have been unable to adapt to their new way of life.

That said, the international manager must at the same time guarantee his intellectual independence, if only to avoid a disastrous complacency toward his surroundings. To enter the world of others does not necessarily entail adopting their whole way of life. "Understand" is not synonymous with "imitate." Lawrence of Arabia, who went a very long way toward absorbing the way of life of the Arabs among whom he was living, found, to his cost, how very much easier it was to rid himself of his own culture than to acquire that of others.

In my opinion, there is only one way for a manager to confront other cultures which the very nature of his work requires him to cultivate, and that is by understanding and liking others whilst remaining true to himself.

CONTACTS AND NEGOTIATIONS

There is no master key to the difficult art of developing contacts and conducting negotiations, even when practised in one's own country. The reader can only be put on his guard against certain tendencies. First, it is most important not to lecture others, especially after the large number of very bad examples the West has thought fit to set for the world. In other words, respect the personality of others and even put yourself momentarily in their place in order to see their point of view and preoccupations. This is the only way to avoid talking at cross purposes and provoking unnecessary misunderstandings. This is the cornerstone of any really intelligent policy, especially when dealing with people from the Third World who have already had to put up with the over-confident attitude of the more developed countries. Such a simple truth, but one which so many men seem to have difficulty in retaining—as if they had not learned anything from history!

But, above all, do not deduce from the above that you should not try to sell yourself. On the contrary. Respect for oneself is requisite in respect for others. You should not be afraid to show who you are and what you want just because you wish to avoid future misunderstandings. The art of negotiation is doubtless in large part knowing when to show one's hand and a certain firmness (naiveté and candor— rarely recognized as such—can also create suspicion and misunderstandings); but it certainly does not consist in trying to deceive one's bargaining partner. And it is here that you must be on the lookout, abroad more than elsewhere, for that complacency mentioned above. Thus, not all local customs can be followed advantageously; they may even be unknown to your particular local contacts. In the first case, some of these "customs" may have been imported by one or another group of the population and may not really correspond to the local character. In these circumstances, they can only represent an artificial element, or even abase the social life of the country.

Secondly, something which occurs frequently is that local tradition is invoked to explain, mistakenly, the absence of certain practices: a local inhabitant may swear in perfectly good faith that in his area such and such a thing "does not exist" or "is not done," without bothering to check because he is sure he knows all the local customs. It is only afterward that you find out that the lack attributed to local usage was, in fact, a lack of knowledge on the part of your informant. Expecting to find yourself sometimes in this kind of situation is one of the ways of showing a good aptitude, rather than a blind acceptance of local customs. The most important factor, in the end, is the impression one gives, and the confidence inspired in others. That is why a certain sort of honesty, implying certain constants of behavior, usually pays off, even if it can be wearing at times. Taken all in all, the weariness is preferable to a clumsy copying of the ambiguous behavior of others.

It goes without saying that the best way to understand and be understood is of course quickly to learn the language of the country. Unless, that is, one has the services of an excellent interpreter, which is a very rare privilege. For an interpreter it is necessary to find someone who not only possesses a perfect mastery of the art of translation but, above all, someone who sets great store by giving an integral and accurate rendering of what is said without yielding to complacency or a polite desire to avoid upsetting one or the other party.

THE MANAGEMENT OF MEN

What has already been said regarding negotiation is also valid for the management of men by imported executives, at whatever level they operate. It has already been seen that they must have a facility for adaptation to local surroundings, not necessarily in order to adopt local usages, but in order better to grasp the basis for those usages and, if called for, to change them. Thus, a responsible chief will not allow his workers to live in insalubrious dwellings, earning a relatively low salary, on the pretext that most of the other local or international managers treat their personnel like that, or because he believes he has to adhere to some possible racist policies of the country in which he finds himself.

In the same way, whatever the local usages, he will try neither to hide his authority behind appearances nor to worry about questions of prestige. Ideally, he will employ a simple and direct approach to his entourage, which is, in fact, easier said than done. Here the manager's personality comes into play. Where, for some, this approach shows itself as a natural familiarity, others only succeed in creating an unpleasant demogogic impression. The manager should always know how to take the personal interests of his collaborators into account, and to foresee their needs, particularly in certain countries where, through shyness or pride, people do not bring such things up of their own accord.

Especially important is that the imported chief should remember that in many ways he is only there as a stop-gap. Which means that one of his principal tasks is to prepare nationals to take over from him. He must also give his people the feeling that their careers are not

blocked by a set top limit (whatever that may be) and that it is possible for capable people to be successful anywhere in the organization.
This is the only way to create team spirit. The manager should also
protect the interests and feelings of nationals by finding opportunities
for them to advance outside their own country. Thus an Argentinian
could take over the management of a Spanish factory whilst his Spanish colleague could be sent to Venezuela. A Swiss would manage the
German branch while a German would take control of the French
one.

By giving executives of all nationalities the possibility to attain
positions of high responsibility one avoids at the same time fostering
in them narrow nationalistic attitudes. Here again, of course, flexibility—*souplesse*—is the keyword, especially at a moment when the
multinational companies are more than ever regarded with suspicion
by many nationalists and an increasing number of governments,
jealous of their sovereignty and perhaps, also, not enough conversant with the dynamics of modern world development.

This is why, in conjunction with the efforts made to create the
team spirit mentioned above, care must be taken not to discourage
local collaborators from taking a part in the political life of their
country, even if that activity would seem at first sight to reduce their
output within the company. In effect, international business, in the
countries in which it is established, must make a contribution to the
forming of political élites. In general terms, companies must know
how to look beyond short-term commercial interests to the general
problems of the societies in the midst of which they are working and
in the development of which they are expected to participate.

RELATIONS BETWEEN THE COMPANY
AND THE STATE

The question of company/state relations has many technical and
practical aspects which do not have their place in this chapter. What
should be stressed here is that these relations have also a subjective,
almost emotional, side which could very often dominate all the
others. This is so especially when the cultural factor comes into the
picture to complicate the basics of the problem. Here, again, instead
of looking for readymade solutions for each government it would be
better to follow, flexibly, certain general rules: Governments and
politicians change, but men are always men, and to work with them

on good terms, it is first necessary to try to understand what they want and what they are doing. The multinational company must, therefore, make an effort to understand government policies and, should the occasion arise and to the best of its ability, should help the government to implement them. For example, planning (a word which makes certain liberal groups shudder!) is *a priori* politically and economically neutral. Well implemented, state-imposed measures do not necessarily go against the interests of the company, as long as the company knows how to take a long-term view. What's more, it can also be involved in the development of the measures—to the advantage of all concerned. At the least, those managers who possess the requisite imagination can advise the government, even in a totally objective manner, and thereby contribute to the well-being of the country and its way of life. They can—to put it succinctly—make themselves *useful*.

It is however most important that managers always bear in mind that such an interest can only be usefully shown as long as they do not let themselves be carried away—even involuntarily—to meddle at the strictly political level of the state. This is a strong, and serious, temptation; free enterprise nearly always encourages a certain liberal political creed. The company must therefore especially guard against siding systematically with the propertied classes. When helping to form the élites, it must take great care not to discriminate against collaborators who hold different political views from its own, and also not to favor representatives of a particular social class (or race) over others of equal talent. Interpolitical relationships change, or can change (especially in the southern hemisphere) and those companies which either purposely or through ignorance favor a rightist, leftist, or any other movement in particular, could well pay dearly for their attitude sooner or later.

In general, a multinational company's relations with the world's different political regimes pose serious problems, and sometimes even require serious soul-searching. Is it possible to work with no matter what regime without becoming tainted? The question remains an open one. However, what can be asserted is that the answer largely depends on the attitude adopted by the businessman toward his bargaining partners and workers. Here, once more, it is essential to follow the openly stated line of action firmly and steadfastly. We would not, after all, think of building new prisons for our subordinates on the pretext of following a government's policies.

THE LEGAL ENVIRONMENT

The law is by definition the expression of a people's character. The law reflects the present and the people's problems; it is also a heritage of the past, even of other cultures from the near or more distant past. In the West, for example, two main legal systems can be traced: first, the Continental system based on the Napoleonic code, the main influence coming from southern usages and northern European Roman law; and, second, the Anglo-Saxon system based on common law. The various bodies of law are as a result varied—at the same time similar and dissimilar—even within a relatively small geographical area (taking Europe as an example).

Apart from variations in basic law with which the international company will be dealing, company law, itself, has developed in a most irregular way from one country to another and is not always in harmony with the economic development of the country concerned. For example, one country has a highly developed system, while another, equally industrialized, has only a rudimentary one.

Over and above the legal implications (and complications) arising out of differences in legislation, the paralegal rules and behavior (which, in turn, vary from country to country) must be taken into consideration. To take just one example: someone has given his word—what value can be attached to this? Here, it is equal to a firm engagement; there, it serves only to feel out the ground and does not in any way bind the giver; elsewhere, it is used to better hide one's thoughts; and so on.

Pursuing this line of thought to the logical consequences, the legal and social areas would soon be left behind and the question for the manager would become one of the behavior of individuals: for, in the end, it is individuals and individual psychology which must be understood. All in all, the international manager must know how to deal with these separate elements in their global sociocultural context.

THE PUBLIC AND PUBLICITY

It is in the realm of advertising that the greatest efforts at adaptation should be made, and where the study of collective attitudes is, of course, most necessary.

The company must be able to adapt itself and its policies to its different markets. In this connection, the capacity of the company to influence the market and to stimulate consumers to adopt new habits (depending on the size of the company and the sort of product) must not be underestimated. But not all peoples are equally open to change. In one country, a product will take a few months to enter the market; in another it will take years. Of course, the capacity for assimilation can also depend on the type of product being introduced, some being accepted everywhere, some only in certain cultural milieux. However, this is part of the vast problem of marketing, which I cannot hope to deal with in a few lines in the framework of this chapter.

THE COMPANY CHIEF'S POWER FOR CHANGE

Deep-down, man is the same everywhere. What I am trying to say is that, whatever the cultural divisions between peoples, the individual and the group from wherever they may come have a similar potential for energy and intelligence. Climate has often been invoked to explain the differences in human behavior; its influence has been greatly exaggerated.

Far more than on climate, the activity of an individual or a group depends on working conditions (both physical and moral), health, eating habits, and housing. To a large extent the modern manager has the possibility to transform the worker's living conditions. This has been proved often enough. Here again, the power to change must be employed with discrimination. The manager must not allow himself to be carried away by a blind faith in all things new, nor to be influenced by fashion, which exists in all domains. To do so will always lay him open to grave disappointment, especially if he neglects the cultural question or, even more simply, if he overlooks the time factor. Just because something is new, it does not follow that it can be introduced everywhere, immediately. Where necessary, the manager will endeavor to create the propitious environment. Patience is a virtue.

It is quite simply a question of being conscious of the fact that, perhaps more than anyone else, the manager holds the key to the behavior and capabilities of his employees. It is up to him to wield his power to the greatest advantage of all.

DEALING WITH FOREIGN GOVERNMENTS

by Pieter Kuin

*Former Director, Unilever N.V., and Unilever, Ltd.**

A CAUTIONARY TALE

"I AM SORRY," the young aide said, "the Minister has been called to the Palace." He looked regretful; but not too much so. My colleagues and I were perplexed. We had a confirmed date, our project would benefit the country, the Cabinet in power needed successes. We did not believe the excuse; it was too glib. "Come back next Monday, at eleven o'clock," the aide said. When we did (it was an hour's driving from where we were staying) the Ministry was deserted except for a few guards. They laughed—it was the Prophet's birthday and nobody was working. "Come back to-morrow," they said. That evening we told our old friend the governor of the city, who had invited us to dinner, that we were going home. It was clear the government was not interested in industry. He was very angry, reached for the telephone, and spoke rapidly into it for about ten minutes. "All right," he said, "the Deputy Minister will see you tomorrow at ten and has all morning for you. It will be a working session and various officials will be at hand." It *was* a working session and the way was cleared for a major expansion of our manufacturing capacity.

What had gone wrong in the first place? We had had introductions from our local management, via their contacts in the Ministry which

---

* [Ed. Note: Pieter Kuin was for many years, until his retirement in 1973, a member of the boards of the parent companies—one Dutch, the other British—of Unilever: "N.V." and "Ltd." On these boards, as an officer of management, he was, as they say, an "executive" director, or as we in the United States would say, an "inside" director. Since 1973, Dr. Kuin has been an "outside" director of N.V. Koninklijke Nederlandsche Petroleum Maatschappij, the Dutch 60 percent parent company of the "Royal Dutch/ Shell Group of Companies." Kuin would like to point out that the experiences he has drawn upon for his chapter occurred while he was with Unilever.]

were quite good. But we had underestimated the political factor. The Minister we had approached was a politician. He wanted the industry, but did not want to be seen with foreign industrialists. He was also an overlord in the Cabinet and probably wanted to demonstrate his own importance and his country's newly-won independence.

Anyway, it gave us food for thought, and impressed upon us the need for careful study and preparation before approaching a foreign government. A *foreign* government? Always remember that *they* are at home, in their own territory, and that *you* are the foreigner. Perhaps the title of this chapter should have read: "How to deal with governments as a foreigner."

COUNTRIES AND SOCIETIES DIFFER

When I review my own and my colleagues' experience of "foreign" countries, what most impresses me is how many different kinds there are. Labels such as "old established," "newly independent," "developing," or "industrialised" are useful but not adequate. Each differs from the others and one has to study a country in some depth before approaching the government with a plan.

It is hardly necessary to enumerate the aspects that have to be studied. An economic analysis will throw light on the country's needs and opportunities. It will also reveal its problems, for instance in the area of foreign exchange. Equally important, and often overlooked, is the social situation. The society's anatomy will show the various categories, groups, and classes, their relative sizes and strengths. Introducing the time element into this picture will show who has gained prominence and who has receded into the background. Some extrapolation may be in order.

Social analysis is a basis for political analysis, but not the only one. Politics reflect ideas, ideals, and idiosyncrasies as well as group or class interests. And sensitivities are not necessarily less in one area than in the other.

Everybody knows the particular sentiments of former colonial territories that have gained national independence. They mostly want to emphasize their independence by choosing as their partners or sponsors countries that are not their former colonial powers. Yet they know the latter best, and after the bitterness of pre-liberation days has worn off they may well return to former friends. This is one reason why the political situation relevant to foreign businessmen is not always entirely determined by social structures. Religion is another "ideological" factor—irrelevant in some countries, but most important in others.

I mention all this because dealing with governments means dealing with countries; their social and ideological situation determines the government's scope, just as the economic situation determines its needs. An understanding of social and ideological change is helpful in knowing what to expect of the future; it saves us from being unpleasantly surprised, as they say some nations are, by the advent of winter when it's November.

Most governments are not entirely free agents. They are deeply rooted in the society and ideology of their people, or parts of it, and though they lead its progress, they are to some extent also led—led to assume, led to expect, led to act, and this more by their own roots and backgrounds than by us foreigners.

POLITICAL ASPECTS

Roots and backgrounds may be important but they are not the whole story. Politics proper is a separate subject, and merits special study. Three aspects can be distinguished: personalities, parties, and procedures.

Personalities

Little need be said about personalities. Whatever the political system, each government party or office has its own "Kremlinology"— the knowledge of whose star is rising and whose is falling. A sober assessment of the relative position of each potential contact person in his own constellation can be very useful.

Parties

However, the politician's loyalty is to his party, and whoever rises to power has to observe its basic laws and propensities. Roughly speaking, the main configurations in the political sphere, from this angle, are one-party systems, alternating party systems, and coalition systems.

The one-party system is, of course, characteristic of dictatorial regimes, whether they be pre- or postrevolutionary. Yet the positions of various single parties are not the same. Some are the real fountains of power in their countries, some mere instruments of juntas or dictators, others somewhere in between. Caution is essential in such surroundings.

Alternating party systems are more familiar to English-speaking peoples. Republicans and Democrats, Conservatives and Labour each have their periods in office and in opposition and their politics are well known to the business community. But the simplicity of the system may be misleading; many of us would be hard put to it when asked to explain the meaning of a changeover in, say, Afghanistan. And even nearer home the attitudes of well-known parties toward such issues as foreign investment (or "penetration") can be most surprising. Anyway, it is necessary, before approaching the government in a two-party country, to find out what each one's relevant attitude is and what chances each party has to maintain power or rise to it.

In such a constellation, the position of the civil service is important. If there is patronage and a changing of the guards in higher echelons with every change of government, politics plays more part in judging foreign propositions than in a system where civil servants hold tenure no matter who is in power. In fact, the permanency of the administration can be a most valuable stabilizing factor in a system which in itself contains the danger of see-saw policies. There have been instances when party A undid what party B had done, and vice versa, and they created great uncertainties for industry.

As a former civil servant, myself, and a citizen of a country with coalition governments, I am inclined to value the stability and security of such a political system. It is true, coalition governments often take a long time to form, after much negotiation about programs, and some of them have too short a lifespan, but with an able and stable civil service the country can stand a lot of apparent indecision.

Procedures

This brings us to the subject of procedures. Apart from the political structure it is relevant to know the mechanics of a country's decision making; or, one step removed, of policy making, since individual decisions have to fit into the broader frame of policies.

In an authoritarian system only the top makes policies—although the role of advisers should not be underestimated. Feudal and military rulers often rely on them. Single parties may have official ideologists. The civil service in such countries is mostly an instrument, rather than a body of administrators—and a poor instrument at that. It can be very dangerous for an official to displease the real rulers, and there is safety in evasion and delay.

In a democracy, ministers are answerable to parliament. This means that party rule and technocracy have their limits. The study of parliamentary politics and power structures is too often neglected by businessmen. But this being said, and keeping within the framework of agreed policies, the merits of individual propositions are mostly studied by civil servants, and their opinion counts for much.

THE FIRST APPROACH

What, then, should the foreign businessman do when he wants to put a project before a government he has not met so far?

It will be clear from the foregoing paragraphs that there is no single answer to this question. It depends partly on the nature of the project, but even more on the economic, social, and political situation in the country in question. I would venture a few general remarks.

The first is that a nation's customs in this respect should be respected. In many a culture the direct approach by an interested party, coupled with a certain degree of insistence, is most unusual and apt to be resented. It recalls the image of a steamroller or a siege.

I remember an instance where a foreign-owned consumer goods manufacturer was threatened with a special, high sales tax, inspired by the domestic makers of a competing product which had suffered market losses. The foreign manufacturer, after having tried every possible plea with the authorities, finally fled into publicity and started an advertising campaign to mobilize the public, out of whose pockets the tax would have to come. The authorities resented this unusual step more than anything else. This was not the way things were done there. If, for the time being, one's allies were less influential than those of one's opponent, one bowed to necessity and searched for as flexible an application of the law as possible. The opinion of the public was neither here nor there; what counted was the political constellation.

In this particular country, it was considered normal to have allies, sponsors, pleaders, or just friends in the right places who could arrange things for the best or make the worst less painful. The firm's alleged fault had been to substitute force for subtlety.

Should the foreign entrepreneur venturing into unknown territory always look for an ally? It depends on the type of country and its system of government. Wherever the civil service has any real influence the approach had better be direct. Never use a lawyer or consultant there, except to tell you where to go, because the experienced civil servant wants only first-hand information. And he wants to see his man.

With more personal rule, be it feudal or political, an introduction may be valuable. Do not try to get yourself introduced to military rulers; they mostly prefer to remain inaccessible. Moreover, they tend to consider themselves above such mundane matters as commerce. For these, they use high class technocrats as ministers, who then rule their own departments as autocrats.[1]

At the time when my colleagues and I were snubbed we had tried too high and too exposed a man. Usually, one or two ranks below is better. For instance, in a European country or in the European Community a director-general of the administration may be more useful, for a first visit, than a minister or commissioner. Similarly, in other countries a junior minister of the technocrat type may be better than his superior if the latter is a "political animal." And if you, Mr. Corporation President, feel that kings speak to kings only, then wait until the time for a royal visit has come.

Generally speaking, all one needs for the first approach, if it cannot be direct, is an effective introduction. Very often your own country's embassy is the place to get such an introduction. It is part of the diplomat's job to know who is who in the government and the administration. He may also be very good, even better than yourself, in summing up your problem and putting it before the competent official. But this latter course should be followed only in exceptional cases, because it gives your proposition a political flavor which can be very dangerous.

Remember, there is nothing government people in other countries are more afraid of than domination. American firms in particular have to reckon with this, partly because of the wealth and advanced technology of the United States, partly because the U.S. government expects some of its laws (antitrust and trading with the enemy acts)

---

[1] Some military leaders *will* see foreigners. I was once in a group received by the late General Qasim of Iraq. But he was of no use—he just preached with a glint in his eye about his mission and past sufferings. The same applies to some other military dictators. Abdul Nasser was one of the few ex-army officers to run his country like a corporation president; but to all intents and purposes he had become a civilian.

to have extraterritorial effect. Domestic industry, which may suffer from competition, is always alert to see that ministers and government officials do not favour foreign enterprise unduly, or bow to the political power behind it.

As I have said, in some cultures it is natural to get in touch with the authorities through a mediator. Depending on the country's social structure and the nature of its government this might be a member of a ruling family, the leading class, or the party in power. Sometimes there is no other way. But even then it is advisable to let the role of the mediator be a temporary one.

The danger of more durable alliances of this kind is that it draws the enterprise into the political sphere and makes it dependent on existing power structures. In an age of coups d'état and political landslides this is like building a house on sand.

Economic usefulness is a firmer foundation. Once the mediator has done his duty the proposition should be judged on its own merits for the economy. The government's agreement or cooperation should not be a matter of kindness or favour but of enlightened self-interest, that is to say for the nation.

It is hardly necessary to say that lack of complete sincerity evokes distrust. The foreign businessman should not suggest that he has come for altruistic reasons. The proposition may indeed be useful to the country, but there is no reason to play down the proposer's own interest. Most government people are mature enough to see that the best transactions are those that benefit both parties.

There may, however, be a fear of harming local interests. For instance, an offer of new products or services, though beneficial to users and also, on balance, to the national economy, may threaten an existing industry. To overrule this, the government must have stronger arguments than the personal recommendation of a mutual friend. In such cases, support by a potential ally in the business world, whose interests run parallel with those of the foreign visitor, may tip the scale. Depending on the social and political situation, such allies may also be sought among labor leaders or regional governors.

ESTABLISHING A NEW BUSINESS

At this point it is difficult to avoid becoming more specific. Rather than continuing about "propositions" in general, I choose as an example direct investment—a project to establish a business in the country in question. It is the kind of thing I am most familiar with; and, also, it is a topical subject.[2]

Let us assume the first approach has been made and the ghosts of domination and undue threats to local business have been laid. There are, of course, many other problems. The effect on the balance of payments—the foreign exchange position—is of major concern to many governments, especially of less-developed countries. It is a subject the foreign businessman must be prepared to discuss in fairly great detail. The reasoning is that over the years a successful enterprise will want to transfer dividends, service fees, pensions, and savings, which—in addition to payments for raw materials and spare parts—will exceed the initial investment of foreign currency many times. It is not unusual in this connection for officials to speak of a "permanent drain" on the foreign exchange position.

There are, of course, arguments to counter this. The new business may replace imports, set free local materials for export, create valuable employment, provide careers for local managers, contribute to general education and vocational training, create a constant influx of new technology and generally help to strengthen the economy and speed up the nation's progress. The balance of payments aspect is after all a very limited one. No business or private household would prosper if it thought that only cash inflow was good, cash outflow bad. What matters is the countervalue and productive effect of the outflow. But granting all this, one cannot blame a government for being very careful with foreign exchange, especially if the proposed production involves luxury goods. The poorer the country, the more strictly priorities have to be observed.

It is one of the complaints heard on behalf of developing countries that they are sometimes pushed (by credits or persuasion) into accepting projects that should really have lower priority for the time being. Pressure of this kind may easily lead to sharp repercussions later.

A preference for national ownership of certain sectors of the economy, considered vital to the national interest, may also be a reason for the government to resist foreign investment proposals. For these and other reasons, the foreign entrepreneur should, in the words of the International Chamber of Commerce *Guidelines,* "ensure in consultation with the competent authorities that the investment fits

[2] See: *Guidelines for International Investment;* Brochure 272 of the International Chamber of Commerce; 38 Cours Albert ler; Paris 8e, France; 1972.

satisfactorily into the economic and social development plans and priorities of the host country."

If it does, there may be further anxieties on the side of the government which the investor must try to allay. One of these is that the foreign enterprise could grow so much out of proportion with the environment that national firms might get squeezed, labor-wise, marketing-wise, and money-wise. Excessive recourse to scarce financial resources is particularly resented. It is, therefore, important to be frank with the authorities about the expectations the entrepreneur himself has of the company's future. Possible areas of friction should be explored beforehand, rather than disguised first and discovered later.

Contributing to exports is one such area. Governments nowadays tend to make it a condition for approval. Some companies can undertake to export part of their production, but others cannot. The potential markets may already be served by other companies of the same group, and it would be rather absurd if A exported to B and B to A, just to comply with the export requirements of both governments—a modern form of kite-flying.

Moreover, the new venture may have too little capacity and its costs may be too high to compete successfully in foreign markets, particularly those served from the world's most efficient and sophisticated industrial centers. If this is so, the entrepreneur should refuse to enter into any export commitments, and say so from the beginning. But this should not prevent him from trying to help the government in other ways. The country may produce goods of a different nature, for which a business with worldwide connections could find profitable outlets abroad.

The possibility of a joint venture, or some other form of local participation, is likely to come up as soon as negotiations with the government start in earnest. In this respect, the International Chamber of Commerce *Guidelines* also point out "that joint ventures are much more likely to be successful if they are entered into voluntarily . . . and that there may be cases where investments which deserve high priority are only feasible on the basis of total foreign ownership." This pertinent reminder was addressed to governments of host countries. But the foreign investor also gets good advice. He "should, in presenting his investment proposal to the authorities of the host country, examine favorably suitable proposals concerning forms of association with local interests, public or private."

I am inclined to subscribe to both statements, with emphasis on the latter. If at all possible, I would advise the investor not to wait until the other party makes the proposals, but show some imagination of his own. True, the difficulties and complications of joint ventures are often overlooked, especially by people without any business experience. Here again, I might refer to an I.C.C. brochure (No. 256, published December 1968) about joint ventures in developing countries. In it, the problems with joint ventures, together with suggested solutions, are set out in some detail, with particular reference to manufacturing industries. I do not intend to review the pros and cons of joint ventures, but I must remind businessmen who consider setting up a company abroad that they will be faced with official pressure in this direction, particularly in less developed countries. More and more, governments and public opinion insist that what has been called "partnership in progress" be practised not only in the public but also in the private sphere.

One particular form of local participation is directly relevant to the subject of this chapter, namely participation by the government itself. I have in mind not so much the imposition of royalties or part nationalisation of existing businesses, but rather a claim made by the government that it must get part of the share capital of a new venture which is still being negotiated.

To many an entrepreneur it is a rather disconcerting thought. Most of us would rather be in business with private partners than with the state. Yet the experience has not been altogether unfavorable. It can be very useful to a company for the supreme power in the state to have a positive interest in satisfactory profits. But, in order to reduce the risks to good management, the foreign entrepreneur must get certain assurances in writing, particularly against patronage and political influence. In fact, he must insist on freedom for the private side to manage the company in accordance with its own standards.

The state (or state bank, or state development agency) should be content with the role of a sleeping partner or at best a minority position on the board. Otherwise, the investor becomes the government's prisoner.

Even so, it may be wise for both partners to consider in advance what will happen when the company grows and requires more capital. Does the government stay put and acquiesce in its share of the capital shrinking? Or will it make more money available, at the expense perhaps of other ventures? The kind of shareholders' agreement which

I.C.C. brochure 256 recommends for private partners should, with appropriate modifications, also be drafted for a joint venture with the government.

In short, once the negotiations start in earnest, the foreign businessman should combine openness about his objectives with precision about conditions.

Obviously, the conditions include assurances for transfer of dividends, service fees, pensions, and savings, and also for labor permits for expatriates and import licenses for spare parts. But the foreign-owned enterprise should not bank too heavily on getting privileges not available to national firms. Treatment as a national is often the best it can obtain, and if this is combined with some consideration of its special position and requirements the owners should be satisfied.

MANAGING AN EXISTING BUSINESS

Those who have had one or more operating companies abroad for a number of years do not, as a rule, need much advice. Most of them have learned about government relations the hard way. Yet, some reminders may be in order.

The first is that social and political conditions are changing rapidly everywhere. Too often, executives at headquarters assume that they know a country because they worked there, or paid frequent visits, some five or ten years ago. Dated knowledge is worse than no knowledge at all, because it masks the need for up-to-date information. So be sure not to rely on memory, and provide for regular surveys.

Secondly, it is becoming more and more important to recognize national sensibilities and aspirations. This may affect not just the management structure but the very foundations of your business abroad.

Traders

Traders will notice that traditional forms of exporting produce and importing merchandise cannot remain in foreign hands for long. Indigenous firms are becoming much better oriented in the world's markets and are keen on taking over profitable business. Governments may help them with currency allocations and by similar methods. Quite a number of governments have taken the export side in their own hands by forming marketing boards. Does this mean there is no place for foreign trading firms any more? Not necessarily. The United Africa Company, a subsidiary of Unilever, found an interesting solution for this problem several years ago when it shifted from fairly simple forms of trade to much more sophisticated ones, including such novelties (for Africa) as running a department store and starting technical divisions which combine imports with assembly, maintenance, customer instruction, and staff training courses. This is the way foreign merchants can prove their worth to host countries: by specializing on things that are still outside the domestic traders' scope.

Manufacturers and Service Industries

Manufacturers may work for the home market or for export. The former are more dependent on the government than the latter. They need import licenses for raw materials and spare parts, and foreign exchange to transfer profits and savings. The fact that they substitute local production for imports is soon forgotten, especially when domestic, national firms learn the tricks and start competing. Good government relations, however necessary in such cases, are no substitute for indispensability. Like the merchant, the foreign manufacturer must therefore stay ahead and offer types and qualities which local people need but cannot yet produce. The same applies to *service industries* working for the local market. They, too, should be aware of the need to make themselves distinctive. Any foreign bank or insurance company, for instance, which merely competes with local firms at the same level of performance is basically in a weak position. It may easily become the victim of anti-foreign feelings. No government relations policy can, in the long run, save a foreign-owned firm which is economically expendable.

Conducting an export industry tends to make a firm popular. Establishing links with world markets and bringing in foreign exchange is quite obviously useful to the country. Yet there are grades of popularity, depending on the kind of business. Understandably, manufacturing goods from homegrown raw materials tops the list; added value, from the host country's point of view, is almost 100 percent, barring transfers for services and dividends. It is not very difficult for managements of such firms to maintain good government relations. Unfortunately, they are a minority.

Mining and Extraction

Mining and extraction, including oil drilling, are a much more difficult area. True, they do provide export revenues, and (this is often overlooked) without their formidable risk-taking and skills the country would not have obtained these revenues. But nowadays the emphasis is on alleged exploitation more than on benefits. Foreign firms in these industries often have to agree to "participation" (government rake-offs) or even nationalization. Their only defense in the long run may be superior skills, making their cooperation indispensable, if only in further processing and marketing. It is useless to try to become more specific about government relations in these highly sensitive areas.

SOME GENERAL COMMENTS

Two general remarks may suffice. The first is that more and more countries are becoming jealous of their allegedly exclusive title to natural resources in their soil. The rightness of this may be debatable, but there can be no doubt about the feelings. Even Americans—critical of Canadians and Venezuelans—might be roused to protests if they saw Japanese or Arab firms staking claims for Rocky Mountain oil shale. This kind of national sensibility will force American and European firms engaged in mining and extraction overseas to prepare themselves for minority positions in quite a number of their own businesses. The essential thing then is to keep the management, and this is possible only if the foreign founder, now a partner, combines superior skill with superior diplomacy.

The second general point is that in many cases there will be pressure to raise the added value accruing to the host country's economy by "forward integration"—establishing processing operations in the country where the raw material is found. This is not always the best place, for a variety of reasons: high capital investment entailing heavy interest and creating little new employment, lack of electricity, high cost of transportation, difficulty in getting skilled managers and operators to move to the new place, distance to markets, dependence on one kind of raw material only, etc. Companies faced with such pressure have a difficult government and public relations job to do, defending the principle of sound international division of labor against national desires and distrust. Distrust, because their story may look more like special pleading than objective analysis. In such cases, it may be useful to propose an independent study by an impartial institution of high repute. But this should imply that the company could be persuaded to abide by the findings of such a study. If it has some noneconomic reason for refusing further commitment in the country in question—e.g., fear of political instability—it had better say so from the beginning.

This said, I feel that international companies should show understanding for the host countries' desire not to be mere suppliers of raw materials for other nations' industries—particularly if these raw materials are found in the less developed areas of the world.

Some of these less developed areas have little else to offer than manpower, but that in abundance. Workers, mostly unskilled, may leave their homeland temporarily to find employment abroad. This creates all sorts of social and political problems, but they are outside the scope of the present chapter. They would belong in an article headed "Dealing with Foreign Workers." The reverse movement also takes place. American, European, and Japanese corporations are establishing operations in areas with abundant manpower, mainly to get a cost advantage. This creates a rather delicate situation. Everything used comes from outside: fixed assets, raw materials, and management; and (almost) everything produced goes outside. Added value consists of wages and taxes mainly. The government of such a host country will appreciate the employment foreign firms are creating, but in the long run a desire for further national involvement is bound to come up.

Government relations in such a country will have to include a readiness on the side of the foreign firm to do more than just exploit the labor situation. Wage differentials with other countries are likely to decrease, anyway, following the pressure of concentrated demand soon facing some form of unionized supply. The foreign-owned firm will be well advised to make additional roots in the country, e.g., by developing a "national" management cadre and using part of its profits for community work and education. Or else, it should be ready to clear out as soon as the wage advantage melts away. But this is not a very good basis for government and public relations.

GOOD CITIZENSHIP

All foreign-owned companies, whether newly established or not, will be expected to behave in a way which is often described as good citizenship. The exact interpretation of these words may differ from country to country, depending on the situation. Consequently, if a transnational corporation encourages its operating companies to assimilate themselves as much as possible to their environment, it may find itself the parent of children with very different lifestyles.

Yet it is not meaningless to try and formulate certain general rules of good behavior. Every enlightened transnational enterprise does this, and the International Chamber of Commerce has done it for the entire business community.

Before specifying some of these rules, I would like to dispel the notion that the foreign or jointly owned company is expected to sit on the government's lap. In most countries of the free world, domestic firms and their governments deal with each other at arms' length. The points of contact are usually defined by law and any idea that the government "controls" the policy of private firms beyond these points is an illusion. The foreign-owned company will, as a matter of course, observe and respect the laws of the country. It can also, within this framework, claim the same freedom to conduct its business as national companies enjoy.

This said, I think that the foreign or jointly-owned company will be wise if it tries just a little harder than domestic firms to earn the government's trust and appreciation. Usually there has been a certain distrust or dislike at the start, and such feelings cannot be dispelled by words but by deeds alone. The company must act right and be seen to act right. It should, in addition to strict adherence to the law:

Show itself ready to explain to the government its commercial, financial and social policies.

Try to shape these policies in such a way that the country's major needs and constraints are taken into account.

Disclose to the government the extent of its interests in the country and, if possible, of its aspirations.

Consider favorably the reinvestment of part of its profits in the country.

Cooperate with the government in establishing and maintaining training facilities for labor and managers.

Take part in regional development programs to the extent consistent with efficient operations.

Try not to disrupt social and family structures more than necessary, and respect the workers' religion and customs.

Inform and consult the government about proposed actions seriously affecting the labor market.

Try not to be an island of advanced management and technology, but radiate knowledge and skills.

Practice fair pricing policies in dealing with associated companies.

If possible give preference to local sources of supply, especially in less developed countries.

Give full scope to local managers to develop and rise to positions of real responsibility, not excluding those on the board of the operating company itself.

In short, the company's business policy should be such that a friendly government can feel its benevolence is fully justified and a hostile government cannot find valid reasons for reproof.

In addition, expatriate managers of wide experience should show themselves prepared to serve as advisers or experts in matters of public interest whenever they are called upon to do so.

It is clear that "good citizenship" means a lot more than donations for worthy causes: It requires a constant effort to understand and, if possible, support the government in serving the public good, without being intrusive and, of course, without detracting from the standards of good management.

Unfortunately, most governments live in the sphere of party politics. At one time or another the company may be asked to give money to some organization or institution belonging to the party in power. For the same reason I gave in connection with allies or mediators, I would be strongly against this. A sponsor of the party in power *now* will be noted as an opponent of the party in power tomorrow. Better to stay outside the sphere of party politics altogether and aim at a good relationship with the government as such.

From the definition I have given of good citizenship it will be clear that much depends on the managerial quality and civic sense of the men on the spot. They, not the board members of the parent company somewhere abroad, are the opposite numbers of the people in government. They are in the limelight and must be seen to have considerable discretion. To put it briefly, for a worldwide enterprise to have good government relations everywhere it must confer real power and status on national managers and maintain a low profile for international headquarters.

SHOWING ONE'S COLORS

This strategy should not lead to dissimulation. For several decades it was considered unwise for transnational corporations to advertise their omnipresence. They preferred to present their companies as national and the links with the parent as unimportant. This policy has turned against them. An attempt to blend into the background is seen as a sign of essential dishonesty.

Whilst maintaining the principle of maximum delegation of responsibility to the men on the spot, the transnational corporation should not hide its members' identity. Openness is the best guarantee for satisfactory relations with the government and the public, wherever one chooses to work.

DOING BUSINESS WITH
THE RUSSIANS

by Dr. Armand Hammer
Chairman of the Board and Chief Executive Officer,
Occidental Petroleum Corporation

SELDOM do corporate executive officers and their staffs have an opportunity to participate in events of historic proportion. It is a matter of
record, not a boast, to state that Occidental has played a significant
role in strengthening the trade detente between the earth's two
greatest powers, the United States and the Soviet Union. Each has the
nuclear armor and delivery systems to destroy the other, and a lot of
nations in between. Each has at times shaken a mailed fist under the
other's nose. But now, almost miraculously, there is a leavening:
commercial rapport. It offends certain groups on both sides of the
rusting Iron Curtain. But it would have pleased Benjamin Franklin
who once tartly replied to a Congress critical of his efforts to make
trade agreements with France, "Trading partners do not make war!"

It takes a bit of doing and limitless patience for a capitalist, as am
I, to deal successfully with Ivan, communist proprietor of the newest
and potentially most rewarding marketplace in the world. The familiar dialogue between Macy's and Gimbel's is not pertinent in any
U.S.-U.S.S.R. trade talk. The overriding objective is understanding
of the other side's traditions and methods of doing business. From
such understanding, once achieved, can come peace in our time. The
profits will take care of themselves.

My unique experiences with the Russians span the more than half
a century between Lenin in the early 1920s and Brezhnev in the middle 1970s, a period during which the largest of all countries emerged
from its czarist Dark Ages, staggered through a political and then an
industrial revolution, and became a great power—with every intention
of growing greater. It is my pleasure to share my know-how of that

past, present, and future with my fellow American chief executives who have entered that challenging arena or have intentions of doing so.

EARLY EXPERIENCES

A brief account of my own incursion, the better part of three generations ago, might be useful. I first went to Russia in the summer of 1921. My reasons were several. I didn't know what else to do with a vacation period between June, when I was graduated from Columbia's School of Physicians and Surgeons, and the following January when I was scheduled to take up my residency at Bellevue Hospital in New York. I was touched by the accounts of widespread typhus and famine in the land of my father and mother. It might be a chance for me to do further research in my medical school majors, immunology and bacteriology. And I could collect the money due my New York pharmaceutical company for the medicines my father, Dr. Julius Hammer, who was sympathetic to their cause, had persuaded me to ship to Moscow a year or two earlier for distribution among the stricken.

(It should be explained at this point that while I was still an undergrad at Columbia my father, a retired physician, put me in charge of a pharmaceutical company in which his lifetime savings were invested and which was badly foundering. Luckily, I came up with promotion ideas, turned the business around, and became a millionaire while still attending classes.)

I went to Russia more or less forearmed. In the hope of easing my entrance—not many individuals were granted visas in those bleak days—I purchased a surplus World War I field hospital from the United States government, ambulance and the lot, to give to the Bolshevik government. I phrased a small speech to the effect that I wanted to volunteer to work among the distressed peoples until the following January 1922.

They could not have cared less. I was assigned to a dreadful room in a wretched rat-infested hotel. When the food I had brought with me ran out, I seriously believed I might die of malnutrition. Fortunately, I ferreted out a food speakeasy, strictly black market, furtively bought a membership, and lived. But not even that windfall relieved the frustration of a young physician with his own hospital whose offer to serve without pay was snarled in appalling bureaucracy.

I was ready to throw up my hands in despair and return to New York when I was invited (perhaps to get rid of me) to join a group about to be sent to the Urals on a month-long junket to report on that area's industrial potentialities.

That trip changed the course of my life, ended a medical career that had never really begun, and moved me, astonishingly, into multinational business.

It was a ghastly trip. I was plunged into a nightmare of famine and pestilence beyond my comprehension. Every glimpse out of the windows of our special train would reveal by day or night countless bodies of the dead and dying. Starving children and their parents pressed pathetic and dirty faces against the windows, causing food to stick in our throats.

It was too much. One day I asked a provincial official what could be done about this human catastrophe. He shrugged and said, "Nothing." The drought had withered the grain fields; the people had no money with which to buy abroad, even if the outside world would sell.

As best I can now reconstruct that talk of long ago, I said I had a million dollars and I would cable my older brother in New York and tell him to buy that much wheat and ship it as quickly as possible to the Soviet Urals. U.S. farmers had a glut of wheat, and were selling it for a dollar a bushel or burning it to save the time and expense of taking it to market.

When the official said sadly that there would be no way to repay me I told him I had seen mountains of furs during our stop in Ekaterinburg and unused stocks of platinum, Ural emeralds, and hides and mineral products at other stops. I asked him to find a person who had the authority to accept the million bushels and permit me to send back by return ship what might be judged a million dollars worth of the unwanted products of the Urals. There is no space here to detail my first barter deal with the Russians, save that it worked to the satisfaction of both sides (and the Russians threw in a *ton* of caviar for good measure).

Today the U.S. and the U.S.S.R. have instant communications via sophisticated satellites and a Trade Hot Line that gets hotter with every passing day. But in the summer of 1921 it took a bit longer. Suffice it to say that about a week or two after I proposed the barter deal to the provincial official, I found myself in a tiny railside telegraph station, where our train had been flagged down, listening to a Morse code exchange between our junket director and, incredibly, the man who had changed the history of the world, Vladimir Ilyich Lenin.

Lenin asked telegraphically if it was true that some young American doctor was willing to gamble a million dollars on helping Russia. When he was assured that this was true, he asked that I return to Moscow. He wanted to see me.

There was nothing routine about my meeting with a man who was old enough to be my father, as well as the most controversial man in the world. He didn't sound much like the Red Dictator he was portrayed to be in much of our press. At one point he picked a copy of *The Scientific American* from his desk, thumbed through it and said (in English), "Look here, this is what your people have done. This is what progress means . . . building, inventions, machines, development of mechanical aids to human hands. Russia today is like your country was during the pioneer stage. We need the knowledge and spirit that has made America what she is today. . . . I heard you wanted to do medical relief work. It is good and greatly needed, but we have plenty of doctors. What we want here is American businessmen. What we really need is American capital and technical aid."

He said much more, but the upshot of it was that he offered me, and I accepted, the concession (first of its kind) to resuscitate (and maybe profit from) an abandoned Czarist asbestos mine I had seen at a place named Alapayevsk, north of Ekaterinburg.

It was a ghostly hole in the gray ground of misery. But it was the beginning of a still hard-to-believe relationship between instinctively hostile philosophies. Under Lenin's wing, and on occasion the protection of Leon Trotsky's Red Army troops, I soon thereafter became the sole representation in Russia of 38 American companies whose products ranged from Fordson tractors to fountain pens.

The first and toughest of these to bring in line was the Ford Motor Company, then totally dominated by its cantankerous founder. Mr. Ford was perhaps the foremost anti-Bolshevist in America in 1921. The strongest editorials in his *Dearborn Independent*, aside from those denouncing "Jewish International Bankers" were directed at Russia and its leaders. But I made the long trip from Moscow to Dearborn anyway and somehow persuaded him to believe that Russia was here to stay, that those leaders he scorned rated him with Tom Edison as the greatest living Americans, and that they would pay him fully for every tractor he chose to send to them.

During the next nine years Henry Ford made millions out of the sale of Ford products to the Soviets. The most lucrative deal of all was the building of the first mass production automobile and truck factory in the U.S.S.R. sometime in 1930 in return for the purchase of 30 million dollars' worth of Ford products and a like amount of spare parts and equipment.

By 1930, with Stalin in power, the official Soviet trade agency AMTORG took over most of my type of Russian-American trade dealings. But someone remembered what I had done to restore the asbestos mines and open trade between the Soviet Union and the United States, and I was granted a final and richly rewarding concession: the manufacture of pencils. That came about by chance. Shortly before that I had bought, for the equivalent of a dollar, a pencil imported from Germany. Inferior pencils made by the state-owned pencil factory could not be sold. They tore the paper when people tried to write. I went to Leonid Krassin, Chief of the Foreign Trade Monopoly Department, showed him the bad pencil, and asked him if it was true that his government intended to see to it that every citizen would learn to read and write. Certainly, he replied. So I said I'd like to obtain a license to manufacture them in Russia, pencils every bit as good as those imported from Germany.

The resultant deal was hard but fair. I had to put up $50,000 as a guarantee that I would build a plant and have it in operation within 12 months, and deliver a million dollars' worth of pencils in the first operating year.

I took the next train to Nuremberg and rounded up some old Faber master technicians. To condense matters, I made a couple million dollars operating the plant and a few million more when I sold it to the State. They asked me to take promissory notes for most of the latter. I agreed instantly. I took the "paper" with me when I moved to Paris, where I planned to establish an international bank, and there I found that my complete faith in the integrity of the Soviets was not exactly shared. A number of American businessmen who had accepted Russian notes offered them to me at panic rates. I bought some 3-year notes for as little as a third of their promised value.

The Russians paid me off right down to the last kopek.

RECENT EXPERIENCES

There was a hiatus of three decades in my association with the Russians, in my case filled with ventures and adventures in fields as varied as art, cattle, whiskey, radio, gold mining, and some tentative approaches to the oil business. I might never have resumed what has been called my "Russian Connection" if President Kennedy had not asked me in 1961 to go on a balance-of-trade fact-finding mission to the United Kingdom, France, West Germany, Italy, Libya, the Soviet Union, India, and Japan.

The journey ended abruptly in Moscow; its appearance and affluence had improved immensely since I last saw it, 31 years before. The journey ended there because of most significant talks I had, first with my old friend from Fordson tractor times, Anastas Mikoyan, and then with Nikita Khrushchev.

Looking back, it seems ludicrous that Khrushchev and Mikoyan were outraged at that time because the Eisenhower Administration had put a boycott on the importation of canned Russian crabmeat. The U.S. charge was that the crabs were harvested, prepared, and packaged by "slave labor." A trivial amount of money was involved. It was the principle of the thing, they told me angrily. (By contrast, recently Occidental had a most amicable $20 billion deal with the Russians.)

What interested Washington in 1961 was that, between explosions, I found Khrushchev tantalizingly receptive to a step-up in trade with the United States. At one point he said in his tough way, "If some people in the United States think that by not trading with us they can crush us, they are mistaken. We don't want you to sell to us unless it is profitable for you to do so, and profitable for us. There are things we want from you—if we can get them we don't have to develop our own industries. If we work together, our economies will thus be tied in together. If you give us credit, you should do so because it is to your benefit and not as a favor. You will earn interest, you will make a profit on the goods you sell, and it will keep your plants busy. There has never been a case when we have failed to pay our commercial obligations and there never will. We will not buy on credit, even for five years, unless we know we can pay for it."

That was the encouraging core of our talk, and the reason why Washington cancelled the last two stops on my trip and brought me home for an expanded report. But the meeting provided other opportunities to get closer to an important man who previously had predicted that his country would "bury" us economically, the man who had brusquely ended the Paris Summit after the U-2 spying incident and withdrawn his invitation to Eisenhower to visit the Soviet Union and speak to its 200 million people. I seized upon every opportunity to dampen his deep-rooted suspicions of us. I promised to do my utmost to lift the ban on their crabmeat. (And did.) I held out the proposition that the two hostile powers, then engaged in a missile and space race, might come to know each other better if we exchanged our separate works of art. After he said stoutly, "We are no longer afraid of the United States," and predicted that by 1980 his country would be producing twice as much steel as the United States, I pleased him by offering to send him a young Black Angus bull by my champion, Prince Eric of Sunbeam. In turn he gave me a handsome pencil with a jeweled red star in the place normally reserved for the eraser. It had been presented to him by the workers of my old plant, by now named the Sacco-Vanzetti Pencil Factory. And he arranged for me and my wife to visit the place and be entertained by old and new employees before we left Moscow.

By the summer of 1972, upon invitation before and after the Nixon-Brezhnev summit in the spring of that year, I returned to Moscow to deal with a new generation of leaders. As a mark of the changing times, our group arrived in our company's 600-mile-an-hour Gulfstream II, the first private jet given permission to land there.

OCCIDENTAL'S NEGOTIATIONS

This was now the era of Leonid I. Brezhnev. Doors began opening for us after I was received by Premier Kosygin. They began opening partly because I speak Russian and particularly because of my record in the U.S.S.R. I knew and was liked and trusted by Lenin. Not even Khrushchev had ever met him, much less Brezhnev, Kosygin, and the remainder of the new regime. There is no way to describe the effect of that friendship except to say that it compares roughly with the reception U.S. firms would give an elderly Russian merchant, who, as a very young man, had done business with Abraham Lincoln.

Most of my meetings that hot week in July of 1972 were with Dr. D. M. Gvishiani, Deputy Chairman of the State Committee for Science and Technology. He is Premier Kosygin's son-in-law and very bright, well-groomed, and sports a Pulsar wristwatch. Others in my party spoke at great length with Gvishiani's associates and put together what is called a trade protocol, a framework for doing business where business had never before been seriously considered between a sovereign state and a private enterprise.

As others have in their dealings with the Russians, my group began to itch with restlessness over the progress of its negotiations. So, in the hope of speeding up matters, I informed Dr. Gvishiani that we planned to leave before dusk on a certain day. In mid-afternoon of that day he called me to his office and presented me with a draft, in Cyrillic, of a proposed protocol. It listed five points. If the terms were acceptable, we at Occidental would be permitted to delve into:

1. Exploration, production, and use of Soviet natural gas and crude oil.
2. Supplying the U.S.S.R. with needed fertilizers and chemicals.
3. Presenting a plan for a trade center and American-style hotel in Moscow that might attract business conventions, provide office space for future firms dealing with the Soviet Union, and offer familiar conveniences to tourists.
4. Providing the Soviet Union with the knowledge to produce sufficient quantities of metal plating.
5. Utilizing Soviet solid wastes.

No business deal with the Russians can be launched without a signed protocol. It provides a base from which all details of the deal are initiated. Under a protocol, visas are issued for continuing visits, government agencies schedule appointments, and meetings are held that lead to the next stage, which is a letter of intent. Once the latter is successfully negotiated, it leads to implementing contracts and global agreements. It is a tedious process which has discouraged more than one impatient chief executive; to his loss. But in our particular case I found a way to circumvent the accustomed delays in reaching agreement.

When Dr. Gvishiani handed the involved document to me, he suggested that I have it translated, study the proposals, and return to Moscow for more discussions. I glanced through it quickly, picked up a pen, and struck out the word "draft."

"Occidental accepts," I told him.

He was stumped. "Don't you want to study it longer and show it to your lawyers?" he asked.

I said, "No, it's something we can work under. It's your draft, not mine. I haven't changed a word, so why don't you sign it?"

He conferred with his associates for a time, smiled, and signed.

That was the beginning of the barter and expertise relationship which was first announced as an $8 billion proposition, but which escalated to the aforementioned $20 billion extending over the next 20 years.

It was not as simple as I have outlined above. There followed many negotiations at home and in the Soviet Union. I made 21 trips to Moscow between July 1972 and January 1975. An executive must be willing to make the long trip to Moscow with little notice. The Soviet chain of command is like any other. It functions best when those who make policy send word down the line that the policy must be implemented with the least possible delay. Many American companies have found themselves caught in a morass of red tape which would have been avoided if the Chief Executive Officer had made one more trip to talk to a proper minister and keep the project from bogging down.

REMAINING THOUGHTS

A few remaining thoughts.

A capitalist can do business with a communist, not as newfound friends but as hard-nosed businessmen making a deal. It should be remembered that whatever document you sign is one which you and your stockholders must be prepared to live with.

A capitalist should always keep in mind that his opposite number in the Soviet Union generally does not have the same freedom of decision that he, the American individualist, possesses. We have many chairmen of the board. In the Soviet Union there is only one chairman—General Secretary Brezhnev—and one corporation, the Union of Soviet Socialist Republics.

All Soviet expenditures are geared to the Gosplan—the Five Year Plan. Thus it is important that American businessmen complete their contracts in time to be included in the current Gosplan. Otherwise, with rare exceptions, there may be a longer period of negotiations required before a major transaction can be put together.

You should not try to butter up the Soviet official or be obsequious in any way. They would not respect you if you were. You must be a hard bargainer because they are consummate negotiators who will hold off an affirmative nod until the last moment, in order to get their points into a contract. On the other hand, you can have the utmost confidence in a contract, once signed.

Our ideologies will always be disparate. I cannot conceive of communism ever veering toward capitalism, any more than I can foresee the United States allowing its democratic system to give way to Marxist-Leninism. But I do believe, to repeat, that we can live together and that if we continue to exist as trading partners the world we share will be a better place.

If it is in your power or sphere I would encourage you to trade with the U.S.S.R. I warn you that the competition is sometimes fierce and the personal requirements great. But so are the profits. The challenge in Occidental's case was well worth the expenditure of our time and efforts. We don't regard our trade with the Soviets at this time as the centerpiece of our profit structure, but we have found that our involvement has led us to a position where our signed deals are becoming a sweet dessert for our future balance sheets. Victor Hugo expressed it best long before there was an Occidental when he wrote, "Nothing is more powerful than an idea whose time has come."

It has come, I can assure you. Don't fail to seize it, not only for the sake of profit, but for the sake of peace.

PART IV-G

Other
Functions
of
the
Business

WHAT THE CEO SHOULD EXPECT FROM HIS GENERAL COUNSEL

by Frank E. Barnett

Chairman of the Board and Chief Executive Officer,
*Union Pacific Corporation**

and William J. McDonald

Senior Vice President—Law, Union Pacific Corporation†

THE SPREADING THICKET OF BUSINESS REGULATION

THE 20th century has been marked by an ever-continuing growth, at both the federal and state levels, of regulation of the American business corporation. Today there are few aspects of business whether involving research and development, production, distribution, employment, financing, or ownership which are free from regulation in one form or another.

The turn-of-the-century-born mandates of the federal antitrust laws, originally the Sherman and later the Clayton (as amended by Robinson-Patman) and the Federal Trade Commission Acts, to preserve and maintain free competition are, of course, of general application to American business. Additionally, a number of industries, with heightened public interest responsibilities, have long been subjected to specific and comprehensive regulation on both the state and federal

---

* Mr. Barnett served as Chief Legal Officer of Union Pacific Railroad Company and its subsidiaries during the period 1951 through 1966.

† Before assuming his duties as Chief Legal Officer of Union Pacific in 1968, Mr. McDonald had been a partner in a New York City law firm with which he had been associated for 16 years.

[Ed. Note: At year-end 1973, Union Pacific and its subsidiaries employed 56 attorneys as full-time corporate law department employees. These lawyers were located in ten cities, including Washington, D.C. The expenditures of the company and its subsidiaries for legal services in 1973 aggregated $5 million, including in excess of $1 million paid to over 40 outside law firms representing the company's interests.]

899

levels. Although the rail transportation industry was the first major segment of American free enterprise to be subjected to this type of regulation under the Interstate Commerce Act (involving restraints on market entry and withdrawal, competition—including mergers—pricing, and financing), other industries later followed that path. Chiefly during the New Deal era, and as a result of the felt needs of those times, there sprang up, primarily on the federal level, a number of laws to establish or strengthen industrially specific regulation in such areas as commercial banking, investment banking, securities brokerage, gas and electric utility service, air transport, and radio and television broadcasting.

The 1970s mark a decade wherein federal and state legislatures appear to be turning more and more to a generic type of business regulation rather than regulation of the earlier industrially specific variety, though with no less pervasive consequences. Just as the earlier enacted antitrust laws have across-the-board applicability to business, so too do the latter-day National Environmental Policy, Clean Air, Water Pollution Control, Equal Employment Opportunity, Occupational Safety and Health, Economic Stabilization, Federal Energy, Consumer Product Safety, and Pension Reform Acts—all at the federal level. The same is true of the several proposals for national health insurance, land use regulation, and renewed economic stabilization laws, all of which appear foreseeable in the near term at the federal level.

The formidable impact of this generic type of regulation of business is illustrated by the Federal Consumer Product Safety Commission which is now "routinely described as the most powerful regulatory agency ever created by Congress." Having the authority to act against hazardous products in a variety of ways, its "jurisdiction covers anywhere from 10,000 to 100,000 products that have been associated with at least 30 million consumer injuries yearly."[1]

The states have been no less active in the area of generic business regulation, evolving their own counterparts of NEPA and other laws designed to preserve aesthetic and ecologic values attached to land and sea areas by controlling or prohibiting development of such areas (e.g., California Environmental Quality Act and Coastal Zone Conservation Act), the strengthening of innumerable state fair employ-

---

[1] Gardner; "Consumer Report—New Product Safety Commission Adopts Tough but Responsible Approach to its Job"; *National Journal Reports*; September 22, 1973; p. 1391.

ment practice acts, and the passage of land use acts, such as industrial siting bills and other measures regulating the use of land.

It was said over 15 years ago in an American Bar Association study of lawyers' economic problems that "there never has been such a need for lawyers as today. Never before has life been so confused, bewildered, beset and upset by laws, rules, regulations, orders, opinions, changing and being changed, almost by the hour, with and without notice."[2] This observation remains currently apt with respect to the day-to-day life of the American business corporation and its need for legal guidance. Businesses even though not subjected to comprehensive regulation of an industrywide nature are nonetheless continually faced with legal problems involving the application and impact of taxes, trade, labor, or other regulatory legislation to their activities. The necessity of doing business within today's complex framework of federal, state, and local laws, regulations, and judicial and administrative decisions requires constant, prompt, expert, and thoroughly reliable legal advice.

The general counsel and his supporting staff, whether employed in-house or retained as outside counsel, supplies this need to the American business corporation. He is in large measure engaged in the practice of preventive law and is continually called upon by the Chief Executive Officer and senior management to advise them as well as the board of directors, respecting the legality of corporate plans, policies, and procedures so as to ensure legally effective corporate action and to avoid or minimize corporate—and in this age of derivative and other shareholder actions—even personal, liability.

In general terms, the answer to the question: "What Should the CEO Expect from His General Counsel?" is twofold. First, direct staff support in terms of creative, strategic, and tactical legal guidance and technical advice to senior management, the CEO, and the board of directors in the exercise of their duty to define corporate goals and make corporate policy and with particular reference to the increasingly important area of federal and state governmental affairs. Second, efficient exercise by the general counsel of his delegated responsibility to manage all of the legal affairs of the company. The CEO should properly expect his general counsel to provide, either

---

[2] "Lawyers' Economic Problems and Some Bar Association Solutions"; American Bar Association Special Committee on Economics of Law Practice; pamphlet no. 2; 1959; p. 4.

through the corporate law department or through outside counsel, competent legal advice to and legal representation for all management levels in the company.

FEDERAL AND STATE GOVERNMENTAL AFFAIRS

Because of the growing tendency on the part of government to increase the degree, and change the nature, of regulatory impact on American business, there is today a greater need than ever before for industry and government to work together in the constructive formulation and implementation of legislative programs. The American business company and its Chief Executive Officer, in particular, must play a more active role in federal and state governmental affairs. Although regulation of private enterprise to safeguard the public interest is an indisputably proper affair of government so, also, is constructive participation in the evolution and application of such regulation a proper responsibility of private enterprise. In short, just as government is more involved in the management of business, so too must management become more involved in the business of government. Today, the American business corporation is faced with a new array of politically potent, highly structured, and sophisticated activist organizations. They are striving to achieve what they perceive to be reasonably-sought reforms in environmental, ecological, tax, consumer-oriented, and other matters. In a political system in which many activist groups express varying values and aspirations, American business has the responsibility to see to it that the Congress, the state legislatures, and the regulatory bodies receive balanced views of matters so as to contribute to political resolutions that are truly responsive to all sides of the issues.

As Bryce Harlow recently said: "We are entering a period of possibly historic realignment of political forces in Washington and across the nation. In the short range, at least, business could suffer."

A primary management responsibility of the Chief Executive Officer is to plan for his company's long-term future. It is no accident that more and more Chief Executive Officers are becoming the principal "Mr. Outside" of their organizations. It seems to us impossible for a CEO to discharge his particular responsibility for long-range planning without himself becoming an "activist" in the areas of federal and state legislation and regulation.

Of course, he cannot do the job himself, but requires direct and substantial functional support from within his organization and, we think, particularly from his general counsel. Although the "Washington rule" should never be the hallmark of a CEO's existence, i.e., "One never writes what he signs nor signs what he writes," yet in this special area a significant degree of supportive apparatus and technical guidance is unavoidably necessary.

The direct supportive role of the general counsel and his deputies can be complex and time consuming. Take federal and state legislation as an example: First, a comprehensive system must be installed to ensure a thorough monitoring of all legislative bills with potential significance to the company. Each bill must be evaluated with respect to its political viability; it is an obvious waste of time to engage in wheel spinning over "perennials" that chronically go nowhere in the legislative process. The "live ones" must be carefully analyzed for a thorough understanding of their real meaning and practical and financial application to the company's business. To the extent necessary or appropriate, position papers must be prepared setting forth the company's views regarding the legislation. To make such positions meaningful, lobbying and formal testimony before legislative committees must be undertaken. These activities, together with the substantive position adopted, must be coordinated with other industry members, whether through a trade association or otherwise.*

Finally, and we believe most significantly of all, it is hard to overestimate the long-term corporate benefits which can be derived from anticipating the "temper-of-the-times" and moving forward in the role of constructive leadership, vis-à-vis legislation, rather than simply taking the traditional reactionary position of either defender of the status quo or a "patch-up" artist.

It is not difficult for today's CEO, given the multifarious burdens imposed on his shoulders, to yield to the temptation to argue against any change, i.e., simply to be "agin it." In the current egalitarian age of future shock and rising political and economic expectancies, we regard this temptation as a dangerous one to play with. Although each situation must necessarily be judged on its merits, as well as with an eye toward the political expediencies of the circumstances, it is well to bear in mind—and to reject—the advice offered by some moral theologians that "if rape is inevitable, relax and enjoy it." That advice should be roundly repudiated because it can only lead to a

---

* [Ed. Note: See the chapter by Roy M. Goodman, "The CEO and State and Local Governments."]

result which one hardly had in mind in the beginning. To the contrary—and if you will forgive a couple of railroad men for saying so—when you see the locomotive coming down the track, at least try to get the car or yourself off the grade crossing.

In 1973, a "locomotive" *was* coming down the track in the minds of many respecting what was then a major national crisis occasioned by the threatened shutdown of service by the Penn Central, the nation's largest rail carrier. The Joint Resolution of the Congress sending the Penn Central men back to work on the railroad, while the Secretary of Transportation was sent to work on a proposal to solve the Northeast rail crisis, ultimately produced two specific legislative proposals. One came from the Administration and one from the Interstate Commerce Commission. Both had serious, practical, and political defects in the eyes of many, within as well as outside the industry. This is not the place to recount in detail the story of what happened in connection with those proposals. That has been done elsewhere.[3] Suffice it to state here that several leaders in the industry, having come to such a conclusion, were faced with the decision whether to leave the matter to final resolution through the "art of the practical" or to attempt, independently and constructively, to advance an alternative solution.

I was inclined in the latter direction. But it was not an easy decision for me—Frank Barnett—to reach, as the Chief Executive Officer of my company. I well realized the long road I was starting down when I first resolved, with the backing of my Board, to embark on such a project. But in the end the game *was* worth the candle. The Congress *did* pass what came to be known as the Regional Rail Reorganization Act of 1973, which some have described as the most important piece of rail legislation since the Pacific Railway Acts of 1862 and 1864. This hyperbole overstates the case. But the statute, the constitutionality of which was recently upheld by the U.S. Supreme Court in a bitterly contested case, comparable in significance to Harry Truman's famous seizure of the steel industry, offers a substantive and procedural basis for solving the Northeast rail crisis within the framework of maintaining a private enterprise rail system.[4] The Act is

---

[3] See, e.g., Loving; "A Costly Rescue for the Northeast Railroads"; *Fortune*; February 1974; p. 118; and Albright; "The Penn-Central Cliffhanger—A Hell of a Way to Run a Government"; *The New York Times Magazine*; Section 3; November 3, 1974; p. 16.

[4] See, *Regional Rail Reorganization Act Cases*; Supreme Court of the United States; Decided December 16, 1974.

substantially reflective of the legislative solution drafted by the general counsel of my company following my basic decision to move forward on the matter. There were, of course, many involved in the legislative process. However, the end result does stand for the principle that a constructively based private industry response to a true public need can be sustained through that legislative process and be reflected in congressional action. It is my view that should the statute ultimately fail to achieve its stated goals, the Congress may in its then agony turn to the alternative, nationalizing the railroads in the Northeast of the country. This, and the consequential ultimate threat of nationwide rail nationalization, was at the heart of my motive in becoming involved in the matter.

THE MANAGEMENT OF THE LEGAL AFFAIRS OF THE COMPANY

Special Duties Owed Directly to the CEO

Typically, the bylaws of the American business corporation charge the chief legal officer with the responsibility for all of the company's legal affairs. This, as is obvious from what we have earlier noted, is saying quite a mouthful; there is virtually no area of company activity free of legal involvements. We can, however, for purposes of considering the particular responsibilities which the general counsel bears to the Chief Executive Officer, lay to one side such legal matters as are routinely handled by subordinates of the general counsel, whether they be attorneys employed full time in the company's law department, or outside retained counsel. This is not to say that such matters as litigation, financings, material contracts, tax law, legal issues affecting employee relations, and other matters of law as are handled by subordinates of the general counsel may not be of material significance to the corporate enterprise. It is to say, however, that the particular duty of the general counsel is to keep the chief executive and his senior colleagues fully informed respecting such matters as may have immediate or future material impact on corporate goals, strategies, tactics, results of operations, financings, taxes, or employee relations. Given the magnitude of all of the items on his plate, as well as the other, and often more compelling, line and staff demands on the sheer time availability of the Chief Executive Officer and his senior colleagues, sorting out *the* most important legal matters and getting them effectively before the top management can often be a difficult assignment.

The Growing Concern over Personal Liability

Among the responsibilities which the general counsel bears to the CEO and his senior colleagues and, in turn, to members of the company's board of directors, is the increasingly important one of advising them respecting possible exposure to claims of personal liability relating to corporate activity. Under this heading, there are three areas requiring special attention by the general counsel and his associates.

Procedural Steps Precedent to Significant Corporate Action. Prior to authorization and implementation of any significant corporate action, the general counsel should be made fully familiar with the contemplated action so that he may consider the procedural steps to be taken by management and develop an independent conclusion respecting the reasonableness of the foundational underpinning for such action. What we are here referring to is not simply the technical question whether all legally required detailed procedures have been properly followed, but rather a more basic evaluation of whether senior management and/or the board of directors of the company may be unduly exposing themselves to a claim of personal liability predicated on alleged mismanagement of the business, including claims of alleged improvident expenditures or disposition or waste of assets, failure to supervise, or such items as improper charitable or unlawful political contributions. It might occur to the general counsel in the course of such an evaluation to recommend to the Chief Executive Officer that an additional legally protective step or two be taken before implementing a particular plan. For example, he might recommend the engagement of independent investment banking counsel to represent separately the interests of minority stockholders (in addition to the investment banking counsel retained by the company itself) in the case of an intended transaction with minority shareholders of a subsidiary of the company. In some cases, he may even recommend against, or suggest corporate procedural safeguards respecting, an action when either fact or appearance of illegality or doubtful propriety might lead to difficulties.

Compliance with Statutory, Regulatory and Contractual Restraints and Requirements. Obviously, in this day and age of heightened investor awareness of the provisions of the federal securities laws and their vigorous enforcement by the Securities and Exchange Commission, a prime item under this category of responsibilities of the general counsel is the company's duty to make full and prompt disclosure of all material facts affecting its business as required by those laws. This, along with other matters of legal compliance, including avoidance of conduct impermissible under the antitrust laws, adhering to the requirements of all regulatory rules and quasi-judicial determinations, and due procedural authorization of all intended corporate activity, are not matters which need directly involve the Chief Executive Officer. The general counsel or his deputies can function effectively in these areas by working closely with other senior line or staff officers. The Chief Executive Officer need become involved only if a problem arises which cannot be resolved to the mutual satisfaction of the legal and other officers. Situations of this type should be infrequent.

Measures to Prevent Conflicts of Interest. In today's post-Watergate climate it would be a particularly poorly advised company that would operate without an explicit written policy against conflicts of interest. Such a policy should clearly delineate illustrative areas where conflicts (or indeed, the appearance of conflicts) will not be tolerated between the personal interests of directors or officers or employees, on the one hand, and the interests of the company on the other. It would be an equally poorly advised company, in our opinion, which fails to remind its directors, officers, and employees periodically of their obligations respecting this area of significant potential liability, including especially the possible misuse of inside information.

The substantive content of the company's stated policy against conflicts of interest should be drafted by its general counsel and, through the CEO, submitted to, and approved by, its board of directors. It should be periodically distributed to all officers and employees who should be required at that time to advise the Chief Executive Officer (perhaps through the corporate secretary) that they are familiar with the company's policy and that they are not in violation of any provision thereof. All questions of doubtful interpretation should be handled by the employee concerned with the general counsel directly.

Today's apprehension on the part of Chief Executive Officers, members of senior management, and the boards of directors of publicly held American business corporations as regards claims seeking to impose personal liability for corporate action is well founded in fact.

In a recent fairly broad-gauged private survey of over 1,300 companies (including about half of the nation's corporations with assets exceeding $1 billion) some 94, or 1 out of 14 surveyed, reported claims made during the 6-year period 1968 through 1973 against their directors or officers seeking to impose personal liability.[5] These claims represented actual or threatened litigation on the part of various of the corporation's "publics" including security-holders, competitors, creditors, customers, and government.

Of the claims filed, some 30 percent alleged mismanagement (in various forms); 42 percent alleged failures on the part of the company to comply with statutory, regulatory, or contractual restraints and requirements (including antitrust violations, which accounted for 16 percent of the claims); and alleged failures to make full and complete disclosure under the securities laws (which accounted for 10 percent); 13 percent involved claimed inadequacies in procedures foundational to corporate action; and 15 percent dealt with matters in the conflict-of-interest area.

Litigation and Other Matters for Outside Counsel

The phenomenon which, in our judgment, is next in significance to what has been characterized as the "widening net of government regulation" is the accelerating volume of litigation involving American business.

According to data furnished by the administrative office of the federal courts, over 26,000 business lawsuits were filed in the federal court system of the United States during 1974, as compared with just over 9,000 ten years earlier. This trebling in the volume of business lawsuits included a particularly explosive growth in so-called civil rights cases which went from 709 in 1964 to 8,443 in 1974 (an increase of about 12 times) while so-called commerce cases went from 271 to 3,925.

In addition to the frequently complex and significant issues raised in the widening burden of litigation, it also presents what is becoming a larger and larger problem: the simple matter of effectively managing the costs of litigation.

Generally speaking, American business does not handle its litigation "in-house." Although there are notable exceptions to this rule,

---

[5] "The 1974 Wyatt Directors' and Officers' Liability Survey Summary Report"; The Wyatt Company; September 1974.

they usually involve companies (1) which are in intensively regulated industries where adversarial proceedings bulk large in the volume of legal work done, and (2) who act as self-insurers in the main. The nation's railroads, which have traditionally handled litigation involving claims based on personal injury or property damage in-house, furnish a good example.

If there is one single functional responsibility which presumptively can be handled more efficiently and effectively by outside counsel than by in-house lawyers, surely it is litigation.

It is our impression that the very nature of both the corporate law department and the type of practice conducted by outside law firms has, for a number of years, been undergoing a profound evolutionary change. It seems to us that litigation—embracing all varieties of adversarial proceedings, both judicial and quasi-judicial (i.e., before federal and state regulatory agencies)—is becoming a more and more significant part of the practice of the outside law firm.

The last 20 years have seen an accelerated growth of corporate internal legal capacity in terms of both numbers of attorneys employed full time and, more importantly, the heightening degree of sophistication reflected by the increasing ability of corporate internal counsel to begin and follow through to finality the legal side of corporate projects. No longer is internal counsel merely expected to perform the routine housekeeping chores of acting as "scrivener" to the corporation (by attending to such duties as drafting contracts and the like) or simply as a "compliance" officer (by preparing and/or reviewing for filing each of the manifold reports required in today's legal regulatory and reporting environment). Corporate law departments are now being looked to, we believe properly, to handle such matters as representing the company in major financings—whether public or private—and even significant corporate acquisitions or dispositions.

This sort of thing was, in earlier years, always handled by outside counsel. Today, the traditional routine corporate legal work is being done inside the company and the work which used to be referred to outside counsel (including, in addition to matters we have already mentioned, such legal concerns as taxes and employee compensation and benefits) are well on the way to becoming matters of routine internal handling.

There has been a correlative change in the "stuff of the practice" of outside law firms. Today, they are substantially out of the routine corporate work. They are devoting themselves more and more to "transactional law" (i.e., they represent the corporation in particularly important transactions); to their traditional role as counsel to the "money men" (whether they be commercial or investment bankers or institutional investors); and, of course, to their most important role as litigators.

In summary, we would say that there are three areas where, presumptively, outside counsel should become involved in particular legal issues having material consequences to the company: (1) where there is a real threat or a clear expectancy that the issue will ripen to litigation; (2) where the problem presented calls for expertise in a particular legal specialty or area not possessed by internal counsel (e.g., antitrust and special aspects of tax law); and (3) where there are legal issues common to a number of companies which can logically and legally jointly engage outside counsel. Typically, if not invariably, the second and third categories will also involve pending or threatened litigation.

We believe it most important to establish the rule that the decisions whether or when to engage outside counsel, and which counsel should be engaged, are matters within the authority and responsibility of the general counsel. We believe it is also important to establish that, in such cases, the reporting relationship, both functional and administrative, runs directly from the outside law firm to the general counsel rather than to the Chief Executive Officer or any of his subordinate line or other staff officers. If these principles are followed, the general counsel will have the authority over—which is correlative to his responsibility for—the handling of matters by outside lawyers.

It has been said that many companies can effect significant savings in the annual cost of legal services by maximizing their in-house capabilities. We are in general agreement with this statement, particularly where a company has been in the habit of permitting outside counsel to handle and accrue substantial chargeable time for the traditional routine type of legal work which otherwise might be done by a young full-time in-house corporate counsel.

As President Lincoln is reputed to have said, "A lawyer's time is his stock-in-trade." Although outside counsel are fond of stating that in arriving at the amounts of billings, all relevant considerations such as the significance, novelty, degree of difficulty, results achieved, and the like, are considered, yet, in this day and age of inflation, large law firms, and computerized accrual of chargeable hours by client and by attorney, the amount of time committed to a particular matter remains the single most important determinant in arriving at the fee. It is customary for law firms to plug in an hourly rate for each lawyer which is designed to provide a satisfactory economic return to the firm overall. These rates are almost unvaryingly departed from only on the up side, where the intangibles, which we have earlier noted, reflect themselves in an added charge over the basic rates and which some firms euphemistically characterize as "progress."

With typical law firm average billing rates ranging upwards (and not infrequently materially so) of $60 an hour in 1974, prudent management requires that companies which have yet to get their internal house in order, respecting at least "routine" legal work, do so with dispatch.

However, the cost factor does not of itself argue in favor of a full blown rush to staff-up totally in-house. Given an assumed average billable rate in the range of, say, $65 and with full recognition of salary costs and of other direct costs (such as fringe benefits which are currently running on the order of 20 percent of base compensation), and of associated overhead, purchased outside legal services may not greatly exceed in cost the in-house alternative buildup. The rate and extent of internal staffing-up must be carefully managed.

It is important to emphasize that the general counsel must, in respect of all matters referred to outside law firms, closely monitor the amount of time being committed to the project as well as the quality of the work product and results achieved. By reason of the combined increasing volume of referred matters and escalating fee schedules, it has become necessary for him to be thoroughly familiar with the billing practices of all outside firms with whom he deals. It is today by no means out of order for the general counsel to seek and obtain from the outside law firm detailed figures as to the several hourly rates assigned to the various attorneys, whether associates or partners, who are working on the referred matter. With associates' time (i.e., those junior lawyers who are not members of the firm) being today charged at rates ranging up to as high as $65 per hour and partners at rates which can exceed $100 per hour, it requires managerial oversight on the part of the general counsel to insure that the average hourly billable rates will be held to an acceptable level. The general counsel must see to it that work which can be effectively handled by a young associate is not being done by a partner and that the firm is utilizing nonlawyer, so-called paraprofessional help for such statistical, research, or other efforts which can be reasonably and responsibly so delegated. In this way, the magnitude of billings by outside law firms can be properly controlled.

The Relationship of Parent Company General Counsel with Subsidiaries and Divisions

In the case of a major business corporation with a number of lines of business, either incorporated as separate subsidiaries or operating under a divisional organization structure, and particularly where the corporate or headquarters office is located in one city and the operating entities are located in one or more geographically separate points, it is necessary to resolve the nature of the relationship of the subsidiary staff services, including the legal service, to the operating component and to their functional counterparts at corporate headquarters. On the one hand, it is possible to establish each subsidiary or division as operationally independent in the sense, for purposes of staff services, that the legal and other staff needs of such entity are furnished with no reporting relationship or functional responsibility running between the head of the subsidiary or divisional staff service and his counterpart at corporate headquarters. The alternative, which we regard to be clearly the more desirable of the choices, is to create what is generally referred to as a functional or "dotted-line" reporting relationship between the staff chiefs of the various subsidiary services, including subsidiary general counsel, and their counterparts at the headquarters office. One corollary benefit to be derived from such a policy is to enable the subsidiary or divisional staff officer to utilize the expertise of another specialist in his field, even though not employed by that particular entity.

Of course, the general counsel of a subsidiary or division must bear responsibility for his client's legal affairs and must necessarily report administratively to the subsidiary or divisional line executive officer in charge. However, we believe it important to require that the general counsel of the operating entities also report functionally to the parent company's chief legal officer (who may, indeed, be charged under the publicly-held company's bylaws with the duty of managing all of the legal affairs of the company *and* its subsidiaries).

By functional or dotted-line responsibility and reporting, we mean that the parent company or corporate headquarters general counsel has the explicit duty: (1) to formulate broad legal policy from the viewpoint of the parent company; (2) to audit and professionally appraise the performance of all corporate counsel, whether directly employed or engaged as outside counsel; (3) with the concurrence of the Chief Executive Officer at the subsidiary or divisional level, to recruit and select attorneys and to establish and change their areas and levels of responsibility; (4) again, with the concurrence of such Chief Executive Officer, to effect changes in law department organization; and (5) in partnership with such Chief Executive Officer to arrive at determinations respecting salary changes, whether normally incremental or promotional in nature, as well as other matters affecting or involving employee compensation. The subsidiary or divisional general counsel must bring to the attention of the company's chief legal officer all legal matters which "rise to the level of material concern" within their own entities and cooperate fully with him in aid of the discharge of his particular and overall legal responsibilities.[6]

CONCLUSION

The company's general counsel is a principal member of the CEO's management team with significant responsibilities in administering the furnishing of a broad array of legal services to the company. He can, when properly utilized, often provide an added dimension to a company's senior management or board of directors in the carrying out of their duties, to set corporate goals and to establish overall policies.

The evolution in recent years of corporate internal lawyers "from one man counseling and referring services to full-fledged law departments,"[7] coupled with the recruitment into corporate employment of attorneys of the highest professional competence and academic achievement, comparable to the levels found in private practice, has been a phenomenon which has measurably benefited the American business corporation in its constant striving to grow and act both responsively and responsibly under our rule of law.

One former colleague in the railroad industry, when once asked what the CEO expects of the general counsel and its law department, put it this way:

---

[6] See Dale; "Organization"; Chapter 3; *Line and Staff*; American Management Association; 1967; p. 61.

[7] Ruder; "A Suggestion for Increased Use of Corporate Law Departments in Modern Corporations"; *The Business Lawyer*; American Bar Association; vol. 23; January 1968; p. 341.

The chief executive expects the law department to do everything superlatively well. He expects it to be courageous, but not rash; vigilant in the protection of the company's assets and property, but not inhumane; firm in representing us but tactful. He expects its members to have opinions but not to be opinionated; he expects the lawyers to be learned but not pedantic; he expects them to be self-confident but not arrogant; he expects the law department to have pride in the law as a profession, but not to depreciate or belittle the professions of others. In short, the chief executive expects that his law department will have all of the virtues—and none of the vices—of mankind in general.[8]

---

[8] Heineman; "What the Corporate Executive Expects from His Legal Department"; *The Business Lawyer*; American Bar Association; vol. 20; January 1965; p. 482.

WHAT THE CEO NEEDS TO KNOW ABOUT LABOR RELATIONS

by John J. O'Connell

Vice President—Industrial Relations, Bethlehem Steel Corporation

INTRODUCTION

THIS CHAPTER describes in broad outline such matters as the organization of the labor relations function, the effect of the political nature of the labor organization on that function, the negotiation and administration of labor agreements, including the ongoing relationship with the labor organization, and the legal framework of the labor relations function. That background leads to certain guides for the Chief Executive Officer in selecting a labor relations executive, appraising his performance, and fitting him into the organizational structure of the company.

THE ORGANIZATIONAL ENVIRONMENT

Close coordination between the labor relations function and other corporate groups is vital. For example, close coordination is absolutely essential with operations and public relations.

The collective bargaining agreement sets forth the basic rights and obligations governing the relationship between the employees and the management. The rights and obligations set forth in the agreement are often limited or expanded by custom or practice and they are, of course, subject to interpretation by arbitrators' decisions. This entire bundle of rights and obligations governs the relationship between the employees and the management primarily at the plant or operating level. Obviously, therefore, there must be close coordination between the labor relations executive and his staff and the operating management and the labor relations office at the plant level. In a multifacility operation, this coordination becomes not only more important but more complex. There are, of course, many different methods by which this coordination can be obtained. The method utilized varies from company to company, depending on its organizational structure and its management philosophy. Regardless of the method adopted, however, close coordination must exist in order to produce a successful administration of labor relations policy.

The labor relations organization is a service organization, not an operating organization. To a large extent, a labor contract and labor unions fetter management's rights in acting for the corporation. Thus, accommodation must frequently be made between two sets of rights and obligations—those of labor and those of management. A primary purpose of such coordination is to create uniformity of contract administration and uniformity of response with respect to similar labor relations problems arising at an operating facility or at different operating facilities. Through such coordination, conflicts between operating needs or desires and labor relations considerations are brought into focus and may be resolved or accommodated at the home office level and, if need be, at the top labor relations executive-operating executive level, thus either eliminating a head-on confrontation at the operating-local union level or properly positioning local operating management in case such confrontation becomes necessary. Communication between the labor relations executive and the top representative of the international union often furthers the advancement of a company's position in situations of this sort.

Basic labor policy is formulated at a company's top level. It is the function of the labor relations executive not only to participate in the formulation of that policy, but to see that it is enforced—firmly, fairly and uniformly—in the administration of the labor agreement. The performance of this latter function is impossible without close coordination with the company's operating organization.

Labor relations and public relations executives must work hand-in-glove in many areas. The timing of public announcements is of the utmost importance with respect to any matter having labor relations overtones. For example, announcements relating to such matters as forthcoming plant expansions and necessary realignment of work forces, acquisitions, force curtailments, and plant or departmental shutdowns should not be made to the news media in advance of advising the union representing the employees to be affected. Furthermore, announcements to the news media of matters involving labor relations should never be made by public relations without clearance by labor relations, not only as to substance but as to form as well.

In the area of potential acquisitions and mergers, there must be close coordination between labor relations and the financial, planning, engineering, and law departments. In such situations, some of the areas of concern are as follows:

1. Are the employees of the company to be acquired or merged represented by a union?
2. Are attempts being made to organize them?
3. What is the nature of the relationship with the union?
4. Is it the type of union which could form an aggressive nucleus for organizing other unorganized units of the acquiring or merging company?
5. What is the rate of grievance filing?
6. When does the union contract terminate?
7. Does the union contract contain a successor clause? What is its effect?
8. Are there National Labor Relations Board (NLRB) decisions or settlements involving payment of back pay to employees?
9. Are there Occupational Safety and Health Act (OSHA) citations and complaints requiring the payment of penalties?
10. Are there union or employee suits under Section 301 of the Labor-Management Relations Act resulting in outstanding judgments?[1]
11. Are there federal, state, or local government civil rights actions involving potential back-pay obligations on the basis of past discrimination?
12. Are there decisions based on grievances which require the payment of monies to the grievants?

When information of the foregoing sort has been assembled, the labor relations executive's knowledge of relevant National Labor Relations Board and court decisions should indicate the course to be followed in order to avoid or minimize organizational and bargaining problems and to avoid or protect his company against liabilities.

---

[1]Section 301 makes labor contracts, including arbitration provisions, enforceable under the law.

The Political Nature of Unions

Labor unions are essentially political organizations. Local union officers and representatives are elected to their positions by the membership. In the course of their campaigns for election, union representatives make commitments and take positions which motivate their activities when they are elected. Needless to say, the fulfillment of those commitments usually creates many problems for management. The phenomenon of the "political" grievance,[2] for example, is well known to all in the field. Likewise, those in the field are well aware of the fact that the filing rate of "political" grievances usually increases as the time for a local union election approaches. Conversely, the rate of disposition of those grievances increases as the political election fades into the past.

The officers of the international union are, like those of the local unions, elected to office by the membership and, as a result, political motivation exists at that level. The political motivation in dealings with companies at that level is, however, less pronounced. This is true for several reasons. At the national level, the union officer is usually more mature and more sophisticated than the average local union representative. Furthermore, he is advised, assisted, and to some extent guided by the nonelected staff of full-time, paid, professional experts who, to a large extent, are outside the political arena.

The labor relations executive must be fully aware of the political motivations and considerations at all levels within the unions with which he deals. Such awareness will enable him to avoid pitfalls and, more importantly, if properly used will quite often enable him to take advantage of those political motivations in solving problems and advancing positions advantageous to his company. As a consequence, the timing of a move which a company wishes to make and the approaches to be used will not infrequently be determined by relevant union political considerations.

NEGOTIATING LABOR AGREEMENTS

At the base of the labor relations function lies the crucial responsibility for the establishment of rates of pay, hours of work, and myriad other conditions of employment through the process of col-

---

[2] A grievance filed and perpetuated principally to demonstrate that the union official pursuing the grievance is actively representing the union's membership.

lective bargaining and the administration of the resulting labor agreement.

The type or format of the bargaining will affect the manner in which the bargaining is conducted. The manner of bargaining will depend, for example, upon whether the employer's spokesmen bargain on behalf of only their own company or as part of a group representing the interests of several companies associated for the purpose of bargaining. Neither bargaining posture is necessarily preferable; each has its advantages and disadvantages; but a clear characteristic of associated bargaining is the limitation placed on the ability of the labor relations executive to bargain on the basis of his own company's unique interests as compared with the possibly differing interests of the associated companies, either individually or as a group.

Another consideration affecting the nature of the collective bargaining process is its emotional environment. Has a crisis atmosphere been created by the likelihood of the use of economic force in the form of a strike or lockout? Or, on the other hand, is there a crisis-free atmosphere created by a long history of strike-free bargaining or by the adoption by the parties of alternative resolution methods, such as binding arbitration? The latter, crisis-free atmosphere, is obviously preferable; achieving it requires a mature management-labor relationship and statesmanship on both sides of the table. If there is a disadvantage inherent in the achievement of crisis-free bargaining, it is that, from the employer's viewpoint, the preservation of a strike-free bargaining history, or the continuation of the alternate means of resolving issues, may become too much of a consideration in the negotiations at the expense of a rational resolution of immediate issues.

In any individual situation, factors ranging from the relative economic strengths of the parties to the personalities of the negotiators may be important influences on the substance of discussions and the outcome of bargaining. There are, however, additional factors, such as other current collective bargaining settlements, government policies, and the conduct of the parties' press relations. Information on the details of collective bargaining settlements is much more readily available than was the case in the past, and neither party can afford to ignore what has been happening in other bargaining situations nationally, in the immediate geographical area, and in the industry or related industries. Government policies in such areas as wage and price control, pension legislation, and the generation and publication of wage-related statistics, such as the Consumer Price Index, are clearly becoming more influential in their effect on bargaining issues. Finally, the nature of the parties' relationship with the press is an important consideration. Little is to be gained by a public airing of the issues involved during bargaining, and it is preferable that the parties agree not to release to the news media any details concerning their discussions prior to a settlement's being reached.

Regardless of the many factors which may affect the manner in which bargaining takes place, the first and very essential step for the employer's representatives is the development of what may be called bargaining goals. Objectives must be established, before bargaining begins, in two major categories. First, it is imperative that the probable demands from the union be determined and that perimeters be set clearly defining the extent to which demands can be realistically accommodated. Second, the changes in the labor agreement which the employer believes must be made must be clearly defined and a logical, factual position must be developed to support the arguments that the changes are necessary. Although the whole of the bargaining process is usually viewed as the province of the labor relations specialist, it is actually the case that the development and revision of bargaining objectives necessarily draw upon the intelligence of other sectors of the corporate organization— the financial and operating staffs, for example. The development of objectives often (perhaps typically) occurs in an informal, evolutionary manner. The more effective course involves deliberate and directed examination of objectives both prior to bargaining and as bargaining progresses.

Administering the Agreement

The administration of the labor agreement, once it has been negotiated, is essentially a continuing process of problem solving. This is because a labor agreement, affecting as it does the interactions of people, is subject to differing interpretations and cannot practicably be so complete as to prescribe the proper course of action in every possible set of circumstances. A large part of the labor relations function is, therefore, the maintenance of an ongoing relationship with the union that will permit the labor agreement to be a viable, working document forming the basis for a stable relationship between the parties.

Typically, most of the activity involved with labor agreement administration occurs within the context of the formal grievance and arbitration procedure provided by the agreement itself. The essential ingredient in a successful grievance procedure is a first-line supervisory staff that has been trained sufficiently to apply the terms of the labor agreement in routine, day-to-day situations and that has been given sufficient authority to dispose promptly of employee complaints arising in those situations.

Minimizing the Adversary Relationship

One reality in present-day labor relations is that management and labor in many industries are becoming (at least away from the bargaining table) less diametrically opposed in all of their objectives than they have been in the past. Economic differences between members of the work force and management have become less distinct, but an even more pronounced influence has been an increase in the number of areas in which the interests of management and labor are identical or at least closely enough aligned to result in a degree of mutuality.

The development of a global market for many products and the resulting importance of foreign trade policy to the domestic economy have resulted in a mutual interest in attempting to shape that policy. The enactment and enforcement of civil rights and environmental legislation have also resulted in a common interest in realistic, reasonable implementation of the law.

The ongoing management-union relationship is, therefore, becoming an increasingly broad one, reaching well beyond the scope of the labor agreement. And, even in the narrower area of labor agreement administration, the relationship between management and the union must lend itself to a cooperative approach to solving problems. In an increasingly complex industrial society such as ours, new approaches to old problems are needed; the specific needs frequently cannot be anticipated during contract negotiations, and solutions frequently cannot be postponed until renegotiation of the agreement.

THE LEGAL FRAMEWORK OF THE LABOR RELATIONS FUNCTION

The basic framework of the legal structure within which the labor relations executive works today consists primarily of four statutes:

The Labor-Management Relations Act, as amended in 1959;[3] the Occupational Safety and Health Act; the Civil Rights Act of 1964, as amended in 1972; and the Age Discrimination in Employment Act of 1967.

In addition to those four basic statutes, there are numerous others with which the labor relations executive must deal. To name a few: the unemployment compensation and the workmen's compensation statutes of each of the states in which his company does business; several veterans' reemployment acts; the Walsh-Healy Public Contracts Act;[4] the Davis-Bacon Act;[5] and the Fair Labor Standards Act.[6] The labor relations executive in certain industries must also be familiar with statutes which are tailored especially for those industries; for example, in the railway and airline industries, the Railway Labor Act. There are also complex regulations issued by the regulatory agencies administering many of these statutes, e.g., the voluminous Occupational Safety and Health Act regulations.

The statutes to which reference has been made form only the skeletal framework of the entire legal structure within which the labor relations executive must work. Many of these statutes, like so many other statutes, are written in the broadest of terms. The flesh is then placed upon these broad definitions by the decisional interpretations issued by the courts and the governmental agencies created to administer them. By way of example, the Labor-Management Relations Act states, in Section 8(a), that it shall be an unfair labor practice for an employer "to interfere with, restrain or coerce employees in the exercise of the rights guaranteed in section 7." Section 7 guarantees the right of self-organization. What constitutes interference, restraint, or coercion is not, however, defined by the act. Those definitions have evolved and will continue to evolve from the constant interpretative processes of the National Labor Relations

---

[3] The Labor-Management Relations Act, as amended in 1959, now includes the Wagner Act of 1935, the Taft-Hartley Act of 1947, and the Landrum-Griffin Act of 1959. The first two of those component Acts are administered by the National Labor Relations Board and govern the rights of employees, employers, and unions in a labor relations context. The Landrum-Griffin Act is aimed primarily at policing internal union activity, but it also governs payments and contributions by employers to unions, and is administered by the Department of Labor.

[4] This act governs wages, hours, and working conditions for work on federal contracts.

[5] This act specifies that prevailing area wage rates and benefits must be provided on federal public works projects.

[6] This act governs wages, hours, and overtime payments for all business activity within the definition of interstate commerce.

Board, its Administrative Law Judges, and the courts. As a consequence of this process, the labor relations executive must be constantly alert to the changes which occur. The process creates a body of law which often makes it difficult to render precise, categorical answers to problems. Answers to problems must often be the result of a combination of knowledge of many interpretive decisions in a given area coupled with professionally trained judgment indicating in which direction the law will finally move and stabilize—at least for a reasonably foreseeable period of time.

Decisions of the National Labor Relations Board are subject to appeal to the federal Circuit Courts of Appeal. Appeals to Courts of Appeal in different circuits from similar decisions by the board may, and often do, result in conflicting decisions by those courts. One must then wait, hopefully, for a resolution of those conflicts by the Supreme Court of the United States. In the interim, there is a period of uncertainty which requires the exercise of sound, trained judgment by the labor relations executive.

What has been said with respect to the state of the law under the Labor-Management Relations Act is equally true with respect to the law under many of the other statutes with which the labor relations executive must deal.

In essence, the field of labor law, like many other fields of the law, is not a static field. It is one of constant change and evolution. To be a labor relations executive in this field requires constant attention and alertness. It is fraught with pitfalls for the unwary and the unalert.

CHOOSING AN EFFECTIVE LABOR RELATIONS EXECUTIVE

The foregoing description of the wide variety of technical and human relations responsibilities of the labor relations executive makes it clear that the Chief Executive Officer must select and appraise his labor relations executive carefully.

Substantial experience in union relations and demonstrably successful performance are particularly important qualities for the top labor relations executive of any company in which a labor organization represents a segment of the work force. They are required by the sensitive relationship which is implicit in the objectives of a union vis-à-vis those of an employer. An experienced labor relations executive recognizes the need for, and strives to attain stable labor-management relations notwithstanding the quasi-adversary nature of the relationship.

The relationship also implicitly requires an executive who is personable but firm. The labor relations executive should be well acquainted with the various statutes outlined above. The degree of necessary knowledge will vary in relation to the technical or legal back-up available to the top labor relations executive either from within the company staff or from accessible outside counsel. Although certainly not essential, legal training can be a valuable asset for a labor relations executive.

If at all possible, the labor relations executive should be selected from within the company's labor relations staff. In addition to the usual good reasons for promoting from within the organization, the ongoing and delicate nature of a company's relationship with the union or unions with which it deals suggests that this policy should be given even greater consideration than usual. If there is not a person from within the labor relations department of the company who has experience in the field and an acquaintance with the union officials concerned, the next best source for a labor relations executive is elsewhere in the company, such as in the personnel or law departments.

If the Chief Executive Officer is forced to go outside the company for his labor relations executive, it is advisable although not essential, that the search focus on either the same industry, a similar industry, or in the labor relations field in other industries that deal with the same union or unions. The method of conducting a search outside the company need not differ from that used to seek any other executive.

The Labor Relations Executive's Organizational Status

To whom the labor relations executive should report within the company structure depends largely on the size and organizational structure of the company and whether it follows a centralized or decentralized philosophy.

Nonetheless, a general approach can be recommended. It is common for the labor relations executive to have overall industrial relations responsibility for a company. This often includes the personnel function in addition to labor relations, safety and health, and security. If such is the case, it is logical that he would report directly to either the Chief Executive Officer or his designate, such as an executive vice president, senior vice president, or administrative vice president. On the other hand, if the labor relations executive is responsible for labor relations alone, he would normally report to a vice president of industrial relations or someone with the broader responsibility of employee relations, which includes other functional areas. Despite the legal ramifications of the labor relations area, the labor relations executive rarely reports through the company general counsel because of the special nature of the statutes and law referred to above. In any event, because of the need to maintain a balance between operating objectives and obligations imposed by a labor agreement, the labor relations executive should not report to the executive with primary responsibility for operations.

The Chief Executive Officer need not normally require his labor relations executive to report to him on a basis any different from that required of those executives charged with other areas of responsibility.

There will, of course, be times when circumstances will require far more frequent reporting, such as during the critical stages of collective bargaining or in the event of a work stoppage. Any variation from regular reporting should simply be a matter of common-sense judgment.

It must be stressed, however, that even in critical situations, increased communications between the labor relations executive and the Chief Executive Officer should not lead to direct personal involvement in the labor-management relationship by the latter. Experience has shown that it is absolutely essential that the Chief Executive Officer remain insulated from exposure to the union. This caveat is based on the fact that, once the union gets wind that someone superior in authority to the labor relations executive is directly concerned in labor relations matters, it will ignore the labor relations executive and attempt to deal directly with the superior official, particularly in critical situations. Unfortunately, the law gives support to the union's predilection in this respect because "bargaining in good faith" requires that the employer representative dealing with the labor organization possess sufficient authority to reach agreements with union representatives. Once the union believes that the real authority to reach agreement is out of the hands of the labor relations executive, it will attempt to bypass him. Furthermore, direct involvement by the Chief Executive Officer eliminates the opportunity to thoroughly discuss and think out the proper response to an unanticipated union demand.

EVALUATING THE LABOR RELATIONS EXECUTIVE'S PERFORMANCE

At the risk of setting forth the obvious, the following are certain judgmental criteria for the Chief Executive Officer's use. The absence, or low incidence, of strikes, may be, but is not necessarily, an indicator of a properly operating labor relations function; it may, however, mean that peace has been obtained at a higher-than-necessary labor rate or by making other costly concessions. On the other hand, a low labor wage rate obtained either with or without strikes may or may not indicate a properly functioning labor relations operation; a low labor wage rate may lead to low worker morale, resulting in poor and inefficient production, thereby actually increasing labor cost. The picture must be appraised as a whole in order to see that it is properly composed and balanced.

What has just been said about the relationship between labor peace and labor cost may be also said about the use of a low filing rate of employee complaints as an index of a properly functioning labor relations operation. If the low filing rate is obtained at the expense of "giving away the store," it is, obviously, a bad sign.

Following, by way of illustration, are a few of many other criteria to be used in judging the effectiveness of the labor relations executive's performance. Are the terms of the company's labor agreements competitive within the industry? Are the company's policies being firmly but fairly enforced or are needless and expensive compromises made? Are causes of unrest among employees investigated and remedial action taken where indicated? Are effective steps taken promptly to remedy breaches of the labor agreement by employees or the union? Is there sufficient flexibility in the face of changes in circumstances underlying policies? Has any part of the supervisory function been permitted to be assumed by the union? Are the negotiated labor costs (as distinguished from labor rates) competitive within the industry? Have compromises been made during the term of an agreement which have resulted in increased labor costs?

CONCLUSION

In summary, the Chief Executive Officer of any company which has a portion of its employees represented by a labor organization should ensure that his staff includes a competent and experienced executive in the labor relations field. The Chief Executive Officer should be adequately informed of significant developments of a labor relations nature. Nevertheless, he should maintain a respectful distance from direct involvement in labor relations.

THE CEO AND PERSONNEL

by Henry B. Schacht
President, Cummins Engine Company

with Ted L. Marston
Vice President—Personnel, Cummins Engine Company

GENERAL OBSERVATIONS

THE ROLE of a personnel group will vary with the organization's perception of the world in which we live. A management that views the world in rather static terms will tend to seek an administratively oriented personnel group; a management that views the world in terms of dominant trends will shape its views and organization to meet the challenges presented by these trends.

It is my view that the world has entered a period of very rapid change sparked by an enormous expansion of knowledge about many things, knowledge spread through modern communications and travel. One result is that individuals in organizations of all kinds, not just business organizations, are more knowing, more self-assured and more self-assertive than ever before. As far as I am concerned, this is all to the good. After all, the key element in any human organization in today's society is the individual; in particular, the response of the individual to the various views he or she perceives to be key.

But what are the kinds of issues which tend to impact most on people in organizations, and which provide a setting for determining just what is the mission of your personnel function? This question is worth the attention of the CEO who is interested in reexamining just what kind of personnel function is appropriate for his (or her) company—and what kind of leadership of that function is called for.

There seem to have been three main issues that have caused our society to reexamine itself during the past 30 years: a survival issue, an equity issue, and the issue of the new generation. These issues

928

have not always affected people in the same way; but, they have touched upon the lives of each of us.

The *survival* issue began on August 6, 1945, with the dropping of "the bomb" on Hiroshima. It was reenforced by the Cold War of the 50s, and the bitter conflict in Vietnam of the 60s and early 70s. It is now underscored by the pollution, population, and energy crisis which make man himself an endangered species.

The *equity* issue in this country had its roots in the Great Depression of the 30s. It submerged during World War II; but it re-emerged in recent years with the increased social sensitivity for the "Other America" of the have-nots. It has taken another giant leap in respect to equal rights for women. And, this issue increases significantly in prominence for organizations active in international business, especially among developing nations.

Finally, there is the issue of the *new generation*—its outlook, values and priorities. Although this issue began with the youth of our country, it has influenced all Americans. What is at issue is a change of consciousness—a consciousness that seeks a new understanding of what it means to be human and, incidentally, less materialistic.

It seems to me that these issues lead us to consider some difficult points.

1. The age of the machine and mass production has caused an "identity crisis." For men and women, black and white, it is difficult for people to develop a satisfying self-image. Many are asking themselves the question "Who am I? What am I? Where do I fit?"

2. There is an increased awareness of self through universal education and communication. This has altered people's expectations. The need for self-actualization is more apparent at all levels of our workforce.

3. When these new expectations have been unmet, they give rise to a sense of alienation as well as estrangement from established institutions. There seems to be an increased resolve by many that they will no longer allow others to determine their lives.

4. The rapid change in technology in this age of information requires, as Peter Drucker puts it, that people work "smarter, not harder."

It seems to me that the worth and growth of modern business in the next two decades, at least in part, will be determined by its ability to deal with these issues. It will be the momentum and creativity of human energy which will distinguish the outstanding company from the "also-rans." Personal creativity, willing human effort, and the capacity for innovation will make the difference.

THE ROLE OF PERSONNEL

If personal creativity, willing human effort, and the full utilization of human potential are what will make a business healthy, then it is essential that the organization must have a strong, competent personnel group. This organization must be as able to deal with the human resources as well as, or better than, the organization that deals with the numbers or the machines. The role of Personnel becomes one of dealing with the total utilization and health of the business and not just the hiring, firing, and compensation issues. This is a changing role and will be changing over the rest of the decade, but it is essential that it take place.

In the following sections I would like to discuss in more specific detail the role that I visualize Personnel must play at Cummins Engine. I hope you may see ways in which these remarks might apply to your own organization.

THE CONSCIENCE ROLE

Since Personnel deals mainly with the human elements of the organization, it must be in a position to speak for the people. One of the toughest jobs of any personnel group is to ensure that the individual rights of each person in the company are protected and that their voice can be heard. Personnel must be able to tap the deepest roots of any group to determine that people are being treated with dignity and respect. They must constantly work with the organization to instill a sense of fairness, openness, and trust. When they see power being misused, they let those who can correct that misuse know and insist it be stopped. The personnel group should be one place—not necessarily the only place—in the organization where a person can come and get a full hearing. They need to have not only the competency to deal with a person's problem, but also the access to influence situations which may be causing the problems. When someone from Personnel comes to a manager and tells him he has a people problem, then that manager should know that it's time to listen.

Within Cummins' personnel organization there is an "Office of Equal Opportunity." A good portion of its time is spent in counseling with minorities and women on problems they feel they have within their various units. Some of these problems are expressed as overt acts of discrimination. When so identified, the personnel counselor has the opportunity to investigate and seek corrective action before the whole matter takes on a legal character. At Cummins we also have a counseling and career planning function that spends all of its time dealing with work related and career problems. In the course of its work this function identifies many problems that are personal in nature or work related. Employees who have a drinking problem are encouraged to join AA (Alcoholics Anonymous). Employees with emotional problems are referred to the Mental Health Association in our community, with which we have a close relationship. Certainly, the Personnel Department misses many situations where the organization has misused an employee; on the other hand, many problems are identified that can be corrected before they become critical.

THE ROLE OF A CHANGE AGENT

In areas of individual development, growth, and learning, the personnel group should have the ability and have earned the respect to act as a change agent for the company as a whole. They need to be on the "cutting edge." They must understand the society in which they operate, and how it is changing.

When an organization is having problems, you can bet that some part of the problem is a result of people in the organization. The personnel group should have the ability to help the head of that organization diagnose the problem and work out a process to correct it. Many times this proces must involve the total organization in order to reach a solution. The personnel group must have the expertise to engage the total group in a problem-solving activity. They are responsible for ensuring that the decision on how to solve people, or organization, problems is not made in a vacuum, but is made on the best data possible, data furnished by the organization itself. This means that the personnel group is well schooled in intervention techniques and knows how to deal with groups and group processes.

At Cummins we have an organizational audit that takes place each year. This audit is sponsored by Personnel, but conducted by the organization. The prime focus is to identify problems that are causing the organization to function less effectively than it should. The audit ranges from discussion of the human talent within the organization to examination of the way the individual units of organization within the company are structured to function best internally and to interface with other organizational units. Overlaps of responsibility are identified and consolidation of functions is discussed. At the end of the audit each organizational unit is required to write an action plan on specific points discussed in the audit. This action plan is then followed up each quarter by the personnel staff. It's Personnel's responsibility to make sure the action agreed to is being carried out. This action plan is also reviewed each quarter by the chief operating officer, the chief financial officer, and the president.

To help each organization deal with the types of problems that are revealed by the audits, there is a personnel staff unit available to work with any line organization that requests their help. This unit normally has 10 to 15 projects going with the line organizations on organizational type problems. These problems range from communications to the redesign of jobs.

THE ROLE OF DEVELOPING FULL UTILIZATION OF THE WORKFORCE

Going back to the first comments of this chapter, one of the ways in which the personnel function can contribute to a company is to do something positive about meeting the self-actualization needs of employees. This means a very strong emphasis on the content of jobs, on the opportunity for each employee to use his/her full potential, and on the developmental system which promotes this. This is by far the toughest area for a personnel function to deal with. By any fair standard, the personnel function at Cummins can only have scratched the surface of what can and might be done. Nevertheless, without a high priority effort to deal with this issue, Personnel could not meet the expectations and concerns they see being expressed at all levels within our company.

The basic fundamentals that need to be put in place in order to deal with the problem of full and proper utilization are a prime responsibility of the personnel group. (Just what these fundamentals are is worth some attention, by the way.) Implementation and on-going activities are the responsibility of the line supervisor or manager. The line manager must be able to look at the work in his area to determine if that work gives people real responsibility, a chance to learn more, and the opportunity to be held accountable and be measured on what they actually do.

Most managers, when asked, will say this is an important part of their job. In fact, most managers spend little time on this part of their job; that is, the role of teacher, coach, and counselor. It falls on the personnel group to provide the knowledge and the systems to try and make this part of the manager's job a priority item.

During the past five years Cummins' personnel people have done some experimentation in what is referred to as "job enrichment" or "quality of work." The initial attempts were in designing work for new college hires. This led to three or four rather small projects in our Columbus, Indiana, plants. The projects involved our engine test-cell operations, the block line, a fabrication shop, and a ware-housing operation. One result has been to expand the concepts to two new plants now in the start-up phase, but operating with unique changes in organization structure and management style. It is too early to evaluate the effectiveness of these changes, but the early results look good.

Therefore, the personnel group has two major responsibilities in developing the fundamentals for full utilization of the workforce.

1. The personnel group must have an understanding of current technology in the behavioral sciences. There needs to be an understanding of how jobs are developed and structured; the reasons people like their work, and the factors that cause them to learn and grow. They need to impart this knowledge to the line organization. Their role is that of supporter, trainer, and measurer of results.

2. A second major responsibility is to ensure that the personnel-related systems of the organization reenforce the concept of people being able to advance in an organization to the maximum of their ability. This means that the performance evaluation system, the man-power planning system, and the compensation system all must complement and support this effort. All too often these systems are developed and carried out totally separate from each other. This can result in: a compensation system that reenforces seniority, not learning; a manpower system that worries about numbers of people, not

the long-range skills necessary in changing technology; or a performance evaluation system that deals only with what a person has learned, not what that person's capability or interest to learn might be.

THE ROLE OF MAKING THE FIRST IMPRESSION

In our organization, the personnel group is normally the first organization to make contact with any person we might hire. This is true from the people we might hire into blue-collar jobs right on up to a top executive. The first impression of Cummins that these people develop is the one left by the personnel group. I think that this first impression is very important; not so much in what is said about the job or the way the company operates, but in how that person is treated. If each person that comes to us for a job is treated with dignity and respect; if each person is listened to, and if we try to fully understand their skills and work expectations; then, if they come to work, they come with an impression and expectation of how they will be dealt with on the job. We want them to come with this expectation. This forces the organization to set standards for itself that already have been established in the hiring process.

THE ROLE OF HIRING

A role related to the foregoing is that of the initial screening of talent entering the organization. This means that the personnel group makes, for the most part, the first assessment of any individual we might hire. In order to do this with any degree of validity, the personnel group must understand the people in the company and must understand their value systems. This also means that the personnel group needs to be aware of both short-term and long-term company objectives, and be able to help the organization translate these objectives into what its people requirements will be.

Making an initial impression and hiring clearly are two of the most important and sensitive jobs in the personnel group. Able and sensitive people need to be in the hiring role, whether for the top or bottom of the organization.

Another important issue in the hiring and first impression role is affirmative action. If any institution wants to ensure that it gives all people an opportunity for jobs, the initial thrust will need to come from the personnel group. They set the tone, they identify the talent, and they help the organization best understand how it can use that talent.

PERSONNEL ORGANIZATION STRUCTURE

At Cummins, most of the people who are in the personnel function are scattered about—internationally—in the various line units. Why? Because that is where the action is. The central staff is kept small in number. The relationship between the line and central staff parts of Personnel is maintained by a flow of communications, periodic meetings and reassignment of personnel people, and common use of personnel information and other systems.

The top personnel officer has responsibility for proposing what his/her organization structure should be. But since the CEO has a lot to say about this matter, there are several points I would like to make regarding the organizational structure of a personnel group.

Line versus Staff

As I have said, where the real action is, so far as personnel matters go, is in the line organizations; this is where the real organizational and human change can take place. Consequently, the personnel department's central, worldwide staff organization is kept small. It is staffed with people having special skills, such as psychologists, for example, and people with direct line experience. The role of the central staff has to do with personnel policy, program development, personnel systems development, and consulting. They need to have the time and ability to know what is on the "cutting edge," and the credibility to be able to impart this to the line organization. We maintain a regular flow of people between on-the-line and on the personnel staff. We seldom have a person with major personnel responsibility who has not had personnel experience in a plant or on the line.

The Focus of Personnel Activity

At both the line and staff levels, the Cummins personnel organization is concerned primarily with two major activities. The first, touched upon earlier in this chapter, has to do with training, development, job structure, and organizational development—more or less, the overall health of the organization.

The second major activity is personnel administration—ensuring that personnel policy and personnel systems operate in the most effective and efficient way. The focus is on the environment in which people do their work, while the focus of the first area of activity is on the work itself and on the growth and learning of people within the organization (in Professor Herzberg's terms, motivation and maintenance[1]).

Labor relations and compensation activities are run with a mixed focus—a little bit of the first above, and a little bit of the second. The top personnel officer is uncertain as to where these fit. He would like to operate labor relations from the motivation perspective, but he runs into the traditional type of union management contracts. This makes it difficult for him to operate other than from a day-to-day traditional mode as regards labor relations and compensation.

Reporting Relationship

I believe that it is vital that each personnel group report directly to the head of each line organization to which it is assigned. Personnel people sit on the operating committees. In order to speak for the health of the organization, a personnel person must have the right platform to speak from and the right communication channel—right to the head person of any of our operating units.

THE TOP PERSONNEL OFFICER

In some firms personnel departments are relegated to a largely administrative role. They are combined with other miscellaneous groups whose day-to-day functioning is important but not critical if done well in a routine fashion. And that kind of personnel department does not call for demanding leadership.

But if a CEO views "people" as the key differentiating factor in the success of a company; if the CEO views the personnel department as the staff group responsible for monitoring the overall health of the organization and for being an agent of change; accordingly

---

[1] Herzberg, Frederick; *Work and the Nature of Man;* Cleveland: The World Publishing Company; 1966.

then, the CEO must be sure the department is led and staffed in an outstanding way.

I believe that CEOs should look to personnel departments as staff advisers and action agents on people just as CEOs look to finance departments on money.

The fully functioning personnel department must be led by a person who is a "professional"—technically competent, dedicated to other people, and not too much worried about "self." The role requires working through other people. Personnel's job is to get the organization to make change; to cause others to be better managers; to foster creativity in others. Personnel people can't do the job themselves; they must work through others. This requires a secure, stable, mature leader.

The administrative areas traditionally assigned to Personnel are important ones; I have mentioned a number of these earlier in this chapter. However, they are *not* critical to the mission of Personnel unless done poorly. Therefore, the senior personnel person should have skills and probably formal training in interpersonal disciplines. There needs to be administrative skill in the department but this need not be the predominant skill of the senior person. The top personnel officer should understand, appreciate, and insist upon proper administrative discipline, but he/she should be a "people person" first.

LOOKING AT THE PERFORMANCE OF PERSONNEL

After all is said and done, you can follow the best, most up-to-date principles and practices—but, still, *results* can be disappointing. Good intentions go only so far. Some hard-headed measures of *performance* are called for. Periodically, I review statistics on turnover, new hires, hiring costs, training, grievances, and productivity, among other indicators as to whether the personnel function is making itself felt. And I question the top personnel officer—as well as other executives—as to the meaning behind the statistics.

True, it is all too easy to view such measures of performance out of context of the organizational situation, and to lose one's time perspective. But that's true for any and all measures of organizational or functional performance. The top personnel officer has the responsibility to recommend just what measures of performance are appropriate, and to provide the necessary data if they are not otherwise available. The CEO has the responsibility—preferably with the advice of the top personnel officer—of understanding how to interpret the data.

SOME KEY GENERALIZATIONS

1. The CEO should turn naturally to the personnel officer for questions about the functioning of any organization or person in the company. Does he know he will get a straight answer, no matter what?
2. The CEO should be confident the personnel officer will "pound the table" over any perceived wrong to any individual at any level in the company anywhere in the world.
3. The CEO should be confident the personnel officer will be equally if not more concerned about the shop and office personnel as about the executives. The personnel department is not there to provide staff services for the bosses.
4. The CEO should naturally include the personnel officer in all strategy and policy meetings. If he doesn't, he is not getting the proper inputs. (Would you exclude the financial officer from long-range planning sessions?)
5. Things that would concern me about a personnel department:
   a. Headed by a lawyer.
   b. Participates in most discussions about administration but excluded from key strategy meetings.
   c. Populated by people by-passed in other parts of the organization.
   d. A place where the senior managers wouldn't think of going for advice on people problems of any dimension.
   e. Head of personnel department one of lowest paid officers or even worse, department not headed by an officer.
   f. Where the senior personnel executives view themselves as spokesmen for management and against labor.
   g. Where an international company's personnel department is populated solely by U.S. citizens.
   h. If the CEO hadn't been caught up short by the senior personnel officer at least once in the past month.
   i. A contented and satisfied senior personnel officer.
   j. A top personnel officer out of tune with problems of minori-

ties, women, and others traditionally disenfranchised by U.S. commercial organizations.

k. The head of the personnel department is someone who couldn't make it someplace else in the company.

A personnel department is a reflection of the company's view of the world. An observer can tell a lot about a company by asking to meet the personnel officer and asking him about the role and calibre of his organization.

CONCLUSION

In this chapter I have tried to draw a picture as to the general approach of my company to the personnel function. There are many areas that I have not covered that are significant; for example, affirmative action, which is of vital importance to Cummins.

The personnel function, I believe, should rank high in a CEO's priorities. This can pay off.

PURCHASING

by J. Donald Rauth

President, Martin Marietta Corporation

INTRODUCTION

THE READER NEEDS to be aware of the author's experience—and biases. Mine are based on long direct involvement with the aerospace industry up until recent years. One valuable segment of my earliest experience involved direction of a sizable purchasing (matériel) department. In later stages of my business life in aerospace, I viewed the purchasing function from other perspectives on the executive ladder. No matter what the perspective, it is a critically important function. In any case, although it certainly is not perfect, the federal procurement process as it has developed for the aerospace industry is one of the most comprehensive yet devised anywhere. It will soon become clear that I have drawn mainly on that system for this set of observations, both general and specific, that may be useful to the chief executive of any modern corporation.

PHILOSOPHY AND ORGANIZATION

The responsibilities of the purchasing function, properly exercised, will touch importantly on all sections of the corporate structure. The fact that the procurement organization spends a heavy percentage of the sales dollar outside of the company has a direct relationship to return on investment, inventories, cash flow, and a variety of other operating results and financial impacts. Especially when one is dealing with corporate fixed price contracts, the efficiency and effectiveness of the procurement function can be directly measured on the bottom line of the income statement. It is an easy step from there to my recommendation that the procurement function in any sophisticated business should answer directly to the president or the chief operating officer of the organization involved.

940

The function deserves, and demands, the best talent. Its personnel and the implementing charter of responsibilities must be strong enough to stand among coequal operating and financial people and departments. It requires sufficient status and support to make aggressive performance possible. For example, it sometimes is difficult to achieve a proper balance between purchasing and engineering in a high technology company. At one extreme, purchasing may become a clerical function; at the other, equally undesirable extreme, it is a barrier to progress. Ideally, it is a coequal vital link in progress and corporate performance. It is important that purchasing not be subordinate to the other functions, at least at the working levels, because when properly performed, it will many times conflict with the strong desires of the other departments. Purchasing certainly must be viewed as one of the mainstream functions in any substantial multiproduct company. In this circumstance, its value to the organization will be reflective of the personal strengths and perceptions of the executive to whom it answers.

Although purchasing is a highly specialized function in detail, it demands a variety of skills in varying degree. My experience suggests that it requires outstanding people; but in purchasing, such people are not as abundant as in other functional specialties. Purchasing as a specialty has some distance to go in achieving the professional stature it deserves, or the attention in the curricula of institutions of higher education that it might be accorded.

There are many industries where this becomes a matter of large concern. Consider purchasing in a high technology industry such as aerospace, where the function clearly involves much more than just the placement of purchase orders for standard commodity items. In different businesses, however, there clearly should be varying degrees of responsibility. In some cases, procurement can be a rather straightforward commodity purchasing service—to handle the staples that are usually obtainable from many and varied sources. Its responsibility can be expanded further to include spare parts, replacement equipment, and off-the-shelf new equipment built by a manufacturer to his own specifications.

Carried one step further, the function now includes procurement of products and services to the purchaser-user's self-generated specifications. And it is here that one is most likely to encounter a bumpy road, for here the opportunities for mistakes are the greatest. Not only the specifications, but also such considerations as the eligible bidders' list, source evaluation, source selection, the monitoring of subcontractors, contract changes, product testing, and warranties all become important. These are items for enlightened sophistication and thorough knowledge.

To expand further, there are two basic kinds of procurement concepts. One includes only the function of purchasing. The other concept, more suitable to the experiences I have had, includes not only the purchasing function but also the matériel control function. This means the purchasing responsibilities do not cease until the "procured item" is placed in the hands of the production worker in the manufacturing process. A production or manufacturing manager generally will care little about problems in the process of procurement. His interest is getting the specified item or items as needed to meet production schedules and budget targets. A matériel control function that is part of purchasing, therefore, should make communications lines shorter. One practical consequence of such an arrangement is that commodity-type items can be more readily kept on a "max-min," or some other consumption basis which will hold inventories at minimum practical levels. Annualized buying becomes easier. Internal matériel handling problems, and the costs thereof, are more easily identifiable. Such is the fiber which makes for increasing efficiencies.

SUPPLY CONTRACTS—ANNUALIZED BUYING

Annual supply contracts are practical considerations in times of relative worldwide economic stability. In periods of economic uncertainty or turbulence, annual contracts are least likely to be viable.

In such circumstance, and we have seen many recent examples, trading or bartering takes on increasing importance. This is not surprising, taking account of the scarcity of energy sources, material shortages that are on the increase, along with escalating costs of transportation, not to mention fluctuating values of money. The effective purchasing organization has, in barter, a useful tool to consider in looking toward effective use of its purchasing power. Many companies have established quite effective trading arms that are profit producers in their own right. Needless to say, working closely with the trading department, the purchasing function may often find unexpected avenues to increase corporate effectiveness.

Speaking of effectiveness, the annual supply contract should not be dismissed lightly. Protective clauses, properly used, make it sometimes attractively possible even in uncertain times.

In these days, the economic environment—with rapidly changing interest rates, rapidly changing availability and costs of energy, unpredictable rules and regulations imposed by multinational, national, or local governments, the yet-to-be-crystalized requirements for ecology, safety and health, and other emerging influential factors— must be evaluated when considering whether satisfactory and assured annual supply contracts can be developed.

In this connection, one should not overlook the importance of *force majeure* provisions. While this type of provision may take many forms, generally the provision provides an excuse to the seller or the buyer in the performance of his contractual obligations. This excuse usually becomes applicable as a result of the happening of events classically referred to as "acts of God," or circumstances beyond the reasonable control of the party to be excused.

Unfortunately, in many instances the importance of this provision is overlooked, misinterpreted, or misunderstood. Seller and buyer should, of course, approach this type of provision with different attitudes. The seller seeks protection against those factors which would preclude his ability to perform his obligations. The buyer should protect himself against those factors which would prevent his timely access to purchased goods. A buyer may also want to provide that any delay—or excuse—in performance by the seller shall be treated as temporary and have the contract automatically extended for such additional time as needed to allow full performance of the seller's obligations.

Over the long term, the test of a good contract is that it is good for both parties. Each is entitled to the opportunity for a reasonable gain as measured by the contractual opportunities and obligations presented.

GOVERNMENT PROCUREMENT

The federal government every year purchases many billions of dollars of goods and services. Effectively, state and local governments buy at about the same level or higher. For many industries, not just for military equipment, of course, governments are among the largest, if they are not *the* largest customers. For this reason, most company executives—and not just those whose principal or sole customer is the government—should be at least generally familiar with some of the principal features of government procurement. There is another reason for becoming at least a little knowledgeable in such matters. Some government procedures and forms of contracts, suitably adapted, can be useful in purchasing by business corporations and nonprofit organizations as well.

Aside from the most obvious requirements of good business practice that are placed on procurement, there are in certain areas other stringent requirements of law, regulation, and the prime contract.

The Law

Various public laws impose special requirements on buying for contracts funded with public funds. Although this subject is most properly in the province of the legal function, procurement functions also must be aware of the antitrust and price discrimination laws as well as the Renegotiation, Truth in Negotiation, and the Cost Accounting Standards Acts, to mention only some of the most prominent strictures.

The Regulations

Almost all government procurement agencies have issued procurement regulations. To mention some major federal ones, there are the Armed Services Procurement Regulation (Department of Defense), National Aeronautics and Space Administration Procurement Regulation, Atomic Energy Procurement Regulation, and the Federal Procurement Regulation. There also exist corollary state and local procurement regulations that require attention. Management must assure that the personnel charged with the responsibility of negotiating, writing, or placing contracts with suppliers be familiar with the requirements imposed by these regulations.

In this regard, an important observation: Legal counsel needs to be involved in the purchasing function at the onset of the negotiating process, rather than into it after its completion. This hand-in-glove sort of arrangement, as a procedural practicality, can save a lot of headaches later on, for it should narrow down the chances for error in not only the original considerations but in subsequent change orders and amendments.

The Prime Contract

The typical master or prime contract with the federal government also mandates that various contract provisions be made applicable to subcontractors, among them such things as security requirements, termination clauses, observance of Defense Matériel Systems ratings, and more.

In addition there are various other provisions that, for the prime contractor's protection, must be included in various subcontracts and purchase orders. For example, reporting requirements in the prime contract may, and most often do, dictate that precise reporting requirements will be imposed on the subcontractor as well. The same applies to inspection, warranties, termination, correction of defects, and myriad other specific and special contractual obligations.

Furthermore, the prime contract will also provide in many cases how a subcontract may be awarded, the form it must (or may) take, the extent of procurement permissible by subcontract, and the governmental authority, if any, to give approval not only to the subcontract subject but also to the supplier and his price.

Type of Contract

Various contract types are available to achieve a desired result. The Armed Services Procurement Act specifies that firm fixed-price contracts should be let as a result of competition. At the same time, however, it wisely provides flexibility by 17 exceptions to this policy. It is unfortunate that from time to time some contract types fall into disfavor while others appear to be regarded as a cure-all. The fact is that each of the contractual forms has a proper application in certain circumstances, and failure headlines very often are a result of failure by the policymakers who opted for an inappropriate contractual vehicle.

Cost Plus Fixed Fee Contract (**CPFF**). This type of contract is best to use "when the uncertainties involved in contract performance are of such magnitude that cost of performance cannot be estimated . . ." with reasonable accuracy.

Basically, this contract owns up to uncertainties in obtaining the goods, services, and quality required. The result is to agree to limit the contractor's profit to a fixed amount, which will not vary, and assures that all allowable and reasonable costs necessary for completion of the contract will be reimbursed.

Cost Plus Award Fee Contract (CPAF). This type is suitable when performance objectives cannot be wholly established in advance by definite targets, milestones, or other goals susceptible of definitive interim measurements. In this important regard, CPAF differs from Cost Plus Incentive Fee contracts discussed later.

Basically it is a cost-reimbursement contract with a minimum fee (profit), which is not based on performance, coupled with an award amount that is based on a subjective evaluation of the quality of the contract performance. Broad criteria set down in the contract are usually the bases for this evaluation.

Cost Plus Incentive Fee Contract (CPIF). This type of contract should be used when uncertainty of performance is not of such magnitude as to require a CPFF contract and when a target and fee adjustment formula can be negotiated.

Basically it resembles the CPFF, except that the fee may be adjusted under a formula based on the relationship that final costs bear to the original estimated, or target, costs. Such a contract may also provide for schedule and performance incentives. The end result may be high maximum fees or low minimum fees, or even zero or negative fees in cases of poor performance.

Fixed Price Incentive Contract (FPI). Fixed-price incentive contracts are most often used when the uncertainty of performance does not warrant a cost-reimbursement type contract. Under this form of contract, costs are not reimbursed as incurred. Generally, there is established a target cost, a target profit, a ceiling price, and a formula for sharing in costs, either over target or under target, at completion. After completion costs are ascertained, the contractor's actual profits are adjusted—either over or under the original target— by application of the cost sharing formula. Schedule and performance criteria can also be the subject of substantial incentives.

Firm Fixed Price Contract (FFP). The firm fixed-price contract should be used when there is little uncertainty in either design or resulting performance. Thus when designs are established and proven, or the items being procured are standard commercial or military products, and when fair and reasonable prices can be established by competition or otherwise, this is the preferred contract form. For emphasis again, when it is used, both parties must be dealing with known and proven products. Frequent changes are not easily introduced into the FFP because of its very nature.

These descriptions of several contract forms are simplified here for purposes of brevity. The reader should note, however, they are arranged in order of their increasing difficulty in administration—to both buyer and supplier. Thus, as the list stands, the risks—of loss of profit; loss due to technical and schedule performance; loss due to correction of defects under warranties—become increasingly greater.

BIDDERS' LIST

A very important decision in the procurement or purchasing cycle involves assembling the list of sources that will be requested or permitted to bid. An independent firm, and this is also true of the prime contractor in government procurement, is not constrained, as is the government, to use "maximum" competition, but rather only *adequate* competition. Thus, there is much more opportunity to limit a solicitation to a reasonable number of competent supply sources, although the prime contractor is often restricted by supplied drawings, qualified bidders' lists, and government approval requirements.

A company's, or a prime contractor's, well-run purchasing organization will have, regarding potential bidders, access to previous facility surveys, performance analyses, talent and facility availability assessments, and judgments on the quality and load of current work under contract. All of these are important. Not the least of them is the effect the new business will have on the attention it will receive from management of each potential bidder. These appraisals, along with detailed understanding of things peculiar to the pending procurement, should be documented and understood before a potential supplier is invited to bid. It is awkward to argue inadequacy of a potential supplier on any grounds once the request for a proposal has been tendered. Such a request, by its very nature, implies a tacit approval of adequacy in all important regards.

So also should a response be viewed as a promise to perform. All too often, not nearly enough weight is given to the proposer's past performance. Having decided that past performance is worth significant weight in the source selection process and having decided to restrict the bidders' list to a judgmental list of "qualified companies," one must be prepared to stand by his conviction against all varieties of political and other pressures, plus the emotional arguments mustered in efforts to support logical conclusions, and challenges that surely will come from many quarters. Being prepared to hold the fort—instead of taking an easier "out" of opening the bidding to good, mediocre, and marginal performers—is a real test for an effective purchasing organization. There is no doubt in my mind that the makeup of the prospective source list is a singularly difficult and probably the most important decision in the purchasing cycle.

SOURCE SELECTION

The nature of the commercial business world requires acknowledgment, freely given, that source selection for nonstandard items or developmental services may be based upon more subjective judgments than in public procurement. Many commercial enterprises, for example, have used one general contractor for all of their construction for years, with good result and a quite happy relationship. The nature of the government procurement process is such that great efforts are made to give source selection unassailable objectivity. The commercial buyer, on the other hand, is relatively unencumbered in the exercise of his best judgment about the past performance and reliability of the supplier. The government prime contractor must follow formal, prescribed procedures involving extensive documentation, justification, reviews, and approvals.

Where "competition" is not present or evident, the federal system requires the buyer to generate it—or else to justify, document, and present a detailed evaluation on its absence. Usually, in such cases discussions are held with all suppliers within a "competitive range," and best and final offers are received in a competitive atmosphere before selection. There frequently exists a real temptation to turn the final phase of contract placement under such circumstance into an auction. When this occurs, the results are quite predictable: less than satisfactory performance, accompanied by increased costs and schedule failures.

MAKE OR BUY

In the commercial environment, the decision to make a component or to buy it from a supplier should be based solely upon the best interests of the company. In government procurement, such is not the case.

The prime contractor often begins his make-or-buy decision process well in advance of the solicitation, often when he enters into a teaming arrangement with another company to obtain a capability or strength his own company lacks. Such agreements usually designate one company as the anticipated prime contractor and the other as a subcontractor. Such team agreements are contingent upon a contract award, and the ultimate performance of them requires approval by the contracting officer.

Generally, the Request for Proposal in very large programs requires explicit make-or-buy programs for important components. These make-or-buy decisions are evaluated by the government to insure that they support such program interests as capability, capacity, competence, cost, schedule, and performance, and such other governmental interests as socioeconomic objectives. The interests of the contractor—such as his internal workloads or acquisition under the contract of certain new or added capability—yield to the interest of government in cases of conflict. Once the make-or-buy agreement is incorporated into the contract, any subsequent change desired by the contractor must be approved by the government. A make-or-buy decision in the aerospace industry, as is clearly seen in this brief narrative, is not bounded by the criteria applicable to such a decision in commercial enterprises.

The executive who introduces his company into the field of government contracts without understanding thoroughly the potential pitfalls is heading for trouble. Among other things, he must appreciate that his control over his procurement function will be substantially limited, for the function will be constrained by the requirements of government contracts, laws, and regulations.

RECIPROCITY

Is reciprocity a useful tool in conducting business transactions involving purchasing and selling, or is it a club used to restrain the free forces of the marketplace?

At the outset, it is useful to bear in mind that there are various degrees of reciprocal dealing. Perhaps the simplest is identified in the concept that one person will purchase products he needs from those to whom he sells, provided other things—such as quality and price—are equal.

From there we proceed to a more restrictive concept, namely that one purchases the products he needs from those to whom he sells irrespective of the equality of other elements in the transaction.

Finally we get to the type of reciprocal dealing where a dominant purchaser *requires* those from whom he purchases to buy his products —irrespective of equality in quality and price, or in reverse where a dominant seller conditions his purchases on the sales he is able to make to his supplier.

Although at first blush the simplest form of reciprocal dealing appears to make sense to the average businessman, upon analysis it can be seen that, even at that level, there is a sacrifice of the free choice which is the bulwark of a free enterprise economic system. Then, as we progress (or regress) into the more advanced types of reciprocal dealing, it can be seen that the reciprocal dealer not only is sacrificing the benefits which he and his customers could derive by purchasing from nonbuying competitors with superior products, but he is also restraining competition between the buying and nonbuying suppliers.

The government has often appeared on this scene with a copy of the antitrust laws in hand. Even though the nonthinking reciprocal dealer may be willing to act inconsistently with his own best interests, the government most decidedly is not willing to tolerate the injury to competition which inevitably results.

In recent years, both the United States Department of Justice and the Federal Trade Commission have filed numerous complaints against companies for allegedly engaging in reciprocal dealing. In most cases, these companies have entered into consent decrees, agreeing to cease engaging in reciprocal dealing, whether systematic or casual. The reason for this "voluntary" cessation of reciprocal dealing lies more in the recognition by management of the disadvantages inherent in such dealing than in fear of protracted litigation. In many instances, results of the practice had not previously been thoroughly analyzed at the level of management where objectivity is best achieved, but rather had grown up at the salesman and purchasing agent level where objectivity is often lost in the hustle of daily activities.

Once the practice of reciprocal dealing is scrutinized, the sensible businessman is unlikely to require assistance from the government in recognizing its pernicious effects and in bringing about its termination.

AUDIT

A well-disciplined purchasing organization, no matter how efficient and effective, should be subject to periodic audits. A corporation's outside auditing firm can be useful, and should be requested, from time to time, to review procurement practices and adherence to policies—in other words, to go beyond usual inventory verifications and other required auditing tests.

The matter of dishonest practices and kickbacks will always be a problem. In government procurement, however, they are a violation of the Anti-Kickback Act and subject violators to criminal penalties. Many, perhaps most dishonest practices are usually well-conceived plots and are not easily detected. However, a formalized approval cycle based on written documentation, if utilized in more than a perfunctory manner, will aid in stopping kickbacks. Competition with sealed bids is a deterrent when this form of contracting is possible.

One's best source of information on rigging or kickback schemes often is a disappointed bidder whose experience indicates that something is amiss. He will usually direct a letter to the company president. Prudence indicates that such complaints be investigated thoroughly and a conclusion developed. The investigation may be done through one's own organization or with outside help.

In the case of government contracting, there are many sources within the government to give assistance. (The specific branch of the government having cognizance over the contract in question has the ability to provide such assistance.) Also the General Accounting Office can be helpful. Under the Anti-Kickback Act it has authority to "audit" any contractor who has a negotiated contract, for the purpose of ascertaining whether kickbacks have been given or received.

SUMMARY THOUGHTS ABOUT THE FUNCTION

The purchasing function in the modern American corporation has sometimes in the past been relegated, in a manner of speaking, to the stockroom, somewhere deep in the recesses of the factory: in short, out-of-sight and out-of-mind in the chief executive's primary order of concerns, priorities, or attentions. If such an approach in the past may have been understandable or defensible, it most certainly is not so any longer.

The chief executive of today, always hard put to find new ways to better results, is giving increasing attention to the purchasing function. How any corporate executive, in actual practice, treats the purchasing function will vary, and properly so, depending upon the organizational structure and the size of his company. A centralized purchasing function, directed by a high-ranked executive, may very well be the ideal arrangement for a company with only one, or just a few plants, operating in a single line of business. On the other hand, such an arrangement might be ineffective or cumbersome in a multi-industry company with operating plants scattered across the face of the nation or even around the world.

A central fact is, however, important to the top executive management of either kind of company, or of any other kind in between the examples mentioned above. That is: The purchasing dollar must be spent efficiently; which is to say with deliberate intelligence, meaning timely procurement at competitive costs with quality as specified from responsible and stable sources of supply.

Evidence abounds that management must no longer take for granted some things that have long been accepted. The consequences are felt by us all. Insofar as those consequences influence our industry and business, the responsibility for adjustment falls upon the executive management. And in the end, the purchasing function is certainly among the places to look for the specific remedy.

In certain of my company's multi-industry operations, data indicate that in recent years an average of 40 to 60 cents for each dollar of sales generated goes "outside" to suppliers of the materials and services (freight and other transport are increasingly important, although perhaps less obvious than, say, raw materials or machines) that are the ingredients of the business lifeblood.

Even in an economy of plenty, it is not sound business practice to put purchasing into the stockroom category. In an economy of scarcity—even spotty scarcities—it can be foolhardy and devastating. Intelligent use of the purchasing instrument may give the alert chief executive's company a competitive advantage. At the least, the executive should expect that the function be carried out so as to prevent his company from finding itself competitively disadvantaged.

What this means to the executive will, to repeat, vary from company to company. But it *is* important.

WHAT IS PUBLIC RELATIONS?

by Jack Valenti
President, Motion Picture Association of America, Inc.

"PUBLIC RELATIONS" is an amorphous term that has come to embrace all sorts of activity. Some people believe it means publicity, gimmickry, trying to lard over the truth, corporate hocus-pocus, the paraphernalia of press relations, junkets, and so on. Mainly, "Public Relations" has become a kind of dirty phrase, suggesting the guile of devilishly clever practitioners of some arcane artform. I remember one old mentor of mine, a self-educated genius who bemusedly described public relations men as "people who bow and smile and spend money." In fact and in purpose, it is no such thing these days.

Perhaps the first need is to disengage the very concept from the old corporate rubric and devise a newer and more meaningful purpose. Public relations is really "public interest." I would, if I were the Chief Executive Officer of a corporation, rid myself of the words or title "public relations" and call my public relations chief official "Vice President in Charge of Public Interest."

Public interest I would define as those activities in which the corporation participates and which involve not only the public (the consumer, the customer, the client, the family, the neighborhood), but the public's evaluation of the corporation's decision, whatever it may be.

By this description, everything the corporation does is connected in some fashion to the public interest. Relocate a plant? Negotiate with the unions? Raise prices? Lower prices? Benefit programs for employees? Vacations, sabbaticals? Investment in new activities? Mergers—horizontal or vertical or conglomerate? Lay off employees? Slacken production or increase it? Personnel changes? Accounting practices? Disclosures or nondisclosures? Equity funding, bond financing, borrowing? Contributions to the community weal? Involvement in community activities by officials and employees? Pollution, conservation? Use of land, resources? Participating in politics and local and state government? Information to stockholders and employees, and to the people of the community in which the corporation does business? The Congress, legislatures, the courthouses, and city halls? Are these "public interest" matters? Of course.

This is the definition of public interest: All that which involves the public or a segment of it in the affairs of the corporation.

Immediately, one is aware that this definition vaults the conduct and management of affairs in the public interest to the highest levels of corporate authority. In short, the official in charge of *public interest* must sit in the high councils of management and must be a part of every public decision that is taken, because nothing—or practically nothing—the corporation does is unhinged to the public interest.

Indeed, one might go further and suggest that the official in charge of the public interest might be an ombudsman of the corporation, skeptical, investigatory, curious, sensitive, alive to what is being done so that the corporation takes no steps which collide with the public interest to the ultimate detriment of the corporation.

No doubt, the observer can detect a frown on the face of the president and chairman as they read this, for this role inserts itself into what is considered their responsibility. Yes, it does. But the public interest demands that the chief executive be constantly and persistently counseled and challenged by his public interest official so that no scrutiny is undimmed and no adventure in the marketplace goes untended by special care that the corporation's interest and the public interest are one and the same.

The fact is that today, when the public's curiosity about business is enlivened, when a growing majority of the citizenry is educated beyond the wildest imaginings of a century ago, when neither governments' nor corporations' motives go unchallenged, the enterprise that determines that it should mingle its thrust for profits with the best interests of the public is the enterprise that will endure.

But, the enterprise must understand that in today's world it is not enough to find one's way by the shine of the corporate ledgers and the profit-and-loss sheet. Increased profits and growth are every year sensible and normal goals. But, sometimes in the public's mind profits translate into avarice, and growth sometimes gets deciphered as sprawl. It is possible to have both profits and public interest linked to the corporation's objective, but it does take time and effort, and sometimes it is discomforting, as well as annoying.

It is the duty of the official in charge of public interest to be the objective counselor, asserting the public interest viewpoint at the management table, keeping the corporate feet to the public interest fire. Once, a president of the United States told his staff a major truth: "It is not enough to *do* good; you must *look* good." Unless the corporation is able to make its position clear and simple, what to corporate officers might seem a logical business step, to the public may seem clogged with self-interest. Therefore, the Chief Executive Officer must rely on his public interest official to give him all he needs to know about the possible action as it concerns the public interest; suggestions as to what the CEO needs to do to shape his decision in both the public's and the corporate interest; and, also important, what the CEO ought to avoid doing. Finally, the public interest official must communicate all this to the community.

No CEO takes any major step without inquiring of his legal staff as to the pitfalls that might entangle the corporation with the law; no major technical move is decided until the engineers, the scientists, and the technicians have had their say; and no important financial move is contemplated without the financial and accounting officers pouring in their judgments. Same thing with public interest; except that public interest entwines itself in nearly all corporate decisions, which is all the more reason why the public interest vice president is there to study, to counsel, and to give his judgment to the CEO.

In this kind of environment, the public interest official should be a member of the corporation's board of directors so that he is privy to ultimate decision-making, and available to produce his judgment on specific problems before the board resolves them.

THE DETAILED SPECIFICATIONS OF THE PUBLIC INTEREST VICE PRESIDENT

Today, the so-called public relations function cannot be isolated from other aspects of company policy which is communicated to others. Therefore, the public interest chieftain should have within his arena of responsibility the following:

Government Affairs. All the apparatus of monitoring the congress, state legislatures, the city councils, and other government installations should come within the ken of the public interest official. Nothing is more troublesome and frustrating than to have two different policies declared, one by the press office of the corporation and one by the liaison officials with the government. Indeed, the corporation should be especially careful to make certain that it is informing the government what it is both doing and communicating in other areas. In many enterprises, government affairs is the province of one official and the public relations function the responsibility of another. But they are in truth mortared together and in the world of instantaneous communication we live in, the CEO must understand he cannot separate them.

Press Relations, Publicity, All the Machinery which Gets the Raw Material of Information to the Media. This is the technical communications staff, men and women trained and skilled in the complexities of dealing with the various forms of the media. Deadlines, special handling procedures, how, when, and where to get the most information to the public; all of this should be handled by craftsmen in the printed and broadcast word.

Public Mood and Attitude Research. To know what the public is thinking about the corporation's business and its ways of doing business is data of the highest moment to the CEO. Or it should be. The CEO's top public interest official needs to be alert to the fragility of public temperment. Indeed, it is a sensitivity to the public mood that is part of the spacious skills an effective public interest official must have. Men in the political arena call it "instinct" or a "feel for the wind of change." Call it what you will, but the bottomline definition of it is knowing in advance how the public will react to a particular decision which affects them. Not to be constantly tapping the community pulse is to ignore the possibilities of corporate error.

There are two brother gods in the Greek pantheon, one of which is eternally famous and the other obscure and unknown. The first is Prometheus, which in Greek means "foresight" and the other is his brother Epimetheus, which means "hindsight." Epimetheus is not exactly a household word. The reason is simple .The Greeks placed store by foresight and very little value in hindsight. It is well for corporations to emulate the Greeks. Therefore, research, constantly learning more about the public attitude, ought to be high on the agenda of the CEO and his public interest official.

Publications, Booklets, Pamphlets, the Annual Report. Again, these communications represent shadings of the corporation face that the public sees, and, thus, command the attention and scrutiny of the public interest official.

Advertising and Sales Promotion. Here we tread on sacred ground. It is a current maxim that the advertising function and the public relations function are not of a piece and ought to be separated officially. If, however, the CEO buys the premise that whatever the public sees, hears, reads, and feels is part of the "public relations" or "public interest" arena, then it is logical to mandate they both report to the same man.

The coordination of the corporate reach to the public is overwhelmingly crucial. Much of the corporate communications dollar is frittered away because there are too many channels to the public which go their separate ways. Impact, continuity, and credibility are linchpinned together. If the enterprise has a public policy, a strategy, grounded in truth and dramatized, then it should be part of the communications synergy, each part gracefully blending into the whole. These are the tactical weapons under the control of the public interest official.

Moreover, there should be close rapport between the public interest official and his industrial relations and training counterparts. Any corporate entity that has a public arm (transportation companies, retail establishments, any organization that has salesmen of any kind, any enterprise that has employees meeting or treating with the public in any way) needs to make certain that those employees who face the public understand the company's overall policy, are carefully trained to gain the public affection and respect, and are motivated to do their very best every time. The public interest official and his organization have to be in daily and intimate coordination with those corporate divisions that select and train employees.

There needs to be constructed within the corporation a spirit of cooperation, which, incidentally, only the CEO can produce by his example and his determination. Again, the reason is clear. The public interest official's judgment should be given entry to problems in other areas of the corporation's activity, activity not normally and usually considered part of the public relations function. But to repeat, in the decade ahead, where the crush of instant communication will become the most noticeable civil intrusion, the alert corporation and its CEO will reshape the corporate posture so that it is both protective and aware, sensitive to the public attitude, and capable of dealing with public and political tangents.

THE DIMENSIONS OF THE MAN OR WOMAN IN CHARGE OF PUBLIC INTEREST

The background of the public interest official within the corporation (if he is promoted from within) is not important. But, the character, instincts, and sensitivity of the person are.

First, he (or she) ought to be a person aware of people as individuals. He must understand and be sympathetic to the human spirit. This is not to say he should be without technical skills, but that given these skills, he should be, foremost, keenly open to the public as a body and as a force in the marketplace.

Second, more than brilliance and quickness of mind, he should have good judgment, the ability to sense forks in the road before they appear, and to be appreciative of error before it occurs. In short, he ought to be a wise man rather than a smart one, though the two are not necessarily incompatible.

Third, he can be a lawyer, an engineer, an accountant, a liberal arts major, a financial analyst, a former foreman, a labor negotiator, a marketing expert, or an advertising professional; he can be any one of these or none of these, for the judgment he brings to bear on a public problem is not so much technically acquired as it is genetically and instinctively present.

Fourth, he should be a person in whom the CEO reposes confidence and respect. It is no good to select a person to head the public interest office and then receive his counsel hesitantly for lack of faith in his purpose or his ability.

Fifth, he needs to be a good administrator for he must manage a large group (depending on the size of his company). He must be able to organize ideas and give lucid expression to the tactics he devises. He must have an innate understanding of how one policy can be channeled to varying groups.

Sixth, he should be a negotiator in the sense that he deals with his people on a level and not on a slant, so that what he proposes to others is proffered with an appropriate civility. Arrogance is a fatal flaw in a public interest official. Respect for his colleagues is an absolute in the public interest official.

Seventh, he should have the mind and tools of a professional, which briefly defined is one who does his homework, is outfitted with detailed knowledge of whatever it is he confronts, and never ventures before he has learned. A professional attitude toward every problem is essential to good management of public interest problems.

In summary, the public interest official is a person who could, if events and circumstance warrant it, become the CEO himself.

PROBLEMS THAT FACE THE PUBLIC INTEREST OFFICIAL IN THE 70s AND 80s

The old slogans are collapsing; the old traditions are being abandoned; and that which we held to be unshakable now becomes misshapen. In short, the marketplace is in radical, avalanching change with new forces intruding and new challenges forming. Today, too many corporations are geared to old rhythms.

Two giant counterthrusts are alive in the marketplace, and the corporation which intends to grow and prosper cannot ignore them. They are government and consumer groups, and they are nourished and enflamed by instant communication. This is not to say these two new challenges are either good or bad, but simply that they *are there* and must be dealt with honestly and intelligently.

Our land, so long used to surplus of materials, energy, and potential now girds itself for shortages, restrictions, and the summons to put the community interest ahead of the corporate objective. When this happens, freedom of action shrinks and the traditional premise of the corporation, which is to do all that it can to increase return on investment to the corporate ledgers and to the stockholders, is in jeopardy. It is not enough to wring one's hands in despair, anger, or frustration. The durable corporation will adjust to change.

When traditional elixirs no longer work, the intelligent corporation fits new solutions to new problems. That is the dominant reason why public support for the corporation's actions is indispensable to corporate survival.

It is the prime task of the public interest official to understand the public's and the government's demands and to construct plain answers for nagging questions as well as counter criticism with evidence of good works (good works of management, financial stewardship, employee loyalty, and community decisions) and then to make sure both the answers and the good works are communicated wisely and believably.

Because the role of the outside director has become much more today than a sinecure or a prestigious place to sit in amiable contemplation, the outside director will welcome a new voice at the directors' table, a new experience of wisdom grounded in the public's reaction and the public attitude.

The effective CEO is one who perceives there is no place to hide in this modern world. There is no such thing anymore as "corporate executive privilege." The vacuum that heretofore existed wherein the corporation's business was its business and no one else's has been filled with a public belief that it has a higher rank in the priority of benefits.

Again, it is a waste of time to debate the merit of such a conviction. It exists and the wise CEO expends little time grumping about the gracelessness of such views. He goes about his duty spending his thinking on how to keep his enterprise intact and muscular.

But, the public view may not be the right view. It may be the public has been misinformed, or that what the corporation is doing is perceived to be what it is really not. That is not unusual. What has to be done is to set the matter right, honestly, clearly, and to make easy to understand what is often not easily understood. Annual reports, balance sheets, income statements, proxy statements—with all their underbrush of footnotes—are many times beclouded with opaque arithmetic. Murky explanations of policy or of operating decisions sometimes sound as though they developed all by themselves in dimly lit, smoky board rooms. What is needed are plain tales plainly told. If the public understands, it is quite possible it will respond rationally.

In this new situation—the world we now live in—oozing with hazard, the CEO's chief ally becomes his public interest office, or as one able CEO put it, his "public awareness cavalry scouting the outer edges of minefields in the marketplace" bringing this vital intelligence to the CEO and the board for responsible action.

EVALUATION OF STAFF PERFORMANCE

by Mortimer J. Fox, Jr.

Vice President (Retired), Schering Corporation

NEED FOR STAFF PERFORMANCE STANDARDS

"STAFF" is considered to include those functions and those people who are primarily engaged in auxiliary or advisory capacities. Their duties are to ascertain actions to be undertaken, sometimes indicating how these actions are to be executed. Staff people usually have authority only to recommend. They may be assistants to managers or supervisors.

Staff personnel have a vital impact on the productivity of the entire organization. Frequently more than 15 percent of total personnel resources participate in staff activities. Because of the magnitude and influence of staff, it is important to be able to measure its performance.

Performance standards will help determine what staff is needed, how well it is utilized, and what benefits are derived from its efforts. Such standards can contribute to better utilization and control of this considerable and important resource. Increase in sales, growth in profits, or improvement in the rate of return on investment, while useful in appraising overall results, are too broad to be useful in measuring the performance of staff functions. How then, is it possible to make objective measures in this critical area?

The following discussion points out some of the weaknesses in measures frequently used by the Chief Executive Officer; suggests specifications for workable staff performance measures; lists typical performance standards for 12 basic staff concepts (see Appendix later in this chapter); and provides some examples of measures in selected staff functional areas.

HOW THE CEO OFTEN MEASURES PERFORMANCE

Often, the CEO bases his judgment of staff performance on the confidence he has in the individual who is responsible for leadership in the particular area evaluated. Frequently, it is a subjective judgment of informal considerations such as: breadth of knowledge of company operations or of outside contacts; the ability to focus on important issues, and to articulate them well; the ability to secure commitments by management and to follow up and get things done; aggressiveness, and the desire to dominate.

For the most part, these are not measurable characteristics. Furthermore, judgments may be based on impressions or feelings, and may well be influenced by personal chemistry. They may not be systematic in their coverage. Such judgments of performance may create disincentives, and may create friction between the CEO and the person involved. They may also constitute a demoralizing factor for the rest of the organization, because the working staff may have a better knowledge of what has been accomplished and of what effort has been extended than does the CEO who is doing the evaluating.

SELECTING STAFF PERFORMANCE STANDARDS

What are some essential elements in developing meaningful measurement standards, where quantification is feasible and relevant? What about standards where only qualitative assessments are feasible and appropriate? How should the CEO go about designating the basis for evaluating staff performance? What are some of the components which might be considered? Some of the factors which are critical to successful staff performance are dramatized in the following dialogue.

The CEO of Worldwide Operations called his Vice President— Finance on the phone: "I would like to make a date to spend about an hour with you to talk about some of the work you and your staff are now doing. I think we might also review some of the more important jobs *you* are planning for next year, and some of the jobs *I* think we should be looking after. I'd particularly like you and your people to help me decide what standards or measures we can use to evaluate how well we are doing. Could you be ready for such a talk by next week?"

The finance vice president's enthusiastic reply was: "I'll be delighted to have the opportunity to go over our program with you. I'm sure we in Finance can do a better job if we know more specifically what you and the directors and officers need, as well as your priorities. Surely we can be ready. When would it be convenient for you to meet?"

(CEO) "How about Thursday of next week at ten o'clock? At that meeting, we might shoot for agreeing on a tentative outline on the major projects and the standards or measures *we* want to use. Then after our meeting, these can be more thoroughly developed and reviewed by your people. We might then be able to have a final go-round, say by the end of the month."

(VP) "Sounds fine. We'll prepare an outline of the projects we think should be done and of some appropriate performance measures. This will give you and us a way to determine whether we are meeting our schedule, whether we are making good use of our resources, and whether—and how well—we are giving service to other operating and staff functions."

(CEO) "If you do that, we'll have a productive session next week. Bear in mind that in the finance area, I'm particularly interested in: reporting systems (quality, timeliness, accuracy, evaluative analysis); operating plans and capital project plans (budgets); cash and portfolio planning and management (including overseas commitments); financial and stockholder public relations; tax management; and risk management (insurance)."

This dialogue illustrates several dimensions which contribute to establishing a favorable climate for the development of appropriate measures of staff performance. It indicates the need to: communicate at the beginning of the planning process; specify desired end results; select specific projects; determine schedules; agree on how results will be measured; encourage staff participation in selection of projects and of performance measurements; determine priorities; establish means of control.

When faced with the opportunity to suggest performance measures, there is often a tendency to present a volume of easily accumulated data which may be superficially impressive, but when considered in relation to the critical aspects of the services required, does not supply what is needed. For example, the finance division may be overwhelming the organization with all kinds of reports, responding to questions which were once posed, but which may no longer be pertinent. Finance may be able to show excellent on-schedule production of these many reports, and in the process, employ many hands for many hours both on the part of the producer as well as on the part of the reviewer. This might be a spectacular performance statistically, but it may not be a really productive use of effort. Critical reviews of the reports and of the circulation list may indicate opportunities to reduce the number of reports as well as the number of recipients.

Performance evaluation would be concerned with the extent and manner of service to users. The speed of availability of reports and their focus on critical developments requiring responsive action are more useful measures of performance than the number of reports or copies issued.

STAFF PERFORMANCE EVALUATION STANDARDS

Twelve standards which have been used to evaluate various aspects of staff performance are shown in the Appendix later in this chapter. These are arranged to show: (1) concept to be evaluated; (2) essential components of the concept which should be considered; and (3) criteria to be used in making evaluations. Staff personnel have a vital concern, especially with the first three concepts listed in the Appendix. Staff not only share the responsibility for developing well-stated corporate objectives, divisional goals, and policies, but also carry much of the burden for the productive use of these management techniques.

Corporate Objectives*

A corporate objective should be significant, specific as to what the company wants to do, where it wants to go, and how it wants to get there. The quality of the statements of corporate objectives (their depth, clarity, realism) and the extent to which operating people use them as guides often is a result of staff work. Staff participation and accomplishment in this effort can be measured.

---

* [Ed. Note: Marvin Bower—see his article "The Chief Executive as Chief Strategist"—might use the word "goal" where Mr. Fox uses the word "objective" and vice versa.]

Goals

Goals can be useful in helping all segments of the organization—headquarters, subsidiaries, divisions, and line or staff—make better use of available resources. A well-thought-through goal will: relate to corporate objectives; have a limited time reference—one to three years; be important, specific, and achievable; state the end result desired as well as the means of measurement; show resources required; include a time schedule for completion of critical components; indicate responsibility for accomplishment; indicate cooperation required—other divisions, other departments; indicate priority.

Performance evaluation is facilitated by the use of goals because they include the end result desired, significant checkpoints for determining whether the work is progressing on schedule, and the means of measurement of the achievement.

A word of caution: goals performance status reports prepared by responsible officers or their subordinates can often be somewhat misleading, intentionally or otherwise. Indicated accomplishment can sound better than actual results. How can a reviewing officer or the CEO avoid being misled by the so-called "snow job"? There are several means available: (1) the CEO can take time to be sufficiently knowledgeable to make such an evaluation, but this doesn't often happen; (2) an independent peer group can review the status reports and secure more penetrating data where needed, but this doesn't happen often either; (3) an operational audit group of subordinate specialists can review the status report against the actual performance, making their findings generally available; or, (4) publication of the performance status reports to other members of the organization will cause the reports to be more realistic. Any of these methods will soon have a subtle impact on the integrity of status reporting.

Policies

Policies express management's philosophy. They constitute the rules within which institutional activity is conducted. They need not be detailed, but their intent should be clearly understood. Staff usually carries the main burden for preparing policy statements. Staff performance in this area can be measured by the number and quality of policy statements issued.

Checklist

A well-developed checklist can speed the preparation of acceptable written material. It can be useful in assuring that critical aspects are considered when making decisions. A good checklist is developed over a period of time and by periodic modification and updating. A checklist is also a good tool for training and instruction and can be useful in orienting people newly transferred into an area. The existence and the quality of checklists covering various phases of staff responsibility can also be used in staff performance evaluation.

SELECTED APPLICATIONS

Some examples in four staff areas may suggest types of performance measures which will be of use to the CEO. They are based on actual experiences. Only in the first and second areas—Finance and Information Systems—has the relation between staff department goals and corporate objectives been indicated. In the other two areas, it is assumed that staff department goals discussed are also in response to appropriate corporate objectives.

Finance

In the fictitious case quoted earlier, the Vice President—Finance's subsequent presentation to the CEO included a *goal* in response to the CEO's corporate objective on improving the reporting system:

> *Goal*—Review the system of reporting to determine: usefulness— action orientation, purpose; preparation—streamlining, eliminating duplication, possibility of combining reports; circulation—limited to those who are responsible for taking action; documentation—written statements of method of preparation and designation of responsibility for producing the report; control—numbering of each report, review-committee authorization before making changes in context or format; and analytical evaluation comments.

The Vice President—Finance suggested assembling an inventory of all reports prepared, cross-referenced by subject, by recipient, and by identification number. Reports having the largest circulation were to be studied first, as they represent the greatest amount of management reading time, and therefore any improvement would have important cost/benefit impact. The Vice President—Finance also indicated the amount of time and resources of *his* as well as the *users'* staff which it would take to complete the inventory and to review the first ten reports.

> *Standards*—Standards which were to be applied to this effort covered: whether a report inventory was completed; whether the selection of the particular reports to be studied was accepted by management and by the users; whether adequate statements of purpose for all of the reports were developed; whether checklists of the types of analytical comments which should accompany the reports covered essential aspects; and whether the resulting revisions in the reports and analytical comments were accepted by the users.

Responding to the CEO's corporate objective regarding interest in operating plans and capital project plans, the Vice President—Finance prepared a goal which called for more emphasis on concepts than on "number-massaging" pencil-pushing, as follows.

> *Goal*—Simplify and standardize the content and process of review of the operating plan; prepare necessary formats and instructions; and hold seminars explaining any changes in formats and instructions, and the reasons for them.
> *Standards*—Standards which could be applied to this effort covered whether there was: adequate justification for the programs proposed in the plan; realistic limitation of programs to a few critical areas; evidence of thorough consideration of the programs, the risks and resources involved, and their impact on the organization; review of programs at various levels of management; a suggested order of priority; coverage of only the most critical variables; meaningful analytical commentary; and a timely, on-schedule presentation of the plans.
> At the end of the period covered, it would be possible to evaluate actual performance against plan. (Sometimes the extent that operations vary from the plan reflects unrealistic planning.)

Information Systems

A corporate objective frequently concerns the economic application of modern data processing techniques to various parts of the organization. Responses to this objective might cover goals on:

equipment lease-or-buy decisions; utilization of in-house or outside services; coordination of computer facilities (hardware and software) throughout the various parts of the organization; establishment of formal top management review procedure for proposed applications; utilization of modernized computer technology to provide increased efficiency and productivity in research, manufacturing, marketing, and financial administration; development of computer-based models for planning and control; post-implementation appraisals; biennial operational audits of all major information systems efforts. More specific examples follow.

> *Goal*—Establish a formal procedure for top-level review of computer application project proposals, complete the processing of two major and five minor proposals in the coming year.
>
> *Standards*—Economic evaluation of end result desired (purpose); scope; benefits (savings) to be derived; development costs; operating costs; personnel resources required; schedule; progress reporting; risks; user participation in systems design; security of data; documentation; means for controlling post-implementation changes in documentation; and post-implementation appraisal by independent (in-house) personnel.

The post-implementation appraisal can contribute much to more efficient design and implementation of programs through learning by experience and avoiding recognized pitfalls in future undertakings. The appraisal can also have an impact on the motivation of users, system designers, and programmers as well as on the various levels of management concerned. The post-implementation appraisal has useful education benefits for those who prepare it, those who participate in the project, and those who review the findings.

> *Goal*—Prepare three post-implementation appraisals to determine the extent of accomplishment of approved project proposals.
>
> *Standards*—Original purposes realized or not realized; changes in scope from original proposal; time-schedule performance; development-cost performance; benefits realized; lessons to be learned from development and implementation experience; actions recommended to benefit future proposals; extent of utilization of the new system; possible additional applications for the new system; documentation; hardware utilization; controls and audit trails; and evaluation of the new system.

Some companies undertake periodic biennial operational audits of all of the work in the information systems area. This produces an objective, independent evaluation of the use of resources devoted to data processing. It can be done either by in-house personnel, provided they have the skill, or by outside consultants. Although costly, such activity does help generate confidence on the part of the officers and board that this sometimes sizable resource and complex area is being satisfactorily managed and productively utilized.

> *Goal*—Evaluate the effectiveness of corporate data processing activities against criteria selected by management to determine the need for changes in: the extent of resources utilized; and priorities or applications.
>
> *Standards*—User satisfaction; cost and schedule adherence; accuracy and timeliness of outputs; hardware utilization; user participation and training; documentation; personnel skills; total resources utilized; cost savings accomplished; control over requests for changes; and multiple use of basic input data.

Personnel

In the personnel area, evaluation of performance will be enhanced by an appropriate statement of specific goals, including an agreement at the outset as to vectors which will be quantified. Four goals and specific standards for each might be as follows.

> *Goal*—Complete a comparative survey of salary and benefits structure of industry or local area companies, and recommend adjustments required to remain competitive.
>
> *Standards*—Extent to which the specified number of companies and of positions in each company are covered; validity of position comparisons—responsibility, skill, experience, fringes, salary ranges; usability of data; number and variety of positions covered; equity adjustments needed to retain managers; cost and acceptance of recommended salary range adjustments; and success in attaining company salary policy objective.
>
> *Goal*—Compile a skills inventory of personnel by major functions indicating promotion potential and back-up candidates.
>
> *Standards*—Quality of the candidate lists produced; criteria used in classification; supervisor cooperation in indicating promotion potential; clarity and focus of inventory form; simplicity and usability of data assembled; thoroughness in canvassing and documenting personnel resources; and track record—recommendations accepted, successful promotion experiences.
>
> *Goal*—Formalize and implement a program for planning individual development.

Standards—Clarity of the component features of the program; the extent management has been oriented and committed to the program; the extent individual initiative for development planning is stimulated; sensitivity to types of new experiences or responsibilities which will stimulate candidates' growth; status reports on number of: in-house training courses offered, number of people attending; outside training courses offered, number of people attending; personnel development plans prepared; people promoted, rotated; people in participating development training; evaluative feedback on courses attended by participants; and evaluative feedback by supervisor.

Goal—To provide required personnel resources, establish an effective, centralized recruitment program.

Standards—Periodic summary of the number of open positions filled, the success in meeting required dates, the number of approved positions remaining open and unfilled, analysis of key problems encountered; track record of recent recruitments including turnover rate after first three months of employment for clerical people, or after one year of employment for middle management people; and progress made by middle management recruits in terms of assignment rotation or promotion, inventory of available in-house candidates.

Legal

Much of the legal staff's activity falls in the unpredictable category. Nevertheless, a substantial content of the workload can be anticipated. Productivity can be increased, and measurement of performance can be accomplished, depending in large measure on the ability to conceptualize in advance what is needed for accomplishment. Five typical goals and possible measures of performance for each might be:

Goal—Negotiate satisfactory settlement (specify range) of the XYZ litigation by (date).

Standards—Supporting facts and documentation, selection of capable in-house and outside counsel, periodic progress evaluation (reports), time spent in preparation versus plan, time spent in negotiation versus plan, final outcome.

Goal—Establish a records management program.

Standards—Determine the existence of, or compliance with: inventory of vital records covered including computer, patents, research notes, payroll, deeds, agreements; retention schedules— compliance with governmental requirements, disposal of records no longer legally required; procedure—operating, evacuation, storage;

protection against catastrophe—retrieval, interim processing; control —licenses, patents; security—access, audit trails; and operational audits—periodic to determine degree of compliance with policy and procedure.

Goal—Follow pending proposals in pension legislation and prepare appropriate changes in pension plan.

Standards—Analysis of the various provisions—preparation of company or industry positions; determine impact on company; evaluate strategy utilized to inform legislators on company or industry position; speed and quality of plan revisions; and understanding and acceptance by plan participants.

Goal—Implement corporate policy in licensing other companies to manufacture and sell patented products in the United States and international markets.

Standards—Third-party bulk or finished product sales and profit; number of agreements negotiated, terms; documentation; number of exchange agreements negotiated; and income from products handled under exchange arrangements.

Goal—Review and approve all publicity statements issued to press, stockholders, financial community, and technical publications to assure compliance with corporate policy and appropriate accounting and regulatory requirements.

Standards—Existence of up-dated policy; checklist summaries of regulatory requirements; control—method, responsibility; evaluate method of handling stockholder communications—extent of management review of content; evaluate method of handling financial community relations—number of meetings, number of analysts attending, preparation and preliminary review of information to be discussed; and evaluate public reaction to official statements—annual reports, quarterly reports, proxy statements, press releases, technical journal publications.

Some of the effort of the legal department will be directed to unanticipated litigation or regulation. Although resources are usually provided for such contingencies based on the experience of prior years, evaluation of performance should be sufficiently flexible to take these developments into consideration. This can be done by periodic review during the year of the accumulation of unanticipated tasks, agreeing as to scope, establishing and documenting responsive actions to be taken, and reassigning priorities and schedules.

There are other standards of performance of the legal department which may be useful: for example, periodic review and evaluation of contacts with regulatory agencies—which usually are carefully minuted. Service extended to other parts of the organization can be evaluated with the benefit of feedback from the user. The degree of success in negotiations can be evaluated. Reevaluation of negotiations with the benefit of hindsight can also be informative. The handling of litigation can be measured by the number and success of actions completed.

SUMMARY

Evaluation of staff performance—including quantification of measures and systematic use of qualitative standards—is possible. Performance evaluation requires careful conceptualization and formal documentation of the nature and scope of major projects to be undertaken, agreement on aspects to be assessed, resources involved, and time schedule for completing significant components. Review of individual plans by staff supervisors encourages better motivation and commitment. Staff performance evaluation can contribute to increased productivity of staff—as well as in other areas of the organization—as a consequence of improved service, better guidance, and less wasted effort. Periodic status reporting improves control and emphasizes accomplishment within predetermined time and monetary parameters. Objective performance evaluation on the part of the chief executive is likely to more highly motivate personnel in the areas concerned.

APPENDIX

Staff Performance Evaluation: Typical Standards*

Concept to Be Evaluated	Essential Components of the Concept	Criteria for Evaluation
Objectives	Significant Specifically stated Responsibility Longer range (beyond next year) Participative development	Extent achieved Resourceful handling Periodic review

---

* It is not the author's intention to suggest that *all* of the concepts, components, and criteria above should be used *all* the time. The exercise of judgment is called for, of course.

Staff Performance Evaluation: Typical Standards (*Continued*)

Concept to Be Evaluated	Essential Components of the Concept	Criteria for Evaluation
Goals	Purpose End result desired Steps	Whether accomplished Variance from plan Unexpected problems
	Resources Schedule	Participants' attitudes Coordination—multi- departmental Cost/benefit
Policies	Guide to preferred course of action Applicability How implemented Responsibility for development Approval levels	Number completed Quality Importance of areas covered Degree implemented Ease of interpretation
Allocation of responsibilities	Clarification for each functional area involved Method of coordina- tion Documentation Control Periodic audit and review	Quality User reaction Streamlined workload Reduction in errors Possible conflicts in leadership
Position descrip- tion	Title—reports to Function—duties Responsibilities Supervises Relationships Requirements	Periodic personnel audit and review Comparison of actual versus description Morale
Workload analysis	Work flow pattern Documentation handling Activity log	Thoroughness—com- prehensive Quality of analysis— focus on essentials

Staff Performance Evaluation: Typical Standards (*Continued*)

Concept to Be Evaluated	Essential Components of the Concept	Criteria for Evaluation
	Report inventory Training—supervision Complaints	Quality of recommendation User acceptance
	Morale—absenteeism Duplication of effort Extent mechanized	Efficient use of resources—study, area covered Sensitivity to constructive opportunities Budget variances
Documentation	Written operating procedures User orientation Standardized, formal Indexing Review and control of procedural changes	Clarity—simplicity Improvement in function Recall "look-up" capability User acceptance
Meetings	Agenda—position papers Presentations—visuals Frequency Behavior—leader, group Action orientation—achievement Minutes—follow-up	Actions taken Tension-free meeting atmosphere Focus, substantive, well articulated Good listening, participation Objective audit of meeting
Operational audit	Soundness of objectives Organizational structure Existing policies and procedures—appropriate, being followed Essential reports—controls Minutes of meetings	Completeness of coverage Recommended method improvements Management acceptance Volume of work performed in relation to manpower utilized

Staff Performance Evaluation: Typical Standards (*Concluded*)

Concept to Be Evaluated	Essential Components of the Concept	Criteria for Evaluation
	Position descriptions— personnel skills Technical aspects Layout—equipment Budget variances	
Reports	Inventory of reports prepared Content—purpose, user needs, action orientation Distribution Analytical evaluation comments Extent of duplication Standards—formats, numbering, headings Control—changes, distribution	Readability—clarity User reaction Duplication Timeliness Variance commentary
Sensitive Ratios	Selected areas critical to successful operation; (i.e., employee turnover, percent of rejects, value added per employee)	Expected performance Historical patterns Industry comparison Recommended corrective action
Checklist for management review	All specific, pertinent and vital aspects List of key questions Points suggested by analysis of previous submissions	Thoroughness of coverage Focus on essential aspects Saving in rework man-hours Reduction in time taken to review and approve projects submitted

PART V

Managing the Company's External Relationships

THE SOCIAL RESPONSIBILITY OF THE BUSINESS LEADER

by Sol M. Linowitz

Partner, Coudert Brothers; Former Chairman of the Board,
Xerox Corporation

"BUSINESS IS FOR THE BIRDS"

TODAY, THERE IS great disenchantment with business and widespread antagonism and suspicion directed toward business leaders in this country. This is particularly true among young people who have, in increasing numbers, turned away from possible business careers because they do not believe they can find such a life satisfying and fulfilling. The epitome of the young people's view of business today was captured in that scene in *The Graduate* when Ben, the anti-hero, is told by a friend of his parents to remember just one word, "plastics." For young people, that word "plastics" has come to be the universal symbol for all things synthetic, vulgar, superficial, and insincere—especially the business world, its products, personnel, and organization. The corporate world has come to represent for much of our youth an unreal "plastic" world insulated and protected from the real world of poverty, disease, hunger, and deprivation. It has come to represent apathy as against empathy; insulation as opposed to involvement; competition as opposed to cooperation. In short, for them, business stands for making money as opposed to creating a better way of life.

All of this came through loud and clear during the White House Conference for Youth in 1971, when hundreds of young people between the ages of 14 and 24 came together and set forth their views of our society and its institutions. An analysis of their conclusions and recommendations is especially relevant. For what they focused on perhaps more than anything else was "humanization." They indicated that they saw the business community as a direct threat to their lives as "total persons" because it tended to develop a superspecialist; to compartmentalize individuals into slots; to dictate their style of dress; to discourage free human interaction; to render work "meaningless"; to segregate employer from employee. They also said that they viewed the efforts of business as a threat to their whole way of life through unbridled proliferation of technology without concern for social or environmental implications. What it all boiled down to was a queasy feeling among a large percentage of our youth that business leaders in particular have failed to evolve concepts of social and moral responsibility in the midst of all of our opulence and technological advancement.

These are the same views I heard expressed again and again on our college and university campuses when I served in 1971 as Chairman of the American Council on Education's Special Committee on Campus Tensions. Our goal was to try to find out what had caused the outbreaks on the college campuses and our committee consisted of educators, university presidents, students, faculty people, and public members. Although there were obviously a number of factors involved, certainly one of the most prominent—repeated again and again—was the disillusionment with our society and its leadership —particularly business leadership. A number of students said quite clearly that, in striking out against their college or university, they were rebelling against our institutions, especially our corporate leaders who, in their judgment, ran our colleges and institutions.

All of this explains why the *Wall Street Journal* started off a piece on business and youth by saying that the word around campuses is that "business is for the birds."

Not only is this a view held by young people, but it is far more widely shared in this country. The impression is that business has not been doing its fair share to help deal with our social problems, that it has been involved in all kinds of hanky-panky with the government, that the allegations surrounding ITT are typical, etc. And this view of the American businessman is, of course, prevalent in other parts of the world. I remember an occasion when as Ambassador to the Organization of American States I talked to a large group of students in Colombia, and we had a rather extensive and probing exchange of opinions. When I got through, I asked them to guess what my occupation had been before I became an ambassador. There were guesses all over the place, but when I told them that I had been in business, there was utter incredulity. One student put it succinctly: "We are smarter than you think. We *know* that you cannot be a businessman, because American businessmen are concerned only for themselves and never for others."

How do we change this image? What does the businessman have to do to establish the fact that he is in fact concerned about the problems of his society and his world and is ready to pitch in and do his fair share in dealing with these problems?

FIRST, LET'S CUT OUT THE DOUBLE-TALK

For a long time, business leaders have been mouthing pious preachments about their "commitments" which are simply not observed in practice. For too many years now, chairmen of boards and presidents have been making eloquent speeches about the responsibilities of business, yet these are often ignored within the very companies they head. This covers the whole range of activities. For example, some business leaders speak with conviction about the need for honesty and integrity, yet their own advertising agencies and departments resort to misrepresentations, exaggerations, and misstatements. Many business leaders speak about the importance of preserving the "quality of life" in this country, and yet their own companies may be peddling products inimical to that goal. A number of businessmen understandably complain that there is a failure to accord business the credit and respect to which it is entitled for its leadership and contributions. Yet when there are allegations as in the ITT case, that corporate executives may have misused their power or abused their trust, these same business leaders remain silent, unwilling to raise their voices to condemn such behavior.

All this has led to the broad feeling that business engages in double-talk and hypocrisy.

Professor Milton Friedman of Chicago leads a school of thought— supposedly *pro* business—which claims essentially that the only obligation of a business is to make money. This approach may be medieval, but it has the virtue of putting on the line precisely what it believes business is all about. It minces no words in saying that business ought to be concerned only with what it can get and gives short shrift to the notion that management ought to pay any attention to its social contribution other than what comes out of running its business. I believe very few business leaders today go along with this view.

But the fact is that the more business leaders talk about social responsibility, but ignore it in practice, the more will people believe that—despite all the fine speeches—business is *really* out to get all it can from society without any real concern as to what it can contribute.

LET'S FACE IT: THE BUSINESS OF BUSINESS IS AMERICA

The simple fact is that we have come a long long way from 1925 when Calvin Coolidge said that "The business of Business is business." For in its own self-interest, business is today deeply and inextricably involved in our social problems in this country, and no intelligent business leader—and no intelligent employee or shareholder—really believes that a business can be successful which ignores the problems of our society. The simple fact is that society is the life support system for business. All the problems which plague and agonize our society—poverty—inadequate health care—lack of education—polarization—racial struggle—the abandonment of cities—all have a direct effect on the future of business in this country, and most business leaders today recognize it.

After the urban riots in 1967, even the most reluctant business leaders had to come down from their executive towers· in the sky and recognize that they had to become involved. This led to the formation of the National Urban Coalition and other organizations such as the National Alliance of Businessmen, all trying to play a part in dealing with the problems of our cities and our broader society. I first became involved in these problems in Rochester in 1965, when the first city riot occurred and when we worked to establish a citywide unit to deal with the problems and try to find answers.

Today, it is simply good business to become involved in the needs of our society. And any businessman who fails to understand it· is not only begging for trouble, but risking the future of his own enterprise.

I think that this involvement by business must go beyond urban problems and extend into virtually every area of society. For example, I think that business has a real responsibility to make sure that our educational institutions, our art galleries, our symphony orchestras are properly supported. At Xerox, we tried to do these things with great generosity—not out of any misguided sense of do-goodism, but because we recognized that to attract the kind of employees we wanted, and to keep them happy in Rochester, they ought to have the kind of intellectual and social climate which a university, an art gallery, a symphony orchestra could provide. This had much to do in bringing us the kind of people we needed in Rochester.

Obviously, corporate enterprises as such cannot, and should not, become involved in politics. There is, on the other hand, every reason why business leaders should be willing forthrightly to take political positions and to identify themselves on behalf of political candidates. Moreover, companies should encourage this kind of political participation—and, especially, activity on the part of employees in both parties. A personal experience in 1956 indicated how much can be done to stimulate activity and participation from the top down. In that year General Eisenhower was running against Adlai Stevenson for the presidency. Joseph C. Wilson, president of Xerox and my closest friend and associate, was a strong Eisenhower supporter and became chairman of the Monroe County Committee for Eisenhower. I had long been a friend and admirer of Adlai Stevenson, and I became vice chairman of the New York State Committee for Stevenson. Joe Wilson and I then undertook debates on television, on radio, and in the newspapers on the merits of our respective candidates. This, predictably, led to a great deal of interest and evoked significant attention—some of it even nationally —but most importantly, it led others in the company (and indeed in other companies of the Rochester area) to announce their own affiliation and to go to work actively for candidates whom they were willing to support. The point that was clearly made, of course, was that it is possible to disagree about politics, and yet work together in friendship and mutual respect, even in the corporate community. I think business leaders have come to recognize increasingly that they have the same responsibility as other citizens to participate, to make their views known, to stand up and be counted.

Recently I had an experience which suggests how far we have yet to go. When President Nixon announced his proposed budget for 1973, I wrote to 12 American business leaders asking them to join me in a statement along these lines: That we recognized the importance of having an overall spending ceiling as recommended by the President; that we believed it would be presently neither feasible nor desirable to attempt to institute a tax increase; but that we felt it was of the greatest importance that the President and Congress together carefully reexamine the allocations of resources as proposed, in order to assure that the great human needs of the nation—in housing, education, welfare, health care, etc.—were given proper prior attention and concern.

Of the 12 business leaders who responded, only one was willing to sign such a statement. Virtually every one of the others agreed with the position set forth, but felt it would be "inappropriate" for him to say so publicly.

THE BUSINESS OF AMERICA IS ALSO THE BUSINESS OF AMERICAN BUSINESS

What is of concern to us as a nation in world affairs is also significant to the future of the American business community.

In the international area—to a gratifying extent—business seems to have recognized this. For example, today when strong isolationist waves are washing over the nation, the American business community is at the forefront of those stressing the importance of internationalism, and emphasizing the fact that good international relations must be a two-way street. Admittedly, part of this arises from the fact that so many multinational corporations are American, and they have a stake in the preservation of peace and the establishment of sound trade relations. But this in itself underscores the point that what is in the nation's best interest in the world today, will also tend to benefit American business. Thus, most of the pressure for quotas and tariffs is coming not from the soundly established, well operated companies, but from those who are by and large hanging on or surviving in the midst of real economic uncertainty.

By the same token, business has a strong stake in assuring the survival of the United Nations. For, clearly, the United Nations is devoted to the goal of helping to bring about a world at peace in which American business can prosper. It was this conviction which led Xerox, in 1962, to sponsor four television films in prime time telling the story of the United Nations in dramatic form. We put $2 million into the project, and presented the hour-long films without any commercials. Involved were the best actors, producers, screen writers, and directors of Hollywood, working in conjunction with Adlai Stevenson, Paul Hoffman, and other United Nations personnel. When we announced the establishment of the television series, we were immediately deluged with attacks from the John Birch Society.

Joe Wilson and I each received almost 30,000 letters, and other members of the Xerox board were also castigated for undertaking to present United Nations programs. But the counterreaction was also strong and, in due course, we came to believe that this had been the best business investment Xerox could have made in the whole field of advertising and public relations. For people from all over the world applied to the company for positions, and we acquired a reputation which paid off in countless ways.

There are many ways business can play an appropriate role in its own best interest in the international area. Thus, in 1964 business leaders founded the International Executive Service Corps. Working in conjunction with the government, there was set up a private organization of American business leaders who would undertake to arrange for American executives, scientists, and technicians to go to enterprises in developing countries for a period of from six months to two years in order to help these ventures as a kind of executive peace corps. Virtually every important American corporation joined in the venture, and today the corps is a flourishing enterprise which has sent almost 5,000 representatives to various countries of the world and has presented the picture of American business as interested in helping make available its managerial techniques, its technology, and its executive and expert competence.

Notwithstanding the fact that business leaders clearly shared the grave concern of most Americans over the Vietnam War, few business voices were raised about it. An exception was Mr. Louis Lundborg, then president of the Bank of America, who testified before a congressional committee that he felt the war was a mistake and had done much to erode the national spirit.* A group of liberal businessmen did undertake to organize in order to express opposition to the war, but none of the members was connected with any of America's important corporations or institutions, and their views were regarded as those of a fringe business group. Quite clearly, when confronted with one of the gravest international adventures in which this country had ever engaged, the nation's business leaders regarded it as unwise and impolitic to express their concern. Interestingly enough, this fact loomed large and strong in the minds of young people who were so deeply disturbed about the war, and

* [Ed. Note: See the chapter by Louis B. Lundborg, "Dealing with Local Action Groups."]

who felt that the whole powerful business community of the nation was lined up on the other side.

WHAT KIND OF BUSINESS LEADERS DO WE NEED?

The clear fact is that, as never before in our history, we will need business leaders in the future of breadth and vision, with a worldview far more expansive than has been required in the past. Especially at this time of increasing sophisticated technology and exploding knowledge, we have to recognize that "splinter specialists" will no longer be able to cope with the great challenges. This means, I think, that American business is going to have to give new emphasis to the importance of a liberal education in the preparation of its business and industrial leaders. We are going to have to look for business leaders who will be able to communicate with one another and with other people in other places, who will know how to transmit and stimulate ideas, who will recognize that things human and humane are even more important than the computer or the Xerox machine, who understand that "know-why" is even more important than "know-how."

This means that the business leaders will have to instruct their personnel departments to look for such broad-gauged people in their recruiting.

Within the corporation, much more has to be done to assure the development process of the individual. In too many companies, the executives rise in responsibility in a directly vertical line—spending years in one function or related functions, such as sales and marketing or finance and control. To get the young people we need as business leaders, there should be progression within the corporation which would be neither lateral nor vertical, but diagonal. People should be given jobs of increasing responsibility and function—enough to sustain interest and curiosity, to challenge ability, and to equip them with the kind of diversified knowledge necessary for executive leadership in the company of tomorrow.

Part of this must involve development in the area of public affairs. No longer can the public policy of the corporation be the sole prerogative of top management, or that of the staff of a specialized department. Increasingly, corporations will have to consider assigning public problems to management at all levels so that those who are charged with responsibility in the future will have some understanding of the complexity of the problems of our time. Incidentally, it is this kind of a program of development for the individual within the corporation that the White House Conference of Youth in 1971 stressed as so important to young people in their consideration as to whether or not to embark upon a business career.

IF IT ASSUMES LEADERSHIP, AS IT CAN AND SHOULD, BUSINESS CAN DO MUCH TO MAKE US THE KIND OF SOCIETY WE CAN AND SHOULD BE

If the business community approaches the future with the vision and thought required, and develops the kind of men who are able to understand the changing and developing human condition, it can help bring into being the kind of free society we have always talked about in this country.

This will mean a willingness on the part of business and industry to recognize that science and technology are tools which can be used effectively to advance the human condition, and that improvements and scientific developments must therefore be evaluated in terms of their social impact. I am not suggesting that American industry take on itself a solitary crusade for the conquest of our problems. What I am suggesting is that a systematic and intimate understanding of the dominant social problems of our day, combined with the firm dedication to public service, will lead to the discovery by businessmen of innovations that will satisfy their direct corporate goals and simultaneously make a contribution to the solution of our pressing human needs.

THE CHIEF EXECUTIVE OFFICER AND GOVERNMENT RELATIONS AT THE NATIONAL LEVEL

by Jayne Baker Spain

Vice Chairman, U.S. Civil Service Commission

THE CHIEF EXECUTIVE OFFICER generally goes to Washington in one of two ways, often in both. If wise, he will assume that he could well try our Capital on for size in the two configurations, and use one to learn about the other. If he does this, he will not only have gotten from government, but also have learned how to give to it.

THE CEO IN WASHINGTON

First, the CEO usually comes to Washington for various congressional and business association affairs, to put salt on the tail of a big contract or to explain his company's shortcomings in carrying it out, or to take protective measures about legislation or regulations which could, on the one hand, ease the way for him, or on the other, make his business survival precarious. Second, many CEOs are persuaded to leave the firms which they have headed so long to accept appointment at great financial sacrifice to some position of responsibility in the machinery of government itself, even though the longevity of such appointments averages only 19 months.

The first CEO role is the traditional one. It is simple because he comes with a company position and objective and a personal philosophy about how he will attend to it. The second CEO course is the sporty one, in that he burns all his bridges behind him, makes something resembling a scorched earth of his previously warm and cordial "old boy network," and faces an uncharted minefield ahead. In neither case does he ever come with a supply of what he's likely to need most—his very own bank of blood plasma. Washington is known for making CEOs shed and sweat a lot more blood than their Creator gave them in the first place.

Most CEOs arrive in Washington, whether to do business or to work in government, with much less of what they thought they had in abundance—*know-how*—and more than enough of what they don't need—*naiveté*.

This is my considered conclusion based on many years' experience in this traffic pattern as a CEO engaged in seeking and delivering to the specifications of government agency contracts; and, in recent years, serving in the hierarchy of national government itself. So I believe I have seen Washington from enough of its sides to say that the so-called business approach to the governing process is an insupportable myth.

My feeling is that the typical CEO courts failure in whatever task he undertakes, including the assault on Washington, for the same reason that generals are defeated in battle. A general can have all the luxuries his office affords, staff brilliance, more "perks" than he will ever need, plus tanks and air support, the best field position, and even the longest reputation for winning. Still he will be bushwacked if he overlooks some small but important element of battle strategy and is taken by surprise. Likewise, a CEO cannot afford to overlook, or be forgiven for overlooking, any aspect of contract hunt and fulfillment that might allow his competitor to surprise him.

Washington, to state the obvious, is forever unpredictable, forever whimsical, forever nerve-wracking, and forever full of surprises. Its cogs and gears are oiled by notions and vogues, by "in things" and innuendo; added lubrication comes from headlines and fulminating rhetoric; and it's a place where the tiniest of tadpoles, given time, has a way of turning into the most formidable of bullfrogs. The CEO will emerge best who treats Washington with respect, knowing it can serve him but that it can also serve him up with lots of salt and pepper and make a meal of him if it so wishes.

Washington is really one thing for sure: the most effective collector of money and probably the most prodigal spender. It tries hardest to improve on its reputation for the former, but is viewed as having absolutely no interest in curing itself of the latter. It is the largest purchaser of goods and services, as any CEO knows, and it throws out the biggest fishhooks through legislation and regulations impinging more and more on the freedom of business to operate. Government regulations tend to be inflexible. They usually apply to all business irrespective of size and nature, without taking into account the particular idiosyncracies with which each business is confronted. Whether the CEO likes it or not, much of this results from an undercurrent of antibusiness sentiment which comes from: people who are misinformed or uninformed about the private enterprise system; those, such as consumers and environmentalists, who sincerely think they have suffered, or are likely to suffer wrong at the hands of business; those who have encountered the arrogance and insensitivity which oftentimes comes with bigness; and others who equate profit with exploitation. There is a never-ending trek to Washington by those who look to it as a power center which can assign corrective actions and social justice missions against other manifestations of power, whether it is equipped to handle such tasks or not, as CEOs and the business community have learned.

THE CEO'S PREP SCHOOL

The CEO's prep school often serves him badly. Whereas the communist world's sainted oracle, Lenin, could call religion "the opiate of the people," the CEO is often lulled and set up for personal disaster in Washington by the broken-record litany of undergraduate business schools and his later executive club room associations. Endless pratings about the sanctity of the bottom line and other wornout platitudes rain on him to reinforce his prejudices and please his ears. There is a tremendous desire to believe such things as ultimate truths in exclusive locker rooms, in penthouse petroleum clubs, élite resorts, and anywhere else the CEO peer groups confront each other and have their coteries of sychophants quite ready to nod agreement on cue. The honest CEO has lost count of how many times in such cloisters he had heard such hoary clichés as:

"What they need down there in Washington is a good, hard-headed businessman to do that job."

"He's a bureaucrat! What the hell does he know or care about meeting a payroll?"

"A business has to make a profit to exist, or it can't employ people or pay taxes. Where would the government be without corporation taxes?"

"What is this *business social conscience* thing anyway? What does it have to do with what I manufacture, and the government's need to have it?"

"Just find out who the key guy is. Romance hell out of him. Don't pay any attention to those clowns around him. That's the way to get that contract and/or legislation we need."

"Promise him anything to get that signature on the line. He'll probably be transferred by the time the stuff hits the fan. We'll most likely have a lot of new faces in the act, too. Let somebody else catch all those cats!"

"That guy over in the White House does nothing for business. Where would he and his party be without employment, production, taxes, and talent if he didn't have business to draw on?"

And so on. It is surely not a very good beginning impression or preconceived notion about Washington and its ramifications, and even less on target for the bureaucracies of other national governments with which major Chief Executive Officers must cope if they have international spread.

DEALING WITH GOVERNMENT

Dealing with government will always range from difficult to insurmountable for one-dimensional chief executives who approach bureaucracy from personal and staff points of view alone. They will be successful in proportion to their capability as chameleons, the ability to wear the other side's coat and see through its glasses, and to understand its accountabilities which are far more severe, exacting, brutal, and ever-present than a once-a-year two-hour confrontation with an audience of shareholders.

Government relations must always be conducted as the country judge observed during an alienation of affections suit: "When you write letters to another man's wife, it's best to start 'em off 'Dear Sweetheart, and Gentlemen of the Jury.' " It is first, last, and always political business, fraught with all the perils attendant thereto, and every approach and every contract should be reviewed as to how it will look as a lure to an adversary position—not that anything has to be done in fear of the adversary position, except to be sure it can be lived with and discounted and is not going to have a disruptive effect.

The CEO

The CEO who hangs on to popular misconceptions because they are soothing and simplistic comes to our capital as a severe arthritic. Flexibility, so vitally needed, will be painful and even impossible for him. He is an Abe Martin kind of victim. As Abe said, the most dangerous men were those "who know so many things for sure that just ain't so." The CEO prone to such assumptions will not only find Washington a bed of nettles, but will be unable to identify which nettle bit him. If his is an international operation, this will probably be upgraded to a bed of nails awaiting him in all those other countries.

The hallowed "good, hard-headed businessman" so often offered as a modern Moses to lead the tribes in Washington to the Promised Land, by taking the "pragmatic" tack, is already in Washington in some numbers. He has been there before, he is there now, and he will come again. He comes initially suspicious that he is now among the Philistines; and the first civil servants he meets, he usually marks down three grades as "people who couldn't cut it in the business world," and any suggestions made by them are suspect. In one week's time, he is using each of them as an indispensable crutch.

The Washington he had though of as a place to do business is also *not* a business; and not being a business, it works in its own way. He will learn how to work within it, or he will leave town. This should be no news to him, but it always is; and it's no different from corporate life, in that one works within the personality of a company, or he leaves it.

The "hard-headed businessman" doing his stint in Washington, the CEO will find, is carried on the shoulders of something called the Civil Service. It is the largest single employee force in the United States, numbering more than 2,800,000 men and women worldwide. Civil servants are the ones who actually assemble the specifications, draw up the requirements for proposals, accomplish procurement, supervise contracts, defend government claims of shortcomings, conduct audits, provide congressional reports and technical testimony, relate to committee heads on Capitol Hill and their staffs, and attend to all the masses of paperwork in which the government "fish" actually "swims."

The CEO who comes to Washington prepared to accept the fact that people are people, no matter what payroll ties they have, and that they will respond to him as people, based on what he puts into that relationship—be they congressmen, administrative assistants, agency representatives, rank-and-file civil servants—will be the successful CEO. The "hard-headed businessman" is really a buzz-word after all, for a hard head suggests its wearer is impervious to a new idea and incapable of change.

The Bureaucrat

The *bureaucrat* is so many, many things in Washington. The CEO may come to town believing him to be synonymous with *obstacle, deadwood,* a *patronage payoff.* The bureaucrat is the business version of an infidel, in that he worships at an idol called the federal budget, when everyone who has been to a graduate business school or was raised correctly knows that God's other name is "Bottom Line." It is absolutely unnerving to some CEOs when they find themselves talking with generals and admirals and high-level bureaucrats who send out for appropriations with almost the same aplomb as they send the office girl to the corner snackbar if they want to stay in and eat at their desks. The CEO is up against a different point of view—one which is arrived at by agencies of government making a case for the programs or responsibilities or responses expected of them for which they list items and the pricetags. Come the appropriations, they're in business.

As far as the question goes about the bureaucrat's not knowing what it means to meet a payroll week in and week out, it is not relevant to his job, so why should he know or care? He expects the CEO to handle all those things which are his concern, and that will be reflected in the contract they make. Knowing how to get the appropriations for the programs *is* the bureaucrat's role. Knowing how to meet the payroll is something required of the CEO. They will work best if they do not get in each other's business. This is not to say that they don't find themselves in each other's yards from time to time, but it's best if they observe fences and proprieties.

It is a rich CEO, indeed, who has access to the bureaucrats who make Washington go. In spite of the synonyms assigned to the bureaucrat by a CEO with no Washington experience, the time may come when the CEO adds another he would never have thought possible—*helper,* and even *friend.* And the bureaucrat will be forgiven the fact that meeting a payroll does not concern him, for he can do many other things, which are his business, and better than anyone else can do them.

Washington agrees almost 100 percent that business has to make a profit to exist, but has little or no concern about business profits because the people who populate Washington have towering respect for the government's ability to tap sources of money transfusion. Businesses may come and go—Washington will continue to exist, and it never writes thank-you notes to anyone who sends it money.

The government would erase the company name from its data file if a company disappeared and was no longer a source of tax funds. No CEO should ever come to Washington expecting sympathy. Tax money is impersonal, and taxes will always be with us. It's better to treat the subject with a sense of resignation and good humor as Bob Hope did when he was asked why he went to Washington so often. "I go down there to visit my money," he said. Not to handle it; not to have the people come out from the Department of the Treasury and wave affectionately for sending it in; just to visit it.

Congress

The CEO who can't find the time to spend seeing and making himself available to Congress, its committees, and the committee staffs—in fact, making it a part of the way he parcels himself and his time up for most effect—is not making proper use of himself. This is one of the finest places to go about that "chameleon school" ritual, and the CEO may be shocked with what he finds. I knew one who went in to talk about a strike of some 20,000 employees at one of his plants, and the congressman never mentioned the word *employees* once. He said he was concerned that 20,000 *voters* in his district were unemployed, and that they expected him to do something about it. The CEO had never been in to see him before, and he soon found that when the measuring stick was *voters* and his standing was in ratio of one to 20,000, any rationale for his position would be weak.

There is no congressman who doesn't like to be on intimate speaking terms with the "power structure" of his district, but CEOs who are oftentimes expert in taking care of headwaiters—"Always make the big tip going in, if you want a fuss made over you during all the courses"—are often the ones who wait until they're in deep, unfixable, and probably inexcusable trouble before going to see "Whatsizname, that fellow in Congress." Congressmen, more than senators, are very constituency-conscious, and the numbers game is the best one they play. The savvy CEO will learn from that. It starts at home, inside the company; a letter on some subject from ten employees expressing themselves strongly in behalf of a regulation or legislation can oftentimes make more impression than the CEO, even if he said the same thing.

One company of my acquaintance built on this very effectively.

The idea came from the employee Christmas party. Every executive in the company was assigned a table, and the employees were allowed to sit with anyone of their choice. All the company charwomen chose to sit with the CEO. He was their favorite, and he couldn't have been more pleased. I never knew that executive ever to have a congressional problem, nor would any of his employees not respond to his request that they, rather than he, express themselves to their congressman on subjects of mutual interest. He was not in the *people business*, buzz-word variety; he had the touch, the real thing.

THE SOCIAL CONSCIENCE OF BUSINESS

The matter of *"business social conscience"* has been a headbumper. How many of us remember the righteous indignation of CEOs who once said, of their interpretation of their executive responsibilities, that they couldn't give profit moneys to charity? And there were dutiful like-minded shareholders who raised hob in annual meetings, and even sued managements who had done such terrible things. There is legitimacy in the contention that corporations do not constitute the vehicle to pay the costs of social change, but this is not to say they shouldn't participate. I know many CEOs who have found participation to be an uplifting of the spirit. Many shareholders feel somewhat warmer when the company they own encourages its people to engage in such activities and they see evidences of such things.

And all that aside, it is my belief that CEOs who are reluctant to talk about what they do in this area are serving the free enterprise system badly; their own company badly; serving badly the employees who give of their time; and in the government contract area, they may well be giving an advantage by their silence to a more vocal competitor who may be doing less.

Congress and funded agencies of government are gung-ho for examples of such works. The *social audit* entrancement of the country's campuses has been growing steadily for two decades. The plain truth is that most CEOs would be flat-out startled if they ran such a social audit, because in doing some of the things they do best—from job training to skill upgrading, to job matching of both handicapped people and those with minimal formal education—they have been doing fantastically well for years and years. They have just never thought about it that way, have not made a pointed analysis of it, and as often happens when people are too close to an old and enduring story, the overlooking CEO is not even aware that he has been up to some very good things, indeed. The name for it may be different, but the fact of *business social conscience* is not.

The CEO should be fully aware that every business decision in today's society can have political overtones, and trigger public clamor or approval depending on how it is done. He should be updated regularly on all legislation which has bearing on what he does, or which may have future implications for him, and get in early with inputs in the right quarter before the corrective process is out of reach.

TO DO—AND NOT TO DO

Keep Informed

With his many other responsibilities, a CEO cannot personally devote a great deal of time to government relations matters, but a key assistant can be designated to be his "eyes and ears" on a full or part-time basis, with the responsibility to alert him to timely and significant information.

As a first means of keeping informed, and depending on the size of the company or corporation, it may be wise to retain a representative in Washington to provide timely intelligence and support for corporate interests. A company's physical presence in Washington greatly facilitates a government relations program. The representative can have immediate contact with key congressmen or staff, and the corporation maintains visibility. The representative may be a lawyer, and in many instances that qualification is a necessity.

A second way in which a CEO can keep informed is by having his government relations assistant scan a variety of publications for information on legislation and actions which affect the organization. These publications include the journals of trade associations, newsletters and news services of trade interest, and—for the most complete coverage—the daily *Congressional Record* and the *Federal Register* (which announces new regulations of government agencies).

The CEO should also be familiar with those government agencies which have programs that relate to his business, especially those agencies with regulatory authority. Information on these agencies is available in the *United States Government Manual*, available from the Superintendent of Documents, Government Printing Office,

Washington, D.C. 20402. A simple letter to an agency from any business office will get attention, although not necessarily an immediate solution to the problem. Don't hesitate to communicate with the appropriate agency official (the *Government Manual* may serve as your directory here) whenever you have specific questions or problems within his or her area of responsibility.

Develop Relationships

It is very important to develop a working relationship with the people in the government agencies closely connected with your company's area of interest *before* any serious problems present themselves. These agencies are not faceless enemies. They are operated by people with human concerns and interests. They exist ultimately to serve the public interest, but they also are keenly aware of the multiple constituency in a pluralistic society. They want to hear *your* side of the story. They appreciate your logical presentation of the facts bearing on issues before them.

The CEO should sense the political pressures and influences which are bearing down on the legislators, and be ready to help them bridge what may be a wide chasm between their positions. The CEO is no stranger to logic, or reasoning, or persuasion, or the soft sell, to have risen to his station, and this is exactly the octave scale on which he should play legislation from inception to passage. A CEO with a reputation for honesty and reliability in this arena will always be worth more than he's paid by his company, no matter what that is.

I would again like to emphasize how essential it is to develop lines of communication to government officials and to members of Congress *before* you face the crisis of a new law or administrative ruling. Informal contact and communication, when there are no specific pressing needs, will lay the groundwork for communications channels when such communication is an urgent necessity. Too often Chief Executive Officers react after the fact, instead of being right in the middle of the action *before* the glue is hardened on a legislative package or agency policy.

Lobbying

I have no qualms about labeling this as "lobbying." There is a widespread feeling that there is something wrong in lobbying. There seems to be too much association of the word with payoffs and big money. Ethically and legally, the "payoff" is wrong, but there are many legitimate means of presenting your position. Not only are these means legitimate, but you have the responsibility to let agency officials and members of Congress know just what a particular policy or piece of legislation is going to do to business. You have the obligation to do this, not just to save your own business, but everyone else's. There is nothing wrong in lobbying except in payoffs and side-dealings. You lobby to fight your case on its merits.

There are several approaches which you may use in concert as a means of achieving legislation favorable to your business interests.

There are occasions when you may find it useful to submit a legislative proposal to a congressman. As a citizen you have a constitutional right to petition Congress. This is an important part of the total democratic process, and you should not be embarrassed by a show of self-interest in this process. However, you will meet with the greatest success if you present your proposal in a well-thought-out manner which suggests that its applicability is not confined to your particular business, but is significant to a broader area of business.

After a bill is introduced in the House of Representatives or the Senate by a member of Congress, it is referred to the standing committee having jurisdiction of the subject matter. If the bill is sufficiently important or controversial, a public hearing is held. During the public hearing, you or your representative may serve as a witness, giving testimony in favor of or against the proposed legislation. In this situation, a Washington representative may be particularly useful in arranging your appearance before the committee.

If a bill is favorably reported out of committee, a committee member is designated to write the committee report which describes the purpose and scope of the bill and reasons for recommended approval. Committee reports are perhaps the most valuable single element of the legislative history of a law. They are used by the courts, executive departments and agencies, and the public, generally as a source of information regarding the purpose and meaning of the law. Your lawyer-lobbyist can assist the committee member in writing this report, and the input given at that point is of great significance in later application of the bill.

Grassroots lobbying can be an effective means of presenting the issues at hand before the public, and ultimately before members of Congress and federal agencies. Letters to editors of local or Washington newspapers, the release of related news stories, and the publication of articles in trade journals on the issues are some of the means by which you can make your point.

Washington Works through Organizations

As to the advice to "romance the key individual and forget those around him," the CEO should pigeonhole that before he leaves home. Washington is a "staffed" community. At the top, someone says "I need thus-and-so," and immediately the staff mill starts grinding: terms of reference, specifications, authorization fund numbers, complementary purpose to existing programs, and very, very importantly, locations of legislator strength and weaknesses should congressional concern or support be required.

None of these staffers should rate the putdown as "clowns" which the business community underlings lay on them. One of the most slipshod areas of business, by comparison, is often in staff work; the CEO frequently finds in Washington's thoroughness that he has been poorly served by his own. And the "key guy," if there is one, is at best but a fraction of the whole decision-making structure; so the CEO who looks for, and thinks he has one, has probably kidded himself. In federal bureaucracy there is a chronic loneliness which requires as a protective measure that no one go it alone toward a decision, or as the longtimers say it, "get several on the hook with you."

Coordination in Washington is of epidemic proportions and I was once warned to be careful about "the words" that go in a document if it is to have any hope of speed at all, because "if you so much as mention a tree, for example, you'll have to coordinate it with the U.S. Forestry Service!"

About Contracts

The CEO who is party to promising anything to get a contract, and assumes he will be able to take care of things by attrition or transfer, new faces on both sides of the table, is really sending out an extensive list of invitations to come to the party later with him as the guest dishonored. Better he understand well the pitfalls of doing business with Washington, which starts with knowing in detail all the procurement laws and regulations that pertain to the business being pursued. He also ought to know his own company well enough so that he goes after that contractual tie for which it is best suited by substance and experience, rather than because it has pretensions to grandeur which can only be accomplished by risky spreading out.

The CEO should guide on the principle that it is relatively simple to make changes in contract drafts as to what is agreed *before* the contract is signed, and that thereafter any afterthoughts are as hard and as costly to fit in as when his wife decides to change the bathroom from its original location on one side of the house to the other, just as the roofing has begun.

A part of that unwitting "invitation" which the careless CEO and his minions send out, if they are at all cavalier about a government contract, goes to the so-called ladies and gentlemen of the Washington press corps. They are ladies and gentlemen of the same genre as Count Dracula and his daughter, with the same fascination for an offending CEO's jugular vein. And if any CEO is ever asked to come to Washington to take a post in government, if he has been other than honest, frank, honoring of agreements, and a producer of reliable product, each of these evidences is the equivalent of handing a sharp, broad-axe to the political opposition which will enjoy recounting them, in or out of context.

"That Man in the White House"

And as to that man in the White House. Whoever he is, the CEO should recognize him for what he is, what he has to do, what he is capable of doing, and what he cannot do. Calvin Coolidge could say that the business of the United States was business, or words to that effect, and get away with it. Then came 1929, and in months the Wall Street which had been the fastest way to easy riches turned into business caught with its pants down, and many sought the quickest way to the street from open windows and the tops of the tallest buildings they could find.

The White House is a location from which expressions march out, such as prosperity and victory in wars being "around the corner"—which come back to haunt the sayer regardless of party. It is everybody's mailbox, everybody's favorite place to be photographed.

In other words, the CEO should see "the man in the White House" as everybody's equivalent of a Wailing Wall, not just his own. And if he truly believes in the "free enterprise" system and thinks it is worth saving (and we all hope he does, and really wants to do something about it besides branding it as the true faith and thinking that's enough), he will make it easier for the president of the United States to stand up for it, extol its virtues, and defend it as the highest hope of all people to achieve all the things and aspirations they may have.

How Business Looks to Washington

No CEO can be unaware that he often encounters coolness in various quarters in Washington when free enterprise comes up for discussion. This is because there are many in influential corner offices and lesser cubbyholes who can accept that it has served our country and the people who live in it well, but that it has been applied freely and enterprisingly on a selective rather than general basis.

In Washington where every known problem, some unknown, and other especially contrived problems eventually come to roost looking for solution, the view from the White House and the Congress, and from the agencies, is that the CEO who may have corporate designs on the whole world wants to play in a small and flowery and profit-making corner of Washington's garden behind a fence so high he can't see the menacing weed patches.

The bureaucratic concept of the businessman, who does so well in the profiles of the commercial press, is that he has a highly-tuned sixth sense for appropriations direction, and orients on available money as the jungle jackals do a fresh kill. The businessman is perceived as waiting for government to identify the problem area, although he may see it even sooner and have ideas about how to deal with it more soundly.

As an example, only some 20 major industrial firms participated in the Task Force which laid the groundwork for what became the Office of Economic Opportunity and took up contracts which would engage them in skill training for high school dropouts. Hundreds of big businesses and their CEOs elected to stand apart and engage in the unproductive game of criticism, all the while offering no discernible alternatives which were as good, and none better.

How the Chief Executive Officer looks by his performance to the man in the White House, to the bureaucracy, to Washington, is what all these nooks and crannies of opinion-making and response add up to. It has nothing to do with the frequency of his presence at black tie dinners and peer associations at expensive tables purchased for effect at Washington functions.

SUMMARY

Looking at things broadly, there are several positive actions you can take to properly influence the political process; and in turn help to create a more responsive government.

1. You may encourage and support your employees' participation on issues and in politics *as individuals.*
2. You may conduct campaigns which give employees an opportunity to register to vote and to contribute to the party of their choice at their place of work. And remember, it is *their* choice.
3. You may wish to send a corporate representative to present your views at party platform committee meetings.
4. As an individual, you may wish to make a private campaign contribution to the extent permitted by law. (A contribution from corporate funds is illegal.)

Along with these suggestions for elements of your government relations program, I must also indicate to you actions which you should avoid.

1. Follow the advice of your legal counsel; avoid actions which could violate laws and regulations relating to conflicts of interest and ethical conduct, particularly in your dealings with members of Congress. There are criminal statutes which prohibit congressmen from receiving compensation to affect legislation, and also prohibit the offering of any thing of value to a congressman to influence his action, vote, or decision on any matter.
2. Understand that there is a distinction between a politically appointed executive in a federal agency and a careerist in that agency. Both groups are often sensitive of this distinction, and you can avoid a misunderstanding of your approach on the part of the agency official if you are also aware of these different roles.
3. When communicating and seeking information, it is important to avoid situations which could be subjected to the criticism of creating the *appearance* of "side-dealings." Offering your company aircraft for travel of key agency officials can create this appearance.
4. Take it easy with traditional business "oratory." The astute

CEO will remember that pontifical and self-serving utterances from what seem to be safe platforms with parochial audiences stamping their feet in approval are as cannonballs fired. No matter how fast the orator runs, no matter how big a catcher's mitt he may employ, he can't get those words back and they can haunt him. The savvy CEO will tell himself that even though individuals in government move around, its files have long and enduring memories.

If I can leave only one point firmly with you, it is that you must establish that working relationship with your government. Let your elected representatives and those in government agencies know how you feel about potential legislation. Do it when it can begin a casual but ongoing dialog. If you do this, you won't face the surprise of a crippling piece of legislation.

So, Mr. CEO, whether you come for a Washington visit with business in mind, or to stay for a period, as a part of government, let me tell you that the Golden Rule is an enduring wicket—"Do unto Others as You Would Have Them Do unto You!" The underlined word in there is *others*, which means everybody, the public body.

Please don't dismiss that as "old stuff," as there's been so little of it in evidence around Washington lately, it would be bright and shiny and a relief to behold.

THE CEO AND STATE AND LOCAL GOVERNMENTS

by Roy M. Goodman

New York State Senator;
Former Corporate President and
New York City Finance Commissioner

INTRODUCTION

ONCE UPON a time, the typical corporate executive could enjoy untroubled sleep if, in addition to discharging his regular corporate responsibilities, he kept generally abreast of developments at the federal government level. The federal government, it seemed, had the real power in most important areas, from taxation to regulation of business.

Today, as a result of the explosion of public interest in the environment, consumer protection, equal opportunity, women's rights, and other potent local movements, the chief executive must now cope, in addition, with a vastly more complex network of problems in business-government relations at the state and local level.

Alert chief executives must now familiarize themselves with the structures of state and local governments, with their operations, and with methods of affecting such operations. Having impact on government involves working not only with those who are elected or appointed to public office, but also with the press, civic organizations, political leaders, labor, and business interests.

Although the governmental structures of the 50 states and the thousands of towns and municipalities throughout the country differ in important details, they have much in common. All have an executive, a legislature, and a judiciary. The names, with the exception of "governor," may differ, but their functions and method of operation generally are similar. For our purposes, and because I am familiar with them, I will use the structures of New York State and New York City to illustrate how local government operates.

THE STATE

The U.S. Constitution gives certain definite powers to the federal government. All other powers are reserved to the states or to the people. Although, over the years, decisions of the U.S. Supreme Court have broadened the powers of the federal government, the states, theoretically, are still supreme. Cities derive their powers from the states, and in almost every instance a city's powers are granted by legislation passed by the state legislature. Even in such matters as municipal regulation of business by the city, that power to regulate had to be obtained from the state.

The State of New York, as do other states, has an executive branch, a legislature, and a judiciary. Although they are separate and independent, they act and interact on each other, especially the legislature and the executive. It is with these two that the chief executive must primarily be concerned.

The State Executive

The executive branch of government in New York State is headed by a governor, a lieutenant governor, a controller, and an attorney general. All are elected for four-year terms. Like the president and the vice president of the United States, the governor and lieutenant governor are joined together on the general election ballot, assuring that they will be of the same political party.

The governor is the head of the executive branch of government and appoints a cabinet whose members head the various departments of state government. All of his—or her—appointments, except for his personal staff, must be confirmed by the state Senate.[1]

The main function of the lieutenant governor is to provide for gubernatorial succession in case of a vacancy caused by death, resignation, or removal from office of the governor. He serves with the full powers of the governor when the governor is out of the state. Aside from this, his other function is to preside over the Senate. Traditionally, although his political ideology may differ from that of the governor, he espouses the policies enunciated by the governor. His strength at meetings which make policy is based on his own public popularity or the power of his political base. In New York State in the

---

[1] In this day and age, the American people frequently elect women to high political office. For purposes of this article, words of the masculine gender include the feminine.

past 42 years, it should be noted, only one lieutenant governor, Herbert Lehman, was ever elected governor.

The controller is the fiscal officer of the state. He supervises vast state borrowing operations through the flotation of tax exempt bonds. He heads a vast Audit and Control Department and has extensive inspectorial and audit powers. He controls the placement of billions of dollars in bank deposits.

The attorney general is the state's chief legal officer and heads a large staff of attorneys in the Department of Law. He represents the state in all litigation in which the state is either a plaintiff or a defendant and also advises the governor on the constitutionality of laws passed by the legislature prior to signature by the governor.

In recent years, the Department of Law has devoted much of its efforts to consumer protection, civil rights, and enforcement of environmental laws. The attorney general also has power to prosecute criminal matters or to appoint special prosecutors in specific areas of alleged criminal activity.

Operation of the State Executive. The four most important aides to the governor of New York State are: (1) his counsel, who advises him on all legislative matters and whose staff carefully reviews every bill passed by the legislature and sent to the governor for signature; (2) the secretary to the governor, a constitutional office equivalent to chief of staff; (3) the director of the budget, the governor's chief financial executive; and (4) his director of communications who supervises all news media relations and speech preparation. The corporate chief executive who has the ear of any one of these key people in effect has the ear of the governor himself.

Bills passed by the legislature and sent to the governor may either be approved or vetoed by him. His veto has been overridden on only the rarest of occasions. Disapproval by any of the four major aides to the governor often results in a veto by the governor. Similarly, a recommendation for approval or veto by the head of the particular state department or agency which has jurisdiction over the subject of the legislation is rarely ignored. When two agencies submit conflicting recommendations, the decision is made by the governor.

Inasmuch as the heads of state departments and agencies are appointed by, and serve at the pleasure of the governor, their function is to carry out the policies of his administration. The head of an agency frequently has enormous delegated powers, especially through the promulgation of rules and regulations which contain the practical ground rules for departmental operation.

Administration policy is developed by the governor, his staff, the comptroller, and attorney General—when members of the same political party—and the legislative leaders of the governor's party. On major issues, a bipartisan policy may be developed by bringing into policy-shaping meetings the legislative leaders of the opposition party. However, this usually happens only when not enough majority party votes are available to pass a bill and help must be sought from "across the aisle."

The State Legislature

New York State and many other states have bicameral legislatures having two houses, the Senate and the Assembly. They have substantially equal power and all bills must pass both houses with a majority vote of the members elected before going to the governor for signature. The Senate also has the power of confirmation of gubernatorial appointments. In New York, there are 60 members of the Senate and 150 assemblymen, the senatorial districts being approximately three times the size of assembly districts. Senators and assemblymen are elected for two-year terms.

Operation of the State Legislature. The most powerful member of the Senate, with the title of "president pro tem," is the leader of the majority party. He is elected by a caucus of the members of his party in the Senate. He appoints the chairmen of all committees and assigns members of the majority party to various committees. The members of the minority party also are assigned by the majority leader in consultation with the leader of the minority party. Except during a period of party unrest, seniority plays the major part in the election of the majority and minority leaders. These two leaders are the de facto spokesmen in their legislative body for their respective parties. They also control the legislative operations budget which in New York is several million dollars, a vast patronage pool.

In the Assembly, the elected leader of the majority party is called the speaker of the Assembly and he presides over that body. He is aided by the majority leader, whom he appoints. The minority party elects its leader, known as the minority leader. The speaker of the Assembly, as does the president pro tem of the Senate, appoints the committee chairman and assigns the members to various committees.

The president pro tem of the Senate and the ex speaker of the Assembly have large legal and research staffs to help them prepare and review legislation proposed by other members of the legislature. Quite often, the leaders have aides who deal with legislation in specific areas and who are experts in their particular fields. These aides also act as liaison with the various state departments and agencies in these areas. The corporate chief executive should always find out who is the key legal and research staff person in any legislative area of concern. Direct communication with such staff people can be most important.

Working closely with the legislative leaders are the chairmen of important committees of each house of the legislature. Ranking next to the president pro tem of the Senate are the deputy leaders and the chairman of the Finance Committee. The Finance Committee staff review the budget submitted by the governor, after it has been prepared by the director of the budget. The counterpart of the Finance Committee chairman in the Assembly is the chairman of the Ways and Means Committee. Other important committees are those of Judiciary and Codes.

Once policy is developed by the governor and the legislative leaders—if they are of the same party—it is the responsibility of the leadership to steer that legislation to passage by both houses.

State Legislative Committees.   Although they may have different names, the committees of the Senate and Assembly function in about the same way. Committees on various subjects—housing and urban development, health, finance, civil service, cities, banking, towns and villages etc.—are created under the rules of each house. Each committee has a chairman and a ranking minority member representing, respectively, the majority and minority parties in that house of the legislature.[2]

All bills introduced in each house by members are assigned to a committee which deals with the subject of the proposed legislation. Often, companion bills are introduced at about the same time in both houses of the legislature—one by an assemblyman and the other by a senator. The bills are printed, distributed to every legislator, and made available to members of the public who desire them. A condensation of the bills introduced to date, the committees to which

---

[2] [Ed. Note: Mr. Goodman, at the time of this writing, was chairman of the Committee on Housing and Urban Development of the New York State Senate.]

they have been assigned, and the action taken to date on each, appear under the appropriate subject title in a weekly publication called the *Legislative Index*. Business firms must subscribe to this book to keep track of the introduction and progress or disposition of bills that affect, or might affect their industry. Alternatively, they can retain a legislative representative who will watch the Index like a hawk and sound early warnings on important legislation when it is filed and keep in close touch as it progresses.

After filing a memorandum with the committee to which his bill has been assigned, the sponsor may request that the committee take action on the bill. The committees, which usually meet each week, act on agenda prepared by the committee chairmen. A bill may be approved or disapproved (killed) by a majority vote of the members of the committee, or action may be deferred.

If a bill is disapproved, that is the end of it—at least for the time being. If it is approved (voted out of committee), it goes on the "calendar" for consideration by the legislative body.

After a required number of days during which it must be on the calendar, the bill may be considered by the entire house. The bill may pass, not pass, or be referred back to committee. It may also be stalled to death. Bills also may be amended on the floor of the house, but this is rare.

If the bill is passed in one house, it then is sent to the other house for action. If it passes the second house of the legislature, it then is sent to the governor for approval or veto. If he signs the bill, it becomes law. If he vetoes the bill, the legislature may attempt to override his veto by a two-thirds vote. This seldom happens.

The State Judiciary

Unlike the legislative and executive branches where businessman's intervention is appropriate, the judiciary is a "hands off" area. The ethical businessman will never try to "influence" a judge. Such action is illegal, immoral, and, in the great majority of cases, doomed to backfire with grave consequences.

As regards legislation and the legislative process that affect business, the role of the state judiciary is largely confined to determining the constitutionality of state laws. For that reason, in the area of legislation, chief executives need not be concerned about the judiciary except in such cases as their attorneys determine the need to challenge the constitutionality of regulatory legislation affecting their firms' business. Such actions are begun in the state Supreme Court, which, despite its name, is a court of original jurisdiction. Ultimately, the constitutionality of state legal action under the constitution of the state—as distinct from the federal constitution—will be decided by the Court of Appeals, the state's highest tribunal.

Supreme Court judges and judges of the Court of Appeals are elected for 14-year terms. Court of Appeals judges are elected state-wide; Supreme Court judges are elected from judicial districts, of which there are 11 in New York State.

THE CITY

New York City, like the state, has an executive branch, a legislative branch, and a judiciary. However, unlike the state, the city's legislative and executive branches are interwoven. Although the judiciary of the city is part of the statewide system of courts, some of the judges who serve in the city courts are elected and others are appointed by the mayor.

As the nation and state are governed by their respective constitutions, the city, too, is governed by basic law called the City Charter. As is true of the state constitution, the charter must be approved by popular referendum. However, the power of the city to tax—its lifeline—and the kind of taxes it may levy are granted and limited by the state. The state can force the city to provide services and the state can restrict the power of the city to regulate. The importance of this to the chief executive will become apparent as we discuss lobbying and lobbyists.

The Mayor and Municipal Top Management

The executive branch of government in New York City is headed by the mayor. He is elected for a four-year term, in a year when there is neither a presidential or gubernatorial election. Other city-wide elected officials are the comptroller and the city council president.

The mayor has enormous powers in New York City. He appoints the heads of city agencies and departments and all of the other departmental executives and staffs, except to positions which are under civil service and which are held by career officers. The mayor's appointees need not be confirmed by any legislative body. The mayor also plays the key role, through his budget director, in promulgating and administering the municipal budget (now in excess of $11 billion in New York City—larger than that of many nations!).

The comptroller—for some reason it is spelled differently from the state controller—heads a huge bureau and has both preaudit and postaudit powers. He has additional power as a result of the votes he casts as a member of one of the city's governing bodies—the Board of Estimate, which I shall discuss in a moment.

The president of the City Council, the other legislative body of the city government, has little power in that body. Like the vice president of the United States or the lieutenant governor of New York, he wields no power in the legislative chamber over which he presides, except to cast a deciding vote in case of a tie. But in New York, the president of the City Council is also a member of the Board of Estimate; and the most important power he wields in the city government is derived primarily from the votes he casts as a member of the Board of Estimate.

The City "Legislature"

The legislative branch of New York City is composed of two bodies, the Board of Estimate and the City Council. Except that they both vote on the city's two budgets—the Expense Budget and the Capital Budget—the two bodies perform different duties. The City Council, composed of 43 members, elected from districts throughout the city, originates laws, and has the power to adopt them. Except for its important action in adopting the budget, it does not have any subsequent power over the financial affairs of the city once the budget is adopted. The City Council's majority leader is the key figure in this body. Normally, he runs the show on most important matters and he is the man to know.

A most important governing body—unique to New York City—is the Board of Estimate, composed of the mayor, the comptroller, the president of the City Council and the presidents of the five boroughs that make up New York City. Some have extended this board to a corporate board of directors. It must approve all contracts and appropriations of city funds. The three citywide executives—the mayor, the comptroller, and the president of the City Council—each have four votes; the borough presidents each have two votes. Approval of most items requires a majority vote, but some items require a two thirds vote.

Any chief corporate executive during business with the City of

New York must clearly understand the workings of the Board of Estimate or, alas, he may find matters of deep concern to him indefinitely pigeonholed by the board.

Few, if any, other cities in the country have a bicameral "legislature," and no other has a legislative body composed of members of the executive branch of government. But aside from such specific differences, all cities and towns have some form of "legislature," be it a New England town meeting, a city council, a board of aldermen.

So much for the structure and functions of state and city government. We now turn to discuss ways whereby interested business executives, along with other interested parties and groups, may have impact on their workings.

THE LOBBYISTS

Although often maligned as a result of untoward acts by unscrupulous people, lobbyists or legislative representatives in general provide an important and welcome service to legislators by supplying them with information on pending legislation. When I say "legislators," here, I mean lawmakers at the local as well as at the state level.

Few legislators have either the time or the knowledge to cope with all of the numerous complex subjects raised in the matters on which they have to vote. They are interested in knowing how legislation will affect the people, industries, or divisions of government to which it will apply. They eagerly await information from those who favor and those who oppose a particular bill. Here, then, is the function of the lobbyist.

A lobbyist may represent a division of government—New York City maintains a full staff of lobbyists in Albany—a labor union, an industry association, a good-government organization, or a private business. The lobbyists may be an executive or an organization, a public relations consultant, a lawyer or one or more chief executives of business firms.

Lobbying

Lobbying is, in effect, presenting a particular point of view in favor of, or against some legislation. A lobbyist may deal directly with legislators; with legislative leaders, with members of their staffs; with the executive—governor or mayor—his counsel or aides; with department or agency heads; or with political leaders.

The lobbyist's arguments, for or against a bill, should be prepared in written form, as clearly and concisely as possible, and enough copies made for distribution to those concerned. Armed with the facts, an effective lobbyist usually makes personal visits to the legislators or their staffs. Conscientious legislators welcome visits from reputable representatives in regard to pending legislation. On technical matters involving detailed discussion, a meeting with the legislators' counsel is often preferable. These men have the ear and, usually, the confidence of their bosses and have a clearer understanding of the "nuts and bolts" of many bills.

There is no substitute for a personal meeting, but if circumstances prevent it, a personal letter, with an attached memorandum presenting your views on the bill or bills, should be mailed or hand-delivered to those concerned.

I cannot stress enough the importance of making your comments concise and to the point, as public officials have so much to read that they may be put off by a memorandum that is overly lengthy. An executive summary at the beginning if a necessarily lengthy memo is a great asset.

Very often the chief executive can be his own best lobbyist. No one is as well qualified to explain to a legislator the problems—or advantages—of a specific piece of legislation than the head, himself, of a company affected by its passage. Then, too, it is natural for a legislator to be impressed by the fact that a chief executive feels the pending legislation is so important that he came to discuss it personally. Even better, several chief executives journeying to the capitol together to make their point really pack a wallop.

Earlier, I pointed out that cities and towns derive their powers from the state, and often local action can be mandated or halted by the state legislature. This is important to keep in mind in those rare instances when the local legislative body may not be responsive to the legitimate needs of business or industry.

Lawyers

If the chief executive has legal problems with any governmental agency, he may wish to retain attorneys who specialize in the particular area. Government regulations have become so complicated that specialists are often needed who can best interpret these rules as they apply to the chief executive's firm.

When a lawyer is being used in a quasi-lobbyist role, it is important that he be an individual who knows his way around and is respected for his expertise and integrity. The chief executive must select his legislative representative as carefully as he selects his key subordinates.

THE POLITICAL LEADERS

The influence of political party leaders in regard to legislation, varies from place to place. In many areas, the days of omnipotent political "bosses" are largely over; in others the senior county chairman of a party may be helpful in arranging meetings with legislators and with governmental agencies. Because party chairman often play a key role in the nomination and election of legislators, they can usually assure a business executive that he will get a fair hearing of his point of view by a legislator. But the executive must be sensitive in not trying to use a party chairman to pressure the lawmaker; this can lead to resentment and be self-defeating.

Watergate has made both public officials and political party leaders wary of exercising what could be construed as undue influence upon legislation and the administrative processes of government, but they can serve as useful liaison for chief executives. They are anxious to gain the support of the business community for their respective parties' candidates. And although the Watergate scandals and exposures should have a salutory effect on financing political campaigns, political leaders still have a natural interest in obtaining from businessmen campaign contributions that are legitimate and comply with campaign spending laws. (In 1974, New York state made it legal for corporations to contribute within specified limits to political campaigns. It had previously been proscribed.)

In major cities, the chief executive should establish a relationship with the county chairmen; in towns and villages, with the town chairmen. He will also do well to be acquainted, at least, with the state chairmen of the major parties.

HELPING TO ELECT CANDIDATES

The chief executive should seriously consider jumping into political campaigns with both feet! It is fascinating, zestful, a welcome change of pace, and—above all—crucially important to making our free democratic system work better.

Although political campaigns, even on the local level, are often highly professional operations, there still is a place in them for the corporate Chief Executive Officer, even if he is a neophyte in politics. Every segment of our population is engaged in electing men and women to public office who, they believe, will represent their respective views on public issues. Organized labor, environmentalists, and tenant groups are just a few of the special interest groups that lend their support, personal as well as financial, to candidates for elective office. Just as these groups do, so also should business and industry take an active part in attempting to gain election of public officials sympathetic to their views.

These are various avenues of entry into politics. One possibility is to identify closely with a party and work with its regular organization in pushing its state of candidates. A visit to the state or county chairman to volunteer one's services could be the way to start.

Or, a chief executive may prefer to identify with a single candidate, an incumbent officeholder, or a newcomer for whom he has some real enthusiasm. He can help by raising money or active direct participation in the campaign at a policy or adminstrative level.

Finances are, of course, the lifeblood of any campaign, and the chief executive who can aid in raising needed funds will become an integral part of the political campaign. No honest politician lets anyone "buy" his way into his inner circle, but the honest helper who can raise money from a variety of legitimate sources is likely to gain an important place in the politician's "campaign cabinet."

Second, the chief executive can aid the candidate in developing policy in the specific area in which the executive, by virtue of his business background, is an expert. The chief executive must realize that it is not enough for him to present his own point of view—which he should do forcefully—but he also must understand all facets of a question objectively and present contrary positions as well. This can be an extremely valuable service to the campaign and win him a place in the candidate's "brain trust."

Third, the executive can play an important role in organizing and administering a key part of the campaign on evenings and weekends that have been set aside. This might involve supervision of advertising, direct mail, or of volunteers who phone or ring doorbells.

WORKING WITH THE COMMUNITY

In the past, most chief executives confined their community activities to participation in philanthropic drives—Heart Fund, Community Chest, and the like—and to organizations such as the Chamber of Commerce. As a result, the "good government" organizations often were dominated by lawyers and academicians who were not so much "anti-business" as they were ignorant of the problems of business. Consequently, the views of these organizations on public matters often were opposed to those held by businessmen.

In recent years, however, an increasing number of chief executives have realized that they cannot stand aloof from activist civic organizations and that their participation in the deliberations of these groups will help their members to understand and be more sympathetic to the problems faced by business and industry.

The chief executive who decides to play a role in these "good government" organizations may find, in the beginning, that many of the members are openly hostile to his views. Patience must be his watchword. What has been caused by neglect over the years cannot be undone in a month or two. He will find, however, that many members are willing to try to understand his point of view and to reconcile it with their own previously held positions.

At the same time, many chief executives, who have been insulated from their critics, will have an opportunity to learn why actions and stances of their companies may be in disrepute with these groups and with other influential organizations in their towns, cities, and states. Such "feedback" may lead to healthy revision of company policies.

In addition to working within these good government groups, the chief executive can participate in other community drives. Too many chief executives have confined their participation to making company financial contributions and have failed to take active part in the direction and conduct of drives.

The participation of the chief executive in these various community organizations—in good government groups with their advocacy of specific public programs and in others concerned with local improvement or cultural activities—not only will improve the public image of the chief executive but broaden his own understanding as well.

CONCLUSION

The private sector of our economy no longer is "private." Both government and the public feel they have a right to intervene in the operations and policies of business and industry insofar as these operations and policies affect the community and the public at large. To meet this challenge, business and industry, through their chief executives, must be prepared to demonstrate that they, too, are part of the American "public." They must demonstrate that they are not solely dedicated to the amassing of profits, that their loyalties are not just to their stockholders, and that they, too, are genuinely concerned with the general well being of their nation and their communities.

The chief executive must learn, as his adversaries have learned, how to present his case most forcefully and logically before his elected representatives. He must realize that it is no longer sufficient for him to make speeches to his colleagues who echo his views, but that he now must try to "sell" his ideas in the open market marketplace and even to hostile audiences.

The corporate chief executive must recognize that times have changed and that he no longer can restrict his activities to the affairs of his own firm, but must devote a portion of his time to community activities. By doing so, he can further the long-range objectives of the company he heads.

One word of warning: Political and governmental activity may be deeply gratifying, stimulating, and habit forming! The Chief Executive Officer may find—as I did—that the tail will someday wag the dog. I started in politics as an avocation and after a few years of escalating activity and responsibility, found I wanted to make it a vocation.

I hope for the good of our society that the same thing will happen to some of you!

CORPORATE INVESTOR RELATIONS

by Roger F. Murray*

S. Sloan Colt Professor of Banking and Finance,
Columbia University

ACHIEVING and maintaining the credibility of the Chief Executive Officer is the unending task of successful investor relations. It is essential that in moments of both success and failure the CEO be believable in the eyes of the investing public. A piece of good news must be presumed to be well supported by facts and figures; a piece of bad news must be accepted with confidence in the completeness and accuracy of the disclosure. Only the CEO can communicate the crucial pieces of information, those that really make a difference, and have them reduce, instead of add to uncertainty.

A "good press" is no substitute, even though an essential resource, in achieving this objective. The mistake most frequently made is to confuse a generally favorable public *acceptance* of both the company and its chief executive with his *credibility*. This is a confusion that few companies can afford.

WHAT IS AT STAKE?

Investors every day in the marketplace revise their expectations about the future and express anew their confidence, or lack of it, in the growth and stability of the earning power of individual companies. It takes an entire organization to produce those earnings, but one man, the Chief Executive Officer, can materially influence the price people will pay for them.

The job of corporate management is to maximize the value of the enterprise over the years. This means producing earnings; but it also

*Professor Murray is a director of banks, life insurance companies, and mutual funds; he is a trustee and chairman of the Finance and Investment Committees of Smith College.

means instilling in investors the confidence that those earnings will recur and grow in the future. Stable growth will command a good multiple (price/earnings ratio), especially if it is expected to persist far into the future. "Earnings visibility" is the desirable characteristic in the minds of security analysts. Even cyclical swings in earning power are acceptable as long as the range of variations are consistent with logically supported expectations.

Performance and credibility are reinforcing. Good earnings will be valued highly in the marketplace when their reliability is accepted and their continuity is expected with confidence. The shortfall in earnings below expectations, when it also shatters confidence, has a devastating impact on the market's valuation of the enterprise. In markets which lack liquidity and continuity of prices, it is not unusual for an unexpected earnings disappointment in the range of 10 or 15 percent to produce a price decline of 40 or 50 percent in a few days. When both the earnings rate and the price/earnings ratio decline at once, of course, the effect is bound to be drastic. Good investor relations cannot eliminate this impact but they can cushion it materially.

THE FORECASTING PROBLEM

A simple way to remove people's feelings of uncertainty about the future is to tell them what that future is most likely to hold in store. In a stable world of peace and tranquillity, a reasonably good job can be done of forecasting the sales of businesses which are characterized by a high degree of stability; but predicting net income is difficult even when compensating errors come to the rescue.

The conflict, then, is between seeking to guide investors' expectations about the future and the risk of impairing their confidence when that guidance proves unreliable. The solution offered by one astute forecaster was as follows: "Don't forecast! If you must forecast, forecast frequently." This thought deserves to be taken to heart by all Chief Executive Officers, who inevitably find themselves forecasting the economy, industry trends, and company prospects in the year-end forecasting season, at annual meetings, and on various other occasions. It is easy to forget earlier predictions and many are best forgotten by all concerned, but the reading and awareness of investors is invariably laced with the last forecast of record.

Recent discussions of the Securities and Exchange Commission, the accounting profession, and the Financial Analysts Federation have given company forecasts a new degree of respectability. (In the past, forecasting has frequently been equated with promoting the stock.) Although still optional and still controversial, forecasts for the coming year are no longer regarded with suspicion. One school of thought, indeed, argues that because security analysts are constantly testing forecasts with corporate managements and eventually circulating the results to large investors, company officials ought to make a public statement about what they see ahead.

The present state of affairs gives the chief executive a wide range of choices. The "we never make forecasts of earnings" line is probably the only one which is truly unacceptable. Any well managed enterprise should be making one-, two-, and five-year projections (forecasts) of sales, earning power, and capital needs on a recurring basis. Goals and budgets are not forecasts but objectives, however, and they should not be communicated to investors. The qualifying statements like "we are budgeting" or "our target level in a favorable environment" are soon lost in the translation into investor expectations.

Analysts will always press for a single estimate, for a precision not possible in the typical case. This pressure must be resisted by explaining the number and possible range of variables. For example, in the third quarter report to stockholders it might be timely for the chief executive to say something about the year ahead along the following lines:

> My present thinking is that 197x offers us opportunities for continued growth in sales and earnings. If we can obtain our material supplies on schedule, we ought be able to manufacture and sell between $100 and $110 million of widgets. Our current programs of cost control are showing good results. On this volume, therefore, I think we ought to earn between $6 and $7 million, which is equivalent to between $3.00 and $3.50 on each outstanding share of stock. As we enter the new year, I shall make a point of updating these estimates in each quarterly report.

This kind of informal statement, showing ranges rather than point estimates and updated on a quarterly basis, avoids the appearance of precision and certainty which so frequently leads to disappointment and loss of credibility. The subsequent revisions, which ought to narrow the range as the year progresses, should serve the admonition to "forecast frequently" and should prevent the shocks of major change in expectations. If major developments indicate that changes should be made between quarterly dates, the news release or published interview may be of assistance.

If no statements have been made in the past, the use of "dry runs" is desirable, by way of experiment, before the practice of issuing them is adopted. Preparation in draft form of a series of forecasts and revisions as they would have been released will provide an idea of what they would have been like to live with during the period of experimentation.

DIVERSE CONSTITUENCIES

Although all investors are interested in estimates of what may lie ahead, not all are equally interested in further details. Many individual stockholders are curious about earnings and dividend prospects but really do not want to go much further. The experienced and knowledgeable financial analyst, on the other hand, will not be satisfied with less than divisional and product line sales and earnings, financing plans, new product developments, competitive factors, and a host of accounting details. The good analyst is like a sponge, soaking up all the facts and forecasts available and deciding later what conclusions they suggest about the future.

So different are these constituencies that investor relations programs must be geared to each. The discrepancies in disclosure must be minimized to avoid giving confidential and significant (so-called "inside") information to selected institutions and maximized to be as responsive as possible to the levels of interest of the different investor groups. Making information available to one or a few, but not all stockholders can be a serious matter as legal counsel will be quick to advise. The best solution is to release immediately any sensitive matters which are about to be discussed with institutional investors or their representatives.

Lawyers will properly warn against premature and incomplete disclosure of the kinds of information which would have an impact on share prices. The significance of any piece of news can be best appraised by corporate executives, with the chief executive acting as the final judge in doubtful cases. This judgment must be of the completely dispassionate variety. Unfavorable developments cannot be withheld in the hope that they will go away, nor can good news be invariably hastened to the mimeograph room.

Commercial and investment bankers, seasoned security analysts, important leaders, and investors can properly be on mailing lists for news releases and special announcements in addition to the usual press and financial reporting services. These professional investors and institutions are not being favored or catered to; they are simply being kept informed of developments clearly of interest to only the most seriously involved analysts.

Other communications with stockholders also involve dealing with diverse constituencies. The small individual investor needs the kind of assistance that the secretary's office or a bank's corporate agency department can supply. It deals with missing dividend checks and changes of address; it involves services which must be performed efficiently but without involving the cheif executive. These services are terribly important to those who use them and should be reviewed periodically by responsible officers to check on performance standards.

The institutional investor and the financial analyst represent a totally different assignment. Scheduling their visits and interviews should be the responsibility of someone in the finance function specifically designated to deal with them. He must know the qualifications and interests of the individuals and be able to decide who should be permitted to take up the time of senior officers. This is partly a matter of whom the analyst represents, but it depends even more on his knowledge and experience. A good analyst, a real "pro," can make a valuable contribution to the thinking of key executives because of his knowledge of industry conditions and his feel for the corporation's standing with investors. In contrast, there is always the poorly-prepared, inexperienced analyst, the "operator" who is looking for a short-term play in the stock. Time spent with him is substantially of no value to the firm. Knowing the pros and the operators is the most important assignment of the person selected to be their point of contact with the company.

Throughout this whole range of investor interests, the atmosphere and the style of the people involved should be the same. This is the tone which the Chief Executive Officer should set. It should be in keeping, not in contrast, with his own style and manner. If it is not, he will be bombarded with questions and requests for interviews. He will find that the investor relations function has gradually shifted to his office. Only if those down the line responsible for investor relations reflect his manner will delegation to them work effectively.

RELATIONS WITH MARKET MAKERS

Still another group to be considered and dealt with effectively is composed of brokers, dealers, stock exchange specialists, and all others involved, not in investing but in providing markets for the corporation's securities. Having good markets to improve the liquidity of the bonds and stocks will add to their value and reduce the cost of raising capital externally. Those who are involved in the securities markets functions should, therefore, be kept informed promptly and accurately of all developments. But, caution: They must not be in a position to act upon information not yet known to the investing public.

As a minimum, someone must be constantly available to respond to stock exchange or dealer inquiries prompted by rapid changes in price and trading volume. There are also circumstances which may call for a cessation of trading until an important announcement is widely disseminated. Some monitoring of the market-making performance is also warranted. This involves a continuing analysis of both price and volume, with daily reports from the transfer agency. This information may be important in understanding changes in share ownership and it also provides the identification of new stockholders to whom a letter of welcome and financial reports may be sent.

Watching changes in institutional holdings, observing how blocks of stock are handled, and appraising the performance of market-makers are all desirable and appropriate. Any good investor relations program must be evaluated against what investors are actually doing. One word of warning: These activities must not be permitted to drift into an intensive market-watching function in which stock price behavior receives more emphasis than the fundamentals of the business. The often irrational aberrations of the stock market in the short run cannot be permitted to influence corporate financial policy geared to long-run objectives.

INFLUENCE ON FINANCIAL AND OTHER POLICIES

Most public companies view the investor relations function as a part of the public relations area in which the communication of information and ideas flows only in one direction. There is amazingly little appreciation of the potential for a return flow from investors.

The classic example is dividend policy. The preferences of share-holders are assumed or hopefully shaped to a pattern preconceived in the minds of corporate executives. Shareholders are delighted and flattered to be asked to express their preferences on cash and stock dividend policies, annual meeting locations, and a host of matters of greater concern to them than to company officials.

Too many chief executives show signs of great insecurity when a self-styled "gadfly" like Lewis Gilbert, Wilma Soss, or Evelyn Y. Davis proposes a change of no real consequence and some merit. The best legal minds are assembled to demolish with legalistic overkill a proposal simply because it comes from a challenger of The Estab-lishment. No better demonstration of poise and confidence can be made than to recommend adoption of a reasonable proposal, even if it did not originate with management. The use of tortured reasoning to oppose an innocuous change in procedures reflects an insecurity which weakens the chief executive's effectiveness in dealing with im-portant issues.

The legal profession, in its diligence to protect and defend the authority and independence of the executives who retain it, can al-ways imagine threats from any form of stockholder expression. Let-ting stockholders decide where they would like to have their annual meeting is somehow regarded as a dangerous precedent. To the in-secure, it seems that to admit that management does not necessarily know best on every subject might encourage challenges on substan-tive issues. There is no need to embrace or study every foolish notion suggested by stockholders or others; but a relaxed and confident ap-proach will help create and maintain the chief executive's credibility.

Investors want to see how decisions are made. They are not per-mitted in the boardroom or in the key conference room. As a result, they must draw their conclusions from the visible instances of con-troversy, most likely to occur at annual meetings. A straightforward response, direct and to the substance of the matter will create the desired impression of confidence.

When the questions of policy become more complicated, there are no such easy answers. For example, doing business under, or with certain governments known for repressive social policies may be questioned. Will the oppressed people really be better off because of withdrawal of an American company? Should shareholders' votes be decisive on the question in spite of their limited knowledge of a very involved situation? How much attention should be paid to a vocal minority if the great majority of shareholders are indifferent to the issues?

Whether to change a financial or other policy should be a question of the merits of the case. The executives who adopt an answer of "never!" make themselves appear insecure, if not even ridiculous, by presenting obviously weak arguments against doing something that everyone knows they are likely to do later or in modified form. The fact is that a strong, effective Chief Executive Officer will accept good suggestions and ideas from any source.

THE ANNUAL MEETING

The rituals to be observed at annual meetings are so completely planned in advance that there is no possibility of giving them meaningful content except, of course, when contests are in process. As a consequence, some have advocated having all this business done by mail ballot. Actually it is a harmless enough exercise and gives a meeting a certain structure which can be useful in introducing an informational session.

As a platform of launching new ideas or reporting on old ones, the annual meeting leaves something to be desired, but it has some distinct advantages. Reporting to stockholders about their company has a broad enough purpose to permit commentary on a wide range of topics, some informal observations, and direct responses to individual inquiries. There is no reason why some questions cannot be planted with employee stockholders in order to bring out current points which do not fit into our opening statement, which should always be extremely brief. Remarks which otherwise might be considered a form of "selling" securities can be made in the give-and-take session with stockholders.

The "gadflies" at such meetings are really not the problem sometimes represented. There is no mystery about their projects and favorite questions of the season. Sending a scout to other meetings is often productive and helpful in anticipating questions. Careful advance preparation for dealing with them is well worth the time and trouble. Fairness and firmness coupled together will work to deal with substantially all of these situations.

On the general run of questions, the advantages of calling upon those officers with specialized knowledge is evident. They should have had a careful rehearsal if they are not old hands at dealing with both extremely good questions and those dismally repetitive and confused observations which arise at almost all sessions.

A novel and refreshing innovation would be to have the presiding officer, on occasion, call upon a well-prepared outside director present to respond or comment. When stockholders have just elected a slate of their representatives, hearing from one or more of them would hardly shake the corporate structure. After all, exhibiting directors who are present but completely silent, rather like figures in a wax museum, can be interpreted as another evidence that the Chief Executive Officer is so afflicted with feelings of insecurity that he is reluctant to relinquish center stage for even an instant.

Corporate staff are not about to make such suggestions to the Chief Executive Officer. They will also wish to "play it safe" by not taking chances on finding someone poorly prepared. Thus, the initiative must rest with the Chief Executive Officer to broaden the participation and visibility of the entire organization.

The carefully planned and studied presentation of the Chief Executive Officer is good for his ego, but not his credibility. The natural style of the individual, speaking from notes if possible rather than from prepared statements, is what must come through. All sorts and varieties of style work well if they are natural and unrehearsed. Anything less genuine will reveal its synthetic qualities early in the chief executive's exposure at annual and special meetings with investors.

MAINTAINING CREDIBILITY

All of these attitudes and efforts to communicate effectively are subsidiary to the central objective of building the confidence of investors in the Chief Executive Officer and his close associates. All of the constituencies look for frank, open disclosure of developments affecting those aspects of the business which are expected to play an important part in shaping the future.

Credibility is a fragile quality. No matter how carefully built over a long period of time, it cannot stand shock. The classic cases of a total loss of credibility have usually been those instances in which the CEO appears to be presenting all of a piece of bad news, perhaps a write-off of an unsuccessful venture, but subsequent events show the announcement to be only a portion of the ultimate damage. Equally lethal is the denial of rumored problems with a new plant, process, or product, followed by the subsequent evidence that problems had indeed emerged even before the denial. Good manners may suggest the use of euphemisms like "electing early retirement to devote more time to personal affairs" to describe the firing of a senior executive, but this must not be confused with providing information to long-term investors concerned about the depth and effectiveness of the top management group.

The illustrative negatives could be listed almost without limit. Most of these mistakes have occurred, even in well-managed companies, because of an ill-founded lack of respect for the investing public. The erroneous assumption is made that the average individual investor of modest size is really not very bright. A steadily rising dividend and some good art work in the annual report are presumed to be all the pacifiers required. Again, there is the notion that the analytical fraternity will be enchanted with carefully "managed" sequences of growth in per share earnings. Yet the daily stock quotation pages are full of what are called "damaged" stocks, those whose chief executives lost their credibility when they were unable to deal with adversity.

THE CHIEF EXECUTIVE OFFICER
AND THE MEDIA

by John P. Fishwick

*President and Chief Executive Officer, Norfolk and
Western Railway Company*

RECENTLY, I attended a conference dealing with the social responsibilities of business. One speaker expressed his pride in the accomplishments of business since the end of World War II and in its role in creating an affluent society. He ended with the lament that business had never been held in such low esteem by the public. Another charged that the media were responsible because of their lack of understanding of and hostility toward business.

A newspaperman replied that business did not understand the mission of the media and that business was largely responsible for the media's lack of credibility. It struck me as paradoxical that two great institutions, each suffering from public distrust and lack of credibility and each needing the other's support and understanding, should be at one another's throat.

Private business exists by public sufferance. In the long run, it cannot exist without public understanding, confidence, and support. To achieve such support, business must know what the public expects of it. The public's expectations are constantly changing. Business must reflect these changing expectations, policies and practices if it is to survive.

The media are the primary communication links between business and the public. The expanding role of the media and the speed of news and communications have resulted in the average citizen's knowing much more about what private business is doing and what impact it has on his life than he knew only a few years ago. There may have been a time when he saw only the cosmeticized picture that business wanted him to see. Now he demands an unretouched picture, warts and all.

Understanding the reasons behind this new, intense interest is necessary if one is to appreciate the role and problems of the Chief Executive Officer in dealing with the media. And, as we shall see, this new climate of closer relationships holds great opportunities for the CEO and for business generally, as opposed to the commonly held belief that the intrusion of the press is a distraction, distasteful and too often a waste of time.

Why this increasing interest? First of all, we live in an open society whose institutions including the media, business, church, and government are responsive to the opinions and wishes of the general public. The responses are often slow and reluctant, but all of the basic changes in our social and economic system for the past 200 years have been taken with the acceptance or encouragement of the general public.

Today's giant corporations have evolved from individual enterprises to organizations in which ownership (stockholders) and management have become separated. The evolution of the large company has recently included an evolution of ideas about what its proper role should be in our society. Its early concentration was on economic performance, the bottom line, maximum profit, and increasing productivity. This was its response to public demand for production. Within the past 20 years, however, the public's concept of the corporation's proper role has changed from major emphasis on economics to one where its "social responsibility" has been added. Equal opportunity, pollution control, and safety are a few of the social responsibilities that business has been forced to accommodate in its operations. These three I have selected because they are all responsibilities which have been made a part of public law. In this sense the public *demands* that business discharge these responsibilities regardless of their effect on the traditional economic side of a company's operation.

This changing social and economic climate is the root of many of the most serious problems of business in dealing with the media. Faced with his role as communicator, the CEO can no longer operate behind a wall of closed doors, deft secretaries, and adroit public relations employees. He, himself, is increasingly called upon to provide not only details of his operations, but the reasoning behind his decisions.

THE NEW BALL GAME

It is a new ball game where the personality and accessibility of the CEO are as important as his company operations. The media which interview and engage in chitchat with these executives in their daily routines are quick to spot a coverup, ignorance, or buck-passing. In the new climate of business today, there is a high premium on openness, frankness, and everyday honesty. This is not only desirable but necessary, often as a matter of law. In addition, a frank opinion and response, which is in the businessman's own self-interest, has greater credibility than an attempt to sidestep potentially embarrassing questions.

The successful CEO of the 1970s and 1980s will be affirmative, less defensive, and more accessible than he has been in past decades. He will recognize that the public and the media are usually more interested in information as such than in his opinions. He will understand that the media and the public are increasingly educated and sophisticated, able to form their own opinions, seeking only the facts and numbers on which to base them.

In brief, he must adjust. It need not be a painful experience. In fact, it can be fun. But understanding the background is not enough. The CEO should also understand the media: what they are, how they work, why they work, and what they expect from the corporate executive, and what *their* problems are.

SHARED PROBLEMS

The public's low opinion of business is not a rifle shot aimed at the corporation alone. The public has used an old-fashioned blunderbuss to spray every institution with assorted criticisms. If misery loves company, the businessman has lots of it. The church, the media, the Congress, the courts and our educational institutions have all been the targets of public disdain and criticism. The media as an institution have suffered fully as greatly as business, so that business and the media, which sometimes see themselves as adversaries peering over embankments at one another, often find themselves fellow victims of the same shot and shell. Both are criticized for lack of credibility, for producing subgrade products, or for ignoring the welfare of their customers and blindly pursuing the bottom line at the expense of other more important responsibilities. And both have thin skins.

The CEO who is successful in his relations with the media will have an understanding of how the media see themselves and their work. Basic to this understanding is the fact that the news media look on the constitutional guarantees of freedom of the press as the great bulwark of our other freedoms and as a guarantee that they will be allowed to pursue any story to its end, subject only to the laws of libel, slander, and good taste.

Joseph Alsop, the noted columnist of the *Washington Post*, put the news media's role in perspective neatly when in one of his farewell columns he wrote:

> I am certain, all the same, that getting the significant facts and publishing them are still the great delights, the real tests, the main burdens and the true public functions of the reporter's trade. I would emphasize particularly the public functions; for these are what justify the pride of good reporters.

Part of the tension between the press and business today is a result of the broader perspective that reporters have been forced to take, the new skepticism they have learned to use. Business has had its share of corporate Watergates, and many unwitting investors have been cheated.

The public's expectations have become very high. The change in the idea of business' real responsibilities has occurred very quickly, in a decade or less. This accounts for much of the confusion of businessmen in accommodating themselves to the new social climate. The average CEO is in his forties or fifties, the product of a childhood when business careers were valued very highly, of an education which reinforced that value, and of a business career in which net profit, "the bottom line," was the chief and usually the sole measure of his company's success. Accustomed to public acceptance and often acclaim for success in this role, businessmen have been a bit dismayed to find themselves blamed for pollution, abandoned cities, growing trash heaps, and ugly landscapes.

Reporters are interested in the *effects* of business actions. This expanded concern for social impact accounts for the fact that news about business can be found in every section of the daily papers and on any TV news program.

The key question for the businessman is not "what are the media?" but "who are they?" They are people with normal faults and strengths. They are professionals. Their tools are words and their product is information that the public will buy. The chances are that they know more about that market than do businessmen.

They are articulate, quick-witted, and generally well informed, but, with the possible exception of a few specialized business writers, they are not well informed about business and business practices. Unless and until you have evidence to the contrary, you should never assume that reporters know very much about business, especially about your business. They are not particularly interested in business as business. If they were, they would have gone into business rather than the media. You should assume, however, that they will catch on quickly to anything that you tell them and that they will dig for further facts to satisfy themselves that they have "the whole story."

What seems important to you about your business may seem unimportant to them. They look for items which will interest the public rather than your stockholders or creditors. A price hike which produces higher net income may delight your stockholders and appear as a squib on the financial page. The same information described as "price gouging" is more likely to end up on the front page and interest the public. The "Iron Rule" is that most news is usually bad news. It is essential that businessmen realize that this rule was not made by the media but by the consuming public. Businessmen cannot change this rule, chagrined as they may be that the media largely ignore what they are doing right and beat the drums for what they are doing wrong.

Newspaper editors and reporters, as well as TV commentators, also tend to see the day-to-day workings of our society and economy in terms of problems unsolved, "needs unmet." There will always be needs and problems so that the business executive can expect no "progress" here either. But understanding that this is the way it is can make it acceptable and in time creates executive-philosophers, and media-columnists and commentators.

OF SHOTGUN MARRIAGES AND HAPPINESS

The shotgun marriage of business and the media is not, as we have seen, an eternally happy one. Both parties have their problems, but the public, with the blunderbuss handy, demands social responsibility from business. From the media it requires both social concern *and* an unbiased account of how business is doing. What can the businessman do? Are there any ground rules beyond candor, respect, and a positive outlook in dealing with the media? Yes, and a summary should include these:

1. The CEO must recognize that business, especially "big" business, has always had its detractors. A part of the media's responsibility, and one they have always embraced with enthusiasm, is to point with alarm, to criticize and upbraid business for its shortcomings and inanities. This is not new; it traces back at least as far as the sixth chapter of Matthew. But CEOs must take this understanding as their only flack jackets.

2. CEOs of large corporations require spokesmen, or public relations representatives, wise in the ways of both the company and the media. These representatives should reflect the company's own commitment to openness, candor, respect for media problems, and the right of the public to a clear knowledge of company activities and prospects. Public relations people and their departments may handle 90 percent of a company's contacts with the media and public through telephone conversations, news releases, speeches, and the like. The CEO is more likely to be dealing with the media at annual meetings, special interviews, press conferences, and open letters outlining some aspect of company business. Both the spokesmen and the CEO contacts are required; the chief executive cannot handle all contacts, nor can public relations provide the "horse's mouth" that media people are assigned to get.

3. There was a time when the old saying "half a loaf is better than none" had some validity in business-media relations. No more. The public blunderbuss is primed to get the whole story. The recent history of class action suits, show-cause orders, and injunctions indicates that the public, through the courts, is quite prepared to get the whole loaf. The media are well aware of this and are quick to punch the alarm button. In fact, nothing galvanizes the media to full hue and cry today so quickly as the sensing of a story half told or, worst of all, a true story cloaked in half truths. Distortion is no longer bad policy; it can be illegal. A few carefully selected facts, though true in themselves, betray the need for public understanding of the company's situation as a whole.

4. Credibility is the touchstone of the CEO's relation to the media. No businessman inherits this quality with his position. It must be established by openness and honesty. This does not mean that you must tell everything, but it does mean that you cannot mislead.

5. The media are not adjuncts to corporate public relations departments. A reporter gets no personal satisfaction from printing a press handout. In fact, he receives it with suspicion. He knows that business does not generally or voluntarily report "bad" news. You should make yourself available for follow-up questions after a press release is distributed.

6. Don't underestimate the power of the media, but don't overestimate it either. Except in rare cases, don't become upset about misquotes. Most people don't remember them, especially if they are buried in the body of an article. Don't develop a vendetta against a newspaper or reporter; in the long run the businessman cannot win. And don't go over the head of a reporter to the publisher. He is concerned with running a business and cannot dictate to reporters who value their freedom to write the truth as they see it and resent interference.

7. See the media not only as your link to the public in getting your facts and views publicized, but also as a feedback opportunity which can relay to you what the public is thinking, how it may react. The information flow through the media, that is, should be a two-way street.

8. The media can be the conscience of business. Chauncey M. Depew advised young men to govern their conduct by a conscientious answer to the ever-present question: "Would my mother approve?" Businessmen might substitute for this question: "Would I mind seeing an account of this in the newspapers?"

9. Don't feel you must limit yourself to talking only about your business and what affects it. Without pretending to be an expert in all directions, speak out on public issues that you think important. If you don't, the media and public will think that all you say is determined by self-interest and lacks credibility. Avoid "no comment." Don't be afraid to say: "I don't know," or "We haven't decided what we will do."

10. Don't try to "buy" favorable comments from reporters. Good reporters won't appreciate excessive entertainment or gifts and will resent your trying to compromise their independence. To some extent, services of the media can be "bought" to transmit an unedited message. This is advertising. It sells products and services; it creates a "corporate image." It also supports the media. But this is an area that the CEO can largely delegate to experts. In fact, he will probably

make a mistake if he goes beyond judging an advertising program by any standard other than results.

11. The CEO should view the media as a constituency just as are employees, stockholders and directors. It is an important group, and the CEO should spend time trying to understand, help, and gain the respect and support of the media just as he does in his relations with employees, stockholders, and directors.

12. Increasingly, business is being drawn under the same regulatory floodlights that the railroads and public utilities have known for decades. Hearings by agencies, legislative committees, and courts place the company and its executives, especially the CEO, under close scrutiny. These are almost always public hearings, open to the public and media, reported and commented on via print and TV. Since these occasions are inevitable, they should be looked on as opportunities to project a full understanding of the company position, its problems, and the alternatives. Hearings usually require a great amount of preparation, but for the company whose operations are dimly understood, such occasions can be one of the best means of showing your company's response to public concerns.

13. Have steady access to good legal advice. Full disclosure requirements for publicly owned companies are complex. A change in outside auditors, for example, is closely reviewed by the Securities and Exchange Commission and the various stock exchanges. Flagrant disregard or simple oversight can bring publicity detrimental to the company, with long-term public relations effects. Corporate finance and company dealings with shareholders have become a minefield for the unwary and badly advised.

14. Until you know otherwise, never assume any reporter fully understands the workings of the American free enterprise capitalist system. The business executive often assumes this to his chagrin. The fact is that some reporters, as well as a large segment of the public, have wildly distorted ideas about profit margins, the role of profits, the need for retained capital, and similar elementary details of company finances. I believe that many executives' public relations problems today stem directly from these misunderstandings.

15. The CEO of the modern corporation is far from the demigod of the past. Where the executive of old held himself aloof from all but perhaps his directors, today's CEO must involve himself with the protocol of the marketplace of ideas. Accessibility to the press and to

his employees is the way of prudence for the man who appreciates the public wish for accountability and the public understanding that top management rarely has a mystique that assures success.

CONCLUSION

Given this rain of restrictions and warnings, and in view of the necessary contacts with the media whether we wish it or not, can business find happiness in the arrangement? Do shotgun weddings ever succeed? I think so, because my experience has shown that a large company can succeed in getting its point across, its information presented accurately on most occasions.

By understanding the problems of the reporters and by getting to know many of them, I feel I have not only helped my company in many instances, but I have established also personal friendships that will last many years. I don't imply that any of this shows a magic touch or that our relationship with the media has been a long stream of unbroken satisfactions. Far from it. Both my company and the media have had our bad moments. But this is beside the essential fact that a satisfactory relationship with the media is not only possible; it is often accomplished more easily than the foregoing might indicate.

Business is not dealing with ogres or lunatic fringes when it deals with the media. They are by and large reasonable people with reasonable expectations. Nor are the laws affecting the publication of business performance and results especially onerous. They are drawn to protect the public, and they are the result of serious lapses by some businesses in the past.

In sum, it is a new world for business, but livable. And if we did not have the media to tie us and our activities to the public in a quick, sustained, and reasonably accurate way, we would have to invent something like the media to do that very job.

THE CHIEF EXECUTIVE OFFICER AND TRADE AND PROFESSIONAL ASSOCIATIONS

by James L. Hayes

President and Chief Executive Officer, American Management Associations

THE CEO'S NEED

THE CHIEF EXECUTIVE's effectiveness is directly related to the attention he gives the world outside his organization. The penalties for misdirecting that attention will eventually be counted in dollars and cents. Guiding even a small business today requires a keen awareness of the economy, legislation, the political situation and the tastes and temperament of at least the nation, if not the world.

Financial reviews, political reports, industry newsletters, environmental briefings—any number of pages can bring the world to the CEO, and with it, a false sense of security, of being "on top of the situation." But he should beware: The world as brought to him in reports is a once-removed image of the real world in which his company operates.

To gain the unique experience that nourishes his decision-making power, the CEO must *go out*, both literally and mentally, into the world. At times he must involve himself in the market, the industry, or with the government. As he does so, he will discover a growing need to make his thoughts known to influential people. A sense of obligation to endorse those ideas he believes in, and to change those he knows would benefit from change will keep his attention properly focused.

The most accessible avenues to the world outside his company are trade and professional associations.

One CEO has underlined this from his own experience. "When

1037

I was a vice president I always promised myself that if I became president I wouldn't let myself get isolated as I'd seen so many others do. It wasn't until our market position slipped drastically because of our unresponsiveness to new trends that I realized that I'd let myself fall into the trap. I had been relying on reports and unconsciously filtered information instead of spreading my own antennae. Today, I wouldn't think of giving up my active participation in at least two professional associations!"

WHICH ASSOCIATIONS TO JOIN?

There is no scarcity of associations wanting a company's (or its president's) membership. It is not unusual for a large corporation to belong to hundreds of associations. Often there is considerable deadwood in these memberships: noninvolvement where there should be active participation, and valuable time spent on ineffectual associations. Deciding which associations are valuable, and which are not, is essential. In addition, the CEO must also decide *who* should be active in which associations—members of the top team, or the lower echelons of management. If he does not take an active interest in these decisions, he risks wasting his company's time and money. He will also miss several opportunities available nowhere else.

A View from Two Sides

The task of reaching these decisions can be reduced to workable proportions if the choices are examined from two sides: subjective and objective.

Subjectively, which associations does he genuinely want to contribute to, and *what* is he willing to contribute? He can offer an association his time, his money, or his support. Some associations warrant all three; many one or two; and a few, none.

Having selected associations from this viewpoint, the CEO should take an objective look at the choices. The question now becomes, what can the associations contribute to the company? Certainly, a national association that conducts legitimate lobbying activities in behalf of the industry offers a great deal, as does an association dedicated to finding new applications of the company's product or new markets. Every company needs influence in its local community; and for that, chambers of commerce, along with other local associations, will be valuable. The CEO may find others that pursue goals consistent with those of his company. It naturally follows that his company will be able to make valid contributions toward these common goals.

This two-fold approach to selection, considering the company's needs and the CEO's own desires, will lead to several obvious choices. The final selection or elimination, however, must consider the health of the individual association.

A Healthy Association

The president of a company must examine the internal health of any association with which he is considering affiliation. He may decide to drop an unhealthy group; or perhaps, he may decide that changing it is worth the time and effort.

A basic operational structure is common to most trade and professional associations. Two groups of people are involved: (1) staff, hired to work for the association; and (2) members, who join and pay the dues.

The policy of the association comes from the *members* who are elected to the board of directors. The *staff's* responsibility is to carry out the members' directives and to provide enough reliable information to develop good policy.

The Importance of the Chief Staff Officer

In contrast to the Chief *Executive* Officer of the typical association (he may be called the chairman of the board), the chief *staff* officer may hold his job for many years. He may have the title of vice president, president, or even executive officer. Whatever his title, his function is that of any operating officer: to insure that the policy of the board is converted into effective results.

Because he usually holds his position for a number of years, he furnishes a continuity. His personality and method of operating will pervade the organization, and much of the public's image of the association depends on his conduct. His name and reputation, therefore, should be examined closely.

Generally, an association with a sound and healthy operation will have these characteristics:

1. The board will have a reasonable amount of turnover. The average limit is three-year tenure, with new membership each year. Board members may return after a period of nonservice.
2. The financial history is steady, normally free from extra assessments.
3. Auditing features are open enough to disclose the full story.
4. The chief operating officer (staff) has a record of having worked well with the various past chief executive officers.
5. The association has a long-term plan, which meets the needs of the membership. The plan has evolved from, rather than been imposed on, the membership.

Warning Signs

Some warning signs are, as follows.

1. A tendency for the chief operating officer to insist constantly on his choice of Chief Executive Officer. Is he afraid of the maverick, the strong man? It is vital that the chief operating officer be able to work effectively with different personalities.
2. Any suspicion of unethical conduct among the paid staff.
3. Any indication that the association is actually run by a clique, politically oriented or otherwise.
4. Any sign of financial instability.
5. Any unwillingness of the most influential people in the trade or profession to join. If there is such unwillingness, why?

These signs can be portents of a downhill reputation that it would be well to stay clear of.

A WORD ABOUT LOBBYING

Unfortunately the word "lobbying" has an unfavorable connotation today, when in fact it is an invaluable part of the lawmaking process. Adjudged to be inherent in the First Amendment, it is carefully described in *United States* v. *Rumely:* "lobbying in its commonly accepted sense—to direct communications with members of Congress on pending or proposed federal legislation." Legislators seldom object to legitimate lobbying, and they often seek the help of reputable associations for facts and statements of an industry's position.

But, be warned. As with any right, the right to lobby is sometimes abused, with unfavorable public consequences for the industry. A reputable trade association is scrupulous in its lobbying activities. The CEO would be wise to reconsider membership in any group that isn't.

AND ANTITRUST

Supreme Court decisions going as far back as 1925 indicate that trade associations may openly gather and distribute information on costs, production volume, and other matters. Antitrust dangers appear if statistical programs go beyond an informative function.

Compliance with antitrust laws is difficult, because legal precedent is not a foolproof guide. This problem was well stated by Earl W. Kintner, former chairman and general counsel for the Federal Trade Commission, who spoke of "The perplexed businessman—who must always obey the law without always knowing what the law is."

How does the corporation president protect himself? He makes sure the association has a good lawyer who will give clear guidelines beforehand on what may be done, what may not be done, and the possible risks involved. The CEO must make the final decision, however, based on his own assessment of legal and other consequences.

In sum, three considerations will give the CEO a sound basis for choosing among trade associations:

1. Which organizations am I willing to contribute my time, money, or support to?
2. Which organizations are capable of making valid contributions to my company, and vice versa?
3. How healthy is each?

USING THE ASSOCIATION TO FULL ADVANTAGE

The Trade Association Division of the Department of Commerce reports that the various industry groups engage in nearly 100 types of activities. Not all engage in that many, of course; but most offer at least these typical services:

1. Functioning as a national information center for their particular industry.

2. Keeping in close touch with all related industries.
3. Issuing bulletins, usually monthly, on business trends, legislation, trade statistics, labor relations, and other specialized subjects.
4. Preparing information booklets relating to the industry, and annual compilations of industry data.
5. Arranging member conferences, with the help of technical experts, on current industry problems, and offering technical training courses.
6. Handling government relations for their industry.
7. Providing smaller companies with staff services they could not normally afford by themselves.

These services are standard, expected, and valuable. A company will do well to use them. But the CEO who wants to get full advantage from an association will look beyond the expected services to find the opportunities unique to that group.

The Benefits of Giving His Time

"There's no quicker or easier way for the president of a company to make important government contacts than by serving on one of our committees," the chief staff officer of a medium-sized trade association maintains. "Years after serving with us, that president will keep his contacts, and chances are, they'll be valuable to him from time to time."

What he says is true. Serving in important positions in associations, local or national, can offer opportunities to meet and mix with influential people seldom encountered in one's office.

This intermixing will not come about if the CEO takes a passive role. He soon learns that only through genuine, active service to the organization will the unique opportunities he is seeking present themselves. To get the most from his association, the astute CEO knows, he must give his service unselfishly.

Those personal relationships are not the only benefits; the association is also an excellent means of self-development. Being the president of a company is no assurance that the business skills once used with regularity will stay as keen as they were. Making a presentation to the board of directors of a trade association may be excellent training for the next presentation to one's own board of directors.

SERVING THE ASSOCIATION

Because of its council-like nature, the trade or professional association will have a set of working dynamics unlike the environment to which the CEO is accustomed. In his office, the people are *hired* by his company; in the association, they are *volunteering* their time. When he leaves his office and joins with his peers, he must be aware that *his* way of being effective in his office may not be effective in the association situation. Often, the association can offer the CEO the opportunity for reflection and self-examination.

MAKING CHANGES

If the CEO feels certain practices in the association should be changed, he should criticize and complain—but about specifics. A general blanket complaint leaves the responsible persons no alternative but to defend themselves, or the practices; it leads nowhere. A specific complaint, however, can lead to changes.

A valuable concept borrowed from the Norwegian and other national governments and used by many associations is that of an "ombudsman." This official's sole duty is to receive complaints, investigate them, and rectify situations where complaints are justified. If the complaint is specific, and a specific person responsible for the oversight singled out, the ombudsman will bring both sides together and expect a solution. It works. With a general complaint, however, little can be done.

Probably one of the most valuable services a member can offer an association is specific, constructive criticism. The truly valuable member will make his voice heard.

RESIGNING

The CEO should not be timid about resigning an association job or from the group itself. At the end of a term on a committee or in an elected position, it is entirely appropriate for a person to offer to resign, to allow another member to gain valuable experience. It is also appropriate for the CEO to offer another association his services. It is common for able men to pass their talents from one group to another.

LEADING AN ASSOCIATION

If elected Chief Executive Officer of an association, the CEO would be wise to determine by mutual agreement with the board the amount of time he will commit to serving in this office. His responsibilities will be executive in nature; he can expect the staff to function operatively.

The association chief executive must:

1. Speak out and inform members of political, social and economic issues, even when his views conflict with popular opinion.
2. Substantiate his views by explaining forcefully and logically why a position on a given issue is in the best interest of the public and his membership.
3. Analyze his own activities and those of his association to determine whether the dues his members pay are being used with maximum effect.
4. Encourage the principals of his industry to take a public stand wherever and whenever their business lives are threatened.
5. Be ready to put aside personal pride when the situation demands that his organization work not alone, but with other groups to achieve common goals.

DEVELOPING IN HIS OWN
PROFESSION—MANAGEMENT

Whether the president of a company was, or is, an engineer, accountant, doctor, or lawyer, he must not fail to recognize his new profession—management. He may be tempted to give time to his old professional association, and if he heads a smaller company, this may have merit. But, generally, he uses his time better if he conscientiously strives to improve his managerial skills.

The president of a large metal-forming company put it this way. "I started off here as an engineer, belonged to every good professional association, tried to keep up with the field. But really, I'm not an engineer anymore, I'm a manager. It's much more important now to know how to manage the engineers I have, every one of them a better engineer than I ever was, than it is for me to know engineering. My profession is management now."

The two main professional management associations for Chief

Executive Officers are the Presidents' Association of the American Management Associations, the Conference Board, and the Young Presidents' Association. All are concerned with the specific problems a CEO encounters; the Presidents' Association of the American Management Associations and the Young Presidents' Association are exclusively composed of CEOs.

These associations offer a CEO exposure to a rich mixture of cross-disciplines. The president of a steel mill may work with the president of a communications company, and both will gain from each other's perspective.

DEVELOPING OTHERS IN THEIR PROFESSIONS

In a similar vein, the CEO can help sharpen the skills of his subordinates. Encouraging his managers to participate actively in relevant groups can bring out their own latent potentialities. Rarely will a CEO who is seriously pursuing his own development overlook the development of his subordinates. Trade and professional associations offer ideal grounds for this development.

The CEO has a responsibility to his company to insure that the members of the top management team are as informed in their professions as possible. His chief engineer certainly should be able to keep him informed of recent technological developments, and his top accountant had better keep abreast of tax changes. His top managers must indeed be top, not only in the company, but in their respective fields and professions.

Few professionals will be able to stay in the vanguard of their field without taking an active role in the main professional associations. A man who shuns his professional groups, and does not offer a cogent reason for doing so, casts suspicion on his own capabilities.

This is not to slight those few men and women who are genuinely ahead of their times, who live and work with advanced concepts, and who have no alternative but to see their associations as lagging behind the times. However, a distinguishing characteristic of those people is their strongly felt sense of personal responsibility to pass on the advanced concepts they have discovered. They will be found either taking active, if perhaps revolutionary, parts, in their professional associations with strong commitment, or isolated in their profession through no fault of their own.

A LAST WORD

The benefits of active participation in trade and professional associations are many, and the man intent on doing the best possible job will take full advantage of them. He will contribute his time and the time of others to those groups he feels deserving, and will use them as valuable training grounds, officially and unofficially, for the development of his subordinates, and himself.

In personal terms, the CEO will gain the most out of associations which recognize his profession of management, and help him reach his fullest potential in this area.

For the convenience of CEOs, there follows a descriptive listing of associations where information can be obtained concerning the kinds of industry and management associations in which they may be interested.

APPENDIX

Where to Learn More about Associations

American Chamber of Commerce Executives
   1133 15th St., N.W.
   Suite 620
   Washington, D.C. 20005

American Society of Association Executives
   1101 16th St., N.W.
   Washington, D.C. 20036

Chamber of Commerce of the U.S.
   1615 H St., N.W.
   Washington, D.C. 20006

The Conference Board
   845 Third Ave.
   New York, N.Y. 10022

Encyclopedia of Associations
   Gale Research Co.
   Book Tower
   Detroit, Mich.

National Association of Manufacturers
   1776 F St., N.W.
   Washington, D.C. 20006

National Industrial Council (of NAM)
1776 F St., N.W.
Washington, D.C. 20006

Presidents' Association
135 W. 50th St.
New York, N.Y. 10020

Professional Institute
135 W. 50th St.
New York, N.Y. 10020

U.S. Department of Commerce
Fourteenth St. between Constitution Ave. and E St., N.W.
Washington, D.C. 20230

United States JAYCEES
(formerly U.S. Junior Chamber of Commerce)
4 W. 21st St.
P.O. Box 7
Tulsa, Okla. 74102

Young Presidents' Organization
201 East 42nd St.
New York, N.Y. 10017

Further Remarks

American Chamber of Commerce Executives. ACCE has a membership of approximately 2,500 leading executives of chambers of commerce, organizations of persons interested in promoting the civic, commercial, and industrial welfare of a single community.

It issues a quarterly *Journal*, a commerce news bulletin, and frequent committee reports on chamber problems.

American Society of Association Executives. ASAE, founded in 1920, has a membership of over 2,200 leading executives of trade and professional associations. Regional chapters, in about 28 cities, hold monthly meetings to discuss current association management problems.

ASAE's quarterly journal has included hundreds of in-depth articles on association organization, financing, and current activities problems. Reprints of these are available.

Chamber of Commerce of the United States. The chamber is the nation's largest association of businessmen, with a direct membership of 4,000 chambers of commerce, 900 trade and professional associations, and 40,000 companies. Among its departments are Agriculture, Association Service, Chamber of Commerce Service, Construction and Civil Development, Domestic Distribution, Education, Foreign Commerce, Institutes for Organization Management, Insurance, International Relations, Labor Relations, and Legal, Manufacture, National Defense, National Resources, Taxation and Finance, and Transport and Communication.

There are departmental newsletters, the monthly *Nation's Business*, and other periodicals.

The Conference Board. Formerly known as the National Industrial Conference Board, this nonprofit institution furnishes information on business, economics, and management activities through research and published studies and by an information service to members. Nine periodic publications are augmented by published statistics, supplements, bulletins, and reports of ongoing research. Members attend meetings to examine business trends. The library contains information on business economics and operations.

National Association of Manufacturers. NAM is the nation's largest association of industrial interests, with a membership of about 20,000 manufacturing companies. Through its affiliate, the National Industrial Council, it also has 12,000 trade-association members.

NAM claims that its direct and indirect membership produces over 75 percent of the annual factory output of the United States.

It issues *NAM News*, a weekly, and many other publications for its members. It is a leading center of information of industrial problems, international economics, labor relations, legislative research, taxation, and related subjects.

New York Chamber of Commerce. It issues the only annual directory of chambers of commerce throughout the United States, covering more than 3,000 cities.

The Presidents' Association. This association is a forum in which chief executives can exchange views on matters of common concern, as well as a source for information on management approaches to the increased effectiveness of their corporations. The objective of the Presidents' Association is to help chief executives do the best possible job of running their companies. The Association sponsors many meetings during the year which provide chief executives with a rundown of general management topics of interest as well as of current business and economic trends. The Association produces a number of publications and especially commissioned studies which are designed to help chief executives enhance their effectiveness as managers.

The Professional Institute of the American Management Associations. Providing customized management services for government, educational, and health organizations, the Professional Institute of AMA offers courses directed at the administrator. It tailors management development programs to the organizational structure of each client. The team planning process is emphasized, to help agencies pinpoint realistic goals and determine how to attain them, within the limitations of their financial, physical, and human resources. Material will be sent on request.

United States Department of Commerce. Associations work closely with bureaus and offices in the Department of Commerce such as Area Development, Business and Defense Services, Business Economics, Census, Coast and Geodetic, Distribution, Field Offices, Foreign Commerce, Industrial Mobilization, International Trade Fairs, Maritime, Patents, Public Roads, Standards, Technical Services, and the Weather Bureau.

Associations and businessmen can contact the Department through any of its 33 field offices in the United States. Also, some 650 chambers of commerce and associations serve as official cooperative offices. A helpful weekly publication, *Business Service Check List* names and describes briefly every publication of every agency within the Department ($1.50 a year; free sample copies are often available upon request.)

United States Jaycees. USJ has a membership of about 300,000 young men, 21 to 35 years of age. There are local chapters in some 3,800 communities, with activities devoted to helping young men become civic and business leaders. Each "Jaycee" local fosters Americanization programs, economic education, local social welfare, and allied efforts.

One of its monthly publications is *Future: The Magazine for Young Men.*

Young Presidents' Organization. Founded in 1950, the YPO is organized on a chapter level. Its membership is composed of executives who have been elected president of their companies before their 40th birthday and who must retire from YPO before their 50th birthday. The organization's goal of helping its members to become better presidents through education and idea exchange is furthered through seminars and courses in business and the humanities for presidents and their spouses.

DEALING WITH LOCAL ACTION GROUPS

by Louis B. Lundborg*
Chairman of the Board (Retired), Bank of America

THE TRADITIONAL APPROACH

IF THIS CHAPTER were being written a generation ago, the emphasis would have been placed on selling the importance of being a good corporate citizen in each plant city and branch-office city in which the company operates.

Being a good corporate citizen that practices good community relations is just as important today as it was in that earlier day; but it does not require the emphasis today that it did then. Community involvement is as standard a part of the management package as personnel administration or cost control; and the manager who does not know this must have spent the past 20 years playing Rip Van Winkle.

In part this step-up of community participation has been induced by the pressures and expectations of the community itself; but in equal part it has resulted from the growing recognition by executives of the value to the company in having its people taking active roles in the organizations, projects, and programs of the community. Where the company has a product or service that is sold locally, the publicity value is obvious. But even when the company has nothing to sell and has no customers in the nearby area, there are other values.

For example, the operation of an industrial plant in an urbanized area involves the company in constant contact and interaction with every kind of public agency, administering every kind of governmental or quasi-governmental program: building codes, traffic regulation, pollution control and other environmental impact issues, industrial safety, public health, employment practices, training programs, etc.,

---

* [Ed. Note: Mr. Lundborg is the author of *Future Without Shock*.]

etc. Some of these agencies and their activities represent potential problems of course. But others represent opportunities, because many of these agencies, both governmental and nongovernmental, have facilities that can be of great value. Schools and colleges, for example, often offer possibilities of cooperative programs that can be valuable in training and in recruiting; chambers of commerce and other civic organizations have research and information services that often help to solve marketing, operating, and other problems. Companies that have entered (often reluctantly) into contracts with federal agencies to train and employ minority workers have often found extra dividends from these efforts: improved effectiveness of their own training techniques, for example, plus some surprises in lower turnover rates among workers so trained.

It is typical of many of the needs for help from public agencies that a company would have that they arise suddenly with no advance warning. This is true of nearly every agency concerned with public safety and protection. They are never needed until an emergency arises—and then they are needed *right now*.

A company should not expect to be treated differently from anyone else just because its regional manager has been active in the United Fund and gotten to know the mayor. But when the crisis comes—when emergency help is needed—the mere matter of time saved by instant identification and instant credibility can be crucial.

IMPORTANCE IN PUBLIC OPINION DEVELOPMENT

Although propaganda may be generated from a central source, public opinion forms at the grass roots.

The agencies that are effective in forming political, social, or economic opinion are always organized from the community level up. Both major political parties are strongly organized locally; and although other factors are at least as important, the failure to carry a particular state has often been traced to a failure to organize strongly at the local level.

The groups that influence legislation nationally are organized strongly at the local level. The farm organizations—Farm Bureau, Grange, Farmers Union, National Cooperative Council—all have strong local units in most states, and maintain frequent contact between congressmen and the farm locals. Labor unions are built on a base of locals, federated into nationals and internationals.

It is surprising that business leaders who would not think of spending money to advertise their products nationally with no provision for local dealer follow-up will try to influence national political, social, and economic thought without giving any attention to the local "point of sale."

Why is the community so important in shaping political philosophies? Why are "home towns" important in the formation of public opinion? Aside from the fact that congressmen and other legislators come from home towns somewhere, and that home towns are a handy place for constituents to buttonhole their representatives, why are the home constituencies the places where movements grow? Because that is where people see each other face to face and exchange ideas by word of mouth.

Public relations, or public opinion, never crystallizes into anything important until one person says something to another person by word of mouth. Publicity, the printed word, may be the raw material of public opinion—the seed—but word of mouth, or "gossip," is the soil that feeds and fertilizes the seed into a living organism.

And the community is the seedbed.

The public opinion that develops within a community may mean opposition from conflicting groups or it may represent support from affiliated and sympathetic interests. The very fact that the community is a blending of divergent interests makes its effects so much more far-reaching. The interlocking and overlapping character of community groups multiplies the effect of every contact.

RELATION TO BUSINESS DEVELOPMENT

The most effective public service is often based on enlightened self-interest. Nowhere is that more true than in the community field. Community relations undertaken solely for selfish purposes may backfire; but where the enlightenment is at least as great as the self-interest, both community and "self" may profit.

But although there is no better business builder, in most lines, than active community contact, it is a paradox that community activity will be a better sales builder if it *isn't* used for that purpose. The same axiom also applies in large measure to the other direct public-relations benefit that can come from community activity: "If you don't try to cash in, you will. And if you do try to cash in, you may fail entirely."

If a company representative, for instance, becomes known as using his community-organization contacts solely to promote sales, he will be resented and so will his company. But for those who approach community relations without any immediate thought of direct sales promotion, it is a rich source of the good will that produces sales.

VALUE AS EXECUTIVE TRAINING GROUND

Community activity has another value that should not be over-looked or discounted: its role in identifying potential executives in a company and in helping to develop their leadership talents. Many a junior employee whose own job had provided no opportunity to test or display executive ability has enrolled in a chamber of commerce committee or a United Fund drive and emerged as an effective group leader.

Even for the already-established executive this type of activity involves a change of pace, a change of perspective, that can have great therapeutic value. It has been demonstrated repeatedly that the bene-fits of this therapy do not stop with the executive himself but have a carryover value in his relations with his own employees.

WHERE TO START—ADOPTING A POLICY

Step one is not to *do* something, but to *decide* something—to adopt a basic policy by which everything thereafter will be measured and tested. Until a basic policy is adopted—until it is decided that the community *is* important, that good community relations are worth making some effort for—no specific efforts will accomplish lasting results. Once the policy is sincerely adopted, specific ways to apply it become easy to find.

The basic policy should have three parts: (*a*) a negative, or "don't," part; (*b*) a passive, or minimum, part; and (*c*) a positive, or aggres-sive, part. It should be decided that:

1. Nothing will be done, knowingly, that is harmful to the com-munity nor, so far as avoidable, that is unpleasant or unwelcome to the community.
2. Everything within reason that is requested by or for the com-munity will be granted, and certain other minimum steps will be taken to establish acquaintance and contact with the community.
3. A positive effort will be made to seek new and additional ways

in which to benefit the community and to identify the company as a good citizen, a good neighbor, and an asset to the community.

WHO IS RESPONSIBLE?

Step two is to make it a major responsibility of a top executive to see that the policy and the program to execute it are carried out. If the community is, as we have suggested, a service arm of the business, an extension of the business plant, then it deserves the continuing attention of an executive with authority, just like any other department of the business.

The responsible executive should analyze the community—its character and traditions, its needs and desires, its assets and opportunities, its organizations and its facilities—and analyze his company's policies, personnel, and practices in relation to the community. He should prepare a program for the company, based upon this analysis and setting forth the things it should do immediately, the things it should undertake later, and the things it should study further.

IMPLEMENTING THE PROGRAM

The foundation stone of human relations, upon which all else must be built, is friendly acquaintance.

The steps by which a company gets acquainted with its community are not materially different from the ways in which a person gets acquainted with any of his neighbors. It recognizes that families of employees, as well as employees themselves, and other "neighbors" around town have a natural curiosity about the company and would like to know more about it. The companies that have been successful in their community relations have approached it in that spirit. Once the decision has been made, the methods that can be used are legion; and each company can adopt and adapt the ones that fit it best.

Some companies have used plant tours, group visits, and open house days for employees, of course, and for others. Others have had organized programs of calls on city, county, school, and other key officials in town. Nearly all that have succeeded have had representatives at chamber of commerce, United Fund, and other community meetings, and have participated in local service clubs and their meetings.

Keeping the Community Informed

If acquaintance is the foundation stone of good community relations, information is its next structural beam. The community must "know" and must "know about" a company or an institution of any kind. What was said above about the natural curiosity of employees' families is equally true, in varying degree, of everyone in a community, including people in positions of influence and responsibility.

Most human beings insist upon having opinions of one kind or another about everything in their communities. If they are not furnished the raw material for the right opinion, they will have the wrong one—about the factories where their friends work; about the stores, banks, and other business firms; about the local government; the schools; the transportation system, utilities, and other services—about everything they see or use that might ever be a topic of a conversation.

So, although information alone will not guarantee proper attitudes of those who might have emotional reasons for prejudices, prejudice can never be removed without information, nor can full understanding be gained even from those without prejudice. The withholding of information not only leaves a vacuum that sucks in distortions of truth; but in the intimate relationship of a community, the very act of withholding tends to create resentment and suspicion.

"If they're so secret about everything, they must have something to hide." Then rumor starts to work.

Once the decision is made to furnish information, the channels for doing it are virtually unlimited in a community. That is one of the reasons why the community is the place to start any public-relations program. The lines of communication fan out endlessly from the community to other segments of the public, and there is no other place where every segment of the public—every "public"—may be so readily reached.

The techniques of disseminating information are so well understood that they already have been made the subject of a vast literature of their own. So we shall not dwell here on those techniques.

Helping Local Causes and Organizations

Recognition of the community, its achievements, and its aspirations is important to good community relations, and the ultimate in that recognition is to help in promoting the local causes, drives, and organizations that are created by the local people to meet their civic and welfare needs.

To the company that wants simply to do its share when asked, and not to make any unusual or imaginative contribution to the community, opportunities will present themselves as a matter of routine in annual appeals for financial help and an occasional request for personal participation.

But to those who want to go a step farther, and to get credit for giving leadership in advancing the community, there is a rich field of unexplored needs. The needs exist in virtually every field of community life; and no matter how many agencies are set up to deal with the local problems, there always seem to be openings for a business firm, with its special know-how and resources, to step in and do a spectacular job that the agency alone would have found difficult or impossible—if it had even thought of trying.

The help that business firms can give to local efforts ranges all the way from a simple lending of company facilities for use in community activities to the planning and directing of community campaigns.

One of the easiest things for a company to do, and yet one of the most valuable to community organizations and movements, is to lend company facilities which already exist to local organizations for their use in meetings, programs, drives, and activities.

In nearly every community adequate meeting-room space is always at a premium, and the struggling local organization cannot afford to spend money for the halls that are available for rent. So if a company has an auditorium or the equivalent (a dining room, cafeteria, gymnasium, conference room, or even the board of directors' room) that is not in constant use, the company can do a useful and warmly appreciated piece of community relations at little or no cost by allowing the room to be used for organization activities. Such a service brings a large cross section of the community, again, into personal contact with the company on a plane of community service. Naturally, some discretion must be used: A women's club might safely use a mahogany-paneled conference room, while a vigorous troop of boy scouts would wisely be assigned to a more rugged space.

Cooperation with schools can take many forms and pays large dividends. The fact that school children grow up to be tomorrow's adults is only part of the story. The extent to which public opinion is affected by ideas and attitudes carried home by school children and relayed to adults in home discussions is probably greater than has been generally recognized.

Helping Local Government

The same type of trained technical and professional personnel and know-how that business firms lend so helpfully to the service of local charitable, civic, school, and other causes can be just as helpful to local governments.

Especially in smaller communities, but sometimes even in larger ones, problems arise on which there is no one readily available to advise the city. Sometimes it is necessary to import an expert at great expense; but often there are specialists in the industries and business firms of the community who could solve the problems just as readily.

Local business firms, in such a case, would be well advised to make their specialists available to help on such assignments.

In a growing city new fiscal and control problems appear, ranging all the way from finding adequate sources of revenues on down to the mechanical problems of preparing and mailing tax bills. Corporation executives well versed in finance, and others well versed in the application of modern business machines and techniques, have counseled their local governments in such matters.

Plant engineers, structural engineers, chemists, and many other technical experts in industry have advised local governments on such matters as location and design of structures, strength of materials, lighting safety, and the like.

SPECIAL PROBLEMS OF PRESENT-DAY COMMUNITY RELATIONS

What has been said up to this point in this chapter was good counsel 25 years ago, and it is still good today. The difference is that today the chief executive is confronted with a kind of community-relations problem that never came to his attention then. All the elements were present then, but they had not risen to the surface with enough force or with enough organized backing to be recognizable as a community-relations problem.

It is the problem of dealing with local-action groups on such issues as minority employment, housing, environmental impact and protection, women's rights, consumerism, and similar causes advanced by special groups or affecting special segments of society.

Many of these issues, such as the employment and advancement of women or of racial minorities, involve the practices of the company within its own four walls and have not in the past been considered community concern. Today, however, they are aired and debated in the public arena with the obvious intent of building public support and backing for whatever cause is being advanced.

What distinguishes today's issues even more sharply from those of the past is that they typically are presented not as suggestions, requests, or proposals but as *demands*. Demands, in turn, beget not discussion but confrontations. Those who pose such demands and raise these kinds of questions are often militant. So the parties to the issues find themselves in an adversary setting.

THE REAL OBJECTIVE

What I am here proposing as a course of action is not intended as advice in how to defeat an adversary. If that were the objective, which, in these circumstances, it rarely is, others could provide better counsel than I on how to do it. But the objective usually is more complex than just victory or defeat. It is more than a platitude to say that the objective should be to settle the issues in a way that is most fair to all the parties and that will in the long run be best for the community; and to handle the confrontation in a way that will maintain the integrity of the company, will preserve the respect of the community for the company, and will leave the fewest scars in the community or among the parties to the issue.

That is a large order, especially when such adversary confrontations tend to be highly charged emotionally. But that very fact makes it important to keep the objective constantly in mind and not to surrender to the temptation to react in blind anger. What is really essential is that executives address themselves not to the legitimacy or stridency of those who pose the question, but to the legitimacy of the question itself.

Importance of Basic Policy

Actually the basic approach to dealing with militant action groups should not be materially different from the traditional approach to community problems. As with any other community relations, the first step is to adopt a policy; but that policy is so much more important here than in any other community involvement that I cannot stress too strongly how basic it is.

Before anyone makes any response on behalf of the company to action-group demands, the responsible executives of the company should make a thorough and objective examination and analysis—not only of the demands themselves, but of the issues involved in them: What does the company *really* believe on each point? What does it think is fair and realistic? What does it think it can do, and what does it think it cannot do in keeping with all its responsibilities to employees, to customers, to stockholders, and to the general public?

On the basis of that examination the company should draft a clear policy statement of what it is and is not prepared to do. Such a statement must be completely honest and without self-deception; it must be in terms the company is prepared to live by, both externally and internally. The policy should be broad enough to envision all likely developments, yet specific enough to avoid the charge of weaseling or "motherhood" protestations.

Once a policy is adopted, the company should measure every action, decision, or statement against it. All interested officers and employees should have been informed of it, so that no one could depart from it out of ignorance. But the company itself, or its principal spokesmen, should not depart from the policy on an expedient basis.

If subsequent developments demonstrate that the policy was in error, or was inadequate, or has been outdated, then the policy should be revised, and all interested parties so informed. Until then, all actions, decisions, and pronouncements should be consistent with the declared policy.

Chain of Command

A "chain of command" is important in dealing with sensitive community confrontations. The Chief Executive Officer must be fully committed, fully and currently informed, and prepared to be directly involved when appropriate. Someone who reports directly to the chief executive must have responsibility and authority for directing everything that is done in connection with the confrontation; and everyone else—including the executive himself—who might have contact with action groups, the media, or other secondary parties should be committed to the practice of coordinating with the designated officer. This does not imply censorship or "management of the news." Quite the contrary: Those who are not in charge and, hence, not in possession of all the facts on everything that has been said or done can easily make statements—particularly answers to questions—that are accurate enough in themselves, but out of context can give so distorted an impression as to prejudice all future efforts at understanding.

BANK OF AMERICA—CORE DISPUTE

An example may serve to illustrate how a policy thoughtfully arrived at and consistently adhered to can guide a company successfully through a potentially damaging confrontation. Early in 1964, Bank of America became the target of demonstrations by a civil rights organization, the Congress of Racial Equality (CORE). CORE and an affiliated group, the Ad Hoc Committee to End Discrimination, had been moving with amazing speed and effectiveness in the San Francisco area. Through a series of large and occasionally unruly demonstrations, these groups had in a period of six weeks extracted agreements from a chain of the largest automobile dealerships in town, from one of San Francisco's oldest and most prominent hotels, from a major supermarket chain and others.

The agreements were ones in which hiring quotas were set forth, in which disclosure of detailed facts relating to hiring practices was demanded, and in which members of the Ad Hoc Committee were given authority to pass judgment on dealer and hotel compliance.

While these demonstrations were going on the Bank received no direct communication from CORE. Instead, there was a series of statements—issued by CORE leaders and carried in the local news media. Within a short time, three facts emerged: (1) the Bank was indeed to be the next target for demonstrations; (2) CORE was to be the striking arm used against it; and (3) the Bank could not remain silent any longer without doing itself irreparable damage.

Bank of America did not discriminate in hiring and had, in fact, a large number of minority employees. It had for years stressed its position as an equal opportunity employer and, as a result, had over 600 black persons on the staff—some in management and supervisory positions. That number does not look impressive today;

but at that point in history, it put the Bank well out in the forefront because few corporations had as many as 600 black employees in other than janitorial or other such jobs. Of its total workforce, over 12 percent were from groups officially designated by the State FEPC as minorities—that is Negro, Oriental, and Latin American. The Bank believed that this record, although it could and should be improved, was defensible.

Management began making plans immediately to put its case before the public. It recognized at the outset that, over the long pull, it would need large-scale public support if it hoped to be successful. It further recognized that, in order to obtain this support, the Bank would have to address the public and take a strong position on two questions: First, it would have to stand up and be counted on the urgent social problems posed by the fermenting unrest in the black community. Second, only if it did this with force and candor could it take the strong stand it wanted to take on the propriety of the agreements being forced from other employers by civil rights organizations.

A series of management committee meetings was held at which the Bank's basic public position was hammered out. That position— which remained the same throughout the controversy—embraced these principal elements.

1. The Bank would publicly and candidly recognize minority group employment as an urgent social problem.
2. The Bank would publicly pledge to do its part as a good corporate citizen toward solving the problem by accelerating its already existent programs of minority recruitment.
3. The Bank would acknowledge that the entire matter was of legitimate public interest and agree to full public disclosure as to the racial composition of our workforce and the steps we were taking and would take to further workforce integration.
4. It agreed that it should welcome the opportunity to sit down with any minority groups, and entertain and put into effect any constructive suggestions they might have.
5. But, with its readiness to do these things, the Bank itself was also committed to an unswerving policy not to sign agreements or provide statistical data to any private group. It would categorically refuse to set up CORE, a White Citizens Council, or any other private organization as its policeman.

6.   Finally, the Bank felt that if the public was to believe its story, it would need to have its position authenticated by a third party. It had already seen the public confusion arising from the contradictory statements issued by civil rights groups and corporations, and its management was determined to secure large-scale public support for its position. Since the CORE plans were for statewide action against the bank, it decided to ask the State of California Fair Employment Practices Commission to serve as a validating agent.

On March 12, an open letter was sent to the State Fair Employment Practices Commission, offering to provide them with information on the Bank's staff and its hiring policies. The same day, the Bank held a press conference for all Bay Area media—including campus and minority-group media—to make clear its willingness to discuss any alleged discriminatory practices with responsible minority groups and indicating our position.

Following this press conference and the subsequent publicity, CORE issued a statement in which it denied plans to demonstrate against the Bank, and wrote the Bank asking for a meeting. The Bank agreed. The first meeting with CORE, a "get-acquainted session," was held March 16.

During the next two months, four more meetings with CORE were held at which relations rapidly deteriorated. CORE presented demands for a signed "quota" agreement, despite the Bank's repeated assertions that it would provide such information only to the FEPC and would sign no agreements with any private organization. At the same time, CORE leaders continued a barrage of statements to the press which were either misleading or false.

CORE broke off discussions with Bank of America on May 18, and announced to the press that the discussions had reached an impasse. It was indicated that picketing would begin soon. A day later, the Bank called its second major press conference and set forth its side of the dispute.

On June 1, 1964, Bank of America and the Fair Employment Practices Commission held a joint press conference announcing a memorandum of understanding regarding the timing and content of information which the Bank would provide to the FEPC and its subsequent handling by the agency.

Following this agreement with the FEPC, CORE continued

picketing throughout most of the summer. During this period, CORE contacted the Bank seeking additional meetings. It was the Bank's position that the meetings could be resumed only if CORE publicly announced that it understood the Bank would not provide it with statistics or sign an agreement. CORE failed to do this, although it continued the correspondence. As a result, no further meetings were held.

Public interest in the picketings declined throughout the summer, as did the size of the picketing groups. Finally, on August 31, CORE announced that picketing would be discontinued.

The great paradox of the entire controversy was that CORE's dispute with Bank of America was not related to the bank's willingness, even eagerness, to hire qualified black applicants.

Rather, the point at issue was whether the Bank, or any other corporation for that matter, should give detailed statistical information about its operations to a pressure group in order that that group might set itself up as a policing agency. For any business to award police powers to a pressure group is dangerous in principle and foolhardy in practice. A Bank spokesman has said:

> Did we succeed? Yes, beyond our most optimistic expectations. To my knowledge, Bank of America is the only picketed corporation in California where ministers, the NAACP and other prominent civil rights leaders were conspicuously absent from picket lines. The CORE–Bank of America dispute stayed just that. The main thrust of the civil rights movement stayed out of the issue. Also, the Bank enjoyed the vocal support of a number of prominent Negroes, a goodly percentage of the Negro press, and a substantial number of clergymen.
>
> If there is any single factor that contributed most to this support, it was our willingness to make a public disclosure of detailed statistical data on a regular basis to the FEPC.
>
> We entered into our agreement with the FEPC to demonstrate beyond any doubt that Bank of America is indeed vitally interested in providing equal opportunity for all of our minority citizens. We entered into the agreement in order to disprove the contention that was made in some quarters that Bank of America has "something to hide." We entered into the agreement because we felt it would be a major step in removing the equal employment opportunity problem from the streets and placing it where it rightfully belongs— in a duly authorized government agency empowered by law to act in this field.

A later chapter in the field of equal-opportunity employment attests to the value of an affirmative policy. In 1971, Bank of America, like hundreds of other employers, was named in a class-action suit filed on behalf of a group of women employees who charged discrimination. The Bank took the position that what the women were seeking was completely consistent with what the Bank itself had set as an objective. As facts were brought to light through pretrial discovery proceedings, all parties became aware that their objectives were basically the same, and that they involved equal opportunity for employment. When a final settlement was reached, it was the first time to my knowledge that in an equal-opportunity case the settlement was forward-looking and corrective in its totality. It was in two parts: one involving goals and timetables by which everyone could measure the Bank's progress toward those goals; and the other monetary. But the monetary element, instead of being punitive and backward-looking, as back-pay settlements typically are, set up trusts to be used to encourage women to seek up-grading training, and to pay their expenses in getting that training.

PART VI

The Personal Side of the Chief Executive

PROFESSIONAL SELF-DEVELOPMENT OF THE CHIEF EXECUTIVE

by Gene E. Engleman

Chairman, Union Bank of Fort Worth

IT SEEMS to me that one of the truly basic concerns of today's chief executive must be that of his own personal and professional growth and development. There is a great deal written about how to help other people grow and develop, and all that. But how about the CEO himself? Just because he's "made it" to the top, does that mean that personal and professional growth are no longer important to him? And to his company and associates? And family and community?

I don't think so! As long as we are active, we all need to continue to grow, to stay alive, even merely to "keep up."

Besides that, I think we all run the danger of getting "set in our ways," or even losing our touch, or just plain losing sight of those things that are really essential in our job. So we have to keep renewing what we do have, just to stay even.

If we are going to grow, develop, or renew—anything like that— it seems to me that we need to have clearly in mind what those *basics* are that we want to work on. Lord knows there are so *many* things we ought to be perfect in! We just can't hope for that, of course. But, at least, if we can keep clearly in mind some of the very basics of the CEO's job, we can surely hope to keep working on those as long as we're active. There's just no risk that we can ever become overly competent in the basics!

First of all, we have to recognize that being a CEO is a profession, and that the basic skills and knowledge of the job need to be kept fresh and to be expanded. Second, we need to keep in mind what the basics are, and to evaluate ourselves periodically against those basics. Third, we need to have some ideas as to how to keep on developing our competence in those basics.

THE PROFESSION OF CEO

For the past ten years I have spent about six weeks each year speaking to Chief Executive Officers and senior members of management in the United States, Canada, Central and South America, Europe, and the United Kingdom. The various subject matters covered have been planning, climate of management, motivation of managerial personnel, control, and other subjects related to the job of the CEO. Usually, these meetings have been sponsored by the Presidents' Association, an affiliate of the American Management Associations, as a "Management Course for Presidents" or "The Presidents' Round Table."

The range of responsibilities of the people attending has varied from large multinational companies with many thousands of employees to small companies with only a few workers. All of these people had enjoyed some degree of success, of course. Some were from old organizations and some from very new ones. The scope of organizational activities included almost every conceivable product and service, such as farming, space travel, education at all levels, manufacturing, retail, churches, hospitals, government, and many others. Some came from publicly held companies, some from private companies; some from family businesses and some from partnerships.

In the give and take of these meetings, there have been many comments on management concepts and techniques, but one recurring theme always comes up for discussion by those participating in these meetings. This theme is a pattern of thought expressed by most of those present in one way or another, which fails to recognize that management is a *profession*, and that as an activity, it meets all the criteria of the recognized professions such as law, medicine, accounting, etc.

I usually get the impression there is some surprise and perhaps mental reservation when I express the opinion that we are members of a profession called "management" and that, as professionals, we must spend a substantial degree of our time on "keeping up and self renewal" in what is going on in our profession—just the way other professionals must do if they are to be worthy. For example, how would you like a major operation to be performed on a member of your family by a surgeon who graduated from medical school 20 years ago and had not kept up with new concepts and techniques of the medical profession, or by a young man who thought he might like to be a surgeon and had just arrived at the hospital to practice a few operations before deciding on his career?

Further, in this exposure to more than 2,000 Chief Executive Officers and other members of top management, I have made an attempt to keep in touch with a number of them. I would estimate only about 30 to 40 percent of those I know are making a serious effort to stay abreast of the changing requirements of management at their level. I have noted that there seems to be a substantially higher percentage of personal and organization success in the ranks of those who have tried to grow with their jobs and who have *not* continued to operate in the same old way as they did when they started the company, or when they were vice-president of sales, chief engineer, or whatever. The successful seem to be those who are working at becoming and remaining competent, professional CEOs.

By any chance, do you know a former chief engineer who is now a CEO, but who still carries a slide rule in his pocket and likes to drop by engineering "just to check a few things out"; or a former vice president of sales who is now CEO but still calls on a few of the major customers? Is that "keeping up" or lingering behind? We should ask ourselves, are we *managing* an organization as best as we possibly can, or are we just practicing our hobby?

In short, being a CEO *is* a profession. That's one point. The other is this: Although it is useful to have been a chief engineer, or a sales manager, or a financial vice president, or whatever, before becoming a CEO, the job—the profession—of the CEO is *different*. That's what we have to work on.

THE "BASICS" OF THE PROFESSION

I would say that of the several "basics" of being a CEO, the first—or, perhaps, the most "basic"—is the ability to manage *change*, and to give leadership to an organization undergoing change.

Management of Change and Change in Leadership and Management

It is generally agreed that the management of change is one of the major challenges of top management. There can be no disagreement as to whether or not the rate of change is accelerating in all areas of human activity and in all bodies of knowledge! Why, then, do some think they can continue as a successful CEO of an organization that must grow and develop by adapting itself to a changing world unless they are willing to change their own concepts of management and style of leadership, as well as their products and services?

Leadership Style for Management Change. I believe that one of the requisites for personal and organizational growth in an era of change, of necessity, must be a changing style of leadership.

Let's discuss the need for changing our style of leadership as the needs of our organization and the needs of our people change. I have heard distinguished speakers on management say, "Management and leadership are synonymous." I disagree! Although there are many definitions of "Management," the one I like best, is very simple. "Management is getting results through the efforts of other people." And getting results out of a complex organization like a business requires many things. I do agree some managers are outstanding "leaders," but I maintain that leadership is only one part of the management job. There are other requirements of an effective manager. This is particularly true of the demanding job of the CEO of a tough-minded, fast-moving management group who share the responsibility of achieving the organization's objectives, not only this year but five or ten years into the future. The management job—besides "leadership"—requires application of all sorts of techniques, too, and a deep knowledge of the business as well.

I don't disagree with Peter Drucker when he says most managers belong to a leadership group within an organization; they aren't just individualistic "leaders." But just the same, giving "leadership," or leading the leaders, is part of the CEO's job. And he has to be as good at this part of his job as he can.

Some people have said that leaders are born. I don't go along with that. My experience and evidence tells me that leadership is a learned skill and achievable by those who want to work hard for it.

Leadership is hard to define in a pat phrase which is easy to remember. But I believe there are attributes of leadership that our professional CEOs ought to recognize and seek to cultivate and maintain in their own actions. Here are some of them, as I see them:

1. The professional leader is easy to follow; he has established a climate in which people will want to achieve. (Have you ever looked back over your shoulder, mentally, and found no one following you?)

2. He knows where he is taking the organization and has an awareness of opportunity. He has a direction in mind, at all times, and he knows when to change direction!

3. He sees to it that people understand where the organization is going (in both tactics and strategy); he gets their participation in developing the plan for getting there; and he gets their participation in helping him make the important decisions which he must make along the way.

4. He has learned to be sensitive to detail but never overwhelmed by it.

5. He has acquired intellectual maturity. He has integrity, is willing to admit mistakes. He has economic acuity; he knows the value of a dollar.

6. He has achieved emotional stability. He has learned how to keep his cool—at least so far as the outside world can see. He has ability to direct his anger, frustrations, and irritations into constructive channels to achieve the full potential of the situation.

7. He knows what he believes in and calls things by their right names.

8. He has an appreciation of human values and understands that he does not motivate people but, rather, that motivation comes from within the person and relates directly to the needs of the individual.

There are times when effective leadership requires an autocratic style. And there are situations where a high degree of permissiveness is the best style for getting the job done. The style of leadership which produces results is not the one "best way," but a changing pattern designed to fit the current needs of the organization as well as the needs of the followers. In my view, the real test of your style of leadership is not what the organization achieves in the short term. Rather, it is how well you launch the organization into the future, into an area where you and your organization have no experience. The test that really counts is whether your organization achieves its short-term goals consistent with a strategy designed to achieve worthwhile long-range objectives three, five, or even ten years out.

Others may specify the essentials and the focus of leadership differently. No matter, these will do. The point is this: In your own candid estimation, where do *you* stand in these dimensions? Are you improving? Frankly, are you deteriorating in these attributes? If you're not satisfied with your answer—and none of us can ever be completely satisfied—what are you going to do about you?

Management for Change.   There is a lot of literature about "management," and a lot of courses in "Programs" and in business schools that is really about managing a *given*, or ongoing business, where the major or almost exclusive concern is getting current sales and getting out current production. But today, many of the toughest problems for managements—and that includes CEOs, especially—is managing so as to bring about change.

I am aware, of course, that "the store must stay open." I fully believe that "if the ox is in the ditch, we must get him out." But I hasten to point out, if we, the CEOs, have to spend our time just "getting out the wash" and "fighting fires," then we have not done the real job of management—figuring out what our options and alternatives are; deciding where we want to get to; getting planning done and controls established to measure where we are, compared to where we said we would be; figuring what our management group is going to do when we are off course; and, sometimes, setting new objectives.

If management were just taking care of ongoing matters, life for the CEO would be pretty simple. But it isn't.

How can you tell what kind, or, better, how good a professional manager you are? When you've done that, you will have a better idea of what you need to do to improve yourself.

If you want to check yourself out as a professional in the job of CEO, here are some questions you might ask of yourself—honestly, "Yes" or "No":

1. Do your people frequently tell you how good you are?
2. Do you often feel you are not appreciated by your people?
3. Do you frequently have personnel problems with the younger managers?
4. Do you get into "win-lose" situations with your people?
5. Do you have to "win" all of the time? (If so, how do you like being surrounded by "losers"?)
6. Do you have frequent communication problems, and difficulty making yourself understood?
7. Do you secretly feel your associates or subordinates are falling short of your expectations?

8. Do you find yourself saying to your management team, "We must do this for the good of the organization?" (Note: No one does much for "the good of the organization" for very long unless doing so also fairly well meets his or her personal needs!)

9. Do you get written reports from your subordinates which *you don't read*, on matters which *you don't need to know about*, on which *they* should have *acted* and gone on to the next job?

10. Do you sometimes wonder why your people are so involved in trivia?

(Note: Subtract 10 from 100 for each honest "Yes" to get your rating as a professional in management!)

Perhaps your answers to the foregoing ten questions triggered some thoughtful analysis of what goes on in your organization, and why it happens that way. At least, I hope so. But don't get too discouraged. The average rating is about 40!

As regards both "leadership" and "management" I would stress that we are what we do—not what we say, think, or hope to do. Our people hear loud and clear what we do, and this pretty much determines what happens in our organization over the long pull.

Let's face it—not many of us have any real understanding of ourselves; and yet, behavioral scientists tell us the core of personal development begins with a substantial degree of self understanding. That's why I started by outlining some ideas about leadership and management and then I invited you to measure yourself against these "specs" to determine for yourself how much professional growth and development you need in these basics.

MANAGEMENT OF CONFLICT

When complex organizations are trying to bring off complex change in a complex world, conflict inside the organization is inevitable. And that is why the ability to manage conflict is one of the "basics" of professional management. What does this consist of? How much of it do you have? How can you improve your abilities along this line?

Conflict between Organization and Personal Objectives

This is a matter with which all managers must deal from time to time, both within themselves and among their people. It is really a problem of the most effective use of our human resources and it involves some basic principles of human behavior which I find convenient to classify under the heading "The Management of Conflict." It involves an understanding and a skill which is most valuable to a CEO in providing effective leadership for his top management team.

It seems to me that the following must be some of the key principles of conflict management.

1. To manage his human resources, the CEO must recognize he does not necessarily need to see the situation or circumstances as the other person does, nor, necessarily, to agree with any of the views to which he may be exposed by other people. But he must—I believe—be able to *understand* the other viewpoints, what the other, or others want to do and why they want to do it. Listening carefully to find out such matters is a vital part of the CEO role. As he listens to find out what people want, and why, he will try to remember that motives are, naturally, very personal; they vary by individuals; and they change frequently. What people want for the organization is almost inevitably related somehow to what they want for themselves. And what they want for themselves may or may not be the very best for the organization.

2. What we want—whether for ourselves or for the organization—is almost sure to be intertwined with emotions of one sort or another. And when we listen to others our own emotions are likely to give meaning to the situation—at least for us, personally. All of us try to "make sense" of situations by relating the present situation to our past experiences. Because our emotions are not necessarily rational, we may find a behavior pattern in someone else appearing irrational; at this point it is useful to recall that the pattern we find hard to understand, let alone agree with, makes sense to the individual concerned. The meaning which the people who are involved in a situation give to the situation affects the results of the whole organizational effort. The meanings they attach to the situation control their behavior and, therefore, their contributions to the results. Differences in perception, emotions, and values in situations of change lead to conflict.

3. Conflict can be reduced if we take the time to discuss together the organization's objectives in terms of what we want to accomplish. Is it worthwhile, realistic, and attainable? What does the situation require in the way of human and physical resources to get the job done? When it is done, how will individual performance be measured?

If we listen more than we talk, and cover the four steps outlined, we can expect a higher degree of acceptance, participation, and good performance. As a friend of mine says, "Most of us CEOs need to remember, if God had wanted us to talk more than we listen, He would have given us two mouths and one ear!"

4. Conflict or differences either in organizational or personal needs are not always all good or bad. It does seem clear, however, that such conflicts deserve the personal attention of the CEO where they occur in senior management levels because they can be most damaging. Getting a satisfactory solution to such conflicts can be helped by clearly identifying the nature of the problem. Is it about the merits and feasibilities of a proposed course of action or one which we are now following, or are we really comparing and contrasting, and disagreeing about our personal value systems? Do we all have the same information or has our information come through our personal "filters" with different meanings? How important is it for the matter to be resolved now? How much time do we have, without endangering an important organizational objective, to really work the thing through?

5. One of the most important things about managing conflicts is to recognize that it exists. Another is to recognize that people care, but see matters differently and "feel" differently about them. If we can admit these simple truths, without "pointing the finger" or being accusatory, maybe we can start to deal with the conflict—as a prelude to getting a decision.

Conflict and the Professional CEO

Now, the question arises: How good are we—how good are you— as a professional in recognizing the existence of conflict? In getting an understanding of its nature and causes? In getting people to admit to its existence? In getting them to help resolve it, and get to a decision? As you think about these matters, if you are like the rest of us, you are likely to realize you have some development, or some self-renewal, to do.

MANAGING FOR RESULTS

Many "managers" don't really "manage." They're busy. But they are just *doing.* They are reacting and improvising. They are responding to externalities or to situations brought on by others. But they *aren't managing.* The CEO's job is to produce results. Just reacting to events and developments isn't a very sure way to produce results. So, the CEO, his team, and his board should agree as to what results they want and the programs that give promise of bringing them about. That's another "basic" in the management of change. How good are you in managing for results? Is this something you need to develop or renew?

Well, there are lots of different kinds of results, but let's look at just a few of the kinds we want, especially in the area of organization building. If, as I think, it is results *achieved* that determine our future, then our principal job as CEO is to project the company successfully into the future. We shall do well to ask ourselves the question, "What are the critical areas which should receive our attention in planning for the future and controlling the action as we get plans implemented?" Here is my own list of the key considerations in doing that:

1. Require objectives to be stated in *quantitative* terms. (If objectives cannot be measured, how will we know when they are achieved?)

2. Plan and control operations and policy for customer satisfaction.

3. Measure productivity in terms of the relation of Output to Input, and if it isn't right, do something about it!

4. Plan and control operations to make the most of the company's resources; plan for their conservation, use, and creation.

5. Plan for management development in a formal manpower plan that specifies results to be achieved. The plan should cover at least the term of your strategic long-range plan. Then, in order to see whether you are on the track of getting the results you want, appraise the managerial performance of your top management people at least annually against predetermined mutually-arrived-at standards of performance. Coordinate these appraisals with your management manpower plan for the long term, and update and revise the long-term plan.

6. Get a written statement of your responsibilities as CEO worked out with the assistance of your top management group, and get it approved by your board of directors. What results are you to achieve, this year? Next? Over a five-year period? Then, develop specific measurable standards of performance for each of your responsibilities, in terms of specific conditions which will exist when

you have done an acceptable job on each one. The idea is to make completely visible to you, your board of directors, and your subordinates, whether or not you have done your job as CEO—whether you have achieved the results desired. If you would like a more formal evaluation of your results (it really is too bad, but not many CEOs sincerely want to be evaluated), appoint a committee of your board to do an evaluation and to review it with you, in the presence of the full board!

7. See to it that a sensible system is adopted for all employees in the organization, at all levels of management, to have written job descriptions of their responsibilities and related standards of performance. Get performance evaluations done by the individual's boss —not by someone from a personnel department, and not on some standard form dreamed up by personnel or by a consultant. It is a basic truth that people cannot do well what they do not understand. They expect to do well what they know will be inspected. Also, while we're on the subject, let's not measure people on anything but key result areas where they are the ones who are responsible for those results. One of the things I believe I have learned about professional management is that performance appraisal of an individual with, and by, his boss at scheduled intervals of time is vital to growth and development of the individual, as well as directly related to getting today's job done today.

8. Plan for the CEO—that's you—to take on and carry out well a significant public responsibility which goes beyond customer satisfaction. I do believe this is a vital part of the CEO's personal self-development job, as well as his management job. If you feel that you just "don't have time" for civic or community activities—or, as some feel, even for your family and your church—take a real close look at your management of time. You won't like the results of such an examination.

Now. How good are you at managing by planning for results along such lines as these? If you're not altogether happy with your answer, what are you going to do about it?

PLANNING FOR YOUR SELF-DEVELOPMENT AND RENEWAL

If, as you think about these things, you get a little uneasy, and feel that, as a professional, you, too, need to do something to "keep up," to develop your management talents, and to renew those you have, you come to a question as to what to do to remedy any short-falls you detect. Well, here are a few ideas.

I think one good place to start is to write out your very own philosophy of life. Define the things you believe in, the values you believe are important. Set down what you intend to do, or not to do, in the way of personal living. What would you like to become and to be?

Your beliefs and your value system determine, of course, what you are. And you are what you do! By working to get them reduced to writing—very frankly, and with no crap—you will acquire some greater self-understanding. It will enable you to examine with some realism your own personal objectives, and to decide whether these are what you really want to achieve. Few people do this; yet, all of us really do have a philosophy of life. By striving to write out our beliefs, define our values, and establish clear-cut objectives which can be measured, we are applying to our own life a fundamental concept of management and a prime requirement of leadership—"Know where you are going and how you are going to get there."

In designing your personal program of self-renewal, I suggest you consider the kind of "image" you would like to have in your organization, your family, your community, the industry. By clearly defining the image you want, you are really outlining the kind of character and reputation you must have if the "image" is to be created. Your image with people will be what you are, because that will be what you do.

When you are reasonably clear as to what you want to be, and the "image" you want to have, then really work on changing your be-havior, your capabilities, and your character along the lines you have in mind. In time, if it's for real, your "image" will come closer to being what you want it to be.

This personal plan for self-renewal, which I am suggesting, needs to be reexamined and updated periodically. Just as the organization's long-range plan needs to be changed and updated, so will your plan for your own life and your role in your company need changing be-cause your values and objectives, as well as the company's needs, will change as time goes by.

After you think you have set down the objectives for your life, as based on your philosophy and have developed written plans for ac-complishing these objectives, examine the whole of it for realism and attainability. In my opinion, more failures develop from attempting objectives which are unattainable than from almost anything else. I am not suggesting one should set objectives that are easy. I am saying they should be realistically attainable within your capacity and time frame. For example: I have always thought I would like to travel to the moon. Probably you would, too. It has been done several times. So why couldn't this be one of my objectives? But, at age 63 and after two minor heart attacks, I know that I would not be able to achieve that objective. So, it isn't one of my personal objectives. My time and effort should be concentrated on more realistic goals, and perhaps yours should too.

SOME PRACTICAL SUGGESTIONS FOR SELF-DEVELOPMENT AND RENEWAL

Although self-development and self-renewal start with an inner desire and are encouraged by the working out of a personal plan, there are any number of other steps that may further the process. I shall mention two.

Management Programs and Seminars

There are all kinds of management programs and seminars being given these days—by industry and trade groups, business schools, and private firms. Do, by all means, get involved with some of these on a regular basis. Inquiries among other CEOs will help you decide which are for you.

But, if I may be forgiven, I have also a couple of specific suggestions. One thing all CEOs need is greater understanding of human behavior, including their own. Too many of us fancy ourselves (perhaps secretly) as amateur psychiatrists. Instead of continuing to go down that easy, misleading road, I think we all need genuine exposure to some of the fundamentals of the behavioral sciences. If you are interested, I suggest you arrange to attend one of the courses given for CEOs by the American Management Associations or the National Training Laboratories for the Advancement of the Behavioral Sciences. Both of these organizations do a good job. I am sure there are others who do it well, but I just don't happen to know who they are. I do know from my own observations and inquiries that these programs have done any amount of good for many, many CEOs.

Leveling—You and Your Board

If you have the right kind of board, you have a first-class instrument for measuring your own personal, as well as professional performance and growth. At least once a year, in a formal session of the board, and preferably with your second-in-command present, you should try, most candidly, to evaluate yourself, your performance, your strengths, your weaknesses, and your plans for future development. After this is done, the second-in-command can proceed to evaluate himself and to set forth his plan for his development. The CEO and his lieutenant can be of tremendous help to each other in this experience.

This suggestion may shock some readers. But I have seen it done. And I know it can work.

Candor—combined with sympathy and goodwill—can work wonders after the CEO has established the atmosphere which permits and encourages this sort of "confessional." Seeking for help and guidance, ideas really can begin to flow. Having colleagues who will go through this process with you is a tremendous help. It can be a real outside check and can lead to useful ideas for future action.

The process is encouraged if this kind of evaluation and dialogue can be a two-way street. Some CEOs meet with each member of their board, privately, and give *him* a candid evaluation and appraisal and suggestions for his improvement as a board member. It is probably useful if these sessions come *after* the session with the top managers. Most board members *want* to do a good job and really appreciate frank appraisals and suggestions for their self-development and self-renewal.

CONCLUSION

Having been a manager of sorts most of my adult life, and a CEO for more years than many others, I have long since concluded that there is almost no other matter that should be of greater concern to a CEO than his own development and self-renewal. When he stops growing, begins to "top-out" or even lose his punch—he'd better do something about it, or start making plans to move out!

OUTSIDE ACTIVITIES AND INTERESTS

by Donald S. Perkins

Chairman, Jewel Companies, Inc.

OUTSIDE INVOLVEMENTS—YES OR NO?

IT IS QUITE possible to make a case for or against outside involvements for a chief executive, but I am comfortable with only one side of the argument. I'm strongly biased in favor of selective not-for-profit and for-profit outside activities for all executives beginning with the Chief Executive Officer.

Our society needs such involvement!

And concern for other human beings demands the outside involvement of chief executives! Most chief executives understand early in their careers that they cannot themselves have a truly successful career if their company does not stay healthy. Further, they appreciate the fact that their company cannot be healthy in the long run if their city, their state, their nation, or their society doesn't remain healthy. Few would argue these points or would question the obvious need for the insight, energy, and ability of business leaders in working toward the maintenance of our key institutions or the solution to our more difficult human problems.

Our own companies need such involvement!

Although it is of course essential that everyone know that our own company's demands on our time have priority at all times, we are obviously living in an era that requires good citizenship on the part of its chief executives. And it seems to be almost invariably true that corporations are good citizens when their leaders are good citizens. I would never suggest that shoddy products should be forgiven because of worthy involvements of a company's chief executive. But in an era when the reputation of business with the public is declining and in an era when young talent is questioning how they should spend their lives, the public, and particularly the young public

1081

does and should expect business leaders to contribute their talents in a variety of worthwhile ways. I personally feel, for instance, that the quality of our company's recruiting and the retention of young talent has been aided by knowledge of the involvement of numerous executives in important activities outside of our company.

We as individuals need such involvement!

A sensible amount of time taken away from our normal pursuits is essential to the growth and development of each of us as individuals. The ideas and stimulation found in thoroughly different outside activities are important in their effect on me as a person. It's more obvious that ideas gathered from membership on outside corporate boards can be put to use in my own company, but I find the same principle surprisingly true for membership on charitable boards. All of the good management and motivational ideas in this country are not confined to corporate executive suites. Importantly, too, no executive whom I truly admire feels fully satisfied with the contribution he is making in his lifetime unless he can combine outside contributions with inside accomplishment. If nothing else, it's a debt that's owed in return for the gifts of ability and energy with which chief executives are fortunate enough to have been endowed.

OUTSIDE ACTIVITIES—OR PITFALLS?

—Every chief executive is susceptible to flattery.
—Every charitable or trade organization wants chief executives on its board.
—Every fund-raising activity knows the value of the involvement of chief executives.
—Every corporation wants successful chief executives on its board.
—Everyone knows that you're supposed to give tough jobs to busy people.
—Every chief executive has too little time.

Put all of these thoughts together and they suggest that outside activities can be a pitfall as well as make an important contribution. None of us are any good to anyone if we overcommit and figuratively or literally kill ourselves trying to live up to our commitments. Perhaps all of us might do a better job of putting outside activities in perspective if we set forth general criteria for outside involvement before saying "yes" to any invitation. Such criteria might include these ideas:

1. Of course make certain that the internal job is organized and operating successfully before anything is ventured on the outside.

2. Make a first—or at least an early, strong commitment to a community not-for-profit involvement.

3. Develop the habit of waiting a day or so before accepting any outside invitation. The delay will help diminish the effect of the flattery which accompanies all invitations.

4. Don't judge an invitation just by the person who delivers it. Every organization sends its better salesmen and most impressive people to invite involvement.

5. Consider asking someone or some group to be an "outside activities committee." I have done this with three outside directors, one of whom was my predecessor. Annually I ask my secretary to review my prior year's calendar and summarize by activity the number of days I spent away from the company on outside activities. With this as background material, I ask this threesome to review any significant invitations whenever I am inclined to want to say "yes." Another good frame of reference for me regarding outside involvements is my wife. Her perspective on the subject of how much I'm trying to do has always been more realistic than my own.

6. Ask for board of director approval before accepting any outside commitment which takes a significant amount of time.

7. Choose those involvements that are most rewarding—with people with whom it is fun to associate—with organizations whose accomplishments give the greatest satisfaction.

8. Whatever the organization offering the invitation, take the time to find out whether it is possible to be truly helpful before saying "yes." Whether the invitation comes from a profit or not-for-profit organization, spending time away from the job or away from home attending nonparticipative, rubber-stamp-type meetings is an insult and a foolish waste of time besides.

9. Be aware of, and monitor, what company associates think about the time you spend away from your company and how that interferes with their access to you.

If you are a chief executive in a reasonably prominent organization in any sizable community, you probably already know that you receive at least five times the invitations you might possibly be able to accept and handle well. Perhaps by starting out with that knowledge as an expectation a new chief executive might be encouraged to learn to say "no" at least four times for each time he says "yes." The first few board invitations are the most difficult to decline but that is certainly the time for each chief executive to think through the types of outside involvements he or she chooses to have.

FLATTERY ONE: CORPORATE BOARD INVITATIONS

Receiving invitations to join corporate boards (including your own) is always flattering. Perhaps for that reason these invitations may require the greatest degree of mature evaluation and restraint. Be patient and wait for those invitations that are right for you.

My own definition of what has been right for me includes:

a. Companies that are in businesses totally different from my own, both because I learn more and because I avoid any conflict of interest.

b. Companies that are financially strong and whose managements are scrupulously honest. Given the legal and financial responsibility of directors and the inadequacies of all directors' liability insurance, I see no wisdom in becoming involved with weak companies or weak managements.

c. Companies that are concerned about communication to directors between meetings as well as at meetings.

My own definition of what I try to avoid includes:

a. Companies that meet monthly. First, I don't have the time. Second, they too often confuse frequency of meetings with communication.

b. Companies that seem to want outside directors as front men for managements who really don't want their help.

c. Companies that regard their board as a very exclusive private club rather than a diverse group of informed counselors.

d. Bank boards, because I do not want to live with the possibility of any semblance of influence on our company's financial executives as they choose between alternate sources of capital.

Serving as an outside director on the board of a company that makes good use of the contributions that can be made by outsiders is both fun and satisfying. The accompanying responsibilities are so great, however, that care must be taken to limit these involvements to those that can receive the full attention they deserve.

FLATTERY TWO: NONPROFIT BOARD INVITATIONS

Every nonprofit organization is quite properly looking for ways to involve the chief executives of prominent companies in every city, both to insure their corporate gift and to enlist their talent. I emphasize "quite properly" because that's the way it should be and needs to be. But it's always better to say "no" than to say "yes" and and do a poor job—and I'm continually surprised by chief executives who are seemingly quite able and dependable in their own company but who fail to complete a nonprofit outside task they accept.

Assuming the general criteria already discussed, there are some particular potential pitfalls worth mentioning which apply to all nonprofit activities—charitable, trade association, government, etc.:

—Generally, it makes sense to avoid having your name used if you aren't involved. It is not always possible but it will often save potential frustration and embarrassment.

—It is important to check out and understand what fund-raising responsibilities are being accepted (even by implication) in joining a nonprofit board. It's very difficult to raise money effectively for more than one or two causes at a time.

—It is probably wise to avoid organizations which use a disproportionately high percent of their income to raise funds. It is a lot more satisfying to work with an organization which spends 5 percent of its funds raised on fund raising than with one which spends 35 percent or 50 percent or more.

—Organizations with weak staffs should be joined with caution unless you have the time, the inclination, and the support of the other board members to strengthen that staff. Working with a good staff multiplies the outside board member's contribution considerably.

—Educational or health agency professionals often try to show their strength by reminding laymen that they are just that. Most organizations need lay boards to remind professionals that for the public good they cannot run their organizations entirely for their own selfish benefit. On the other hand, discretion and realism about suggesting the application of "business methods" to nonbusiness problems is essential.

Four specific types of involvement are presented to most chief executives and are worthy of a comment or two—at least to give me a chance to suggest my own personal feelings about them.

1. *Trade and industrial association* involvements are hard to avoid and often frustrating. Many associations seem to be run for the benefit of the lowest common denominator of their membership as picked up on the politically tuned antenna of the association's professional executives. Unless trade associations are willing to limit their membership by imposing standards of performance as a membership requirement, this is not likely to change.

2. *Governmental part-time service* can be very helpful and rewarding but *not* if you believe that all governmental workers are bumbling bureaucrats. If you feel that way, stay away for you'll do more harm than good. On the other hand if you're willing to spend considerable time and effort understanding what a particular governmental agency sees as its job and who it sees as its constituency before trying to advise it, you may be able to be quite helpful indeed.

3. *Political campaign involvement* can be exciting and rewarding, win or lose—*if* you'll select a candidate with the same care with which you would select a business partner. Assume that your reputation is at least partially on the line when you support a candidate for office and avoid involvement unless you know for a fact that he or she is a first-class person in every way. Incidentally, I have not found it detrimental to my company to have personally worked for a political candidate even when we have lost.

4. *Fund-raising dinners in your honor* are perhaps the most highly developed form of chief executive flattery and in my judgment the least desirable. To each his own, but I firmly refuse to be the honoree on any occasion that is designed to raise funds. I do not want our management people twisting suppliers' arms to make sure that I'm "honored" by a big attendance.

OUTSIDE INVOLVEMENTS: YES!

Two overall impressions occur to me as I think generally about this subject. First, from the point of view of the individual, the pluses clearly outweigh the minuses for the chief executive who picks and chooses from among the most rewarding and effective alternatives for outside involvement. Second, from the point of view of organizations that want and need the involvement of chief executives, they would be wise to listen more carefully to busy chief executives who answer an invitation by saying, "Yes, I'd like to have our company involved, but I personally do not have the time